This catalogue is published in conjunction with the exhibition *Art et Liberté: Rupture, War and Surrealism in Egypt (1938-1948)*, presented at Tate Liverpool from November 10, 2017 to March 11, 2018

EXHIBITION TOUR

Centre national d'art et de culture Georges Pompidou, Paris
19.10.2016 - 09.01.2017

Museo Nacional Centro de Arte Reina Sofía, Madrid
14.02.2017 - 28.05.2017

Kunstsammlung Nordrhein-Westfalen, Düsseldorf, K21 Ständehaus
15.07.2017 - 15.10.2017

ISBN 978-2-37074-031-1

The spelling of the artists names in this publication respects, when applicable, their signatures on their works, and the way they appear in the majority of primary sources.

TATE LIVERPOOL

Albert Dock, Liverpool Waterfront
Liverpool, L3 4BB
UK

T. +44 (0)151 702 7400
www.tate.org.uk

ART REORIENTED

Sam Bardaouil and Till Fellrath
New York
244 5th Ave #2906 New York
NY 10001
USA

Munich
Corneliusstrasse 20
80469 Munich
Germany

ÉDITIONS SKIRA PARIS

14 rue Serpente
75006 Paris
www.skira.net

Senior Editor
Nathalie Prat-Couadau

Editorial coordination
María Laura Ribadeneira
assisted by Auriane Kolodziej
and Anissa Mahdaoui

Graphic Design
Sophie Dupriez

Copyediting
Chrisoula Petridis

Color Separation
Litho Art New, Turin

Cover:
RAMSES YOUNANE
Untitled (detail), 1939
Oil on canvas
46.5 x 35.5 cm
H.E. Sh. Hassan M. A. Al Thani collection, Doha

ART ET LIBERTÉ

RUPTURE, WAR AND SURREALISM IN EGYPT (1938-1948)

EDITED BY SAM BARDAOUIL AND TILL FELLRATH

ACKNOWLEDGEMENTS

SAM BARDAOUIL AND TILL FELLRATH

Over the last five years, we have undertaken the challenging task of putting together an exhibition about the significant, yet little known story of the *Art and Liberty* Group, and their reworking of Surrealism in Egypt. In assembling the pieces of this art-historical puzzle, we have seen our research take us all around the world to cities as diverse as, Paris, London, Rome, Thessaloniki, Doha, Beirut, Dayton, New York, Los Angeles, Chicago, or Tokyo. In Egypt, where it all began, we spent substantial time tracing the individual stories of *Art and Liberty* members, talking with family descendants and revisiting the locations where their activities unfolded. We unearthed and analyzed hundreds of archival materials and primary documents written in Arabic, French, English, Greek, Italian and German, mirroring the cosmopolitanism of the group.

In 2012 / 2013, we presented a preview of our ongoing research on the *Art and Liberty* Group within our international traveling exhibition *Tea with Nefertiti*. Today, we are honored and proud to present the result of our work, and would like to thank all those who contributed towards it. Our exhibition *Art et Liberté : Rupture, War and Surrealism in Egypt (1938 - 1948)* is the first comprehensive museum exhibition on the *Art and Liberty* Group, reuniting for the first time over 125 artworks and 150 archival documents, most of which are seen and published for the first time. These are testimony to *Art and Liberty*'s legacy, not only within the context of modern Art in Egypt, but to a distinct chapter in the history of Surrealism at large.

Throughout our journey, we were very fortunate to have had the support of so many individuals and institutions that we would like to acknowledge and thank wholeheartedly.

Exhibition Lenders

First and foremost, we would like to thank all of the fifty lenders of artworks and documents to the exhibition whose trust and generosity have made it possible to unearth and exhibit so many rare paintings, works on paper, photographs, publications and archival materials.

We are delighted to thank the following private lenders: Waleed Abdulkhalek, Soraya Antonius, Mona Barakat, Alexandre Bideau, Christophe Bouleau, The Chafik Charobim Estate, Mai El-Dib, The Abdel Hadi El-Gazzar Estate, El-Telmissany Family, Nadim Elias, The Henein – Farhi Collection, Sergio Grossetti, Michael Holter, Fatenn Mostafa Kanafani, The Robert Medley Estate, The Laurent Marcel Salinas Estate, Naguib and Ghada Sawiris, Sherwet Shafie, Hassan Al Thani, Kareem Wissa, Evelyne Yeatman, The Younan Family, Kamal Youssef, Yasser Hashem.

We would like to thank the following institutional lenders: The Rateb Seddik Museum, Cairo, The Egyptian Ministry of Culture of the Arab Republic of Egypt, the Sector of Fine Arts, The Dominican Institute for Oriental Studies, Cairo, The Library at the American University of Cairo, The Bibliothèque Georges and Boula Henein at the Institut Français au Caire, The Centre d'Études Alexandrines (CEALEX), Alexandria, The Arab Image Foundation, Beirut, Mathaf: Arab Museum of Modern Art, Doha, Qatar Museums, Doha, Qatar Foundation, Doha, The Barjeel Art Foundation, Sharjah, The European Cultural Centre of Delphi, Athens and Delphi, The National Portrait Gallery, London, The Lee Miller Archives / Roland Penrose Art Collection, Farley Farm House, Chiddingly, The Library at the Scottish National Gallery of Modern Art, Edinburgh, The Bibliothèque Kandinsky at the Centre Pompidou, Paris, The Bibliothèque de Documentation Internationale Contemporaine, Nanterre The Universities of Paris – The Bibliothèque Littéraire Jacques Doucet, The Bibliothèque Interuniversitaire Sainte-Geneviève, Paris, The Museum of the Institut du Monde Arabe, Paris, The Musée Nicéphore Niépce, Chalon-sur-Saône, The Beinecke Rare Books and Manuscripts Library at Yale University, New Haven

Exhibition Collaborators

We would like to acknowledge the numerous individuals and institutions who supported this project in a wide array of ways from acting like a sounding platform for the exchange of ideas, to assisting in various research aspects, and to being generous interlocutors connecting us to various institutions, collections and artist estates: Mona Abaza, Reda Abdel Rahman, Nabil Abou El-Hassan, Emad Badr El-Din Abu Ghazi, Wafik Chammaa, Jean Colombain, Ahmad El-Dabbaa, Esmat El-Dawastashy, Chris Dercon, Laila Effat El-Gazzar, Hager El-Hadidi, Mostafa El-Razzaz, Bashir El-Sibai, Tarek El-Telmissany, Catherine Farhi, Hesham Geshta, Samir Gharib, James Gifford, Valerie Hess, James Hyman, Jean-Roch Giovachini, Daniel Lançon, J.R. LeShufy, Karen LeShufy, Nazli Madkour, Nuria Medina, Samia Mehrez, Elizabeth Miller, Yasser Mongy, Mandy Prowse, Hussam Rashwan, Markus Richter, Francesca Rondinelli, Irene Rustom, Mona Saïd, Mohamed Salmawy, Sarah Salmaway, Hala Sarofim, Taya Sawiris, Ola Seif, Nicholas Serota, Nada Shabout, Avinoam Shalem, Ragy Soliman, Przemyslaw Strozek, Mohammad Talaat, May Telmissnay, Mecerdes Volait, Nadia von Maltzahn, Anna Wallace Thompson, Annie White, Doreen Wenzel, Mai Yannie, Sonia Younan, Sylvie Younan

Our gratitude goes to Ines Bouaillon, project coordinator for the exhibition at Centre Pompidou for her assistance in procuring a number of research materials from various libraries in Paris. We also would like to thank her and Dorothée Lacan, head of production for the exhibition at Centre Pompidou, for their assistance in procuring a number of HD images for this publication. We would like to thank Véronique Sorano-Stedman, chief restorer at Centre Pompidou, Cinzia Pasquali from the restoration laboratories Arcanes, and their respective teams for their tireless diligence in restoring and preparing the artworks and documents for this exhibition. We would like to thank architect Julie Boidin for her assistance in transforming our vision for the exhibition design into a real spatial experience, and for all the creative solutions she brought along the process. We also would like to thank the audiovisual department at the

Centre Pompidou for their assistance in the making of the projections and films for the exhibition. We would like to thank Ronan Prigent, cultural attaché of France in Egypt for placing his diplomatic skills and endless patience at the disposal of this project. We also would like to thank Mr. Michael Schischke, head of external relations at Centre Pompidou, for his attentive care in liaising with the French ministry of culture.

We would like to thank the team at Skira, in particular Francesco Baragiola, Nathalie Prat-Couadau, María Laura Ribadeneira, and Sophie Dupriez for their diligence and commitment in simultaneously producing five separate language editions of this publication.

A very special thank you goes to Sama Waly and Amy Arif, our research assistants and project coordinators in Cairo for their phenomenal dedication to the project from beginning to end.

Our sincere gratitude goes to Mai El-Dib who so willingly gave from her time and energy, and introduced us to a network of individuals and institutions who became partners to this project in various capacities.

Exhibition Venues

We are delighted that four of the most renowned museums worldwide have honored the unique contributions of the artists, writers and affiliates of the *Art and Liberty* Group. Therefore, we would like to thank the directors of these four institutions for relying on our expertise in the topic, and for inviting us to present this historic exhibition as part of their programs.

For Centre Pompidou in Paris, we particularly wish to thank Bernard Blistène and Catherine David for the opportunity to showcase Surrealism in Egypt within the museum's special programs on the occasion of the 50th anniversary of the death of André Breton. For the Reina Sofia in Madrid, we would like to thank Manuel Borja-Villel for providing us with the unique opportunity to unite Pablo Picasso's *Guernica* with its reproduction on the cover of *Art and Liberty*'s 1938 manifesto, in our exhibition that illustrates the group's political engagement with the Spanish Civil War. For the Kunstsammlung K21 in Düsseldorf, we would like to thank Marion Ackermann and Doris Krystof for making it possible to highlight *Art and Liberty*'s anti-fascist stand and solidarity with Entartete Kunst. And for Tate Liverpool, we wish to thank Francesco Manacorda for enabling an unprecedented exploration of the links between the surrealism in Egypt and Great Britain.

Exhibition Donors

At a time when many cultural institutions are facing increasing challenges to fund comprehensive and complex exhibition and research projects, the support of dedicated partners has become indispensible.

Throughout the project, we have been fortunate enough to build strong relationships with a number of genuine patrons, who became primary stakeholders of this exhibition. Beyond their generous financial contributions towards the exhibition's international tour and its Arabic, English, French, German and Spanish catalogues, they have tirelessly continued to garner all their resources towards advancing the project in countless additional ways.

We would like to thank Casa Arabe in Madrid whose support made it possible to have a Spanish edition of this catalogue.

Our particular gratitude goes to Yasser Hashem, who in the spirit of *Art and Liberty*'s belief in the value of education for all, underwrote the Arabic edition of this catalogue and supported its circulation at no cost to a wide number of schools, universities and art spaces in Egypt.

We express our profound gratitude for the considerable support of Samih Sawiris, which made it possible to include some of the masterpieces that are on view in this exhibition. It is due to his guidance and advice that we have managed to realise some of the complex aspects of this project.

We are grateful to the considerable support of the Montblanc Cultural Foundation, and for recognizing the project's ambition to rewrite a chapter in the history of Surrealism; an ambition that echoes the foundation's faith in the value of Knowledge and innovation.

Last, but most certainly not least, our most heartfelt gratitude goes to Hassan Al Thani for his enduring friendship and support. What he has singlehandedly done for the preservation and promotion of modern art from the Arab world, over the last three decades, has been an inspiration for so many. It is this personal passion that has been guidance throughout the project. It is with unwavering generosity that he has supported the international exhibition tour. He has also provided additional support towards the publication of the English, French, and German editions of the catalogue. For all of this, we are wholeheartedly grateful.

Our final thanks goes to the members of the *Art and Liberty* Group and their advocacy for the liberation of artists from the confines of geographical boundaries and political propaganda. At a time when the world is becoming increasingly divisive, their uncompromising faith in the social, economical and cultural empowerment of humanity, sets an example to us all. ■

Sam Bardaouil and Till Fellrath,
Exhibition Curators

FOREWORD

FRANCESCO MANACORDA AND ANDREA NIXON

Art et Liberté: Rupture, War and Surrealism in Egypt (1938-1948) is the first ever comprehensive survey of the activity of the *Art and Liberty* group in Cairo. It brings together a wide and varied range of artworks — paintings, photographs and printed matter — which trace the history of the group from 1938 when it was established to its dismantling in 1948, as well as investigating its legacy and influence on a younger generation of Egyptian artists. The exhibition also highlights the group's international connections, inscribing it in a wide network of artists from around the world who shared ideas, eagerness to experiment and political views that shifted the path of global modernity.

At Tate we are committed to expanding the art historical canon and inverting the dominant historical narratives. We are therefore thrilled to introduce this underrepresented yet extremely rich aspect of twentieth-century art history to our audiences in Liverpool. Joining a major exhibition tour, we hope to add another layer of interpretation to the phenomena of Egyptian Surrealism by exploring the relationship between the artists who formed the *Art and Liberty* group and those who were at the forefront of parallel avant-garde practices in Britain.

We present *Art et Liberté: Rupture, War and Surrealism in Egypt (1938-1948)* as part of our autumn 2017 season, alongside a retrospective of John Piper (1903-1992) a major contributor to the artistic landscape of twentieth century Britain. He is renowned for his landscape, architectural and abstract compositions which combine a sensitivity to the physical characteristics, atmosphere and history of his native landscape with the visual language of European abstraction, creating a distinctly British vision of modernity that was deeply engaged in the history of his home country. Together, the two shows unveil the complexities of constructing narratives around geographies and art.

We are very grateful to Sam Bardaouil and Till Fellrath, who under the auspices of Art Reoriented curated *Art et Liberté: Rupture, War and Surrealism in Egypt (1938-1948)* and generously shared with us their in-depth knowledge and expertise throughout the preparations of the show. It is thanks to their enthusiasm and efficiency that their project evolved into an international exhibition tour. Collaborating with colleagues in our partner institutions in Paris, Madrid and Düsseldorf was a highly rewarding experience. We are, as ever, immensely grateful to our team at Tate Liverpool for the skill and commitment with which they have made this project possible. We thank Kasia Redzisz, Senior Curator, and Tamar Hemmes, Assistant Curator, who organized the exhibition with Till and Sam for Tate Liverpool. Dan Smernicki, Ken Simons, Barry Bentley and Roger Sinek managed the shipping and installation, and our colleagues in collections care and conservation provided the project with their considerable expertise. Our Learning team, headed by Lindsey Fryer, has planned a wide-ranging programme of activities for children, young people and adults to enable the exhibition's themes to reach the widest possible audience. The Development team led by Jo Warmington have ably supported and fostered Tate Liverpool's roster of patrons, sponsors and donors. For managing the press and marketing of the exhibition we thank Alison Cornmell and Jennifer Collingwood, together with Mike Pinnington, who has overseen the development of the interpretation materials.

Crucially, we extend our deep thanks to the supporters of this exhibition, in particular to the University of Liverpool. We would also like to thank H.E. Sh. Hassan M. A. Al Thani for his main contribution that made the exhibition tour possible, and to acknowledge the additional support of the Montblanc Cultural Foundation, and the Sawiris Foundation for Social Development. Finally, the exhibition has been made possible by the provision of insurance through the Government Indemnity Scheme. Tate would like to thank HM Government for providing Government Indemnity and the Department for Culture, Media and Sport and Arts Council England for arranging the indemnity. ■

Francesco Manacorda, Artistic Director
Andrea Nixon, Executive Director

CAIRO TO CALIFORNIA: *ART ET LIBERTÉ* TO ANARCHIST POST-SURREALISM

JAMES GIFFORD

The story of *Art et Liberté* is rich, but perhaps more importantly, also enriching. From their exhibitions and manifestos in Egypt, the artists of *Art et Liberté* connected outward around the globe and drew in an extraordinary range of other artists and writers. They were transformed by the experience and shared it from Cairo to California.

Where we are accustomed to thinking of their relationships as a roadway to—or rather, *from*—Paris, Surrealism, and André Breton, we may instead see them spiraling outward among their own generation with a politics of the personal rich in mutual support and distribution. The crux is the unexpected relationship between Egyptian radical art and literature of the 1930s and 40s and what *Harper's Magazine* in America called in 1947 "The New Cult of Sex and Anarchy" in Big Sur and Berkeley, California. Both have surprising affinities to the development of English Post-Surrealism after the 1936 London International Surrealist Exhibition but also earlier ties to the Villa Seurat group in Paris.

Georges Henein and Albert Cossery, both of *Art et Liberté*, were involved in the anti-Fascist Egyptian Surrealist movement inaugurated by their 1938 manifesto "Long Live Degenerate Art!" They refuted Adolf Hitler's racist and propagandist attack on modern art during the 1937 "Entartete Kunst" exhibition in Munich, and their exhortation gave Europeans a way to respond outside of Fascist, Communist, and Capitalist paradigms. The Nazi exhibition featured works by Pablo Picasso, Henri Matisse, and Max Ernst, all mocked as degenerate and the product of Jewish Bolsheviks. Over 4,000 of the artworks were eventually burned in anti-Semitic and anti-Communist campaigns. The next year, *Art et Liberté* released the "Long Live Degenerate Art" manifesto in Cairo signed by several Egyptian authors and artists, including Henein and Cossery, who used a variant anglicized spelling of his name. This manifesto was translated and published in periodicals across Europe, including England in the *London Bulletin* through E. L. T. Mesens, who had co-organized the 1936 London exhibition. Later, in 1944, the poet George Leite founded the magazine *Circle* in Berkeley, California. It was an Anarchist, anti-Fascist project, which he co-edited with Bern Porter, a physicist who had been involved in the Manhattan Project but became a publisher of West Coast poetry. Leite also opened daliel's bookshop and gallery in Berkeley, which prefigured the famous City Lights Books and was an early venue for the authors of the San Francisco Renaissance. This was the so-called "cult of sex and anarchy." The great surprise, however, is to find Leite in California publishing Henein's poetry as well as the first

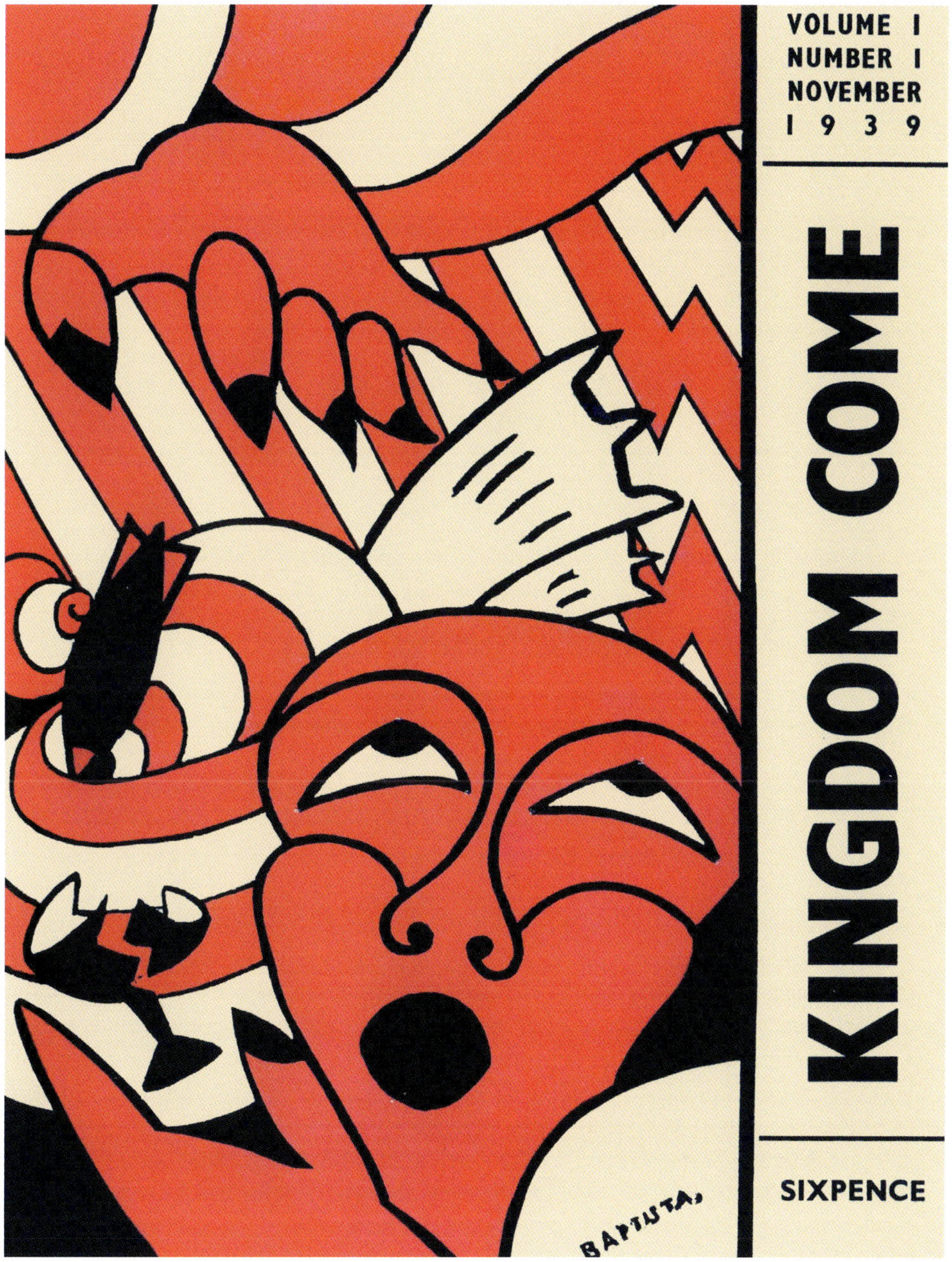

BAPTISTA GILLIAT-SMITH
Cover illustration
for *Kingdom Come*
no. 1.1, November 1939
Printed journal
McPherson Library,
University of Victoria

English translation of Cossery's novel *Men God Forgot.* Even more surprising is the densely entangled network of artists from Cairo and Alexandria who brought their work through Athens, London, Paris, New York, and San Francisco. The bridge between these two worlds, it turns out, was composed of the English Post-Surrealists who were scattered by the war after formulating an anarchist vision of Surrealism that marked their difference from (and rejection of) the politics of the Parisian Surrealists and the then dominant Auden Generation of authors, perhaps best seen in relation to Christopher Caudwell and Breton's collaboration with Leon Trotsky.

The American novelist (and later also painter) Henry Miller moved into 18 villa Seurat, Paris, in 1934. He took over Antonin Artaud's rooms in the villa named for Georges Seurat, where he was surrounded by other artists and writers. The next year, his infamous *Tropic of Cancer* led him into a correspondence with the British art critic and writer Herbert Read about art, Surrealism, Communism, and finally Anarchism. It was Miller's reaction to the Communist affinities of the 1936 London International Surrealist Exhibition that gave Read one of his final prompts to declare himself for Anarchism, and Miller's essay "An Open Letter to Surrealists Everywhere" outlined what an anarchist Post-Surrealism might take up for its concerns. The confluence of thought and circumstance shaped much work that followed and redirected many of the English Surrealists by giving them a pathway to an Anarchist Post-Surrealism. In the same year that *Art et Liberté* published "Long Live Degenerate Art," the novelist Lawrence Durrell published his Post-Surrealist novel *The Black Book,* the English poet and translator of the Surrealists David Gascoyne left the Communist Party and Spain to increasingly fall under Miller's influence (reading both the "Open Letter" and *Black Book* in manuscript), and by 1940 the New Apocalypse movement in Britain was disseminating an Anarchist Post-Surrealist movement to develop forward from Miller's provocations and with Read's vital support in the art world and among London publishers.

This might seem coincidental, and we cannot be sure if these English-language Post-Surrealists actually read the French or English versions of "Long Live Degenerate Art" that appeared in the *London Bulletin,* although their own works appeared there as well, and it was the most important surrealist publication in England after Roger Roughton's *Contemporary Poetry & Prose.* We do know, however, that when World War II began and Durrell fled from Greece to Egypt barely ahead of the Nazi invasion, and when a number of English poets from these movements were also sent to Cairo (with Miller's works, shockingly, held in the Servicemen's libraries), their activities exploded. Amy Smart (née Nimr), in whose salon *Art et Liberté* exhibited works, also translated and wrote about the Greek poet C. P. Cavafy for the English poets' journal in Cairo, *Personal Landscape.* Durrell would later lament not including Henein and Cossery in the same publication, though he wrote a tribute to Henein in 1974 and during the war defended Cossery from unwanted attention from American intelligence while lending him financial support. When Henein's poem "There Are No Pointless Jests" later appeared in Leite's anarchist magazine *Circle* in California after the war, it was in the same issue as Henry Miller's boost for Cossery's novel *Men God Forgot,* which was published by Circle Editions and sent to California for publication by Durrell. Miller made the pathway clear when he praised Cossery's depiction of the poor of Cairo and the book's irreligiosity that made it unpublishable in Egypt as "This terrible breviary, dispatched to us from Alexandria by Lawrence Durrell." The English poets in the same network, Erik de Mauny and Harold Edwards, both translated Cossery into English, publishing him in Cairo, London, and San Francisco during and after the war.

For Henein, these ties run deeply as well. His "There Are No Pointless Jests" was translated for *Circle* by the British surrealist painter Ithell Colquhoun, who had broken with the English Surrealists at the same moment as the New Apocalypse poets began in London. This fracture led to her poetry appearing through the *Fortune Anthology* along with Durrell and Miller as well as other writers from the New Apocalypse and Villa Seurat group, edited by the Apocalyptic poet Nicholas Moore. Colquhoun's role as translator is doubly complicated by her credit identifying her as "the wife of Toni del Renzio," who also broke with Mesens and the Surrealist core in London. After 1940, not only was this wide younger generation of Post-Surrealists breaking new ground through anarchist paradigms and open form based on their different understanding of subjectivity and social life, they were doing so in a widely distributed yet resilient network of mutual support spanning the globe.

These deep ties between the English Post-Surrealist movements and the Egyptian *Art et Liberté* are especially striking since they trace the outlines of *Art et Liberté*'s internationalism: both its distribution and the sympathetic resources on which it could draw during the war years in Egypt. This outward reach also places Henein and Cossery in a network made up of a younger generation of authors than the French Surrealists. It was a generation dispersed by the war and without access to the same kind of editorial authority their seniors could command after the end of the war. But at the same time, they were connected and prepared for an unprecedented dissemination of new literature around the world through personal networks that shared an antiauthoritarian if not openly Anarchist ethos and sympathies. Amidst the Europeans and Egyptians there were also Chinese artists tied to the New Apocalypse while students in Oxford, such as Xiao Qian and Xiao Gongquan, who publishing through the experimental student journal *Kingdom Come* and other Apocalyptic venues before revolution would bring them back to China and close the Shanghai journal *Tianxia Monthly.* This is a very different Surrealism than had come to London in 1936. And the network was also American.

While Henry Miller's Anarchist provocations had sparked a change in Herbert Read's thinking, which in turn led to his role as intellectual father of the New Apocalypse, Miller was also provoking others in America with Post-Surrealist interests. The young poet Robert Duncan began to publish Miller and Durrell in his journal *Experimental Review* out of Woodstock, New York, before the war. The connection was again through anarchism, and Duncan repeatedly planned editions of Durrell's Post-Surrealist stories "Zero" and "Asylum in the Snow" and novel *The Black Book* with illustrations by the painter Virginia Admiral, although these only came to fruition through the same Circle Editions in Berkeley as published Cossery. Durrell signed the contract with Circle in Alexandria on September 24, 1945, and Leite signed his on November 20, 1945, with a copy from Curtis Brown dispatched on January 3, 1946, which makes the entire process precisely the same timeframe as Circle's production of Cossery and Henein, with all of their works appearing within the span of a handful of months. The interaction between British translators and correspondents with American publishers and boosters and the Egyptian *Art et Liberté* draws tight. Duncan remained actively involved with *Circle* and Leite with his major poem "The Years as Catches," which first appeared in the same issue as Henein and Miller's review of Cossery, and while this is three years before Duncan's relationship with the artist Jess Collins, visual art increasingly played a role in the magazine as well. The Anarchist poet Kenneth Rexroth also supported the journal and anthologized the British Anarchists while identifying their internationalism in his major work *The New British Poets.* Likewise, Jean Varda, whose Anarchist artist commune in France has influenced Miller, was also a contributor. He gave work for *Circle*'s cover and the issue with Henein, he was featured in it for a study of his work, and he showed his own and his students' work in exhibitions as Leite's daliel's bookshop gallery. That Miller had lived in Varda's Anarchist commune in France and again in Big Sur, for a time with Leite as well, narrows the group considerably.

This network around *Art et Liberté* alters our approach to their art and writings. It privileges their extensive network of connections to Anarchist late modernist movements—it becomes, for instance, impossible not to notice the absence of Georges Henein's Anarchist writings from his *Œuvres. Poésies, récits, essais et articles* (2006). This otherwise excellent collection gives readers a vision of Henein in relation to André Breton without Anarchism, it removes Herbert Read's understanding of open form as antiauthoritarian in abstract art, and it leaves an activist art in the same moment as the Spanish Civil War with a very different set of allegiances. The sense of art as a hammer to make change rather than a mirror to gauge the world would seem to set *Art et Liberté* closer to Trotsky, especially given Breton and Trotsky's 1938 manifesto "For An Independent Revolutionary Art." And indeed, this is generally how it has been interpreted. Yet it demands more.

When Henein writes "that modern society looks with aversion on any innovative creation in art and literature which threatens the cultural system on which that society is based," this sense of art as an agent of change is clear. What does not appear in his *Oeuvres,* however, is the antiauthoritarian impulse that is made clear in 1945 by his further contention in "Manifesto." While "Long Live Degenerate Art!" could be read by the light (or under the shadow) of Trotsky and Breton's "For an Independent Revolutionary Art," Henein's later articulation makes the distinction plain: "Our position regarding Marxism is the inverted reflection of that adopted by Marxist groups towards the individual, freedom and the activities arising from literary or artistic creation in general." The individual as a unit of value, an active agent with self-possession, is the link to the English Post-Surrealists displaced to Egypt and the "Personalists" under the sway of Miller's Villa Seurat group who had fled from Greece and founded the poetry journal *Personal Landscape* in Cairo (astonishingly, with virtually no direct reference to the war in any of its eight issues, which sets the personal outside of the political). The matter is resolute in Henein's call to action and reflects the fracture between anarchists and Marxists after Spain:

> Our grievance against Marxism lies not in its leaning towards revolution, but on the contrary, to its taking a starchy, stagnant, reactionary stance . . . We consider the individual as the only thing of worth, yet today, seemingly, it is under relentless fire from all sides. We declare that the individual is in possession of largely unexplored inner faculties, the most important of which is imagination . . .
> The individual against State-Tyranny.
> Imagination against the routine of dialectical materialism.
> Freedom against terror in all its forms.

This 1945 clarification of "Long Live Degenerate Art!" does not so much open new terrain as it stresses what "freedom" had meant in *Art et Liberté*—"liberty" had been closer to Bakunin and Proudhon than to Marx and Lenin or even Trotsky. Ramses Younane added his signature to the declaration, and while Cossery did not, his own anarchism became increasingly overt in his novels after *Men God Forget*, such that the radical revolutionary in *The Jokers* clarifies the focus of his critique of poverty and the urban slum in his earlier *The House of Certain Death*, a work again translated by the British poets displaced to Egypt during the war and trumpeted by their Anarchist colleagues in America. Henein renewed the same sentiments in tandem with pacifism in "The Prestige of Terror," again in 1945.

There is, of course, even more that stitches these seemingly disparate groups together. John Waller was a student in Oxford before the war, where he founded the journals *Bolero* and *Kingdom*

Come, the latter succeeding the former and including a cover image on all issues of revulsion over war—after publishing Anarchist works in their pages, he turned the project over to the Anarchist New Apocalypse when he left for Egypt. From Cairo and with de Mauny, Waller included Cossery in his *Middle East Anthology* using a story previously published by the New Apocalypse's essayist and poet G. S. Fraser's—Fraser had published it in his servicemen's journal *Orientations.* Cossery's "The Human Sound of the Street" and "The Postman Gets His Own Back" appeared in Waller's collection between the contributions of the two editors. Cossery's work was also placed between two stories by Stefano Terra, whom both Waller and Fraser knew well and with whom Fraser worked in intelligence and propaganda. "Terra" was the pseudonym of Giulio Tavernari, the Italian anti-fascist activist who edited the journal *Quaderni di Giustizia e libertà* in Cairo in affiliation with the Italian Justice and Freedom movement, which supported the Anarchists in the Spanish Civil War. Tavernari later served Italian radio in Belgrade at the same time as Durrell's post-war service in Yugoslavia, both of them subverting Tito's communist regime, and the stories were most likely translated by Fraser's friend Hamish Henderson who was also translating Antonio Gramsci while in Egypt.

But where does this leave us when we encounter *Art et Liberté*? Like Henein's iconic self-photograph strewn across a rail track and smoking, the lone individual may confront the seemingly irresistible force racing toward him. Or he may derail it. Regardless of which, the individual demands our attention and leads our eye down a path that is ever winding, moving abroad in connection with other individuals, each down the track, independent yet connected. It is rich, but it also makes us look differently to the Post-Surrealisms in London, in San Francisco, in Shanghai, in Berkeley, in New York, in Paris, in Athens, and on down the long tracks vanishing to the horizon. It enriches. It shows an Egyptian movement that drew from far more sources than just Trotsky and Breton as well as a fecund Egyptian influence outward to the world, planting seeds of provocation that grew and spread to germinate again and again. ■

BIBLIOGRAPHY

Brady, Mildred Edie. "The New Cult of Sex and Anarchy." *Harper's Magazine* 194 (April 1947).

Cossery, Albert. *The House of Certain Death.* Translated by Erik de Mauny. London: Hutchinson International, 1947.

——. "The Human Sound of the Street." *Orientations* (September 1943).

——. *Men God Forgot.* Trans. Harold Edwards. Berkeley: Circle Editions, 1946.

——. "The Postman Gets His Own Back." *Middle East Anthology.* Edited by John Waller and Erik de Mauny. London: Lindsay Drummond, 1946.

Durrell, Lawrence. *The Black Book.* Paris: Obelisk Press, 1938.

——. "Georges Henein." *Hommage à Georges Henein: dernier cahier de littérature appliquée.* Cairo: La part du sable, 1974.

Gifford, James. *Personal Modernisms: Anarchist Networks and the Later Avant-Gardes.* Edmonton: University of Alberta Press, 2014.

Miller, Henry. *Max and the White Phagocytes.* Paris: Obelisk Press, 1938.

Nimr, Amy. "The Poetry of Cavafy." *Personal Landscape* vol. 2, no. 4 (1945).

Rosemont, F., et al. *Black, Brown, & Beige: Surrealist Writings from Africa and the Diaspora.* Austin: University of Texas Press, 2009.

Henein, Georges. "Long Live Degenerate Art!" *London Bulletin* 13 (April 1938).

——. "There Are No Pointless Jests." *Circle* 7–8 (1946).

Waller, John, and Erik de Mauny, eds. *Middle East Anthology of Prose & Verse.* London: Lindsay Drummond, 1946.

THE *ART AND LIBERTY* GROUP: RUPTURE, WAR AND SURREALISM IN EGYPT (1938 – 1948)

SAM BARDAOUIL

To curate an exhibition on the *Art and Liberty* Group is to imagine anew the definition, expression, and the overall canon of Surrealism. The mechanisms of visual and literary display by which artists are framed and through which knowledge is created ultimately lead to the creation of the canon.

With increasing stature that is multiplied by the passage of time, the canon becomes tradition. As Keith Moxey has expressed it: "The conviction underlying these attitudes, which continue to be widespread, if not even prevalent in art history today, is the commitment to tradition. . . . we are often unwittingly engaged in the unthinking reproduction of culture: reproducing knowledge, but not necessarily producing it."[1] One of *Art and Liberty*'s most striking attributes is their refusal to succumb to tradition and the passive reproduction of inherited canons: both the internal one that exalted Egypt's modern hero-artists as necessitated by the local national project, and the external one, which in advancing a fixed notion of what Surrealism is and looks like, relegated them to the margins, or excluded them all together.

Ever since such narratives have been set, there have been several corrective interventions that have sought to remedy this historical injustice, to re-insert the achievements of the so-called "Other" into the mainstream canon, often perceived as exclusively written by the so-called "West." This is where historicism could become problematic. Therefore, for an "aesthetic re-creation," to use Panofskian terms, of *Art and Liberty*'s work and consequent contributions to be achieved, art historians and curators must be cautious not to allow their participation in the contemporary polemical positions that are driving the discourse surrounding history and its wiring today, to encroach upon and dictate their evaluation of former artists and movements subscribing to a set of cultural and political parameters that were the product of their own distinct era.[2]

A thorough investigation of *Art and Liberty*'s achievements is a timely initiative necessary to remedy the blurred historicisms from which they have suffered. For instance, in moments of heightened Nasserite Egyptian nationalism and pan-Arabism, Egyptian art historians had located them at opposite ends of the spectrum, either as "imitators and followers of European thought"[3] or as "genuine upholders of Egyptian identity," while, all along, *Art and Liberty* had considered themselves members of an international network of artists who were immersed in shared artistic

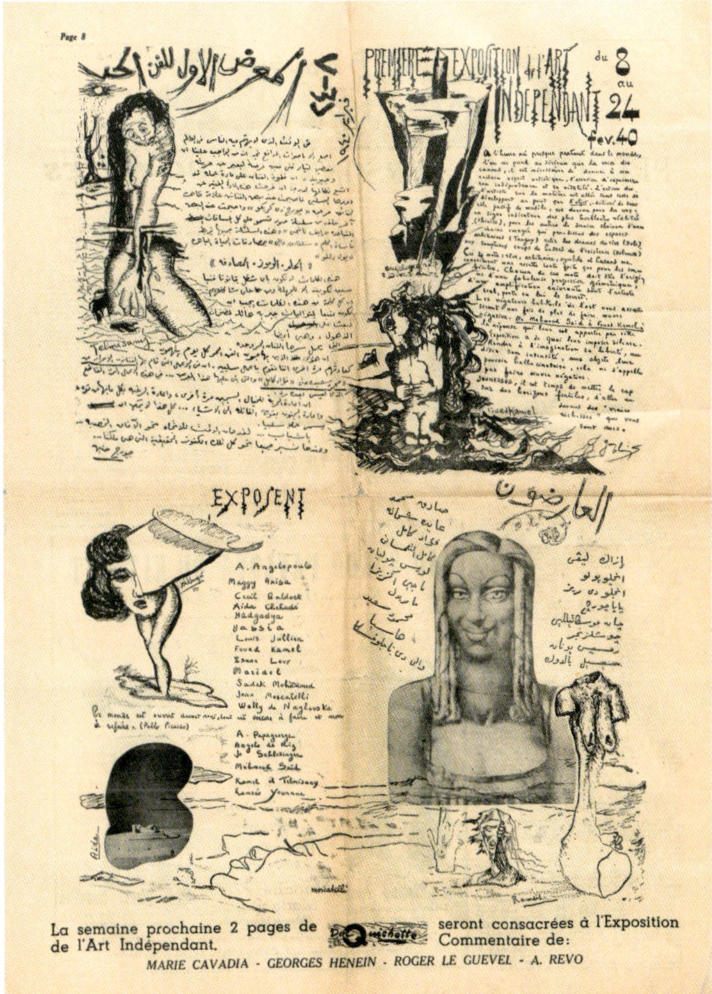

Page 8

PREMIERE EXPOSITION de l'ART INDEPENDANT du 8 au 24 fev. 40

EXPOSENT

La semaine prochaine 2 pages de l'Art Indépendant. seront consacrées à l'Exposition Commentaire de:
MARIE CAVADIA - GEORGES HENEIN - ROGER LE GUEVEL - A. REVO

1

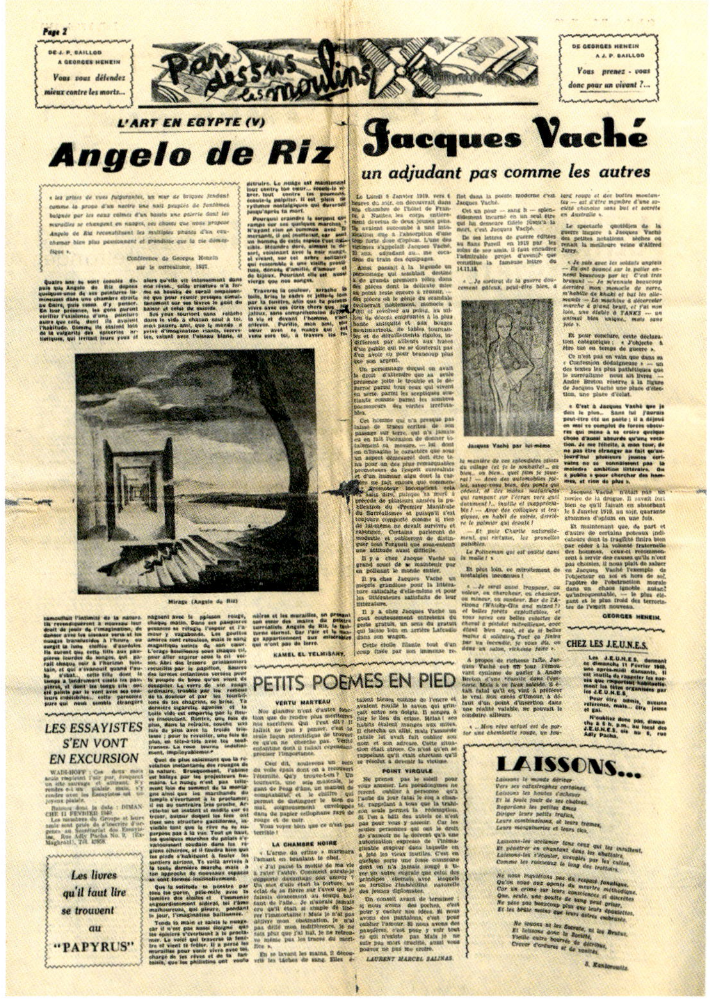

Page 2

DE J.-P. SAILLOR A GEORGES HENEIN Vous vous défendez mieux contre les morts...

Par dessus les moulins

DE GEORGES HENEIN A J.-P. SAILLOR Vous prenez - vous donc pour un vivant ?...

L'ART EN EGYPTE (V)

Angelo de Riz

Jacques Vaché
un adjudant pas comme les autres

Mirage (Angelo de Riz)

PETITS POEMES EN PIED

LES ESSAYISTES S'EN VONT EN EXCURSION

Les livres qu'il faut lire se trouvent au "PAPYRUS"

CHEZ LES J.E.U.N.E.S.

LAISSONS...

2

and intellectual pursuits, social and political implications not withstanding, and who were simultaneously engaged, from Cairo, with the modernist challenges that were being discussed in a number of locations such as New York, Mexico City, and Paris, just to name a few. Failing to recognize these central qualities, opting to coerce the example of *Art and Liberty* into the polemics of post-colonial rhetoric, seems to me contradictory to the way that they actually perceived themselves, and would be rendering them grave disservice. Instead of picturing them as victims to a marginalizing Western-centrism, it is more adequate to highlight their role as active catalysts who contributed to the evolution and widening up of the formalistic qualities of Surrealism at the time. This timely exhibition, for which Till Fellrath and I have put together more than two hundred artworks and archival documents assembled over more than five years of research and drawn from across the globe, is an attempt to do just that.

What is *Art and Liberty*'s story, who were its protagonists, why did they embrace Surrealism as their modus operandi, what could we learn from their legacy, and how, like all good stories must, did theirs come to an end? There are no better, simpler, and more straightforward words with which to begin answering these questions than the ones uttered by Georges Henein in 1945 as part of a performance act through which he greeted the baffled visitors to *Art and Liberty*'s fifth exhibition of independent art: "Begin at the beginning."[5] And so we shall . . . The beginning here is befittingly located on February 8, 1940, the date on which the group's first exhibition opened its doors to the Cairene public. In one of the exhibition's several pamphlets, *Art and Liberty* declared:

1
Don Quichotte, hebdomadaire d'actualité paraissant le jeudi,
no. 10, February 8, 1940. Page 8
Bibliothèque de Documentation Internationale Contemporaine (BDIC), Paris

2
Don Quichotte, hebdomadaire d'actualité paraissant le jeudi,
no. 10, February 8, 1940. Page 2
Bibliothèque de Documentation Internationale Contemporaine (BDIC), Paris

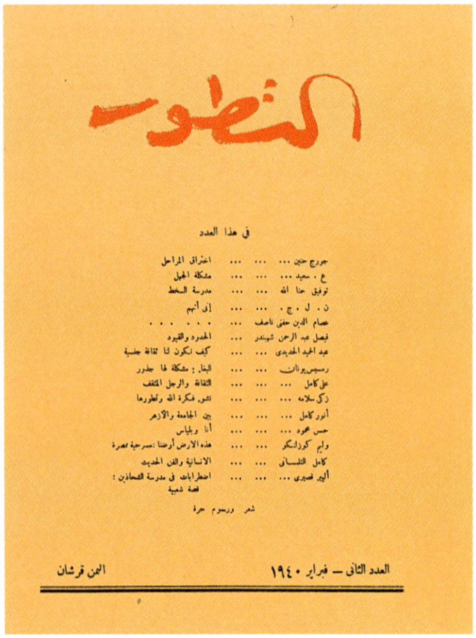
التطور

في هذا العدد

جورج حنين ... ... اختراق المراحل
ع. سعيد ... ... مشكلة الجيل
توفيق حنا الله ... ... مدرسة السخط
ن. ل. ج. ... ... إلى أيهم
عصام الدين حفني ناصف ... .
فيصل عبد الرحمن شهبندر ... الحدود والقيود
عبد الحميد الحديدي ... ... كيف نكون لنا ثقافة جنسية
رمسيس يونان ... ... البغاء: مشكلة لها جذور
علي كامل ... ... الثقافة والرجل المثقف
زكي سلامه ... ... نشوء فكرة الله وتطورها
أنور كامل ... ... بين الجامعة والأزهر
حسن محمود ... ... أنا وبلياس
وليم كوزلنكو ... ... هذه الأرض أرضنا: مسرحية مصرية
كامل التلمساني ... ... الانسانية والفن الحديث
ألبير قصيري ... ... اضطرابات في مدرسة الشحاذين: قصة شعبية

شعر ورسوم حرة

العدد الثاني — فبراير ١٩٤٠ الثمن قرشان

3

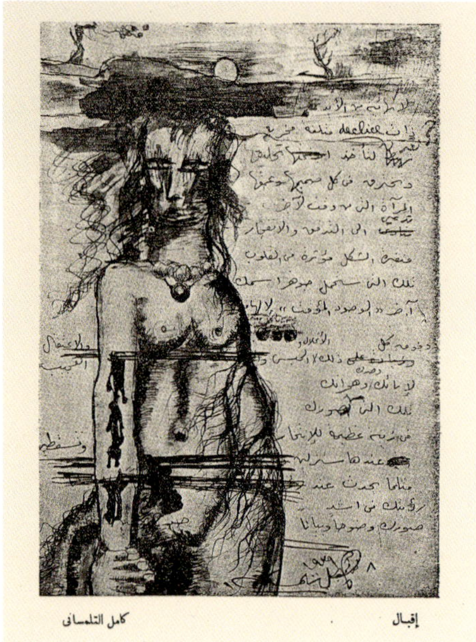

4

In this hour, when the entire world cares for nothing but the voice of canons, we have found it our duty to provide a certain artistic current with the opportunity to express its freedom and its vitality.[6]

With these words, from the margins of the local cultural mainstream, a group of young and determined artists and writers, women and men, Egyptian and otherwise, were communicating one of their central tenets, one that was unmistakably artistic, yet equally political. They called themselves the *Art and Liberty* Group. With these words, they introduced the first of their five seminal exhibitions (1940–45), all mounted in the thick of World War II (ill. 1–2). This was happening in Cairo, a city of many cities, and of clusters of astonishingly dissimilar neighborhoods where the disparity between rich and poor was unfathomable, and the widening gap between a worldly bourgeoisie and a marginalized working class was increasingly unbridgeable. Merely six months after Britain and France had declared war on Germany on September 3, 1939, this unruly bunch made it a point to conjure the perils of combat (*voice of canons*).

Through a few, but evocative words, *Art and Liberty* were reiterating a complex social project they had been articulating from the mid-1930s onward, and that they would continue to uphold for the better part of the remaining decade. From across the far side of the eleventh hour, this group of "misfits"[7] as the photographer Lee Miller used to call them, were expounding a conviction in an art that stems from a sense of responsibility instead of a position of privilege (*we have found it our duty to provide a certain artistic current*), that asserts its alignment against any form of confinement (*its freedom and its vitality*), and that does so right now, in the very present (*in this hour*). *Art and Liberty* rejected what they perceived as an imported academicism endorsed by a propaganda-seeking state/monarchy, rebelled against an oppressive colonial power, and broke away from a conservative bourgeois morality that celebrated art for art's sake. A decade later, not without scandal, several of the group's members would already end up in prison or in exile.

Art and Liberty was founded on December 22, 1938, by a predominantly young generation of Cairo-based artists, writers, and activists who were in the process of articulating a distinct vision for the correlation between art and social engagement. The main protagonists who gave *Art and Liberty* its initial thrust were the poet Georges Henein, and painter/critic turned-filmmaker Kamel El-Telmisany. They were accompanied by the Trotskyite writer Anwar Kamel and his younger brother, the painter Fuad Kamel. The theorist and painter Ramses Younane would soon

3
Al-Tatawwur, monthly periodical of the Art and Liberty Group, 1940
Print journal
Henein - Farhi collection, Neuilly-sur-Seine

4
Al-Tatawwur, monthly periodical of the Art and Liberty Group, no. 1, January 1940
Illustration by Kamel El-Telmisany of Georges Henein's poem
Henein - Farhi collection, Neuilly-sur-Seine

join them. Together, they would become the main face of the group. Each would bring to it a different yet complimentary attribute. While Henein secured the group with proliferating international networks comprising fellow Surrealist writers and artists, El-Telmisany, Younane, and Fouad Kamel bestowed on it the rootedness that it needed to take wing within its local cultural milieu. Anwar Kamel would serve as the editor of its short-lived periodical *Al-Tatawwur* (Evolution) and mainly spearhead the group's political and social reform program. (ills. 3–4) Surrealism, a movement that *Art and Liberty* considered to be "still in the phase of experimentation"[8] would be the tool that they would use to achieve their reformatory aims. The group's deliberation of Surrealism allowed them to achieve a contemporary pictorial and literary language that was as much globally engaged as it was rooted in local artistic and political concerns. In doing so, they opened up the Surrealist canon, infusing it with a broader range of pictorial and literary styles. They also coined new terms for Surrealism such as "Free Art" and "Subjective Realism," providing the movement with a renewed definition vis-à-vis its theory and expression. But, how did Surrealism arrive to Egypt, and who were the main protagonists responsible for its dissemination?

SURREALISM IN EGYPT: THE EARLY PROTAGONISTS

There is no doubt as to the central position of Surrealist poet Georges Henein when it comes to the introduction of Surrealism to Egypt. Every respective historiography, and there are not many of them, locates or at least references the seminal lecture entitled *Bilan du Mouvement Surréaliste* that he delivered in Cairo on February 4, 1937, as a quasi-official inauguration of Surrealism in Egypt.[9] It is, however, important to note that Henein's Surrealist and leftist leanings begin to surface in 1935 through his contributions to two publications: *Un Effort,*[10] a monthly periodical published in Cairo by *Les Essayistes*, a Francophone literary group, and *Les Humbles,*[11] a Marxist-Leninist journal that was printed in Paris. Henein, who also dabbled with photography and installation art (ill. 8), had started introducing Surrealist ideas into Egypt from as early as 1934 through various publications such as his Surrealist play *Suite et Fin* (1934). This was followed in 1935 by his collection of Surrealist poems *Le Rappel à l'ordure* (1935), a collaboration with Jo Farna (Joseph El-Habachi), and various articles appearing in *Un Effort.* (ill. 5–6).

Henein's father, Sadek Henein Pacha, was an Egyptian diplomat. His mother was Italian-Egyptian Mary Zanelli. His father's career meant that Henein would spend his childhood between Cairo, Madrid, Rome, and Paris where he eventually completed his secondary education at the Lycée Pasteur de Neuilly and went on to study at the Sorbonne (ill. 7). This early cosmopolitanism allowed him to equally master Arabic, Italian, Greek, English, and French. This in turn enabled him to navigate the various worlds in which he roamed with the ease and confidence of a "*flâneur des deux mondes*."[12]

In 1936, Henein met Breton. In a letter dated April 8, 1936, Breton already revealed to Henein his awareness of the latter's efforts to promulgate Surrealism in Egypt: "The imp of the perverse, as he deigns to appear to me, seems to have one wing here, the other in Egypt."[13] From there on, Henein would become the main conduit for developments on the international scene into the local circuit. Beyond his countless publications in tens of Surrealist and political reviews

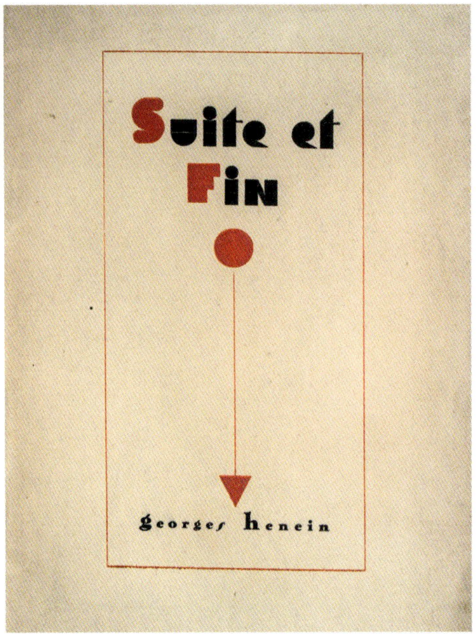

5

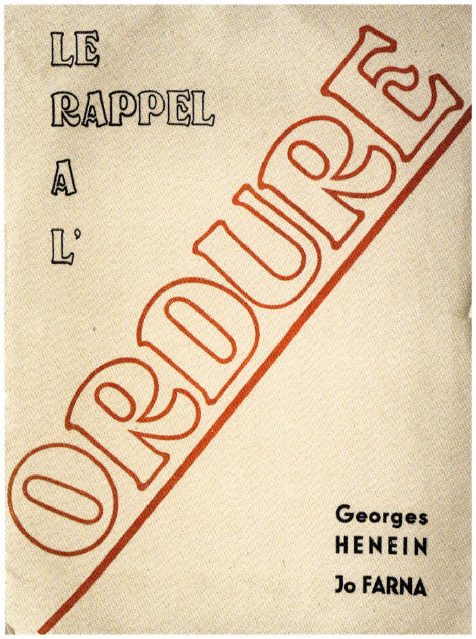

6

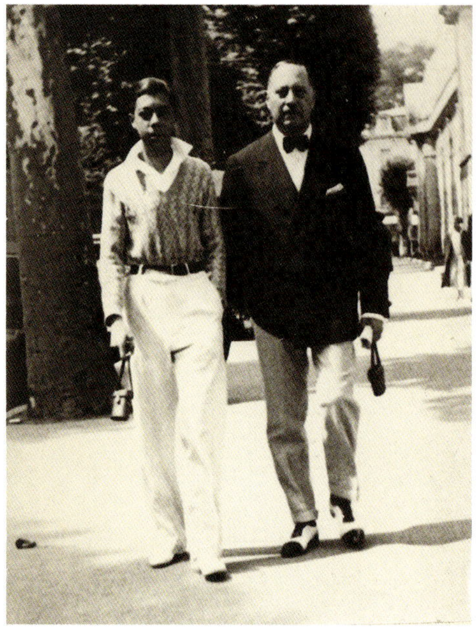

7

abroad, correspondence with a large number of fellow Surrealist writers and artists, one could cite numerous examples that reveal Henein as a pivotal link between *Art and Liberty* and their international counterparts. I am going to list but a few.

During a sojourn in Paris in 1936, Henein attended the Surrealist meetings that Breton called for to discuss and take a stand towards what became known as the Moscow Trials. A manifesto, or more precisely a declaration, entitled *La Vérité Sur Le Procès de Moscou* was read by Breton in a meeting on September 3, 1936, and was signed by those present. Henein was one of the signatories. So was Yves Tanguy, one of the main organizers whose famous poem "L'Évidence poétique" would later appear in the first issue of the *Art and Liberty* Group's periodical *Al-Tatawwur.* In a letter to Henri Calet from December 1938, Henein asks his friend if he could pass on *Art and Liberty*'s manifesto of December 22, 1938, entitled *Long Live Degenerate Art* that was circulated "yesterday" to the *Nouvelle Revue Française.*[14] Calet obliged and a short announcement was printed in the issue of February 1, 1939, with the heading "The East is working for the defense of Western culture." Similarly, in February 1939, a short text announcing the founding of *Art et Liberté* appeared in the second issue of *Clé*, the Fédération Internationale de l'Art Révolutionnaire Indépendant (FIARI) bulletin that was published in French from Paris[15]. The same issue included a text of literary criticism on Franz Kafka's *The Castle* by Henein.[16] The previous issue also included a text by Henein, this time a review of Marcel Jouhandeau's book *Chroniques Maritales* (Marital Chronicles).[17] *Art and Liberty*'s manifesto would also get republished in the April 15, 1939 issue of *The London Bulletin* due to Henein's friendship with Roland Penrose, one of the journal's founders and a leading figure in British Surrealism. All of the above citations are but a few indicators of an ongoing trail of correspondence, publication, travel, and participation that points towards a simultaneous involvement with Surrealist matters on both sides of the Mediterranean that was made possible through a close network of friendships and personal acquaintances. Henein was undoubtedly at the center of that network.

Besides Henein, and in some ways preceding him, there were two other seminal protagonists who played an integral role in the introduction and diffusion of Surrealist thought, literature, and art in Egypt. These were the artists Antoine Malliarakis, otherwise known as Mayo, and Lee Miller. Their connections with various Surrealist figures, and their own artistic practices that were rooted in Surrealist aesthetics, paved the way for Henein's activities allowing for Surrealism's seeds to flourish in Egypt.

5
Georges Henein, *Suite et Fin*, 1934
Hardback book
Institut Dominicain d'Études Orientales, Cairo

6
Georges Henein and Jo Farna,
Le Rappel à l'ordure, 1935
Hardback book
Institut Dominicain d'Études Orientales, Cairo

7
Georges Henein and his father in Rome,
c. 1926
Photographer unknown,
Vintage gelatin silver print
Henein - Farhi collection, Neuilly-sur-Seine

8
GEORGES HENEIN
Surrealist Portrait of Ikbal El-Alaily, c. 1945
Vintage gelatin silver print
8.7 x 13.9 cm
Henein - Farhi collection, Neuilly-sur-Seine

From as early as 1934, Surrealist painter Mayo created the illustrations for *Pieds en l'air* (Cairo: Éditions de La Semaine Égyptienne, 1934) by *Art and Liberty* affiliate Edmond Jabès. Mayo provides us with a significant example of the entry of Surrealism into the Cairene art scene in the years preceding the formation of *Art and Liberty*, and as such deserves special attention. Born in 1905 in Port Said into a Greek-Egyptian family (ill. 10), Mayo spent most of the 1920s in Paris where his true artistic education, apart from the formal courses that he followed at the École des Beaux-Arts, took place at the Académie de la Grande Chaumière in Montparnasse, the heart of the Parisian avant-garde. It was in 1926 at 16 rue Jacques Callot, the address of the Surrealists' first gallery in the adjacent neighborhood of Saint-Germain-des-Prés, that Mayo made the acquaintance of Man Ray and in 1927 of Yves Tanguy.[18] There he witnessed, firsthand, the birth of Surrealism, and would forge a close friendship with two of its founding members, Robert Desnos and Georges Duhamel. By the time that Mayo would have his first exhibition in Egypt, which took place at the Cercle du Canal du Suez in Ismailia in December 1933 (ill. 9), he would have been already quite established among the Surrealist circles in Paris with several exhibitions to his name alongside some of the leading figures of the time such as André Masson and Giorgio de Chirico. One of Mayo's illustrations adorn the front cover of the November 30, 1933 issue of the Egyptian cultural review *La Semaine Égyptienne* accompanied by a note from the editors confirming that "Mayo, who comes to us from Paris, has been in contact with the best Surrealists"[19]. It was only a matter of time before Mayo and Henein's circles would begin to overlap, first in Cairo and then in Paris as the latter's Surrealist network was expanding, with several common friends between them such as the Serbian Jewish Surrealist poet Monny de Boully with whom Mayo was a member of the quasi-Surrealist group *Le Grand Jeu*.[20]

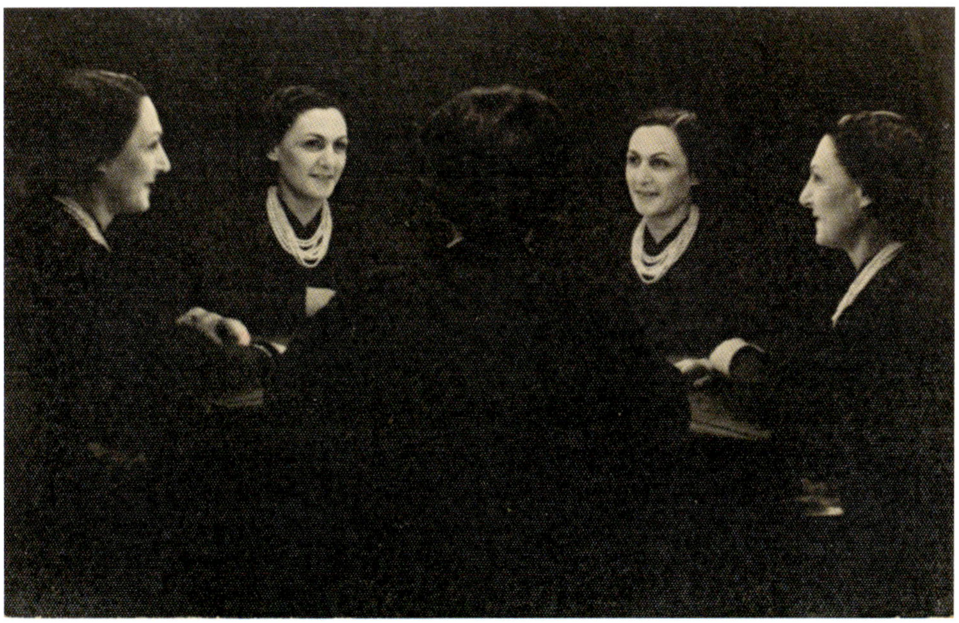

8

Mayo would spend the early years of the war from 1937–38 until 1941 in Cairo where he would continue to exhibit independently, creating some of his most striking Surrealist paintings such as *Portrait*, *Composition surréaliste*, *Coups de batons*, and *Dessin cruel*—all from 1937, *L'Union* from 1938, and *Souvenir de Sonia* from 1939. Upon the conclusion of the war, both Mayo and leading *Art and Liberty* painter Ramses Younane would exhibit at the Galerie Nina Duasset in Paris, another pointer to a tight circle of shared personal and professional acquaintances. Throughout his stays in Egypt, Mayo would continue to provide illustrations, Surrealist and otherwise, taking on a more dramatic and macabre character during the war years, to a number of writings by *Art and Liberty* members and affiliates such as Ivo Barbitch and Édmond Jabès, as well as to various articles of literary and art criticism.[21]

Photographer Lee Miller was the second artist to occupy an important position within this proto-Surrealist chain. She played an equally important role in introducing Surrealism to the Cairene arts scene. In 1933 Miller moved to Cairo upon marrying the wealthy Egyptian businessman Aziz Eloui Bey (ill. 11). For the last three years that Lee was in Cairo, she was actively engaged in introducing her Cairo friends to Surrealist ideas through "presenting the subject" by disseminating a broad range of Surrealist literature and reviews of Surrealist exhibitions supplied to her by Roland Penrose, with whom she had been having a long-distance love affair since the summer of 1937: "I have lent my Surrealist library to everyone in town and they are beginning to have ideas on the subject."[22] Kamel El-Telmisany's direct quote from an English translation by Penrose of Jean Scutenaire's article on Paul Delvaux that appeared in the June 1938 issue of *The London Bulletin* is a good example of how successful Miller was in placing

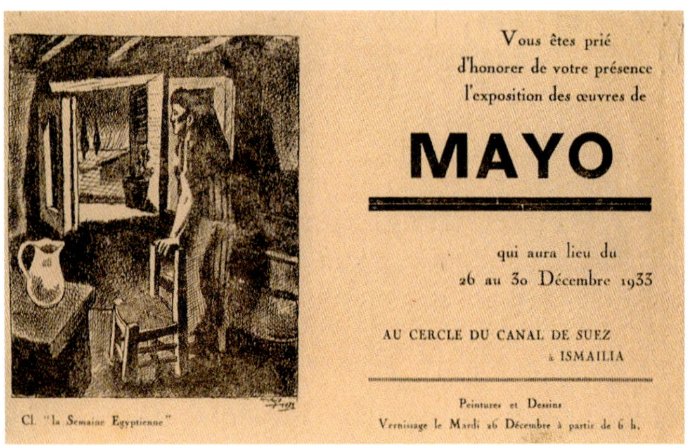
Vous êtes prié
d'honorer de votre présence
l'exposition des œuvres de
MAYO
qui aura lieu du
26 au 30 Décembre 1933
AU CERCLE DU CANAL DE SUEZ
à ISMAILIA
Peintures et Dessins
Vernissage le Mardi 26 Décembre à partir de 6 h.
Cl. "la Semaine Egyptienne"

9

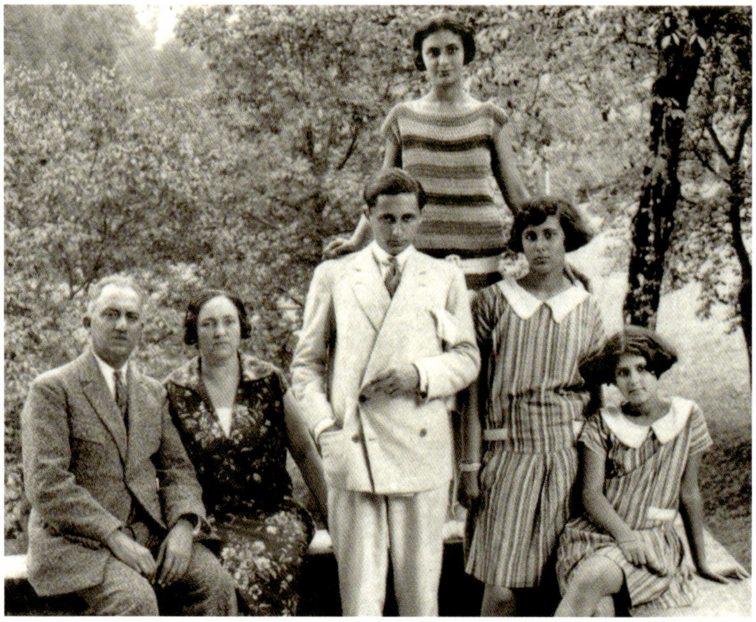

10

some of the latest Surrealist publications in the hands of *Art and Liberty* members.[23] Miller and various *Art and Liberty* members would also spend time in the western desert, which with its sand dunes, hot springs, rocky formations, and clusters of remote villages with ancient citadels and mud-brick dwellings, would serve as a creative pool inspiring several works of painting and photography (ill. 13). Furthermore, in several letters between Miller and Penrose, mostly throughout the years 1937 to 1939, we learn of a number of nighttime events where Miller, who was planning to launch a "Surrealist review with Maria Riaz [also known as Marie Cavadia], Henein and Santini,"[24] would engage in spontaneous drawing exercises and clairvoyance sessions with members and affiliates of the *Art and Liberty* Group.[25] On some of these occasions, some of them would come dressed in "Surrealist costumes which included gas masks and piss pots full of flowers."[26] There is enough evidence to suggest that these performances transcended the formal confines of the exhibition space or opening nights and were connected to a broader interest in investigating various means of unlocking the subconscious mind.

Through Miller, Roland Penrose, a leading figure within British Surrealism, would become acquainted with Henein and the *Art and Liberty* Group. It is evident, for instance, through his appointments diary from that period that he was a regular at the households of Amy Nimr, leading *Art and Liberty* artist and patron, and Surrealist poet and critic Marie Cavadia Riaz referred to in Miller's letter earlier. Cavadia had moved to Cairo upon marrying Egyptian minister Mamdouh Riaz.[27] She would actually be the one who would introduce Henein to Miller in January 1939, and in doing so, indirectly to Penrose[28] (ill. 12). Upon their introduction, Penrose would continue to meet with Henein on several occasions during the latter's frequent visits to Paris. Given their close connection, it comes as no surprise, therefore, that Penrose would preside over *Art and Liberty*'s general assembly of March 8, 1939, as we learn from the group's second bulletin of May 1939 (ill. 14). For the occasion, Penrose delivered a speech on the correlation between art and political activism against Fascism.[29] Penrose would then ensure that the full French and Arabic texts of *Long Live Degenerate Art, Art and Liberty*'s manifesto of December 22, 1938, get republished in the April 1939 issue of *The London Bulletin,* the periodical of the British Surrealists, with a preface entitled "From Egypt", penned by Penrose, that read: "The victories of Fascism do not fail to provoke reactions and awaken an activity which is creative as well as defensive. In Cairo a newly founded group *Art et Liberté* led by the Surrealist poets Georges Henein and Georges Santini and the painter Telmisany has recently published a manifesto in Arabic and French entitled 'Long Live Degenerate Art' containing a reproduction of Picasso's Guernica. (Overleaf is reproduced a facsimile of the Arabic, also the French text). It is signed by thirty-six intellectuals and has been widely distributed. In spite of a press boycott the group is constantly active, holding meetings and protesting vigorously when a new menace to their liberties becomes apparent. A Surrealist review is also in preparation."[30]

The multiple channels through which *Art and Liberty* and the British Surrealists exchanged ideas in their common search for a reworked version of Surrealism could not have happened without the role that Lee Miller played in connecting the two. Her dissemination of Surrealist ideas and practices, and the holding of Surrealist sessions whereby a young generation of Egyptian artists and writers could engage in games centered on the unlocking of the subconscious mind, fostered an environment that allowed *Art and Liberty* members to explore and experiment with various

9
Invitation Card to Mayo's first solo exhibition in Egypt from 16 to 30 December 1933 at the Circle du Canal de Suez in Esmailia
Ink on Carton
Yani Malliarakis collection, Paris

10
Mayo with his parents and sisters Hélène, Marguerite and Calliope, 1924
Photographer unknown,
Vintage gelatin silver print
Yani Malliarakis collection, Paris

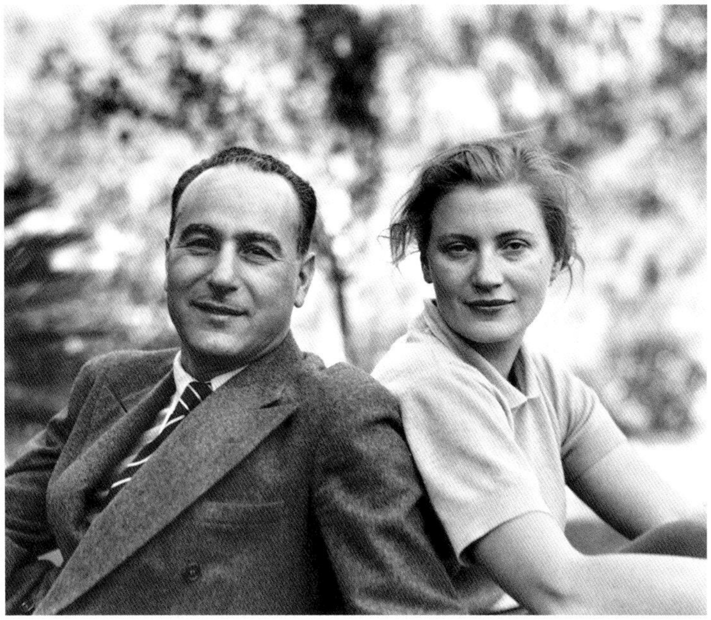

11

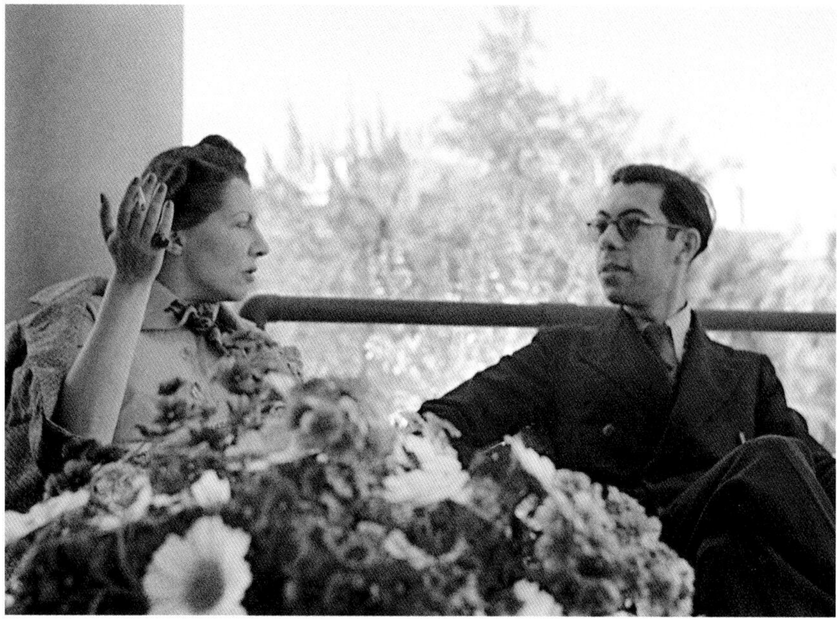

12

modes of performative events that would form a small part of a larger activity that they would go on to further explore in their controversial exhibitions.

Through such and various other activities whereby they employed a range of Surrealist tactics, *Art and Liberty* would launch their project of cultural and socio-political liberation. To better comprehend the reasons for this alignment, we need to briefly outline some of Surrealism's main tenets, tracing its trajectory since its formation from the late years of the 1910s and early 1920s until the onset of World War II, by which point it had arguably dissolved as an organized chapter in Europe and proliferated into a truly international movement. We equally need to shed light on the political and cultural environment within Egypt at the time when *Art and Liberty* emerged onto the local arts scene.

WHY SURREALISM . . .

It had taken a while for the Surrealists with whom *Art and Liberty* were in close dialogue, to arrive to where they were at by the late 1930s. From the early 1920s, the Surrealists had been articulating an aesthetic vision that was closely connected to social awareness: one that found its ultimate manifestation in the sphere of the real. They were initially primarily rebelling against the rational traditions that had hurled the world into the throws of World War I. At first, they found, or so they had thought, the perfect remedy in the exhibitionism and uncompromising nihilism of Dada through which they could unleash their "violent disgust at the old, narrow security" that governed all social orders.[31] "Violently disturbing"[32] was Breton's opinion of Tzara's 1918 manifesto. To the Dadaists, art and literature represented "the very image of society, consecrated by habit and smug self-satisfaction. How better to awaken men to a new awareness than by subjecting to ridicule the techniques and attitudes reflected in their art forms?"[33]

The opening up of language to elements of chance in challenging the exclusive authority that the poet had over the act of creation was completely overthrown by the collaborative poems of Tzara, Arp, and Serner.[34] Tzara's instructions on how to write a poem by randomly selecting snippets of jumbled words that had been cut out from a newspaper article would force the reader to look for meaning beyond the logic of syntax and semantics. The magazines and newspapers that constituted the bourgeois repertoire of printed communication would be irrevocably dis-

11
Aziz Eloui Bey and Lee Miller, Egypt, 1939
Photographer unknown
Modern digital print
Lee Miller Archives, England 2016

12
Georges Henein and Marie Cavadia, 1939
Photographer unknown
Vintage gelatin silver print
Lee Miller Archives, England 2016

torted, as they would get recruited for the creation of iconoclastic collages and photomontages.[35] Perhaps no other work better exemplifies Dada's attack on conservative tradition and stale academicism than Francis Picabia's 1920 *Natures Mortes: Portrait de Cézanne, Portrait de Renoir, Portrait de Rembrandt* in which he attached a stuffed monkey to the center of a canvas around which he wrote clockwise starting from the upper side: *Portrait de Cézanne, Portrait de Renoir, Natures Mortes,* and *Portrait de Rembrandt*, all of which could be read as conventional titles for paintings that the museum-going bourgeoisie would nd perfectly respectable.[36] All such subversions, along with scandalous performances such as, just to name a few, Picabia's *Festival Manifeste Presbyte* on March 27, 1920, where Breton appeared dressed up as a sandwich made of two boards with impertinent text written on them, or Festival Dada at Salle Gaveau on May 26 of that same year where the event was interrupted by an outraged audience hurling eggs and pennies at the Dada provocateurs, were to leave a major imprint on the psyche of the would-be-Surrealists.[37] Most significantly, it would instill in them a deep-seated awareness of the power of provocation through the summoning of the absurd in order to generate revolution; something that *Art and Liberty* excelled at through unconventional mechanisms of visual display and Surrealist performances that turned their independent solo and group art exhibitions, all mounted between 1938 and 1948 into platforms of protest that took Cairo by storm. Nevertheless, the Surrealists would soon be of the opinion that Dada's version of revolt did not exceed the level of instant gratification, and the pursuit of scandal for scandal's sake.

In 1922, Breton would publish a manifesto entitled *Après Dada* in which he declared: "I deplored the stereotyped character our gestures were assuming, and wrote as follows: After all there is more at stake than our carefree existence and our good humour of the moment. . . . It seems to me that the sanction of a series of utterly futile 'dada' acts is in danger of gravely compromising [our] attempt at liberation."[38] Breton and fellow Surrealists such as Philippe Soupault and Paul Éluard had come to the conclusion that Dada, having become trapped in an inventory-like stock of prescribed techniques, was no longer capable of bringing about the type of revolution that they saw increasingly pressing.[39] It was time for a change of strategy. In 1924 Breton published *Le Manifeste du Surréalisme,* clearly aligning Surrealism with the psychological theories of Sigmund Freud about dreams and the subconscious. Surrealism began strictly as a literary movement. Relying on Freudian techniques of free association, Surrealist literature drew upon the private terrains of the mind, resulting in unpredicted forms and images. The Surrealists believed that the protracted processes of making an artwork, be that a drawing, a painting, or a sculpture, was inherently opposed to the spontaneous, unbridled spontaneity of expression one could achieve through literature. Therefore, they were initially reluctant to align themselves with the visual arts. However, several artists such as Max Ernst, André Masson, and Joan Miró would soon join the movement heralding a number of new techniques such as automatic drawing, frottage, and decalcomania. Through *dépaysement,* meaning displacement, they fragmented familiar objects, depicting them within settings that were alien to their natural environments allowing them the possibility to be interpreted differently. The Surrealists also developed the *cadavre exquis* (exquisite cadaver), a technique of collective writing or drawing by which words or images are sequentially assembled where each collaborator builds on the contribution of the preceding one, while only allowed to see the end part of the previous input. A number of *Art and Liberty* artists would employ some of these techniques in their literary and pictorial work.

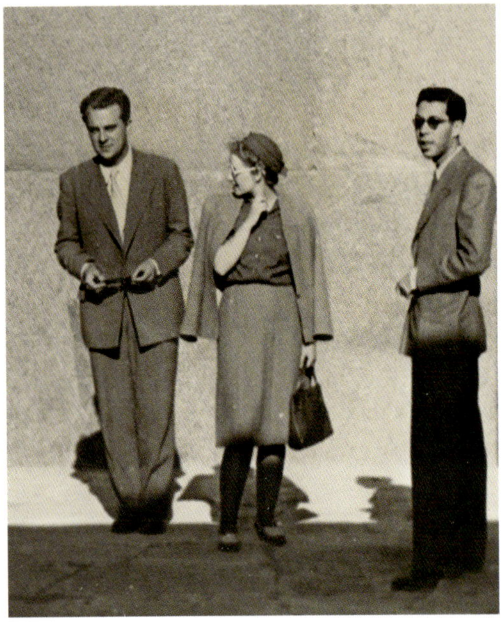

13

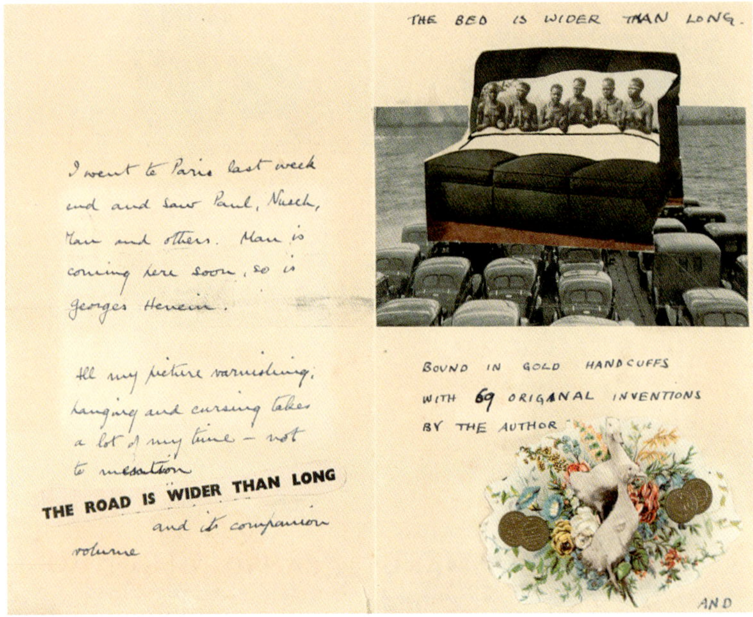

14

In 1929 the Surrealists ceased the publication of their main journal *La Révolution surréaliste* (1924–29), substituting it with *Le Surréalisme au service de la révolution* (1930–33). This was soon followed by the second manifesto of Surrealism, published by Breton in 1930. Surrealism was undergoing a shift in its political position from a complete non-alignment with a specific political ideology or party to an embrace of Marxism.[40] This was demonstrated in the joining of the French Communist Party by several key Surrealist figures. Breton himself had officially joined the party in 1927. The Surrealists endorsement of Stalinist Communism would prove very short. On one hand, the party never fully embraced the Surrealists as reliable members, disregarding them as an uncommitted bunch of flighty poets and artists. The Surrealists, who were more interested in the concept of revolution rather than the discipline required to achieving it, resented and ultimately rebelled against any form of literary and artistic censorship that the party dictated. By the mid-1930s, the Communists were imposing Social Realism as the official art form to be followed by artist party members. For the Surrealists, this was nothing but another form of fascism.

Beyond their artistic counter positions, the Surrealists and Stalinists would find themselves equally opposed on the question of the Moscow Trials to which I have already referred. Initiated by Stalin in 1936 and lasting until 1938, these were staged trials that Stalin used to purge his government from any oppositionists, with Leon Trotsky becoming the most emblematic. On September 3, 1936, in condemnation of these abominable acts, the Surrealists published their declaration *La Vérité sur le procès de Moscou.* Twelve leading Surrealists signed the tract. Georges Henein, as we have seen earlier, was one of them, along with Breton, Benjamin Péret, and Yves Tanguy, just to name a few. *La Vérité* marks a decisive rupture between Surrealism and Stalinism ushering in a new phase in the movement's rocky trajectory. It illustrates Surrealism's espousal of Trotskyism from the mid-1930s onward. This culminated in Breton's visit to Trotsky, now exiled in Mexico, in the summer of 1938. The result was the founding of FIARI (and the publication of its manifesto of July 25, 1938, *Pour un art révolutionnaire indépendant* ["For a Revolutionary, Independent Art"]. The manifesto was co-penned by Trotsky and Breton and signed by Breton and leading Mexican painter Diego Rivera. The FIARI manifesto and *Clé,* its monthly political bulletin, reflected the common grounds on which Surrealism and Trotskyite doctrine converged during the months leading up to the outbreak of World War II. They both insisted on the complete freedom of art and argued that no true revolutionary political program could dictate the form and content of a work of art, or impose a certain style or school on an artist. It was these emancipatory traits of Trotskyite Surrealism that made the movement appealing to *Art*

13
Georges Henein and Lee Miller in Siwa, c. 1939
Photographer unknown
Vintage gelatin silver print
Henein-Farhi collection, Neuilly-sur-Seine

14
Postcard from Roland Penrose to Lee Miller, 23-27 January 1939
Letter typed on paper
Lee Miller Archives, England

and Liberty, as well as to a wide range of artists and art collectives who, on the eve of World War II, were looking to initiate their own revolution.

By the late 1930s, what had started as an offshoot of Dada had proliferated into a truly international movement. The creative intersection that occurred between Surrealism, in and by itself defined by rupture and metamorphosis, and a heterogeneous array of distinct literary and artistic centers, resulted in the formation of places of encounter that fostered a renewed interpretation and application of Surrealism. Writers and artists in far-flung cities from across the globe were simultaneously re-envisioning Surrealism through the dual lens of literary and artistic innovation and political action. As far as *Art and Liberty* were concerned, the movement was not a fixed, static entity. On the one hand, it was a faltering art movement of different schools whose various evolving styles and methods had not arrived yet at one conclusive definition. On the other, it was a project of social revolution that was still figuring out how to articulate, in concrete terms, the tangible role that art could play in the implementation of that revolution. This is perhaps best expressed in the words of Ramses Younane, who, in describing Surrealism in 1938, wrote: "Since Surrealism is still in the phase of experimentation, it has not managed to discern its abilities and limitations, and is constantly hesitating in its methods. For sometimes it deviates towards the right and at other times to the left. It makes advances in one direction, but eventually retracts—like an archeologist who does not fully know where treasures hide or what treasures will the belly of the earth surprise him with."[41] Most significantly, Surrealism in 1938 was a movement in flux whose renewal *Art and Liberty* members felt as entitled to as any other Surrealists anywhere in the world. As a matter of fact, the movement had already been transplanted, negotiated and translated in several cities across the globe.

In Japan, for instance, from as early as 1925, translations of French Surrealist literature appeared in Japanese literary anthologies and reviews. Horiguchi Daigaku's survey of French poetry entitled *Gekka no ichigun* (A Multitude at Midnight), which included various Surrealist works by Soupault, Cocteau, and Goll, comes to mind. In 1937 Tokyo would host the second International Surrealist Exhibition, organized by the art journal *Mizué* and held at the Nippon Salon from June 9–14.[42] Around the same time, a group of self-confessed Surrealist writers such as Teófilo Cid, Enrique Gómez-Correa, and Braulio Arenas were self-organizing in Santiago de Chile around the literary journal *La Mandrágora.* On July 12, 1938, they would officially found a Surrealist group under the same name, which within the predominant socialist atmosphere that permeated Chile back then, would adopt a strong anti-Fascist stand.[43] Concurrently, Mexico was formulating its own engagement with and departure from Surrealism. Two years after the publication of the well-known FIARI manifesto of July 5, 1938, the fourth International Surrealist Exhibition would take place in Mexico. Opening on January 17, 1940, at the Galería de Arte, the exhibition would trigger a heated debate around the complex convergences of art, national identity, and political action vs. political propaganda.[44] Another significant example of the international proliferation of Surrealism is its appropriation by the Négritude movement of Martinique, a French colony at the time, which found in Surrealism a counterargument to the Hegemony of European colonial ideals. Recruiting Surrealism's revolutionary praxis, Négritude's leading journal *Tropiques*, first published in 1941, featured the work of Lucie Thésée, Aimé and Suzanne Césaire, Aristide Maugée, and René Ménil, among many others.[45]

When considered within the numerous contemporaneous instances of appropriated Surrealisms, albeit within heterogeneous cultural, geopolitical, and temporal contexts, the *Art and Liberty* Group assumes a notable position within a fluid network of pivotal intellectual hubs. These were operating in tandem, both formally and organically, and were of a geographical scope that was multiplied due to the displacement of writers, artists, and all sorts of cultural practitioners who were either forced into exile, or were turned into refugees escaping the perils of World War II. Cairo was no exception.

CAIRO ON THE EVE OF WORLD WAR II

Cairo may not have experienced the blitzkrieg, yet it was de facto a city at war. According to Article VII of the Anglo-Egyptian treaty of 1936, in the case Great Britain should ever go to war, Egypt would be obligated to put its national resources along with its entire infrastructure at the disposal of the Empire.[46] Despite granting the nation further autonomy in certain domains, and thus paving the road towards full self-governance, many considered the 1936 accord as favoring British interests and hindering national sovereignty. Egypt was a "veiled protectorate"[47] where the final word often laid within the hands of the British consul-general. This could not have been made any clearer when, in what would become known as the incident of February 4, 1941, British troops occupied the periphery of Abdin Palace, the royal residence, and coerced King Farouk to endorse the British-backed Mustafa El-Nahhas Pasha for prime minister of Egypt. Between granting his consent or the humiliating recourse of abdicating his throne, the king had no choice but to submit. Sir Miles Lampson, later Lord Killearn, Britain's ambassador who had engineered the affair, noted: "this show of force worked without a hitch."[48]

This demonstration of power had already begun manifesting itself on the streets of Cairo since the early months of the war when Britain, in taking Egypt up on its word in regards to the aforementioned Anglo-Egyptian treaty, began the deployment of Empire troops on Egyptian territory. Within a span of one year, the one and a half million strong populace of Cairo would see the number of Commonwealth soldiers multiply from 35,000 in the spring of 1940 to an overwhelming 140,000 around the end of 1941.[49] Both troops and tanks swarmed the city streets (ill. 15). With war came the men, and men needed entertainment. The movie theaters never were so popular. Some even organized special screenings for war soldiers based in Cairo (ill. 16). The hundreds of thousands of troops that would pour in from every corner of the world looked for various diversions, and when the movies failed to distract, they sought solace in the arms of prostitutes. The image of the prostitute, expressed through the motif of the deformed female figure, would become one of the most recurring themes in the work of several *Art and Liberty* writers and painters.

Along with the military came a sizable number of administrative personnel, and a considerable variety of British subjects transiting or seeking refuge from nearby war zones, such as Greece or the Balkans, that were either under heavy bombardment, or had fallen behind enemy lines altogether. Cairo was bursting at the seams. To cite Morris who comments on this issue in his book *Farewell the Trumpets: An Imperial Retreat*: "There were kilts and turbans and tarbooshes, slouch hats and jodhpurs. There were Kenyan pioneers, and Indian muleteers, and Australian tank crews, and English gunners, and New Zealand fighter pilots, and South African engineers. There

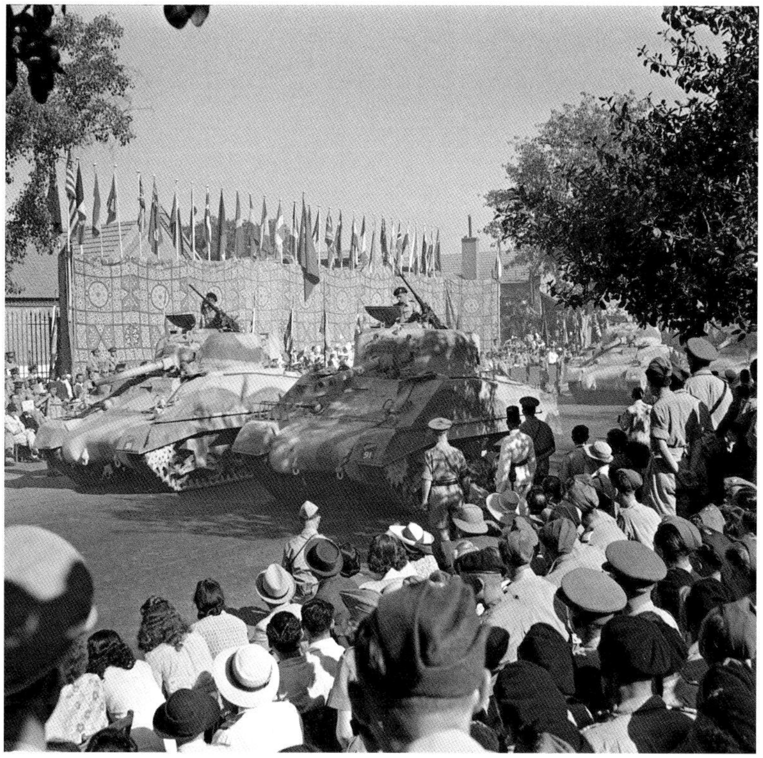

15

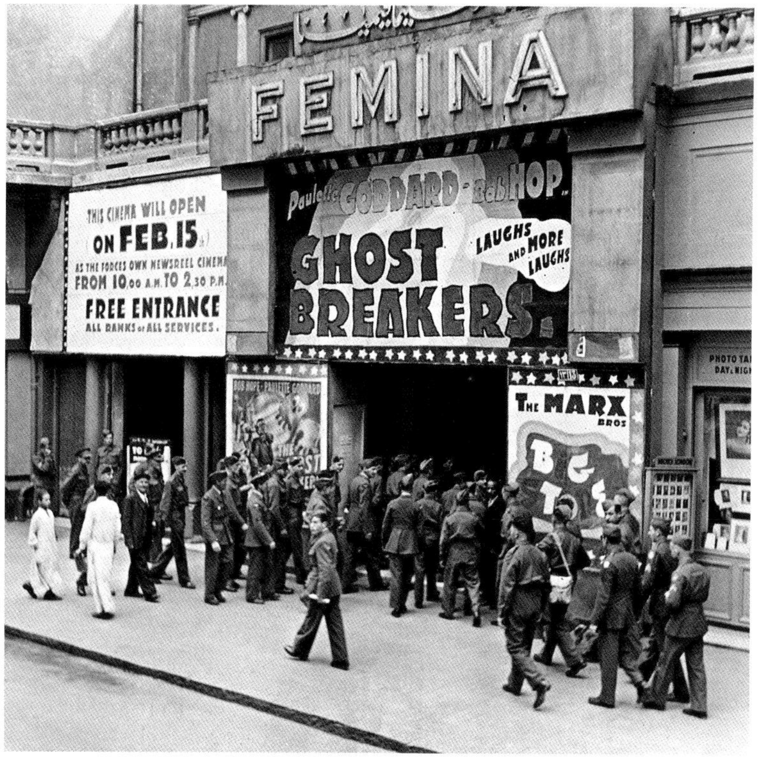

16

15
Two Sherman tanks taking part in the United Nations parade in Cairo on 14 June, 1943
Captain Cash of the No. 1 Army Film & Photographic Unit
Imperial War Museum, UK

16
Entertaining the Troops, 1943
Sgt. Mott of the No. 1 Army Film & Photographic Unit
Imperial War Museum, UK

were scholarly staff officers straight from their Oxford colleges, and swaggering extroverts back from secret missions in the Balkans, and rumbustious troopers of the sheep-station and the surfing beach."[50] But these were not the only ones.

THE FORMATION OF INTERNATIONAL NETWORKS OF DISPLACED WRITERS AND ARTISTS

The war had driven a disparate number of writers and artists to Cairo. Some were refugees like writers Lawrence Durrell and Olivia Manning who in mid-spring of 1941, when the Nazi troops were marching onto Athens, fled by boat from Greece to Alexandria. Durrell would be posted to the press office at the British Council in Cairo. There, he would meet Bernard Spencer who had also been evacuated from Athens three months earlier. Together with Robin Fedden, a professor of English at Cairo University, they would start the literary journal *Personal Landscape*[51] on whose pages writer and painter Amy Nimr, an *Art and Liberty* Group artist and patron, would in 1945 publish a literary critique of the Greek-Alexandrian poet Constantine P. Cavafy. Nimr was an accomplished painter who had studied at the Slade in London in the late 1920s. By the time *Art and Liberty* emerged onto Cairo's arts scene, she had become quite established both locally and internationally with several solo shows to her name in a number of renowned galleries in Paris and London, and a prolific painting trajectory evidencing, besides Surrealism, a heterogeneous stylistic language (ills. 17–18).[52] Besides her exhibiting with *Art and Liberty*, Nimr played a pivotal role in the their formative phases through providing the group with a cultural salon in her Zamalek home, as well as introducing them to the intellectual trends that were emanating from the Henry Miller circle at the Villa Seurat in Paris.[53] Nimr kept a studio at 101 bis rue de La Tombe Issoire within Villa Seurat's alley of sprawling modernist buildings that by then had become the place to be for the artists and writers of the avant-garde.[54] There, she would create some of her most striking Surrealist paintings.[55]

Another refugee, a Brit who had been living in Riga, was Cambridge graduate Lawrence Lovett-Turner. He also worked at the British Council, and had escaped with his wife, the Latvian painter Natalija Tile (ill. 19).[56] Nata, as her friends knew her, who also had her own solo exhibitions, would take part in the *Art and Liberty* Group's fifth independent show from May 30 until June 9, 1945. Only a few weeks earlier, Lovett-Turner had exhibited, to critical acclaim, at Nobilis, a bookstore in downtown Cairo and a staple gathering place for many of *Art and Liberty*'s members and affiliates. The show was particularly well received due to a series of portraits and double self-portraits entitled *Self-Realization* (ill. 20) that were hailed as "a play in colour of profound intention and expressive attitude."[57] Running for one week from April 7 until April 14, it coincided with another solo exhibition for one of the group's leading members, Ramses Younane, which was staged at the Lycée du Caire, the site for *Art and Liberty*'s third and fourth group exhibitions. Nata's 1945 show was one of several that would continue to take place until the artist and her husband moved to Baghdad in 1951[58]. There she would be a regular exhibitor among the pioneering figures of modern art from Iraq such as Jewad Salim, Hafidh al-Drubi, Ismail Fattah, and Faïk Hassan.[59]

Another non-Egyptian who arrived to Cairo as a British soldier and would take part in the fifth *Art and Liberty* exhibition was Robert Medley, an English painter who had exhibited at the London International Surrealist Exhibition of 1936. Prior to Egypt, Medley was an active member of the London Surrealist circle, and a close friend of Roland Penrose, who—along with Mesens—was the group's foremost leader. Penrose's diary from 1930 to 1940 reveals that the two met on a regular basis. Medley, beyond his artistic ties with the English Surrealists, was also actively involved in the organization of various types of Surrealist activities as evident, for instance,

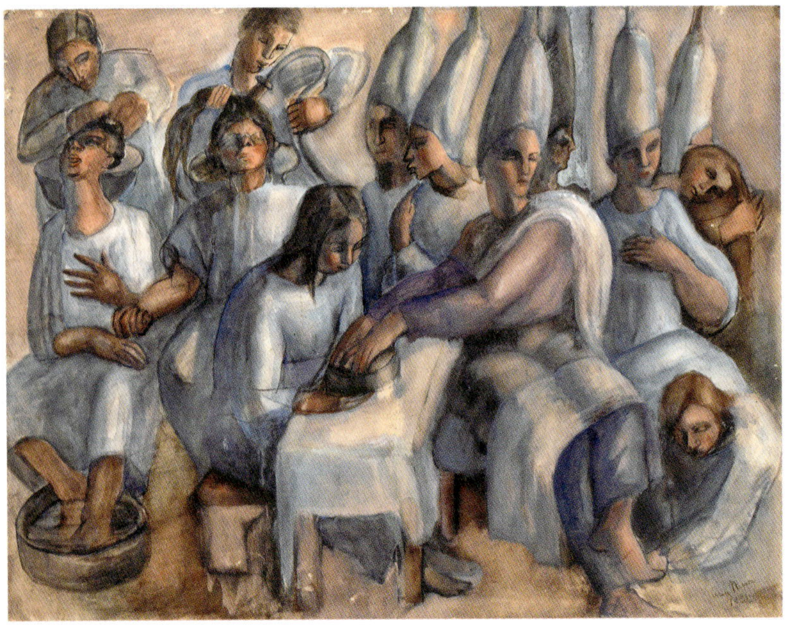

17

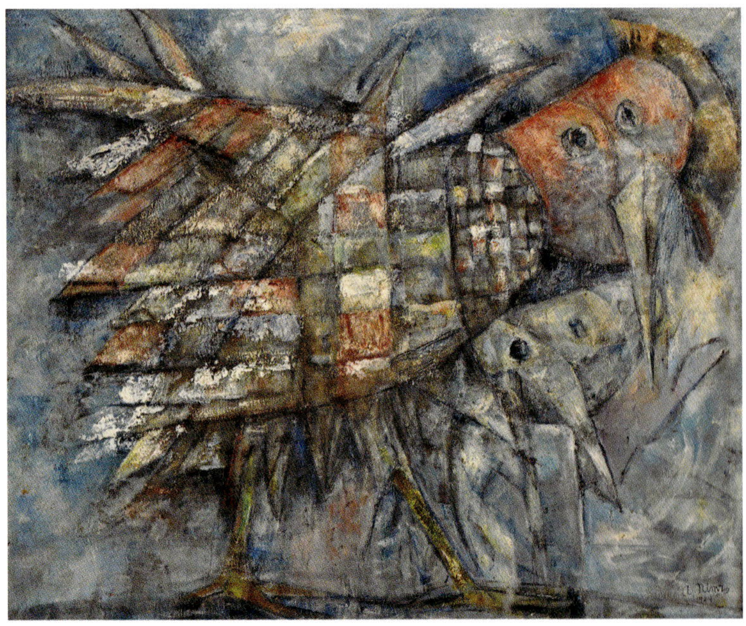

18

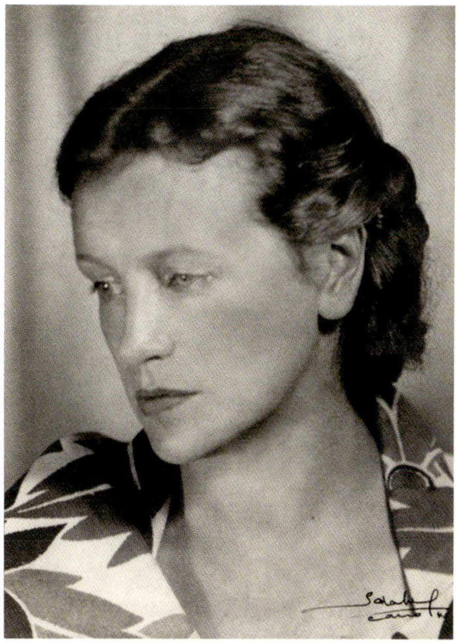

19

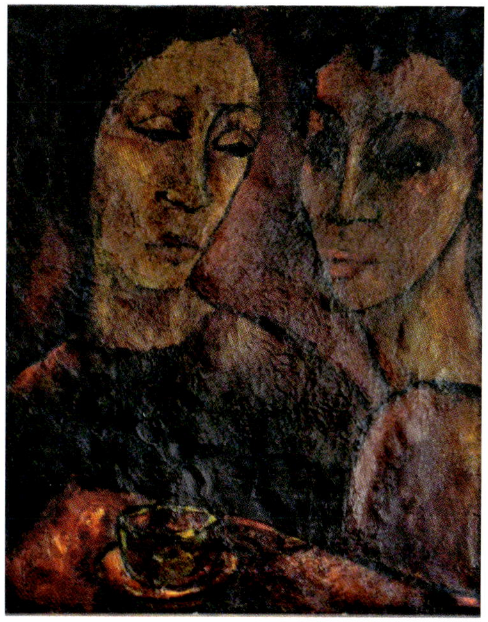

20

in a report that appeared in the first issue of *The London Bulletin* of April 1938 where we learn that "On the evening of Wednesday the 26th of March, Mr. Robert Medley and a full moon presided over a debate between Realists and Surrealists."[60] Moreover, before the war, Medley had taught painter Rateb Seddik, one of *Art and Liberty*'s members at the Chelsea College of Arts.[61] Like many other artists such as Anthony Gross, Edward Bawden, and Edward Ardizzone, just to name a few, Medley arrived to Cairo with the deluge of British and Commonwealth troops that were stationed in Egypt and along the North African coastline.[62]

During World War II, Cairo provided a relatively safe haven for a wide assortment of political activists ranging from anti-Fascist anarchists to Jewish intellectuals fleeing from the ever-expanding Nazi sphere. There was Angelo de Riz, for instance, an art teacher at the Lycée du Caire. An ardent anti-Fascist, de Riz had left Italy at some point in the mid-1930s.[63] Having established himself as a regular on the Cairene gallery scene, he had "opened the voice for the Surrealists in Egypt,"[64] and was among the first artists to sign *Art and Liberty*'s manifesto of 1938. He would continue to exhibit with them throughout the entire war period. So central was de Riz to *Art and Liberty* that, when founding group member Kamel El-Telmisany embarked on a series of articles entitled *L'Art en Égypte* that appeared in the group's affiliate review *Don Quichotte* he dedicated one of them to him[65].

There was also Étienne Sved, a Hungarian Jewish photographer and graphic designer who, through his friendship with writer and Intellectual Georges Henein, worked as a photographer at the French paper *Le Progrès Égyptien*.[66] In 1945, when Sved executed a series of posters for a local brand of cigarettes called Setos, Henein was the director of Gianaclis, the company that owned it. During his years in Cairo, besides his photography, Sved created a series of anti-Nazi caricatures that were republished many years later in a bound volume entitled *Adolf ou à quand le crépuscule des odieux*. Sved would go on to illustrate Jean Cocteau's *Maalesh*,[67] a journal inspired by Cocteau's 1949 stay in Egypt.

All of the individuals cited above illustrate one of the very few positive, albeit collateral benefits of a war that was otherwise devastating. However, the formation of these fluid networks and hubs of displaced intellectuals coincided with another less favorable phenomenon that was rapidly gaining momentum, the detrimental repercussions of which played a significant role in triggering the foundation of *Art and Liberty*.

17
AMY NIMR
Untitled, 1931
Ink and watercolour on paper
40 x 60 cm
Private collection

18
AMY NIMR
Untitled, 1949
Oil on canvas
75 x 100 cm
Private collection

19
IDABEL (IDA KAR AND EDMOND BELALI)
Portrait of Nata Lovett-Turner, 1946
Vintage gelatin silver print
22 x 16 cm
Mandy Prowse collection, London

20
NATA LOVETT-TURNER
Self Realization, 1945
Oil on canvas
26 x 22 cm
Annie White collection, London

THE RISE OF LOCAL FASCIST SENTIMENT

From the mid-1930s onward, Egypt experienced a rise in local totalitarian sentiment, evidenced in the proliferating debate about the virtues of Fascism as opposed to democracy was underway. As one browses through the pages of the daily papers and weekly magazines from the mid-1930s onward, the contours of a proliferating argument about the benefits and shortcomings of Nazi and Fascist ideology begin to emerge. The discussion assumes a much fiercer dimension during the months leading up to the outbreak of World War II. This was caused as much by a considerable instability at home, as by the events that were simultaneously unfolding in Europe.

In Egypt, frustration about the political and social conditions was felt among the population, blue and white collar alike. In the span of four unsteady years from 1935 until 1939, Egyptians saw as many as five prime ministers come and go. They all hailed from one of the two leading rival political parties at the time: the liberal *Al-Wafd* (The Delegation), founded in 1919 and considered by most as the one most in step with the national sentiment on the streets, and the more conservative Palace-controlled *Al-Ittihad* (The Union), founded by King Fouad in 1925 to maintain control over parliament, and seen by many as anti-democratic.[68] The enmity between the two parties meant that as soon as a government formed, it would seek to undermine the accomplishments of the one that preceded it. The many Egyptians witnessing this game of political chess began to question the viability of the political establishment. The momentous rise of Italy and Germany, their perception as new great nations to contend with, and the propagandist strategies that denied any dissent and demonstrated nothing but euphoric mass adulation, compelled those who were seeking an alternative model of governance to contemplate a local appropriation of Fascist and Nazi ideals as a potential solution. "*Hal tanjah al-dicatatoriyyah 'indana?*" (Could Dictatorship Succeed within Our Midst?) asked one writer on the pages of *Al-Hilal* in February 1939.

In March of that year, a writer by the name of Ali Adham published a lengthy critique of the philosophy of Fascism in *Al-Muqtataf* outlining its causes and applications, intellectual protagonists, and its conflicting perception by both its adherents and opponents. A few months later in June, Al-Majallah Al-Jadidah published a nine-page article entitled "Al-imbratoriyyah al-almaniyyah al-naziyyah" (The Nazi German Empire).[70] The same magazine had published, from as early as June 1936 a lengthy article translated from English and entitled "Adolph Hitler and the German Government."[71] It is worth noting that the writer was James Vincent Murphy, an English teacher who, until his departure from Berlin in 1938 after he had fallen from the grace of the National Socialists, was the party's only authorized translator of Hitler's *Mein Kampf*.[72] Predictably, the article chosen by the editors of the magazine had a rather positive tone to it. In a translation from an Italian article that also appeared on the pages of *Al-Majallah Al-Jadidah* on February 1, 1936, under the title "Al-fashiyyah kama yaraha du'atuha" (Fascism through the Eyes of its Advocates), the author states:

> And it is worth mentioning that Mussolini, through his recreation of Italy, has positioned himself among the ranks of the greats upon whom all eyes are fixed, and has made of himself an example of leadership desired by so many for the advancement of their own countries.

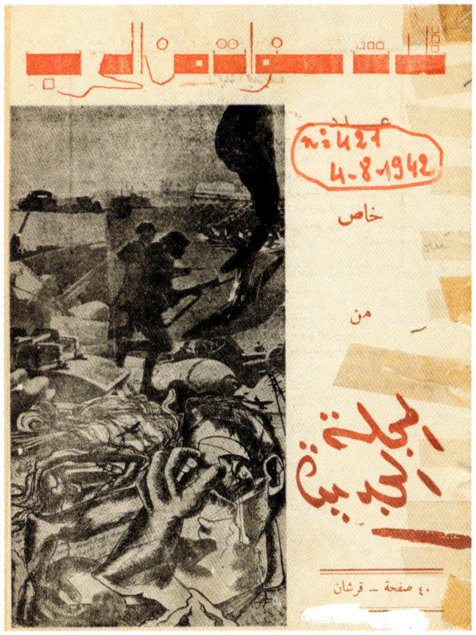

21

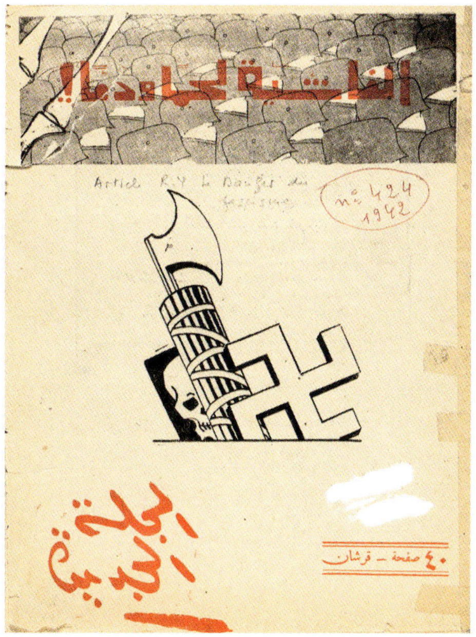

22

> It is because of his efforts that Italy has assumed its position at the front rows of the great nations to which all look with great respect.[73]

For many, Fascism and what it might offer within the local political sphere was not to be dismissed, at least not yet. It suffices to say that the debate was rife, and that it was unresolved. *Art and Liberty* were equally embroiled in the public debate and continued to publish various anti-Fascist tracts and articles throughout the war period (ill. 21–22).

Beyond the pages of magazines and newspapers circulating across the nation, this ideological debate was simultaneously manifesting itself in a highly felt manner on the actual streets of Egypt. For several years now, pictures of military parades, proudly showcasing the mobilization efforts and the armed might of Nazi Germany and Fascist Italy had become staples in the local press. These were the visual counterparts to the ideological discussions that were expressed in the type of articles that we had been exploring so far. As striking as these images may have been, a different type of mobilization had been taking place at home that would continue until the late 1930s, one that *Art and Liberty* would have been witnessing in person. On January 10, 1936, a one thousand-strong parade of uniformed youth marched through downtown Cairo declaring their allegiance to the king and to their party.[74] These were *Al-Qumsan Al-Zarqa'* (The Blue Shirts), a paramilitary organization belonging to the Wafd (ill. 23). After having been Egypt's foremost political institution for a good two decades, the Wafd had been grappling with a marked drift away from its leadership, especially among the youth. This was due, in part, to the not-so-successful Anglo-Egyptian treaty in which the Wafd, residing over government at the time, was the official state partner signing on behalf of the Egyptian people. The Blue Shirts would prove to be, even if temporarily, an effective remedial course to resuscitate the party's dwindling popularity. Named after the color of their shirts, these units of quasi-soldiers would take to the streets, infiltrate demonstrations, and, if needs be, even resort to acts of public violence in order to quell the rise of anti-Wafd sentiment. By the summer of 1936, reports were circulating that the number of Blue Shirts had reached as many as twenty thousand.[75] Resorting to the mobilization of high school and university students as a means of turning political tides was not exclusive to the Wafd.

The Muslim Brotherhood had their roving troops, too, organized into an elaborate hierarchical structure and highly focused on athletic activity and physical training.[76] Even the Italian

21
Al-Majallah Al-Jadidah,
n° 421, 4 August, 1942
Printed journal
Centre Pompidou Paris, MNAM-CCI,
Bibliothèque Kandinsky,
Ramsès Younan Archives

22
Al-Majallah Al-Jadidah,
n° 424, 15 August, 1942
Printed journal
Centre Pompidou Paris, MNAM-CCI,
Bibliothèque Kandinsky,
Ramsès Younan Archives

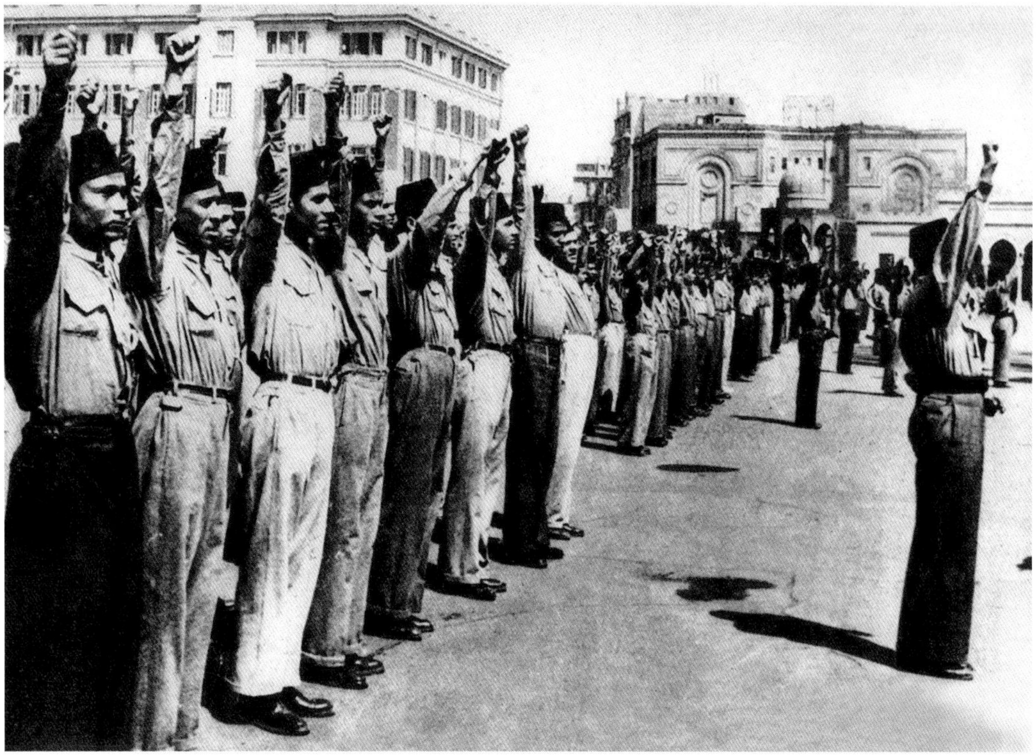

23

communities in Egypt, primarily in Alexandria and Cairo, had their own version of Mussolini's Camicie Nere (Black Shirts) roaming about their neighborhoods. Misr al-Fatat (Young Egypt), another leading rightwing movement had its own *Al-Qumsan Al-Khadra'* (The Green Shirts). Ahmad Hussein, who founded the organization in 1933, was known to be a pro-Fascist and Nazi sympathizer. In 1936 Hussein and a delegation of Green Shirts took part in the Reichsparteitag, the Nazi's annual rally and a monumental propaganda event.[77] Misr Al-Fatat's Green Shirts fashioned themselves after Nazi Hitlerjugend. They were the arch rivals of the Wafd's Blue Shirts. Violent clashes between the two were not uncommon. However, what the two did have in common was a penchant for Fascist salutes, army-like uniforms, and torchlight parades. For the Blue Shirts, for instance, "various badges were prescribed, and the salute was to be a clenched right hand placed on the heart and then thrust to the sky (presumably with vigor)"[78].

Art and Liberty's sense of freedom was augmented by the realities of a raging war, and articulated with a pressing awareness of the growth of Fascist and totalitarian ideologies within Egypt. Emerging against the backdrop of World War II, *Art and Liberty* would reject Fascism, which beyond its firm grip over Europe, had been on the rise in Egypt since the early 1930s and was beginning to pose a highly felt threat at home. On December 22, 1938, their founding was announced through their bilingual, Arabic-French manifesto *Yahya al-fann al-munhatt / Vive l'Art Dégénéré* (Long Live Degenerate Art). A first interpretation of the manifesto could frame it as a reaction to the Fascist and Nazi crusade against the avant-garde in Europe. One could also read in it an echo of the July 25, 1938 manifesto of FIARI. While not entirely misguided, such readings are certainly not sufficient. The ideologies that were designating the movements of the avant-garde as *entartete Kunst* were simultaneously at play in Egypt, and were manifesting themselves, albeit in different conditions, through an authoritative, hegemony over the arts by state-related associations on the one hand, and a rigorous local chapter of Futurists that was highly connected with the Fascist party on the other. In March 1938, *Art and Liberty*, following a lecture by F. T. Marinetti in Cairo, would reveal their uncompromising rejection of any alignment between Fascism, nationalism, and art. Alexandria-born Marinetti, the father of Futurism, had arrived to Cairo as a delegate of the Fascist government of Italy. By then, he had already been elected by Mussolini as a member of the regime-aligned Reale Accademia d'Italia. Marinetti's

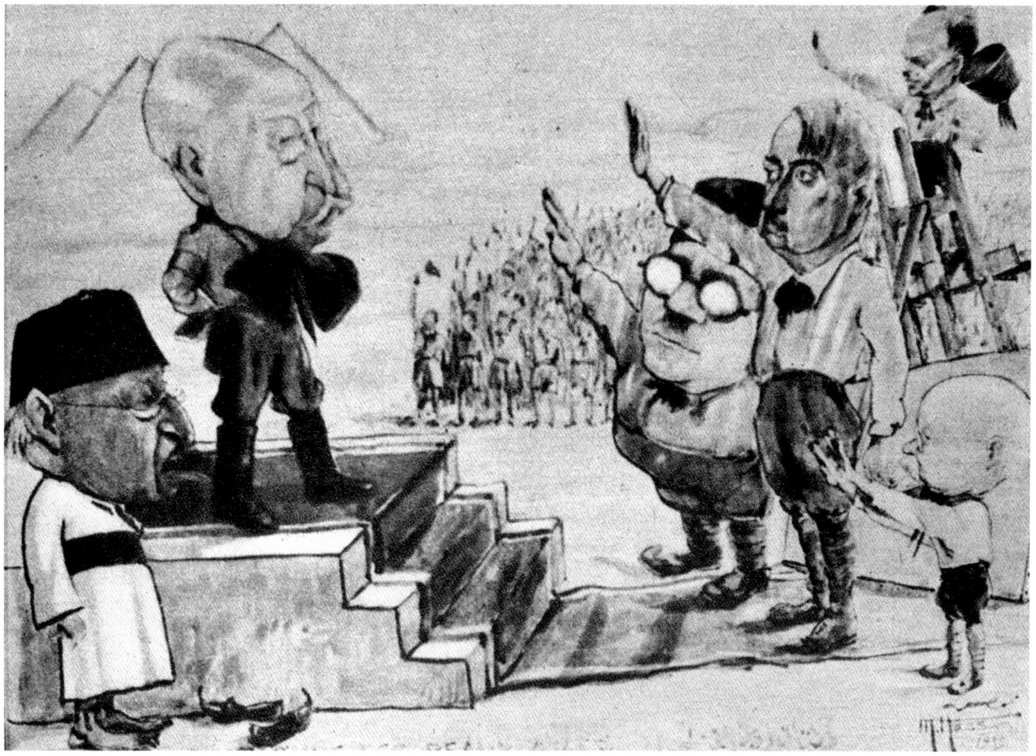
24

visit to Cairo a few months before the outbreak of World War II, which coincided with the simmering of local Fascist sentiment, is by far one of the most relevant occurrences to consider when constructing the immediate background against which *Art and Liberty*'s Manifesto was penned and the group was founded. *Art and Liberty*'s mockery on the evening of March 24, 1938, was targeted at a legendary figure who had revolutionized the artistic landscape of Europe upon publishing his *Manifesto of Futurism* in 1909. Marinetti would find himself on the receiving end of some of the future members of *Art and Liberty*'s most insolent attacks to date, turning what had started as a conference on Futurist poetry into a scandalous brawl.

In placing *Art and Liberty* and their 1938 manifesto against this local backdrop, their vision of a reworked version of Surrealism, not only as a form of artistic emancipation, but a political one as well, begins to emerge. What remains to be uncovered is the extent to which Fascist ideology had seeped into the fabric of the official art institution. To further shed light on this, we will turn to an unexpected clue, which despite its professed humor, is quite telling of a far more serious rift within the local arts community in Egypt.

THE *SOCIÉTÉ DES AMIS DE L'ART*, OR THE DICTATORSHIP OF THE ARTS

On the eve of World War II, Cairo's cultural institutions were undergoing a crisis of orientation. Several younger artists were self-organizing into autonomous art collectives that sought an existence beyond the academic stylistic confines and institutionalized practices of the formal arts establishment, mainly the *Société des amis de l'art* (*Jam'iyyat muhibbee al-funoun al jameelah*).

The *Société* was founded by Fouad Abdel Malek, a onetime artist turned art and furniture dealer and connoisseur. Abdel Malek, upon his return to his native Egypt in 1919 after receiving his art education at the Academy of Fine Arts in Munich, opened a showroom that would serve at once as a sales outlet for fine and decorative arts, as well as a gallery space for art exhibitions. He called it Dar al-funoun wal sana'i'a (The House of Arts and Crafts). Without going into details, the *Société* arguably emerged from this institution, and would assume the organization

23
The Blue Shirts Roam the Streets of Cairo
Al-Lata'if Al-Musawwara, March 23, 1936, p. 4. Newspaper print
Al-Lata'if Al-Musawwara Archives, Cairo

24
MOHAMMAD HASSAN
The Dictatorship of the Fine Arts, 1939
Al-Musawwar, n° 1164, 31 January 1947
Bayerische Staatsbibliothek, Munich

of the annual, highly conservative, Salon du Caire. Contrasting historiographies have placed the date of the Salon's foundation, as well as that of the *Société* between 1919 and 1923.[79]
In its January 31, 1947 issue, the illustrated weekly society magazine *Al-Musawwar* (The Illustrated) published the picture of a caricature painting that was included in the Salon du Caire of that year. Entitled *Dictature des Beaux-Arts* (The Dictatorship of the Fine Arts), the work at hand was by the renowned painter and sculptor Mohammad Hassan (ill. 24). The central figure in Hassan's caricature is the arts mogul Mohammad Mahmoud Khalil. Khalil was one of the main patrons of the *Société des amis de l'art*, of which he was one of the main founders and lifelong president until his death in 1953.

Significantly influential over the arts establishment and an avid collector of mostly classical and late nineteenth-century French art and sculpture, Khalil's lack of appreciation for modern Egyptian art was no secret, and he did not shy away from expressing his disdain, publicly scorning most Egyptian artists of the time and expressing his predilection for European art.[80] This disdain is further substantiated in an article from the May 1935 issue of a local cultural review, *Un Effort*, about that year's annual salon. The unnamed author speaks of the impossibility of securing any financial support from the patron Mohammad Mahmoud Khalil for local Egyptian artists whose works he would never allow into his home. He continues to irreverently explain to the readers that if such a thing were ever to happen, Khalil would "*se taper le derrière par terre au son de l'hymne du Vénézuela*"[81] (would roll on the floor to the sound of the Venezuelan national anthem). The author openly acknowledged that he borrowed his crude depiction of Khalil from one of the many insolent statements that could come from Georges Henein.
By 1935, Henein had become the ultimate enfant terrible among writers on the local literary circuit. And, by the time Hassan painted his caricature, Henein's position as the champion of all things avant-garde in Egypt had been quite established, locating him at an irreconcilable pole, not only to Khalil, but the entire official establishment. In *La Peinture moderne en Égypte*, Aimé Azar's seminal 1961 book on the history of modern art in Egypt, he describes Henein in the mid-1930s as "a poet and polemicist, adventurous and curious of spirit, who would soon rally the members of the avant-garde."[82]
The reference to Henein highlights the counter position that he, as well as *Art and Liberty* maintained towards the *Société* and Khalil who, for them, were the representatives of outdated bourgeois taste, which championed conservative art styles that no longer reflected the reality of the time. This is an important point that was equally alluded to in the opening statement of the 1938 manifesto: "It is well known that the present society looks with aversion on any innovative creation in art and literature which threatens the cultural system." This is my own translation, and not the one found in Rosemont's mostly cited *Black, Brown and Beige* where the word "present," expressed as "*al-hali*" in Arabic, and "*actuelle*" in French in the original Manifesto, has been mistranslated into the word "modern."[83]
Khalil was also notorious for his open Fascist leanings. From the early 1930s and well into the War, Khalil was quite forthright about his admiration for Mussolini and the Fascist party. He was also called upon regularly to exclusive functions at the Vichy Club, the wartime Cairo residence of Vichy government diplomats and high-ranking officials. So outspoken Khalil was about his political leanings that in 1942 Sir Miles Lampson, British ambassador to Egypt, described him as "a poisonous snake that makes propaganda for the enemy and spreads defeatism." Lampson's

apprehension of Khalil's sway over the political elite in Egypt was serious enough to make him ask Wafdist Prime Minister Nahhas Pasha to place Khalil under house arrest, to which the latter, in words that were quite telling of his great contempt for Khalil, dismissively replied: "Khalil is a senator and a completely worthless creature, therefore not deserving of incarceration."[84] Hassan depicts Khalil as a pontificating dictator standing on an elevated platform in a mass rally that brings Fascist military parades to mind.[85] Several figures from the official art establishment hailed him with a Nazi/Fascist salute. The alignment of personalities in Hassan's caricature is telling of a contemptuous rift between the *Société des amis de l'art* on one hand, represented by its totalitarian president Mohammad Mahmoud Khalil, and the official artistic establishment.[86] The placement of the three Pyramids of Giza in the background of Hassan's caricature reminds us that this race for control was located right here in Egypt. In fact, the question of "Egyptianness" lies at the very heart of this fissure.

In an article that appeared in the May 1929 issue of *Al-'Ousour* (The Times), a monthly journal of political commentary and cultural and literary criticism, under the title *Haqiqat al-nahdah al-fanniyyah al-masriyyah fi al-naht wal tasweer* (The Truth about the Egyptian Artistic Renaissance in Sculpture and Painting), artist Zaki Sha'ban accusingly declares that the *Société*, while claiming to serve the interest of Egyptian artists, had long abandoned the interests of those who it had been supposedly established for. To substantiate his criticism, Sha'ban cites the local artists' conclusive dismissal of the *Société* and self-organization into various other bodies such as, to quote one of Sha'ban's examples, *Al-rabitah al-masriyyah li al-fannaneen* (The Egyptian League of Artists). Later, art historians speak of a *Rabitat al-fannaneen al-masriyyeen* (Egyptian Artists' League) and ascribe its founding date sometimes to 1933, and at other times to 1936.[87]

A second article that was published in the March 1930 issue of *Al-'Ousour,* took the more threatening form of an official petition entitled *Taqrir 'an il-nahdah al-fanniyyah* (A Report on the Artistic Revival).The report asserts, that the *Société des amis de l'art* was created for "the encouragement of the fine arts through the organization of exhibitions, lectures, and any other means."[88] However, the report continues, "instead of directing its care towards Egypt, the society limited all its efforts to the service of Europe, and instead of working towards creating a sympathetic relationship with Egyptian artists, it favored the foreigners with its consideration and embraced them with all kinds of encouragement."[89] The report concluded with a detailed agenda directed to the Office for the General Administration of the Fine Arts that was founded in 1927, proposing that the ministry relieve the *Société* from the responsibility of organizing the annual exhibition. In addition, the petition demanded amongst other things, that Egyptian artists oversee all cultural affairs, that they take on the administration of exhibitions and museums and that the acquisitions for the museum of modern art focus primarily on Egyptian artists maintaining a section dedicated for works by foreign artists.

This quasi-nationalization of the arts that several local artistic voices were demanding would continue to make itself heard for the better part of the decade, and is ultimately an important backdrop to *Art and Liberty*'s manifesto of December 22, 1938. The coalition between art and nationalism that would give birth to the notion of a genuine "Egyptian" art would become one of the main issues that *Art and Liberty* would vehemently argue against and seek to dismantle.

As a matter of fact, that was one of the main stipulations in their 1938 manifesto: "And we believe it absurd and ridiculous the fanatic racism, religiousness, or nationalism that some individuals seek to align the destiny of modern art with."[90] The disentanglement of art from the confines of "Egyptianness," in particular, would prove to be one of *Art and Liberty*'s main battles.

THE FORMATION OF INDEPENDENT ARTIST COLLECTIVES

By the late 1930s, a growing sense of alienation, triggered by the favoritism of the *Société des amis de l'art*, had driven several artists to form their own independent groups. Consider the example of *Rabitat al-fannaneen al-masriyyeen* (The Egyptian Artists League), a group of artists who, upon feeling sidelined by the *Société* took it upon themselves to organize their own art exhibitions promoting the works of lesser-known emerging Egyptian artists. Soon, however, the group would become a demagogical mouthpiece for the alignment of art with nationality, unlike *Art and Liberty* whose members came together based on shared intellectual affinities, rather than nationality.

Art and Liberty was by far the most long-lived of the independent groups of the time who found in the revolutionary tactics embedded within the Surrealists attack on bourgeois aestheticism, as well as the movement's stand against Fascism and championing of freedom, a mirror reflection, not only of the reality of their own context and nature of their position, but also of the lines of attack that they felt were most suited to bringing about the radical cultural and political change that they desired for their society. Two of *Art and Liberty*'s leading members hailed from two independent art groups in which they were deeply implicated. Disgruntled with the hegemony of the official institutions, and believing in the value of articulating and disseminating a relevant art form, unlike the imported academic styles championed by the *Société*, both collectives, despite variances in expression and application, considered the edification of the individual as one of their main objectives. Ramses Younane was actively involved with a group that went by the name Jama'at al-di'ayah al-fanniyyah (loosely translates as The Arts Advocacy Group). Gathered around the art educator Habib Gorgui, the group was quite robust organizing its own art exhibitions and publishing its own books well into the late forties[91] (ill. 25). For example, Younane's 1938 treatise on modern art entitled *Ghayat al-rassam al-'asri* (The Purpose of the Contemporary Painter), in which he provides a contemporary critique of Surrealism and which I had cited earlier, was published by the group.

Kamel El-Telmisany was a founding member among a group of artists who called themselves the *Néo-Orientalistes* / Al-mustashriqoun al-judud (*New Orientalists*). El-Telmisany, who would be one of the first artists to be discovered by Henein locally and presented to Breton in a letter from as early as May 1937,[92] believed, along with several other artists who belonged to the *Néo-Orientalistes* group like Ali Kamel El-Dib, Kamal William El-Mallakh, and Jean Moscatelli, "that their personal ideas and feelings, those that are of an oriental nature, can bring about a true form of art, only upon developing a truly oriental sensitivity, unobstructed by occidental concepts."[93] At first glance, one might misinterpret these lines, drawn from the *Néo-Orientalistes*; manifesto of January 1, 1937, as a calling for a national art form. This could not be further removed from the truth. The interest by El-Telmisany and his fellow *New Orientalists* in mining their native visual traditions, referred to as oriental in this case, for the articulation of an art form that relies on a locally-inspired vernacular, was a response to what they perceived as a passive aping of European academic styles, mostly impressionism and realism, by almost all the established artists from their senior generation, who upon traveling to study in Europe, to quote El-Telmisany, "felt inferiority running through their veins until they started to copy the images of the dominant and strong . . . prisoners of museums and churches, and of church-like academies, you could easily see the features of the saints and characters that were inscribed by Raphael and Michelangelo and others . . . behind the characters that were drawn by these enslaved copiers."[94]

In a special arts issue from the architectural magazine *Al-Emara* from June 1939, the author writes favorably about the group of *New Orientalists* designating its main tenet as a form of "painted literature . . . a modern trend that relies heavily on each artist's overall artistic cultivation. . . . Each artist, in guarding their individual personality and the atmosphere surrounding them, can innovate their own personal style where one artist could, for instance, consult negro (tribal African) art, and another one could look at ancient Egyptian art learning from its spirit, lines and simplicity, while a third could be influenced by Persian art with its distinguished patterns and motifs. This does not mean that they are imitating ancient Oriental art forms, but that they are channeling them based on profound study and an understanding of the spirituality inherent to them. This, in turn, enables these artists to dwell in a world of powerful imagination."[95] A few years later, Ahmed Rassim, a leading art critic and would-be supporter of *Art and Liberty*, would contribute an article about the *New Orientalists* to issue no. 7–8 of *Al-Emara* in 1945. By then several of the group members such as Kamel El-Telmisany and Kamal William El-Mallakh, were already integrated within *Art and Liberty*. Rassim had written favorably about the group in two earlier articles from 1938 that appeared in the daily papers *Al-Ahram and Al-Balagh* on September 17 and October 15 respectively, almost a year after the *New Orientalists* were established. Through these articles, he disclosed an essential clarification to what the term "oriental" truly meant to these artists "who have taken upon themselves the study to the core of the popular arts propelling them towards a contemporary cultural expression."[96]

The use of the term "popular" first appeared within the context of a heated debate that unraveled during the summer of 1939 between the editors and writers of *Al-Risalah,* a weekly literary, scientific, and artistic journal, and three members of the *Art and Liberty* Group, Anwar Kamel, Ramses Younane and El-Telmisany himself. An article that appeared in *Al-Risalah* on July 10, 1939, that announced the imminent disintegration of a circle of Egyptian artists, who called themselves the Group of Degenerate Art, had initially prompted this entire debacle. In a polemical defense of Surrealism's unalien nature vis-à-vis the Egyptian context, El-Telmisany outlines some of the most central theorems, not only of what popular art meant, but how *Art and Liberty* envisioned Surrealism as a non-contradiction to a local aesthetic tradition. In responding to critic Aziz Ahmad Fahmi, El-Telmisany writes:

> Have you never seen, my dear sir, the four-fingered dolls that are special to the saints' days holidays (*'aroussit el-moulid el-halawah*)? Have you never come across the small rag puppets? Have you never listened to the stories of *Oum el- shou'our, el-shater Hassan* and other such folk fables of our local popular literature? All of this my dear sir is Surrealism . . .

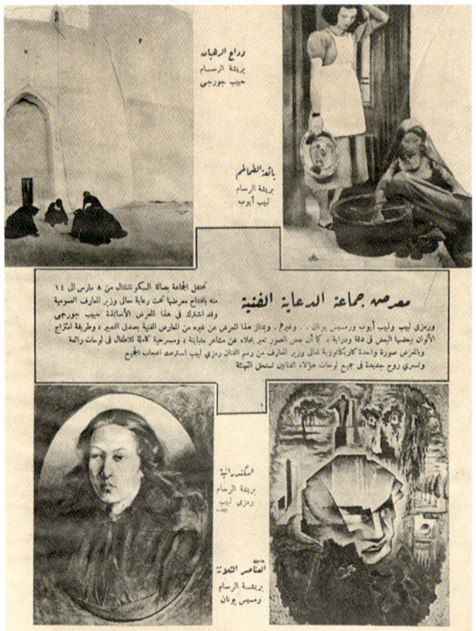

25

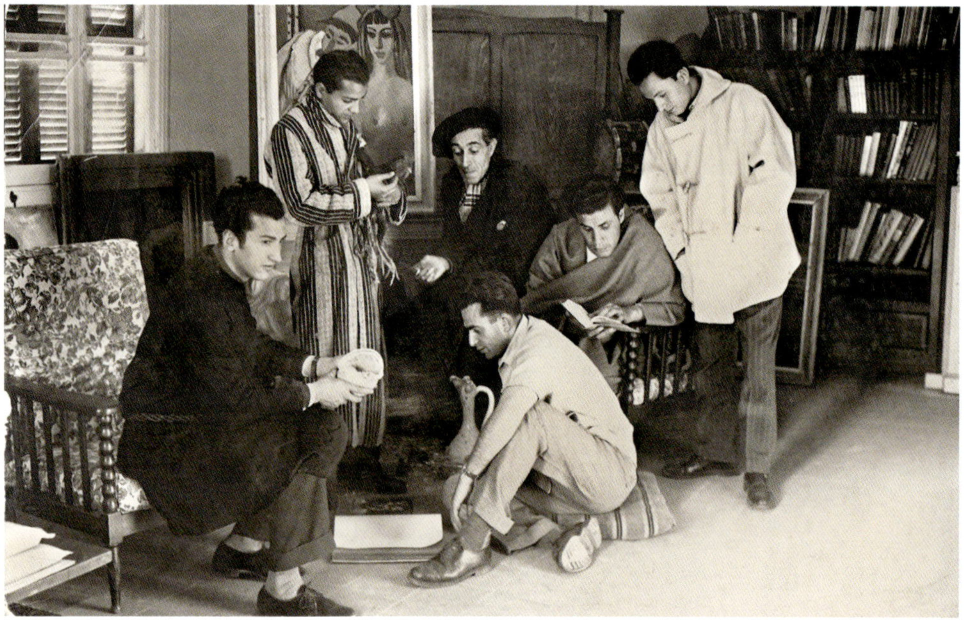

26

Have you never been to the Egyptian museum . . . Much of what you see there of Pharaonic art is Surrealism.
Have you not been to the Coptic museum . . . Much of Coptic art is Surrealist. We do not imitate foreign schools but create an art form that has emerged from the tanned soil of this land and that has been running in our veins from the day we used to live by unrestrained free thought until this very hour. . .
The word "Surrealism" is nothing but the modern technical term to what we have always referred to as free imagination: the freedom of expression, the freedom of style, and the orient, since eternity, has been the dwelling to all of this.[97]

The intellectual premise from which the New Orientals, and concurrently *Art and Liberty*, built their position reveals a reconciled correlation between the local and international, the familiar and the foreign to an extent where such categorizations becomes almost marginal. Surrealism, once its definition, geography, appearance, application, and even its temporality are opened up, becomes a manifestation of an ongoing process of expression that can be equally at home in Paris as in Cairo, and could exist as legitimately in a Magritte painting as much as in a locally crafted hand puppet.

Suffice to say, *Art and Liberty* appeared on the Cairene artistic scene at a time when there was an increasing desire for an alternative platform. Radicalized by the events of the World War II, and disillusioned with the cultural ancien régime that was associated with it, *Art and Liberty* evaded national rhetoric, alignments with academic schools, and conservative bourgeois taste and gathered around concepts and styles that echoed the more recent avant-garde currents, namely Surrealism, as well as the turbulent times in which they found themselves. *Art and Liberty* were quickly finding an application to their intellectual and artistic cache that, while reflective of their international nature, was nonetheless informed by and focused on the immediate social, political, and artistic context in which they existed. Through their bulletin, entitled after the group's name, and their two periodicals, *Don Quichotte* and *Al-Tatawwur,* all published in 1939–40, the several works of prose and poetry they released through their two publishing houses Éditions Masses and La Part du Sable, and the numerous interventions and exhibitions of independent art that they mounted, including five seminal group shows between 1940 and 1945, *Art and Liberty* provided a generation of disillusioned generation of artists and writers with a heterogeneous platform for cultural and political reform. For the better part of an entire decade

25
Newspaper *Al-Radio Al-Masry*, no 208, 11 March 1939, image taken from a work of Ramses Younane
Hamdi Hamed Archives, Cairo

26
The Contemporary Art Group, c. 1946
Photographer unknown
Gelatin silver print on paper
Kamal Youssef Archives, Dayton PA

(1938–48), they were unwavering in instigating a revolution against all the stale cultural and political structures that had been put in place by a conservative bourgeois society. However, if all good things must come to an end, *Art and Liberty* most certainly did.

During the second half of the 1940s, there were factors at play that would contribute to the next, and arguably the last chapter of *Art and Liberty*'s life. In an ironic twist of fate, the times were burdened with issues and concerns that were not all that different from the ones that had initially led to the formation of the group. Granted, the war had ended, but with its closing, a host of issues opened up demanding, with pressing urgency, swift and decisive action. Once again, these had to do with the repercussions of an increasingly militant nationalism locally, and an intensifying crisis of orientation within Surrealism internationally. By 1948, the discrepancy between *Art and Liberty* and most notably the Breton-centric Surrealists and how they viewed the movement along with its applications had come to an unbridgeable gap, so much so that it resulted in irrevocable rupture. Henein wrote a formal letter dated July 26, 1948, to André Breton declaring withdrawal from the Surrealist movement: "I write these lines with no humour, and no spite."[98]

Locally, despite their resilience and ferociousness, both the soil and the tools that were needed for the seeds that *Art and Liberty* had planted to flourish, were simply not there. That is not to say that the group would disappear without a trace. On the contrary, their impact would resonate through the work of many leading painters from the generation to follow. The issue, however, was that *Art and Liberty*, did not themselves consider the younger artists who implied, if not even maintained, to be their offspring, to be their successors or a legitimate continuation of what they stood for. These artists, such as Samir Rafi, Kamal Youssef, and Ibrahim Massouda to name a few, who had on occasion exhibited with *Art and Liberty*, moved on in 1946 to create, with a few others such as Abdel Hadi El-Gazzar, Mahmoud Khalil, and Salim Al-Habschi what they called the Contemporary Art Group (ill. 26).[99] Several leading *Art and Liberty* protagonists had serious doubts about both their talent and politics. In a letter from Henein to Younane, the former would go as far as accusing them of "pretending" to be the continuation of *Art and Liberty*, while in their search for an "Egyptian art" they had in reality become a deplorable mouthpiece for the "new Fascists in uniforms," referring to Abdel Nasser and the Free officers who conducted the Revolution of 1952.[100] With several of its original members in prison or in exile, a disappointment in a younger generation with whom the relationship was becoming increasingly concerted, and a succession of ideological ruptures within a Surrealist movement struggling to remain relevant in a post-war world, there were simply too many factors placing *Art and Liberty*'s existence at risk.

Yet, while one legacy was interrupted, several others began as each of the original group members went on to develop their own artistic and literary paths. The El-Telmisany brothers would become leading filmmakers with Kamel moving to Lebanon almost until the end of his life.[101] Hassan, the younger of the two, would continue to paint, but his real fame would be as a pioneer in the field of documentary film[102] (ill. 27). Ramses Younane and Fouad Kamel would switch to an almost exclusively abstract style of painting. In the 1960s, true to form, they would play a leading role along with Rateb Seddik in securing governmental legislation for professional artist stipends allowing artists to pursue their work on a full-time basis.[103] Inji Efflatoun, who began her artistic career as a student of El-Telmisany and first exhibited with *Art and Liberty* in 1942, would embark on a life of feminist and social activism spending several years in prison where she would articulate a distinct painting style triggered by the experience of light through the bars of her prison cell[104] (ill. 28). Her muse Albert Cossery moved to Paris in 1945 where he checked into La Louisiane, a non-descript hotel on Rue de Seine in Saint-Germain-des-Prés and would remain there until his death in 2008.[105] After the 1952 revolution and the sequestering of their family assets and property by the government of Abdel Nasser, several of the artists like Laurent Marcel Salinas and Amy Nimr, who hailed from wealthier backgrounds, left the country altogether and settled in different cities.[106] Some would persevere, others would quit art altogether for the sake of making a living through more reliable means. Henein and his wife Boula did not leave until 1960. The first two years of their reluctant exile were spent in Greece and Morocco, followed by four years in Rome from 1962 until 1966 when they would move to Paris and remain there until their passing, Georges in 1973 and Boula in 1984.[107] It was a few hours before his death that Henein would utter his last words to his wife, in a touching statement that could be adequately considered a description of the shared destiny that befell most *Art and Liberty* members: "Baby elephants die alone."[108]

WHY *ART AND LIBERTY*

The contemporaneity of *Art and Liberty* reflects a temporal progression whereby the particular—i.e., the local evolution of style in a location commonly perceived as marginal and derivative—was in tandem with and at times transcending that of the universal, the latter conventionally allocated the stature of grand centre of innovation. I would like to refer this as multiple temporalities. The timeliness of *Art and Liberty*'s contributions, both vis-à-vis their immediate context, as well as their international associations, implies a convergence of multiple temporal speeds, and therefore art histories, signifying a synchronization in pace between the time along which both, local and global artistic contributions evolved. In that sense, as Keith Moxey would argue many years later in his inquiry into notions of multiple modernities, *Art and Liberty* is a case in point for how the reconstruction of an alternative canon can be possible without forcing the art history of the marginal to operate in tandem with that of the dominant centre.[109]
With all the preceding in mind, as we explore *Art and Liberty*'s example of modernism, I would like to invite us to, first, consider a paradigm that operates beyond the lens of Saïdian Orientalism, and second, to allow *Art and Liberty* to challenge our preconceived notions of what we have come to take for granted about Surrealism.

INTERNATIONALISM VS. ORIENTALISM

In seeking to instigate a rupture away from national constraints, *Art and Liberty* conceived of an artistic domain that transcended the rigid regionalist categories by which artists were classified and judged, a sphere of creativity that was driven by considerations of an artistic rather than a nationalistic nature. In taking advantage of the influx of international artists and writers into Egypt due to World War II, and through putting into use a multi-latticed network of fluid hubs spread over a disparate number of cities across the world, they embarked on their artistic and

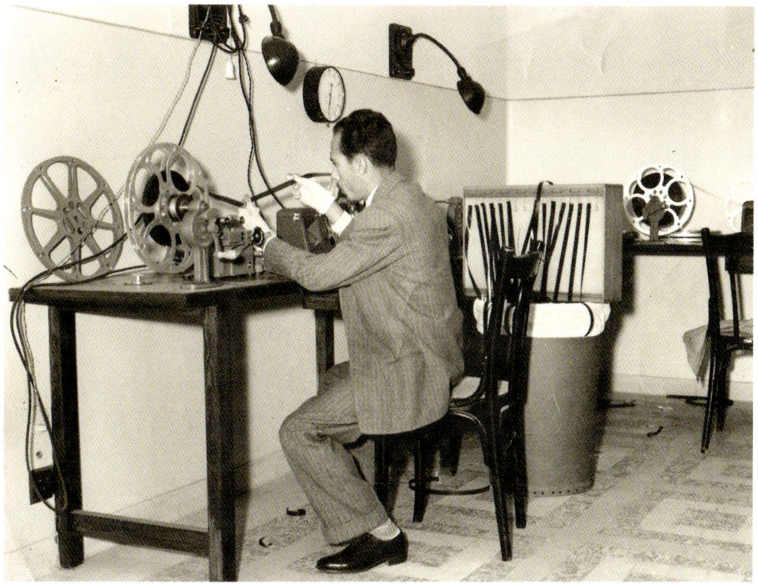

27

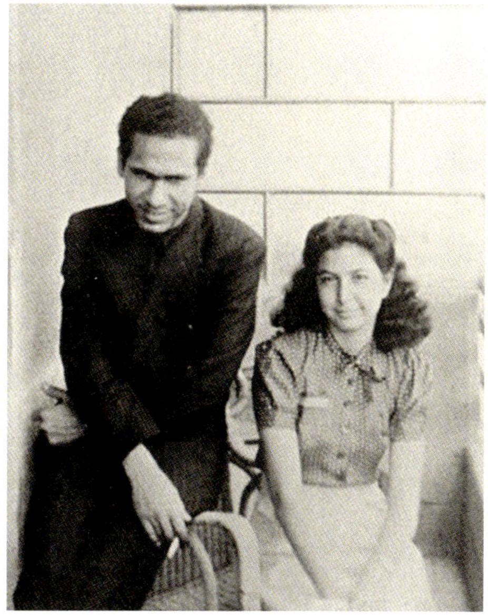

28

political project with the awareness that liberty comes from ideas, while geographic and national affiliations can only lead to the demise of the individual's unfettered evolution.
Years after the dissolution of the group, Ramses Younane would declare: "Although it was essentially a Surrealist movement, '*Art and Liberty*' welcomed other different artistic trends. It also helped relate the Egyptian artist to the contemporary world . . . Therefore cultural invasion is not the issue, it is rather cultural response, expressed in breaking out of the boundaries of national tradition into the international heritage."[110] Ramses Younane's advancement of the notion of cultural response can be considered as one of *Art and Liberty*'s main contributions towards affecting a shift in the discourse on art and regionalism. Breaking out beyond national boundaries to partake in a contemporary international network of artists, was in a sense the modus operandi that underpinned all of *Art and Liberty*'s activities. Alongside Younane, from as early as 1939, El-Telmisany had already spoken of how significant it is for artists in Egypt "to be in sync with the world and not fall behind while everybody else marches forward."[111] In that same article written in defense of *Art and Liberty* and their association with Surrealism, El-Telmisany demonstrated a truly global grasp of the movement, not only through quoting some of its seminal figures and important affiliates such as André Breton, Roland Penrose, Herbert Read, Max Ernst, Henry Moore, Salvador Dali, Paul Klee, Giorgio de Chirico, and Paul Delvaux, but through listing some of the many places where Surrealism has caught on with countries as far flung as Mexico, the United States, England, and Belgium. El-Telmisany exhibited an equal awareness of the main Surrealist publications like *Minotaure*, *Clé*, and Herbert Read's *Surrealism* and *The London Bulletin* all of which would at one point or another publish writings and news by and about *Art and Liberty*.

The group's insistence on the internationalism of art signifies a conviction in an ongoing process of cultural transfer, of appropriation and negotiation that allows for a cross-germination of ideas and practices allowing the artist possibilities for growth and creation that far outweigh the consequences that result from a much-contested nationalism. In an article that appeared on the pages of the leftist political and cultural review *Al-Majallah Al-Jadidah* on September 15, 1943, with Ramses Younane by then at the helm of its editorial office, Fouad Kamel provides a heartfelt defense of modern art that exemplifies the group's commitment to internationalism and rejection of nationalism. He writes:

> Internationalism is one of Modern art's most brilliant characteristics, for all those who contributed towards its construction— especially when it comes to the school of Paris—

27
Hassan El-Telmisani in the editing suite, c. 1950
Photographer unknown
Digital print on paper
El-Telmissany family Archives, Cairo

28
Inji Efflatoun and Kamel El-Telmisany, c. 1942
Photographer unknown
Digital print on paper
El-Telmissany family Archives, Cairo

belong to various nations and races. Therefore, whenever we go through such painters as the ones who settled in Paris and acquired fame we will find Chagall, di Chirico, Ernst, —, Miro, Modigliani, —, Picasso, Soutine, and —, all strangers to French blood. . . . Once we concede to the fact that Modern Art resulted from the participation of all nationalities, we cannot but admit that modern art is equally a pure mirror that reflects the overall decay within western societies. . . . Modern art can only be assessed as a response against these conditions and as a means of resistance against them. Therefore, Surrealism is in reality nothing but a hard slap in the face replete with all the rational and literary meanings that the revolution against these fake traditions has come to signify.[112]

Kamel's reasoning, which was in line with that of El-Telmisany and of Younane, further reveals the extent to which *Art and Liberty*'s practice was informed by a network of complex and current nodes, rather than the reductive and binary notions largely adopted within the discourse on nation and heritage. *Art and Liberty*'s example, therefore, provides us with an alternative paradigm for art historical construction, or more accurately reconstruction, that transcends the confines of geotemporal linearity, and the regionalist designations employed when attempting to write histories of multiple modernities.

What *Art and Liberty* were calling for, and what seems to me an appropriate paradigm for us to follow as we look back and attempt to comprehend the particularity of their position, is an awareness that all art has been informed in one way or another by an ongoing process of cultural transfer. When the field of art history continues to be singular or region-centric, and museum displays, even if only for the sake of pragmatism and popularity, keep with inherited classifications and hierarchies, the artwork can never be anything but an anomaly: a syncretic object that is ironically denied the promiscuity of its attributes by the same discipline that is supposedly meant to reveal its heterogeneity. Kitty Zijlmans has proposed a solution to this conundrum through an approach to art history that she refers to as the intercultural perspective. I find the part in which she tackles the notion of centre and periphery especially relevant in that it reflects *Art and Liberty*'s critical thinking about these issues: "The centre/periphery model is taken as a flexible one. There is no fixed centre, the centre is (or in historical research, was) where the action is (was), as seen from the perspective of the art in question. Centre/periphery can also apply to the canon. An intercultural perspective rejects the idea of a fixed canon; it is static neither in place nor in time."[113]

Many years earlier, when discussing the *Art and Liberty* Group within an argument about the attributes of modern art, and in foreshadowing Zijlman's notion of Interculturalism, Ramses Younane wrote:

> We can safely say that the *Art and Liberty* Group was like a seed from which—directly or indirectly—have emerged the various innovative trends that appeared amongst our artists since the last war. The benefit of the movement was not limited to linking us with the sources of an art that is alive at a time when our connection to European art was confined to its deteriorating images; for in connecting us to these living fountains, Surrealism has led us to a global cultural heritage which is one of modern art's fundamental constituents. In doing so, Surrealism has brought us full circle making us rediscover our heritage of popular legends

inspiring our artists to evoke it in their work. . . . Many will say that modern art is nothing but one of colonialism's many fruits; that colonialism, having invaded the world with its armies, has also invaded its cultures wiping out its traditions and arts. Yet we cannot but notice that European art had already been influenced by the arts of the orient and Africa long before any Oriental or African artist were influenced by European art. Modern art began—at least in regards to some of its most important aspects—as a revolution against the European heritage represented in the Greco-Roman tradition and the norms of the Renaissance. One of the factors that contributed to this revolution, there is no argument about it, was the interaction with the arts of the Far East, followed by the old orient, African Art and Islamic Art . . . This is not a matter of cultural invasion, but of profound cultural revolution, represented here in transcending the circle of national tradition to enter into the perimeter of global heritage. This is what Malraux has spoken about in his 'imaginary museum.' This museum that can be built nowhere, but is constructed in the mind due to the monographs of modern art that can include between its front and back covers the caves of Lascaux with its primitive paintings, the temple of Luxor, the Indian cave of Ajanta, the Parthenon, the Mexican Pyramids and Chartres Cathedral, not to mention the endless wonders that can be found in the museums of Cairo, Rome, Florence, Paris, Moscow, Beijing, London, Madrid, and New York.[114]

Besides putting forward a prototype for the "Intercultural Perspective" that Zijlman's proposed years later, Younane's thesis touches upon several other notions that were to be articulated by a number of art historians and theorists when broaching the question: "Can Art History be Global?" Younane, and the *Art and Liberty* Group, seem to have pondered these questions foreshadowing the very similar ones that historians like James Elkins would ask, when he writes: "What is the shape, or what are the shapes, of art history across the world? Is it becoming global—that is does it have a recognizable form wherever it is practiced? Can the methods, concepts, and purposes of Western art history be suitable for art outside of Europe and North America? And if not, are there alternatives that are compatible with existing modes of art history?"[115] Elkins's questions could have their answer, albeit retroactively, within Younane's early vision of an art history that is able to transcend the geographical boundaries and chronological lineages of source and copy to provide us with a model of perpetual fluidity and exchange by which a so-called European movement such as Surrealism could enable artists in Egypt to rediscover and imagine anew a local vernacular of popular imagery, and at the same time, Islamic art or African art could equip Surrealist artists in Paris, to give but one example, with the creative impetus to articulate a new aesthetic that they can then put at the service of their own cultural revolution.

Younane's comparative analysis does not assign any judgment and is able to see artistic traditions on par with each other within a context of cross-germination and fluid transplantation. What is even more remarkable is Younane's refusal to use the facile narrative by which the so-called periphery, in this case Egypt, is the victim of the so-called center, represented in his argument by Colonialism. Younane evades the static roles whereby the art of the colonized can be legitimized only if it aligned itself with nationalism, or emulated the art of the colonizer. In doing so, Younane rejected, many years earlier, what would become the prevailing rhetoric of both Saïdian Orientalism and post-colonial studies, which in their desire to empower the other, one could

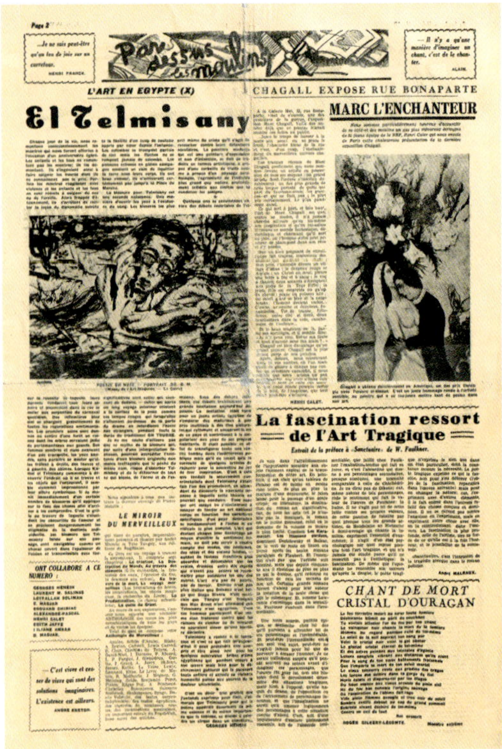

Par dessus les moulins

L'ART EN EGYPTE (X)

El Telmisany

CHAGALL EXPOSE RUE BONAPARTE

MARC L'ENCHANTEUR

La fascination ressort de l'Art Tragique

LE MIROIR DU MERVEILLEUX

CHANT DE MORT CRISTAL D'OURAGAN

29

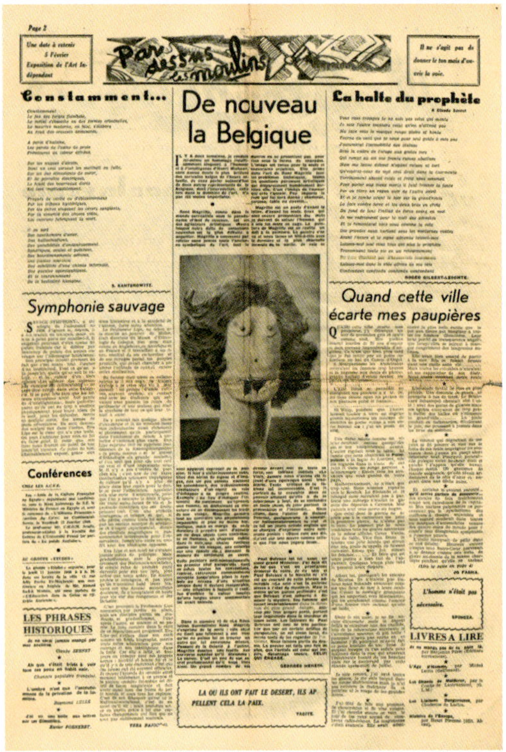

Par dessus les moulins

Constamment...

De nouveau la Belgique

La halte du prophète

Symphonie sauvage

Quand cette ville écarte mes paupières

Conférences

LES PHRASES HISTORIQUES

LIVRES A LIRE

30

argue, have inadvertently contributed to its othering. Instead, he and his fellow *Art and Liberty* artists and writers, have striven to articulate a notion of art history where multilateral exchanges assume primacy over identity politics and contested geographic boundaries that are usually reflective of ongoing power struggles. (ills. 29–30).

While the discipline of post-colonial studies that owes much of its logic to Saïdian Orientalism has been often employed as an intellectual counter position to an arguably prevalent Eurocentric canon, the assessment of *Art and Liberty*'s contributions and position within the canon of Surrealism might be better achieved through adopting another approach; one that is not framed by the polemics of Orientalism. Although such a theoretical notion might seem the most valid, I would like to propose that, perhaps in the case of the *Art and Liberty* Group, it might be counterproductive. As Patricia Almarcegui has put it: "Orientalism obliged binary thinking or, in other words, the assumption that Westernism also existed. In this way, the West was considered a homogeneous entity lacking in heterogeneity. Neither was Westernism the answer to Orientalism. As stated by the anthropologist James Clifford, possibly one of the most lucid critics of Orientalism, Saïd was dichotomizing and, therefore, essentializing, what had always been a continuum: East and West."[116] Clifford's, Almarcegui's, and several recent scholarly projects that seek a new position towards the study of modernity beyond the lens of Saïd's Orientalism seem to me the better way to go when it comes to analyzing the example of *Art and Liberty*, not only for how they perceived themselves, but equally so, for the way in which they could not perceive an "other," in this case that other being their European Surrealist counterparts.[117] Saïd's notion was a pioneering light that paved new entry points into the disciplines of cultural and literary theory that have all culminated, so to speak, in the vast discipline of post-colonial studies. This has become the field of choice for art-historians seeking the expiatory rhetoric with which they could exonerate the other. Yet, while *Art and Liberty* were well aware of such tilted narratives, they never perceived themselves, as victims to their hegemony. To use the words of James Clifford, "rather than considering the tautological art of identity lost and regained, we would instead be attending to real spaces filled with relational knots that are always difficult to untangle and that in any case cannot be reduced to a confrontation between self and other, past and present."[118]

29
Don Quichotte, hebdomadaire d'actualité paraissant le jeudi,
no. 17, March 29, 1940, p. 2
Print journal
Bibliothèque de documentation internationale contemporaine (BDIC), Nanterre

30
Don Quichotte, hebdomadaire d'actualité paraissant le jeudi,
no. 6, January 11, 1940, p. 2
Print journal
Bibliothèque de documentation internationale contemporaine (BDIC), Nanterre

Through a decade spent in making art, exhibiting it and writing about it, all within a dialogical framework that favored a conceptually disposed internationalism over a locally contrived nationalism, *Art and Liberty* had in effect manifested a prototype for several philosophical and theoretical positions that would not be articulated until decades later. Through their cultural and artistic polyglotism, they were able to enter a process of negotiation, hybridization, and ultimately metempsychosis propelling them to develop the type of malleability and mobility that predate, to cite a few examples, Zygmunt Bauman's "Liquid Modernity,"[119] Césaire's "Créolization,"[120] Anderson's "imagined communities,"[121] and Bourriaud's notion of the "Semionaut or Radicant"[122] artist. Therefore, in retelling their story, it is mandatory that *Art and Liberty* are presented neither within an orchestrated "Arab" art history that reinforces the notion of periphery and otherness, nor within the dialectics of Orientalism and Postcolonial Studies. Conversely to their exonerating objectives, these have framed their subjects within a binary that risks reducing them into passive victims, while contrarily, *Art and Liberty* provides us with a timely lesson in how an artist can be politically active without politicizing their work, belonging to a place and relevant to their time, but never at the mercy of their geotemporal grip.

THE RECONSIDERATION OF SURREALISM AND ITS CANON

Art and Liberty's self-perception as central to the discourse and formulation of a new chapter in Surrealism's trajectory, provides us with an example in late modernism that challenges one of art history's most contested meta-narratives; that modernity, in this case represented by the Surrealist movement, was a Western (French) invention that took place in Europe (Paris and to a lesser extent London) to then be simulated decades later by the non-West, but to lesser effect, in this case Egypt. This notion still underlines the much-contested binary correlations of centre vs. periphery, the metropole vs. the colonies, the West vs. the non-West (ill. 29–30).

None of these dichotomies hold ground as far as *Art and Liberty* are concerned, for they envisioned themselves as partners within a fluid movement comprising of international networks whereby their role in instigating change and contributing artistically and intellectually was as valid and legitimate as that of any other Surrealist chapter anywhere else in the world. Their nationality and geographic location were not even a question. However, it was perhaps the time in which *Art and Liberty* emerged onto the Surrealist stage that was to be the biggest disadvantage. The rise of modern nation states, responding to the colonial past/present, was unfolding. Many artists were mining their visual heritage in search for iconic forms, through which they could communicate a vision of national identity. At home, these artists' legacies would be coerced into the nationalist project. When exhibited abroad, they would be equally enmeshed within a rigid system of hierarchical classifications elaborated through the reductive labels of ethnicity and geography. However, in contradiction, the artists who hailed from the so-called centers of artistic production, even when drawing their creative impulse from the same aesthetic objects and visual sources, were praised as the instigators of the avant-garde. Nada Shabout has coined this as a form of cultural "Occidentalism" emphasizing that the problematic of "self" and "other" is not the sole domain of the West, that questions regarding cultural appropriation were a reflection of a conscious, global, theoretical reworking of aesthetics, and that "it is the inequality

of power that allows Matisse's and Klee's adaptation and philosophical reformulations of Islamic aesthetics [and the Surrealists' of Primitive or traditional Mexican art, for instance] to pass without commentary thus far, while a comparison to a European counterpart is always deemed necessary when speaking of Arab artists [*Art and Liberty* included])."[123]
In reflecting on the downfalls of comparison as a prevalent conceptual tool through which artists and artworks from different parts of the world have usually been designated into art-historical narratives and hierarchies, Mieke Bal has stated that "(comparison) quickly becomes a ground for (relative) judgment and establishing hierarchies, and it distracts from looking. Indeed, art thus seems to be an area where judgment is compulsory. Instead of 'just looking,' the ordinary as well as the expert viewer feels compelled to judge. . . . There are, however, other forms of comparison, not built on a logic of oppositional judgment. Comparison can be a tool for analysis as long as one of its terms is not established as normative. . . . As soon as comparison promotes judgment and one term is instituted as the norm, there will always be the lesser work, and we are discouraged from taking a good look at it because we already 'know' it is less valuable, less pleasurable, less intelligent—in short, less masterly (and we may add less worthy of entering into the canon)."[124]

Bal's insightful dissection of the disadvantageous purposes of comparison as a vantage point from which to assign value is a good alternative even to the most honourable of polemical defenses aimed at rescuing the helpless "other" from the marginalising effect of the powerful centre. The studies that have been conducted on *Art and Liberty*, as well intended as they may have been, have one short sightedness in common. In all of their discussions about the Surrealism of the group, none of them stopped to question the canon of Surrealism in its European manifestation. The underlying assumption that has been maintained until the present, and against which the authenticity of *Art and Liberty*'s Surrealism continues to be assessed, is that Surrealism looks a certain way, signifies a specific set of tenets, espouses a particular political project, has its conclusive bona fide canon and begins and ends within clearly marked dates and in very specific places. It is exactly this type of a priori uncontested knowledge that would in as early as 1951 lead art collector and amateur art critic Comte d'Arschot to the somehow essentializing conclusion that "in matters of the plastic arts, Surrealism has not opened up any new perspectives for Egyptian artists. Those who have allowed themselves to be seduced by this school have only adhered to it in a superficial manner; their subconscious having certain complexities that Surrealism cannot address in the same manner that it has managed to resolve in the Occident. Fact is, there is between oriental sentiments and ours, a frontier that only someone with a profound knowledge of the two sensibilities can manage to cross with ease. Therefore, in order to avoid running into the danger of being imprecise, we cannot apply the label of Surrealism on all forms of expression that attach themselves to it from near or from far."[125]

This kind of binary thinking that designates the Orient as irreconcilable with the Occident and therefore unable to adequately respond or utilize an art movement that has ostensibly resulted from the cultural and geographical terrain of the latter is contradictory to how *Art and Liberty* viewed and conducted themselves. This limited and limiting approach by which Surrealism, and in consequence art history at large, is not allowed to be anything other than what has been canonically established, is the reason behind the narrative that has ironically cemented the notion of the centre that *Art and Liberty* had attempted to shift. This "commitment to tradition,"[126] to refer to Moxey's "Motivating History" again, is a blind spot within the discipline of art-history that continues to hinder new possibilities of seeing that designate *Art and Liberty* as a derivative imitation of an otherwise monolithic European movement, while all along, *Art and Liberty* perceived Surrealism as an expression of an artistic language, responding to the cultural and political needs of its time, still in flux, hesitating in its methods, and far from being rigid or complete.[127] They saw themselves to be capable of articulating, with confidence, a new direction, along with a visual and literary language to go with it, for a movement that was going through a crisis of orientation. As far as they were concerned, this was neither a matter of geography or race, but urgency for artistic expression and cultural relevance.

Based on the above, and in using the words of Craig Clunas from a study on Chinese art, "therein lies the central issue. Far from simply arguing for inclusion in the art-historical canon of hitherto neglected or disregarded material, we need to lay down the discipline's claim that we already know everything [about Surrealism] . . . if we wish to learn anything at all."[128] In other words, a full understanding of the contributions of the *Art and Liberty* Group can only become possible once we allow ourselves to shed our pre-established knowledge of what we have come to "know" in advance of Surrealism and, therefore, of what it must look like and how it must be expressed. Only then can we fully grasp *Art and Liberty*'s significant position, not only in regards to the evolution of modernism in Egypt, but towards the construction of a new definition of Surrealism, one that contributes to an inclusive vision of art history where the particularities of the peripheral are no longer seen as dichotomous with the authority of the central, and perhaps even to an extent where such oppositions are no longer visible.

Art and Liberty's deliberation, alteration, and implementation of Surrealism while simultaneously conversing with the global and attending to the local, highlights the great benefits that were reaped from the literary and artistic networks of the 1930s and 1940s; networks that transcended national and geographical barriers and loyalties to include a younger generation of international writers and artists, such as the ones in Cairo. Within this prolific and far-reaching network, enhanced to its peak by to the diasporic effects of World War II, a new generation of Surrealists could connect on an international scale. This was a generation that was intent on questioning all the givens of the movement in search for relevance and renewed artistic and political agency. The example of *Art and Liberty*, therefore, and the entanglement of their activities with a complex network of literary and artistic hubs dispersed in cities as far-flung as Cairo, Athens, Paris, London, New York, and San Francisco—and in the case of Surrealism we can easily add Prague, Mexico City, Fort-de-France, Santiago de Chile, and Tokyo just to name a few— challenges the regionalist approach to the study of modernity demonstrating that it is ultimately the power of an idea to inspire and rally people around it, that triggers the significant shifts that mark the course of history. ■

NOTES

1 Keith Moxey, "Motivating History," *The Art Bulletin,* vol. 77, no. 3 (September 1995): 392.

2 For more on Panofsky's theories of art-historical interpretation see Erwin Panofsky, "The History of Art as a Humanistic Discipline," in *The Meaning of the Humanities,* ed. T. Greene (Princeton, NJ: Princeton University Press, 1940), 89–118.

3 Kamal al-Mallakh and Rushdi Iskandar, *Thamanūn sana min al-fann* (Cairo: General Egyptian Book Organization Press, 1991), 118.
4 Naïm Atiyyah, *Al-'ayn la tazal 'ashiqah* (Cairo: Al-hay'ah al-'aammah li qusour al-thaqafah, 1998), 38.
5 Georges Henein, "Le *III*e Salon de l'Art Indépendant," *La Bourse Égyptienne* 121, May 22, 1942.
6 Georges Henein, *The First Exhibition of Independent Art, February 8–24,* exhibition catalog published in conjunction with the exhibition which took place at the Nile Club Talaat Harb Square (Midan Soliman Pasha at the time). *Art and Liberty* Group, Cairo, 1940.
7 Lee Miller to Roland Penrose, Cairo, January 23–27, 1939, Lee Miller Archives at Farley Farm House, Chiddingly, UK.
8 Ramses Younane, *Ghayat al-rassam al-'asri* (Cairo: Jama'aat al-di'aayah al-fanniyyah, 1938), 50.
9 The references are simply too many to cite, but here are some of the ones that are most commonly referred to: Samir Gharib, *Al-suriyāliyya fi miṣr* (Cairo: General Egyptian Book Organization Press, 1998), 54; Don LaCoss, "Egyptian Surrealism and 'Degenerate Art' in 1939," *Arab Studies Journal* 18, no. 1 (Spring 2010): 78–117.
10 Georges Henein, *De l'irréalisme,* from *Un Effort* (Cairo, 1935) as cited in Alexandrian, *Georges Henein,* 11–12.
11 Georges Henein, *Le chant des violents* (June 1935), *Vive la Catalogne* and *Si on ne le pend pas* (December 1936), *Projet d'un monument international* (November 1937), from *Les Humbles* (Paris, September–October 1936).
12 Sarane Alexandrian, *Georges Henein,* from the collection *Poètes d'aujourd'hui* (Paris: Seghers, 1981), 67.
13 Alexandrian, *Georges Henein,* 17.
14 Georges Henein, *Lettres: Georges Henein – Henri Calet (Grandes Largeurs)* Letter 14 (Association Henri Calet, Fall–Winter 1981), 26–27.
15 "Art et Liberté," *Clé* 2 (February 1939): 12.
16 Georges Henein, "Franz Kafka: le Chateau," *Clé* 2 (February 1939).
17 Georges Henein, "Marcel Jouhandeau: Chroniques Maritales," *Clé* 1 (January 1939): 2.
18 For more on the Surrealist gallery at 16 rue Jacques Callot, see Nathalia Brodskaïa, *Surrealism* (New York: Parkstone International, 2012), 123; for more on Mayo, see Gérald Messadié et al., *Mayo* (Paris: Association Mayo/Evelyne Yeatman-Eiffel, 2012).
19 "Exposition Mayo," *La Semaine Égyptienne,* year 7, no. 35–36 (November 30, 1933): front cover.
20 Along with de Boully, Mayo is listed as one of the contributors the cover of the Spring 1929 issue of le Grand Jeu's review entitled after the group's name. Boully inscribes his book *Er l'Armenien* (Paris: Éditions Sagesse and Librairie Tschann, 1938), with a signed dedication to Henein that reads: "À mon ami : Georges Henin avec la joie toujours renouvelée de le rencontrer par hazard (le plus heureux des hazards), bien cordialement, Monny de Boully – otherwise: Henein). The book can be found in the Bibliothèque Georges Henein at the Institut Français du Caire.
21 Some examples of texts that were illustrated by Mayo include: Ivo Barbitch, "Faiblesse," *La Semaine Égyptienne,* Christmas issue, year 8, no. 1–2 (1934): 9; Edmond Jabès, "Quatrains," *La Semaine Égyptienne,* year 8, no. 3–4 (January 15, 1934); Marietta Minotou, "Près du Puits," *La Semaine Égyptienne,* year 7, no. 33–34 (November 18, 1933): 14; Costis Palamas, "Alexandre Papadiamandis," *La Semaine Égyptienne,* year 7, no. 31–32 (October 31, 1933): 5; Jeanne Arcache, "Sur une maison morte," *La Semaine Égyptienne,* year 7, no. 29 – 30 (October 15, 1933): 6; For Mayo's wartime illustrations see Jacques Prévert and others, Mayo (Paris: Éditions Jacques Damase, 1978), 42–81.
22 Ibid., November 9, 1937–December 29, 1937–March 9, 1938.
23 Kamel El-Telmisany, "Naḥwa fann hurr," *Al-Tatawwur* 38–40. 1
24 Lee Miller to Roland Penrose, London, January 30, 1939 (unpublished letter), Lee Miller Archives at Farley Farm House, Chiddingly, UK.
25 Ibid., January 23–27, 1939.
26 Ibid., March 9, 1938.
27 Several entries from the unpublished diaries of Roland Penrose (1937–39), (Ref. GMA A35/1/1/RPA200), Roland Penrose Archives at the Library of the National Gallery of Scotland in Edinburgh.
28 Lee Miller in Cairo to Roland Penrose in London, January 6, 1939 (unpublished letter), Lee Miller Archives at Farley Farm House, Chiddingly, UK
29 "Activités De Art et Liberté," *Art et Liberté* 2 (May 1939): 4.
30 Roland Penrose, "From Egypt," *The London Bulletin* 13 (April 15, 1939), 15.
31 Robert Motherwell, "Some Memories of Pre-Dada: Picabia and Duchamp," *The Dada Painters and Poets* (New York: Wittenborn, Schultz, Inc., 1951), 255.
32 André Breton, *Entretiens 1913-1952* (Paris: Gallimard, 1952), 52.
33 J. H. Matthews, *An Introduction to Surrealism* (University Park, PA: Pennsylvania State University Press, 1965), 20.
34 For more on this topic see Anna Katharina Schaffner, "Dissecting the Order of Signs: On the Textual Politics of Dada Poetics" in Elza Adamowicz and Eric Roberson, *Dada and Beyond,* vol. 1, *Dada Discourses* (Amsterdam: Rodopi Brill Editions, 2011), 37–50.
35 For more on this topic, see Sarah Ganz Blyth and Edward D. Powers, *Looking at Dada* (New York: Museum of Modern Art, 2011).
36 For more on this topic, see George Baker, *The Artwork Caught by the Tail: Francis Picabia and Dada in Paris* (Cambridge, MA: MIT Press, 2007).
37 For more on this topic, see Marius Hentea, *TaTa Dada: The Real Life and Celestial Adventures of Tristan Tzara* (Cambridge, MA: MIT Press Books, 2014), especially chapter six: "Tours and Season", 153–76.
38 André Breton, "Après Dada", *Comœdia* (March 1922), in Robert Motherwell, *The Dada Painters and Poets,* trans. Ralph Manheim, 2nd ed. (Cambridge and London: The Belknap Press of the Harvard University Press, 1989), 205.
39 For more on this topic, see André Breton, *Les Pas Perdus* (Paris: Gallimard, 1924).
40 Fore more on Surrealism and its relation to Communism, see Helena Lewis, "Surrealists, Stalinists, and Trotskyists: Theories of Art and Revolution in France between the Wars," *Art Journal,* vol. 52, no. 1 (Spring 1993): 61–68.
41 Ibid., 51.
42 For more on Surrealism in Japan, see Miryam Sas, *Fault Lines: Cultural Memory and Japanese Surrealism* (Stanford: Stanford University Press, 1999); Vera Linhartová, *Dada et Surréalisme au Japon* (Paris: Publications Orientalistes de France, 1987)
43 For more on *La Mandrágora* and Surrealism in Latin America, see Melanie Nicholson, *Surrealism in Latin American Literature: Searching for Breton's Ghost* (Basingstoke: Palgrave Macmillan, 2013).
44 For more on the repercussions of Surrealism in Mexico, see Luis M. Castañeda, "Surrealism and National Identity in Mexico: Changing Perceptions, 1940–1968," *Journal of Surrealism and the Americas,* vol. 3, no. 1–2 (2009): 9–29.

45 For more on Surrealism and the Négritude Movement, see Michel Hausser, *Pour une poétique de la negritude,* vols. 1 and 2 (Paris: Silex, 1988); Michael Richardson and Krzysztof Fijalkowski, eds., *Refusal of the Shadow: Surrealism and the Caribbean* (London and New York: Verso Books, 1996).

46 For more on this topic, see Laila Morsy, "The Military Clauses of The Anglo-Egyptian Treaty of Friendship and Alliance, 1936," *International Journal of Middle East Studies 16,* no. 1 (March 1984): 67–97.

47 Peter Mansfield, *The British in Egypt* (New York: Holt, Rinehart and Winston, 1972), 58–59.

48 Trefor E. Evans, ed., *The Killearn Diaries 1934–46* (London: Sidgwick and Jackson, 1972), 215.

49 Quarterly medical reports for the Cairo area, July 1941–December 1946. WO 222/1337, British National Archives.

50 James Morris, *Farewell the Trumpets: An Imperial Retreat* (New York: Helen and Kurt Wolff Books, 1980), 419.

51 For more on this topic, see Roger Bowen, *Many Histories Deep: The Personal Landscape Poets in Egypt, 1940–45* (Cranbury, NJ: Associated University Presses, 1995).

52 With a French mother, Amy had a strong connection to France. From the early age of seventeen she had two paintings, *Passion* and *Scéance du Café* exhibited at the *Salon d'Automne* of 1925. After studying at London's Slade School of Fine Art between the years 1926 and 1929, she frequented the studio of Walter Sickert. During the 1930s, Amy exhibited in various Paris galleries such as Galerie Vignon and Bernheim Jeune. Her first close encounter with a young generation of British Surrealists would take place in 1930 when she would be invited by Lucy Wertheim, to participate in a group exhibition at her newly opened Gallery at 3–5 Burlington Gardens in Mayfair. The exhibition was to include a number of young English artists and would constitute the nucleus for the significant yet short-lived *Twenties Group.* Amy, who was twenty-three years old at the time, would see her paintings alongside works by Barbara Hepworth and Robert Medley. He would eventually be stationed in Cairo as a war artist and would participate in *Art and Liberty*'s fifth exhibition of 1945. Around the same time, Amy also exhibited at the Warren Gallery in London. The gallery owner Dorothy Warren Trotter was one of the most daring London dealers of the time who gave Henry Moore his first solo exhibition in 1928, exhibited the explicit paintings of D. H. Lawrence whose raw sexual content caused a huge outrage upon the opening on June 14, 1929, and the artists and life-partners Dorothy Hepworth and Patricia Preece who had studied at the Slade with Nimr. For more on Amy Nimr's biography are drawn from two primary sources: Jean Moscatelli, "Chez Amy Nimr," *La Semaine Egyptienne,* year 11, no. 3–4 (February 1937): 3–4; Aimé Azar and Philippe d'Arschot, *Femmes Peintres d'Égypte* (Cairo: Imprimerie Française, 1953), 64. More information was provided by Ms. Soraya Antonios, Amy Nimr's niece, on Friday, February 6, 2015, in Nicosia, Cyprus, and on Saturday and Sunday, October 17 and 18, 2015, in Gadencourt, France. Further sources include Morik Brin and André de Laumois, *Peintres et sculpteurs de l'Égypte contemporaine* (Cairo: Les Amis de la culture française en Égypte, 1935), 26; Henry Moore, *Henry Moore: Writings and Conversations,* ed. Alan Wilkinson (Oakland, CA: University of California Press, 2002), 59; D. H. Lawrence, *The Cambridge Edition of the Works of D. H. Lawrence: Late Essays and Articles,* vol. 2, ed. James T. Boulton (Cambridge: Cambridge University Press, 2004), 182; Claude J. Summers, ed., "Hepworth, Dorothy and Patricia Preece," *The Queer Encyclopedia of the Visual Arts* (San Francisco, CA: Cleis Press, 2004), 168–69.

53 Situated at 101 rue de la Tombe Issoire in the 14th arrondissement of Paris, Villa Seurat was a quiet cul-de-sac, which during the 1920s and the 1930s, served as a hub for many avant-garde artists and writers such as Chaïm Soutine and Salvador Dalí, Henry Miller, and Anaïs Nin. For more on this topic, see Douglas Stone, *Henry Miller and the Villa Seurat Circle* (Irvine: University of California Press, 1973).

54 Amy Nimr (Paris) to Paul Vanderborght (Brussels), July 6, 1934, ref. ML 07738/0005/007, Paul Vanderborght Archives, Archives et Musée de la Littérature, Bibliothèque Royale, Brussels.

55 In describing her visit to Nimr's atelier at Villa Seurat perched on the top of a crooked wooden stairway, we learn from Surrealist port Marie Cavadia, a main patron of *Art and Liberty*, that Nimr was at her most accomplished Surrealist phase: " And lastly, two small mysterious paintings representing a stampede of prisoners in a dream-like atmosphere, would be the latest works of Amy Nimr. These horses that have arrived from the end of life to stop at the far reaches of death, neigh at our souls opening the floodgates to magic. Here the surrealism is intended, premeditated and accomplished." For more on this, see Marie Cavadia, "Une Exposition d'Amy Nimr," *La Semaine Égyptienne,* no. 3–4, (February 11, 1937): 16.

56 Mandy Prowse (granddaughter of Natalija Lovett-Turner), in discussion with the author, London, July 9, 2015.

57 H. Soulon, "Nata Lovett-Turner," *La Semaine Égyptienne* 19, no. 9–10 (April 1945): 26; Eric de Nemes, "Nata Lovett-Turner's Paintings," *The Sphinx*, April 14, 1945.

58 One of the many other Lovett-Turner exhibitions that was widely covered in the local press took place at the Cairo British Institute from March 14 until March 20, 1948, and was reviewed by leading critics such as Ahmad Rassim, Étienne Meriel, and André Raymond, and covered by leading papers and reviews such as *The Egyptian Mail*, *Le Progrès Égyptien*, *La Semaine Égyptienne*, and *Al-Balagh.* This was confirmed in an interview with Mandy Prowse (see note 10), during which I consulted the said press clippings.

59 Alan Neame and Jabra Ibrahim Jabra, *The Baghdad Exhibition of Painting and Sculpture,* exh. cat. (Baghdad: The Trading and Printing Co. Ltd., 1956); *The Baghdad Exhibition of Painting and Sculpture,* exh. cat. (Baghdad: The Trading and Printing Co. Ltd., 1957); *Iraq and Britain: Sixth Annual Exhibition of Paintings,* May 14th to 24th, exh. cat. (Baghdad: The British Institute Club, 1957).

60 "Discussion Between Realists and Surrealists," *The London Bulletin* 1 (April 1938): 20.

61 Muhammad Rateb Seddik, *Tajribāt fi al-fann wa al-ḥayat,* part 1 (Cairo: Al-hay'a al-maṣriyyah al-'ammah lil kitab, 1989), 14.

62 For more on this, see Brian Foss, *War Paint: Art, War, State and Identity in Britain, 1939–1945* (London: The Paul Mellon Centre for Studies in British Art, 2007); works by Edward Bawden and Edward Ardizzone were included in the exhibition of contemporary British art that was organized in 1945 by the British Council in Cairo. More on this in section II, chapter 3 of this study.

63 Very little biographical information exists on Angelo de Riz. In the novel *25, Rue Soliman Pacha,* Gerald Messadié (Paris: Jean-Claude Lattès, 2001), 216, he is portrayed as the local Surrealist painter who has decorated a fresco for the house of Louis Hanafi, another character based on Georges Henein. For more biographical information see Aimé Azar, *La peinture moderne en Égypte* (Cairo: Les Éditions Nouvelles, 1961), 340.

64 Azar, *La peinture moderne en Égypte,* 340.

65 Kamel El-Telmisany, "L'Art en Égypte V: Angelo de Riz" *Don Quichotte* 10 (February 8, 1940): 1.

66 Maria Golia, *Photography and Egypt* (Chicago: University of Chicago Press, 2010), 146–47. This information was further verified with the curators at the Musée Nicéphore Niépce in Chalon-sur-Saône, France.

67 Jean Cocteau (text) and Étienne Sved (photographs), *Maalesh: Voyages en Égypte* (Marseille: Le Bec en l'air, 2008).

68 For more on this topic see Selma Botman, *Egypt from Independence to Revolution, 1919–1952,* (Syracuse, NY: Syracuse University Press, 1991).
69 Ali Adham, "Falsafat al-fāshiyya," *Al-Muqtataf* 3 (March 1, 1939): 290–94.
70 Ahmad Khaki, "Al-imbratūriyya al-almāniyya al-nāziyya," *Al-Majallah Al-Jadidah* 6 (June 1, 1939): 33–41.
71 James Murphy, "Adolf Hitler wa-l-hukūma al-almānniya," *Al-Majallah Al-Jadidah* 6 (June 1, 1936): 19–32.
72 For more on this topic and the controversy surrounding the translation, see Michael Ford, *Mein Kampf: A Translation Controversy* (Elite Minds Inc., 2009).
73 Ghali Ameen, "Al-fāshiyya kama yaraha du'ātuhā," *Al-Majallah Al-Jadidah* 2 (February 1, 1936): 45.
74 *Al-Ahram,* January 11, 1936, 10.
75 *The Manchester Guardian,* July 21, 1936, 12, and *Times,* August 18, 1936, 19.
76 For more on this topic, see Richard Paul Mitchell, *The Society of the Muslim Brothers* (Oxford: Oxford University Press, 1993), 199–202.
77 Bernd Philipp Schröder, *Deutschland und der Mittlere Osten im zweiten Weltkrieg* (Göttingen: Musterschmidt, 1975), 58.
78 James P. Jankowski, "The Egyptian Blue Shirts and the Egyptian Wafd, 1935–1938," *Middle Eastern Studies* 6, no. 1 (January, 1970): 82.
79 In his *Tarīkh al-ḥaraka al-fanniyya fi misr ila 'ām 1945*, Mohammad Sidqi El-Gabakhangui presents us with a chronology that sees the *Société* as a natural continuation of the activities of the Egyptian Association of Fine Arts that was founded two years earlier in 1921.This is not what Al-Mallakh and Iskandar tell us in their *Khamsūn sana min al-fann*. In contradiction they insinuate that Fouad Abdel Malek falsely attributed the 1921 spring exhibition that he organized under the auspices of his House of Arts and Crafts as the fourth in a series of annual exhibitions that first took place informally in 1918 upon the call of several local Egyptian artists who then went on to found in 1919 the Egyptian Association of Fine Arts. In highlighting its birth as a response to the call in 1918 for an annual exhibition of Egyptian artists, the authors contend that Abdel Malek sought to ascribe the *Société*'s existence to as early as 1919. For more on this see Mohammad Sidqi El-Gabakhangui, *Tarīkh al-ḥaraka al-fanniyya fi misr ila 'ām 1945* (Cairo: The General Egyptian Authority for the Book, 1986), 38–44; Al-Mallakh and Iskandar, *Khamsūn sana min al-fann* (Cairo: Dar al-ma'ārif, 1962), 108–10.
80 Salmawy and El-Razzaz, *Mohammad Mahmoud Khalil,* 32.
81 "Choses à dire. A propos du XVeme Salon," *Un Effort 54* (May 1935): 7, as cited in Francesca Rondinelli, "Continuité et rupture dans Un Effort, Revue culturelle et intellectuelle de l'entre-deux-guerres" (paper presented at the Centre d'Études Alexandrines, Alexandria, June 4, 2011), 20.
82 Aimé Azar, *La Peinture moderne en Égypte* (Cairo: Les Éditions Nouvelles, 1961), 52.
83 This is my own translation, and not the one found in Rosemont's mostly cited *Black, Brown, and Beige* where the word "present", expressed as "*al-hali*" in Arabic, and "*actuelle*" in French in the original Manifesto, has been mistranslated into the word "modern." This error has transformed the sentence into an open-ended statement stripping it from its immediate temporal, and spatial urgency. "It is well known that modern society looks with aversion" in Rosemont and Kelley, eds., *Black, Brown, and Beige,* 148.
84 These accounts have been confirmed in several sources: *Aujourd'hui l'Égypte* 27–29 (1995): 66; Mohamed Salmawy and Mustafa El-Razzaz, *Mohammad Mahmoud Khalil* (Cairo: Ministry of Culture, 1995), 13; Samir Raafat, "The House of Mohammed Mahmoud Khalil and How It Became a National Museum," *The Egyptian Mail,* May 6, 1995.
85 Worth mentioning here is that the caricature was considered briefly in Patrick Kane's significant and expansive book *The Politics of Art in Modern Egypt.* Kane cites the caricature's source as al-Mallakh and Iskandar's *Khamsūn sana min al-fann* (Fifty years of Art) as reproduced in their 1962 edition. He does not acknowledge, however, the original review in which the caricature appeared in the in the January 31, 1947 issue of *Al-Musawwar.* For more on this, see Patrick Kane, *The Politics of Art in Modern Egypt: Aesthetics, Ideology and Nation Building* (London: I.B. Taurus, 2012), 45.
86 Beneath Khalil to the right, we recognize in the guise of a servant, the person of Kamel El-Mawardi, secretary to the Office for the General Administration of Fine Arts. The advisory committee, of which Khalil was president, was in principle set up to counsel the general administration office, which out of the two bodies was the one that technically possessed official ministerial authority. Hassan's portrayal of the administrative office's secretary as a servant to Khalil reveals who it was that in reality had the upper hand. In further indicating Khalil's uncontested authority, Hassan brings in Georges Raymond, the presiding director of the Ministry's Office of the General Administration of Fine Arts, and shows him conducting the Nazi salute to Khalil. El-Mawardi, who in principle should be reporting to Raymond, is in confrontation with him, standing subserviently instead on Khalil's side. Hassan, who would eventually succeed Raymond as director of the General Administration office, paints himself standing next to Raymond performing the same gesture. Next to him, we identify French painter Pierre Beppi Martin who had settled in Egypt from as early as 1890, taught at the School of Fine Arts that was established in 1908 by the arts patron prince Youssef Kamal, and where he had occupied a number of administrative positions. Behind them, raised on an aisle was painter Ahmad Youssef, who at the time was the Dean of the School for Applied Arts, which back in 1919 had been co-founded by Hassan as the School for Decorative Arts.
87 Mustafa al-Razzaz, *Al-fann al-masri al-hadīth – al-qarn al-'ishrīn* (Cairo: The Fine Arts Sector, Egyptian Ministry of Culture, 2007), 40; Al-Mallakh and Iskandar ascribe the founding date to 1936 and speak of three major exhibitions that were hosted in the Ministry of Trade. Amongst the participants was Mohammad Hassan, the creator of the Dictatorship of the Fine Arts caricature and Ahmad Youssef whom Hassan depicted within his camp in the said painting. The League also exhibited other groups such as *Jamā'at al-di'āya al-fanniyya* that was founded in 1938 by Habib Gorgui and of which Ramses Younane was an active member (the group published his *Ghāyat al-rassām al-'asri* in 1938); Kamal al-Mallakh and Rushdi Iskandar, *Thamanūn sana min al-fann* (Cairo: General Egyptian Book Organization Press, 1991), 93–95, 103, 113, 143–145.
88 "Taqrīr 'an il-nahda al-fanniyya," *Al-'Usūr* 31–32 (March 1, 1930): 395.
89 Ibid.
90 This is my own translation. For the translation that has been often cited by English-speaking scholars, see Rosemont and Kelley, eds., *Black, Brown, and Beige,* 148.
91 For more on this, see "Ma'raḍ jamā'at al-di'āya al-fanniyya," *Al-Radio al-Masry,* year 4, no. 208 (March 11, 1939): 17; Mohammad Youssef Hammam, "Ma'raḍ al-ustadh Habib Gorgui," *Al-Thaqafah* 337 (June 12, 1945): 21–22; Mohammad Youssef Hammam, "Ma'raḍ al-ustadh Habib Gorgui," *Al-Thaqafah* 388 (July 4, 1946): 16–17; Ellen Michaeleson, "Al-fannan al-thā'ir Habib Gorgui," in Ahmad Maher al-Ziftawi, trans., *Al-Majallah* 87 (March 1, 1964): 61–63.
92 Georges Henein (Cairo) to André Breton (Paris), ref. BRT.L.948, Breton Archives, La Bibliothèque Littéraire Jacques Doucet, Paris.
93 Excerpt from the January 1, 1937 Manifesto of Neo-Orientalists as cited in Daniel Lançon, "Le Caire (1934 – 1941): le défi des avant-gardes

européennes pour les écrivains égyptiens et pour Georges Henein en particulier" in Edith Kunz and Thomas Hunkeler, eds., *Les Métropoles des avant-gardes* (Bern: Peter Lang Publishers, 2009), 164.

94 Kamel El-Telmisany, "Nahw fann ḥurr," *Al-Tatawwur* 1 (January 1940): 34.

95 "Ila al-fann al-hadīth," Al-'Imāra 4, no. 7–8 (July 1939): 377–78. The article includes a reproduction of th+ree drawings by Kamal El-Mallakh; a painting by Ali Kamel El-Dib, and an engraving entitled *The War* by Kamel El-Telmisany.

96 Ahmed Rassim, "Al-fannānūn al-misriyyūn fi tariqihim ila fann maṣri," *Al-Ahram,* year 64, no. 19402 (September 17, 1938): 2; Ahmed Rassim, "Jamā'at al-sharqiyyūn al-judud," *Al-Balagh,* October 15, 1938, 7.

97 Kamel El-Telmisany, "Hawl al-fann al-munḥatt," *Al-Risāla* 321 (August 28, 1939): 1702–3.

98 Georges Henein in Cairo to André Breton in Paris, July 26, 1948 (unpublished letter), ref. BRT.L.962 1/3, Georges Breton Archives, La Bibliothèque Littéraire Jacques Doucet, Paris.

99 Samir Rafi, unlike the dominant narrative that places the founding of the Contemporary Art Group in 1946 under the leadership of Hussein Youssef Amin, an art educator and artist who exhibited with *Art and Liberty*, maintained that he founded the group from as early as 1940 with Chafik Rizk. For more on this, see Abd El-Razek 'Oukashah, *Dhikrayāt wa a'amāl Samir Rafi'* (Cairo: General Egyptian Book Organization Press, 2012), 14.

100 Georges Henein in Cairo to Ramses Younane in Paris, December 10, 1953 (unpublished letter), Georges Henein Archives, Farhi Collection, Paris.

101 From an interview with Tarek El-Telmisany, the nephew of Kamel El-Telmisany, with the author in Cairo on Saturday, February 14, 2015.

102 For more on this, see Moukhtar al-Suwaifi, *Hassan el-Telmisany: Fannan Hafatha 'ala sharaf al-kamera* (Cairo: Dar al-Ghadd, 1987).

103 For more on this, see Muhammad Rateb Seddik, *Tajribati fi al-fann wa al-hayat,* part 1 (Cairo: Al-hay'a al-masriyyah al-'ammah lil kitab, 1989); Rateb Seddik, Fouad Kamel, and Ramses Younane, *Tafarrogh al-fannan: mas'alah mulihhah* (Cairo: Rabitat al-fannaneen, 1963)—this is a four-page leaflet that was disseminated to highlight the urgency of artist stipends: consulted at the Esmat Dawastashy Archives, Alexandria, on March 29, 2012.

104 For more on this, see the letters from Inji Efflatoun to her sister Polly in which she describes on several occasions the influence of the prison experience on her painting style in Inji Efflatoun and Saïd Khayyal, ed., *Muthakkarat Inji Efflatoun* (Cairo: Dar al-thaqafah al-jadeedah, 2014), 233–47.

105 For more on this, see Michel Mitrani, *Conversation avec Albert Cossery* (Paris: Gallimard, 1995).

106 For Salinas: an interview with Ms. Karen LeShufy and Mr. J. R. LeShufy, the estate owners of Marcel Salinas on June 22, 2012, and September 9, 2013, in New York and Paris respectively. For Nimr: an interview with Ms. Soraya Antonius, Amy Nimr's niece on Sunday, October 18, 2015, in Gadencourt, France.

107 From an interview with interview with Bertho Farhi, close friend of Georges and Boula Henein and collaborator with *Art and Liberty*, on Thursday May 10, 2012, in Paris.

108 Based on a statement by Boula Henein in an interview with Abdel Kader El-Janabi in Abdel Kader El-Janabi, *The Nile of Surrealism: Surrealist Activities in Egypt, 1936–1952* (Paris: Arabie-sur-Seine, 1991), 14. The paper was first presented on September 26 at a conference entitled *The Triumph of Pessimism,* held at the University of British Columbia, Vancouver.

109 For more on this, see Keith Moxey, *Is Modernity Multiple?* www.columbia.edu/cu/arthistory/courses/Multiple-Modernities/moxey-essay.html

110 Ramses Younane, *Dirāsāt fi al-fann,* ed. Louis Awad (Cairo: Dār al-kātib al-'arabi li-l-tiba'ah wa-l-nashr, 1969), 276–80.

111 El-Telmisany, "Hawl al-fann al-munḥatt," 1702.

112 Fouad Kamel, "Maṣīr al-fann al-hadīth ba'da inhiyār faransa," *Al-Majallah Al-Jadidah* 434 (September 15, 1943): 19–21.

113 Kitty Zijlmans, "An Intercultural Perspective in Art History: Beyond Othering and Appropriation," in James Elkins, ed., *Is Art History Global?* (New York and London: Routledge, 2007), 296.

114 Ramses Younane, "Al-ḥaraka al-fanniyya bayn al-maḥaliyya wal 'ālamiyya," *Al-fikr al-mu'aṣir* 17 (July 1, 1966): 48–49.

115 James Elkins, "Art History As A Global Discipline," in *Is Art History Global?*, 3.

116 Patricia Almarcegui, "Orientalism and Post-Orientalism. Ten Years without Edward Said," *Observatory of Euro-Mediterranean Policies,* 2014, http://www.iemed.org/observatori/arees-danalisi/arxius-adjunts/qm20/Orientalism%20and%20Post-Orientalism%20Ten%20Years%20without%20Edward%20Said%20Patricia%20Almarcegui.pdf/view

117 For more on post-Saidian theory, see Gyan Prakash, "Writing Post-Orientalist Histories of the Third World: Perspectives from Indian Historiography," *Comparative Studies in Society and History 32,* no. 2 (April, 1990): 383–408; Joshua Muravchik, "Enough Said: The False Scholarship of Edward Said," *World Affairs* (March/April 2013), http://www.worldaffairsjournal.org/article/enough-said-false-scholarship-edward-said; Ella Shohat, "The 'Postcolonial' in Translation: Reading Said in Hebrew," *Journal of Palestine Studies* 33, no. 3 (Spring 2004): 55–75; John D. Rogers, "Post-Orientalism and the Interpretation of Premodern and Modern Political Identities: The Case of Sri Lanka," *The Journal of Asian Studies* 53, no. 1 (February 1994): 10–23.

118 Francois Pouillon, "150 Years of Algerian Painting: Relevance for Understanding the Postcolonial Situation," *French Politics, Culture and Society* 20, no. 2 (2002): 141.

119 Zygmunt Bauman, *Liquid Life* (Cambridge: Polity, 2005).

120 Petrine Archer-Straw et al., *Créolité and Creolization: Documenta11_Platform3* (Ostfildern: Hatje Cantz, 2003).

121 Benedict Anderson, *Imagined Communities: Reflections on the Origin and Spread of Nationalism* (London and New York: Verso Editions, 2006).

122 Nicolas Bourriaud, *The Radicant* (Berlin and New York: Lukas and Sternberg, 2009).

123 Nada Shabout, "The Challenge of Arab Modern Art," *The Future of Tradition—The Tradition of Future,* ed. Chris Dercon, Leon Krempel, and Avinoam Shalem (Munich: Prestel Publishing Ltd., 2010), 45–46.

124 Mieke Bal, "Grounds of Comparison," *The Artemisia Files: Artemisia Gentileschi for Feminists and Other Thinking People,* ed. Mieke Bal (Chicago and London: University of Chicago Press, 2005), 128–29.

125 Comte d'Arschot, *Peintres et sculpteurs de l'Égypte contemporaine* (Brussels: Éditions des Arts Plastiques, 1951), 19–20.

126 Moxey, "Motivating History," 392.

127 Ramses Younane, *Ghāyat al-rassām al-'aṣri* (Cairo: Jamā'at al-di'āya al-fanniyyah, 1938), 50–51.

128 Craig Clunas, "The Art of Global Comparison," *Writing the History of the Global: Challenges for the 21st Century,* ed. Maxine Berg (Oxford: Oxford University Press, 2013), 174.

"THE PERMANENT REVOLUTION"

Art and Liberty Group, *La Séance continue*, 1945

In the 1930s, by the time *Art and Liberty* emerged on the Cairene arts scene, the prevailing nationalist project was consciously appropriating the past through the promulgation of a unified history centered on the legacy of Pharaonic art. In line with Surrealism's rejection of the alignment of art with political propaganda, *Art and Liberty* rebelled against the conflation of art with national sentiment, for to cite the words of Kamel El-Telmisany, "there is no crime bigger in the world of art than for an artist to limit his work within a specific piece of land."

Art and Liberty equally rejected the notion of art for art's sake whereby pictures had become a platform for the recycling of the same pictorial allegories and literary metaphors that did nothing to challenge the world. The two institutions, as far as *Art and Liberty* were concerned, responsible for the promulgation of this form of stale academicism and bourgeois conservatism were: the School of Fine Arts in Cairo and the *Société des amis de l'art*. The first was founded by Prince Youssef Kamal in 1908 and would produce some of the most esteemed Egyptian artists of the time. The *Société*, which was founded around 1923, organized the annual Salon du Caire. It would not be surprising therefore that some of *Art and Liberty*'s most polemically charged writings were directed against the artists who belonged to this camp, these "enslaved copiers", who had become fundamental to a local canon that *Art and Liberty* would seek to reshuffle, if not eliminate altogether.

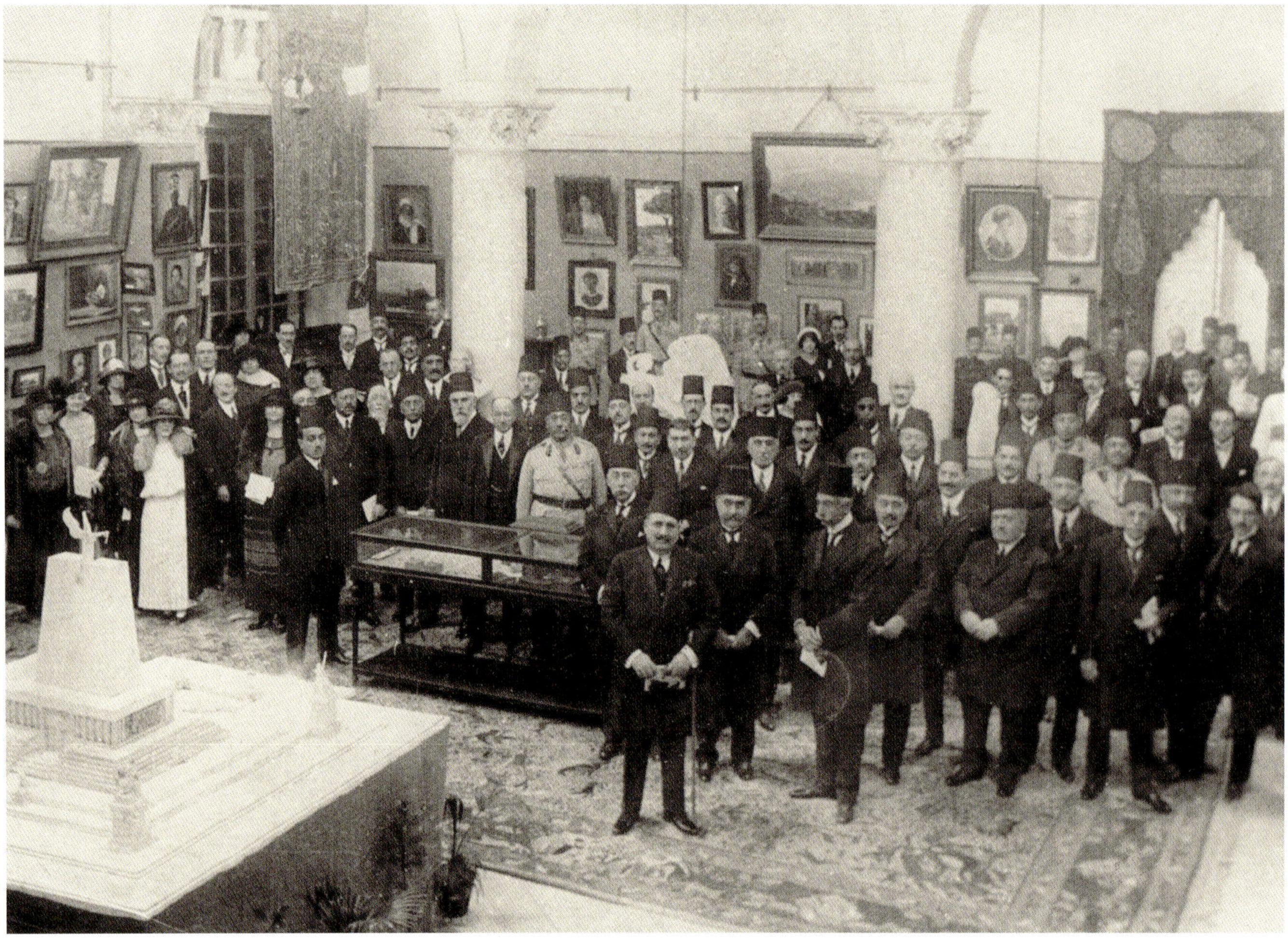

1

"His Majesty the King, inaugurated last week
the annual Egyptian exhibition of the friends of fine arts society...
And the top floor has been dedicated for oil paintings
and pastels where almost every nation has its own gallery
with the largest for the Egyptians."

Exhibition review of the annual Salon du Caire, *al-Musawwar* magazine, December 20, 1927

1
Inauguration of the Salon du Caire
Société des amis de l'art, 1927
Photographer unknown
Silver gelatin print on paper
Estate of Chafik Charobim, Cairo.

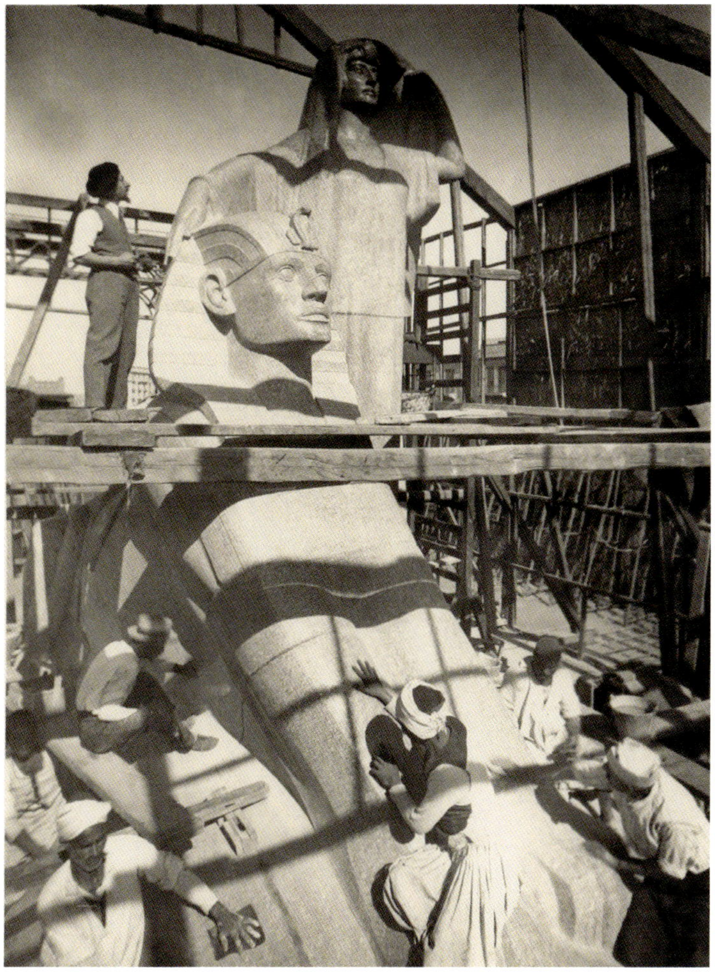

2

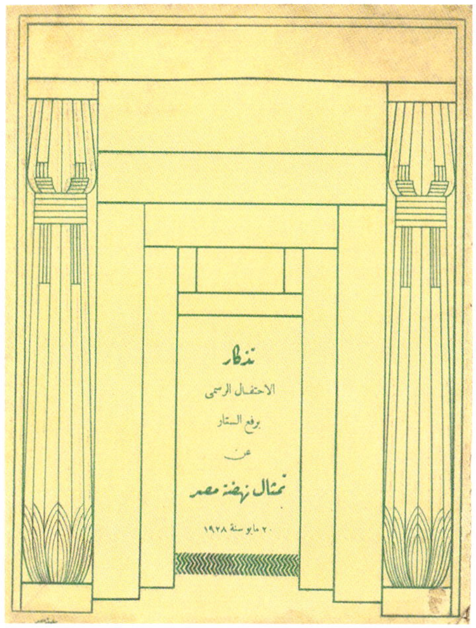

3

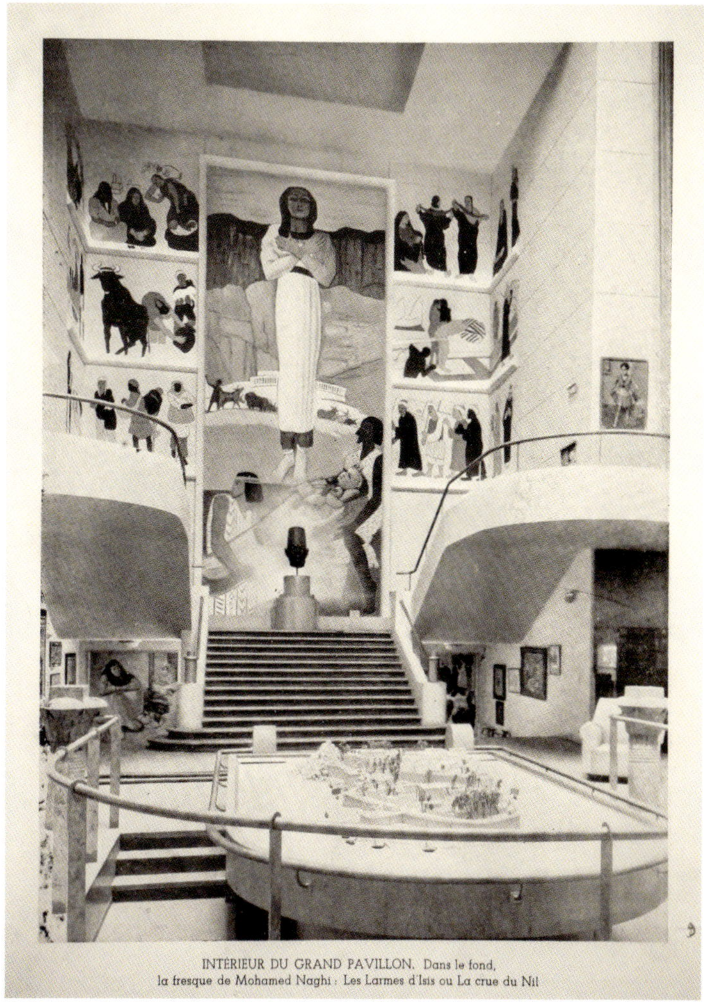

4

2
Mahmoud Moukhtar at the work site
of his sculpture *Egypt Awakening*, c. 1928
Photographer unknown
Gelatin Silver Print
Emad Badr el-Din Mahmoud Abu Ghazy
Archives, Cairo

3
Card of invitation to the inauguration
ceremony of Mahmoud Moukhtar's public
sculpture *Egypt Awakening*, May 20, 1928
Cardboard
Emad Badr el-Din Mahmoud Abu Ghazy
Archives, Cairo

4
View of the main hall
within the Egyptian pavilion at the 1937
Paris International Exhibition
Image taken from the pavilion catalogue
Issmat Dawastashy collection, Alexandria

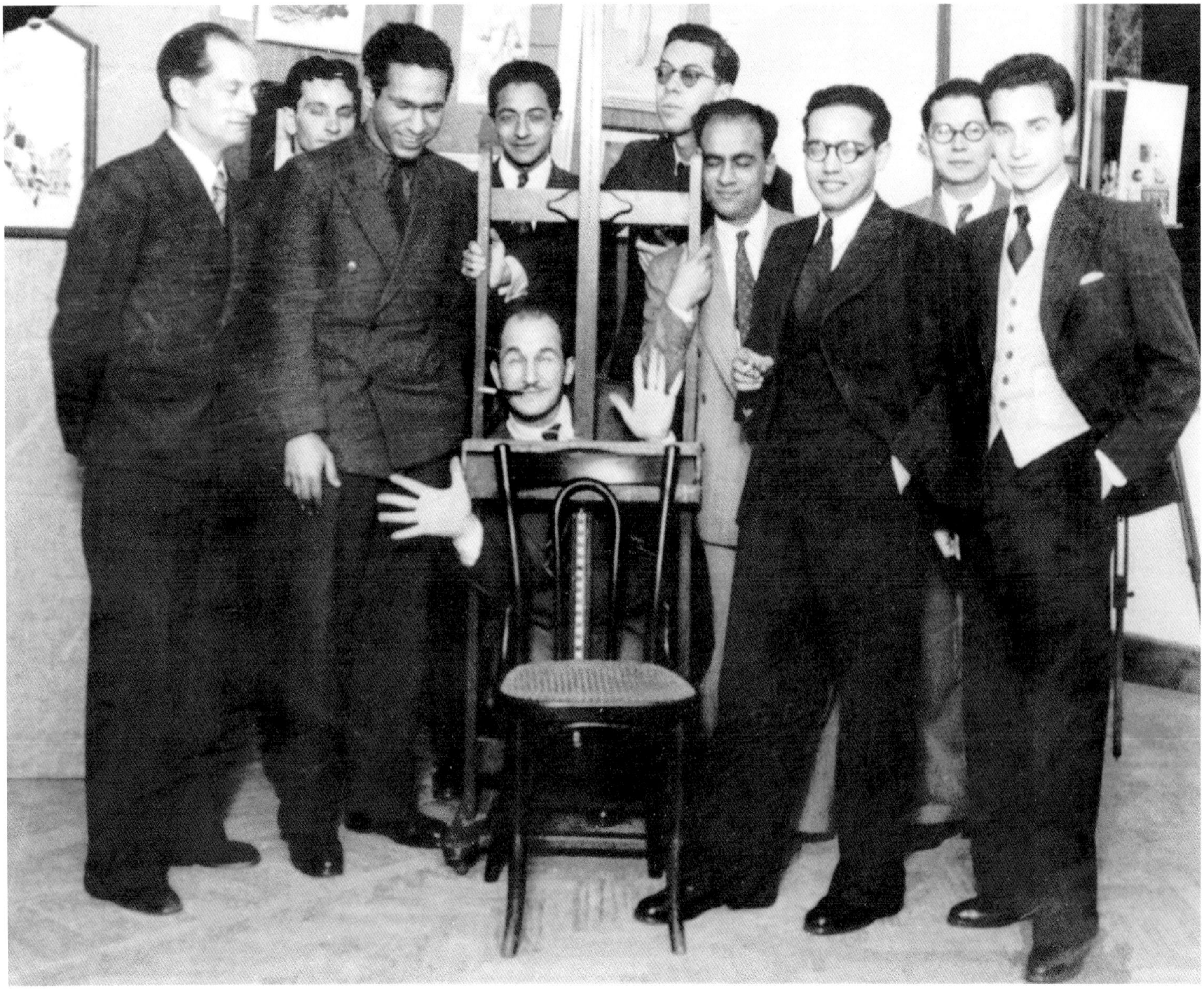

1

“*It is necessary to state here that advertisement of any American shoemaker is infinitely more moving than the best paintings exhibited at the annual Salon of Cairo... These poor souls will never understand that painting is a way of thinking, loving, hating, fighting and living.*”

Art et Liberté, “The second exhibition of independent art,” 1941

1
Members of the *Art and Liberty* group
during the 1941 exhibition
Front (from left to right): Jean Moscatelli,
Kamel El-Telmisany, Angelo de Riz,
Ramses Younane, Fouad Kamel
Back (from left to right): Albert Cossery,
unidentified, Georges Henein,
Maurice Fahmy, Raoul Curiel
Photographer unknown
Vintage gelatin silver print
Sylvie and Sonia Younan collection, Paris

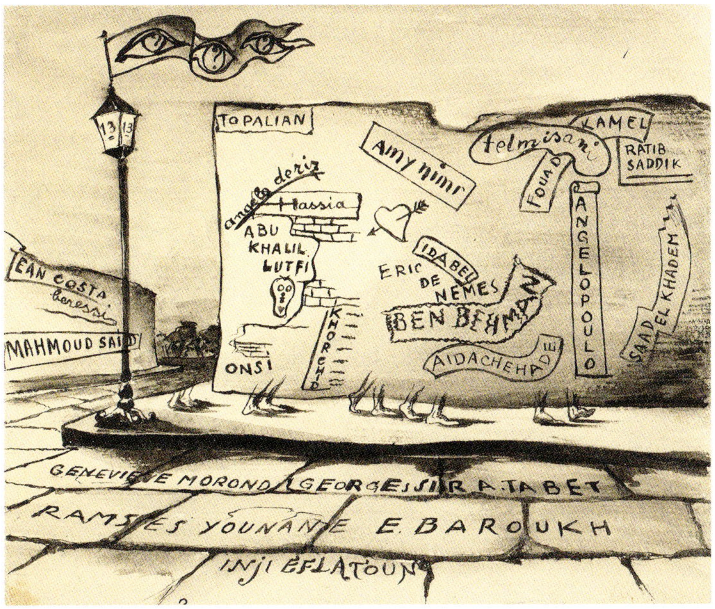

2

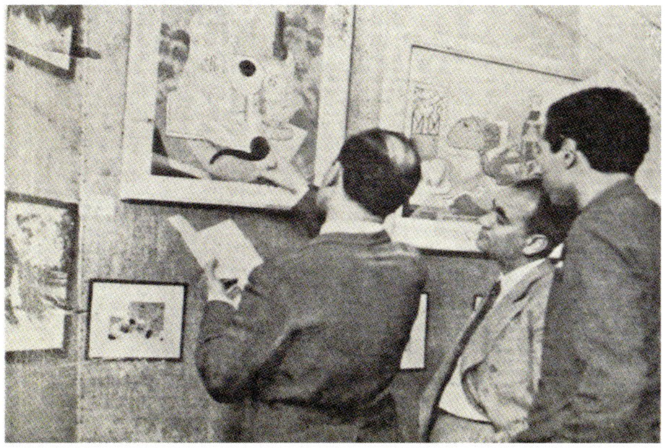

3

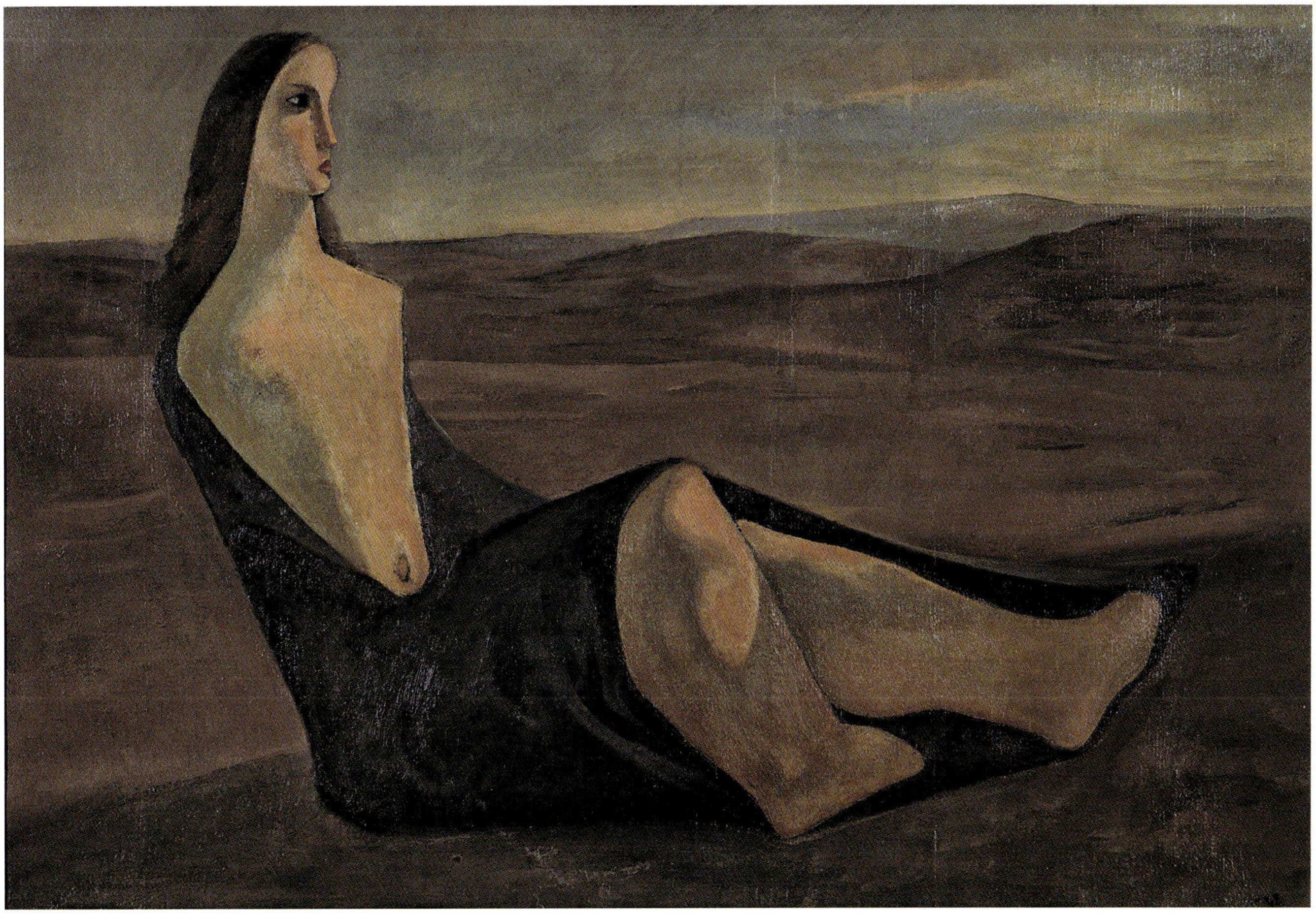

4

2
Invitation to the third exhibition of the *Art et Liberté* Group, 1942
Folded card
Henein - Farhi collection, Neuilly-sur-Seine

3
Visitors and members of the *Art and Liberty* group at their second exhibition of independent art, 1941
Photographer unknown
Le Progrès égyptien, March 17, 1941, p. 6

4
RAMSES YOUNANE
Untitled, 1942
Oil on canvas
50 x 73 cm
Private collection

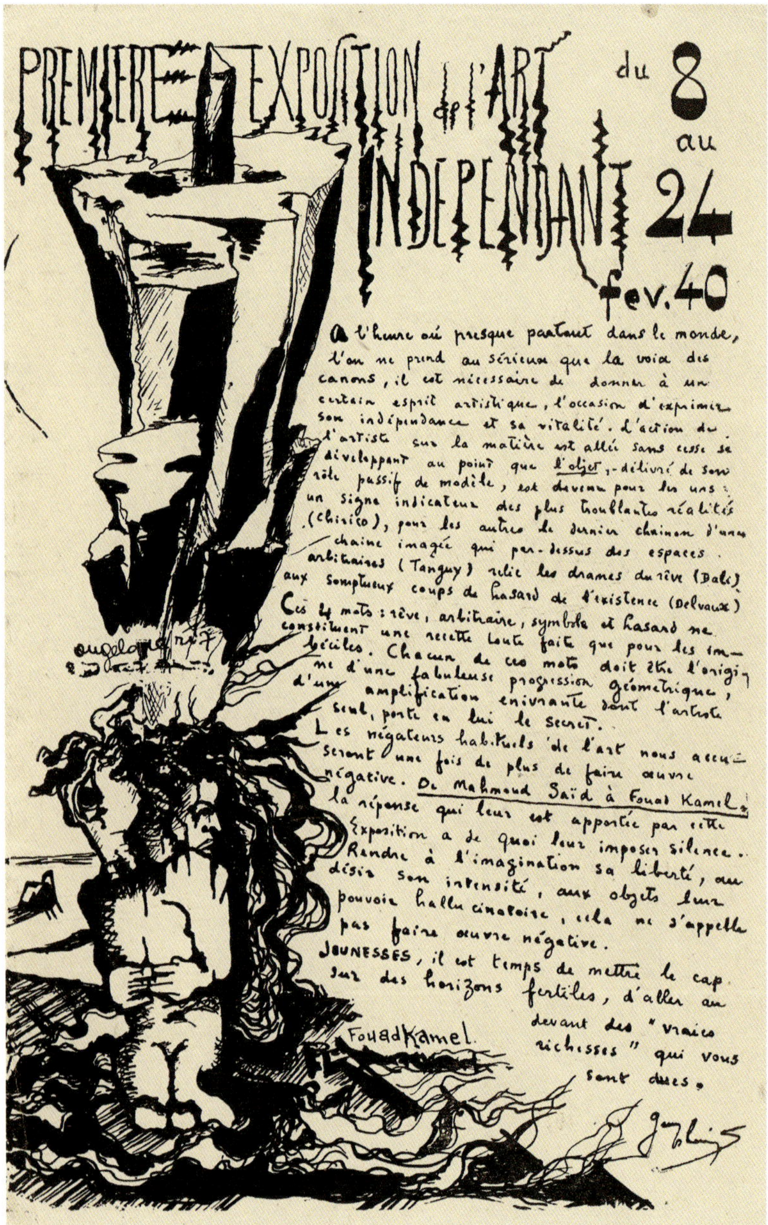

1

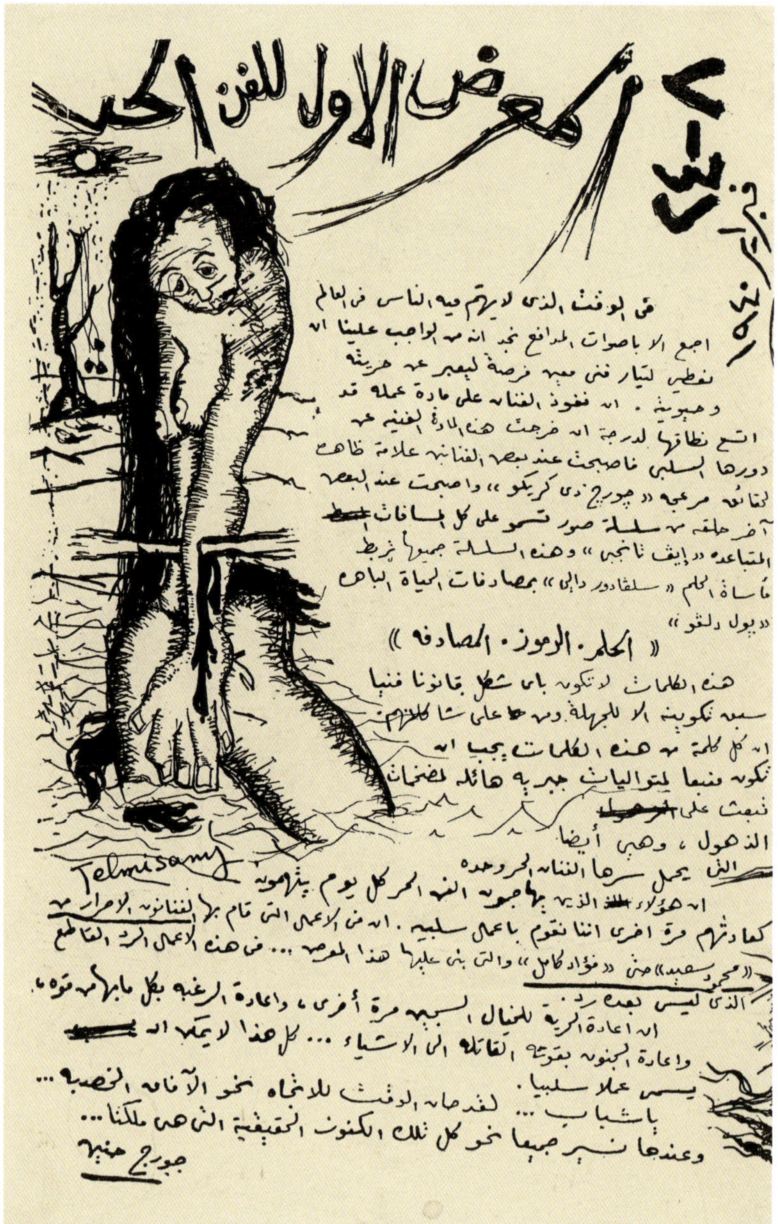

2

1
Back cover of the catalogue
of the first *Art and Liberty* exhibition, 1940
Printed paper
Centre Pompidou Paris, MNAM-CCI,
Bibliothèque Kandinsky, Sylvie Younan gift, 2015

2
Front cover of the catalogue
of the first *Art and Liberty* exhibition, 1940
Printed paper
Centre Pompidou Paris, MNAM-CCI,
Bibliothèque Kandinsky, Sylvie Younan gift, 2015

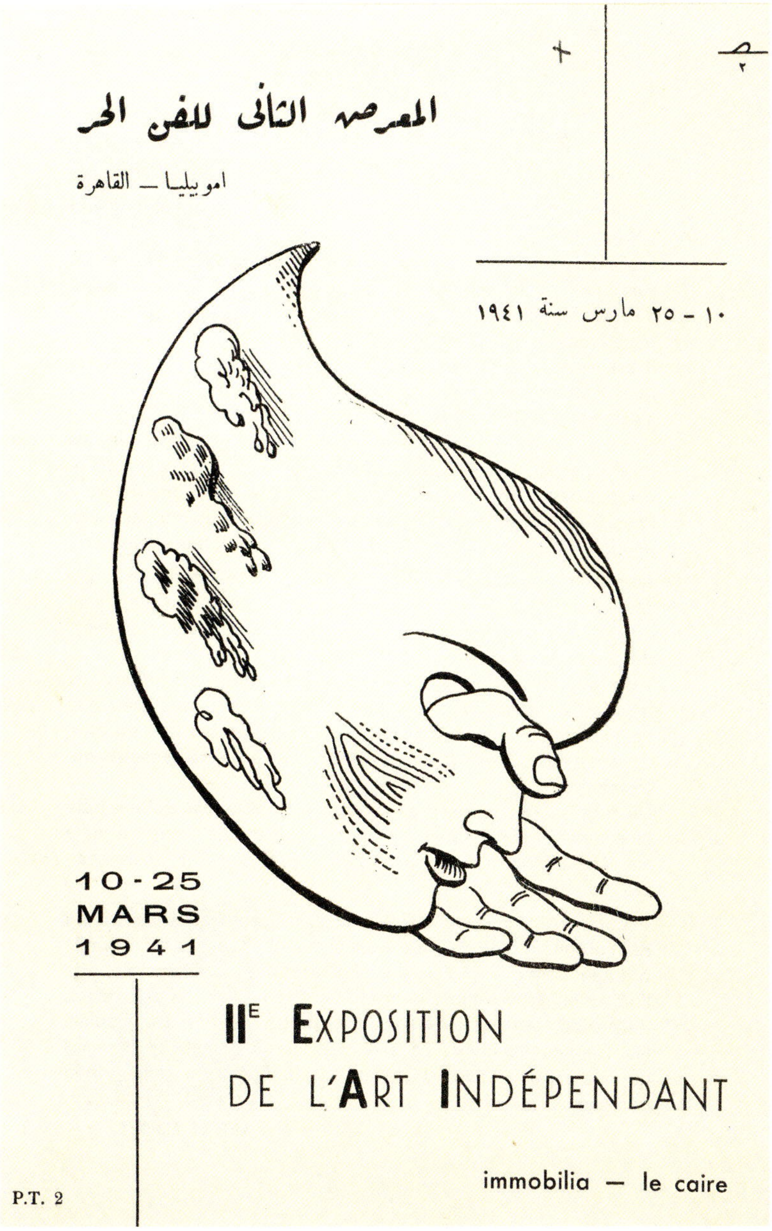

3

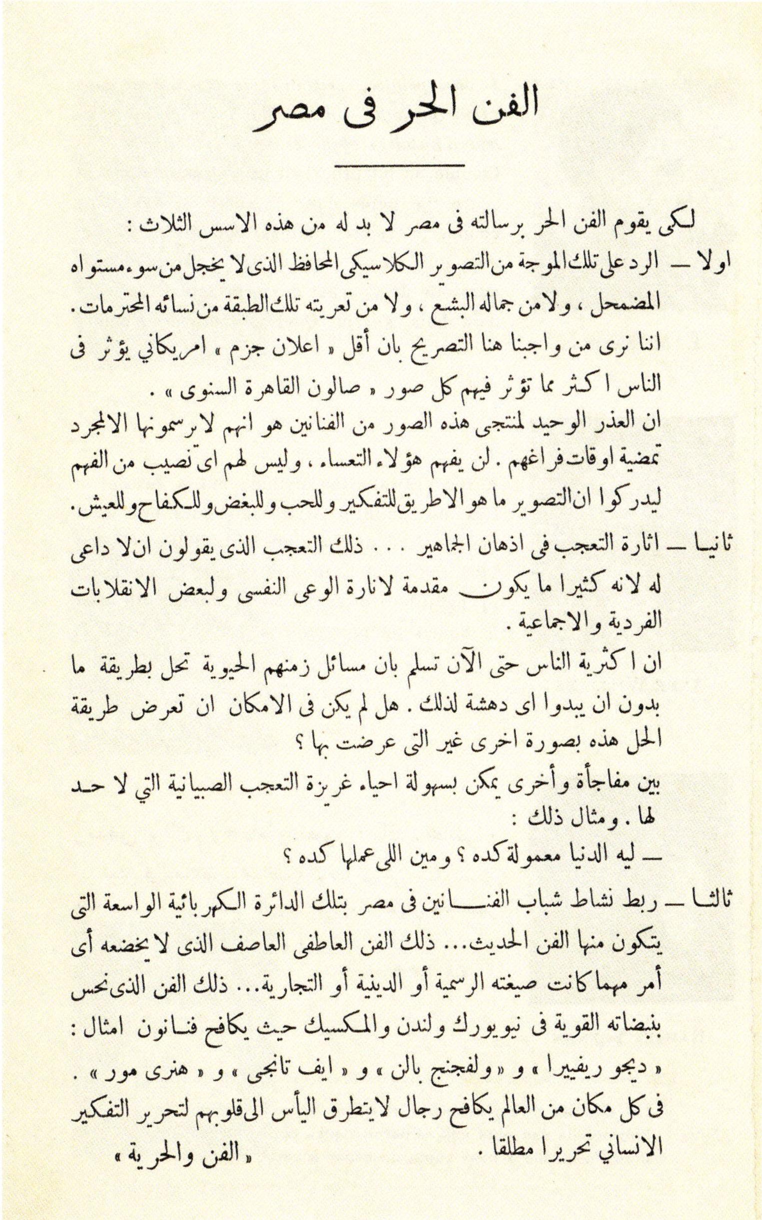

الفن الحر فى مصر

لكى يقوم الفن الحر برسالته فى مصر لا بد له من هذه الاسس الثلاث :

اولا — الرد على تلك الموجة من التصوير الكلاسيكى المحافظ الذى لا يخجل من سوء مستواه المضمحل ، ولا من جماله البشع ، ولا من تعريته تلك الطبقة من نسائه المحترمات.

اننا نرى من واجبنا هنا التصريح بان أقل « اعلان جزم » امريكاني يؤثر فى الناس اكثر مما تؤثر فيهم كل صور « صالون القاهرة السنوى » .

ان العذر الوحيد لمنتجى هذه الصور من الفنانين هو انهم لا يرسمونها الا لمجرد تمضية اوقات فراغهم . لن يفهم هؤلاء التعساء ، وليس لهم اى نصيب من الفهم ليدركوا ان التصوير ما هو الا طريق للتفكير وللحب وللبغض وللكفاح وللعيش.

ثانيا — اثارة التعجب فى اذهان الجماهير . . . ذلك التعجب الذى يقولون ان لا داعى له لانه كثيرا ما يكون مقدمة لانارة الوعى النفسى ولبعض الانقلابات الفردية والاجماعية .

ان اكثرية الناس حتى الآن تسلم بان مسائل زمنهم الحيوية تحل بطريقة ما بدون ان يبدوا اى دهشة لذلك . هل لم يكن فى الامكان ان تعرض طريقة الحل هذه بصورة اخرى غير التى عرضت بها ؟

بين مفاجأة وأخرى يمكن بسهولة احياء غريزة التعجب الصبيانية التي لا حد لها . ومثال ذلك :

— ليه الدنيا معمولة كده ؟ ومين اللى عملها كده ؟

ثالثا — ربط نشاط شباب الفنانين فى مصر بتلك الدائرة الكهربائية الواسعة التى يتكون منها الفن الحديث... ذلك الفن العاطفى العاصف الذى لا يخضعه أى أمر مهما كانت صيغته الرسمية أو الدينية أو التجارية... ذلك الفن الذى نحس بنبضاته القوية فى نيويورك ولندن والمكسيك حيث يكافح فنانون امثال : « ديجو ريفيرا » و « ولفجنج بالن » و « ايف تانجى » و « هنرى مور » . فى كل مكان من العالم يكافح رجال لا يتطرق اليأس الى قلوبهم لتحرير التفكير الانساني تحريرا مطلقا . « الفن والحرية »

4

3, 4
Brochure extract from the second exhibition of independent art, 10 – 25 March 1941, Immobilia, Cairo
Stapled paper booklet
Centre Pompidou Paris, MNAM-CCI, Bibliothèque Kandinsky, donated by Sylvie Younan, 2015

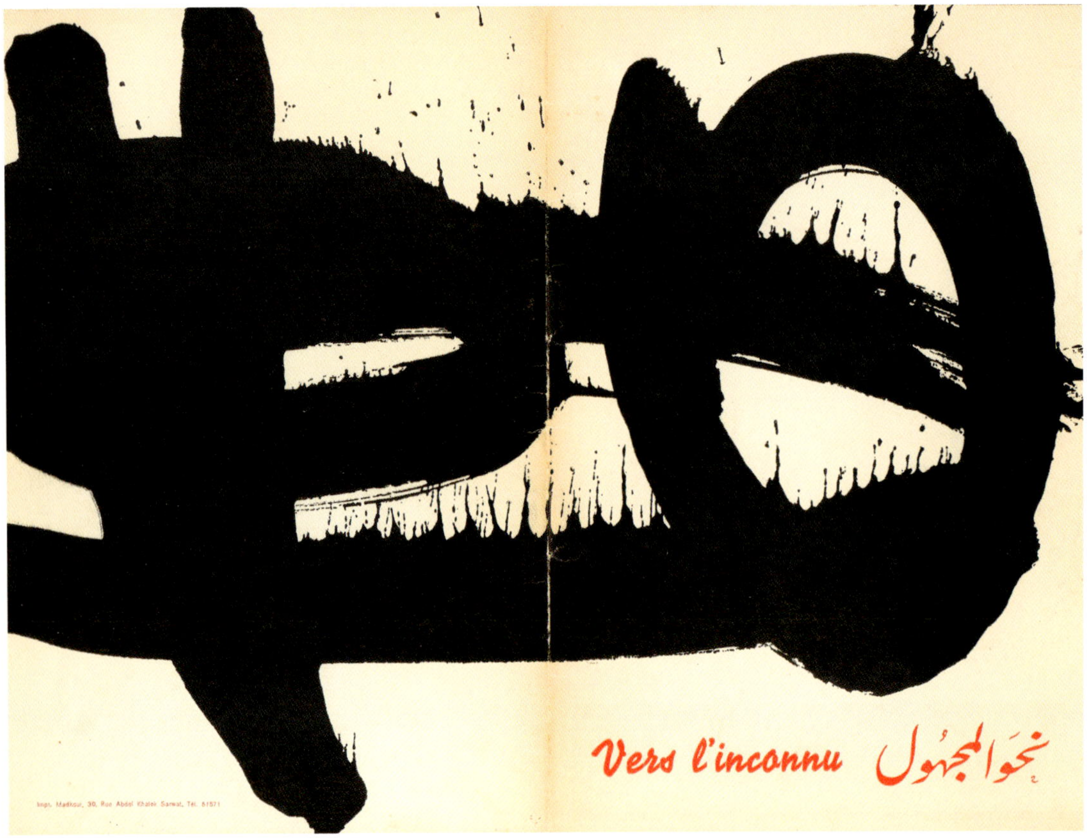

1

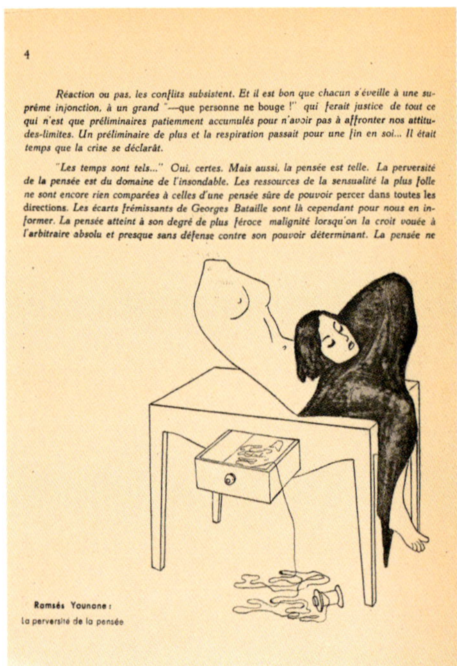

4

Réaction ou pas, les conflits subsistent. Et il est bon que chacun s'éveille à une suprême injonction, à un grand "—que personne ne bouge !" qui ferait justice de tout ce qui n'est que préliminaires patiemment accumulés pour n'avoir pas à affronter nos attitudes-limites. Un préliminaire de plus et la respiration passait pour une fin en soi... Il était temps que la crise se déclarât.

"Les temps sont tels..." Oui, certes. Mais aussi, la pensée est telle. La perversité de la pensée est du domaine de l'insondable. Les ressources de la sensualité la plus folle ne sont encore rien comparées à celles d'une pensée sûre de pouvoir percer dans toutes les directions. Les écarts frémissants de Georges Bataille sont là cependant pour nous en informer. La pensée atteint à son degré de plus féroce malignité lorsqu'on la croit vouée à l'arbitraire absolu et presque sans défense contre son pouvoir déterminant. La pensée ne

Ramsès Younane :
La perversité de la pensée

2

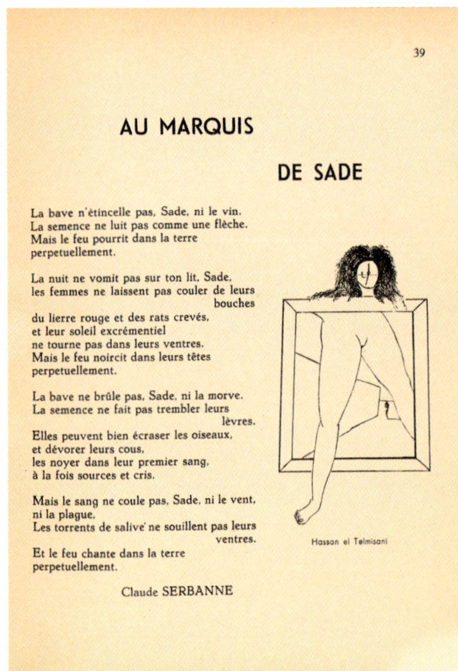

39

AU MARQUIS

DE SADE

La bave n'étincelle pas, Sade, ni le vin.
La semence ne luit pas comme une flèche.
Mais le feu pourrit dans la terre
perpetuellement.

La nuit ne vomit pas sur ton lit, Sade,
les femmes ne laissent pas couler de leurs
bouches
du lierre rouge et des rats crevés,
et leur soleil excrémentiel
ne tourne pas dans leurs ventres.
Mais le feu noircit dans leurs têtes
perpetuellement.

La bave ne brûle pas, Sade, ni la morve.
La semence ne fait pas trembler leurs
lèvres.
Elles peuvent bien écraser les oiseaux,
et dévorer leurs cous,
les noyer dans leur premier sang,
à la fois sources et cris.

Mais le sang ne coule pas, Sade, ni le vent,
ni la plague.
Les torrents de salive ne souillent pas leurs
ventres.
Et le feu chante dans la terre
perpetuellement.

Claude SERBANNE

Hassan el Telmisani

3

1
Vers l'inconnu, 1950
Softcover book
Henein-Farhi collection, Neuilly-sur-Seine

2
RAMSÈS YOUNANE
La Perversité de la pensée
La Part du sable, Vol. 1, 1947
Paperback
Centre Pompidou Paris, MNAM-CCI, Bibliothèque Kandinsky

3
HASSAN EL-TELMISSANI
Illustration for Claude Serbanne's poem *Au Marquis de Sade* in *La Part du sable*, Vol. 1, 1947
Paperback
Centre Pompidou Paris, MNAM-CCI, Bibliothèque Kandinsky

4, 5
JO FARNA
A Project for a Monument in Honor of Those Who Are Not Dead

WADID SIRRY
Untitled

Illustrations in *La Séance continue*, The fifth exhibition of independent Art exhibition catalogue, 1945
Centre Pompidou Paris, MNAM-CCI, Bibliothèque Kandinsky

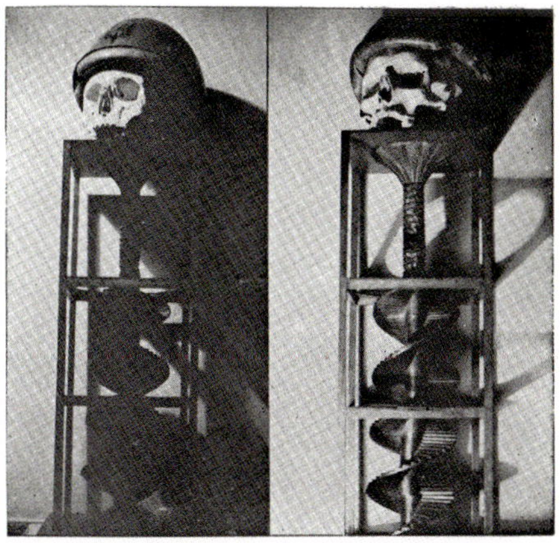

4

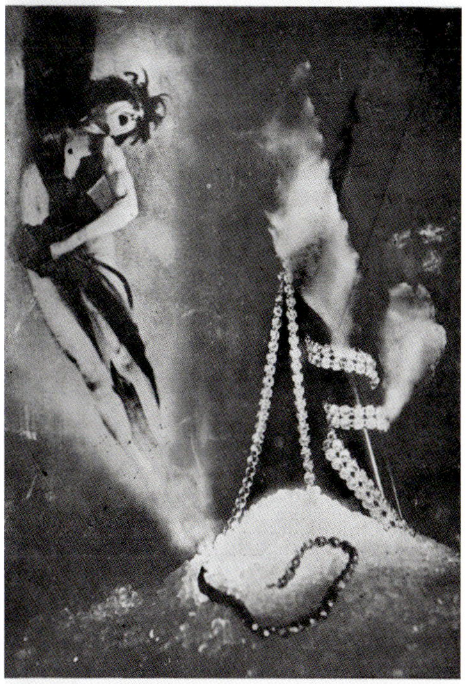

5

6
La Séance continue, 1945
The fifth exhibition of independent Art exhibition catalogue
Centre Pompidou Paris, MNAM-CCI, Bibliothèque Kandinsky, Destribats Archives, French national treasure acquired thanks to the patronage of the Lagardère group, 2005

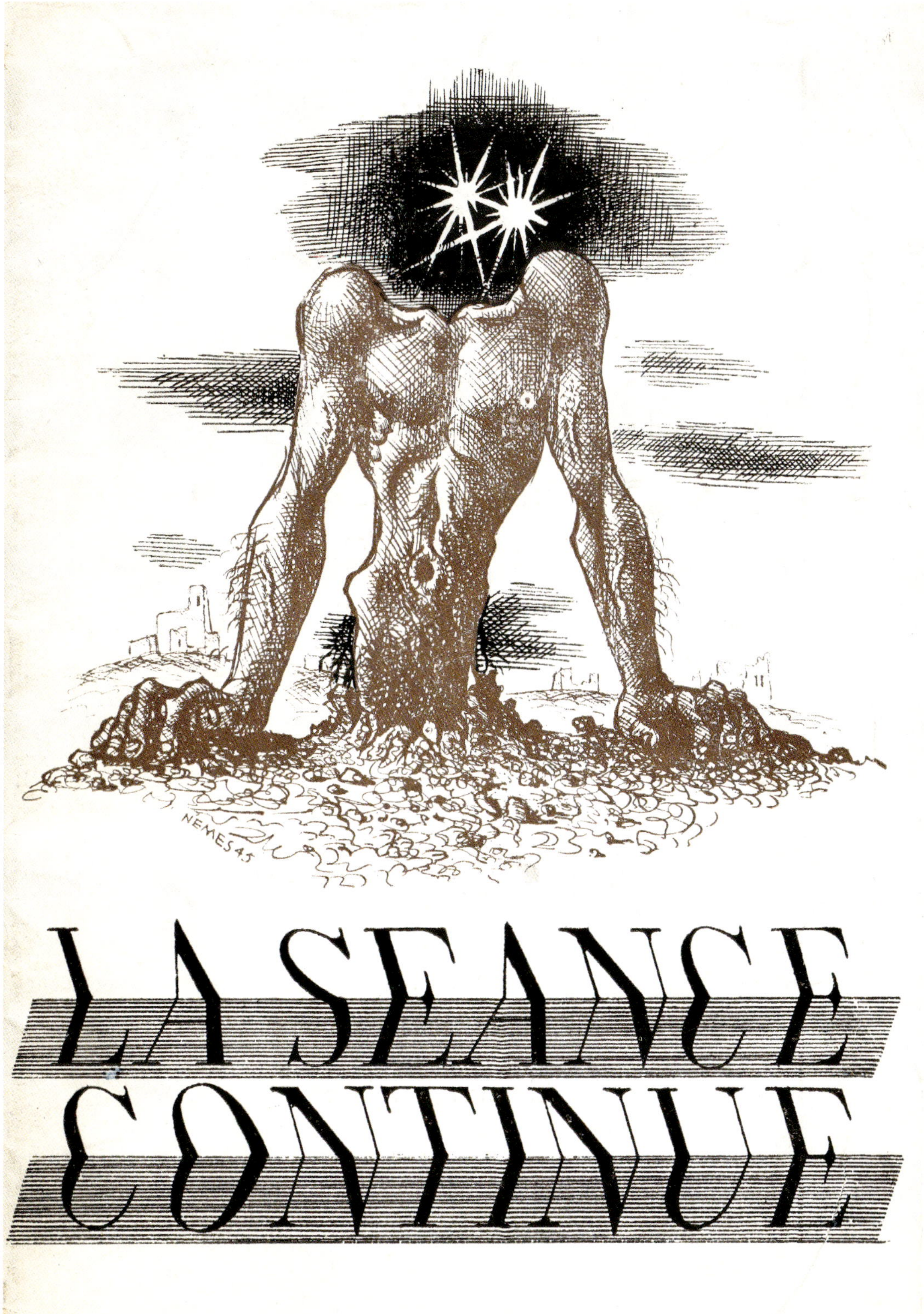

6

"THE VOICE OF CANONS"

The catalogue of *Art and Liberty*'s first exhibition, 1940

The *Art et Liberté* Group appeared onto the Cairo culture scene at the onset of the Second World War. A profound engagement with the course of its events, the destruction that it begot, and the poverty that it fuelled, is a leitmotif that runs across the whole spectrum of the group's literary and visual production. War-related themes such as the Apocalypse and scenes of combat and destruction appear in the works of artists such as Marcel Laurent Salinas and Hassan El-Telmisani respectively. Surrealist depictions of battle fields and symbols of death, such as we see in the works of Mayo, evoke the state of anxiety that was felt upon the eve of the war. Some artists such as Amy Nimr, who lost her eight-year old son in a bomb explosion, created haunting imagery of death that was derived from their personal experience of loss.

Art et Liberté's sense of freedom was augmented by the growth of Fascist ideologies, which beyond their firm grip over Europe, had been on the rise in Egypt since the early 1930s. It was their stand against Fascism that ultimately led to the formation of the Group. This was prompted in March 1937 by a confrontation with a local chapter of Fascist-leaning Futurists. Founded in 1920 by the Italian-Egyptian lawyer and poet Nelson Morpurgo, the local Futurists had a close connection with the founder of the movement, F. T. Marinetti. Born in Alexandria to an immigrant Italian Family, Marinetti kept close ties with his birthplace throughout his life. In 1929, he gave a series of lectures on *parole in libertà* in Cairo and Alexandria. Marinetti's visit to Egypt as a delegate of the Fascist state was captured on the cover of *Maalesh*, a local satirical weekly review, which depicted him gesturing forcefully with Mussolini hovering above. On March 24, 1938, during a second visit to Egypt and while lecturing on *La poesia motorizzata* in Cairo, several anti-fascist intellectuals such as Georges Henein, Georges Santini and Jean Moscatelli interrupted the conference causing a scandal. They then published several articles attacking Marinetti and Futurism. On December 22, 1938 they published their manifesto *Vive L'art Dégénéré* marking the birth of *Art et Liberté.*

"In this hour, when the entire world
cares for nothing but the voice of canons,
we have found it our duty to provide
a certain artistic current with the opportunity
to express its freedom and its vitality."

Georges Henein, "The first exhibition of independent art," 1940

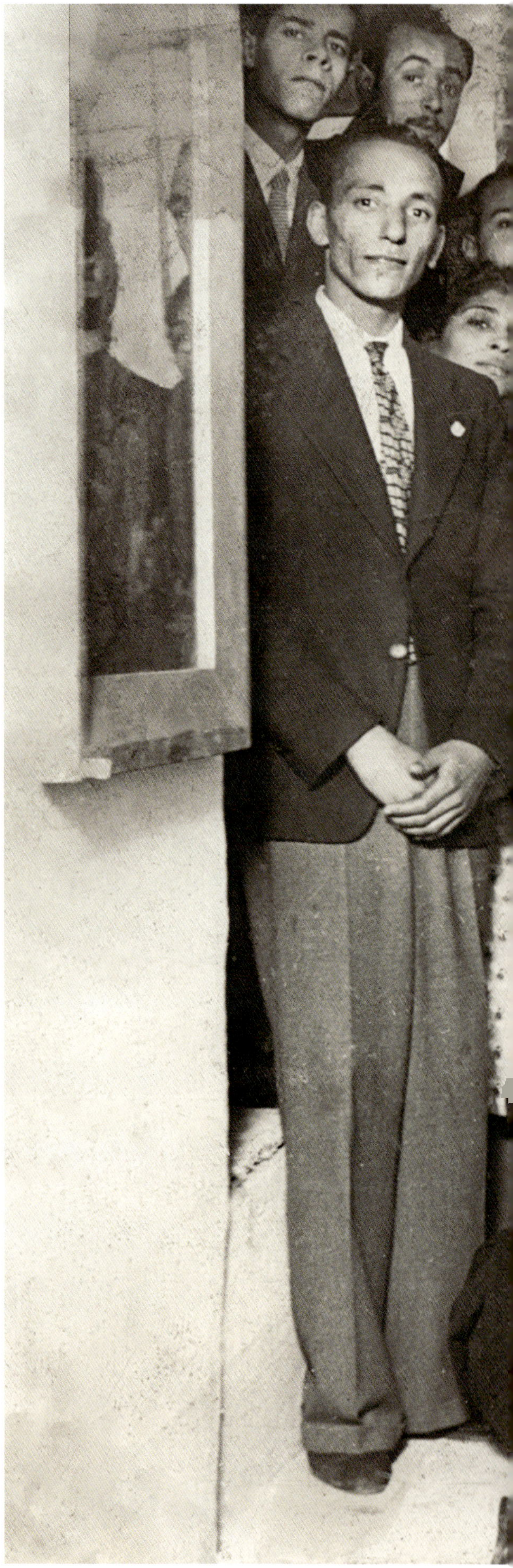

Members and Affiliates of the Art and Liberty Group at the Maison des artistes, Darb el-Labbana, Citadel, c. 1945
Photographer unknown
Vintage gelatin silver print
Christophe Bouleau collection, Geneva

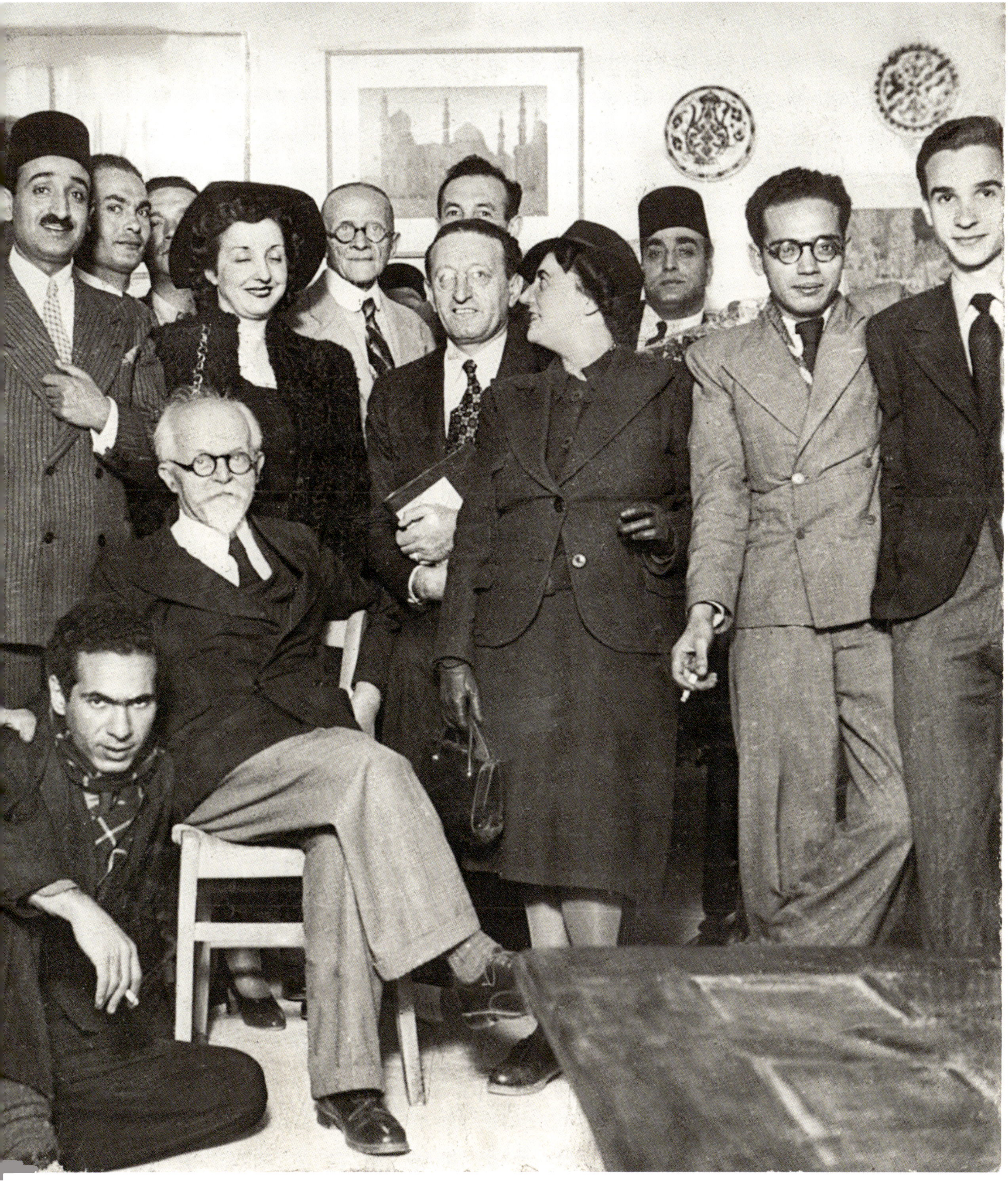

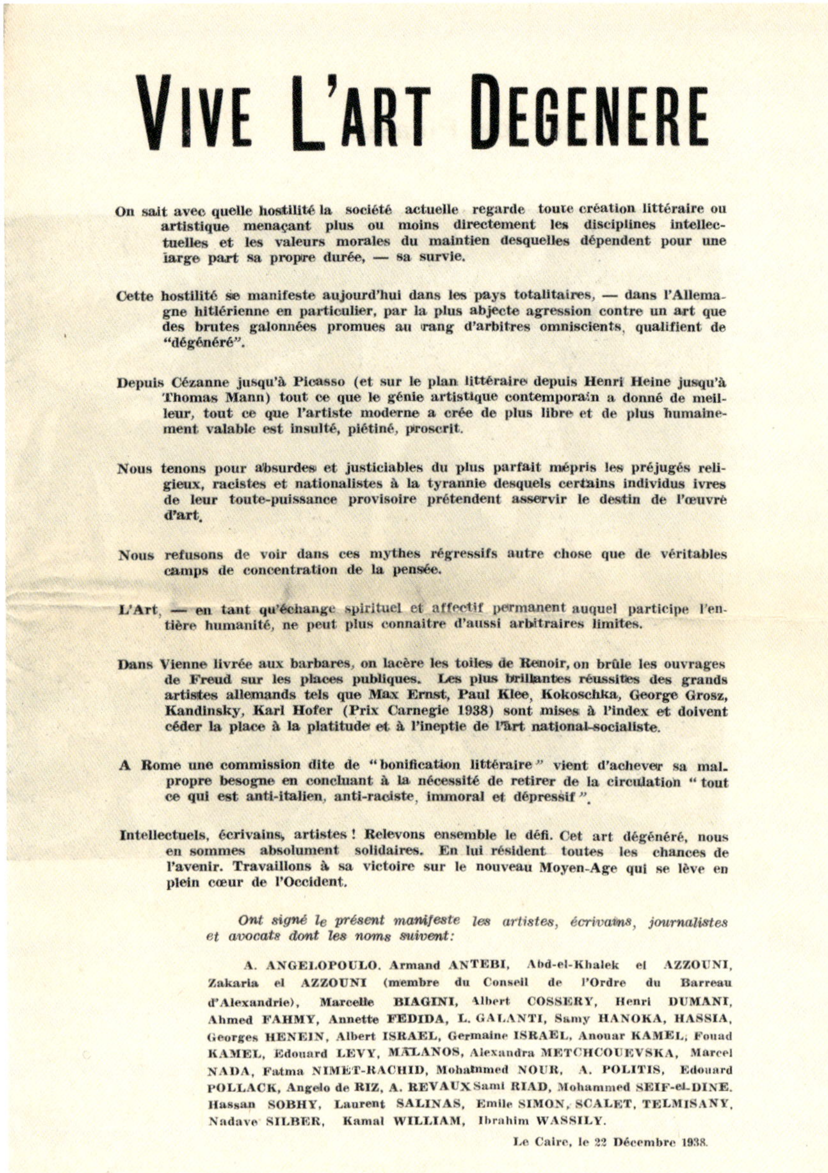

VIVE L'ART DEGENERE

On sait avec quelle hostilité la société actuelle regarde toute création littéraire ou artistique menaçant plus ou moins directement les disciplines intellectuelles et les valeurs morales du maintien desquelles dépendent pour une large part sa propre durée, — sa survie.

Cette hostilité se manifeste aujourd'hui dans les pays totalitaires, — dans l'Allemagne hitlérienne en particulier, par la plus abjecte agression contre un art que des brutes galonnées promues au rang d'arbitres omniscients, qualifient de "dégénéré".

Depuis Cézanne jusqu'à Picasso (et sur le plan littéraire depuis Henri Heine jusqu'à Thomas Mann) tout ce que le génie artistique contemporain a donné de meilleur, tout ce que l'artiste moderne a crée de plus libre et de plus humainement valable est insulté, piétiné, proscrit.

Nous tenons pour absurdes et justiciables du plus parfait mépris les préjugés religieux, racistes et nationalistes à la tyrannie desquels certains individus ivres de leur toute-puissance provisoire prétendent asservir le destin de l'œuvre d'art.

Nous refusons de voir dans ces mythes régressifs autre chose que de véritables camps de concentration de la pensée.

L'Art, — en tant qu'échange spirituel et affectif permanent auquel participe l'entière humanité, ne peut plus connaitre d'aussi arbitraires limites.

Dans Vienne livrée aux barbares, on lacère les toiles de Renoir, on brûle les ouvrages de Freud sur les places publiques. Les plus brillantes réussites des grands artistes allemands tels que Max Ernst, Paul Klee, Kokoschka, George Grosz, Kandinsky, Karl Hofer (Prix Carnegie 1938) sont mises à l'index et doivent céder la place à la platitude et à l'ineptie de l'art national-socialiste.

A Rome une commission dite de "bonification littéraire" vient d'achever sa malpropre besogne en concluant à la nécessité de retirer de la circulation "tout ce qui est anti-italien, anti-raciste, immoral et dépressif".

Intellectuels, écrivains, artistes ! Relevons ensemble le défi. Cet art dégénéré, nous en sommes absolument solidaires. En lui résident toutes les chances de l'avenir. Travaillons à sa victoire sur le nouveau Moyen-Age qui se lève en plein cœur de l'Occident.

Ont signé le présent manifeste les artistes, écrivains, journalistes et avocats dont les noms suivent:

A. ANGELOPOULO. Armand ANTEBI, Abd-el-Khalek el AZZOUNI, Zakaria el AZZOUNI (membre du Conseil de l'Ordre du Barreau d'Alexandrie), Marcelle BIAGINI, Albert COSSERY, Henri DUMANI, Ahmed FAHMY, Annette FEDIDA, L. GALANTI, Samy HANOKA, HASSIA, Georges HENEIN, Albert ISRAEL, Germaine ISRAEL, Anouar KAMEL, Fouad KAMEL, Edouard LEVY, MALANOS, Alexandra METCHCOUEVSKA, Marcel NADA, Fatma NIMET-RACHID, Mohammed NOUR, A. POLITIS, Edouard POLLACK, Angelo de RIZ, A. REVAUX Sami RIAD, Mohammed SEIF-el-DINE. Hassan SOBHY, Laurent SALINAS, Emile SIMON, SCALET, TELMISANY, Nadave SILBER, Kamal WILLIAM, Ibrahim WASSILY.

Le Caire, le 22 Décembre 1938.

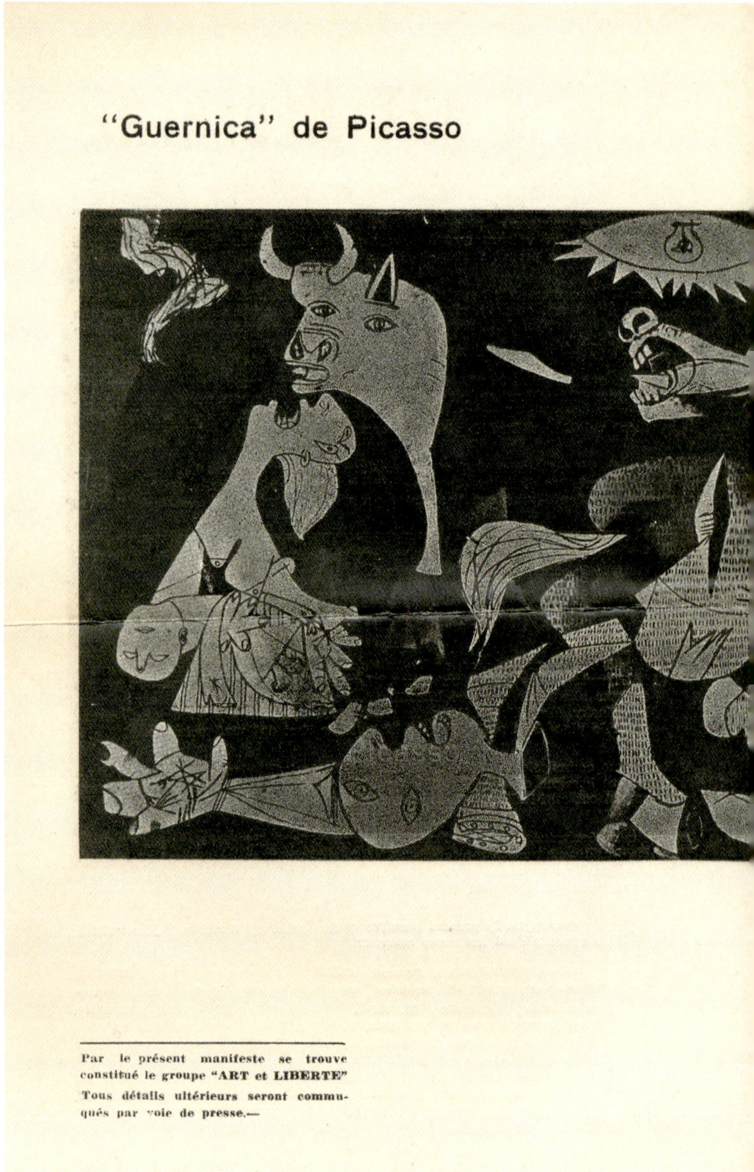

"Guernica" de Picasso

Par le présent manifeste se trouve constitué le groupe "ART et LIBERTE"
Tous détails ultérieurs seront communiqués par voie de presse.—

Manifesto "Vive L'Art Dégénéré", 1938
Printed paper
Scottish National Gallery of Modern Art Archives, Edinburgh

LONG LIVE DEGENERATE ART
We know with what hostility current society looks upon any new literary or artistic creation that directly or indirectly threatens the intellectual disciplines and moral values of behaviour on which it depends for a large part of its own life—its survival.
This hostility is appearing today in totalitarian countries, especially in Hitler's Germany, through the most despicable attacks against an art that these tasselled brutes, promoted to the rank of omniscient judges, qualify as degenerate.
All the achievements of contemporary artistic genius from Cézanne to Picasso—the product of the ultimate in freedom, strength and human feeling—have been received with insults

جارنيكا « الحرب الاسبانية » لبيكاسو

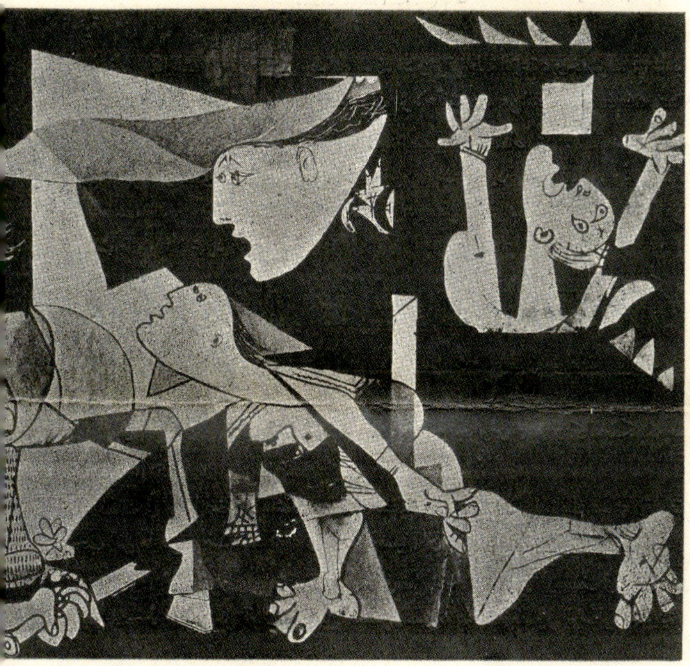

بهذا البيان الحاضر قد تكونت جماعة : —
« الفن والحرية »
وسنعلن التفاصيل الخاصة بالجمعية
بنشرها على صفحات الجرائد

يحيـــا الفن المنحط

من المعروف أن المجتمع الحاضر ينظر بعين الاشمئزاز الى كل خلق جديد فى الفن أو فى الأدب طالما يهدد النظم الثقافية التى تثبت قدم المجتمع سواء أكان من ناحية التفكير أم من ناحية المعني .

ويظهر هذا الشعور بالاشمئزاز جليا فى البلاد الاوتوقراطية النزعة ، وخصوصا في المانيا حيث يتجسم التعدى الشنيع ضد الفن الحر الذى دعاه هؤلاء الغشم :ـ الفن المنحط l'art dégéneré

فمن « سيزان » الى « بيكاسو » وكل ما انتجته العبقرية الفنيه المعاصرة . . . . هذا الانتاج الكثير الحرية والقوى الشعور بالانسانية ، قد قوبل بالشتائم وديس بالاقدام . ونحن نعتقد أن التعصب للدين أو الجنس أو الوطن الذى يريد بعض الافراد أن يخضع له مصير الفن الحديث ما هو الا مجرد هزء وسخرية .

نحن لا نرى فى هذه الاساطير الرجعية إلا سجونا للفكر . ان الفن بصفته مبادلة فكرية وعاطفية دائمة تشترك فيها الانسانية جمعاء لن يقبل مثل هذه الحدود المصطنعة .

فى فينا المتروكة الآن للهمج ، يمزقون صور « رنوار » ويحرقون مؤلفات « فرويد » فى الميادين العامة. إن المع منتجات كبار الفنانين الألمان أمثال « ماكس أرنست » و « بول كلى » و « كارل هوفر » و « كوكوشكا » و « جورج جروس » و « كاندنسكى » قد صودرت وأحل محلها الفن النازى العديم القيمة .

كذلك فى روما أخيراً قد شكلت لجنة « لتنظيف » الأدب !!. وقدقامت بمهمتها وقررت سحب كل ما هو « ضد القومية » و « ضد الجنسية » وكذلك كل ما يدعو الى التشاؤم .

يارجال الأدب ويارجال الفن . لنقف معا ونقبل التحدى . يجب أن نقف فى صف هذا « الفن المنحط » ففيه كل آمال المستقبل. لنعمل لنصرته ضد « العصور الوسطى الجديدة » التى يحاولون بعثها فى قلب أوربا مرة أخري .

وقدوقع الفنانون والكتاب والصحافيون والمحامون على هذا البيان وأسماؤهم كمايلي : ـ

ابراهيم واسيلي ـ احمد فهمي ـ ادوار بولاك ـ ادوار ليفى ـ ارمان انتيبي ـ البير اسرائيل ـ البير قصيري ـ التلمسانى ـ الكسندرا ميتشكويفسكا ـ اميل سيمون ـ انجلوبولو ـ انجلو دريز ـ انور كامل ـ انيت فديدا ـ ا . بوليتس ـ ل . جالنتى ـ جرمين اسرائيل ـ جورج حنين ـ حسن صبحي ـ ا . رافو ـ زكريا العزونى « عضو نقابة المحامين » ـ سامى رياض ـ سامى هانوكا ـ سكاليت ـ عبدالخالق العزوني ـ فاطمه نعمت راشد ـ فؤاد كامل ـ كمال وليم ـ لوران سالينس ـ مارسل بياجيني ـ مارسل ندا ـ مالانوس ـ محمد سيف الدين ـ محمد نور ـ نداف سيلبر ـ هاسيا ـ هنرى دوماني

القاهرة في ٢٢ ديسمبر سنة ١٩٣٨

and repression. We believe that it is mere idiocy and folly to reduce modern art, as some desire, to a fanaticism for any particular religion, race or nation.
Along these lines we see only the imprisonment of thought, whereas art is known to be an exchange of thought and emotions shared by all humanity, one that knows not these artificial boundaries.
Vienna has been left to a rabble that has torn Renoir's paintings and burned the writings of Freud in public places. The best works by great German painters such as Max Ernst, Paul Klee, Karl Hoffer, Kokoschka, George Grosz and Kandinsky have been confiscated and replaced by Nazi art of no value. The same recently took place in Rome where a committee was formed to purge literature, and, performing its duties, decided to eliminate works that went against nationalism and race, as well as any work raising pessimism.
O men of art, men of letters! Let us take up the challenge together! We stand absolutely as one with this degenerate art. In it resides all the hopes of the future. Let us work for its victory over the new Middle Ages that are rising in the heart of Europe.
The following artists, writers, journalists and lawyers have signed this manifesto:
A. Angelopoulo, Armand Antebi, Abd-el-Khalek El Azzouni, Zakaria El Azzouni (Member of the Bar Association of Alexandria), Marcelle Biagini, Albert Cossery, Henri Dumani, Ahmed Fahmy, Annette Fedida, L. Galanti, Samy Hanoka, Hassia, Georges Henein, Albert Israel, Germaine Israel, Anouar Kamel, Fouad Kamel, Edouard Levy, Malanos, Alexandra Metchcouevska, Marcel Nada, Fatma Nimet-Rachid, Mohammed Nour, A. Politis, Edouard Pollack, Angelo de Riz, A. Revaux, Sami Riad, Mohammed Seif-el-Dine, Hassan Sobhy, Laurent Salinas, Emile Simon, Scalet, Telmisany, Nadave Silber, Kamal William, Ibrahim Wassily.
Cairo, December 22, 1938.

القمصان الزرقاء المصرية

تجوب شوارع القاهرة

في يوم ١٥ مارس احتفلت فرق الشباب الوفدية « أصحاب القمصان الزرقاء » بعيد الاستقلال احتفالا رياضياً نظامياً لم يسبق له مثيل ، فقد اشتركت فيه بعض فرق القاهرة وفرق عديدة من المنصورة وطنطا وبلقاس وبنها والجيزة والمنيا والاقصر ودمنهور وغيرها من مدن القطر ، وكانت هذه الفرق تتوافد في صباح ذلك اليوم التاريخي الى معسكرها العام بجوار بيت الامة حتى اذا ما بلغ عدد اعضائها بضع مئات واكتمل عقدها ، نظمت صفوفها بنظام بديع ، ثم سارت في خطوة رياضية وعرض رائع يتقدمها موكب من الدراجات مخترقة الشوارع في نظام عسكري حتى وصلت الى ساحة السراي الملكية العامرة ، وهنا صدحت موسيقاها بالسلام الملكي وهتف (البقية الى اليسار)

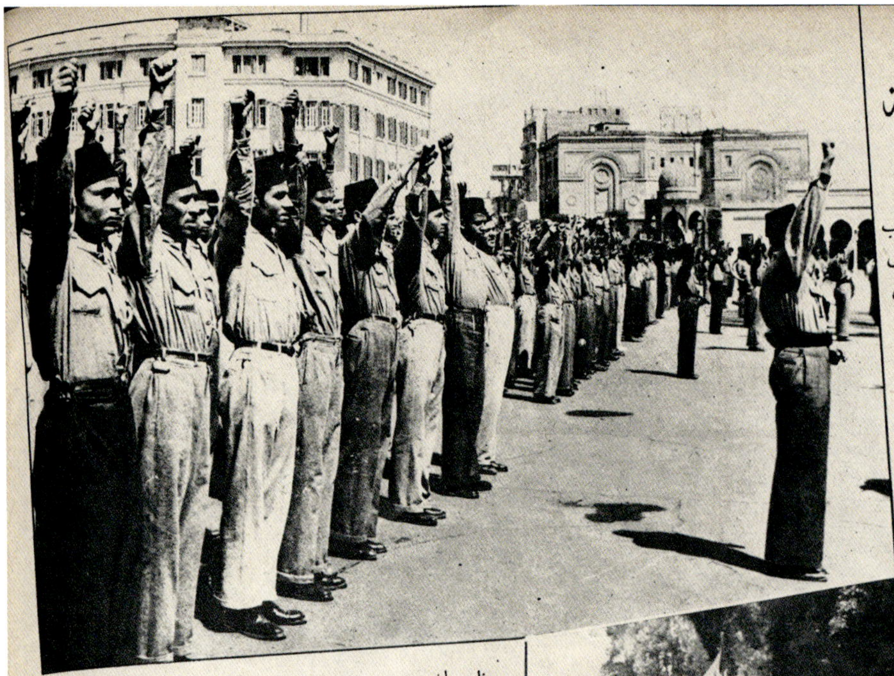

منظر جانب من فرق الشباب الوفدية وهم مصطفون بنظام عسكري بديع امام القصر الملكي العامر في يوم ١٥ مارس لمناسبة عيد الاستقلال وقد رفعوا ايديهم مؤدين التحية الوفدية لحضرة صاحب الجلالة الملك في اثناء عزف السلام الملكي وقد كان عددهم في ذلك اليوم يزيد علي ١٥٠٠ شاب وفدي بارك الله فيهم

(تابع المنشور اعلاه من اليمين) اعضاؤها هتافاً يشق عنان السماء بحيا جلالة مولانا الملك ودخل قائدها العام الى السراي العامرة فرفع تحية هذه الفرق الوفدية ووفاءها وولاءها الى صاحب العرش المفدى . . . وبعد ذلك اتجهت الفرق نحو شارع الملكة نازلي فشارع عماد الدين فبعض شوارع القاهرة تحييها الجماهير من الشرفات والطرقات ثم قصدت الى بيت الامة حيث حيت الزعيم الخالد سعد زغلول وشريكة جهاده صاحبة العصمة أم المصريين الجليلة . . وانتهى هذا العرض (البقية الى اليمين)

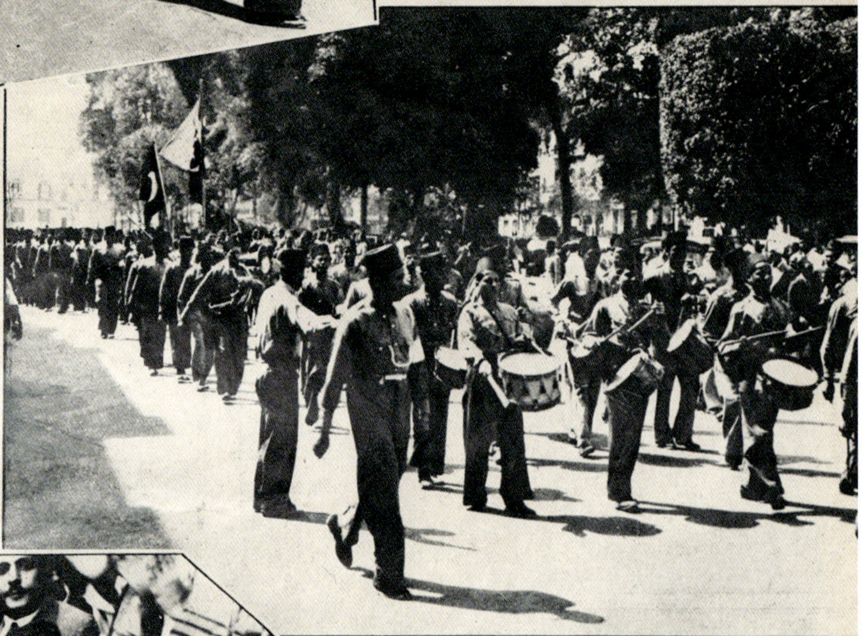

فرق الشباب الوفدية ذوو القمصان الزرقاء في أثناء عرضهم التاريخي يوم عيد الاستقلال وهم يجوبون شوارع القاهرة يحملون أعلامهم وتتقدمهم موسيقاهم وتتألف كل فرقة من ٤٤ جندياً يتقدمها ضابطان ويسير الى جانبها مدربها الرياضي

(تابع المنشور أعلاه من اليسار) التاريخي بين أجل مظاهر النظام والروعة وبهذه المناسبة نقول ان فكرة تنظيم الشباب تنظيما رياضياً اجتماعياً تحت لواء الوفد قد لاقت ترحيباً عاماً بها في جميع مدن القطر وأقاليمه لسمو معناها وجلائل فائدتها في بعث روح النشاط والحياة في شباب البلاد فهي فكرة اجتماعية نظامية حيوية من شأنها تلقين الشباب أصول النظام العلمي وهي ليست عسكرية أو فاشستية كما أشاع خصومها فيما قبل . . فتهنئة صادقة للقائمين بها ولاعضائها والمتطوعين تحت لوائها ونسأل الله تعالى أن يباركها وينميها

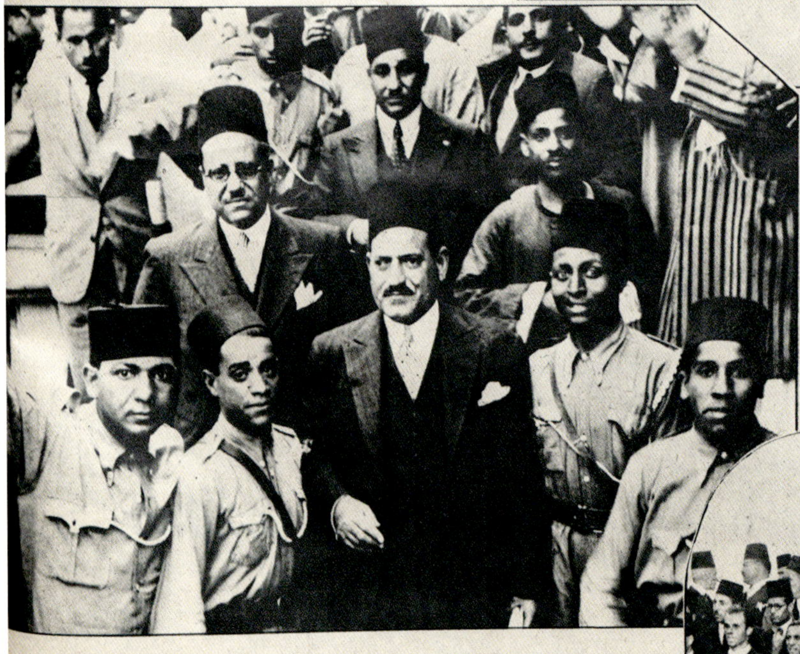

صورة حضرة صاحب الدولة والزعامة الرئيس الجليل مصطفى النحاس باشا القائد الاعلى لفرق الشباب الوفدية ويرى بين ابنائه شباب هذه الفرق وخلفه المجاهد الكبير الاستاذ مكرم عبيد وحضرة الاستاذ مأمون الريدي سكرتير بيت الامة وذلك في يوم ١٥ مارس عقب انتهاء العرض الرياضي لذوي القمصان الزرقاء واجتماعهم بقائدهم الأعلى

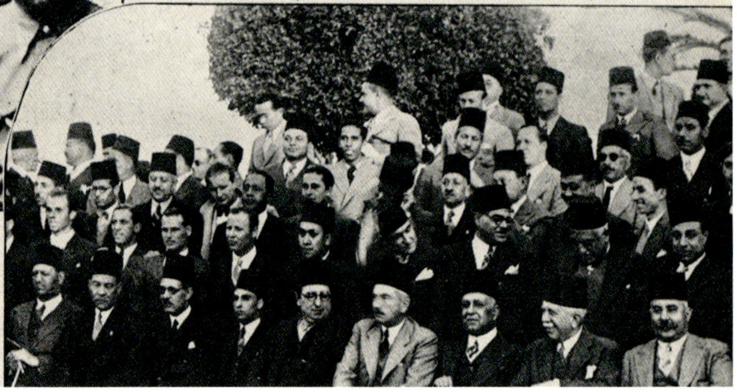

1

"For Futurism, nothing is the same. The exhibitionist character of Mr Marinetti's manifestations, the spectacular and artificial dynamism that he advocates, have earned him the legitimate contempt of the Surrealists. Furthermore, the aeropainting which they currently favor belongs to the realm of decorative art rather than art itself".

Georges Henein, "Bilan du mouvement surréaliste," 1937

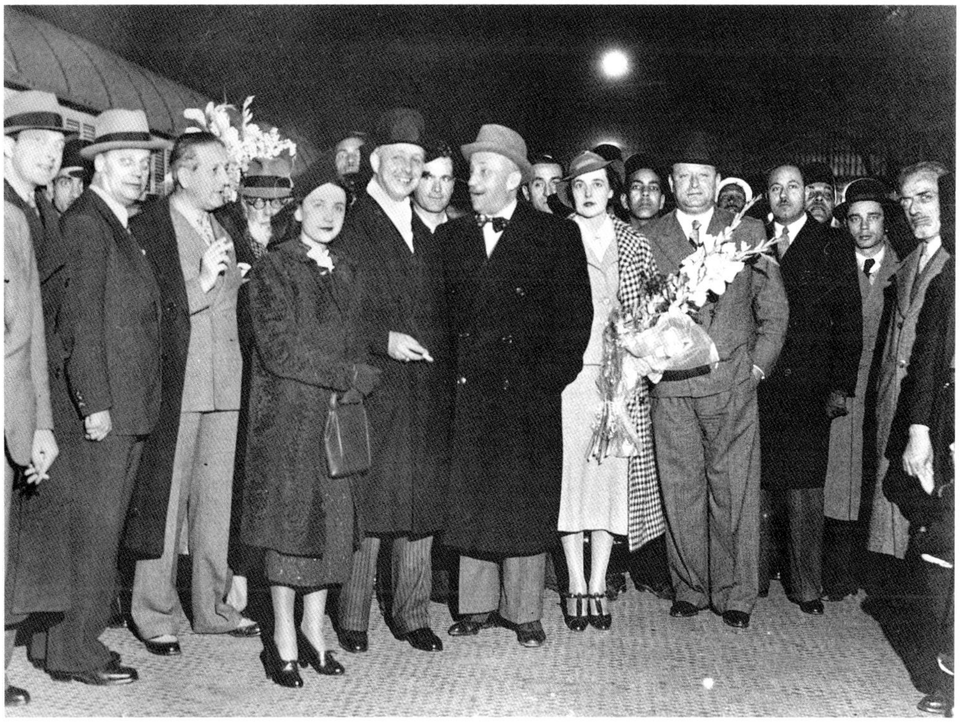

2

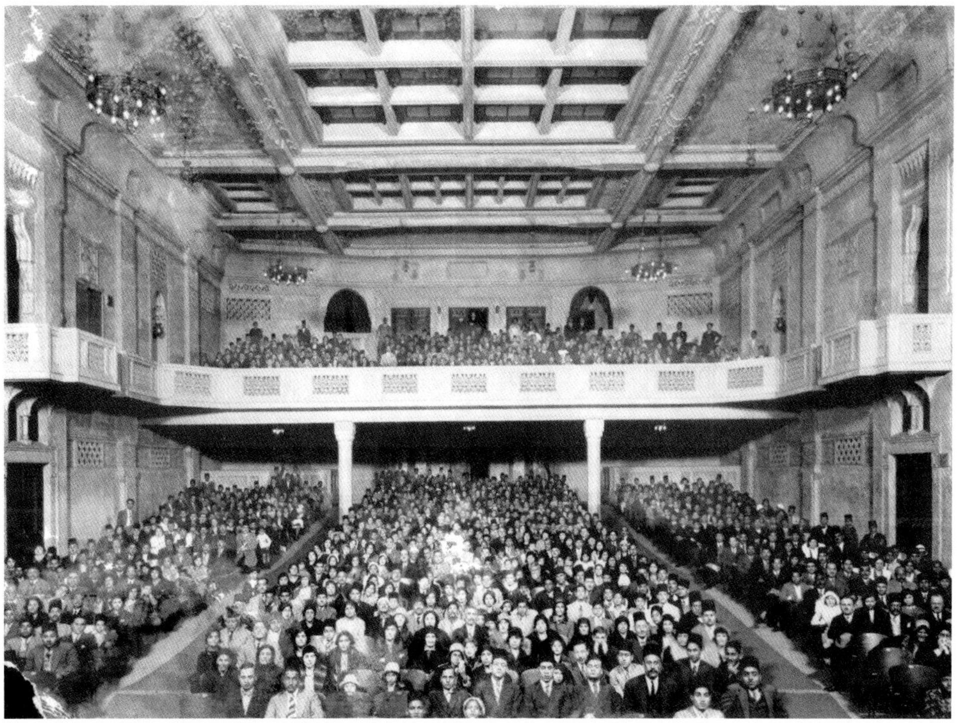

3

1
The Blue Shirts Roam the Streets of Cairo
Al-Lata'if Al-Musawwara, March 23, 1936, p. 4. Newspaper print
Al-Lata'if Al-Musawwara Archives, Cairo

2
Filippo Tommaso Marinetti and Benedetta Cappa Marinetti, 1938
Photographer unknown
Vintage gelatin silver print
Filippo Tommaso Marinetti Papers, Beinecke Rare Book and Manuscript Library, Yale University, New Haven CT

3
View of a conference audience at the Ewart Hall, the American University in Cairo, c. 1930s
Photographer unknown
Vintage gelatin silver print
Rare Books and Special Collections Library, American University, Cairo

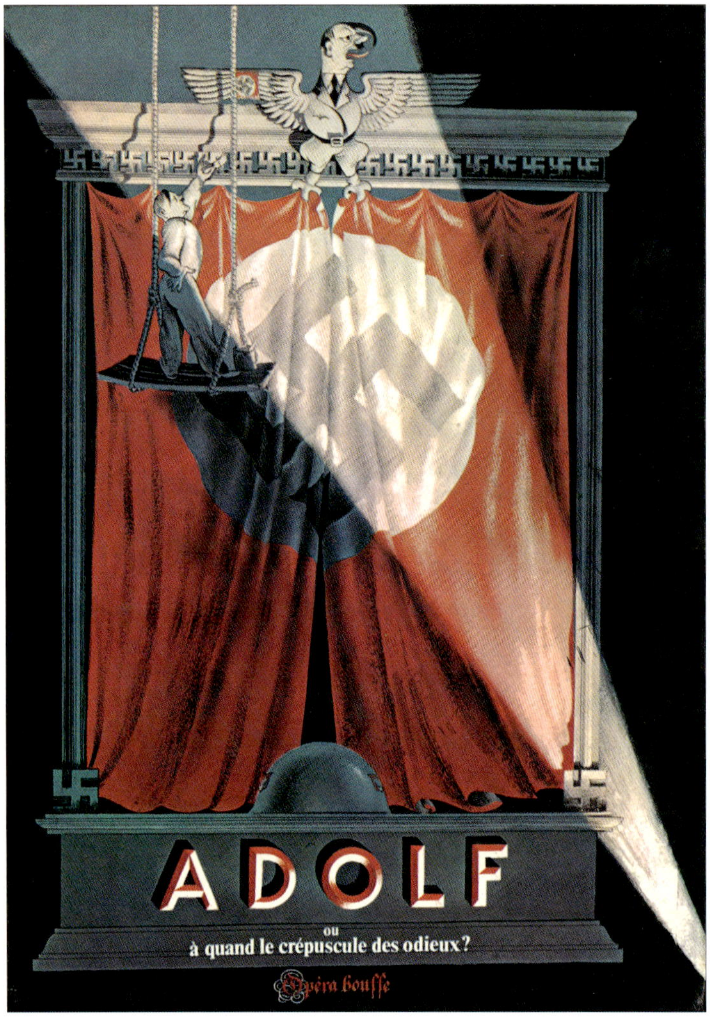

1

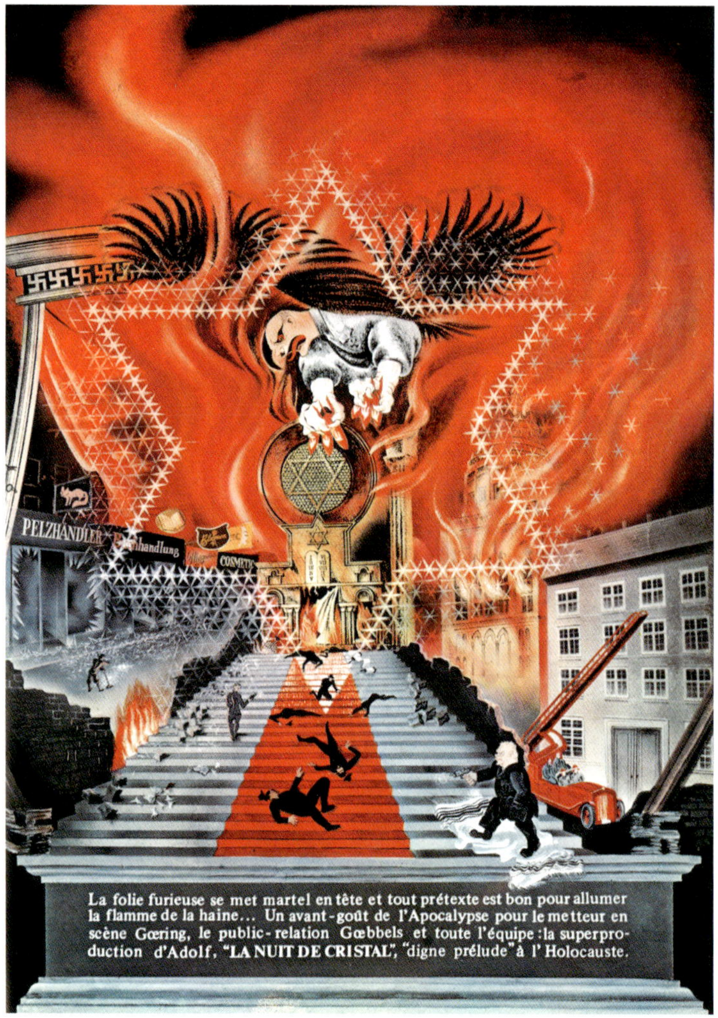

2

1
ÉTIENNE SVED
Adolf ou À quand le crépuscule des odieux?, 1980
Cover illustration
Reprinted in 1980 by Nesle/Sved Publishing
Private collection

2
ÉTIENNE SVED
Adolf ou À quand le crépuscule des odieux?, 1980
Page 43
Reprinted in 1980 by Nesle/Sved Publishing
Private collection

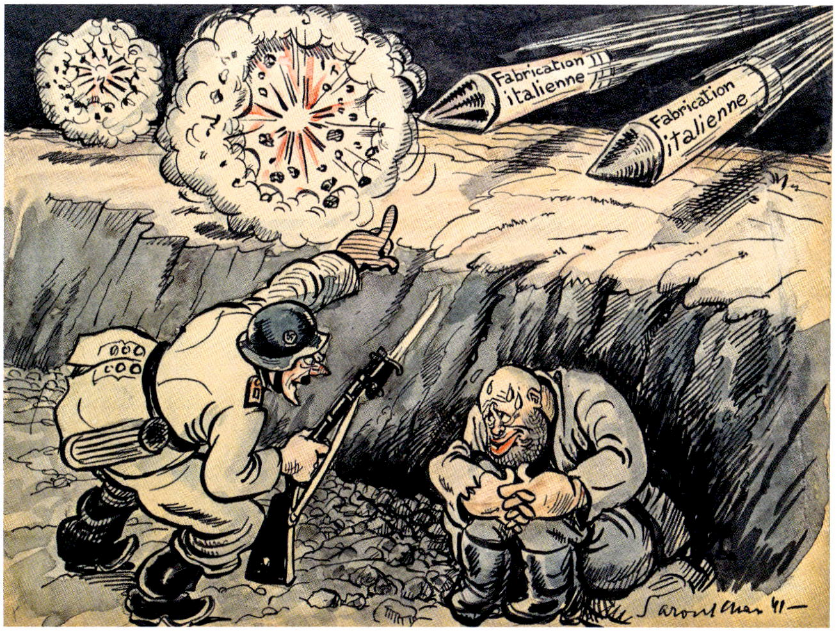

3

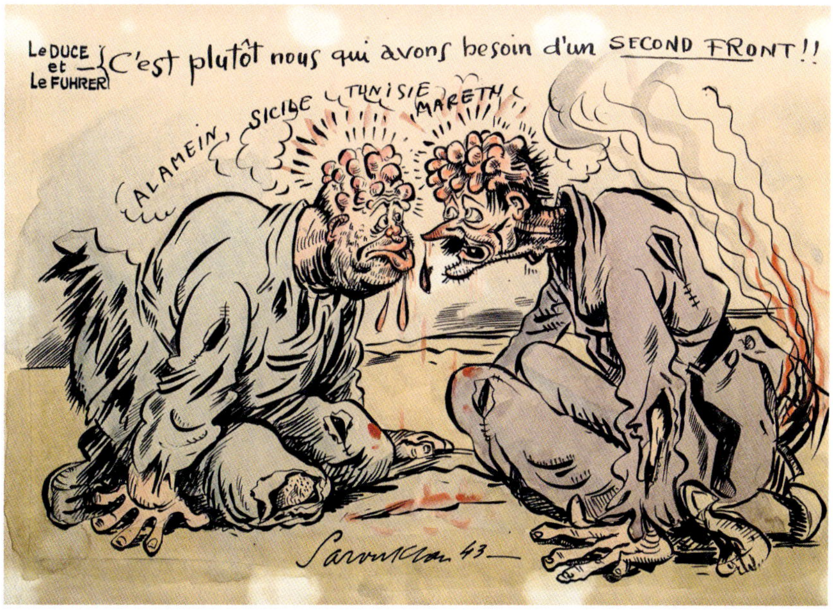

4

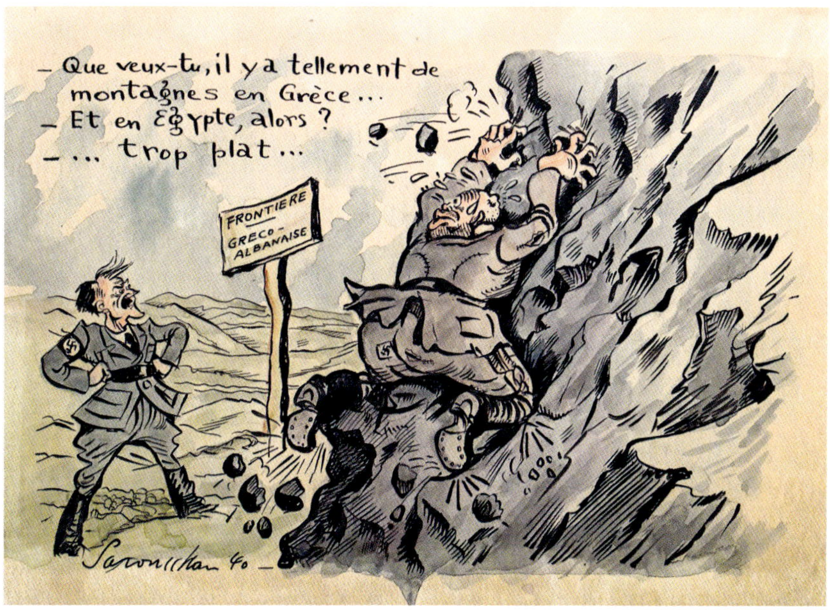

5

3
SAROUKHAN
A Worthwhile Collaboration, 1941
From the series *Cette guerre*
Watercolour and ink on paper
22.3 x 30 cm
Al Masar Gallery for Contemporary Art, Cairo

4
SAROUKHAN
Le Duce et le Führer, 1943
From the series *Cette guerre*
Watercolour and ink on paper
30 x 44.7 cm
Al Masar Gallery for Contemporary Art, Cairo

5
SAROUKHAN
Frontière Gréco-Albanaise, 1940
From the series *Cette guerre*
Watercolour and ink on paper
29 x 43 cm
Al Masar Gallery for Contemporary Art, Cairo

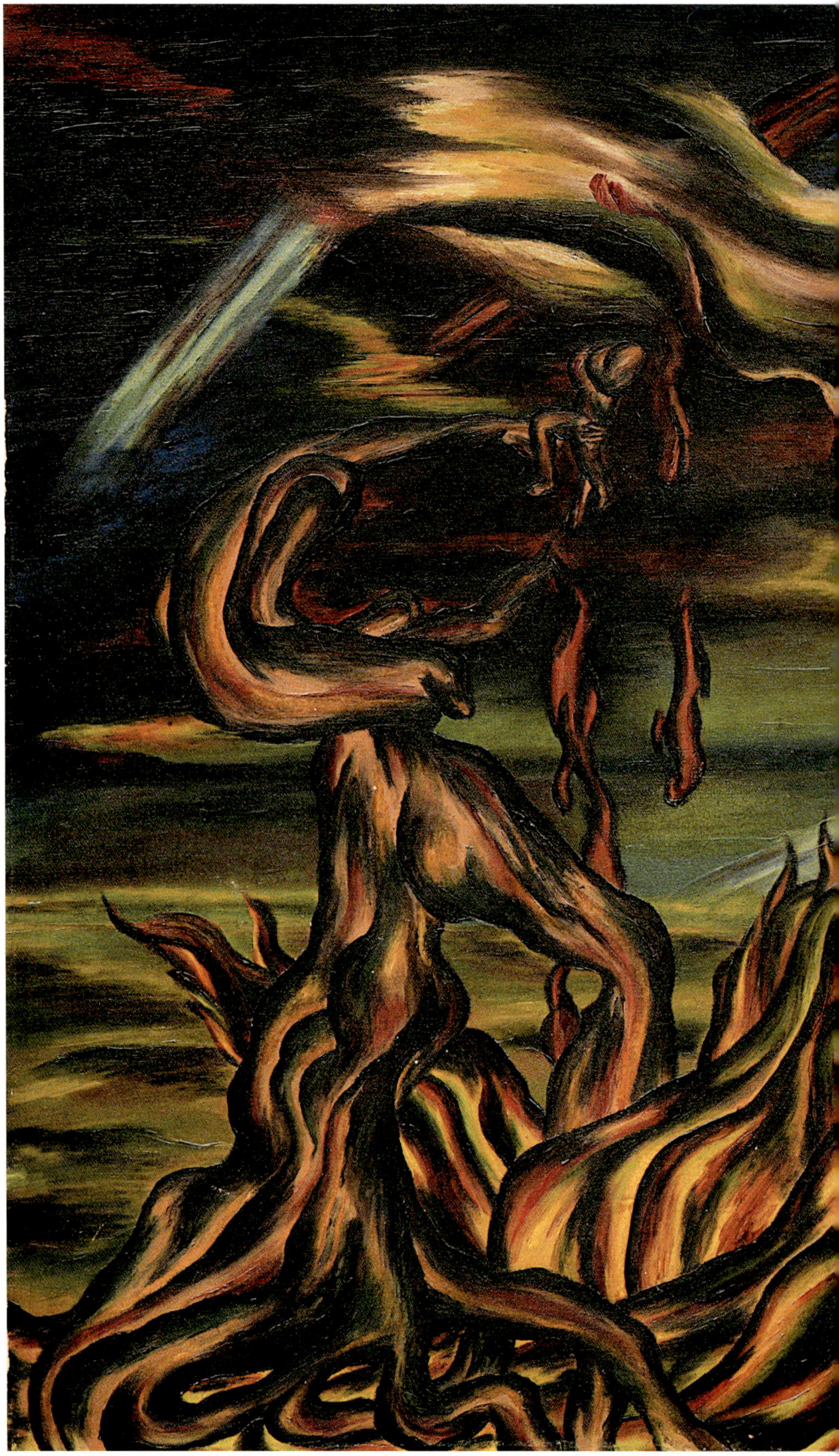

INJI EFFLATOUN
Girl and Monster, 1942
Oil on canvas
80 x 130.5 cm
Private collection

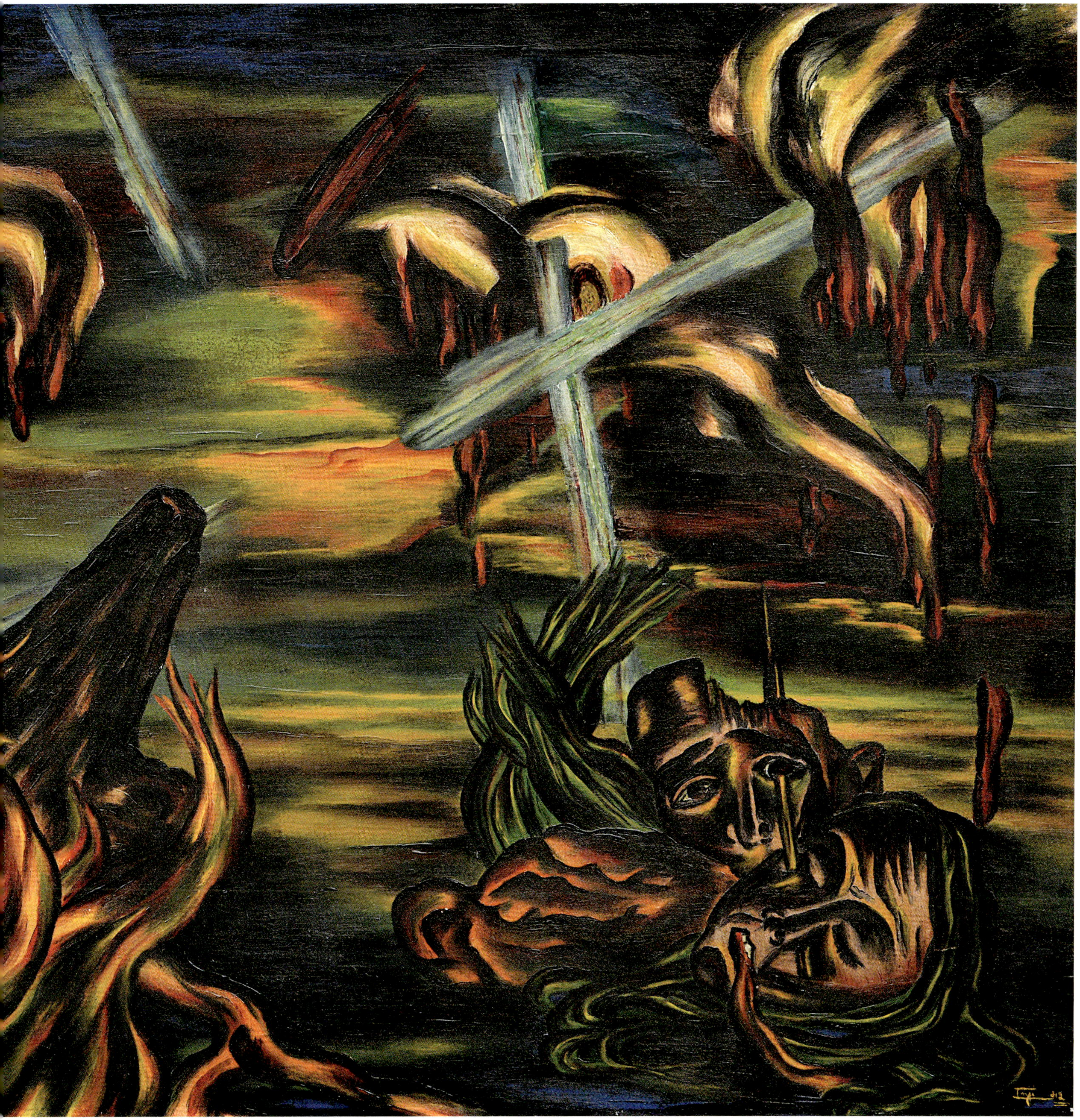

"The salutes of the cracks in your forehead
filter the jewels that come heralding the capital orgies
reserved for those grand parallel desires…

Here rings the exact hour where chance shuts down
the parentheses it had offered us,
where absolute weariness unravels the constant couples…"

Georges Henien, *À contre-cloison*, 1939

INJI EFFLATOUN
Girl and Monster, 1941
Oil on canvas
50 x 43 cm
Private collection

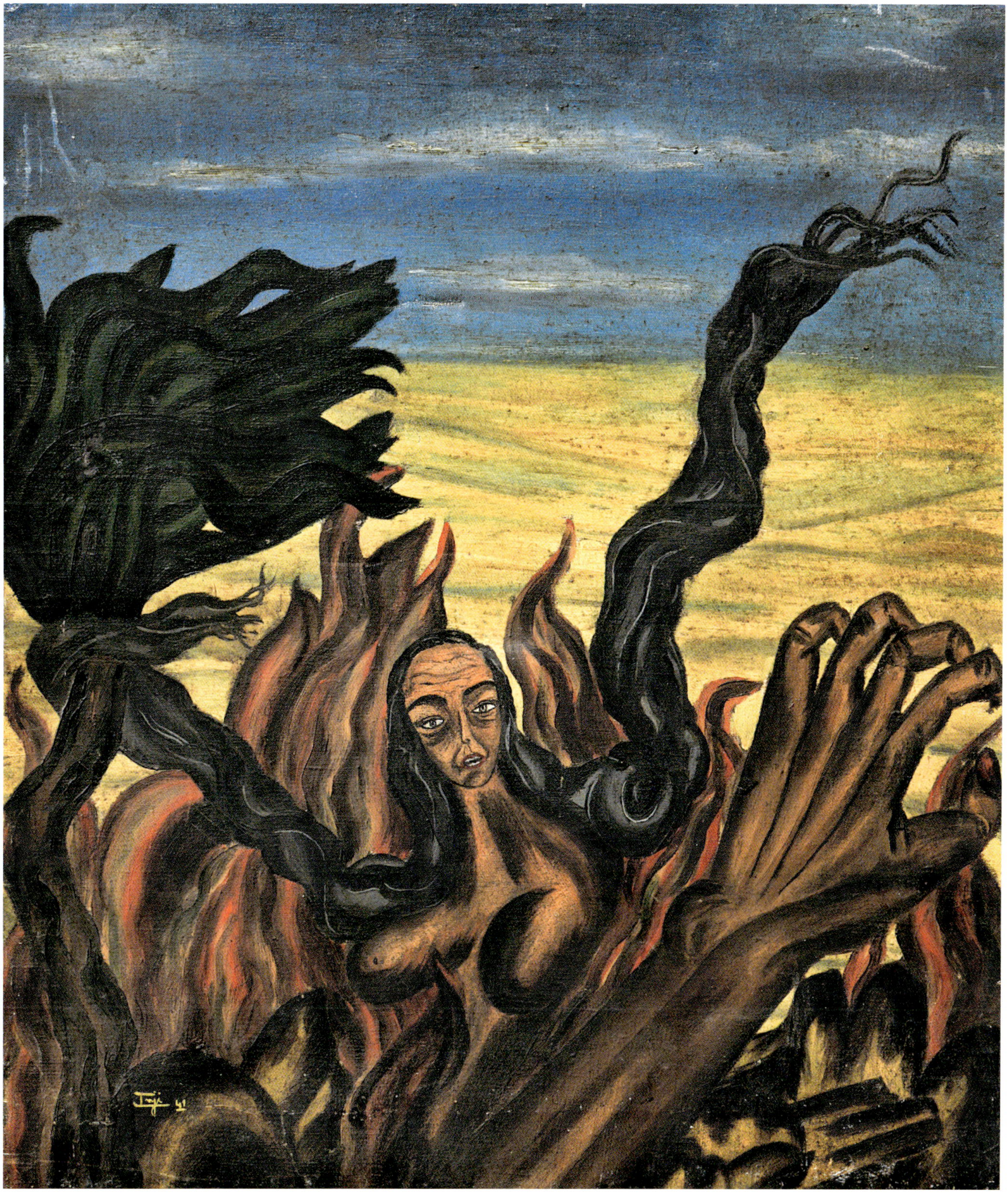

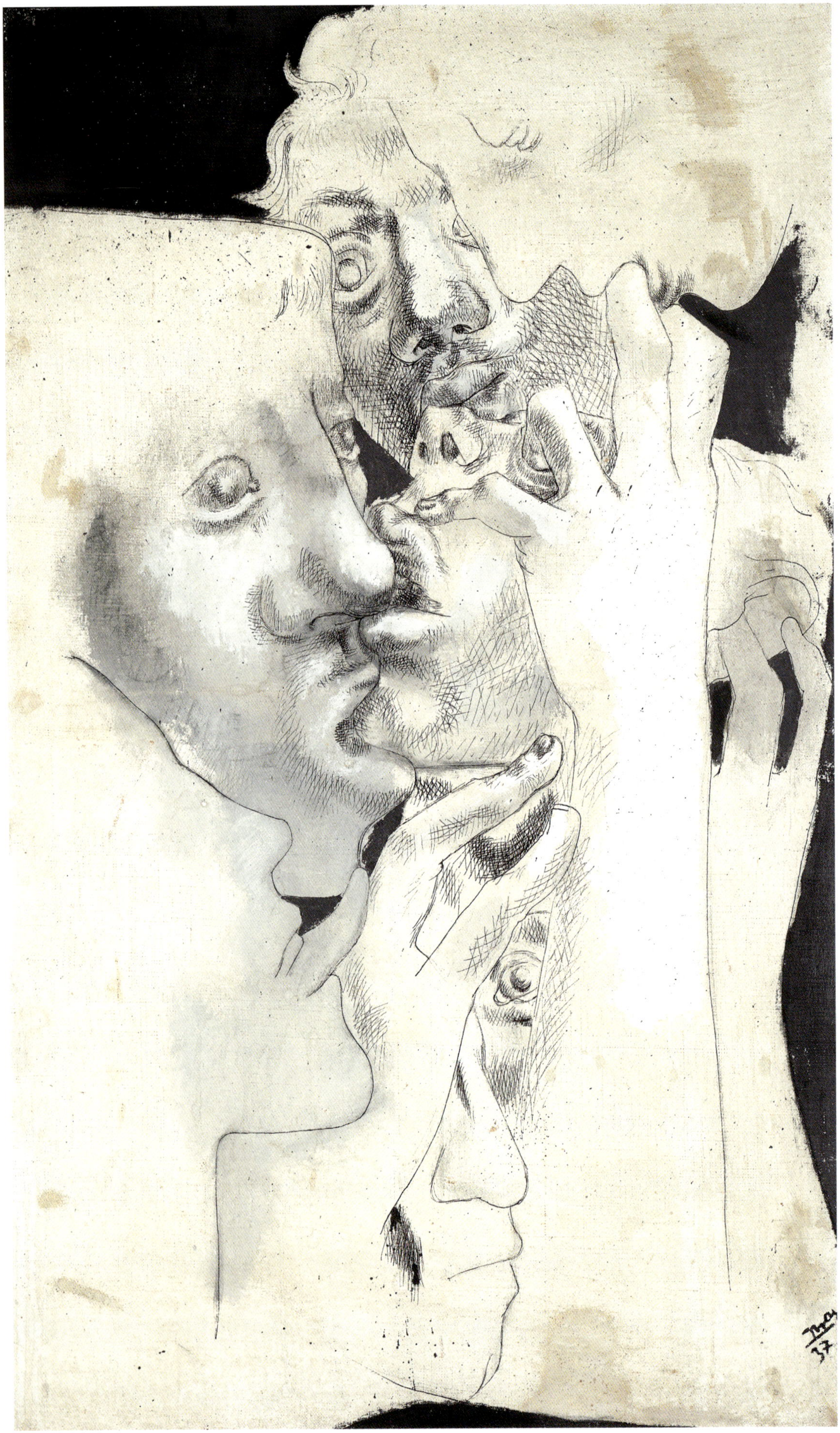

MAYO
Dessin Cruel, 1937
Mixed media on canvas
145 x 90 cm
Yeatman-Eiffel collection, Paris

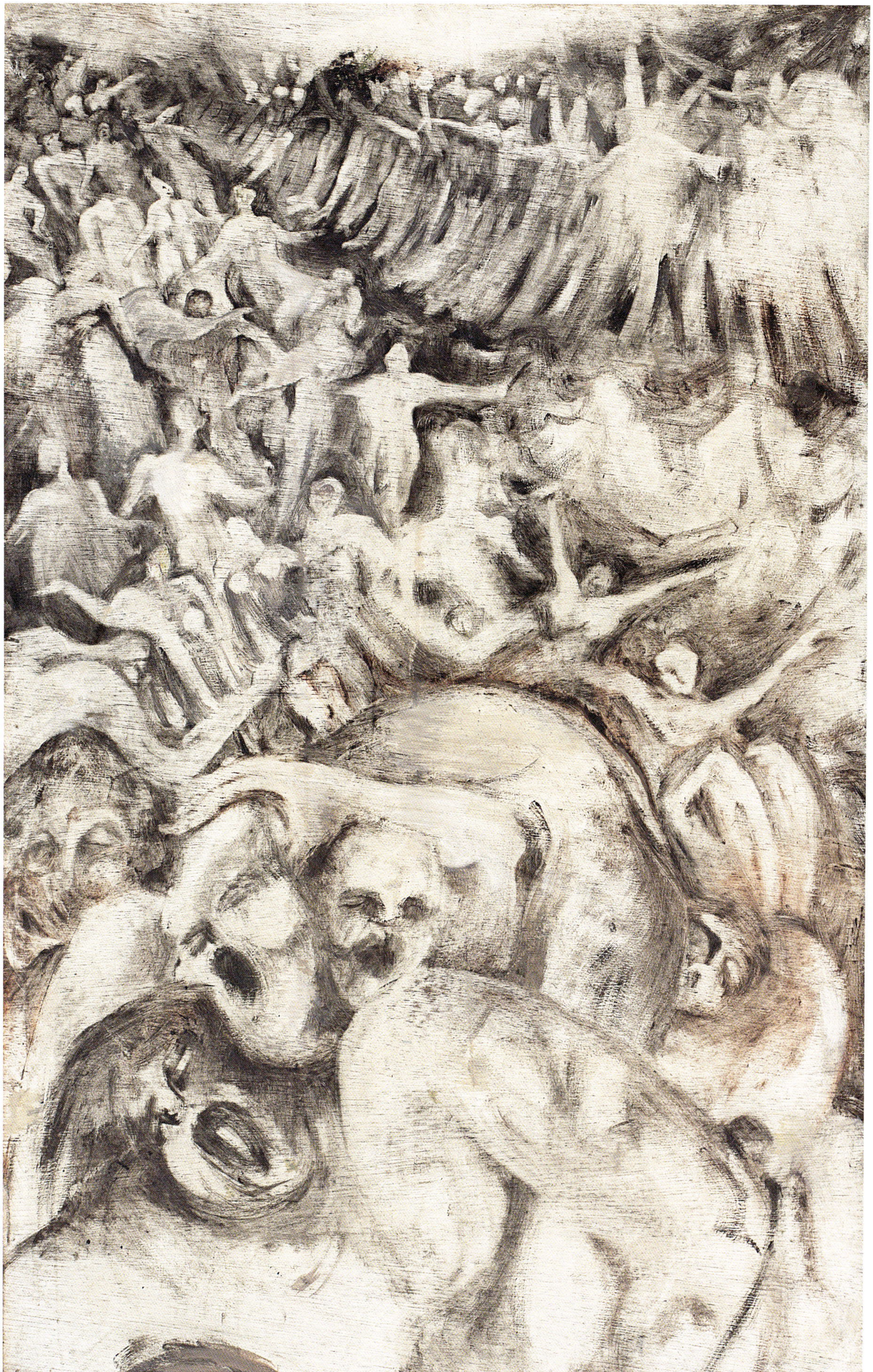

RATEB SEDDIK
Untitled, c. 1940
Oil on wood
120 x 79.5 cm
Rateb Seddik Museum, Cairo

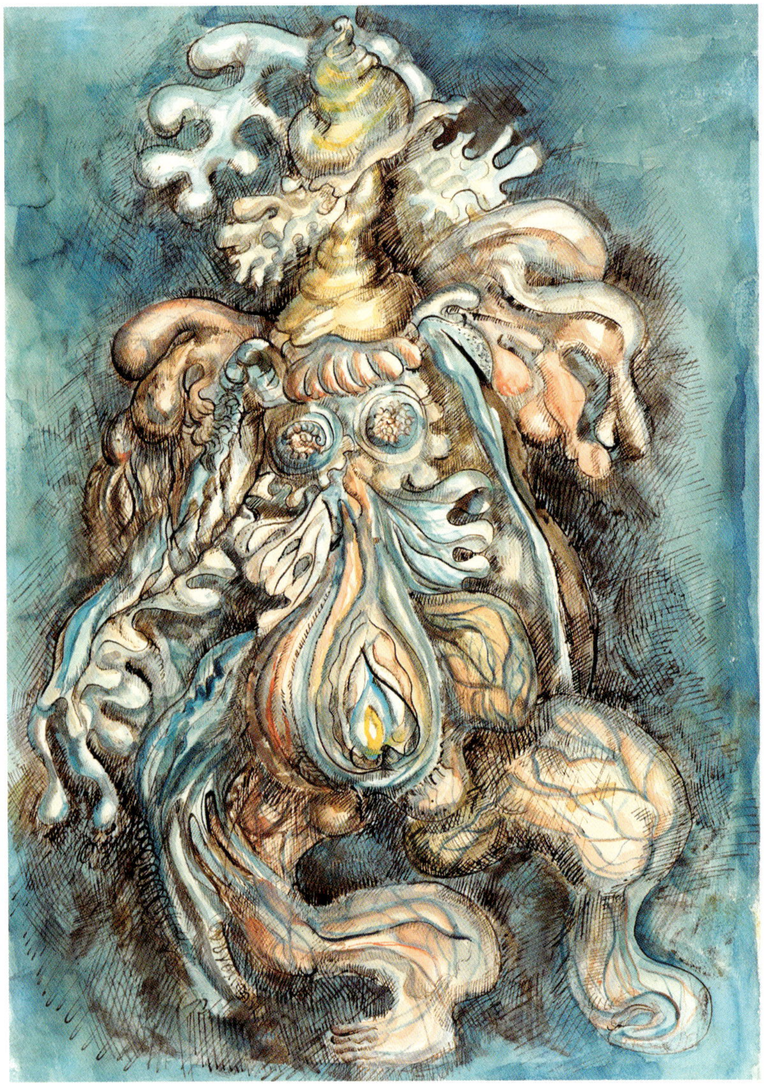

1

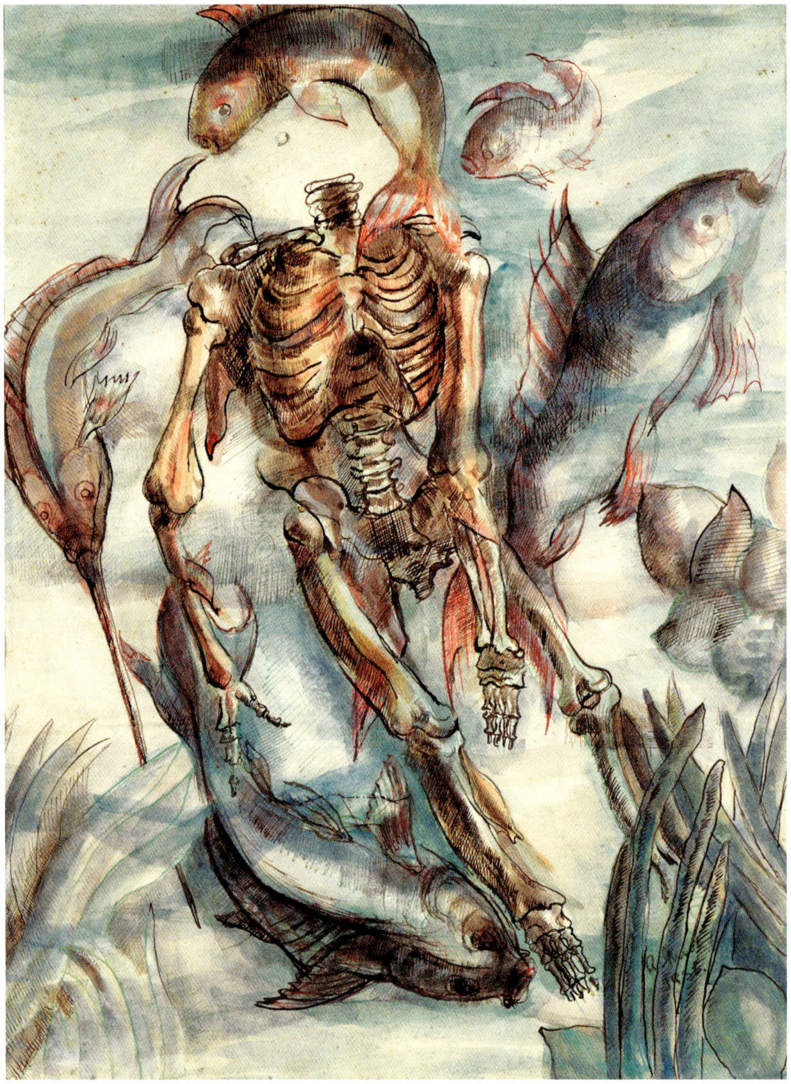

2

1
AMY NIMR
Untitled (Anatomical Body), c. 1940
Gouache and ink on paper
36.5 x 27.5 cm
H.E. Sh. Hassan M. A. Al Thani collection, Doha

2
AMY NIMR
Untitled (Fish and Skeletons), 1936
Gouache and ink on paper
41 x 31.5 cm
H.E. Sh. Hassan M. A. Al Thani collection, Doha

3
AMY NIMR
Untitled (Underwater Skeleton), 1943
Gouache on wood
54 x 45.5 cm
H.E. Sh. Hassan M. A. Al Thani collection, Doha

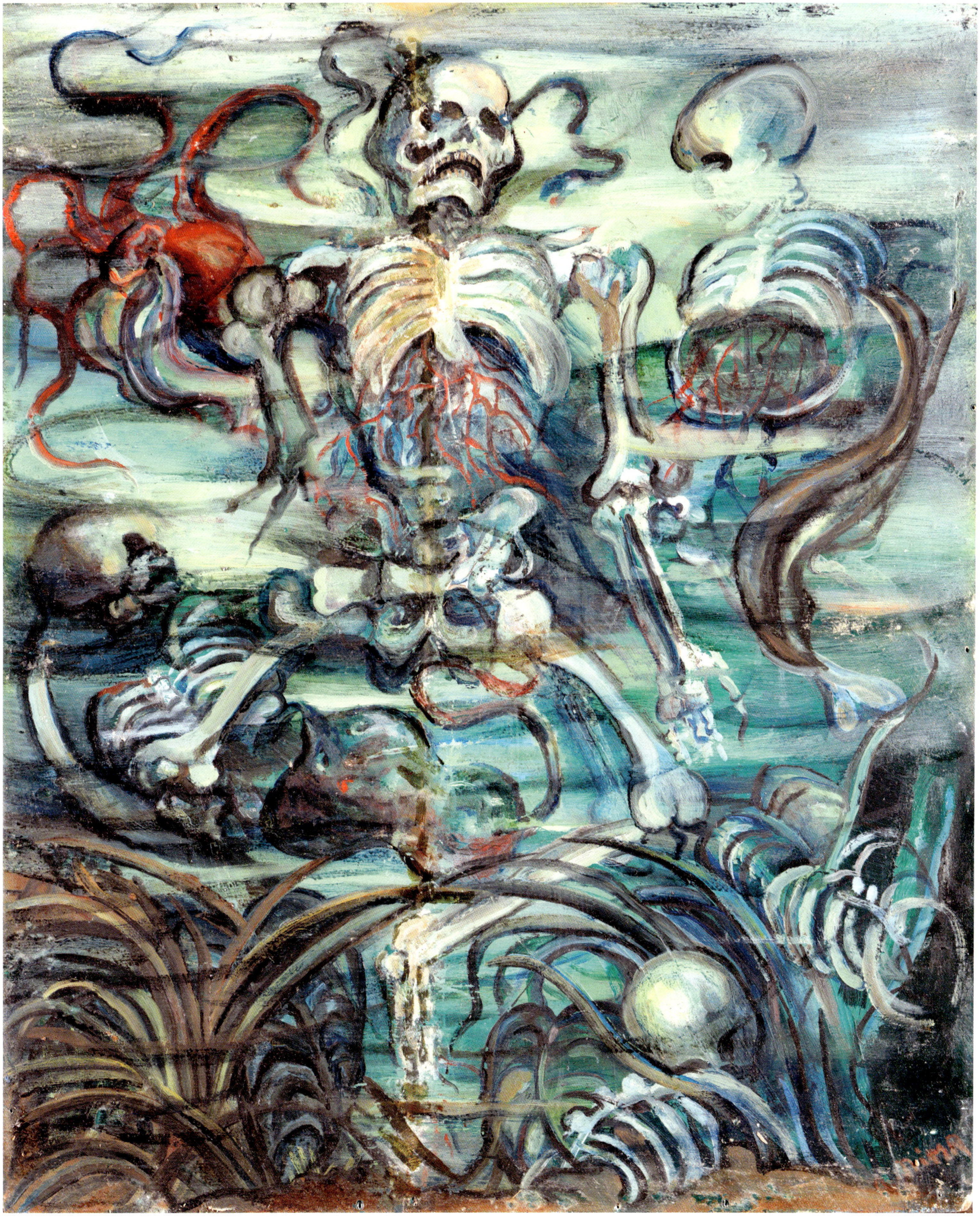
3

RAMSES YOUNANE
La nature appelle le vide, 1944
Oil on canvas
49 x 49 cm
Museum of Modern Egyptian Art, Cairo

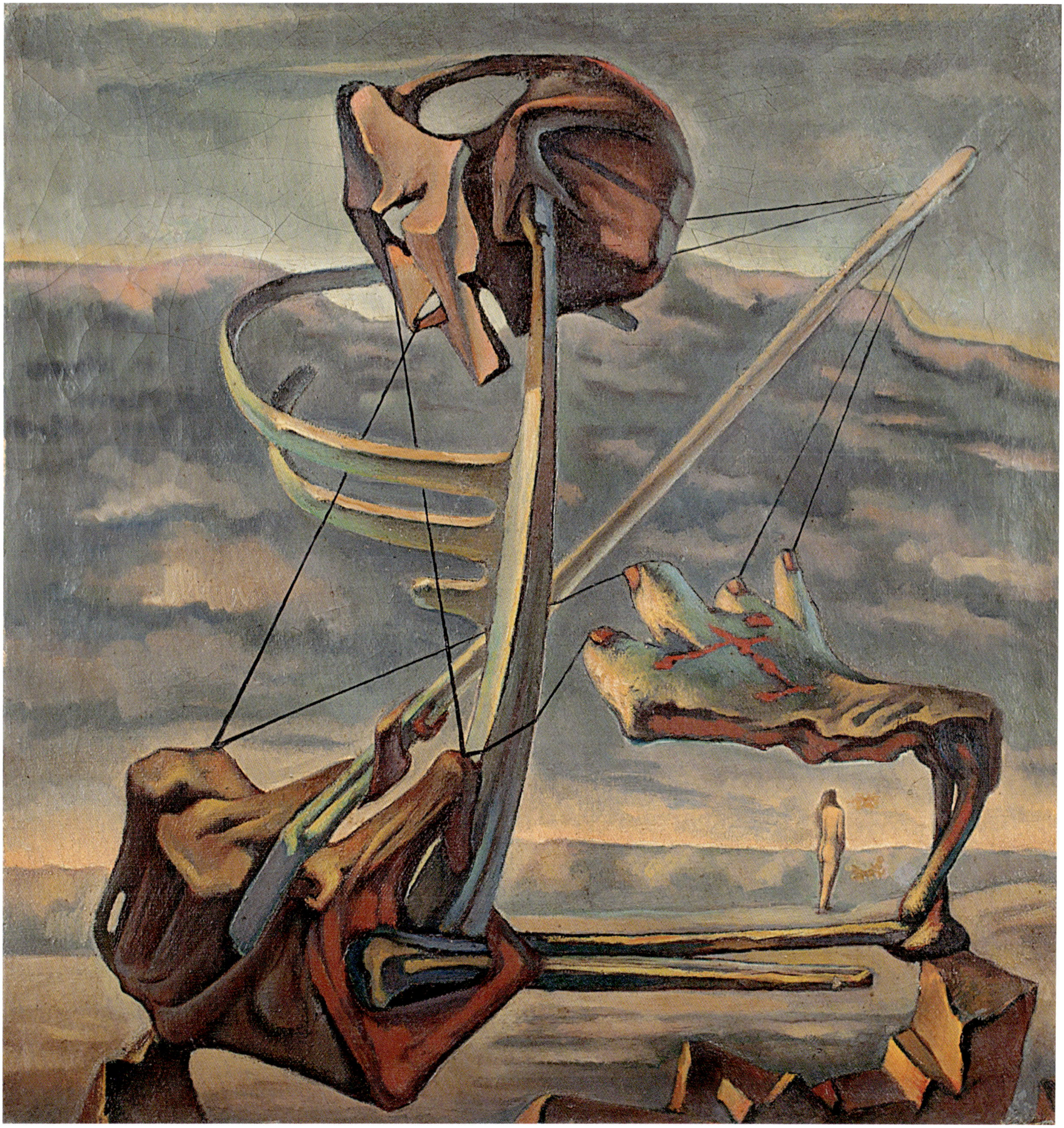

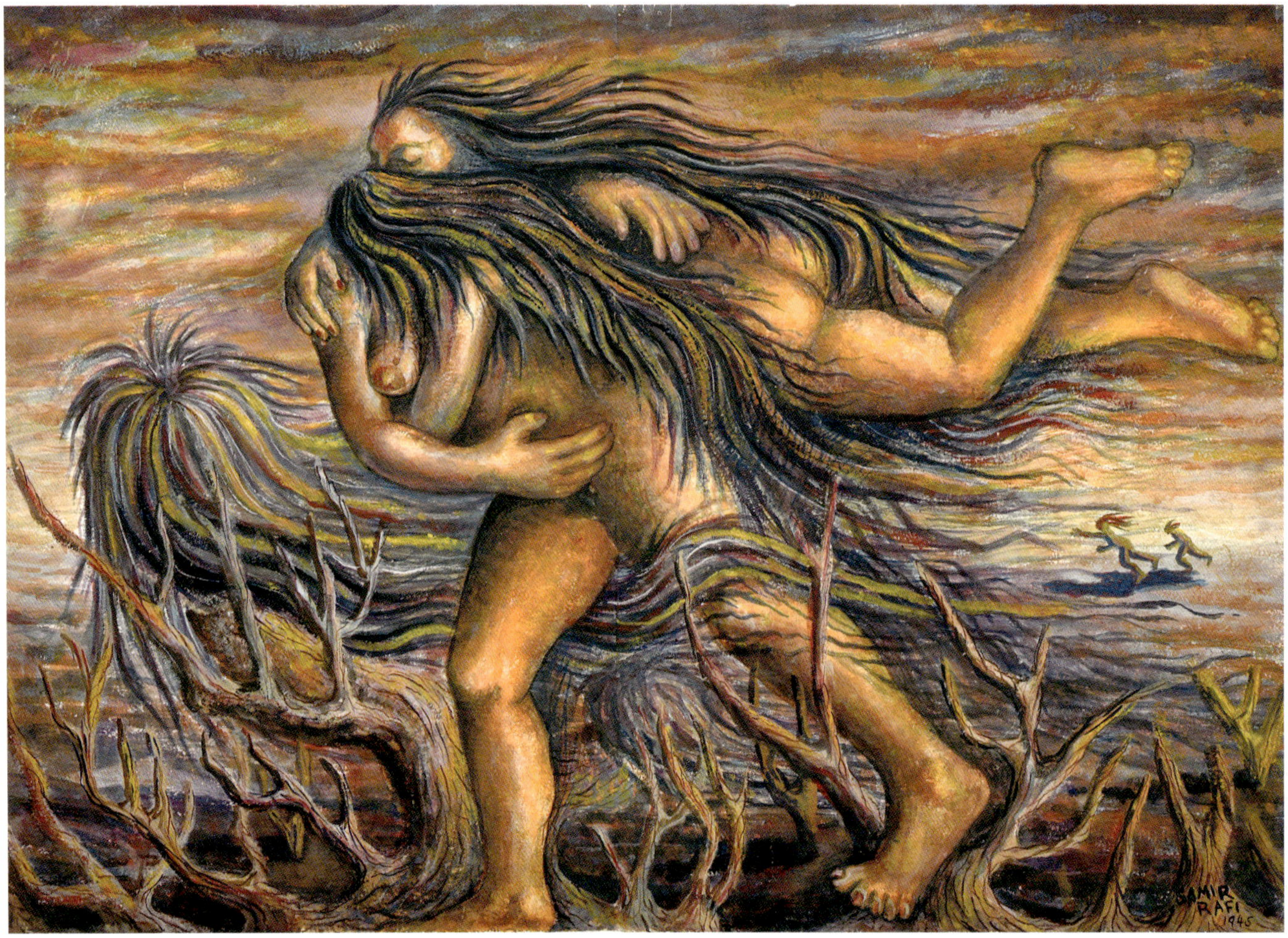

1

1
SAMIR RAFI
Untitled, 1945
Acrylic on paper
69 x 99.8 cm
Private collection

2
SAMIR RAFI
Nudes, 1945
Oil on canvas
177 x 163 cm
H.E. Sh. Hassan M. A. Al Thani collection, Doha

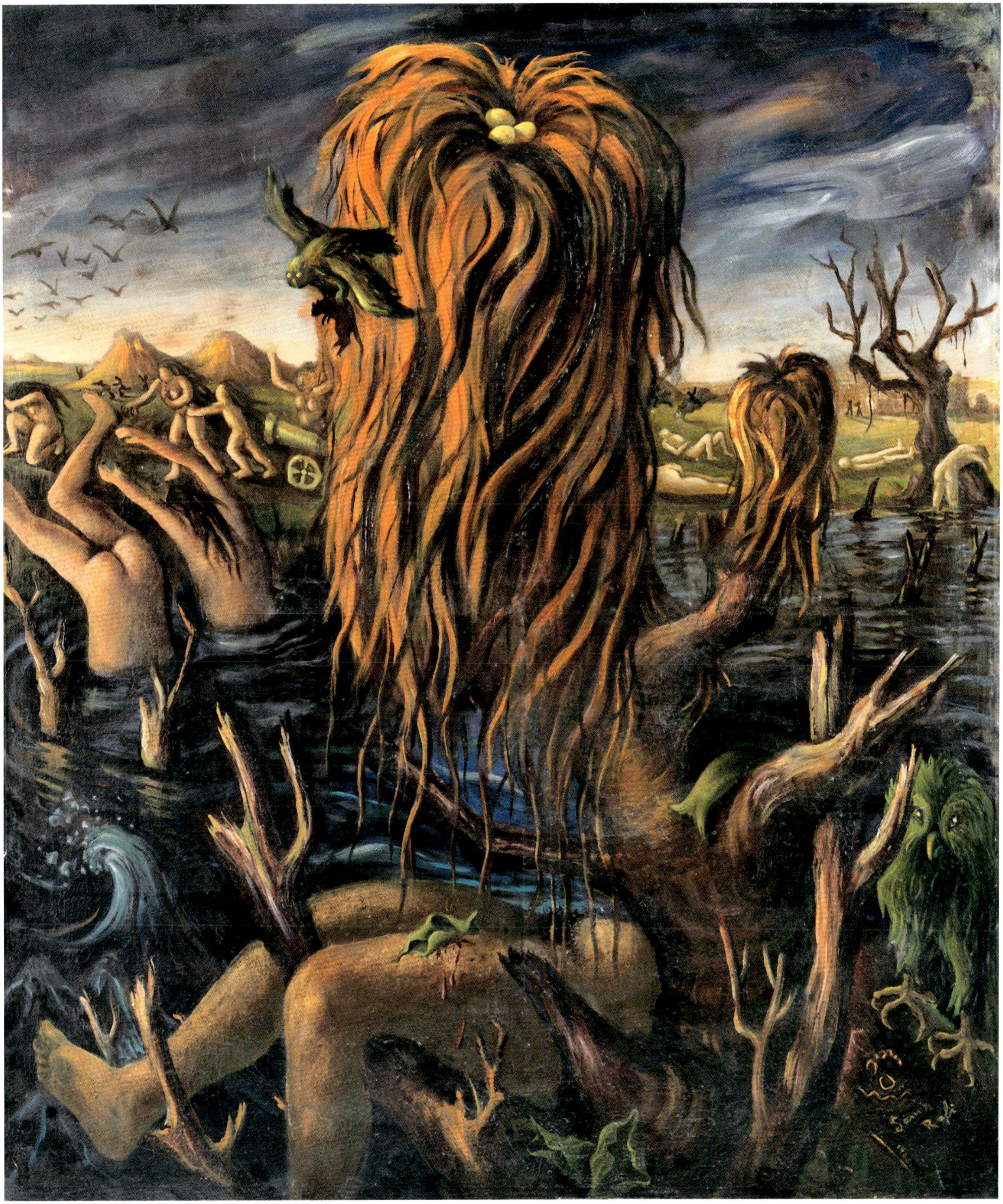

2

"FRAGMENTED BODIES"

Kamel El-Telmisany, *Don Quichotte*, no. 12, February 1940

During the time of *Art et Liberté*, Cairo was a city marked by extreme economic inequality. The majority of wealth was held by a small percentage of feudal landowners and business magnates, while more than half of the population, mostly rural labourers and urban workers, suffered from dire poverty. *Art et Liberté* believed that this unfair distribution of resources was largely due to the bourgeoisie who obstructed the evolution of the lower classes. Revolution was therefore a necessary tool to destroy the hegemony of bourgeois mentality: economically, socially and artistically. In fragmenting the human figure, *Art et Liberté* harnessed Surrealism's revolt against the bourgeoisie's championing of Symbolism and Naturalism. In these traditional styles, the bodies of even the most wretched of characters were portrayed in an idealized fashion. In contrast, *Art et Liberté* painted deformed, dismembered or distorted figures in order to poignantly illustrate the harrowing economic injustice that plagued their society. The motif of the fragmented, or emaciated body, as *Art et Liberté* called it, became a site of social as well as artistic protest. Through paintings that ranged from the miniscule to the monumental, *Art et Liberté* portrayed the body in a state of anguish within violent settings that undoubtedly gained in resonance given the simultaneous unfolding of World War II and the increased circulation of images of maimed soldiers and scenes of battles and destruction.

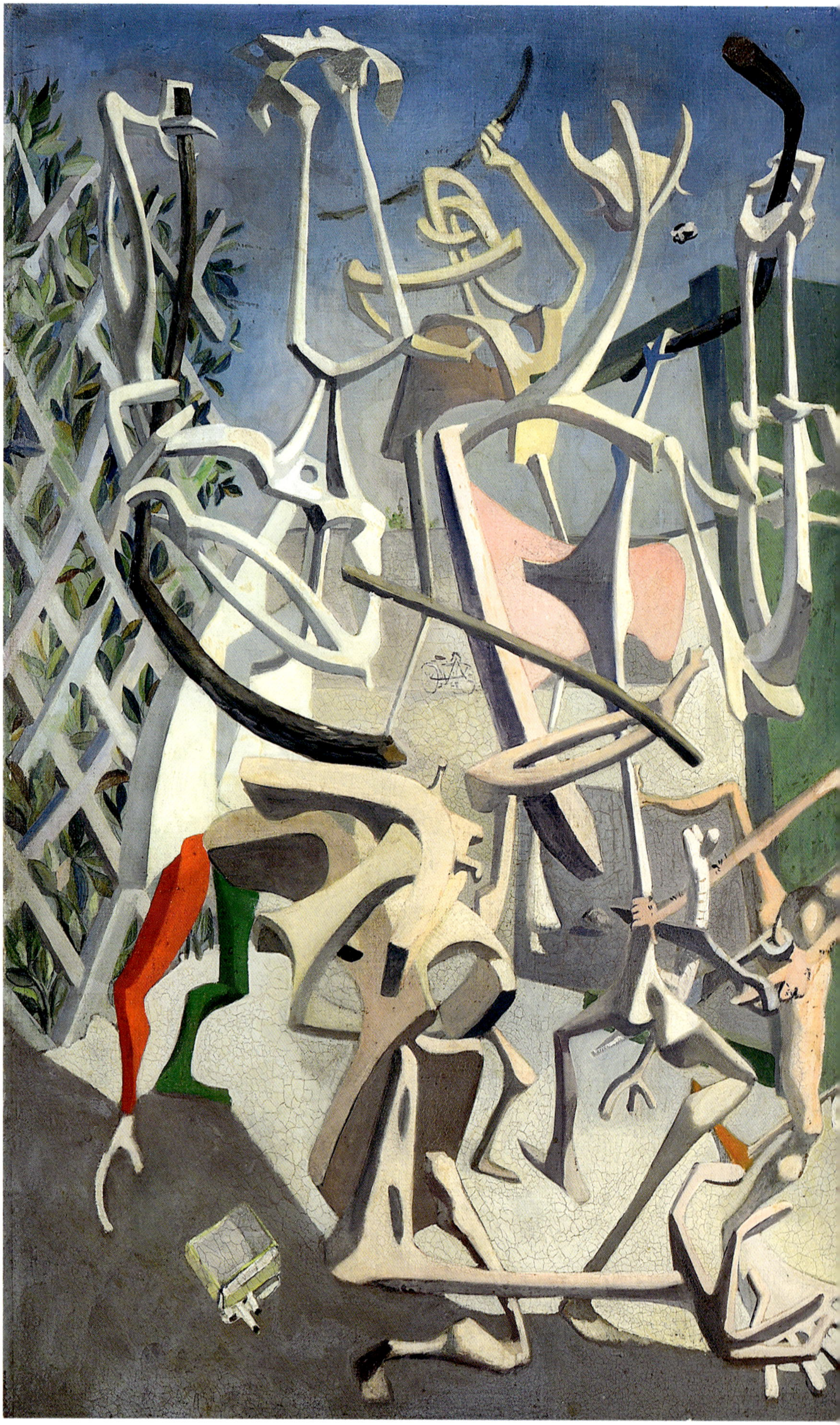

MAYO
Coups de Bâtons, 1937
Oil on canvas
167 x 243 cm
Private collection, Milan

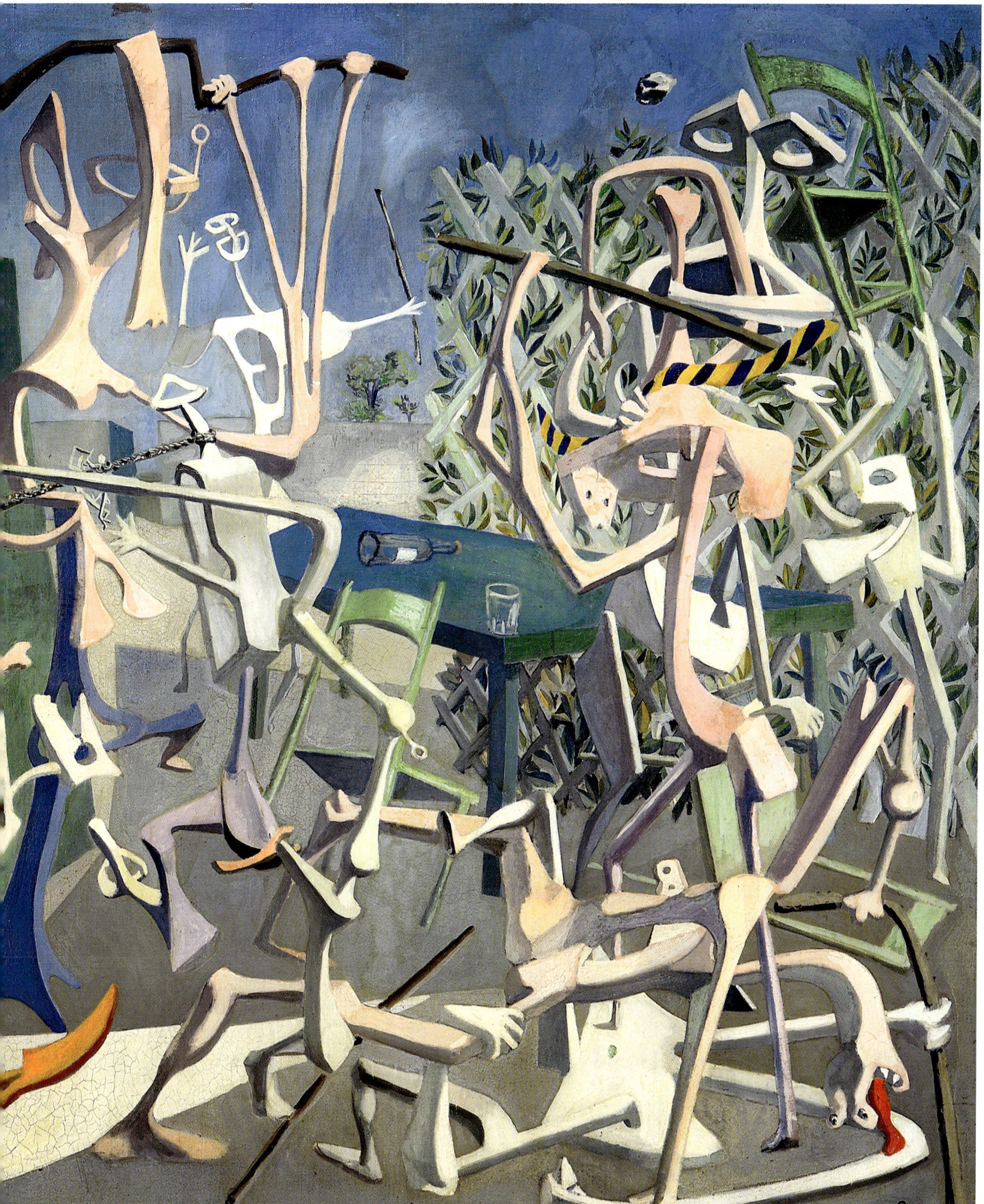
mayo
22 x 37.

MAYO
Portrait, 1937
Oil on canvas
46 x 36 cm
European Cultural Centre of Delphi, Greece

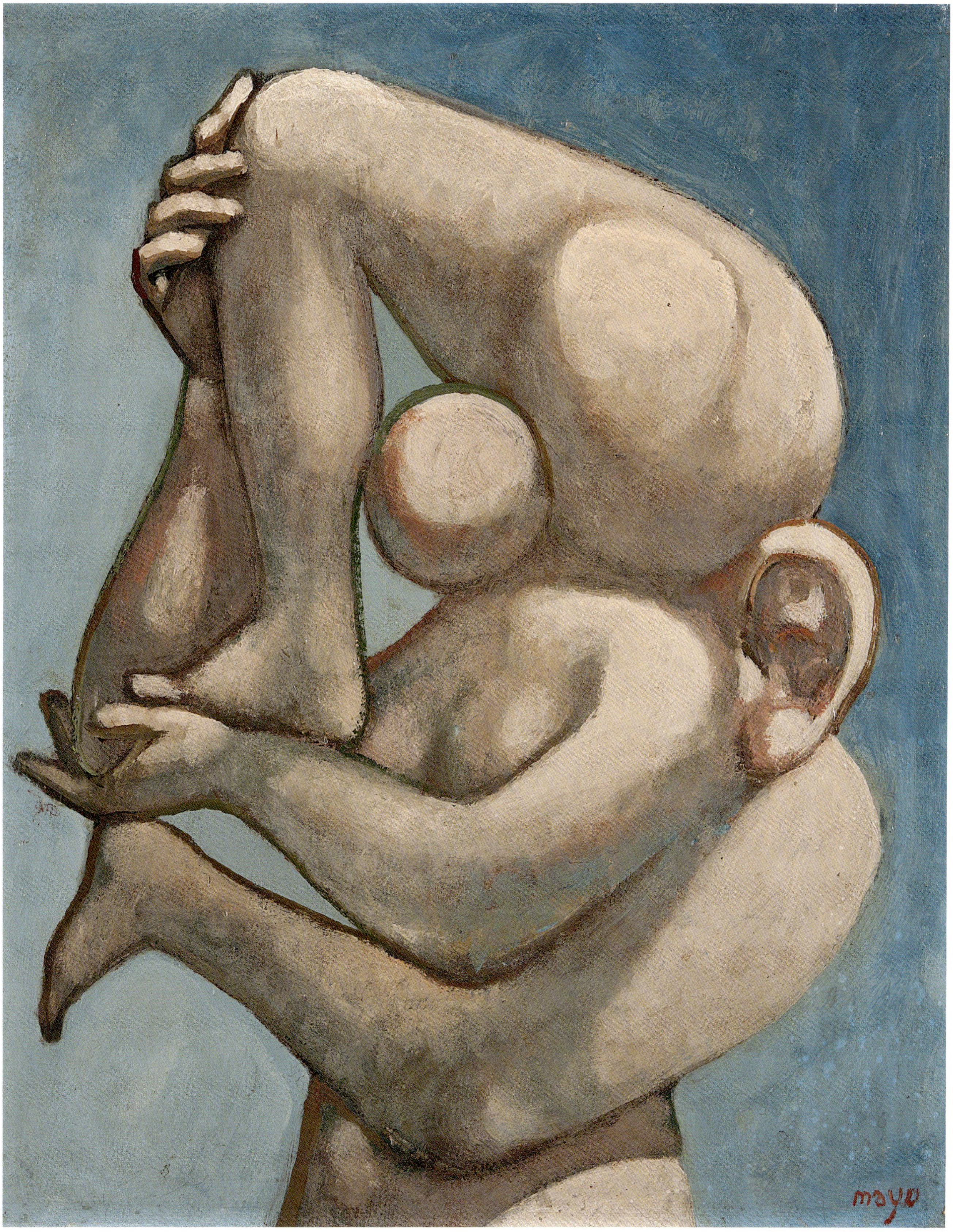
mayo

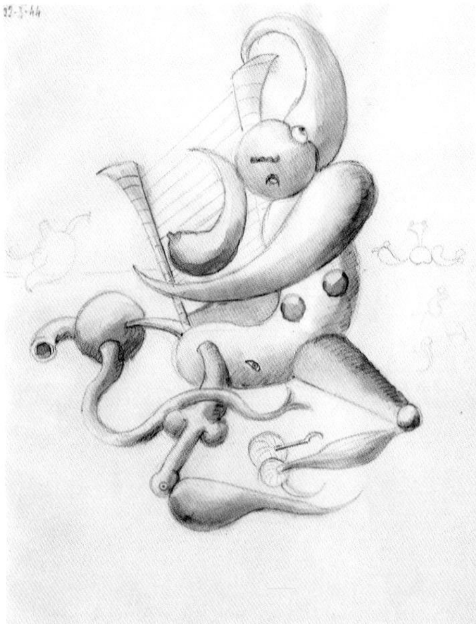

1

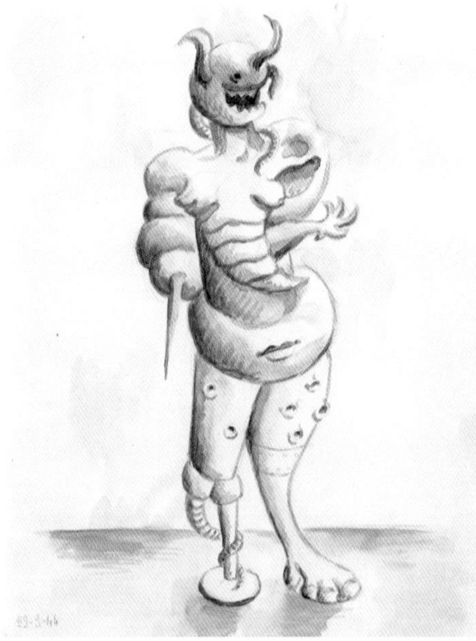

2

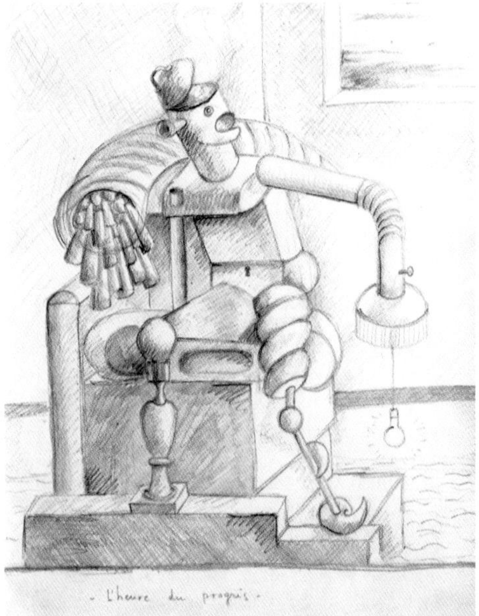

3

1
LAURENT MARCEL SALINAS
Youth, 1944
Charcoal on paper
31 x 23 cm
J. Robert LeShufy collection, New York City

2
LAURENT MARCEL SALINAS
L'Heure du progrès (fête), 1944
Charcoal on paper
31 x 23 cm
J. Robert LeShufy collection, New York City

3
LAURENT MARCEL SALINAS
L'Aviateur, 1944
Charcoal on paper
31 x 23 cm
J. Robert LeShufy collection, New York City

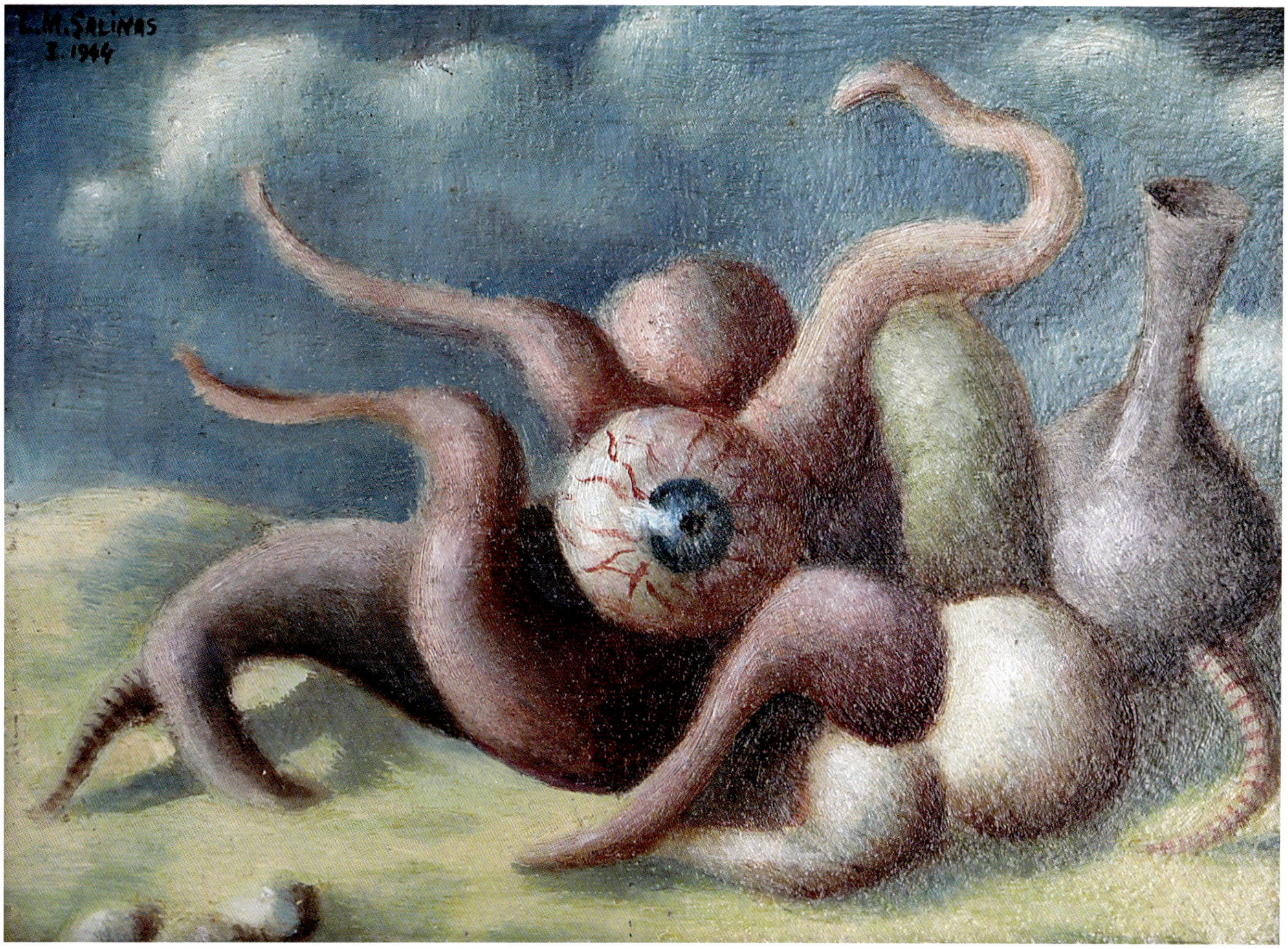

4

4
LAURENT MARCEL SALINAS
Naissance, 1944
Oil on cardboard
16.5 x 22 cm
Estate of Laurent Marcel Salinas

HASSAN EL-TELMISANI
Untitled, 1947
Oil on canvas
50 x 37 x 2 cm
H.E. Sh. Hassan M. A. Al Thani collection, Doha

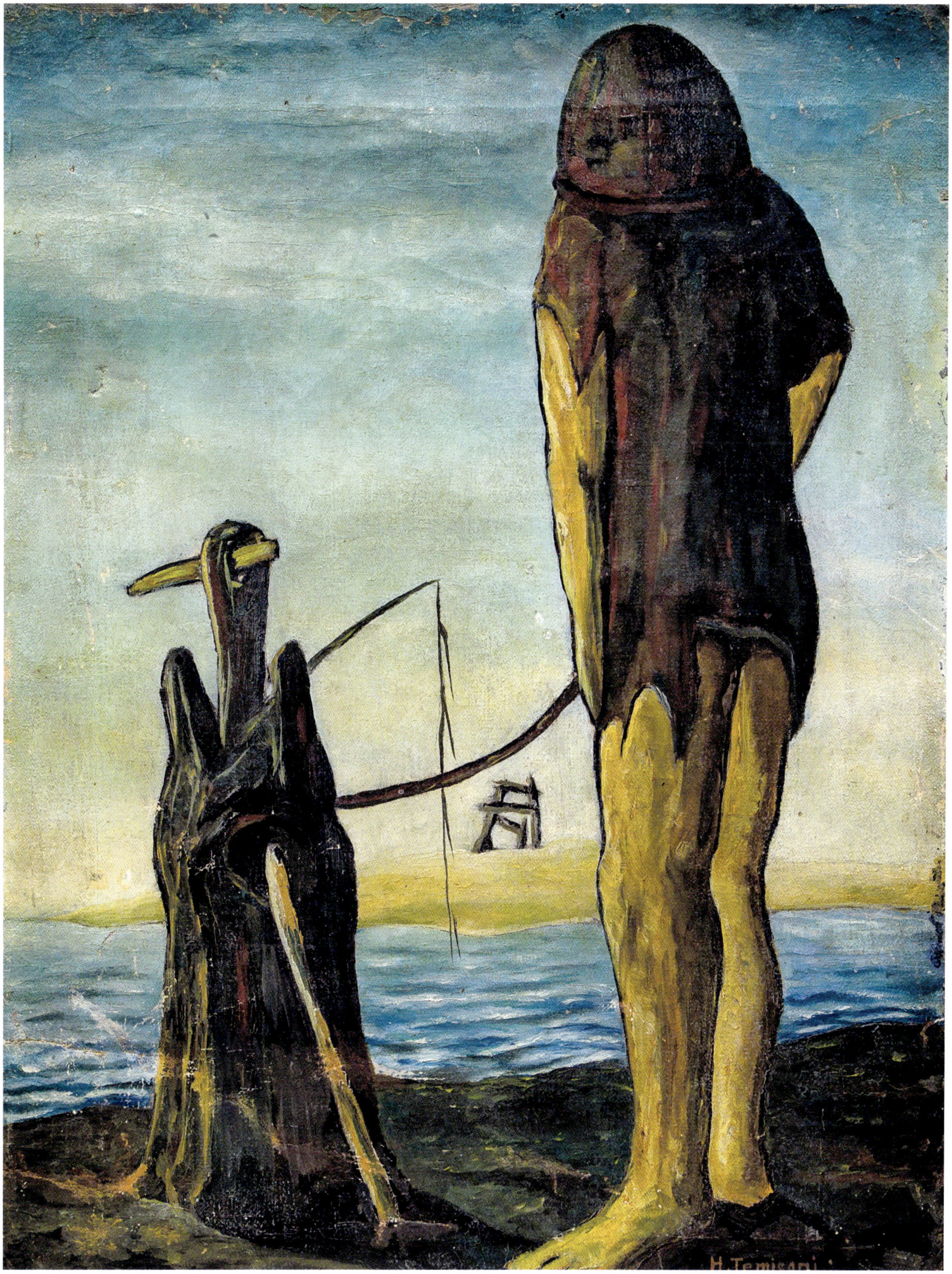

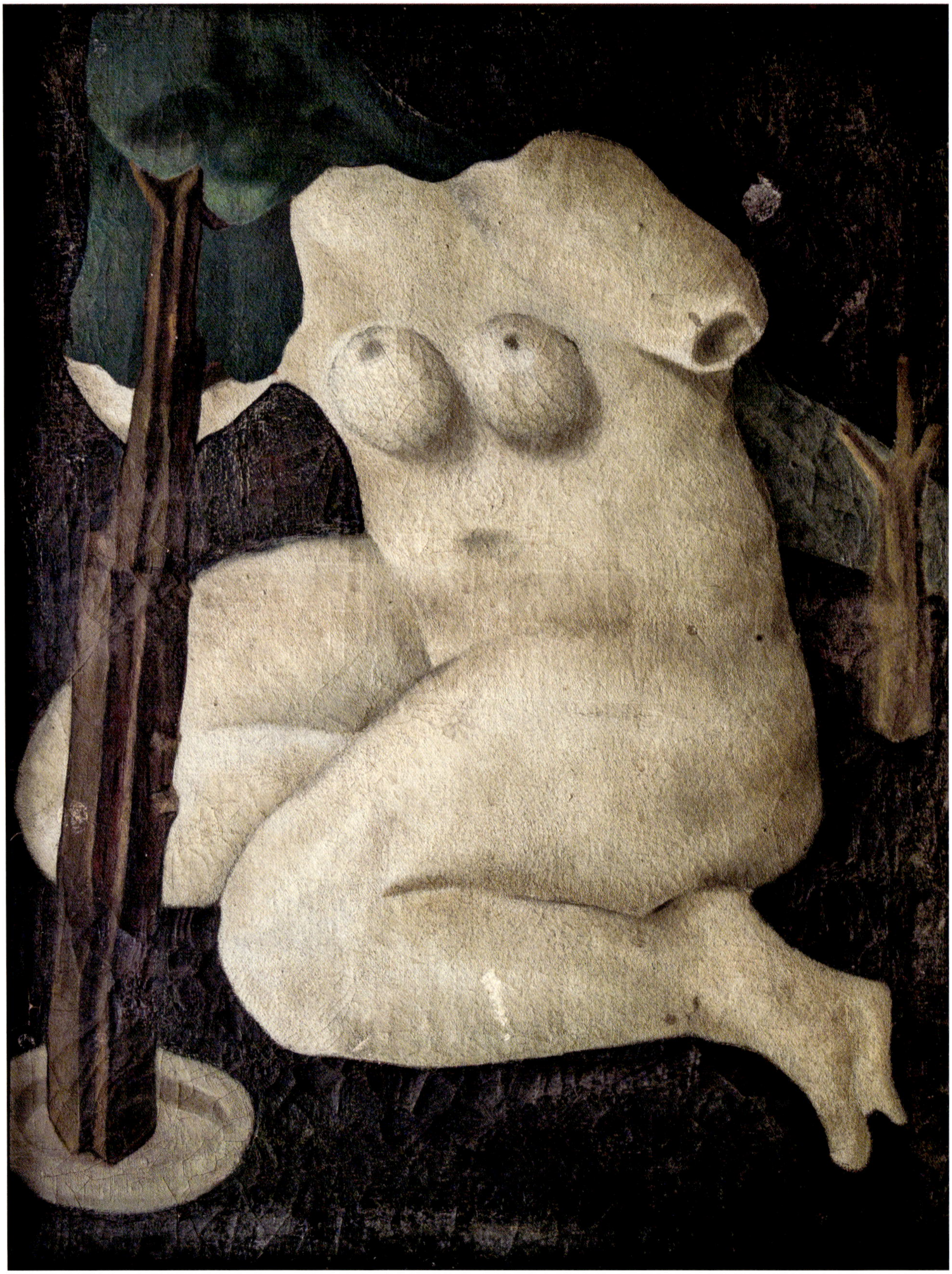

1

1, 2
HASSAN EL-TELMISANI
Untitled, c. 1940
Oil on canvas, double sided
50 x 39 cm
El-Telmissany family, Cairo

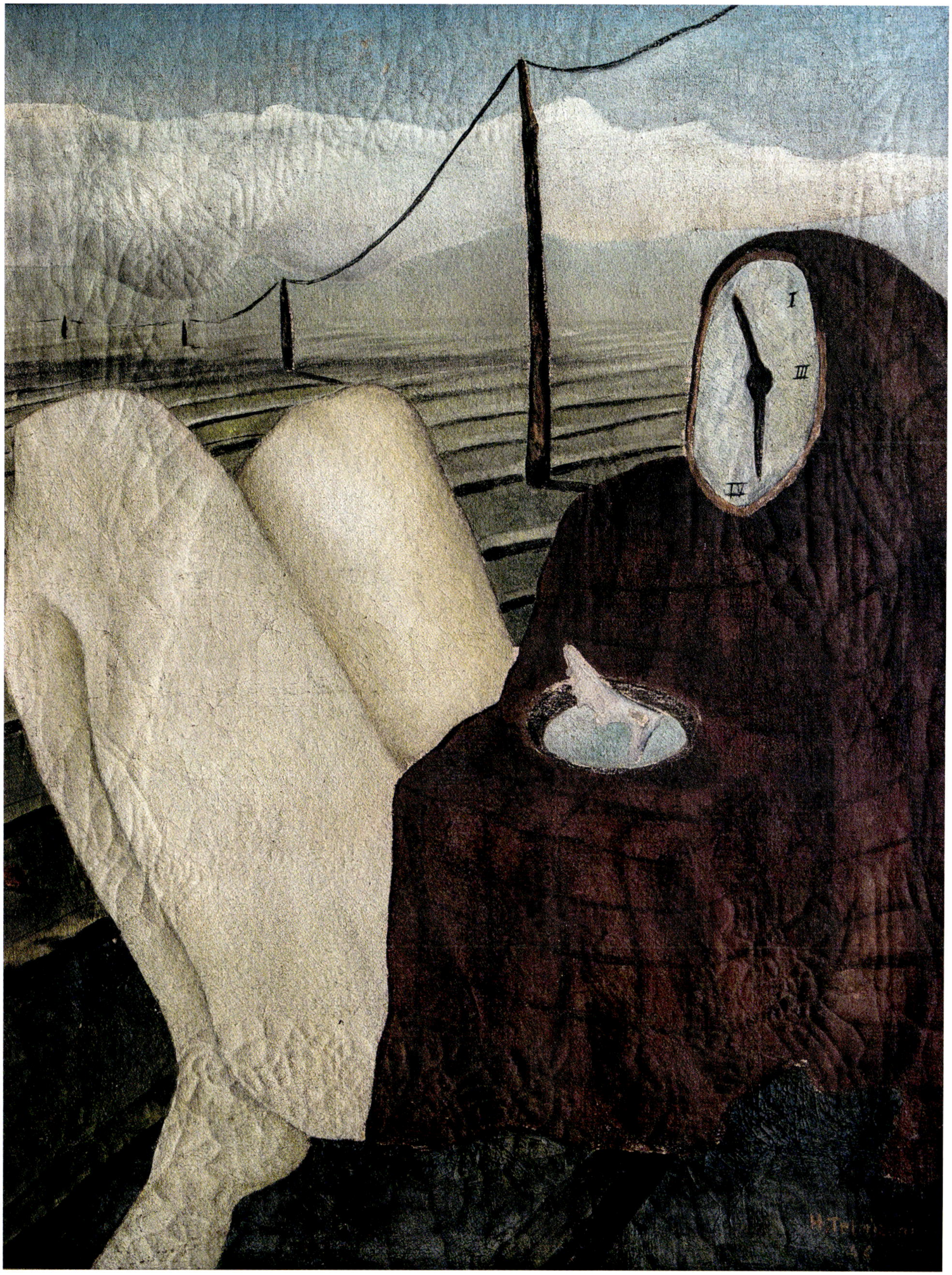

2

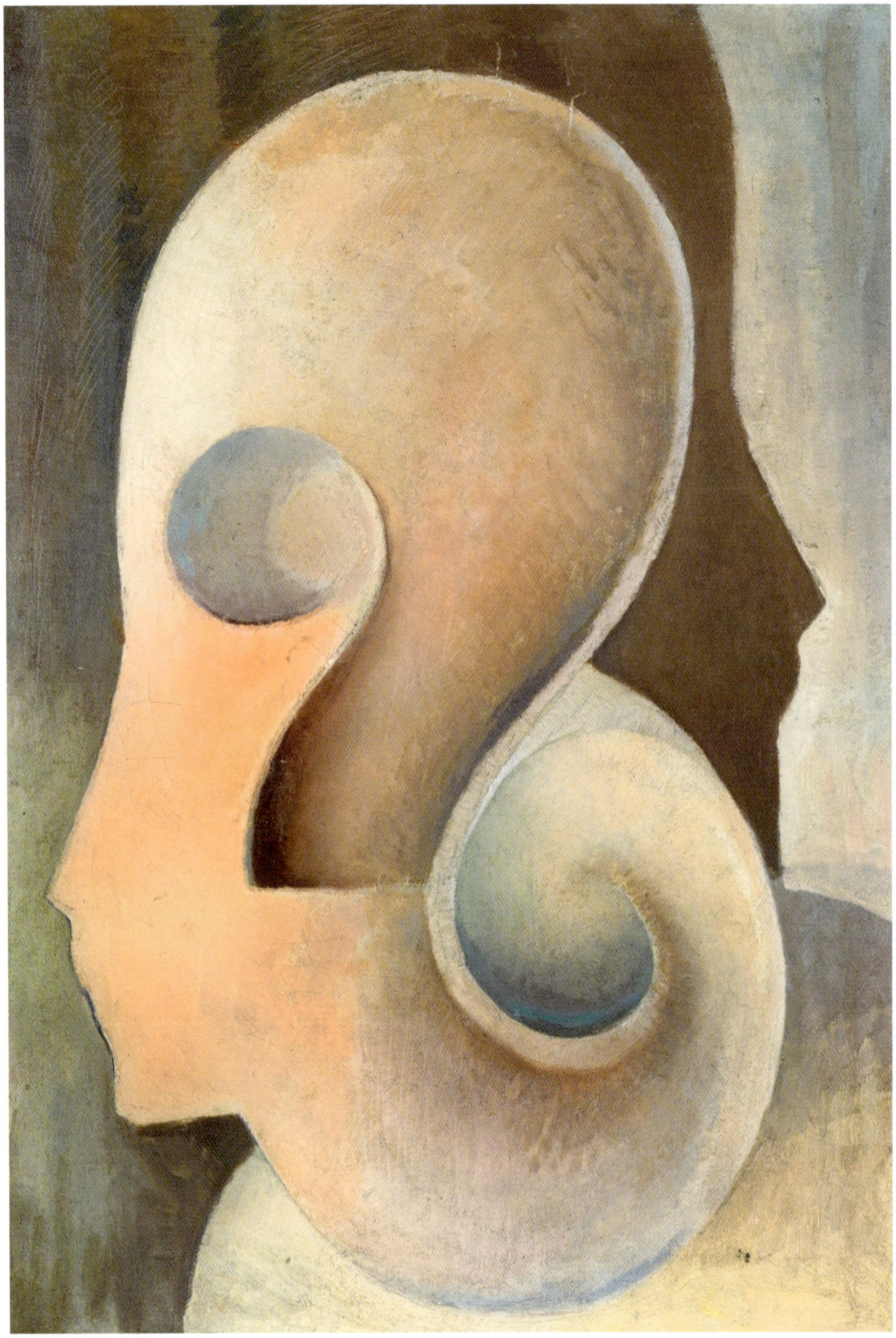

RAMSES YOUNANE
Portrait, 1933-1938
Oil on canvas
50 x 35 cm
Barjeel Art Foundation, Sharjah

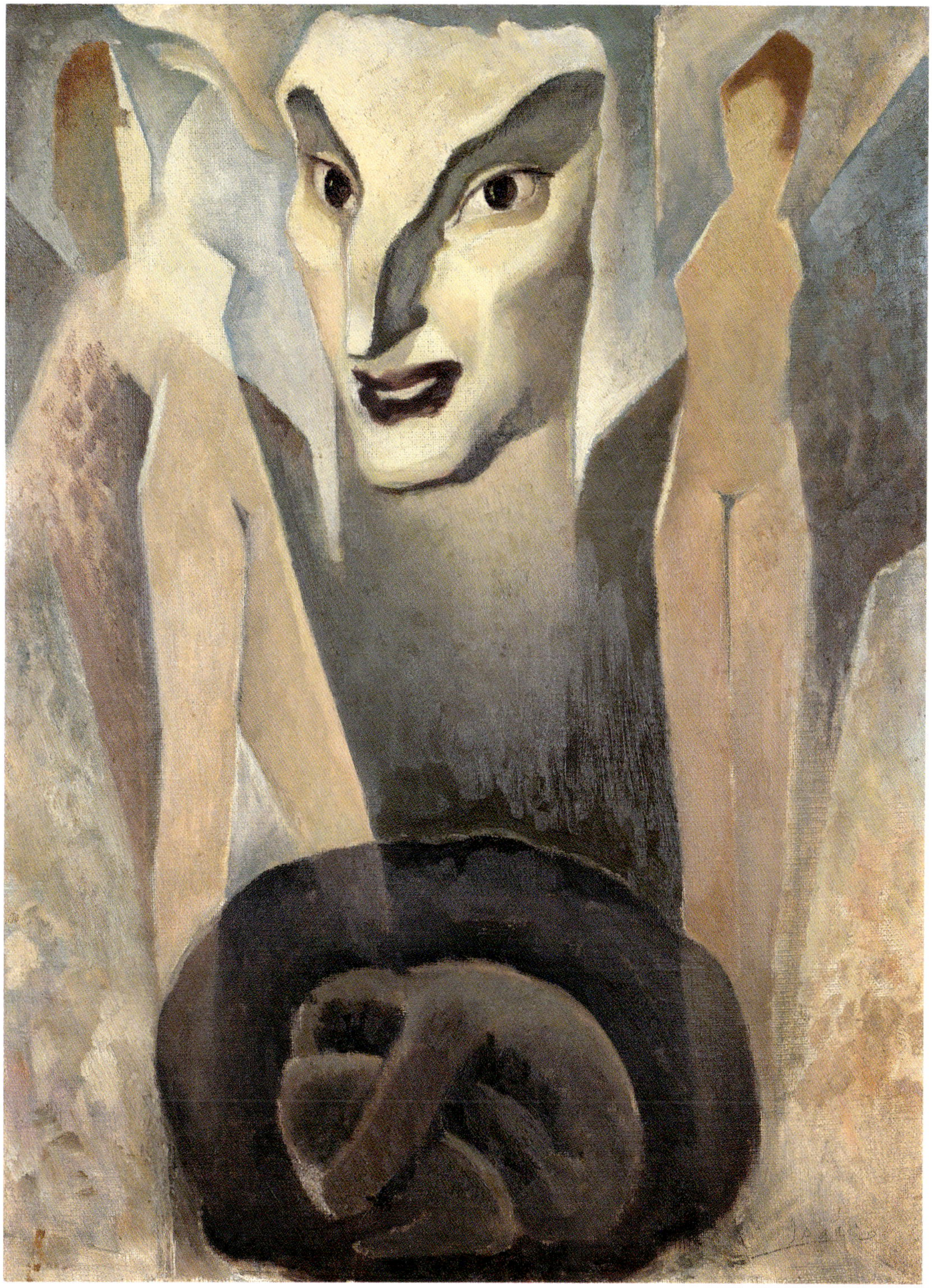

RAMSES YOUNANE
Untitled, c. 1935
Oil on canvas
49 x 37 cm
Private collection, Paris

KAMEL EL-TELMISANY
Nude with Arm, c. 1940
Oil on cardboard
55 x 39 cm
H.E. Sh. Hassan M. A. Al Thani collection, Doha

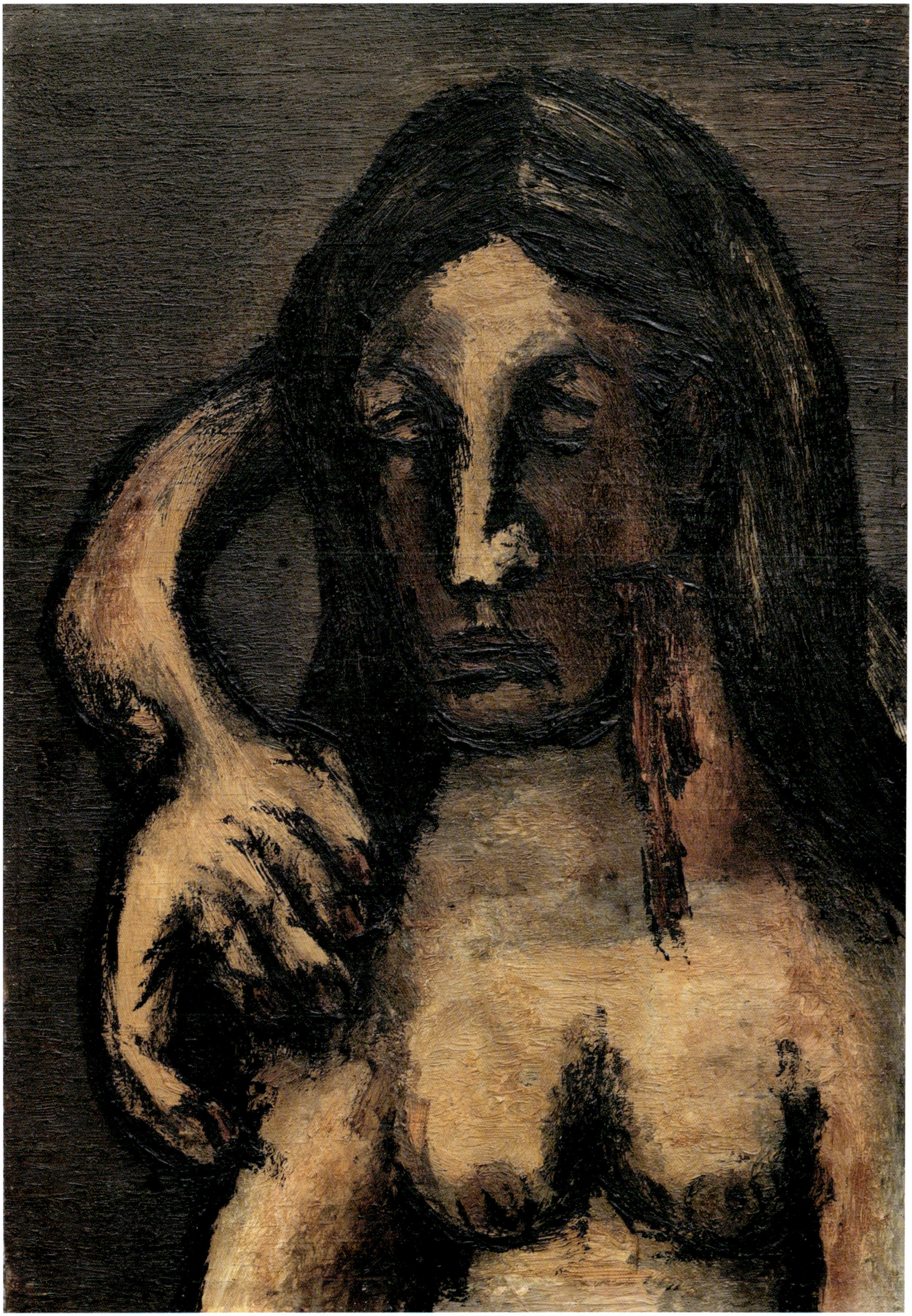

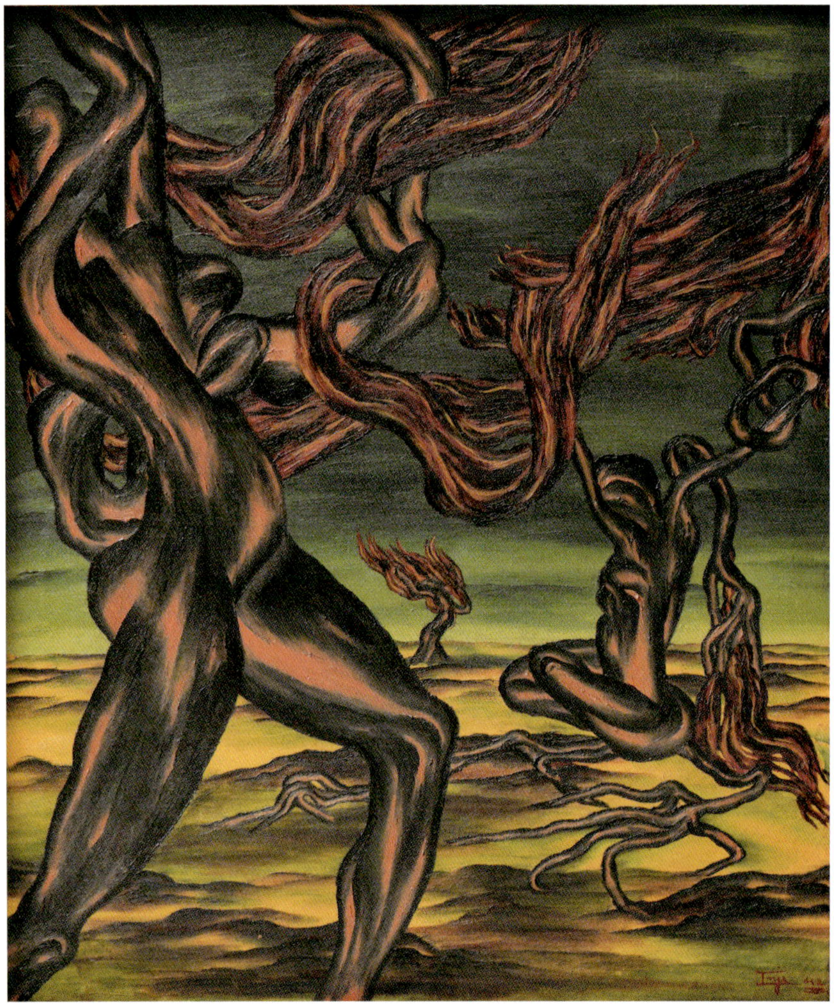

INJI EFFLATOUN
Composition surréaliste, 1942
Oil on canvas
71 x 60.5 cm
Private collection

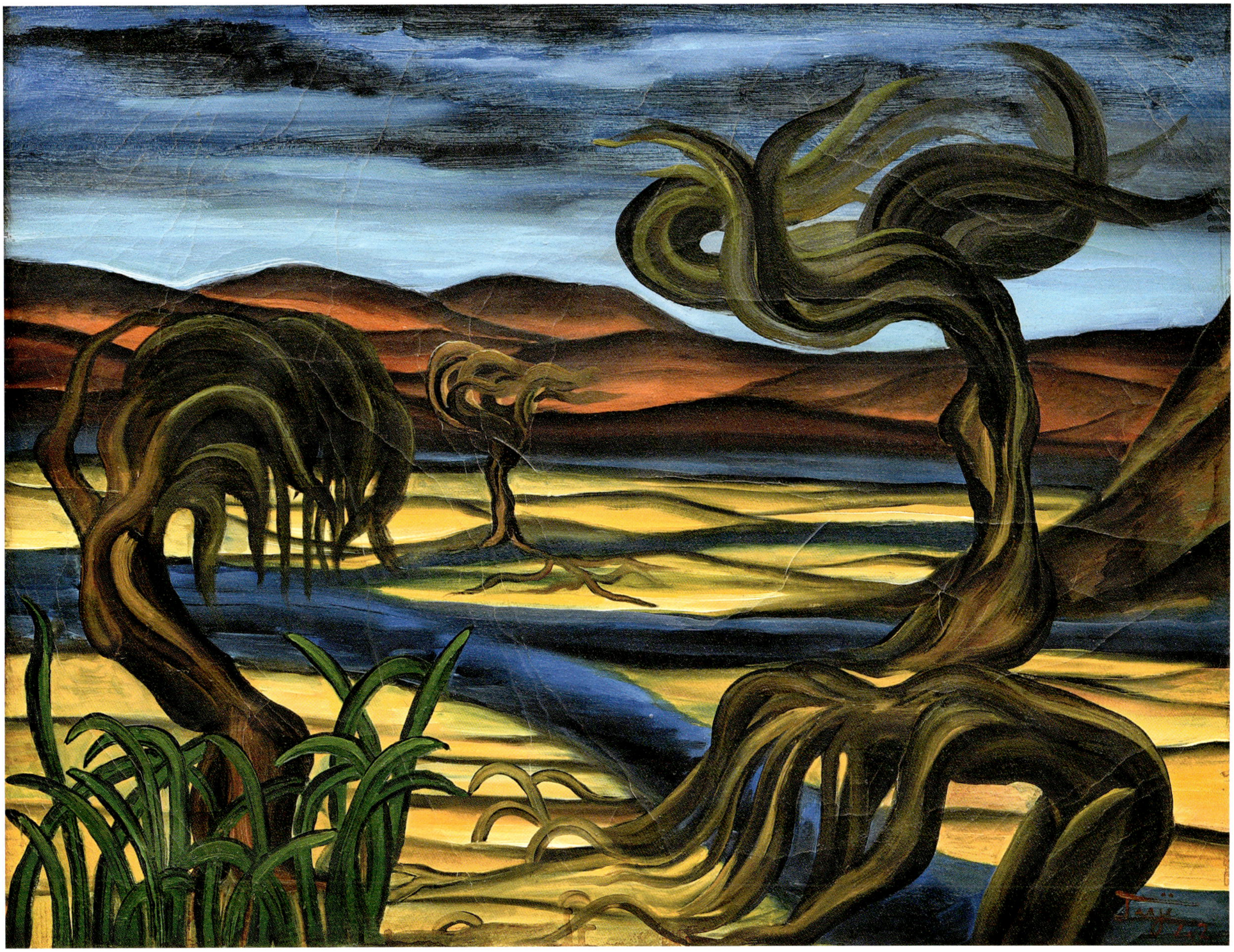

INJI EFFLATOUN
Untitled, 1942
Oil on canvas
60 x 80.2 cm
H.E. Sh. Hassan M. A. Al Thani collection, Doha

"THE WOMAN OF THE CITY"

Georges Henein, *Déraisons d'être*, 1938

In works of prose and poetry, through painting, photography, and installation, *Art and Liberty* managed to capture the concerns of a restless, often sarcastic generation, one that was consumed by the overwhelming proximity of anguish and death. Besides the war, the distortion of the human form reflects *Art and Liberty*'s treatment of the problem of prostitution. Throughout the war years, poverty in Egypt was at such a high that even "wives and sisters," as Kamel El-Telmisany wrote in a letter to Georges Henein in 1937, were being forced into the brothels. With war came hundreds of thousands of troops pouring in from every corner of the world. Prostitution was rampant. The image of the prostitute, or the woman of the city as Georges Henein wrote in his poem *Saint Louis Blues* of 1938, expressed through the motif of the deformed female figure, was one of the most recurring themes in the art and literature of several *Art and Liberty* members. Younane's paintings from that period are often inhabited by the mutilated figures of women, often portrayed as solitary figures within Surrealist landscapes, at times full of mirrors, at others of carcasses and skeletons. Kamel El-Telmisany's prostitutes are pierced with nails, their breasts and navels transformed to constitute the features of a face residing within their contorted bodies, and the girls in Inji Efflatoun's paintings are ravaged by monster-like forests of anthropomorphic trees. Alongside their pictorial output, *Art and Liberty* responded to the severity of the situation by tackling the problem of war prostitution in several reform-driven articles that appeared in *Al-Tatawwur* (Evolution), their short-lived journal that appeared in six issues from January 1940 until September of that year when it was closed by the censor's office. Ramses Younane's article *Al-bagha' mushkilah laha juthour* (Prostitution Is a Problem with Roots) from the periodical's February issue is one of several examples.

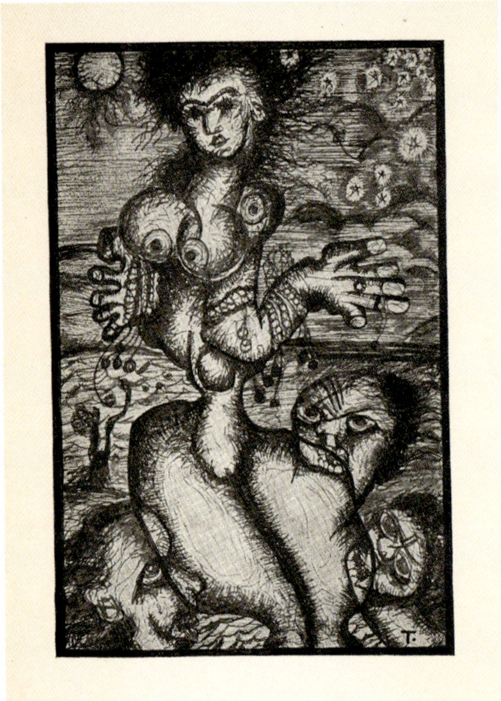

1

"The peasants stop to take a look and one of them whispers:
I would really like to cross this thing for on the other side there surely exists a woman of the city that I would love.

...

The voice of the woman of the city now sounds across the horizon covering the entire plane.

She says that she has an overwhelming urge to see her river again.

She would like to tell him about some fabulous secrets known neither to the priest nor to the pharmacist.

She wants to explain to him the story of these bracelets that burn her arms.

And the ardent insomnia that drains her eyes
and that would only go away with the temptation of killing certain lovers who can understand nothing other than her body".

Georges Henein, "St. Louis Blues," *Déraisons d'être*, 1938

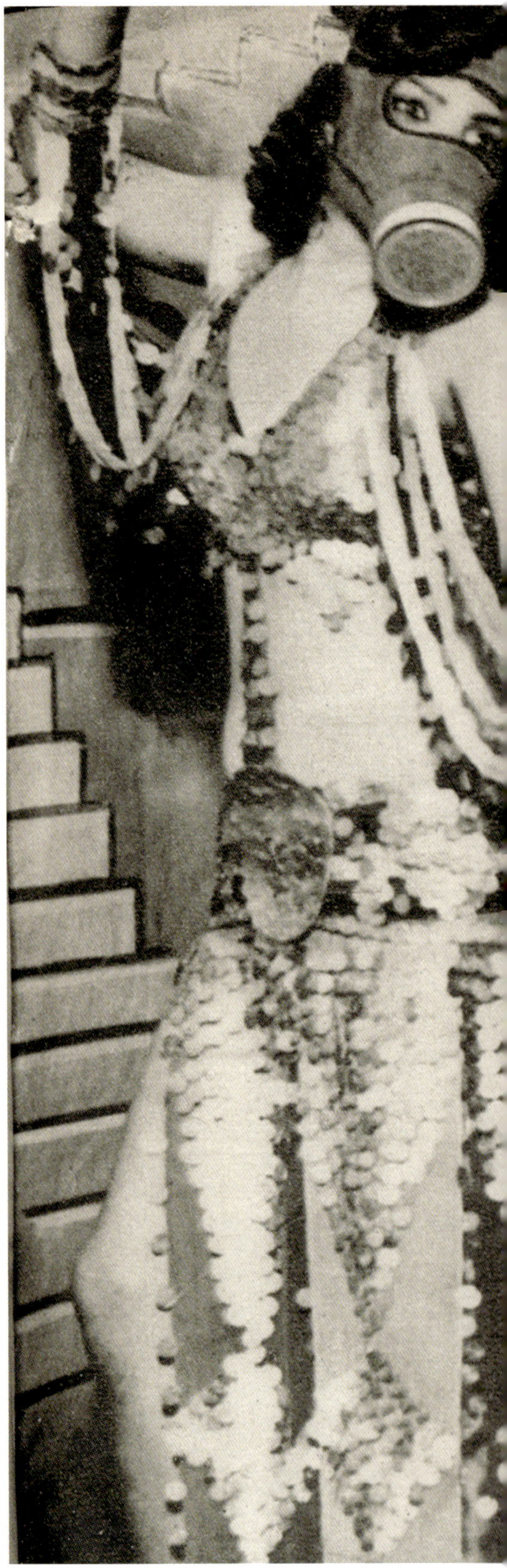

2

1
KAMEL EL-TELMISANY
Illustration of the poem "St. Louis Blues" in Georges Henein's *Déraisons d'être*, 1938
Paperback
Papier imprimé
Bibliothèque Sainte-Geneviève, Paris

2
Belly dancers wearing gas masks as part of a wartime cabaret act
Photographer unknown,
Al-Lata'if Al-Musawwara,
November 18, 1939, p. 24
Al-Lata'if Al-Musawwara Archives, Cairo

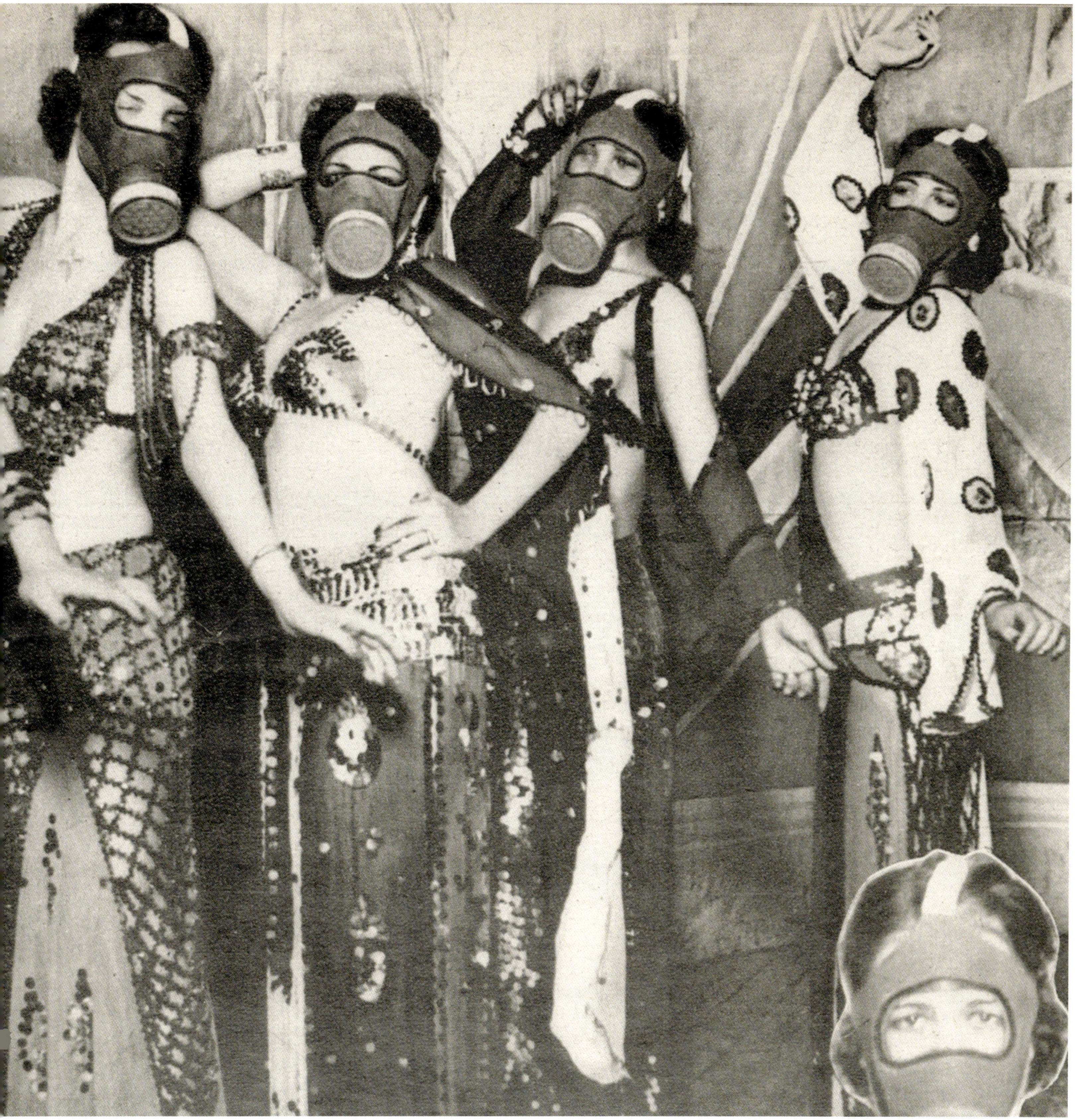

THE WOMAN OF THE CITY

MAHMOUD SAÏD
La Femme aux boucles d'or, 1933
Oil on canvas
81.3 x 60 cm
Private collection

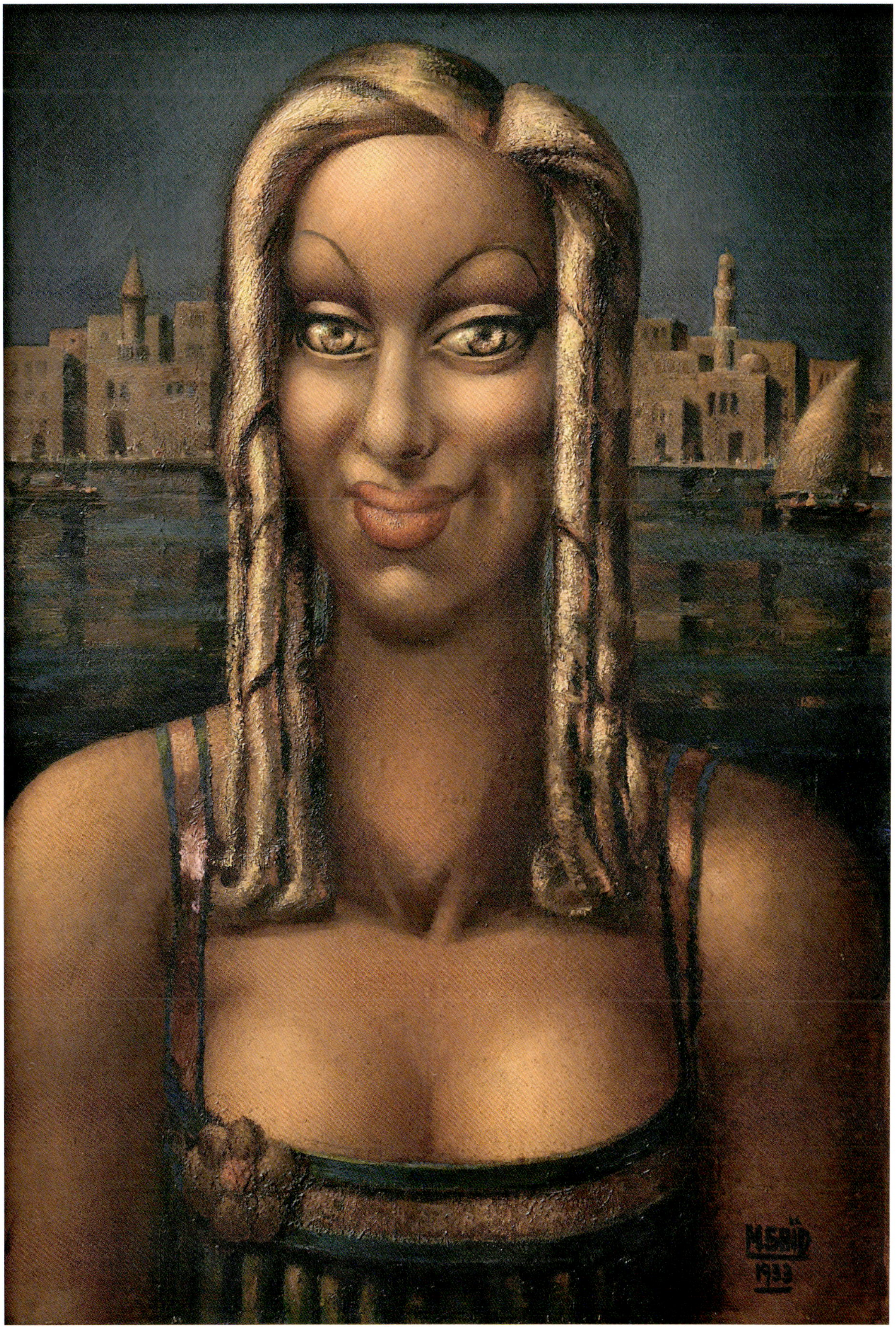
M.SAID
1933

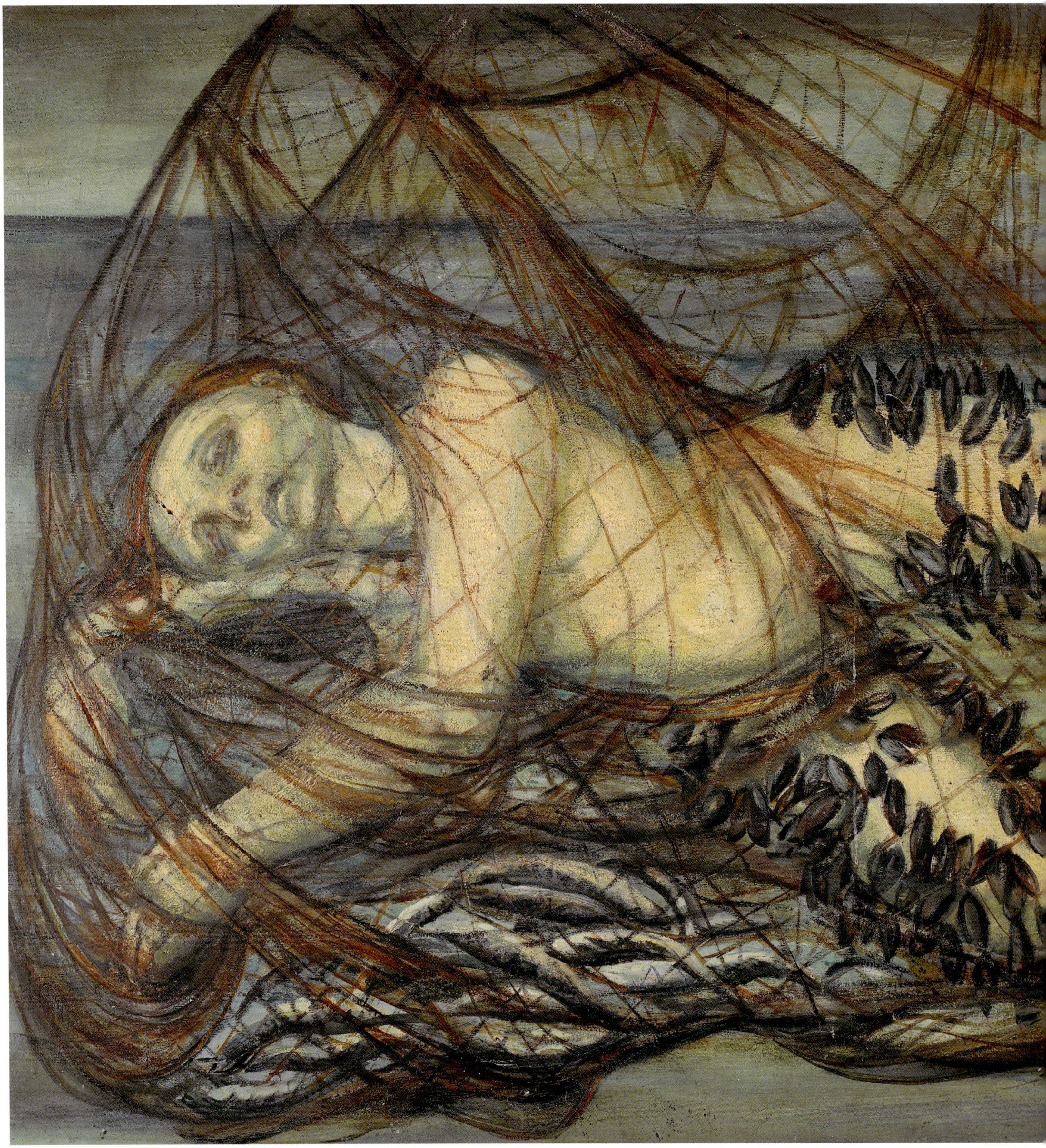

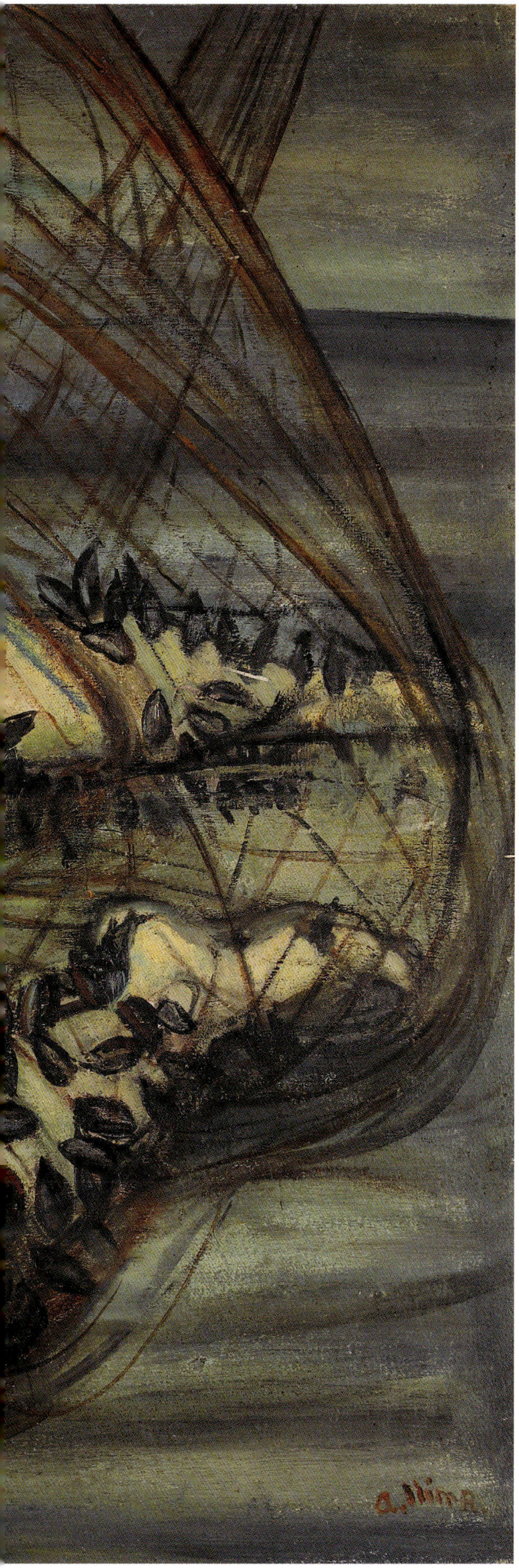

1

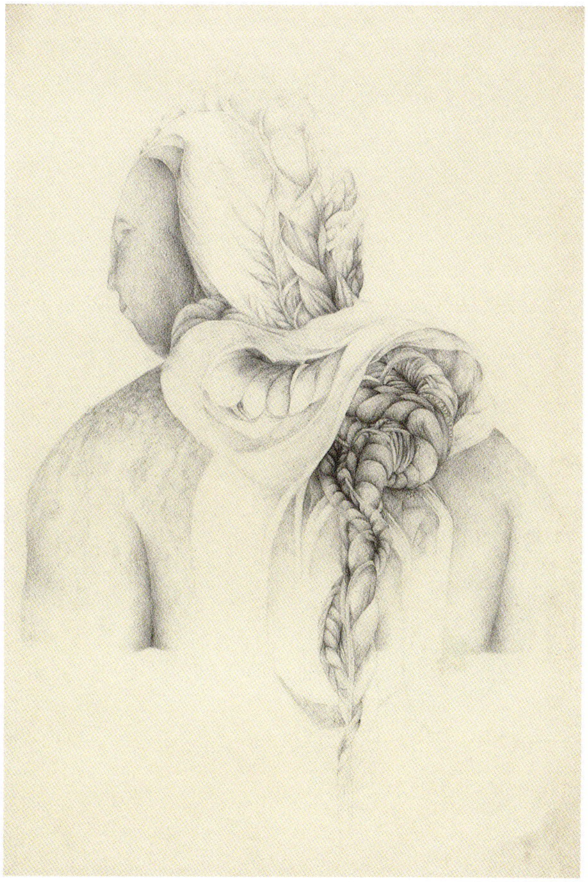

2

1
AMY NIMR
Untitled (Girl with fishnet), c. 1928
Oil on canvas
100 x 140 cm
Private collection

2
RATEB SEDDIK
Head from Behind, c. 1937
Pencil on paper
73 x 55.5 cm
Rateb Seddik Museum, Cairo

RATEB SEDDIK
Liliane Brook et son orchestre aveugle, c. 1940
Oil on wood
120 x 79.5 cm
Rateb Seddik Museum, Cairo

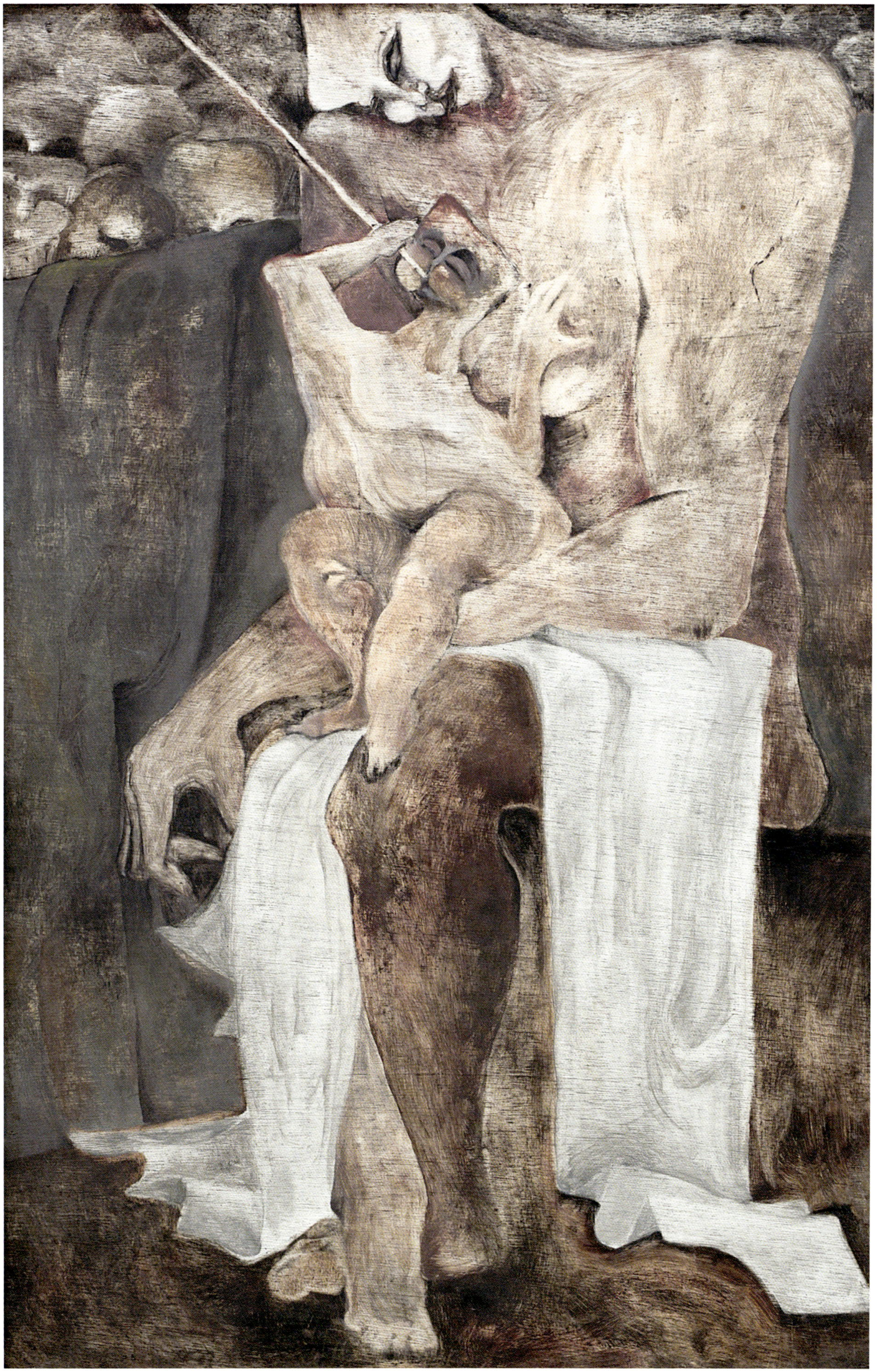

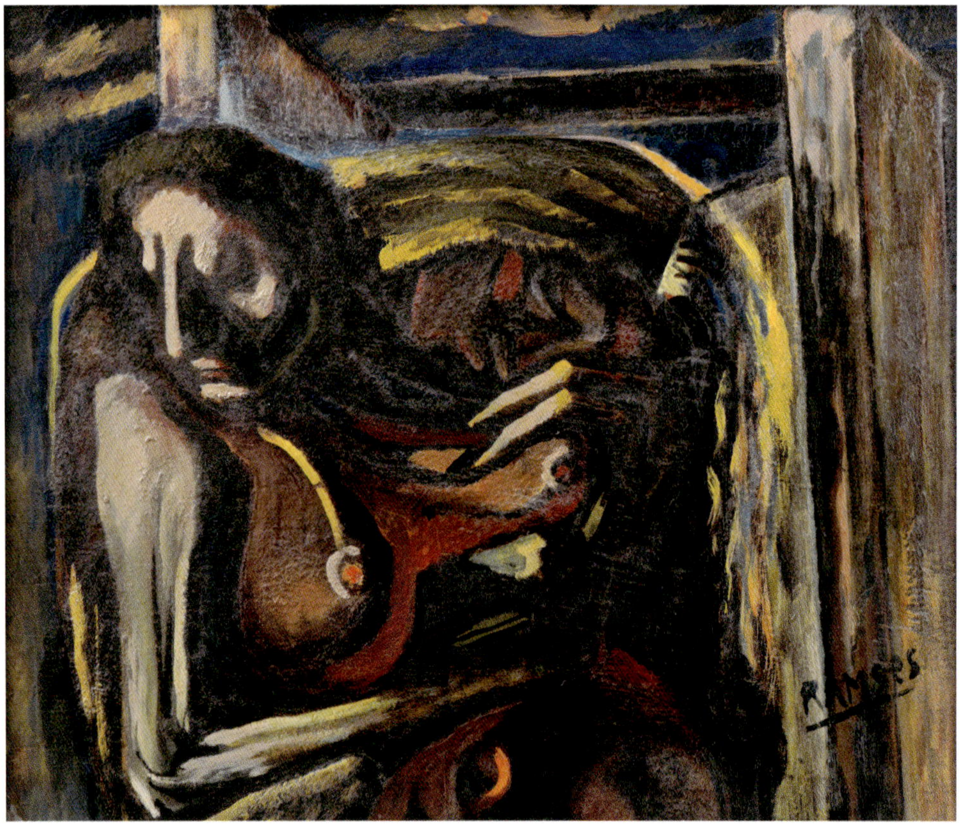

1

1
RAMSES YOUNANE
Untitled, c. 1940
Oil on board
42 x 50 cm
Private collection

2
RAMSES YOUNANE
Untitled, 1943
Oil on canvas
60 x 85 cm
Institut du Monde Arabe, Paris

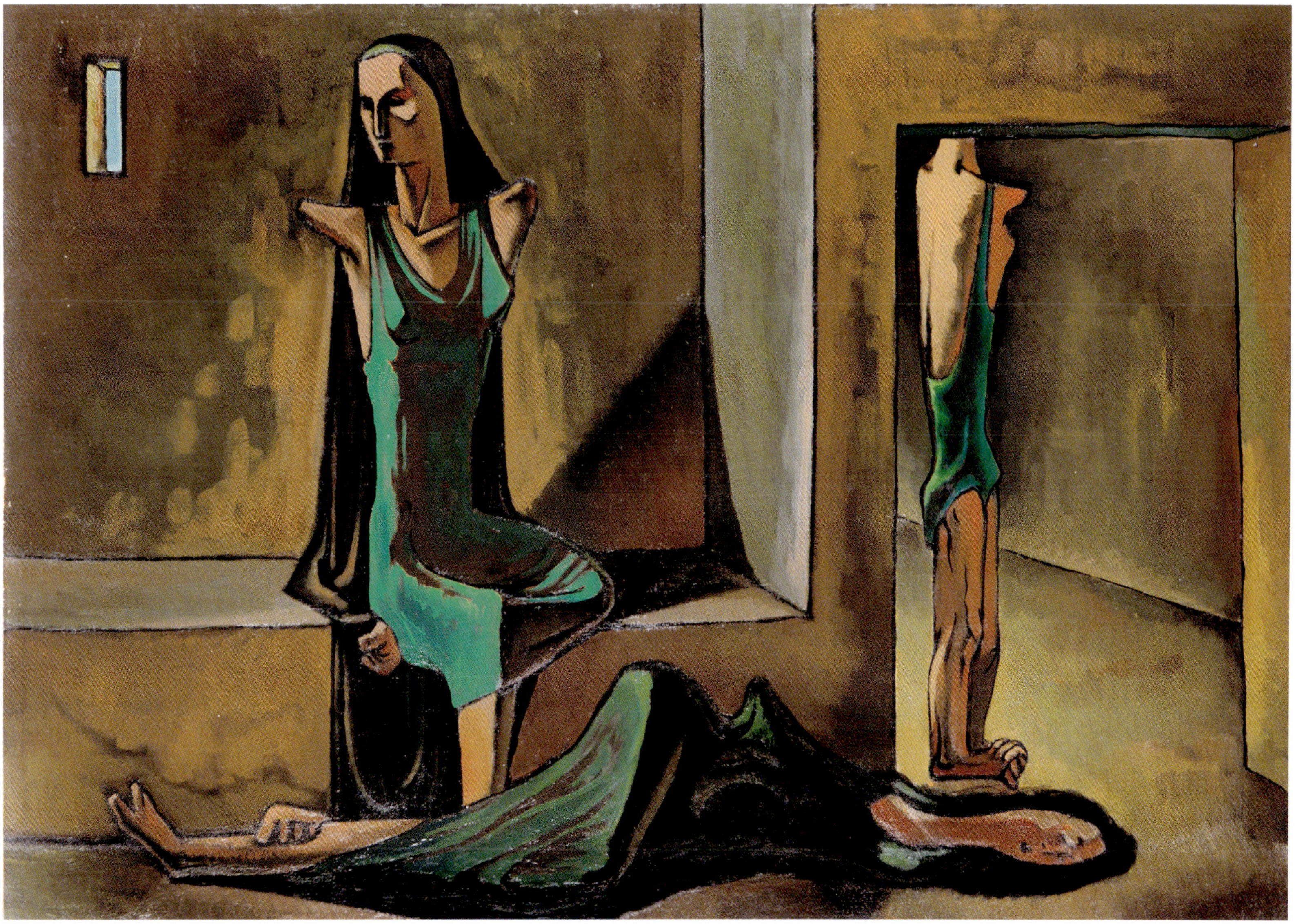

2

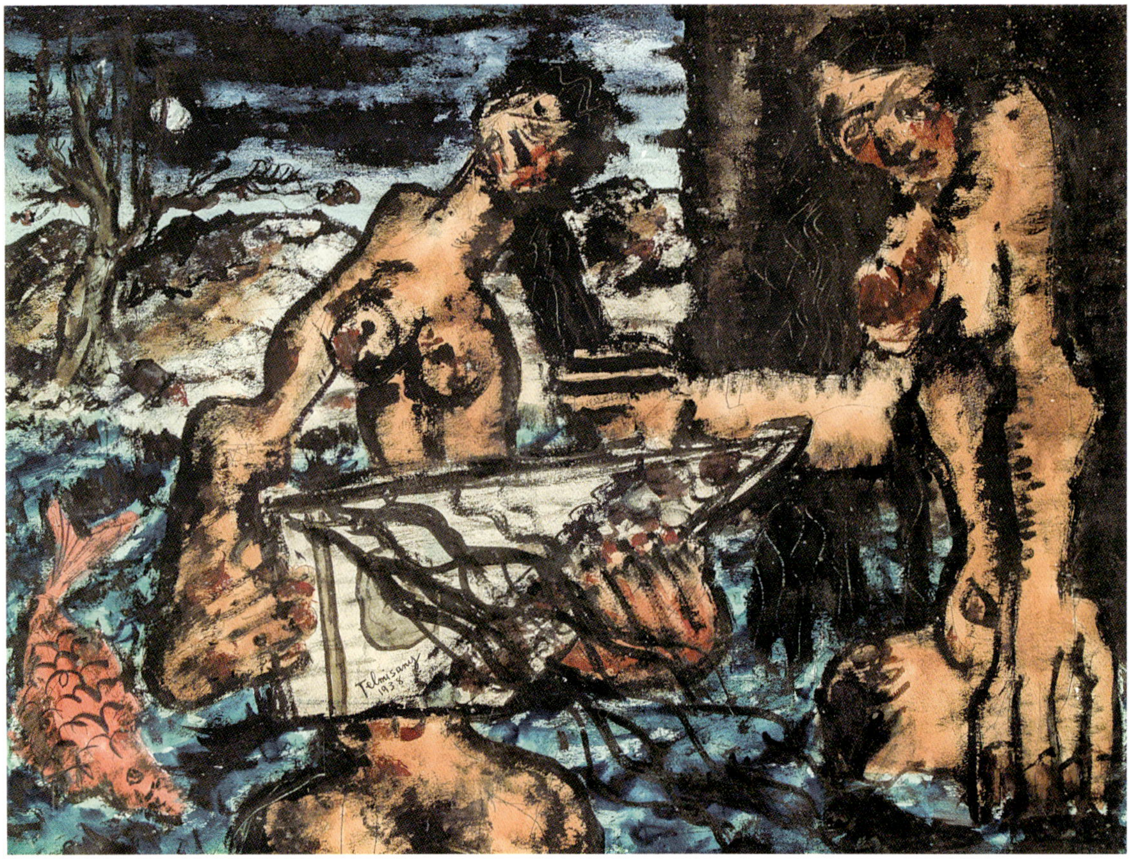

1

1
KAMEL EL-TELMISANY
Untitled, 1938
Gouache, charcoal and wax on paper
39 x 52 cm
Yasser Hashem collection, Cairo

2
KAMEL EL-TELMISANY
Untitled (Wounds), 1940
Gouache, charcoal and wax on paper
75 x 50 cm
El-Telmissany family, Cairo

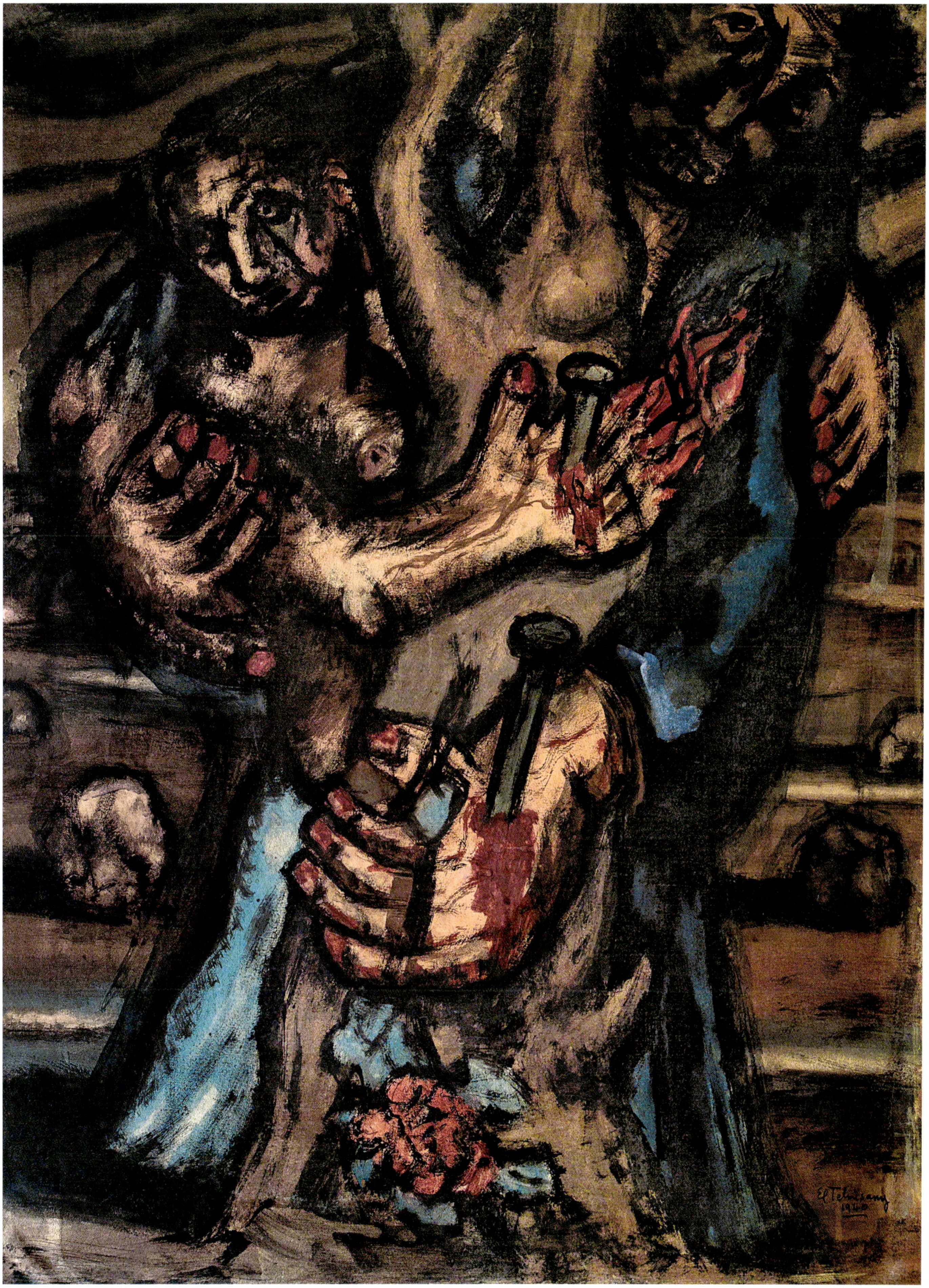

2

KAMEL EL-TELMISANY
Nude, 1941
Oil on canvas
47 x 67 cm
Fatenn Mostafa Kanafani collection, Cairo

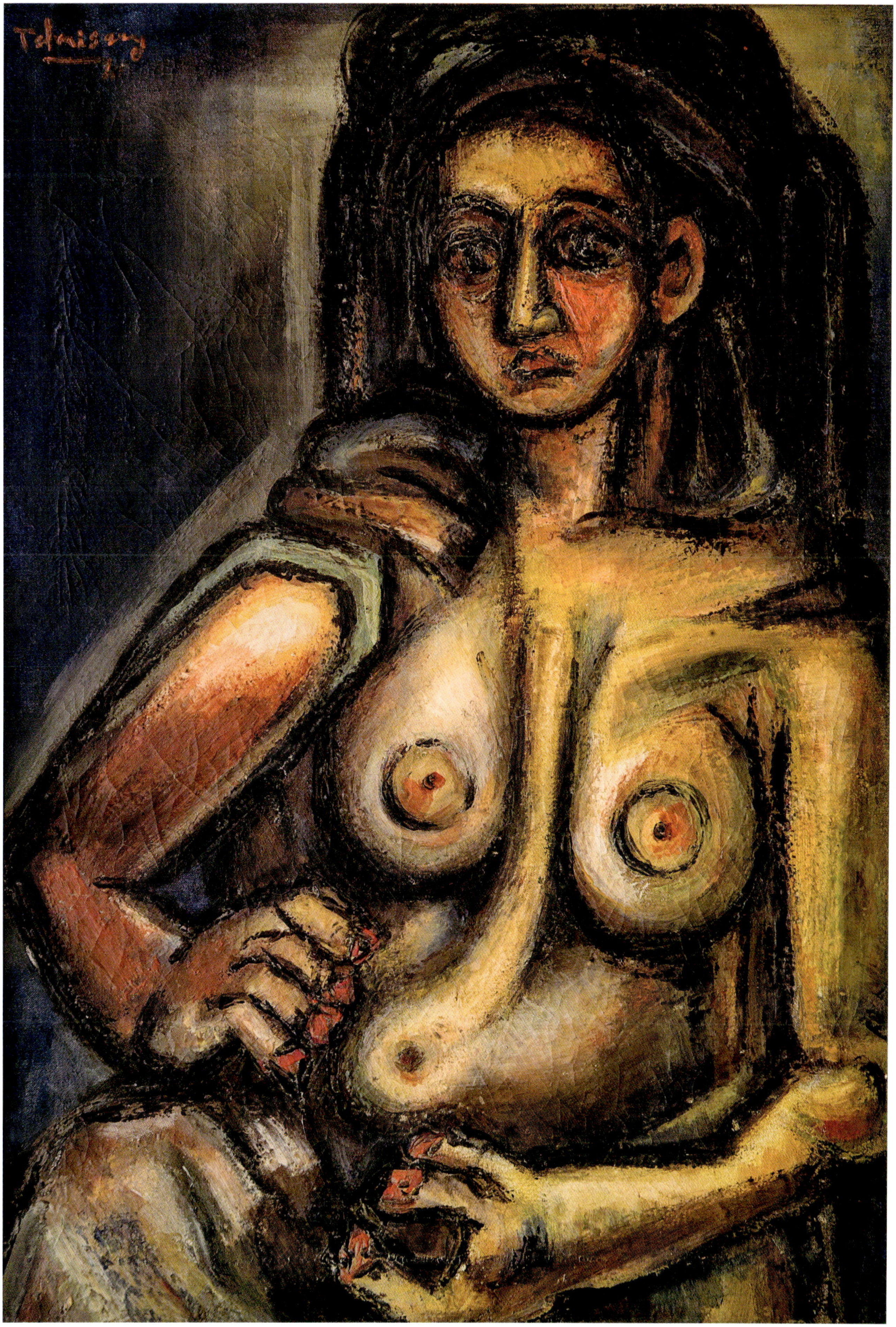

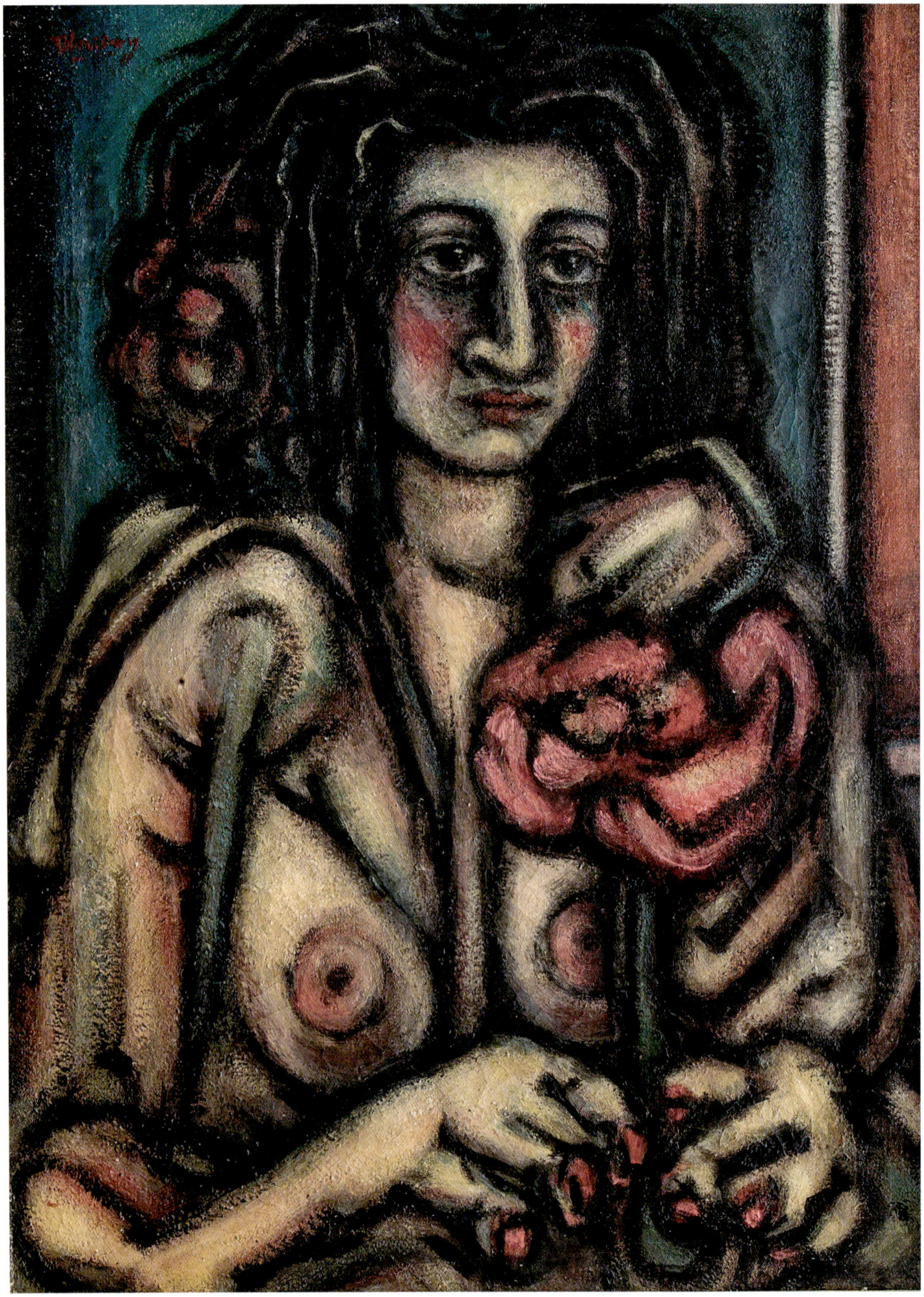

KAMEL EL-TELMISANY
Nude with a Rose, c. 1940
Oil on canvas
55.5 x 41 cm
Yasser Hashem collection, Cairo

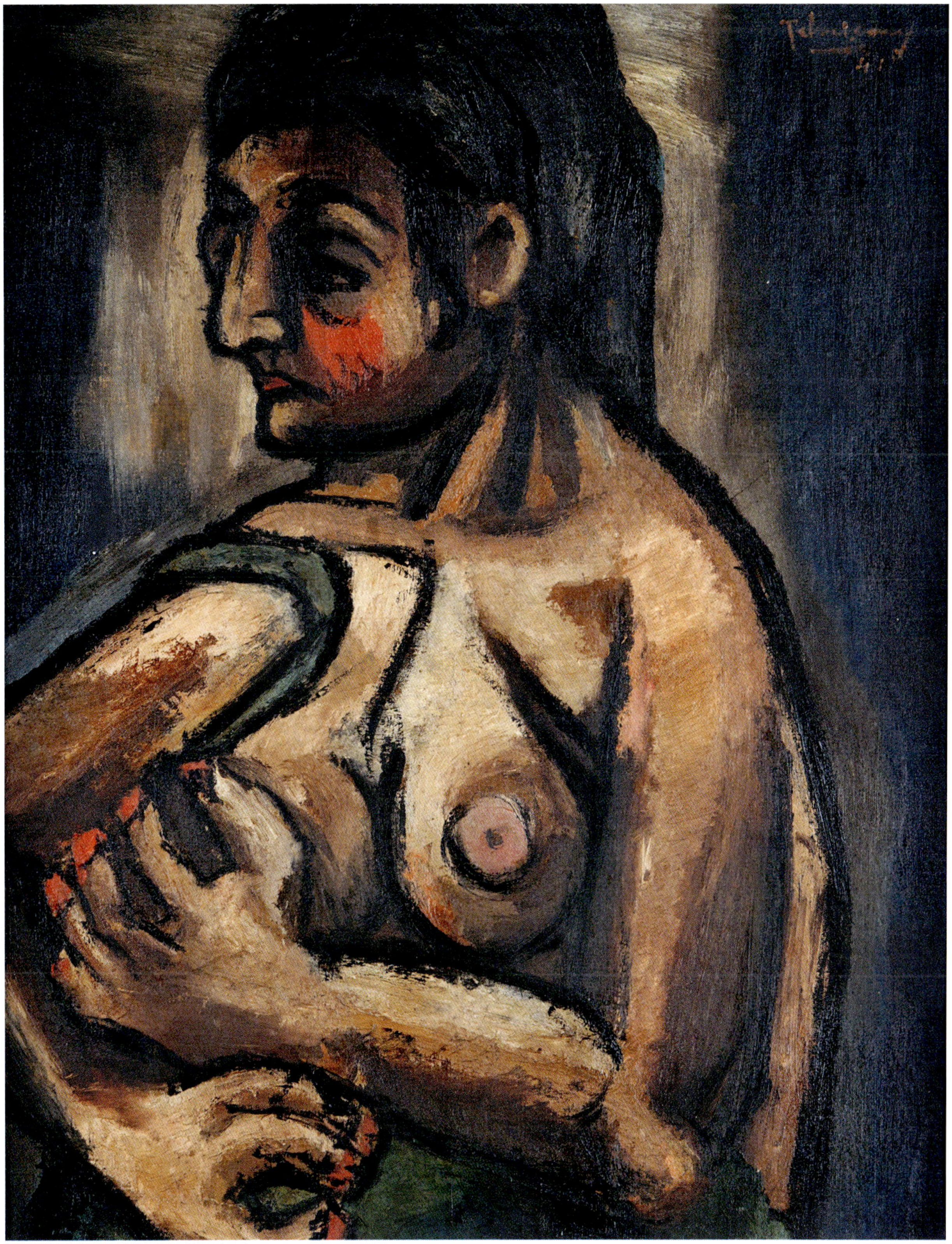

KAMEL EL-TELMISANY
Nude, 1941
Oil on canvas
64 x 49 cm
Barjeel Art Foundation, Sharjah

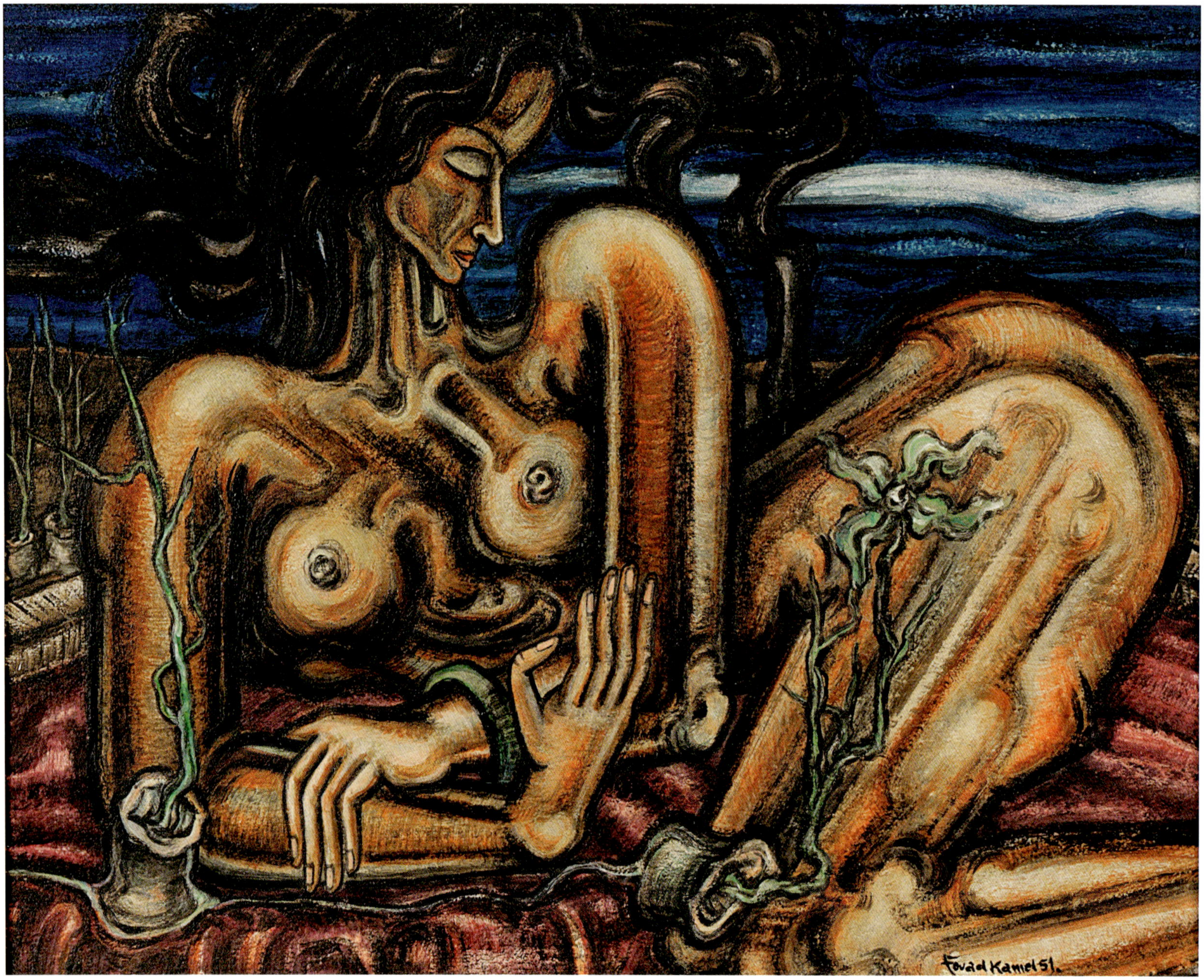

1

1
FOUAD KAMEL
Untitled, 1951
Oil on cardboard
67 x 47 cm
Mai El-Dib collection, Alexandria

2
FOUAD KAMEL
Untitled, undated
Oil on cardboard
70.5 x 50 cm
Private collection

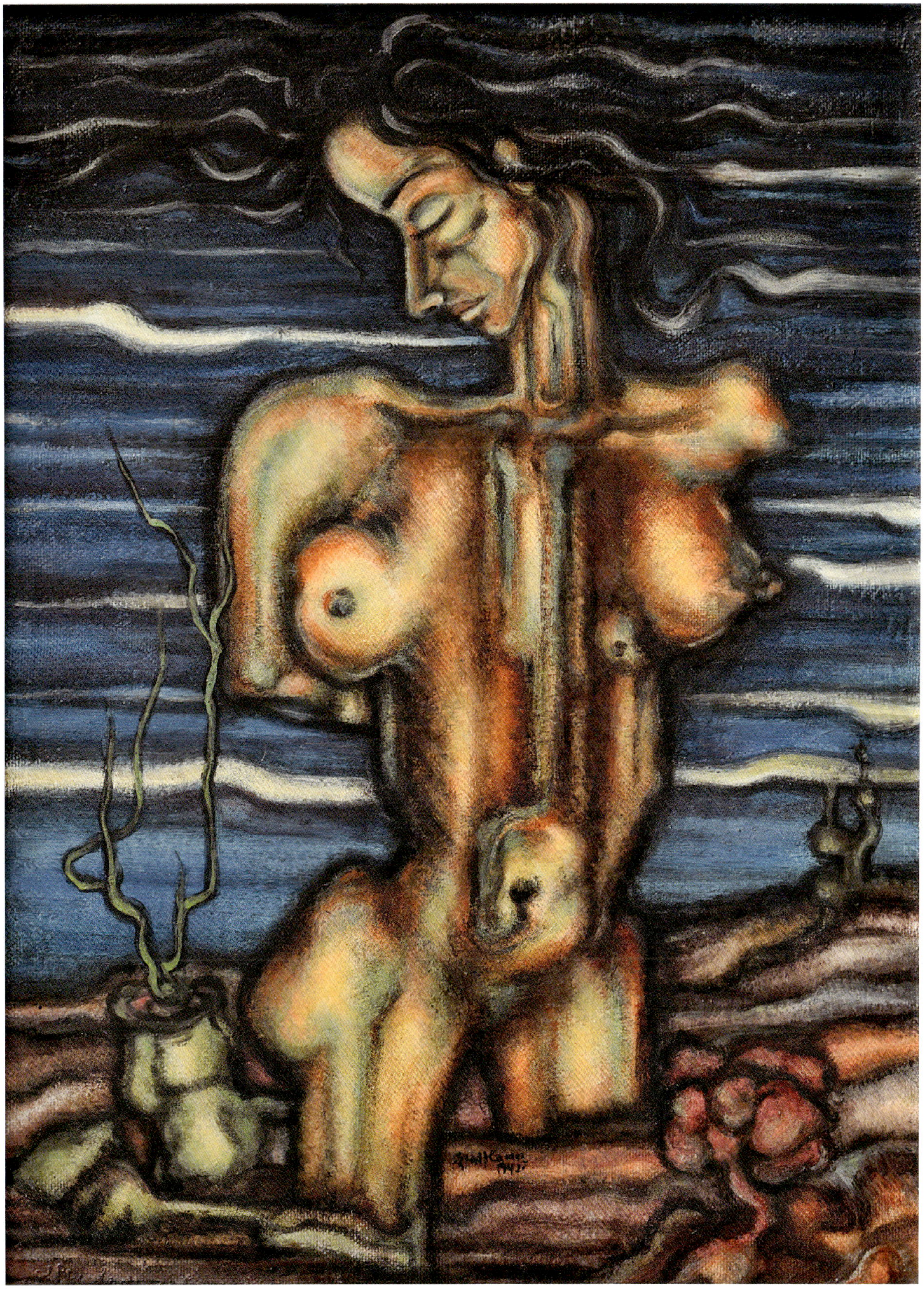
2

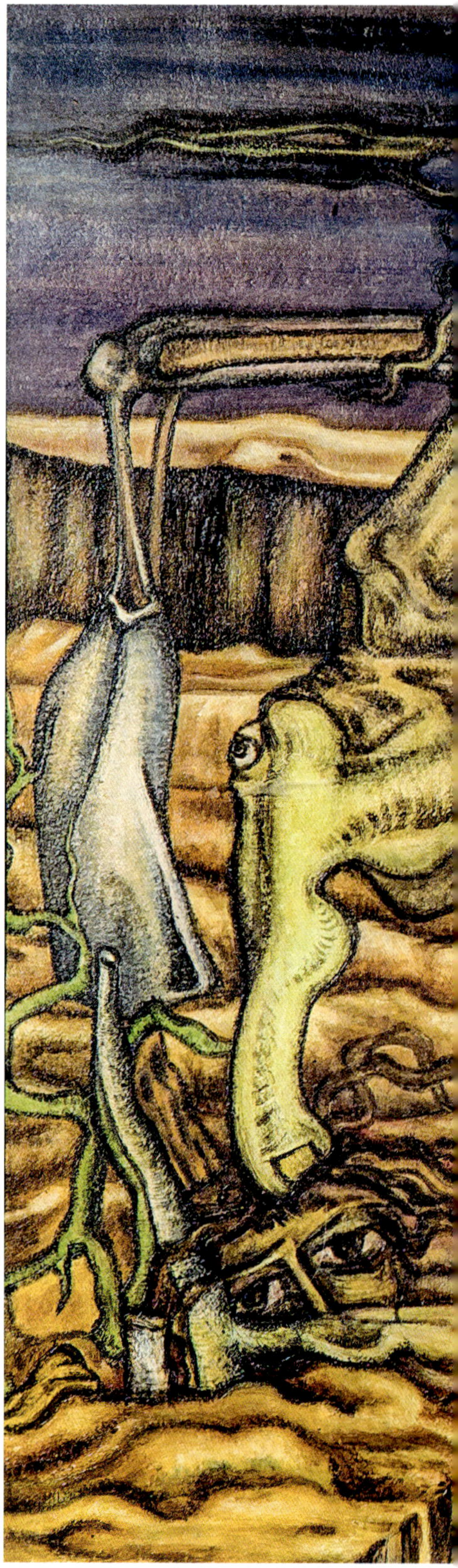

FOUAD KAMEL
Nude, 1950
Oil on cardboard
55.5 x 67 cm
Fatenn Mostafa Kanafani collection, Cairo

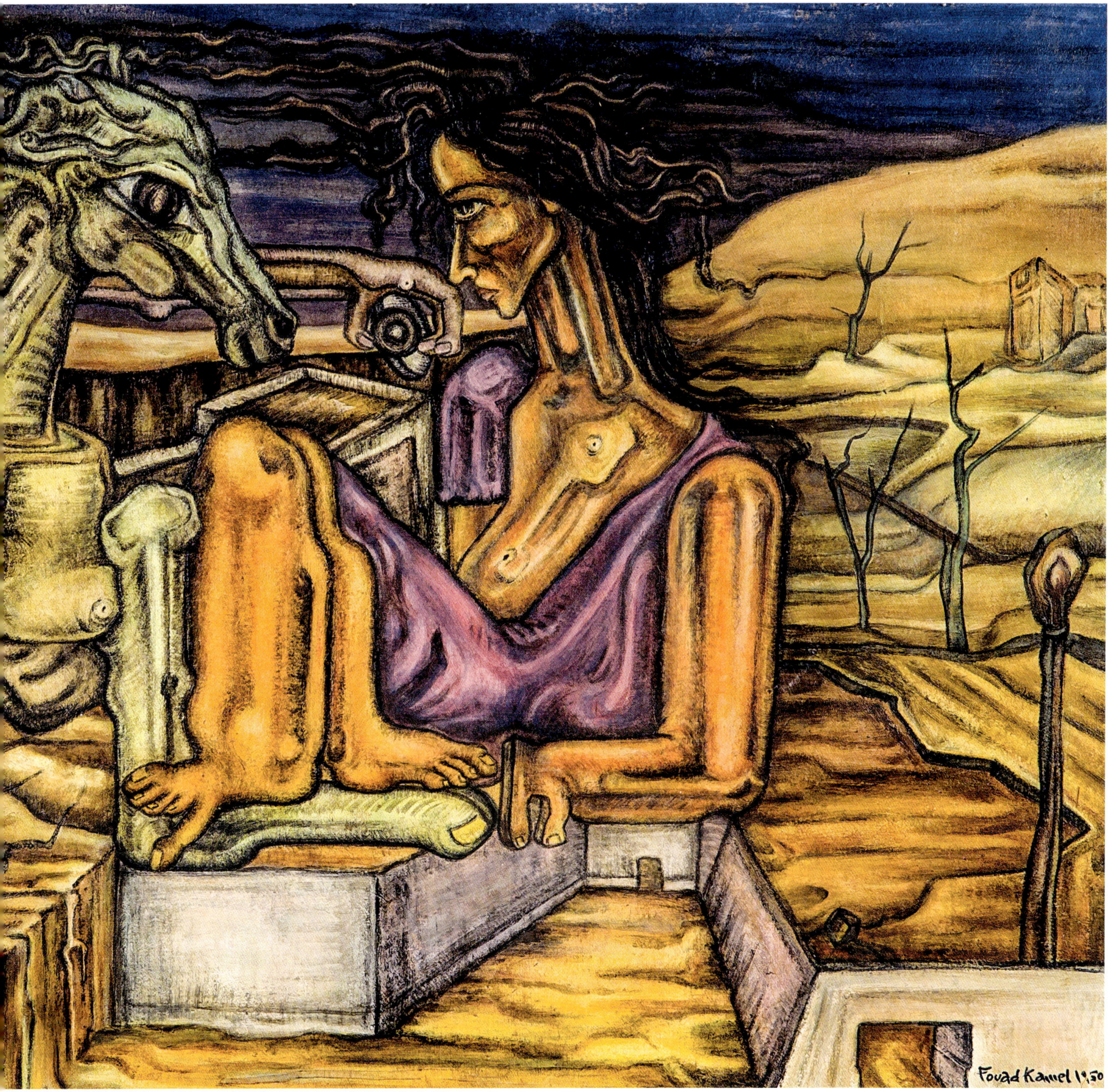
Fouad Kamel 1950

"SUBJECTIVE REALISM"

Ramses Younane, *The Objective of the Contemporary Artist*, 1938

A*rt et Liberté* believed that Surrealism, at its core, is a calling for a social and moral revolution as well as an art movement. They coined a new term for Surrealism: Subjective Realism. Writing in 1938, theorist and painter Ramses Younane depicted Surrealism as a movement in crisis, and divided it into two categories. The first, best exemplified by Dali and Magritte's absurd juxtapositions, was considered excessively pre-meditated, leaving no space for the uncontrolled imagination. The second, consisting of automatic writing and drawing, was deemed too self-centred and not geared enough towards collective empowerment. Younane identified the need for a new type of Surrealism, which he called Subjective Realism, by which artists deliberately incorporated recognizable symbols into works that were initially driven by the subconscious impulse. Kamel El-Telmisany, another *Art et Liberté* theorist and artist referred to this method as Free Art. Group members used these two terms interchangeably as they sought to develop their distinct visual language.

While drawing upon ancient inscriptions, magical talismans, animal fables, and Pharaonic and Coptic symbols to create their own negotiated form of Surrealism, *Art et Liberté* still made use of the subconscious. Besides surrealist games in members' homes, they organized Sufi meditation séances referred to as *dhikr*. These took place in their ateliers in the old Mamluk quarter within Cairo's citadel, and would last until the early hours of dawn. In order to enter a trance-like state, members would whirl in place while repeatedly reciting short phrases or prayers. This was *Art et Liberté*'s equivalent to the self-induced state of sleep-wakefulness used by other Surrealists to achieve their automatic writings and drawings. This new "collective mythology" as Younane described it, expressed with full lucidity the responsibility of the artist within his or her own society.

MAYO
L'Oiseau, 1937
Oil on board
46 x 22 cm
European Cultural Centre of Delphi, Greece

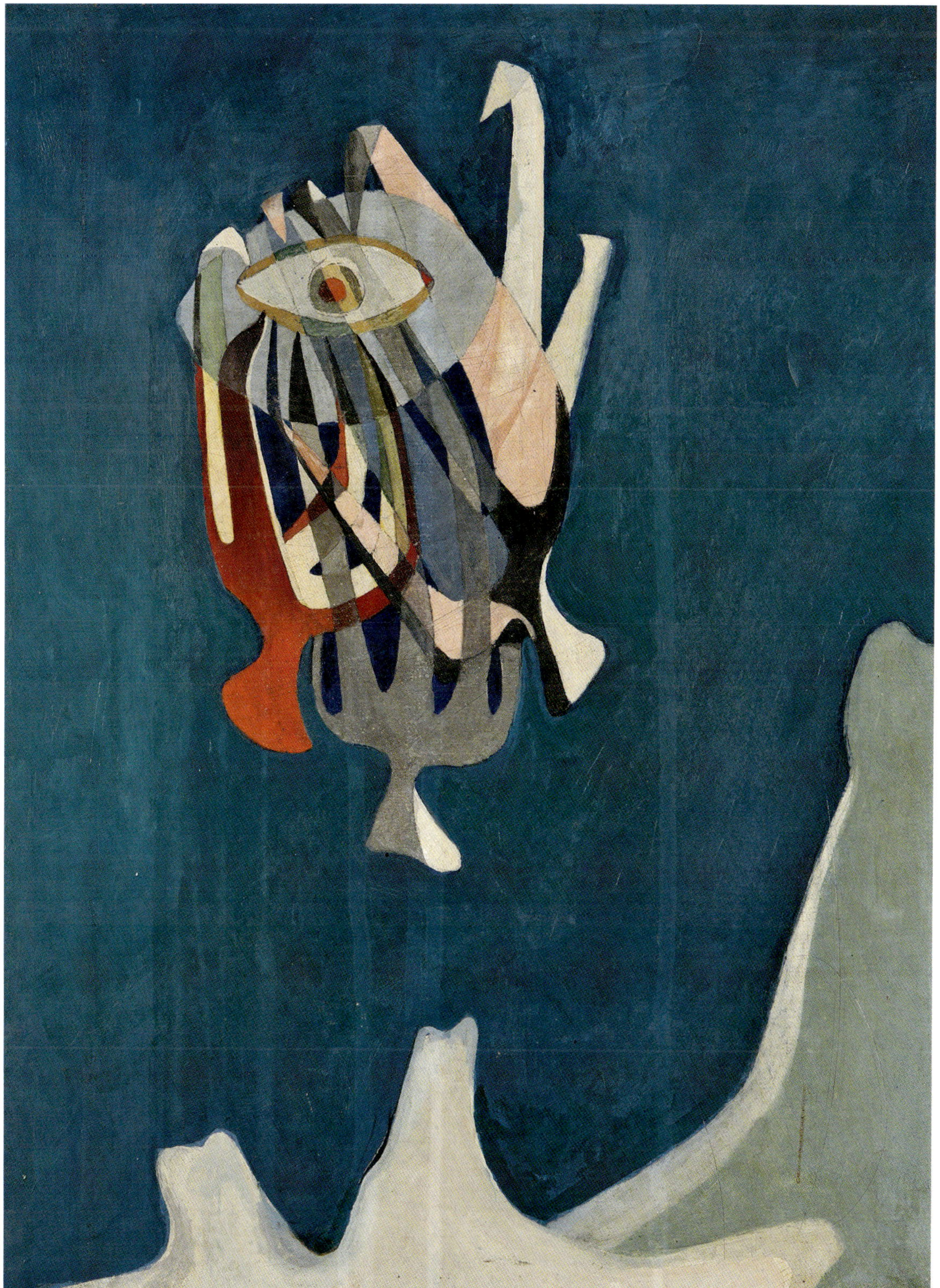
mayo

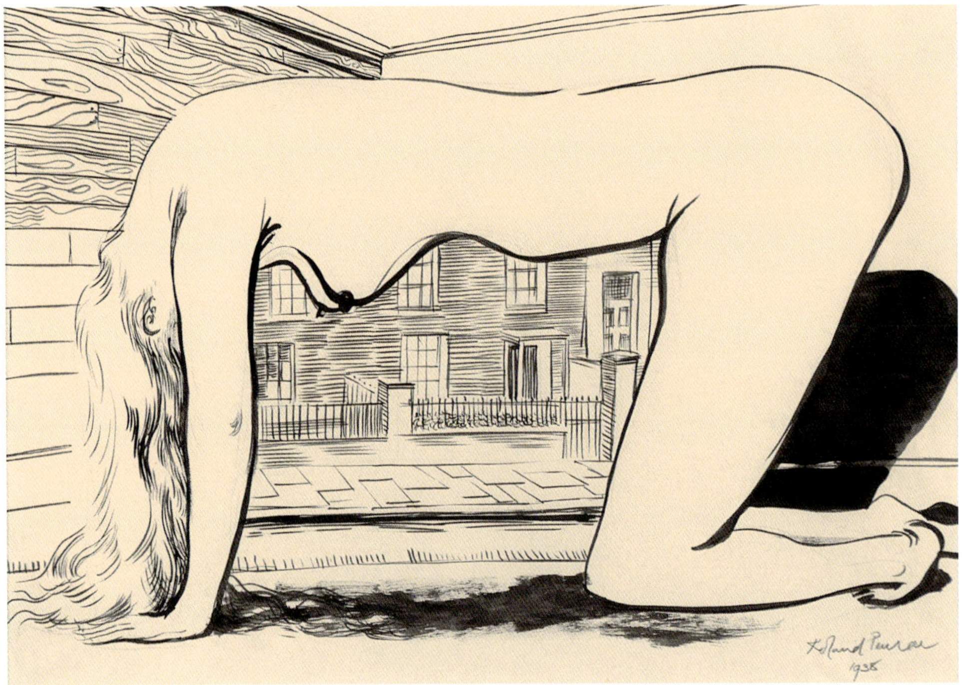

1

1
ROLAND PENROSE
Lee as Nut, 1938
Ink on paper
24.3 x 35.3 cm
Roland Penrose Estate, England 2016
The Penrose collection

2
ROLAND PENROSE
Egypt, 1939
Oil on canvas
62.3 x 74.4 cm
Roland Penrose Estate, England 2016
The Penrose collection

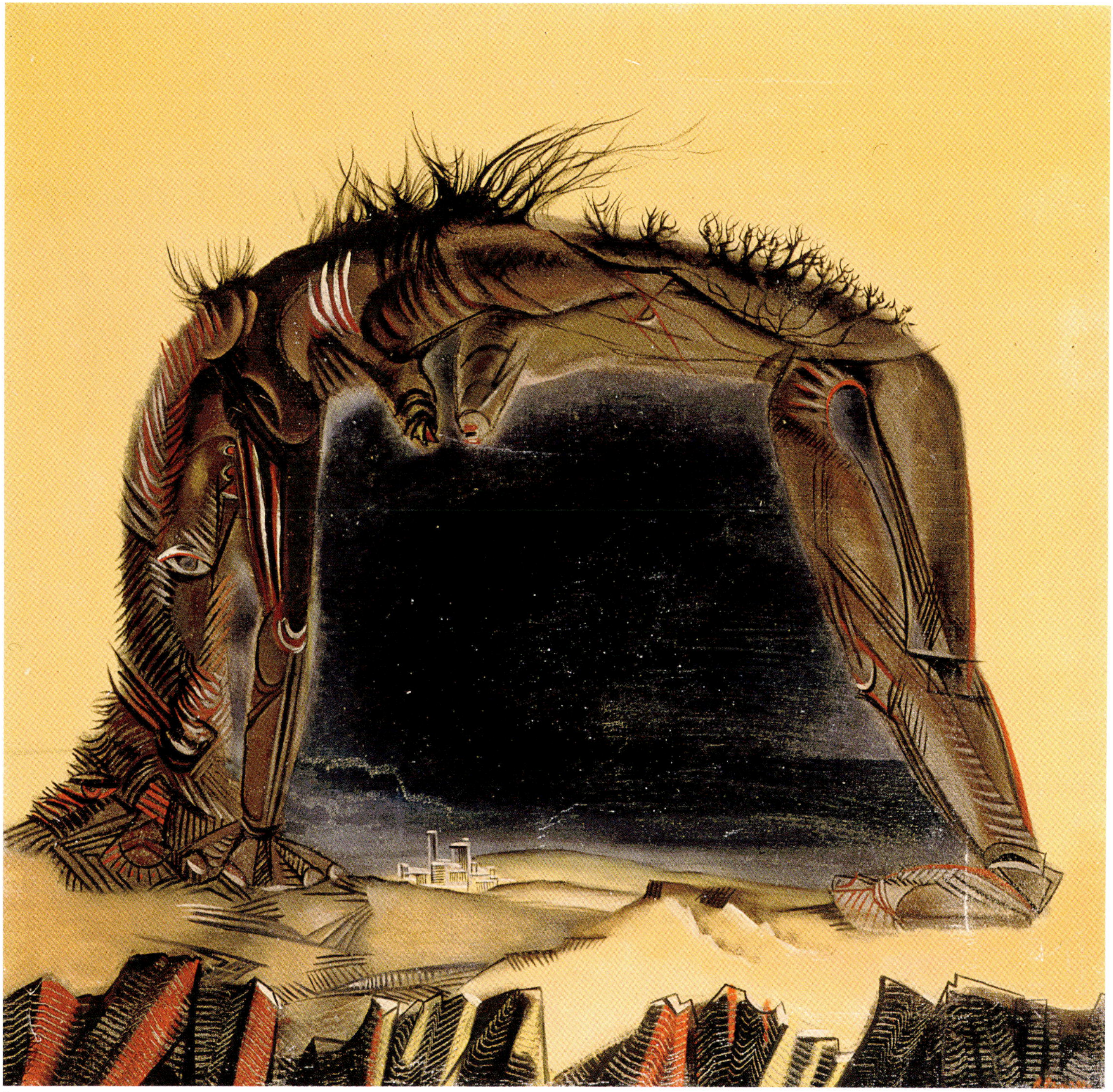

2

RAMSES YOUNANE
Untitled, 1939
Oil on canvas
46.5 x 35.5 cm
H.E. Sh. Hassan M. A. Al Thani collection, Doha

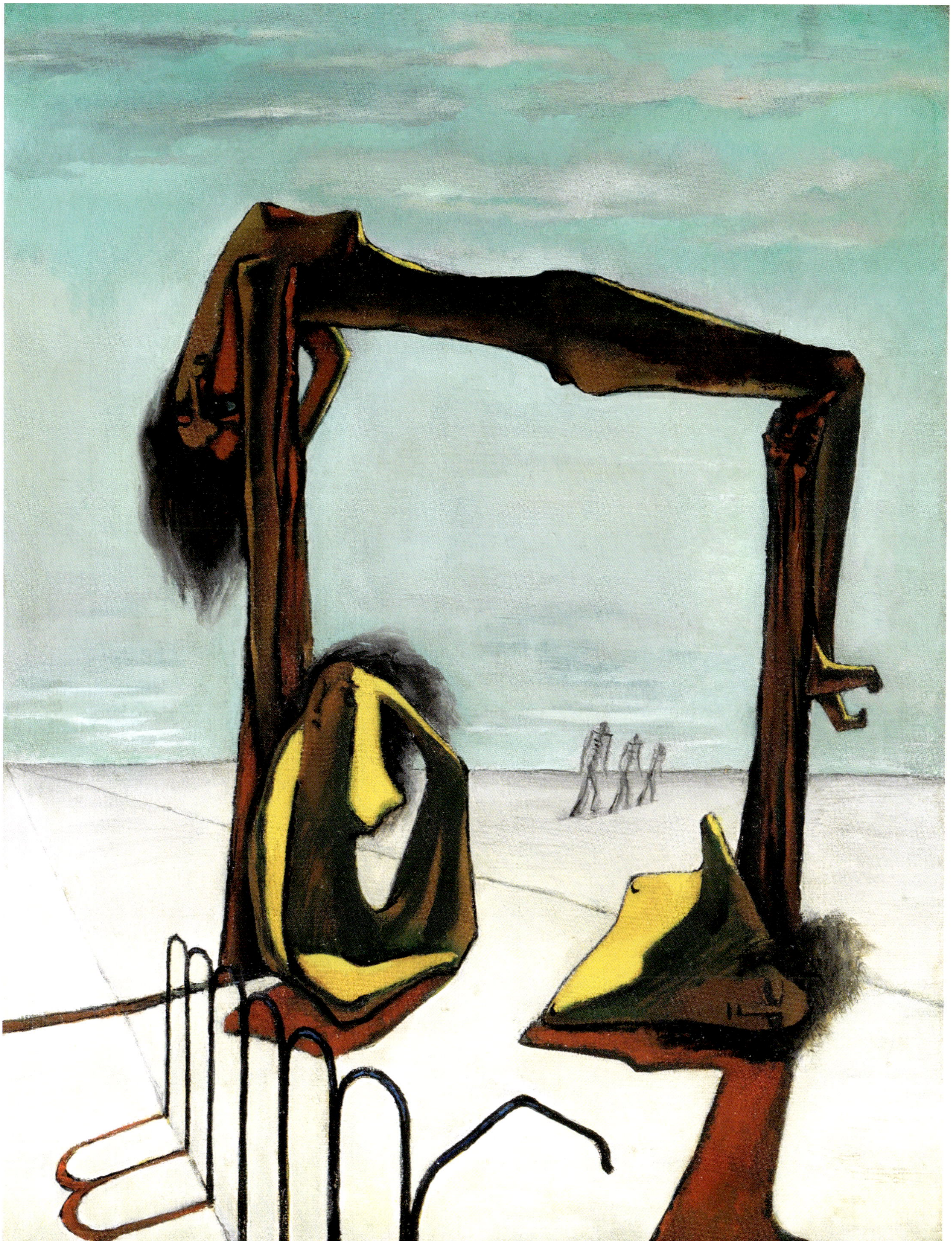

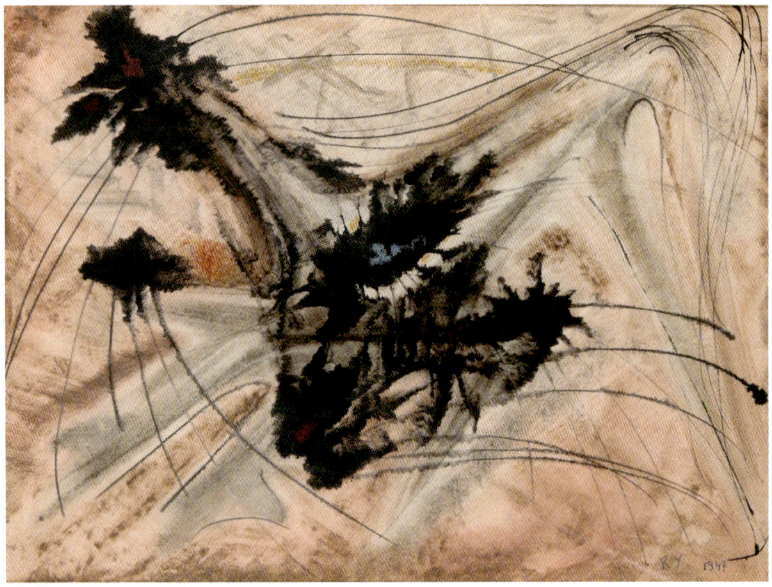
1

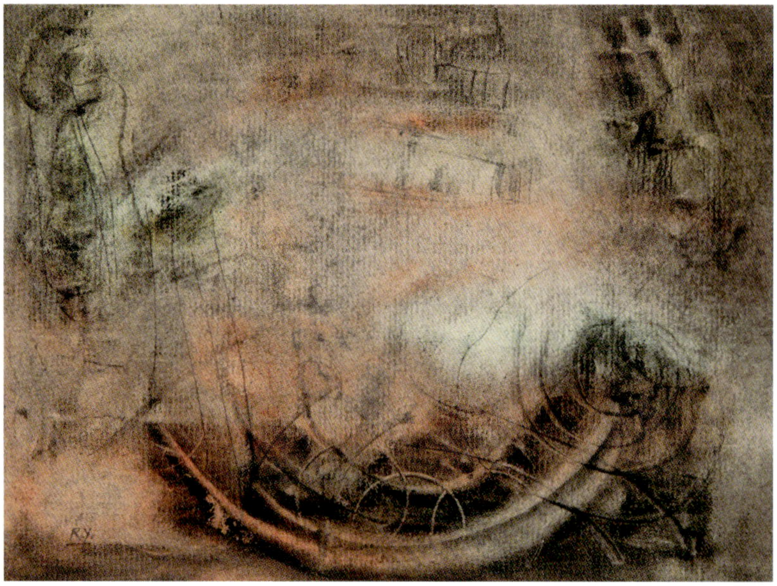
2

1
RAMSES YOUNANE
Untitled, 1947
Gouache on paper
25 x 35 cm
Sylvie and Sonia Younan collection, Paris

2
RAMSES YOUNANE
Untitled, 1947
Gouache on paper
20 x 26 cm
Sylvie and Sonia Younan collection, Paris

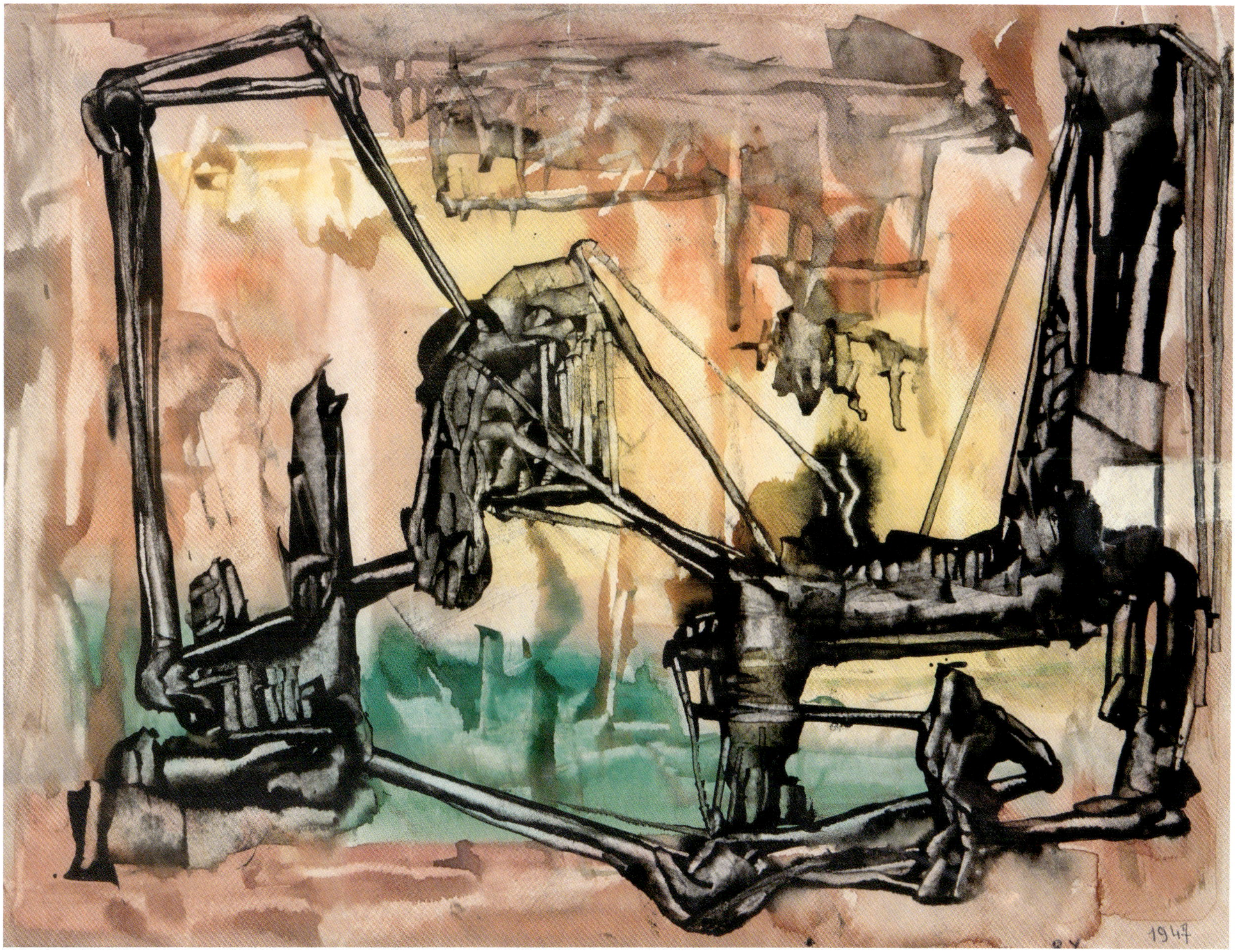

3

3
RAMSES YOUNANE
Untitled, 1947
Gouache on paper
25.5 x 34 cm
Sylvie and Sonia Younan collection, Paris

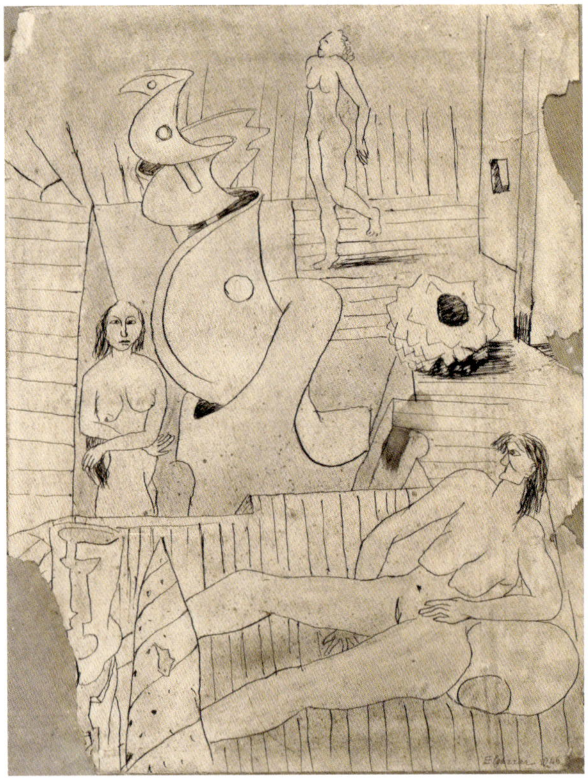
1

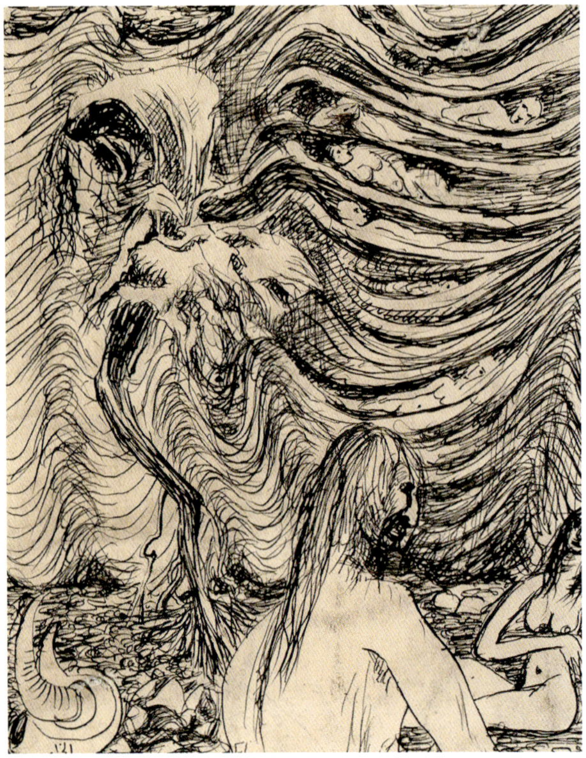
2

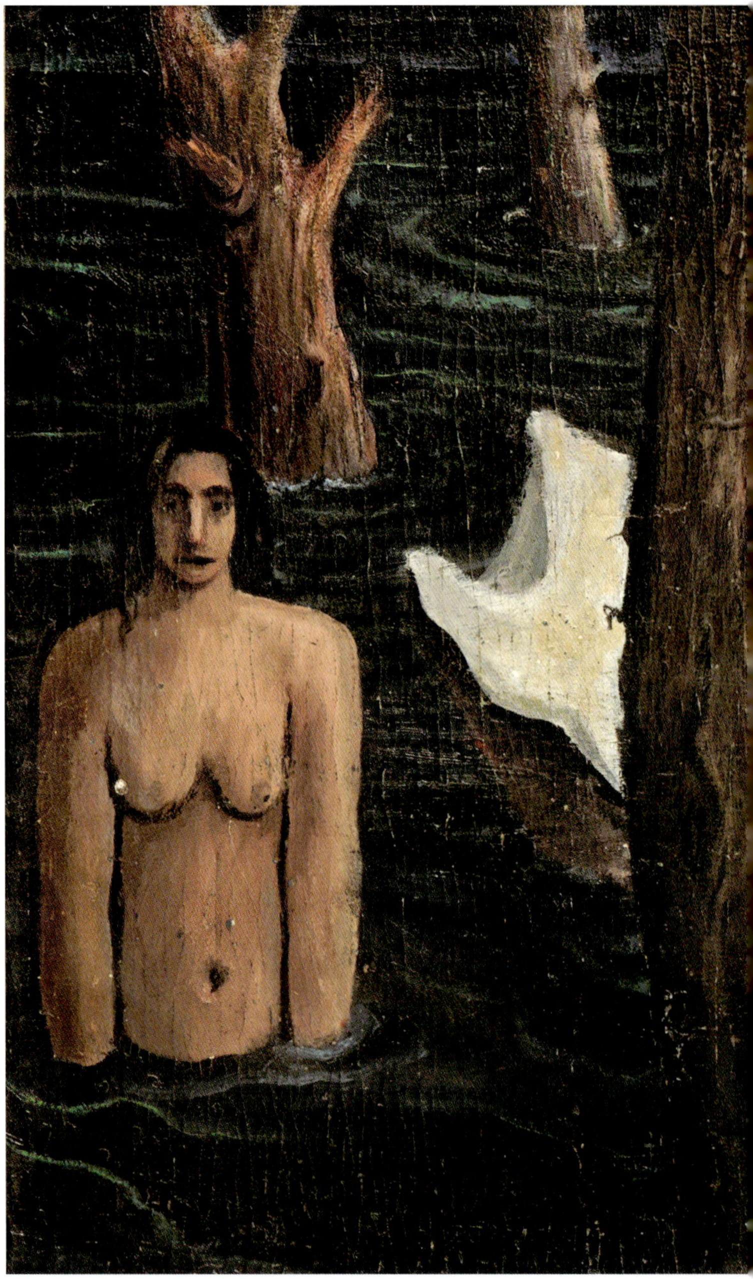
3

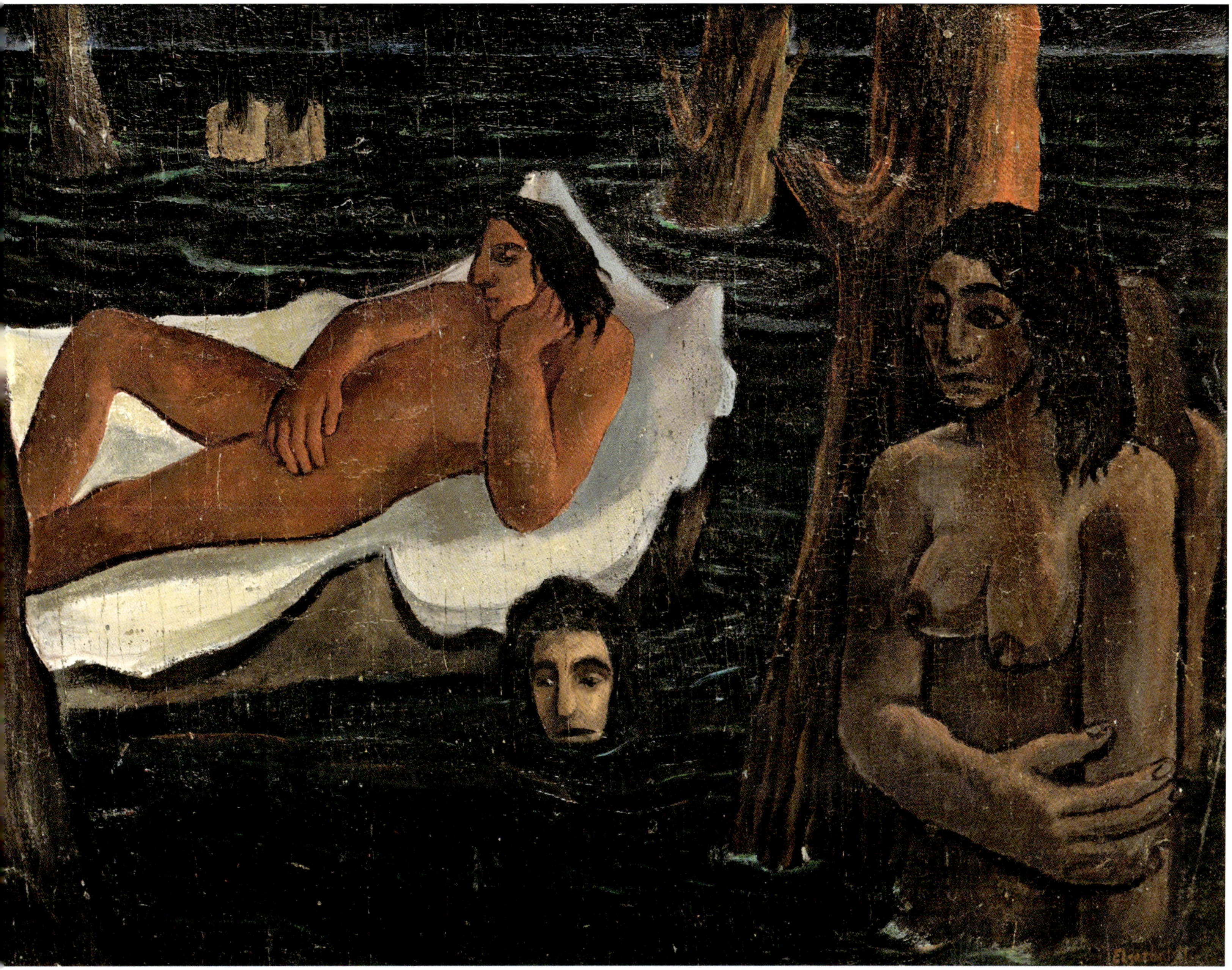

1
ABDEL HADI EL-GAZZAR
Untitled, 1945
Ink on paper
35 x 27 cm
Fairouz El-Gazzar collection, Cairo

2
ABDEL HADI EL-GAZZAR
Untitled, 1946
Ink on paper
22 x 17 cm
Fairouz El-Gazzar collection, Cairo

3
ABDEL HADI EL-GAZZAR
Man in Shell, 1948
Oil on hardboard
78 x 144 cm
H.E. Sh. Hassan M. A. Al Thani collection, Doha

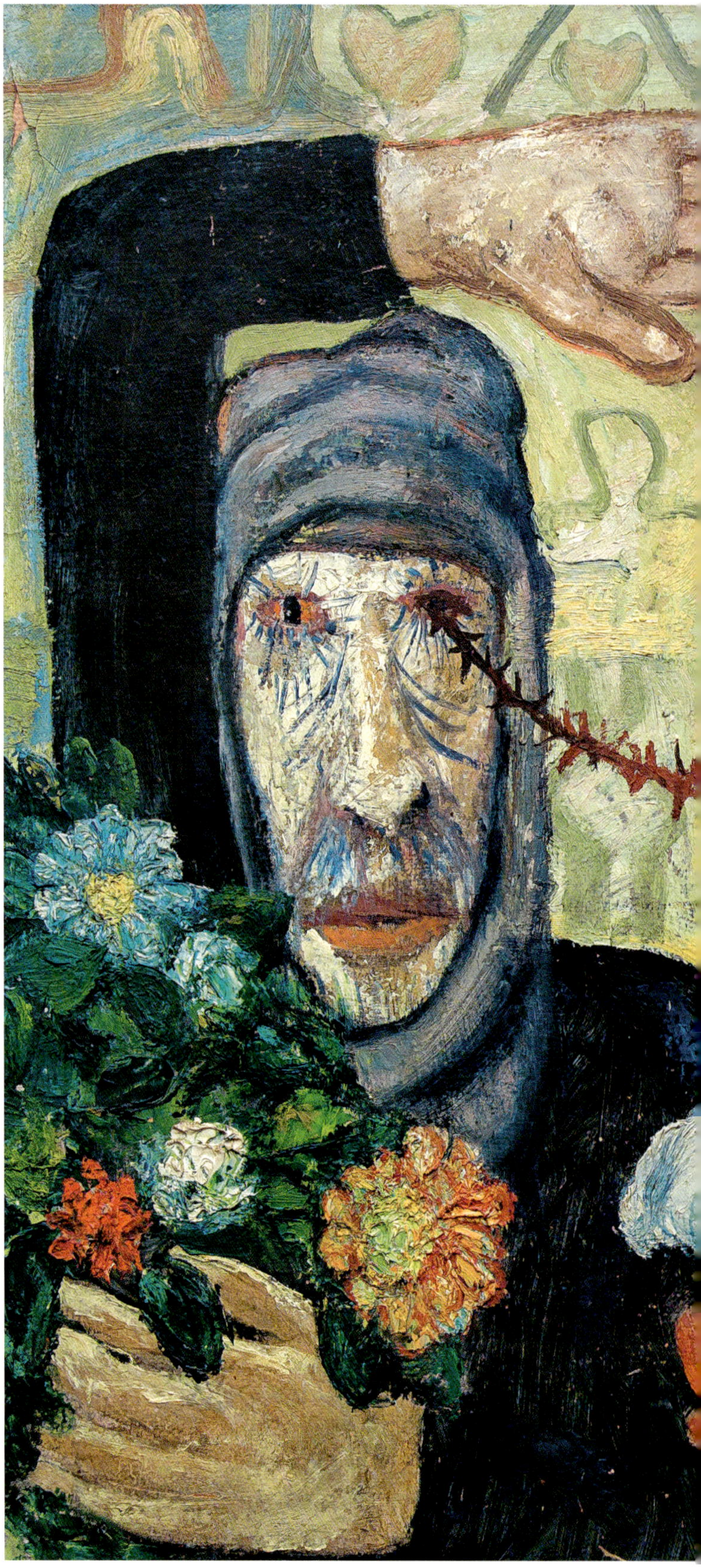

ABDEL HADI EL-GAZZAR
Mahasseb Il-Sayyidah
(The Beloved of the Sayyidah), c. 1950
Oil on cardboard
60.5 x 92 cm
Yasser Hashem collection, Cairo

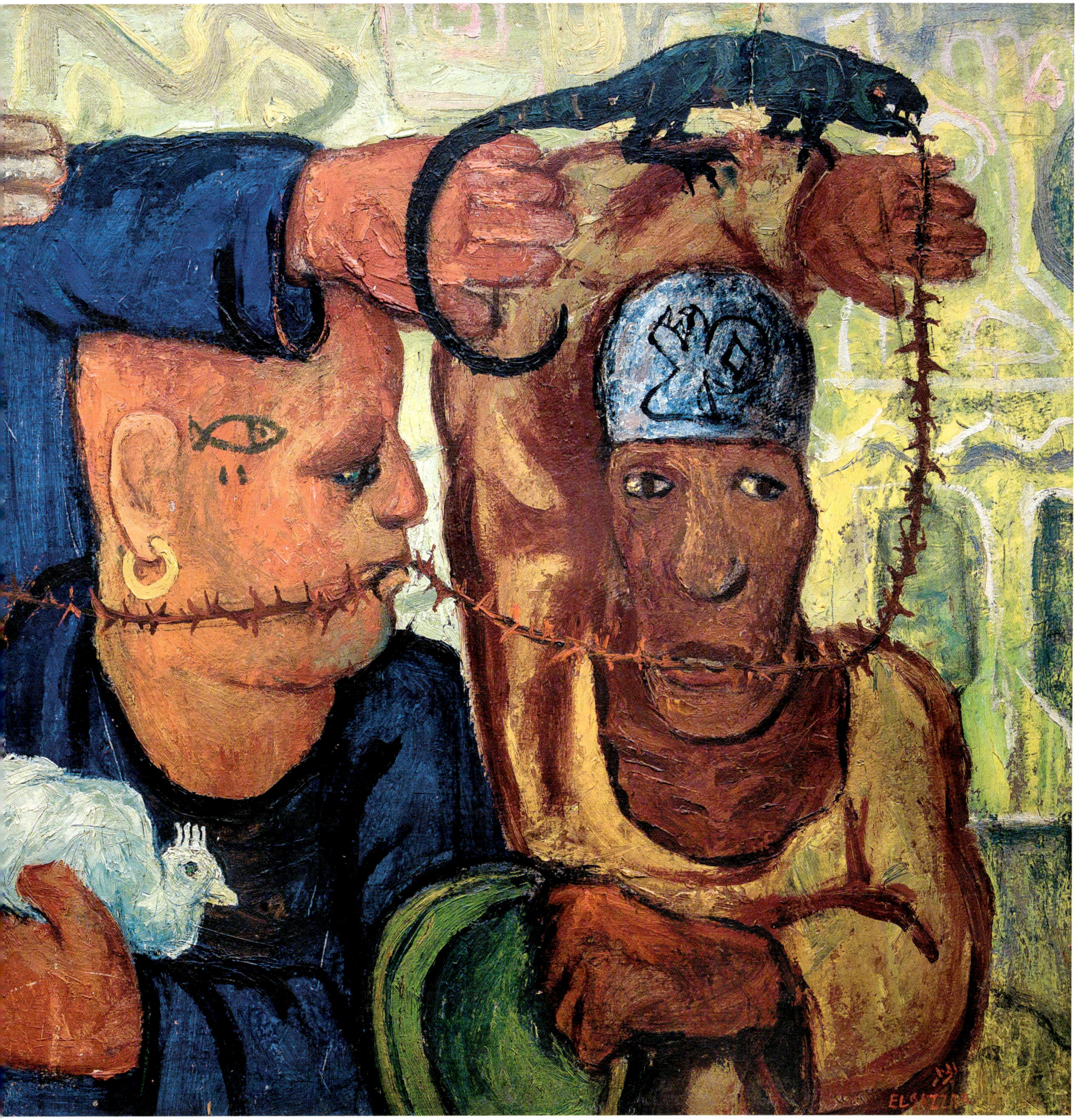

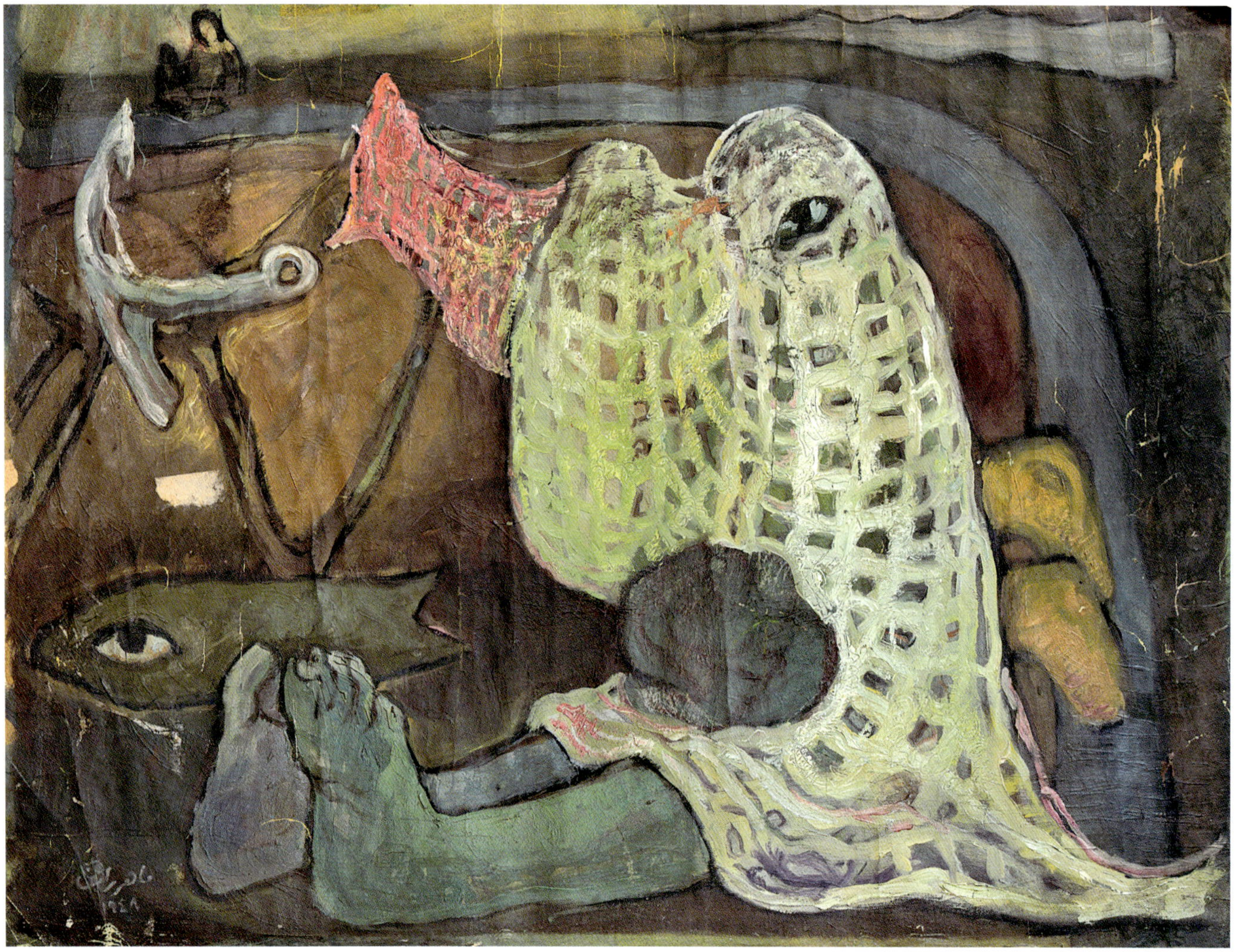

1

1, 2
MAHER RAEF
Untitled (The Fisherwoman and the Net),
c. 1948
Oil on canvas, double-sided
60 x 85 cm
Private collection

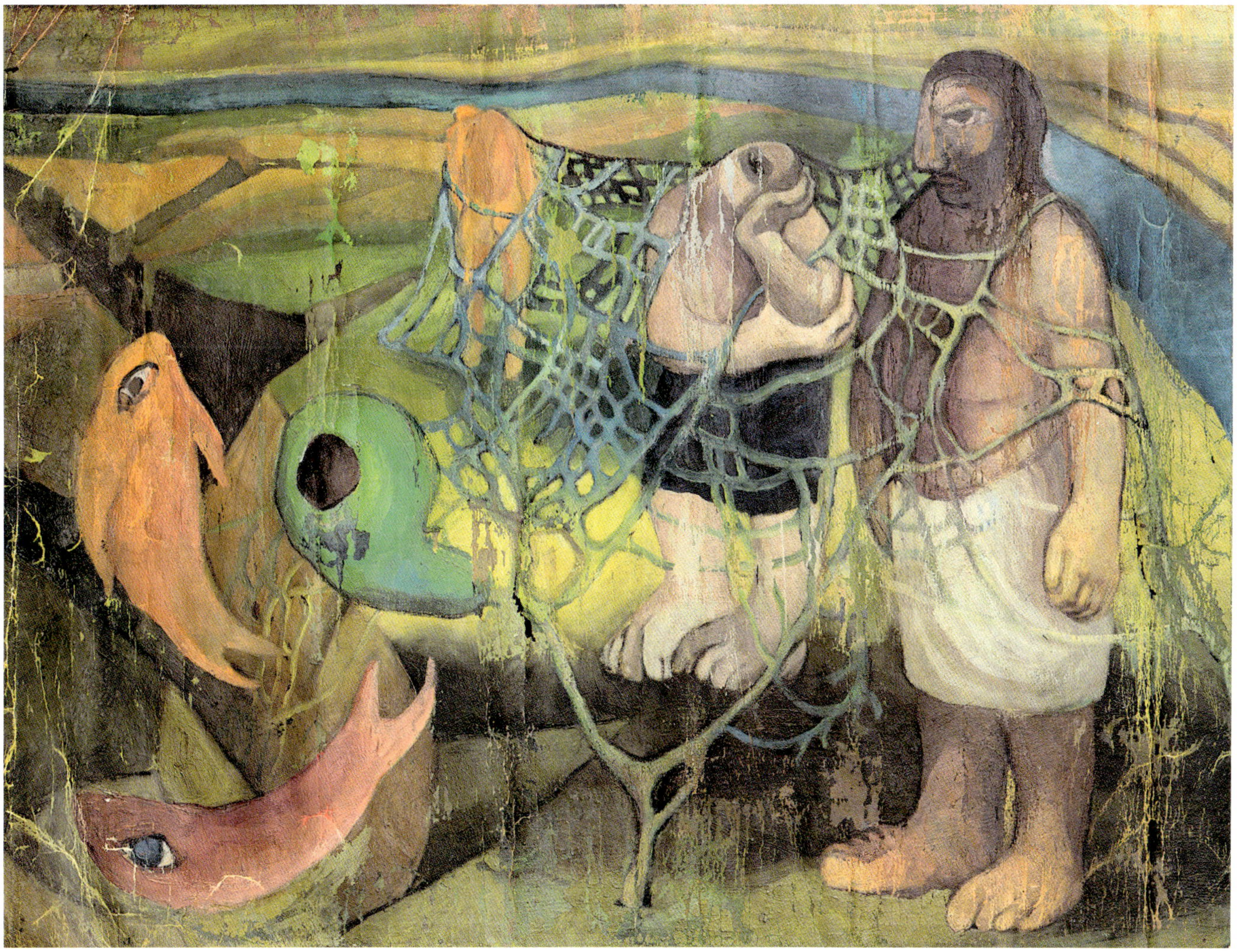

2

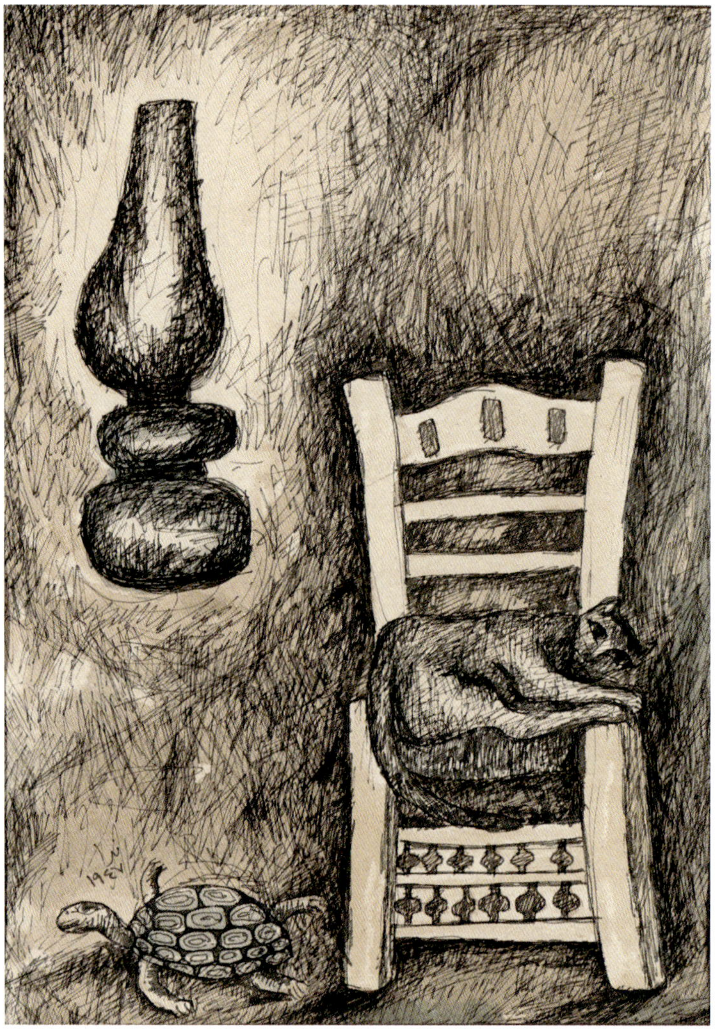

2

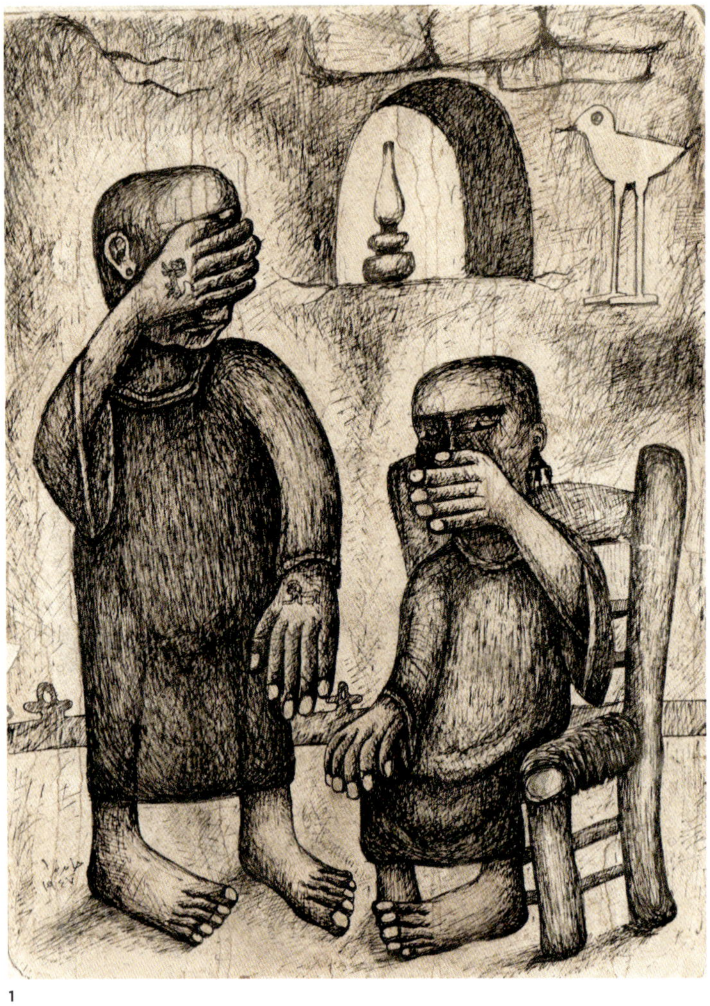

1

1
HAMED NADA
Figures, 1947
Ink on paper
35.5 x 27 cm
H.E. Sh. Hassan M. A. Al Thani collection, Doha

2
HAMED NADA
Nature morte, 1947
Ink and watercolour on paper
35 x 26 cm
H.E. Sh. Hassan M. A. Al Thani collection, Doha

3
HAMED NADA
Man and Cat, 1947
Ink and watercolour on paper
35 x 26 cm
H.E. Sh. Hassan M. A. Al Thani collection, Doha

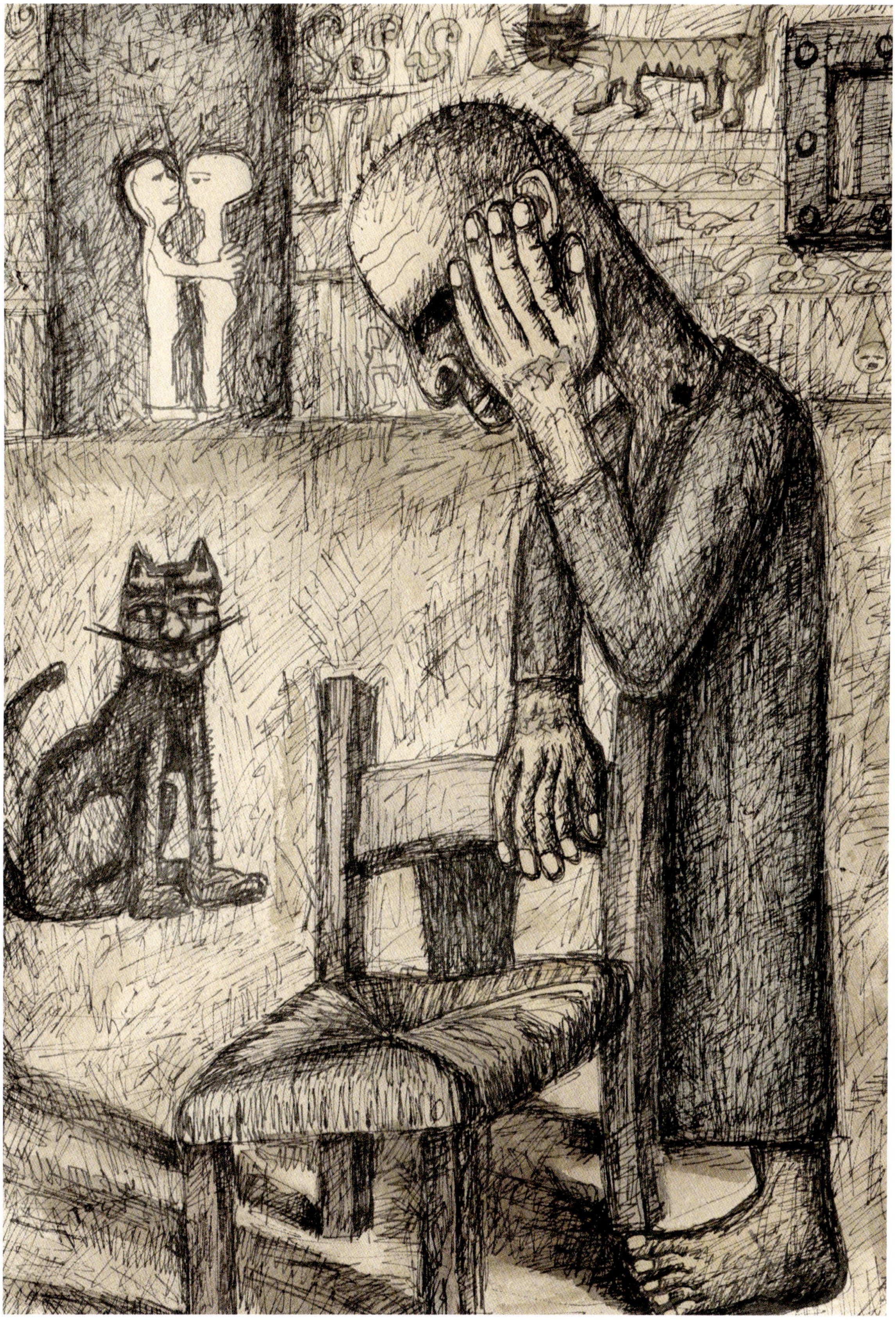
3

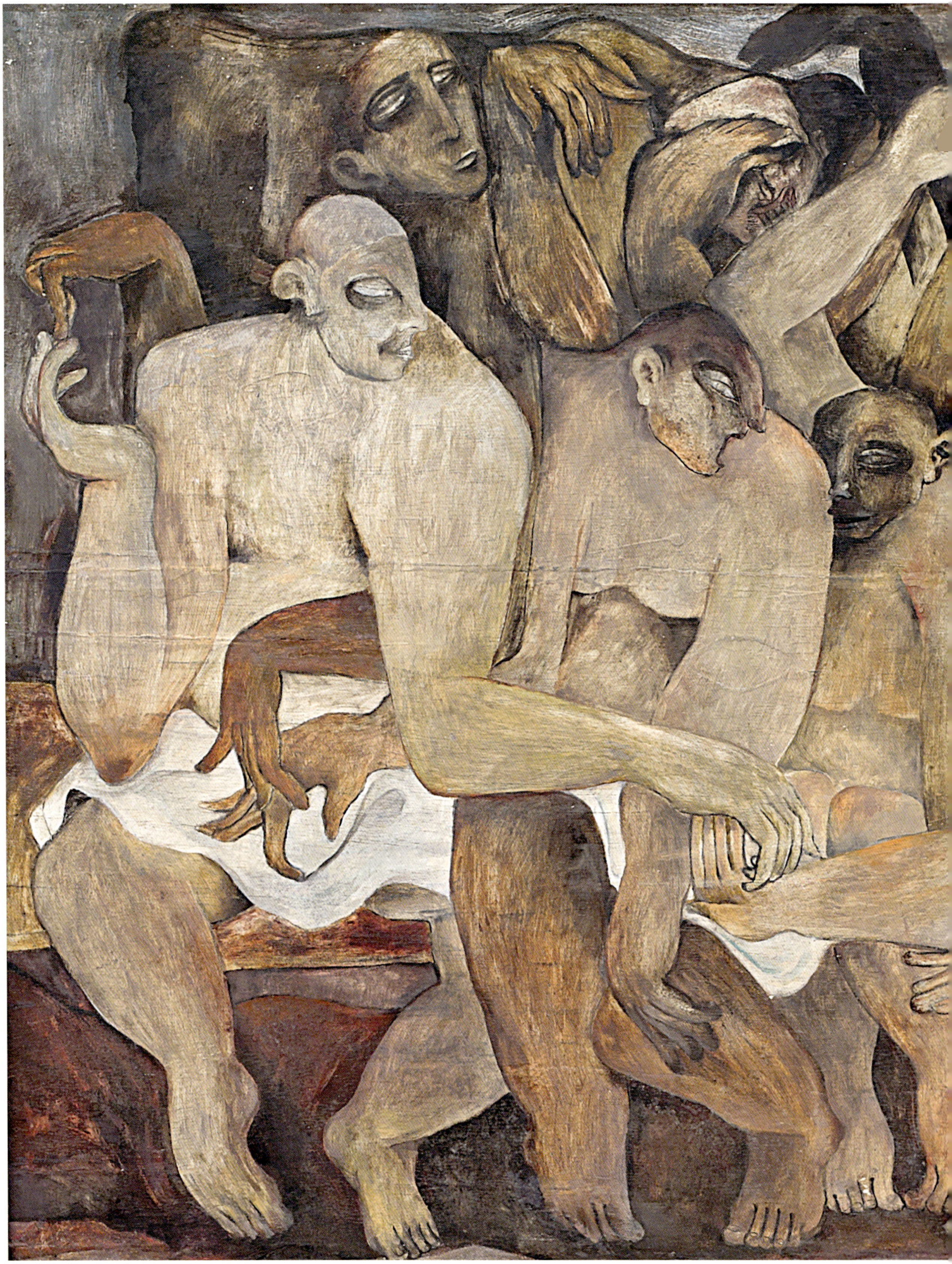

RATEB SEDDIK
Untitled, c. 1940
Oil on wood
120 x 220 cm
Rateb Seddik Museum, Cairo

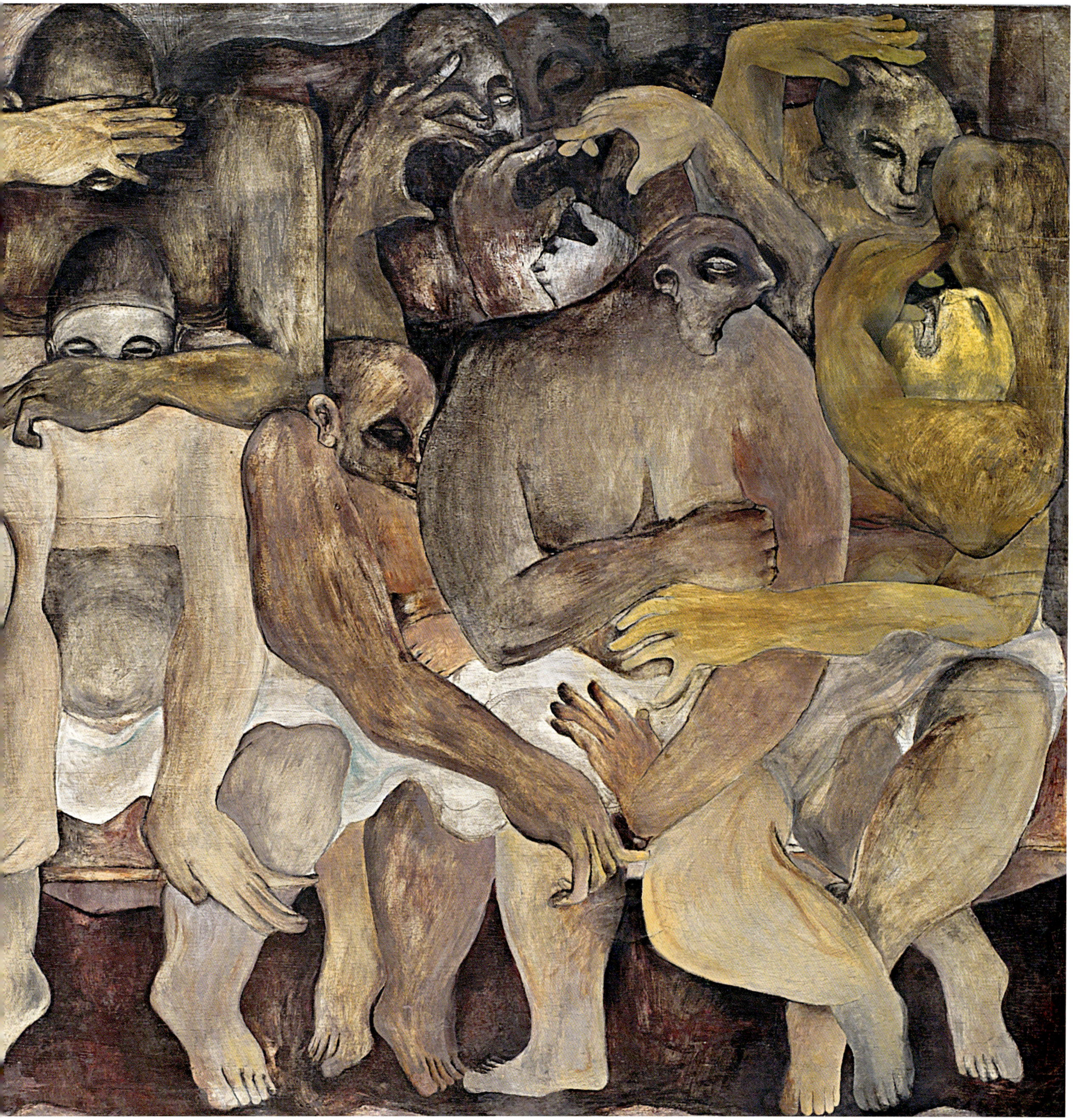

MAYO
Un Soir à Cannes, 1948
Oil on canvas
137 x 144 cm
European Cultural Centre of Delphi, Greece

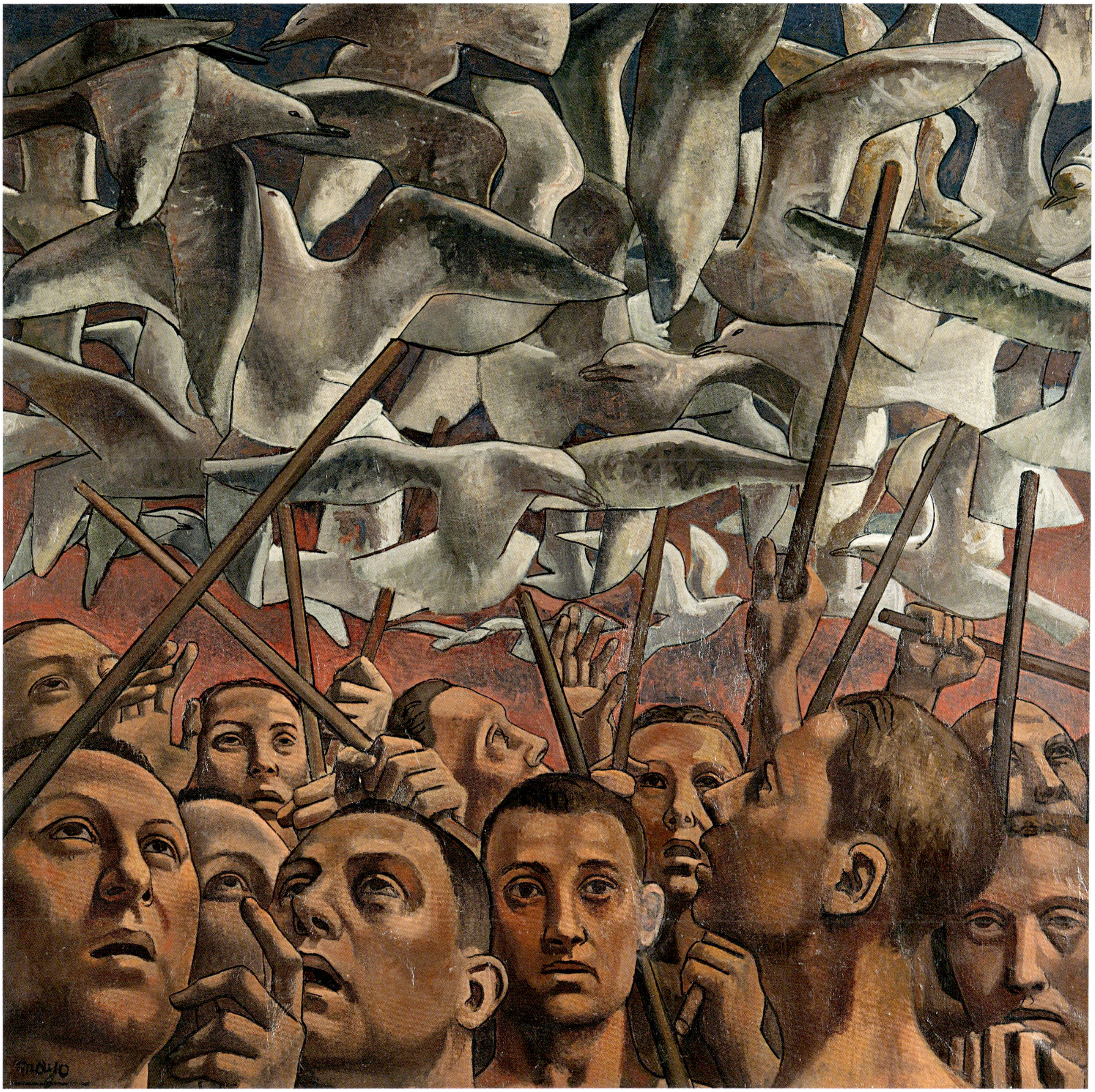

THE CONTEMPORARY ART GROUP: "AN EGYPTIAN ART"

Abdel Hadi El-Gazzar, *Loisirs*, no. 21, Spring 1950

During the second half of the 1940s, *Art and Liberty* manifested a divergence in artistic position, with the Contemporary Art Group, a collective of slightly younger artists of whom some had on occasion participated in some of *Art and Liberty*'s exhibitions of independent art. In the late 1940s and throughout the early decades following the Revolution of 1952, the concern for how to make art Egyptian—very different from the notion of making art for Egypt—becomes a staple in the theoretical ruminations and stylistic experiments of numerous historians and artists respectively. This is where the Contemporary Art Group succeeded in being perceived as a genuinely Egyptian movement that invented the first truly Egyptian art. In order to do so, they mined the visual vernacular of a popular tradition of folk superstitions, myths and fables that had been orally passed on for generations, and articulated a language in which the old and the new, the Pharaonic and the Islamic, the real and the imaginary, and perhaps most importantly, a living repository of forms dwelled side by side. However, as far as *Art and Liberty* were concerned, they feared that these younger artists, who at one point provided them with the blank pages on which they could inscribe the words of their next chapter, were becoming a mouthpiece for a new form of nationalism. Yet despite this divergence, some members of the Contemporary Art Group such as Abdel Hadi El-Gazzar, Hamed Nada, and Samir Rafi, all initially impacted by the Surrealism of *Art and Liberty*, would go on to become some of Egypt's leading modern artists, while several *Art and Liberty* artists would fall into oblivion.

"There exists currently in Egypt various artistic currents that aim to develop a national movement in art.

It is not difficult to create an Egyptian national art if the artist understands our current special problems and traces them with the elements of a modern environment and mentality."

Abdel Hadi El-Gazzar, "Vers un art spécifiquement égyptien," *Loisirs*, Spring 1950

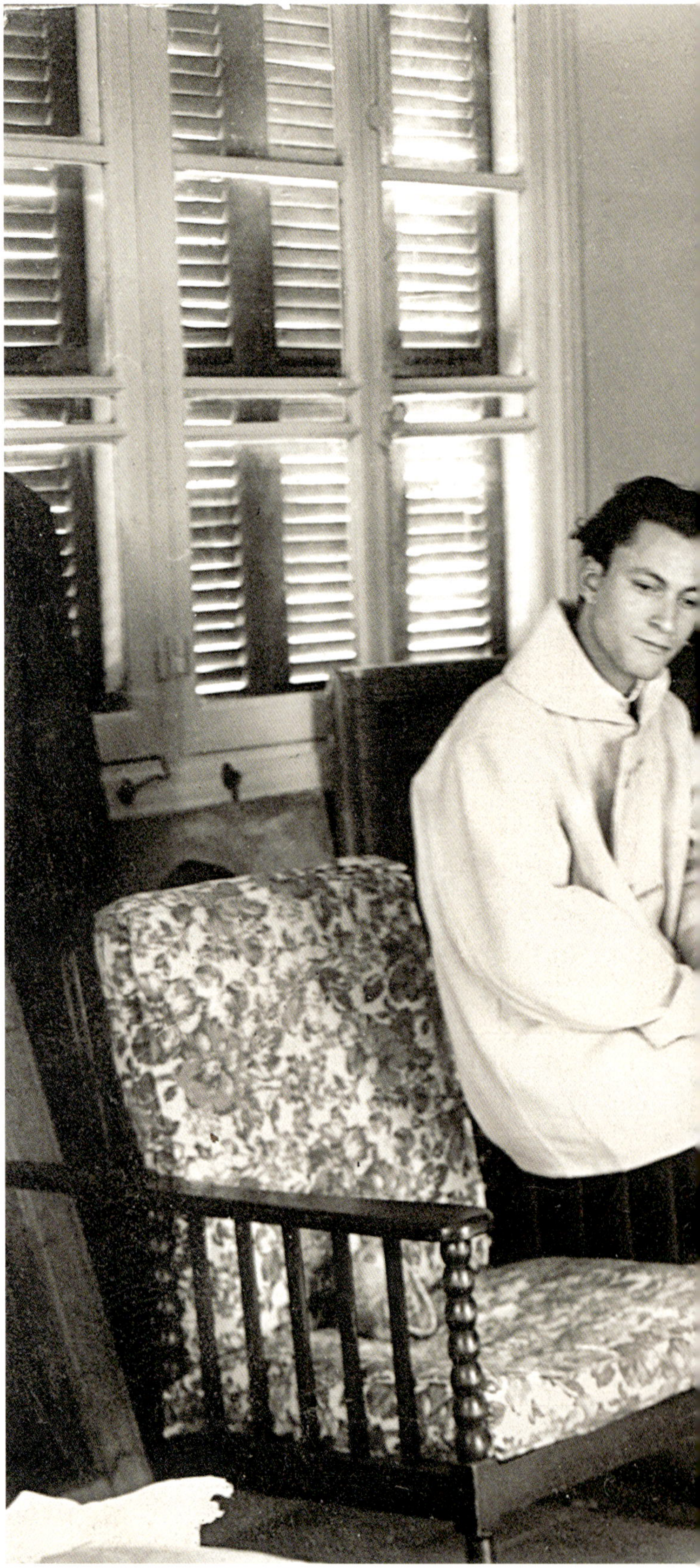

The Contemporary Art Group, c. 1946
From left to right: Hamed Nada, Abdel Hadi El-Gazzar, Hussein Youssef Amin, Mahmoud Khalil (in the back), Kamal Youssef and Samir Rafi
Photographer unknown
Gelatin silver print on paper
Kamal Youssef Archives, Dayton PA

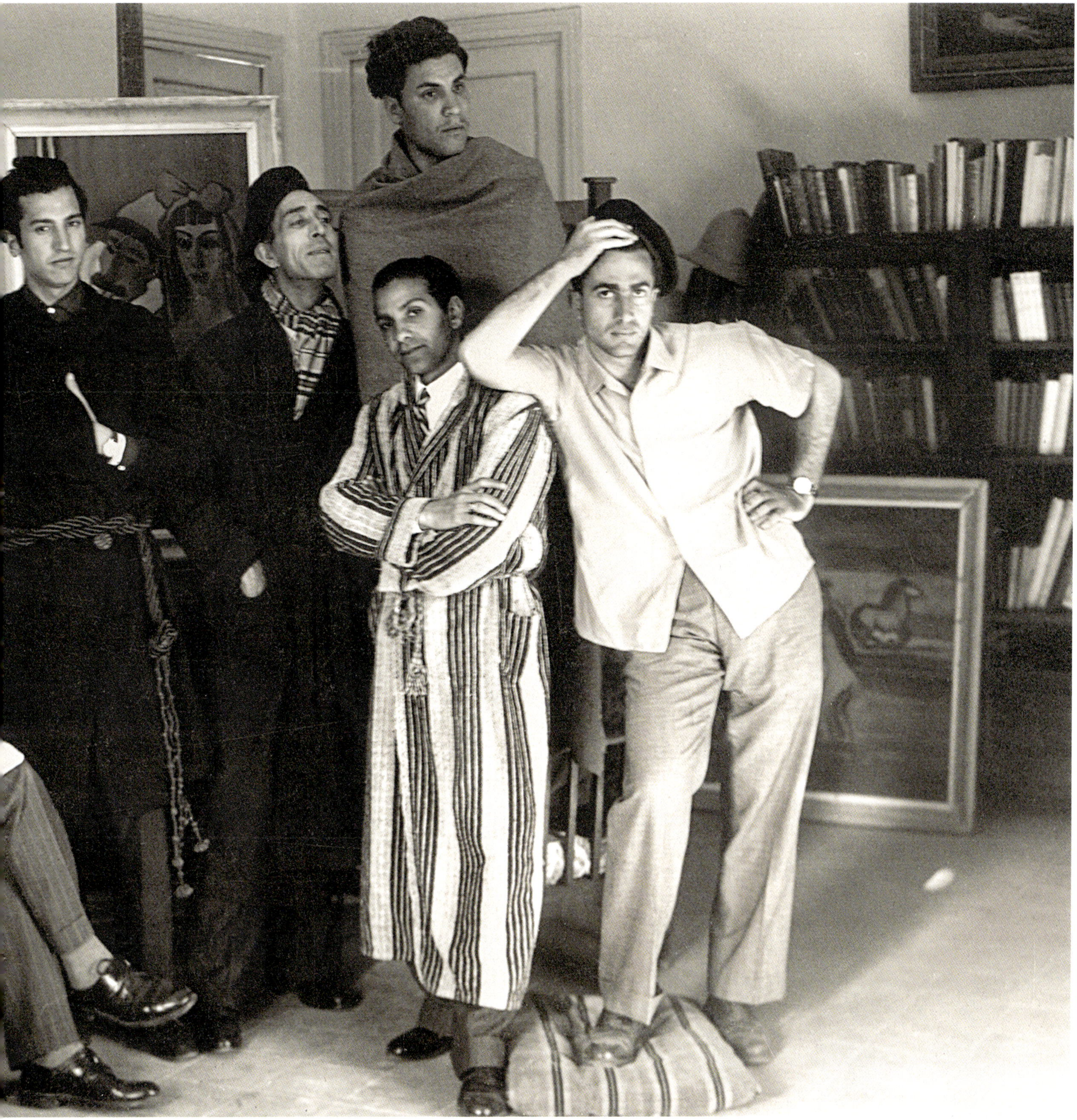

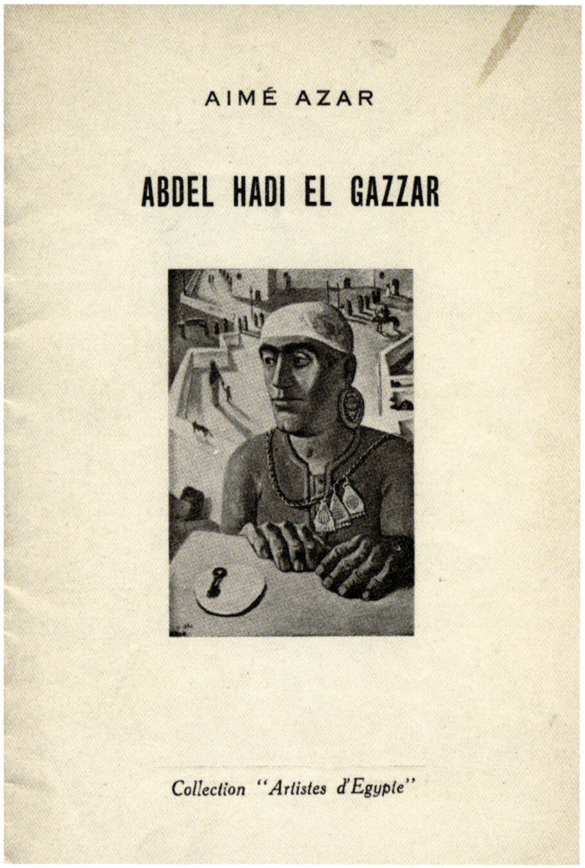

1

1
Aimé Azar
Abdel Hadi El Gazzar, 1952
Paperback
Kamal Youssef Archives, Dayton PA

2
ABDEL HADI EL-GAZZAR
The Green Fool, 1951
Oil on cardboard
63 x 70 cm
Naguib Sawiris collection, Cairo

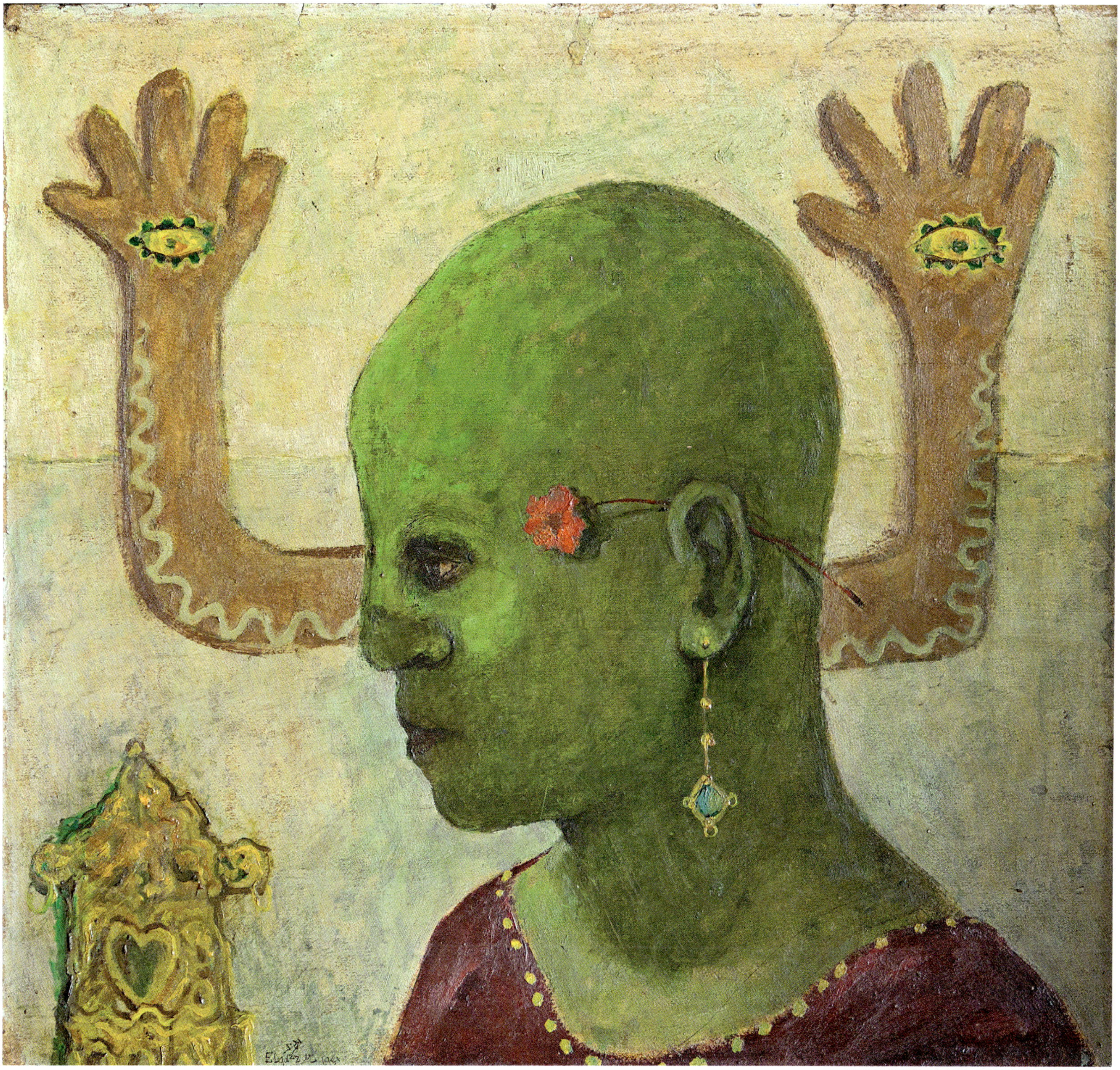

2

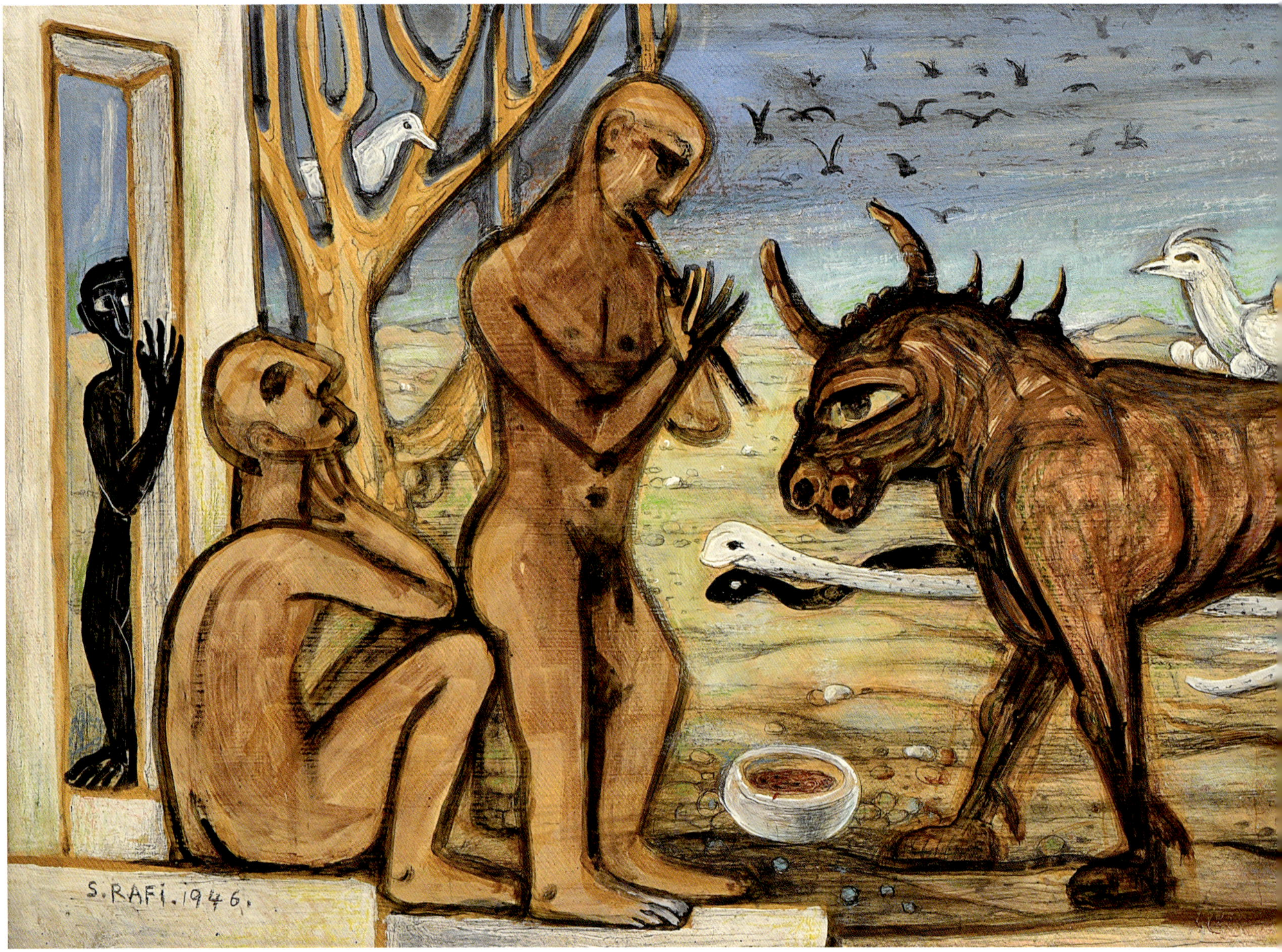

SAMIR RAFI
Untitled, 1946
Mixed media on cardboard
41 x 116 cm
Private collection

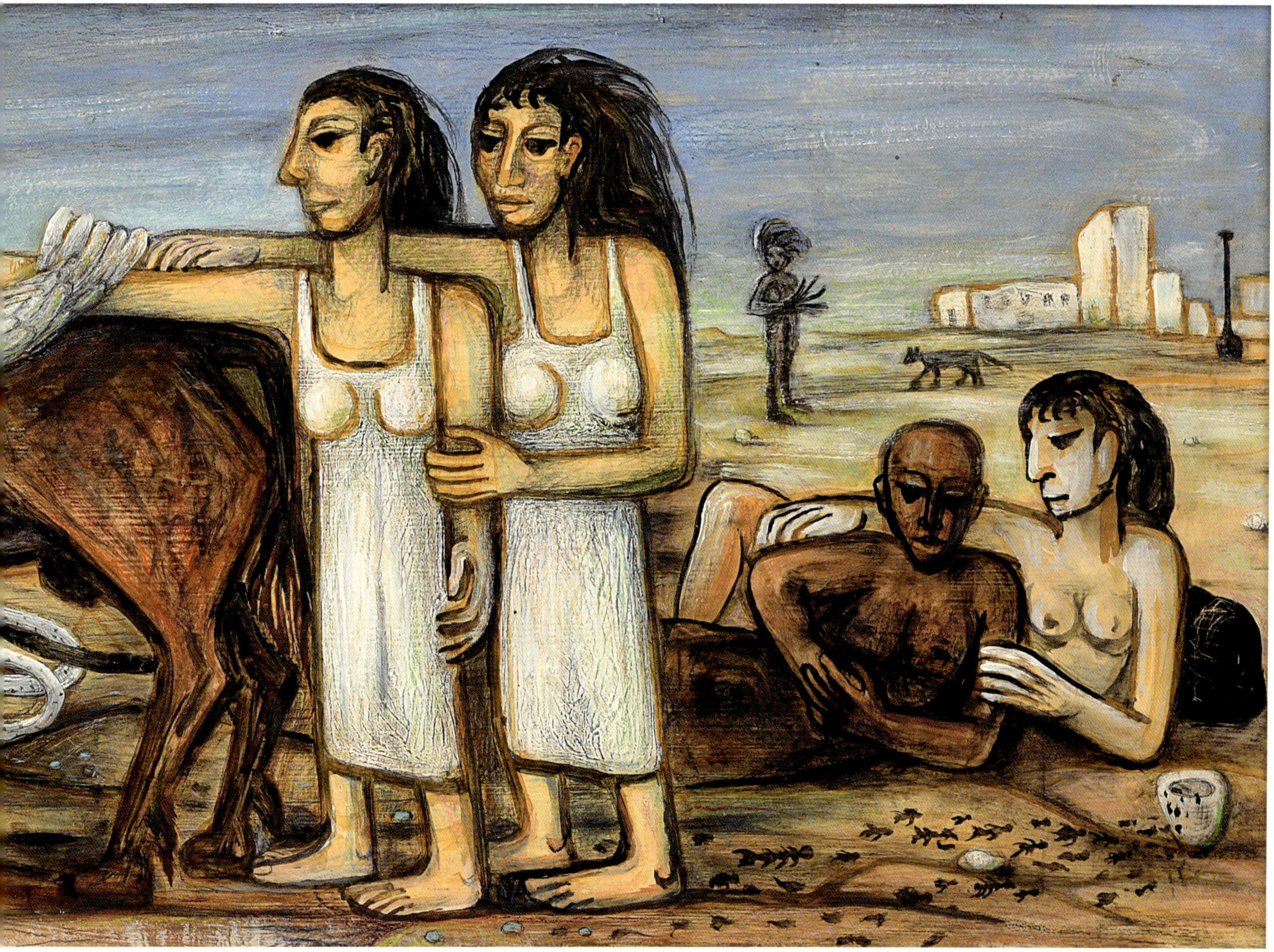

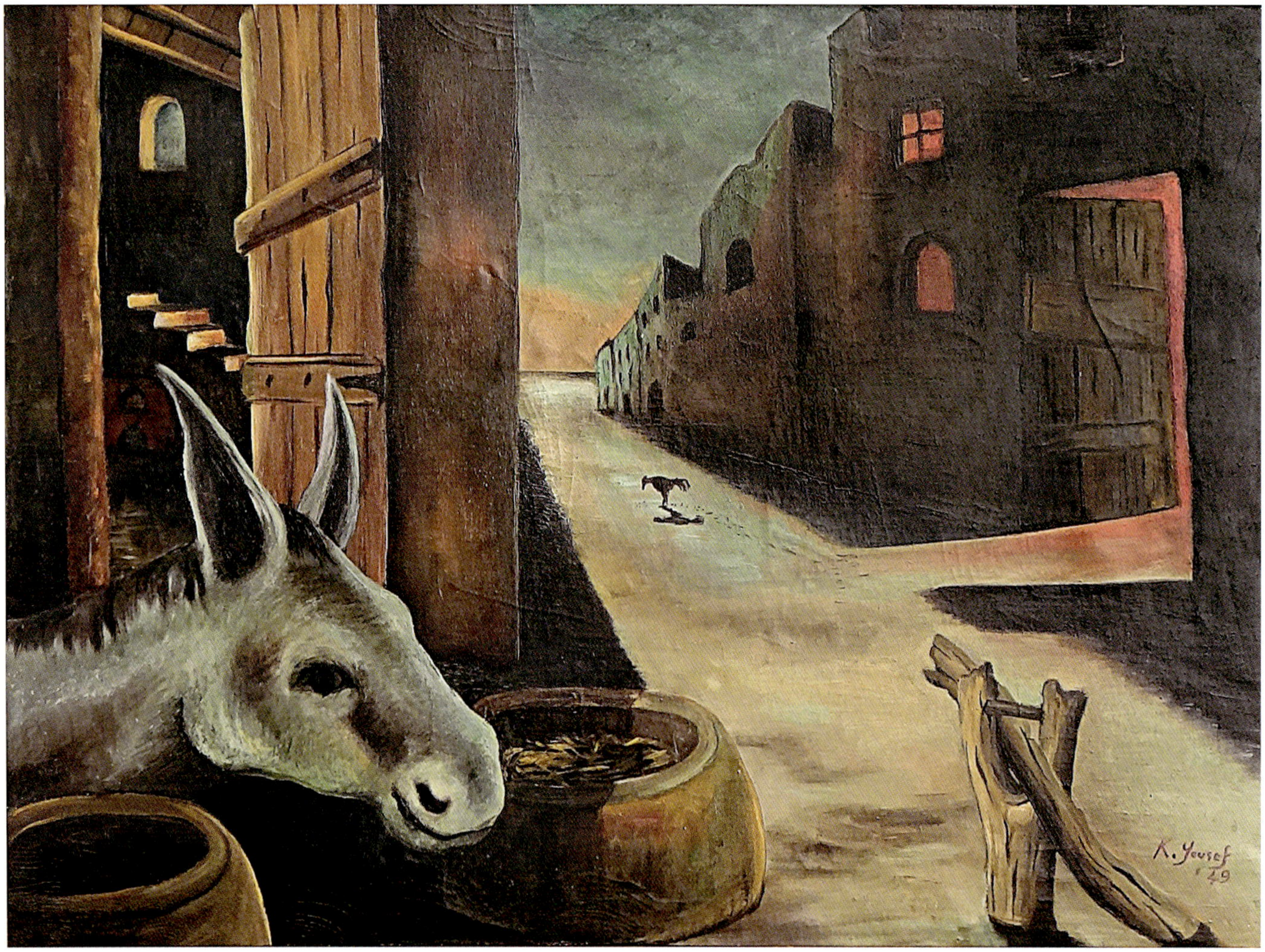

1

1
KAMAL YOUSSEF
The Sunset in the Village, 1949
Oil on canvas
74 x 108 cm
Private collection

2
HAMED NADA
The Possessed, 1952
Oil on canvas
132.2 x 79.4 cm
Private collection

2

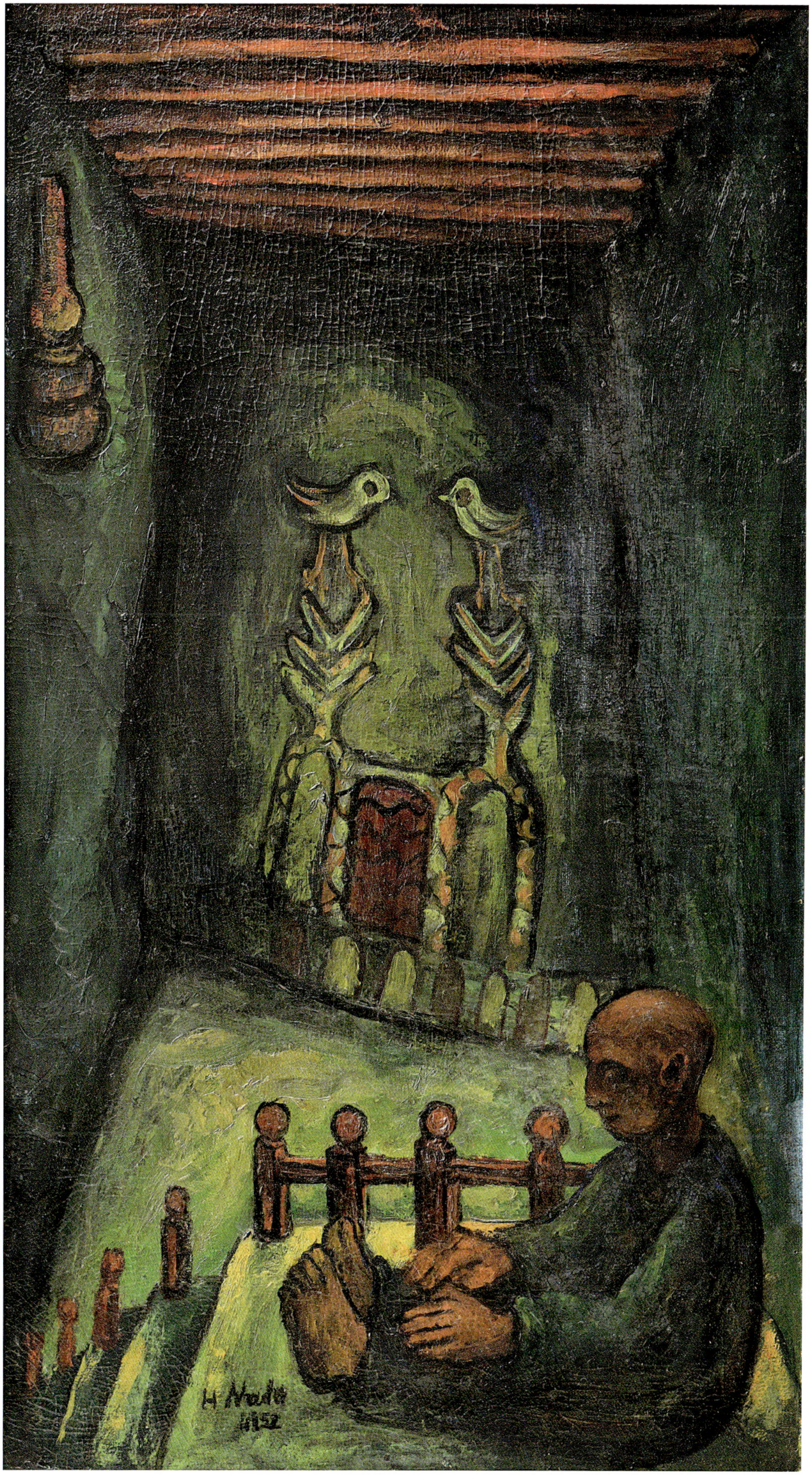

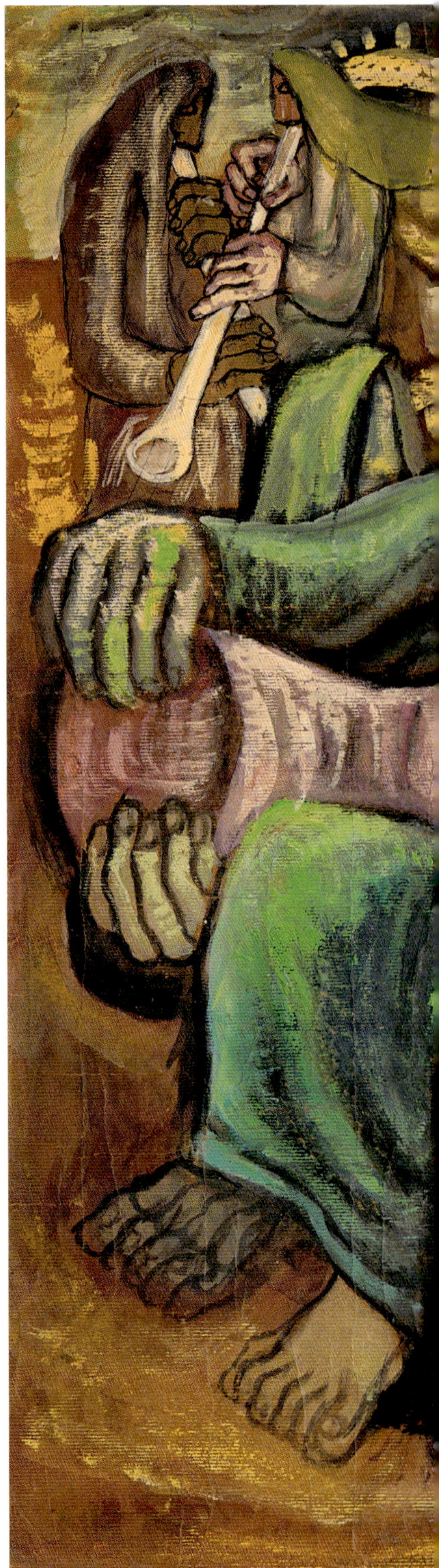

MAHER RA'EF
Untitled, 1948
65 x 74 cm
Gouache and ink on paper
Private collection, Cairo

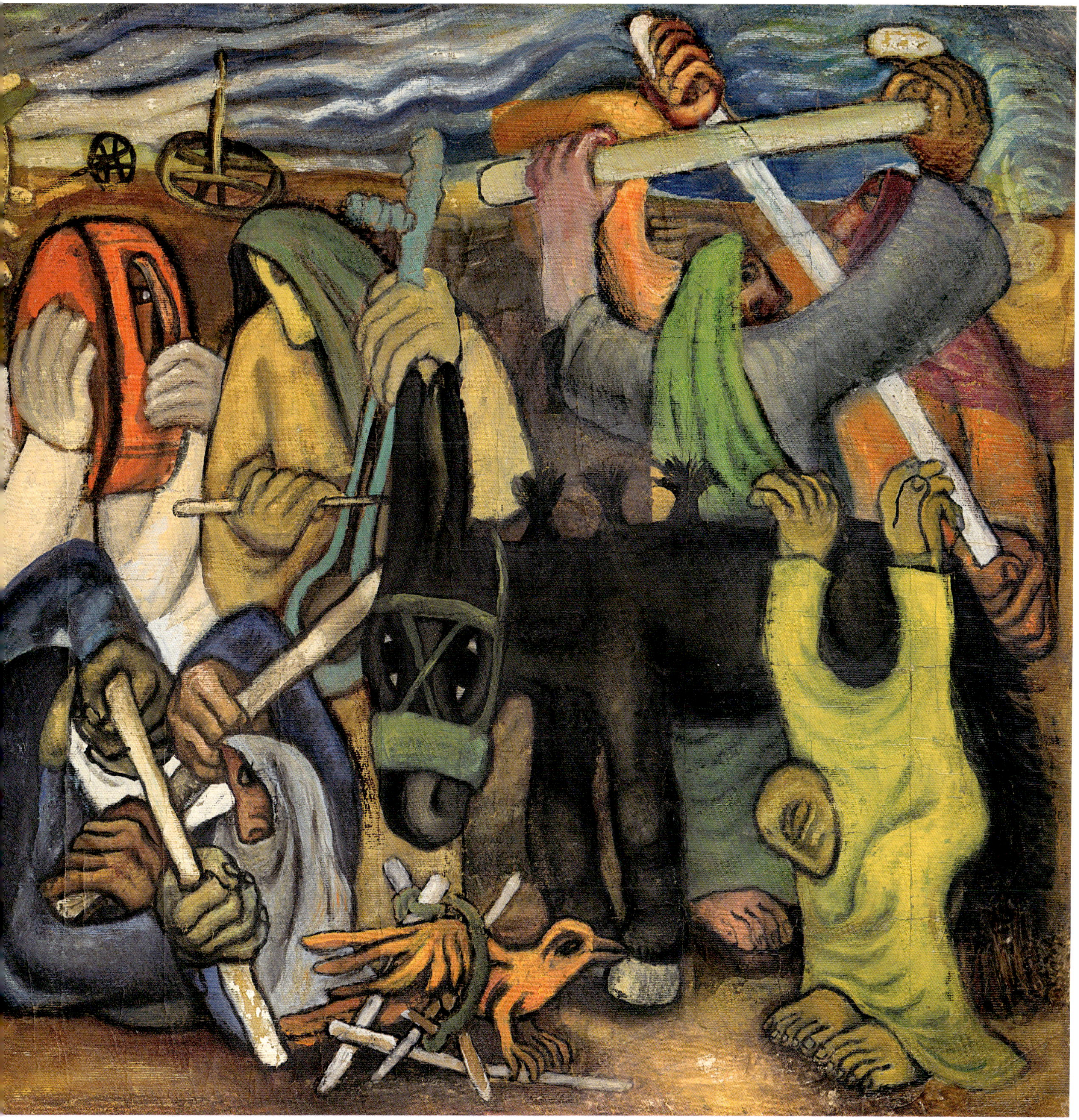

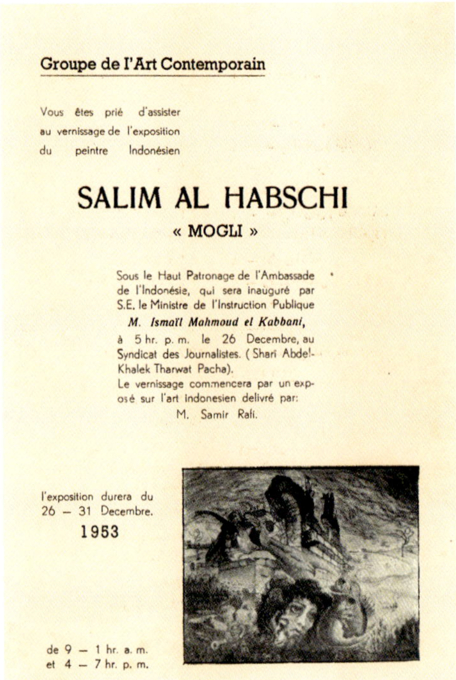
Groupe de l'Art Contemporain

Vous êtes prié d'assister
au vernissage de l'exposition
du peintre Indonésien

SALIM AL HABSCHI
« MOGLI »

Sous le Haut Patronage de l'Ambassade
de l'Indonésie, qui sera inauguré par
S.E. le Ministre de l'Instruction Publique
M. Ismaïl Mahmoud el Kabbani,
à 5 hr. p. m. le 26 Decembre, au
Syndicat des Journalistes. (Shari Abdel-
Khalek Tharwat Pacha).
Le vernissage commencera par un exp-
osé sur l'art indonesien delivré par:
M. Samir Rafi.

l'exposition durera du
26 – 31 Decembre.
1953

de 9 – 1 hr. a. m.
et 4 – 7 hr. p. m.

1

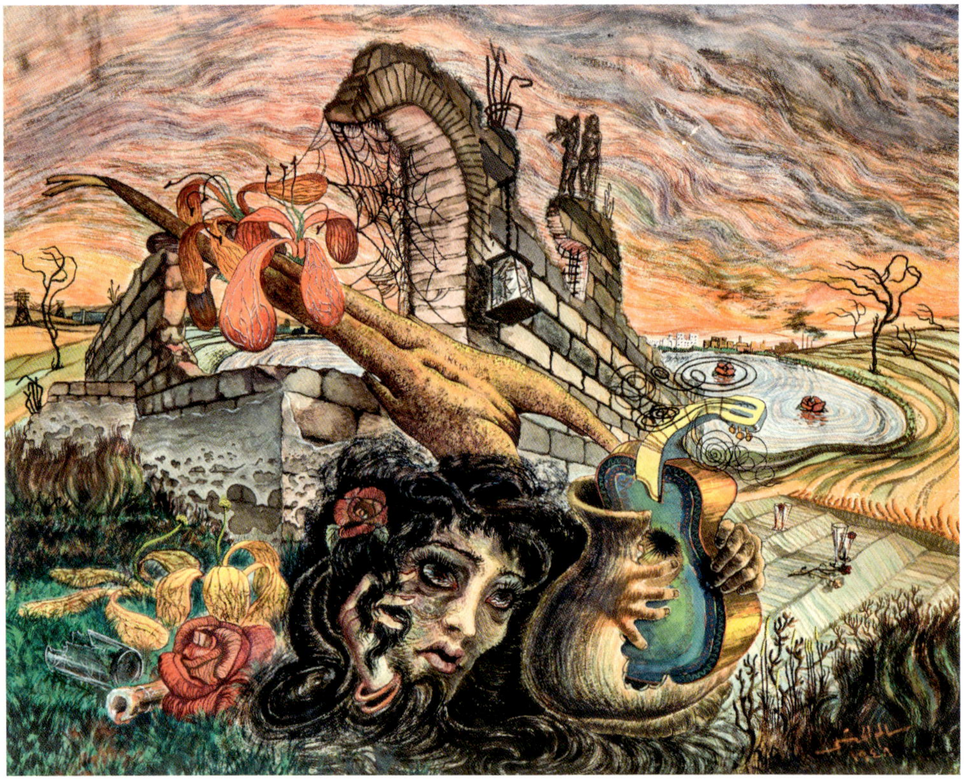

2

1
Catalogue cover of an exhibition
for Salim Al-Habschi (Mogli),1953
Cardboard
Al Masar Gallery for Contemporary Art, Cairo

2
SALIM AL-HABSCHI
Untitled (Au Bord du Lac), 1948
Ink and pastel on paper
47 x 60 cm
Al Masar Gallery for Contemporary Art, Cairo;
private collection, Cairo

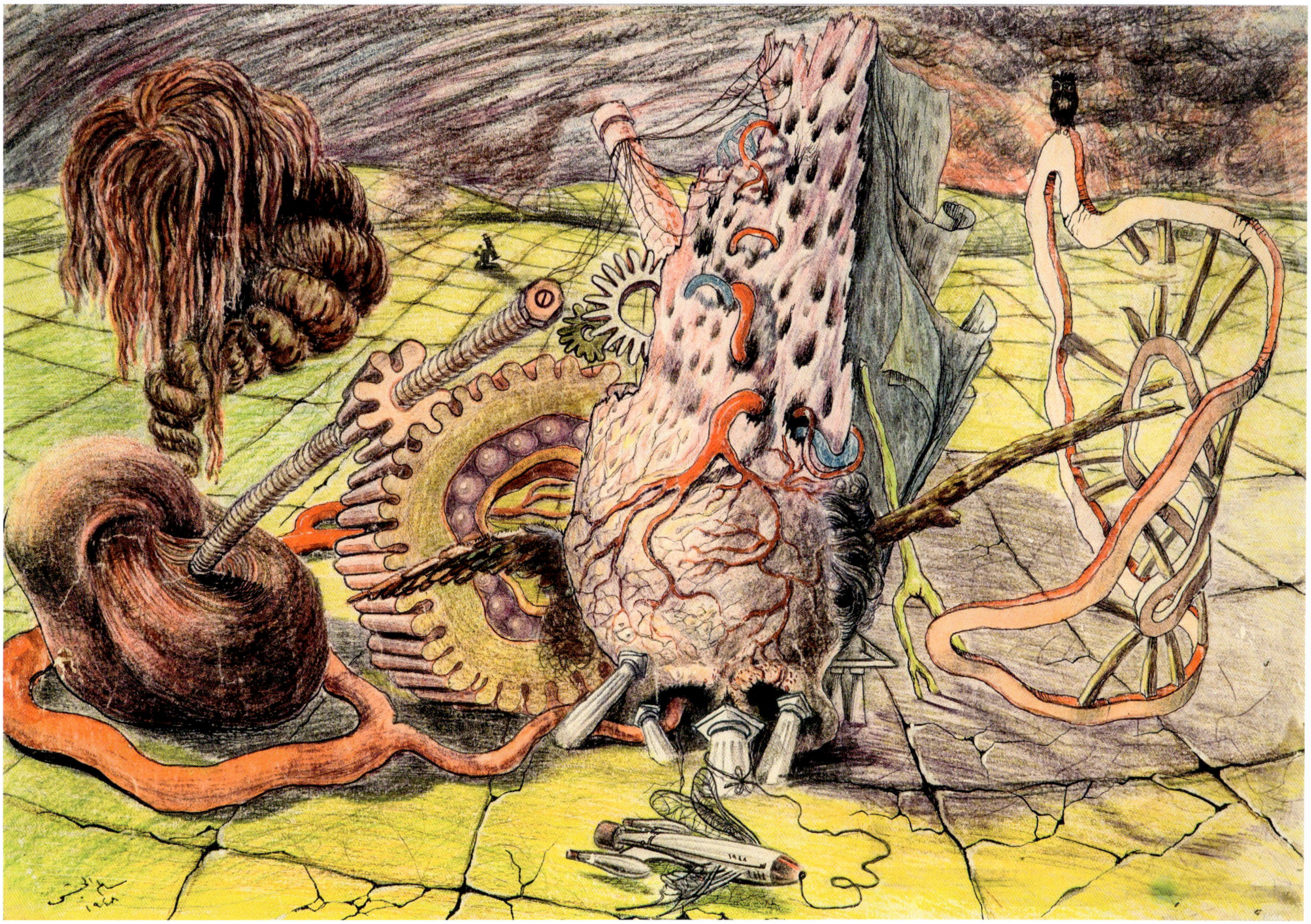

3

3
SALIM AL-HABSCHI
Untitled (Naufrages), 1948
Ink and pastel on paper
37 x 54 cm
Al Masar Gallery for Contemporary Art, Cairo;
private collection, Cairo

IBRAHIM MASSOUDA
Adam and Ève, 1950
Oil on board
41 x 42 cm
Fatenn Mostafa Kanafani collection, Cairo

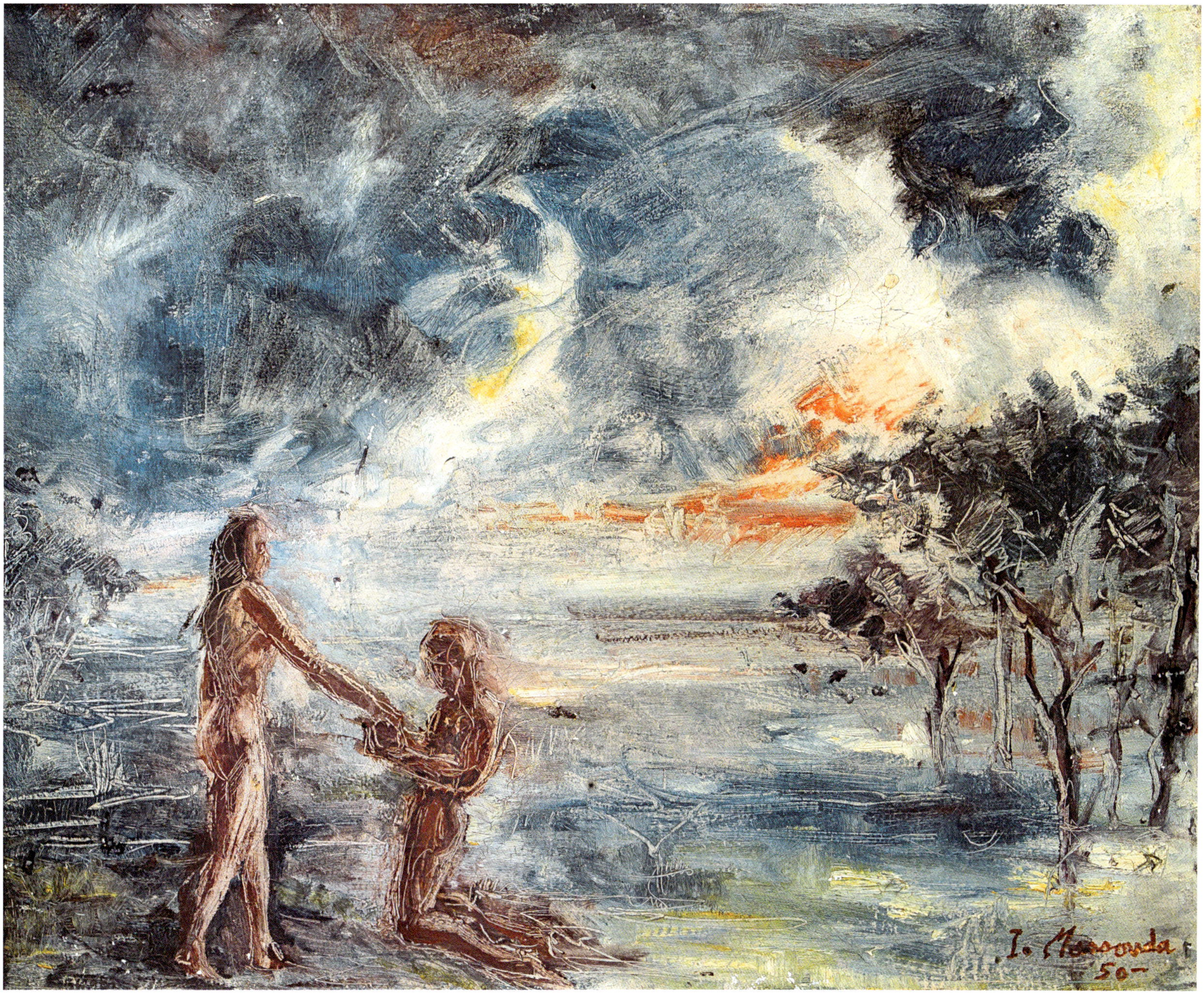

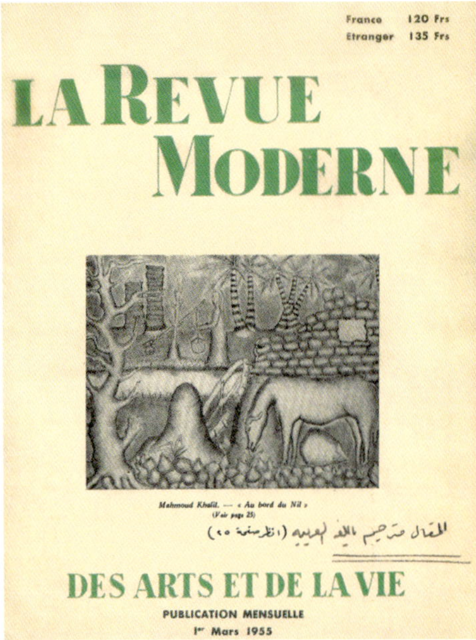

1

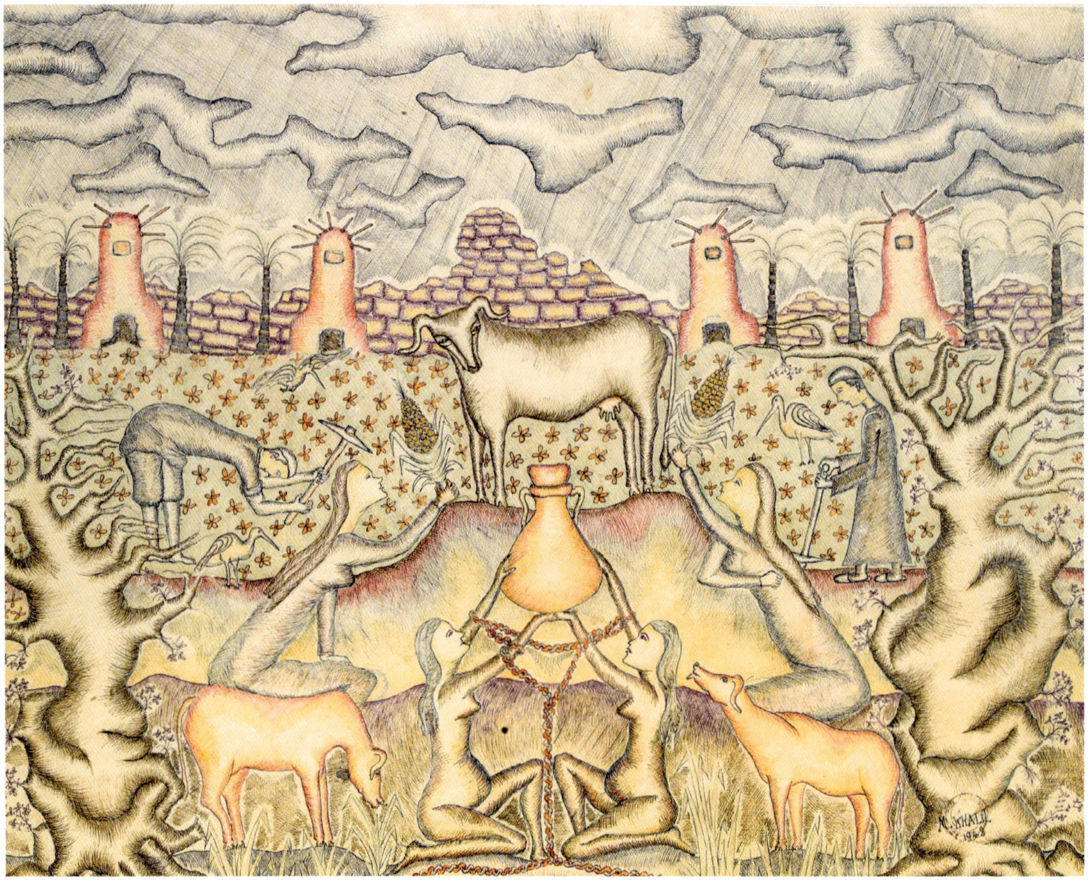

2

1
MAHMOUD KHALIL
Au bord du Nil
Cover illustration for *La Revue Moderne*,
March 1, 1953.
Printed paper
Al Masar Gallery for Contemporary Art, Cairo

2
MAHMOUD KHALIL
Campagne, 1948
Coloured ink on paper
55.5 x 71 cm
Al Masar Gallery for Contemporary Art, Cairo;
private collection, Cairo

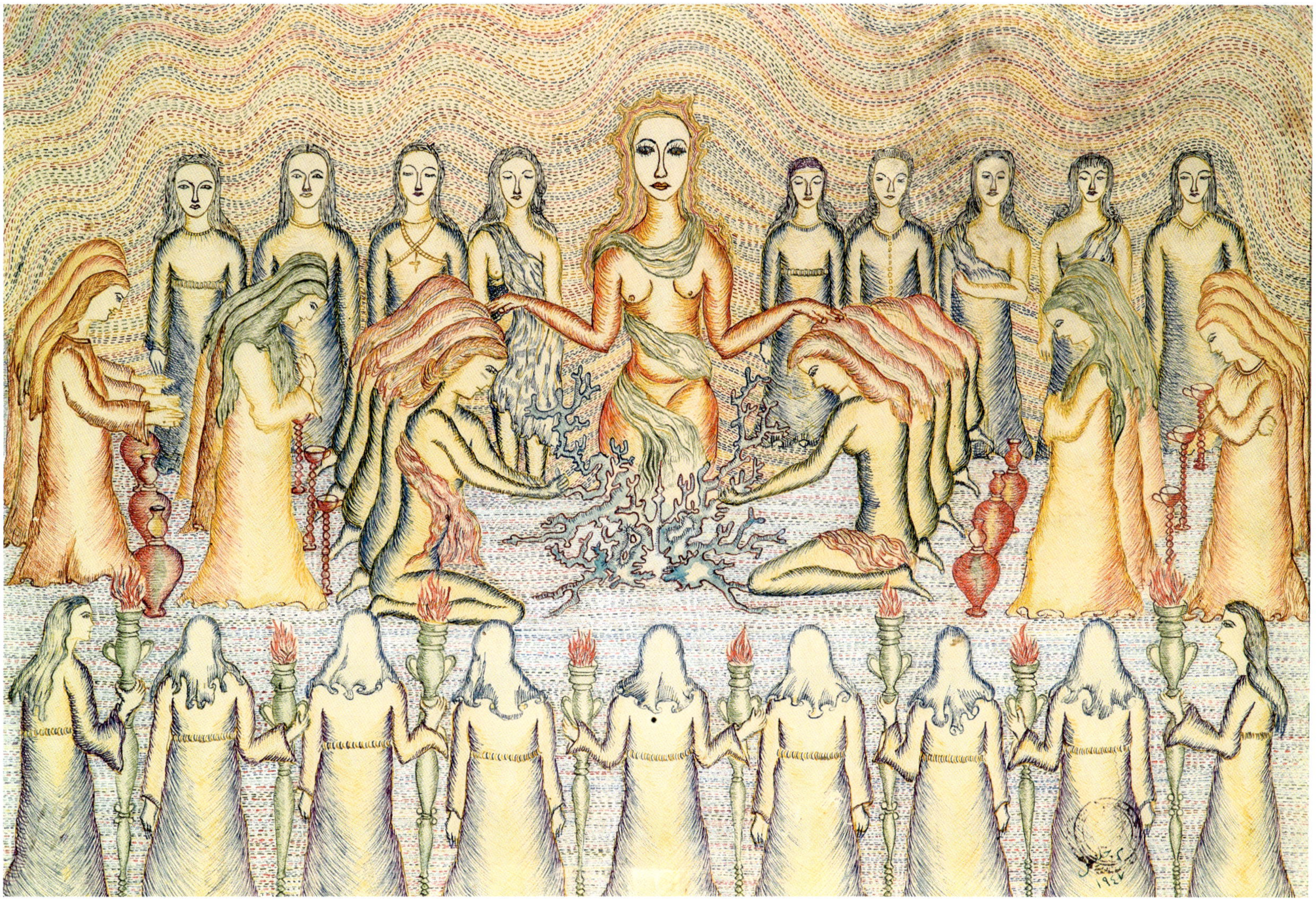

3

3
MAHMOUD KHALIL
Vertu, 1947
Coloured ink on paper
36.5 x 54.7 cm
Al Masar Gallery for Contemporary Art, Cairo;
private collection, Cairo

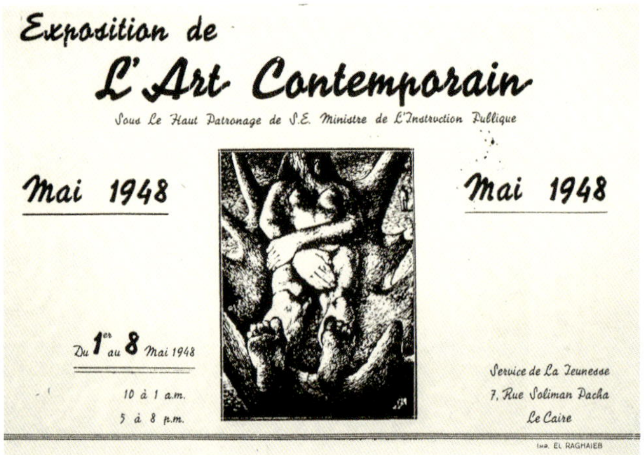

1

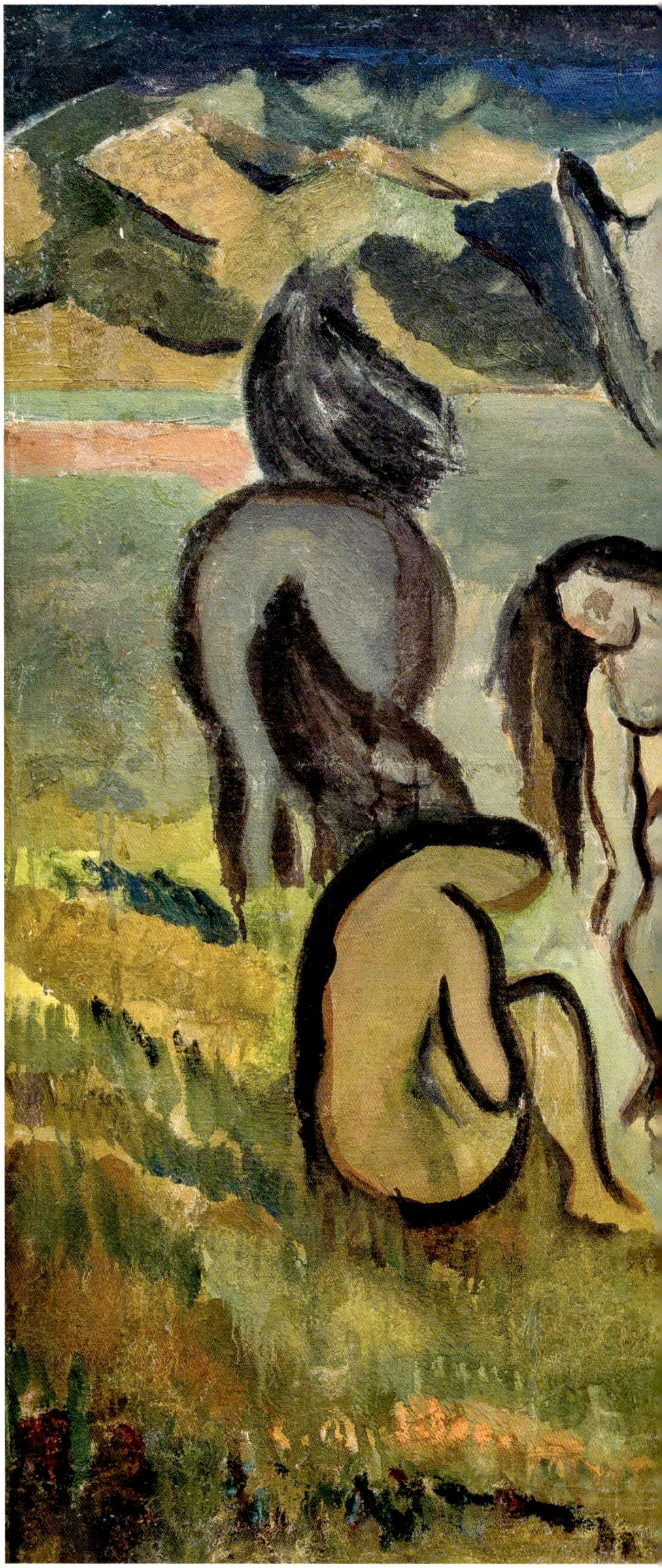

2

1
The Contemporary Art Group
second exhibition catalogue, 1948
Paper booklet
Safarkhan Art Gallery, Cairo

2
HUSSEIN YOUSSEF AMIN
Nude on Shell, 1948
Oil on canvas
89 x 118 cm
Al Masar Gallery for Contemporary Art, Cairo;
private collection, Cairo

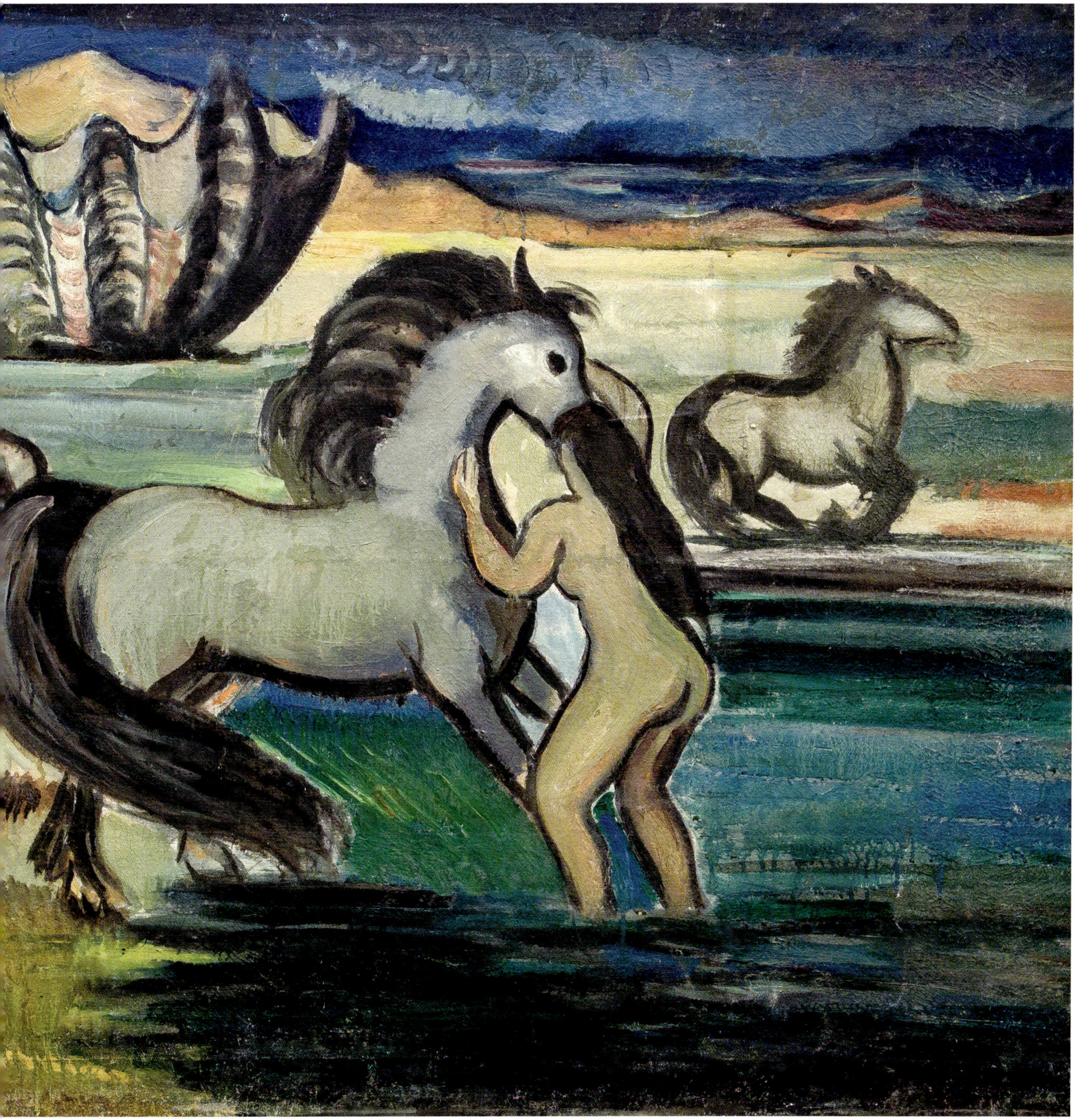

"WRITING WITH PICTURES"

Albert Cossery, *La Semaine Égyptienne*, March 17, 1941

The correlation between the written word and the pictorial image is one of the exceptional attributes of *Art and Liberty* and evidence to the fact that they were mining their own immediate artistic and intellectual circles for pictorial and literary stimulation. *Art and Liberty* ran two publishing houses, Les Éditions Masses and La Part du Sable, which in a span of just under two decades published more than thirty books including such significant authors like Yves Bonnefoy, Jean Grenier, Edmond Jabès, and Philippe Soupault.

It was not uncommon for the writers amongst the group to seek out their fellow artists in order to illustrate their publications. Kamel El-Telmisany executed the illustrations for both, Georges Henein's *Déraisons d'êtres* (Paris: J. Corti, 1938), and Cossery's *Les hommes oubliés de Dieu* (Cairo: Éditions de La Semaine Égyptienne, 1941). Fouad Kamel provided the illustrations for *Phantasmes* (Cairo: Éditions Horus, 1942) by Horus Schenouda, a writer loosely affiliated to the group, as well as to numerous articles in the leftist magazine *Al-Majallah Al-Jadidah* that would serve as a mouthpiece for *Art and Liberty*'s artistic and cultural position. The Hungarian Eric de Nemes who had moved from Beirut to Cairo in 1939–40 completed a series of fourteen drawings that were meant to illustrate John Waller's unpublished *The Lovely and the Dead*. Reversibly, the Surrealist poetry of Henein fueled the imagination of his fellow group members resulting in some of *Art and Liberty*'s most striking artworks. Equally so, Cossery's treatment of the destitute in the book of short stories *Les hommes oubliés de Dieu,* present the reader with a condemnation of the tragedy of immobile fates with meticulous naturalism and poetic sobriety. This dialogical dynamic reflects the truly multidisciplinary nature of *Art and Liberty*.

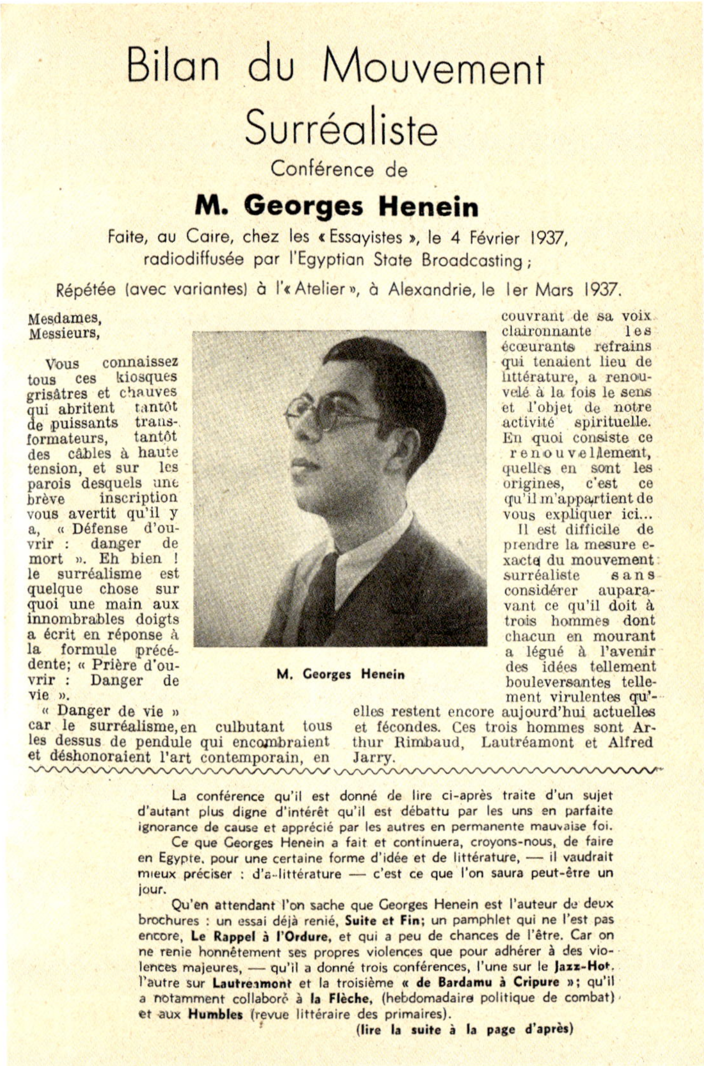

Bilan du Mouvement Surréaliste

Conférence de

M. Georges Henein

Faite, au Caire, chez les « Essayistes », le 4 Février 1937, radiodiffusée par l'Egyptian State Broadcasting ;

Répétée (avec variantes) à l'« Atelier », à Alexandrie, le 1er Mars 1937.

Mesdames,
Messieurs,

Vous connaissez tous ces kiosques grisâtres et chauves qui abritent tantôt de puissants transformateurs, tantôt des câbles à haute tension, et sur les parois desquels une brève inscription vous avertit qu'il y a, « Défense d'ouvrir : danger de mort ». Eh bien ! le surréalisme est quelque chose sur quoi une main aux innombrables doigts a écrit en réponse à la formule précédente; « Prière d'ouvrir : Danger de vie ».

M. Georges Henein

« Danger de vie » car le surréalisme, en culbutant tous les dessus de pendule qui encombraient et déshonoraient l'art contemporain, en couvrant de sa voix claironnante les écœurants refrains qui tenaient lieu de littérature, a renouvelé à la fois le sens et l'objet de notre activité spirituelle. En quoi consiste ce renouvellement, quelles en sont les origines, c'est ce qu'il m'appartient de vous expliquer ici...

Il est difficile de prendre la mesure exacte du mouvement surréaliste sans considérer auparavant ce qu'il doit à trois hommes dont chacun en mourant a légué à l'avenir des idées tellement bouleversantes tellement virulentes qu'elles restent encore aujourd'hui actuelles et fécondes. Ces trois hommes sont Arthur Rimbaud, Lautréamont et Alfred Jarry.

La conférence qu'il est donné de lire ci-après traite d'un sujet d'autant plus digne d'intérêt qu'il est débattu par les uns en parfaite ignorance de cause et apprécié par les autres en permanente mauvaise foi.

Ce que Georges Henein a fait et continuera, croyons-nous, de faire en Egypte, pour une certaine forme d'idée et de littérature, — il vaudrait mieux préciser : d'a-littérature — c'est ce que l'on saura peut-être un jour.

Qu'en attendant l'on sache que Georges Henein est l'auteur de deux brochures : un essai déjà renié, **Suite et Fin**; un pamphlet qui ne l'est pas encore, **Le Rappel à l'Ordure**, et qui a peu de chances de l'être. Car on ne renie honnêtement ses propres violences que pour adhérer à des violences majeures, — qu'il a donné trois conférences, l'une sur le **Jazz-Hot**, l'autre sur **Lautreamont** et la troisième **« de Bardamu à Cripure »**; qu'il a notamment collaboré à **la Flèche**, (hebdomadaire politique de combat) et aux **Humbles** (revue littéraire des primaires).

(lire la suite à la page d'après)

1

"Ladies and Gentlemen, you all know these grayish bland kiosks that sometimes contain powerful transformers or high voltage cables, and on whose doors a brief inscription warns you: 'Do not open: danger of death.'

Well! Surrealism is something on which a hand with countless fingers has written in response to the previous formula: 'Please open: danger of life.'"

Georges Henein, "Bilan du Mouvement Surréaliste," 1937

1
Georges Henein, « Bilan du mouvement surréaliste », 1937
Hardback book bound in leather
Henein - Farhi collection, Neuilly-sur-Seine

2
THIERRY FORMINTELLI
Surrealist Portrait of Georges Henein, undated
Mirror and plaster in wooden frame
39 x 23.5 x 3 cm
Henein - Farhi collection, Neuilly-sur-Seine

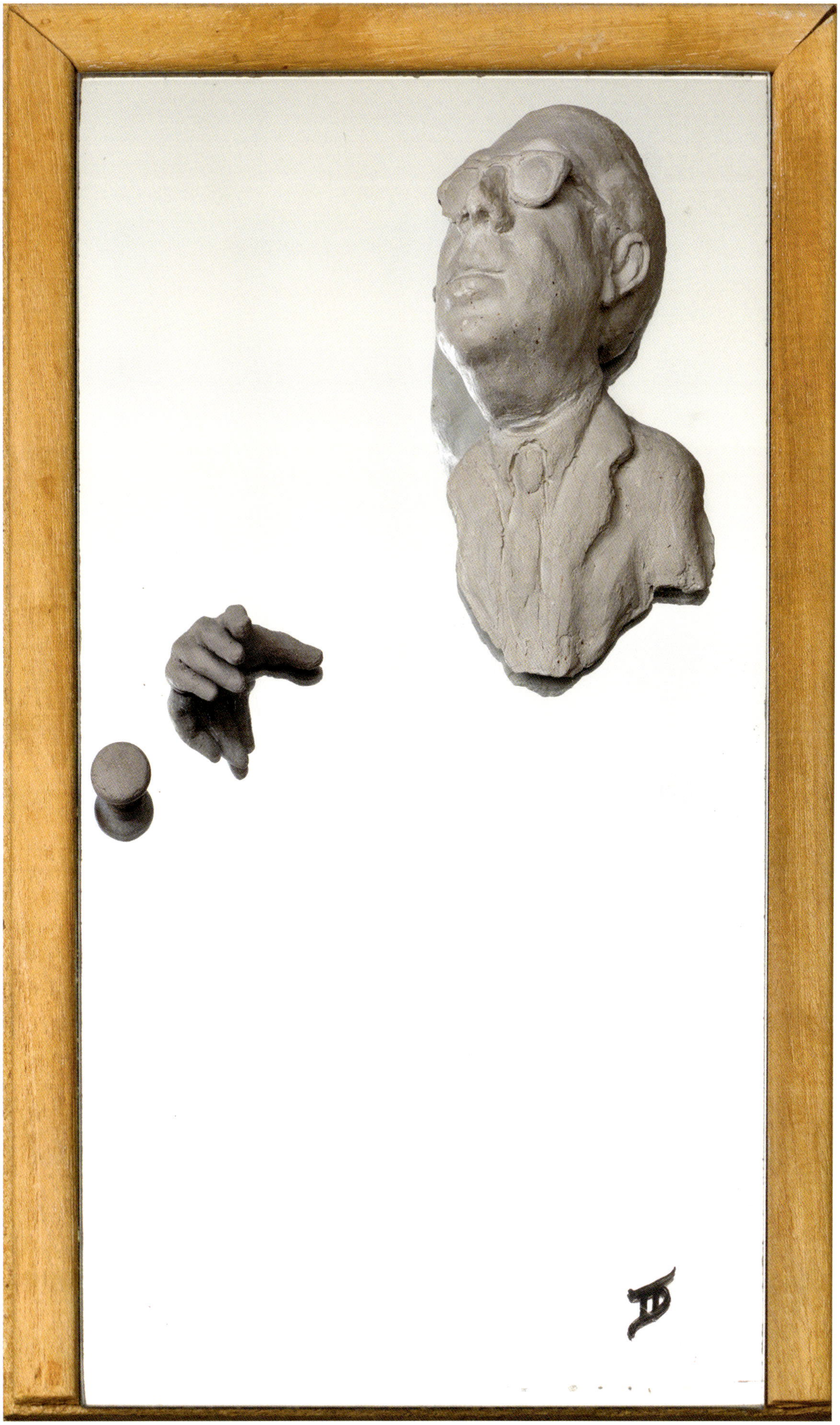

2

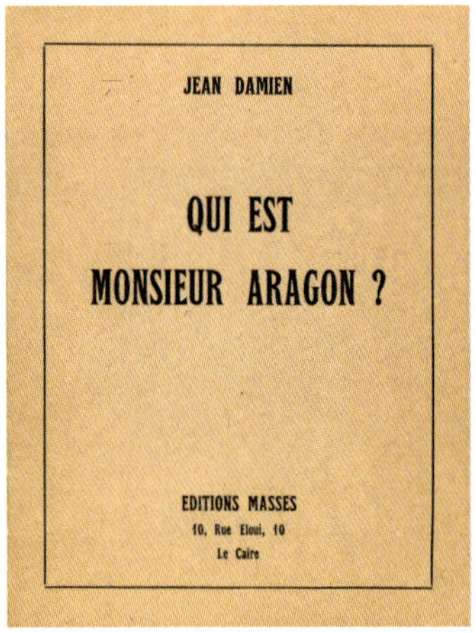

1

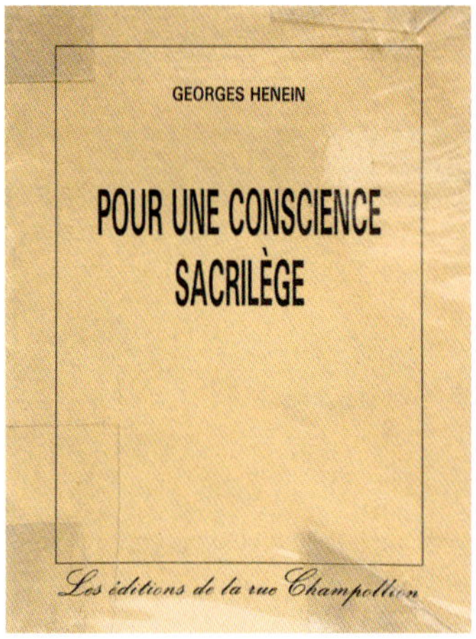

2

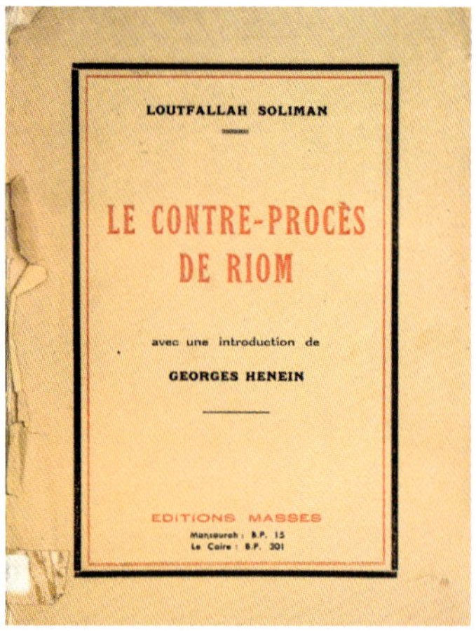

3

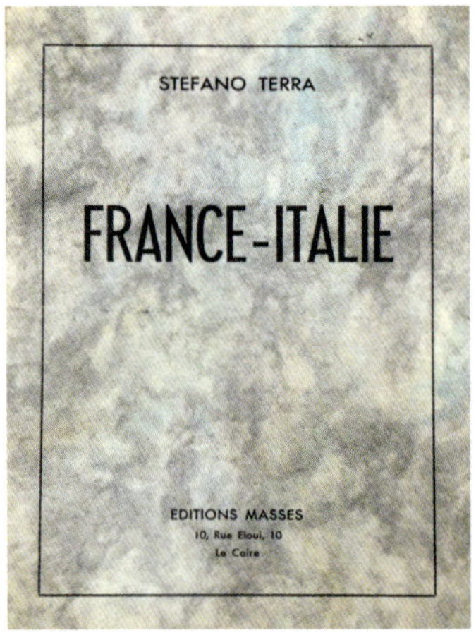

4

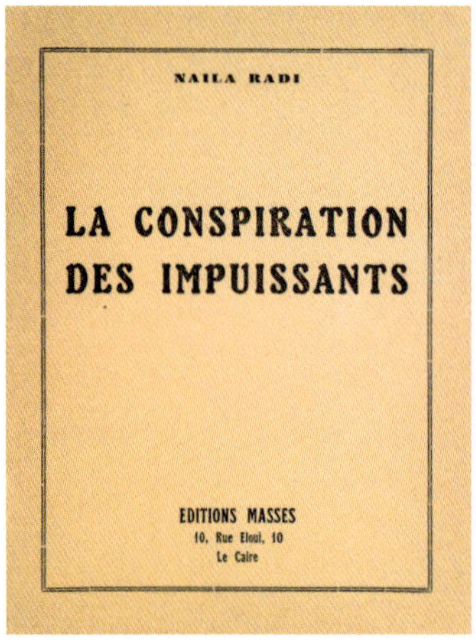

5

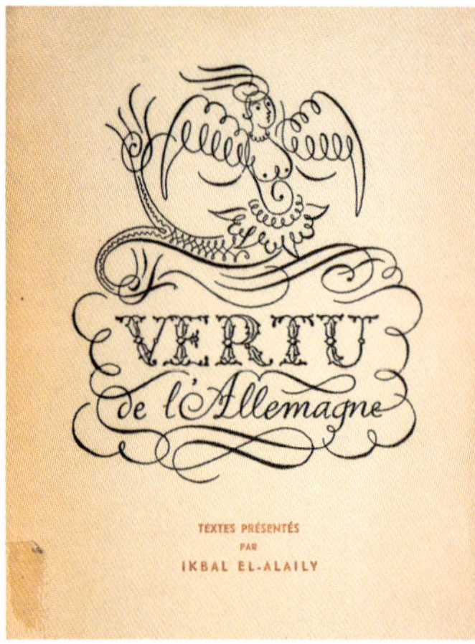

6

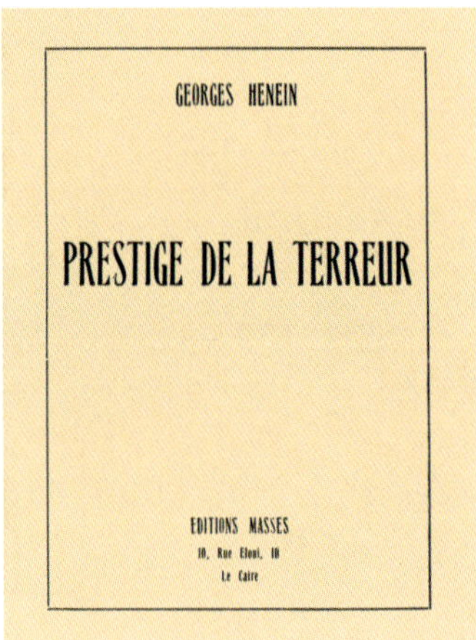

7

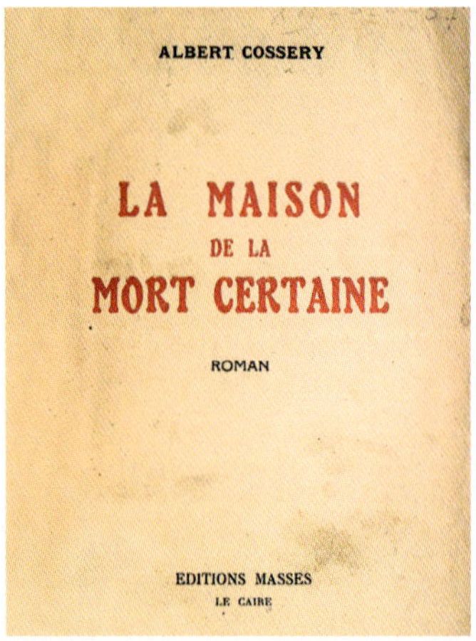

8

1-8
Publications by Editions Masses, 1944-1947

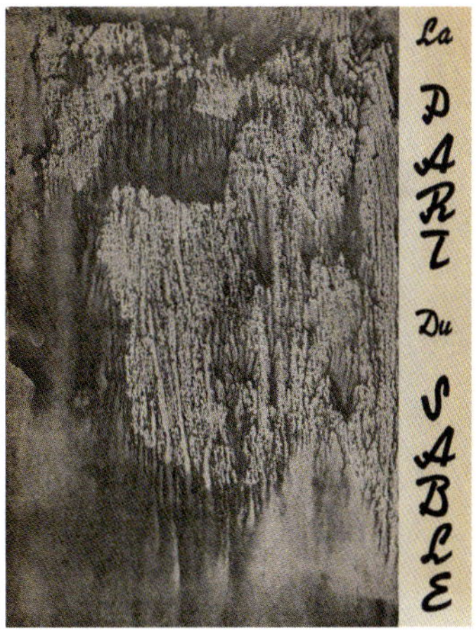

9

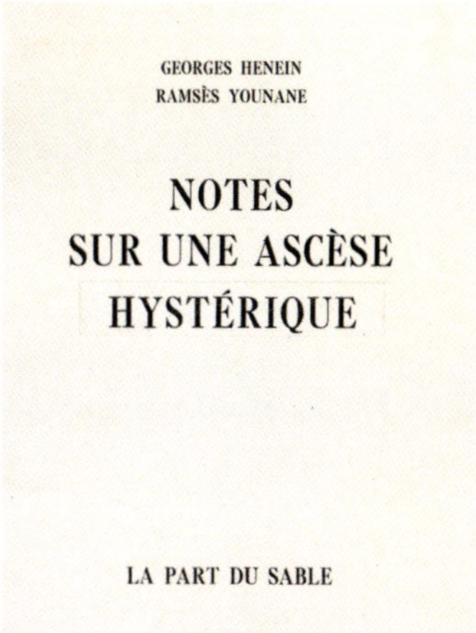

10

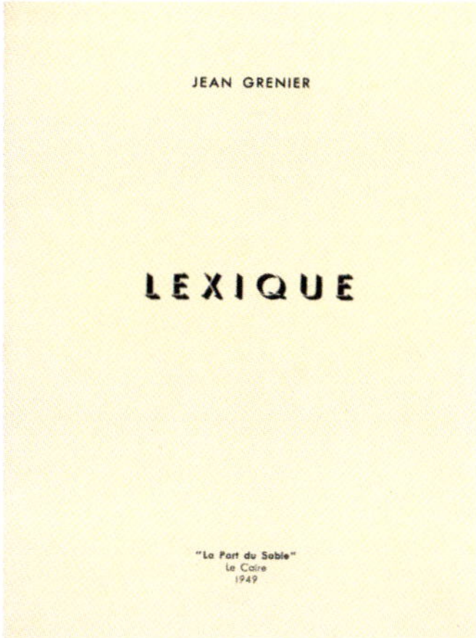

11

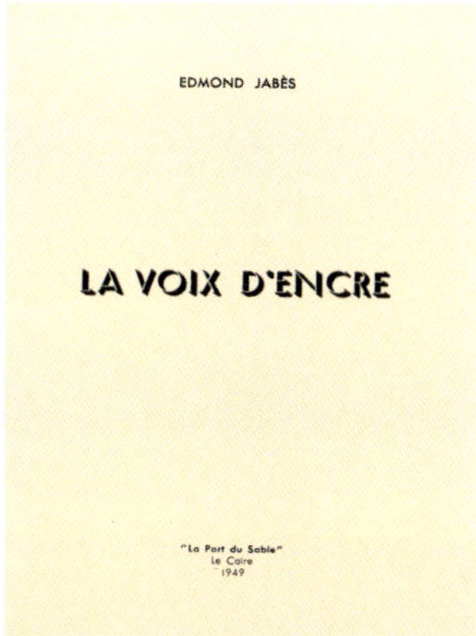

12

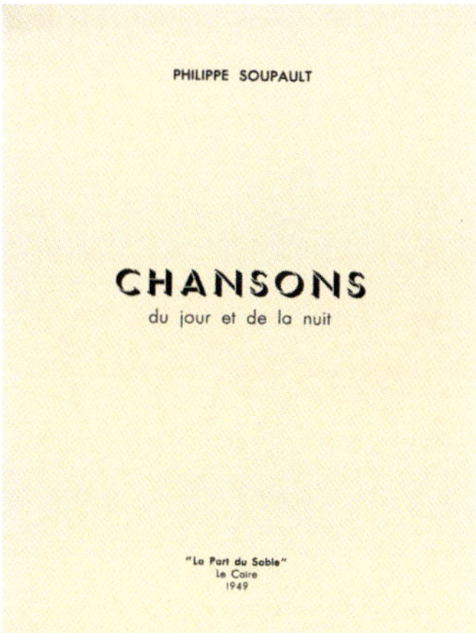

13

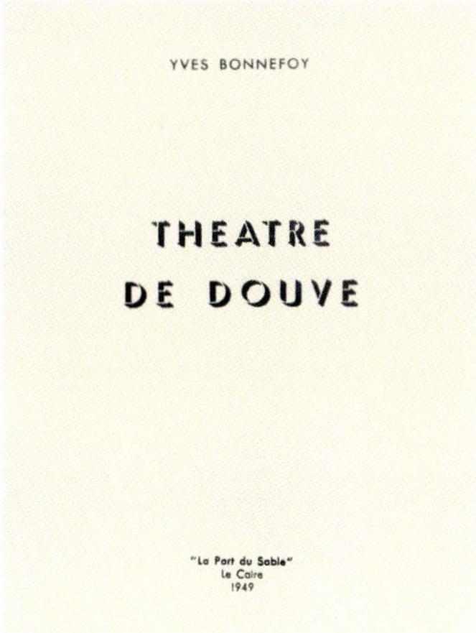

14

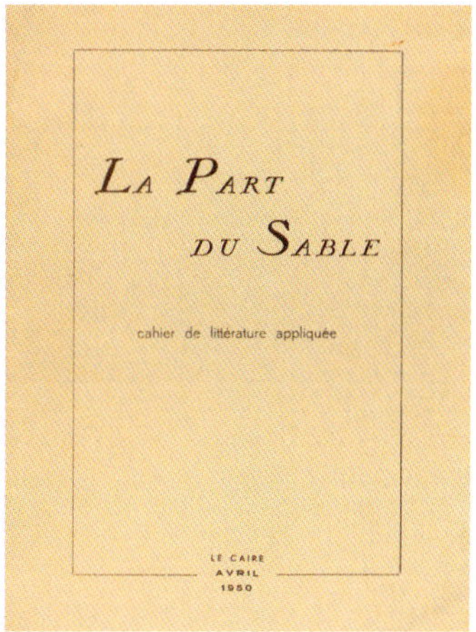

15

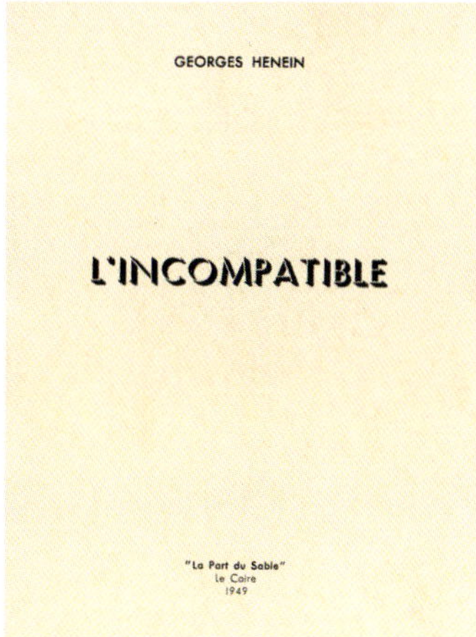

16

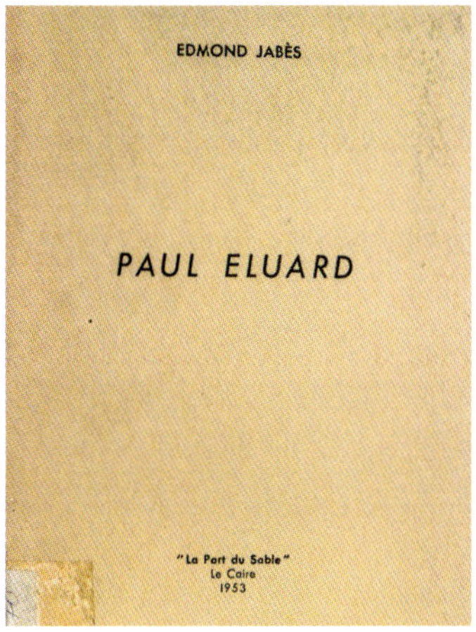

17

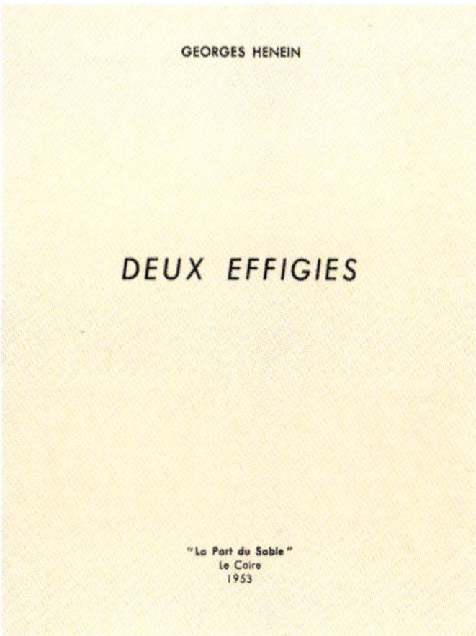

18

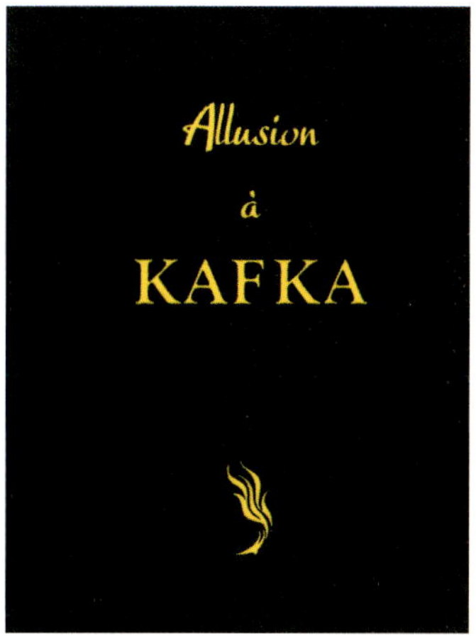

19

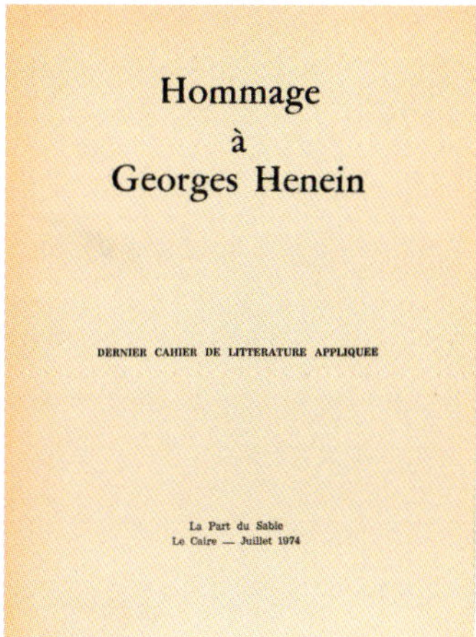

20

9-20
Publications by La Part du Sable, 1947-1973

"Watch the cities loose their veins one after another
The country side withers from rapacious warts
Watch the ultimate wounds settle into open people."

Georges Henein, "Non-Intervention," 1938

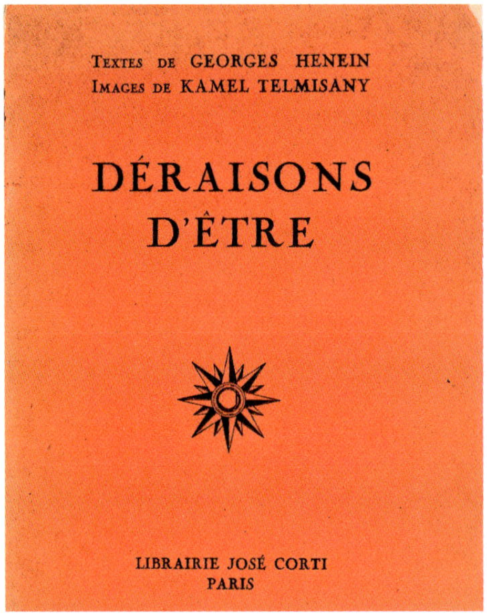

2

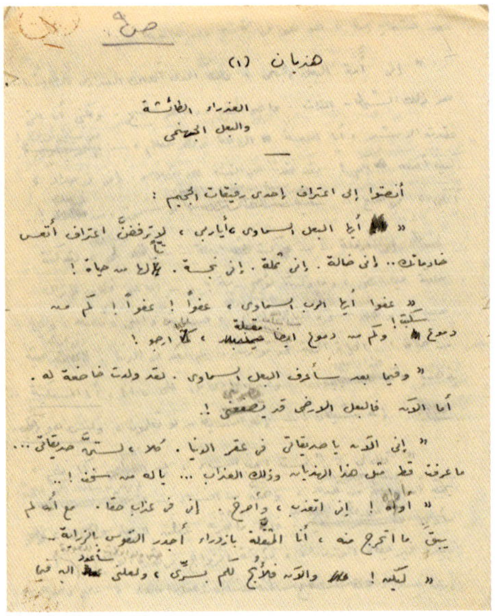

هذيان (١)

العذراء الطائشة
والبعل الجهنمي

أنصتوا إلى اعتراف إحدى رفيقات الجحيم :
« أيها البعل السماوي ، أيا رب ، لا ترفضنّ اعتراف أتعس
خادماتك .. إني ضالة . إني ثملة . إني نجسة . يا لها من حياة !
« عفواً أيها الرب السماوي ، عفواً ! عفواً ! كم من
دموع ! وكم من دموع أيضاً مقبلة ، كما أرجو !
« وفيما بعد سأعرف البعل السماوي . لقد ولدت خاضعة له .
أما الآن فالبعل الأرضي قد يصفعني !.
« إني الآن يا صديقاتي في قعر الدنيا . كلا ، لستنّ صديقاتي ...
ما عرفت قط مثل هذا الهذيان وذلك العذاب ... يا له من سخف ! ..
« أوّاه ! إني أتعذب ، وأصرخ . إني في عذاب حقاً . مع أنه لم
يبق ما أتحرج منه ، أنا المثقلة بازدراء أجدر النفوس بالزراية .
« لكنه ! والآن فلأبح لكم بسرّي ، ولعلني سأعود إليه فيما

1

"I am weary, I die. This is the grave and I'm turning into worms,
horror of horrors! Satan, you clown, you want to dissolve me
with your charms. Well, I want it. I want it!
Stab me with a pitchfork, sprinkle me with fire."

Arthur Rimbaud, *Une saison en enfer*, 1873
(translated by Paul Schmidt, and published in 1976 by Harper Colophon Books, Harper & Row)

1
RAMSES YOUNANE
Translation of Arthur Rimbaud's *Une saison en enfer*, c. 1940
Original handwritten manuscript
Centre Pompidou Paris, MNAM-CCI,
Bibliothèque Kandinsky,
donated by Sylvie Younan, 2015

2
Georges Henein, *Déraisons d'être*,
illustrations by Kamel El-Telmisany, 1938
Paperback
Bibliothèque Sainte-Geneviève, Paris

3 (not exhibited)
RAMSES YOUNANE
A la surface du sable, c. 1939
Pencil on paper
27 x 22.5 cm
Museum of Modern Egyptian Art, Cairo

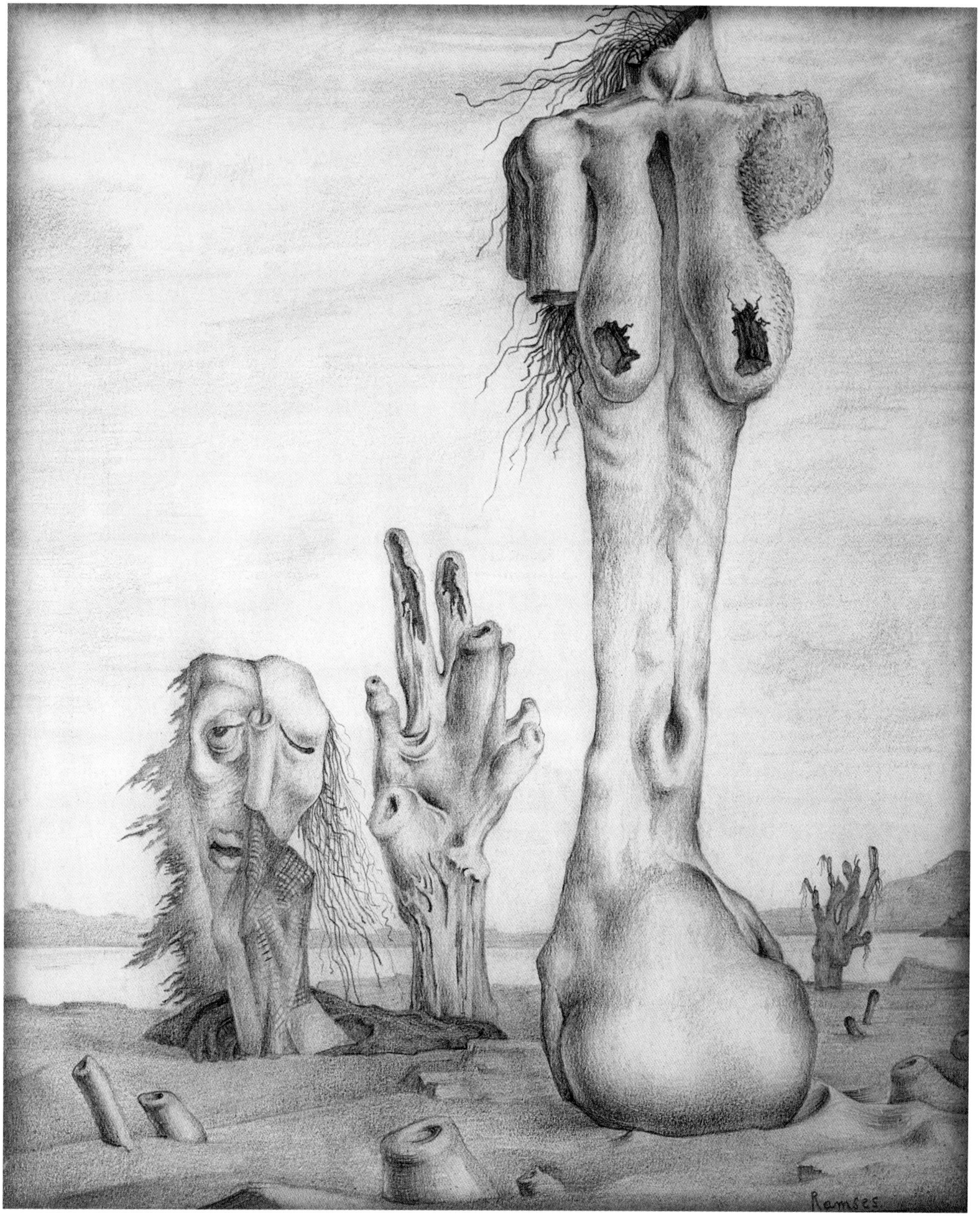

3

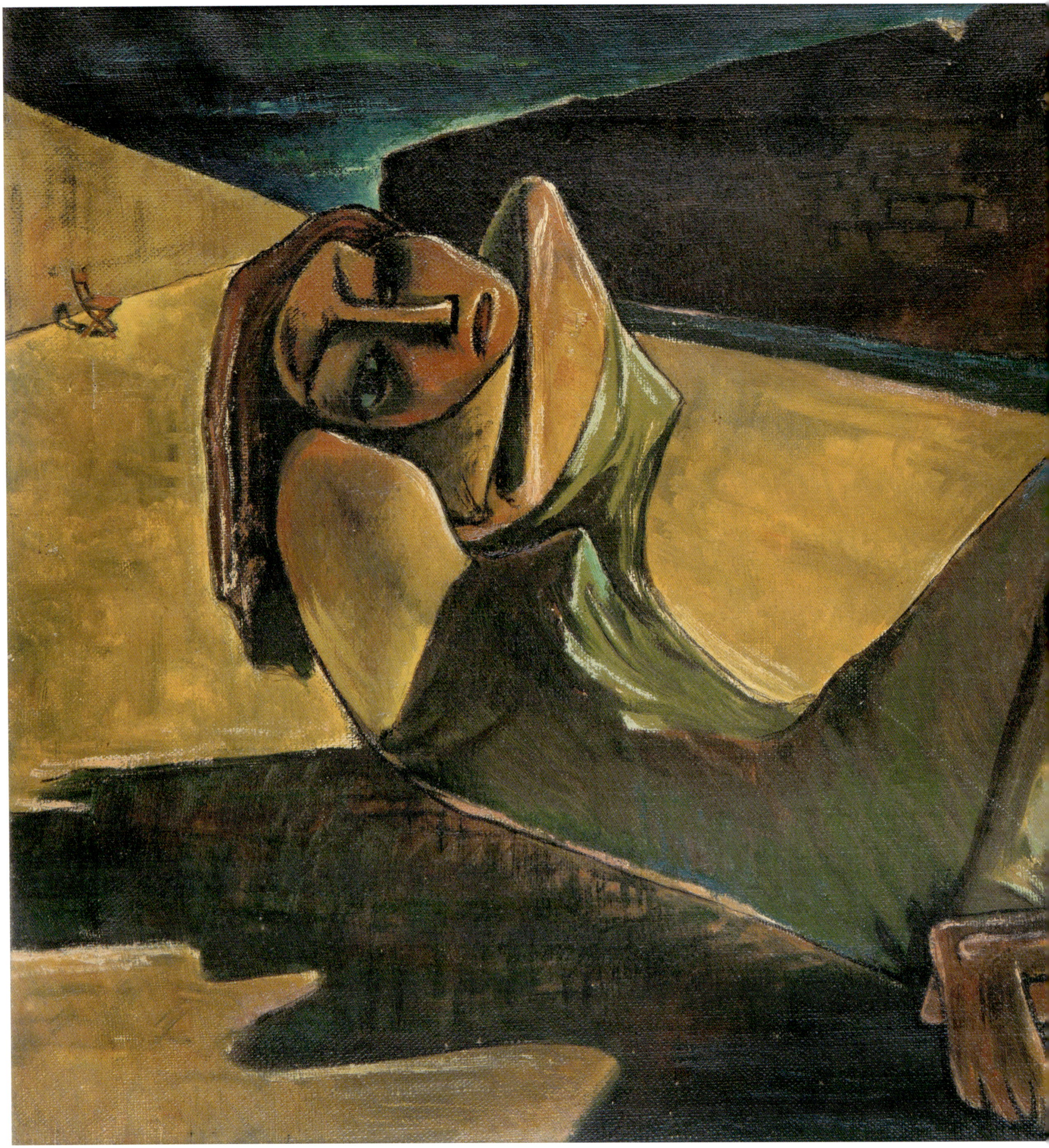

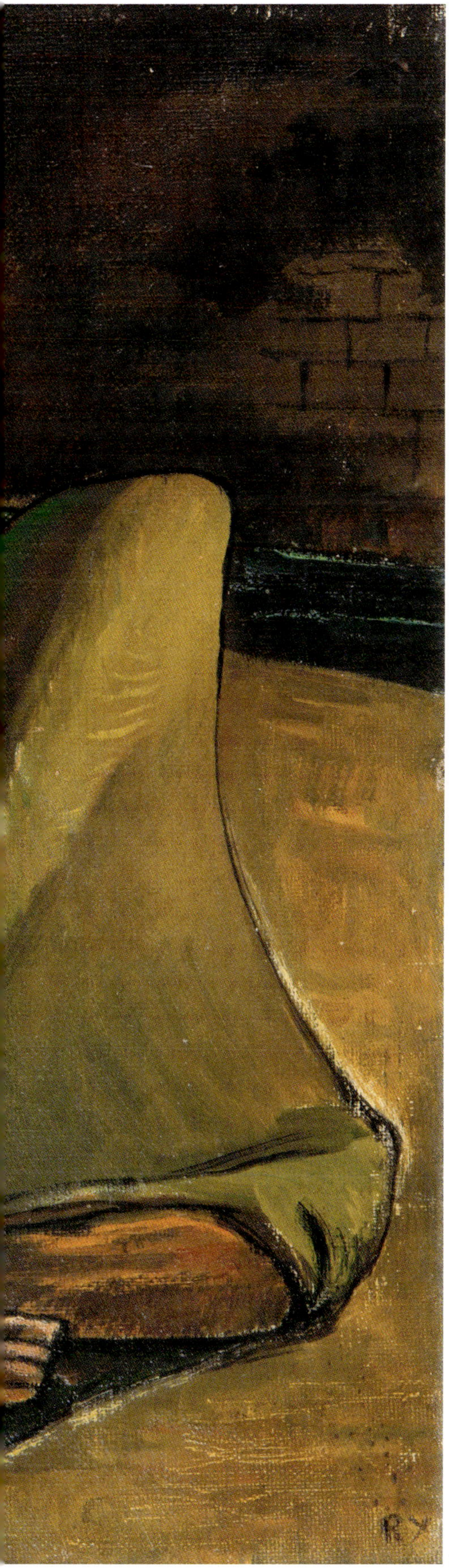

1

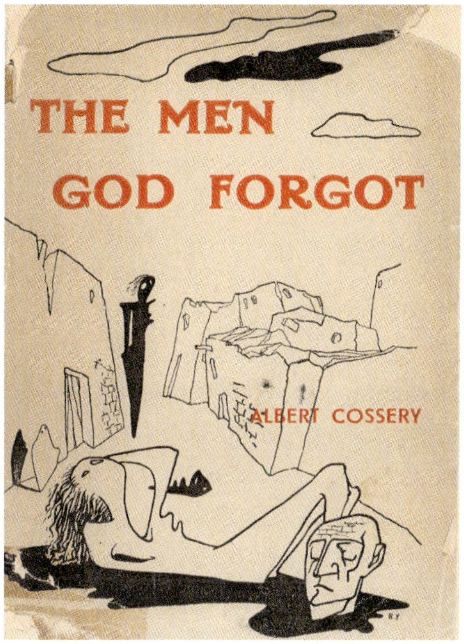

2

"There was always a woman cursing her children in a high and strident voice.

And everywhere, more or less, without preference, garbage was scattered."

Albert Cossery, "The Barber Has Killed his Wife," 1941

1
RAMSES YOUNANE
Contre le mur, 1944
Oil on canvas
37 x 47 cm
Sylvie and Sonia Younan collection, Paris

2
RAMSES YOUNANE
Cover illustration for Albert Cossery,
The Men God Forgot, 1944
Private collection, Paris

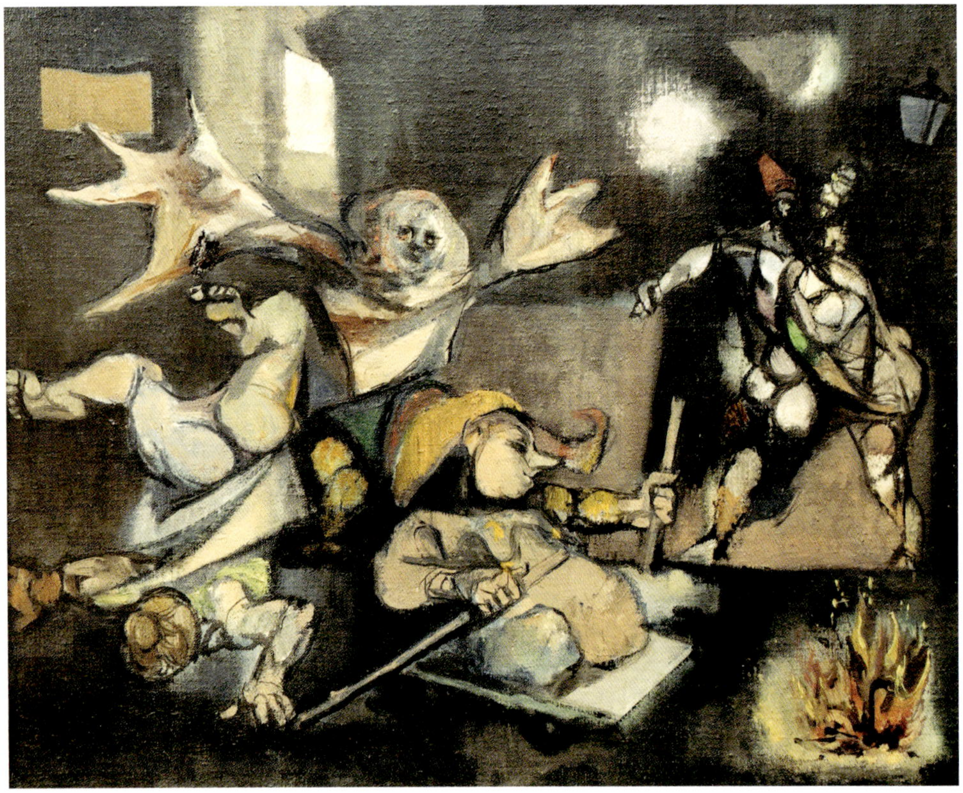

ROBERT MEDLEY
Cairo at Night, 1946
Oil on canvas
43.2 x 53.2 cm
James Hyman Gallery collection, London;
private collection

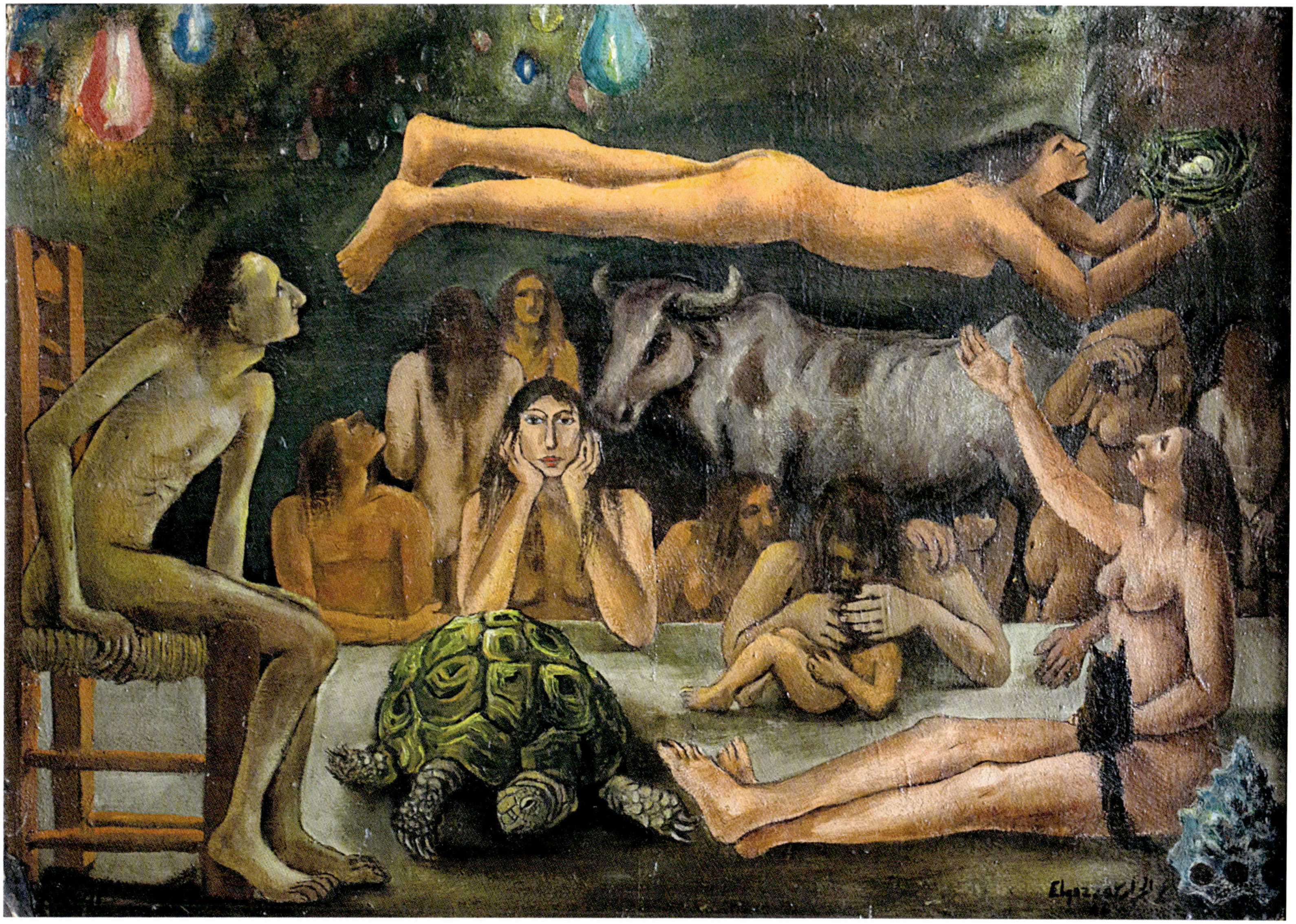

ABDEL HADI EL-GAZZAR
Carnival of Lovers, 1948
Oil on cardboard
70 x 99 cm
Naguib Sawiris collection, Cairo

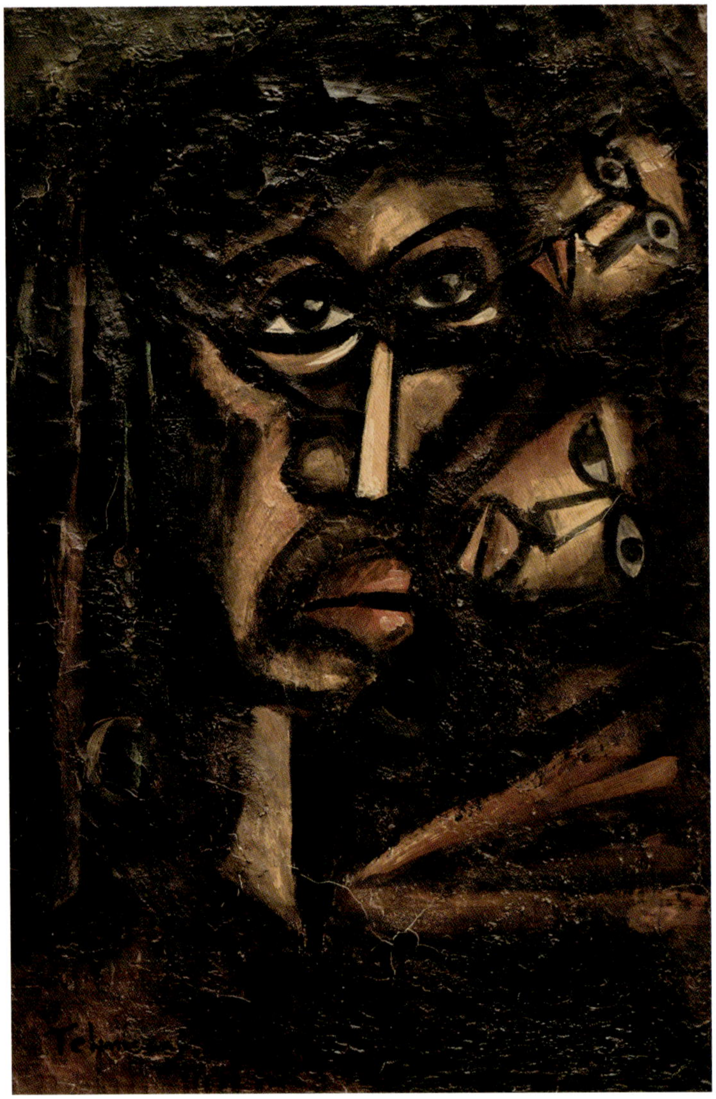

1

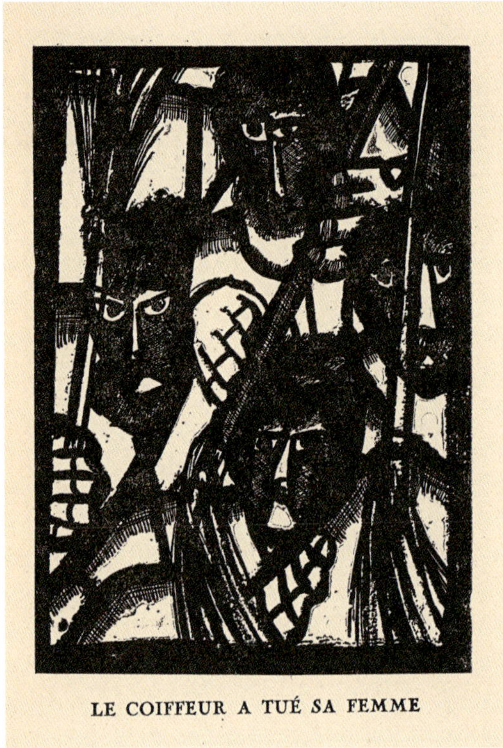

2

*"It was in Black Lane. [...]
Opposite the shop was street lamp No. 329, which squandered its official brightness over the entire lane."*

Albert Cossery, "The Barber Has Killed his Wife," 1941

1
KAMEL EL-TELMISANY
Untitled, 1942
Oil on canvas
68.5 x 46 cm
H.E. Sh. Hassan M. A. Al Thani collection, Doha

2
KAMEL EL-TELMISANY
Le coiffeur a tué sa femme, 1941
Illustration for Albert Cossery,
Les Hommes oubliés de Dieu, 1941
Henein - Farhi collection, Neuilly-sur-Seine

3
INJI EFFLATOUN
Boy and Lamp, 1941
Oil on canvas
64 x 42 cm
Yasser Hashem collection, Cairo

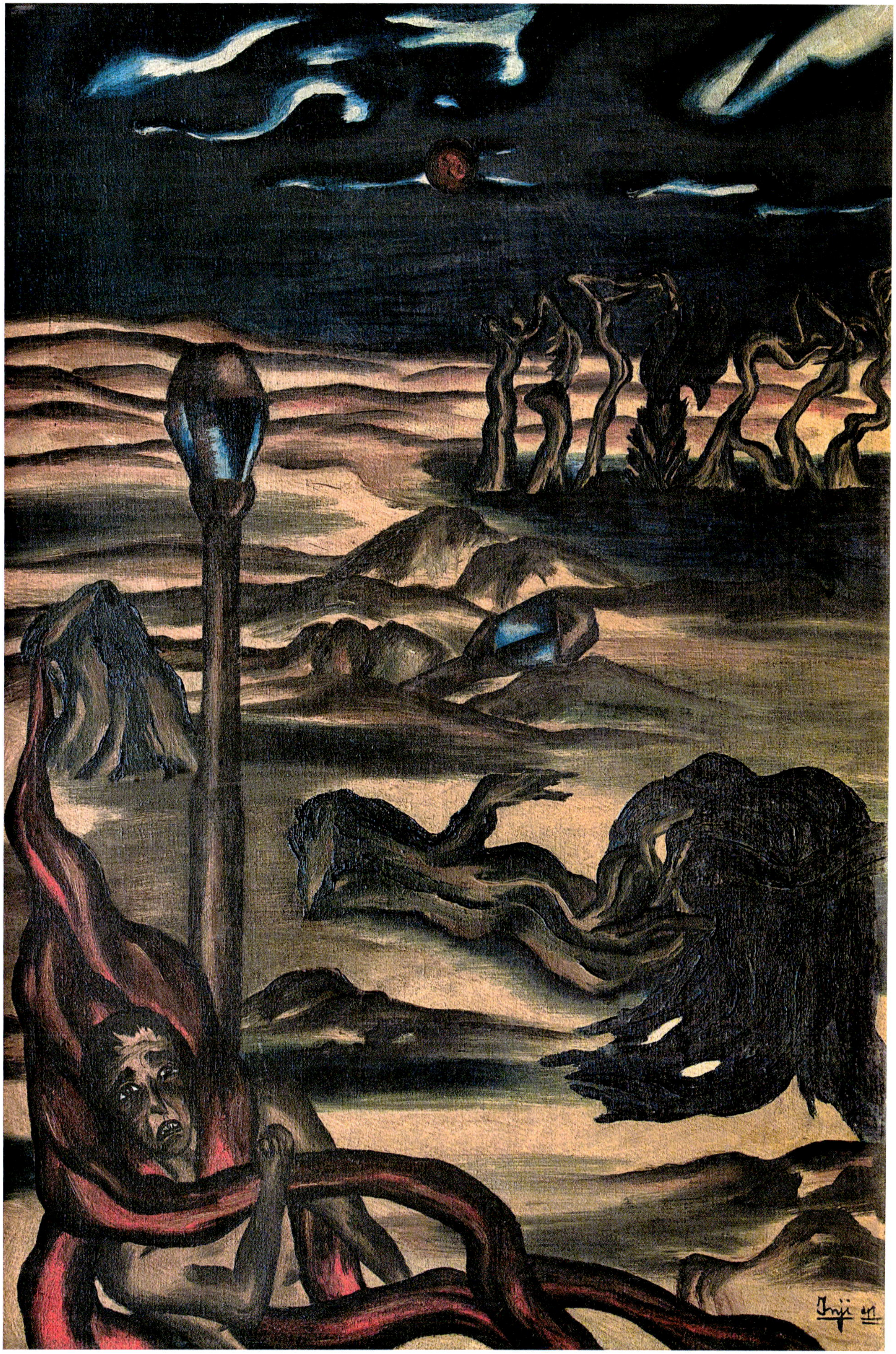

3

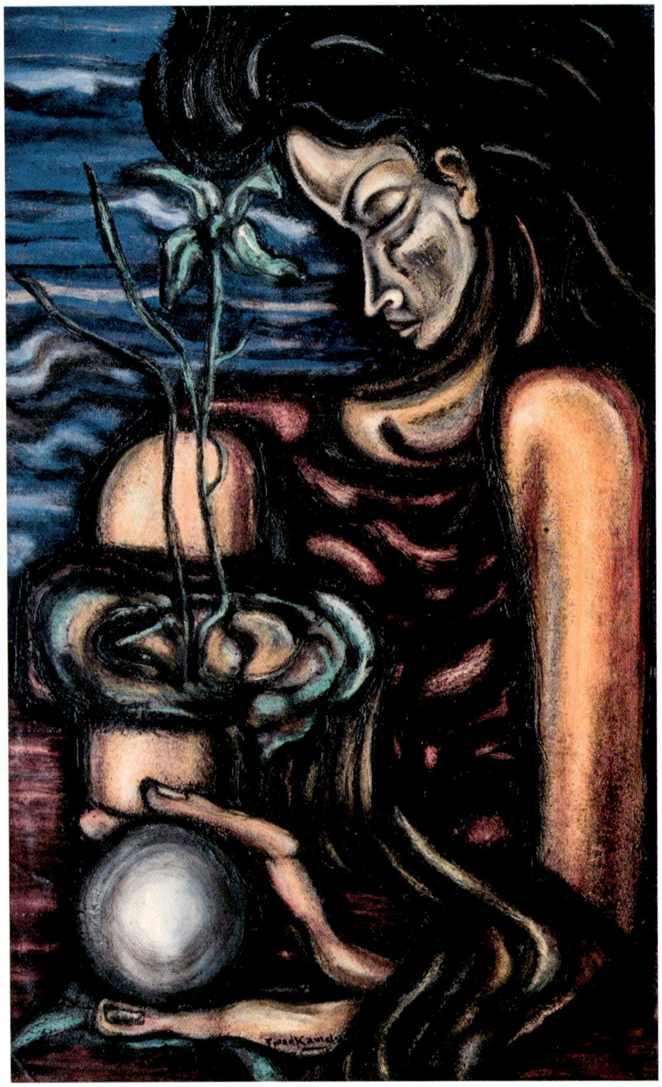

1

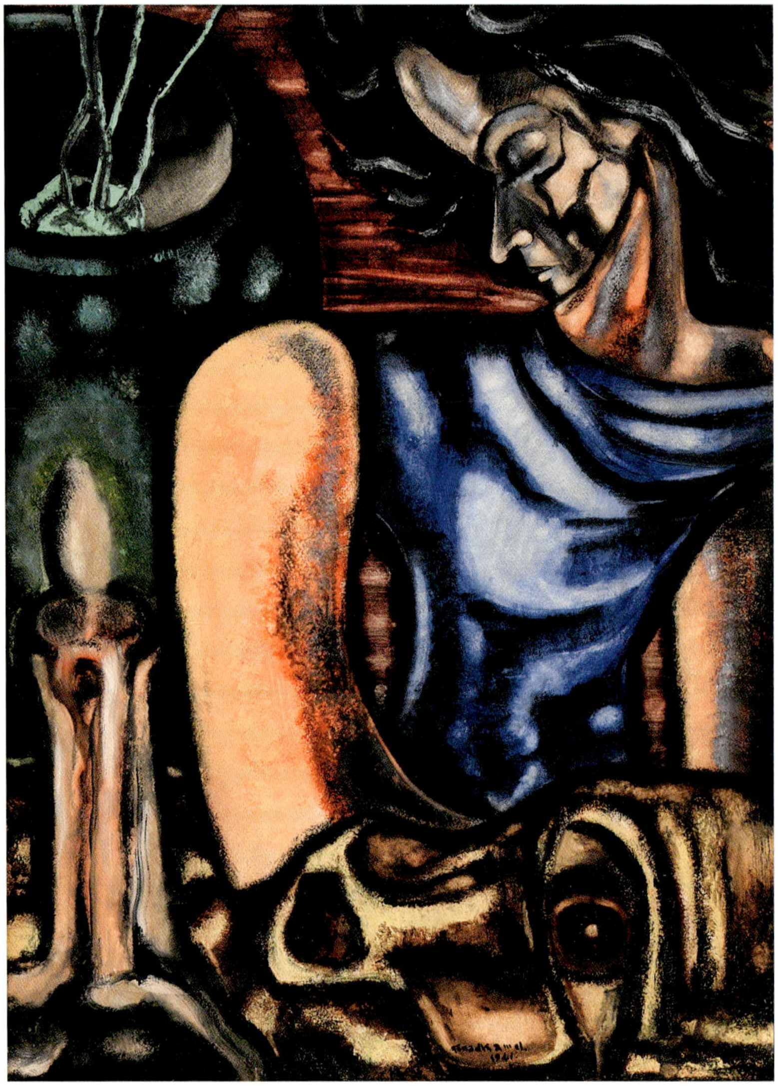

2

1
FOUAD KAMEL
Untitled, c. 1940
Mixed media on cardboard
55 x 35 cm
Yasser Hashem collection, Cairo

2
FOUAD KAMEL
Untitled, undated
Oil on canvas
54.5 x 40 cm
Private collection

"Faiza was completely carried away by the sudden tumult off her senses of delirium...

The flame of the candle nearly out, produced a black smoke..."

Albert Cossery, "The Girl and the Hashash," 1941

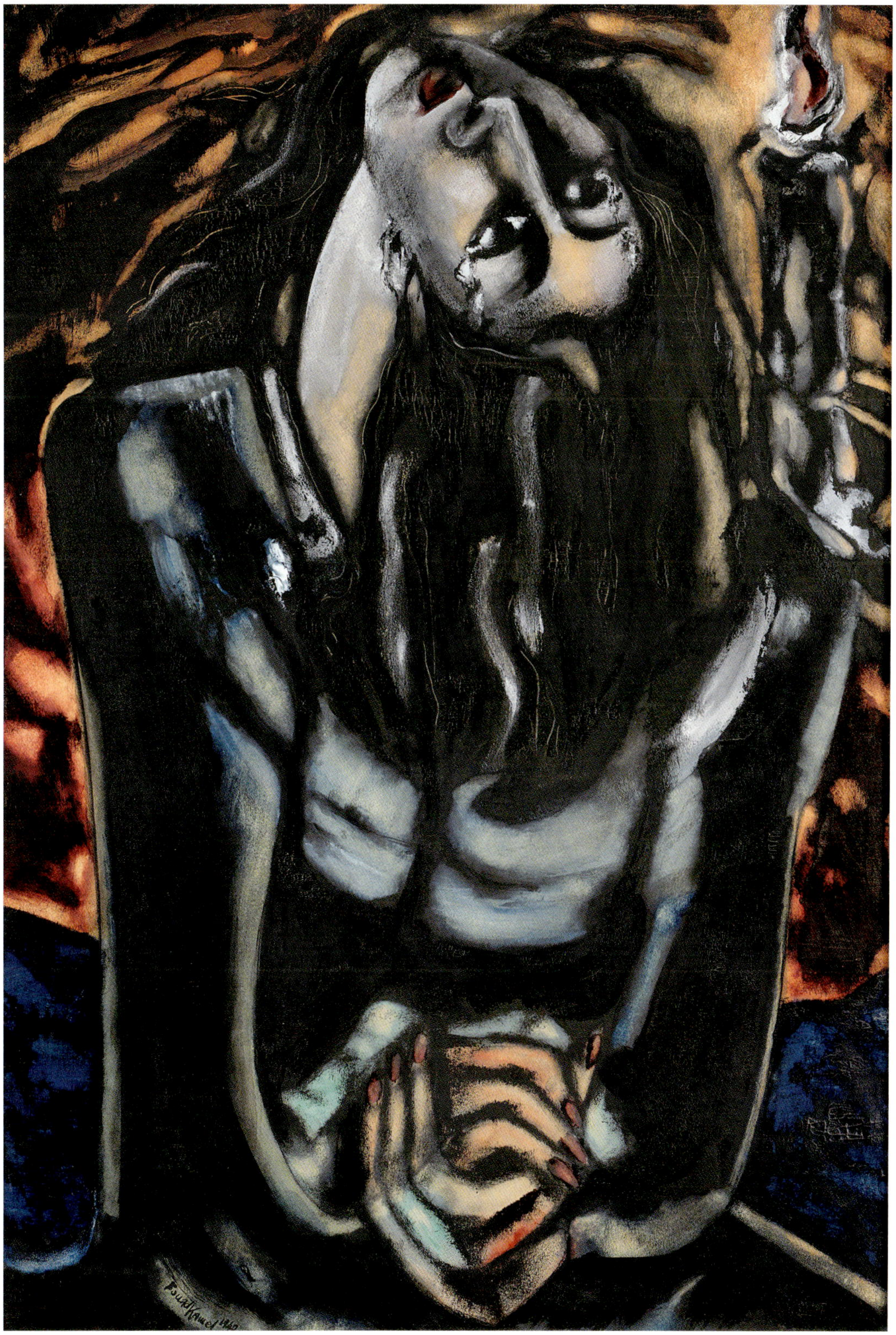

3

3
FOUAD KAMEL
Untitled, 1940
Oil and mixed media on canvas fixed on board
47.5 x 33.3 cm
Private collection

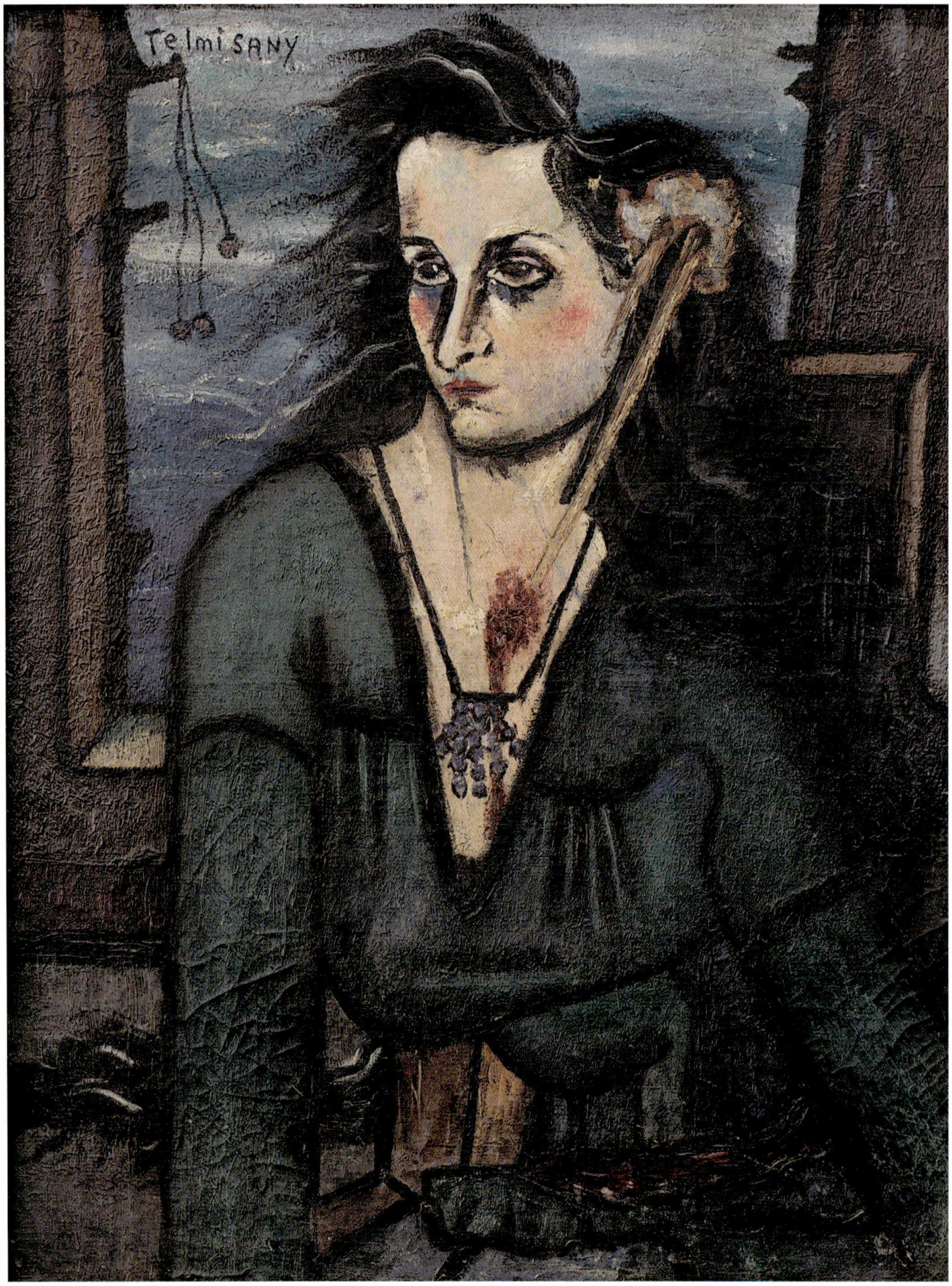

KAMEL EL-TELMISANY
Aïda, c. 1940
Oil on canvas
59 x 47 cm
Rateb Seddik Museum, Cairo

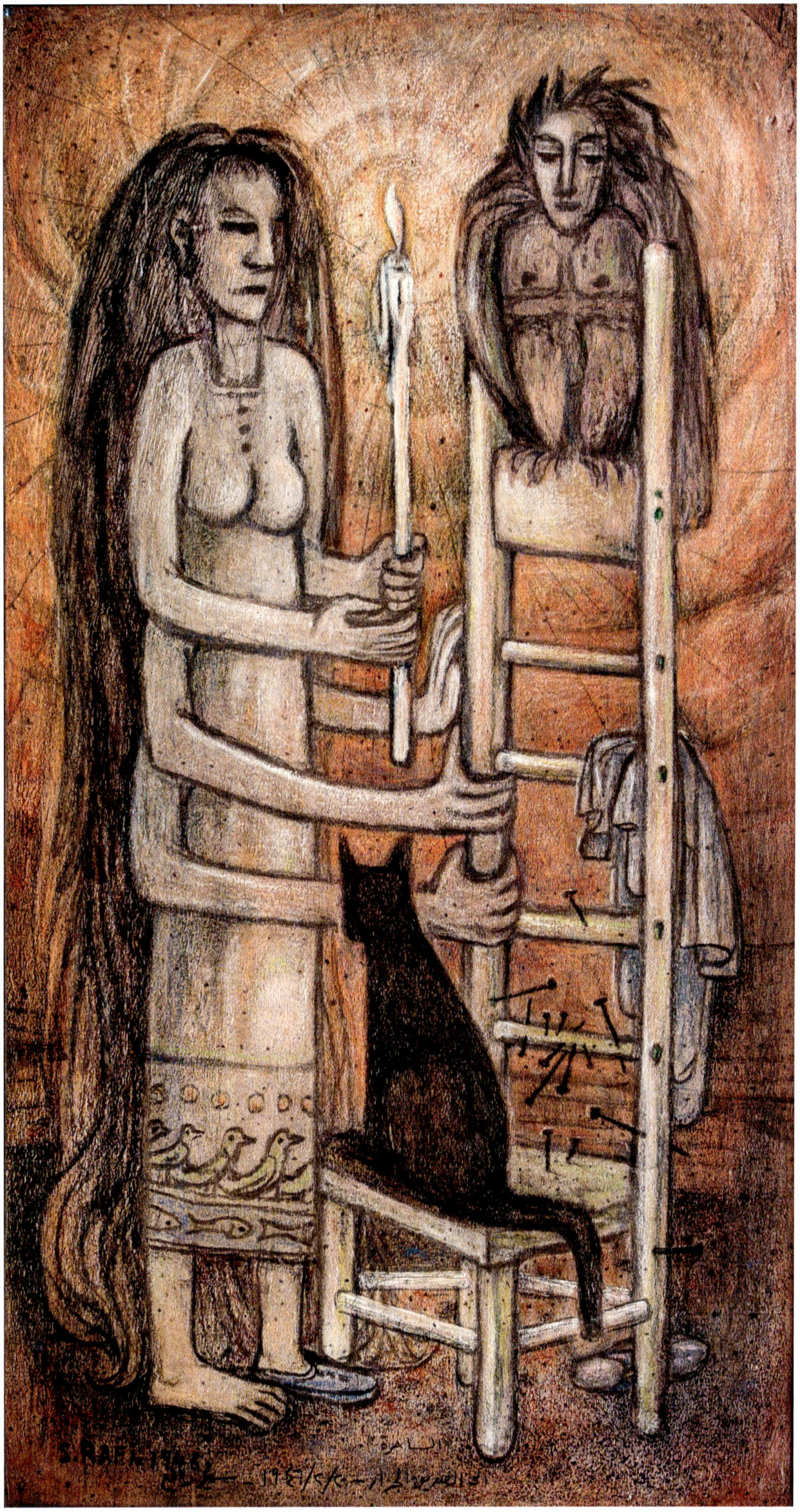

SAMIR RAFI
The Witch, 1946
Oil on canvas
77 x 42.5 cm
Nadim Elias collection, Cairo

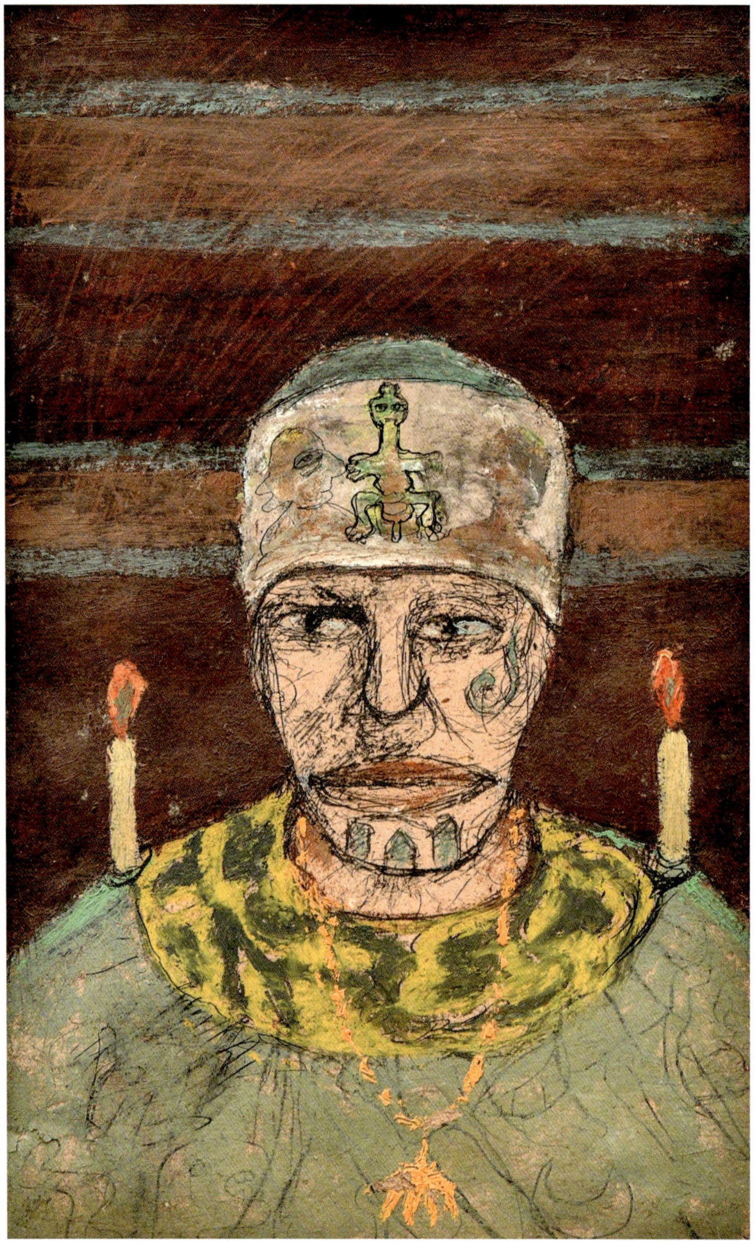

1

1
ABDEL HADI EL-GAZZAR
Portrait (Man with candles), c. 1950
Pastel on paper
42 x 30 cm
H.E. Sh. Hassan M. A. Al Thani collection, Doha

2
ABDEL HADI EL-GAZZAR
Incantation, 1948
Watercolour on paper
90 x 69 cm
H.E. Sh. Hassan M. A. Al Thani collection, Doha

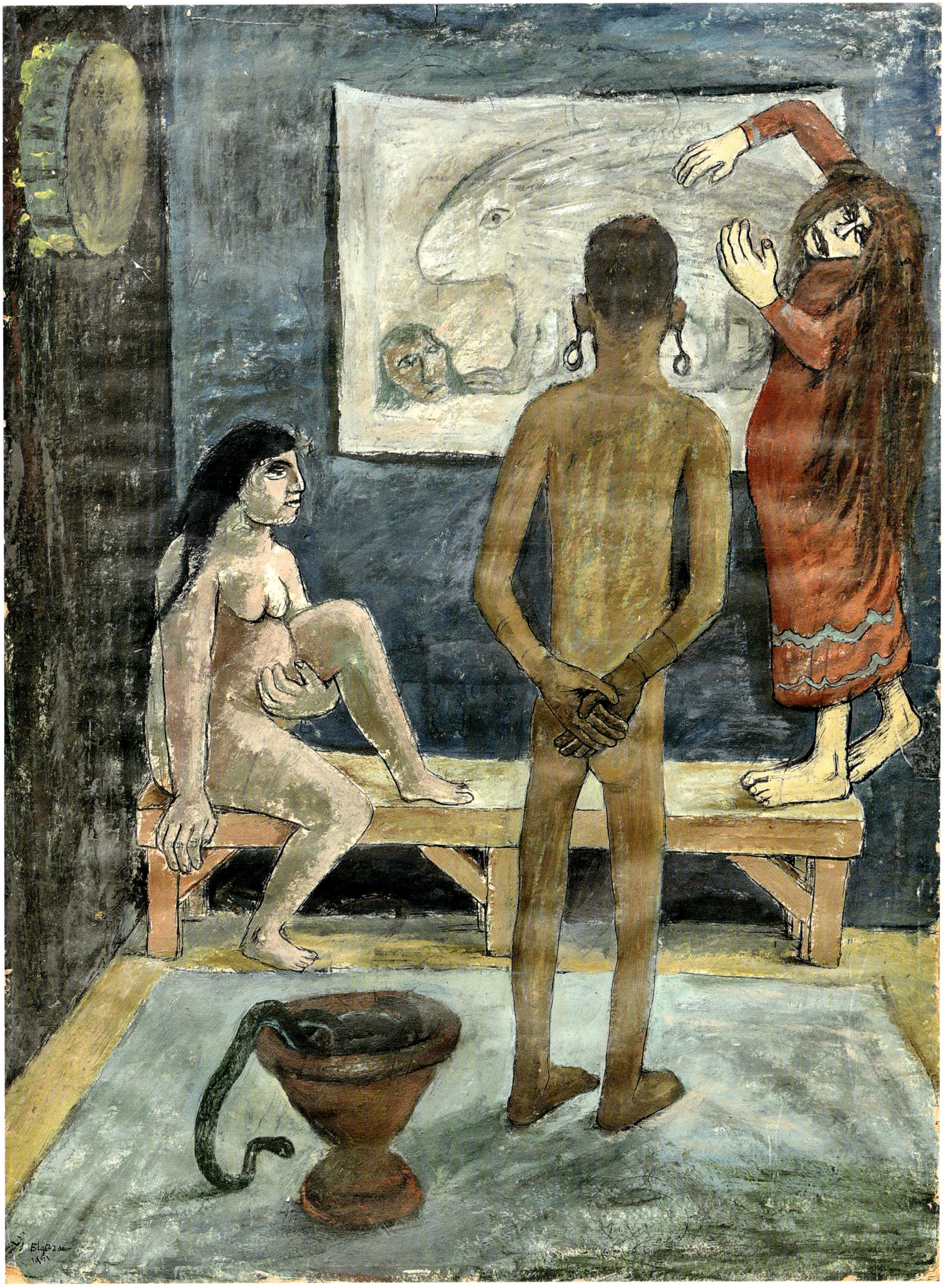

2

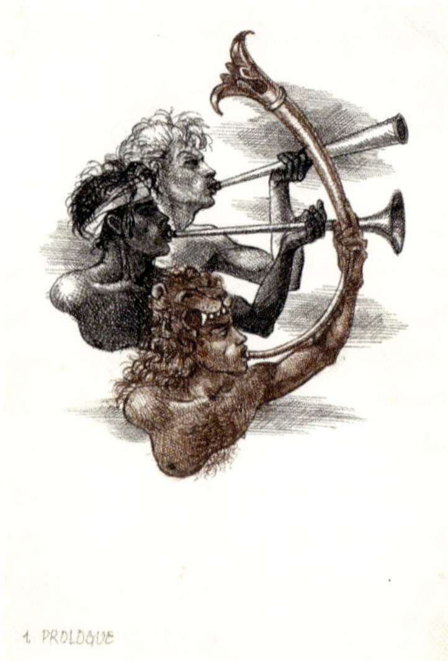

1

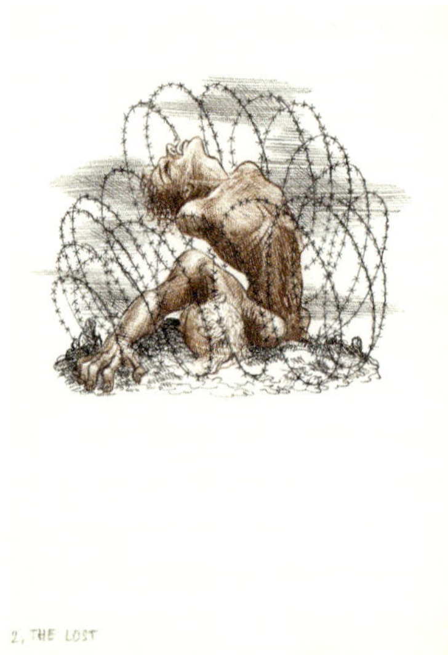

2

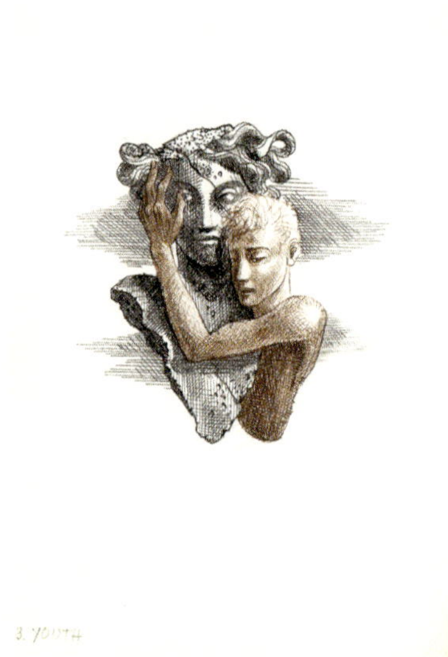

3

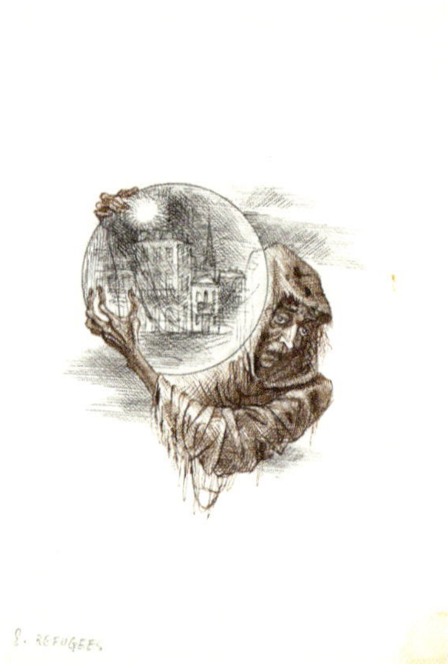

8

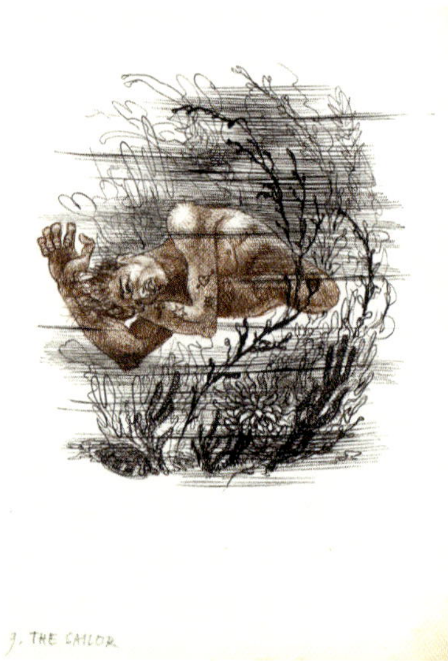

9

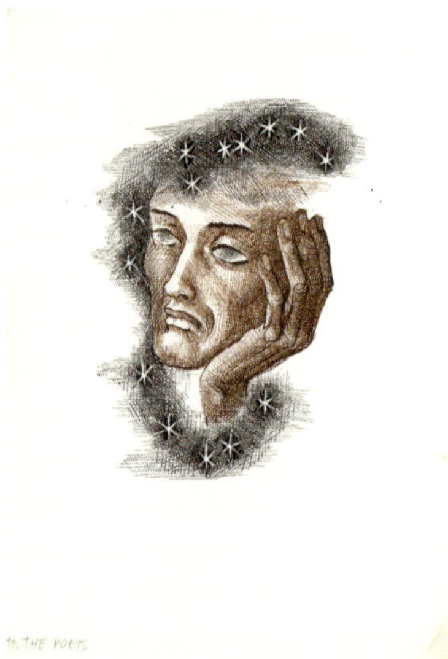

10

1-14
ERIC DE NEMES
Series of illustrations from the book
The Lovely and the Dead
by John Waller (unpublished), 1945
Ink and pencil on paper
28.5 x 19.5 cm
H.E. Sh. Hassan M. A. Al Thani collection, Doha

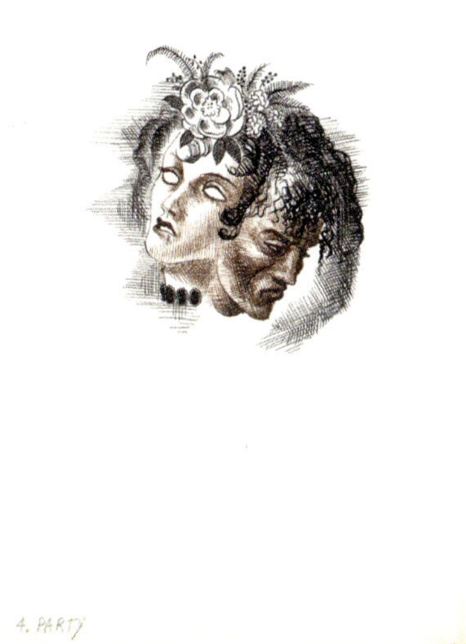

4

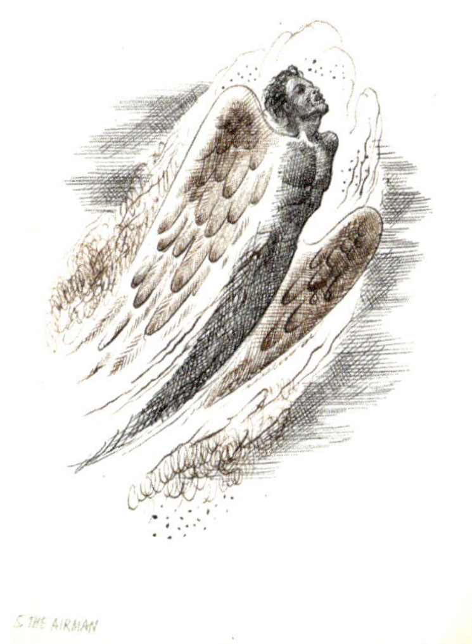

5

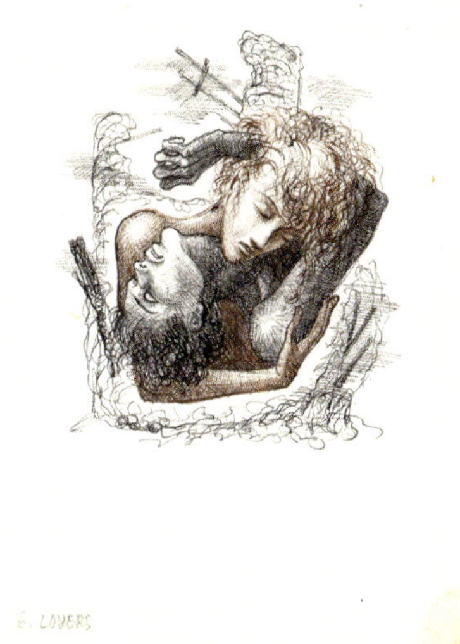

6

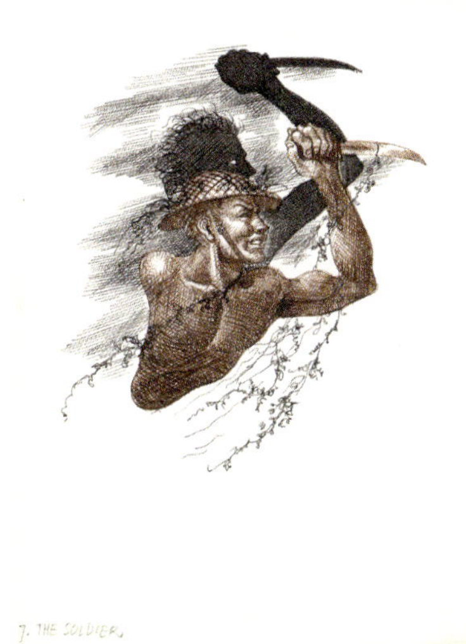

7

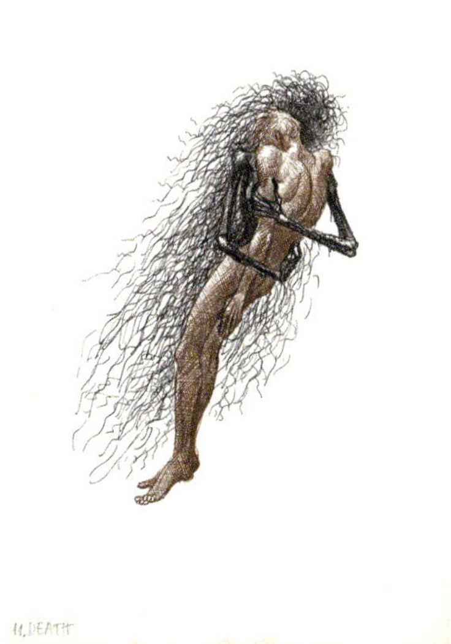

11

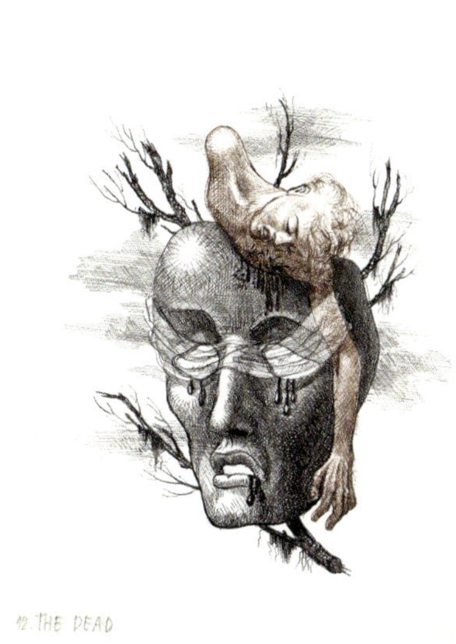

12

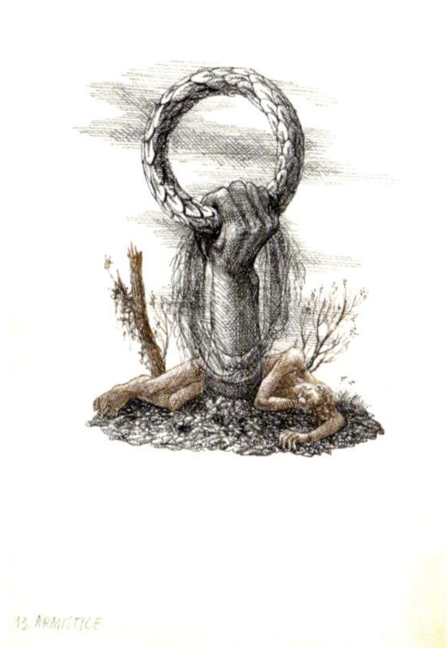

13

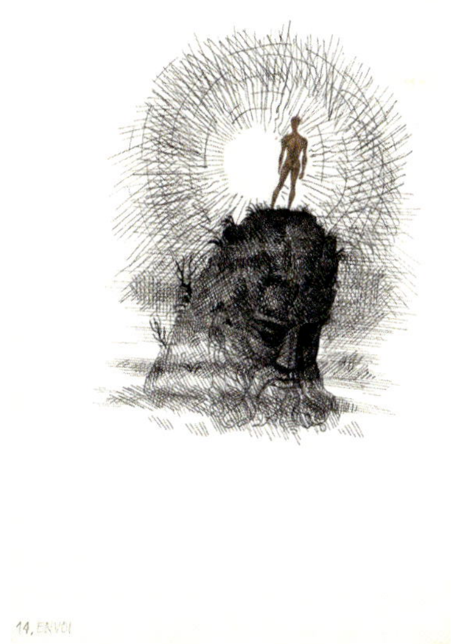

14

"THE SURREALIST PHOTO"

Ahmed Rassim, *Le Progrès Égyptien*, June 7, 1945

In the late 1930s, there were numerous Surrealist photographers emanating from the *Art and Liberty* circle, such as Angelo de Riz, Hassia, Ida Kar, Edmond Belali (Idabel), Lee Miller, Ali Khorchid, and Rami Zolqomah. These would be soon followed by other established figures such as van Leo and Khalil Abduh. Even Georges Henein dabbled with Surrealist photography. They experimented with various techniques that had become staples within Surrealist photography such as solarization, alienation, collage, and photomontage. Through excursions to the Western desert, they were confronted with powerful settings that fed their most striking Surrealist photographs of the time. Miller's *Portrait of Space* from 1938 remains one of the most powerful examples. Similar to how other Surrealist photographers elsewhere, such as Man Ray and Hannah Höch, in such iconic works as *Noir et Blanche* (1926) and *Die Sübe* (1926) respectively made use of primitive masks and objects in order to criticize the rigid hierarchies embedded within Eurocentric art-historical classifications resulting from the contested colonizer-colonized dynamic, *Art and Liberty* artists like Ida Kar and Étienne Sved, in a number of photographs and photomontages, would make use of Pharaonic elements in playful compositions that, instead of colonialism, evaded the associations with Egyptian nationalism. In *Still Life (Pharaoh and Doll)* (ca. 1940.), Kar juxtaposes what looks like a handmade child's rag doll with a sculpture of a pharaoh's head. The insignificant toy trumps the glorified museum artifact. In a similar manner, Étienne Sved confronts the body parts of ancient Egyptian sculptures with their human equivalents. Egypt's Pharaonic past is portrayed free from the burden of neither the imperialist nor the nationalist projects. The technological possibilities embedded within the discipline of photography enabled *Art and Liberty* to push even further their emancipatory project by which artistic expression would become a means of social and political critique.

MOHAMMAD ABDEL LATIF
Untitled, c. 1938
Vintage gelatin silver print
39.5 x 40 cm
Private collection

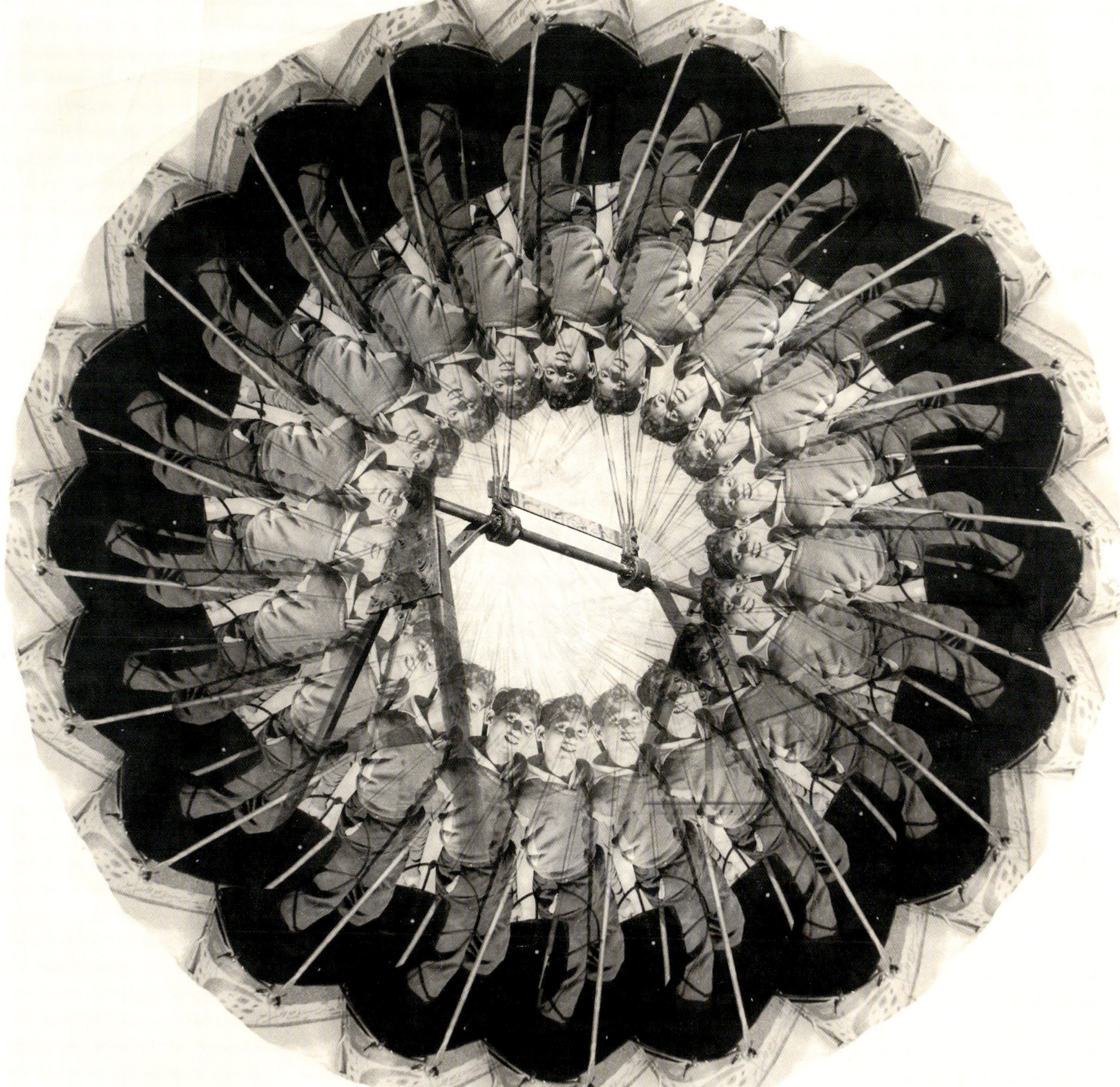

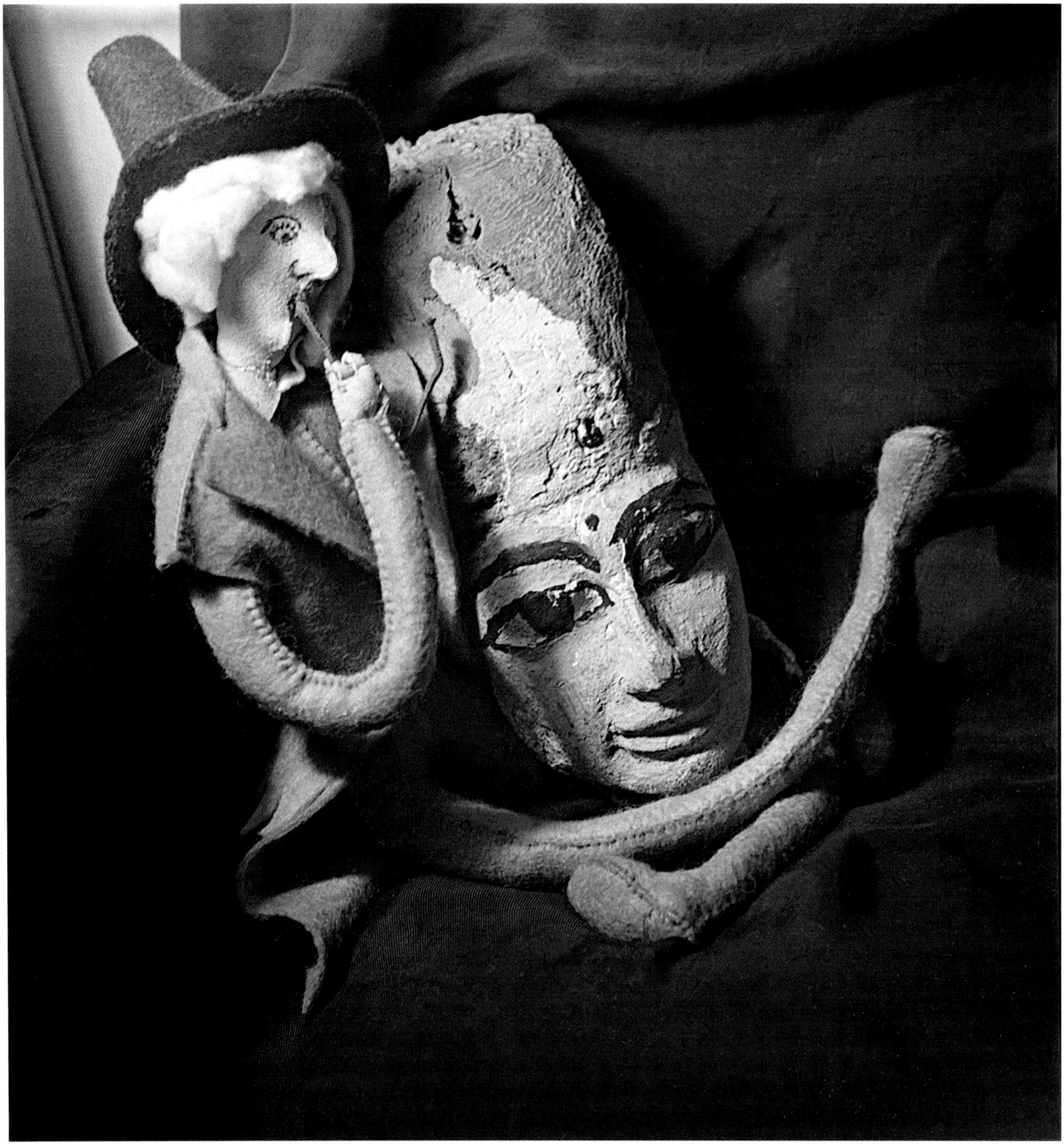

1

1
IDA KAR / IDABEL
Still Life, c. 1940
Vintage bromide print
23.4 x 22.8 cm
National Portrait Gallery, London

2
IDA KAR / IDABEL
Surrealist Study, c. 1940
Vintage bromide print
25.4 x 20.6 cm
National Portrait Gallery, London

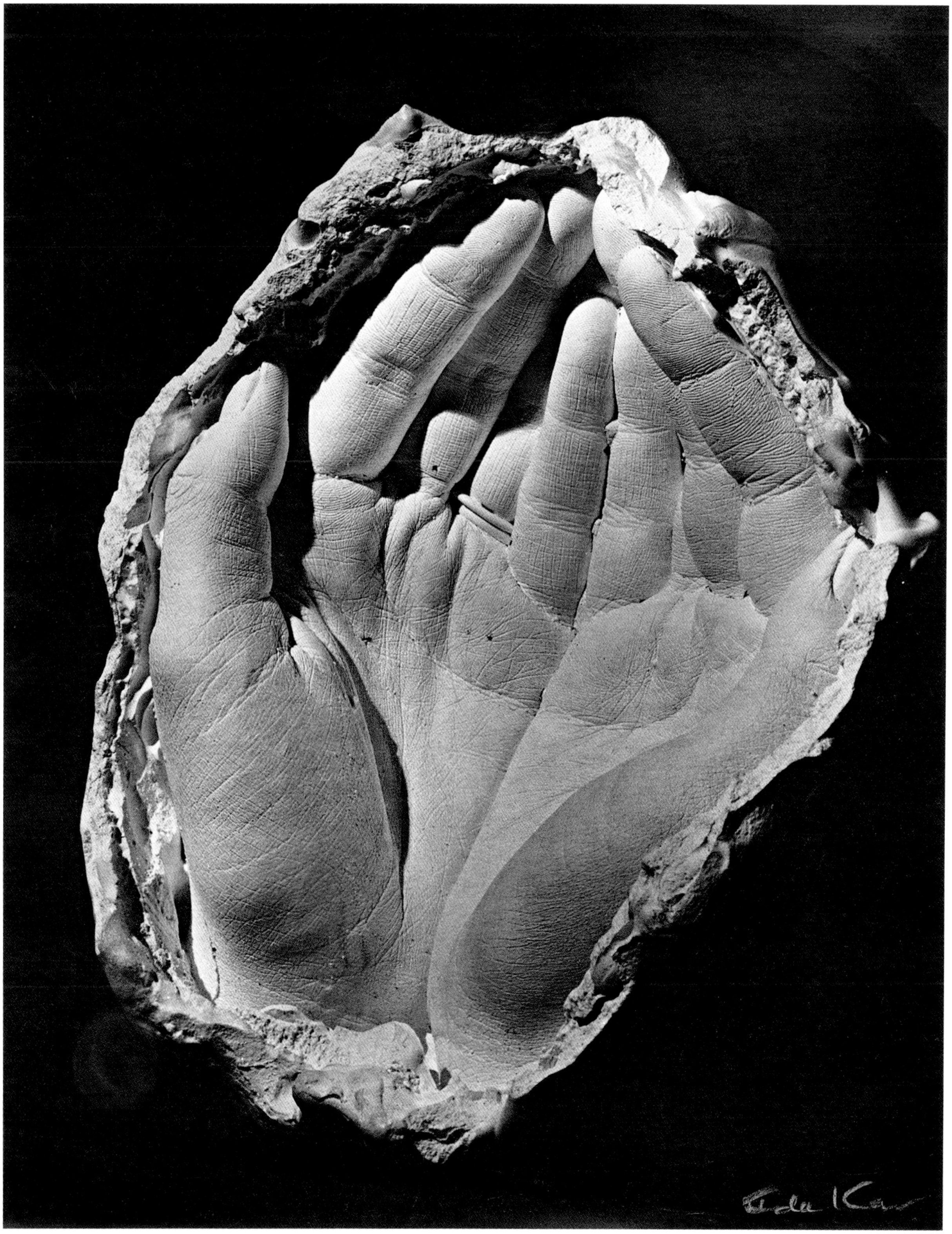

2

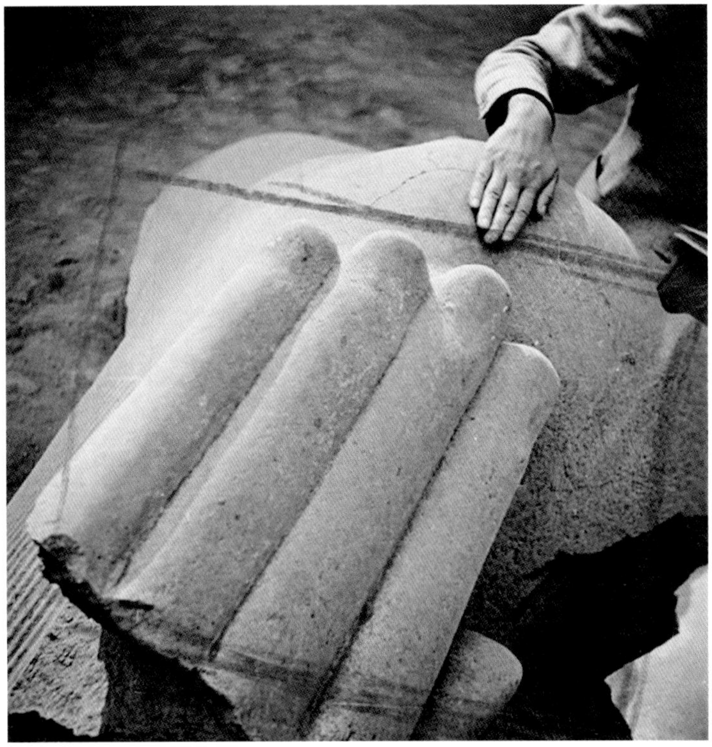

1

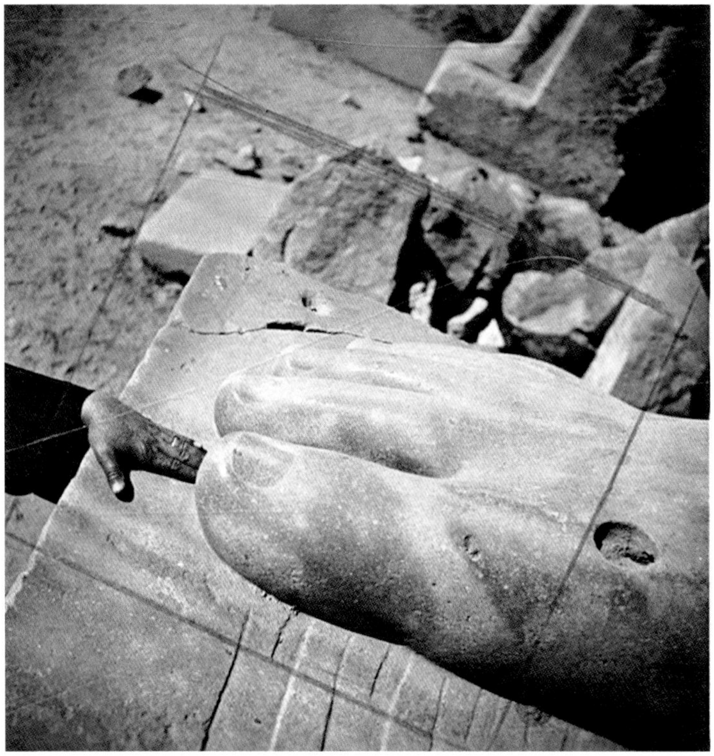

2

1
ÉTIENNE SVED
Untitled, c. 1945
Vintage gelatin silver print
6 x 6 cm
Musée Nicéphore Niépce, Chalon-sur-Saône

2
ÉTIENNE SVED
Untitled, c. 1945
Vintage gelatin silver print
6 x 6 cm
Musée Nicéphore Niépce, Chalon-sur-Saône

3
ÉTIENNE SVED
Untitled, c. 1945
Vintage gelatin silver print
6 x 6 cm
Musée Nicéphore Niépce, Chalon-sur-Saône

3
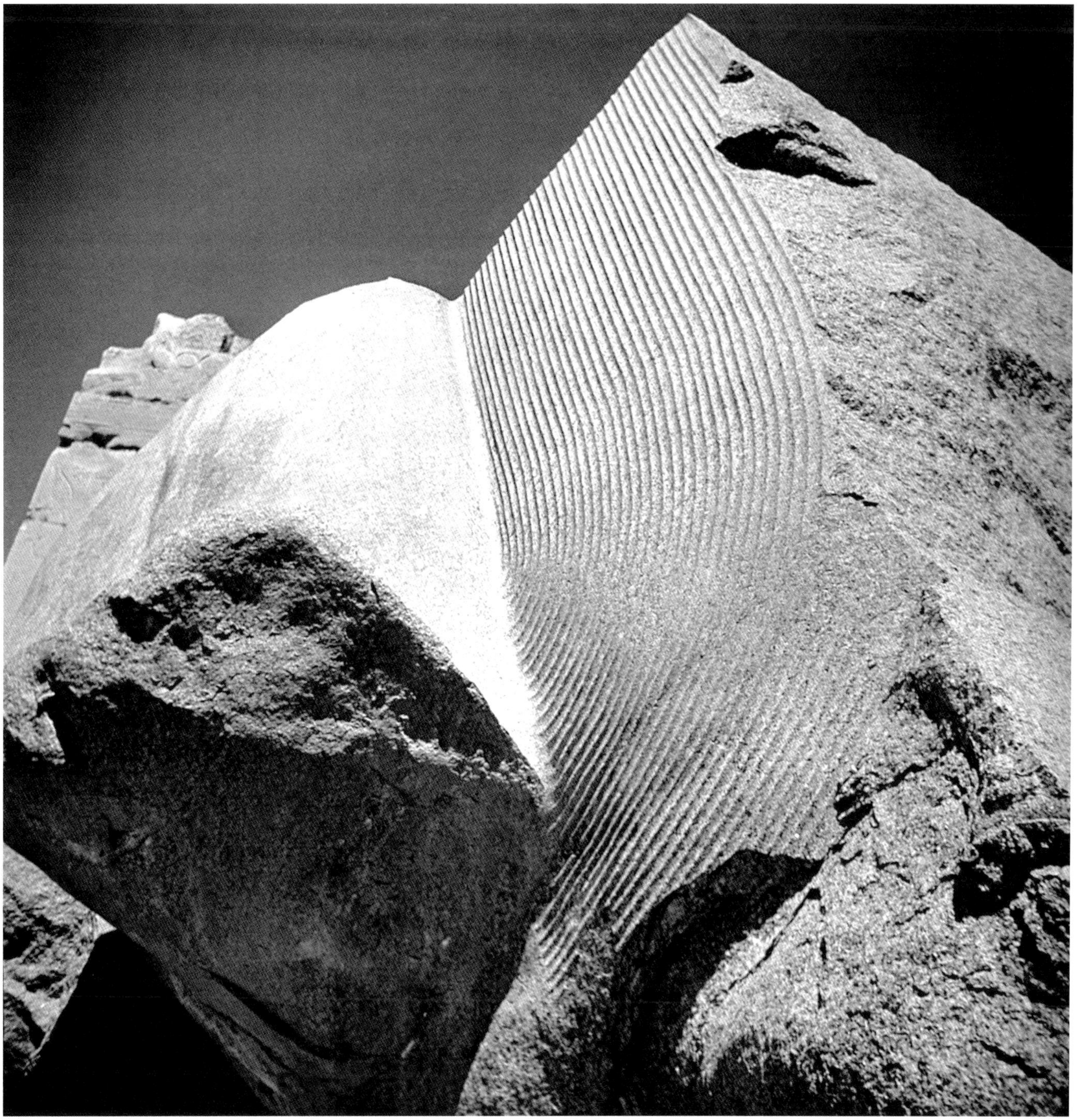

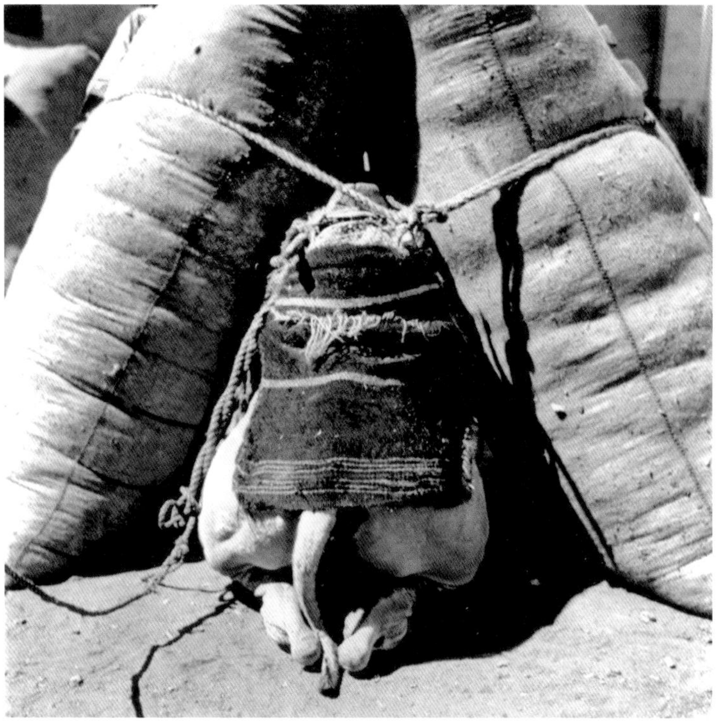

2

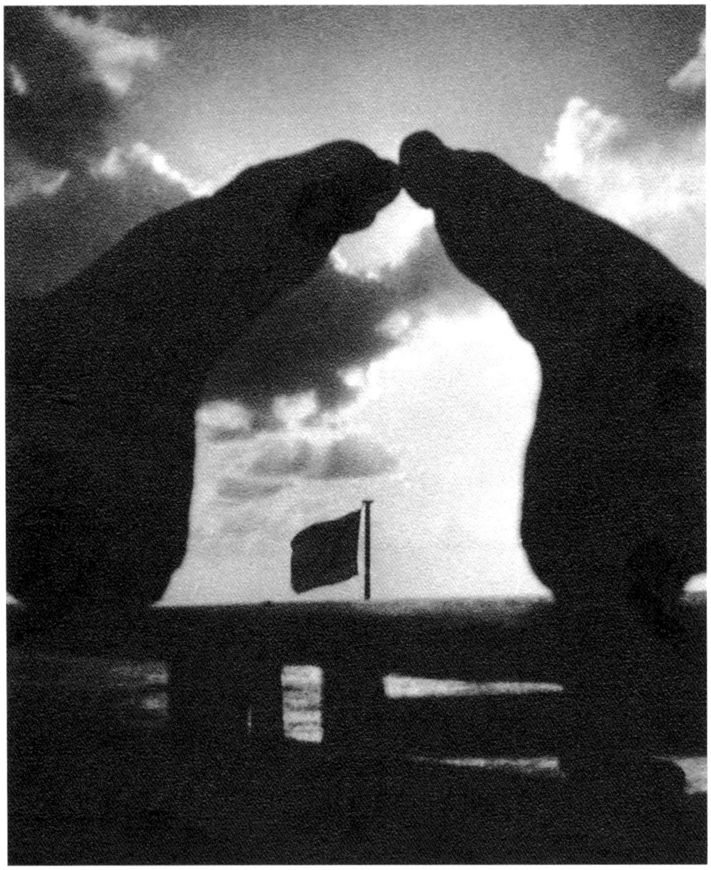

1

1
MAMDOUH MUHAMAD FATHALLAH
Peak – Photographer's feet framing the flag, c. 1944-1945
Vintage gelatin silver print
9.7 x 8.1 cm
Mamdouh Muhamad Fathallah collection, Arab Image Foundation, Beirut

2
LEE MILLER
Camel loaded up with supplies, Egypt, 1936
Vintage gelatin silver print
5.3 x 5.4 cm
Lee Miller Archives, England 2016

3
LEE MILLER
Portrait of Space, Al Bulwayeb, Near Siwa, Egypt, 1937
Modern print from vintage gelatin silver print
30.5 x 27.5 cm
Lee Miller Archives, England 2016

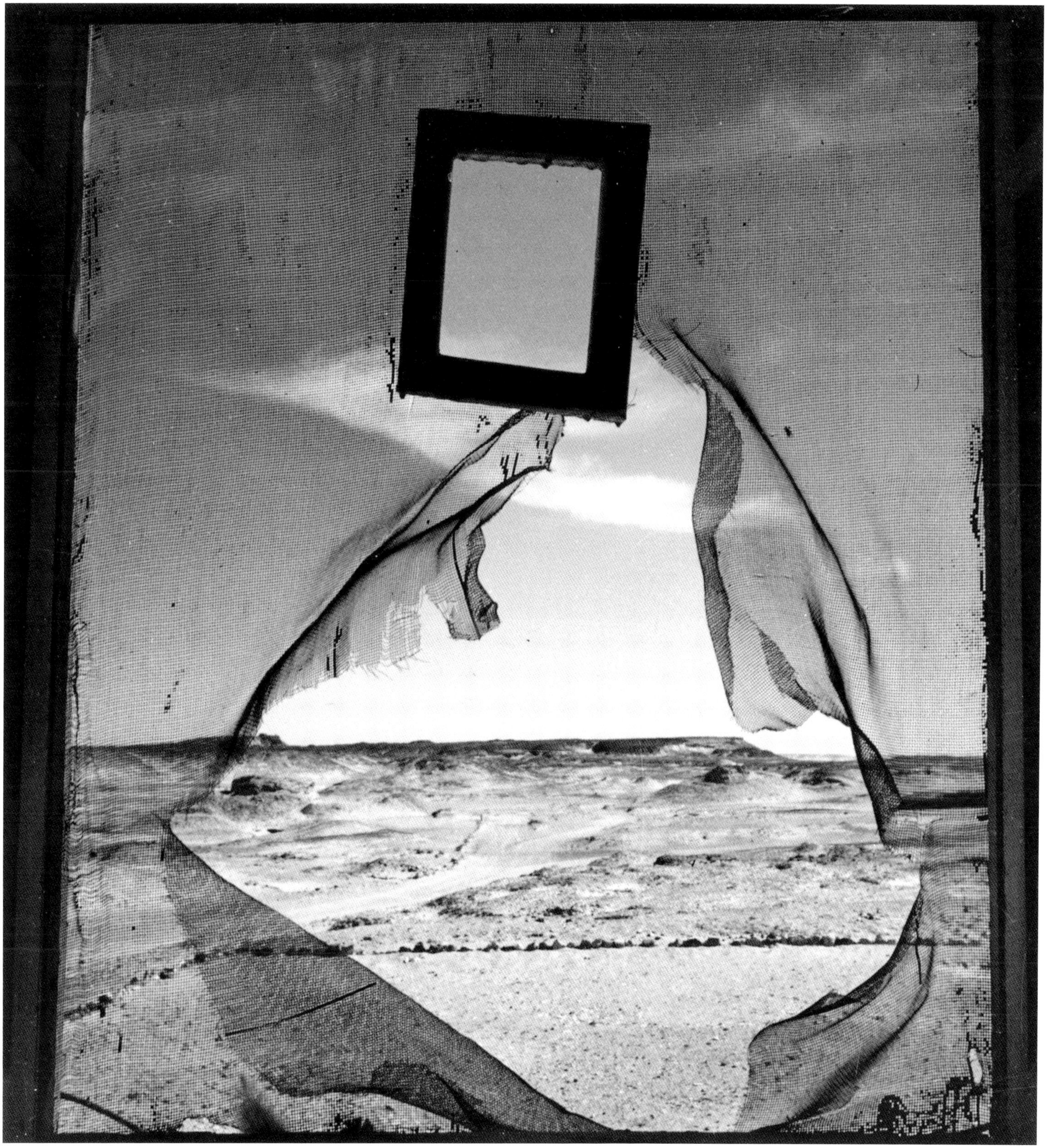

3

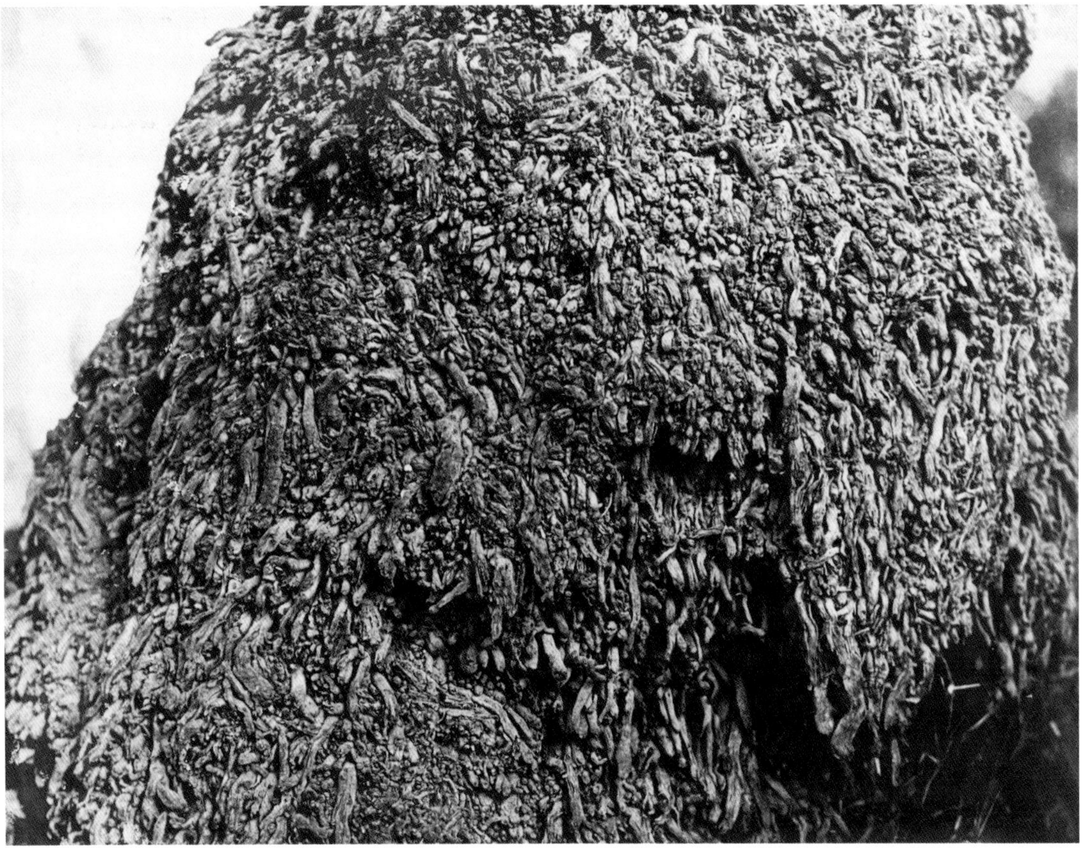

1

1
RAMZI ZOLQOMAH
Untitled, c. 1939
Vintage gelatin silver print
30 x 39.7 cm
Private collection

2
ABDUH KHALIL
Untitled, c. 1949
Vintage gelatin silver print
31 x 29.5 cm
Private collection

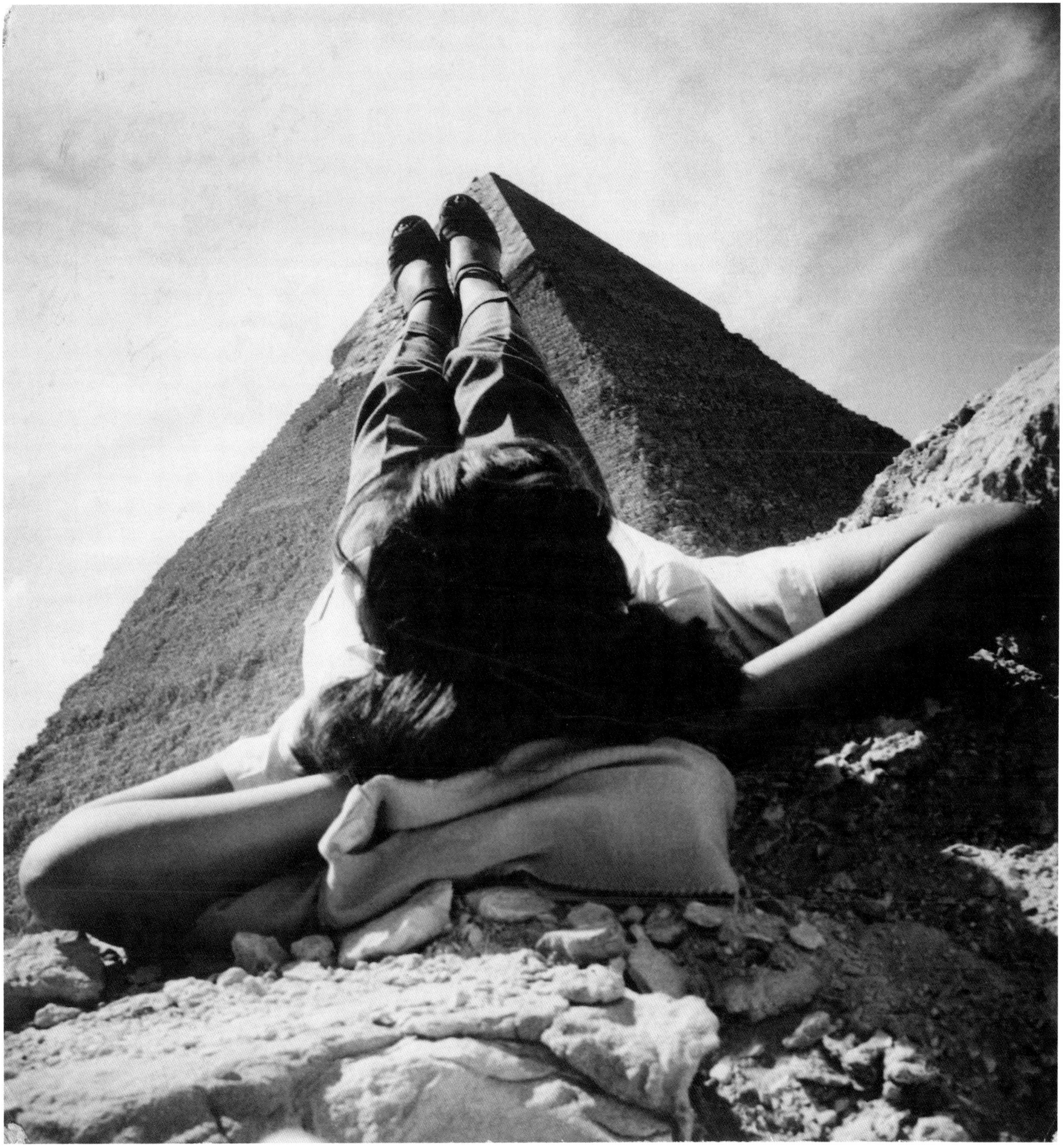
2

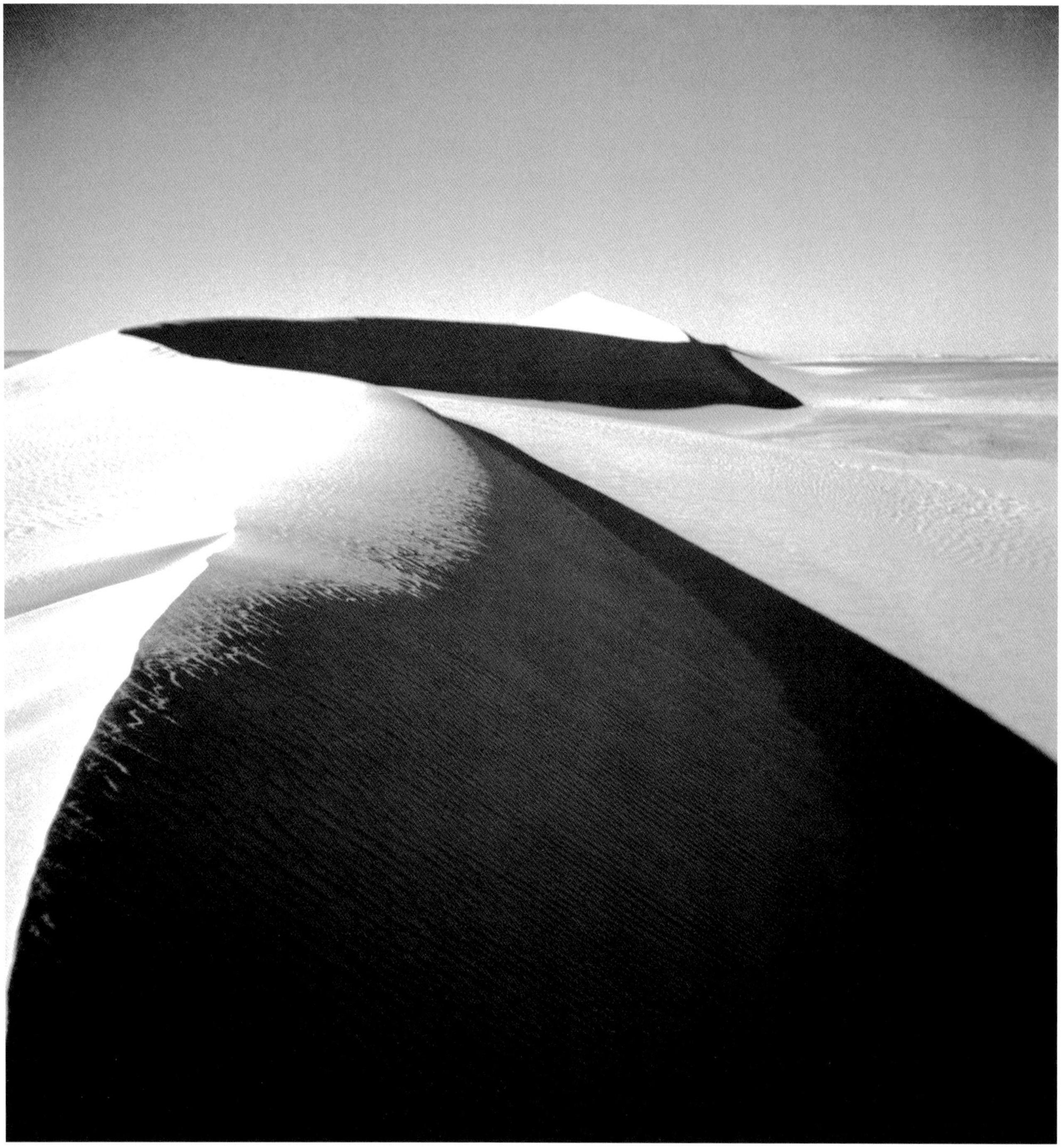

LEE MILLER
Sand dunes, Egypt, c. 1936
Vintage gelatin silver print
5.4 x 5.4 cm
Lee Miller Archives, England 2016

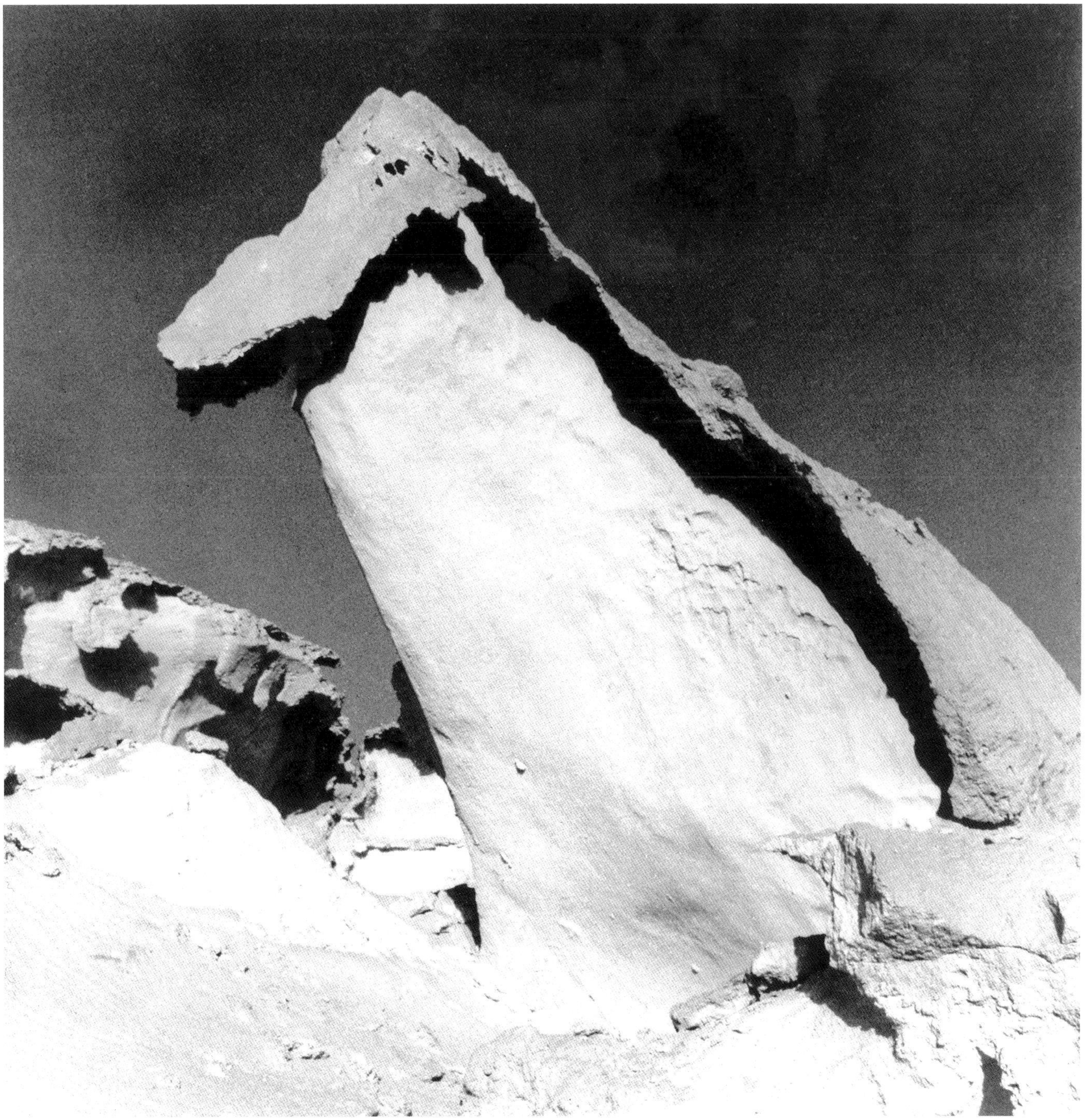

LEE MILLER
Cock Rock (The Native), Near Siwa, Egypt, 1939
Vintage bromide print
5.8 x 5.9 cm
Lee Miller Archives, England 2016

IDA KAR / IDABEL
L'Etreinte, 1940
Vintage bromide print
52 x 41 cm
Private collection, Paris

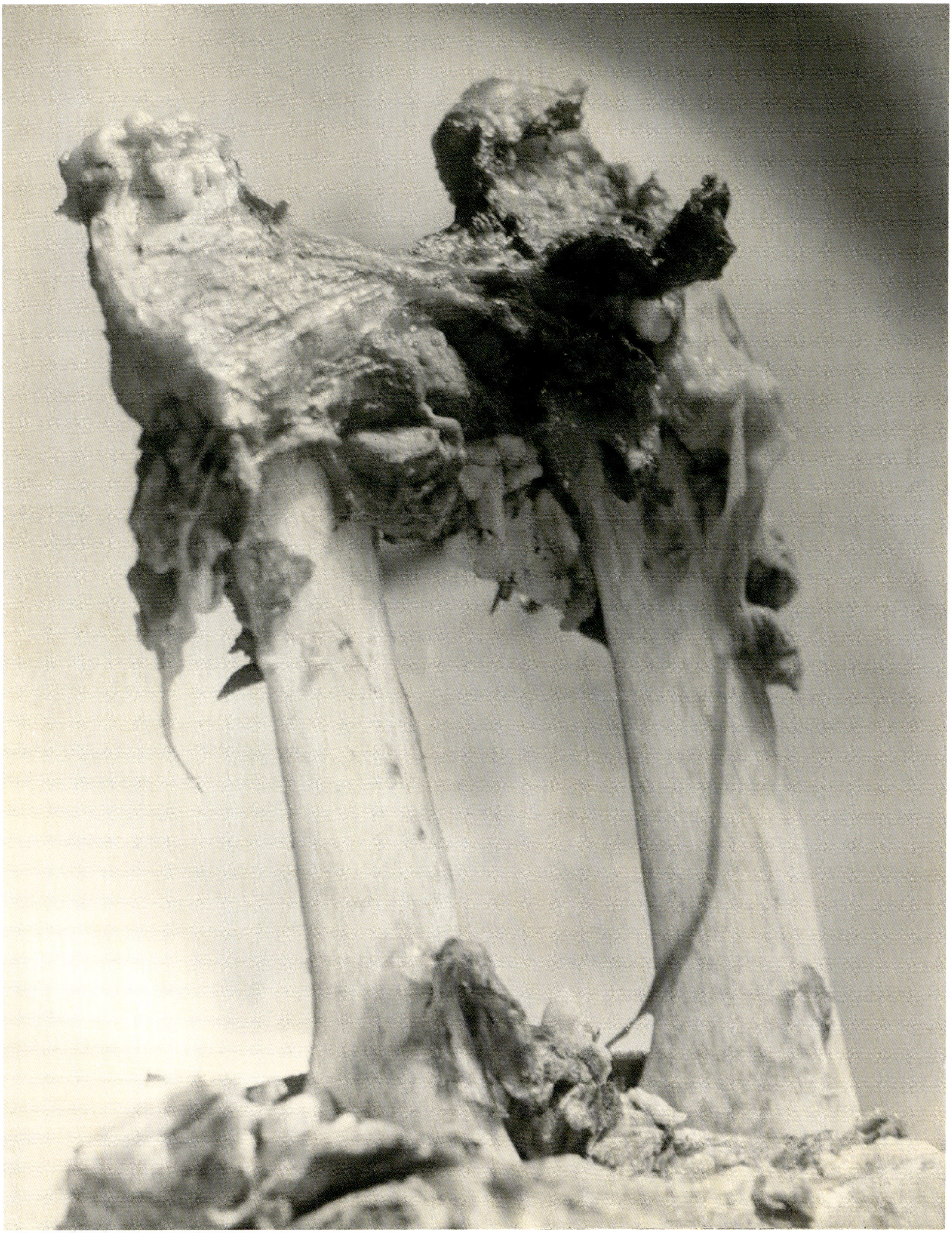

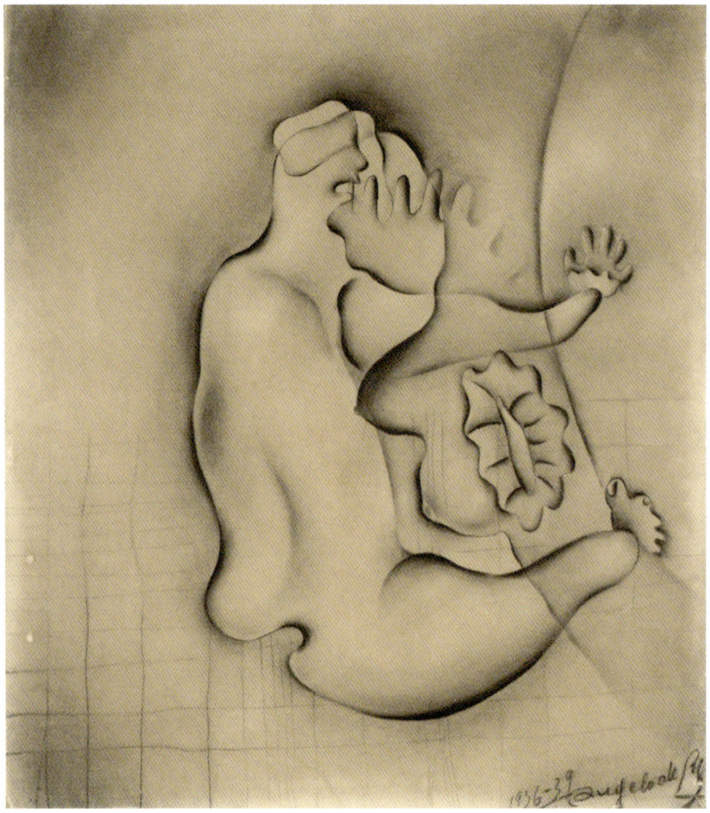
1

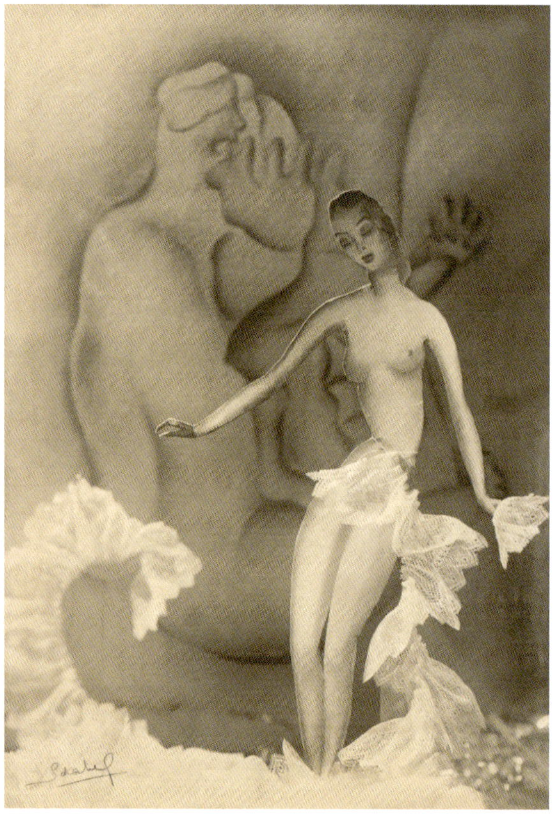
2

1
ANGELO DE RIZ
Untitled (Surrealist Study), 1936
Charcoal on cardboard
50 x 43 cm
Private collection, Paris

2
IDA KAR / IDABEL & ANGELO DE RIZ
Untitled (Surrealist Study), c. 1936
Vintage bromide print
53 x 38 cm
Private collection, Paris

3
IDA KAR / IDABEL
Untitled (Surrealist Study), 1936.
Vintage bromide print
22 x 17 cm
Private collection, Paris

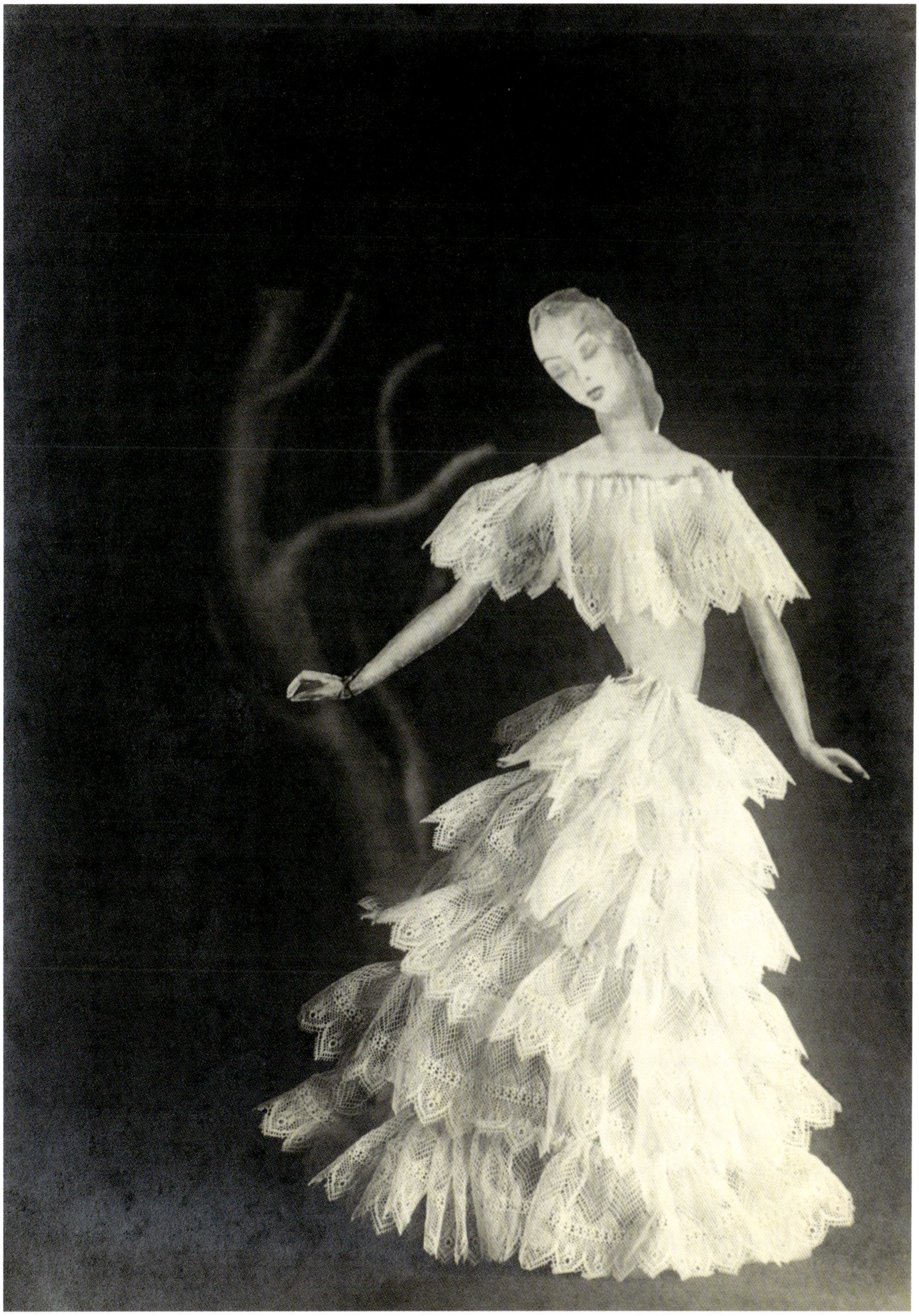

3

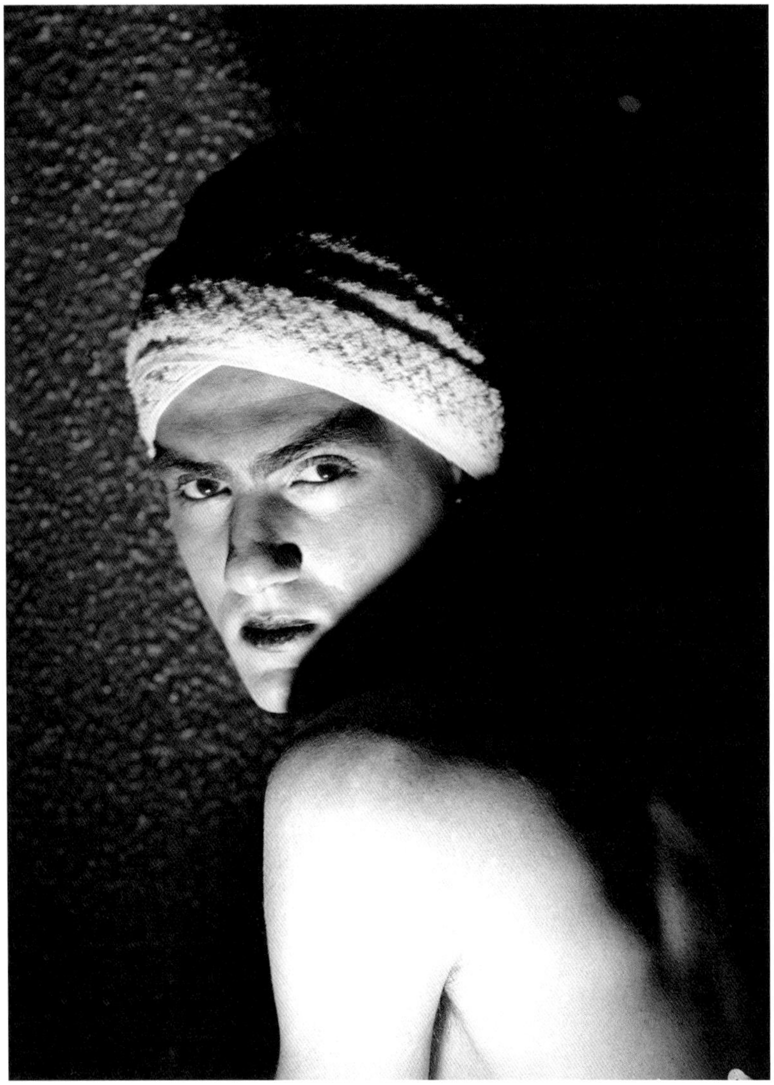

1

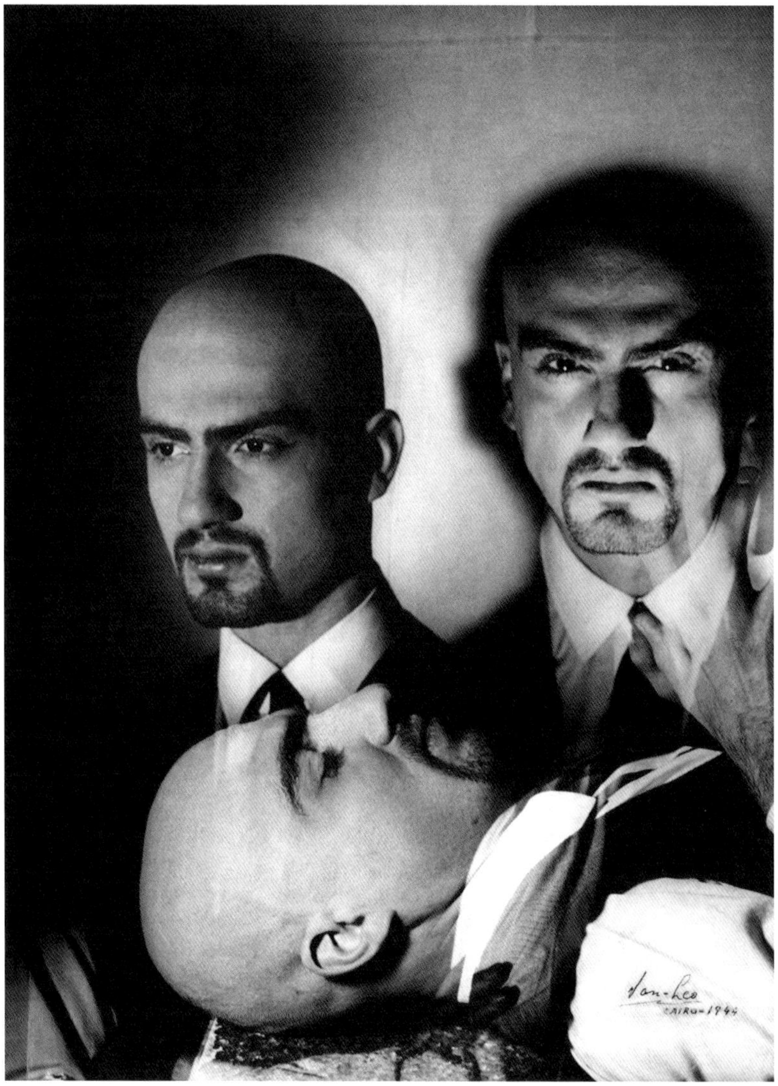

2

1
VAN LEO
Untitled, 1945
Modern gelatin silver print
28 x 21 cm
Van Leo collection, Arab Image Foundation, Beirut
American University in Cairo

2
VAN LEO
Untitled (Self-portrait), 1945
Modern gelatin silver print
40 x 30 cm
Van Leo collection, Arab Image Foundation, Beirut

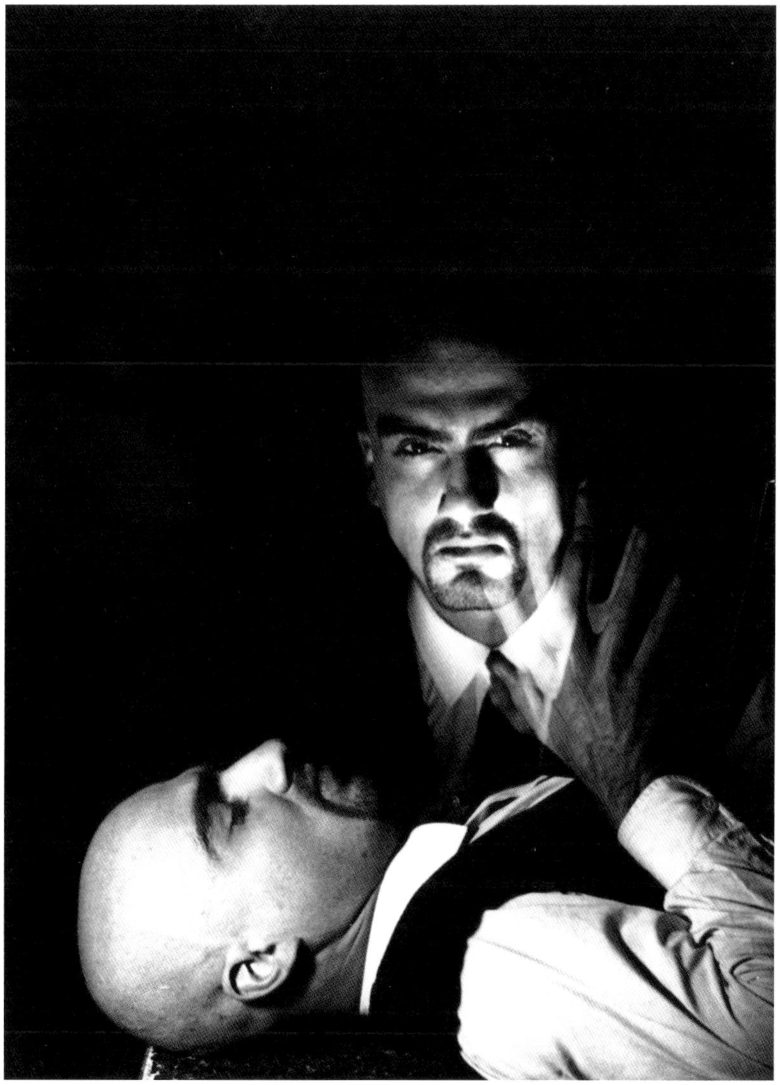

3

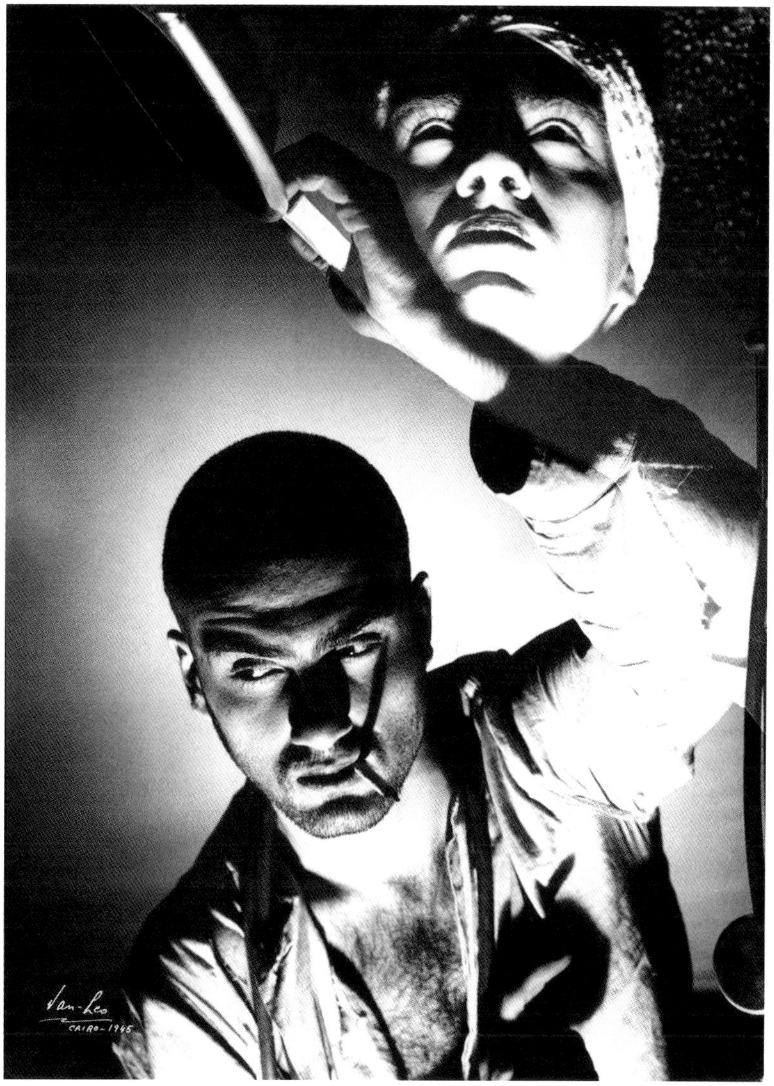

4

3
VAN LEO
Untitled, 1946
Modern gelatin silver print
40 x 30 cm
Van Leo collection, Arab Image Foundation, Beirut
American University in Cairo

4
VAN LEO
Untitled (Self-portrait), 1945
Modern gelatin silver print
40 x 30 cm
Van Leo collection, Arab Image Foundation, Beirut

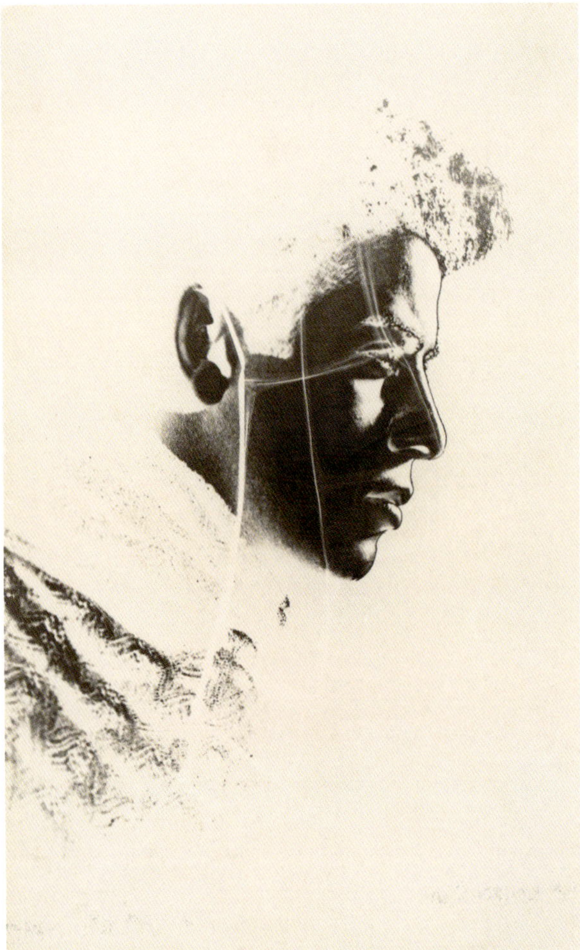

1

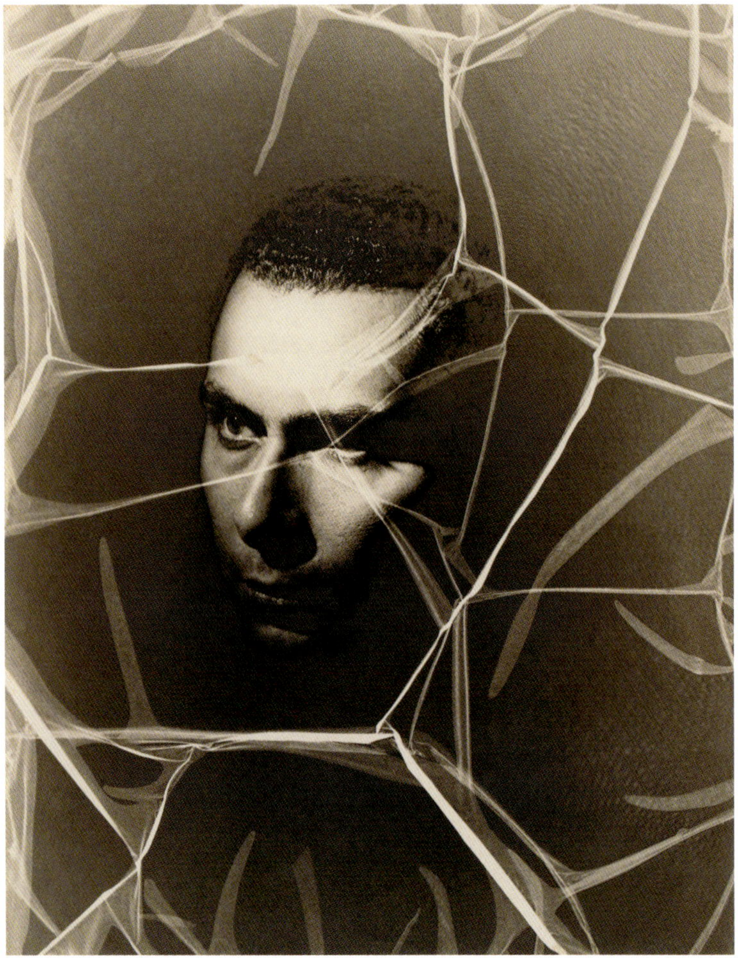

2

1
RAMZI ZOLQOMAH
Untitled, 1938
Vintage gelatin silver print
47.5 x 30.1 cm
Private collection

2
RAMZI ZOLQOMAH
Untitled, 1938
Vintage gelatin silver print
48.7 x 38.1 cm
Private collection

3
AHMED SAWWAN
Untitled, 1938
Vintage gelatin silver print
38.8 x 29 cm
Private collection

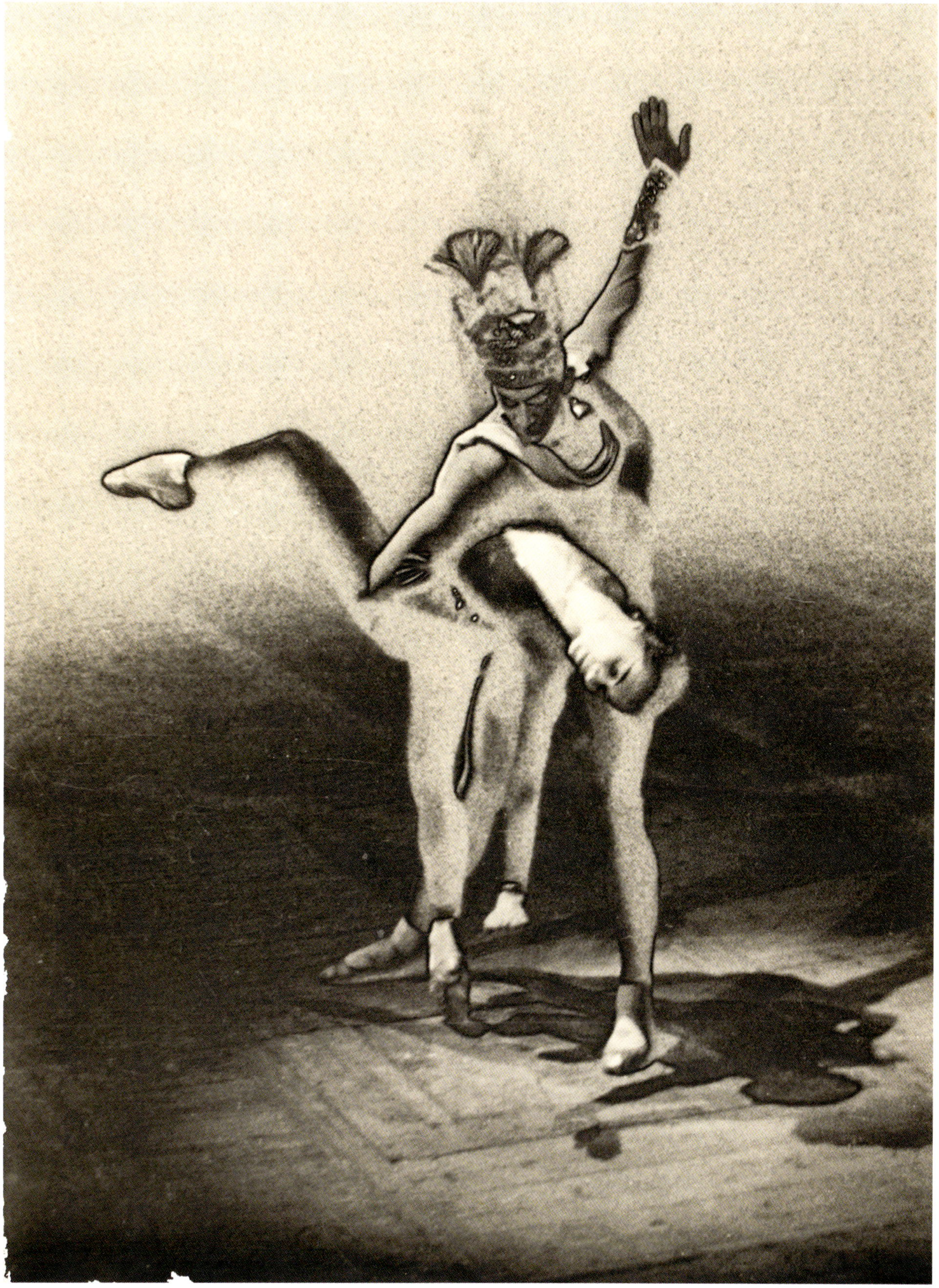

3

BIOGRAPHIES

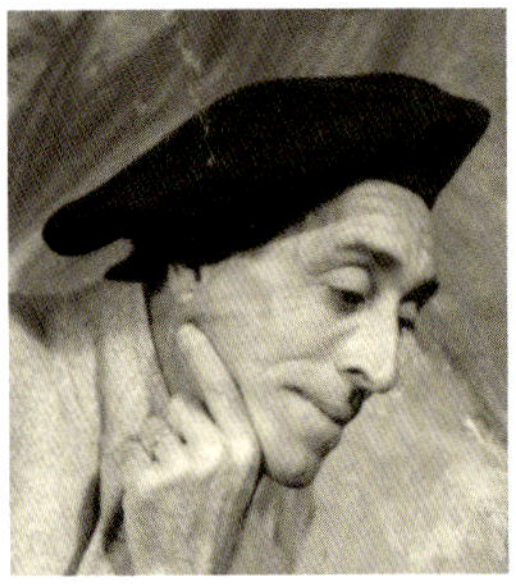

HUSSEIN YOUSSEF AMIN
(1904-1984)

Hussein Youssef Amin was an Egyptian painter and pioneering art educator. He was born in Cairo and received his diploma from the Florence Academy of Art in Italy in 1930. After spending some time in Europe upon graduation, he travelled to São Paolo, Brazil, to assist his then professor in teaching art.

Upon Amin's return to Egypt via Italy, he decided to apply new pedagogical techniques he had acquired in Sao Paolo. He established the Association of Art Teachers together with Youssef Afifi in 1937 and began mentoring a number of young artists such as Abdelhadi El-Gazzar, Hamed Nada, Samir Rafi', Maher Ra'ef, Youssef Kamel, Ibrahim Massouda and Salim Abdallah Al-Habschi (also known as Mogli), around whom he would eventually establish the Contemporary Art Group in 1946. Nevertheless, newly published segments of Samir Rafi's memoirs contend that it was he who founded the group from as early as 1940 (see biography of Samir Rafi'). Some of the artists from Contemporary Art Group were also members or affiliates, though junior ones, of the *Art and Liberty* Group. However, the Contemporary Art Group set itself apart in its use of surrealism to primarily convey Egyptian subjects and themes, attempting to develop a thoroughly "Egyptian" art versus their more universally-minded predecessors.

In addition to his art practice, Amin also specialized in art history, criticism and the psychology of art pedagogy. He was awarded the first Modern Art Prize at the São Paolo Biennale in 1951 and exhibited internationally throughout his life. He died in 1984.

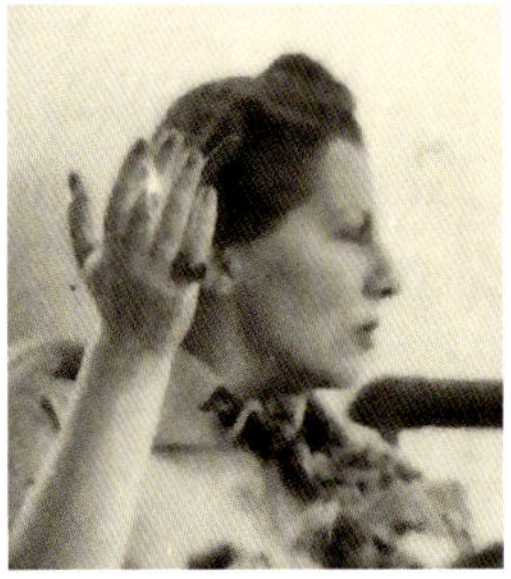

MARIE CAVADIA-RIAZ
(1901-1970)

Marie Cavadia was a Romanian poet and writer of Greek origin. She was born in Romania in 1901, spent her childhood and studied in Paris, and was first married to French filmmaker Marcel L'Herbier. Later, in 1929, she moved to Egypt and married Mamdouh Riaz Bey, a prestigious politician and minister and the grandson of Egypt's former Prime Minister Riaz Pasha.

Cavadia was an important figure in the Surrealist movement in Egypt, both as a writer and as one of its first patrons and supporters in the country. In addition to her own writings, she is known for having hosted one of the prominent cultural salons of Cairo from 1930s to the 1950s in her home in Zamalek, where she owned a significant collection of ancient Egyptian Ramesside objects. Hers was a Surrealist literary salon where many figures from this movement met regularly, including writers Georges Henein, Edmond Jabès, and Joyce Mansour. She introduced Henein to Lee Miller in 1939. Her home was also open to painters, dancers, musicians, as well as foreign, mostly francophone cultural figures passing through Egypt, such as André Gide and Roland Petit, who also brought his ballet ensemble. As such, her salon offered a true platform for cultural exchange between Egyptian and foreign intellectuals.

In addition to being on the committee of *La Revue du Caire*, where she printed surrealist texts, reviews and poems, she also published a number of poetry volumes, including a collection, *Printemps*, and another one of Surrealist tales in 1944 entitled *Peau d'ange*. Her poems and stories were also published in a number of local magazines such as *Don Quichotte*, the *Art and Liberty* Group's affiliate review. She wrote praising reviews of the Art and Liberty exhibitions, advocating for Surrealism as the only poetic movement that could encapsulate contemporary life.

Cavadia left Egypt in 1956 after the Suez Canal crisis and moved to Switzerland. She died in 1970.

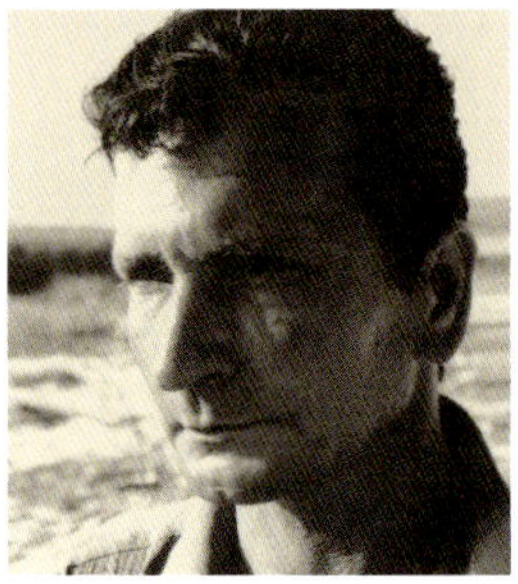

ALBERT COSSERY
(1913-2008)

Albert Cossery was an Egyptian francophone writer who lived in Paris. Born in Cairo into a Greek Orthodox family of Levantine origin, he was educated at the Jesuit School and traveled to France in 1917, where he spent a considerable amount of time before moving there permanently in 1945.

Cossery was highly moved by the poverty and destitution he witnessed in Egypt in the interwar years and during World War Two, particularly with the influx of rural workers to Cairo who, in the capital, found only neglect and poverty. He became a founding member of the *Art and Liberty* Group and his writings inspired many of the group's visual artists in their drawings and paintings, specifically Inji Efflatoun, Fouad Kamel and Kamel El-Telmisany. This literary-artistic cross-pollination is undoubtedly one of *Art and Liberty*'s hallmarks.

Cossery published short stories in *Al-Tatawwur,* the collective's Arabic-language periodical, which would later be published as a book of short stories entitled *Les Hommes oubliés de Dieu* (*Men God Forgot*, 1941). *La Maison de la mort certaine* (1944) is another one of his major works from the *Art and Liberty* era, telling the story of a crumbling house and its impoverished inhabitants in a poor area of Cairo. Cossery was generally interested in society's disregarded underbelly, writing mainly about figures such as smalltime prostitutes, thieves, and beggars. He wrote a total of eight novels during his lifetime, of which *Mendiants et Orgueilleux* ("Proud Beggars," 1955) is sometimes considered his masterpiece.

In 1945, Cossery moved to Paris and lived in the hotel La Louisiane until his death in 2008 from throat cancer. He became a known figure in the circles of Paris's Left Bank, socializing with Camus, Lawrence Durrell, Mouloudji, and Tristan Tzara.

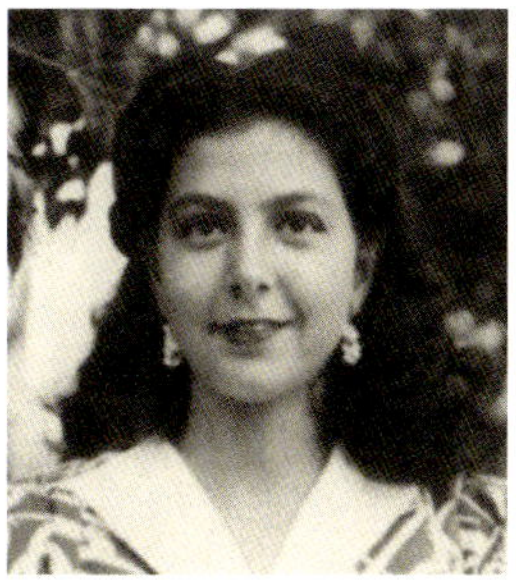

INJI EFFLATOUN
(1924-1989)

Inji Efflatoun was an Egyptian painter, feminist, and political activist and one of the most important figures in modern Egyptian art history. Efflatoun was born in 1924 to an aristocratic Cairene family and educated at the Lycée Français du Caire. Along with her sister, poet and writer Gulperie, Efflatoun was raised by a divorced and working mother, Salha Efflatoun, a fashion designer who, by providing for her family and raising her children alone, defied traditional gender norms and would thus later have an immense impact on Efflatoun's feminism.

Efflatoun showed an early interest in art and was tutored by Kamel El-Telmisany, who introduced her to surrealism, cubism, and the *Art and Liberty* Group. At 18, she was the youngest to ever exhibit in the group's "Expositions d'Art Indépendant," namely in its third installment in 1942. Her work from that period shows a dark torment, where she was greatly influenced by the literary output of the Group, especially Albert Cossery's writings about the plight of poor. She then became one of the first women to attend the free section of the Faculty of Art in Cairo and went on to have her first solo show in 1952. She later studied under Margo Veillon, Hamed Abdallah, and Ragheb Ayyad, and spent time in Upper Egypt to paint local scenes.

A noted Marxist, outspoken and politically active feminist, and writer of three politically progressive short books, Efflatoun's activism landed her in prison in 1959, when she was arrested during Nasser's campaign against Communists. She was in contact with international communist artists including Mexican muralist David Alfari Siqueiros and the Italian painter Renato Guttuso. Efflatoun continued to paint during and beyond her prison sentence, which ended in 1963. Her paintings during her prison time are marked by a somber, harsh quality, though her work gradually became lighter, airier, and of a more joyful quality after her release. She went on to curate a number of exhibitions, including "Visages de l'art contemporain égyptien" at the Musée Galliera in Paris in 1971 and "Ten Egyptian Women Artists" at the Arab Socialist Union in Cairo gallery in 1975 among others. Furthermore, she organized an important personal exhibition that toured in 1970 in East Berlin, Dresden and the USSR. Efflatoun went on to become one of the most widely exhibited Egyptian artists.

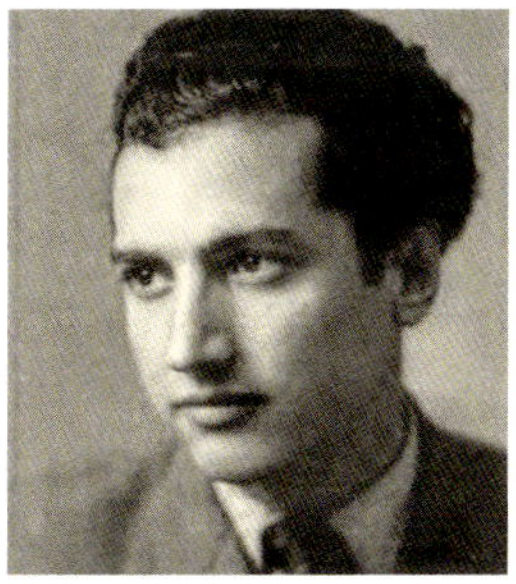

ABDEL HADI EL-GAZZAR
(1925-1966)

Abdel Hadi El-Gazzar is one of Egypt's most revered and well-known artists of the post-war era. The son of an Islamic scholar, El-Gazzar was born in Alexandria in 1925. In 1936, his father was given a position at Al-Azhar, upon which he relocated to Cairo and settled in Sayeda Zeinab, a working-class Cairene neighborhood near Islamic Cairo. There, he witnessed the *moulids* or celebrations of saints and other religious and folkloric rituals that would leave their imprint on his work.

El-Gazzar studied medicine at Cairo University briefly and then enrolled in the Faculty of Fine Arts 1945. He was taught by pioneering art educator Hussein Youssef Amin and would later join him, along with Samir Rafi', Hamed Nada, and others, in the Contemporary Art Group, which is commonly believed to have been founded in 1946. This has been recently contested by newly published segments of Rafi's memoirs in which he contends to have founded the group from as early as 1940. Before joining the Contemporary Art Group however, El-Gazzar had also exhibited with *Art and Liberty* on occasion, becoming a junior member of the collective. His paintings of the time were of a mystifying and surreal nature, and he developed unique imagery to depict magical and imaginary scenes portraying essentially Egyptian rituals or folkloric narratives. Many of his works show an inspiration with the writings of Albert Cossery, illustrating the hardships of the poor. One particular example is *The Queue of Hunger* from 1948, which caused him to be arrested on the opening night of its exhibition. El-Gazzar enjoyed a prolific exhibiting career, showing his work in Egypt and internationally. He participated in the São Paolo Biennale in 1957, for which he won a Bronze Medal Award.

In 1958, El-Gazzar travelled to Rome to attend the Central Restoration Institute, where he gradually abandoned the depiction of typically Egyptian and surreal folkloric scenes and turned to images of fantastical industrialization and complex machines alluding to the nation-state and to Nasser's endeavors. He died in 1966 after his return from Italy at the age of forty, making his career a very short but deeply rich one.

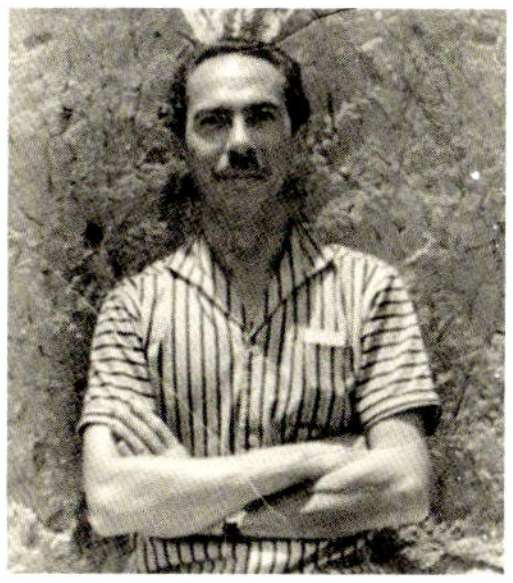

HASSAN EL-TELMISANI
(1923-1987)

Hassan El-Telmisani was a painter and illustrator, and the younger brother of Kamel El-Telmisany. He was born in 1923 and received his diploma in decorative arts in 1938. However, Hassan was enamoured with painting and drawing and followed his older brother's footsteps in visual art, learning to paint under the tutelage of Ramses Younane. Hassan began exhibiting his work in a number of group shows, including the *Société des amis de l'art* as well as the *Néo-Orientalistes.*

Deeply influenced by the outbreak of war and the economic destitution he observed in marginalized segments of Egyptian society, Hassan would join his brother and become a member of the *Art and Liberty* Group. In1943, at the age of 22, he would create some of his most emblematic works reflecting a preoccupation with the devastation of war. Hassan exhibited with the group from 1944 onwards, and in 1942, he joined Fouad Kamel's Bread and Liberty Group, a socialist quasi sister organization of *Art and Liberty* that was more focused on street activism. Together with his brother, Ramses Younane and Anwar Kamel, they were arrested during the Egyptian government's crackdown on communists in 1946 and spent several months in prison. Hassan was later affiliated but never a formal member of the Contemporary Art Group, which included innovators such as Abdel Hadi El-Gazzar and Hamed Nada. They were interested in depicting typically Egyptian scenes but also folkloric narratives of superstition and magic in a surrealist manner.

Hassan later abandoned a professional career in painting and went on to become a pioneer in the documentary filmmaking industry. He died in 1987.

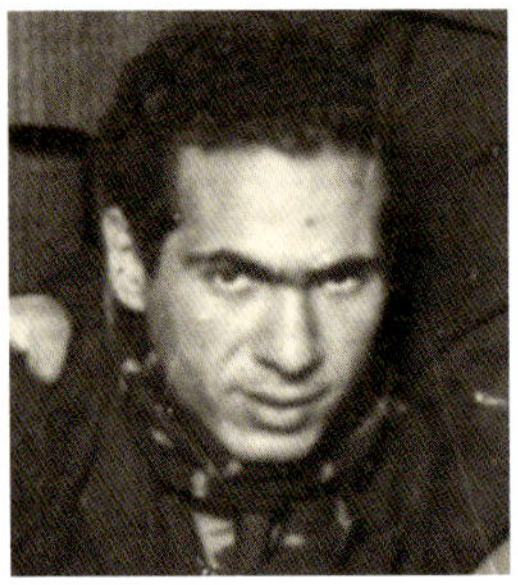

KAMEL EL-TELMISANY
(1915–1972)

El-Telmisany was born in Qalyubiyeh, Egypt, in 1915, and studied veterinary medicine. Passionate about painting, he abandoned his studies and pursued visual art when his family moved to Cairo. There, he met young experimental writer Georges Henein and artist and critic Ramses Younane, and together with them lent *Art and Liberty* its impetus, becoming one of its founders and protagonists.

El-Telmisany's painting career was very short lived, lasting only ten years. His work is a vigorous manifestation of all of *Art and Liberty*'s ideas, exhibiting a particularly violent and dark but poetic nature. In addition to painting, El-Telmisany was a prolific writer and critic, publishing a number of articles in *Al-Tatawwur*, *Art and Liberty*'s Arabic-language review, as well as *Don Quichotte*, a French-language avant-garde artistic and literary review established by Henri and Raoul Curiel with several *Art and Liberty* members and affiliates including Georges Henien serving on its editorial board. El-Telmisany designed the headers for *Don Quichotte* and wrote a series of articles entitled "L'Art en Égypte", for every installment of which he showcased the work of a fellow *Art and Liberty* member and wrote fantastically poetic and surrealist texts to accompany them.

With time, El-Telmisany became more preoccupied with Marxist ideologies and turned to cinema in 1945 to promulgate his message. Like his brother, he excelled in the field and directed the highly controversial and anti-capitalist Al-Souq Al-Sawda' in 1945, one of Arab cinema's most important films and perhaps its first of the neo-realist kind. It was banned from theatres for four years. El-Telmisany died in 1972.

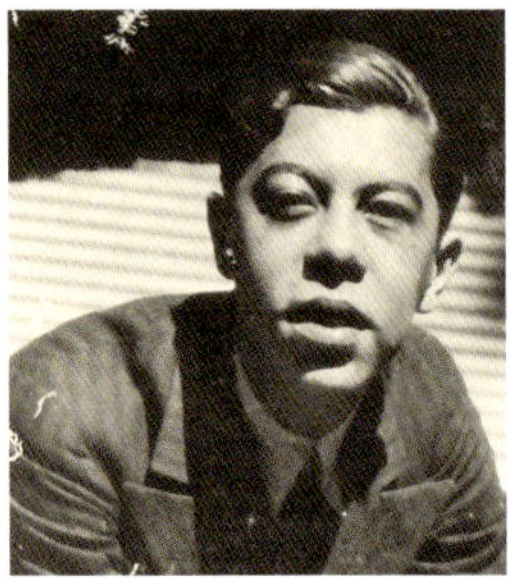

GEORGES HENEIN
(1914–1973)

Georges Henein was an Egyptian Surrealist poet and literary critic. Born in 1914 to an elite Coptic family, Henein's father, Sadik Henein Pasha, was a diplomat, and his mother was an Egyptian-Italian named Maria Zanelli. Growing up in a cosmopolitan home, Henein mastered many languages and spent his childhood years between Cairo, Madrid, Rome, and Paris thanks to his father's diplomatic work. He completed his studies at the Sorbonne and mixed with Surrealist circles in 1930s Paris. He contributed to *Un Effort*, a Cairene monthly published by Francophone literary collective *Les Essayistes*, and to *Les Humbles*, a Marxist-Leninist journal printed in Paris.

In 1936, Henein met André Breton, the so-called father of Surrealism. It was the beginning of a long correspondence and friendship between the two that would encourage Henein to form the *Art and Liberty* Group in Cairo. He finally achieved this upon the publication on December 22, 1938, of the famed Manifesto of Degenerate Art in reaction to the Nazis' persecution of artists in Europe. "Long Live Degenerate Art" signaled the beginning of a movement in art and literature, comprising thirty-nine artists and intellectuals of different backgrounds. The subsequent independent art exhibitions organized by the group, which challenged mainstream ideas about art in every way, saw the growth of Surrealist painting and photography in Egypt. Henein also financed *Al-Tatawwur, Art and Liberty*'s Arabic-language review, and established *La Part du Sable* together with poet Edmond Jabès and painter and theorist Ramses Younane.

In 1948 Henein broke away from the Surrealists in a letter to Breton, citing disagreement in direction and vision. *Art and Liberty* had already disintegrated in the preceding couple of years, and Henein's efforts to imbue it with a second wind by attempting to counsel artists who would later form the Contemporary Art Group, failed. Henein was forced into exile by the Egyptian government in 1962. With his wife Iqbal El-Alaily, also a writer, he settled in France, where he wrote for *Jeune Afrique* and *L'Express*, focusing on journalistic writing until his death in 1973.

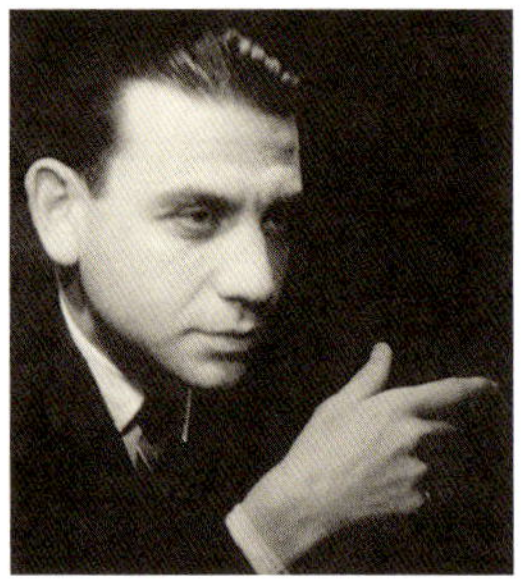

EDMOND JABÈS
(1912–1991)

Edmond Jabès was born in Cairo in 1912 to a comfortable Jewish family established in Egypt from at least the nineteenth century. He would later become one of the most important literary figures of post-World War Two France. From an early age he was interested in theater and in his twenties wrote surrealist poetry. He later became associated with the *Art and Liberty* group. He collaborated with surrealist artists even before the official formation of the collective, notably, with Mayo, the *Art and Liberty* affiliate and surrealist painter, who contributed drawings to Jabès's *Les pieds en l'air* (Éditions de la Semaine Égyptienne, 1934).

Strongly committed to the fight against fascism, Jabès established the League of Youth Against Racism and Anti-semitism in Cairo. He formed friendships during this time with Paul Eluard, André Gide and above all Max Jacob, and published their correspondence after Jacob's death (Éditions du Scarabée, 1945). His poems appeared in the short-lived *La Part du Sable*, the surrealist journal and imprint founded by Georges Henein and Ramses Younane. Edmond Jabès never formally joined a surrealist group and he contributed to the debate on surrealist aesthetics in the wake of death camps. Before fleeing Egypt and settling in Paris in 1957, he founded the imprint Le Chemin des Sources, in which short works by Gabriel Bounoure, Jean Grenier, and René Char appeared.

Jabès published prolifically in France and received many prizes, including the Grand Prix National de la Poésie in 1987. One of his best-known books is *The Book of Questions* (Gallimard, 1963), a long poem about two young lovers living through the Nazi and Vichy persecutions. Jabès was generally preoccupied with the fate of the Jew as always remaining in exile and showed an intense melancholy in his writings. In 1972, Jacques Derrida said of him, "In the last ten years, nothing of interest has been written in France that does not have its precedent somewhere in the texts of Jabès." He died in Paris in 1991.

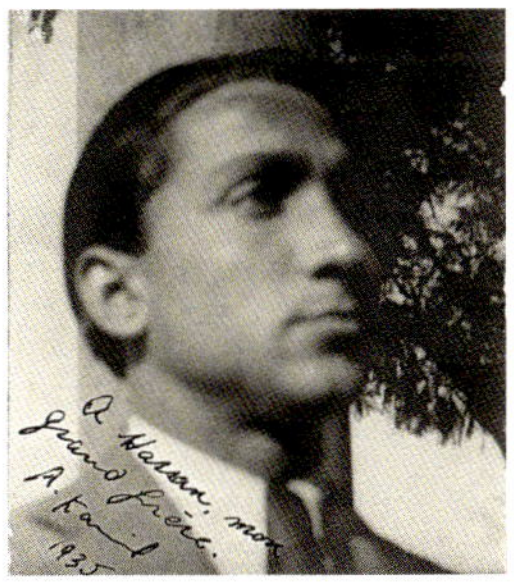

ANWAR KAMEL
(1913-1991)

Anwar Kamel was an Egyptian poet, writer, and political activist. Together with artists and writers Georges Henein, Kamel El-Telmisany and Fouad Kamel, his younger brother, he established the anti-Fascist *Art and Liberty* Group calling for social and expressive freedom and liberation of the imagination through Surrealist values.

A noted Communist, Kamel was already advocating Surrealist and fundamentally anti-fascist ideas before the formation of *Art and Liberty*. In 1936, at the age of twenty-three, Anwar published *Al-Kitab Al-Manbuz* (The Outcast Book) a work of prose poetry wherein he called for the liberation of desires from the repressive ideals of the bourgeoisie. Soon, a group of intellectuals calling themselves Al-Manbuzin (The Outcasts) formed itself around Kamel. It included Ramses Younane and the Telmissany brothers. Down the line, this led to the formation of the *Art and Liberty* Group.

January 1940 saw the publication of the first issue of Al-Tatawwur, *Art and Liberty*'s Arabic-language Socialist review. Kamel was its editor in chief until it was banned by the government for incendiary content in its seventh issue. Fallouts with members of the *Art and Liberty* Group, as well as divergences in vision led Kamel to form Bread and Freedom, a Communist and militant group of intellectuals that helped mobilize worker and student demonstrations. After a growing crackdown on the group, Kamel was arrested along with the Telmissany brothers. He continued to write during his time in prison and published works such as *Al-Sahyuniyya* (Zionism, 1944) and *La Tabaqaat* (A Society Free of Class, 1945). Kamel continued to write after his sentence ended, and in 1948, he published *Afyoun Al-Shu'ub* (The People's Opium), a scathing anti-Stalinist work of sociopolitical criticism.

Kamel died in 1991. The full contents of *Al-Tatawurr* were later republished by the poet Hisham Geshta in *Al-Kitabah Al-Ukhrah*.

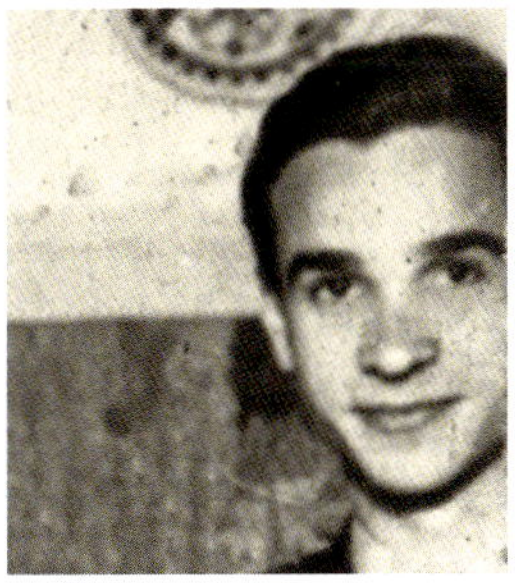

FOUAD KAMEL
(1919-1973)

Fouad Kamel was an Egyptian painter, poet, and illustrator, and one of the founders of the *Art and Liberty* Group. Born in Beni Suef, Egypt, on April 28, 1919, he went on to study art and art education in Cairo and graduated from the Fine Art School in 1942. He subsequently taught drawing in public schools.

Throughout his prolific career, Kamel joined a number of artistic groupings and movements including the Neo-Orientalists along with Kamel El-Telmisany in 1937. Of a rebellious nature, he would later band with Kamel El-Telmissany and Georges Henein to form the *Art and Liberty* Group in 1938, with whom he exhibited throughout the entire war period. His paintings and drawings from that period show an affinity to the writings of Albert Cossery, which dealt with the plight of the impoverished and destitute of Egypt. He also participated in an exhibition of automatic drawing at the Lycée Français du Caire in 1947, together with Ramses Younane and Kamel El-Telmisany. He was included in *Le Surréalisme en 1947,* which was curated by Breton at the Galerie Maeght in Paris in 1947.

Kamel also created a number of illustrations for *Al-Tatawwur, Al-Majallah Al-Jadida*, and *La Part du Sable*, which he helped establish with Henein and Younane in 1947. Even after *Art and Liberty* parted ways, Kamel continued to organize exhibitions of Surrealist art into the late 1940s. His paintings moved toward complete abstraction later in his life. Kamel died in Cairo on June 25, 1973.

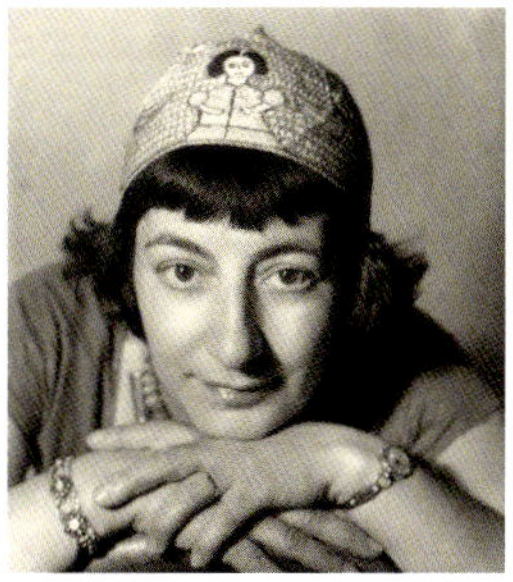

IDA KAR
(1908-1974)

Ida Kar, born Karamian, was a photographer of Armenian origin born in Russia. She spent her childhood in Iran, Armenia, and Russia, before her family moved to Alexandria where she attended the city's Lycée Français.

After having graduated from the Lycée, Kar left Alexandria to study chemistry and medicine in Paris and later interrupted her studies to learn singing and violin. It was during that time that she met German experimental photographer Heinrich Heidersberger, who introduced her to Surrealist photography.

In 1933, Kar returned to Egypt and later married Edmond Belali, a government official and amateur photographer. Together they founded Idabel, a photography collective and studio in Cairo, and went on to exhibit their work in three of the *Art and Liberty* exhibitions to favorable reviews by critics such as Ahmed Rassim Bey. She collaborated with different photographers and artists on photomontage series, including fellow *Art and Liberty* member and Surrealist painter Angelo de Riz. As with Étienne Sved, Kar would also photograph ancient Egyptian monuments and artifacts without according them the heavy burden of national symbolism as opposed to her more traditional contemporaries.

Kar later divorced Belali and married British poet Victor Musgrave, who was stationed in Egypt during World War II. Together they moved to London in 1949, where Kar would embark on a remarkable career in photography, producing portraits of high profile intellectuals throughout the continent. Until her death in 1974, she worked in London and Paris and exhibited throughout Europe and Russia, garnering much critical acclaim and success, and had prominent role in furthering the place of photography within fine art. Kar was the first photographer to have been given a retrospective at a major London gallery, the Whitechapel Art Gallery in 1960.

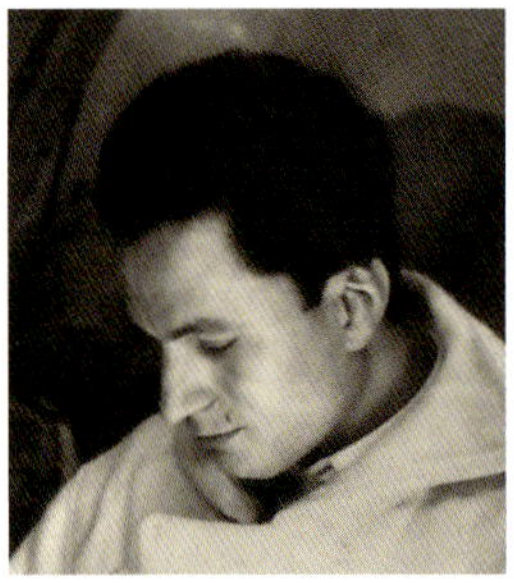

MAHMOUD KHALIL
(1929-1955)

Mahmoud Khalil was an Egyptian painter and poet born in 1929. Scarce information is available on this artist who is known to have been the youngest student of Hussein Youssef Amin and the youngest member of the Contemporary Art Group.

Khalil studied philosophy under the prominent existentialist philosopher Abdel Rahmn Badawi (1917 – 2002). He corresponded with famed Egyptian Romantic writer Mahmoud Taymour and executed his first drawings and paintings in his early twenties. The recipient of a prize for drawing and a grant from the Egyptian government, Khalil participated in the Contemporary Art Group's inaugural 1946 exhibition as well as its second installment in 1948, in addition to an exhibition held under the auspices of the *Amitiés françaises* in the mid 1950s among others.

Described as "completely original" by critic Étienne Meriel in the latter's 1954 booklet about the artist, Khalil's work is said to have set itself apart from the other members of the Contemporary Art Group due to its "naïveté, spontaneity, persuasiveness and mysterious quality." He used China ink in many of his drawings, which almost always depict figures in the midst of a ritual, though in a static form, drawn either from the side or from the front, similar to ancient Egyptian art. His treatment of composition, consistently filling the page and often abandoning depth and classical perspective, led critics to describe his work as being influenced by an "Oriental atavism."

Khalil participated in the Venice Biennale in 1952 along with Abdel Hadi El-Gazzar and Hamed Nada, his colleagues from the Contemporary Art Group, and his works were collected by the Museum of Modern Egyptian Art as well as by private collections. It is known that he spent time in Sudan to focus on art and live in simplicity.

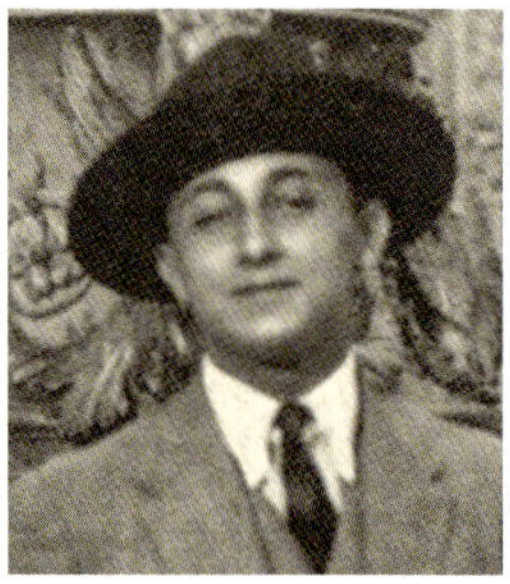

MAYO
(1905-1990)

Antoine Malliarakis, better known as Mayo, was born to a Greek Suez Canal engineer and a French mother in Port Said, Egypt in 1905. Although he neither officially joined Breton's Surrealist group, nor the *Art and Liberty* Group in Egypt, he was an important member of the movement.

Mayo studied at the École des Beaux-Arts de Paris between 1923 and 1927. There, he spent a lot of time in Montparnasse and socialized with prominent Surrealists such as Tristan Tzara, Man Ray, Yves Tanguy, and later Jacques Prévert and Robert Desnos. He went on to exhibit in several group shows as well as solo shows all over Europe and collaborated with the para-Surrealist group *Le Grand Jeu* on their literary review. He returned to Egypt in 1933–34, and again from 1937 to 1941, where he exhibited with the *Art and Liberty* group and was very well received. Mayo also illustrated several writings by *Art and Liberty* group members including Ivo Barbitch and Edmond Jabès and made drawings for a number of other literary reviews. His illustrations took on a more somber tone during the war years and include works for Camus and Prévert. He is also known for his work as a costume and set designer for theater and films, most notably Marcel Carné's *Les Enfants du paradis*.

After 1942, Mayo moved back to Europe, first settling in Paris and then in Rome in 1966 where he continued to actively produce paintings and drawings, exhibiting mainly in Italy as well as Paris, until afflicted by an eye infection in 1984. He returned to Paris in 1986 and was honored as a commander of the French Ordre des Arts et des Lettres. He died in Seine-Port, France, in 1990.

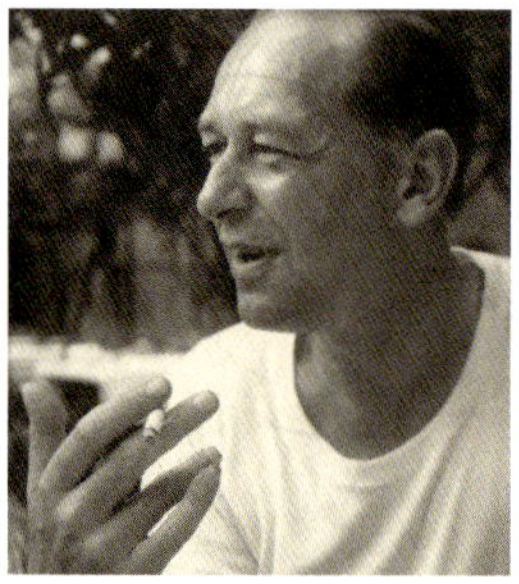

ROBERT MEDLEY
(1905-1994)

Robert Medley was an English painter, theatre set designer, and art educator. He was born in London to a well-known copyright lawyer and studied art at the Slade School of Fine Art, later completing his studies in Paris.

In 1931 Medley began exhibiting his work and also started teaching at the Chelsea School of Art, where by coincidence he taught Egyptian painter Rateb Seddik, who later became an *Art and Liberty* Group member. Medley participated in the International Surrealist Exhibition in London in 1936 and was an active member of the British Surrealist scene, helping organize exhibitions and even moderating a debate in 1938 between Surrealists and realists.

Medley was sent to Cairo as a war artist during World War Two. There, he became acquainted with the *Art and Liberty* Group and participated in their fifth exhibition of independent art in 1945. Like several of his colleagues, Medley was highly influenced by the writings of *Art and Liberty* member Albert Cossery. *Cairo at Night*, which Medley began in 1944 while stationed in Cairo but completed after returning home after the war, is an example of this, with its vividly contorted and morphing figures.

After his return to England, Medley continued to paint prolifically and held a number of teaching positions. He was Head of Painting at Camberwell School of Art for many years and also taught at the Chelsea Art School and Slade School of Art. He is considered as one of the most important English painters of the 20th century.

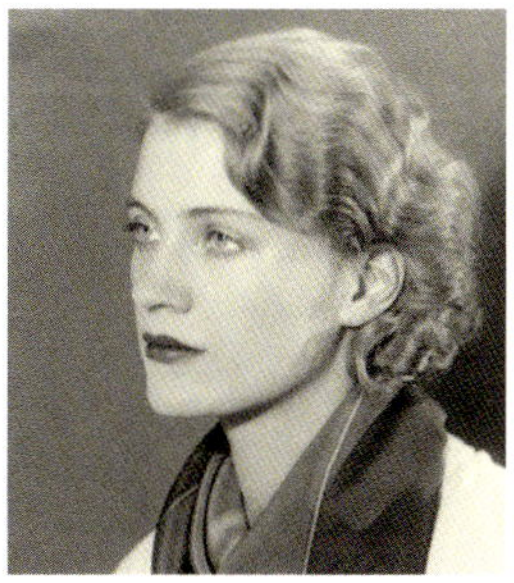

LEE MILLER
(1907-1977)

Born in Poughkeepsie, New York, an American of Canadian and German descent, Lee Miller was a photographer, model, and one of the most famous free-spirited figures of the twentieth century.

Miller began her career in photography modelling for prominent artists such as Edward Steichen and Arnold Genthe. In 1929 she moved to Paris to study under Man Ray, whose muse, apprentice-collaborator, and lover she would become. She then established her own studio in New York in 1932 and ran it successfully until she married Aziz Eloui Bey, a wealthy Egyptian businessman and relocated to Cairo in 1934. There, she formed close ties with the surrealists of Cairo and the *Art and Liberty* Group. Her role was seminal in aiding the dialogue between the group and the British Surrealists in London, as well as the Villa Seurat circle in Paris. By making surrealist exhibition reviews and literature accessible to the Group via her lover Roland Penrose, Miller helped develop the local artistic surrealist scene.

At the same time, her own Surrealist photographic practice flourished as she was captivated by desert landscapes and ruins, of which she made beautiful, almost abstract depictions in works such as *Portrait of Space* (1937).

In 1939, Miller moved to London with the British Surrealist painter Roland Penrose, who would later become her husband and father of her only child. In World War Two, Miller became a freelance fashion photographer and photojournalist for *Vogue* Magazine, covering everything from the London Blitz to the death camps at Buchenwald and Dachau. Returning to England, she and Penrose made their home Farley Farm House in East Sussex a mecca for visiting artists, such as Man Ray, Moore, Dubuffet, and Ernst. She died on her farm in 1977.

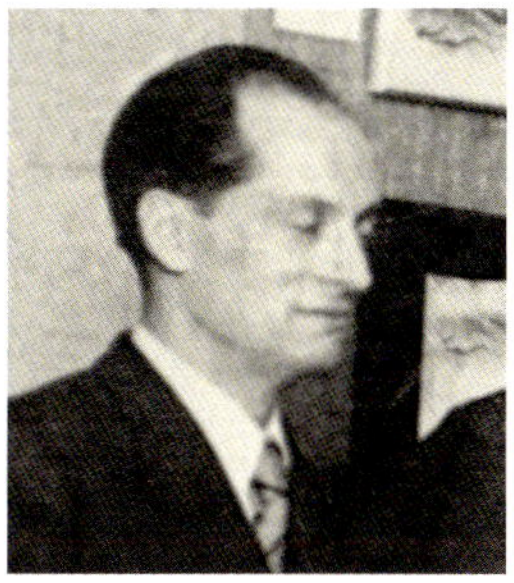

JEAN MOSCATELLI
(1905-1965)

Jean Moscatelli was a French-speaking Italian poet, artist and journalist born in Egypt. Early in his career, Moscatelli was an active member of a number of literary groups. These include the *Salamander Society*, of which art and literary critic Ahmed Rassim and journalist Erik de Mauny were also members, as well as *Les Essayistes*, a francophone literary society based in Cairo that published the review *Un Effort*.

In 1933, Moscatelli translated to French the futurist poem collection *Per le mie donne* ("For My Women", Éditions de La Semaine Égyptienne, Cairo) by the Italian Nelson Morpurgo, at the time a young Egypt-based futurist writer whose avant-garde poetry Moscatelli admired. But with the Futurists' increasingly glaring fascist agenda, Moscatelli would later write an article for *La Semaine Égyptienne* in October of that year critiquing the same poet as well as the Futurist movement, claiming Morpurgo's language was incomprehensible across social classes. It was after Filippo Tommaso Marinetti's visit and lecture in Egypt in 1938, organized by *Les Essayistes*, which led to a controversy following Henein's attack of the latter's fascist propaganda, that Moscatelli, along with Henein and Jo Farna (Joseph Habachi), would break ties with both the futurists and *Les Essayistes* in 1938 altogether.

After his break with *Les Essayistes*, Moscatelli became a founding member of *Art and Liberty* along with Georges Henein and even participated as an artist in the group's inaugural exhibition *L'Exposition de l'art indépendant* at the Lycée français in 1940. Throughout his career, he would go on to write many positive reviews of *Art and Liberty*'s endeavours for a number of publications, including the illustrated periodical *Images* and the weekly French-language *La Semaine Égyptienne*.

Moscatelli's published works include the anthology *Poètes en Égypte* (L'Atelier, Cairo, 1955) and a number of books and poetry collections including *Moi sans toi* (Éditions de La Caravelle, Paris, 1927), *Poèmes maudits* (Éditions de La Caravelle, publication year unknown, and Le Livre et l'Image, 1929), *Dix sonnets* (Éditions de La Semaine Égyptienne, Cairo, 1935) and *Akhénaton ou la religion la meilleure* (Imprimerie Paul Barbey, Cairo, 1936).

In 1956, Moscatelli won the bronze medal for the French language category of the Prix de l'academie française. He died in Egypt in 1965.

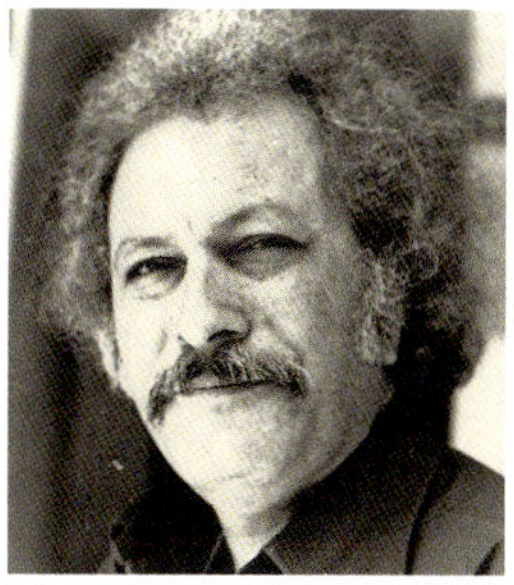

HAMED NADA
(1924-1990)

Raised in a religious household in the Al-Qal'a district of Cairo, Hamed Nada, whose paintings manifest a deep inspiration with the rituals, superstitions, and folkloric narratives present in common Egyptian life, went on to become one of Egypt's foremost Surrealist artists.

Nada's interest in art from a young age led him to be tutored by Hussein Youssef Amin, an art pedagogue known for his rejection of traditional art teaching techniques, as well as being generally accepted as the founder of the Contemporary Art Group, whose main interests were surrealism and a concern for social issues. However, the founding of the Group has been recently contested through newly published material (for more see Samir Rafi' biography in this section). Nada eventually had his first exhibition with the Contemporary Art Group in 1946 and went on to participate in all of their shows until 1951, becoming one its most integral members along with Abdel Hadi El-Gazzar and Samir Rafi'. In addition, he had fifteen more exhibitions across Egypt, France, Italy and Spain during his lifetime.

Nada graduated from the Faculty of Fine Arts in Cairo in 1951 after having been taught by both prominent Egyptian artists Ahmed Sabry and Youssef Kamel. Simultaneously, he wrote and illustrated for the literary review *Al-Thaqafah*, where other noted writers such as Taha Hussein and Louis Awad published their works. After studying in Luxor and Madrid, he later became head of the painting department at the School of Fine Arts in Alexandria, and successively in Cairo in 1977, after which he continued to teach painting on a part-time basis until his death in 1990.

The paintings of Hamed Nada are unique in their approach to Surrealism, combining a profound knowledge of folkloric tales and magicalness together with symbolic elements depicting the life of Egypt's working class.

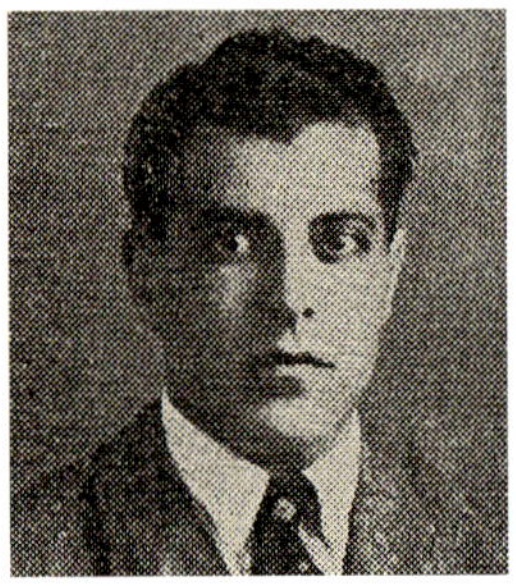

ERIC DE NEMES
(Birth and death dates unknown)

Eric de Nemes was a Hungarian illustrator and writer who moved from Beirut to Cairo in 1939 or 1940. Although not much is known about this artist, it is known that he acquired the Egyptian nationality later in his life.

De Nemes can be considered the most prolific illustrator within the *Art and Liberty* Group. Even though he did not sign the original Manifesto of Degenerate Art in 1939, he joined the group soon afterward, and as one of the many foreigners in the group, his membership is a testimony to *Art and Liberty*'s true cosmopolitanism. He exhibited with the group in 1941 during their second exhibition for independent art. His artist statement in the exhibition catalogue stated that for him, art is like a lucky bag, whose "silver paper and artificial flowers hide a bomb that explodes in the hands of the public."

De Nemes's mastery of illustration can be seen in a range of publications. These include *Poetry of Our Times*, an anthology of Cairo-based Anglophone poets published by Thoth Bookshop in Cairo in 1943. In 1945 he illustrated *La Vertu de l'Allemagne* by Iqbal El-Alaily, George Henein's wife. *Cœurs Doubles* (Alexandria: Éditions du Scarabée, 1948), a literary and cultural review established in 1945 by René Étiemble, is another example of De Nemes's brilliance. De Nemes also produced a series of fourteen illustrations in 1945 for a book entitled *The Lovely and the Dead* by John Waller; however, the book was never published.

In terms of writing, De Nemes contributed to *Sphinx*, an English-language illustrated weekly published in Cairo. He writings ranged from exhibition reviews to short stories.

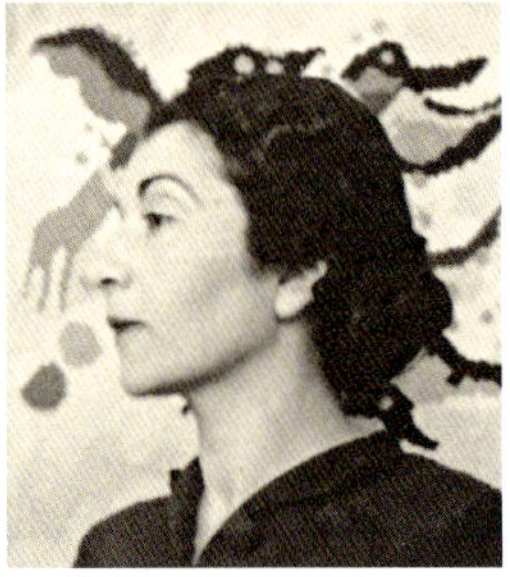

AMY NIMR
(1907–1974)

Amy Nimr, also known as Amy Smart, was a painter and writer, and was the daughter of prominent Egypt-based Syrian media mogul Faris Nimr. Born in Cairo, Nimr travelled to Paris and Rome in her youth and studied fine arts at the Slade School in London. She also studied briefly under Walter Sickert. Nimr began exhibiting her work in Paris and London in the 1920s and became well acquainted with the British surrealists and the artists of the Villa Seurat in Paris. Back in Cairo in the early 1930s she married Walter Smart, a high ranking British official and well-regarded scholar of Arabic and Persian. Nimr would enjoy critical acclaim of her work in Egypt, exhibiting regularly at the annual Salon du Caire among the likes of Mahmoud Saïd.

Nimr and her husband were known for their hospitality, hosting at their cultural salon guests from around the world ranging from royalty and celebrities to cash-strapped artists and intellectuals. She became known for her generosity as she was a patron of the arts and helped many needy artists, including Lawrence Durrell when he landed in Egypt. She played an important role in strengthening the dialogue between European surrealists and the local scene.

Together with her colleague Mahmoud Saïd, Nimr was praised equally by the *Société des amis de l'art* as well as the avant-garde *Art and Liberty* Group, an acclaim that only these two painters of their generation could enjoy. In 1943 however, Nimr's only son, Micky, was killed by a landmine during the family's picnic in Wadi Degla. Her paintings following this accident are described as her most surrealist and dark phase. She exhibited these works in the mid 1940s at the Expositions de l'Art Indépendant to great praise. Finally, it is worth nothing that Nimr is the only Egypt-based surrealist who would later contribute to surrealist war poetry journal *Personal Landscape* with a critical essay on Cavay's poetry in 1945.

Nimr left Egypt after the 1956 Suez War. She died in Paris in January 1974.

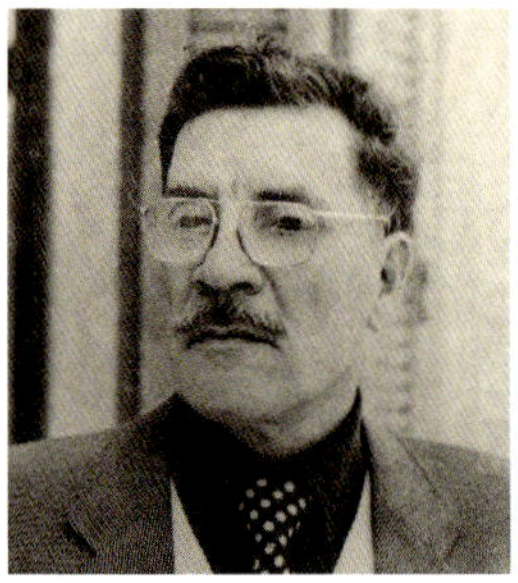

MAHER RA'EF
(1926–1999)

Maher Ra'ef was born in the Shubra district of Cairo. His father was a visual artist and a contemporary of the so-called Pioneers or First Generation Egyptian artists. His grandfather was an Azhar scholar.

Ra'ef spent many years of his life studying and was passionate about research. He studied printmaking at the Fine Arts Faculty in Cairo, graduating in 1950 and later philosophy at Cairo University, earning a degree in 1954.

Ra'ef joined the Contemporary Art Group (for more on the Contemporary Art Group, see biography of Hussein Youssef Amin) and exhibited with them in their inaugural show of 1946. The group was concerned with developing an essentially Egyptian art by examining themes of folklore and popular culture using heavy symbolism. Ra'ef was later awarded a residency in Luxor, and then received two scholarships to study in Germany. He studied printmaking in Düsseldorf, receiving a degree in 1960 and another one from the Wuppertal Academy in 1961. He also earned a PhD in aesthetics from the University of Cologne. When he returned to Egypt, he had become a Sufi and abandoned figurative painting, turning to calligraphy and geometric forms for his work.

Ra'ef exhibited his work throughout Egypt, including the Alexandria Biennale, as well as in Germany, Switzerland, France, and Sweden. He held a number of teaching positions at the Alexandria and Cairo faculties of fine art including dean of graduate studies at the Alexandria Faculty of Fine Arts in 1979. Ra'ef moved to New Jersey to live with his daughter after retiring in 1986. He died in the United States in 1999.

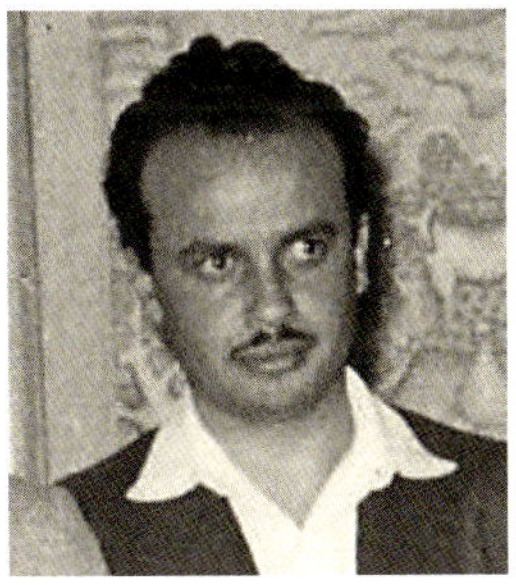

SAMIR RAFI'
(1926-2004)

Samir Rafi' was born in the Sakakini district of Cairo in 1926 to a well-off, multi-faith household. His father was a Muslim lawyer of a severe nature, and his mother was a warm Christian woman who taught Rafi' to speak French.

During his secondary school years, Rafi' was tutored by Hussein Youssef Amin, a pioneering art educator at the Faruk I School who had spent time in South America and Europe and returned to Egypt espousing novel teaching methods. Rafi' went on to study decorative arts at the Fine Arts School in Cairo and graduated in 1948. He had begun exhibiting his work much earlier however, having been encouraged by his teacher Amin to partake in an exhibition at the Qattan Library in Cairo in 1943 when he was only seventeen.

Rafi' was influenced by the surrealists and eventually went on to exhibit with the *Art and Liberty* Group. Georges Henein was aware of his talent and had even suggested him to André Breton in their correspondence regarding the *Surréalisme en 1947* exhibition, even though he was only a junior member of *Art and Liberty*. In any case, it was not long until *Art and Liberty* dispersed, and in 1946, Amin founded the Contemporary Art Group of which Rafi' would become a prominent member, alongside Abdel Hadi El-Gazzar and Hamed Nada. However, Amin's founding of the group has been recently contested by newly published segments of Rafi's memoirs in which he contends to have founded that group from as early as 1940. The group was concerned with depicting Egyptian life and popular culture through a surrealist lens, often using folkloric narra- tives and magic as a central theme.

Rafi' relocated to France in 1954 to study for a PhD in art history at the Sorbonne. He continued to produce inexhaustibly and died in Paris in 2004, leaving behind a significant amount of drawings and paintings.

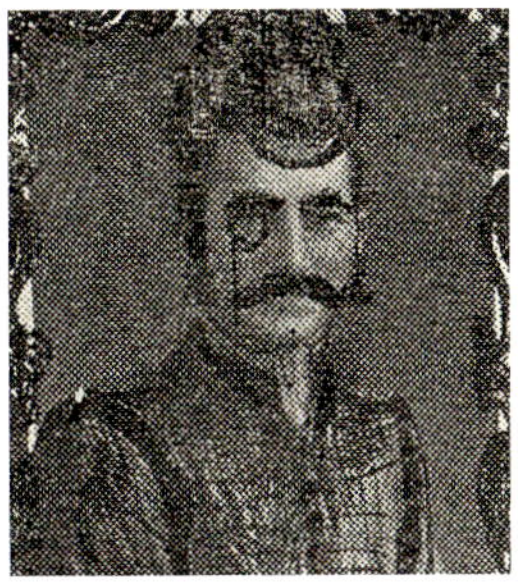

ANGELO DE RIZ
(Birth and death dates unknown)

Angelo de Riz was an Italian Anarchist and anti-Fascist painter active in Egypt between the 1930s and 1950s. Much of this artist's biography and life remain a mystery, however he is known to have fled Mussolini's Fascist regime and landed in Alexandria as a refugee sometime in the mid-1930s. De Riz later moved to Cairo, where he taught at the Lycée du Caire in Bab el-Louq and practiced as a painter, muralist, and decorator.

De Riz can be considered one of the original purveyors of Surrealism in Egypt. In 1937, with the leadership of Georges Henein and together with Ramses Younane and writer Émile Simon, he co-organized a conference that was to introduce Surrealism to Egyptian audiences. In that year, he exhibited with Jo Schlesinger, another *Art and Liberty* artist, at the gallery Nistri in Cairo. He was also a member of the *Art and Liberty* group and one of the first signatories of the Manifesto of Degenerate Art in 1938. He exhibited together with *Art and Liberty* throughout the entire war period and was highly praised by Georges Henein for his paintings dealing with dreams and dream-like narratives. A number of his drawings also appeared in the short-lived artistic and literary review *Al-Tatawurr,* which was published in Cairo in 1940.

In addition, De Riz executed murals for ballrooms in Alexandria and one in the Cinema Rivoli in Cairo. He lived in Beit el-Dahabieh, a house across from the famous Maison des Artistes in Dar el-Labbanah. It was demolished when he moved out in the late1950s.

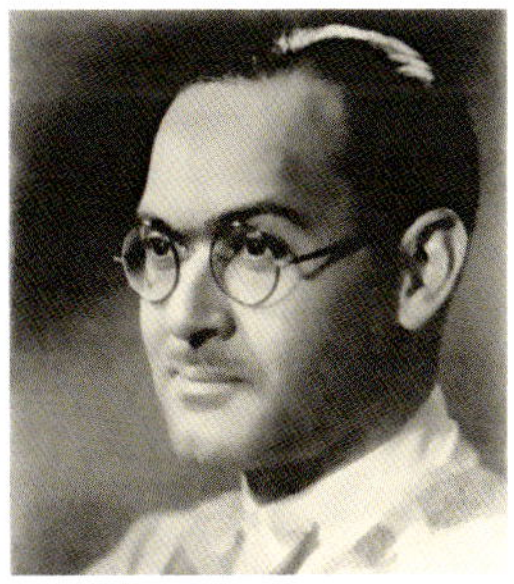

MAHMOUD SAÏD
(1897-1964)

Mahmoud Saïd was born in Alexandria in 1897 to a wealthy and powerful landowning family. His father, Mohammed Saïd Pasha, would later become Egypt's prime minister, and his niece would become Queen Farida of Egypt.

Saïd graduated from the Cairo School of Law in 1918 but had been studying painting under Italian artists Amelia Cassonato and Arturo Zanieri beforehand. Upon receiving his law degree, he traveled to Paris to continue his studies and simultaneously enrolled at the Académie de la Grande Chaumière in 1919.

He worked in the Mixed Courts upon his return to Egypt and continued his legal career until he retired in 1949, devoting his time to art exclusively. Throughout his parallel artistic career, Saïd created works highly praised by both state-backed groups such as the *Société des amis de l'art* as well as the rebellious and Surrealist *Art and Liberty* Group. He was the only artist from the so-called Pioneers to exhibit with *Art and Liberty*, who considered his strange and mystifying portraits, such as *Thaat Al-Jada'il Al-Thahabiyya* (The Woman with the Golden Locks, 1933), to be of a surreal and Freudian quality, probing the realm of the subconscious. Saïd also produced many society portraits as well as nudes.

He participated in the Alexandria Atelier and the Salon du Caire organized by the *Société* every year and also represented Egypt at the Venice and Mediterranean Biennales many times throughout his career. He also received the gold medal for his representation of Egypt in the 1937 International Exhibition in Paris. Saïd died in 1964.

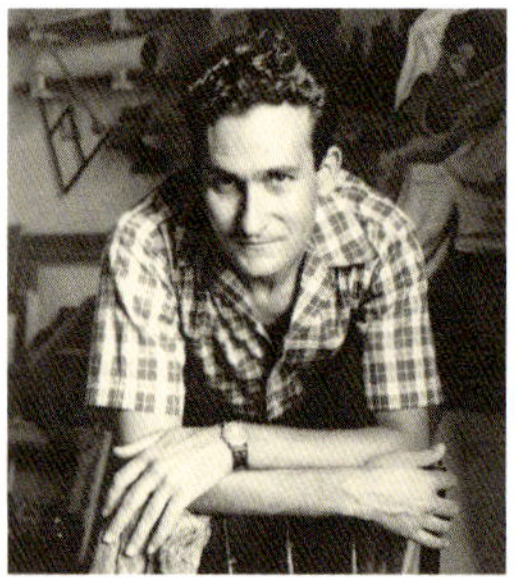

LAURENT MARCEL SALINAS
(1913-2010)

Born to a French mother and an Italian father in Alexandria in 1913, Laurent Marcel Salinas spent his early career years between the Mediterranean port and Aix-en-Provence, France, where he studied law.

However, his interest lay in painting, and he was involved with the *Art and Liberty* Group extensively, being one of the original signatories of its Manifesto for Degenerate Art and also exhibiting his Surrealist paintings known for their hybridization of man and machine in the group's exhibitions of independent art. He also exhibited together with Mahmoud Saïd and Ahmed Nagi at the Alexandria Atelier. Salinas was not only a painter but also an art critic and he contributed regularly to the literary reviews such as the French-language *Valeurs* and *Don Quichotte,* both platforms for many of the *Art and Liberty* Group members.

In the aftermath of the 1952 Egyptian revolution, Salinas and his family were forced into a financially disastrous exile, during which many of his paintings were lost. In the following years, Salinas continued painting and expanded his practice into lithography and photography in Paris, quickly becoming a leading expert of both mediums to the point of earning Picasso's formal recognition for a lithographic rendition of his *29 Portraits Imaginaires* as well as Henri Cartier Bresson's acknowledgment and admiration. He died in 2010.

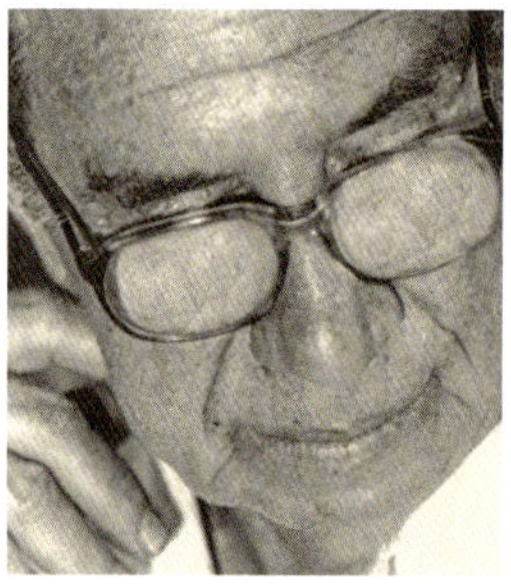

RATEB SEDDIK
(1917-1994)

Rateb Seddik's early artistic training took place under two pioneering Egyptian artists: Mohammad Saïd El-Gharably, and later on Youssef El-Afifi at the Saadiyyah Secondary school. There, he would meet his life-long friend and *Art et Liberté* member Kamel El-Telmisany. In 1936, Seddik moved to London to study at the Chelsea School of Art. Coincidentally, one of his teachers was the surrealist painter Robert Medley who moved to Cairo as a soldier during WWII and participated in *Art et Liberté* exhibitions.

In 1937, Seddik enrolled at the more liberal Amédée Ozenfant Academy of Fine Art, where fellow Egyptian artist Hamed Saïd was a student. In 1938, upon Ozenfant's announcement that he was assuming a teaching position at Yale University, Seddik moved to Paris to study under Fernand Léger. In 1939, he met Georges Henein who encouraged him to adopt a Surrealist style, and invited him to join the *Art et Liberté* Group. The war broke out, and the two found themselves on the same ship headed back to Cairo from Marseilles.

Seddik's first solo exhibition in Cairo was in 1940. He exhibited with the *Art et Liberté* Group until 1942. His work from that period is of a dark nature with apocalyptic scenes, and Surrealist variations on Renaissance religious genres. In 1942, he married a fellow Art et Liberté artist, the sculptor and poet Aïda Schéhadé (1922 - 1981). Together they moved to Sudan where they would teach art, and remain until 1951.

In the 1960s, Seddik's work became more esoteric, depicting mythological figures and prophets. In 1964, he was elected as the director of the Cairo Atelier, and remained so throughout his life. Before his death in 1994, Seddik bequeathed his home, which was completed in 1970 by the legendary Egyptian architect Hassan Fathi, to the Egyptian Ministry of Culture. It is now the Rateb Seddik Museum in Al-Mounib.

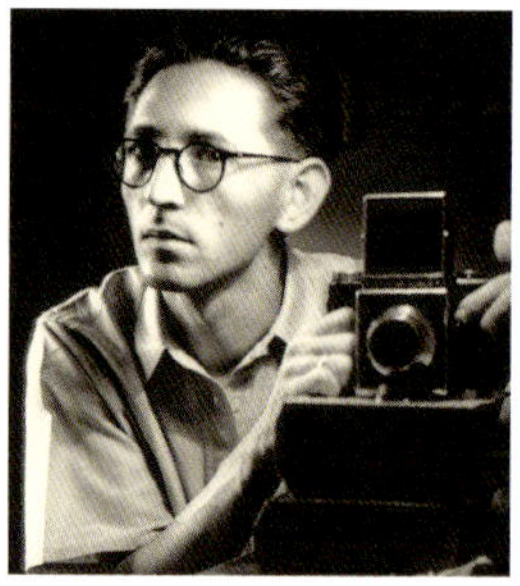

ÉTIENNE SVED
(1914-1996)

Étienne Sved was a Hungarian-born Jew and later a French-naturalized photographer and graphic designer. He studied design in Budapest under Bauhaus professors fleeing Nazi Germany and worked as a commercial poster designer.

Sved fled an increasingly Fascist Eastern Europe in 1938 and settled in Egypt. There, he held jobs as an illustrator at *Al-Ahram* newspaper, and then at the *Société Orientale de Publications*, where he published political caricatures, including a series of anti-Nazi caricatures that were republished many years later in a volume entitled *Adolf ou à quand le crépuscule des odieux.*

Sved also worked for the daily *Le Progès Égyptien,* a position he likely obtained through his friendship with Georges Henein. There, he discovered photography and went on to produce an immense portfolio of works. In concert with local Surrealist and anti-Fascist tendencies, Sved created a series of Surrealist photomontages in the early 1940s depicting ancient Egyptian monuments while stripping them of the national symbolism accorded to such motifs, in direct opposition to lauded national artists such as Mahmoud Moukhtar, who used these symbols to reinforce narratives of national identity.

In 1954, he published a collection of photographs from his trip on donkey-back throughout Egypt with a text written by Tristan Tzara entitled *L'Égypte face à face.* He also later illustrated Jean Cocteau's *Maalesh,* a journal inspired by the latter's stay in Egypt in 1949.

Sved later settled in France, where he founded his own marketing agency as well as his own artistic press. Until his death in 1996, he continued oscillating between editing and graphic design—for which he won numerous international prizes—and his eclectic passions for semiology, therapeutic arts, and illustration.

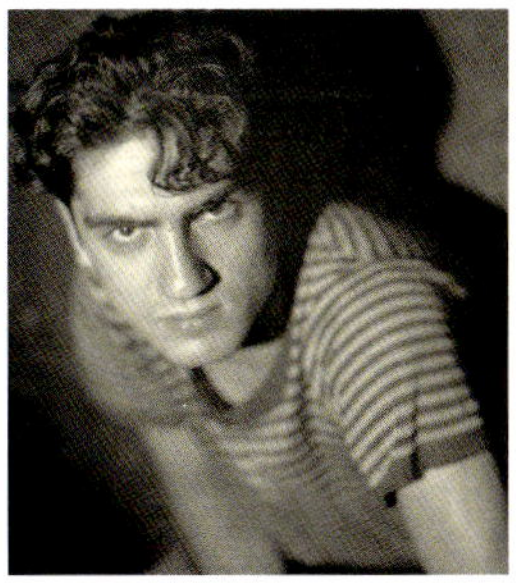

VAN LEO
(1921–2002)

Van Leo was an Armenian-Egyptian photographer who gained fame for his glamorous and striking portraits of celebrities. Born Levon Alexander Boyadjian in 1921 to an Armenian family that had moved to Cairo in the 1880s, Van Leo showed an interest in photography from an early age. He enrolled at the American University in Cairo in 1940 but halted his studies in order to focus on photography since he was a failing student, and apprenticed himself at Venus studio, which was owned by a fellow Armenian named Artinian. At the time, studio portraiture was a field largely dominated by Armenians. From 1941 onwards, Van Leo produced photographs with his brother, which together they signed Studio Metro, and then Studio Angelo.

Van Leo made surrealist self-portraits in the early 1940s, earning him a place in the *Art and Liberty*'s Expositions d'Art Indépendant of 1944 and 1945. He collaborated with *Art and Liberty* member and painter Angelo de Riz to create surrealist photomontages and frequented the latter's home in Dar Al-Labbanah near the Citadel on Sunday mornings to discuss aesthetic concepts. His Surrealist period was brief, however, and in 1947, he opened his own studio in Fouad Street in Downtown Cairo, now called 26th July Street, rebranded himself as Van Leo, and went on to produce works from there for more than 50 years. He is thus better remembered for his glamorous society portraits, capturing the likenesses of Egypt's famous cinema stars and other figures such as Taha Hussein. Van Leo bequeathed his archive to the American University in Cairo prior to his death in 2002.

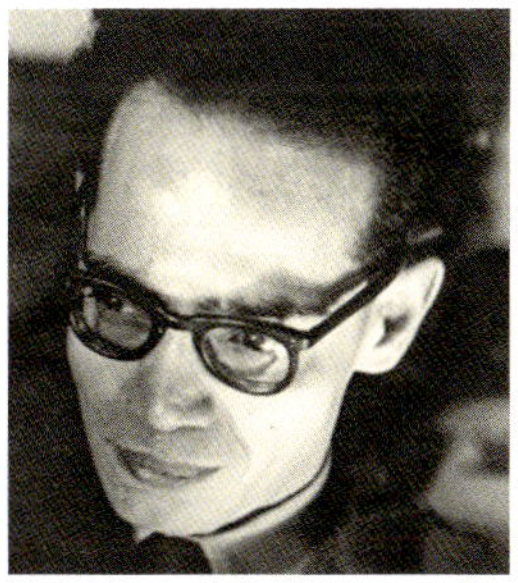

RAMSES YOUNANE
(1913–1966)

Ramses Younane was an Egyptian painter, writer, and translator central to the surrealist movement in Egypt. He was born to a modest family in Minyah and graduated from the Faculty of Fine Arts in Cairo in 1933 and taught art at a number of public schools around the country after having obtained his teaching certificate in 1934.

The following year, Younane joined *Jamaa'at al-di'aya al-fanniyya* (The Society for the Promotion of Art), a collective established by artist Habib Gorgui calling for the importance of art in education. The collective published Younane's book *Ghayat al-rassaam al-'asri* ("The Aim of the Contemporary Artist") in 1938. In January 1939, Younane joined Georges Henein in the newly established anti-Fascist *Art and Liberty* Group, who had voiced, only a few weeks earlier, in their Manifesto for Degenerate Art their condemnation of the persecution of artists in Europe by the Nazis. The manifesto was published in *Al-Majallah Al-Jadidah* and signed by 37 Egyptian and foreign artists, writers, and intellectuals. Thus began the period of the avant-garde and surrealist series of *Expositions de l'Art Indépendant* organized by the group in the early 1940s, showcasing a range of Surrealist and experimental painting, drawing, sculpture, and photography—highly unusual for the time—by artists mostly shunned by mainstream and state-backed art collectives of the time such as the *Société des amis de l'art*. Throughout this time, Younane exhibited his work regularly and published many articles outlining the ideas behind surrealism and calling for social justice. He also translated Arthur Rimbaud's *Une saison en enfer*, Franz Kafka's *Un médecin de campagne*, and Albert Camus' *Caligula*.

In 1942, Younane became the editor-in-chief of *Al-Majallah Al-Jadida*, a review of Trotskyist leanings and a platform for many *Art and Liberty* members, and remained at its helm until it was banned by the Egyptian government in 1944.

He relocated to Paris in 1947 after a short time spent in prison, upon which *Art and Liberty* disbanded, and worked for the French National Radio and then briefly at the press office of the Egyptian Embassy. He returned to Cairo in 1956 after having been exiled by France for political reasons. In 1960, Younane received a grant from the Egyptian Ministry of Culture that allowed him to devote his full time to painting. His work assumed a predominantly abstract style until his death in 1966.

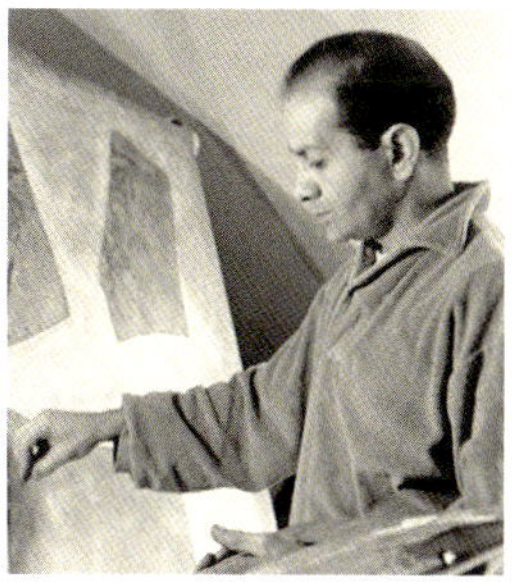

KAMAL YOUSSEF
(B. 1923. Lives in Pittsburgh, Pennsylvania)

Kamal Youssef is an Egyptian painter and civil engineer. Born in 1923 to a well-to-do family, Youssef studied engineering at Cairo University, while cultivating a solid artistic practice at the same time. At sixteen, he joined the *Art and Liberty* Group and partook in their Expositions d'Art Indépendant on several occasions. Like his colleague Inji Efflatoun, Youssef was particularly influenced by the writings of *Art and Liberty* member Albert Cossery and his portrayal of a neglected and underprivileged part of Egyptian society. His paintings often dealt with the struggles of Egyptian peasants, which he was able to witness having spent time in his father's native village of Masjid Al-Khadr.

Later on, Kamal Youssef would also join the Contemporary Art Group, whose main interests lay in a type of surrealism dealing with specifically Egyptian life and native themes of folklore. He also studied under Rateb Seddik, represented Egypt in a number of international biennales, and was given a solo exhibition with the Egyptian Museum of Modern Art.

In the aftermath of the 1952 revolution, Youssef moved to Paris, where he stayed for two years before relocating to the United States, where he has retired and continues to paint. His œuvre spans six decades, and has been heavily influenced by his love of land, his acute awareness of socio-economic disparities, and his work with computers as a civil engineer.

BIBLIOGRAPHY

COMPILED BY SAM BARDAOUIL

Abaza, Mona. *Twentieth Century Egyptian Art: The Private Collection of Sherwet Shafei.* Cairo: American University in Cairo Press, 2011.

Abbas, Raouf, Assem El-Dessouky, and Peter Gran. *The Large Landowning Class and the Peasantry in Egypt, 1837–1952.* Syracuse, NY: Syracuse University Press, 2011.

Adams, Christopher, et al., eds. *Piety and Pragmatism: Spiritualism in Futurist Art.* Rome: Gangemi Editore, 2010.

Alexandrian, Sarane. *Georges Henein.* Paris: Éditions Seghers, 1981.

Almarcegui, Patricia. "Orientalism and Post-Orientalism. Ten Years without Edward Said." *Observatory of Euro-Mediterranean Policies,* 2014. http://www.iemed.org/observatori/arees-danalisi/arxius-adjunts/qm20/Orientalism%20and%20Post-Orientalism%20Ten%20Years%20without%20Edward%20Said%20Patricia%20Almarcegui.pdf/view

Ameen, Ghali. "Al-fâshiyya kama yaraha du'âtuhā." *Al-Majallah Al-Jadidah,* 2 (February 1, 1936).

Amin, Hussein Youssef. "Al-fann al-mu'aṣir." *The Second Exhibition of the Contemporary Art Group.* Cairo: Ministry of Public Instruction, 1948.

Anderson, Benedict. *Imagined Communities: Reflections on the Origin and Spread of Nationalism.* London and New York: Verso Editions, 2006.

Apollinaire, Guillaume. *Les Mamelles de Tirésas.* Saint Julien en Genevois: Éditions Arvensa, 1917.

——. "Le Poète Assassiné." *Œuvres en prose complètes.* Vol. 1. Paris: Gallimard, 1991.

Aragon, Louis. "Communisme et révolution." As cited in Nadeau, Maurice. *Histoire du Surréalisme.* Paris: Éditions du Seuil, 1944.

"Art et Liberté." *Clé* 2 (February 1939).

Art and Liberty Group. *Vive L'Art Dégénéré.* Cairo: Art and Liberty Group, 1938. Roland Penrose Archives, Library of the National Gallery of Scotland in Edinburgh, ref. GMA A35/1/1/RPA200.

——. *La Scéance Continue.* Cairo: C. Tsoumas & Co., 1945.

'Atiyyah, Naïm. *Al-'ain la tazāl 'āshiqa.* Cairo: Al-hai'a al-'āma li qusūr al-thaqāfa, 1998.

Azar, Aimé. *L'Éveil de la conscience picturale en Égypte.* Cairo: Imprimerie Française, 1954.

——. *La peinture moderne en Égypte.* Cairo: Les Éditions Nouvelles, 1961.

Baker, George. *The Artwork Caught by the Tail: Francis Picabia and Dada in Paris.* Cambridge, MA: MIT Press, 2007.

Bal, Mieke. "Grounds of Comparison." *The Artemisia Files: Artemisia Gentileschi for Feminists and Other Thinking People.* Edited by Mieke Bal. Chicago and London: University of Chicago Press, 2005.

Balakian, Anna. *Surrealism, the Road to the Absolute.* Chicago: University of Chicago Press, 1986.

Bardaouil, Sam. "Dirty Dark Loud and Hysteric: The London and Paris Surrealist Exhibitions of the 1930s and the Exhibition Practices of the Art and Liberty group in Cairo." *Dada/Surrealism* 19 (2013). http://ir.uiowa.edu/cgi/viewcontent.cgi?article=1273&context=dadasur.

——. "From Monsieur to Effendi: Reflections on Georges Sabbagh, His Art and A Life Spent Between Two Worlds." In Bardaouil, Sam, and Till Fellrath. *Tea with Nefertiti: The Making of the Artwork by the Artist, the Museum, and the Public.* London and Doha: Bloomsbury Qatar Foundation Publishing, 2012.

Bauman, Zygmund. *Liquid Life.* Cambridge: Polity, 2005.

Beinin, Joel. "Formation of the Egyptian Working Class." *MERIP Reports* 94 (February 1981).

Beinin, Joel, and Zachary Lockman. *Workers on the Nile: Nationalism, Communism, Islam and the Egyptian Working Class, 1882–1954.* Cairo: American University in Cairo Press, 1998.

Berque, Jacques. *Egypt: Imperialism and Revolution.* Translated by Jean Stewart. London: Faber and Faber, 1972.

Blyth, Sarah Ganz, and Edward D. Powers. *Looking at Dada.* New York, NY: Museum of Modern Art, 2011.

Boidard-Boisson, Cristina. "Georges Henein y el surrealismo." PhD diss., University of Cadiz, Spain, 1991.

Botman, Selma. *Egypt from Independence to Revolution, 1919–1952.* Syracuse, NY: Syracuse University Press, 1991.

——. *Egypt from Independence to Revolution, 1919–1970.* Syracuse, NY: Syracuse University Press, 1991.

Bouleau, Christophe. "Les peintres de la Maison des Arts." *Photograph, early 1940s.* In Santelli, Serge, ed. Hassan Fathi: Une Ambition Égyptienne. Cairo: L'Institut Français d'Égypte, 2012.

Bowen, Roger. *Many Histories Deep: The Personal Landscape Poets in Egypt, 1940–45.* London: Associated University Press, 1995.

Breton, André. "Alentours 1 1931 – 1935." *Œuvres complètes.* Vol. 2. Paris: Gallimard, 1992.

——. "Après Dada." *Comœdia,* March 2012. In Motherwell, Robert, The Dada Painters. Translated by Ralph Manheim. 2nd ed. Cambridge, MA, and London: The Belknap Press of the Harvard University Press, 1989.

——. *Entretiens 1913–1952.* Paris: Gallimard, 1952.

——. *Manifestoes of Surrealism.* Translated by Richard Seaver and Helen R. Lane. Ann Arbor: Ann Arbor Paperbacks, University of Michigan Press, 1972.

Brosdkaïa, Nathalia. *Surrealism.* New York: Parkstone International, 2012.

Cannistraro, Philip V., ed. *Historical Dictionary of Fascist Italy.* Westport, CT: Greenwood Press, 1982.

Cavadia, Maria. "Une Exposition d'Amy Nimr." *La Semaine Égyptienne* 3–4 (February 11, 1937).

——. "La 2ème Exposition de L'Art Indépendant." *Images* 601 (March 18, 1941).

Clunas, Craig. "The Art of Global Comparison." *Writing the History of the Global: Challenges for the 21st Century.* Edited by Maxine Berg. Oxford: Oxford University Press 2013.

Cocteau, Jean (text), and Étienne Sved (photographs). *Maalesh: Voyages en Égypte.* Marseille: Le Bec en l'air, 2008.

Cole, Juan R. I. *Colonialism and Revolution in the Middle East: Social and Cultural Origins of Egypt's Urabi Movement.* Cairo: American University in Cairo Press, 2000.

Colla, Elliott. *Conflicted Antiquities: Egyptology, Egyptomania, Egyptian Modernity.* Durham, NC: Duke University Press, 2007.

Cooper, Artemis. *Cairo in the War: 1939–1945.* London: Hamish Hamilton, 1989.

Corner, Paul. *The Fascist Party and Popular Opinion in Mussolini's Italy.* Oxford: Oxford University Press, 2012.

Cossery, Albert. *Men God Forgot.* Berkeley: Circle Edition, 1946.

Cossery, Albert. *Men God Forgot.* Translated by Harold Edwards. San Fransisco: City Lights Books, 1963.

David, Deirdre. *Olivia Manning: A Woman at War.* Oxford: Oxford University Press, 2012.

Davidson, Michael. *The San Fransisco Renaissance: Poetics and Community at Mid-Century.* Cambridge: Cambridge University Press, 1991.

Deeb, Marius. "Labour and Politics in Egypt, 1919–1939." *International Journal of Middle East Studies* 10, no. 2 (May 1979).

Desvaux-Mansour, Marie-Francine. "Le Surréalisme à travers Joyce Mansour: Peinture et Poésie, le miroir du désir." PhD diss., Paris I-Sorbonne Panthéon, 2014.

Durrell, Lawrence. In *Hommage à Georges Henein La Part du Sable.* Cairo: La Part du Sable, 1974.

E. Evans, Trefor, ed. *The Killearn Diaries 1934–46.* London: Sidgwick and Jackson, 1972.

Efflatoun, Inji. *Mudhakkarāt Inji Efflatoun.* Edited by Saïd Khayyal. Cairo: Dar al-thaqafa al-jadīda, 2014.

El-Janabi, Abdel Kader. *The Nile of Surrealism: Surrealist Activities in Egypt, 1936–1952.* Paris: Arabie-sur-Seine, May 1991.

Elkins, James. "Art History as a Global Discipline." *Is Art History Global?* New York and London: Routledge, 2007.

Fahmy, Ziad. *Ordinary Egyptians: Creating the Modern Nation through Popular Culture.* Palo Alto, CA: Stanford University Press, 2011.

"Al-fann al-masrī wa al-mujtama'a al-hahder." *Al-Tatawwur* 1 (January 1940).

Fargues, Nicolas. "Incidences d'un parcours consenti." master's diss., Paris IV-Sorbonne University, 1995.

"Al-fāshiyyūn fi maṣr." *Al-Majallah Al-Jadidah* 410 (April 14, 1942).

Filipovic, Elena. "Surrealism in 1938: The Exhibition at War." In *Spiteri, Raymond, and Donald LaCoss,* eds. Surrealism, Politics and Culture. Burlington: Ashgate Publishing Limited, 2003.

Forrest, Andrew. *The Spanish Civil War.* London: Routledge, 2000.

Frank, Pierre. *The Fourth International: The Long March of the Trotskyists.* London: Ink Links, 1979.

Franklin, Rosemont. *André Breton and the First Principles of Surrealism: A Companion Volume to What is Surrealism?: Selected Writings of André Breton.* London: Pluto Press, 1978.

El-Gabakhangui, Mohammad Sidqi. *Tarīkh al-ḥaraka al-fanniyya fi misr ila 'ām 1945.* Cairo: General Egyptian Authority for the Book, 1986.

Gascoyne, David. "Henry Miller." In *Selected Prose: 1934–1996.* Edited by Roger Scott. London: Enitharmon Press, 1998.

"Georges Henein: hommage: Études de S. Alexandrian, Marcel Berthie, Raymond Beyeler, Yves Bonnefoy…." *Le pont de l'épée* 71–72 (1981): 106.

Gershoni, Israel. "The Evolution of National Culture in Modern Egypt: Intellectual Formation and Social Diffusion, 1892 – 1945." *Poetics Today* 13, no. 2 (summer 1992).

Gershoni, Israel, and James P. Jankowski. *Redefining the Egyptian Nation, 1930–1945.* Cambridge: Cambridge University Press, 2002.

Gharib, Samir. *Al-suriyāliyya fi miṣr.* Cairo: General Egyptian Book Organization Press, 1998.

Gifford, James. *Personal Modernisms: Anarchist Networks and the Later Avant-Gardes.* Edmonton: University of Alberta Press, 2014.

Golia, Maria. *Photography and Egypt.* Chicago: University of Chicago Press, 2010.

Greely, Robin Adèle. "For an Independent Revolutionary Art." In *Spiteri, Raymond, and Donald LaCoss,* eds. Surrealism, Politics and Culture. Aldershot: Ashgate Publishing Limited, 2003.

"Hal tanjaḥ al-diktatūriyya 'indanā?" *Al-Hilāl* 4 (February 1, 1939).

Hanna, Nelly. *Artisan Entrepreneurs in Cairo and Early-Modern Capitalism (1600-1800).* Syracuse, NY: Syracuse University Press, 2011.

Henein, Georges, and Jo Farna [Joseph Habachi]. "La guerre qui revient." *Le rappel à l'ordure.* Cairo, 1935.

Henein, Georges. "À contre-cloison." *London Bulletin* 17 (June 15, 1939).

——. "Bilan du mouvement surréaliste." *Revue des conférences françaises en Orient* 8 (October 1937).

——. "Letter 14." *Lettres: Georges Henein – Henri Calet (Grandes Largeurs).* Association Henri Calet, Autumn–Winter 1981.

——. "Lettre à André Gide." *Combat.* October 30, 1947. In Sarane Alexandrian, Georges Henein. Paris: Éditions Seghers, 1981.

——. *L'Esprit frappeur: Carnets 1940–1973.* Paris: Éditions Encre, 1980.

——. *The First Exhibition of Independent Art, February 8–24.* Exh. cat. Cairo: Art and Liberty Group, 1940.

Henein, Georges, to André Breton, February 16, 1947. Unpublished letter, ref. BRT.L.950 (1/2), Breton Archives, La Bibliothèque Littéraire Jacques Doucet, Paris.

Henein, Georges. "Les Judas de L'Espagne." *Art et Liberté* 1 (March 1939).

Henein, Georges, in Cairo to André Breton in Paris, July 26, 1948. Unpublished letter, ref. BRT.L.962 1/3. Georges Breton Archives, La Bibliothèque Littéraire Jacques Doucet, Paris.

Henein, Georges, to André Breton, 1936. In Kober, Marc, "Georges Henein, reporter de l'universel." Mélusine, no. 25, *L'Universel reportage.* Lausanne: L'Âge d'homme, 2005.

Hentea, Marius. *TaTa Dada: The Real Life and Celestial Adventures of Tristan Tzara.* Cambridge, MA: MIT Press Books, 2014.

Hopkins, David. *Dada and Surrealism: A Very Short Introduction.* Oxford: Oxford University Press, 2004.

"Ila al-fann al-hadīth." *Al-'Imāra* 4, no. 7–8 (July 1939).

"Ila aṣhāb al-abrāj al-'ājiya." *Al-Tatawwur* 1 (January 1940): 30.

Ismael, Tareq Y., and Rifa'at al-Sa'id. *The Communist Movement in Egypt, 1920–1988.* Syracuse NY: Syracuse University Press, 1990.

Jabès, Edmond. "Le Caire quitté." Interview with Carole Naggar and Jacques Hassoun in *Mille et une villes.* Paris: Autrement, 1985.

Jackson, Ashley. The British Empire and the Second World War. London: Hambledon Continuum, 2006.

"Jama'āt al-fann wal ḥurriyya, al-qanūn al-asāsi." Al-Tatawwur 1 (January 1940).

Jankowski, James P. "The Egyptian Blue Shirts and the Egyptian Wafd, 1935–1938." *Middle Eastern Studies* 6, no. 1 (January 1970).

Kamel, Anwar. *Al-kitāb al-manbūz.* Cairo: Majallati Publishers, 1936.

——. "Al-fikr fi khidmat al mujtmama'." *Al-Tatawwur* 1 (January 1940).

——. *Afyūn al-shu'ūb.* Cairo: Al-Risāla Publishers, 1948.

Kamel, Fouad. "A Pain Waiting to Be Found." *Art et Liberté* 2 (May 1939).

——. "Maṣīr al-fann al-hadīth ba'da inhiyār faransa." *Al-Majallah al-Jadida* 434 (September 15, 1943).

Kane, Patrick. *The Politics of Art in Modern Egypt: Aesthetics, Ideology and Nation Building.* London: I.B. Taurus, 2012.

Kantarovitz, Sam. "Yasna'ūn al-mawt." *Al-Tatawwur* 3 (March 1940).

Karnouk, Liliane. *Modern Egyptian Art.* Cairo: American University in Cairo Press, 2005.

Kober, Marc. "The Magic Powers of Ancient Egypt: Georges Henein, André Breton and Horus Schenouda." *Dada/Surrealism* 19, 2013. http://ir.uiowa.edu/cgi/viewcontent.cgi?article=1272&context=dadasur.

Kober, Marc. *Georges Henein: L'éclat de la ténacité – Itinéraire d'un écrivain francophone entre Égypte et Europe au xxe siècle.* Paris: Honoré Champion, 2014.

La Part du sable. Cairo: Éditions Masses, 1947.

LaCoss, Don. "Egyptian Surrealism and 'Degenerate Art' in 1939." *Arab Studies Journal* 18, no. 1 (spring 2010).

Lançon, Daniel. "Le Caire (1934 – 1941): le défi des avant-gardes européennes pour les écrivains égyptiens et pour Georges Henein en particulier." In *Les Métropoles des avant-gardes.* Edited by Edith Kunz and Thomas Hunkeler. Bern: Peter Lang Publishers, 2009.

——. *La Semaine Égyptienne, de 1926 à 1939 ou la littérature comme ailleurs.* HAL Archives Ouvertes, 2011. doi: hal-00872925.

Lewis, Helena. *The Politics of Surrealism.* New York, NY: Paragon House, 1988.

Luthi, Jean-Jacques. "Le Mouvement Surréaliste en Égypte." *Mélusine: Cahiers du centre de recherches sur le surréalisme,* no. 3: *Marges Non-Frontières,* 1982.

Al-Mallakh, Kamal, and Rushdi Iskandar. *Khamsūn sana min al-fann.* Cairo: Dar al-Ma'ārif, 1962.

——. *Thamanūn sana min al-fann.* Cairo: General Egyptian Book Organization Press, 1991.

Matthews, J. H. *An Introduction to Surrealism.* University Park: Pennsylvania State University Press, 1965.

Miller, Henry. "An Open Letter to Surrealists Everywhere." *The Cosmological Eye.* New York: New Directions, 1939.

Mitchell, Timothy. "The World as Exhibition." *Comparative Studies in Society and History* 31, no. 2 (April 1989).

Morris, Jan. *Farewell the Trumpets: An Imperial Retreat.* New York: Harcourt, Brace Jovanovich, 1978.

Morsy, Laila. "The Military Clauses of the Anglo-Egyptian Treaty of Friendship and Alliance, 1936." *International Journal of Middle East Studies* 16, no. 1 (March 1984).

Motherwell, Robert. "Some Memories of Pre-Dada: Picabia and Duchamp." *The Dada Painters and Poets.* New York: Wittenborn, Schultz, Inc., 1951.

Moxey, Keith. "Motivating History." *The Art Bulletin* 77, no. 3 (September 1995).

Muravchik, Joshua. "Enough Said: The False Scholarship of Edward Said." *World Affairs,* March/April 2013. http://www.worldaffairsjournal.org/article/enough-said-false-scholarship-edward-said

Naddaf, Sandra. "Mirrored Images: Rifa'a al-Tahtawi and the West." *Alif: Journal of Comparative Poetics* 6 (spring 1986).

Naguib, Ezz El-Deen. *Fajr al-taswīr al-masri al-hadīth.* Cairo: Dar al-mustaqbal al-'arabi, 1985.

Nimr, Amy. "The Poetry of Cavafy." *Personal Landscape.* Vol. 2. 1945.

Ostle, Robin. "Egyptian Renaissance Man." *Bulletin of the School of Oriental and African Studies* 57, no. 1 (1994).

'Oukashah, Abd El-Razek. *dhikrayāt wa a'amāl Samir Rafi'.* Cairo: General Egyptian Book Organization Press, 2012.

Palermo, Lynn E. "L'Exposition Anticoloniale: Political or Aesthetic Protest?" *French Cultural Studies* 20, no. 1 (February 2009).

Panofsky, Erwin. "The History of Art as a Humanistic Discipline." *The Meaning of the Humanities.* Edited by T. Greene. Princeton, NJ: Princeton University Press, 1940.

Penrose, Roland. "From Egypt." *The London Bulletin* 13 (April 15, 1939).

Perrault, Gilles. *A Man Apart: The Life of Henri Curiel.* London: Zed Books, 1987.

Pollard, Lisa. *Nurturing the Nation: The Family Politics of Modernizing, Colonizing, and Liberating Egypt, 1805–1923.* Berkeley and Los Angeles: University of California Press, 2005.

Al-Quwaidi, Youssri, and 'Esmat Dawastashy. *Mohammad Naghi kama lam na'rifhu min qabl.* Cairo, 2009.

Rassim, Ahmed. "Jamā'at al-sharqiyyūn al-judud." *Al-Balagh,* October 15, 1938.

Al-Razzaz, Mustafa. *Al-fann al-masri al-hadīth – al-qarn al-'ishrīn.* Cairo: Fine Arts Sector, Egyptian Ministry of Culture, 2007.

Read, Herbert. "Children's Art." *Exhibition of Contemporary British Art.* Cairo: Le Scribe Égyptien, 1945.

——. *To Hell with Culture.* London: Routledge Classics, 2002.

Reid, Donald Malcolm. "Cultural Imperialism and Nationalism: The Struggle to Define and Control the Heritage of Arab Art in Egypt." *International Journal of Middle East Studies* 24, no 1 (February 1992).

——. *Whose Pharaohs? Archeology, Museum, and Egyptian National Identity From Napoleon to World War I.* Cairo: The American University in Cairo Press, 2002.

Renton, Dave. *Dissident Marxism: Past Voices for Present Times.* London: Zed Books, 2004.

Roche, Gérard. "Breton, Trotsky: une collaboration." *Pleine Marge* 3 (1986).

Rogers, John D. "Post-Orientalism and the Interpretation of Premodern and Modern Political Identities; The Case of Sri Lanka." *The Journal of Asian Studies* 53, no. 1 (February 1994).

Rosemont, Franklin. *Black, Brown & Beige: Surrealist Writings from Africa and the Diaspora.* Edited by Robin D. G. Kelley. Austin: University of Texas Press, December 7, 2009.

Roux, Pascale. "Georges Henein: écritures polémiques." PhD diss., Paris III–Université Sorbonne Nouvelle, 2009.

Roux-Cassuto, Pascale. "Georges Henein. Une grande opacité veille sur les êtres." *Le nouveau recueil* (July–August 2006).

Safran, Nadav. *Egypt in Search of Political Community: An Analysis of the Intellectual and Political Evolution of Egypt, 1804–1952.* Cambridge, MA: Harvard University Press, 1961.

Said, Edward W. *Culture and Imperialism.* New York: Vintage Books, 1994.

Al-Saïd, Rif'at. *Tarīkh al-ḥaraka al-shuyu'iyya al-maṣriyya.* Vol. 2. *Al-saḥafa al-'alaniyya, 1925–1952.* Cairo: Sharikat al-'amal lil-tiba'ah wa-l-nashr wa-l-tawzee', 1987.

Salmawy, Mohamed, and Mustafa El-Razzaz. *Mohammad Mahmoud Khalil.* Cairo: Ministry of Culture, 1995.

Schaffner, Anna Katharina. "Dissecting the Order of Signs: On the Textual Politics of Dada Poetcs." In Adamowicz, Elza, and Eric Roberson. *Dada and Beyond.* Vol. 1. *Dada Discourses.* Amsterdam: Rodopi Brill Editions, 2011.

Seggerman, Alexandra Dika. "Al-Tatawwur (Evolution): An Enhanced Timeline of Egyptian Surrealism." *Dada/Surrealism* 19 (2013). http://ir.uiowa.edu/cgi/viewcontent.cgi?article=1269&context=dadasur

Shabout, Nada. "The Challenge of Arab Modern Art." In *The Future of Tradition – The Tradition of Future.* Edited by Chris Dercon, Leon Krempel, and Avinoam Shalem. Munich: Prestel, 2010.

Shohat, Ella. "The 'Postcolonial' in Translation: Reading Said in Hebrew." *Journal in Palestine Studies* 33, no. 3 (spring 2004).

Short, Robert. "The Politics of Surrealism, 1920–36." *Journal Contemporary History* 1, no. 2. *Left-Wing Intellectuals between the Wars* (1966.)

Spiteri, Raymond, and Donald LaCoss, eds. "Introduction: Revolution by Night: Surrealism, Politics and Culture." In *Surrealism, Politics and Culture.* Aldershot: Ashgate Publishing Limited, 2003.

Stone, Douglas. *Henry Miller and the Villa Seurat Circle.* Irvine: University of California Press, 1973.

"Al-suriyalism." *Al-Majallah Al-Jadidah* 420 (June 28, 1942).

"Surrealism and Its Others." *Yale French Studies* 109 (July 11, 2006).

Sus, Nasri 'Atallah. "Fann munḥatt biraghm dhalik." *Al-Risāla* 316 (July 24, 1939).

——. "Ḥawl al-fann al-munḥatt – kalima akhīra." *Al-Risāla* 319 (August 14, 1939).

Al-Tahtawi, Rifa'a. *Al-a'māl al-kāmila.* Vol. 2. Beirut: Al-mu'assasa al-'arabiyya li-l-dirasat wa-l-nashr, 1973.

El-Telmisany, Kamel. "Ḥawl al-fann al-munḥatt." *Al-Risāla* 321 (August 28, 1939).

——. "Nahw fann ḥurr." *Al-Tatawwur* 1 (January 1940).

——. "Al-insāniyya wa al-fann al-hadīth." *Al-Tatawwur* 2 (February 1940).

——. "Al-ma'raḍ al-awwal lil fann al-ḥurr." *Al-Tatawwur* 3 (March 1940).

Vilar, Pierre, in collaboration with Marc Kober and Daniel Lançon. *Georges Henein, Œuvres.* Paris: Denoël, 2006.

Volait, Mercedes. "La requalification d'un ensemble urbain créé au xxe siècle en Égypte, Héliopolis (1905–2005)." In *Conquérir la ville.* Edited by Ziad Akl and Nabil Beyhum. Beirut: Académie Libanaise des Beaux-Arts, June 2006 and Université de Balmand 2009.

Volait, Mercedes, and Jean-Baptiste Minnaert. "Héliopolis: Création et assimilation d'une ville européene en Egypte au xxe siècle." *Villes rattachées, villes reconfigurées: xvie-xxe siècles.* Edited by Denise Turrel. Tours: Presses de l'Université François-Rabelais, 2003.

Williams, Caroline. "Twentieth Century Egyptian Art: The Pioneers, 1920–52." *Re-envisioning Egypt: 1919-1952.* Edited by Arthur Golschmidt, Amy Johnson, and Barak A. Salmoni. Cairo and New York: American University in Cairo Press, 2005.

Younane, Ramses. *Ghāyat al-rassām al-'asri.* Cairo: Jamā'at al-di'āayah al-fanniyya, 1938.

——. "Ḥarakat al-suriyalism." *Al-Risāla* 322 (September 4, 1939).

——. "Al-faqr mas'ala 'ijtima'iyya." *Al-Risāla* 427 (September 8, 1941).

——. "Al-ḥaraka al-fanniyya bayn al-maḥaliyya wal 'ālamiyya." *Al-fikr al-mu'aṣir* 17 (July 1, 1966).

——. *Dirasāt fi al-fann.* With an introduction by Louis Awad. Cairo: Dār al-kātib al-'arabi li-l-tiba'ah wa-l-nashr, 1969.

Younan, Sonia (daughter of Ramses Younane). In conversation with the author. Paris, November 24, 2011.

Zijlmans, Kitty. "An Intercultural Perspective in Art History: beyond Othering and Appropriation." In *Is Art History Global?* Edited by James Elkins. New York and London: Routledge, 2007.

Zouari, Fawzia. "En débatant du futurisme." In *Entre Nil et sable: Écrivains d'Égypte d'expression française (1920 – 1960).* Edited by Marc Kober, Irène Fenoglio, and Daniel Lançon. Paris: Centre national de documentation pédagogique, 1999.

Photo Credits

© Waleed Abdelkhalek
p. 150-151

© Emad Badr El-Din Mahmoud Abu Ghazy Archives, Cairo
p. 57 (2,3)

© Al Masar Gallery for Contemporary Art, Cairo
p. 164, 165

© Annunciata Galleria, Milan
p. 88-89

© Arab Image Foundation, Beirut,
p. 198 (1), 208, 209, 221

© Barjeel Art Foundation, Sharjah
p. 121

© Bayerische Staatsbibliothek, Munich
p. 34, 35, 70, 107

© Bibliothèque de documentation internationale contemporaine (BDIC), Nanterre
p. 17, 46

© Christophe Bouleau collection, Geneva
p. 67

© Nabil Boutros
p. 83, 175

© Centre Pompidou, Paris / Georges Meguerditchian
p. 26 (13), 173, 177

© Centre Pompidou, Paris / Philippe Migeat
p. 30, 110, 114, 193, 200, 201, 210, 211

© Centre Pompidou, Paris / Anne Paounov
p. 33, 60, 63

© Centre Pompidou, Paris / Bertrand Prévost
p. 18, 59 (2), 61, 62, 78, 98, 99, 106, 170, 171, 174 (2), 180 (2), 183, 205, 206, 207

© Chafik Charobim Estate, Cairo
p. 56

© Mai El-Dib collection, Alexandria
p. 122

© European Cultural Centre of Delphi
p. 91, 147

© Hamdi Hamed Archives, Cairo
p. 40

© H.E. Sh. Hassan M. A. Al Thani collection, Doha
p. 80, 81, 85, 101, 103, 133, 137, 142, 143, 180 (1), 186, 187, 188, 189

© Henein–Farhi collection, Neuilly-sur-Seine
p. 20, 21

© James Hyman Gallery, London
p. 178

© The Imperial War Museum, London
p. 29

© Institut dominicain d'études orientales, Cairo
p. 20

© Institut du monde arabe, Paris
p. 115

© Timothy Kaldas
p. 79, 111, 113, 140, 141, 144-145, 153, 159, 163, 179, 184

© J. Robert LeShufy collection, New York
p. 92

© Mayo Estate
p. 22

© Lee Miller Archives, England
p. 24, 26 (14), 198 (2), 199, 202, 203,

© Musée Nicéphore Niépce, Chalon-sur-Saône
p. 196, 197, 220 (3)

© National Portrait Gallery, London
p. 194, 195, 215 (3)

© Roland Penrose Estate, England
p. 130, 131

© Mandy Prowse collection, London
p. 31 (19)

© Rare Books and Special Collections Library, American University, Cairo
p. 71 (3)

© Hesham Salama
p. 43, 57 (4), 73, 95, 96, 97, 116, 117, 119, 210, 125, 129, 136, 138-139, 160, 161, 166, 167, 181, 182 (1), 185

© Laurent Marcel Salinas Estate, New York
p. 93

© Viken Seropian
p. 59 (4), 74-75, 77, 84, 102, 109, 123, 154-155, 157, 182 (2)

© Scottish National Gallery of Modern Art Archives, Edinburgh
p. 68-69

© Annie White collection, London
p. 31 (20)

© Yale University, Beinecke Rare Book and Manuscript Library, New Haven
p. 71 (2)

© Sylvie and Sonia Younan collection, Paris
p. 58, 59 (3), 134, 135, 176

© Kamal Youssef Archives, Dayton
p. 40, p. 152

Printed by Graphuis - Geers Offset
in Ghent, Belgium
October 2016

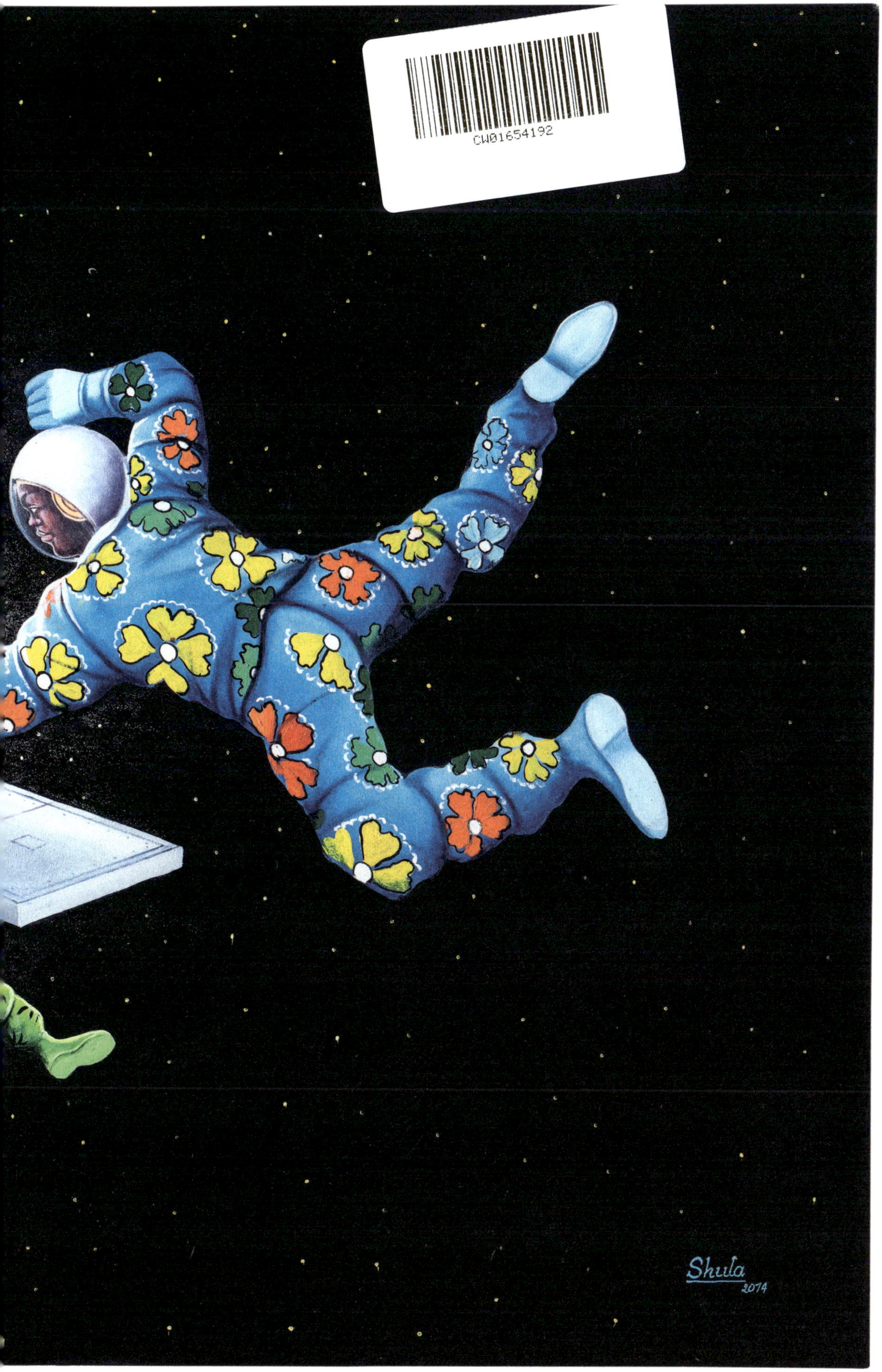

Monsengo Shula
Ata Ndele Mokili
(Tôt ou tard le monde changera)
2014, acrylic and sequins
on canvas, 130 × 200 cm
Henri and Farida Seydoux
Collection

Congo as Fiction

To all the artists from the Congo,
in the past, present, and future

CONGO AS FICTION

ART WORLDS BETWEEN PAST AND PRESENT

Edited by
Nanina Guyer and
Michaela Oberhofer

Museum Rietberg Zürich
Scheidegger & Spiess

EXPLORING, PHOTO-GRAPHING, AND ACQUIRING ART

DESIGN AND ELEGANCE

POWER AND POLITICS

PERFORMANCE AND INITIATION

FOREWORD — The first exhibition of Congolese art at Museum Rietberg opened in 1993. Called *Zaire 1938/39*, it displayed photographs that Hans Himmelheber had taken during his extensive travels through the territories of the Yaka, Pende, Chokwe, and Kuba peoples before the outbreak of the Second World War. I was fascinated by the vitality and dynamism of the dance and mask performances that Hans Himmelheber captured with his Leica. The ethnologist Himmelheber also documented intensive contemporary culture in his artist portraits of mask carvers at work. Just how immediately they processed recent impressions is described by Himmelheber in his article in the journal *Brousse* from 1939. According to this, the Yaka artists carved mask crests adorned with figural scenes, for example a clerk on a motorbike. Today, eighty years after Himmelheber's journey to the Congo and twenty-six years after the *Zaire* show, the present *Congo as Fiction* exhibition once again focuses on the culture of the late 1930s as documented by Himmelheber. At the same time, and again following in Himmelheber's footsteps, we are also interested in the work of the country's contemporary artists. The art world in Kinshasa and Lubumbashi is blossoming; it is dynamic and has international connections. Artists from the Democratic Republic of the Congo exhibit in biennials and in museums and galleries all over the world. In our exhibition we show works by two female and twelve male contemporary artists; seven artists have created works especially for this exhibition. A prominent position has been given to the installations by Sammy Baloji and Sinzo Aanza, who explored the objects and photographs in our museum's collection as artists-in-residence. These artworks should be understood on the one hand as the result of research into the country's colonial past. On the other, they are statements about everyday life—but also about exploitation and social inequality in the modern-day DRC. Including the present in the form of contemporary art is imperative for a museum that intends to continue to play an instrumental role in exhibiting and educating about African art and culture in the future.

Naturally, our museum's collection is and remains the foundation of all our research and educational work. The Congo collection along with Hans Himmelheber's photographic and written estate that is preserved in the museum provide a unique opportunity to gain deeper insight into the art and culture of the 1930s, a time when the Congo was under Belgian colonial rule (until 1960). This estate documents the view of a German art anthropologist who studied various ethnic groups and acquired numerous objects in the course of his intensive fieldwork. It is thanks to this comprehensive and revealing source material that the Museum Rietberg and the Historisches Seminar of the University of Zürich were awarded financial support by the Swiss National Science Foundation for a long-term research project. By investigating and publishing the material collected by Himmelheber eighty years ago, we are also making a contribution to the current debate about decolonization and restitution, as well as creating the foundation for dialogue with the country of origin, the Congo. Launched with this exhibition, we aim for a cooperation and will maintain a dialogue in the future with the Congo.

It is thanks to Hans Himmelheber (1908–2003) and his wife Ulrike Himmelheber (1920–2015), as well as the munificence of their children Eberhard Fischer, Susanne Himmelheber, and Martin Himmelheber, that we are able to preserve and research Hans Himmelheber's estate—which consists of 750 objects, 15,000 photographs, and a written archive of diaries, letters, and notes—in our museum. We would like to thank the ethnologist and friend of the museum Clara Himmelheber, Hans Himmelheber's granddaughter, for her unfailingly generous assistance. Thanks to the financial support of Eberhard Fischer, the former director of our museum, and his wife Barbara Fischer, we have been able to inventory and digitize these documents over recent years. Furthermore, their donations have enriched our museum's African collection for many years. Another occasion for this exhibition was the Congo collection—comprising 484 artworks and objects—gifted to us by Martin Himmelheber in 2018 from his father's effects. We express our heartfelt gratitude to them all.

For a close, productive collaboration with the University of Zürich in the context of the research project supported by the Swiss National Science Foundation, we would like to thank Gesine Krüger, who holds a modern history chair at the Historisches Seminar and specializes in teaching and researching modern African history. Michaela Oberhofer, our curator of African and Oceanian art, and Nanina Guyer, our curator of photography, have embraced this exhibition with burning enthusiasm and boundless energy. Both curators have focused on African art and history in the course of their longstanding research and exhibition work, whether in the field of ethnology or in the field of the history of photography. I extend my sincere thanks to them both for their tireless and superb dedication to this project. Finally, I would like to thank the board and the members of the Rietberg Society who made a substantial contribution to this exhibition. *Congo as Fiction* combines traditional art, historical photography, and contemporary art in equal measure while also raising issues of provenance and restitution. As such, the exhibition adopts an innovative approach—an approach for the future. I wish the exhibition great success and its visitors lasting impressions and deep insights. Finally, I am delighted to pass the torch to my successor Annette Bhagwati with this exhibition. She will take over the management of the museum from December 2019.

Albert Lutz, Director

ACKNOWLEDGMENTS — With *Congo as Fiction*, we are entering new territory in many respects. Although we have already realized several exhibitions at Museum Rietberg, for the two of us as a curatorial team, this is the first major exhibition on Africa in this museum. For the first time, artworks and photographs are exhibited alongside one another as equals. Starting point is the archive of Hans Himmelheber, comprising his exceptional private collection as well as his extensive photographic and written estate, which has arrived at the museum over the past five years thanks to his family. In the exhibition, several of the impressive artworks and black-and-white photos will be shown to the public for the first time. At the same time, we are presenting the initial results of the new research project financed by the Swiss National Science Foundation (SNF) on Hans Himmelheber's archive. The extensive source material, first and foremost the diary he kept on his Congo journey in 1938/39, allows us to show not only his art ethnological research, but also to reconstruct how Himmelheber acquired artworks on site. The critical work on the history of the collection is not only a personal matter, but is more important than ever precisely now in an era of contemporary debates on restitution and decolonialization. Another novelty is the commissioning of contemporary artists from the Congo and the diaspora to create new artworks for *Congo as Fiction* in reaction to the archive from Himmelheber. We are very thankful to all involved, inside and outside of the museum, for venturing into this experiment with us.

First and foremost, we would like to thank Hans Himmelheber's family for their generosity, trust, and good will. Barbara and Eberhard Fischer, Susanne Himmelheber and Peter Pausch, Martin Himmelheber and Clara Himmelheber, as well as all other family members, have supported our project in a variety of ways, whether through gifts and loans, tips and transcriptions, in discussions and interviews, or through their voices, such as in the case of Martin Himmelheber, a trained radio and newspaper journalist whose voice recordings for the exhibition provide his father's direct quotes.

Our thanks go to the international museums for their generous loans—notably, the Museum der Kulturen in Basel, the AfricaMuseum in Tervuren, the Virginia Museum of Fine Arts in Richmond, and the Musée d'ethnographie de Genève—as well as the private collectors and galleries—including Jan Calmeyn, Nuno Crisostomo, Christraud Geary, Marc Felix, Boris Kegel-Konietzko, Wally and Udo Horstmann, François Mottas, MAGNIN-A, CAAC – The Pigozzi Collection, Nomad Gallery, Henri and Farida Seydoux Collection—and all lenders who prefer not to be named. For their substantial support during our research, we thank Isabella Bozsa, Bambi Ceuppens, Anne Brandstetter, Mathieu Zana Aziza Etambala, Sarah Ferracuti, Bernhard Gardi, Beatrix Heintze, Markus Himmelsbach, Floriane Morin, Jan Raymaekers, Pascal Martin Saint Léon, Sarah Van Beurden, Julien Volper, Albrecht Wiedmann, and Richard Woodward. Extremely valuable in the conception of the exhibition were, internally, the suggestions from colleagues of the curatorial board and from Lorenz Homberger; and externally, dialogue with the students in the courses we teach at the University of Zürich, as well as discussions among professionals at the two workshops in the context of the SNF project. Special thanks go to our colleagues in the Himmelheber project, Gesine Krüger, Anja Soldat, and Esther Tisa Francini, for the solid and inspiring collaboration.

This catalogue would not have been possible without the other authors, including Sandrine Colard, Laura Falletta, Nzomba Dugo Kakema, David Mannes, Constantine Petridis, and Jens Stenger. Christraud M. Geary and Z. S. Strother not only contributed essays to the catalogue, but also assisted us with their expertise during the entire preliminary phase, and have eagerly supported us in many ways. We would like to thank them sincerely for their contribution to the success of the catalogue and the exhibition. We thank the Paul Scherrer Institut in Villigen for the enlightening look into the interior of the artworks. Our thanks also go to Claudio Barandun who was responsible for the contemporary and carefully conceived catalogue design, and Muriel Blancho from Verlag Scheidegger & Spiess and our publication coordinator Mark Welzel. Jonathan Bret Maney's translations of the poetic texts by Sinzo Aanza and Fiston Mwanza Mujila deserve special mention. We thank Rainer Wolfsberger for the wonderfully fresh photographs of our own objects.

Representative for all of the others at our museum, we would like to thank Andrea Kuprecht, our registrar, as well as Nanny Boller and Martin Ledergerber for conservation and restoration; Elena DelCarlo, Alain Suter, and Nicola Morgan for marketing and communication; Maya Bührer, Linda Christinger, and Caroline Spicker for the educational program; Michael Busse and Patrizia Zindel for finances and personnel; Silvan Bosshard and Mesut Kara for facility management. For the successful design and graphics, our thanks go to Martin Sollberger and Jacqueline Schöb. We thank Masus Meier as well as Robbert van Rooden and Robin Burgauer from Inlusio for the impressive multimedia projections. Our sincere gratitude also goes to our two assistants Laura Falletta and Daniela Müller; what would we have done without you? Furthermore, we would like to mention, in particular, our director, Albert Lutz, who has graciously supported us and our work over the past several years.

We found the close exchange and discussions with the exhibition's artists from the Congo and the diaspora extremely enriching, both intellectually as well as personally. Our sincere thanks go to Sammy Baloji and Fiston Mwanza Mujila, Sinzo Aanza and David Shongo as well as Yves Sambu and Michèle Magema, whose newly created works enhance the exhibition, as do those by Angali, Steve Bandoma, Hilary Kuyangiko Balu, Aimé Mpane, Chéri Samba, Monsengo Shula, and Pathy Tshindele. For the part of the Congolese diaspora in Switzerland, cited first and foremost is the artist Fiona Bobo, representatively, we also thank Fabrice Mawete, Hardy Nimi, and the Swiss *sapeurs* for their support.

Our most heartfelt thanks go, in the end, to our families without whom we would not have been able to achieve this intense phase of thinking, curating, organizing, and writing.

Michaela Oberhofer and Nanina Guyer

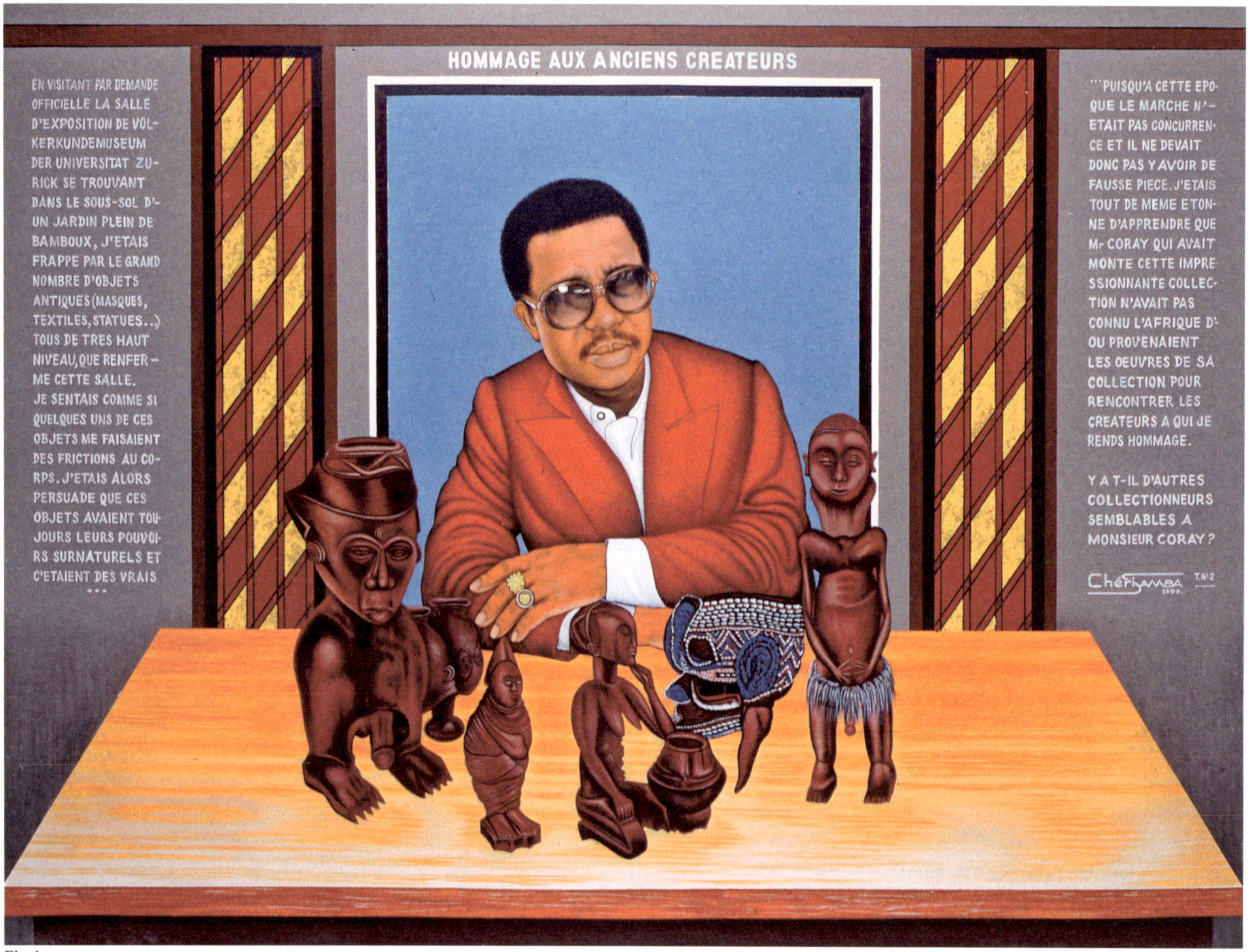
HOMMAGE AUX ANCIENS CREATEURS
EN VISITANT PAR DEMANDE OFFICIELLE LA SALLE D'EXPOSITION DE VOLKERKUNDEMUSEUM DER UNIVERSITAT ZURICK SE TROUVANT DANS LE SOUS-SOL D'UN JARDIN PLEIN DE BAMBOUX, J'ETAIS FRAPPE PAR LE GRAND NOMBRE D'OBJETS ANTIQUES (MASQUES, TEXTILES, STATUES...) TOUS DE TRES HAUT NIVEAU, QUE RENFERME CETTE SALLE.
JE SENTAIS COMME SI QUELQUES UNS DE CES OBJETS ME FAISAIENT DES FRICTIONS AU CORPS. J'ETAIS ALORS PERSUADE QUE CES OBJETS AVAIENT TOUJOURS LEURS POUVOIRS SURNATURELS ET C'ETAIENT DES VRAIS ...
...PUISQU'A CETTE EPOQUE LE MARCHE N'ETAIT PAS CONCURRENCE ET IL NE DEVAIT DONC PAS Y AVOIR DE FAUSSE PIECE. J'ETAIS TOUT DE MEME ETONNE D'APPRENDRE QUE Mr CORAY QUI AVAIT MONTE CETTE IMPRESSIONNANTE COLLECTION N'AVAIT PAS CONNU L'AFRIQUE D'OU PROVENAIENT LES OEUVRES DE SA COLLECTION POUR RENCONTRER LES CREATEURS A QUI JE RENDS HOMMAGE.
Y A T-IL D'AUTRES COLLECTIONNEURS SEMBLABLES A MONSIEUR CORAY?
Chéri Samba
1999.
T.Nº2
Fig. 1

Fig. 1
Chéri Samba
Hommage aux anciens créateurs
1999, acrylic on canvas, 151 × 201 cm
CAAC—The Pigozzi Collection, Geneva

INTRODUCTION: FICTIONS AND ART WORLDS OF THE CONGO BETWEEN PAST AND PRESENT

Michaela Oberhofer, Nanina Guyer

In view of current debates about colonial collections, the question is posed today, more so than ever before, of the appropriate treatment of objects from Africa that have been separated from their cultural surroundings and their original voices. As these objects were never intended for a museum context, it therefore creates a curatorial dilemma, which was also present at the start of deliberations on *Congo as Fiction—Art Worlds Between Past and Present* [fig. 1].[1] Hans Himmelheber's extensive archive—the starting point for this exhibition—has recently been given to the Museum Rietberg by the community of heirs to Himmelheber's estate. It comprises his private collection, unrivaled for its uniqueness, as well as his photographic and written legacy. Himmelheber (1908–2003) was a German art ethnologist who, in his research in Africa, propagated an approach to art and artists that was innovative for its day, and remains influential until the present. The focus of this catalogue is on the 100 colorful masks, filigree figures, woven and embroidered cloths, and everyday objects as well as the roughly 200 historical photographs that he brought back to Europe from his journey in 1938/39 to the Belgian Congo, which in 1971 became the Republic of Zaire, and from 1997, the Democratic Republic of Congo or DRC. Many of these artworks and black-and-white photos have never been publicly shown or published. In light of current questions regarding restitution and identity, as well as the global challenges of migration and digitization, what is the appropriate way of dealing with museum objects and photographs from Africa? Is there a single, correct way? Or aren't, instead, a multitude of perspectives with complementary and also contradicting interpretations required for approaching the archives as witnesses to the colonization of the African continent and the interlocked history of Africa with the rest of the world?

1 For their valuable and thought-provoking comments, we would like to thank Christraud Geary, Gesine Krüger, Anja Soldat, and Esther Tisa Francini. On the curatorial dilemma, see Kasfir 1997.

Since the 1980s, African intellectuals, such as Valentin Mudimbe, Achille Mbembe, and Felwine Sarr, have pointed out what the global North's monopoly and the asymmetry in the production of knowledge about Africa mean. Decolonizing thought and historiography necessitate recognizing the African perspective.[2] The exhibition *Congo as Fiction* presents a possible way—at least to some extent—to breach the interpretive dominance of Western art discourse and expand the view to include alternative narratives and realms of imagination related to the Congo's past and present. The images by Monsengo Shula in the style of popular painting offer a contemporary symbol for this change in perspective: "Afronauts" in luminous wax-printed textiles float around satellites, which are crowned by figures from traditional art. With this, the Kinshasa-based artist not only refers to the Congo's ambitious space program of the 1970s, but also envisions a new world order with the Congo, that is, Africa, as the center of the cosmos [see figs. on the endpapers].

2 Mbembe 2015, Mudimbe 1988, and Sarr 2019.

Exhibitions on the Congo are frequently devoted to either historical or contemporary art.[3] In the past, a masterpiece discourse commonly prevailed, meaning that on the basis of a Western art canon "the seminal" artworks from renowned museums and collections were brought together and exhibited.[4] In doing so, they were classified according to the "one tribe equals one style" paradigm based on regional or ethnic styles.[5] At the forefront was often the representative art by powerful kingdoms, such as that of the Kongo, Kuba, or Luba [figs. 2/3]. In exhibition catalogues, the pieces were illustrated sideways in front of a monochrome, usually gray or black background in conformance with Western viewing habits, in order to fabricate a certain aura and aesthetic. Historical photographs were used—if at all—to show the "authenticity" of the objects. The presentation of the objects in space and in book form often reinforced the stereotype of Africa as ahistorical and traditional.

For quite some time, a dynamic art scene—long ignored by Western art critique—has existed in the Congo, which comprises artists from the successful art schools dating back to the colonial era in Kinshasa and Lubumbashi, as well as young artist collectives and art initiatives. Currently, there is a proper hype in the West with regard to contemporary art from the Congo, as evident by the growing number of exhibitions in Europe and the USA. Popular painting, in particular, emerged in the environment of the art academies founded by colonial officers and missionaries in the 1930s. The colorful images of everyday scenes from urban and folkloristic Congo after all corresponded, despite their inherently political messages, with the widespread stereotype in the West of a festive, colorful Africa.[6] Currently, exhibitions are increasingly devoted to young, often women, artists and feature alternative genres and media, such as photography, performance, literature, installation, sculpture, and digital art.[7] Ever more frequently, Congolese curators are taking over the conception of the exhibitions and foregrounding themes such as urbanity, migration, and utopia,[8] as evident, for example, in the motto of this year's biennale in Lubumbashi: *Future Genealogies: Tales From The Equatorial Line.*

Hans Himmelheber was one of the first in the 1930s to recognize and study the individual authorship behind African objects. Just as he worked together in his day with living artists of his era, we are doing the same now in this exhibition. For *Congo as Fiction,* our curatorial team—Nanina Guyer, curator for photography and Michaela Oberhofer, curator for Africa and Oceania at the Museum Rietberg—envisioned the connection between two art worlds and time periods: the 1930s of the colonial era and the postcolonial present. Congolese artists have always referred in their art to current events and cultural memory, and they comment on social and political situations then as well as now.[9]

At the turn of the twenty-first century, in the course of the archival turn, the extensive colonial archive shifted into focus for artists who, based on the historical sources, became critically occupied with their own history and the archives' inherent knowledge production and materiality [see fig. 1]. This turn to the past opened up the colonial archives—texts, photos, objects, and sound documents—for artistic practice, and led to a series of im-

3 We speak of "art" and "artists" although we are aware that the carvers and sculptors, weavers and embroiderers, ritual experts and potters in the Congo of the 1930s described their activities with other words and concepts, which have less to do with our understanding of these terms as shaped by European art history. Nevertheless, these terms refer to a culturally specific aesthetic that must be described, and to the special role of artists in many societies.

4 Only a few exhibitions focused on the history of collections such as *Exit Congo Museum*, AfricaMuseum, Tervuren 2000.

5 For a critique of the "one tribe equals one style" paradigm in the art history of Africa, see, for example Kasfir 1984 or Gagliardi 2015.

6 Exhibitions on popular painting from the region were, for example, *An/Sichten: Malerei aus dem Kongo,* Museum für Völkerkunde, Vienna, 2001; *Congo Art Works: Popular Painting,* Garage Museum of Contemporary Art, Brussels, 2017; and *Beauté Congo,* Fondation Cartier, Paris, 2015/16.

7 See, for example, the exhibition *Kinshasa Chroniques,* Musée international des arts modestes, Sète 2018/19; or *Multiple Transmissions: Art in the Afropolitan Age,* WIELS, Brussels 2019.

8 Recent examples are Sammy Baloji and Fiston Mwanza Mujila as co-curators of *Congo Stars* at the Kunsthaus Graz and Kunsthalle Tübingen 2018/19, In Koli Jean Bofane as curator of the festival *Kongo am Rhein* in Basel 2017, and Eddy Ekete and Freddy Tsimba as curators of *Megalopolis*, Grassi Museum für Völkerkunde, Leipzig 2018/19.

9 For historical art see, for example, Strother 2016.

pressive works, first and foremost, the works of the artist Sammy Baloji who is represented in the exhibition. For Sandrine Colard, art historian and curator of the Biennale 2019 in Lubumbashi, this archival turn initiated a dialogue between Africa and Europe about a shared colonial history [see Colard/Guyer].

In this spirit, for *Congo as Fiction*, we invited six contemporary artists from the Congo and the diaspora to engage critically with Himmelheber's archive from their own perspective. Sinzo Aanza, Fiona Bobo, Michèle Magema, Yves Sambu, and David Shongo, along with Sammy Baloji (and indirectly Fiston Mwanza Mujila), participated in a dialogic process in the form of brief artist residencies. They created artworks in reaction to the historical objects, photographs, and texts from Himmelheber; works that focus, comment on, and thereby update the older art and its acquisition as well as the archive and its origins in the context of colonization. Added to that were further works by Angali, Steve Bandoma, Hilary Kuyangiko Balu, Aimé Mpane, Chéri Samba, Monsengo Shula, and Pathy Tshindele. The artists all refer formally and in terms of content to historical art and thereby to their own cultural heritage and firmly, but in entirely different ways, confront the colonial past and the social practice of remembering as well as the exploitation and inequality persisting until today in the Congo.

During the intense talks with the artists, we continued to critically question our own perspective. One statement repeated especially often was: “Le Congo, c'est une fiction.” This implicit challenge to perceive the past and present of the Congo as constructed and imagined, depending on the specific actor, time, and location, became the central theme of our project.

GLOBAL ENTANGLEMENT AND LOCAL ART PRODUCTION IN THE CONGO

Although the Congo is the product of a fictitious drawing of borders and, then as now, also a projection surface for Western and Congolese imagination, it is nonetheless a real, existing space whose history and art creation is shaped by a relationship of exchange with the West.[10] The natural wealth and resources of the huge and diverse land, whose area is roughly seventy-nine times larger than that of the former colonial power—Belgium—play a decisive role in this. Artists in the past as well as present focus on the themes of the country's colonial exploitation and the unequal power relations between the global North and South and process them in their own works with satire, seriousness, and humor.[11]

Already in the fifteenth century, through trade, missionary work, and conquest, the Congo was part of early globalization. The former Kingdom of the Kongo on the lower course of the eponymous river had a close relationship to Portugal, delivered ivory, copper, and slaves to Europe, and their upper class adopted the Christian faith. These relations also played an important role in the creation of art: on the one hand, local artists appropriated the newly available materials and forms for their own works; for example, Christian motifs, such as crosses and depictions of saints, were integrated into syncretic religious movements and the associated visual imagery [figs. 4/5].[12] On the other hand, a production for the Western art market began just a short time later; the best-known example being the fine ivory carvings with scenic depictions, which European seafarers, explorers, and deal-

10 Van Reybrouck 2012 provides an overview of the history of the Congo.

11 See on this Strother 2016.

12 See Fromont 2014 for a study on the Christian art in the Congo between the sixteenth and eighteenth centuries.

ers purchased or commissioned from local artists [fig. 6]. Global interdependencies also influenced local art production in areas located further inland. When the Portuguese abolished slavery in neighboring Angola in 1830, the entire region reoriented itself economically and politically, which also became noticeable in the art. For example, Chokwe chiefs, who had become powerful through the ivory trade, commissioned the carving of memorial figures depicting themselves as invincible hunters in the style of the legendary Prince Chibinda Ilunga [fig. 7].[13]

The violent conquest of large parts of the African continent began in the final third of the nineteenth century. From 1876, the Belgian King Léopold II, who reigned from 1865 to 1909, pursued primarily his own personal economic interests in the area of the Congo under the pretext of civilizing and economic efforts. He contracted the British-American journalist Henry Morton Stanley to use unrelenting discipline in convincing local rulers to sign contracts that assured Léopold land and labor power. In the Congo, Stanley was given the name Bula Matari (breaker of rocks) for his brutality. His travelogues and memoirs became bestsellers in Europe and the USA. They made Stanley famous throughout the world, and permanently shaped the perception of the Congo in the West.

At the Berlin West Africa Conference 1884/85, which was tellingly also called the Congo Conference, the major European powers agreed among themselves on "their" areas of influence on the African continent, in order to avoid costs and conflict. The Belgian king, with his *Association Internationale du Congo*, was promised the huge territory of today's DRC as a sovereign area of power. The history of the Congo Free State, which existed from 1886 to 1908, but whose exact borders were first determined in 1910, was one of the bloodiest chapters of colonization. Companies given concessions used armed soldiers to exploit the population with extreme cruelty and extorted huge harvests of rubber. From these early days of the Congo Free State is Joseph Conrad's grim tale *The Heart of Darkness,* about the soulless world of the colonial trade, which until today has contributed to a one-sided reception of the Congo as defined by crisis and conflict. In her work *Under the Landscape,* the artist Michèle Magema focuses on forced labor on the plantations and fictitious borders drawn during the colonial era [fig. 8]. On eighty-one rubber panels, in fine lines she engraves the borders of present-day Congo with its nine neighbors.

After missionaries and human rights activists made the atrocities public—through photography, especially—Léopold II ultimately had to surrender his Free State to the Belgian state in 1908. But the new colony of Belgian Congo, too, was based on exploitation and forced labor under inhumane conditions [fig. 9]. The colonial government further expanded the system of indirect rule in that they divided the huge area into administrative "chiefdoms," each ruled by a *chef indigène.* Often without any backing from the population, these *chefs* were given medals as a sign of their new post [see story, p. 80]. The *chefs médaillés* were important cooperation partners and middlemen for the Belgian colonial power, as were the *évolués,* who were educated Congolese raised mainly in missionary schools, who lived in the cities and had adopted European clothing and attitudes and were often active in the colonial administration.

13 LaGamma 2011, pp. 182–223.

Fig. 2
Artist of the Luba region
Bow stand
Before 1939, wood, iron, plant fibers, 95.7 × 21.5 × 8 cm
Collection Kegel-Konietzko
Acquired by Hans Himmelheber

Fig. 3
Artist of the Luba region
Figure of a sitting woman with bowl
Before 1939, wood, glass, 28.5 × 17.2 × 17.5 cm
Museum Rietberg Zürich, 2018.1109
Gift of Barbara and Eberhard Fischer
Acquired by Hans Himmelheber

Fig. 4
Artist of the Vili region
Crucifix
Nineteenth century, brass, wood, 28.5 × 23 × 5.5 cm
Museum Rietberg Zürich, 2007.144
Gift through mediation by Novartis
Restiau Collection

Fig. 5
Artist of the Songye region
Figure with crown of thorns
Before 1938, wood, 28 × 15 × 14.5 cm
Museum der Kulturen Basel, III 6550
Acquired by Hans Himmelheber

Fig. 6
Artist of the Kongo region
Walking stick of Robert Visser
Late nineteenth century, ivory, silver 96 × 6 × 6 cm
Horstmann Collection

Fig. 7
Artist of the Chokwe region
Figure of Prince Chibinda Ilunga
Nineteenth century, wood, 49.3 × 12.9 × 13.2 cm
Museum Rietberg Zürich, 2007.1
Gift through mediation by Novartis

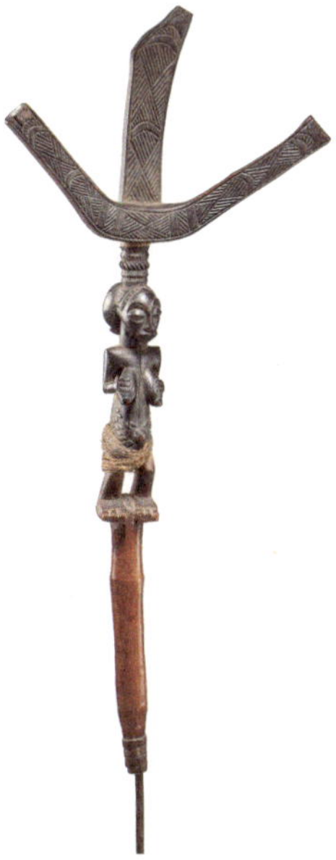

Fig. 2

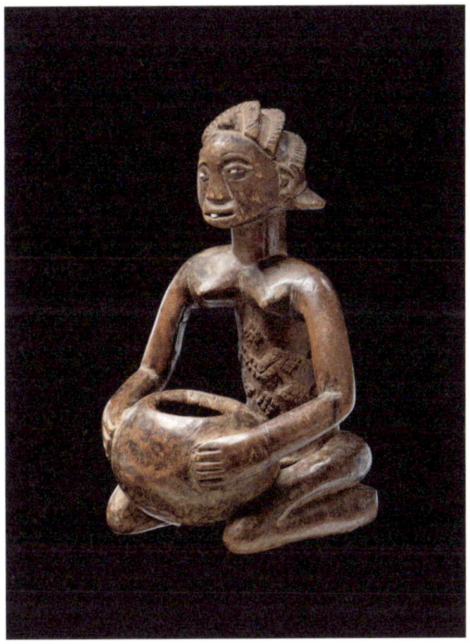

Fig. 3

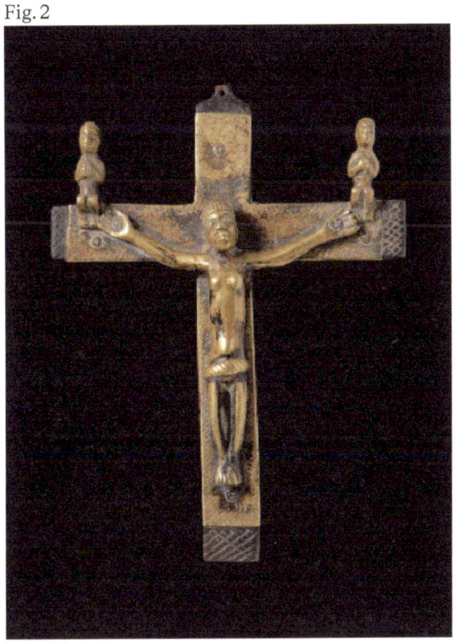

Fig. 4

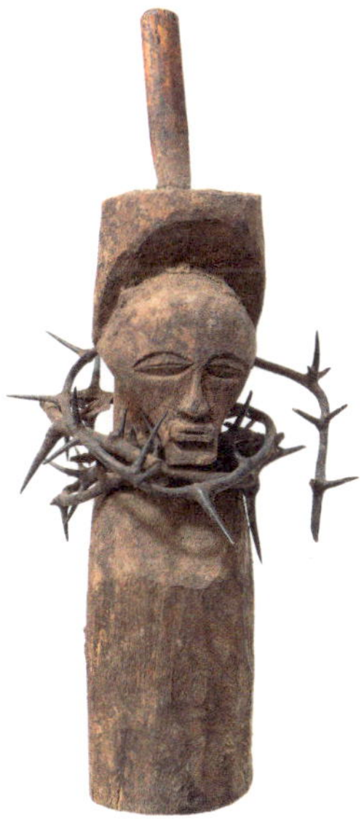

Fig. 5

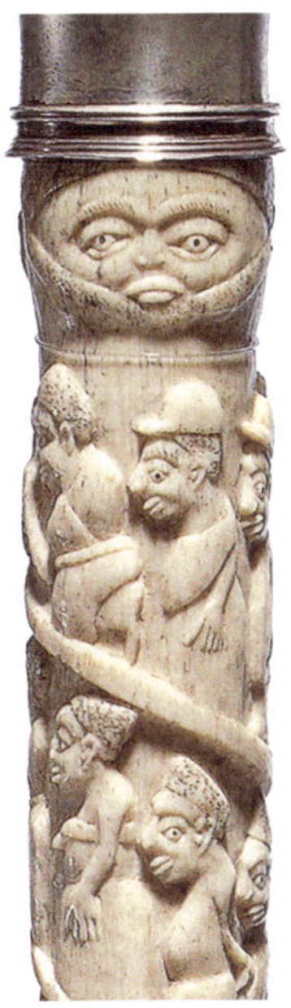

Fig. 6

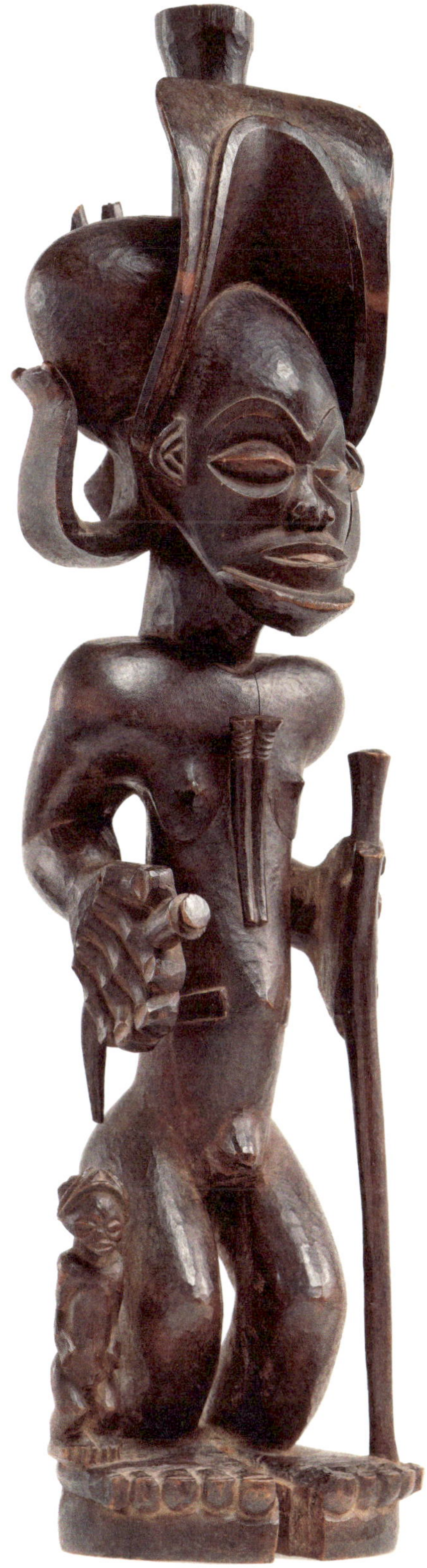

Fig. 7

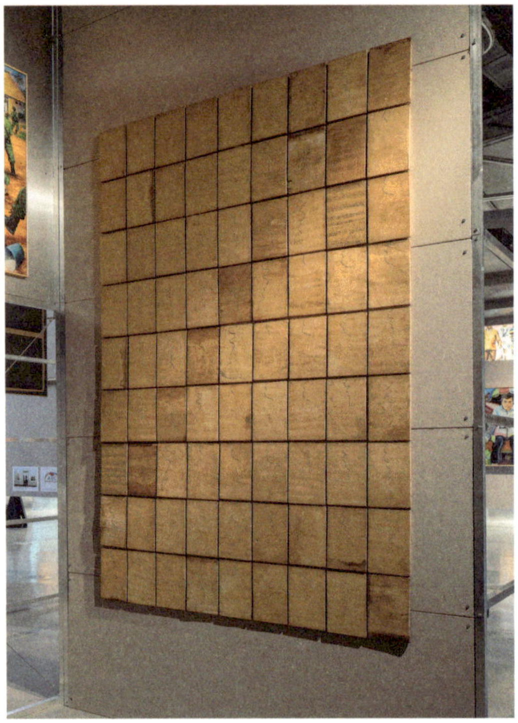
Fig. 8.1

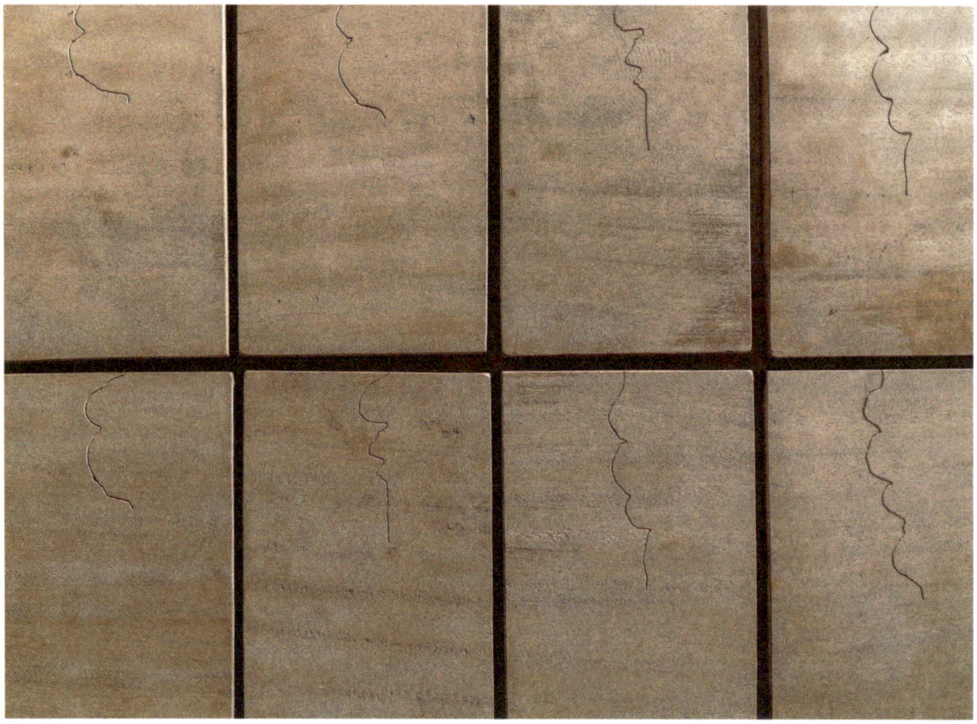
Fig. 8.2

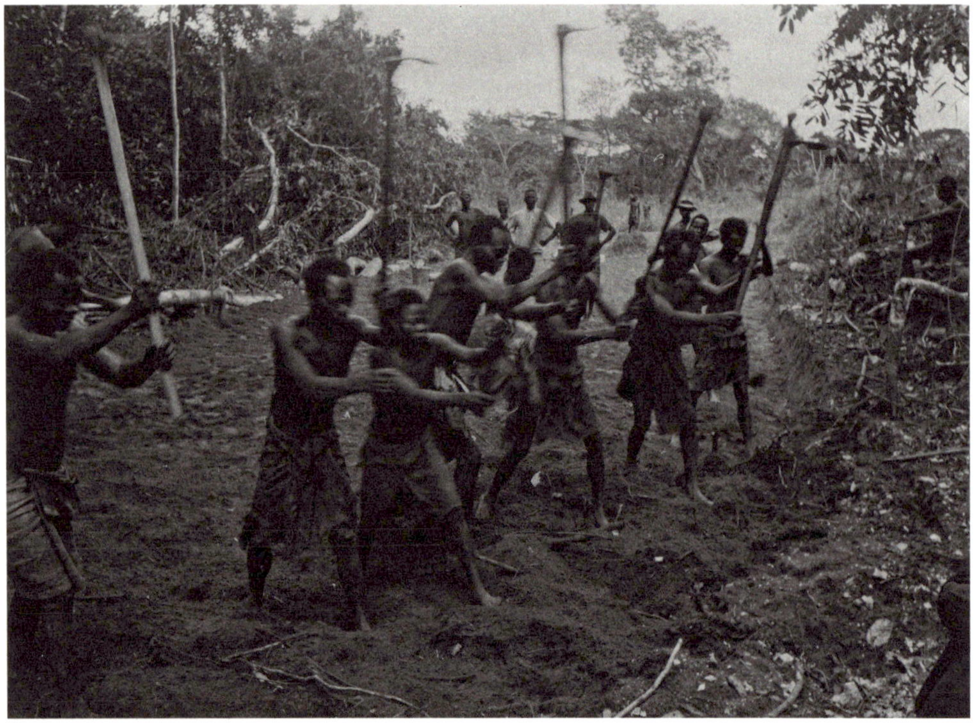
Fig. 9

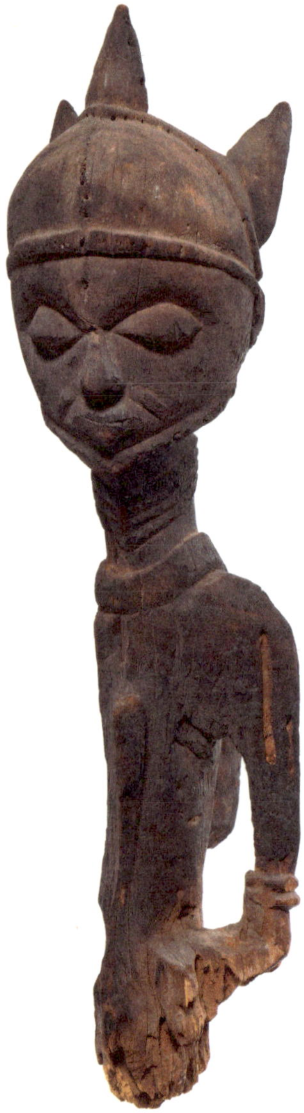
Fig. 10

Fig. 8
Michèle Magema
Under the Landscape
2015, rubber, 300 × 200 cm
Michèle Magema

Fig. 9
Hans Himmelheber
Men working on street construction
Luluwa region, 1939, b/w negative
Museum Rietberg Zürich, FHH 186-20

Fig. 10
Artist of the Luluwa region
Half-burned figure as example of iconoclasm *bwanga bwa bukalenga*
Before 1939, wood, 55 × 18 × 22 cm
Museum Rietberg Zürich, HH 14
Gift of Barbara and Eberhard Fischer
Acquired by Hans Himmelheber

With the help of the administrative system and the companies granted concessions, the population was once again ruthlessly exploited by the Belgian colonial state in order to increase production from agriculture and mining. The interwar years were characterized by growing unrest and mutual mistrust. The population revolted again and again, such as in the case of the Pende Revolt, which was brutally struck down by the colonial government. Through religious movements, the population attempted to liberate itself from the iron grip of the Belgian colonial rule [fig. 10]. At the same time, art was also a symbol of resistance [see story, p. 206].

In the early twentieth century, an abundance of natural resources, such as copper, uranium, and gold, were found and mined to meet the worldwide demand for raw materials.[14] Even after the Congo's independence from Belgium in 1960, global economic interests and local exploitation continued to shape the country's history. The mining of the mineral coltan, in particular, is responsible for the brutal armed conflicts that have erupted repeatedly since 1994, especially in the east of the country. Nearly every electronic device—mobile phones, electronic motors, and computers—requires coltan. Contemporary artists such as Sammy Baloji and David Shongo also address in their works the conflicts surrounding the mining of raw materials.

Not only the colonial conquest of the African continent came to a climax in the late nineteenth and early twentieth centuries, but also the "hunt" for Africas' material production. Explorers, colonial officials, missionaries, and traders brought back from their travels extensive collections, which very quickly filled the newly founded ethnology museums.[15] At the same time, they took thousands of photographs, which led to a distorted image of Central Africa that continues to influence our perception of the region until today.[16] In Paris, but also in Brussels and New York, a lively art market for works from the African colonies became established in the 1920s and 1930s. The objects, which in the nineteenth century were still considered curiosities, colonial trophies, or ethnographica, were now elevated to works of art as so-called primitive art or *art nègre*. Along with the avant-garde, also museums, galleries, collectors, and art critics were involved in the Western canonization of African art.[17] At the same time, awareness developed within colonial circles in the Congo that "traditional" art was worthy of being promoted, collected, and exhibited in its own museum [see essay Oberhofer]. Just a few months before Himmelheber's arrival in Kinshasa, the Musée de la vie indigène, today's National Museum, was created on the initiative of the *Association des Amis de l'Art indigène*.

HANS HIMMELHEBER'S ARCHIVE

Himmelheber was integrated within this transatlantic network of the art worlds—between the collecting and exploring in the colonial South and the art market and art canon in the global North.[18] Between 1933 and 1976, the German art ethnologist undertook a total of fourteen expeditions to the Côte d'Ivoire, Liberia, the Congo, and Alaska. His innovative studies on African aesthetics and artists provide important impulses until today for work with the art of Africa. He was among the first to study Africa's material culture by interviewing the artists about their

14 In the era of industrial and military expansion around the turn of the century, copper was important, then, during the Cold War, uranium. The atomic bombs that were dropped on Hiroshima and Nagasaki in the Second World War contained uranium from the Congo.

15 See Schildkrout and Curtis 1998. The Musée Royal de l'Afrique centrale, or AfricaMuseum, in Tervuren owns the largest collection, which emerged in 1910 from the World's Fair (Van Beurden 2015). But also other European and American museums own extensive inventory from Central Africa.

16 For a comprehensive study on the origins, co-authorship, and logic of this image world, see Geary 2002.

17 Monroe 2012.

18 Based on the concept of the "art worlds" from the American art sociologist Howard S. Becker (2017, first edition 1982) we understand art not as a product of an individual person—the artist genius—but rather, as a collective process of a network that extends beyond regional borders. In the case of the Congolese art world in the past and now, various actors are involved in production and use, sales and marketing, as well as knowledge production and imagination of the same.

careers, their work, techniques, and their aesthetic ideas, rather than focusing on the museum objects; he was interested in the artists' personalities and photographed and described their creative processes.

Himmelheber was born in Karlsruhe in 1908 and earned a degree in ethnology and medicine. In order to finance his studies, already as a young man he began in 1929 to trade in African and Oceanic objects. In Paris he established contact with the French gallerist and collector Charles Ratton, who also supported his journey to the Congo and became an important business partner. He was also able to make a name for himself internationally as a scientist and art dealer after his first two expeditions to the Cote d'Ivoire (1933 and 1934/35) for research and collecting. He supplied numerous museums in Germany, France, and Switzerland and also sold to private collectors. At the same time, he built up a network of universities, museums, and the art trade in North America. He provided loans to the iconic *African Negro Art* exhibition at the Museum of Modern Art in New York (1935). During a stay in the USA between 1935 and 1937, he held academic lectures on his studies on African art.[19] In 1936/37 he spent the winter on the Nunivak Islands in Alaska and studied artists of the Yupik peoples.[20] His friendship with Erhard Weyhe, born in Germany, whose gallery was the main financer of the Congo journeys, also stems from this time [see essay Oberhofer].

Only one week after his return from the USA, Himmelheber, who was just thirty years old at the time, set off on a two-year journey to Cameroon, Gabun, and the Belgian Congo, which was not typical for him, as he would never return there again [fig. 11]. The catalogue and exhibition *Congo as Fiction* focus on the time period from May 1938 until June 1939, when Himmelheber traveled the region between the rivers Kwango, Kwilu, and Kasai through to Sankuru and Lomami, which are now the provinces Kwango, Kwili, Kasai, Kasai-Central, and Kasai-Oriental as well as the adjacent areas of the provinces Sankuru, Lomami, and Lualaba [fig. 12].[21] Whereas mainly the courtly art of the Luba, Congo, and Kuba enjoyed great popularity in Europe, Himmelheber concentrated—along with the Kuba—also on less-explored art regions, such as the Byombo, Chokwe, Luluwa, Pende, Songye, Suku, and Yaka.

Himmelheber had two reasons for his Congo journey: for one, he wanted to continue his research on art and artists that he had begun on the Ivory Coast and in Alaska; for another, he took the Congo journey for financial reasons. As an independent ethnologist who would never be permanently employed as a professor or curator by a university or museum, Himmelheber was forced to rely on the acquisition and trade of artifacts from Africa to finance his scientific work and personal expenses [figs. 13/14]. In the case of the Congo, he was there to collect, as commissioned by the Swiss ethnology museums in Basel and Geneva, as well as the Weyhe Gallery in New York and the Galerie Charles Ratton in Paris.

At the same time, Himmelheber set aside for his private collection particularly impressive artworks that were never intended for sale. In 1993, the Museum Rietberg offered the first showing of parts of the collection, together with his photographs, in the exhibition *Zaire 1938/39*, curated by his granddaughter Clara Himmelheber, the current curator for Africa at Rautenstrauch-

19 He lectured, for example, at Universities in Cambridge, New Haven, Washington and New York. In the USA he met American ethnologists such as Ruth Benedict, Margaret Mead, and Franz Boas. The latter advised him on his research stay in Alaska.

20 Resulting as pendant to his doctoral dissertation *Negerkünstler* (1935) was his book *Eskimokünstler* (1938).

21 Before the reform of the area, between 1988 and 2015 this region corresponded to the old provinces Bandundu, Kasai-Occidental, and Kasai-Oriental. In the Belgian Congo, after 1935 these provinces were called Léopoldville and Lusambo with the districts visited by Himmelheber, Kwango, Kasai, and Sankuru.

Fig. 11
Unknown photographer
Hans Himmelheber with a group
Yaka region, 1938, b/w negatives
Museum Rietberg Zürich,
FHH 167-12 to 167-14

Fig. 12
Hans Himmelheber's itinerary in the Belgian Congo
Continuous line = Precise route
Broken line = Assumed route
Dotted line = Visited region, exact route not known

Stage 1: visited region, exact route not known 2.5.1938–24.12.1938

Stage 2: ship's route from Kinshasa to Basongo 24.12.1938–1.1.1939

Stage 3: itinerary from Basongo to Kananga 1.1.1939–28.3.1939

Stage 4: tour from and back to Kananga 28.3.1939–4.4.1939

Stage 5: tour from and back to Kananga 4.4.1939–18.51939

Stage 6: return journey from Kananga to Kinshasa 18.5.1939–9.6.1939

YAKA, PENDE etc.
Names of language groups visited by Hans Himmelheber

Itinerary reconstructed on the basis of Hans Himmelheber's diary and publications

Concept: Daniela Müller

Fig. 13
Artist of the Yaka region
Male figure
Pre-1938, wood, 56 × 11 × 13 cm
Musée d'ethnographie de Genève,
ETHAF 015945
Acquired by Hans Himmelheber

Fig. 14
Hans Himmelheber
Hans Himmelheber photographs a village square, the acquired figure in front of him
Yaka region, 1938, b/w negative
Museum Rietberg Zurich, FHH 166-19

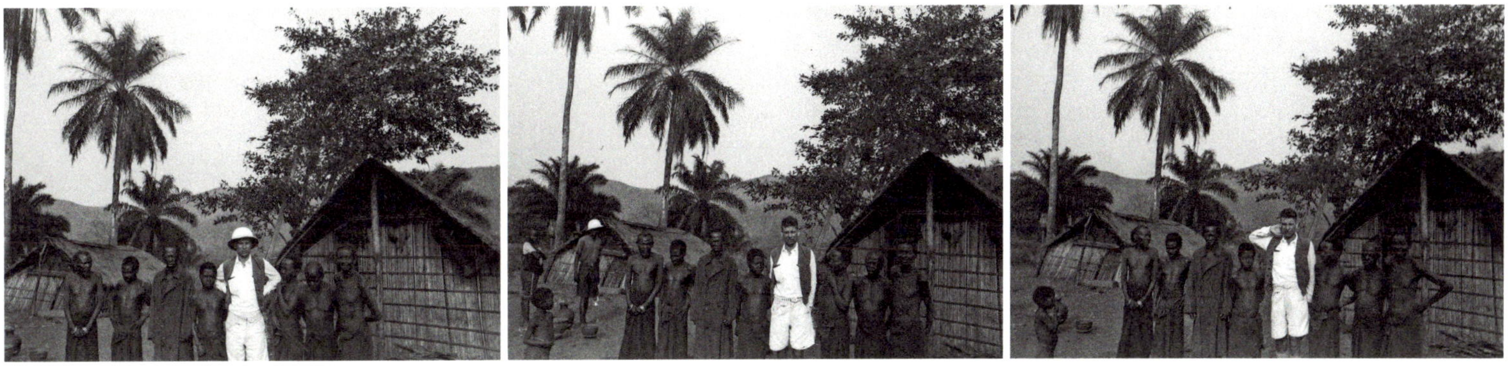

Fig. 11

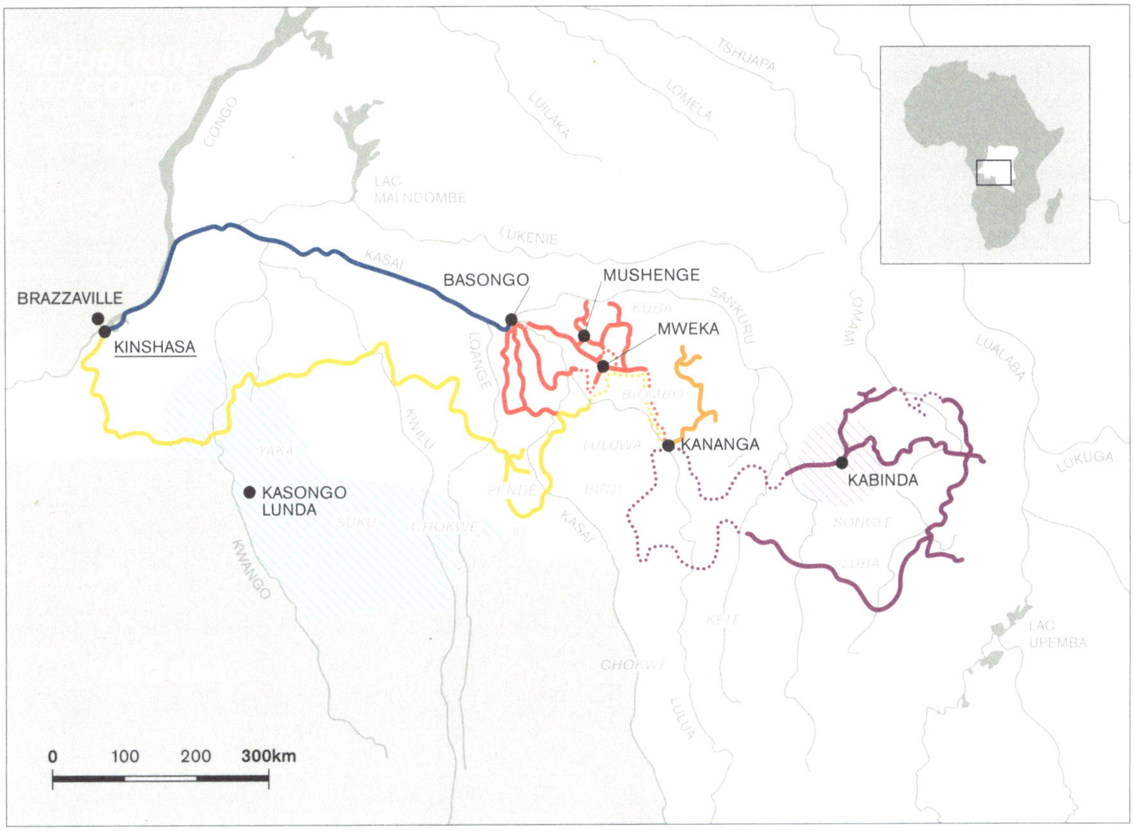

Fig. 12

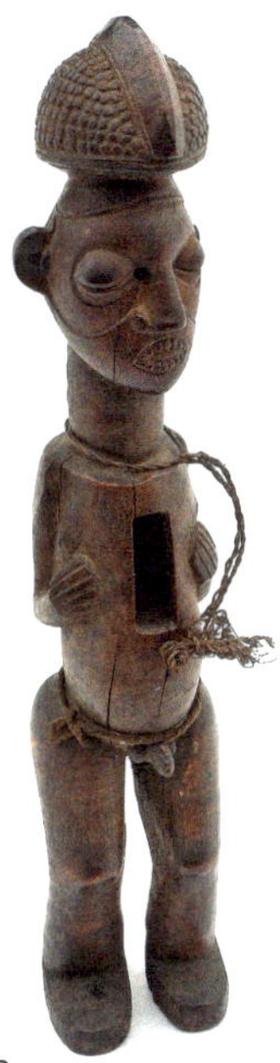

Fig. 13

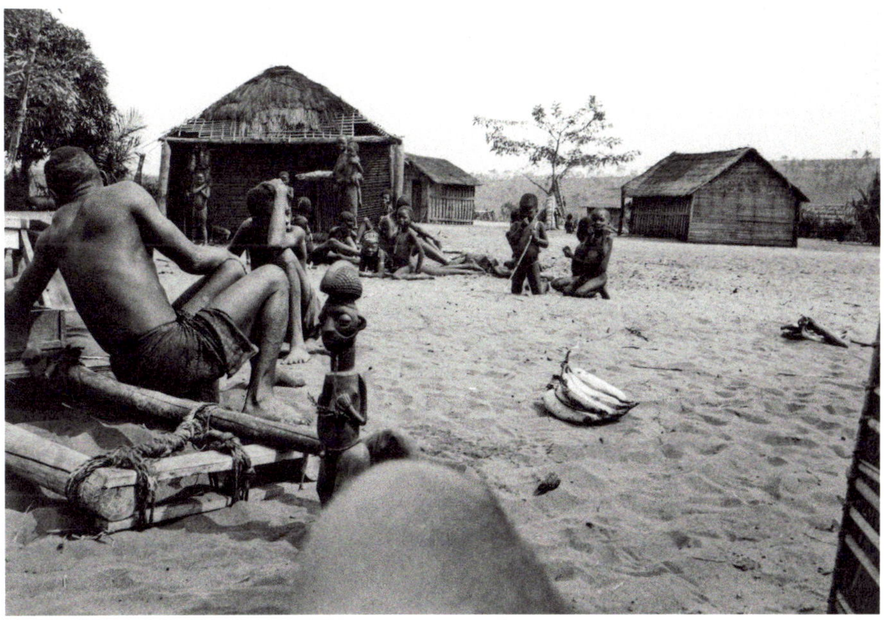

Fig. 14

Joest-Museum, and his son, Eberhard Fischer, the former director of the Museum Rietberg.[22] A selection from the nearly 1,500 photos that Himmelheber took on his Congo journey was published for the first time in the accompanying catalogue [fig. 15].

In the last five years, thanks to the Fischer/Himmelheber family, his collection, which is considered a "family treasure," has arrived at the Museum Rietberg—for the most part in the form of gifts. The collection meanwhile comprises more than 750 objects, whereby almost one-third are from his journey to the Congo. Among them are finely carved sculptures, elaborately embroidered textiles, richly decorated everyday objects, and particularly rare ensembles of initiation masks from former times. Added to that is the photo archive with 15,000 black-and-white negatives from all of his journeys. Himmelheber was a gifted photographer who always took his camera with him and used photography systematically during his art-ethnological journeys as a working tool. Thus, together with the extensive written estate, which has been at the Museum since 2016, a unique "archive" has been created, which is being explored in the context of a project financed by the Swiss National Science Foundation.[23] Among other things, *Congo as Fiction* presents the initial results of this collaborative research process, which is planned for four years.

Although Himmelheber's academic field study notes (also those on the Congo) were lost during the Second World War to a bomb in Karlsruhe, by a stroke of luck a copy of his diary on the Congo journey has been preserved [fig. 16]. Beginning with New Year's Day 1939, every day for the last seven months of his stay, Himmelheber used a typewriter to record his experiences, usually working until late in the night. What arose is a thick description of the journey, which contains his personal emotions, desires, and evaluations, the imponderability of everyday life while traveling, his collecting activity, but also everyday colonial life on the eve of the Second World War in the Belgian Congo. Also evident in his writings is the contradiction and ambivalence between Himmelheber's enthusiasm for certain artworks or artists and his ideas—characteristic of his era—about the hierarchy between the colonial masters and the colonized people. In addition to the archives in Basel and Geneva, in which Himmelheber provided detailed information on the acquired pieces, important as sources are also his scientific articles in the journal *Brousse*, the newly founded journal at the time of the *Association des Amis de l'Art indigène* in Kinshasa.[24] Moreover, for the analysis of his photographs, helpful are the extensive keyword catalogues and notes on the contact prints [fig. 17]. With its wealth of sources, Himmelheber's archive, can, at the same time, be categorized within the larger context of the global art market, the concept of authenticity, and the thereby implied contradiction between tradition and the modern era [see essays Guyer and Oberhofer].

The linking of the various media in the archive—object, image, and text—offers important starting points for researching the objects' biographies and the accompanying reinterpretation process. For example, the path of a Yaka mask can be traced from its creation and use to its purchase in the Congo through to its being placed in museum and aesthetic contexts. Initially created by a Yaka mask maker for the *mukanda* initiation, together with a mask costume, used for dancing in a performance accompanied by drums in front of an audience [fig. 18], the mask then became

22 See on Basel also Gardi 1986.

23 The research project "Hans Himmelheber – Kunst Afrikas und verflochtene Wissensproduktion," which has been running since October 2018, is a collaboration between the Museum Rietberg and the Chair of Professor Gesine Krüger at the Historisches Seminar of the University of Zürich.

24 In addition to the three published articles is also a fourth, which was no longer printed due to the war, but is available in draft form in the archive of the Museum Rietberg.

Fig. 15
Cover photo of the photo catalogue
Zaire 1938/39: Hans Himmelheber. Photographic documents on the arts of the Yaka, Pende, Tshokwe and Kuba. Zürich 1993

Fig. 16
Hans Himmelheber
Page from Hans Himmelheber's Congo diary
Kuba region, January 22 and 23, 1939
Archive Museum Rietberg Zürich

Fig. 17
Hans Himmelheber
Contact prints
B/w positive on paper
Museum Rietberg Zürich, FHH 194-21b

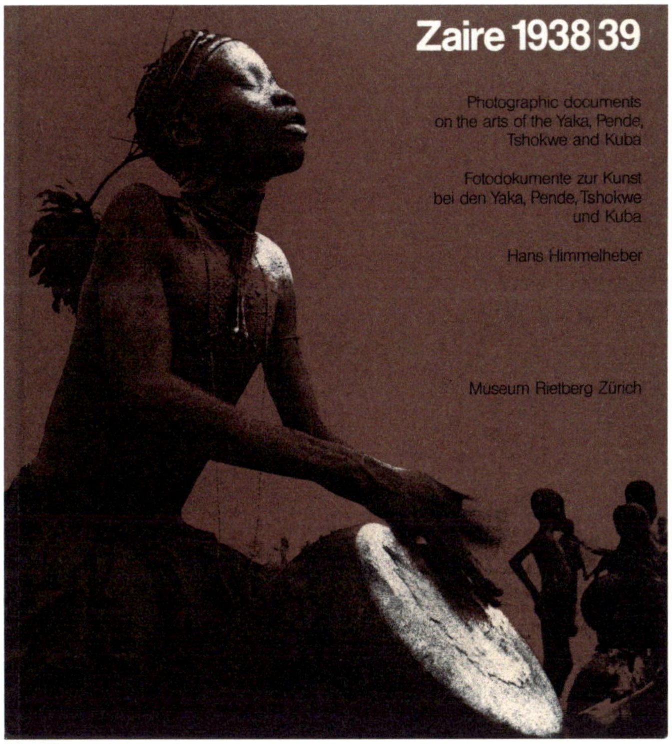

Fig. 15

Tagebuch 11

22.Januar 1939

Sonntag. Morgens weit die Strasse nach Lodi hinauf und in 4 oder 5 Doerfern zusammen 20 Stueck gekauft. Morgen mache ich eine aehnliche Tour gegen Domiongo zu. Dann zum Mittagessen bei den Patres, die eine herrliche Kopie einer Koenigsfigur haben. Ich erfahre, dass noch mindestens 2 Kuenstler diese machen koennen. Sie arbeiten teils aus dem Kopf, teils nach Fotos. Jeder Koenig hat bestimmte Attribute. Der Frère ist ein Englaender, der kein Wort franzoesisch aber flaemisch kann.

Nachmittags grosse Tanzvorstellung. Ich ueberrasche den einen von beiden Taenzern bei der Auftackelung. Er traegt eine herrliche, mit Kupfer beschlagene alte Maske, den Bombo die ich zu kaufen hoffe, obwohl der Haeuptlingssohnsagt, sie koste 150 frs. Sie waere es schliesslichwert. Das Kostuem ist gaudy, mit vielen Graswuscheln, roten Lederhandschuhen und Sandalen.
Im Dorf ist eine zweite Maske, der bekannte perlgestickte Moasambojo, wie ich einen (Moadi) bei den Bakete gekauft hatte, die ihn hier gestohlen haben. Dieser sieht wirklich praechtig aus, ueber und ueber mit Glasperlen behaengt, einem riesigen Rad aus Adlerfedern auf dem Kopf. Es sind viele Zuschauer da und Kwete erscheint nun auch als Eingeborener mit sehr schoener Matte statt seiner wohlgebuegelten Kakihose. Er sieht sehr gut aus. Drei Trommler mit alten Bakubatrommeln. Es sind drei alte Leute, ausnahmsweise, denndas Trommeln ist sehr anstrengend. Es tanzen abwechselnd der Moasambojo und der Bombo, als ob es ein Wettstreit waere. Jeder Tanz ist nur ganz kurz, vielleicht 2 Minuten, und eigentlich nur ein Geschuettel der Feder- und Perlenpracht ohne Schrittartistik. Wenn der Tanz vorbei ist, geht die Maske in ihre Ecke, wird dort von zahlreichen Sekundanten auf einen Hocker gestzt und mit einem xxxxxx Korbdeckel angefaechelt oder mit einer Flasche gesaeugt, genau wie unsere Boxer. Der andre Taenzer sitzt davon entfernt, d.h. nun wird er vonseinen Sekundanten zum Tanzen angespornt und begibt sich zu den Trommlern.

23.Januar 1939

Morgends wieder in die umliegenden Doerfer, auf der Strassen nach Domiongo (Eisenbahnstation). Ca 20 Stueck bekommen, und zu Hause dann nochmal ebensoviel sodass ich jetzt 180 habe seit der Abreise in Mweka vor 6 Tagen. Es macht Spass mit den Bakuba so auszuziehn, weil sie froehliche Leute sind und gut singen. In den Doerfern nehmen meist ein paar Dorfburschen die Tipoye bis zum naechsten Dorf, ohne daran zu denken, einen Matabish zu verlangen, wie sonst stets. Ebenso rennen die Kinder und Halbwuechsigen zum Spass mit, manchmal drei Stunden lang. Es ist unglaublich, wie lange sie's so im Dauerlauf aushalten, aber das singen und das aufstampfen im Takt (und uebrigens im gleichen Schritt) macht es eben zu einer Art Tanz, sogar fuer die Traeger, die jeder die Haelfte meiner 62 kg auf dem Rueck en haben. Sie fuehren alle moegkichen Tanzfiguren auf, waehrend sie so mit ihrer Last dahinrennen, und manchmal gehne sie sogar zum Spass ein paar Schritte zurueck, dann wieder wei

Fig. 16

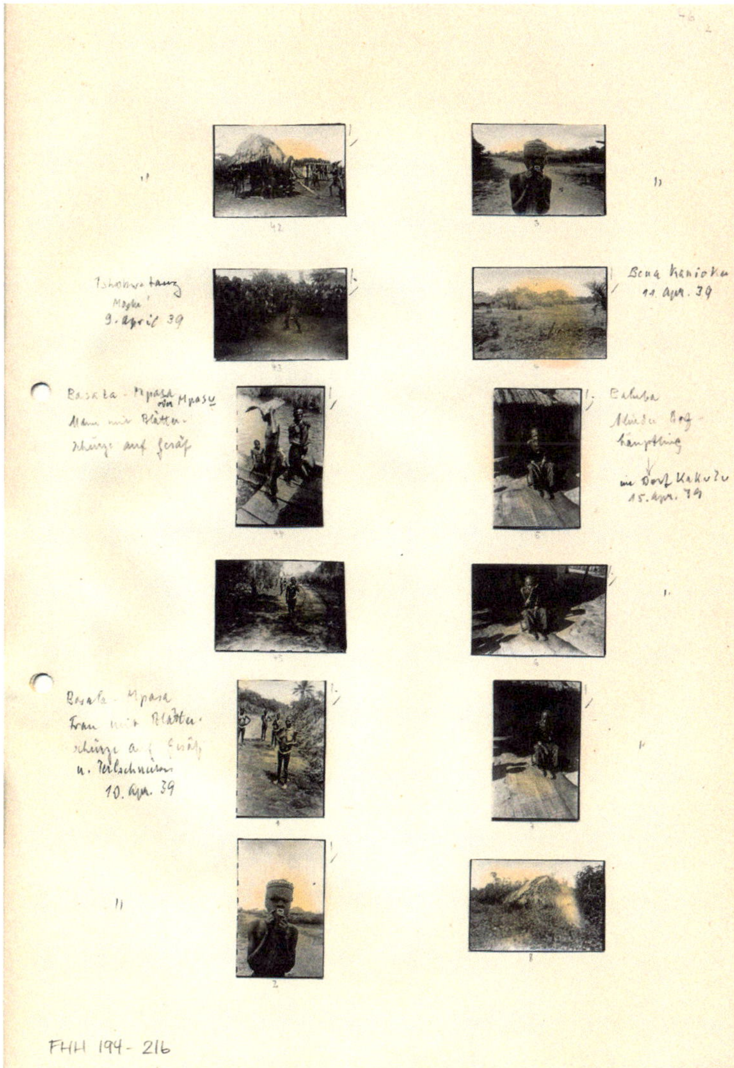

Fig. 17

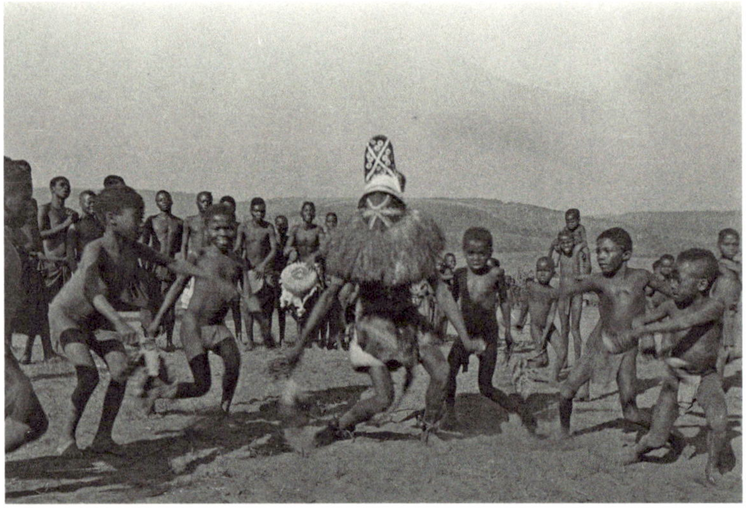
Fig. 18
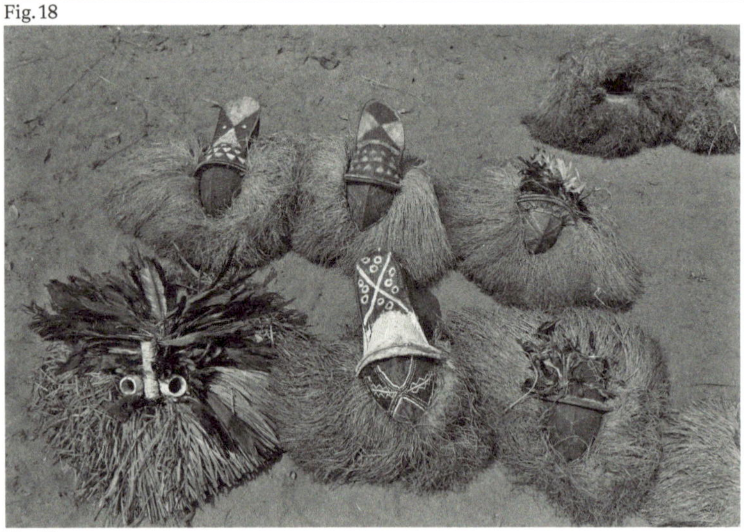
Fig. 19
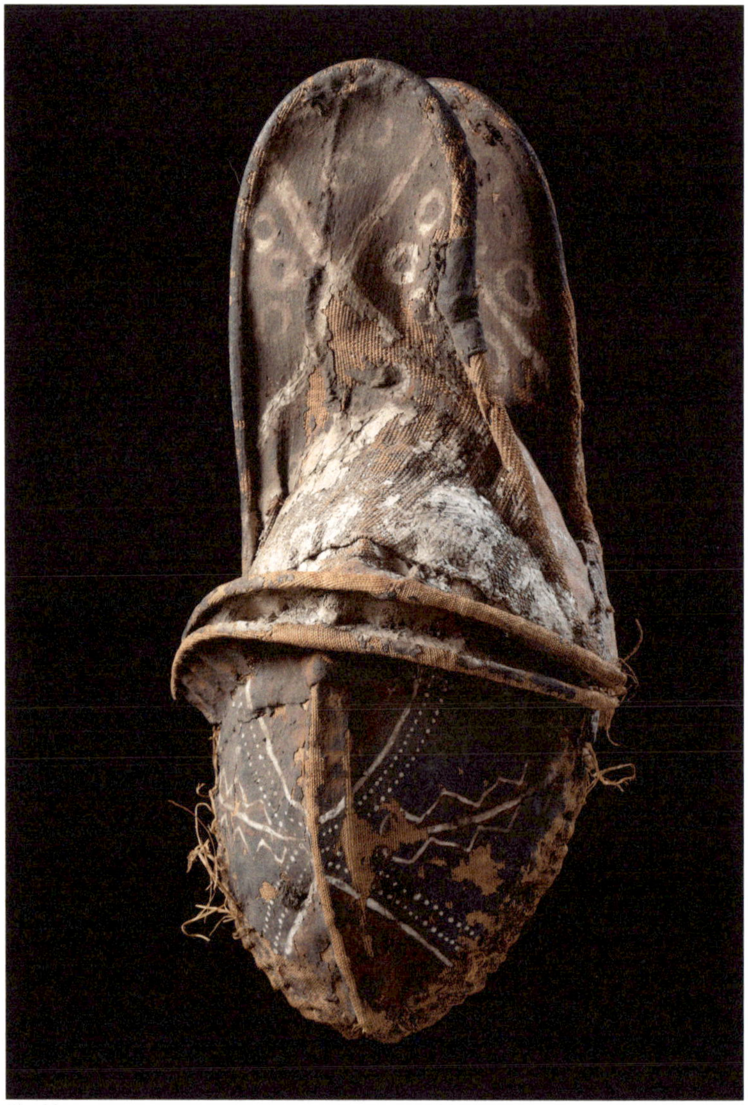
Fig. 20

Fig. 18
Hans Himmelheber
The Yaka masks in dance
Kingulu, June 20, 1938, b/w negative
Museum Rietberg Zürich, FHH 155-39

Fig. 19
Hans Himmelheber
The Yaka masks in overview on the ground
Yaka region, 1938, b/w negative
Museum Rietberg Zürich, FHH 158-18

Fig. 20
Artist of the Yaka region
The Yaka mask as museum object
Before 1938, plant fibers, color pigments, circa 44 × 22.5 × 18 cm
Museum Rietberg Zürich, EFA 7
Gift of Barbara and Eberhard Fischer
Acquired by Hans Himmelheber

the commodity of a dealer, with field photos testifying to its "authenticity" [fig. 19]. Now it is an aesthetically staged artwork—whose colors have meanwhile faded—in the context of a museum [fig. 20]. Detailed essays and short stories are devoted to the intersections in the archive and the dense narratives that arise from them.

ON THE STRUCTURE OF THE BOOK

Congo as Fiction comprises four chapters illuminating the art worlds of the Congo in the past and present; Hans Himmelheber's archive and the art world of the 1930s are the starting points throughout. The first section, "Exploring, Photographing, and Acquiring Art" shows how the purchase of the objects and the on-site transport—whether in a type of hammock (*tipoye*) or in a car [see stories, pp. 72 and 84]—took place, and which actors were involved [see stories, pp. 88 and 92]. During his expeditions to the Congo, Himmelheber attempted to do justice to both his scientific ambitions as an art ethnologist, as well as his duties as a collector and dealer [see essay Oberhofer]. He employed the camera, which he always had with him, in very different ways, for example to articulate his intentions with regard to the village population, as a tool for his studies, and for the construction of a particular visual fiction of the Congo [see essay Guyer]. Both the acquisition of the art and Himmelheber's photographs are characterized by an imbalance of power between the colonists and the colonized, yet at the same time, moments of African agency can also be pointed out: for example, when Himmelheber documents the role of the artist or the production for the art market, or when the local elite use photography as a means of self-portrayal.

The artists Michèle Magema and David Shongo interpret the visual world created by Himmelheber in entirely different ways. In his *BLACKOUT POETRY, IDEA'S GENEALOGY* series, the Lubumbashi-based musician, composer, and artist David Shongo (born 1994) focuses on the colonial gaze that resonates in Himmelheber's photos. In impressive collages, Shongo discloses and at the same time exponentiates this gaze by subjecting the photo's subjects to an update using elements that we all know well, such as astronaut helmets, barcodes, electrical panels, virtual reality glasses, or machine guns, which not only allude to the exploitation and conflicts surrounding raw materials, but also make those depicted appear both familiar and remote [see p. 104].

The performance, video, and photo artist Michèle Magema (born 1977) created *EVOLVE*, an installation composed of photos, drawings, and texts, marked by her own specific interpretation of Himmelheber's photo archive [see story, p. 96]. In the years between the wars, when Himmelheber was traveling through the Congo, her paternal grandfather was among the educated urban elite, the *évolués*, who lived like Europeans and welcomed the goals of the colonial project with regard to education and economic modernization.[25] The France-based artist, who is among the few internationally successful women in Congolese art, combines her personal biography with the colonial past and considers her work a ritual of redressing the history of her family and her country.

25 *EVOLVE* is to some extent a continuation of the work *Mémoires Hévéa* (2015), in which Magema's maternal family history is foregrounded.

In the next section, focus is on "Design and Elegance" as important aspects of the Congolese art worlds—beyond temporal and regional borders. In the past, prominent were the Kuba with their elaborately designed common objects and objects of prestige made of wood, glass pearls, and cowries [see stories, pp. 128, 144 and 156]. Similar to others before and after him, Himmelheber was excited by the Kuba's creativity and "art, for transforming the world based on aesthetic principles."[26] Particularly impressive are the more than six-meter-long dance skirts made of raffia cloth, whose abstract patterns inspired artists such as Paul Klee, Pablo Picasso, and Henri Matisse. In both the past as well as the present, luxurious accessories and designs are associated with pompous and elegant appearances. For example, for public appearances, the kings of the Kuba wore richly decorated garments with head coverings and jewelry that were so heavy they could hardly move in them. Based on this visual repertoire, the contemporary painter Pathy Tshindele (born 1976) created his own vision of an idealized Kuba king with his series *It's my kings* [see story, p. 136].

26 Himmelheber 1940, p. 22.

Just as it does now, in the past, the medium of photography played an important role in self-staging. For example, the Kuba elite used their European visitors' cameras to show their cultural wealth and superiority to others—corresponding with the image of the Kuba in the West [see essay Geary]. Himmelheber's camera, too, was used during his 1938/39 journey by individual men and women as a platform for self-representation. When the Congolese photographer and artist Yves Sambu (born 1980) saw these historical images for the first time, he exclaimed, astonished, *"Mais, c'est contemporain!"* In a dialogue with the black-and-white photos from Himmelheber, Sambu chose particular motifs from his *Vanité apparente* series [see p. 166]. These show portraits of *sapeurs* in Kinshasa who are characterized by their luxurious clothing and eccentric lifestyles. With their looks and way of performing, the *sapeurs* articulate an identity that is uncommon in the harsh conditions of the megacity Kinshasa.

The young Zurich artist Fiona Bobo (born 1992) thematizes the self-confident appearance of the *sapeurs* living in Switzerland. The title of her multimedia installation *Mvuatu-Mboka Na Biso—et la Suisse* can be translated as "clothing style, our country—and Switzerland." Using photographs and videos of Swiss *sapeurs*, Bobo documents the immense importance of the extravagant clothing, style, and fashion in the Congolese diaspora [see p. 173]. The juxtaposition of Himmelheber's, Sambu's, and Bobo's photos links phenomena such as self-staging, fashion, and elegance in the past and present, city and countryside, tradition and the modern era.

The section "Power and Politics," forefronts the agency and political dimensions of artworks. In the past, colonization and missionary work influenced the religious and political relations of power as well as the arts associated therewith. This also resulted in the illegalization of secret societies, such as *kifwebe* and its masks [see story, p. 212]. In some cases, such as with the Pende Revolt, art served to symbolize resistance against the colonial power [see story, p. 206].

With the *mankishi,* the power figures of the Songye, and those of other groups, a ritual specialist charged the wooden sculptures with substances, thereby empowering them with the ability to heal disease and ward off evil powers [see story, p. 232]. In the case of the Luluwa, the finely carved power figures (*manga*) were also characterized by their ambivalence and complexity and possessed both positive as well as negative qualities [see essay Petridis]. The inner lives of the power figures was thereby just as important as their outer lives, which is made visible in the catalogue and the exhibition through the latest imaging techniques [see essay Oberhofer/Mannes/Stenger].

With power figures, too, artists refer to political power relations. In many locations, the meaning of such figures initially increased during the colonial era. Chiefs and the local population used them to try to maintain control over trade and politics in the colonial system, or to regain it [see story, p. 218]. As a reaction, colonial officials and also missionaries had the sculptures destroyed in an effort to prevent the practices associated with them. The fact that this did not entirely succeed can be seen by the recent power figures equipped with Chinese door locks. Also contemporary artists, such as Hilaire Balu Kuyangiko (born 1992), have discovered the subject for themselves. In his work *Nkisi numérique,* the Kinshasa-based artist charges such a power figure using electrical scrap. Balu thereby formulates a grim vision of the future of the world economy, characterized by consumption, capital, and exploitation.

For *Congo as Fiction,* the internationally renowned artist Sammy Baloji (born in Lubumbashi in 1978) created the installation *Kasala: The Slaughterhouse of Dreams or the First Human, Bende's Error* [see p. 242]. The multilayered work of mirrors, photos, sounds, and projections refers to Himmelheber, but also poses timely questions about dealing with colonial collections and archives: What happens with objects from Africa that have been robbed of their cultural context and have landed in museums of the global North? To what extent is it legitimate to expose the secret inner lives of power figures? How can objects be reanimated, to get back their voices? What alternative forms of commemoration exist? For Baloji's installation, the Graz-based writer Fiston Mwanza Mujila composed a remembrance poem (*kasala*) in Luba style, in which he not only poetically captures the brutality of the exploitation of raw materials, but likewise embarks on a search for his cultural roots.

The "Performance and Initiation" chapter focuses on the central significance of movement, music, and interaction in the mask performances in the art of the Congo. Among the Pende, Yaka, Chokwe, and Byombo, colorful masked figures perform during the *mukanda* initiations, a period of tests and deprivation in which, until today, young men prepare for their future roles as men [see stories, pp. 273 and 298]. Himmelheber visited the camp in which the circumcisions were carried out and photographed the masked dances. American art historian Z. S. Strother followed in his footsteps exactly fifty years later [see essay Strother]. The dynamics of the dances captured in the photographs, emphasize the importance of performance and spectacle in this art, entirely opposed to the static art at the royal courts. After their use, such initiation masks were often deemed worthless, which meant that collectors such as Himmelheber were able to acquire them.

The mask ensembles with costumes that Himmelheber acquired captivate through their diversity of colors, forms, and materials [see story, p. 288]. The creators of the Yaka masks, for example, were expected to be as creative and innovative as possible in order to surprise and amuse the audience with consistently new subjects. Local beauty ideals and concepts of masculinity and femininity were expressed in the performances, but eroticism and humor also played a role. The masks' iconography sometimes also referred to current events and offered, for example, a humorous look at the demeanor of the colonial administrators. The *mukanda* camp outlived both the colonial era as well as the current conflicts; in the Pende region, the most recent *mukanda* camp was carried out in 2018 with an increase in the number of participants [see essay Strother].

Contemporary artists have become involved in different ways with the legacy of the masked figures and their performances. The artists Steve Bandoma and Aimé Mpane refer to the unusual, asymmetrical *mbangu* initiation masks of the Pende. While Steve Bandoma, in his painting *Papotage*, questions the message of salvation found in Christianization or missionary work; Aimé Mpane, in his double portraits *La Demoiselle Picasso,* comments on the reception of African art in the avant-garde [see story, p. 284].

The young writer and artist Sinzo Aanza (born 1990) uses a masked figure in the form of a priest's robe hung on a rope in his poetic installation *The lord is dead, long life to the lord* [see p. 222]. In his work, Aanza pursues the continuities and discontinuities of colonial and postcolonial history and politics as well as the issues of restitution and reparation. The soundtrack was created as a mix of his own text together with sound recordings that he made in the villages visited by Himmelheber.

"LIKE CONGO, I AM FICTION AND FUTURE"

The starting point for *Congo as Fiction* is the archive of Hans Himmelheber containing objects, photographs, and texts, which led to various interpretations from curatorial and artistic perspectives, and their interweaving with one another. At the same time, precise borders between objects and photos, whether modern or traditional, past or present, are dissolved. On the one hand, the historical artworks are combined with the photographs that Himmelheber took on his journey in 1938/39, as complementary media of knowledge production. On the other hand, the Congolese art world of the colonial era is confronted with the present, and vice versa. This gives rise to an interlacing of diverse practices and positions across temporal and regional borders, with old and new art, fine arts and photography, scientific and poetic texts, design and performance becoming intertwined in a kaleidoscope of fictions and imaginations of the Congo. A photo by the young artist David Shongo [fig. 21] is representative of this; he wears a self-constructed mask with the portrait of a chief photographed by Himmelheber on it. Similar to our exhibition, the artist's statement "Like Congo, I am fiction and future" draws an arc spanning from the past to the present—and beyond, into the future.

Fig. 21
David Shongo
Like Congo, I am fiction and future
Instagram-Post, August 23, 2019
https://www.instagram.com/p/B1glT8XHrKZ/
(accessed on September 5, 2019)

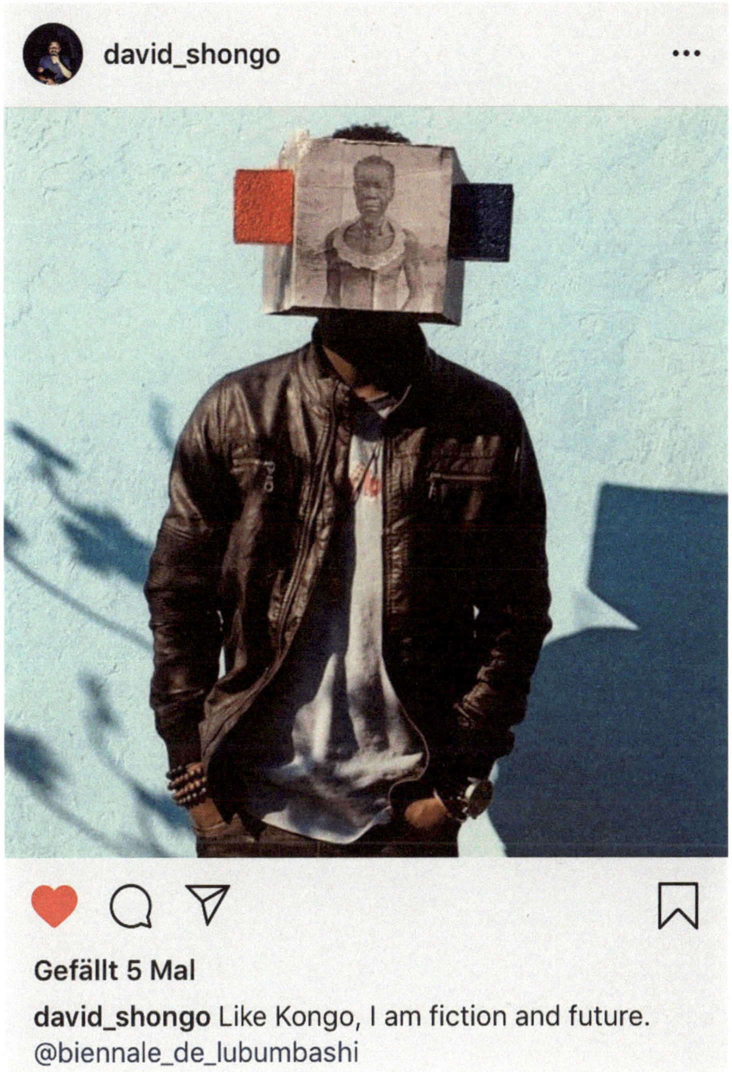
david_shongo
Gefällt 5 Mal
david_shongo Like Kongo, I am fiction and future.
@biennale_de_lubumbashi
Fig. 21

EXPLORING, PHOTOGRAPHING, AND ACQUIRING ART

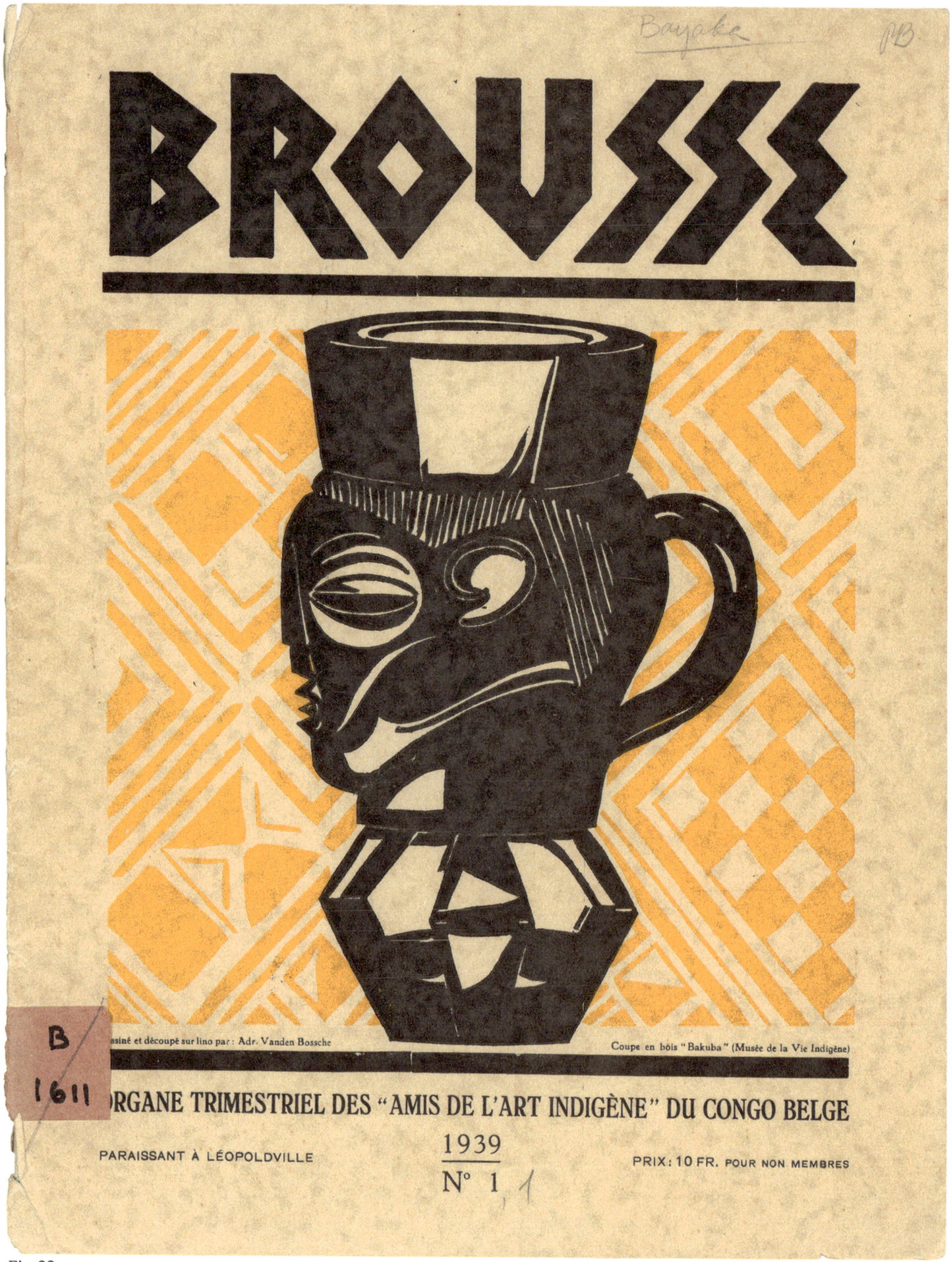
Bayaka
PB
BROUSSE
ssiné et découpé sur lino par : Adr. Vanden Bossche
Coupe en bois "Bakuba" (Musée de la Vie Indigène)
B
1611
RGANE TRIMESTRIEL DES "AMIS DE L'ART INDIGÈNE" DU CONGO BELGE
PARAISSANT À LÉOPOLDVILLE
1939
N° 1, 1
PRIX: 10 FR. POUR NON MEMBRES

Fig. 22

Fig. 22
Cover of the magazine *Brousse*, in which Himmelheber published the results of his research
Kinshasa, 1939
Museum Rietberg Zürich

BETWEEN RESEARCHING AND COLLECTING: HANS HIMMELHEBER IN THE CONGO, 1938/39

Michaela Oberhofer

> "Today, New Year's Day 1939, I have decided for the second or third time to keep a diary, because for a while now I have been determined to work more systematically. [...] I am in Basongo, the administrative center of the Bashilele, to study the art and artists here for the journal Brousse, for which I must write a series of four articles."[1]

When Hans Himmelheber started the diary of his sojourn in the Congo with these words in early 1939, he had already been traveling in Africa for sixteen months. On September 3, 1937, he had arrived by ship in Victoria (Nigeria), now Limbe (Cameroon), and from there he had traveled for six weeks predominantly around the British-controlled Cameroonian grasslands. In mid-November 1937, he continued his journey—this time under much more difficult conditions—in Gabon, at the time part of French Equatorial Africa. Both the transportation on site and the acquisition of art objects proved to be more complicated than expected. After five months he left Gabon disappointed and, in April 1938, headed for Brazzaville. Shortly before the outbreak of the Second World War, Himmelheber was frequently confronted with reservations toward Germans. Only thanks to the intervention of the French governor-general of French Equatorial Africa, François-Joseph Reste, whom Himmelheber knew well from his sojourns in the Côte d'Ivoire between 1933 and 1935, did he finally receive a permit to enter the Belgian Congo from its governor-general Pierre Ryckmans.[2]

In late May 1938, Himmelheber reached the true objective of his journey: the colony of Belgian Congo, now the Democratic Republic of the Congo. From Kinshasa, then still known as Léopoldville, he initially ventured south along the border to Angola. After traveling by boat from Léopoldville to Basongo, he visited the central province of Lusambo before returning to Léopoldville via the Kasai region. The easternmost place that Himmelheber visited was Kabongo and environs; the southernmost was roughly Mato northwest of the then province of Elisabethville. He never found his way into the economically important city of Elisabethville, modern-day Lubumbashi, in the Katanga region. In total he spent thirteen months in the Congo before boarding the Woermann shipping company's cargo ship Togo on June 8, 1939, sailing to Hamburg and returning to his homeland after almost two years in Africa.

Hans Himmelheber's intentions in the Congo can be inferred from the first lines of his diary: he wanted to conduct systematic field research into art and artists and publish his scientific findings in the new magazine *Brousse* [fig. 22], which had been

1 Hans Himmelheber, diary, Basongo, January 1, 1939 (archive of the Museum Rietberg).

2 Letter from Himmelheber to Eugen Paravicini, Brazzaville, May 22, 1938 (archive of the Museum der Kulturen Basel).

founded by Belgian art enthusiasts in the Congo. A few years prior to this he had realized similar projects among the Baoulé in the Côte d'Ivoire and among the Inuit in Alaska.[3] The focus of his investigations in the Congo would be the production, use, and significance of objects, as well as the artists themselves, their biographies, and their beliefs. Unlike colleagues who only studied material culture in museums, Himmelheber considered himself one of the few ethnologists who actually went into the field themselves and researched African art on-site.[4]

Yet he was not motivated by science alone. As Hans Himmelheber was never permanently employed at a university or museum, throughout his life he had to rely on trading artifacts to finance his research. This applies particularly to his Cameroon-Gabon-Congo journey, which was conceived as a collecting tour and commissioned by the ethnological museums in Basel and Geneva, as well as the Weyhe Gallery in New York and Charles Ratton's gallery in Paris. He believed he had a special obligation to the two museums, because in his opinion he had not brought enough ethnographic artifacts back to Europe from his Alaska sojourn, which had been supported by Basel and Geneva.[5] With the comprehensive collection that he sent to Germany and Switzerland from the Congo, Himmelheber hoped for a "turning point in my career" so that he would no longer have to depend on benefactors.[6]

This essay discusses Himmelheber's Congo journey in 1938/39 at the intersection of his scientific work as an anthropologist of art and his obligations as a collector and art dealer. The objects he acquired, his photographs, notes, and publications, and primarily his diary from the last seven months of his sojourn in the Congo serve as sources. The combination of these various levels of analyses provides new insights into his research questions and methods, as well as into his acquisition of and trade in artworks.[7] Himmelheber's detailed observations are an impressive reflection of everyday colonial life and the tense political situation on the eve of the Second World War, but they also testify to his somewhat paternalistic attitude toward Congolese men and women. This essay attempts to reconstruct their agency within the colonial system, although there are no sources from an African perspective. In the sense of Howard S. Becker, the archive of Himmelheber lays bare the connection between the "art worlds" and their protagonists at the intersection of local art production and acquisition, as well as between colonial politics and the global art market.[8]

ANTHROPOLOGIST OF ART AND AESTHETE

"How did you start making these things out of wood?"[9] It was with this question that Hans Himmelheber started his conversations with the artists he met on his research trips in North America and West Africa. During his time in the Congo Hans Himmelheber interviewed at least two dozen mask makers, carvers, and weavers in the region of the Chokwe, Kuba, and Yaka. He would ask them about their training and their careers and meticulously documented the artistic creative process. In his publications he named the artists, compiled biographies, and documented their work. To his sponsors, too—like the museum in Basel—he delivered not only information about the function

3 The findings were incorporated into his dissertation in 1935 and in the monograph from 1938.

4 As further exceptions, Himmelheber also named, e.g., Franz Boas (North America), Augustin Krämer (New Ireland, Samoa), and Joseph Maes (Congo) (manuscript of the lecture "Les Esquimaux et leur art," Kinshasa, July 25, 1938, archive of the Museum Rietberg).

5 His Inuit collection is now considered in its entirety to be unique evidence of the material culture of the period.

6 Hans Himmelheber, diary, Port Francqui/now Ilebo, March 13, 1939 (archive of the Museum Rietberg).

7 For their valuable feedback on this essay, I would like to express my heartfelt thanks to Eberhard Fischer, Christraud Geary, Clara Himmelheber, Nanina Guyer, Marko Scholze, and Esther Tisa Francini. I alone am responsible for any errors that may have found their way into the text.

8 Becker 1982.

9 Himmelheber 1939b, p. 25. *"Wie hast Du angefangen, diese Sachen in Holz zu machen?"* Here Himmelheber used the colonial "Du" (informal "you"), which was an expression of Europeans' perceived superiority over Africans.

and production, local designation, and regional and ethnic provenance of the works he acquired, but also the names of their creators, to the extent that he knew them. Especially in the case of the Yaka, Himmelheber noted down in his inventories the names of numerous makers of masks or arrows, such as Bunila, Hukunga, Kaakambu, Kapalulu, Katomi, Futikissa, Kwatebo, Magaza, Monizaku, and Ngendele [fig. 23].[10]

In anticipation of his book *Negerkunst und Negerkünstler*, which would only be released in 1960, even during his Congo tour Hans Himmelheber was already interested in questions of the aesthetics and art of Africa. It is striking that the dichotomy between art and craft was immaterial to him. As such he avoided the classification into allegedly higher and lower artistic forms of expression that was customary during the colonial period and that went hand in hand with an evolutionistic viewpoint, which elevated the culture of the geographic north to the measure of all things. On the contrary, Himmelheber wanted to prove that there were art and artists in the modern Western sense in Africa. Underlying this idea was a universalistic concept of art as expressed in avant-garde, aesthetic modernism, and not least the founding of the Musée du Quai Branly. In his second *Brousse* article from 1939, in which he addressed art historians and artists, he discussed the question of whether realistic portraits existed in African art as in European art.[11] In his opinion the female dance masks of the Chokwe approximated this, considering that they were modeled on the facial features of particularly beautiful women. Another concept that repeatedly occupied him was *l'art pour l'art*. In contrast to the specific purpose for which masks and figures were created, he felt that "decorative art" objects were produced according to purely aesthetic principles. Alongside the carvings of the Baoulé, he includes the sculptures created by Kuba women from redwood powder *bongotol* in this category [see story, p. 156]. He considered this decorated but nonfunctional objects as "independent artworks." Himmelheber's understanding that there are objects created and enjoyed purely for the sake of art was entirely consistent with that of Western modernism.

Putting the social role and personal histories of the male and moreover female artists at the heart of his research was both exceptional and innovative [fig. 24]. In the literature on the Congo that Himmelheber had reviewed (e.g., Baumann, Maes, Planquaert, Torday, Wissmann), artists were not perceived as individuals.[12] Their works were attributed to an allegedly homogeneous ethnic group; their creators were considered committed to a traditional, "tribal" style and remained anonymous—partly because the Western researchers did not ask for their names, partly because they presumed they were irrelevant. The latter may well have been accurate for some art forms and regions—for example, if an object was produced by a group or as an everyday object, such as the raffia textiles of the Showa that were made by a male weaver and a female embroiderer. However, the opposite was also the case: a work that was considered particularly well made could be closely connected to the name of its producer. For example, the Bashilele chief Niamandele was known for his ornamented drums, and Himmelheber observed Prince Georges Kwete Mwana making borders. Among the Yaka, highly regarded mask makers were awarded the honorary title

10 Yaka collection inventory, August 16, 1938 (archive of the Museum Rietberg). In addition to this initial inventory of his collection from 1938, other lists were probably burned in the war along with the other documents.

11 See also his article on the unusual series of experiments about the issue of the portrait (1972), as well as Boeck 2019.

12 In the late 1930s or in the 1940s, Frans Olbrechts, the director of the museum in Tervuren, started to classify art styles for the Congo, yet he was only marginally interested in individual artists (e.g., the "Master of Buli").

kimvumbu by the chief, and among the Pende they were permitted to adorn themselves with a decorative axe [fig. 25]. Throughout his life, Himmelheber was interested in the question of artistic license and innovative ability. Instead of paying attention merely to what was typical of a regional style, Himmelheber also appreciated what was unusual or surprising about an artistic depiction. In the process, he always took into consideration the possible influence of cultural contact and interethnic relations in the groups he visited.

Himmelheber's approach differed in yet another regard from that of the collectors and dealers of his age.[13] In the art market of the 1920s and 1930s, age and authenticity were important criteria for elevating African objects to works of art. Signs of use and patina were considered features of an "authentic" work from precolonial times, prior to contact with foreign influences. These alleged "antiquities" and "antique treasures"—even if they were actually recent—were associated with long-lost cultures and hence disconnected from the present and its contemporary producers or owners. Johannes Fabian referred to this interpretive framing as the "denial of coevalness."[14]

That this was not the case with Hans Himmelheber is extremely unusual. Even if he sometimes extolled an object as old and attempted to acquire it, age was not the only evaluation criterion for him, neither in his texts nor in the face of his sponsors. On the contrary, he dedicated his third article in the magazine *Brousse*, "Art et Artistes 'Bakuba'," to a specific readership—dealers, collectors, and museum directors. In it he referred in no uncertain terms to the fact that the dating of African sculptures was often "ridiculously exaggerated."[15] Indeed, in two-thirds of cases the creators of works on the art market were still alive. Another example Himmelheber names are Yaka masks, which were frequently burned or sold after their performances in the circumcision camp, which is why the pieces—far from museums' claims—could only be a couple of years old at most.[16] He also challenged patina as a sign of age. During his research he documented cups destined for the art market being intentionally given a shiny patina with the aid of copal smoke and body fat [fig. 26]. Conversely, the old pieces feature a matte, dark shade due to their many years of use. Himmelheber did not judge this and emphasized that what mattered was that the patina made an object more beautiful regardless of its age.

For Himmelheber beauty and quality were far more important criteria than age when assessing Africa's material culture. Everything that he saw and observed, he judged by whether it was "beautiful" or "bad" or rather "ugly," or by whether it had "no charm" in his eyes. Here it was irrelevant whether he was judging the appearance of a person, landscape and architecture, or objects. Himmelheber was an aesthete with a Western-informed universalistic concept of art and beauty. He staged "beauty competitions" in order to have a selection of masks or other objects assessed by his African attendants during his travels. Only after they had expressed their points of view did he also make his opinion known. In his experience, his judgment always aligned with that of the locals, which he took as important evidence of a universally valid aesthetic. That his employees had possibly already adapted themselves to the taste of their employer or other Europeans is not something he took into consideration.

13 On the art market in Paris and New York, see Monroe 2012. On Leo Frobenius, see e.g., Oberhofer 2016.

14 Fabian 1983.

15 "C'est superflu d'introduire ce facteur d'ancienneté dans l'appréciation de l'art primitive" (Himmelheber 1940, p. 28).

16 Himmelheber 1939a, pp. 22 f.

Fig. 23
Hans Himmelheber
Himmelheber documented the names of artists like the pipe maker Kwatebo
Kungasi, June 8, 1938, b/w negative
Museum Rietberg Zürich, FHH 154-13

Fig. 24
Hans Himmelheber
Hans Himmelheber also took portraits of women artists like this potter
Suku region, 1938, b/w negative
Museum Rietberg Zürich, FHH 170-5

Fig. 25
Artist of the Pende region
Decorative hatchet for artists
Before 1939, wood, metal, 36 × 7 × 31.5 cm
Museum Rietberg Zürich, 2019.438
Gift of Barbara and Eberhard Fischer/Susanne Himmelheber
Acquired by Hans Himmelheber

Fig. 26
Hans Himmelheber
Carver blackening a cup for the patina
Lele region, 1938/39, b/w negative
Museum Rietberg Zürich, FHH 178-9

Fig. 27
Artist of the eastern Pende region
Expressive mask
Before 1939, wood, pigments, plant fibers, and metal, 43 × 23 × 28 cm
Museum Rietberg Zürich, 2017.27
Gift of Barbara and Eberhard Fischer
Acquired by Hans Himmelheber

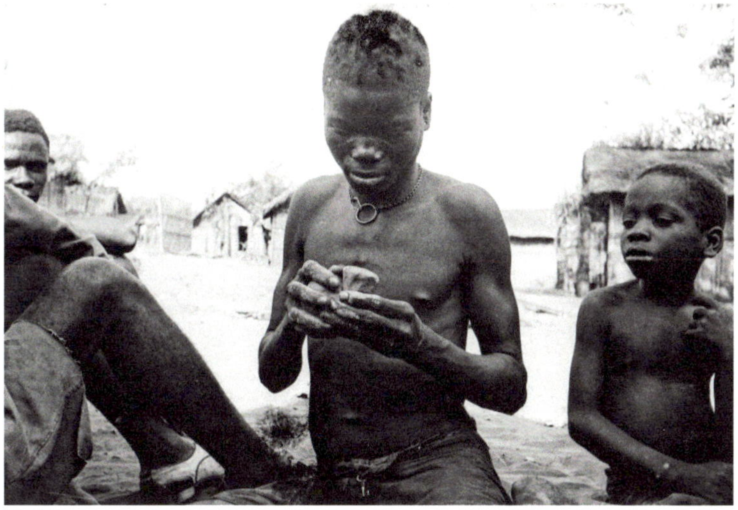
Fig. 23

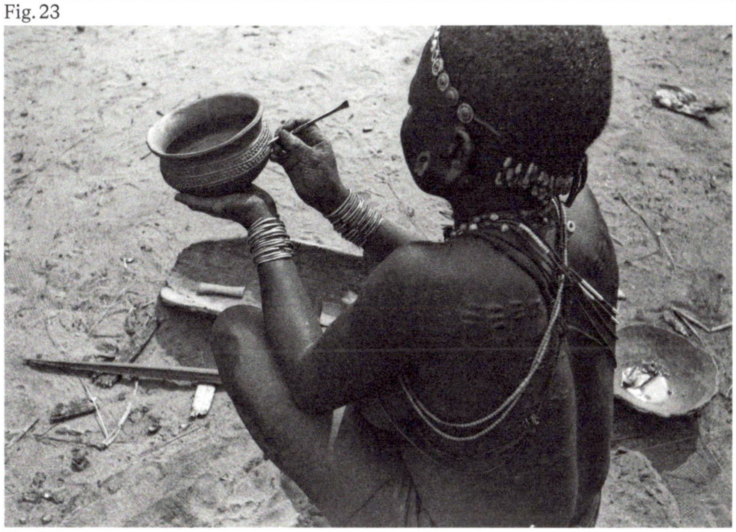
Fig. 24

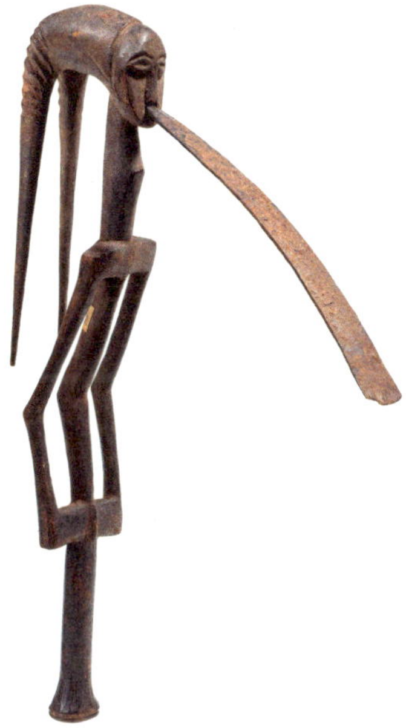
Fig. 25

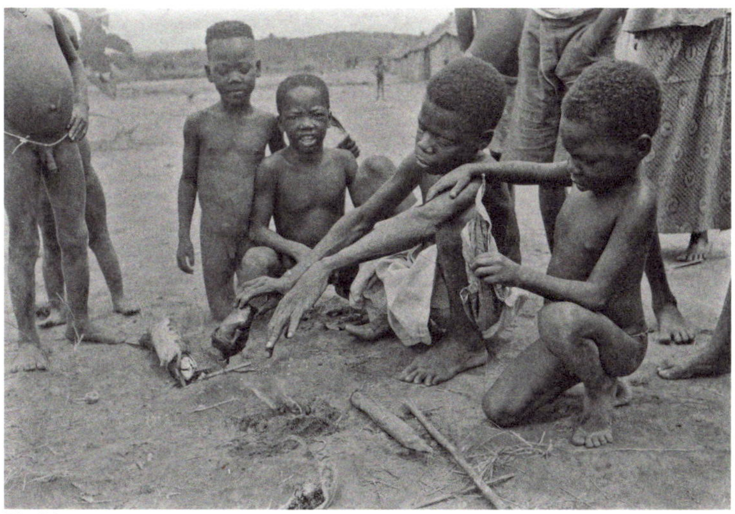
Fig. 26

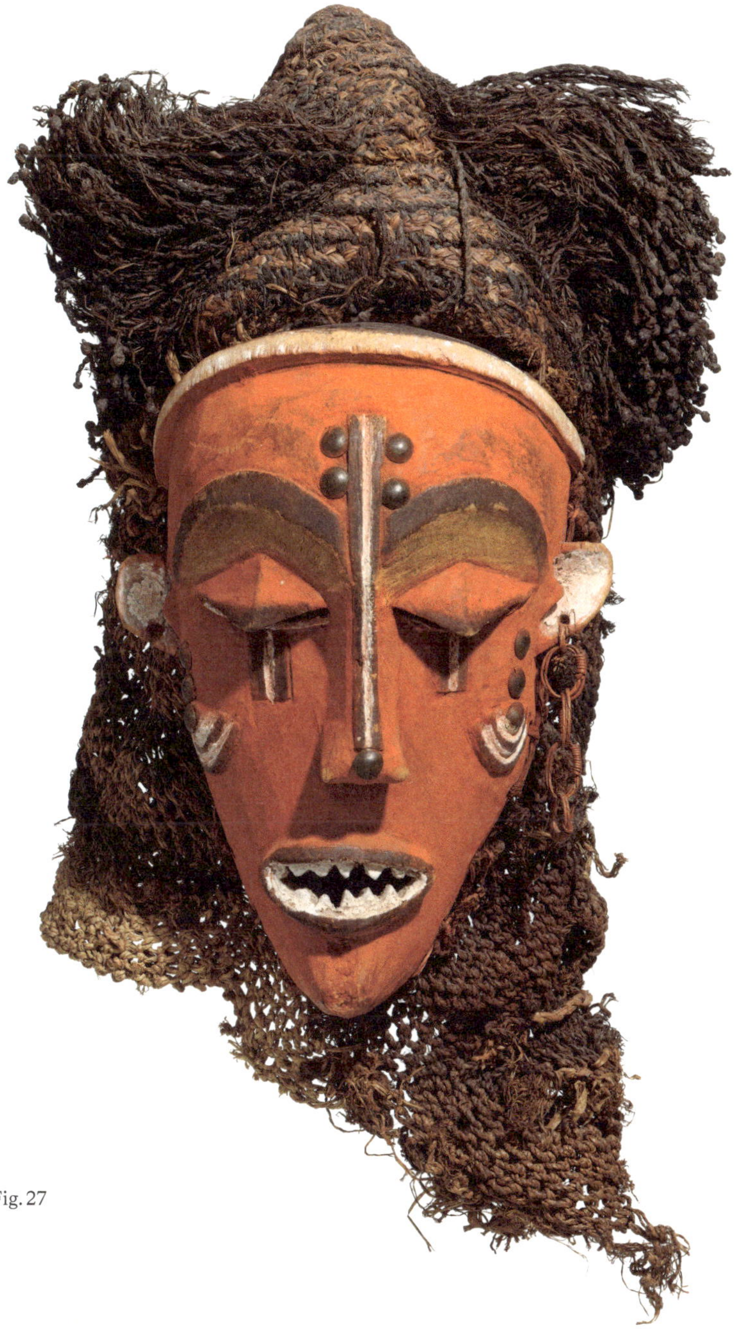
Fig. 27

For Himmelheber a thing was "beautiful" if it had been made with care and was ornamented. He equated this with artistic quality. The decisive factor in his assessment was an artist's craft skill, mastered techniques, and creative ability—and not an object's age. Even a new object that had been carefully carved or that featured balanced proportions and a certain harmony, could be "beautiful." At the same time, as an ethnologist he attempted to allow for regional differences in artistic expression and understanding. For example, he advised against misinterpreting as threatening the open mouth of a Pende mask in which the filed teeth can be discerned. Quite the reverse: the Pende would see in this a laughing mouth [fig. 27].

However, Himmelheber's sojourn in the Congo was not exclusively devoted to research into the anthropology of art; above all, it was a collecting tour.

Fig. 28
Hans Himmelheber
The port of Léopoldville, from which Himmelheber took a steamer east
Kinshasa, 1938, b/w negative
Museum Rietberg Zürich, FHH 160-12

Fig. 29
Hans Himmelheber
One of the *tipoye* that initially served Hans Himmelheber as a means of transport
Yaka region (?), 1938/39, b/w negative
Museum Rietberg Zürich, FHH 162-32

Fig. 30
Hans Himmelheber
Two of Himmelheber's employees ironing and preparing food
Lele region, 1938/39, b/w negative
Museum Rietberg Zürich, FHH 178-25

Fig. 31
Hans Himmelheber
Two panniers with parceled boxes and cups
Kuba region, 1939, b/w negative
Museum Rietberg Zürich, FHH 184-37

TRANSPORT AND THE EVERYDAY LIFE OF TRAVELING

> "I am horrified when I think of the five months in the green tunnel in the Gabonese jungle, and of the fact that I went everywhere there by foot, always with wet shoes (boots were broken after a month), and how one had to balance one's way up—or, even worse, down—the slippery mountain paths there, and through the swamps, etc., etc. The Congo really is a paradise."[17]

After his strenuous travels through Gabon, Hans Himmelheber found the everyday life of traveling in the Congo virtually heavenly. Again and again he appears deeply impressed by the beauty of the Congolese landscape. He mostly used the colonial transport network and his travel route was oriented toward the most important centers of trade in the Belgian Congo [fig. 28]. After having arrived in Basongo via the river paddle steamer *Berwine* from Léopoldville, he visited numerous places to the southeast along the railroad between Port-Fancqui/Ilebo and Luluaburg/Kananga. Until he purchased a delivery truck from an oil plantation owner for the last five months, Himmelheber had to rely on being transported by *tipoye*. This entailed two or more men carrying a wooden pole onto which a hammock or wooden frame with a chair was attached [fig. 29]. Himmelheber's caravan contained four to eight *tipoye* bearers, who often had to take turns due to the physical exertion, as well as several porters for his equipment and panniers or crates containing the newly acquired objects. From his notes it emerges that the porters were given between thirty and seventy centimes for four to six hours of work. In 1939 pieceworkers at a coffee or oil plantation could earn two to four francs a day according to Himmelheber. The traders in roadside shops earned up to fifty to sixty francs a month, while the annual income of whites living in the Congo amounted to at least 2,000 francs.[18] With the car—a 1936 Chevrolet worth 10,000 francs (approximately 800 reichsmarks)—Himmelheber's range grew, but so did his fixed costs. The gas cost roughly four francs per liter, meaning that his daily expenses increased to approximately forty francs.

In addition to the porters, his staff also included a chef and a "boy," who was responsible among other things for washing laundry, ironing, setting the table, packing, and pitching the tent [fig. 30].

17 Hans Himmelheber, diary, Domiongo, February 2, 1939 (archive of the Museum Rietberg).

18 According to his statements at the time, 10 francs were worth roughly 80 pfennig and 1 reichsmark = 12.5 francs. 1 reichsmark in 1937 corresponded to approximately € 4.10 as of January 2017 (https://de.wikipedia.org/wiki/Reichsmark#Kaufkraft, accessed on July 20, 2019).

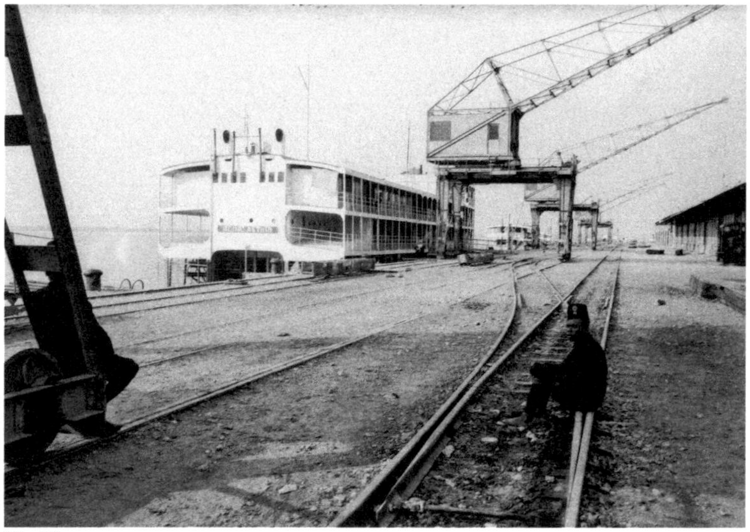
Fig. 28

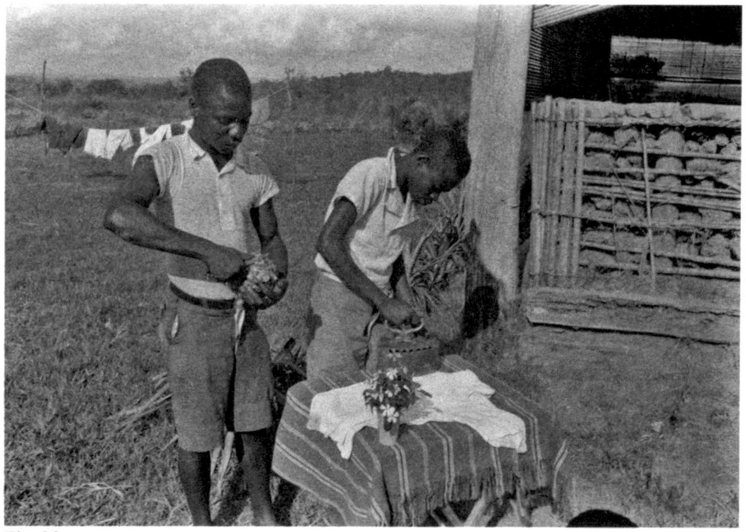
Fig. 30

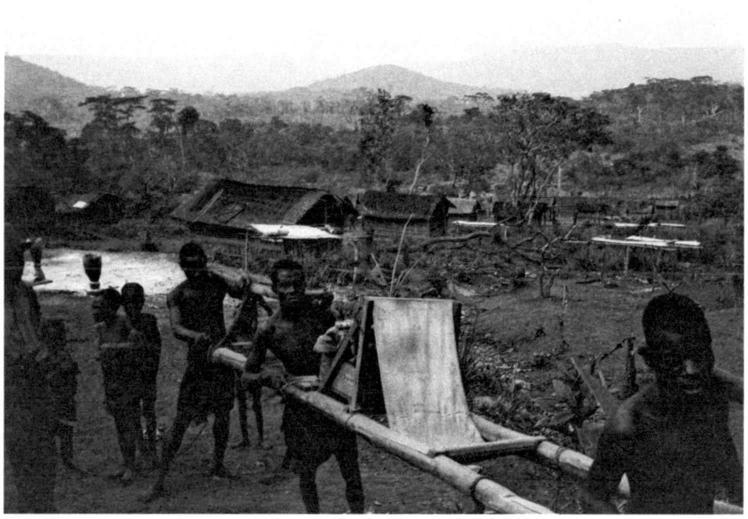
Fig. 29

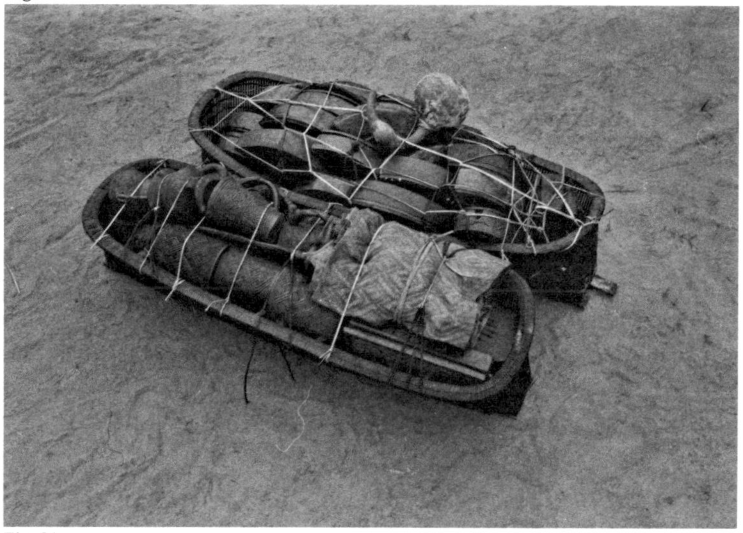
Fig. 31

Furthermore, Himmelheber mentioned his "police officer," who guarded him and above all his collection and gathered together the objects after their purchase. He frequently had problems with his employees and they in turn with him: within half a year five employees had deserted him. In his diary he expressed his discontent with their work and accused them of theft or fraud. While he documented the names of artists, chiefs, and informants in precise detail for his research, the people with whom he had daily dealings remain curiously vague and anonymous [see essay Guyer]. Even the interpreters who made an important contribution to the success of his studies and acquisition of objects are not mentioned by name. He must also have had a teacher who helped him to learn the trade language of Tshituba (a pidgin of Tshiluba).

To organize his everyday life while traveling, Himmelheber resorted to colonial infrastructure just like all other travelers.[19] He arranged the delivery of his collection by rail or ship via trading companies such as Hellebau M.A.S., yet even competent storage in the damp climate was a challenge—in a missionary building part of his collection started to grow mold. Moreover, the fragile, occasionally voluminous works also needed to be well packed [fig. 31].

19 Due to the lack of manpower, he advocated three years of colonial service.

Mostly Himmelheber used the rest houses (*gites*) of the colonial administration and stayed overnight with colonial officials, missionaries, and plantation owners—at times to his vexation, as the associated invitations kept him from his work. Sometimes he spent the night with his caravan in the villages that he visited. That this could lead to conflicts is illustrated by an episode after his arrival in a Kuba village:

> "In every village there is a chief and a kapita. The chief has the majesty, the kapita the work. He has to bring me water and wood and is in charge of the collection. Evidently he is obliged to always be in or near the village, because we always find him straight away. Once today 'only' the chief was there, and most unusually the villagers did not want to carry the crates. Disgusted, the chief picked up a crate himself. But an old dignified advisor forcefully hindered him from doing such ignoble work and then the young men felt ashamed and came after all. I gave one of them a kick and sprained my foot. One should never do that in low shoes."[20]

20 Hans Himmelheber, diary, Mubanga, February 4, 1939 (archive of the Museum Rietberg).

Inflicting physical violence on Africans had not just been part of the brutal regime of the Congo Free State but was still common in the Belgian Congo. In this quotation it emerges that Himmelheber vented his anger about the disrespectful conduct toward the elder generation. However, in his detailed diary this is the only passage in which he mentions having become physically aggressive. That he retrospectively redacted his diary by cutting out the passage, shows the extent to which he was obviously ashamed by his behavior.[21] At another point he criticizes the violent appropriation of objects about which other collectors reported.[22]

21 However, the missing passage survived on a copy. There is another redacted section in which he reports for example that he had left a street sign that had fallen over on the floor so that as many Belgians as possible would be led astray.

22 Hans Himmelheber, diary, Sumiamunene, January 13, 1939 (archive of the Museum Rietberg). Here he is citing a report in the magazine *Art et métiers indigènes dans la Province de Léopoldville* (1938, 9, p. 16), according to which, in the Bas-Fleuve region, a traveler forced the owner of a work in ivory to exchange it for a worthless old umbrella.

In addition to the traditional village chiefs, the Belgian colonial government appointed especially cooperative chiefs as *chefs médaillés*. Furthermore, the colonial administration and the trading companies collaborated with agents (*kapita*; from the Latin *caput*, "the head") who were responsible for collecting taxes or funds and who exploited their position to climb the colonial hierarchy. Not only in the aforementioned village but also on two other occasions Himmelheber was not received as he had expected; for example, he received no water. It remains unclear whether this was an act of passive resistance or, conversely, an expression of fear of being oppressed by the colonial system. The episode cited above reveals that disagreement and conflicts existed between traditional and colonial authorities regarding how hostile or cooperative and hospitable one should be to foreigners in the colonial power structure.

ACQUISITION AND TRADE

> "And thus the most beautiful old things arrived from morning to evening."[23]

The aim of Himmelheber's Congo sojourn was to compile comprehensive collections of ethnographic artifacts and artworks for his sponsors. According to his diary, in mid-March 1939 Himmelheber sent 1,736 objects packed in eighteen large crates by rail from Port Francqui (now Ilebo) to Europe. In his subsequent notes, exact quantities are named only occasionally and therefore, this is merely an estimate; however, in the space of just over a year Himmelheber acquired at least 2,500 to 3,000 artifacts for himself and his sponsors in the Congo.[24] As his sojourn lasted longer than intended, Himmelheber frequently experienced financial difficulties and wrote to his sponsors for an advance. They had high expectations of him and their words left no doubt that they were putting him under pressure. For example, he received a letter from Charles Ratton in the field "in which he very coolly writes that I had undoubtedly returned to Europe and he was expecting a detailed report of my travels and several good items."[25] Even when purchasing or packing the collection, Himmelheber presorted the objects for his various sponsors.[26] The majority of the masks and figures that were considered art in the West went to Erhard Weyhe in New York as his most important sponsor, then it was the turn of Ratton in Paris. However, Himmelheber also kept important collections for himself. Beyond this, the two ethnographic museums in Basel and Geneva—the latter provided the smallest purchasing budget—demanded more ethnographic items, tools, and everyday objects.

A comparison with other collections reveals what is unique or typical about Himmelheber's acquisitions. Instead of purchasing objects from regions that were already represented in European museums and informed the artistic canon in the West in the early twentieth century, Hans Himmelheber avoided the region along the Loango coast and did not visit the Yombe, Kongo, Bembe, Teke, Mangbetu, Hemba, nor the southern Luba. Instead, during his collecting tour he concentrated on the region between the rivers Kwango and Kwilu—which was entirely atypical of the period—where he bought pieces by the Chokwe, Pende, Suku, and Yaka. It was a happy coincidence that he was able to acquire and photograph a series of masks from the circumcision camps that were taking place and coming to an end there. It is likewise unusual that he not only acquired the wooden head crest—as was common—but also entire mask ensembles with raffia collars and costumes [figs. 32/33].

In contrast, the objects Himmelheber purchased from the Kasai and Sankuru conformed to classic Western artistic tastes.

23 Hans Himmelheber, diary, Tenambange, January 31, 1939 (archive of the Museum Rietberg).

24 Of these some 276 objects can now be found in the Museum Rietberg, 137 in the Museum der Kulturen in Basel, and 52 in the Musée d'ethnographie de Genève (MEG).

25 Hans Himmelheber, diary, Port Francqui/now Ilebo, March 13, 1939 (archive of the Museum Rietberg). Further, it says of Ratton: "It will be embarrassing for him now when he gets my airmail announcing the collection, and maybe then he will be more likely to decide to send me more funds."

26 In the 1980s he furnished his private collection from the Congo, which can now largely be found in the Museum Rietberg, with the white inscription "H. Himmelheber." With this label he wanted to make clear that this family treasure was not intended for sale.

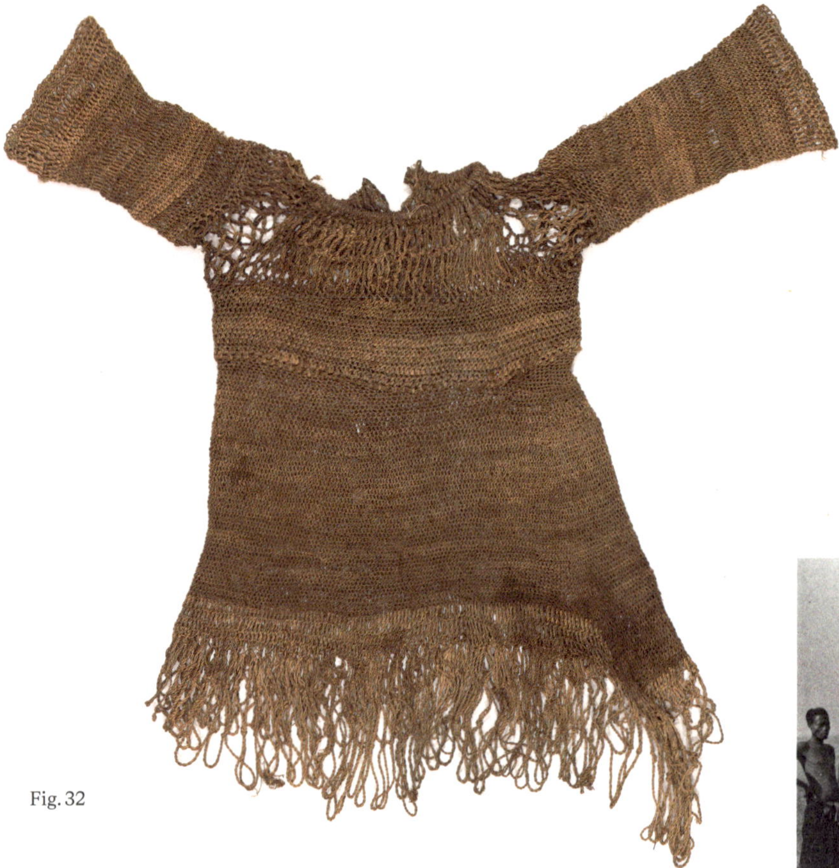

Fig. 32

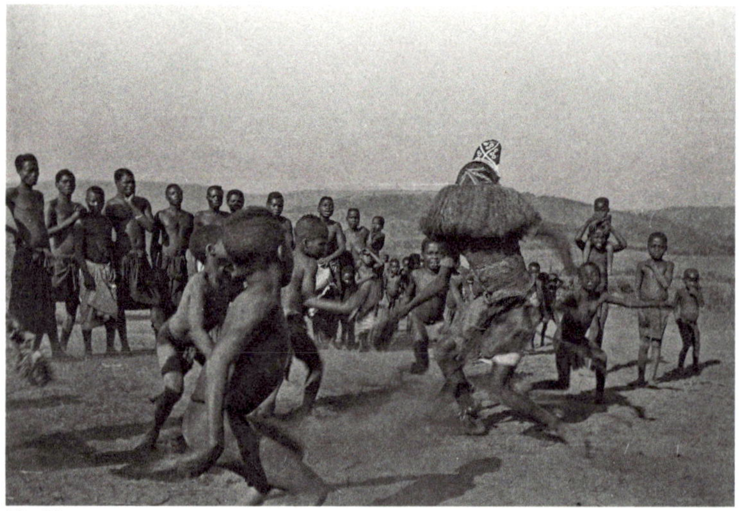

Fig. 33

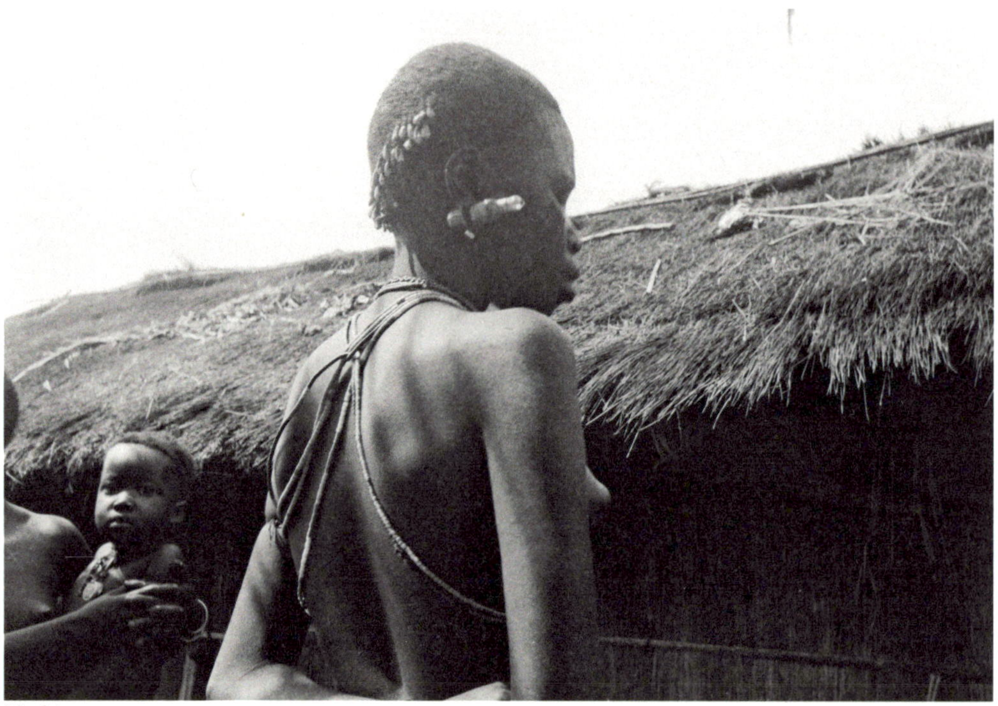

Fig. 34

Fig. 32
Artist of the Yaka or Suku region
Dance shirt *kivuvu*
Before 1938, woven cord, 75.5 × 78 × 5 cm
Museum der Kulturen Basel, III 1354
Acquired by Hans Himmelheber

Fig. 33
Hans Himmelheber
Performance of the Yaka mask with costume
Kingulu, June 20, 1938, b/w negative
Museum Rietberg Zürich, FHH 155-37

Fig. 34
Hans Himmelheber
Woman with a small pharmacy bottle imported from Europe as an earring
Suku region, 1938/39, b/w negative
Museum Rietberg Zürich, FHH 169-35

Among the Songye he purchased the *kifwebe* masks and power figures that were highly sought-after abroad. His enthusiasm for the applied art of the various Kuba groups also corresponded to the Western reception of Kuba art as something unique. In the minds of the Europeans, the Kuba set themselves apart from neighboring groups as a result of their hierarchical society with a king at the helm and their outstanding artistic skills [see essay Geary]. While regalia like the royal *ndop* figures are lacking in Himmelheber's Kuba collection, it does contain their universally popular cups, boxes, and textiles in great quantity and quality.

His acquisitions stood out for their diverse materials (feathers, wood, metal, plant fibers, etc.) and comprised the object categories considered in the West to be art, such as figures, masks, and prestigious objects. Furthermore, Himmelheber was commissioned by the two ethnographic museums in Basel and Geneva to also buy the things of everyday life, including tools, dinnerware, vessels made of clay, wood, or calabash, hygiene products like rectal syringes and razors, as well as clothing. Compared to the obsession of some other collectors, Himmelheber showed little interest in weapons, perhaps because he was a civilian and not a colonial officer.[27]

When viewing Himmelheber's images [fig. 34], it is striking that, despite often photographing men and women with jewelry, he rarely purchased any. This may have been a personal preference but can also be explained by the fact that many pieces of jewelry were made from materials like glass beads or safety pins, which had been imported from Europe and hence were not "traditional" in the eyes of Western collectors and thus not worth collecting.[28]

But how did Hans Himmelheber purchase the artifacts? Even in the early twentieth century collectors took European wares with them as mediums of exchange; they neither shied away from using force nor—like Leo Frobenius—occasionally furtively stealing an item. If one analyzes the detailed descriptions in his diary, none of this applied to Hans Himmelheber, who instead paid for all objects with money. He entered the villages quite openly as a potential buyer of "beautiful old" objects. As a result, both higher-ranking people like chiefs and kings and average villagers—especially in the region of the Kuba including women—offered him their property for sale.

A process of commodification in the sense of Kopytoff (1986) was taking place here. In the moment of transfer the things previously used in an everyday or ritual context became a commodity for which one received money in exchange. While local currencies like cowries and copper crosses (*katanga*) or copper bars (*mitakos*) were still commonplace in the early twentieth century, the monetary economy prevailed from the 1920s with advancing urbanization and proletarianization.[29] Initiated by the Belgian colonial government, this process of monetarization had wide-reaching consequences. Every transaction between people, and above all the per capita taxes, had to be paid with money. Money was likewise necessary to buy the European products that were flooding the country. At the same time, objects were given away or destroyed in the course of Christianization. As such it is not surprising that many people jumped at the chance or felt compelled to part with their old things for a few coins. Himmelheber's collecting coincided with this period of social and economic upheaval triggered by colonization and proselytization.

27 An exception were approximately one hundred arrows and twenty bows that he bought from the Lele. Here he was interested primarily in the production of the arrows.

28 On the later recognition of jewelry as an art form, see Oberhofer 2018.

29 Cf. Van Reybrouck 2012, p. 156 f.

Hans Himmelheber himself saw the objects as a commodity with which to finance his travels. The prices varied greatly depending on how valuable the object was deemed to be in the eyes of the Western art market. Everyday objects like bows and arrows could be bought for just twenty centimes. For an unusual Kuba mask he was even prepared to pay 150 francs on one occasion. For the Kuba's elaborately made raffia mats or carvings adorned with abstract motifs, Himmelheber paid between three and five Congolese francs. This was roughly ten times his porters' daily wage. At the same time, when one considers that he wanted to sell on the Kuba textiles and carvings to his customers for thirty to forty reichsmarks, this was a hundred times the purchase price—though he did have to cover his travel costs, too.

At the sales exhibition in the Weyhe Gallery, which took place with Himmelheber's pieces in New York in 1940, the Kuba fabrics were offered for thirty-five to sixty US dollars (eighty-eight to 150 reichsmarks), meaning three- to fourfold the price that Himmelheber had received for them.[30] The price for wooden boxes and wooden cups by the Kuba was even higher; the top item, a figural cup, was priced at 150 US dollars. Such a high discrepancy between the reward paid to the creator for his work and the proceeds realized for it by gallerists and auctioneers, is typical of the art market then as now. Interestingly the decorative art, for example a small Chokwe chair and Kuba carvings and textiles, were valued much more highly in the Weyhe catalogue than the masks offered by the Kuba, Chokwe, or Yaka, which look more expressive and comprise materials other than wood. In contrast to today, a Yaka mask without a raffia collar was actually worth more than one with this collar. Conversely, the masks of the Suku, Byombo, and the helmet masks of the Pende—all more reserved in their design—were valued slightly higher. These preferences reflect the classic taste of collectors at the time who preferred harmonious, naturalistic faces, and a shiny patina.[31]

BETWEEN BROKERING AND REFUSAL

"So they hesitate to hand over the pieces."[32]
A characteristic of Himmelheber's research and collecting was his great mobility in the Congo. The ethnologist never stayed more than a couple of days in any one place and covered long stretches on an almost daily basis. Mostly there was only time to observe the externals of public life like architecture or clothing. There was often not enough time for more in-depth studies on religion and culture. Himmelheber's research aim was very often at odds with the necessity to collect. Much was a matter of coincidence, such as when he came across a masked dance, a burial, or a circumcision camp en route. Nevertheless, Himmelheber attempted to proceed more systematically, for example, by having masked performances given especially for him or by showing around a sketch of the object he was searching for—such as a Luluwa figure with scarifications [fig. 35].[33]

To research and purchase objects, Himmelheber relied on cultural brokers. When he arrived in a village, he first addressed the local authorities and openly stated his desire to meet artists and buy objects for money. He was keen to establish a good relationship to these key figures, and he gave them gifts like money,

30 See catalogue *African Negro Art* by the Weyhe Gallery in 1940. At the time one US dollar was equivalent to roughly 2.5 reichsmarks (https://www.historicalstatistics.org/Currencyconverter.html, accessed on July 20, 2019).

31 Rubin attributes this "classic taste" to the art dealer Paul Guillaume, who had a formative influence on many collections, such as those of Eduard von der Heydt and Han Coray (Oberhofer and Tisa 2016).

32 Hans Himmelheber, diary, near Galikoko, January 12, 1939 (archive of the Museum Rietberg).

33 About the role of photography during the collecting see essay Guyer.

tobacco, or alcohol. In many cases he was offered objects for sale immediately by the traditionally recognized chiefs themselves, some of whom were also *chefs médaillés*, and by notables, as well as by Congolese agents (*kapita*), or they brokered contact with the appropriate people for him.

Where possible Himmelheber had his arrival announced a day in advance so that he could be certain that the items' owners would be present in the village during the day and not working on the fields. On some days he succeeded in acquiring up to seventy, eighty, or over one hundred objects. Occasionally he would return to a place a second time. Once the car was available to him as a means of transport toward the end of his journey, he added another purchasing strategy that depended even more on chance. On the road he would give a ride to passersby who then introduced him to the nearby villages and announced his request [fig. 36].

> "While traveling along, I now often pick up people who I drive a couple of villages down the road so that upon arrival they can convince their fellow countrymen of my honest intentions and most importantly my paying power."[34]

34 Hans Himmelheber, diary, in the vicinity of Bakwa Mue, May 19, 1939 (archive of the Museum Rietberg).

Now and then he remained in the background and surrendered the transfer to these spontaneously recruited middlemen, as this case of purchasing a number of Pende masks proves:

> "I buy an array of them with the aid of a Butshiok we picked up on the way who continued to acquit himself splendidly until the evening. I remain [...] sitting in the car while he brings out the masks in just a few minutes—something that often costs me an hour."[35]

35 Hans Himmelheber, diary, in the vicinity of Bakwa Mue, May 24, 1939 (archive of the Museum Rietberg).

It is interesting that this cultural broker was a Chokwe man who purchased masks by the Pende for Himmelheber in the mixed settlement zone. There is also evidence that he sometimes found it easier to purchase objects as an outsider—as he repeatedly asserted—because with foreigners it was guaranteed that one's fellow countrymen would learn nothing of the transfer.

A unique acquisition situation—between control and self-interest, between open and covert—was found by Himmelheber among the various Kuba groups. Here, too, Himmelheber initially approached the highest authority with his request, the Kuba king *nyim* Kot Mabiinc, called Lukengo by him as in the literature of the time. At their second meeting in his residence near Mweka, the king assigned him a "constant companion." For two months there are notes in Himmelheber's diary time and again saying that his companion or "minister" had helped him as a broker upon his arrival and welcome in a village, as well as when purchasing art. Even the monarch's son, Prince Georges Kwete Mwana, not only offered Himmelheber objects for sale but also organized a dance performance for him and had his photograph taken by him [see essays Geary and Guyer]. On the one hand, King *nyim* Kot Mabiinc had a certain control over the ethnologist and his actions via his closest confidants. On the other, the unnamed middleman took control himself and afforded Himmelheber access to the king's wives behind his back:

> "I have now stoked a palace intrigue because Lukengo does not want to allow me to come near his wives' treasures. My minister, who accompanies me at Lukengo's behest, has established ties to the harem and the women

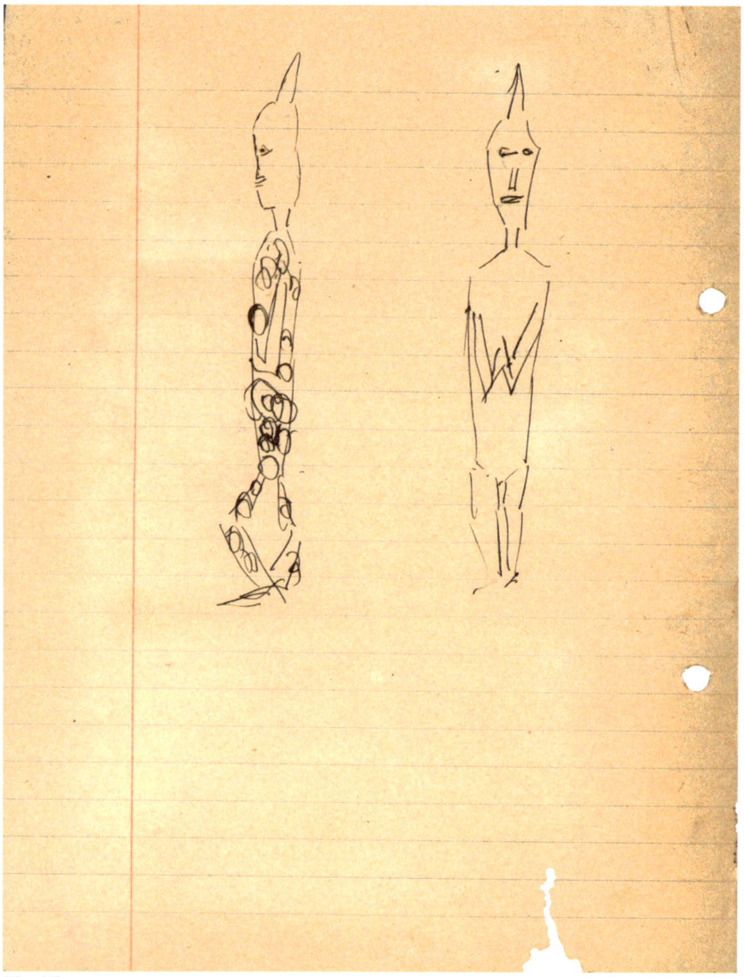

Fig. 35

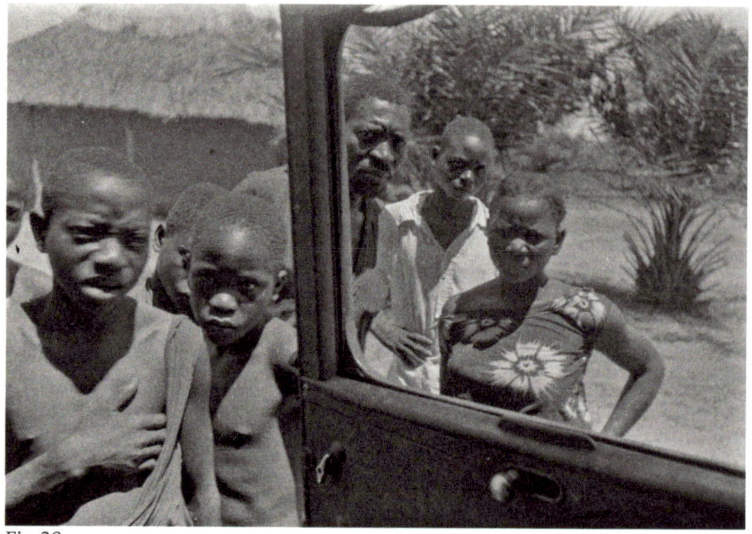

Fig. 36

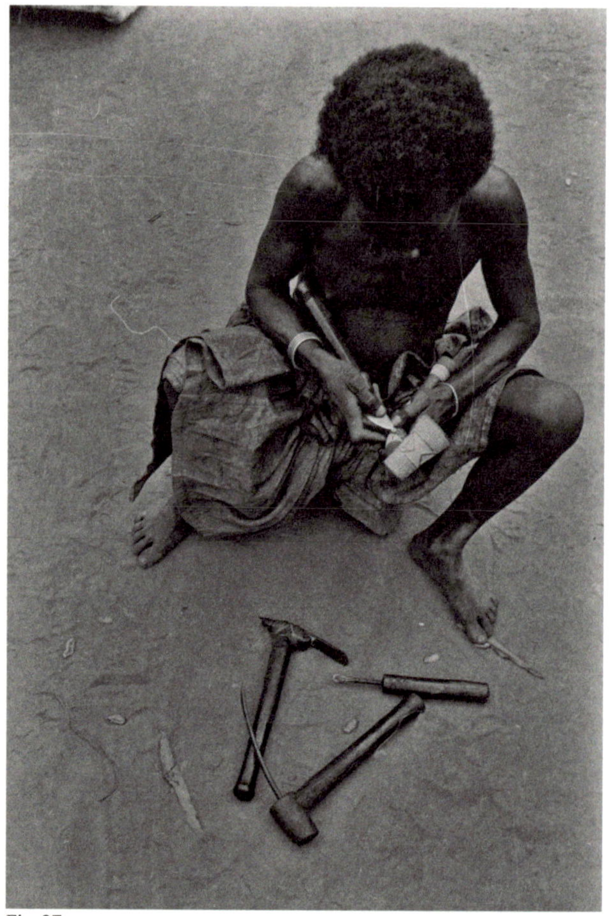

Fig. 37

Fig. 35
Hans Himmelheber
Sketch of a Luluwa figure enclosed in Hans Himmelheber's diary
1938/39
Museum Rietberg Zürich, HH.01-02.01

Fig. 36
Hans Himmelheber
The car attracted the attention of many passersby
Byombo region, May 20–22, 1939, b/w negative
Museum Rietberg Zürich, FHH 188-1

Fig. 37
Hans Himmelheber
Himmelheber photographed a Showa carver with his tool
Tenambange, January 31, 1939, b/w negative
Museum Rietberg Zürich, FHH 184-31

sneak over to me with their boxes under their low-waisted skirts before they go to the plantations."[36]

As a broker, Himmelheber's companion used his high rank and associated contact to the women at court to secretly set in motion the objects' sale for the collector. Similarly, the women also sold their pieces on their own initiative without the monarch's knowledge [see story, p. 212].

Himmelheber spoke positively about how willingly the various Kuba groups offered him objects for sale. According to Western perception, also in his eyes, the Kuba were "something better" [see essay Geary]. Additionally, they were "very open, they do not hesitate to present their things for sale and never flee at the sight of a white man."[37] Very unusually, this was also true of women. Many of the objects belonged to them, like the decorated wooden bowls, or had been made by them, like the *mboong itool* and the embroideries for the raffia textiles. This readiness among many Kuba owners to sell their objects to Western collectors already had a long history. Often they were objects of everyday use and applied art. The elaborately adorned wooden boxes or wooden cups, for instance, were used for mixing redwood powder and for drinking water or palm wine. Consequently, they neither had a ritual function nor were they preserved for specific groups of people.

In the late 1930s Himmelheber was still able to witness active art production in many Kuba villages. Both men and women and even children worked as carvers, weavers, embroiderers, or sculptors alongside their work in the fields. "The desire to transform the world according to aesthetic principles" was part of daily economic life.[38] Stocks could therefore be replenished in the event of a sale. The large quantity of textiles and carvings that Himmelheber was able to purchase while traveling through the region suggests that the art objects were also produced in reserve. By his own admission, Himmelheber could have bought hundreds of modern raffia mats in a short space of time from the Kuba villages between Lodi and Mushenge.[39] Furthermore, he documented the production of art targeted at the Western market. For instance, a Showa carver produced a pipe while the ethnologist watched, took photographs of the working steps, conducted an interview about the production process, and finally purchased the objects and even some of the tools (fig. 37).[40]

Himmelheber saw in the various Kuba groups cultural guardians (*conservateurs*) who successfully resisted missioniaries and would preserve their cultural heritage.[41] Some of the Kuba were aware of the high value and popularity of their art objects among the Europeans. "Even the Bakuba speak of the old things with respect and in contrast to all other tribes visited thus far they set a higher price on them."[42] While Himmelheber was able in many cases to agree on a lower price with the sellers, there were also cases in which the price offered was too low for the owner and the transaction did not take place.

However, it was not just the financial value but also the emotional and historical value that kept some owners from selling their art objects. In the following unsuccessful transaction, a high-ranking Kuba man emphasized the significance of the work as a family memento:

"A minister [...] has a stunning rectal syringe that he stores reverently in a sack and wants to sell to me for

36 Hans Himmelheber, diary, Mushenge, March 6, 1939 (archive of the Museum Rietberg).

37 Hans Himmelheber, diary, Mushenge, January 28, 1939 (archive of the Museum Rietberg).

38 "Le désir de transformer le monde extérieur selon des principes esthétique" (Himmelheber 1940, p. 22).

39 In view of the fact that several days or—in the case of the older pieces—even months or years were necessary for their production, the immediate availability of the textiles when Himmelheber was passing through means that they had been produced beforehand.

40 This would be much more pronounced in later field research than during the Congo tour.

41 Letter from Hans Himmelheber to Eugène Pittard, Bakwa Kengo, February 17, 1939 (archive of the Musée d'ethnographie de Genève).

42 Hans Himmelheber, diary, Mushenge, January 20, 1939 (archive of the Museum Rietberg).

forty francs as something very special. I want to barter, but nothing can be done. He says it is his father's rectal syringe, I would not get it any cheaper."[43]

The age of the works and their associated history were valued particularly highly by the Kuba. Another reason why Himmelheber could not acquire something was because it was still needed or used for rituals.

"The chief has a Bakuba mask of the type moadi but does not want to sell it to me. Because he needs it to die. Then it will be placed on him when he is laid out and in the grave, too. I interview him about the history of the Bakete."[44]

Rather than harassing the owner, Himmelheber accepted his refusal and conducted an interview with him instead.

The aforementioned examples are active refusal tactics by the local actors who did not sell their objects to the Western collector for financial, emotional, historical, or cultural reasons. In a long passage in his diary, Himmelheber described another form of refusal. Although the inhabitants of a Luba village had promised Himmelheber a large figure, they made him wait so long—five hours—that he lost patience and drove away incensed. Despite having clearly stressed his desire for the object, Himmelheber was unsuccessful. Delaying the guest rather than giving in to his will can be interpreted as a passive act of resistance to the supremacy of the Europeans acting in the colonial system.

In the region of the Songye, Himmelheber was also not very successful and was only able to acquire a few of the *kifwebe* masks that were sought-after by the West due to their Cubistic forms and colorful striped pattern. Yet here the destructive politics of the missions and the colonial administration already reveal their consequences. In the area of Kongolo the villagers explained the absence of masks with the fact that the missionaries and colonial administrators had confiscated and destroyed the masks of the powerful *kifwebe* secret society.

"They are extremely rare because the administration has destroyed many of them, and the missions, Catholic and Protestant, continue to burn any they can find. I was able to buy a few last examples, but the locals were careful not to disclose any information about them that goes beyond 'That is for playing/C'est pour jouer.'"[45]

The quote suggests that the owners of the few masks that had not been destroyed by the colonial government attempted to conceal their actual purpose and hence control the production of knowledge. The colonial actors likewise controlled the production of art and associated knowledge.

COMPETITION AND CONTROL

"And yet he has not even noticed that the country is full of treasures."[46]

Hans Himmelheber was not the only one acquiring objects in the Congo. In addition to explorers and art dealers like him, there were also numerous colonial officials and officers, employees of plantations or mines, as well as missionaries, who were working as collectors. Among the various groups of collectors there was rivalry, distrust, and competition. In his diary Himmelheber criticizes the private collections he is shown, which were mostly new

43 Hans Himmelheber, diary, Mushenge, March 4, 1939 (archive of the Museum Rietberg).

44 Hans Himmelheber, diary, Kambungu, January 14, 1939 (archive of the Museum Rietberg).

45 Unpublished manuscript of the fourth *Brousse* article by Hans Himmelheber, which was not released due to the war (archive of the Museum Rietberg).

46 Hans Himmelheber, diary, Mweka, March 23, 1939 (archive of the Museum Rietberg).

or of poor quality: Thanks to his regional and specialist knowledge, but also thanks to his mobility and associated lack of commitment, he was far more successful at collecting than the African and European population who lived there.[47] In his research and publications it was important to him both to acquire knowledge about the objects and to demonstrate his interpretive prerogative as an expert on African art.

In the 1930s some Belgian institutions and organizations were established to support the production of material culture, to preserve the associated knowledge, and to channel and control both as part of the colonial project.[48] From 1935 they included the *Commission pour la Protection des Arts et Métiers Indigènes* of the Belgian colonial ministry. In 1939 a law was passed to protect primarily the colonial sites and monuments, as well as indigenous art as a side note. Far more significant in the Belgian Congo was the *Association des Amis de l'Art indigène*, which was instituted in 1935 by enthusiastic volunteers, among them high-ranking colonial officials.[49] In order to reduce the export of artifacts abroad and promote art production in the Congo itself, the Musée de la vie indigène was founded in Léopoldville in March 1938. Up until independence, further regional museums were added on the initiative of the enthusiasts' association. Other activities by the association included running workshops to teach old and new art, and the publication of the magazine, *Brousse*.[50]

To safeguard his position as a collector and researcher in the country, Himmelheber endeavored to establish a good relationship with the *Amis de l'Art indigène*. He also had a good connection to the artist and art historian Jeanne Maquet-Tombu, the driving force behind the association, and to Adrien Vanden Bossche, the future director of the museum. Shortly after his arrival in Léopoldville, he gave an illustrated lecture about his studies in the anthropology of art among the Inuit. In it he commended the association's attempt to promote indigenous art on various levels (research, conservation, and workshops for artists). After his successful lecture, he took stock: "So now I have their full protection and can continue to work undisturbed."[51] In return for 300 free copies each, in 1939/40 Himmelheber published three detailed articles in French about his most recent research into the art of the Yaka, Chokwe, and Kuba in *Brousse* magazine. In addition, he supported the Musée de la vie indigène with several donations. Even though there was no legal export ban for art, Himmelheber chose the official path and presented his collection to those in charge at the museum before its export so that a few pieces could be selected for the Musée de la vie indigène [fig. 38]. Among the ten objects he donated were five masks by the Yaka and Suku, two Chokwe masks from the village of Mavamba in the Kahemba region, one Chokwe chair from Mwakango, and two dignitaries' staffs by the Suku from the Feshi region. The most impressive piece was the large, painted *mbawa* mask with horns from Menikongo, which Himmelheber captured in front of a flat hut on a field photo in 1938 and which was still exhibited in the museum in the 1940s but is now part of the Virginia Museum of Arts in the USA [figs. 39/40].[52]

Furthermore, there were close connections between Himmelheber and the *Amis de l'Art indigène* in terms of the history of ideas. Both Himmelheber and the museum attempted to document artists' names where possible. At the same time, they both

47 A passage was envisaged on this in his fourth, unpublished *Brousse* article (archive of the Museum Rietberg).

48 See Van Beurden 2015, chapter 2.

49 Cf. Raymaekers 2017.

50 See Halen 1994. *Brousse* (1939–1959) magazine's precursor was called *Arts et métiers indigènes dans la Province de Léopoldville* (1936–1938).

51 His lecture was attended not only by the members of the association but also high-ranking representatives of the colonial state and the Church (letter to Basel, Léopoldville, July 28, 1938, archive of the Museum der Kulturen Basel; as well as the article "Précieuse collaboration" on his lecture in *Arts et métiers indigènes dans la Province de Léopoldville* 1938, 9, p. 4f.). See also the unpublished manuscript of the lecture "Les Esquimaux et leur art," July 25, 1938, Kinshasa (archive of the Museum Rietberg).

52 See the reference to Himmelheber's donation in *Arts et métiers indigènes dans la Province de Léopoldville* (1938, 8, p. 5). On the history of the Musée de la vie indigène, which was handed over to the Congolese government after independence and closed in 1965, as well as the scattered fates of Himmelheber's donations on the art market, see Raymaekers 2016. According to Sarah Van Beurden, who cites an interview with Mobutu (2015, p. 129), many museum objects in Kinshasa were sold by the mayor in the 1960s.

believed that "traditional" African art was being destroyed by the effects of Western modernity and European influence and was in danger of disappearing. As such, collecting could be legitimized as "rescuing" an allegedly collapsing "authentic" culture and history. Photography could also be used to preserve the image of allegedly "traditional" Africa [see essays Geary and Guyer]. This perception of the demise of "genuine" Africa often went hand in hand with a promotion of African culture in the form of colonial humanism. In the workshops run by the *Amis de l'Art indigène* association, which Himmelheber endorsed, the intention was to return modern African artists to their roots—yet it was deemed necessary for Europeans to teach them how to do so.[53]

Not only the cultural policy in the Belgian colony but also the global political situation shortly before the outbreak of the Second World War had an impact on Himmelheber's collecting. In the Congo Himmelheber was constantly monitored by the colonial administration. He had to register with the competent territorial agent whenever he changed location. Moreover, Himmelheber suspected that this was why the Luxembourgian territorial agent Albert Hoffmann or the Belgian colonial official Delcroix were so generously driving him around: to control his collecting and research. Even the local population with whom Himmelheber came into contact was interrogated about him:

> "In Mweka the reception by the administrators was noticeably cool. In the meantime, the Chef de District had been here and spent two days in Mushenge. There the king's son [probably Kwete] told me this morning that he had interrogated him about me. Whether I buy a lot? Yes, more than all other white people. And whether I pay well? Yes, very well. So everyone is happy? Yes, said the prince, and now they could all pay their taxes."[54]

In addition to this sideswipe at the colonial taxes that were paid with the money from selling objects, this quotation also indicates the colonial administration's distrust of Hans Himmelheber as a German citizen. Rumors circulated that he was a spy, and more than once Himmelheber was greeted with a hostile welcome due to his German nationality. Shortly after Himmelheber had returned to Germany in late July 1939, the Second World War broke out and he was drafted into the army. The second transport with his collection—four crates weighing 336 kilograms in total—was detained in Genoa. To avoid its confiscation, he asked the museum in Basel for help; the collection ultimately arrived in neutral Switzerland after the approval of the Ministry of Economic Warfare in London. Only after the end of the war in 1948 was the collection divided, with Himmelheber and Basel alternately selecting one item each. It was in this way that Basel received such impressive pieces as the imposing Songye power figure [see fig. 111] or the *kakungu* mask by the Suku with its long eyelashes [fig. 41].

CONNECTED ART WORLDS

In line with Howard S. Becker's concept of art worlds, art should not be understood as the product of a single creator but as the result of a network of different actors. Spread across several continents, they are involved in art's production, use, and—like Hans Himmelheber—its transfer and marketing, as well as knowledge

53 See also Monroe 2012, pp. 469–472.

54 Hans Himmelheber, diary, Mweka, February 7, 1939 (archive of the Museum Rietberg).

Fig. 38
Hans Himmelheber
Presentation of his first Yaka collection before transport
Yaka region, 1938, b/w negative
Museum Rietberg Zürich, FHH 158-29

Fig. 39
Hans Himmelheber
Field photo of the *mbawa* mask on the right, made by Tata ka sila from Menikongo, which Himmelheber donated to the Musée de Léopoldville in 1938
Mukumbi, June 25, 1938, b/w negative
Museum Rietberg Zürich, FHH 158-4

Fig. 40
Photographer unknown
Musée de Léopoldville's exhibition space with the *mbawa* mask on the wall
Kinshasa, 1940s
Private collection of Angelo Turconi

Fig. 41
Artist from Tsambotseke
in the Suku region
***Kakungu* mask**
Before 1938, wood, fur, plant fibers, ocher, 132 × 80 × 41 cm
Museum der Kulturen Basel, III 1358
Acquired by Hans Himmelheber

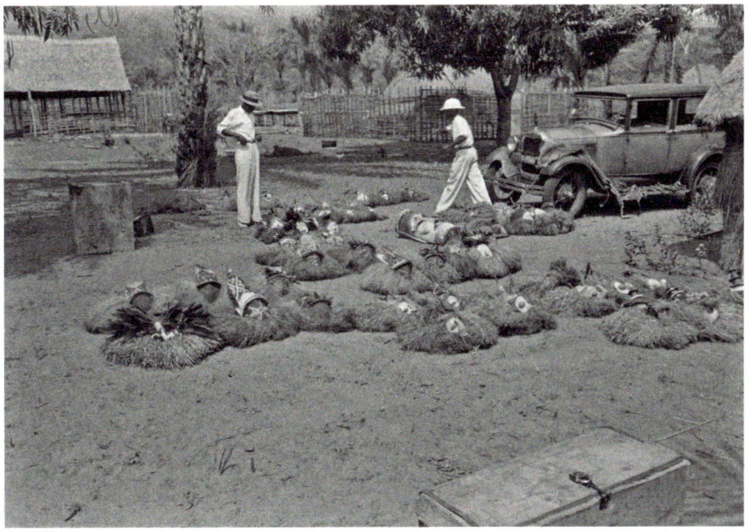
Fig. 38

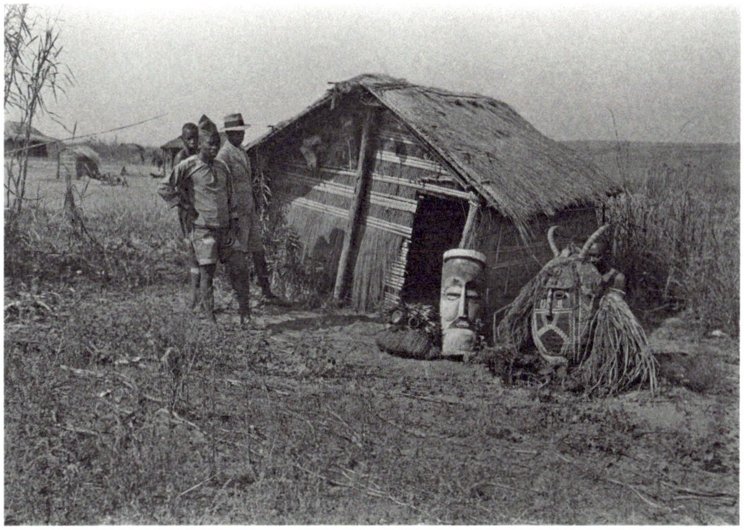
Fig. 39

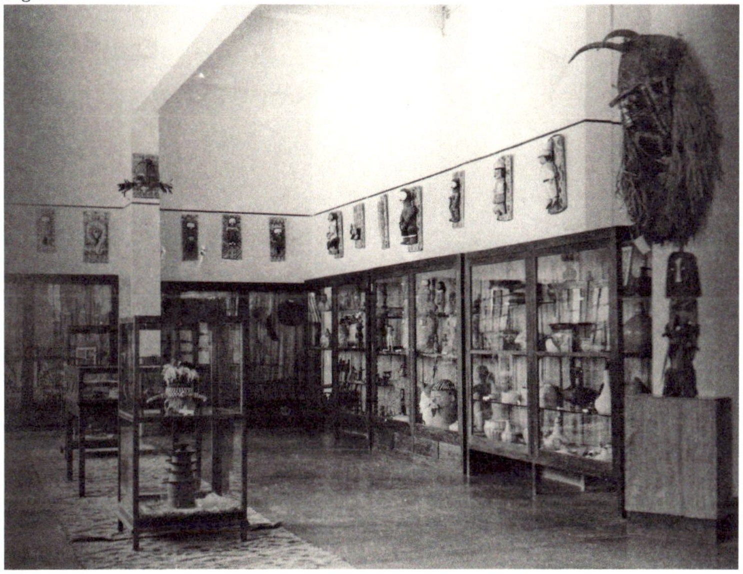
Fig. 40

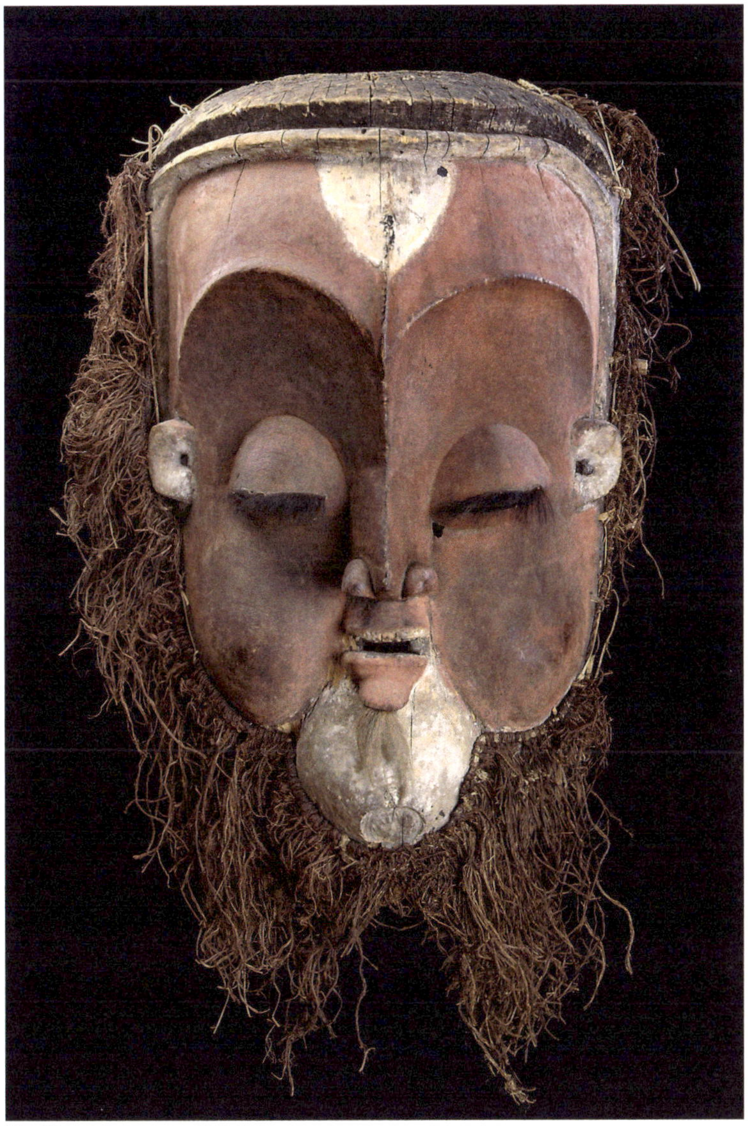
Fig. 41

production and imagination. As this essay has demonstrated, Hans Himmelheber's Congo sojourn in 1938/39 had two motivations. On the one hand, Himmelheber acquired thousands of objects for his sponsors in his role as a collector and dealer. With his contacts to the museums in Basel and Geneva, as well as to the art dealers Charles Ratton in Paris and Erhard Weyhe in New York, Himmelheber was actively involved in the global market for African art. On-site he was dependent for both his research and collecting on the cooperation of African actors who had a wide range of passive and active strategies—from producing for the art market to delaying tactics to silent resistance—in their dealings with European collectors. Nevertheless, the power imbalance between the colonized and the colonizers remained intact. The acquisition of objects and the associated production of knowledge in the case of Hans Himmelheber were actively influenced by the cultural policy of the Belgian colony of the Congo and simultaneously by global politics on the eve of the Second World War.

On the other hand, Himmelheber conducted anthropological analyses of Congolese art and its artists that provide important insights into artistic production in the late 1930s in artistic regions that had hardly been researched prior to that point. His universalistic understanding of art in the Western sense tied in with notions of aesthetic modernism. In contrast to his repeated sojourns in Liberia and the Côte d'Ivoire, Himmelheber's Congo journey remained a singular undertaking due to the political instability in the Congo after independence. To Himmelheber's lasting credit, and especially thanks to his later research, he steered the research interest toward questions of authorship and aesthetic principles in African art.

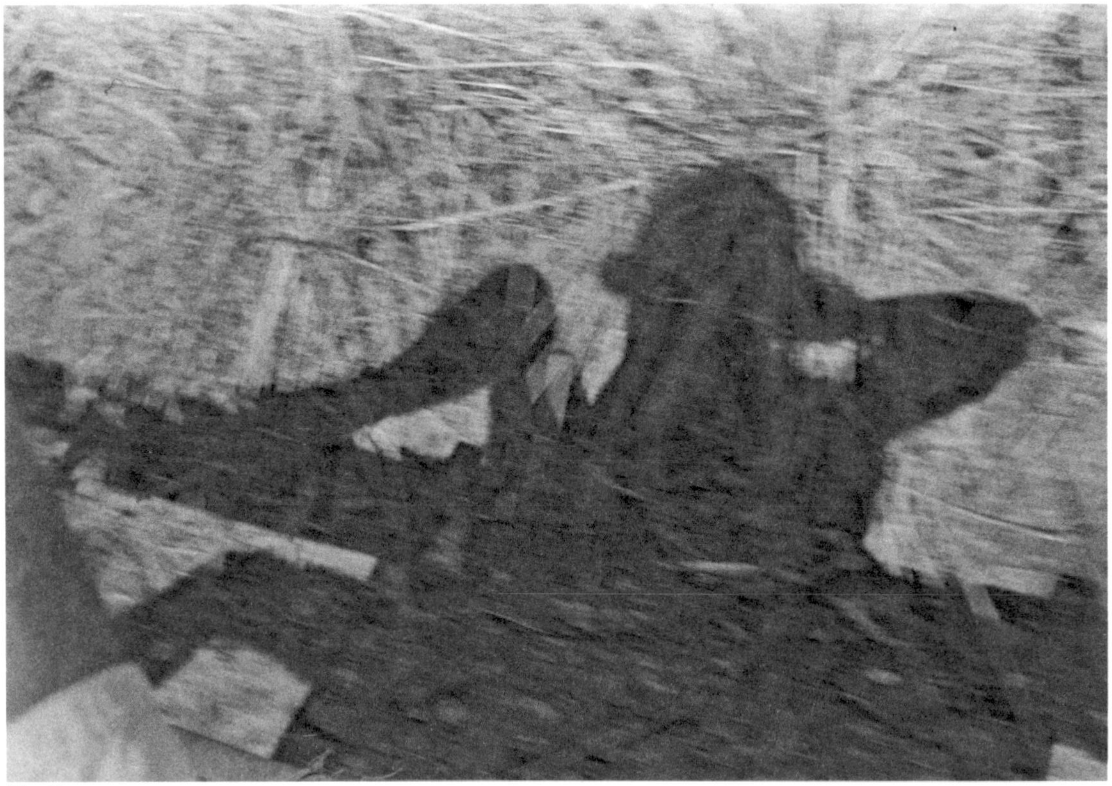
Fig. 42

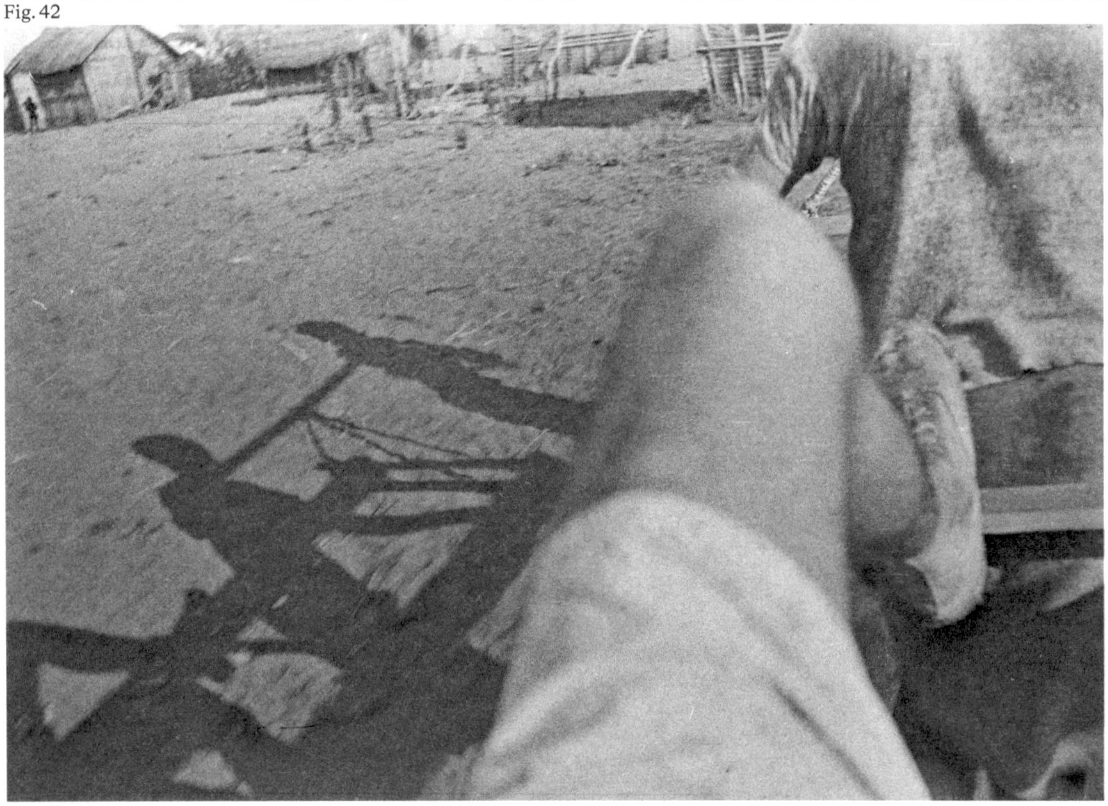
Fig. 43

Fig. 42
Hans Himmelheber
Portrait of his shadow
Kingulu, June 18, 1938, b/w negative
Museum Rietberg Zürich, FHH 155-26

Fig. 43
Hans Himmelheber
"Big Chief's village of Kingulu"
Kingulu, June 18, 1938, b/w negative
Museum Rietberg Zürich, FHH 155-30

*
Captions in quotation marks are translations of Hans Himmelheber's original descriptions, which can be found on the contact prints (archive of Museum Rietberg).

FACTUAL MOMENTS, VISUAL FICTIONS: NOTES ON THE CREATION OF HANS HIMMELHEBER'S CONGO PHOTOGRAPHS[1]

Nanina Guyer

On June 18, 1938 the inhabitants of Kingulu, a village in the Belgian Congo (now the Democratic Republic of the Congo), are met with the spectacle of a white man in a boonie hat being carried forward on a *tipoye*. His face is covered by a Leica camera with which he is photographing his shadow and hence capturing his arrival in the village [figs. 42/43]. The man is the German ethnologist Hans Himmelheber (1908–2003), who had entered the Congo from Gabon only a few days earlier. In the meantime he had obtained permission in Léopoldville (now Kinshasa) to travel further into the region southeast of the capital and not only purchase art unhindered but also take photographs. That he received this authorization was thanks to a letter of recommendation from the governor-general of French Equatorial Africa François Reste de Roca, formerly governor of the Côte d'Ivoire, whom he knew from his previous travels in West Africa. Over the following months Hans Himmelheber will insert some forty roll films with thirty-six pictures each into his Leica camera and take almost one and a half thousand photographs.

The visual archive of Hans Himmelheber's Congo expedition comprises some 1,400 black-and-white negatives taken between spring 1938 and summer 1939 in the area around the rivers Kwango, Kwilu, Kasai, Sankuru, and Lomami [see map, p. 19], as well as contact prints with handwritten notes and fourteen prints by the Congolese itinerant photographer Antoine Freitas. During his Congo expedition, Himmelheber published three articles in the specialist journal *Brousse* featuring fourteen of his photos, six of which bear masked figures, five are pictures of craftwork, and two show art that he has purchased *in situ*.[2] Himmelheber planned to sell his photographs of the Congo upon his return.[3] For this purpose he organized his photographic archive by topic and furnished individual pictures with captions whose wording was intended to appeal to the readership of illustrated magazines like *Die Umschau*. In spite of his efforts, he was not ultimately able to generate widespread sales.[4]

Despite not being a trained photographer, Hans Himmelheber succeeded in producing iconic and impressive pictures that are still being reproduced today. In them we encounter masked dances, craftwork, and portraits of Congolese men and women.[5] At first glance we see documentary snapshots of the rural Congo in the years 1938 and 1939. The same can be said of these images as of photographs in general: they possess a unique aura of authenticity and veracity that is virtually inescapable; their constructed

1 My thanks to Christraud Geary, Michaela Oberhofer, and Eberhard Fischer for their feedback on earlier versions of this text. The initial results of the subproject "Abseits der grossen Narrative. Hans Himmelhebers Kongo-Fotografien als Quellen für alternative Geschichte(n)," financed by the Swiss National Science Foundation, are published in this essay.

2 Himmelheber 1939a, b; Himmelheber 1940. Himmelheber sent the rolls of film to Germany to be developed by the company Foto Kino Veittinger and then had the developed negatives and/or prints sent back to the Congo. That means that he could not give his sitters any pictures, as earlier photographers had often done.

3 Himmelheber, diary, January 6, 1939 (archive of the Museum Rietberg).

4 However, he did sell individual pictures via the Artikeldienst für Zeitgeschehen in Hamburg.

5 A great number of the photographs that document cultural practices were published in 1993 in the photographic volume *Zaire* (Fischer and Mayer-Himmelheber 1993). In addition, Himmelheber took many photographs of the traditional architecture in villages and in modern Kinshasa. These are not the subject of this essay and present a fascinating topic for future research.

nature does not reveal itself to the casual eye. This would have far-reaching consequences for the external perception of Africa at the time. A seemingly timeless and traditional Africa could be portrayed through a photography that evaded the question of Africans' active role in constructing such pictures.[6] The late Nigerian curator Okwui Enwezor remarked that "no medium has been more instrumental in creating a great deal of the visual fictions of the African continent than photography."[7] Thanks to its density, its serial nature, and good source material, Hans Himmelheber's photographic archive conversely grants us second glances, serial glances, intermediate glances, and side glances—and hence the opportunity to spotlight various moments, mechanisms, and actors that contributed to the creation of these photographs. The aim of this essay is to release these photos from their ethnographic present and to locate them instead in the historical context of their creation.

6 Thoss 2000, p. 8.

7 Enwezor 1996, p. 20.

Fig. 44
Hans Himmelheber
"Woman with calabashes in her ear"
Pende region, 1939, b/w negative
Museum Rietberg Zürich, FHH 190-3

Fig. 45
Hans Himmelheber
People at the entrance to the village
Yaka region, 1938, b/w negative
Museum Rietberg Zürich, FHH 155-7

Fig. 46
Hans Himmelheber
A group watches Himmelheber
Songye region, 1939, b/w negative
Museum Rietberg Zürich, FHH 188-8

Fig. 47
Hans Himmelheber
Men looking into the car
Pende region, 1939, b/w negative
Museum Rietberg Zürich, FHH 191-7

PHOTOGRAPHING AND BEING PHOTOGRAPHED SOUTHEAST OF KINSHASA, 1938/39

In the fourteen months that he spends in the Congo, Himmelheber often takes photographs while approaching villages, initially sitting in the *tipoye* and later from his car. Around ten percent of his photographs emerged in the context of approaching a subject. They elude any categorization; they are neither ethnographic photos nor does Himmelheber use them in his later publications.[8]

The population of the Congo was being exploited and oppressed by the Belgians in the late 1930s. In order to successfully purchase and research art under these conditions, Himmelheber had to communicate his role clearly to the population and distance himself from other Western actors in the region. He is not coming to preach; he is not an administrator nor a vaccinator; he is not there to trade nor to recruit workers; he is not a tourist with a cheap camera. He is coming to document and collect. This is precisely what he declares with his camera and the act of taking photographs.[9] Once he has arrived in the village, Himmelheber emphasizes his buying power by introducing himself as a "rich white man."[10]

For him the photographs that emerged from such situations were merely a means to an end, a by-product. Nevertheless, from a modern-day perspective these pictures are valuable and impressive testaments to the first meeting between Himmelheber and Congolese men and women, because he also captures the expressions of the inhabitants upon his arrival. They look friendly, wary, and approachable [see figs. 44–47].

Himmelheber regarded photography as a symbol that the village populations found easy to read. This implies the region's familiarity with photography at the time. Even in the early twentieth century, travelers, ethnologists, and African photographers like Herzekiah Shanu took, brought, and showed photographs in what is now the DRC.[11] Hans Himmelheber likewise had a photograph in his luggage, probably a portrait of his father Gustav Himmelheber, which was helpful when making contact with future sitters for his photographs [fig. 48].

There was a local market for photographs in West and Central Africa by the last third of the nineteenth century.[12] In the 1930s

8 Himmelheber himself tags the pictures of his arrival as "Expedition" (subject index photos, archive of the Museum Rietberg).

9 In the early twentieth century, Western ethnographers and travelers frequently used photography as a Western technological achievement with which to articulate their superiority. See Vansina 1992, p. 201 for an overview of this topic.

10 Himmelheber, diary, February 5, 1939 (archive of the Museum Rietberg).

11 Mack 1991, p. 65. For an excellent overview of the history of photography in Central Africa, see Geary 2002.

12 Schneider 2013, p. 53.

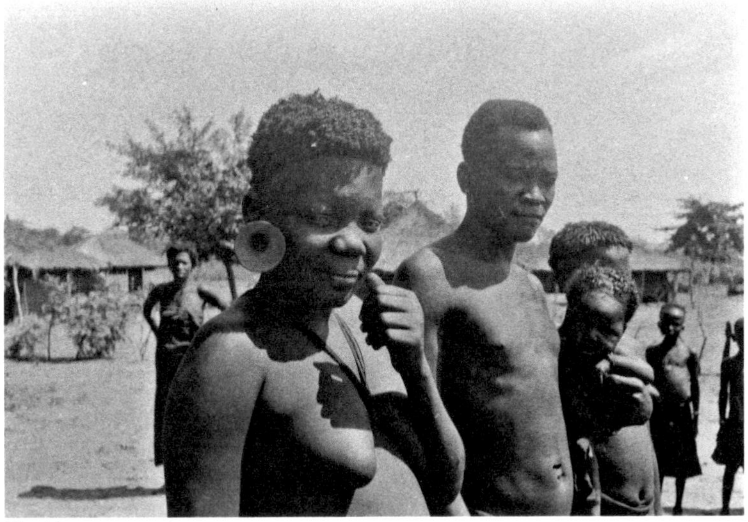
Fig. 44

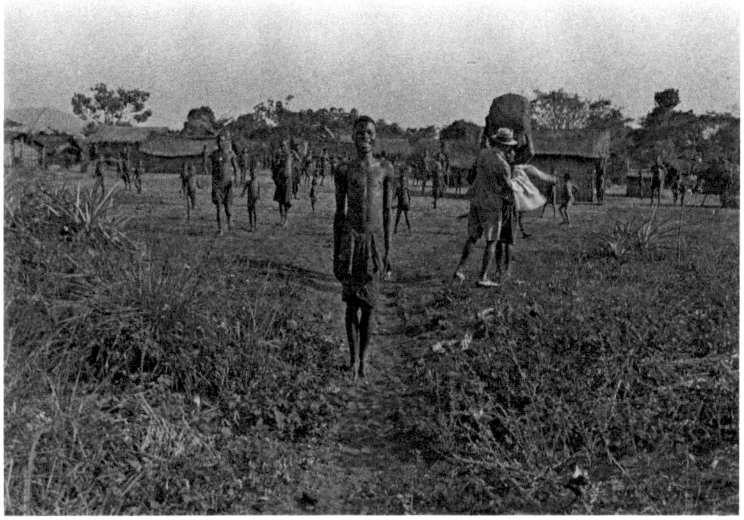
Fig. 45

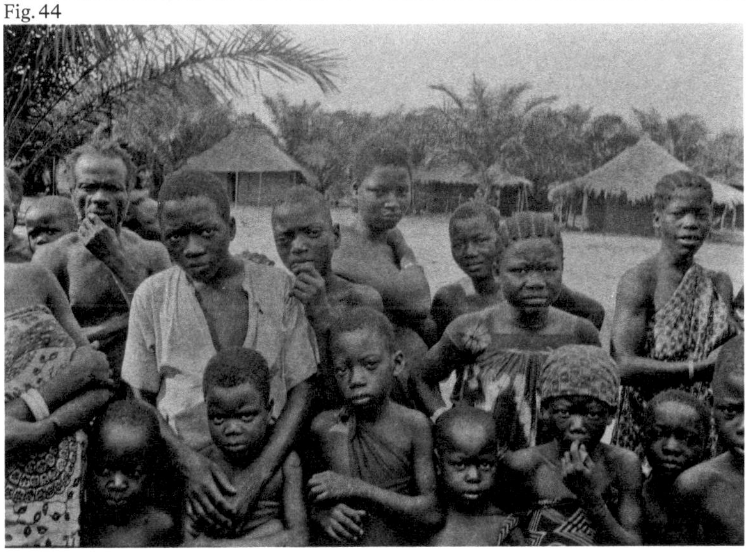
Fig. 46

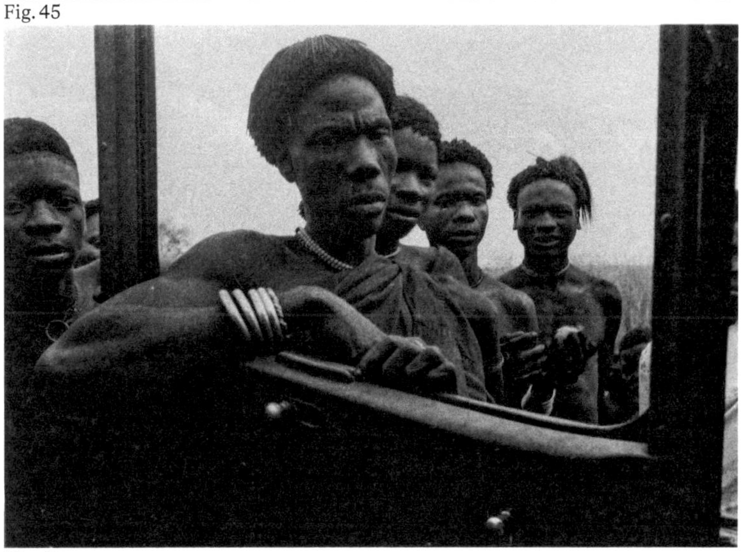
Fig. 47

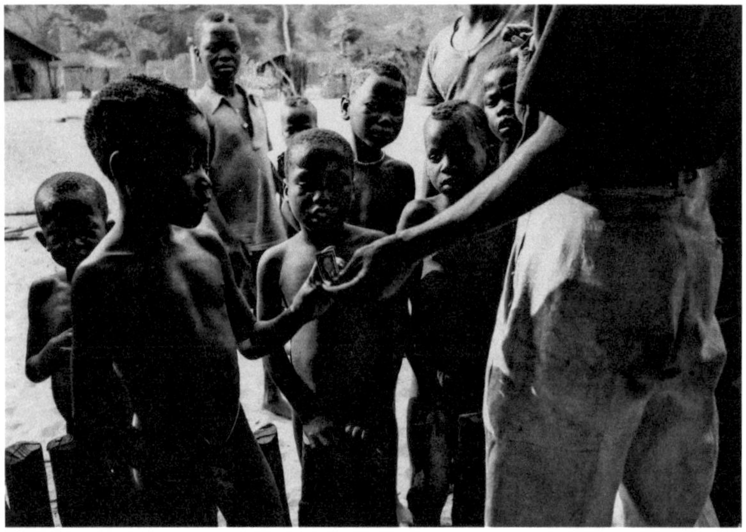
Fig. 48

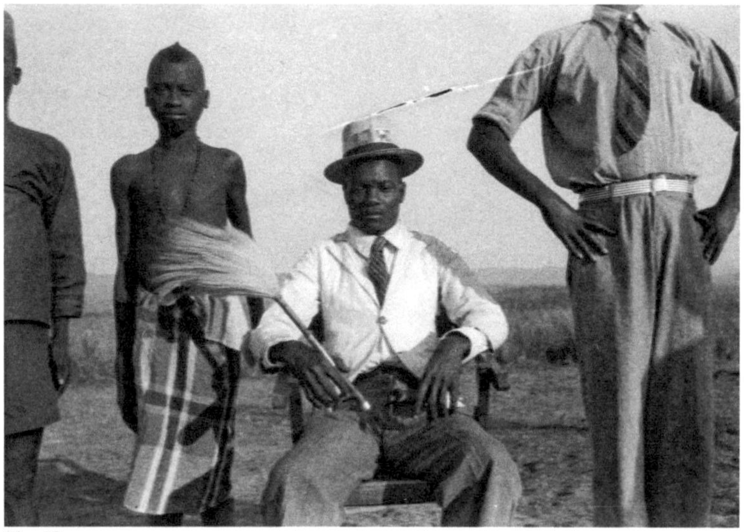
Fig. 49

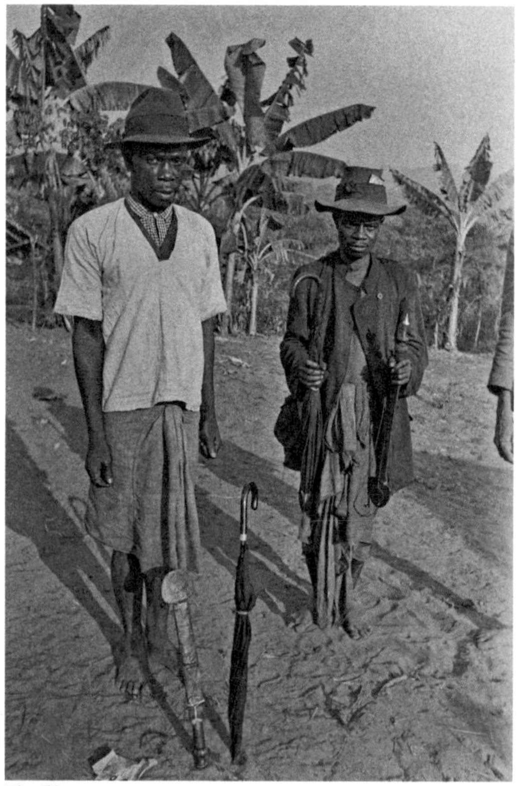
Fig. 50

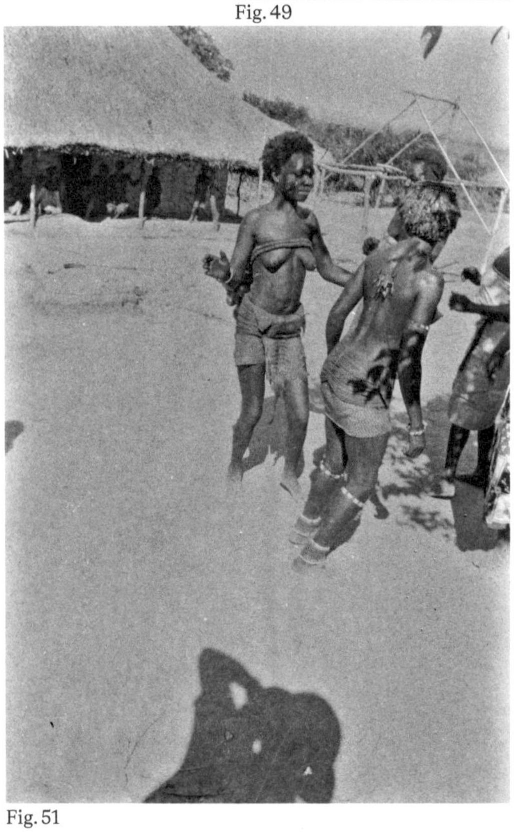
Fig. 51

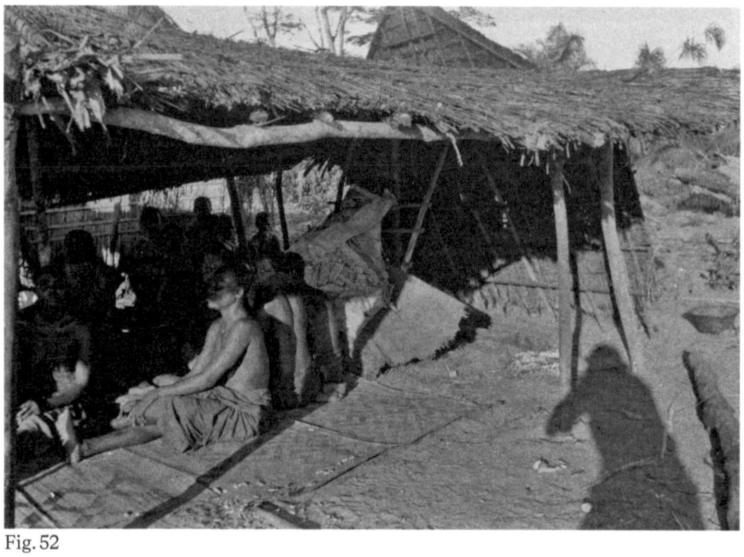
Fig. 52

Fig. 48
Hans Himmelheber
Children looking at a photograph
Yaka region, 1938, b/w negative
Museum Rietberg Zürich, FHH 169-10

Fig. 49
Hans Himmelheber
Portrait of a chief
Kingulu (?), 1938, b/w negative
Museum Rietberg Zürich, FHH 157-3

Fig. 50
Hans Himmelheber
"2 Bayaka chiefs with insignia (sword & umbrella)"
Yaka region, 1938, b/w negative
Museum Rietberg Zürich, FHH 155-22

Fig. 51
Hans Himmelheber
Approaching dancing women
Byombo region, May 20, 1939, b/w negative
Museum Rietberg Zürich, FHH 188-40

Fig. 52
Hans Himmelheber
"Bakuba Festival of the Dead"
Ichala, January 10, 1939, b/w negative
Museum Rietberg Zürich, FHH 181-30

they were considered—at least by wealthier sections of society—a modern means of self-representation. Himmelheber's portraits of chiefs who had pinned photographs onto their hats [figs. 49/50] prove this. Photos could be found in the homes of better-off Congolese people and were a feature of burial rituals. The following photographers visited the region in the years 1938/39 alone: the missionary and doctor Émile Muller, the professional photographers Casimir Zagourski and Antoine Freitas, travelers like the Italian American Attilio Gatti, as well as various tourists who took home pictures as souvenirs of their experiences in the Congo. A film was even being shot with local extras in the Kuba region during Himmelheber's time there [see essay Geary]. Himmelheber also mentions the existence of a movie theater "screened by a man who travels along the railroad with his program."[13]

Chiefs who were familiar with photography were happy to have their photograph taken by Himmelheber. Sometimes they even demanded that he did so in return for permission to document the Yaka's *mukanda* dances, for example [fig. 49]. The chiefs orchestrated these shots themselves and the photographer had little say.[14] The local posing conventions presented a problem for Himmelheber, as can be inferred from his account of a photographic encounter with two chiefs [see fig. 50 for the resulting photograph]: "That reminds me of my difficulties with the natives when taking photographs; when I had finally found an appealing scene, for example two chiefs in the council, and I approached them with my Leica, my chef or a policeman would shout: 'Stand up straight, the white man is going to take a photo.' As if given an electric shock, both chiefs would straighten up, every expression would drain from their faces, their legs and arms would become motionless, and I would take this photo out of politeness 'for the attention of the two natives.' "[15]

Unlike the chiefs, Himmelheber understood the camera as a documentary tool for capturing a timeless, traditional Africa. This approach demanded as truthful, as genuine, pictures as possible. Himmelheber's colleague Hugo Bernatzik, who had ambitions of becoming an ethnologist, also attempted to achieve this ideal. Bernatzik recommended stealth, deception, and snapshots to obtain the most "authentic photographs" as possible.[16] Where he could, Himmelheber also took spontaneous photographs. Such pictures sometimes came about with the sun behind him, as his own shadow in the picture indicates [figs. 51/52]. The length of the shadow cast both by Himmelheber and his subjects reveals that these pictures were taken early in the morning or late in the afternoon. During the day Himmelheber would travel and the people would work outside the villages. He gave his subjects little time to prepare for being photographed. This is evident in the portrait of a man who is still holding the bill in his hand that he had obviously received as payment for the photo [fig. 53].[17] On the other hand, a series of four pictures shows Himmelheber's interpreter asking a man for permission to take his photograph [fig. 54].

The diverging interpretation of photography's purpose—documentary tool versus means for self-representation—is expressed in a series of pictures that Himmelheber took of King Pero. Despite being only a fleeting visitor in most places, Himmelheber spent three days in the king's village—enough time to build trust. Pero sells Himmelheber a cup and a mask. "Very unusually

13 Himmelheber, diary, March 12, 1939 (archive of the Museum Rietberg).

14 Around 1910 King Okondo of the Mangbetu used a mirror to control his appearance in front of an audience and the camera. See Schildkrout 1991, p. 82, and Geary 2002, pp. 85–86.

15 Translated from French. Himmelheber 1939b, unpaged.

16 Bernatzik 1947; Theye 1989, p. 260.

17 Previously salt, nails, or beads were offered in the Congo in return for photographs (Schildkrout 1991, p. 76).

for Africa, where at night one dances at most, he comes at 9 p.m. and stays until 10:30, telling me the history of the Bashilele—see my notes."[18]

Pero makes an appearance in several of the photographs that Himmelheber took during these three days. In one, for example, he can be seen as a passerby in the background while Himmelheber is photographing a cup carver [fig. 55]. When Pero arrives for his own photo session, Himmelheber documents his approach from a different perspective than normal: it is Pero who is coming toward him, not the other way around. We can see Pero being handed a pipe as a symbol of his majesty with which he subsequently poses [figs. 56/57]. The day after, Pero makes another appearance; now he is wearing jewelry and ceremonial dress and portrays himself as a powerful leader by sitting on a chair directly in front of the camera [fig. 58]. This imagery is consistent with local portrait conventions.

18 Himmelheber, diary, January 4, 1939 (archive of the Museum Rietberg).

Fig. 53
Hans Himmelheber
"Bapende ivory pendant"
Pende region, 1939, b/w negative
Museum Rietberg Zürich, FHH 191-17

Fig. 54
Hans Himmelheber
Approaching a man
Lele region, 1939, b/w negatives
Museum Rietberg Zürich, FHH 179-23, 179-24, 179-27, 179-28

Fig. 55
Hans Himmelheber
"Behind the cup carver King Pero of the Bashilele"
Lele region, January 4, 1939, b/w negative
Museum Rietberg Zürich, FHH 177-16

Fig. 56
Hans Himmelheber
King Pero being handed a pipe
Lele region, January 4, 1939, b/w negative
Museum Rietberg Zürich, FHH 177-25

Fig. 57
Hans Himmelheber
"King Pero of the Bashilele"
Lele region, January 4, 1939, b/w negative
Museum Rietberg Zürich, FHH 177-26

Fig. 58
Hans Himmelheber
"King Pero of the Bashilele"
Lele region, January 5, 1939, b/w negative
Museum Rietberg Zürich, FHH 178-21

LIKE PHOTOJOURNALISM: MASKED DANCES AND CRAFTS

Hans Himmelheber's photographs can be located at the intersection of scientific documentation and photojournalism, which was emerging in the 1930s. When selecting his subjects, Himmelheber was informed by the preexisting pictorial arsenal of the region that had been created by the ethnologists who had gone before him. He was extremely well read and during his travels he also occupied himself with specialist literature, such as Emil Torday's standard ethnography of the Kuba or Hermann Baumann's study of the Lunda.[19] Unlike photographers like Emil Torday with whom he was acquainted, Himmelheber eschews arranged group scenes and static full-body portraits—and hence the continuation of nineteenth-century type photography.[20] Rather, in his compositions he imitates the visual culture of illustrated magazines. Photojournalism about foreign peoples was a permanent feature of these periodicals and was an additional source of funding for ethnologists' expensive travels. Himmelheber reports that he would flick through numerous illustrated magazines to pass the time during his travels in the *tipoye*.[21]

19 Himmelheber, diary, March 5, 1939 (archive of the Museum Rietberg); Baumann, 1935; Torday 1925.

20 Edwards 1992.

21 Himmelheber, diary, January 28, 1939 (archive of the Museum Rietberg).

The new visual culture of these magazines demanded high narrative quality in the photos, an avoidance of staged pictures, and photojournalism's serial character, in other words the descriptive portrayal of the respective events in a series of individual pictures.[22] These design principles are identifiable in Himmelheber's visual archive and can be demonstrated with the aid of a series of photos of masked dances.

22 Theye 1989, pp. 32–33.

Himmelheber traveled to the Congo at precisely the moment when the *mukanda* circumcision camp for the boys' initiation was about to take place—a ceremony that only takes place once every ten years [see essay Strother]. It took place at the same time among the Yaka, Chokwe, and Pende peoples. It is thanks to this happy coincidence that Himmelheber was able to purchase numerous masks and to photograph masked dances and other rituals that occurred in the context of the *mukanda*. The conclusion and culmination of the time in the camp was a dancing tour of the villages by an orchestra, masked figures, and the boys to raise funds. Only shortly after his arrival Himmelheber came across such a masked ensemble of Yaka on tour in Kingulu near Kinshasa.

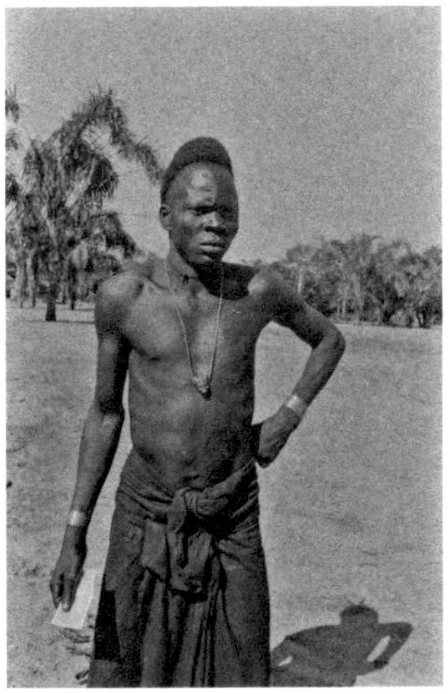
Fig. 53

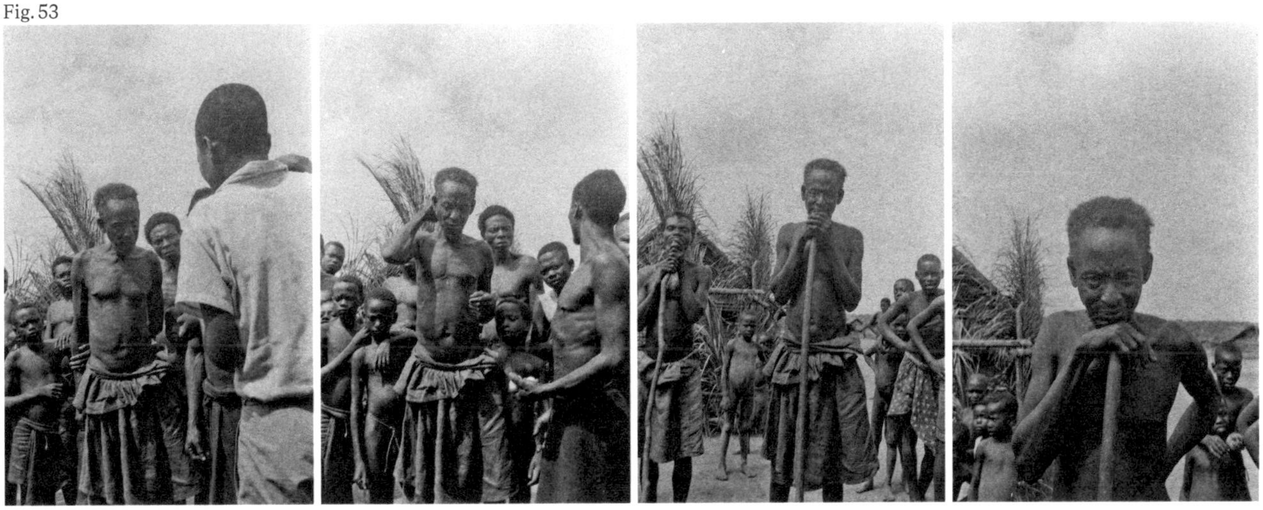
Fig. 54

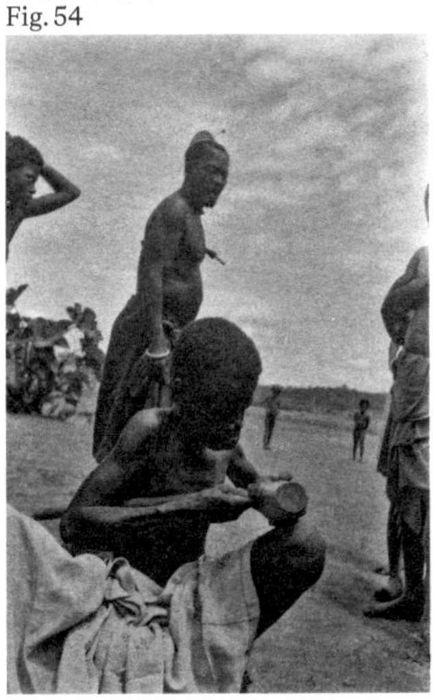
Fig. 55

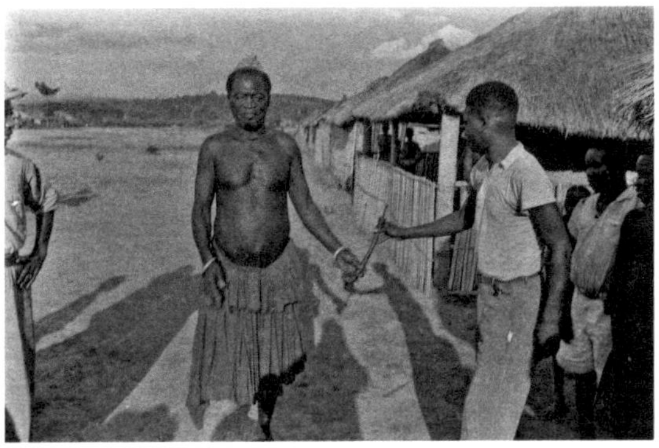
Fig. 56

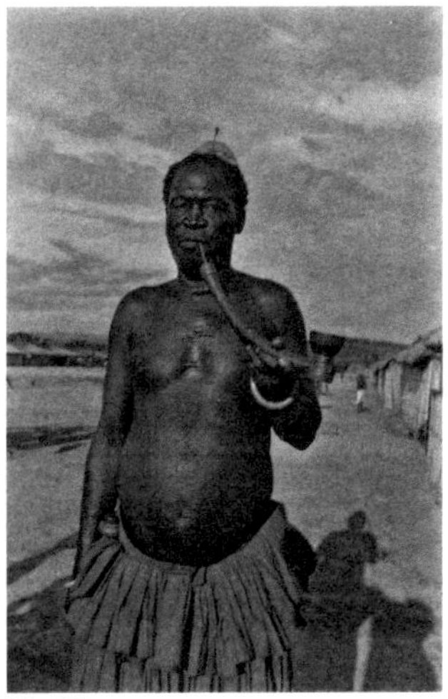
Fig. 57

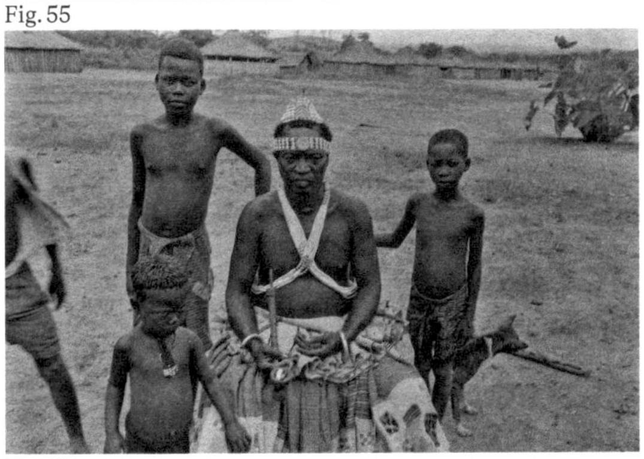
Fig. 58

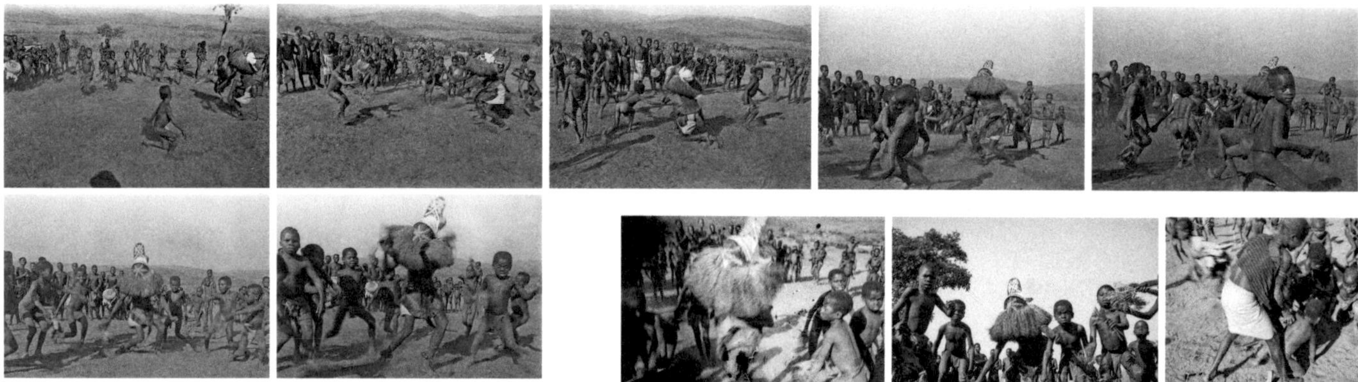

Fig. 59.1

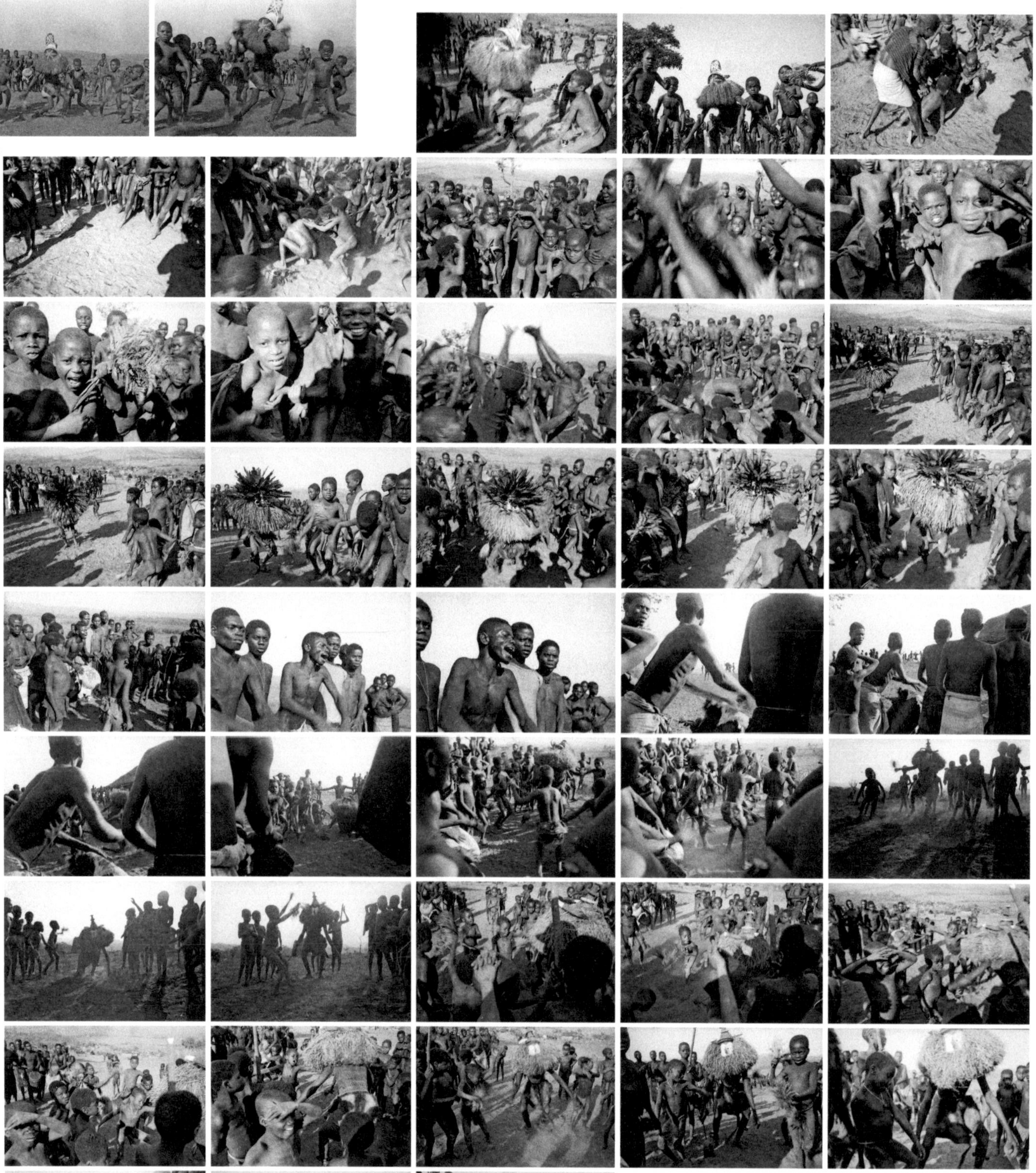

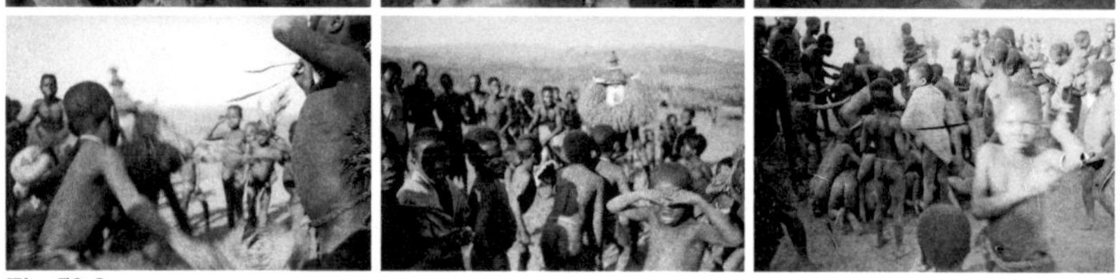

Fig. 59.2

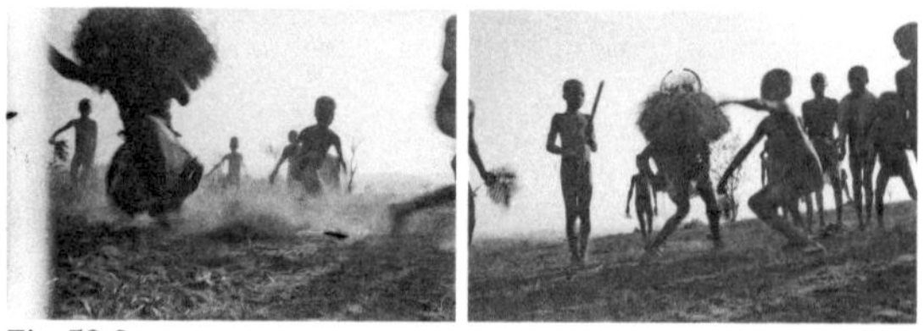

Fig. 59.3

Fig. 59
Hans Himmelheber
"Dance in Kingulu"
Kingulu, June 20, 1938, b/w negatives
Museum Rietberg Zürich, FHH 155-34 to 155-40, 156-1 to 156-41, 157-1, 157-2

Once he had presented the chiefs and singers with gifts, he was able to "attend the dances and take photographs at will."[23] Subsequently he experiences another masked dance performed especially for him. Himmelheber systematically documents these two dances with his camera. He succeeds in creating iconic pictures whose dynamism and perspectives are striking [fig. 59]. If we look at the pictures of the dances in series, we can reconstruct how Himmelheber took photographs on such occasions. Unlike the male spectators who remain seated in the shade,[24] Himmelheber actively partakes in the goings-on as a photographer. He occupies various positions and hence repeatedly changes the perspective while approaching the masked figures and dancing initiands, gradually moving from the periphery into the center. In this way he also documents his movement as a social actor in the ritual space.[25] The masked figures also interact with the camera, thereby helping to create the photographs. They are aware of the photographer's presence and are intentionally turning their bodies toward him.

In Mushenge, the residence of the king of the Kuba, masked dances that deeply impress Himmelheber are performed twice at his behest [fig. 60].[26] Though he always avoided close-up portraits, Himmelheber photographs these dances in unusually close proximity. For example, he shows himself "surprising one of the two dancers while he is dressing up"[27] [fig. 61] or an exhausted masked figure being fanned and water being poured down his throat [fig. 61.1].

It is interesting that there is no discernable difference for the viewer between the dances that Himmelheber photographed spontaneously and those that were performed especially for him.[28] This is probably because their appearance before an audience—with or without a camera—was part of the actors' task.[29] Nevertheless, the staged and candid performances differ in terms of their audience. At the Kuba dance that was arranged especially for Himmelheber, only a few spectators are present; seemingly impassively they are standing in a line at some distance [fig. 60.2]. It is quite possible that the majority of the audience was behind the photographer and a select few men were posed as spectators for the photograph.

The photographic documentation of manufacturing processes is similar, a discipline that Himmelheber would refine and develop over the course of the four decades during which he documented the production of art in West Africa. In the Congo he photographs craft techniques like making pottery, weaving, embroidering raffia textiles, producing borders, carving a pipe stem and masks, cleaning wooden boxes, as well as weaving mats and sewing. A series of nine pictures of a Yaka artist reveal the pattern that underlies Himmelheber's documentation of craftwork [fig. 62]. The series depicts an artist improving a mask and being given instructions by the person who commissioned it. With his camera Himmelheber approaches the artist who is sitting on a deck chair, circles him, and ends with a shot over the artist's shoulder. At the time artists were used to working in public and in front of an audience.

23 Himmelheber 1939a, p. 13.

24 Fischer and Mayer-Himmelheber 1993, p. 148; Himmelheber 1939a, pp. 28–30.

25 Morton 2012, p. 48.

26 Himmelheber, diary, March 6, 1939 (archive of the Museum Rietberg).

27 Himmelheber, diary, January 22, 1939 (archive of the Museum Rietberg).

28 Himmelheber 1939a, p. 30; Himmelheber 1960, p. 323.

29 See also Guyer 2014.

PORTRAITS: TRADITIONAL MEN, MODERN WOMEN

During his travels in the Congo, Himmelheber took portraits of many people, mainly as head-and-shoulders portraits. As when buying art, the aesthete Himmelheber was guided by what was "beautiful" when selecting his subjects—and what he found beautiful was often traditional [see essay Oberhofer]. He searched for men and women with "old" hairstyles and tattoos who reminded him of portraits on cups, figures, and masks. Then he would note in his diary: "One thing is immediately apparent: the women have the proper old Bakuba hairstyle that is on the cups"[30] [fig. 64]. In order to show the people and their features from every side, Himmelheber photographs them from various angles. While the way he approaches people at the beginning of his Congo expedition is still rather tentative [see fig. 54], nearing the end of his journey he advances toward them more resolutely. In the Pende region he comes across some chiefs who impress him: "The men frequently very tall and handsome, [...] lean, slender face, beards, clear-cut features. They frequently wear old glass necklaces and attractive hairstyles [...]."[31] With these men he organizes photo shoots on village squares in front of at times deserted backdrops [fig. 63].

Many of the women whom Himmelheber met on his travels adorned themselves with Western attributes like perfume bottles, empty cartridge cases, or sardine can openers as body jewelry, or wore European clothing. Himmelheber had a hostile attitude to such appropriations. Highlighting what were believed to be corruptive influences of Western civilization on indigenous cultures was a common stereotype in the photojournalism of the time. Himmelheber likewise addressed this issue in many of his pictures. It was not least the readership of illustrated magazines whom he had in mind when doing so. When selling such pictures he supplied captions in which he names examples of modernity being falsely interpreted, virtually caricatures—an interpretive scheme that had been commonplace in the geographic north since the nineteenth century.

That other factors besides finance—such as eroticism—also played a part in the creation of such pictures, is demonstrated by three photographs that Himmelheber takes on May 20, 1939.[32] From the car he catches sight of a young woman [fig. 65.1] who subsequently poses for him in various positions [figs. 65.2/65.3]. This photo shoot is reminiscent of those by local professional photographers, as described for Ghana by Tobias Wendl: the male photographers' sessions with young women resemble a ritual comprising looking, joking, and touching.[33] It is easy to imagine that similar dynamics were at play in the case of the unmarried, just thirty-year-old Himmelheber and the young woman.

"PHOTOBOMBING": UNINTENDED SYMBOLS OF MODERNITY

Photography had a documentary value for Himmelheber. On the one hand, this means shooting spontaneously to produce "candid" photographs; on the other, the point was to capture those snippets of village life that were untouched by outside influences, that were traditional and harmonious. This also corresponded with the Belgian colonial administration's official visual politics,

30 Himmelheber, diary, February 13, 1939 (archive of the Museum Rietberg).

31 Himmelheber, diary, May 24, 1939 (archive of the Museum Rietberg).

32 Fabian 2000 and Hahn 2018 make a case for including the emotional factors that played a part in the creation of knowledge and photographs in the field.

33 Wendl 1998, p. 13.

Fig. 60
Hans Himmelheber
"Ngedemoasch mask, worn by a woman"
Mushenge, March 6, 1939, b/w negative
Museum Rietberg Zürich, FHH 185-20

Fig. 61
Hans Himmelheber
"Masked performance in front of the paralyzed king"
Mushenge, March 6, 1939, b/w negatives
Museum Rietberg Zürich, FHH 182-28, 182-32

Fig. 62
Hans Himmelheber
"Painting a mask's hairstyle that has been woven from bast"
Yaka region, 1938/39, b/w negatives
Museum Rietberg Zürich, FHH 167-3 to 167-11

Fig. 63
Hans Himmelheber
"Old Bakuba hairstyle as on king figures!"
Kuba region, February 2, 1939, b/w negatives
Museum Rietberg Zürich, FHH 185-7, 185-8

Fig. 64
Hans Himmelheber
Male portraits
Pende/Chokwe region, May 24, 1939, b/w negatives
Museum Rietberg Zürich, FHH 190-11 to 190-14, 190-25, 190-26, 190-35

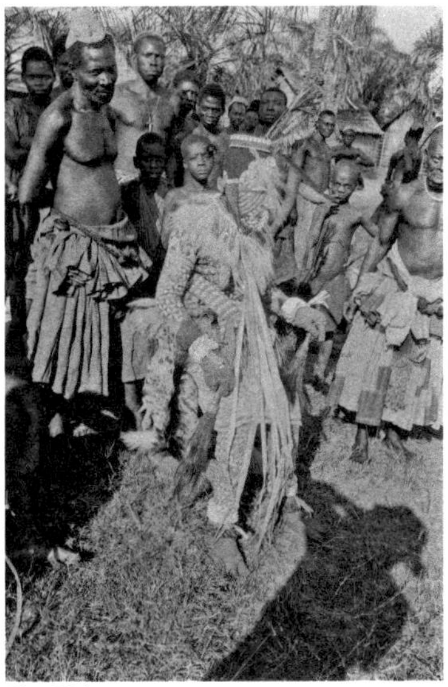
Fig. 60.1

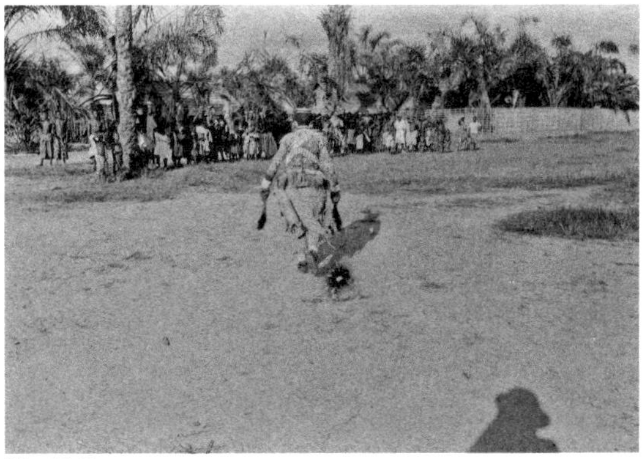
Fig. 60.2

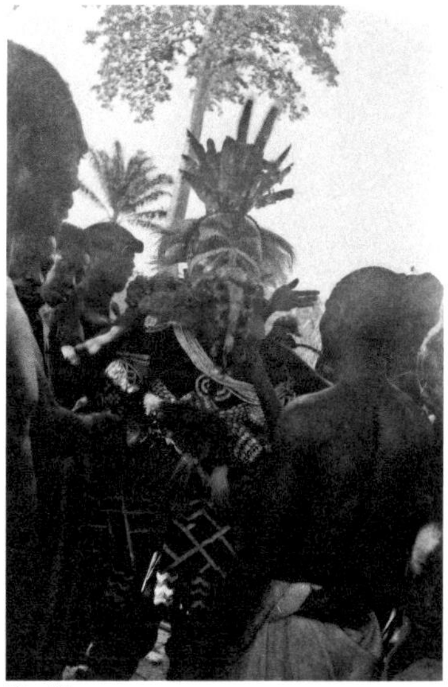
Fig. 61

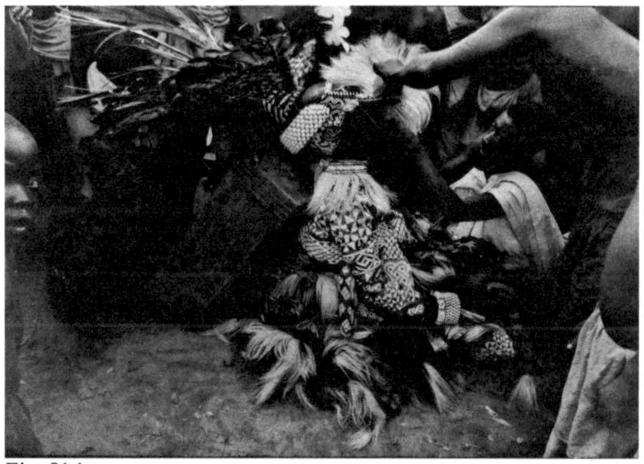
Fig. 61.1

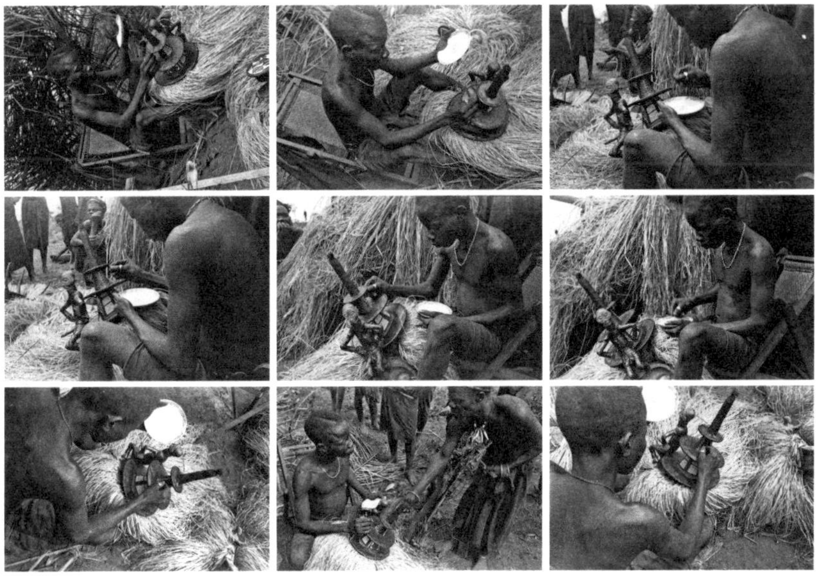
Fig. 62

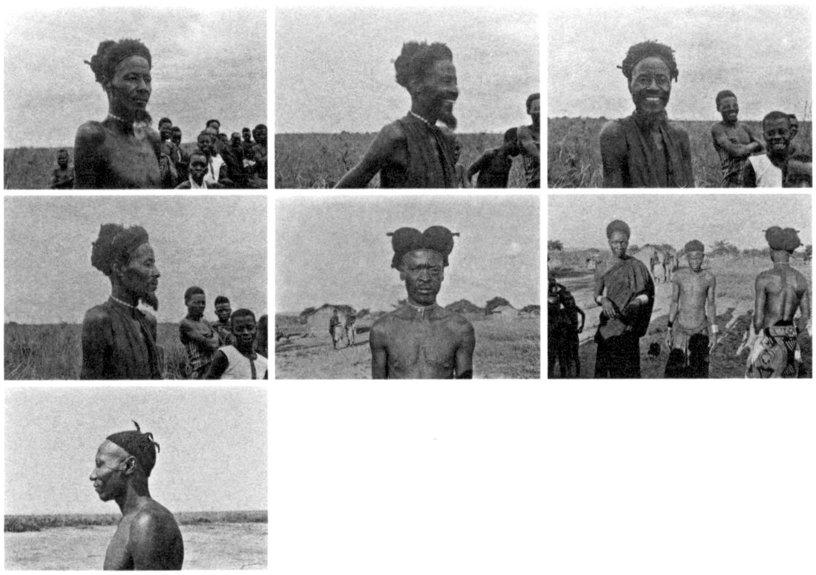
Fig. 63

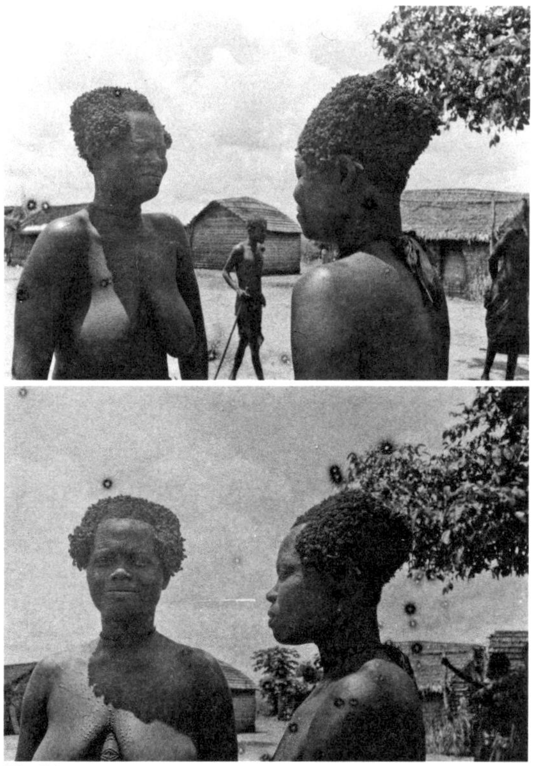
Fig. 64

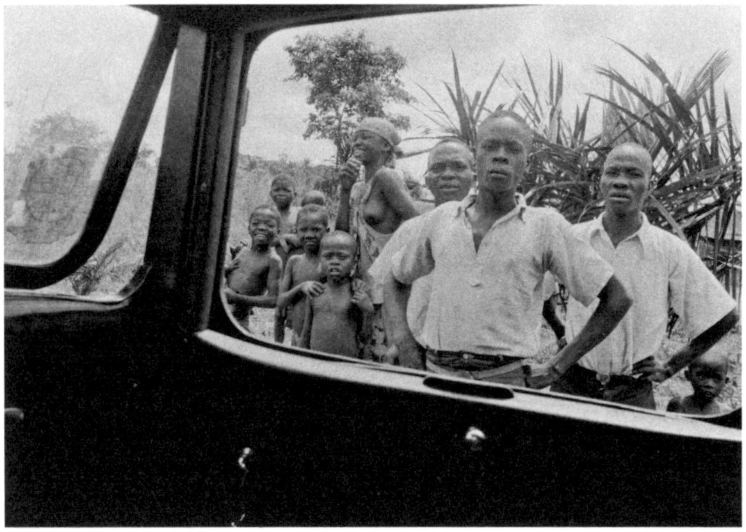
Fig. 65.1

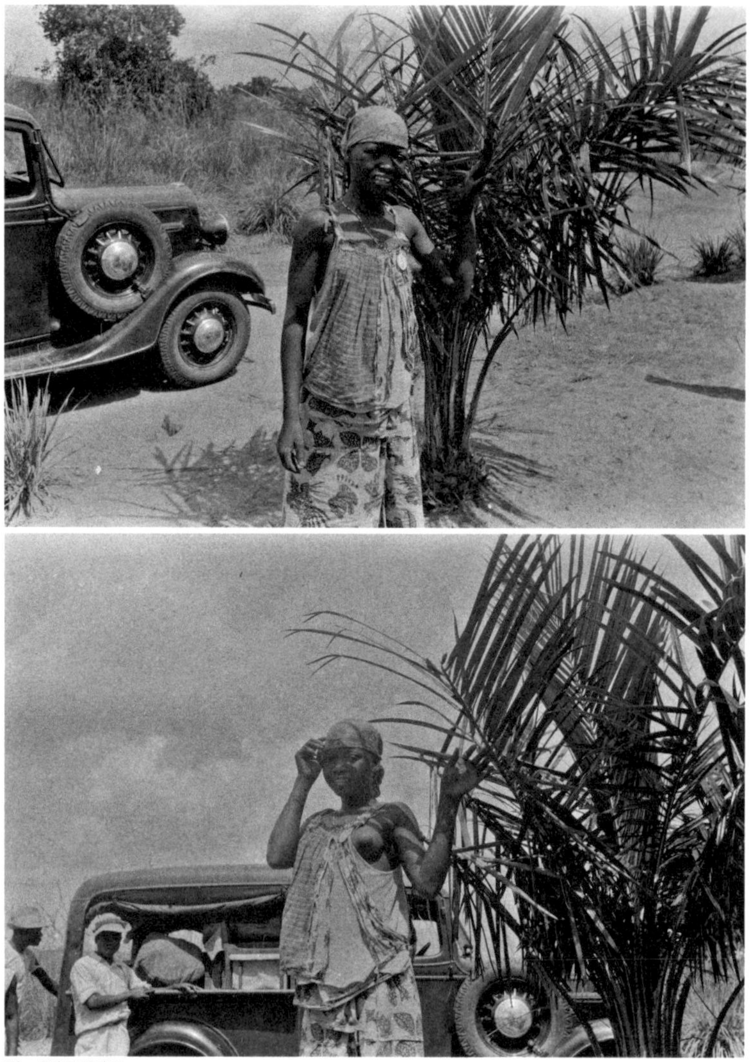
Fig. 65.2/65.3

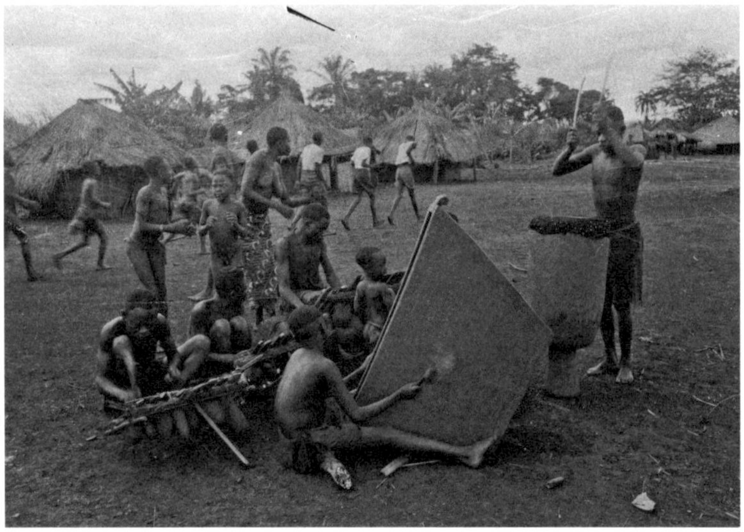
Fig. 66

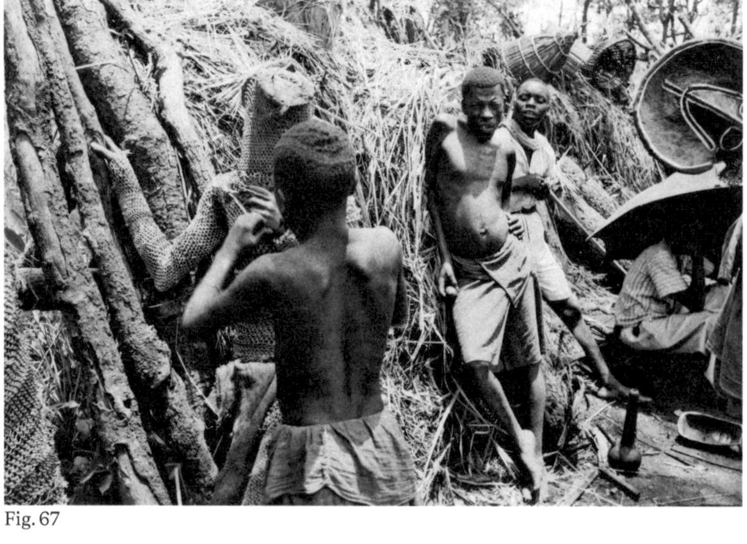
Fig. 67

Fig. 65
Hans Himmelheber
Photo session with a woman
Byombo region, May 20–22, 1939,
b/w negatives
Museum Rietberg Zürich, FHH 189-15 to 189-17

Fig. 66
Hans Himmelheber
Orchestra
Luluwa region, April 9, 1939,
b/w negative
Museum Rietberg Zürich, FHH 186-39

Fig. 67
Hans Himmelheber
"Chokwe boys' circumcision camp"
Chokwe region, 1938/39, b/w negative
Museum Rietberg Zürich, FHH 174-24

which propagated the ideal of a village population untouched by the modern era, timeless and harmonious, versus the modern city with its forward-looking population.[34] Akin to "photobombing," elements nevertheless crept into his pictures that point to the way in which tradition and modernity, city and countryside were closely intertwined in the Congo at that time. By "photobombing," I mean the intentional or unintentional action while the photograph is being taken, such as when a person pushes their way into the foreground or is clearly visible in the background, or an object unintentionally attracts the attention of the viewer.[35] In a photograph of an orchestra in the Luluwa region, three young men in modern dress—perhaps pupils at a mission school—can be seen in the background running through the picture at precisely the moment when Himmelheber released the shutter [fig. 66]. Judging by their cowering posture, they had clearly just been told to leave the background as quickly as possible. This example shows that Himmelheber was indeed anxious to lend his pictures as traditional an atmosphere as possible.

Two such "photobombs" can be identified in a photo from inside a Chokwe *mukanda* camp [fig. 67]. Here Himmelheber wanted to document a masked figure's costume being laced up—but at the same time a mask appears unexpectedly on the right edge of the picture. Most important, however, is the man in Western clothing sitting under a parasol in the background who seems uninvolved in the action; he was not part of Himmelheber's intended visual narrative. This example shows quite plainly that a wealth of readings is possible, some of which have the potential to undermine a picture's original intention and purpose. In this case the desired visual fiction—a *mukanda* practice unaffected by modernity—is deconstructed at second glance by the picture itself [for a recent description of *mukanda*, see essay Strother].

34 Geary 2002, p. 52. The visual politics of the Belgian colonial government posed a counter-movement to the photographs taken by the English missionary Alice Seeley in 1904, which captured the mutilation of the Congolese by soldiers from the Force Publique and made a broad public in the USA and Europe aware of the abuse of the population in the Congo Free State.

35 https://en.wikipedia.org/wiki/Photobombing, accessed on August 23, 2019.

TENTATIVE PRESENCE: REPRESENTATIVES OF COLONIAL POWER, LOCAL HELPERS, AND ACQUIRING ART

"Back to Mushenge by camion with Mr. Delalois in the morning where collection remains at the mission. Bathing with brother in the afternoon," writes Himmelheber in 1939.[36] From the diary we can gather how heavily he depended on the infrastructure of the colonial administration, concession companies, and missionaries for the logistics and organization of his expedition and occupation. Yet hosts, companions, and forerunners—missionaries, colonial agents, interpreters, chefs, etc.—rarely make an appearance in his photographs.

In order to visualize the colonial power's presence in the photographic archive, we must look at series such as that which Hans Himmelheber took in Dibanga on January 9, 1939. In this region Albert Hoffmann, representative of the *Huileries du Congo Belge*, was commissioned to accompany Himmelheber[37]. In the pictures we see Hoffmann approaching the camera on a deserted square with the village leader [fig. 68]; meanwhile the chief appears to be negotiating the payment for the photograph. The square subsequently serves as the stage for the following compositions that show, in one, Himmelheber [fig. 69.1] and in another, Hoffmann [fig. 69.2] having the chief explain arrows to them,

36 Himmelheber, diary, February 6, 1939 (archive of the Museum Rietberg).

37 Himmelheber, diary, January 2, 1939 (archive of the Museum Rietberg).

which Himmelheber then purchases. The series resembles a theatrical display of colonial power. Various actors enter the stage and the two Europeans take turns photographing the action. Another man appears on the stage and poses with a cane [fig. 70]. He is still holding the bill that has been handed over for the shot; later a nearby police officer is standing alongside him as an extra [fig. 71]. Although police officers and other assistants often make an appearance on these pictures, they are rarely in focus. They mostly remain unnamed in Himmelheber's archive and have only a peripheral presence in his photographs, such as when he takes a picture of the richly decorated daughter of one of his employees and captures the interaction between father and daughter [fig. 72].

Another subject that only surfaces here and there in Himmelheber's photos is the acquisition of artworks [see essay Oberhofer]. Himmelheber purchased thousands of objects in the Congo and his diary provides unique insights into their acquisition. He photographs the art objects he has purchased arranged in an overview on Congolese soil, hence proving their authentic provenance [fig. 73]. Portraits of local salespeople can be found in just two series in his photographic archive. They show art being purchased in the village of a female Kuba chief and the acquisition of a power figure [see stories, p. 88 and p. 92]. In these series Himmelheber stages the purchase as a picture story for a readership whom he already had in mind while taking the photographs. He published the picture with the Kuba chief in a specialist article on the art of the Kuba that was aimed at collectors and that can also be read as a guide to the best way to buy art. Later he sent the photos of the power figure being bought to the Museum der Kulturen in Basel, which also acquired the figure.[38]

DELIBERATE FICTION: THE PHOTOGRAPHS OF ANTOINE FREITAS (1901–1966)

Hans Himmelheber's visual archive contains fourteen black-and-white photographs printed on postcard paper that he had bought in Kinshasa and/or Port Francqui (now Ilebo) from the local professional photographer Antoine Freitas [figs. 74–82]. Antoine Freitas migrated to the Congo from Angola in 1919 and learned photography from an English missionary in M'Banza-Kongo. From 1935 he traveled around large parts of the Congo with a homemade camera in the role of a mobile instant photographer before opening the Antoine Photo studio in Kinshasa in 1947.[39] An astonishing picture shows Freitas taking a photograph of four women in front of a backdrop in the village of Bena Mulumba in 1936 [fig. 83]. The picture illustrates the spectacle that a photo shoot entails. Himmelheber's photography sessions would have been similar. The painted backdrop hung on the left edge of the picture is also identifiable in the photos purchased by Himmelheber. Such pictures were commissioned by private individuals, but simultaneously served the photographers as "postcard material."[40] The creative visual constellations and the sitters' playful poses make Freitas's pictures captivating. They testify to the fun had by the photographic subjects during the shoot. The intention behind these pictures stands in direct contrast to that of Himmelheber: Freitas's customers consciously wanted to orchestrate an idealized image. In Freitas's open-air studio his subjects could

38 Index card III 9510, archive of the Museum der Kulturen Basel and Himmelheber 1940.

39 For information on A. Freitas, see Saint Léon 1999 and Fall 2001.

40 Geary 2001, p. 110.

Fig. 68
Hans Himmelheber
"Chokwe chief with administrator Hoffmann"
Chokwe region, 1938/39, b/w negative
Museum Rietberg Zürich, FHH 180-3

Fig. 69
Hans Himmelheber and A. Hoffmann (?)
"Chokwe chief explaining arrows to me, admin. Hoffmann"
Chokwe region, 1938/39, b/w negatives
Museum Rietberg Zürich, FHH 180-13, 180-14

Fig. 70
Hans Himmelheber
Man with staff
Chokwe region, 1938/39, b/w negative
Museum Rietberg Zürich, FHH 180-24

Fig. 71
Hans Himmelheber
Kneeing man and policeman
Chokwe region, 1938/39, b/w negative
Museum Rietberg Zürich, FHH 180-25

Fig. 72
Hans Himmelheber
"Pipe-smoking girl"
Yaka region, 1938, b/w negatives
Museum Rietberg Zürich, FHH 166-23, 166-24

Fig. 73
Hans Himmelheber
"My collection"
Yaka region, 1938, b/w negative
Museum Rietberg Zürich, FHH 158-23

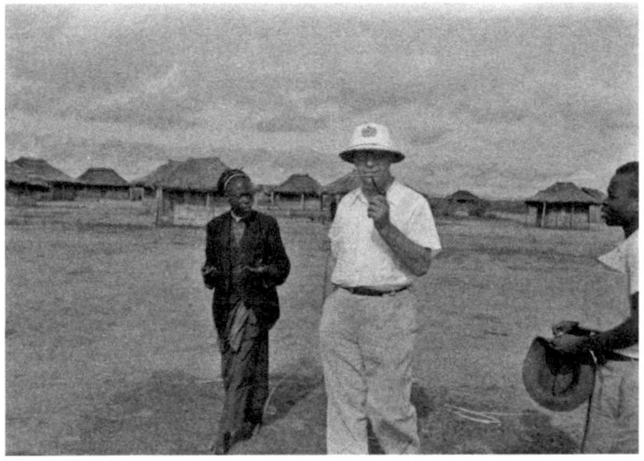
Fig. 68

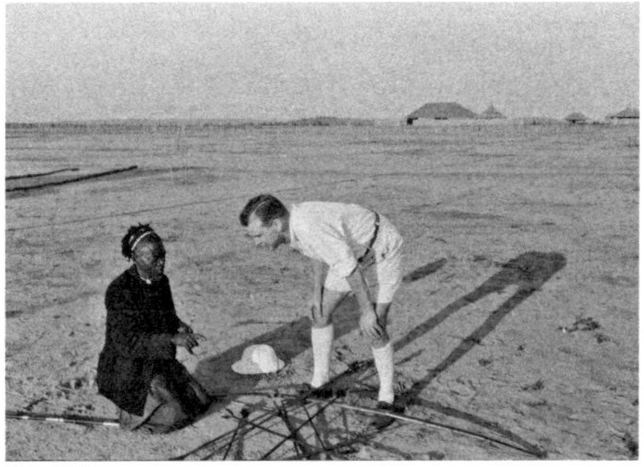
Fig. 69.1

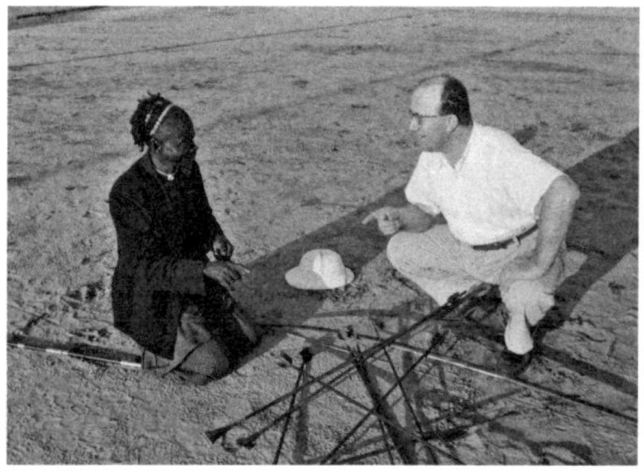
Fig. 69.2

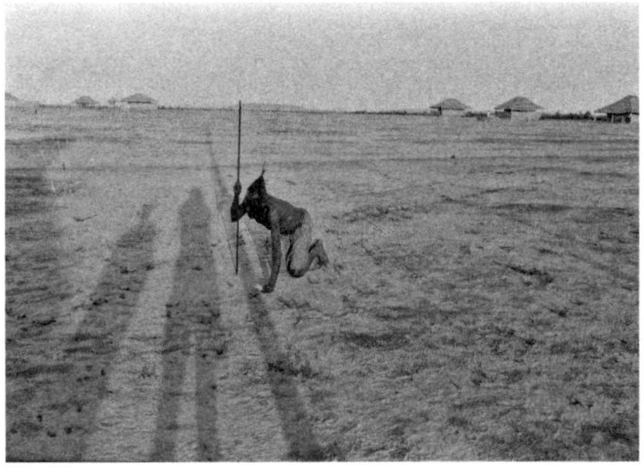
Fig. 70

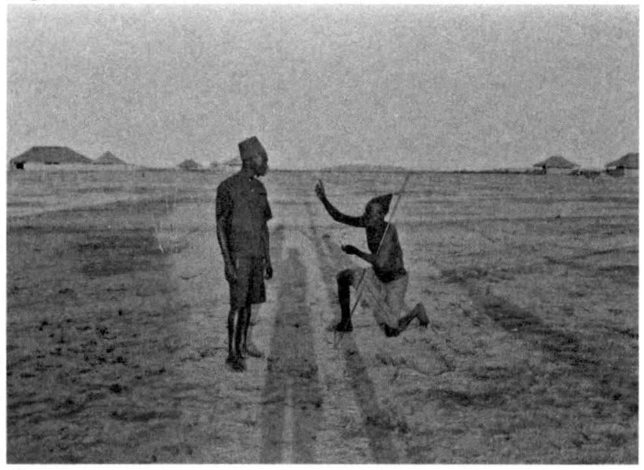
Fig. 71

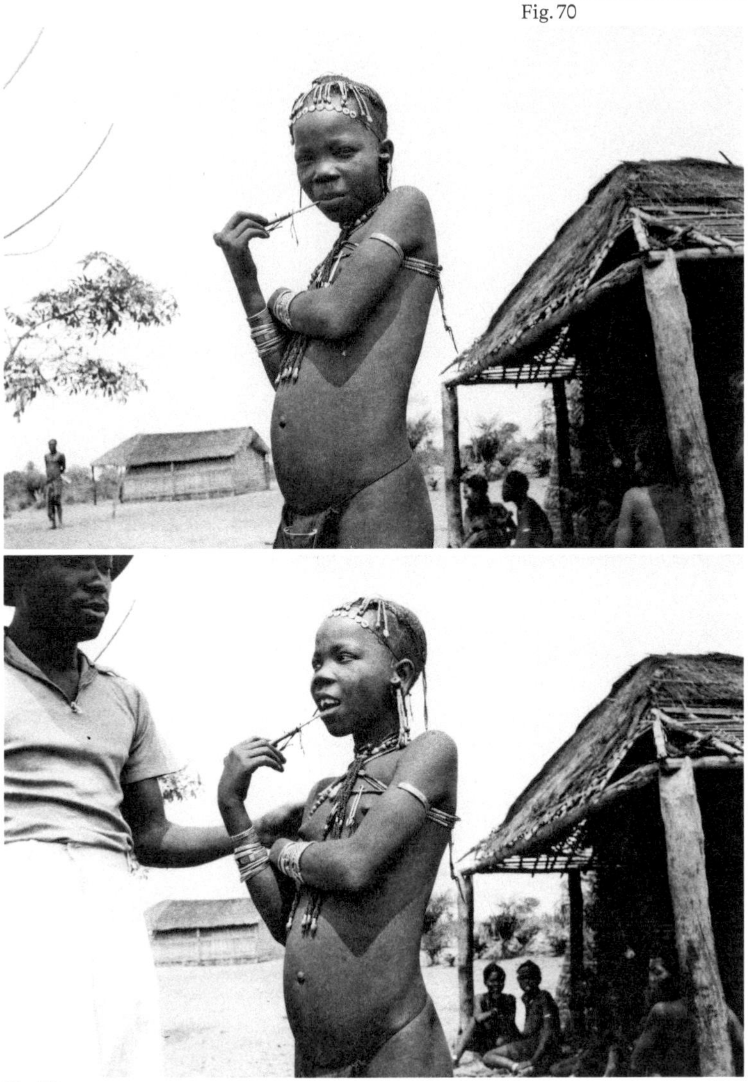
Fig. 72

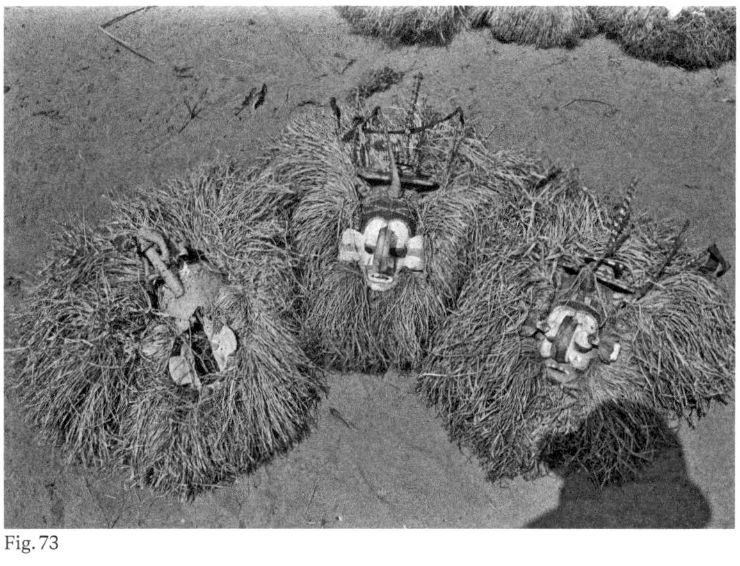
Fig. 73

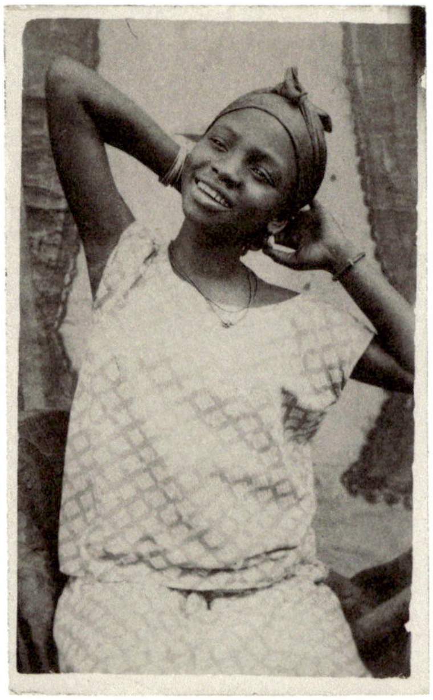
Fig. 74

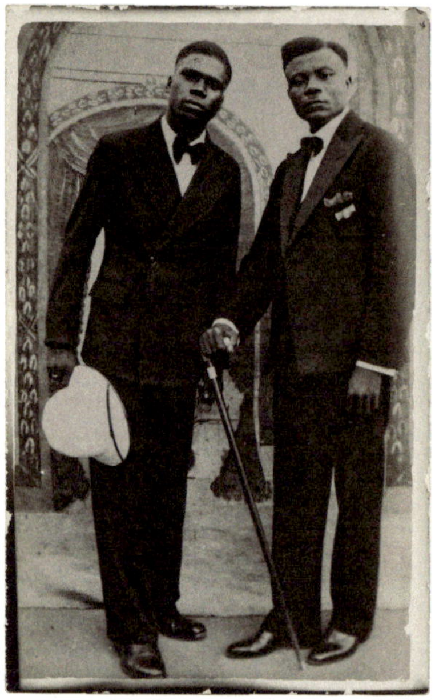
Fig. 75

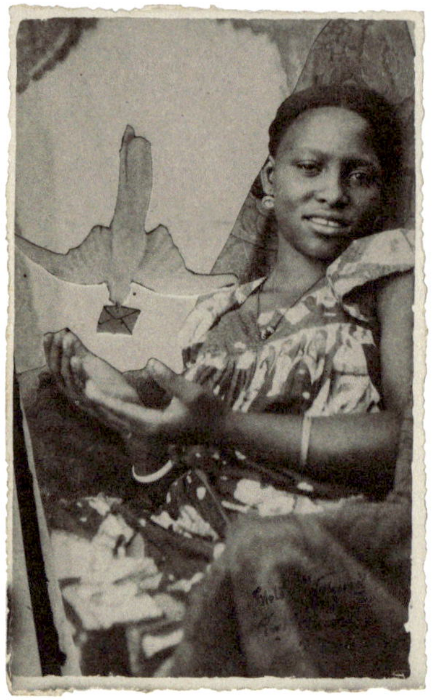
Fig. 76

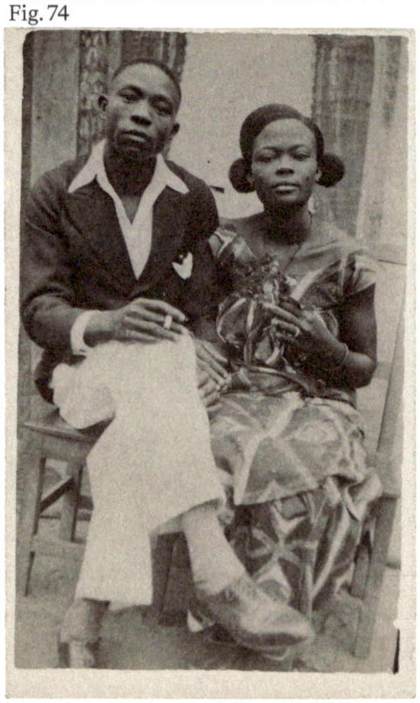
Fig. 77

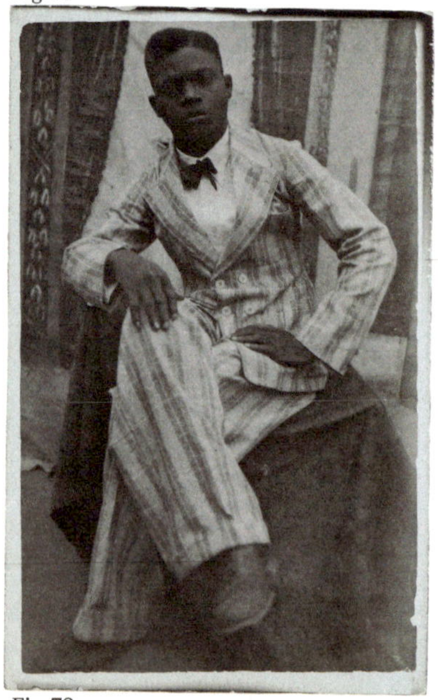
Fig. 78

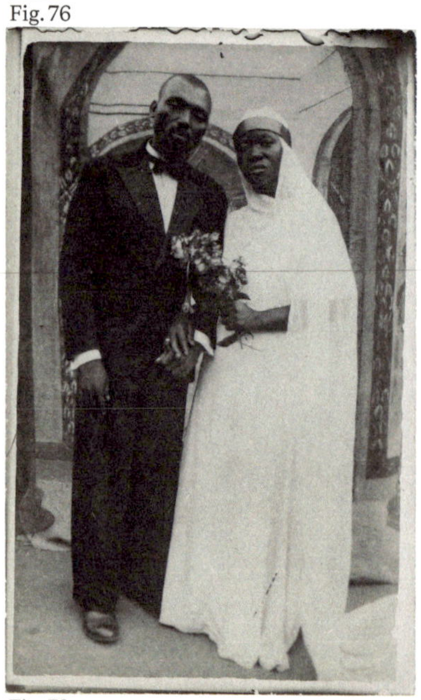
Fig. 79

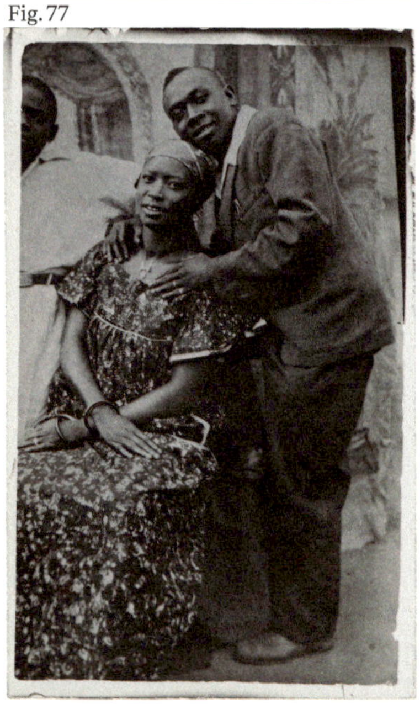
Fig. 80

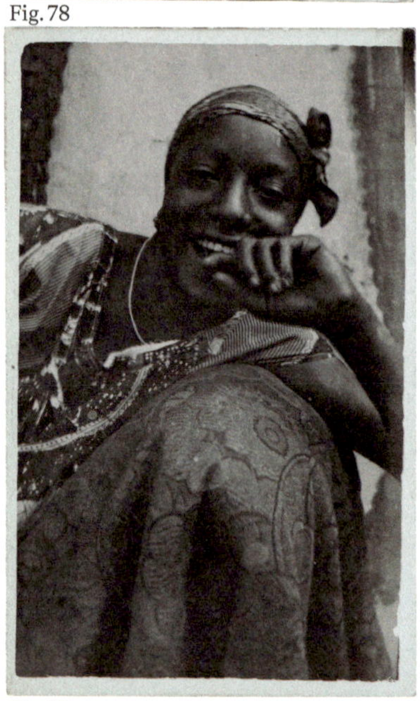
Fig. 81

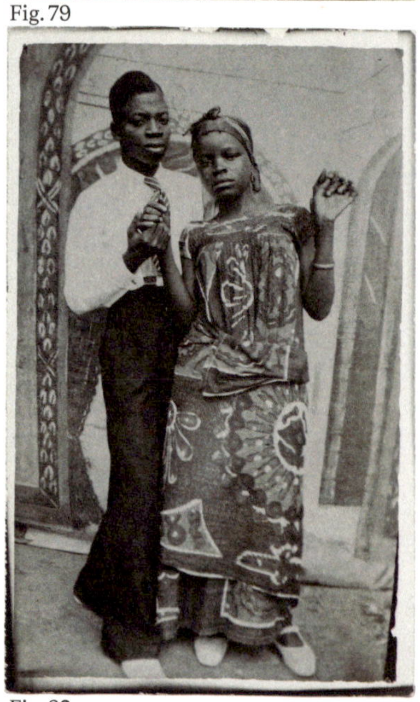
Fig. 82

Figs. 74–82
Antoine Freitas
Portraits
Various places in the Kasai region, 1936–1939, gelatin silver print
Museum Rietberg Zürich

present themselves as they wanted to be remembered by posterity.[41] To achieve this, Freitas also used artistic techniques like collage. This can be seen in the portrait of a young woman signed "Photo Antoine, Port Franqui, July 22, 1938," to which the depiction of a messenger pigeon has been attached [fig. 76].[42]

Himmelheber felt a similar aversion to such photos as to his own portraits of women in European clothing and with European jewelry. He bought Freitas's works to demonstrate that local photography was a manifestation of urban "pseudo culture"; he described the poses of the people depicted as "not free, in marked contrast to the villages where the genuine cultural property was to be found."[43] From today's perspective the fourteen photographs taken at the same time as Himmelheber's pictures and in similar places, show a parallel visual universe and clearly prove the constructive nature of photography. Such pictures illustrate why, in Africa, photographers are now referred to as authors of a parallel historiography.[44]

KWETE AS THE NEXUS OF LOCAL PHOTOGRAPHIC HISTORY

Georges Kwete Mwana (1913–1970), a son of the King of Mushenge, posed for both Himmelheber and Antoine Freitas. On January 20, 1939 Himmelheber photographed Kwete in Mushenge [fig. 84].[45] In the photo, Kwete, who mostly wore European clothing at official appearances from 1936, is shown in ceremonial dress.[46] For Freitas, too, Kwete posed in traditional regalia [fig. 85]. In the photograph he is wearing a simple wraparound skirt, as well as a sword and small hat, thereby articulating his identity as a dignified Kuba [see also essay Geary]. Regarding the composition, however, the two pictures differ considerably. In Himmelheber's photograph, Kwete appears from a distance with a proud, aloof bearing, his gaze turned away from the camera, and his arms crossed. In Freitas's picture, in contrast, Kwete looks out at us with an open, friendly expression, his hands resting on his hips. Kwete's body language makes him seem much more approachable and relaxed. Freitas nevertheless emphasizes Kwete's status as the king's son and an important partner of the colonial administration by shooting him slightly from below, a perspective that makes people look dominant.

> "Ironically, in attempting to defuse the power of these historicist fictions, we must rely upon photography and its vast array of signs, which also stand at the juncture of this refutation."[47]

This essay has attempted to analyze a visual archive using the example of Hans Himmelheber. The results show which thought patterns and visual cultures—both local and European—as well as which economic factors, emotions, mechanisms, and genuine moments, had an influence on Hans Himmelheber's photographic archive of the Congo. By reconstructing some photographic moments, we have clarified the contribution made to the creation of these pictures by the photographs' subjects, in this case the inhabitants of southeast Congo. Indeed, studies on the photographic history of Central Africa have demonstrated that the Congolese people who were photographed were instrumental in creating

41 On the memory function of portraits in Africa, see, e.g., Wendl 1998.

42 The collage technique was also mastered by professional photographers in West Africa (Guyer 2016).

43 Caption for sale purposes, archive of the Museum Rietberg.

44 On the parallel imagery of colonial and local photography in 1950s Congo, see Colard 2019.

45 Himmelheber, diary, January 22, 1939 (archive of the Museum Rietberg).

46 On Kwete's biography, see Kwete 2010.

47 Enwezor 1996, p. 20.

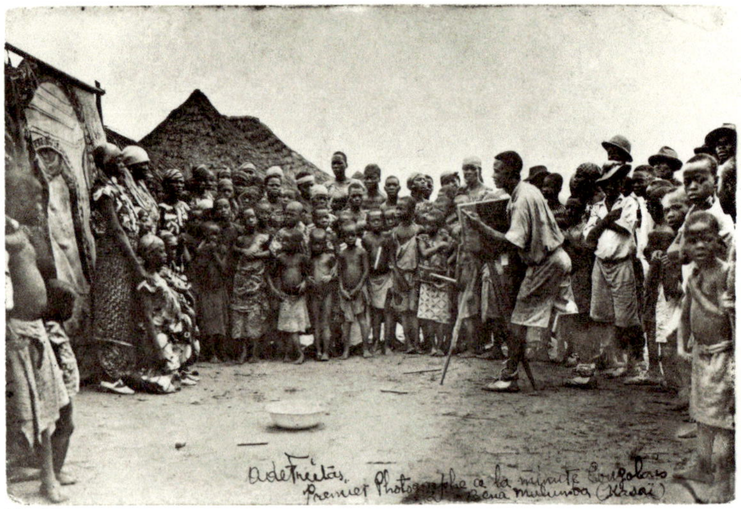

Fig. 83

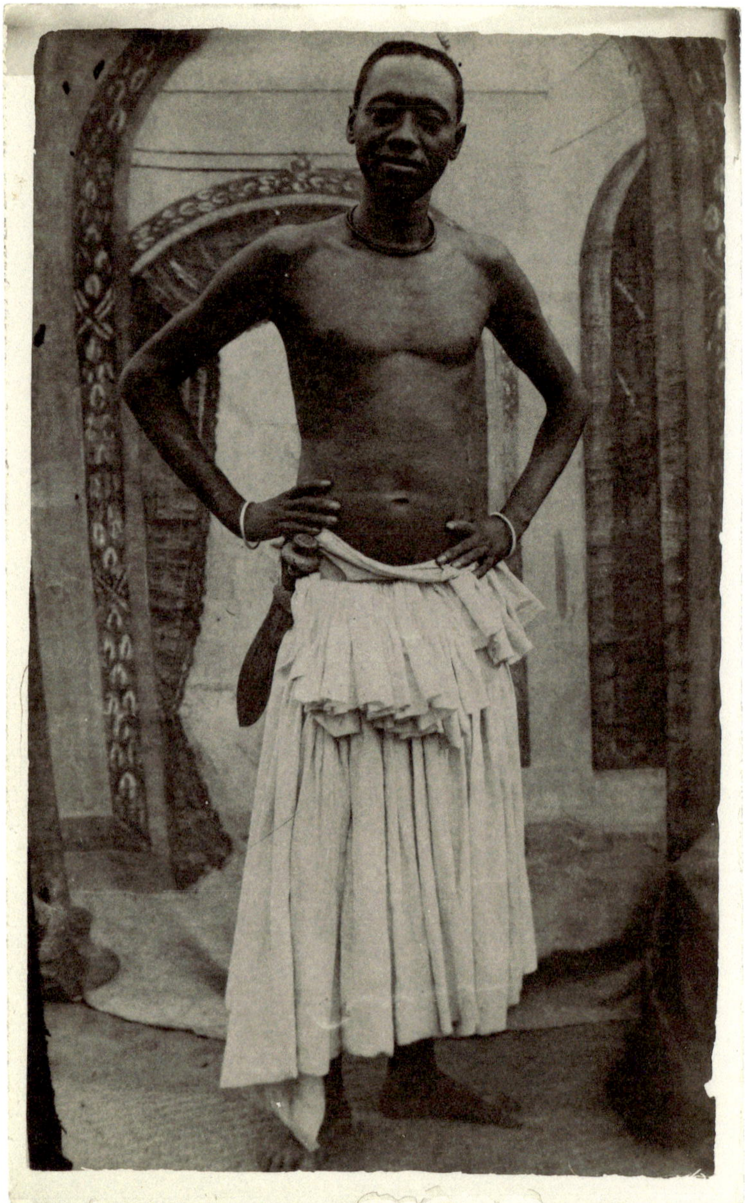
Fig. 85

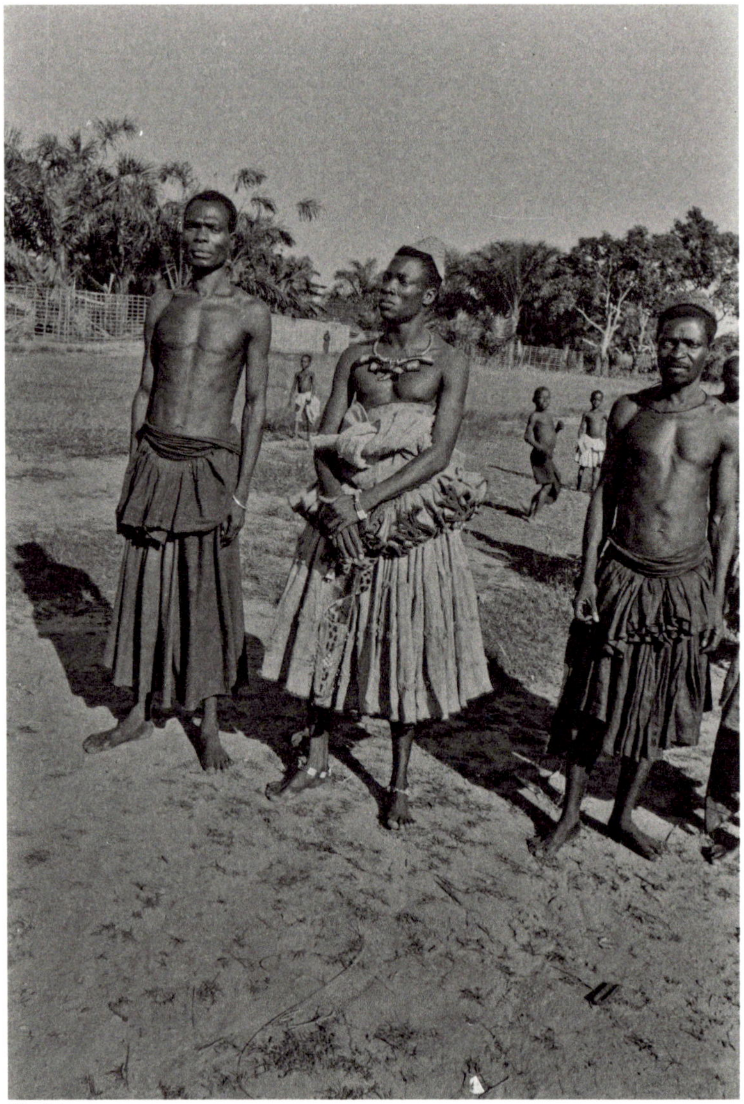
Fig. 84

Fig. 83
Unknown photographer
Antoine Freitas with his box camera in the Kasai
Bena Mulumba, 1936, picture postcard
Revue Noire

Fig. 84
Hans Himmelheber
"King's son called Kwete"
Mushenge, January 22, 1939, b/w negative
Museum Rietberg Zürich, FHH 182-38

Fig. 85
Antoine Freitas
Portrait of Kwete
Kasai, 1936–1939, gelatin silver print
Museum Rietberg Zürich

the pictures taken by ethnologists and other photographers and were themselves also active producers of pictures.[48] By drawing attention to the coauthorship of the photographers' sitters, we aim to counteract the desubjectification of these individuals that goes hand in hand with ethnographic photography. Moreover, visual subjects that are entirely missing or only marginally represented, give us an insight into the selective nature of photographic archives. This became all the more apparent in light of Freitas's pictures, which reveal a parallel photographic universe at the same time and in the same places as Himmelheber's works.

Today, Congolese artists like Sammy Baloji, David Shongo, and Michèle Magema are reappraising Hans Himmelheber's ethnographic photographs [see stories, p. 96 and p. 104]. In the process they are bringing these photographs into the here and now, and creating new fictions for the future.

48 Schildkrout 1991; Mack 1991; Geary 2002.

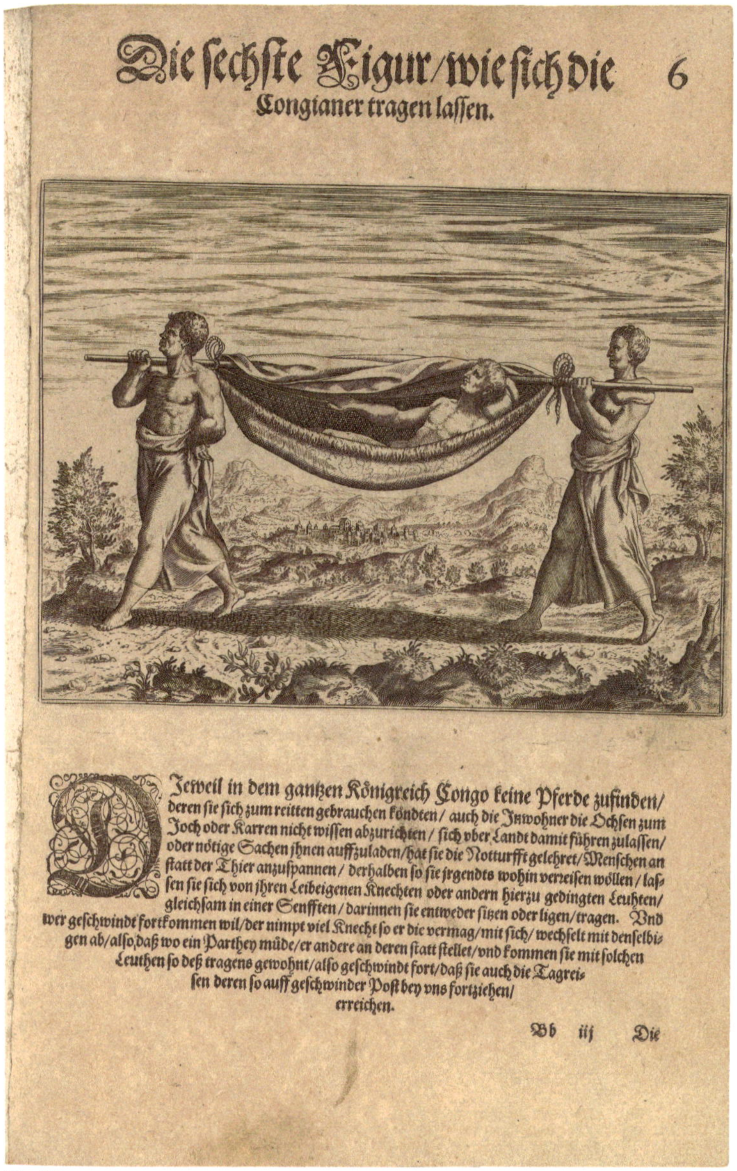

Die sechste Figur/wie sich die Congianer tragen lassen. 6

DIeweil in dem gantzen Königreich Congo keine Pferde zufinden/ deren sie sich zum reitten gebrauchen köndten/ auch die Jnwohner die Ochsen zum Joch oder Karren nicht wissen abzurichten/ sich vber Landt damit führen zulassen/ oder nötige Sachen jhnen auffzuladen/hat sie die Notturfft gelehret/Menschen an statt der Thier anzuspannen/ derhalben so sie jrgendts wohin verreisen wöllen/ lassen sie sich von jhren Leibeigenen Knechten oder andern hierzu gedingten Leuhten/ gleichsam in einer Senfften/ darinnen sie entweder sitzen oder ligen/ tragen. Vnd wer geschwindt fortkommen wil/der nimpt viel Knecht so er die vermag/mit sich/ wechselt mit denselbigen ab/also/daß wo ein Parthey müde/er andere an deren statt stellet/vnd kommen sie mit solchen Leuthen so deß tragens gewohnt/also geschwindt fort/daß sie auch die Tagreisen deren so auff geschwinder Post bey vns fortziehen/ erreichen.

Bb iij Die

Fig. 86

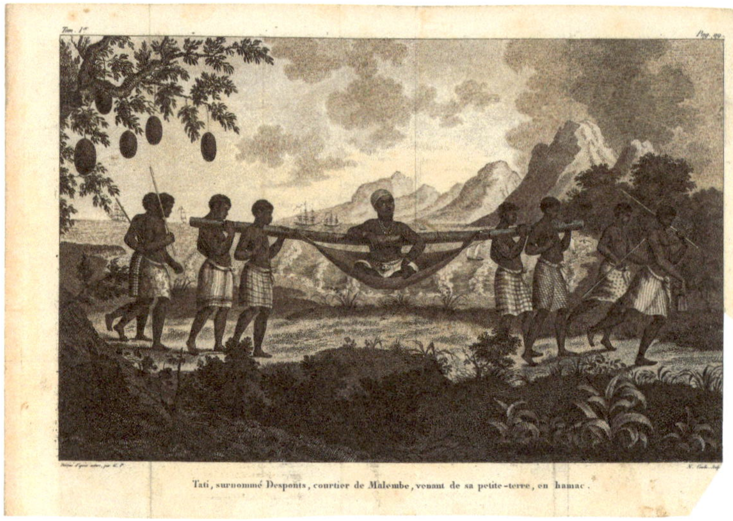

Fig. 87

"Mwaleta lunanda, mwaleta lunanda
Wazunga masambazi, mwaleta lunanda
Wazunga ma lunanda!"

"You brought us the white people
But with them so much misery
Because the whites are always on the move!"[1]

1 De Bouveignes 1948, p. 100.

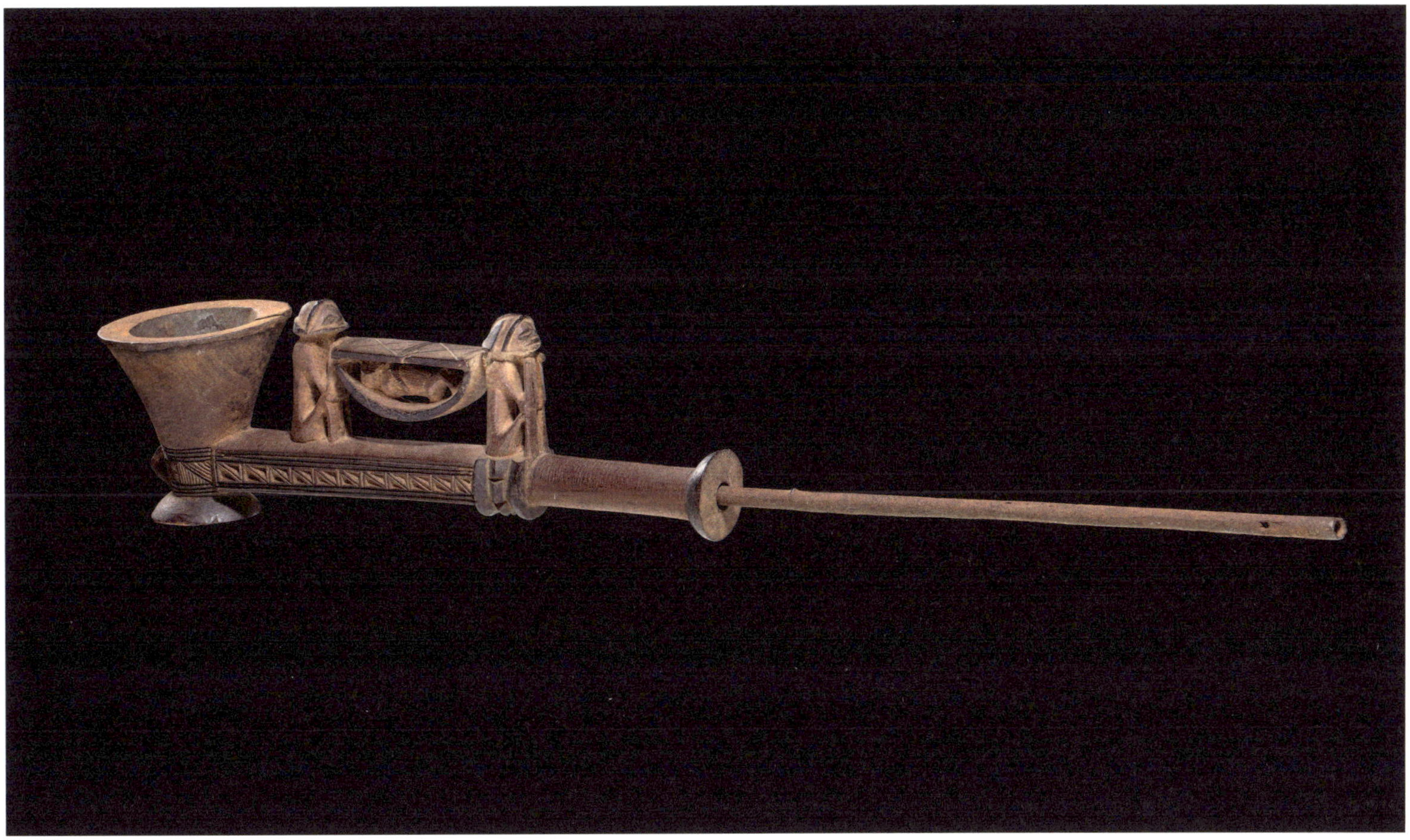

Fig. 88

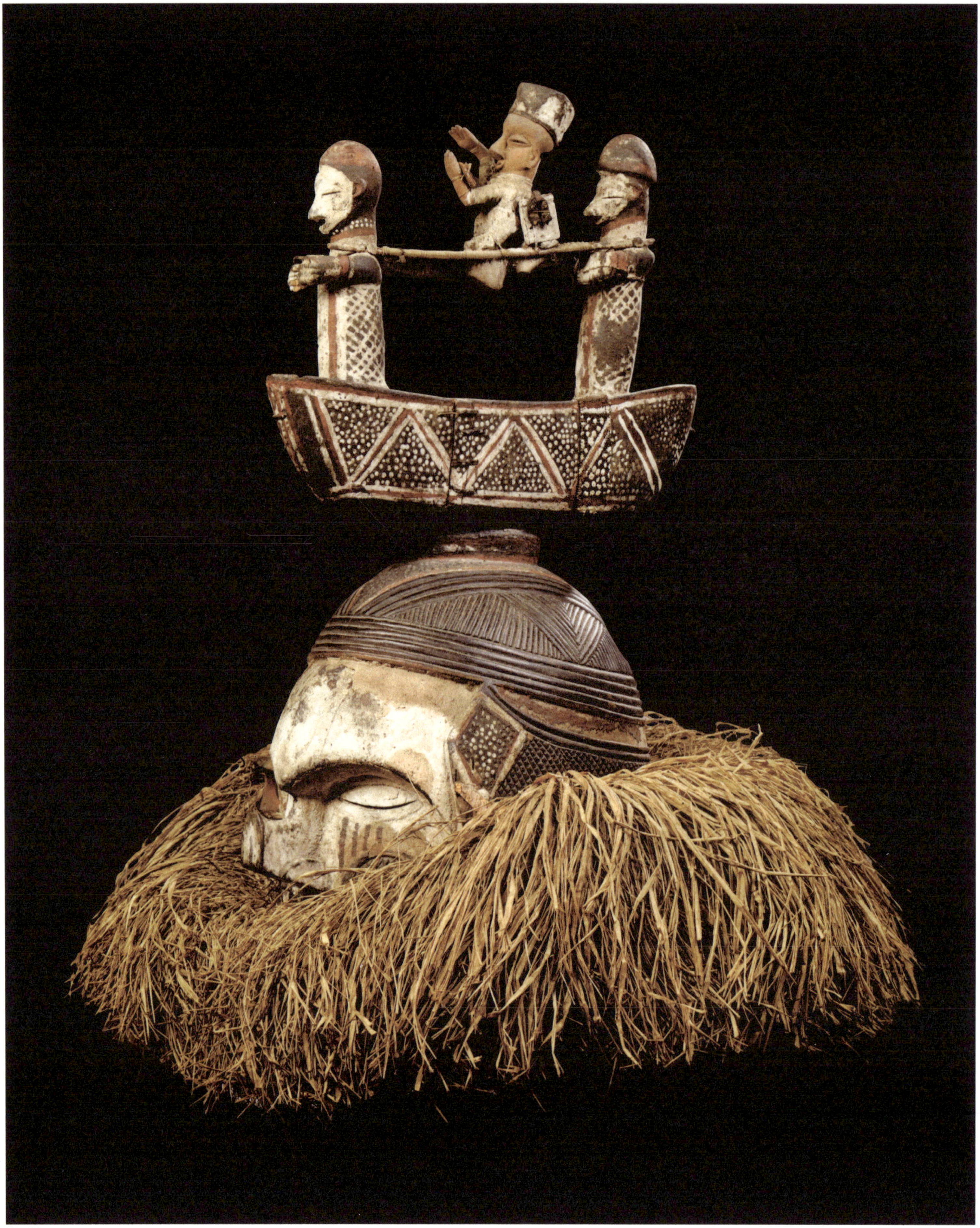

Fig. 89

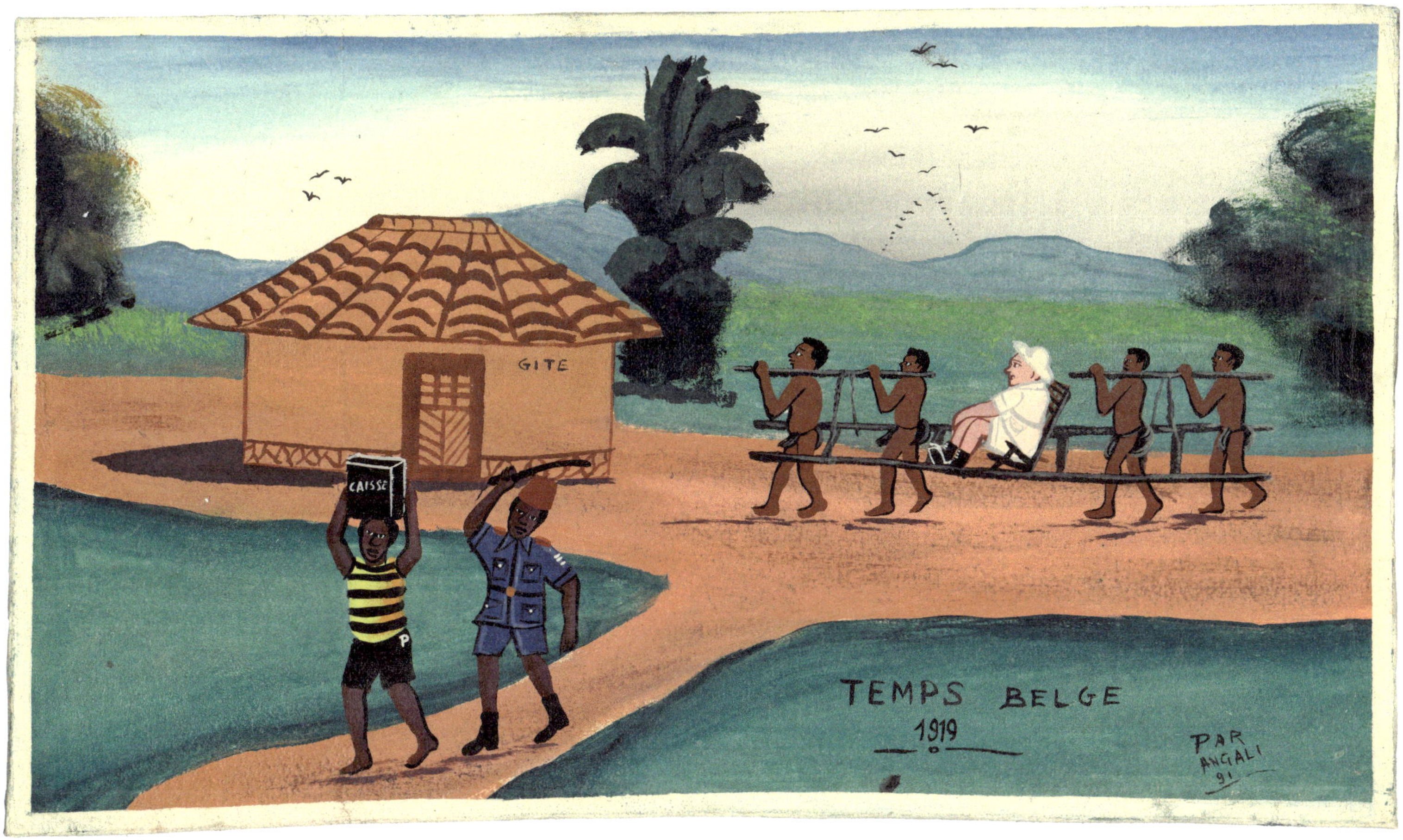

Fig. 90

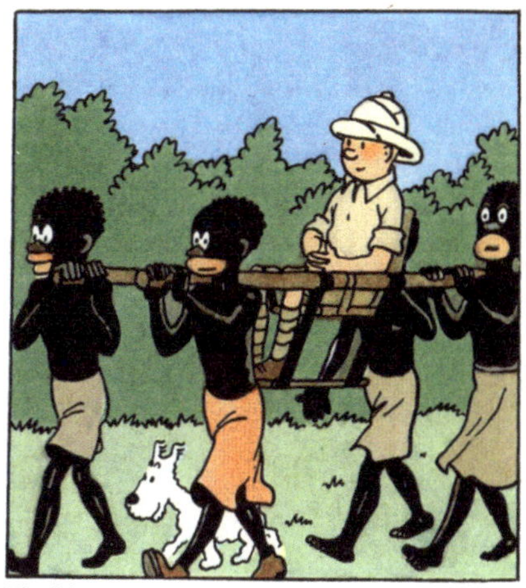

Fig. 91

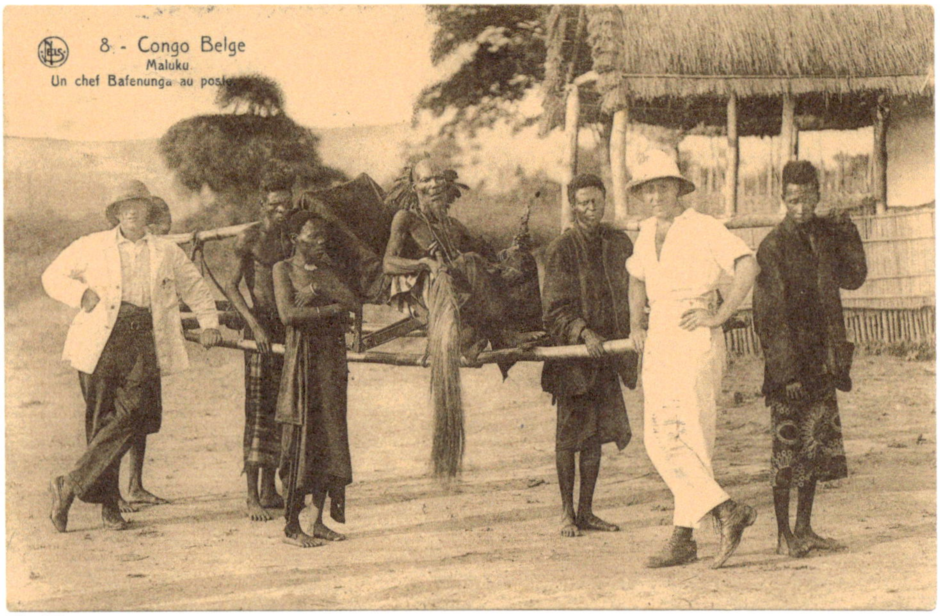

Fig. 92

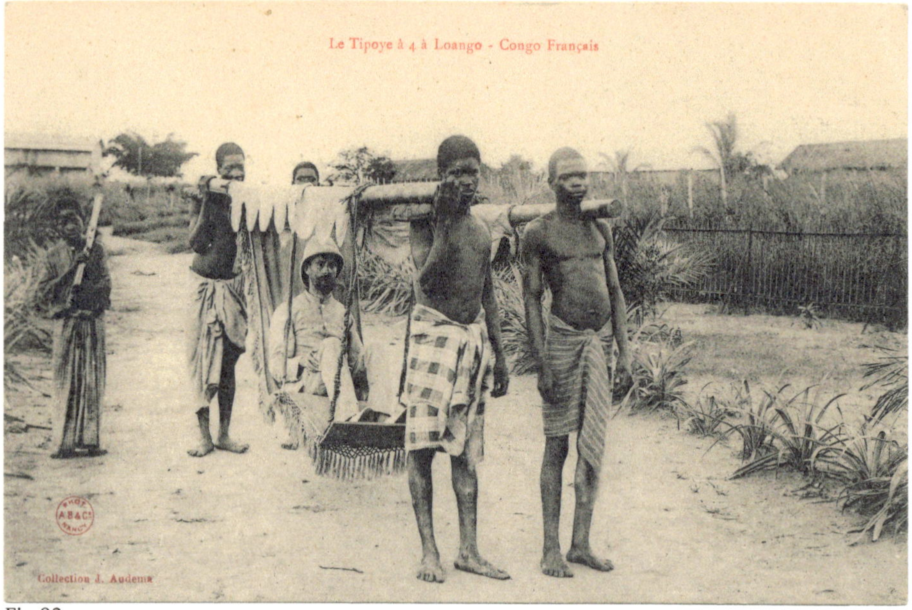

Fig. 93

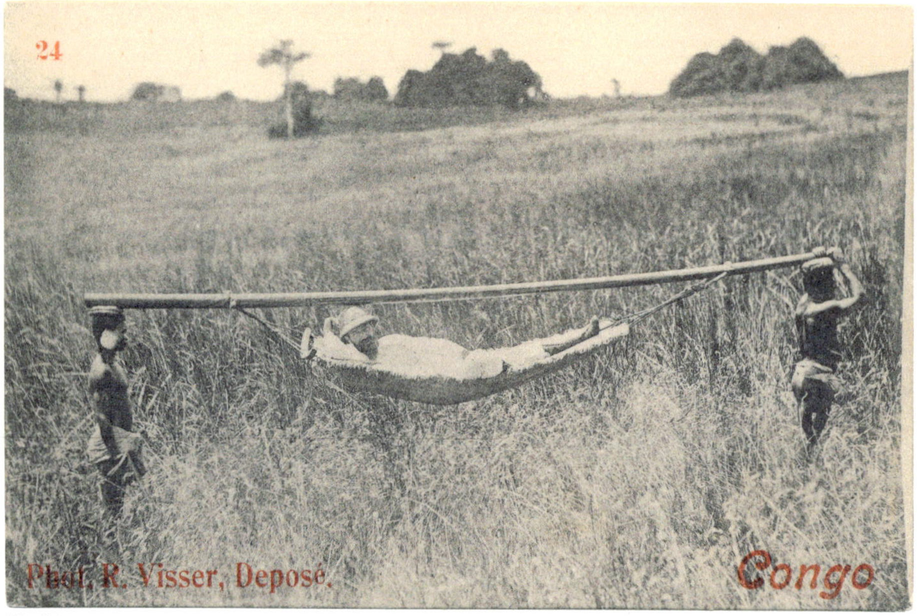

Fig. 94

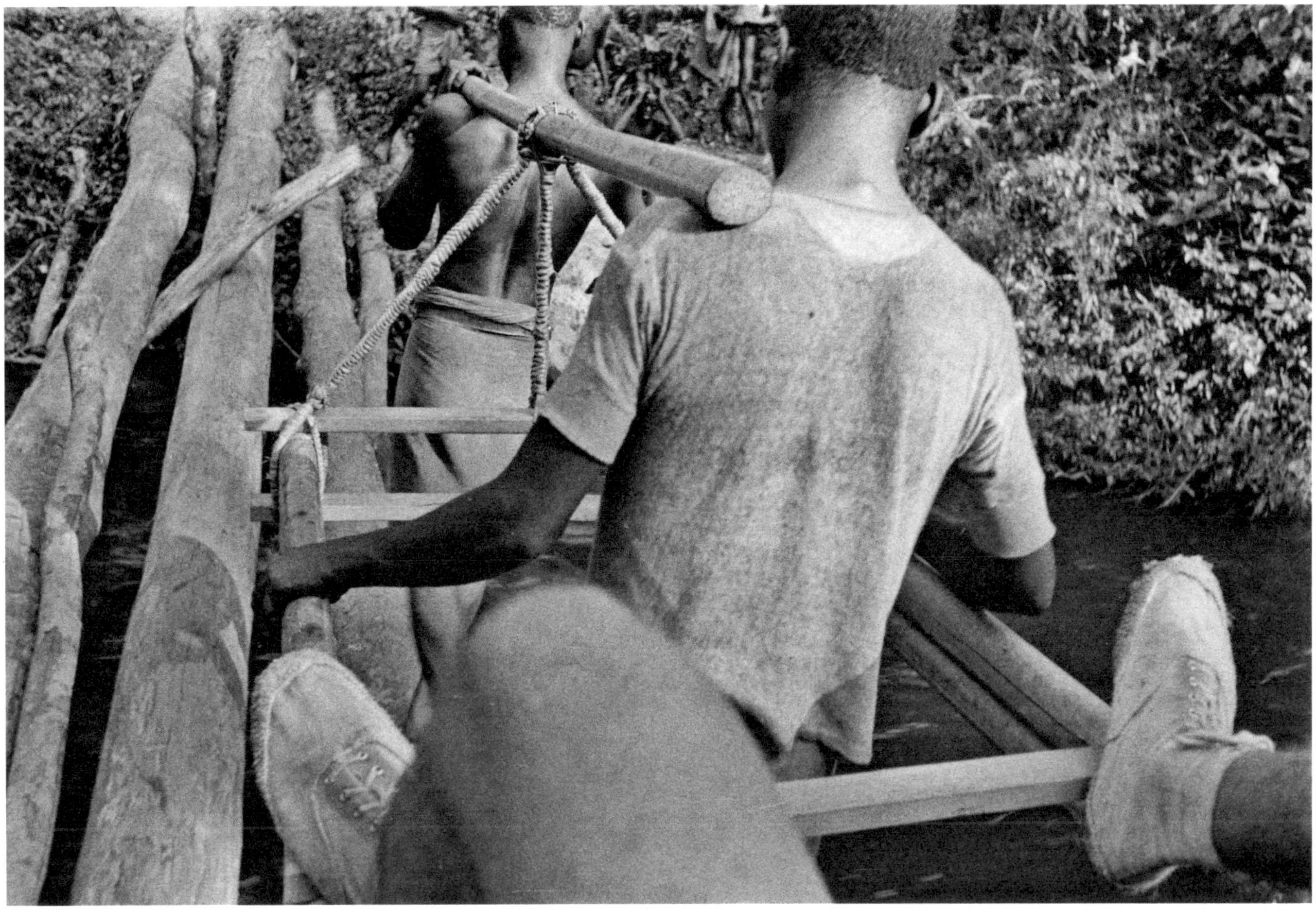
Fig. 95

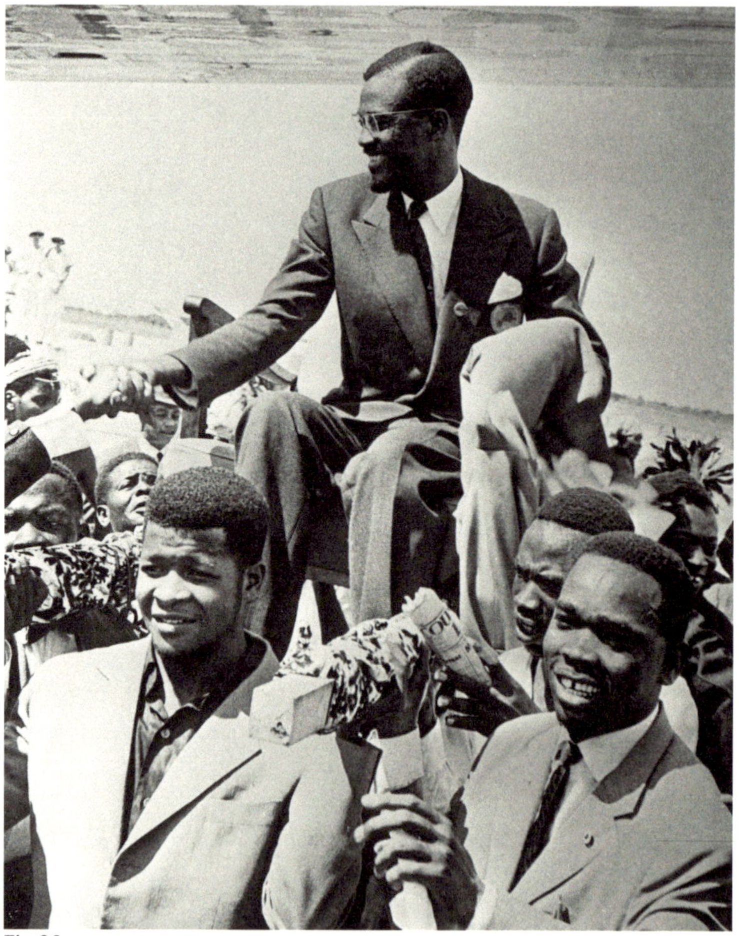

Fig. 96

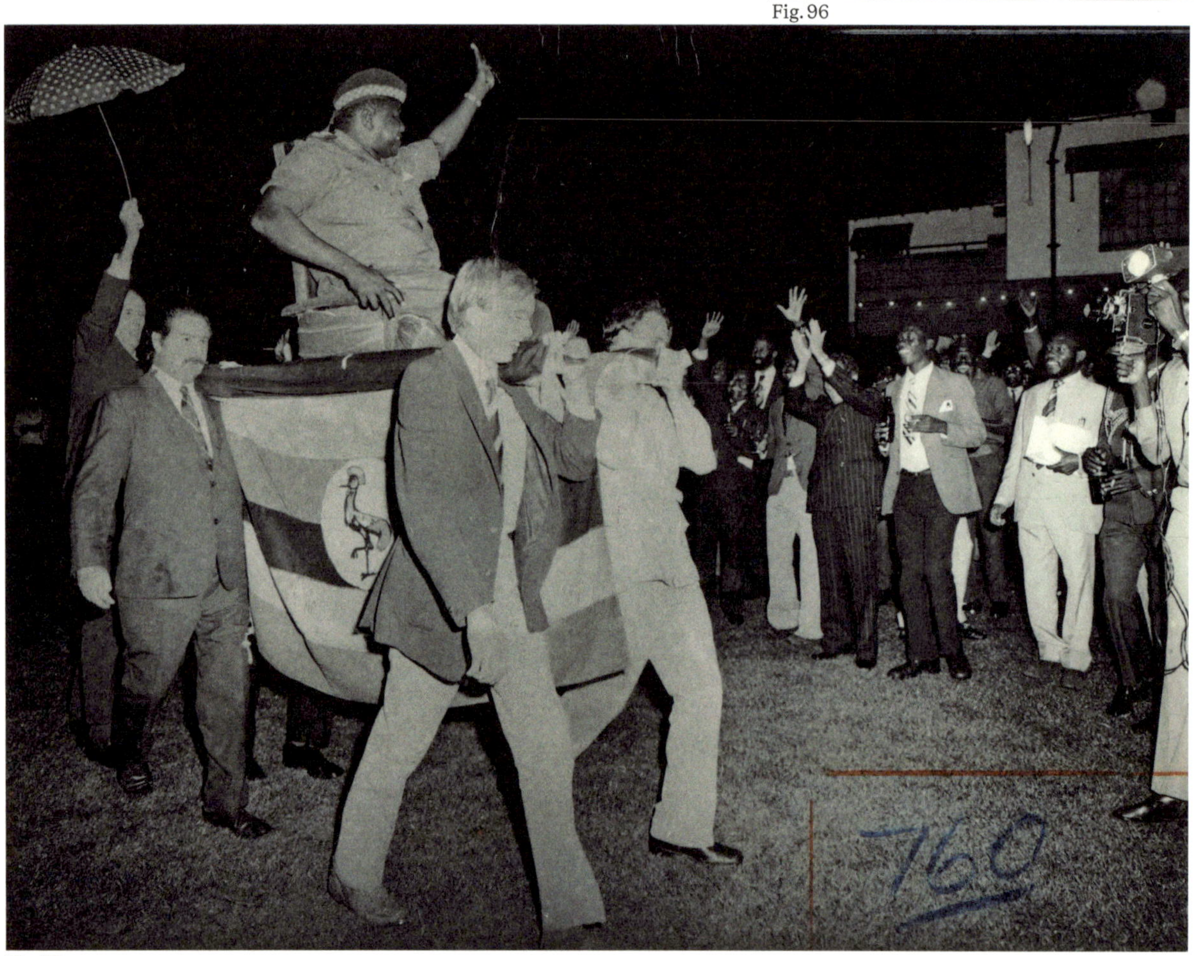

Fig. 97

TRANSPORTING THE POWERFUL: *TIPOYE* THROUGH TIME

—— The *tipoye* is a means of transport that has been used in Central Africa for over 500 years.[1] The *tipoye* is a litter in the form of a hammock or palanquin, which was attached to one or two long pieces of wood and carried on the shoulders of two or four people. Its name comes from the Portuguese word *tipóia*, which in turn is borrowed from a language native to Brazil and originally referred to a sling for carrying children. Even the earliest travelers and missionaries in the sixteenth century reported that dignitaries and kings were carried around in a kind of hammock by slaves or servants [figs. 86/87]. The subject—a chief being transported in a hammock—was also frequently found in local art, as in the case with the Chokwe's prestigious pipe [fig. 88].

In the late nineteenth century the *tipoye* became a symbol of Africa's conquest and colonization by Europe. Colonial agents, officers, and missionaries had themselves transported from place to place by African bearers, some of whom were forced to carry out this hard work. The Suku mask portrays a white man sitting in a hammock that is being carried by two people who are standing in a canoe. In his hands the man is holding a book in which a piece of paper bearing Flemish words has been affixed [fig. 89]. The modern picture by Angali in the popular painting style depicts the power imbalance between the colonizers and the colonized [fig. 90]. While the Belgian man in his white suit is being carried by four men, another bearer is transporting the box containing the collected taxes. The picture of the supposedly superior white man and the servile African can also be found on postcards and in comics—as in Hergé's *Tintin in the Congo* [figs. 91–93].

Travelers and collectors like Robert Visser and Hans Himmelheber also used this means of transport [fig. 94]. According to Himmelheber, it was expected of him as a white man not to walk but to arrive by *tipoye* [fig. 95]. Being carried underlined his prestige and his economic superiority. Furthermore, he took numerous photographs of the landscape, the people, and the villages from this raised and simultaneously detached position.

Frequently the bearers sang special caravan songs during this hard work.[2] While they often served to entertain and followed the rhythm of their steps, there were also lyrics that referred directly to the person in the *tipoye*. The strenuousness of the work was criticized in particular. As the Europeans mostly did not understand the songs that were being sung about them in the local languages, it is possible to speak of a subversive form of criticizing the colonial power structure.

After independence, African politicians like Patrice Lumumba used the *tipoye* as a traditional and yet modern symbol of power [fig. 96]. The Ugandan ruler Idi Amin Dada even turned the situation on its head and had British businessmen carry him around [fig. 97]. —— Michaela Oberhofer

1 On the history of the *tipoye*, see Etambala 2011/12.
2 De Bouveignes 1948. pp. 95–100.

Fig. 86
Duarte Lopez and Filippo Pigafetta
The sixth figure, how the Congolese are carried
From: *Regnum Congo hoc est Warhaffte vnd Eigentliche Beschreibung dess Königreichs Congo in Africa*. Frankfurt am Main 1609.
Zentralbibliothek Zürich, EE 1505

Fig. 87
Louis O'Hier de Grandpré
Tati, surnommé Desponts, courtier de Malembe, venant de sa petite-terre, en hamac
From: *Voyage à la côte occidentale d'Afrique, fait dans les annés 1786 et 1787*. Paris 1801
Zentralbibliothek Zürich, NR 1710

Fig. 88
Artist of the Chokwe region
Tobacco pipe with *tipoye* motif
Before 1939, wood, metal, 51.5 × 8.5 × 7.2 cm
Kegel-Konietzko Collection
Acquired by Hans Himmelheber

Fig. 89
Artist of the Suku region
Mask with depiction of a *tipoye*
First half of the twentieth century, wood, plant fibers, pigments, paper, 60 × 45 × 50 cm
Marc Felix Collection
Dr. de Winter, Jacques and Denise Schwob

Fig. 90
Angali
Temps Belge 1919
1991, oil on canvas, 46 × 80.5 × 2 cm
RMCA Tervuren , HO.2013.57.794

Fig. 91
Hergé
Tintin being carried in the *tipoye*
From: *Tim und Struppi. Tim im Kongo*, Hamburg 1997 (first edition 1931/46)

Fig. 92
C. De Bruyne
Congo Belge. Maluku. Un chef Bafenunga au poste
Postcard c. 1925, dated July 6, 1931, Maluku, collotype, 13.8 × 18.7 cm
Christraud M. Geary Collection

Fig. 93
Jean-François Audema
Le Tipoyé à 4 à Loango—Congo Français, Collection J. Audema
Photograph c. 1895, postcard c. 1904, printed by A. Bergeret et Cie (Nancy, France), Loango, Republic of the Congo, collotype, 24 × 19 cm
Christraud M. Geary Collection

Fig. 94
Carl Friedrich Wilhelm Robert Visser
Congo. Phot. R. Visser, Deposé
Photograph before 1900, postcard c. 1905, Republic of the Congo, collotype, 24 × 18.9 cm
Christraud M. Geary Collection

Fig. 95
Hans Himmelheber
Photographed from the *tipoye*
Yaka region, 1938, b/w negative
Museum Rietberg Zürich, FHH 155-28

Fig. 96
Unknown photographer
Patrice Lumumba on a *tipoye*
Kisangani, May 1, 1960
Alamy Stock Photo, B9RM15

Fig. 97
Unknown photographer
The Ugandan president Idi Amin Dada being carried by four British businessmen
Uganda, 1975
Alamy Stock Photo, E115H9

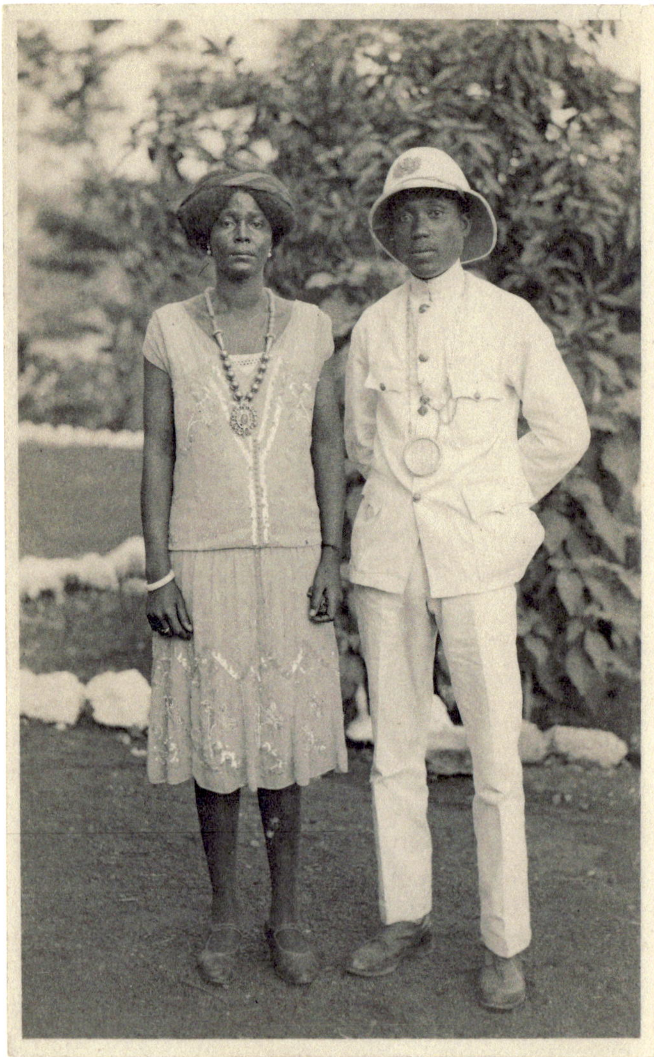
Fig. 98

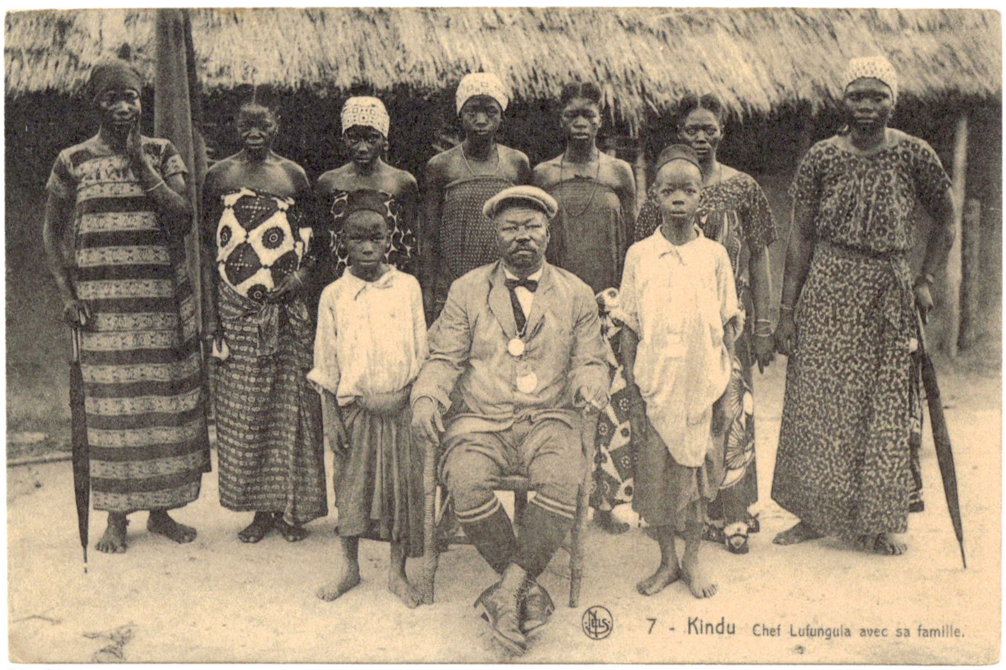

Fig. 99

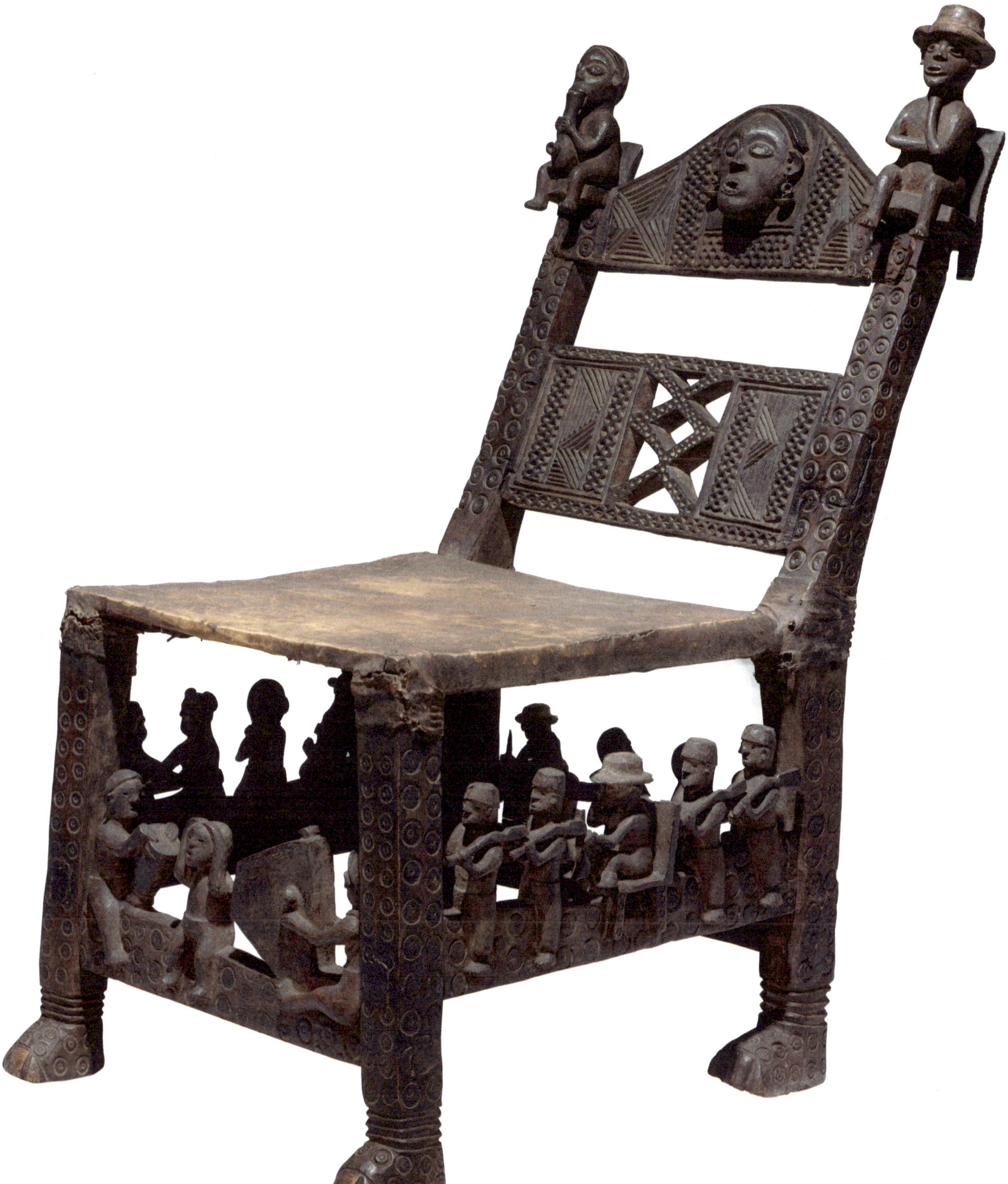

Fig. 100.1

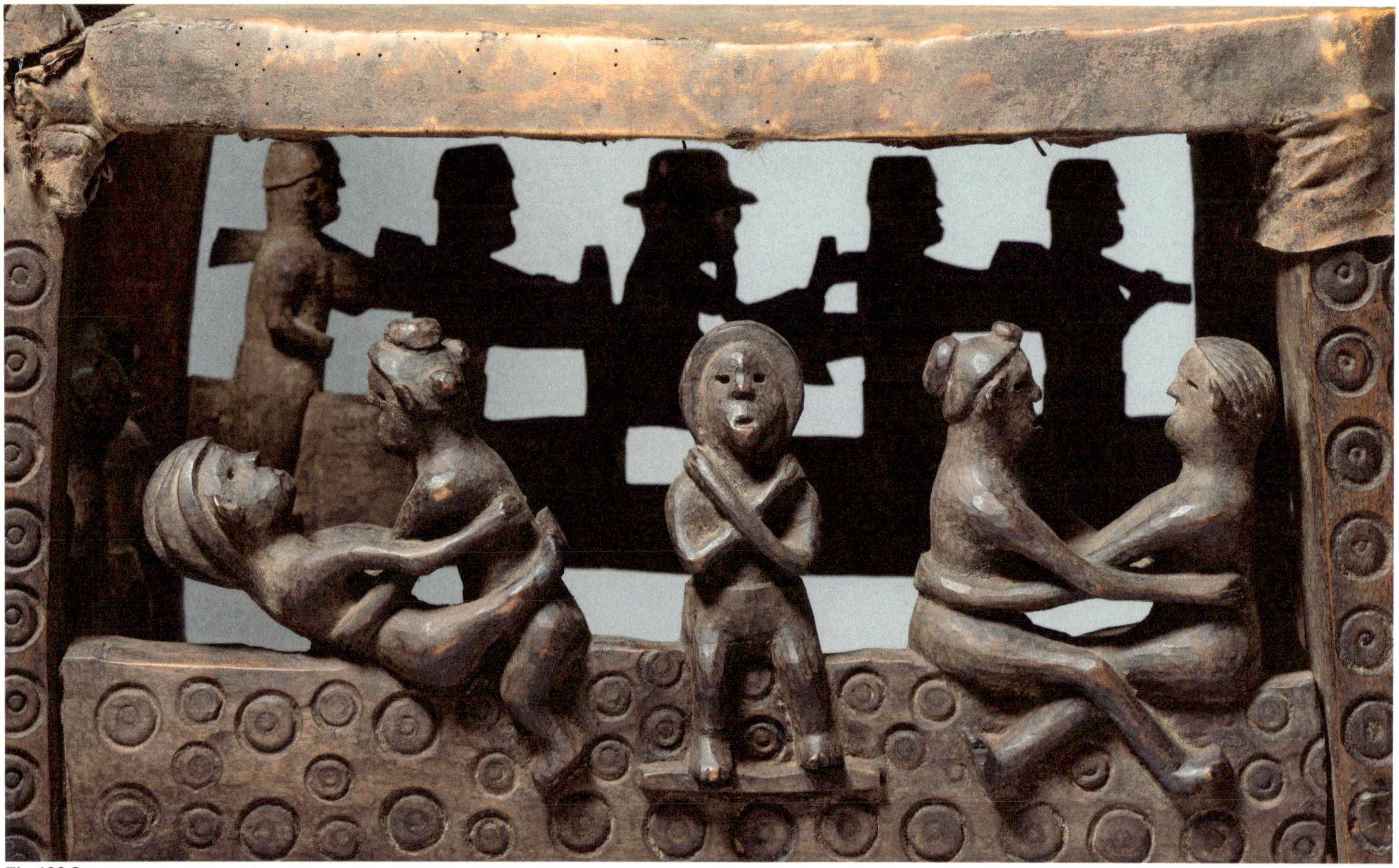
Fig. 100.2

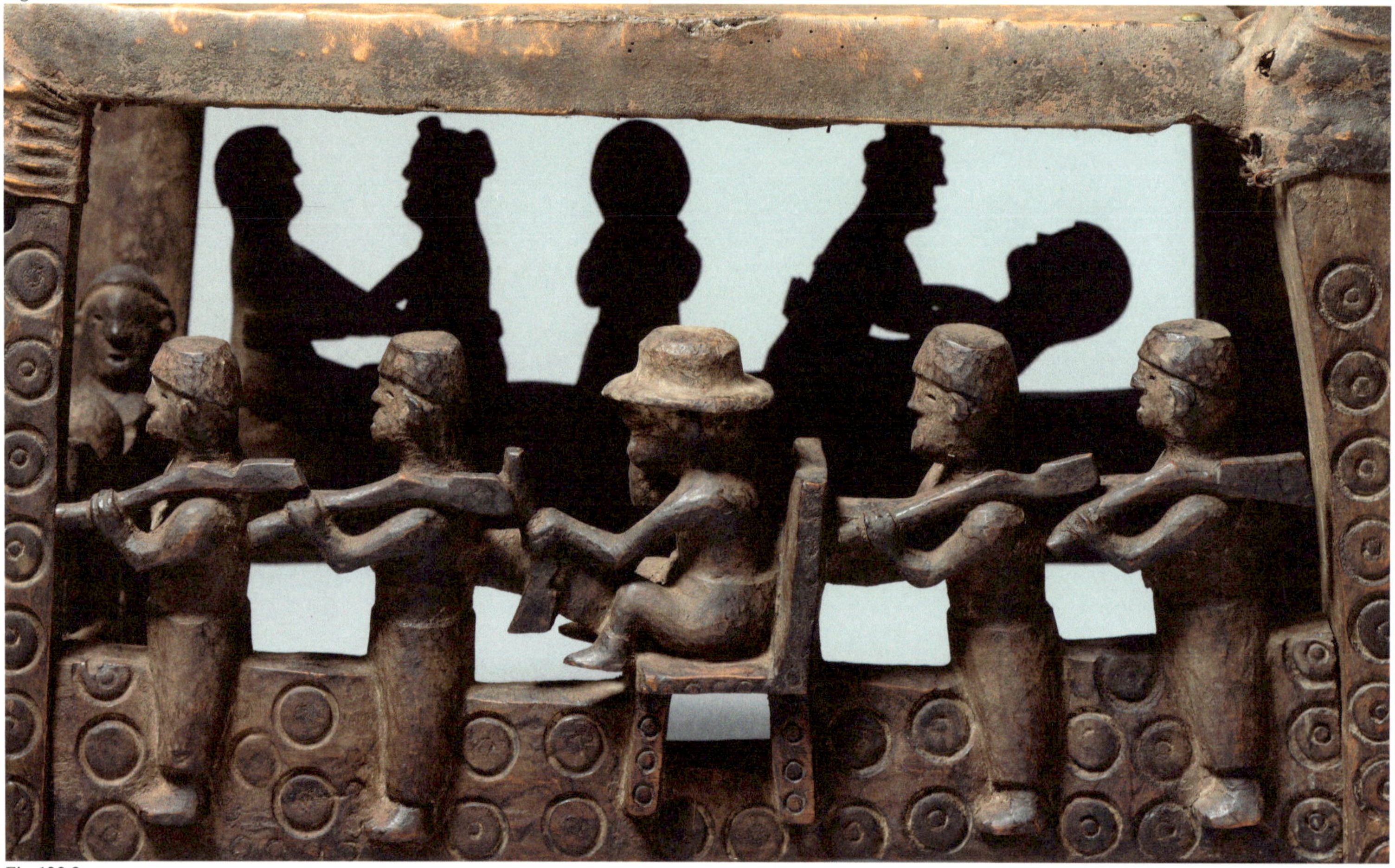
Fig. 100.3

Fig. 98
Léopold Gabriel
[Untitled] *Chef médaillé* with his wife in the Belgian Congo
Postcard c. 1930, Katanga Province (?), gelatin silver print, 13.9 × 8.9 cm
Christraud M. Geary Collection

Fig. 99
S.N. Wellington
Kindu. Chef Lufungula avec sa famille
Photograph c. 1930, postcard published c. 1935 by Nels, Brussels, Kindu, Maniema Province, collotype, 13.7 × 8.7 cm
Christraud M. Geary Collection

Fig. 100
Muledi from Mukulu-Nzambi
Prestigious chair of a *chef médaillé*
Early twentieth century, Kwilu-Pende region, wood, leather, metal, and glass, 97 × 49.5 × 70 cm
Museum Rietberg Zürich, RAC 804
Gift of Eduard von der Heydt

ART AT THE SERVICE OF THE COLONIZER: THE PENDE CHAIR OF A *CHEF MÉDAILLÉ* — Art was not only used to oppose colonization but also to support the colonial power. Among the traditional chiefs, the colonial administration in the Belgian Congo appointed so-called *chefs médaillés* who wore a medal on a chain as a distinguishing feature [figs. 98/99]. In the Belgian colonial system of indirect rule, these medal-wearing chiefs collected taxes and ensured that colonial law was enforced. Those who did not participate or who revolted were severely punished. In contrast to traditional chiefs, who were considered mediators between the population and the world of the ancestors, the "chiefs for the whites" possessed no ritual insignia of power. In the Kwilu region, where their position was especially contested, *chefs médaillés* consequently had bulky chairs made with carved backrests and feet that were intended to underline their social standing and their newly acquired political status.

The Chokwe are in fact more famous for their richly carved chairs than the Pende. Chokwe carvers reinterpreted Portuguese chairs as aesthetic emblems of chiefs' power and adorned them with scenes of social and political life. Soon after Chokwe groups had settled in the Pende region in the 1890s, Pende carvers copied their style and adapted it for the emblems of the new political class. Later they also produced such chairs for the Western art market.

This chair is a particularly impressive example. Carved for his patron by the renowned artist Muledi from the village of Mukulu-Nzambi [fig. 100],[1] the chair's imagery emphasizes the power of the new holders of office and their proximity to the colonial government. The mask and figures on the backrest have their eyes wide open, and as with *mangaka* power figures they are highlighted with glass. Their aggressive expression is a reference to the occult powers that *chefs médaillés*—so the chair implies—knew how to use to their own advantage. In this way the new chiefs came close to witchcraft. The dots spread over the entire chair and the chair's paw-shaped feet refer to leopards and hence to the ambivalent position of the *chefs médaillés* as tax collectors and colonial agents: like a leopard they seized everything for themselves without doing anything in return. On the side of the chair, two scenes depict adultery, a dispute likewise arbitrated by the "chiefs for the whites." Their identification and collaboration with white people are further stressed by the portrayal of one of the power figures on the backrest as a hat-wearing European. On the base another colonial official can be seen sitting in a *tipoye* and being carried by several armed soldiers. The chair's menacing message is clear: the chief is acting on behalf of the colonial government and has its full support. — Michaela Oberhofer

1 See Strother 2016, pp. 207–219, as well as Strother 2008, pp. 41ff. Muledi died in 1946. Another chair from the AfricaMuseum in Tervuren is also attributed to him.

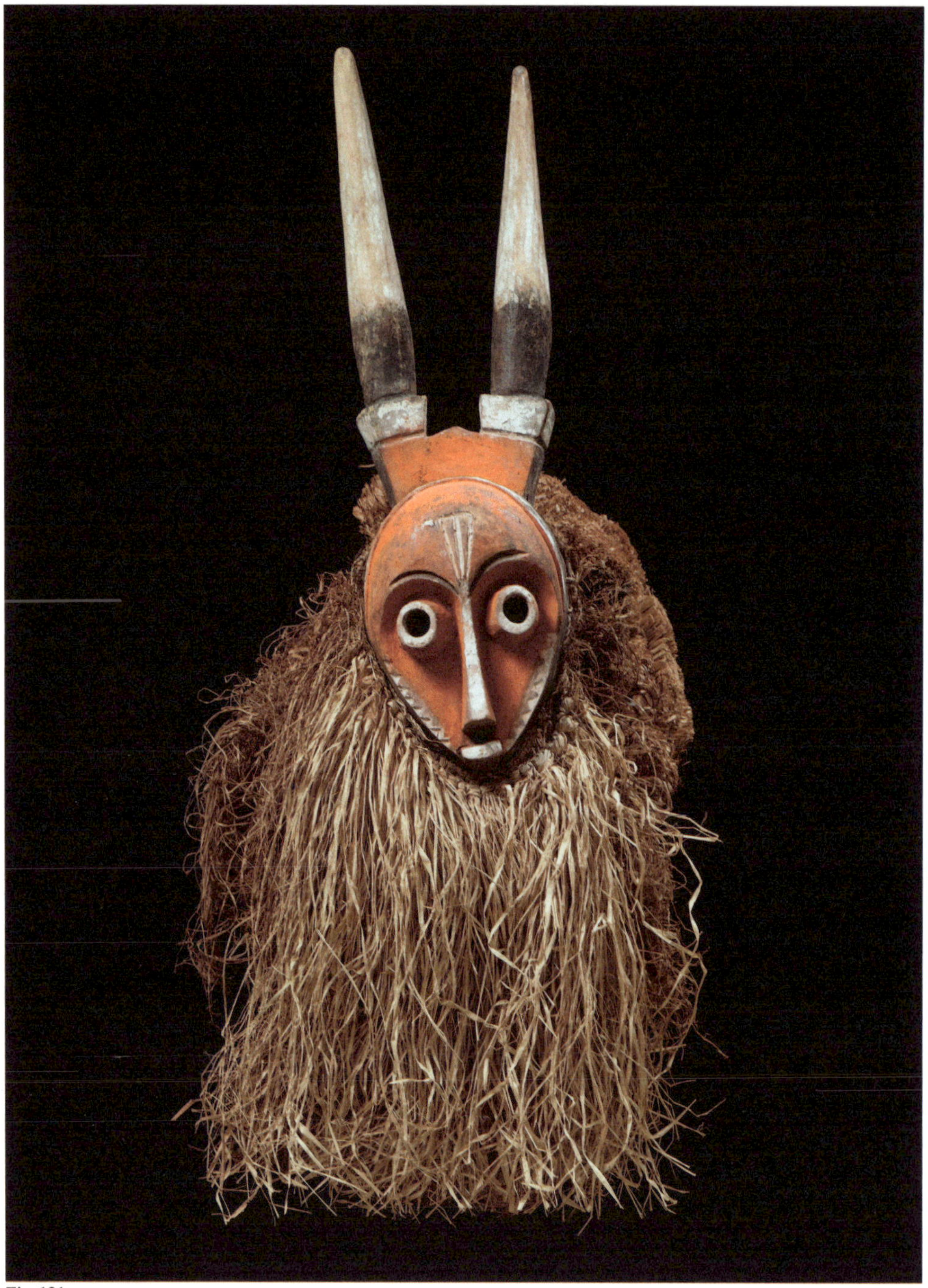

Fig. 101

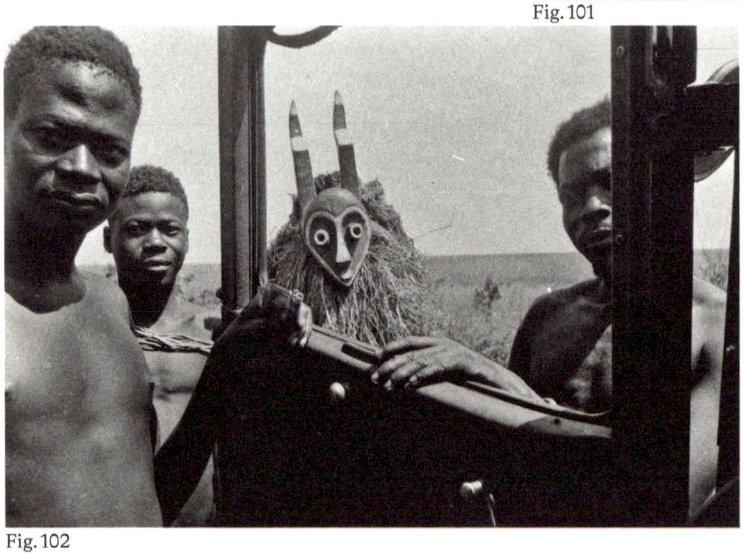

Fig. 102

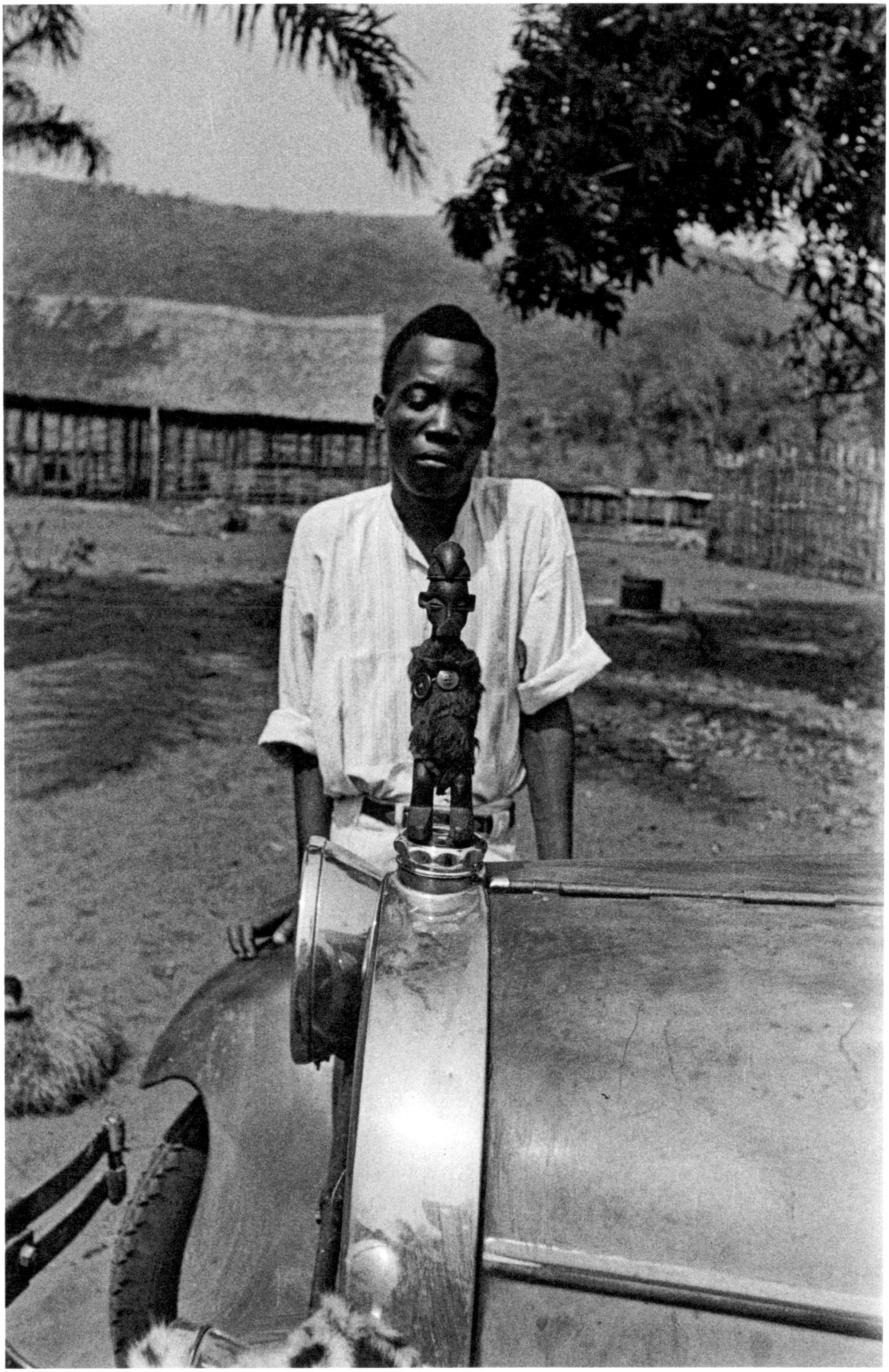
Fig. 103

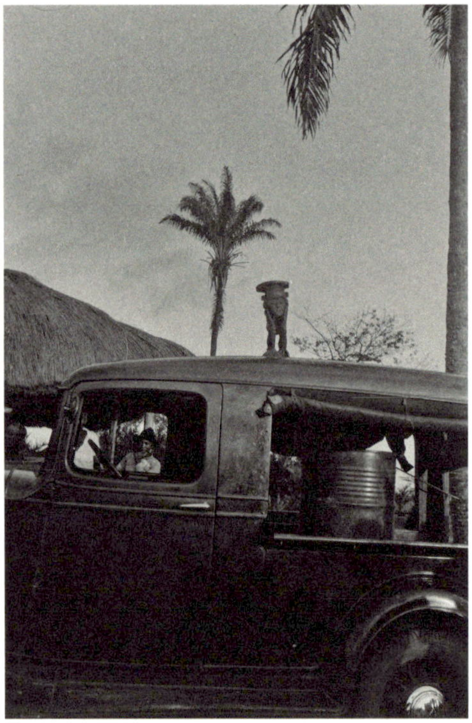
Fig. 104

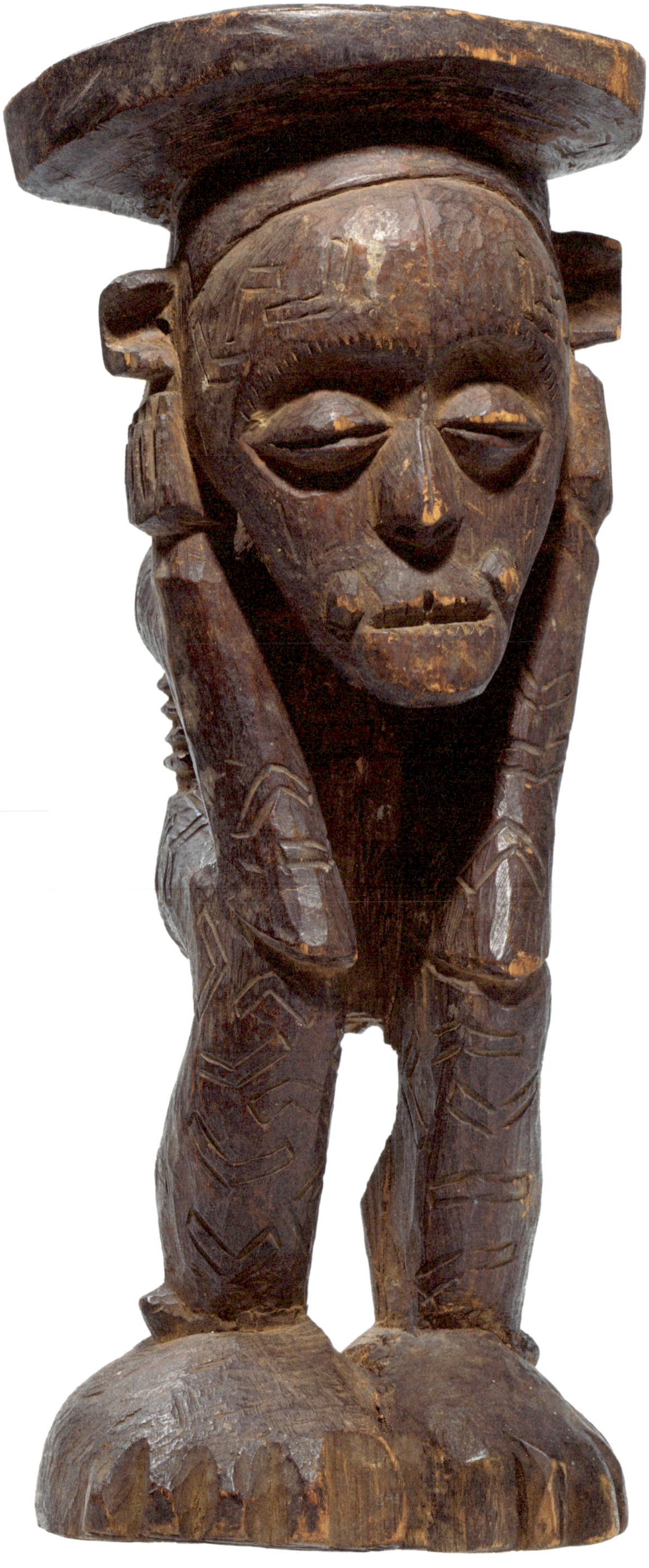
Fig. 105

Fig. 101
Artist of the eastern Pende region
***Ngolo* mask with horns**
Before 1939, wood, plant fibers, pigments, 67 × 29 × 36 cm
Museum Rietberg Zürich, HH 19
Gift of Barbara and Eberhard Fischer
Acquired by Hans Himmelheber

Fig. 102
Hans Himmelheber
Masked figure and men
Pende region, 1939, b/w negative
Museum Rietberg Zürich, FHH 190-37

Fig. 103
Hans Himmelheber
Yaka figure on car hood
Yaka region, 1938, b/w negative
Museum Rietberg Zürich, FHH 158-28

Fig. 104
Hans Himmelheber
Figure on the roof of Himmelheber's car
Luluwa region, 1939, b/w negative
Museum Rietberg Zürich, FHH 186-3

Fig. 105
Artist of the Luluwa region
Stool in the form of a human figure
Before 1939, wood, 42 × 19 × 18 cm
Museum Rietberg Zürich, 2018.110
Gift of Martin Himmelheber
Acquired by Hans Himmelheber

MAN AND MACHINE, AUTOMOBILE AND ART — "So stupid that I don't have a car. I know that there's nothing to be got from being here, but I'm stuck ..."[1]

For over half a year Hans Himmelheber tried to buy his own vehicle—to no avail. Instead he had to rely on chiefs, colonial officials, and missionaries offering him a ride. Only in January 1939 was he successful, becoming the owner of a Chevrolet 1936. Himmelheber now covers up to 270 kilometers a day on potholed roads in his search for art, systematically working his way through the road network using a map from the automobile club. On his way he takes photographs from his car of whatever he encounters, for example, a masked figure from the Pende people's *mukanda* circumcision camp [fig. 101/102].

His preoccupation with and concern about the car, which was constantly in need of repair due to the bad roads and dust, becomes the main theme in the thirty-year-old's diary. In a broader context, Himmelheber's intensive preoccupation with the car can also be situated in the contemporary zeitgeist.

In the interwar period, car rallies that crossed Africa became fashionable. Such modern versions of the nineteenth century's great expeditions symbolized the subjugation of foreign lands and the superiority of Western technology.[2] One of the most famous rallies was the *Croisière Noire*, which took eight cars from Algeria to the Cape of Good Hope on South Africa's southern tip in 1924/25. The 8,000 photographs taken during the expedition include the portrait of a woman from the Congo, Princess Nobosodrou. The picture served as the model for a well-known Art Deco hood ornament designed for Citroën by François Bazin (1897–1956).[3]

Similarly, Hans Himmelheber also adorned cars in the Congo with art. When presenting the pieces he had acquired in the Yaka region, he mounted one of the figures on the hood of a car in the style of the *Croisière Noire* car mascot and photographed it [fig. 103].[4] On another photograph leopard skins can be seen draped over the car [fig. 38]. There are other photographs of automobiles and art in Himmelheber's photographic archive, including the picture of a stool on the roof of his Chevrolet, which is now in the collection of the Museum Rietberg [figs. 104/105].
— Nanina Guyer

1 Himmelheber, diary, January 14, 1939 (archive of the Museum Rietberg).
2 Geary 2002, p. 49.
3 My thanks to Sammy Baloji for this reference.
4 The figure was later sold to Weyhe Gallery in New York. See the catalogue *African Negro Art*, Weyhe Gallery 1940.

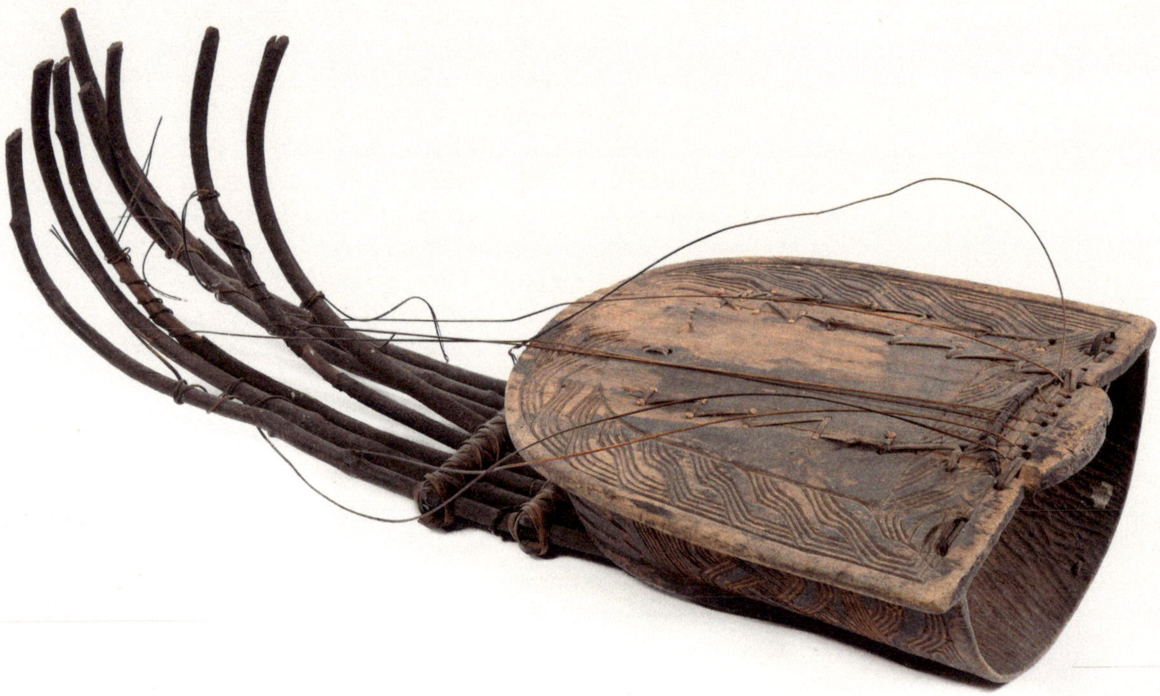

Fig. 106

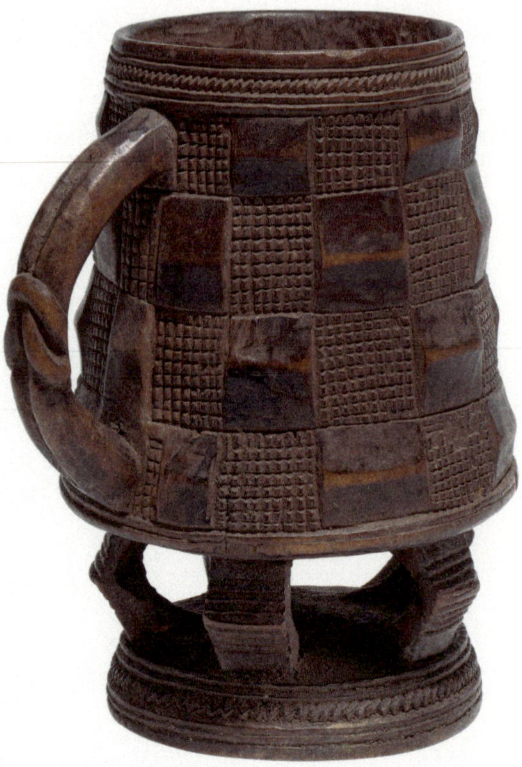

Fig. 107

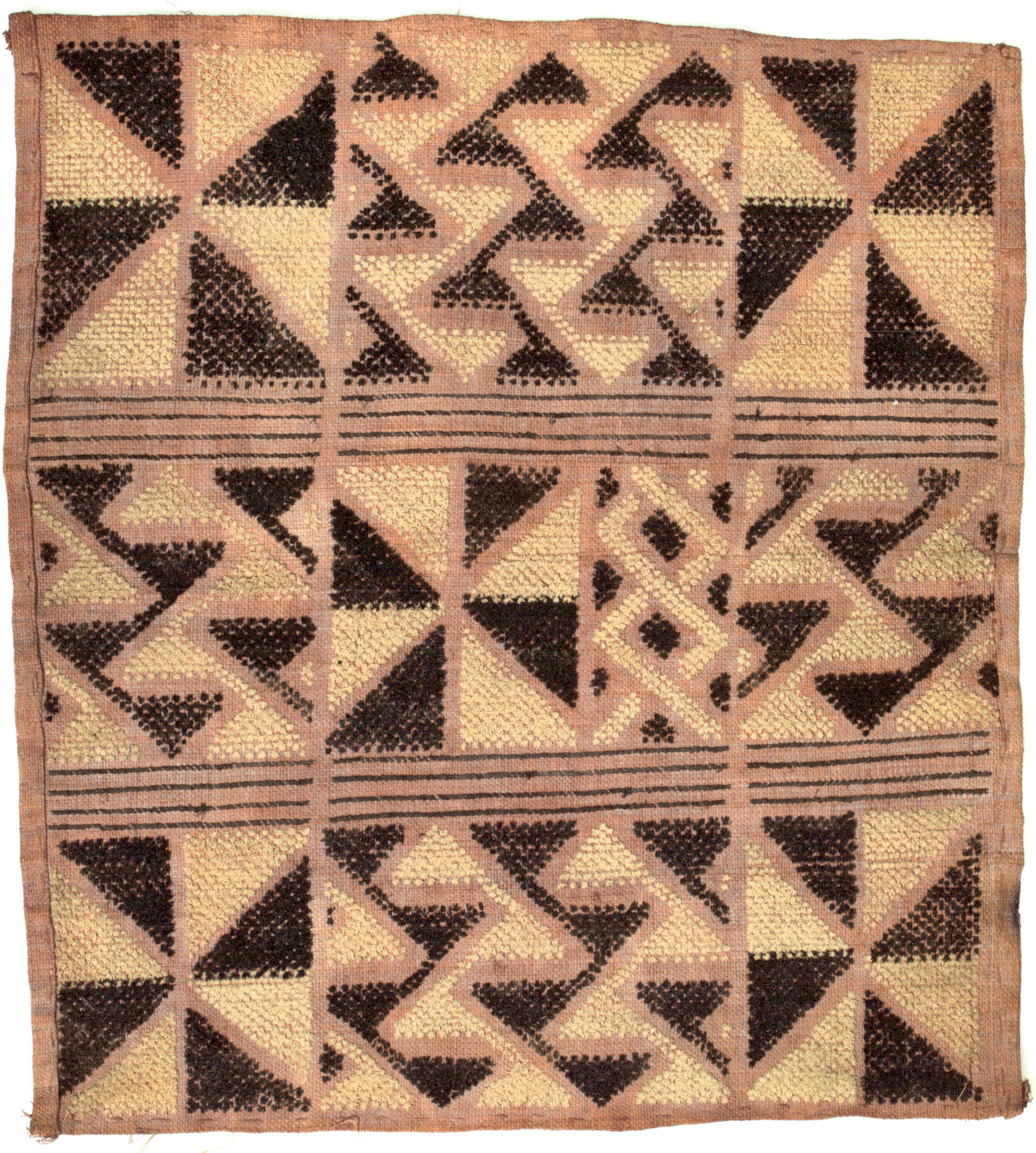

Fig. 108

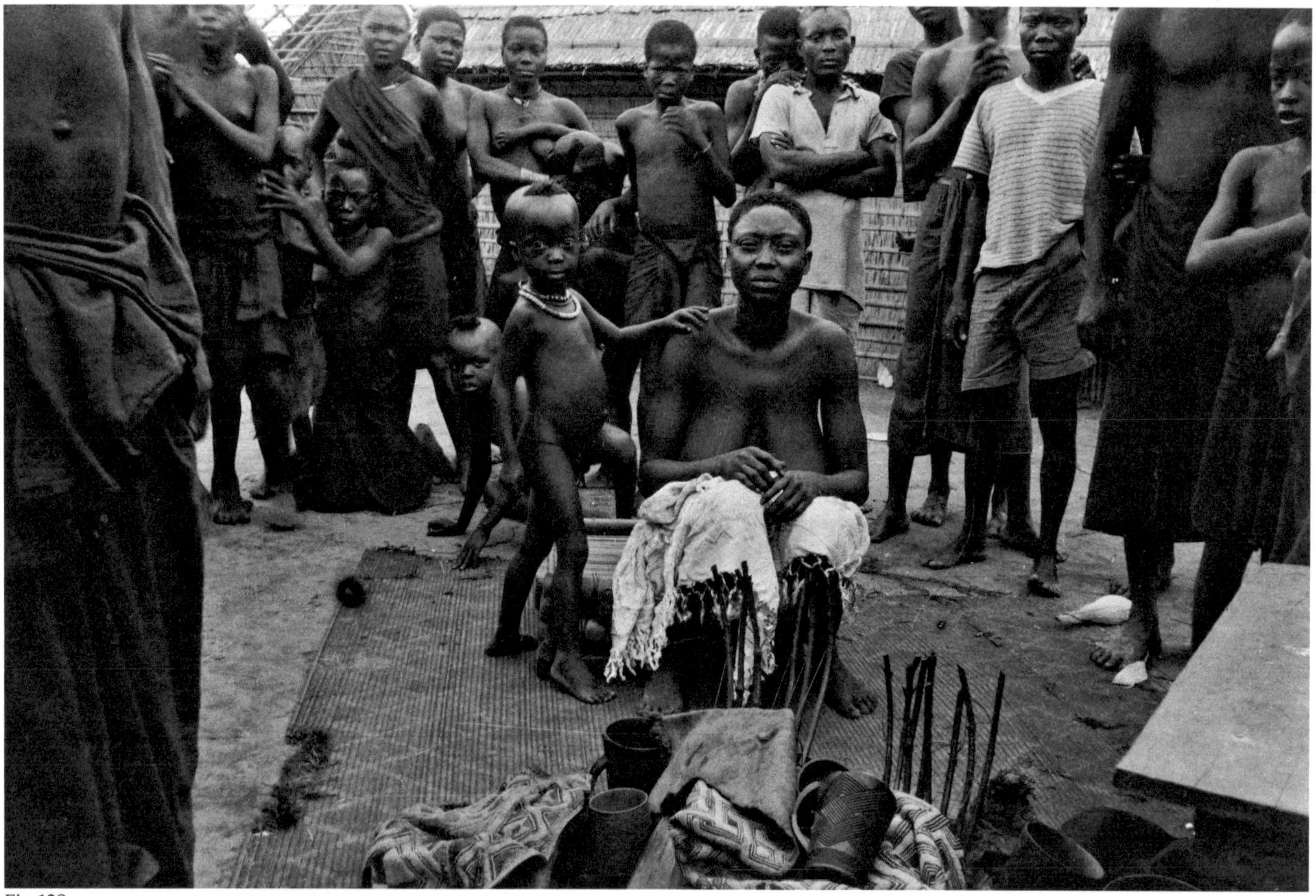

Fig. 109

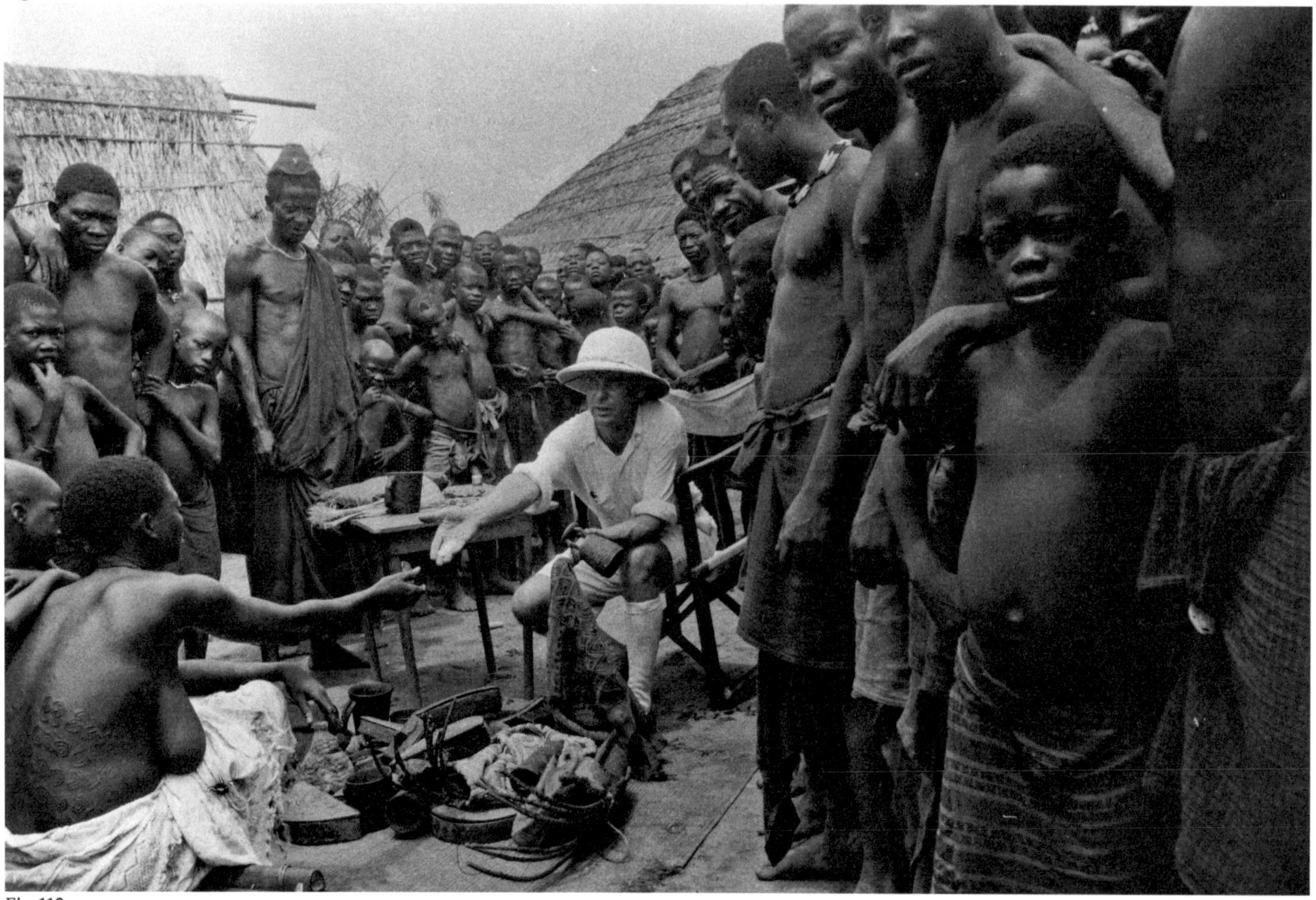

Fig. 110

Fig. 106
Artist of the Kuba region
Harp
Before 1939, wood, plant fibers, 66 × 24 × 20 cm
Museum Rietberg Zürich, 2018.101
Gift of Martin Himmelheber
Acquired by Hans Himmelheber

Fig. 107
Artist of the Kuba region
Cup for palm wine
Before 1939, wood, 19 × 15 × 12 cm
Museum Rietberg Zürich, 2018.14
Gift of Martin Himmelheber
Acquired by Hans Himmelheber

Fig. 108
Male and female artist of the Kuba region
Textile with embroidery
Before 1939, raffia, 66 × 62 cm
Museum Rietberg Zürich, 2014.138
Gift of Barbara and Eberhard Fischer
Acquired by Hans Himmelheber

Fig. 109
Hans Himmelheber
Portrait of a Kuba woman selling art with son
Kuba region, March 8, 1939, b/w negative
Museum Rietberg Zürich, FHH 185-30

Fig. 110
Hans Himmelheber
A Kuba woman and Hans Himmelheber in a staged purchasing scene
Kuba region, March 8, 1939, b/w negative
Museum Rietberg Zürich, FHH 185-35

THE FEMALE CHIEF, ART, AND PHOTOGRAPHY — In quest of everyday art, such as cups, boxes, or fabrics, Hans Himmelheber visited a large village between Mushenge and Port Francqui on March 8, 1939. There he met a female chief of the village who impressed him. Himmelheber documents this encounter in his diary:

> "She is a very impressive aristocrat, tall and reserved with elegantly lowered eyelids. She sat down in front of me. All the others have to stand, and she was greeted like the male chiefs by the assembly, with everybody kneeling down and clapping in the familiar way while she sat still and didn't reply."[1]

In the portrait Himmelheber takes of her and her son, an aloof, dignified woman looks out at us while the men in the background critically observe the goings-on [fig. 109]. Women in the Kuba region were held in high esteem and many of the artworks Himmelheber was looking for were owned by women [see essay Oberhofer]. In the village Himmelheber purchased two harps, several carved cups, crescent-shaped boxes, and raffia textiles [figs. 106–108]. Himmelheber has this transaction reenacted for a photograph and chooses the female chief as his sales partner [fig. 110]. This he also describes in his diary:

> "Afterward I tried to have a photograph taken by one of my men of me with the female chief in a staged purchasing scene. However, while the semi-educated boys did not grasp in the slightest why we were taking this photograph, she immediately understood what it was all about and stretched out her hand for the money I was offering her as if we were bargaining."[2]

The photograph shows Himmelheber sitting on a chair, a cup and textiles in his one hand, a coin in the other. The purchased works of art are spread out in front of him. The woman is seated lower than Himmelheber on a broad stool and is stretching out her hand toward the money he is offering. The male population of the village serves as a kind of frame around the main action.

This is one of the few times Himmelheber handed over his camera and had a photo taken of himself. The fact that he would do this while purchasing art, an activity to which he normally does not necessarily draw attention, is significant. What was Himmelheber's intention with this photo? Himmelheber staged the image for the readers of the magazine *Brousse*, in which he would soon publish an essay on the art of the Kuba that was targeted explicitly at the collectors of Congolese art. He also printed this picture in the essay and gave it the caption "Achat d'objets par l'auteur, chez les Bakele" ("Purchase of objects by the author from the Bakele").[3] The photograph can be viewed as a visual instruction on how to buy art "correctly," i.e., with money, publicly, and by mutual agreement.

And the woman whose name we do not know? The image can be interpreted in many different ways. Although the art was purchased and the photograph taken in a climate of general suppression, she was in fact able to increase her own standing with this performance as a salesperson and actor. — Nanina Guyer

1/2 Himmelheber, diary, March 8, 1939 (archive of the Museum Rietberg).
3 Himmelheber 1940.

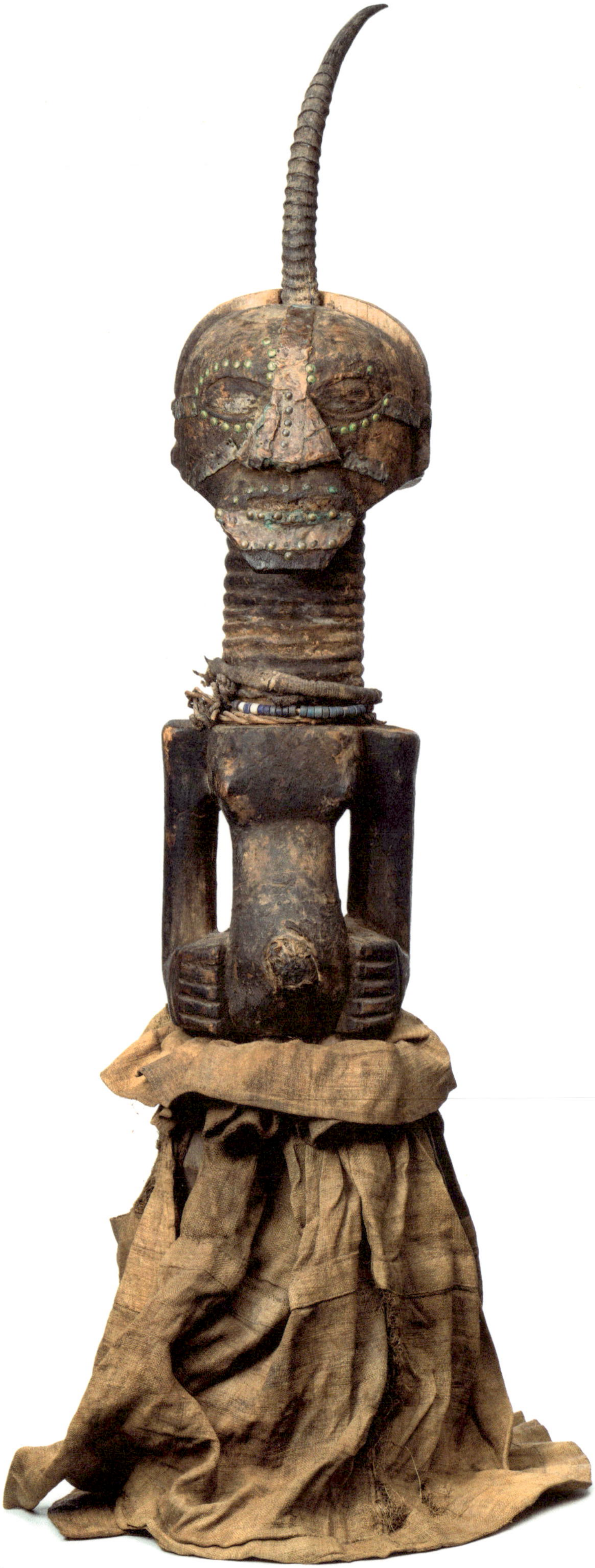

Fig. 111

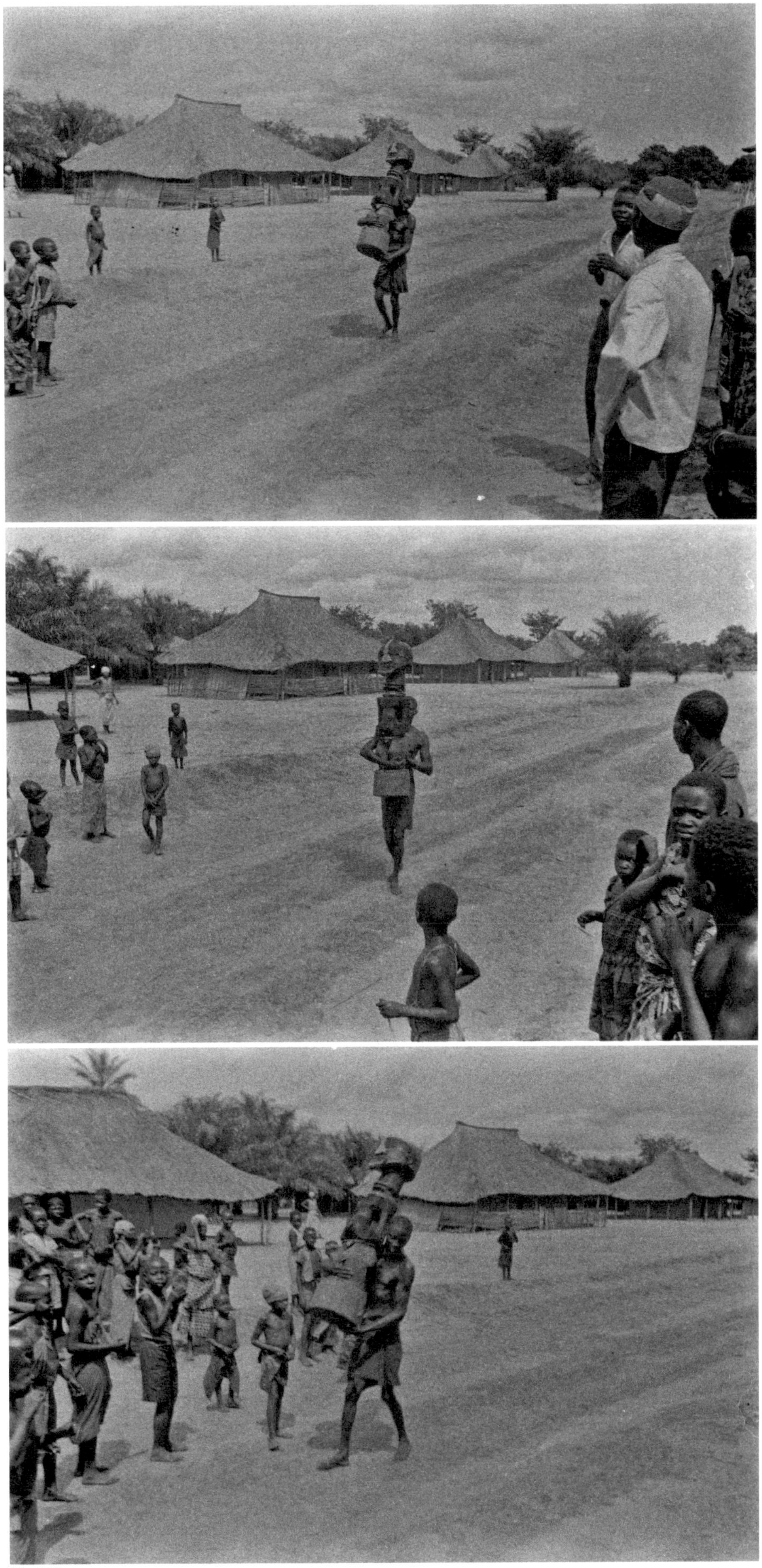

Fig. 112

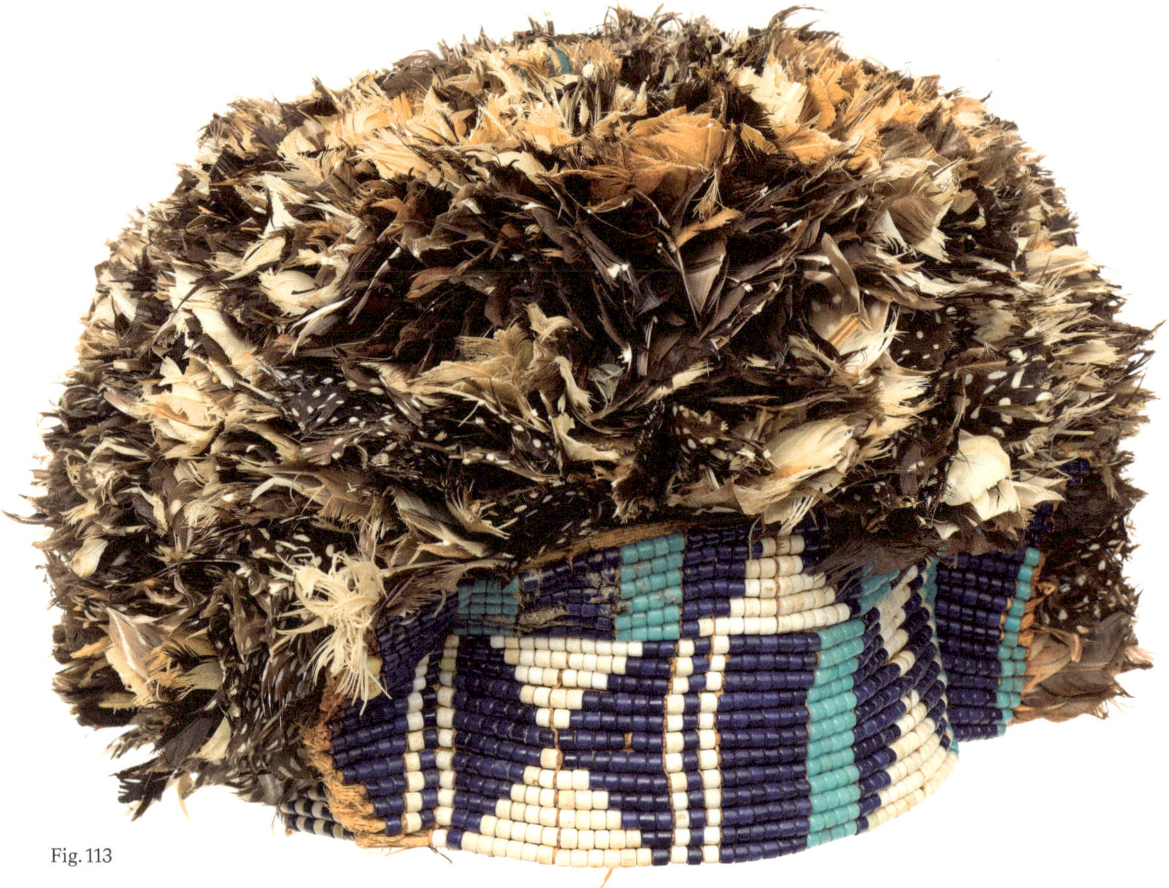

Fig. 113

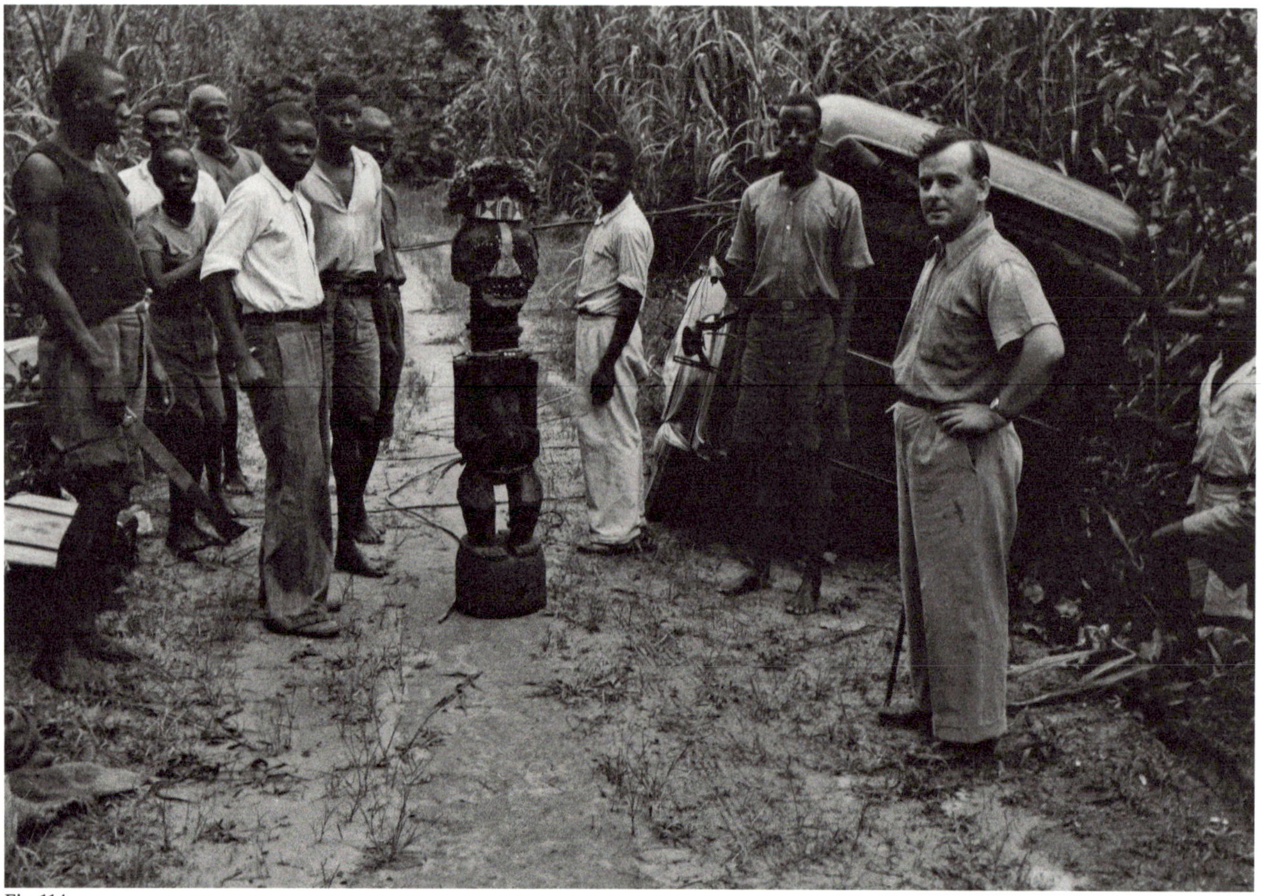

Fig. 114

Fig. 111
Artist of the Songye region
Power figure "Yankima"
Before 1939, wood, antelope horn, plant fibers, sheet copper, brass studs, snakeskin, cord, 164 × 65 × 54 cm
Museum der Kulturen Basel, III 9510
Acquired by Hans Himmelheber

Fig. 112
Hans Himmelheber
The power figure is carried over
Songye region, April 28, 1939, b/w negatives
Museum Rietberg Zürich, FHH 188-21, FHH 188-22, FHH 188-18

Fig. 113
Artist of the Songye region
Cap
Before 1939, feathers, glass beads, plant fibers, 21 × 16 × 18 cm
Museum der Kulturen Basel, III 9496
Acquired by Hans Himmelheber

Fig. 114
Hans Himmelheber
The Chevrolet in a ditch, the figure in focus
Songye region, 1939, b/w negative
Museum Rietberg Zürich, FHH 188-23

FROM POWER FIGURE TO MUSEUM PIECE: THE TURBULENT HISTORY OF "MITEMBE'S YANKIMA" [1] — Hans Himmelheber's archive offers the opportunity to link together objects, photographs, and texts to create object biographies. This can be demonstrated by the example of the power figure called Yankima [fig. 111]. From Himmelheber we know that this imposing and unusually large figure's task was to help Chief Mitembe's village to produce a large number of children. He states: "They literally say he brings the children into the world."[2] It follows that the object was a charged figure that was believed to have agency. The materials affixed to the figure like copper, upholstery nails, beads, snakeskin, or the medicine in its navel served to activate the object [cf. the essay by Oberhofer/Mannes/Stenger]. According to Himmelheber, as a rule he was only able to purchase power figures that had become ineffective.[3]

Hans Himmelheber bought the Yankima figure from Chief Mitembe on April 28, 1939 in a village on the main road not far from Kabinda. Like a film sequence, he documents how the figure is carried along the main road [fig. 112, see also p. 222]. The ethnologist leaves the village around three o'clock. Beforehand he is warned that there is disagreement in the village about whether the Yankima's power really has expired.[4] Shortly afterward, his vehicle leaves the road and slides into a ditch. In his diary he writes: "The natives said to themselves that it was because the great Mukishi doesn't want to let me cross the bridge (twenty meters away)."[5]

The scene with the car in the ditch is also captured by Himmelheber on camera [fig. 114]. The photograph shows a missionary who has rushed to his aid with personnel, the unloaded car, and the large figure in focus. For the photo the figure has been adorned with an unusual cap made of glass beads and clipped feathers, only two examples of which Himmelheber encounters on his travels [fig. 113].[6]

Hans Himmelheber acquired the figure for the Museum der Kulturen in Basel. A comparison between its modern-day appearance and the way it looked in 1939 reveals that it was further manipulated after its arrival at the museum in Basel. Today the power figure wears a raffia skirt and an antelope horn that has been affixed to its head the wrong way around. As such the figure has been aligned with Western notions of the artistic canon of Songye figures, which are customarily adorned in this way.[7] — Nanina Guyer

1 Himmelheber, diary, May 12, 1939 (archive of the Museum Rietberg).
2 Index card III 9510, (archive of the Museum der Kulturen Basel).
3 Index card III 9510, (archive of the Museum der Kulturen Basel).
4 Himmelheber 1960, p. 406.
5 Himmelheber, diary, April 28, 1939 (archive of the Museum Rietberg).
6 Index card III 9496, (archive of the Museum der Kulturen Basel).
7 Index card III 9510, (archive of the Museum der Kulturen Basel).

EVOLVE: MEMORIES OF AN *ÉVOLUÉ*

Michèle Magema

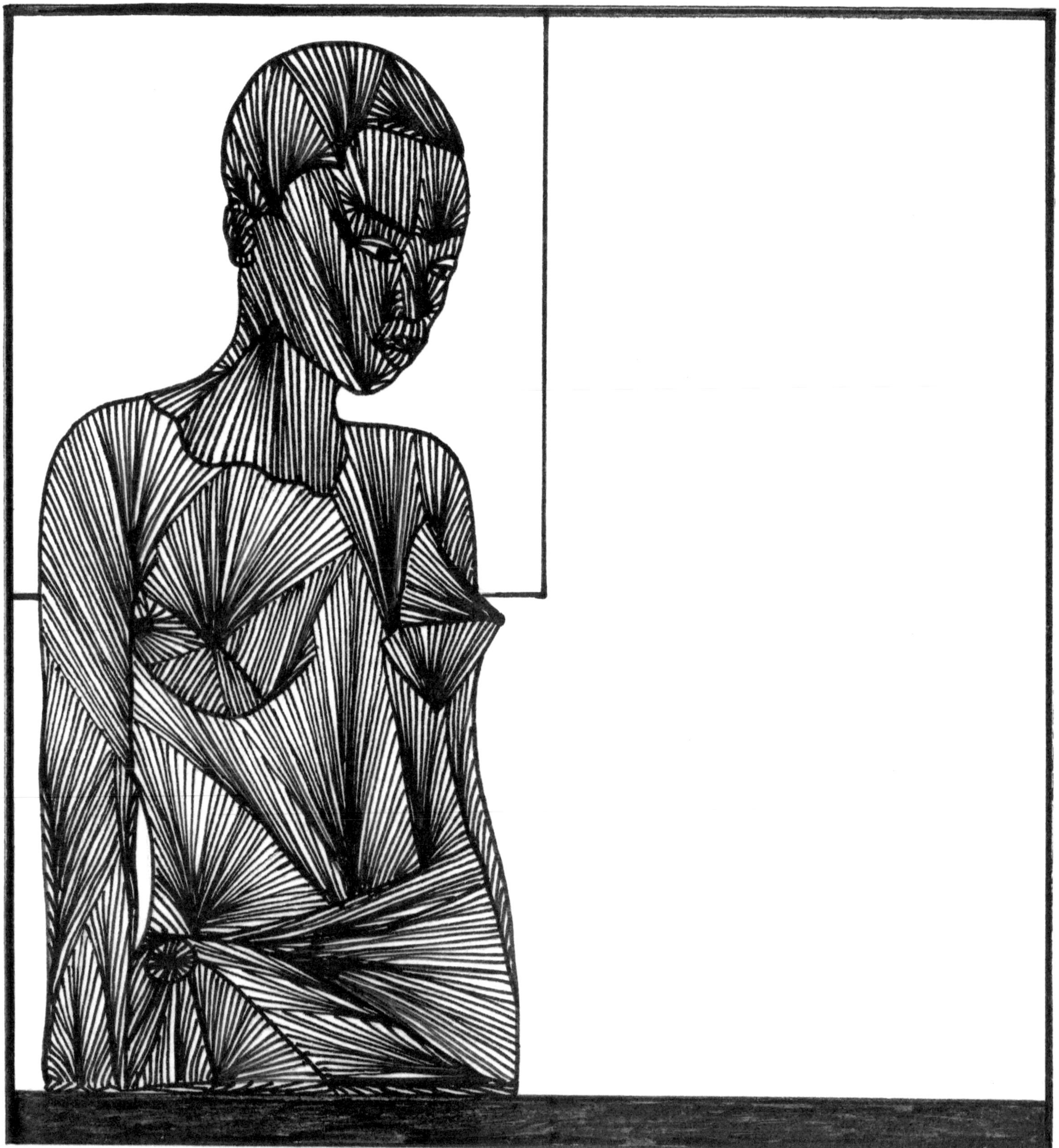

Fig. 115

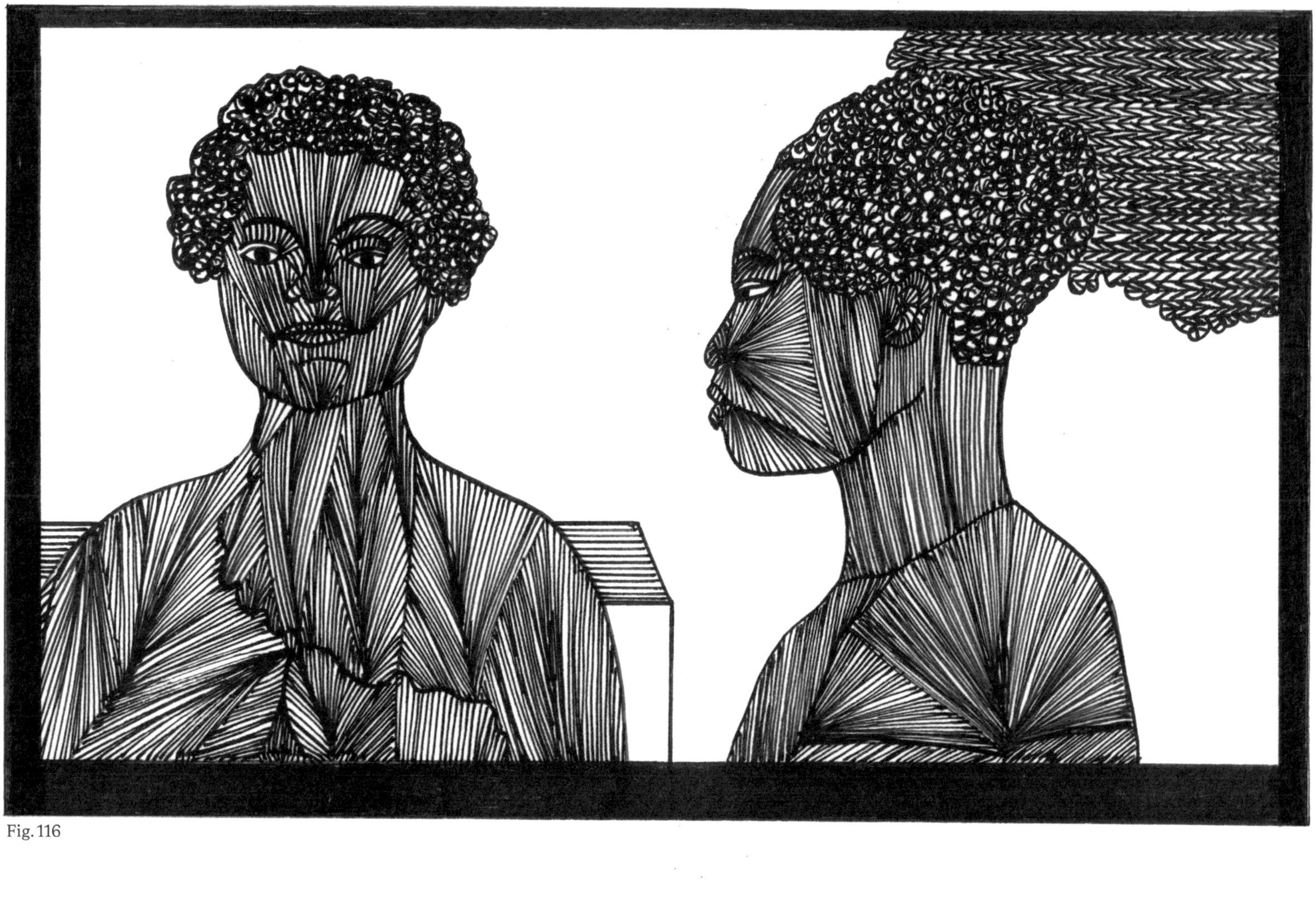

Fig. 116

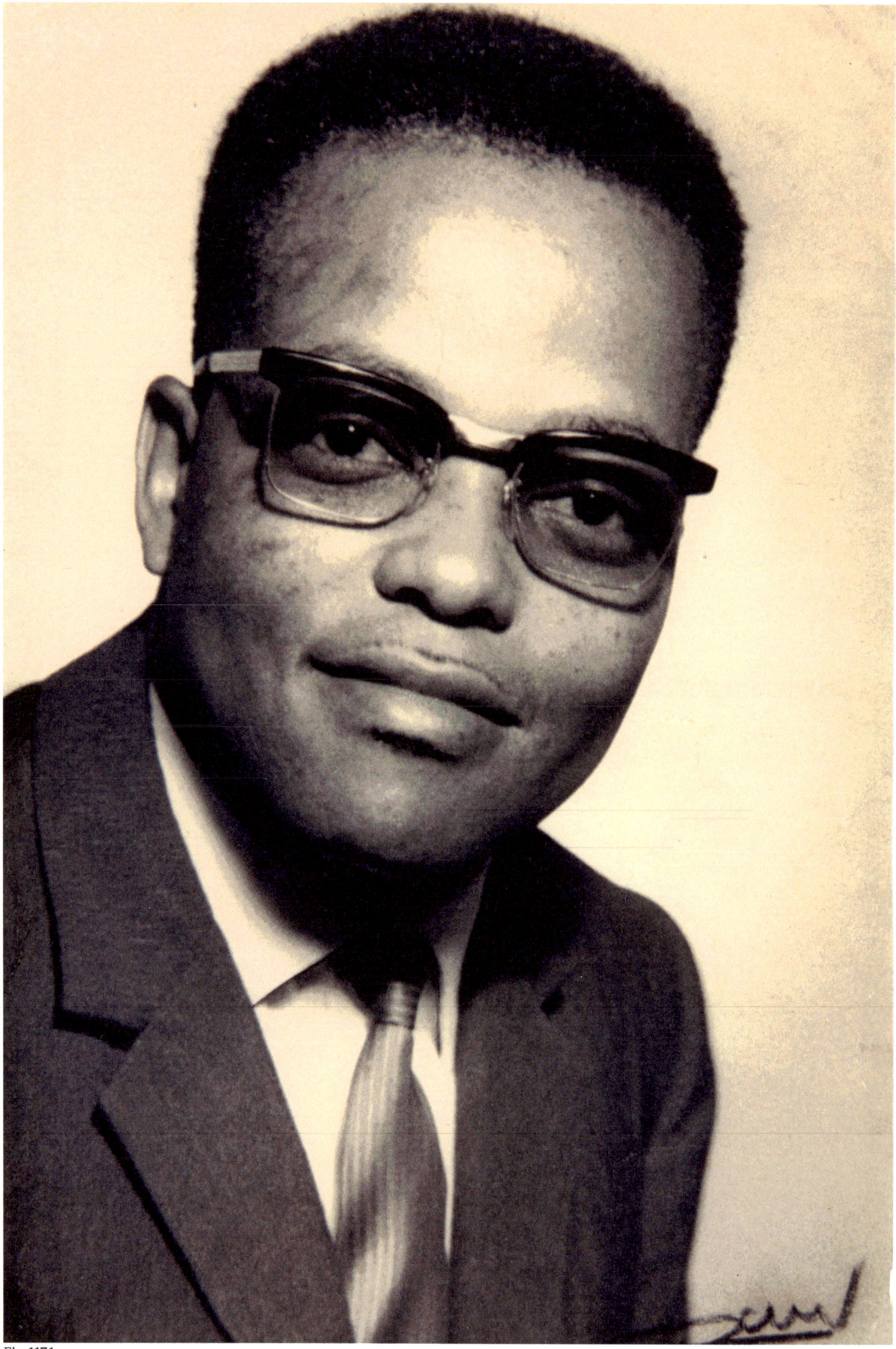

Fig. 117.1

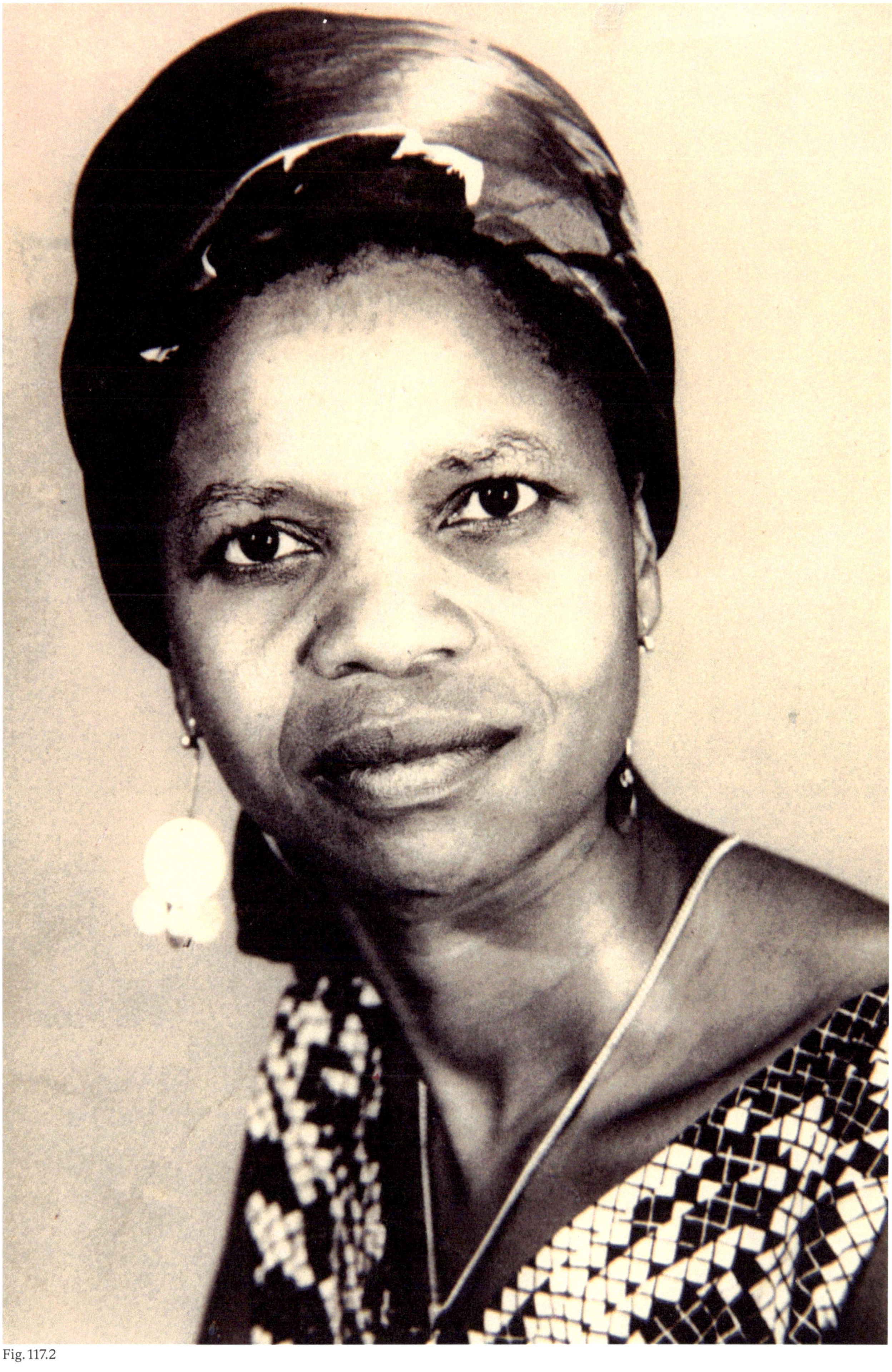

Fig. 117.2

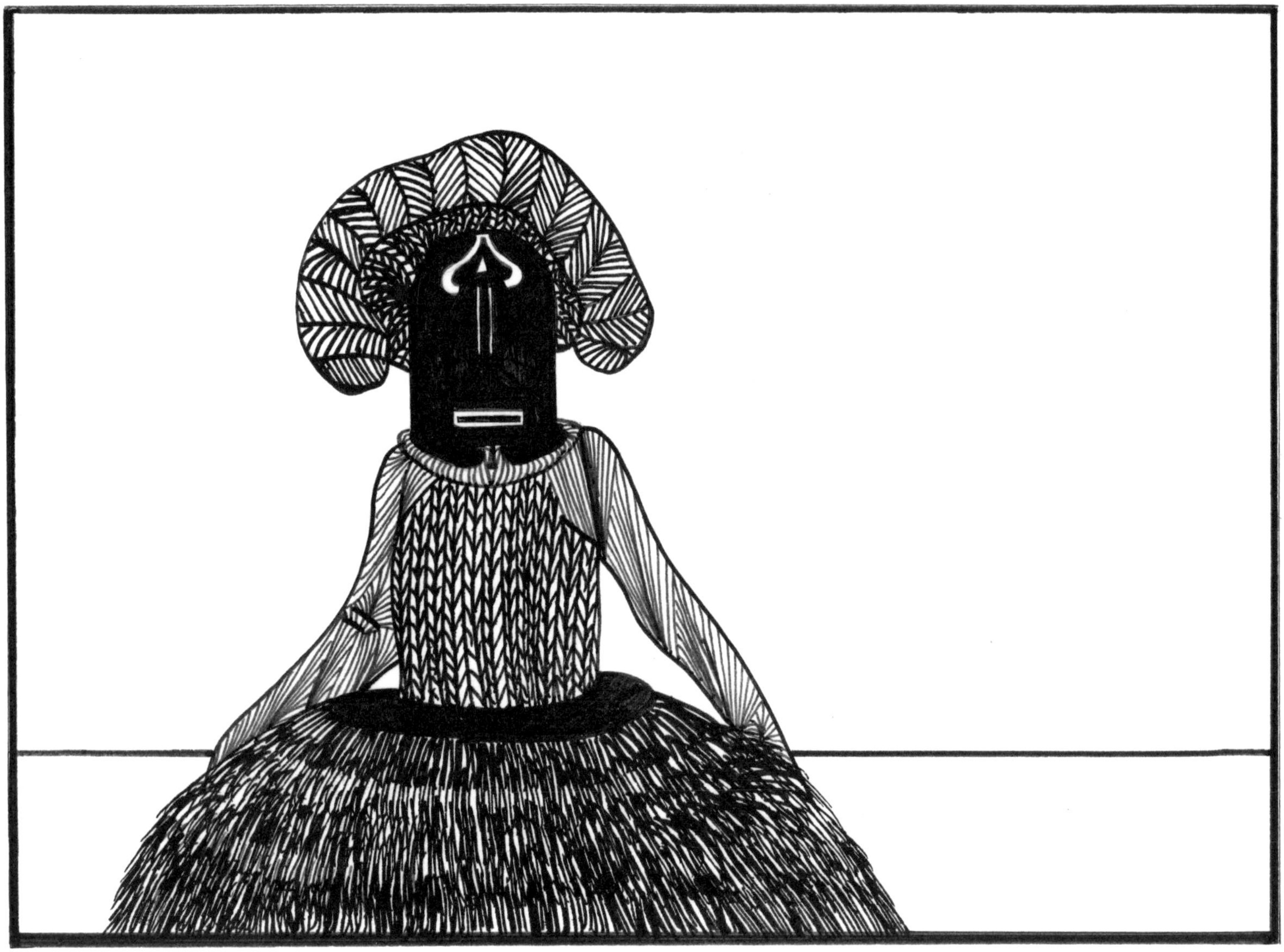

Fig. 118

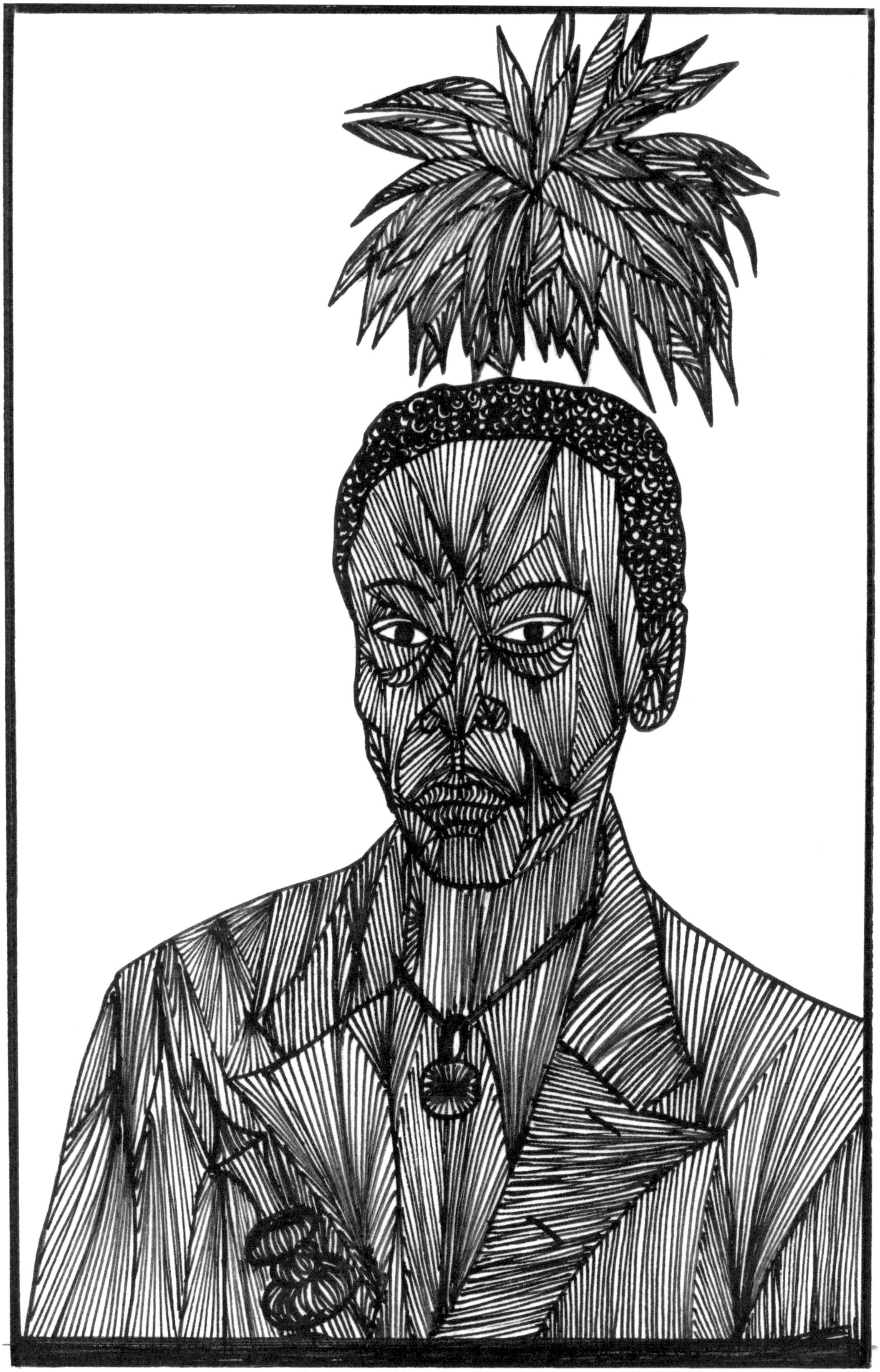
Fig. 119

Fig. 115/116/118/119
Michèle Magema
EVOLVE
2019, drawings
Michèle Magema, commissioned by Museum Rietberg Zürich

Fig. 117
Studio Photo Guye, Kinshasa
Malongo Isaac Magema and Ndenga Mpuntu Marie
1967, photo paper, 20 × 30 cm
Personal archive – Michèle Magema

Fig. 120
Hans Himmelheber
Portrait of a young woman
Kuba region, January 1939, b/w negative
Museum Rietberg Zürich, FHH 182-13

Fig. 121
Hans Himmelheber
Women with traditional hairstyles
Kuba region, February 2, 1939, b/w negative
Museum Rietberg Zürich, FHH 185-8

Fig. 122
Hans Himmelheber
***Chihongo* guardian mask**
Lele region, January 6, 1939, b/w negative
Museum Rietberg Zürich, FHH 178-32

Fig. 123
Hans Himmelheber
Chief with feather cap and sword
Yaka region, 1938, b/w negative
Museum Rietberg Zürich, FHH 155-23

In *Le Monde d'hier: Souvenirs d'un Européen*, Stefan Zweig traces the destiny of a generation brutally confronted with a changing history and to some extent with the failure of civilization. The conflicts in Germany, which would change Europe with the Second World War, climaxed in 1938. Hans Himmelheber carried out his ethnological journey to the Belgian Congo in this charged situation, in 1938/39. At this point in time, when colonial ideology had reached its peak, racist thinking dominated, which preached the inequality of colonists and the colonized.

In 1938/39 Michèle Magema's grandfather Malongo Isaac Magema was twenty years old and worked for the Belgian Congo administration, where he strove to become what was known by the colonial government and the colonized population as an *évolué*. Did Hans Himmelheber and Malongo Magema cross paths in Congo? No! So what sort of view could an ethnologist have had of a colonized civilization while his own was in the process of sinking? What sort of opinion, as a future *évolué*, could Malongo Magema have been expected to form of Hans Himmelheber?

For the exhibition *Congo as Fiction*, Michèle Magema has chosen to create an installation that explores the complex legacies from the Belgian colonization on the *évolué* generation. Michèle Magema has delved into the ethnologist Hans Himmelheber's photographs and created an installation combining drawings, photographs, and texts.

The *EVOLVE* project explores the years 1938/39 within a colonial context and, in doing so, connects Himmelheber's ethnologic travels and the history of the Magema family. The artist gathers therein Himmelheber's ethnological photographs, her own drawings, photographs of her (educated) grandparents, and pieces written by her father, the son of an *évolué*.

The drawings are inspired by Hans Himmelheber's photographs, including the one from the *Zaire* catalogue, 1938–1939 [figs. 120–123]. Each photograph is drawn in Indian ink. The drawings are always composed of tightly drawn continuous lines depicting bodies or spaces. Each of these scarrings of the "paper/skin" is evidence of the artist's repeated gesture. Michèle Magema draws as if carrying out a ritual designed to repair a truncated, forgotten, obliterated ... colonized history.

"At that time being an *évolué* was the tops! We knew our *évolué* parents were going to wrest the country from the whites." — Dieudonné Isaac Magema

"I did not inherit any of the pride my father might have felt during the colonial period, I did not inherit the shame of being the granddaughter of an *évolué*. I feel neither shame nor pride. I incorporate the plurality of my forebears—they are what makes me who I am. My name is Malongo, like my grandfather. This Christian name has been passed down to me along with a thirst for knowledge, a constant need to question the world and its societal components, and art has become their permanent receptacle." — Michèle Magema

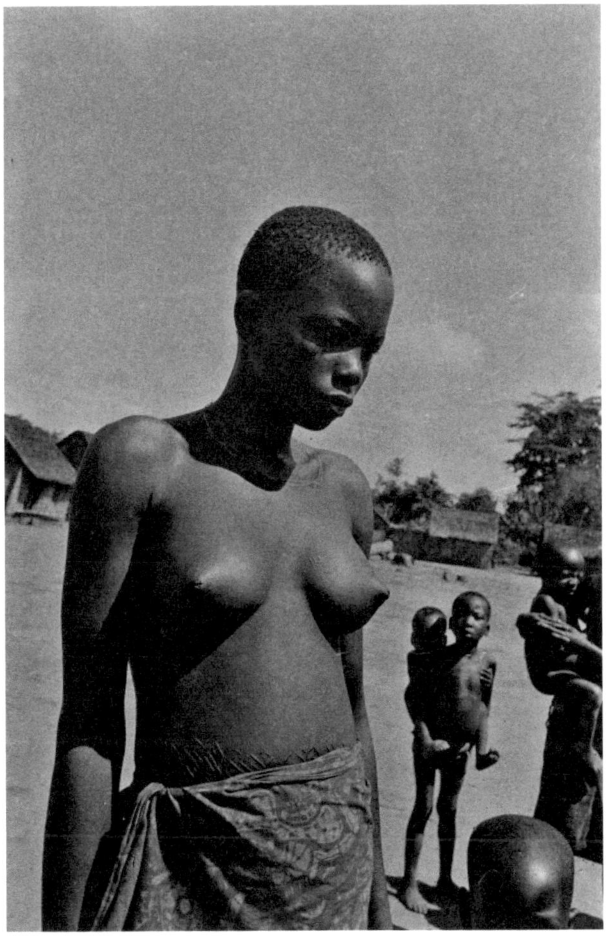
Fig. 120

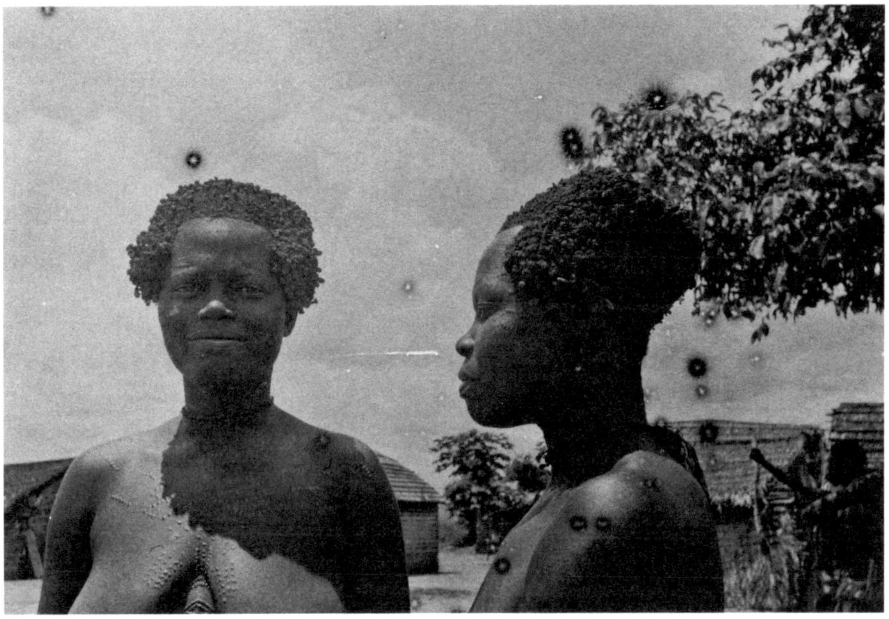
Fig. 121

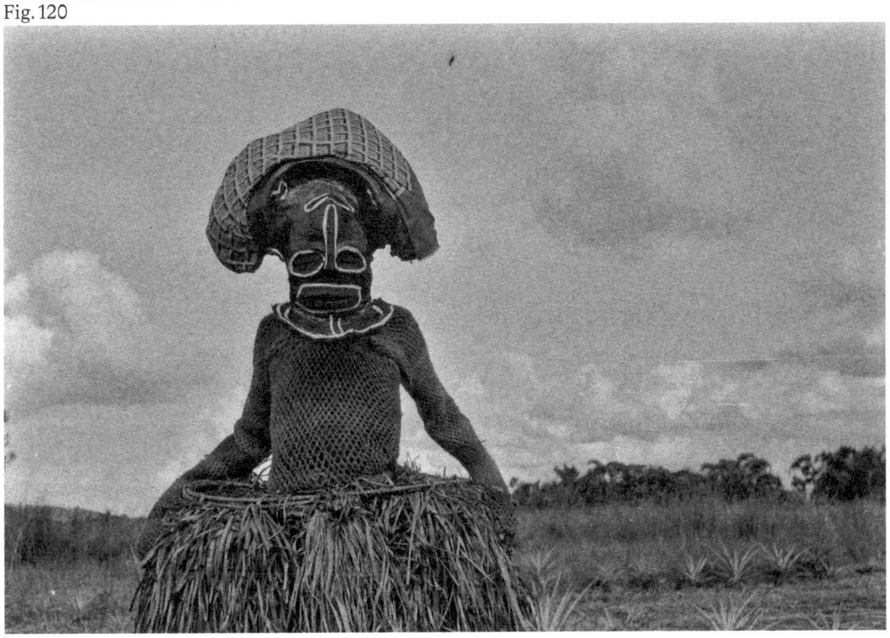
Fig. 122

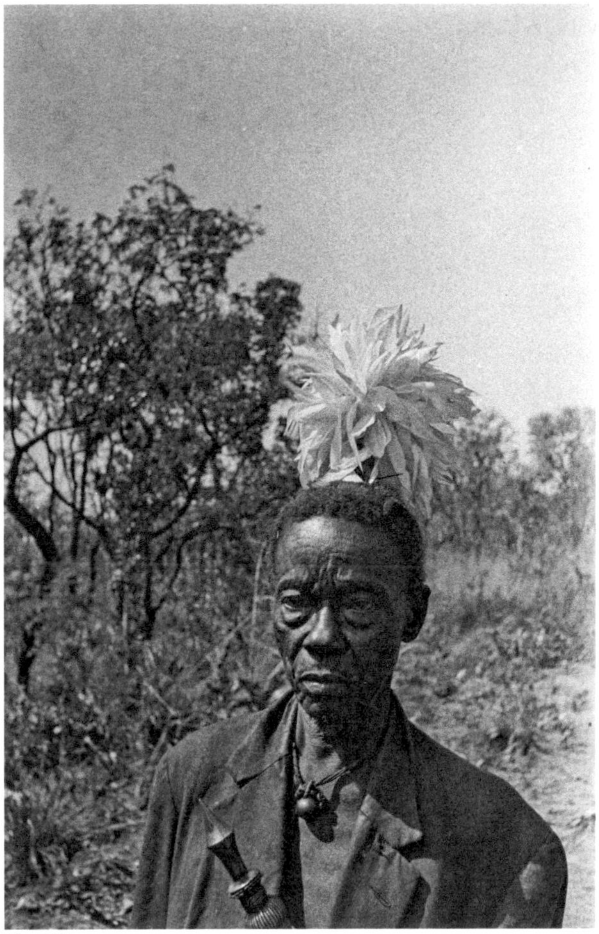
Fig. 123

BLACKOUT POETRY, IDEA'S GENEALOGY

David Shongo

Fig. 124.1

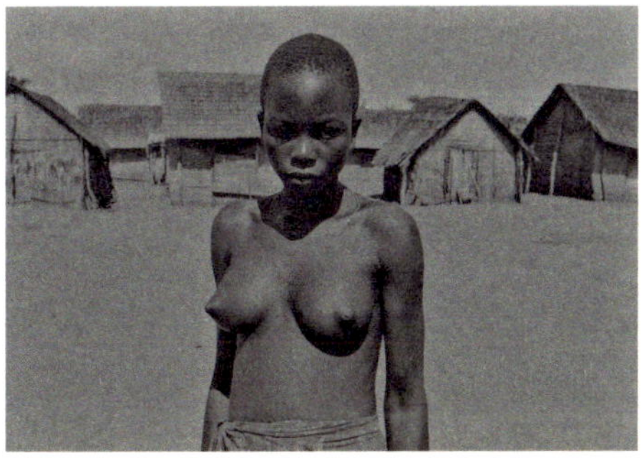
Fig. 124.2

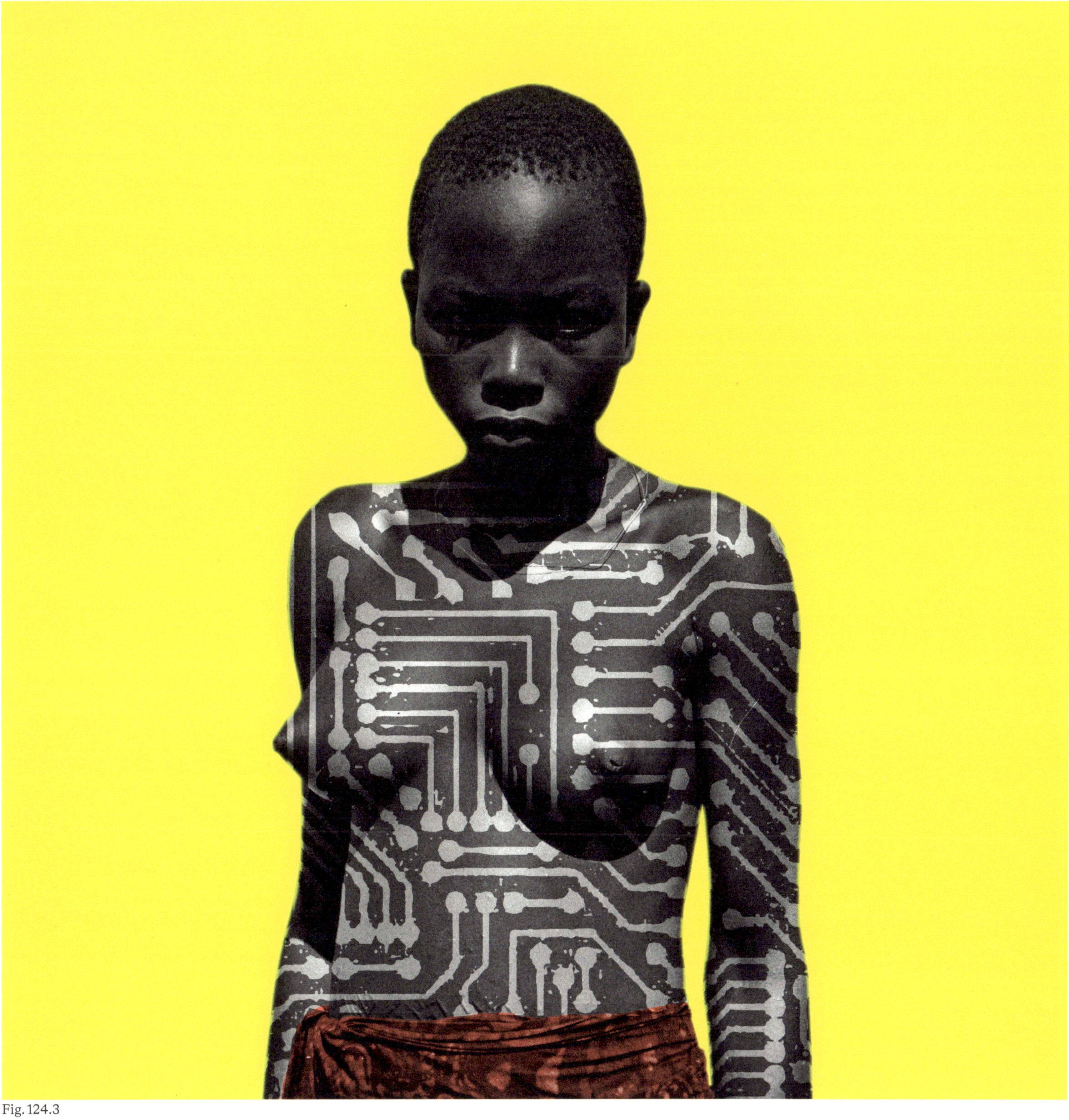
Fig. 124.3

I was in contact with the archives at the Salesians of Don Bosco in Lubumbashi for the first time in 2017. At that time, I began my research on the link between languages and ethnic musical harmonies of the Congo. Father Léon Verbeek, with whom I worked, had presented to me the hunting songs of southeastern Upper Katanga also preserved at the AfricaMuseum in Tervuren, and photos of the colonial era. After listening to the songs and seeing the pictures, I was fascinated as a musician, composer, and visual artist, to see how the contents of the archives were 'encrypting' and complex for me. Very quickly, my research turned to the issue of the decomposition of memory and the colonial inheritance. That is how I started to focus on super-centenary archives. By this, I mean archives of the Congo that have lived and carried data of 100 years or more.

For me, archives are not only tools that carry values and information, but are also benchmarks for understanding problems related to the colonial past. They are traces of history and a guiding thread back and forth. In parallel, they served and serve colonialist and anti-colonialist propaganda and continue to be used to shape the image of Congo in the world. As a Congolese artist, manipulating archives thus amounts to disrupting the psychology of thinking about the colonial Congolese image constructed by colonial narratives.

It was in this process that I first became interested in the photographs of Himmelheber. Himmelheber's photographs, in particular, carry an interesting contradiction. Although this material expresses the will to highlight the art and the people photographed, it still inherently carries Himmelheber's colonial gaze. It is from this perspective that I began to break down the colonial perspective on the photos, erase it in order to leave the photos a power of questioning, and also build a genealogy of ideas from these photos. — David Shongo

Fig. 124.1+3
David Shongo
Bugs
From the series *BLACKOUT POETRY, IDEA'S GENEAOLOGY*
Lubumbashi, 2019, digital print on aluminium, David Shongo, commissioned by Museum Rietberg Zürich

Fig. 124.2
Hans Himmelheber
Portrait of a young woman
Kuba region, January 1939, b/w negative
Museum Rietberg Zürich, FHH 182-11

Fig. 125.1
Hans Himmelheber
Dignitary
Yaka region, 1938, b/w negative
Museum Rietberg Zürich, FHH 163-35

Fig. 125.2
David Shongo
Colonial Binary
From the series *BLACKOUT POETRY, IDEA'S GENEAOLOGY*
Lubumbashi, 2019, digital print on aluminium, David Shongo, commissioned by Museum Rietberg Zürich

Fig. 126.1
Hans Himmelheber
Woman with cartridge cases as necklace
Yaka region, 1938, b/w negative
Museum Rietberg Zürich, FHH 158-10

Fig. 126.2
David Shongo
Ma Nkaki
From the series *BLACKOUT POETRY, IDEA'S GENEAOLOGY*
Lubumbashi, 2019, digital print on aluminium, David Shongo, commissioned by Museum Rietberg Zürich

Fig. 127.1
Hans Himmelheber
Male portrait
Pende/Chokwe-Region, 24.5.1939, b/w negative
Museum Rietberg Zürich, FHH 190-35

Fig. 127.2
David Shongo
Untitled
From the series *BLACKOUT POETRY, IDEA'S GENEAOLOGY*
Lubumbashi, 2019, digital print on aluminium, David Shongo, commissioned by Museum Rietberg Zürich

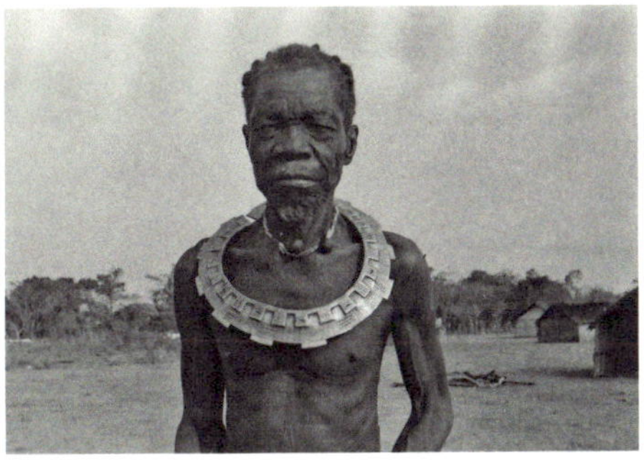

Fig. 125.1

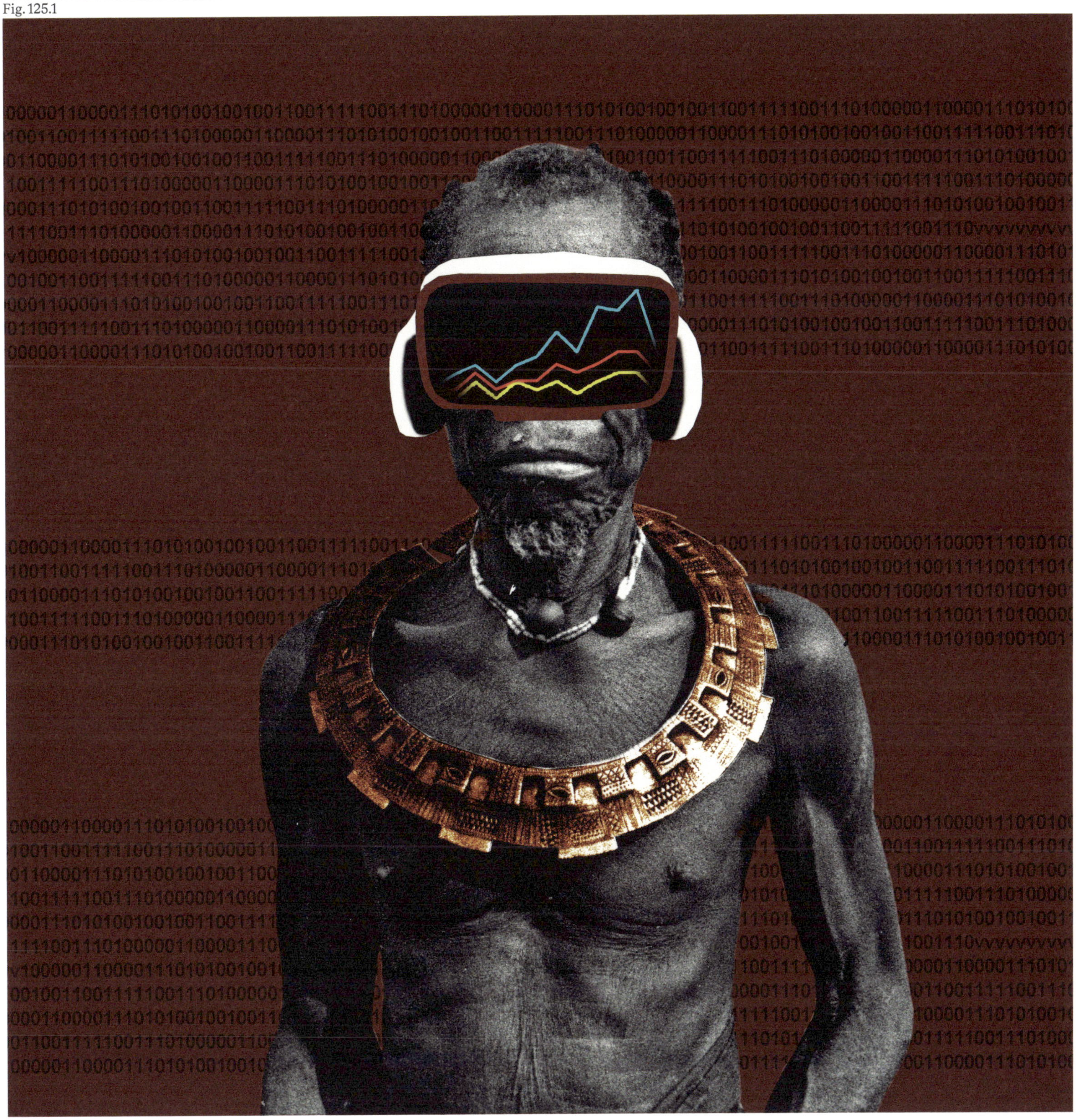

Fig. 125.2

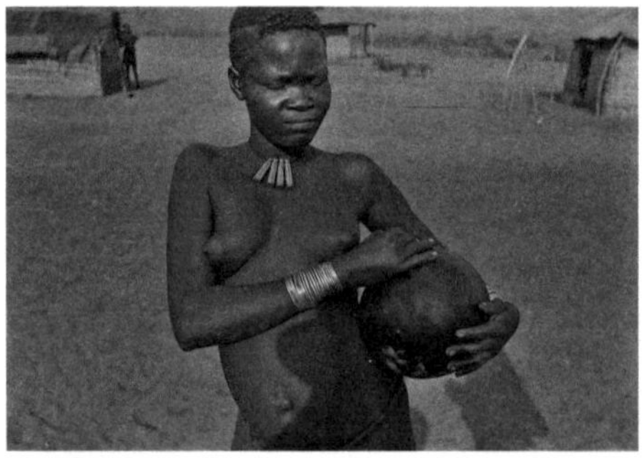

Fig. 126.1

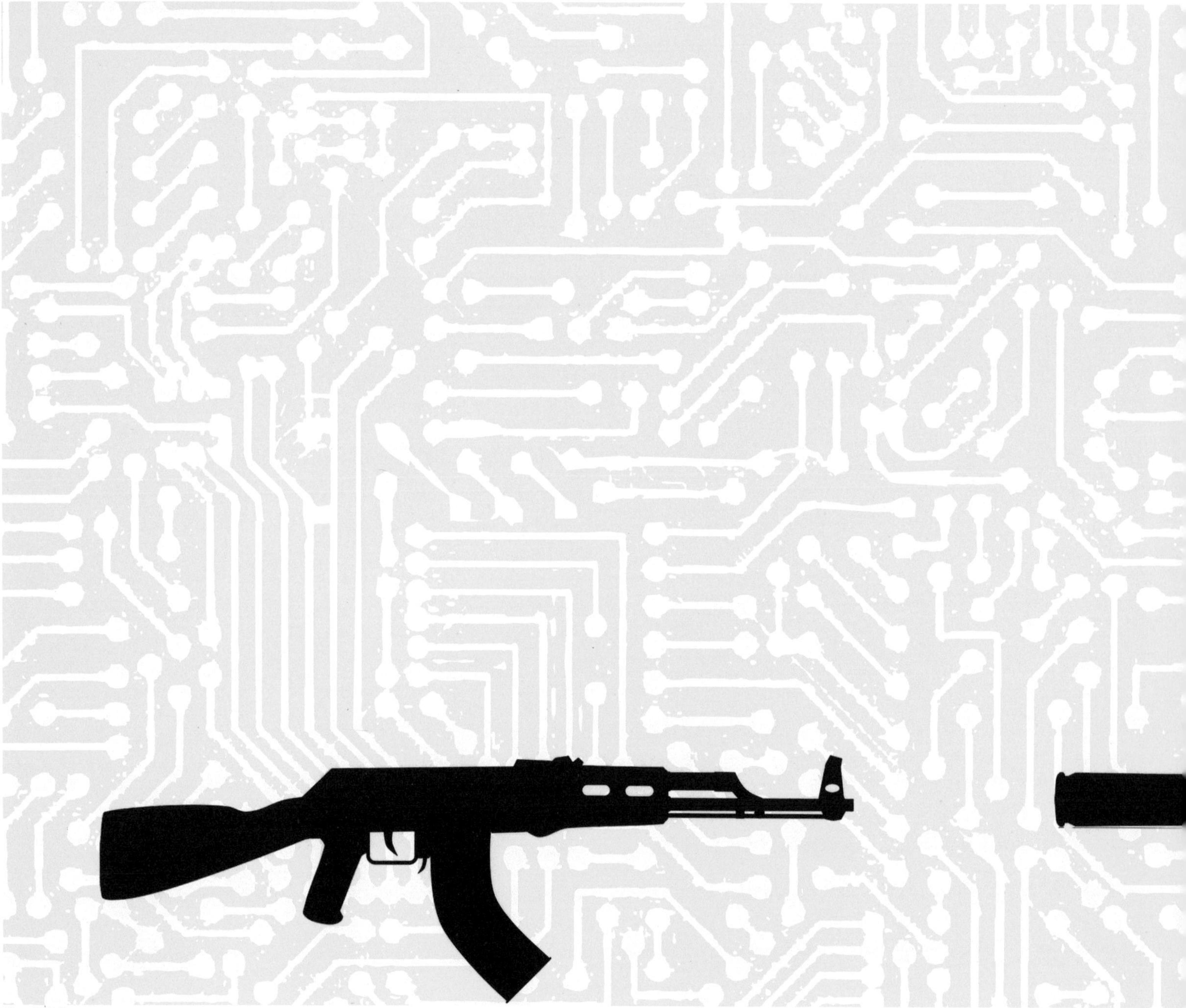

Fig. 126.2

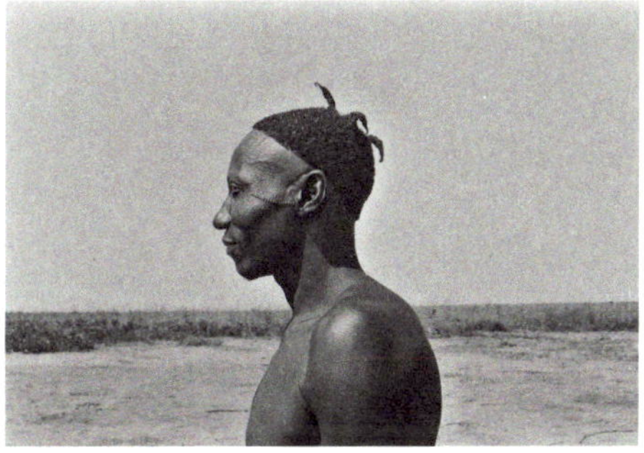

Fig. 127.1

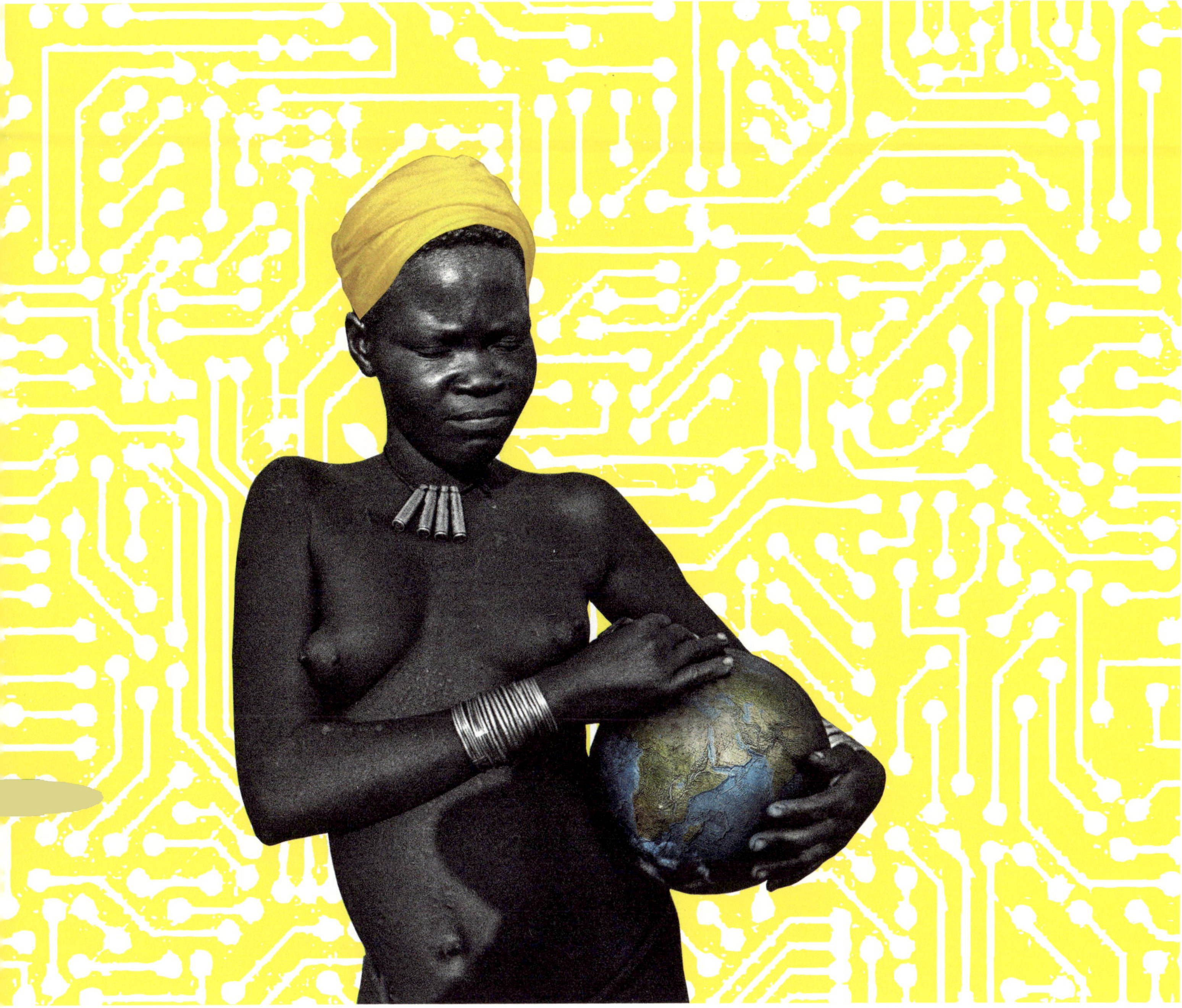

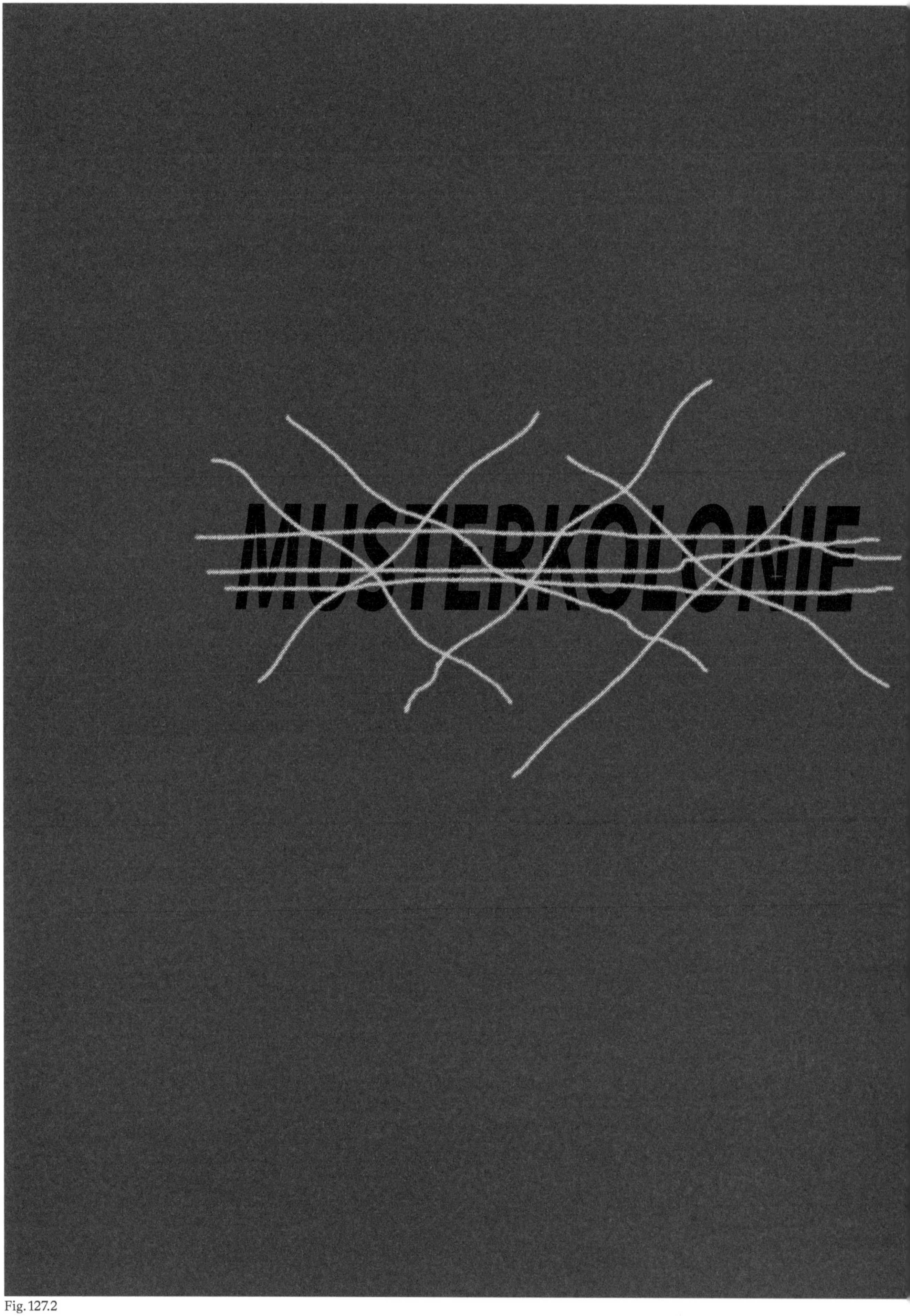

Fig. 127.2

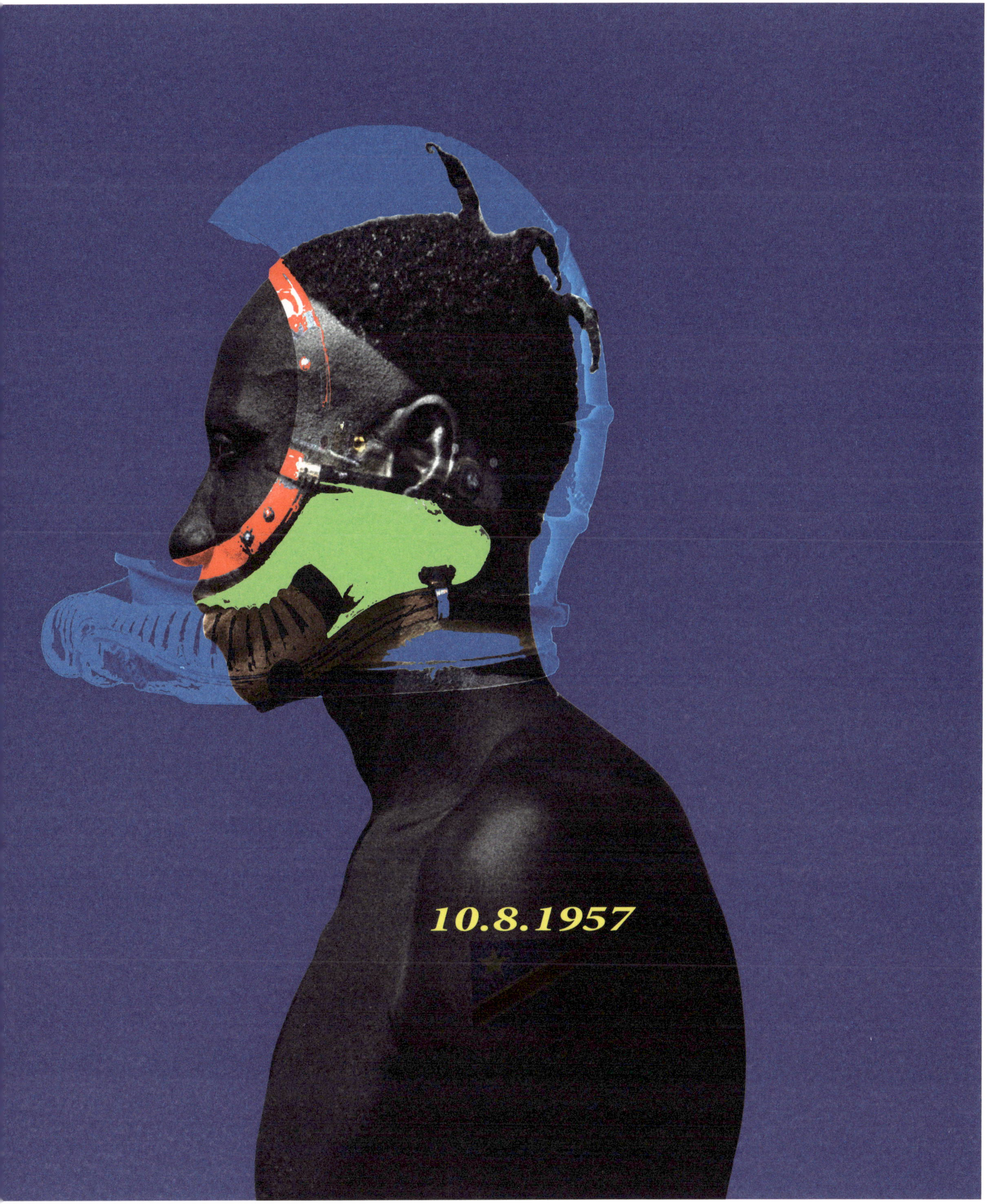
10.8.1957

DESIGN AND ELEGANCE

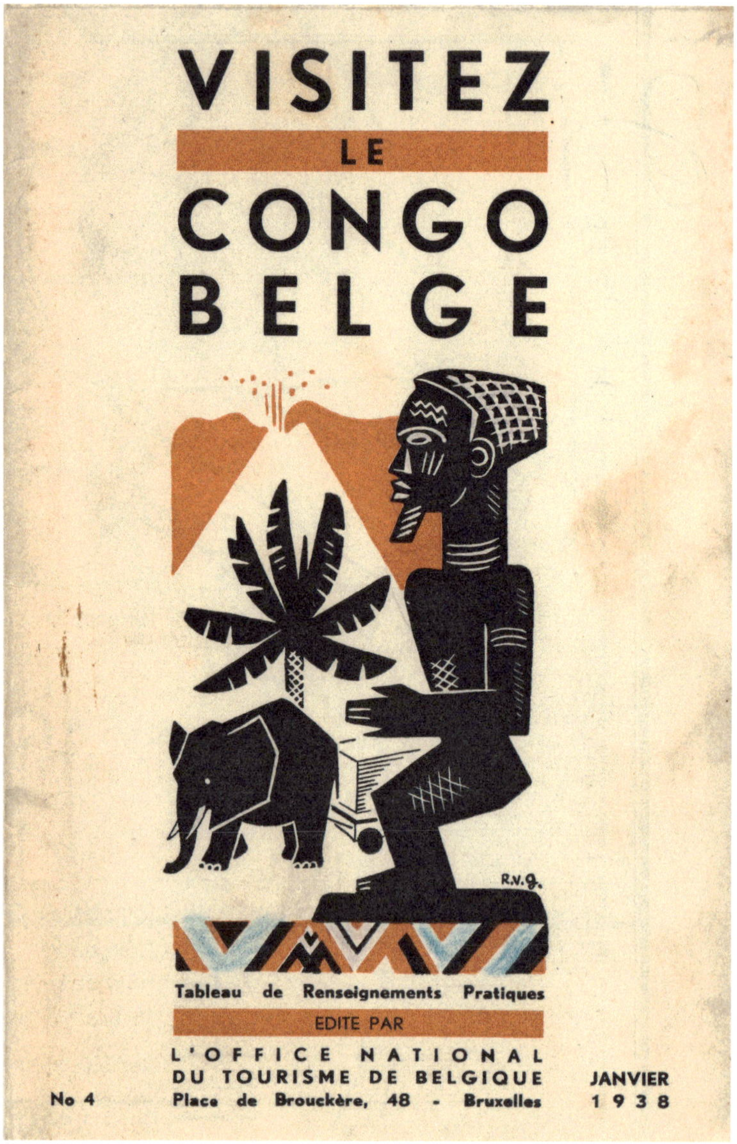
VISITEZ
LE
CONGO
BELGE
R.V.G.
Tableau de Renseignements Pratiques
EDITE PAR
L'OFFICE NATIONAL
DU TOURISME DE BELGIQUE
Place de Brouckère, 48 - Bruxelles
No 4
JANVIER
1938
Fig. 128

Fig. 128
Roger van Gindertael
Visitez le Congo belge
DR Congo, 1928, lithograph on paper
Courtesy Christraud M. Geary
Christraud M. Geary Collection

PERPETUATING A MYTH: IMAGES FROM THE KUBA KINGDOM AND WESTERN FANTASIES (1920s TO 1950s)

Christraud M. Geary

In January of 1938, five months before Hans Himmelheber embarked on his collecting endeavor to Central Africa, the *L'Office national du tourisme de Belgique* in Brussels issued a map brochure titled *Visitez le Congo belge* (Visit the Belgian Congo). It belonged to a series of publications stimulating tourism to and in the Belgian colony [fig. 128]. The cover design by painter Roger van Gindertael (Belgian, 1899–1982) presents iconic sights and works of art associated with the colony. The black and white rendering of a towering male sculpture is modeled on a master carving by an unidentified artist of the Teke people; an elephant pulling a cart in front of a palm tree reminds viewers of ongoing projects to domesticate African elephants; and a lava-spewing volcano in the colony's northeast looms in the background. A strip resembling the patterns of decorated textiles from the realm of the Kuba kingdom stretches across the bottom of the cover.[1]

The inclusion of the wooden figure and the textile strip reflected the fame and reputation of several iconic peoples and their art in the colony and abroad. Among them were the Bushoong, in older writings Bushongo, whose kings in the capital of Nsheng, also Mushenge, ruled over a confederacy of related peoples in the Kasai Province. Their indigenous neighbors and foreigners referred to the confederacy as the Kuba or Bakuba kingdom. Its fame in the geographic north dated back to the late nineteenth century, when explorers and missionaries heard from neighboring peoples about this large kingdom in little traveled parts of the Congo Free State, established in 1888 as a private holding under the harsh rule of Léopold II, King of the Belgians. Stories about the mythical kingdom soon told of a people superior to others in Africa. Such tales resonated with age-old stereotypes according to now debunked hierarchies of race and political organization, which classified Africans as ranging from "ignoble savages" at the lowest level to "noble savages" at the apex.

Under King Léopold's regime, the Kuba peoples and their rulers experienced hard times. Unwilling to open the kingdom to the cruel exploitation of resources, and the abuses and atrocities by some of King Léopold's agents, the monarchs rejected any outside interference. The first foreigner to enter the forbidden kingdom and its capital Nsheng in 1892 was the African-American Protestant missionary Dr William Henry Sheppard.[2] Soldiers of King Léopold's Force Public attacked Nsheng in 1900,

1 *Visitez le Congo belge. Tableau de Renseignements Pratiques*, no. 4, Brussels: L'office national du tourisme de Belgique, January 1938.

2 Sheppard 1917.

and further efforts by the Belgians to subjugate the kingdom followed. Inhabitants of the Kuba realm and elsewhere were pressed into labor for European companies that had opened establishments in the area in order to capitalize on the riches of rubber, palm oil, and minerals; they were forced to build roads, provide porterage, and many other services.[3] After the Belgian parliament annexed King Léopold's private fiefdom, which became the Belgian Congo in 1908, the storied Kuba kingdom and its capital were impacted by various reforms in the expanding colonial administration.

3 Geary 2002, pp. 29–43.

While these momentous changes occurred, prolific writing by visitors, among them German ethnologist Leo Frobenius who traversed the Kasai central region in 1905 and the Hungarian ethnographer Emil Torday who did so in 1907/08, nevertheless contributed to consolidation of the Kuba myth and promotion of Kuba arts.[4] Before turning to ethnology, Torday had worked as a trader for the Belgian Compagnie du Kasai and was thus familiar with the Congo Free State. When he reached the Kuba kingdom, he was received by King Kot aPe (ruled 1902–1919), an indication that the relationship between the Kuba, foreigners, and the Belgian colonial administration and economic enterprises was changing. Books, popular reports, and visual media such as illustrated magazines, picture postcards, and even trade cards contributed to the longevity of the myth and its elements in the following decades.[5]

4 Torday 1925; Torday 1925a; on Torday see Mack 1990; Sheppard 2017.

5 About the visualization of the Kuba myth, see among others, Darish 2015, pp. 14–20; Geary 2002, pp. 97–102; Geary 2015, pp. 56–67.

What elements shaped the core of this myth fostering Westerners' belief in the exceptional nature of the Kuba, and according to eminent historian Jan Vansina contributed to the survival of the kingdom through turbulent times?[6] One narrative focused on the all-powerful paramount rulers (sing. *nyim*, referred to as *lukengo* in older literature), who possessed sacred attributes and governed an orderly and hierarchically structured state. The arts, which included stunning dances and performances of maskers, also played a major role in these constructions [see story, p. 128]. Unique wooden sculptures (*ndop*), thought to be portraits of ancient kings, and utilitarian artifacts of wood with rich surface decoration created in the kingdom gained attention in Europe and the USA early on. Kuba fine palm fiber textiles with bold geometric designs resonated with artists of the Art Nouveau and the Jugendstil movements such as Gustav Klimt, and drew the attention of Paul Klee and Henri Matisse [figs. 166/167]. The artists were inspired by and admired the Kuba aesthetics of abstraction, which broke with Western representational practices.[7] By the 1930s, Kuba cloths were all the rage among collectors including Matisse, who actually owned Kuba textiles. Hans Himmelheber was aware of this fascination when he remarked, "Every collector is familiar with the beautiful raffia fabrics, which the Bakuba decorate in various techniques."[8]

6 Vansina 2007, pp. 5–29, esp. p. 7.

7 On Klimt see Traeger 2015, pp. 68–79. On Matisse see Mack 2012.

8 "Jedem Sammler sind die schönen Raffiastoffe vertraut, die die Bakuba in verschiedenen Techniken verzieren." Himmelheber 1960, p. 365; see also Fischer and Mayer-Himmelheber 1993, p. 101, figs. 133/124.

ENCOUNTERING DIFFERENT CIRCUMSTANCES

Hans Himmelheber, who departed on his trip some thirty years after Frobenius's and Torday's ethnological and collecting missions, was familiar with the writings and illustrations in their books. According to his diary, he considered Torday's and the others' undertakings as roadmaps for his own efforts, when he traveled to the kingdom in order to acquire objects and textiles for his various clients and sponsors financing the stay.[9] However, by the time of his voyage, the infrastructure in the region had changed considerably since earlier days. The establishment of rail services between Port Francqui (now Ilebo) and Luluaburg (now Kananga) in 1928 presented a watershed, and smaller connecting lines facilitated movement for non-Africans. Railroad stops, which offered economic opportunities, developed into settlements where African peoples of many ethnic origins congregated.[10]

9 Himmelheber, diary, January 19 and March 5, 1939 (archive of the Museum Rietberg Zürich). At times, though, he corrected errors in Torday's earlier accounts.

10 Yelengi 1997, pp. 182–211.

Auto routes existed as well, although their condition during the dry and rainy seasons was unpredictable. Initially, Himmelheber relied on transportation from European and American residents who owned vehicles, until he finally acquired his own car, which—due to its frequent breakdowns—caused him constant headaches [see story, p. 84]. Travel to smaller places in the so-called *brousse* (bush) off the main routes remained difficult, and Himmelheber often conducted such excursions either on foot or in a *tipoye*, that is, a litter carried by indigenous porters [fig. 95]. European companies had expanded their enterprises and reach, while churches and stations of various missionary societies dotted the landscape. As Himmelheber reported in his diary, Europeans and Americans accommodated him privately throughout his travels. He also stayed in rest houses (*gites*) established by the colonial administration, in hotels, or in lodgings provided by local chiefs.

One wonders whether under these different circumstances Himmelheber's and other visitors' accounts, and in particular their photographs and films, reinforced or challenged preexisting notions about the Kuba peoples and their arts. The following explorations in this essay suggest that many travelers remained determined to document their encounter with a mythical people. And how did local Kuba actors, including the king, respond to these desires? Did they fulfill their visitors' expectations, thus consciously reinforcing Western fantasies? In other words, did they become coproducers and create scenarios that helped maintain the myth? We will see that this was indeed the case, for they profited from reenacting and perpetuating the myth.

VISITING THE KUBA REALM IN THE 1920s AND 1930s

In the interwar years, visitors and collectors of various backgrounds arrived in the kingdom and its capital Nsheng, the residence of its monarch *nyim* Kot Mabiinc who had succeeded his predecessor *nyim* Kot aPe in 1919. The colonial administration had supported his enthronization even though he was paralyzed, and made him a *chef médaillé* by awarding him the medal bestowed upon traditional leaders in recognition of their authority over their subjects. Their loyalty helped the administration in the effort to establish indirect rule over indigenous peoples.[11] Foreigners yearned to meet or just see this famous paramount ruler, bought carvings, textiles, and metal objects, and witnessed splendid performances, which included dances and at times performances by maskers [fig. 129].

11 Vanhee 2005, pp. 79–82, esp. p. 79.

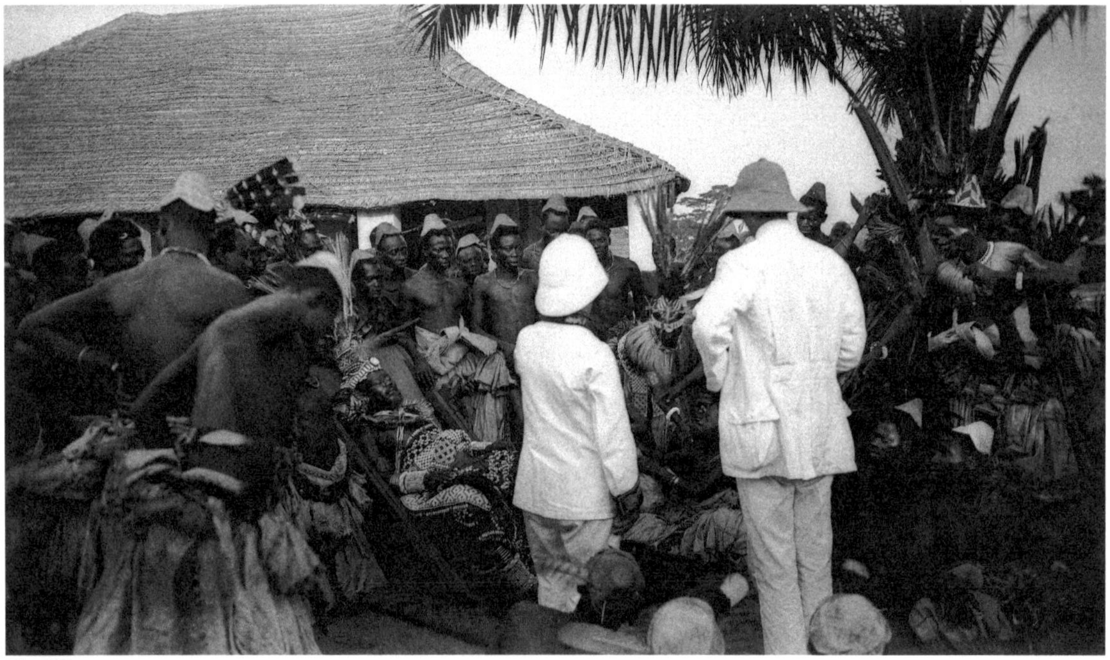
Fig. 129

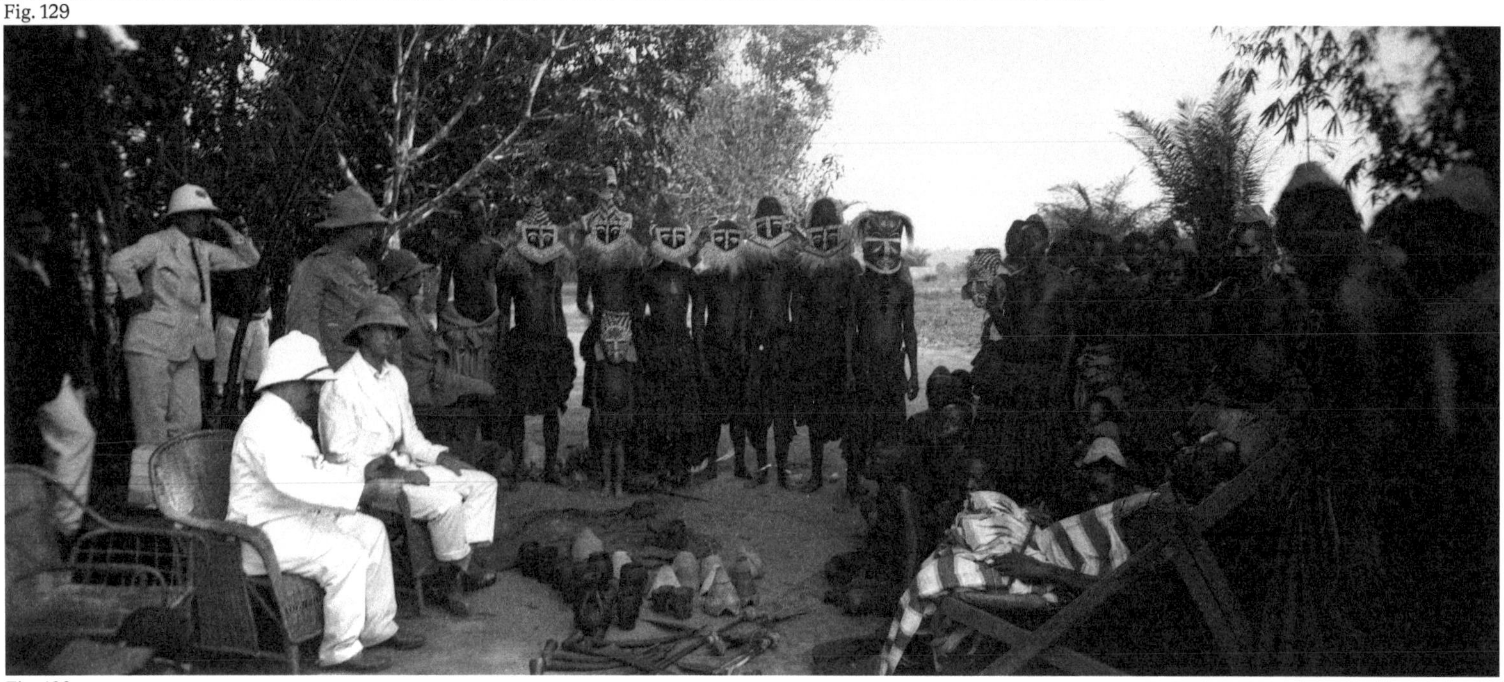
Fig. 130

Fig. 129
Unidentified photographer, provided by Émile Muller
The king with dancers
Mushenge, 1927–1935, b/w negative
Pierre Loos, Brussels

Fig. 130
Unidentified photographer, provided by Émile Muller
The king with display of objects and maskers
Mushenge, 1927–1935, b/w negative
Pierre Loos, Brussels

Among the image makers attracted to the Kuba realm were Émile Muller or professional photographer and amateur ethnographer Casimir d'Ostoya Zagourski (1883–1944), a Polish émigré in the Congo, who had established a photographic business in Léopoldville (now Kinshasa) around 1925. By the mid-1930s, he began to offer photo prints and a series of around 400 postcards titled *L'Afrique qui disparaît* ("Vanishing Africa"), featuring peoples in the Belgian Congo and neighboring colonies. He traveled the colony by car and took images of the Kuba sometime between 1929 and 1937.[12] Beautifully exposed and composed, the black-and-white pictures of his visit to Nsheng have been widely published to this day, among them a famous portrait of *nyim* Kot Mabiinc [fig. 138].

When Himmelheber arrived in Léopoldville in late 1938, Zagourski was at the peak of his career. A year earlier he had displayed his images at a colonial exhibition in Paris and also won a Medaille d'Or, Grand prix (Gold Medal, Grand Prize) for his work during a show in Brazzaville in the neighboring French Congo. It remains an open question whether Himmelheber saw Zagourski's widely distributed postcards while in Léopoldville and throughout his travels. He was aware of the work by other image makers living in the Congo, among them African photographer Antoine Freitas [see essay Guyer].[13] One can be certain that many pictures and postcards made their way back to Kuba country, where rulers, local people, as well as residents from various countries in the geographic north became familiar with them.

Other image makers included the Americans Ray Garner (1913–1989), a documentary filmmaker, and his wife Virginia Garner (1915–2007), a photographer. Together they produced several short propaganda films for the African Motion Picture Project (AMPP) established by the American Emory Ross of the Disciples of Christ Mission in order to find donors and recruits back home in the USA for Presbyterian missions abroad. The couple arrived in the Congo in May 1938 and left in August 1939, overlapping almost entirely with Hans Himmelheber's stay, although they apparently never met. Virginia Garner's diary and other project notes, published in 2011, provide important insights into the social conditions and everyday life in an era of consolidated colonialism.[14] Similar to Himmelheber's diary, these private writings present an unfiltered look at challenges and realities, among them the ways in which Congolese at the time responded to being photographed and filmed.

The Garners' silent movies, which were the public and carefully edited results of their project, celebrated progress and the civilizing aspects of missionary activity according to scripts mostly prepared for them by a writing team in the USA. While in Kuba country, the couple enjoyed the support of the Reverend Hezekiah M. Washburn (1884–1972) of the American Presbyterian Congo Mission in Bulape, located in the kingdom of the Kete peoples, who were closely associated with the Kuba. The missionary became the main white protagonist in two short movies filmed in Nsheng and Bulape. Besides enlisting missionaries, the Garners hired mission-educated Congolese to act in the filmic episodes and paid in kind or with money for their and other local people's services.[15]

12 Pluskota 2002, pp. 58–67.

13 My special thanks to Nanina Guyer for sharing this fascinating information with me.

14 Garner 2011; Reynolds 2010, pp. 459–479. Reynolds's introduction to Garner's *Diaries* is a reprint of this article.

15 Garner 2011, pp. 211–212; Reynolds 2010, p. 472.

The Garners' focused on visualizing the progress of converting the Kuba to Christianity and demonstrating the advance of Western civilization. Their agendas differed from those of Himmelheber and others, who sought to create images of a primordial people, thus maintaining part of the myth. Some elements in the Garners' films nevertheless reflected and reenacted the Kuba myth, such as the opening passage of the film *The Light Shines in Bakubaland. An Epic of the Mission Field,* Part I. It presents the intertitle "Bakubaland is a unique African kingdom in south-western Belgian Congo" with scenes of landscapes, a masker dancing, weavers, and some of *nyim* Kot Mabiinc's "900 wives" singing and rhythmically striking gourds while the king looks on. Another intertitle—"The arts and crafts of the Bakuba excel those of most African tribes"—precedes scenes of weaving and the making of mats and baskets. Yet a third intertitle—"For over four hundred years, the kingdom has had its own established laws and courts of justice, including higher courts of appeal"—alludes to the centralized state with the omnipotent ruler.[16] In the following, comparisons of Himmelheber's experiences with those of the Garners, Zagourski, and various other contemporaries cast an interesting light on image-making among the Kuba and their reaction to being photographed. Our focus here will be on the visualization of two elements of the myth: the dances and performances by maskers and the efforts to portray *nyim* Kot Mabiinc.

16 *The Light Shines in Bakubaland. An Epic of the Mission Field,* Part I. Short film, *images commercialisées par l'atelier des archives* (http://www.atelierdesarchives.com; https://www.youtube.com/watch?v=SwvOBqDwl-8, accessed April 20, 2019).

WITNESSING PERFORMANCES

Staging spectacular displays was one of the local actors' strategies to satisfy the visitors' desires and preconceived notions about the mythical Kuba. Dances with and without maskers often occurred during holidays and official events, such as visits by administrators and high-ranking officials, and even royals from Belgium. Both Belgian and other foreign professional and amateur photographers were present to record them. In these displays, local men, women, and youngsters in splendid costumes followed prescribed choreographies and expected to be photographed. Among the pictures of such events are images in the personal archive of Belgian medical doctor Émile Muller (1891–1976) who lived and worked in the Congo from 1923 to 1938. Sometime after 1928, he and several other Belgians officials visited Nsheng for a "ceremonial interview" with *nyim* Kot Mabiinc, likely in Muller's capacity as a doctor. In one of the encounters, the king, surrounded by a group of dancers, rested in a deckchair and wore exquisite ceremonial attire. A performer in a beaded costume with an elaborate headdress can be seen between two pith-helmeted Europeans standing close to the ruler [fig. 129]. A picture of another meeting shows the king receiving the official delegation while sitting behind a display of metal and wooden objects in front of the visitors—likely royal gifts or perhaps items for sale. Seven young men and a child, wearing new masks without costumes, line up while a man at the side holds a mask in his hand [fig. 130].[17] The masks could also be purchased.

17 Loos and Buch 2007, pp. 74–79.

Occasionally, the hopes of visitors to document such stunning festivities were dashed. This may have been the case when Zagourski traveled through the core Kuba region. Actual performances and dances in the kingdom's capital are missing in his series *L'Afrique qui disparaît*. There are, however, at least three photos of a Kuba performance that can be attributed to Zagourski. The event seems to have taken place during a public spectacle—perhaps in Elisabethville (now Lubumbashi) or even in Léopoldville—judging by the stand filled with spectators in the background and other performers at a distance, directed or perhaps photographed by a European man [fig. 131].

Himmelheber had good luck when he arrived in a village called Ichala on January 10, 1939, where he came upon a woman's funeral. He was allowed to photograph the ceremonies, which included dances accompanied by an orchestra. Whether all participants in the ongoing funerary rites welcomed his presence remains open, given the way women in mourning, who surrounded the corpse, looked at him and the camera [fig. 132]. From Ichala, he continued on to Mweka, a multi-ethnic settlement in Kuba territory, which had sprung up around a railroad stop and was the seat of the Belgian territorial administration. During another chance encounter near Mweka, on January 16, Himmelheber witnessed and photographed a second funeral, this time the commemorative rites for a deceased man, which included dances [fig. 133]. Here, the local participants were well aware of the photographer's presence and actually played to his camera. An image in a series of postcards distributed by the publishing company Photo Home in the early 1950s offers an interesting comparison because it resembles Himmelheber's photographs of the man's funerary celebration. It, too, captured a spectacle in town, perhaps organized just for the photo shoot. The performers aptly staged themselves for the camera [fig. 134].

Nyim Kot Mabiinc had a residence near Mweka where Himmelheber's first brief encounter with him took place. By early 1939, the monarch was gravely impaired and passed away ten months later, a death that caught the attention of the Belgian public.[18] René Van Deuren, the *administrateur territorial* (territorial administrator) for the Kuba kingdom, who was stationed in Mweka, introduced Himmelheber to the ruler. Four months earlier, the Garners had enjoyed the help of the Reverend Washburn, when he arranged for an audience with the king so that they could get the monarch's consent to film in Nsheng.[19] Himmelheber, too, may have sought royal permission to continue on to Nsheng in order to buy Kuba artworks and take photographs. Two days later, he saw *nyim* Kot Mabiinc again, and was informed that the king had sent a message to the capital about his visitor's imminent arrival and delegated an attendant to accompany him on the voyage.[20]

When Himmelheber reached Nsheng on January 20, 1939, he was greeted by a man named Kwete, who arrived on a bicycle and sported Western garb. In his diary he describes him as a young, smart lad, son of the king and his designated successor. Kwete is none other than Georges Kwete Mwana (1913–1970), a prince of the Kuba whose memoir appeared in 2010.[21] Prince Kwete, an experienced guide, immediately offered Himmelheber works in metal, fiber textiles, and a few carved items for purchase, which, however, did not meet the new arrival's expectations of authenticity and age.[22]

A couple of days later, Prince Kwete organized one of the famous dance performances with maskers for the visitor and collector—a perfect photo op, although the king was absent. How-

18 Wannijn 1939, pp. 7612–7614

19 Himmelheber also spent time with Washburn and appreciated his knowledge about the Kuba: "Washburn ist ein hervorragender Kenner der Bakuba und gibt mir allerhand wertvolle Informationen (Washburn is highly knowledgeable about the Kuba and gives me all sorts of valuable information)." Himmelheber, diary, January 19, 1939 (archive of the Museum Rietberg).

20 Himmelheber, diary, January 18, 1939 (archive of the Museum Rietberg).

21 Himmelheber, diary, January 20, 1939 (archive of the Museum Rietberg); Kwete Mwana 2010.

22 Himmelheber, diary, January 20, 1939 (archive of the Museum Rietberg); in his 1960 book Himmelheber refers to the crown prince as Kwete Moana, who knew how to made fiber borders used for wrappers and shirts. Himmelheber 1960, p. 371.

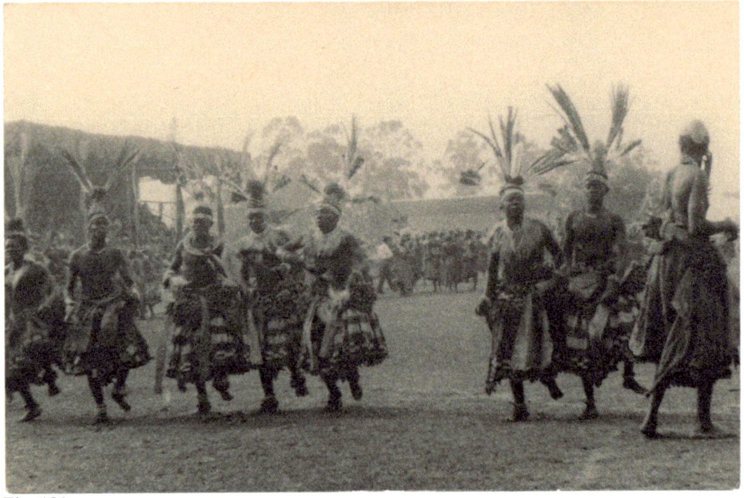
Fig. 131

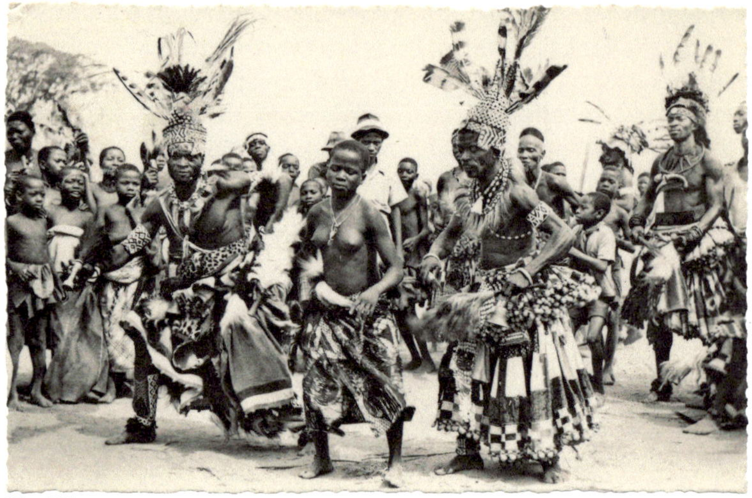
Fig. 134

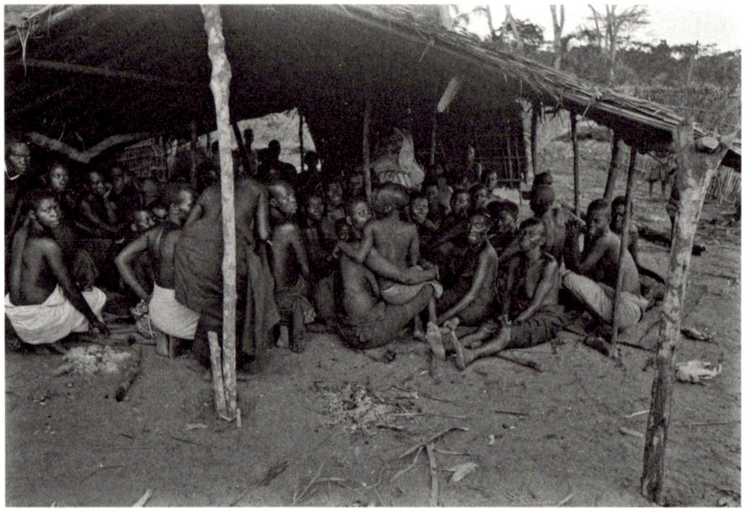
Fig. 132

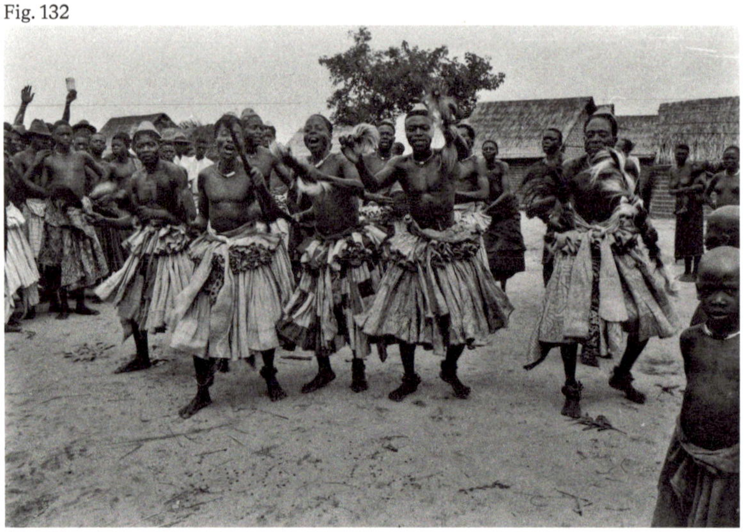
Fig. 133

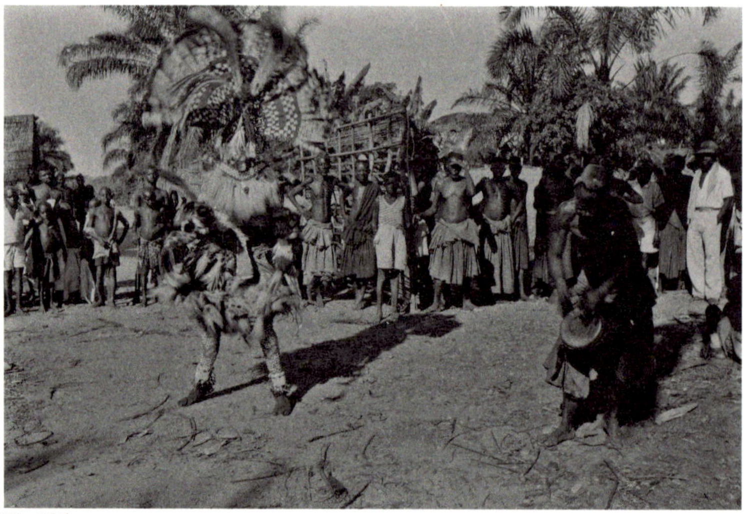
Fig. 135

Fig. 131
Attributed to Casimir d'Ostoya Zagourski
Performance by Kuba dancers during an official event
Kasai, Katanga, or Léopoldville, 1937, postcard, gelatin silver print
Christraud M. Geary Collection

Fig. 132
Hans Himmelheber
Dead body of a woman at a funeral
Ichala, January 10, 1939, b/w negative
Museum Rietberg Zürich, FHH 181-20

Fig. 133
Hans Himmelheber
Dancing men at a funeral
Mweka, January 16, 1939, b/w negative
Museum Rietberg Zürich, FHH 182-24

Fig. 134
Unidentified photographer
Danses chez les Bakuba
Mweka, c. 1952, gelatin silver print
Christraud M. Geary Collection

Fig. 135
Hans Himmelheber
Masker *mwaash a mboy*
Mushenge, January 22, 1939, b/w negative
Museum Rietberg Zürich, FHH 182-34

ever, in some pictures of the shoot one notices local spectators in European style dress, intrusions which did not please photographers [fig. 135]. The prince finally presented himself in local attire, much to Himmelheber's delight, who noted in his diary "There is a large audience here and Kwete appears now, too, as a native with very beautiful woven overskirt rather than his well-ironed khaki pants. He looks quite good." [see fig. 84].[23] Like many of his contemporaries, among them Zagourski, Himmelheber preferred to depict a timeless, unchanging universe of the Kuba with no disruption and perceived degradation of these noble Africans through modern ways of life. During a second stay in Nsheng from March 3–6, Himmelheber witnessed and photographed another display with maskers, this time in the presence of the ruler. Since the event was similar to the earlier performance, he took fewer pictures. In his 1960 book *Negerkunst und Negerkünstler*, he praised these two spectacles and wrote "The [Kuba] mask dancers thus offer a fantastical-grand view; I have never seen anything like that in Africa."[24]

23 "Es sind viele Zuschauer da und Kwete erscheint nun auch als Eingeborener mit sehr schoener Matte statt seiner wohlgebuegelten Kakihose. Er sieht sehr gut aus." Himmelheber, diary, January 22, 1939 (archive of the Museum Rietberg).

24 "Die [Kuba] Maskentänzer bieten so einen phantastisch-prächtigen Anblick; ich habe in Afrika nie dergleichen gesehen." Himmelheber 1960, pp. 367–68. See also Himmelheber 1940, pp. 17–30, esp. p. 25.

PORTRAYING THE KING

According to many observers, *nyim* Kot Mabiinc was in charge of his image and one would assume had seen many pictures of himself sitting in state, which circulated widely in the colony and abroad.[25] In 1923, for instance, Belgian Commandant Charles Godefroid Félix Delhaise (1872–1932) captured an iconic portrait of the king, which to this day appears in publications [fig. 136]. It shows him in his deckchair, carefully dressed in a fine cowrie-trimmed skirt and belt and wearing a small hat (*laket*) with an eagle feather, denoting Kuba cultural identity[26]

In 1928, the king, many of his wives, and his noble entourage traveled to Domiongo, a small railroad stop some twenty kilometers from Nsheng, to greet Albert I and Elisabeth, King and Queen of the Belgians, during their tour of the Congo. Pictures of the event show the Kuba monarch dressed in the ceremonial state ensemble that he donned for official and ritual occasions.[27] The famous state attire of the Kuba kings, which was so heavy that they could barely move, appeared on a trade card published by the Liebig Extract of Meat Company in a 1955 series titled *Les peuplades du Congo belge* (The Peoples of the Belgian Congo). It depicts *nyim* Kot Mabiinc's successor *nyim* Mbop Mabiinc maMbeeky, who ruled from 1939 until he joined ancestors in 1969 [figs. 137/149]. To return to the images of *nyim* Kot Mabiinc: A postcard with another classic photograph of *nyim* Kot Mabiinc portrays him reclining in his deckchair surrounded by attendants. He did not appear in one of his sumptuous outfits for this occasion, although copper anklets adorned his legs and he wore necklaces. He looked directly at the camera, placed at a low angle by the photographer—none other than Casimir Zagourski [fig. 138]. This portrait is now one of the photographer's *and* the monarch's best-known pictures.

The Garners were also determined to film *nyim* Kot Mabiinc in full regalia. Virginia Garner's diary reveals the painstaking efforts to accomplish this task with the help of the Reverend Washburn. After they had received the king's consent for their movie project while in Mweka, he informed them that they could only film when he was back in Nsheng.[28] The ruler finally met them in

25 He was among several prominent African kings and leaders in the late nineteenth and twentieth centuries who embraced photography as a means to further their own agendas. See Geary 2018, pp. 85–97.

26 Geary 2015, p. 60, fig. 2; Vanhee 2005, p. 80.

27 *Le voyage de leurs Majestés le Roi et la Reine des Belges; 5 Juin–31 Août 1928*, Brussels: L'Illustration Congolaise, 1920, pls. LVII, LVIX.

28 Garner 2011, p. 123.

the capital eleven days later, insisting that he had to give renewed approval for scenes in the movie. Then they waited for the king to appear outside in daylight for filming. Frustrated, Virginia Garner wrote in her diary, "No king ... It seems the king wanted to wear a certain costume for the picture and no other would do. His attendants brought him twenty before he found the one he wished to wear. With all his fancy clothes to choose from he had to keep us cooling our heels for so long that the sun went in. And it [the sun] stayed [in] for the rest of the day!! We did not even expose one foot of film." The next day, the Garners "got the king out this afternoon" and also filmed so-called "idols" [fig. 139].[29] They finished their shoot a few days later when the monarch, who by then had grown weary of their presence, appeared once more for a staged display with his wives, which became part of the opening scenes of *The Light Shines in Bakubaland. An Epic of the Mission Field*, Part I, mentioned above. The film's Part II depicts dances and an audience of the Reverend Washburn with "King Lukenga" [sic] whom the intertext describes as the "most powerful African monarch in all Congo." The storyline presents the scene as the king granting the missionary permission to build a mission station in the Kuba realm.[30]

Himmelheber's experiences in Nsheng were similar. During his first stay in the capital in January, he had eagerly awaited the arrival of the king, but was also disappointed.[31] Finally, he encountered the monarch in the capital during the above-mentioned performance of maskers and dances in March, but left without a picture of the ruler, which would have been an important addition to his photographs. According to his diary: "Lukengo was carried here, and everyone kneeled and clapped their hands in beat to the drum, three or four times, every third or fourth time with decreasing strength. It somehow sounded celebratory."[32]

CONCLUSION

This brief exploration of visual and written records left behind by Hans Himmelheber and some of his contemporaries demonstrates that elements of the Kuba myth remained influential during the interwar period, even though conditions had changed since the beginning of the twentieth century. From the perspective of Kuba leaders, perpetuating the myth enhanced the reputation of the kingdom in the colony and the geographic north, and consolidated its prominent position in the colonial state. Within this framework, the production and circulation of visuals, such as photographs that illustrated print media and were reproduced on postcards, supported the kingdom's political and economic agendas.

Performing Kuba identity and resurrecting the past for visitors and their cameras during large and small stagings in and outside of the kingdom required careful preparation under the guidance of men and women aware of the importance of such events. The participants had to execute choreographed routines to the accompaniment of an orchestra and appear in traditional attire, even though many of them no longer wore such clothing in everyday life. Even in remote areas, ordinary folks had learned how to dress and pose for images and often expected remuneration for their services. Dances and masquerades had also developed into marketing events for Kuba arts because foreign visitors

29 Garner 2011, p. 127f.

30 *The Light Shines in Bakubaland. An Epic of the Mission Field*, Part II. Short film, *images commercialisées par l'atelier des archives* (http://www.atelierdesarchives.com; https://www.youtube.com/watch?v=yOS-Qcn9B64, accessed April 18, 2019).

31 Himmelheber, diary, January 24, 1939 (archive of the Museum Rietberg).

32 "Lukengo wurde hergetragen und alle hockten hin und klatschten im Takt zur Trommel in die Haende, 3 oder 4 mal, je drei oder viermal mit abnehmender Staerke. Es hoert sich irgendwie feierlich an." Himmelheber, diary, March 6, 1939 (archive of the Museum Rietberg).

Fig. 136
Commandant Charles Godefroid Félix Delhaise
Le roi des Bakubas et une partie de cour à Mushenge
Mushenge, 1923, gelatin silver print
AfricaMuseum, A.P.O.O. 27794
RMCA Tervuren

Fig. 137
Published by the Liebig Extract of Meat Company
Les Bushongo
(*nyim* Mbop Mabiinc maMbeeky)
Circa 1955, chromolithograph trade card
Christraud M. Geary Collection

Fig. 138
Casimir Zagourski **Le Roi Bakuba Lukengo**
(*nyim* Kot Mabiinc)
Mushenge, 1929–1937, gelatin silver print on postcard
Museum of Fine Arts, Boston, 2012.3269

Fig. 139
Virginia Garner
Ray Garner filming *nyim* Kot Mabiinc
Mushenge, September 17, 1938
Gay Garner Mackintosh

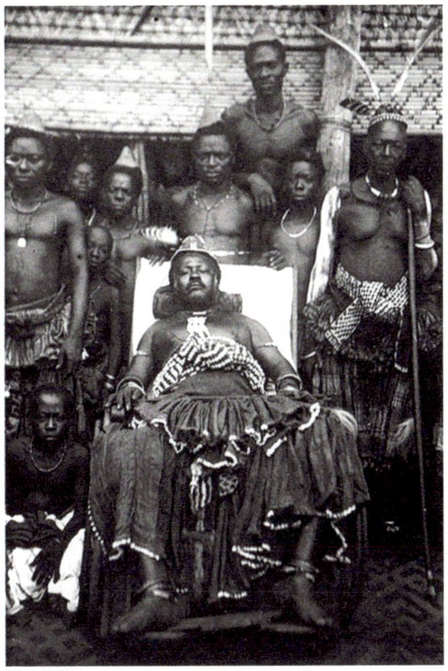

Fig. 136

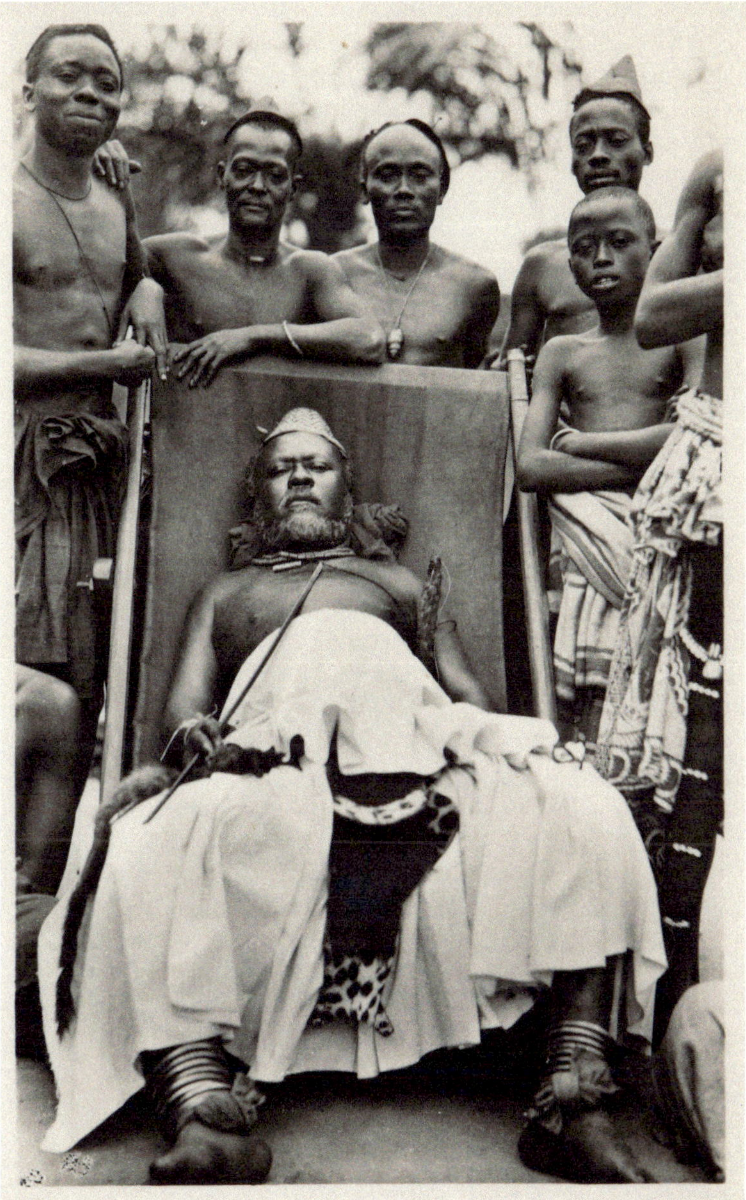

Fig. 138

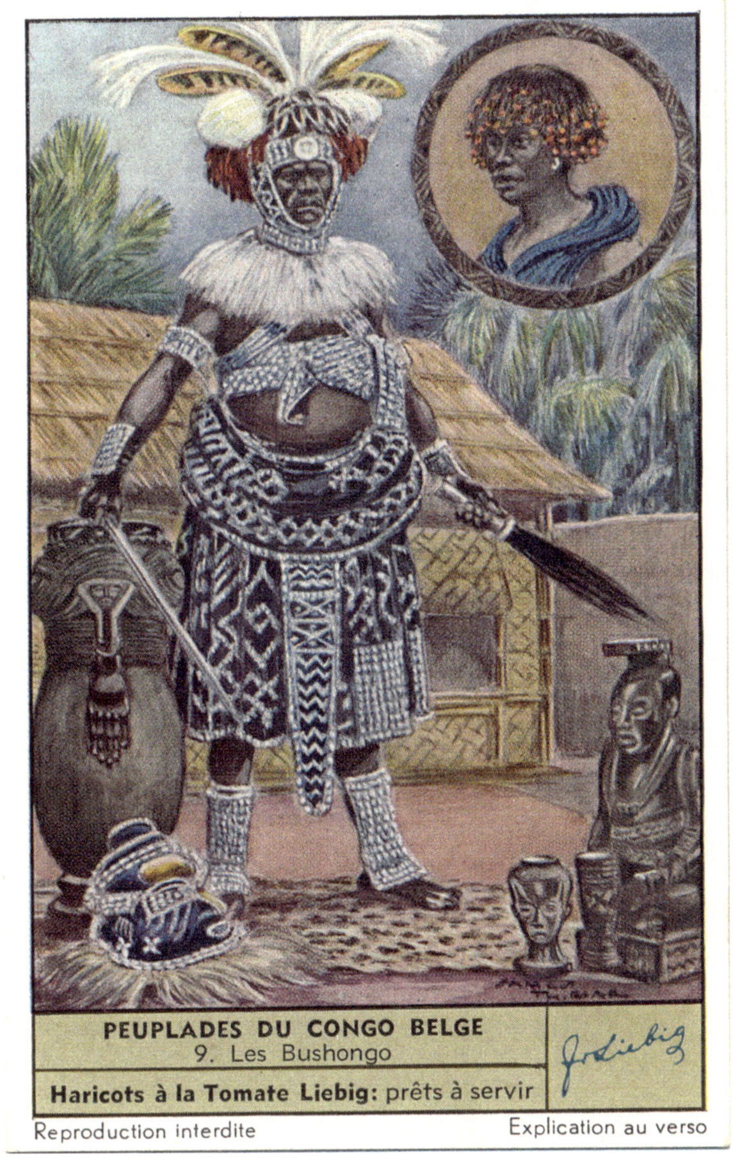

Fig. 137

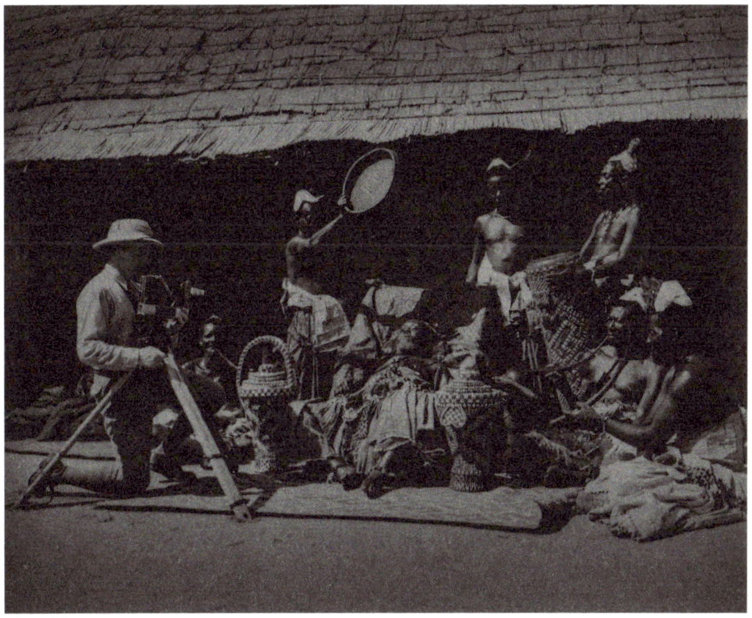

Fig. 139

could often acquire masks and other objects at the end of the festivities. The fact that newly produced pieces appeared during such performances lent them an aura of authenticity in the eyes of spectators unfamiliar with ongoing discourses among collectors such as Hans Himmelheber, who preferred and searched for ancient works made for local use. For the buyers of new creations and foreign viewers, the photographs depicting spectacles cum sales events became reference points of authenticity. For the Kuba and their leaders these pictures played an important role in promoting the arts to the economic benefit of the kingdom.

Nyim Kot Mabiinc embodied the Kuba state and reinforced the myth whenever he appeared in public to be seen and photographed by audiences from Europe and the USA. At the same time, his public appearances helped him to bring together the peoples within the kingdom and elevate his role in the colony. He was fully cognizant of, and controlled the power of visual representation. The ruler's presences and absences during grand displays and special photographic occasions were well-timed and orchestrated. In fact, his perceived "failures" to show up may have heightened anticipation and his impact as a leader, when he finally sat in state and met the expectations of visitors and image makers.

These observations confirm the suggestions at the beginning of this essay, that the king and Kuba actors of all backgrounds had become coproducers of the myth. Indeed, they had! As far as Hans Himmelheber is concerned, the strategies of *nyim* Kot Mabiinc and his subjects in the Kuba kingdom had the desired effect. When Himmelheber compared the Kuba to some of their neighbors such as the Yaka and Chokwe, he mused: "It is twice as nice with the Bakuba, because they are so kind and approachable."[33]

33 "Doppelt so schoen ist es bei den Bakuba, weil sie so nett und zugaenglich sind." Himmelheber, diary, February 1, 1939 (archive of the Museum Rietberg).

Nanina Guyer shared images and the diary of Hans Himmelheber with me, and she and Michaela Oberhofer provided helpful suggestions and comments throughout the writing process. Elisabeth L. Cameron kindly identified the design of the figure on the cover of the 1938 travel brochure as based on sculptures by Teke artists. Publications coordinator Mark Welzel oversaw the production, copy-editor Lisa Rosenblatt, translator Kurt Rehkopf and Laura Falletta, who took care of ordering the images, helped with finalizing the essay. My sincere thanks go to all.

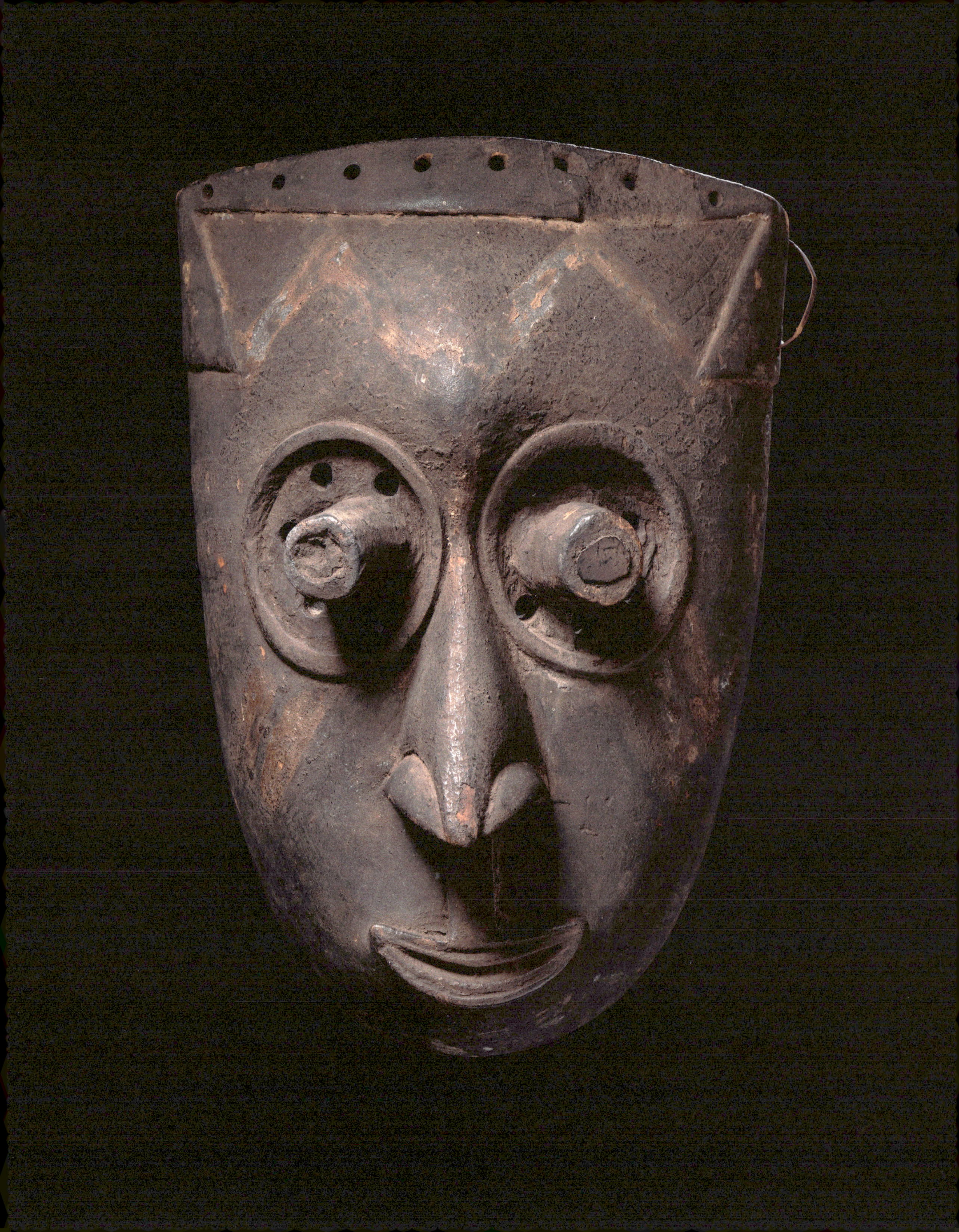

Fig. 140

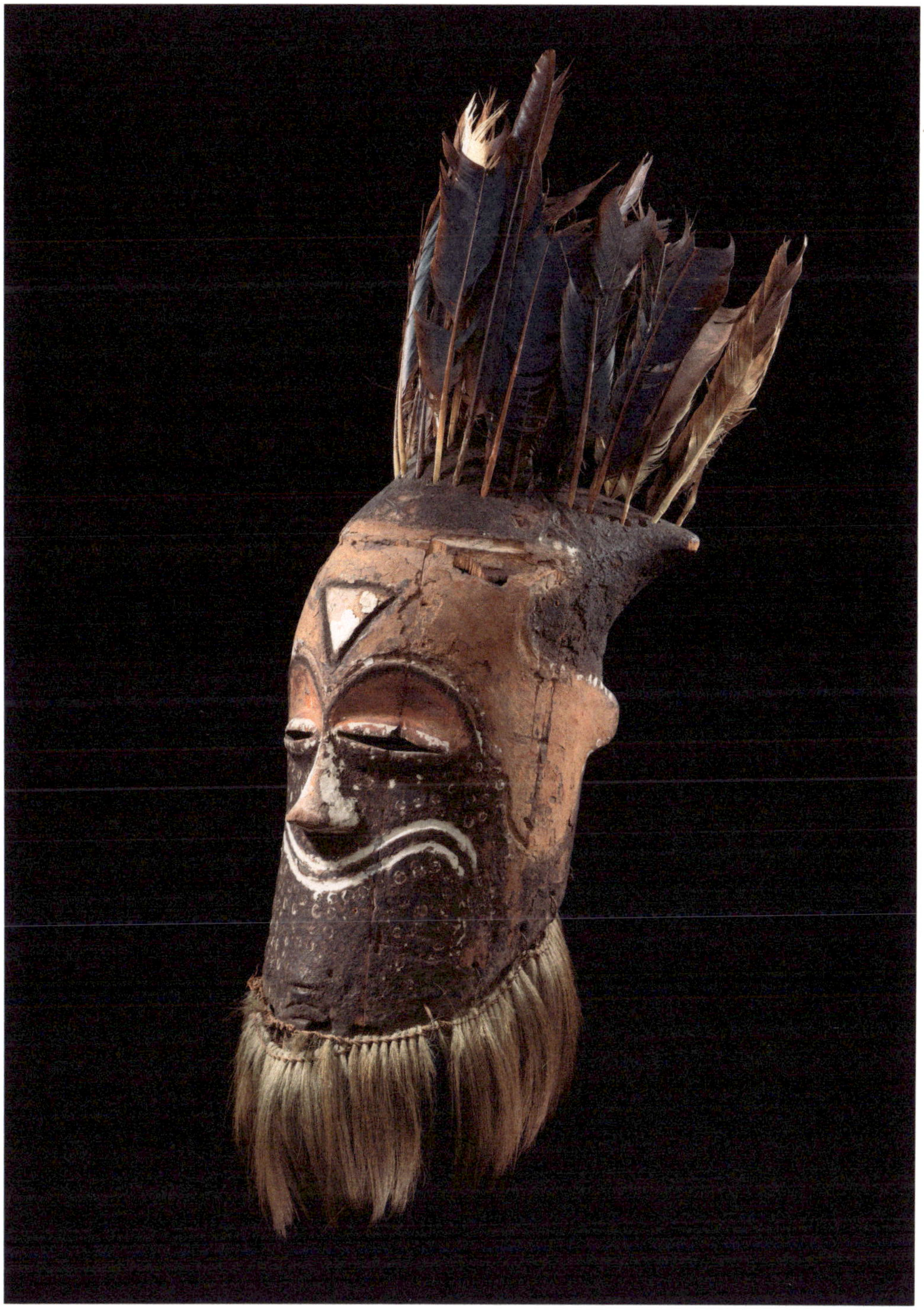

Fig. 141

Fig. 142

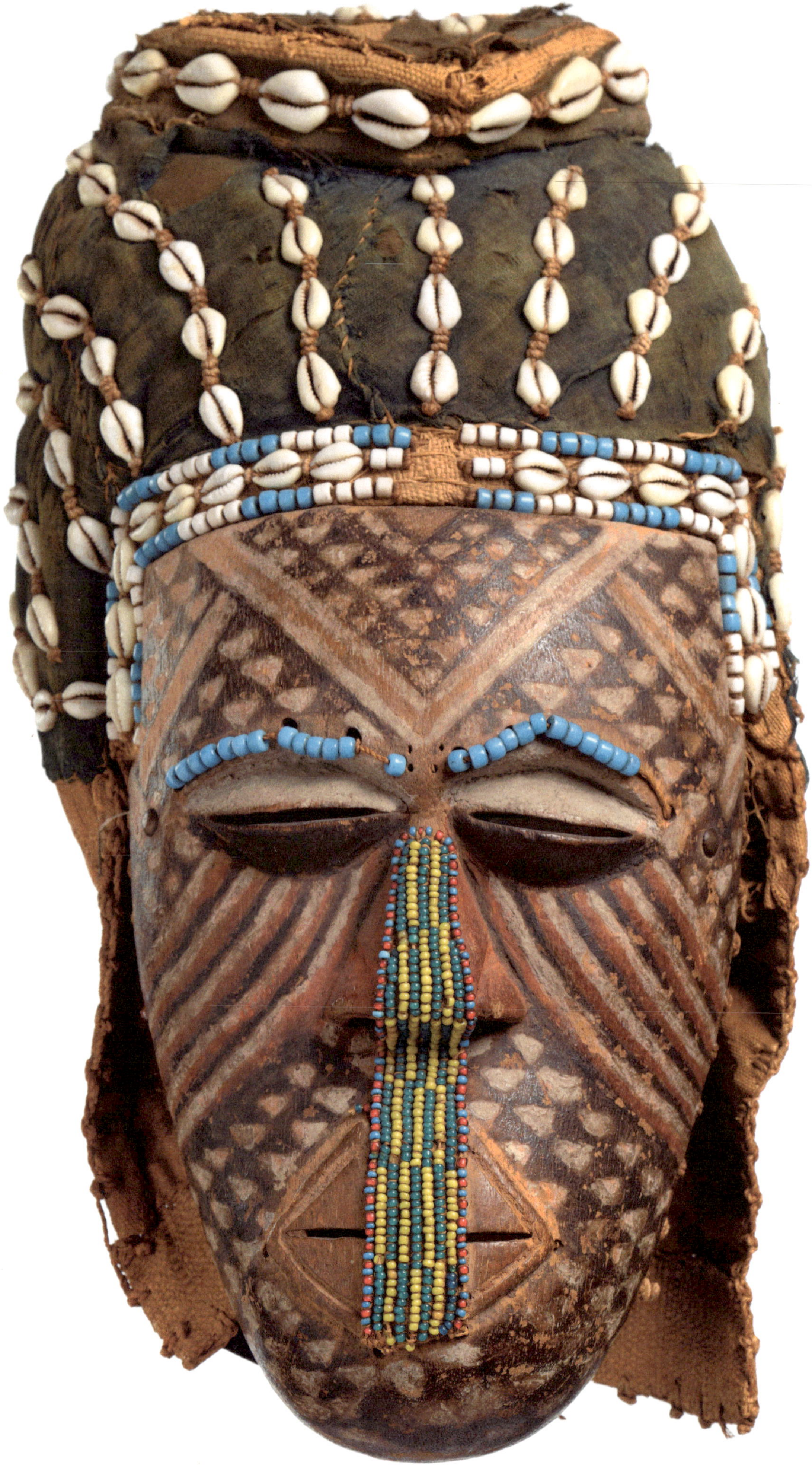

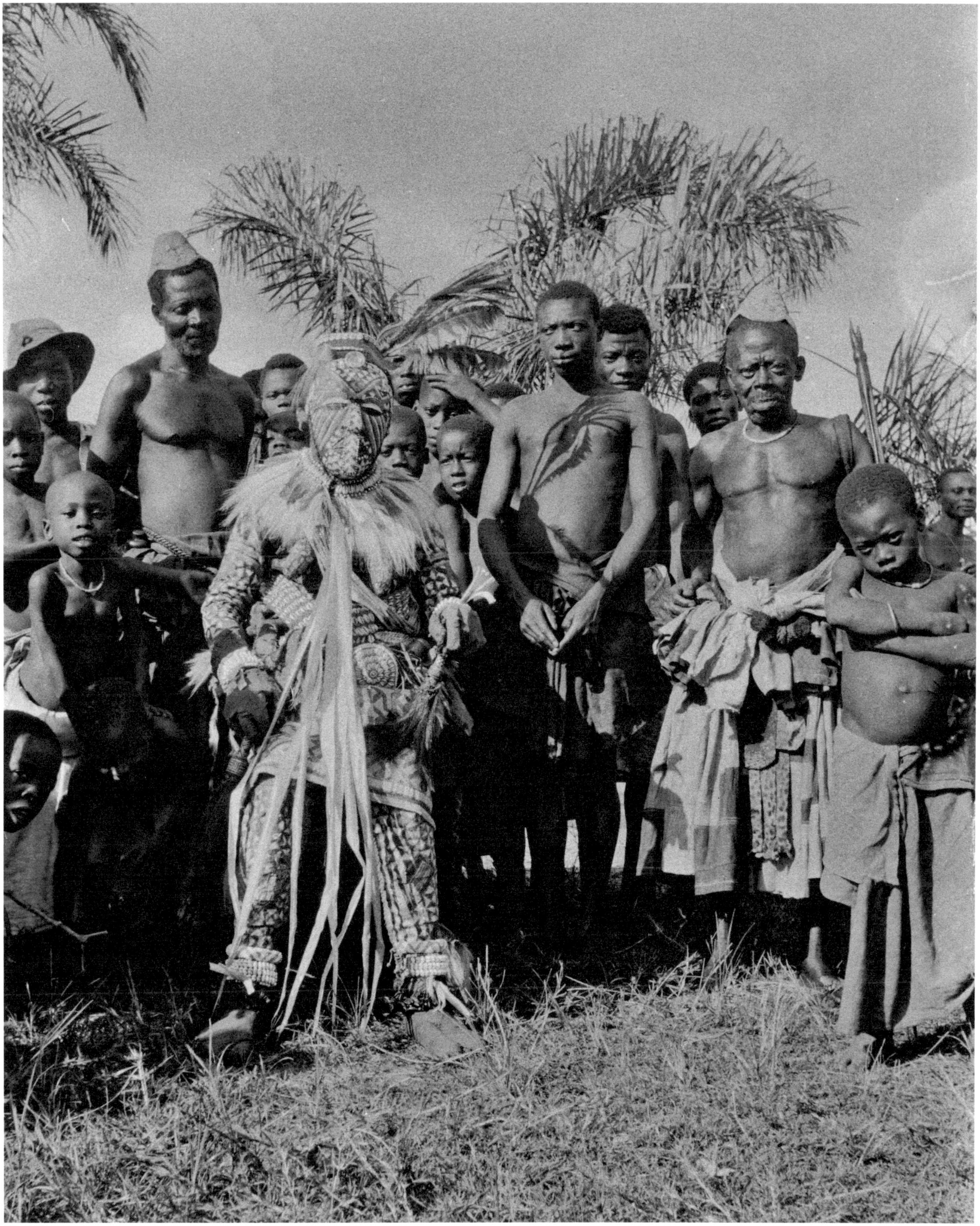

Fig. 143

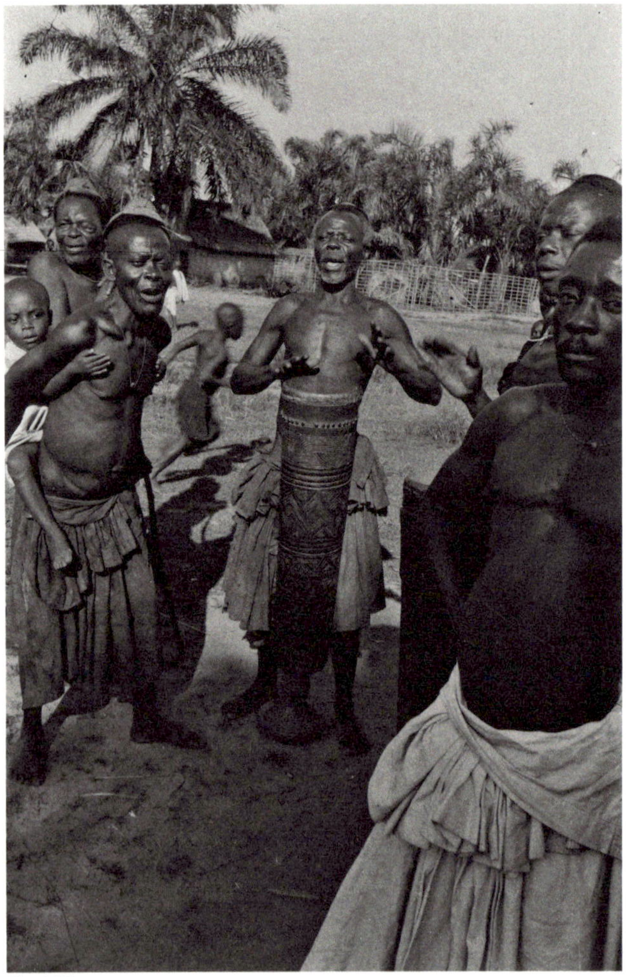

Fig. 144

Fig. 145

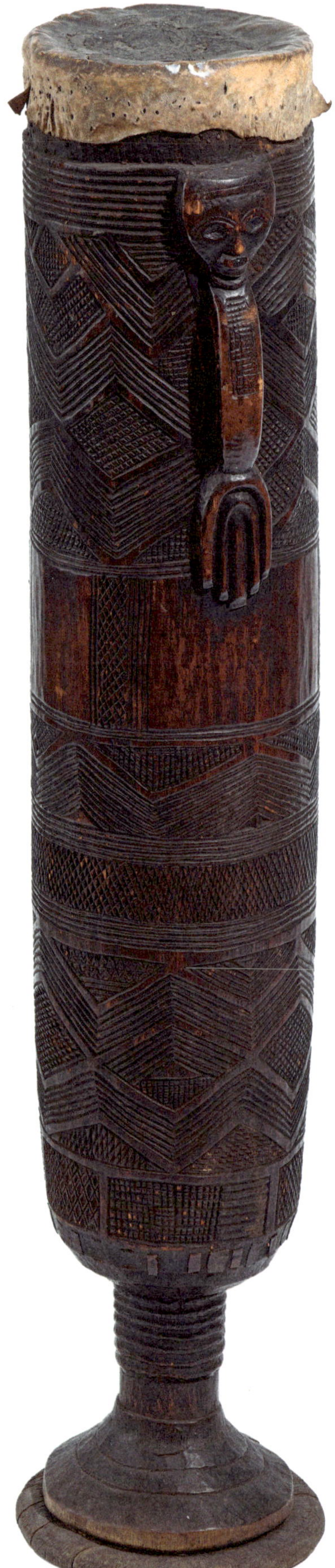

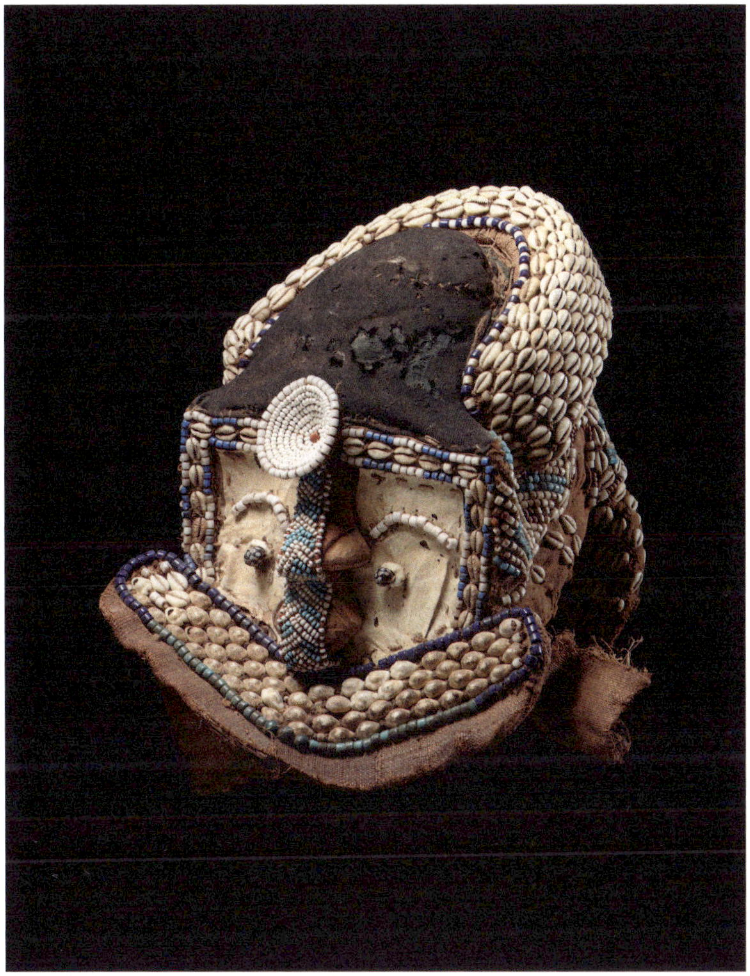

Fig. 146

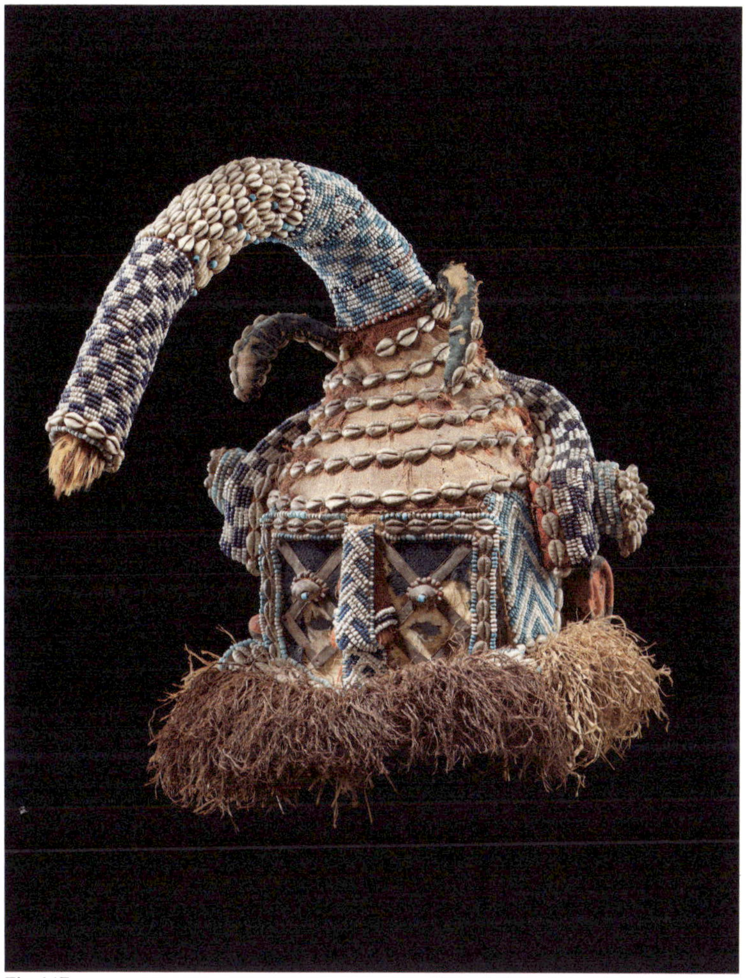

Fig. 147

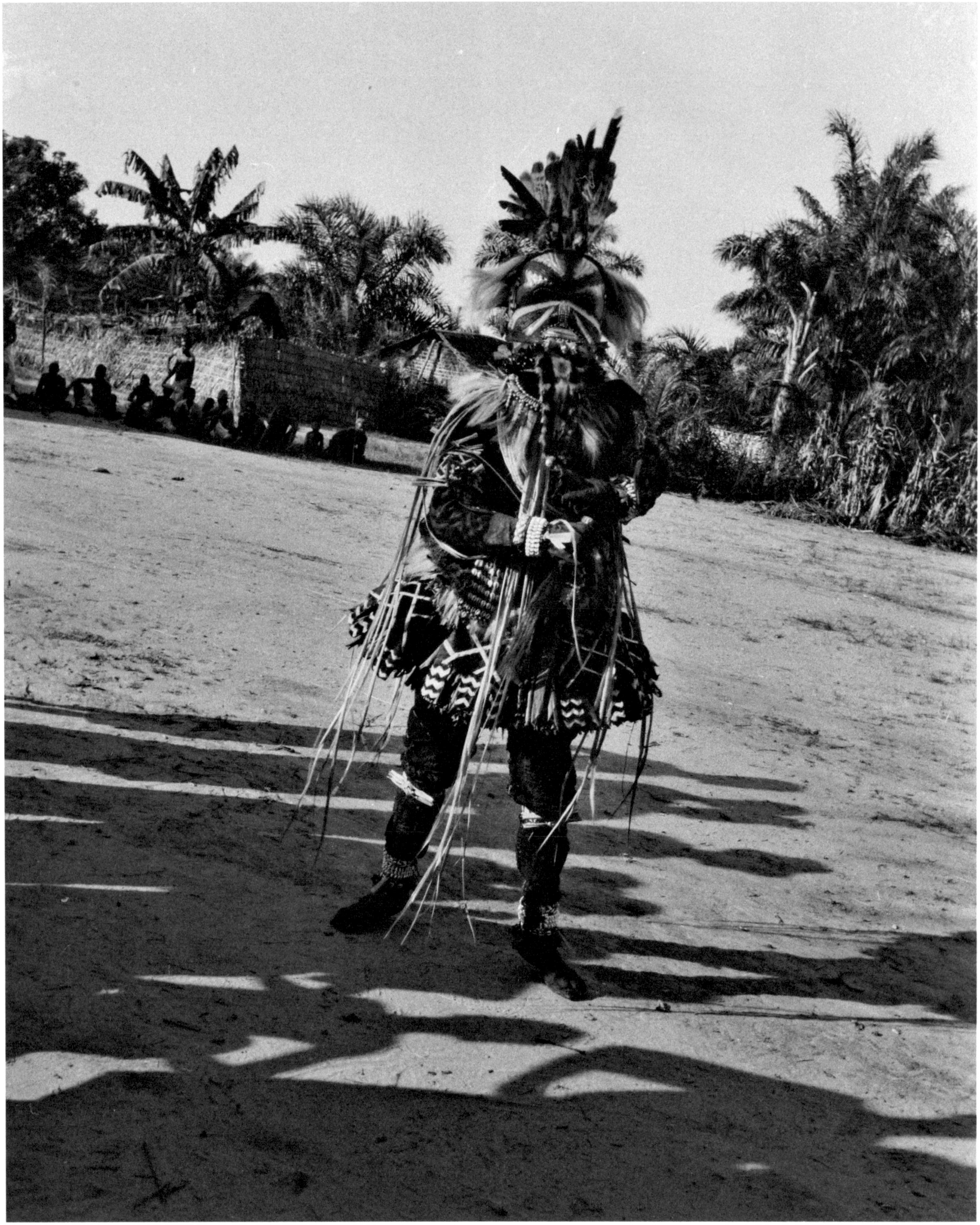

Fig. 148

Fig. 140
Artist of the Bindji region
***Ishyeen imaalu* mask with protruding eyes**
Before 1939, wood, 26 × 19 × 11.5 cm
Museum Rietberg Zürich, HH 15
Gift of Barbara and Eberhard Fischer
Acquired by Hans Himmelheber

Fig. 141
Artist of the Kuba region
Helmet mask
Circa 1900, wood, feathers, hair, pigment, plant fibers, 81 × 30 × 40 cm
Museum Rietberg Zürich, RAC 401
Gift of Eduard von der Heydt

Fig. 142
Artist of the Kuba region
***Ngady mwaash* female mask**
Circa 1900, wood, glass beads, cowries, textile materials, plant fibers, pigments, 39.5 × 21 × 22 cm
Museum Rietberg Zürich, RAC 404
Gift of Eduard von der Heydt

Fig. 143
Hans Himmelheber
***Ngady mwaash* masked figure**
Mushenge, March 6, 1939, b/w negative
Museum Rietberg Zürich, FHH 185-21

Fig. 144
Hans Himmelheber
Drummer
Mushenge, January 22, 1939, b/w negative
Museum Rietberg Zürich, FHH 182-39

Fig. 145
Artist of the Kuba region
Tall drum
Circa 1900, wood, leather, 108 × 22 cm
Museum Rietberg Zürich, RAC 473
Han Coray collection

Fig. 146
Artist of the Kuba region
***Mwaash a mboy* mask**
Before 1939, wood, plant fibers, textile, leather, cowries, glass beads, 31 × 27.5 × 29 cm
Museum Rietberg Zürich, EFA 26
Gift of Barbara and Eberhard Fischer
Acquired by Hans Himmelheber

Fig. 147
Artist of the Kuba region
***Mukenga* mask**
Circa 1900, wood, plant fibers, glass beads, cowries, leather, 47 × 33 × 43 cm
Museum Rietberg Zürich, RAC 402
Gift of Eduard von der Heydt

Fig. 148
Hans Himmelheber
Masked figure
Mushenge, January 22, 1939, b/w negative
Museum Rietberg Zürich, FHH 183-4

STRATEGIC SPECTACLE: THE ROYAL MASKS OF THE KUBA — The royal dances of the Kuba with their brightly colored masked figures were one of the highlights of Hans Himmelheber's journey. The helmet mask *ngady mwaash* was, rather unconventionally, danced by a woman [fig. 142]; *mwaash a mboy* had a face depicted with beads on leopard or elephant skin and was richly decorated with eagle feathers [figs. 146/147]. Their costumes resemble a "shield" made of glass beads with furs, a feather headdress, beaded gloves, and shoes.[1]

Accompanied by a drummer [figs. 144/145], such masked figures danced for Himmelheber twice in the capital Mushenge and deeply impressed him [figs. 143/148]:

> "I have never encountered anything comparable in Africa; it is simply magnificent! Two or even more masked figures always perform at the same time and engage in a kind of competition. Every masked dancer is supported by his surroundings, is surrounded by his accomplices and cheered on by their calls. Then he gets up and dances a few steps to the beat of the drums but the heavy, pompous costume makes actual dancing impossible. After merely a few artful jerks, the dancer soon retreats to the care of his two helpers, stretches out on the ground, catches his breath, and is fanned and handed water by his companions. Then, after a few minutes, he again prepares to dance."[2]

The Kuba were aware of the fascinating effect of these dances, which were not only a colorful spectacle for travelers but, first and foremost, served to display the power of the king, the princes, and the aristocrats [see essay Geary].[3]

The Kuba allowed Himmelheber to photograph these performances. However, it was not easy to acquire the rare masks. The dignitaries were not willing to sell them as the masks would lend them splendor and prestige at the performance for their own funeral.[4] — Nanina Guyer

1 Himmelheber 1960, p. 367.
2 Himmelheber 1940.
3 Vansina 2010, p. 47.
4 Himmelheber 1960, p. 368.

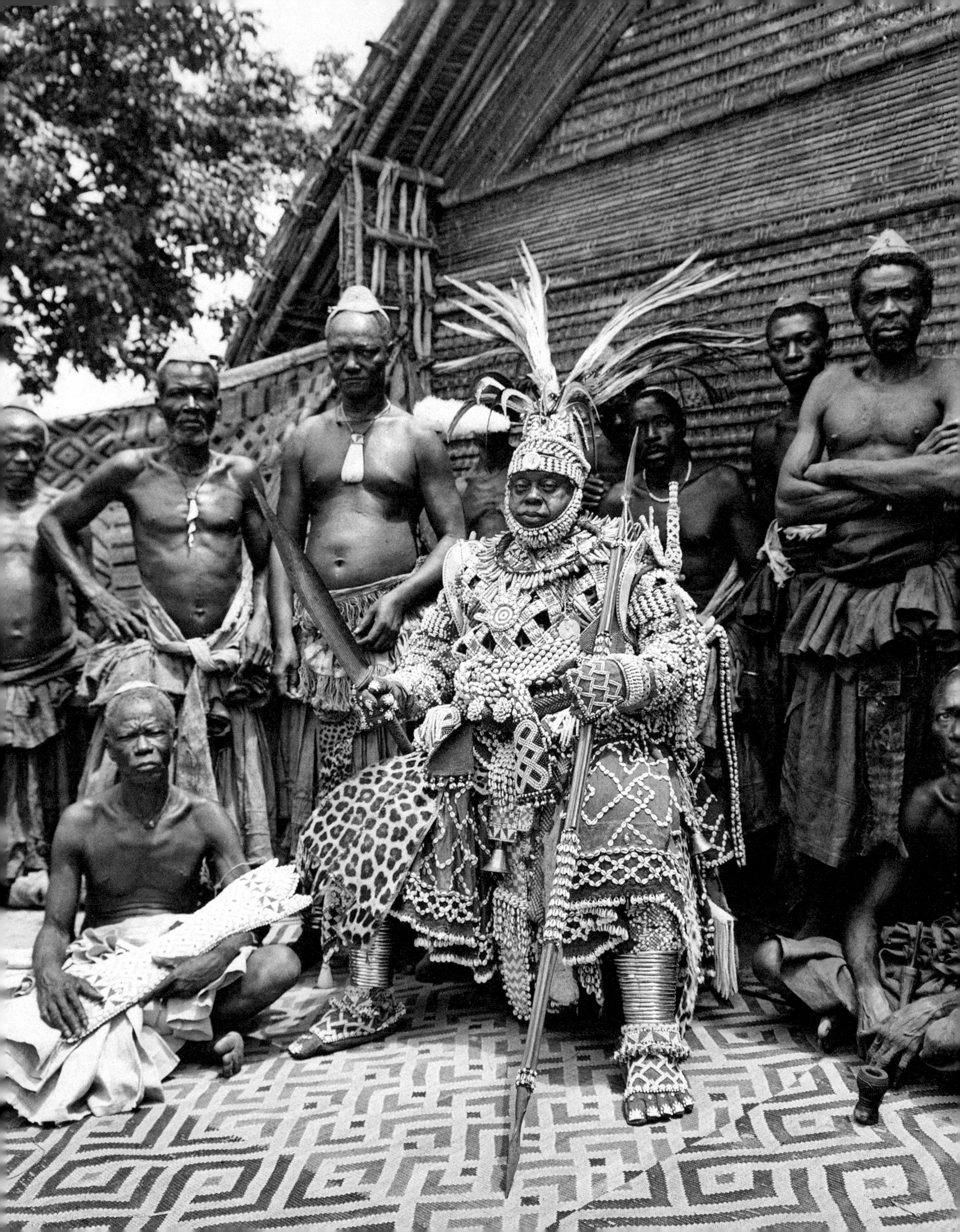

Fig. 149

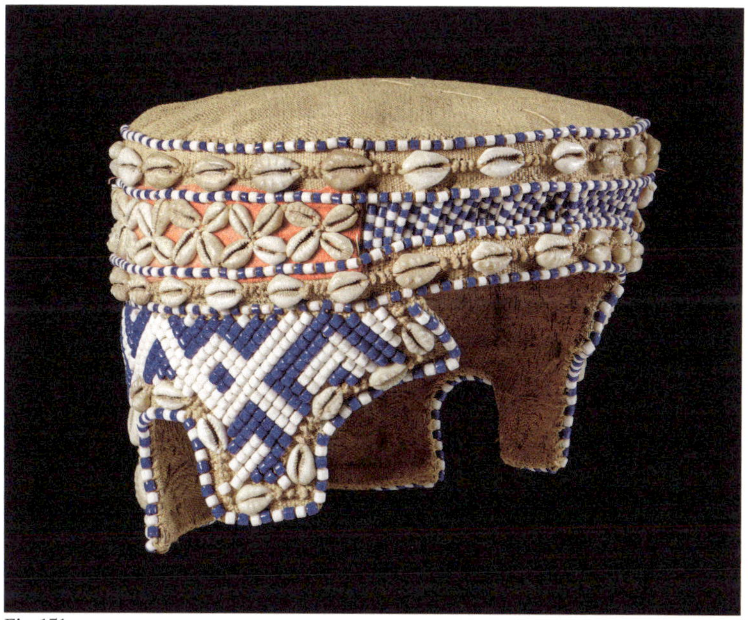

Fig. 151

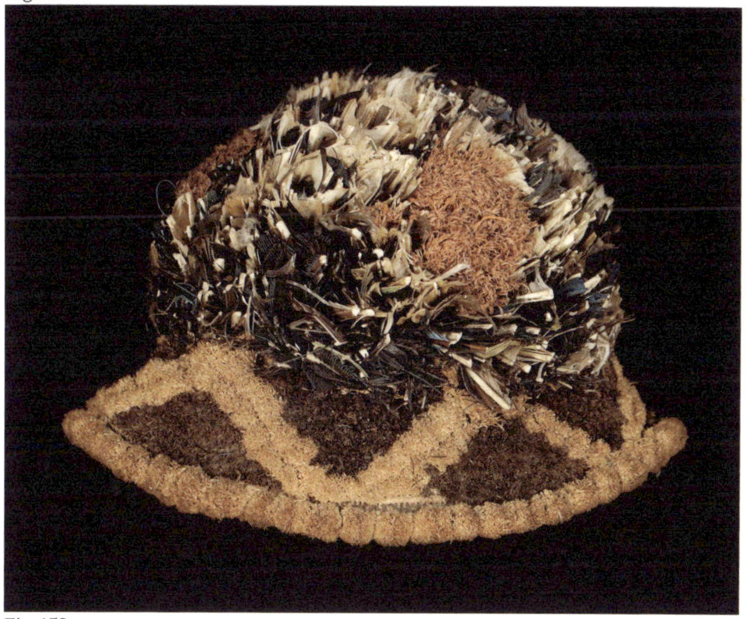

Fig. 152

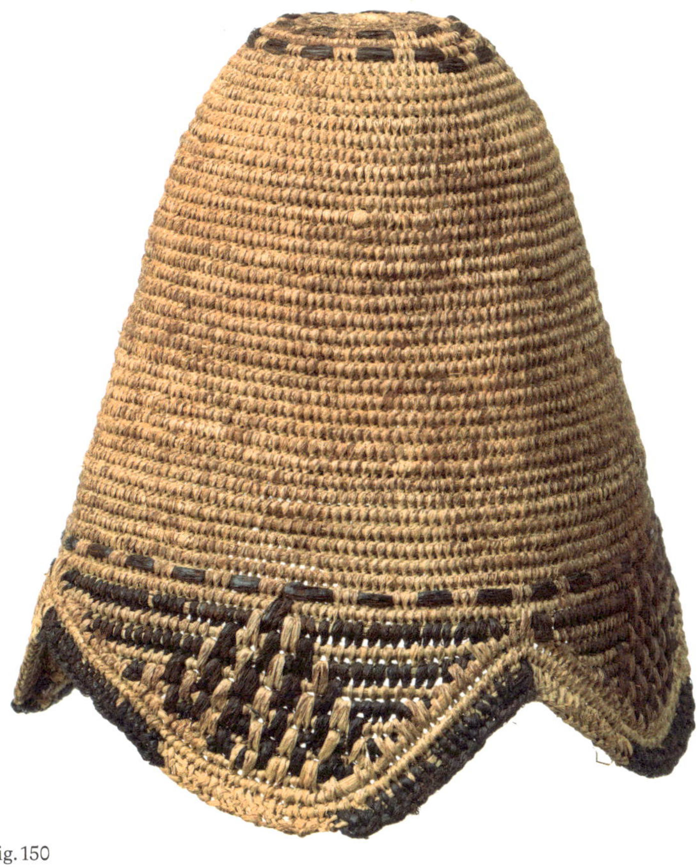

Fig. 150

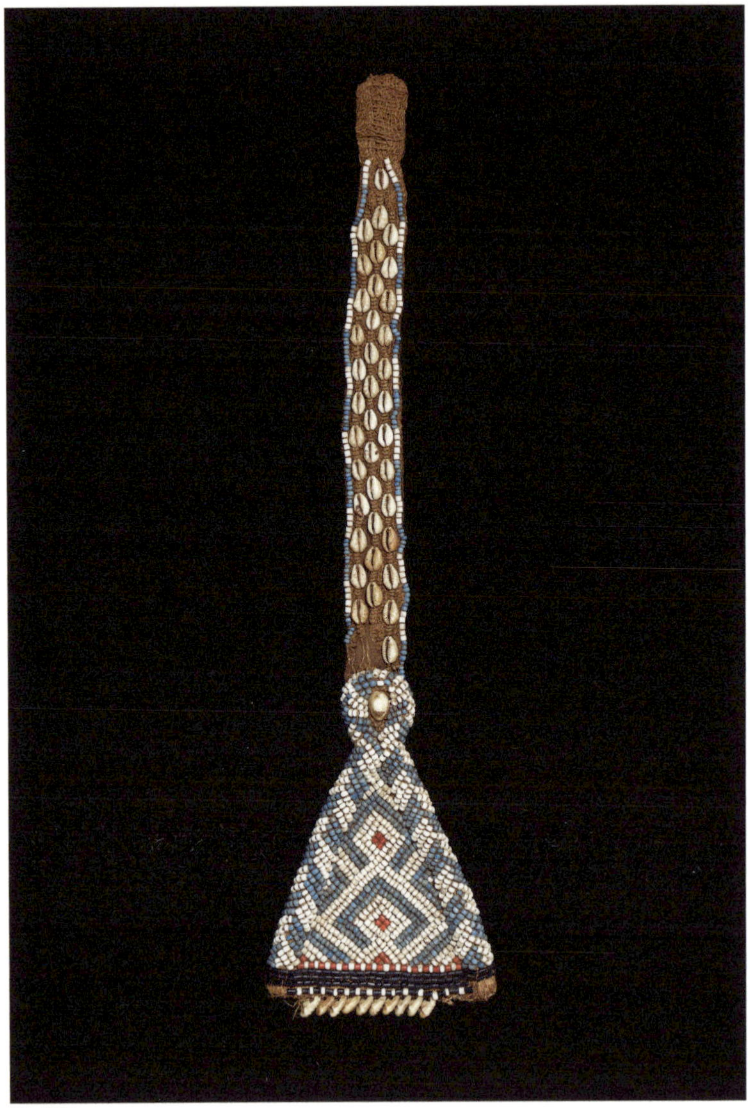
Fig. 153

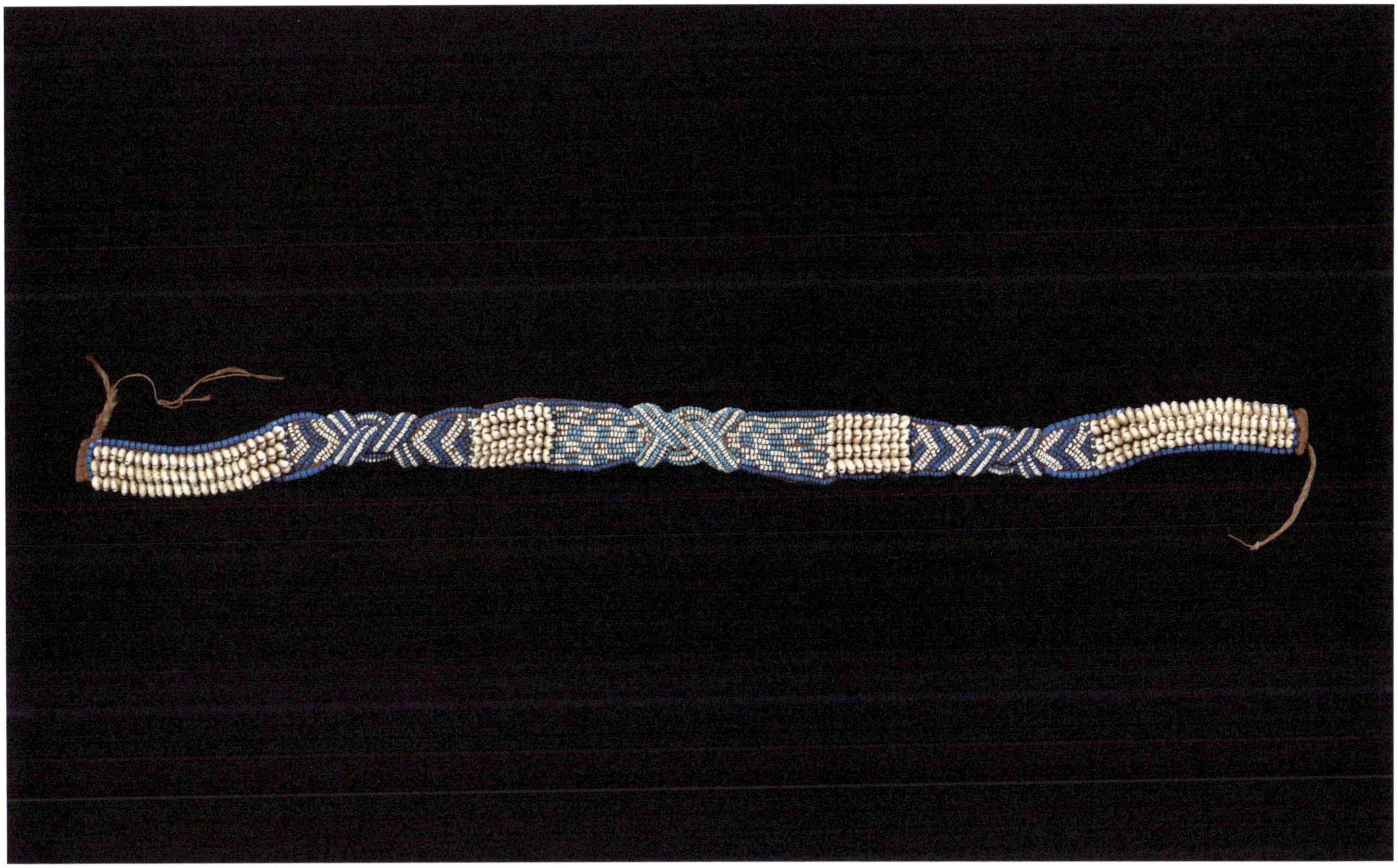

Fig. 154

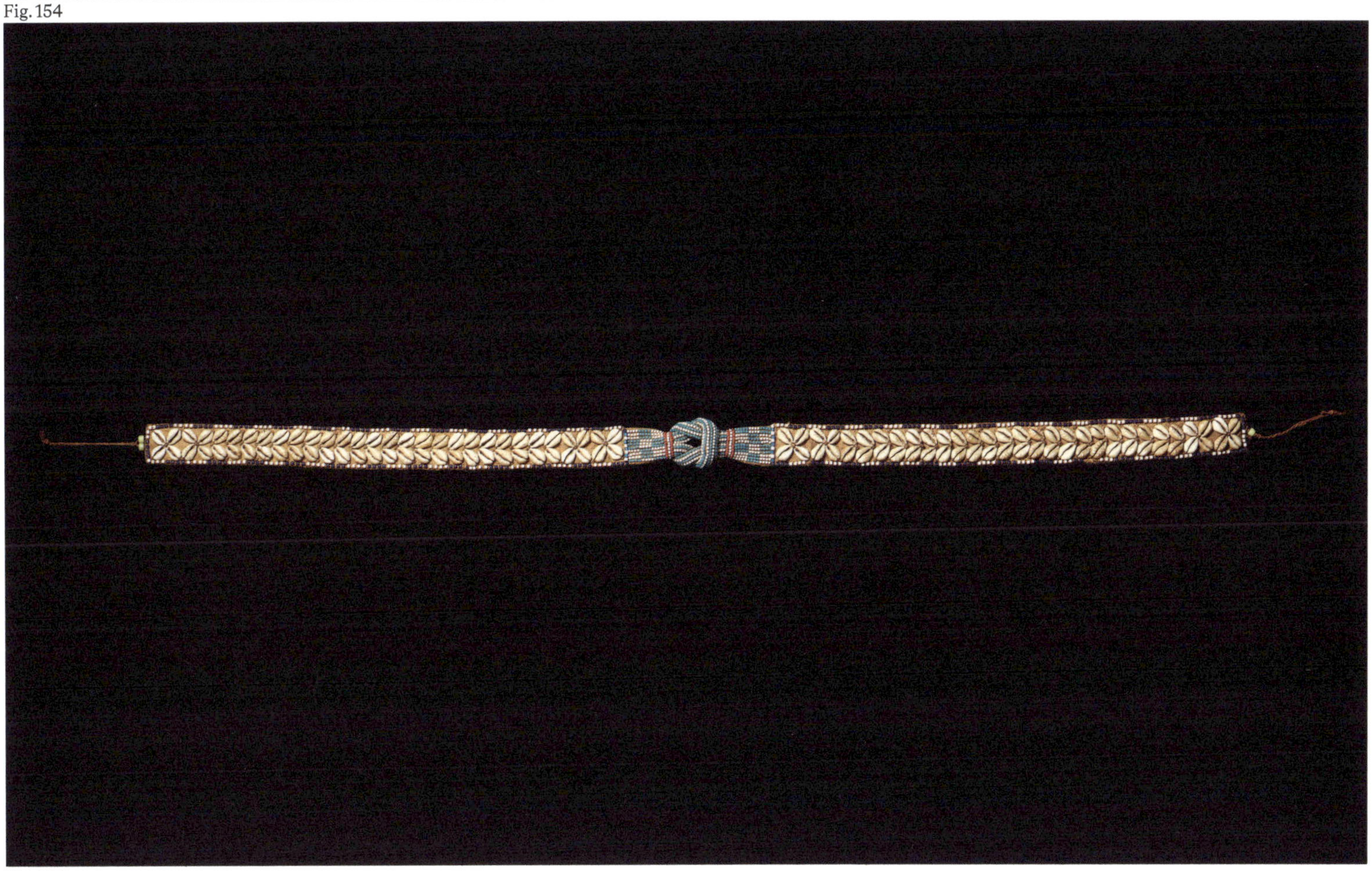

Fig. 155

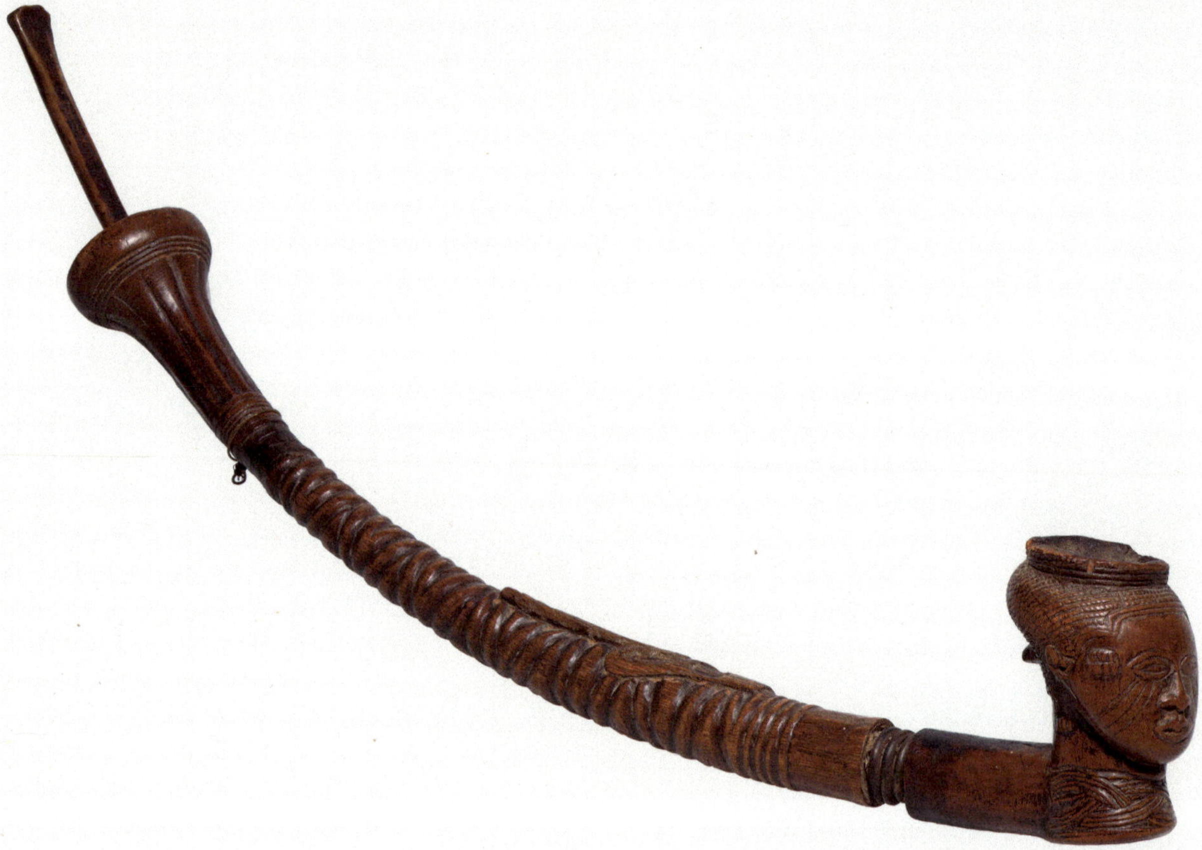

Fig. 156

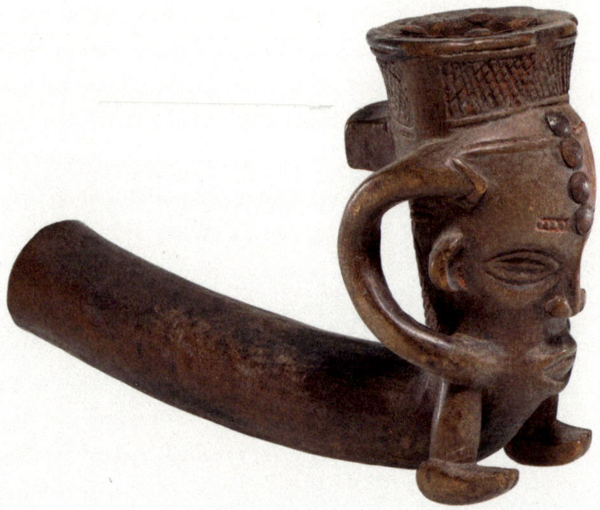

Fig. 157

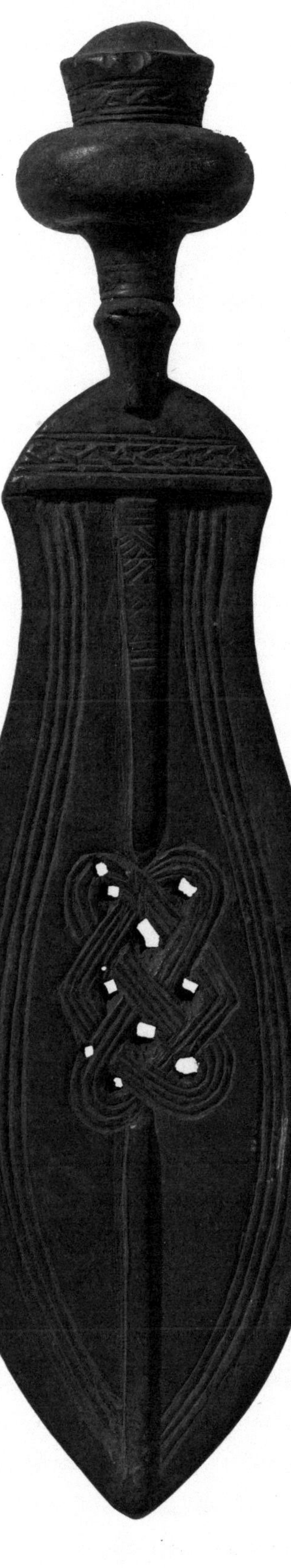

Fig. 158

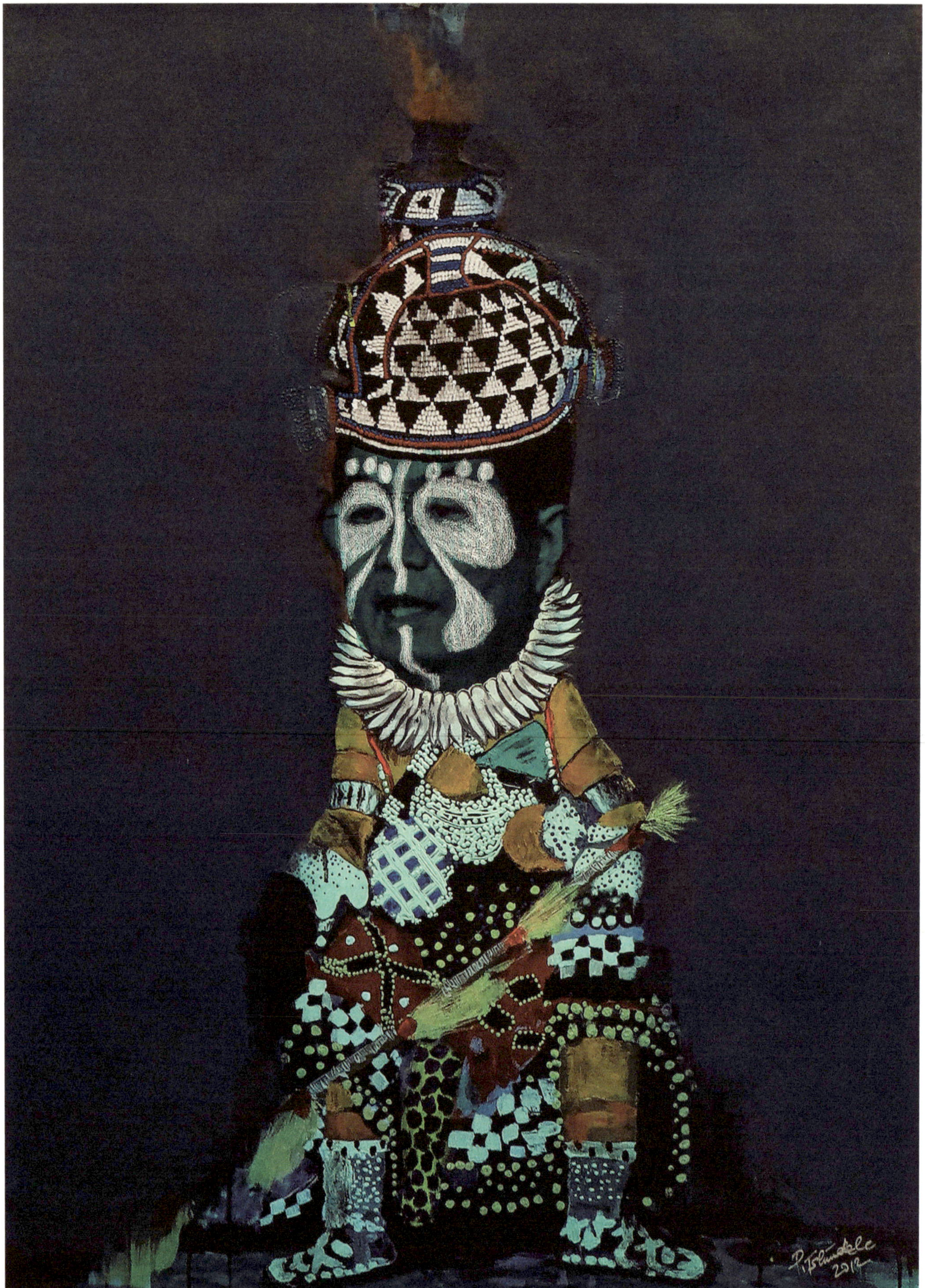

Fig. 159

Fig. 149
Eliot Elisofon
Kuba *nyim* Mbopey Mabiintsh ma-Kyeen
1947, gelatin silver print
Eliot Elisofon Photographic Archives, EEPA EENG 01138
National Museum of African Art
Smithsonian Institution

Fig. 150
Artist of the Kuba region
***Laket mishiing* men's cap**
Before 1939, plant fibers, 15 × 14 cm
Museum der Kulturen Basel, III 9495
Acquired by Hans Himmelheber

Fig. 151
Artist of the Kuba or Lele region
***Mpaan* headdress**
Before 1950, plant fibers, cowries, glass beads, cotton, 14.7 × 19 × 19 cm
Museum Rietberg Zürich, 2017.253
Gift of François and Claire Mottas

Fig. 152
Artist of the Kuba region
Hat with feathers
Before 1939, plant fibers, feathers, 15 × 17 cm
Museum Rietberg Zürich, 2013.175
Gift of Barbara and Eberhard Fischer
Acquired by Hans Himmelheber

Fig. 153
Artist of the Kuba region
***Nkody mupaap* pendant for a belt**
1890–1930, plant fibers, cowries, glass beads, 2 × 13.5 × 52.5 cm
Museum Rietberg Zürich, 2017.123
Gift of François and Claire Mottas
Guy Smal

Fig. 154
Artist of the Kuba region
***Nkody mu-ikup lakiing* belt**
Before 1981, fabric, plant fibers, cowries, glass beads, 2.5 × 85 × 5 cm
Museum Rietberg Zürich, 2017.282
Gift of François and Claire Mottas
Dorothy Wiseman

Fig. 155
Artist of the Kuba region
***Nkody mu-ikup lakiing* belt**
1930–1960, plant fibers, cowries, glass beads, 2.8 × 110 × 4 cm
Museum Rietberg Zürich, 2017.124
Gift of François and Claire Mottas
Guy Smal

Fig. 156
Artist of the Kuba-Bushoong region
Tobacco pipe
1890–1930, wood, 8.5 × 53 × 5.5 cm
Private Collection Lausanne
Baptist Missionary Society, Thomas Hooper

Fig. 157
Artist of the Bindji region
Tobacco pipe
Before 1939, wood, metal, 57 cm
Barbara and Eberhard Fischer
Acquired by Hans Himmelheber

Fig. 158
Artist of the Kuba region
Prestigious sword
Before 1939, wood, 41 × 11.5 × 5.8 cm
Museum Rietberg Zürich, 2018.118
Gift of Martin Himmelheber
Acquired by Hans Himmelheber

Fig. 159
Pathy Tshindele
Untitled [Portrait of the former president of the People's Republic of China, Hu Jintao]
From the series *It's my kings*
2012, acrylic on canvas, 127 × 90 cm
MAGNIN-A gallery, Paris

OLD AND NEW KINGS: PORTRAIT OF MBOPEY MABIINTSH MA-KYEEN AND PATHY TSHINDELE'S *IT'S MY KINGS* — For the series *It's my kings*, the artist Pathy Tshindele Kapinga investigated the history and culture of the Congo from colonial times to the present. While doing so, he came across the various kings and dignitaries who shaped the history of the Congo.

In *It's my kings* Tshindele refers directly to the appearance of the kings of the Kuba, a once powerful kingdom in today's Kasai province. In the Kuba kingdom there was a longstanding tradition of portraying monarchs that ranged from *ndop* carved wooden sculptures of kings to photographic portraits.[1] The Kuba king Mbopey Mabiintsh ma-Kyeen, whose reign lasted from 1939 to 1969, for example, posed in his spectacular robe for American photographer Eliot Elisofon in 1947 [fig. 149]. The king is wearing a costume embroidered all over with beads, a leopard skin is lying on his knee, and in his hand he is holding a lance and a sword. It took three hours and numerous assistants to put on the costume.[2] Members of the royal court also demonstrated their status with various attributes, such as belts, pipes, and headdresses richly adorned with beads, or a sword [figs. 150–158].

For *It's my kings* (2012) Tshindele portrayed the ruling heads of state of international great powers at the time—such as Nicolas Sarkozy, Barack Obama, David Cameron, and Hu Jintao—in the brightly colored robes of the Kuba kings and in the style of Congolese popular painting [fig. 159]. Just as in the photograph, Tshindele's king is wearing a magnificent costume and is holding a kind of scepter in his hands. However, the artist decorates the face—here that of the former president of the People's Republic of China, Hu Jintao—with face painting that is unusual for the Kuba. The past visual repertoire of the Kuba is linked to elements from the present and to others from the artist's imagination to create a vision of future kings. In doing so, Tshindele is criticizing the dubious role played by rulers from the geographic North in African politics and, at the same time, claiming a voice in future politics of the Congo with the title of the series *It's my kings*. — Nanina Guyer

1 Geary 1993, pp. 72–77.
2 Geary 1993, p. 72.

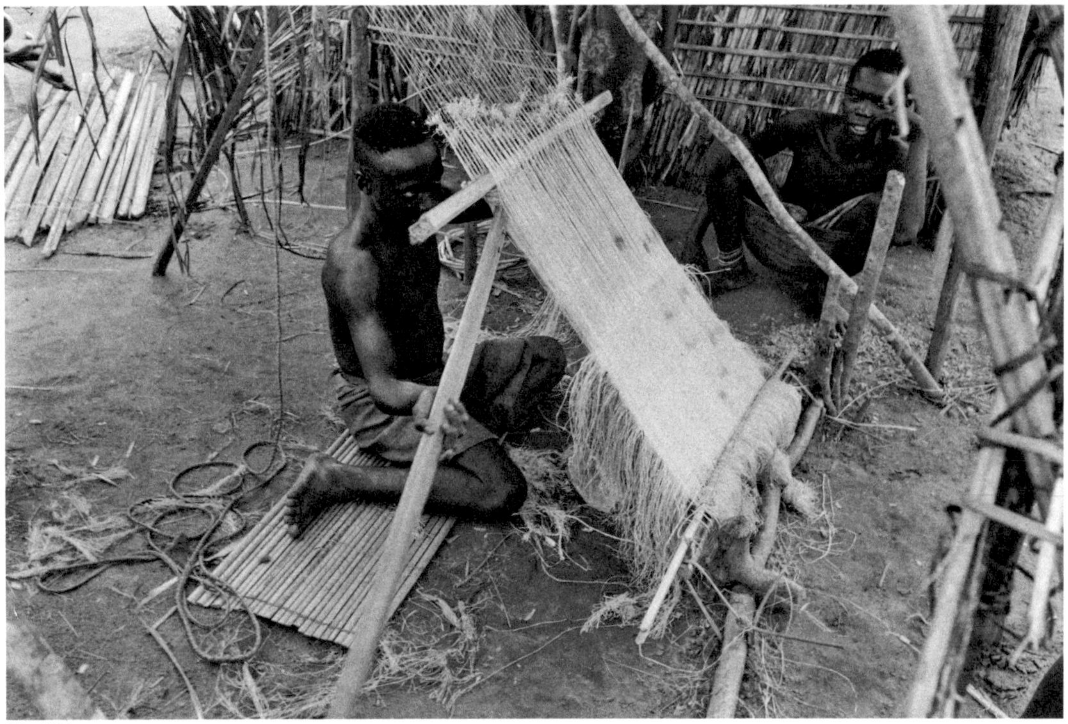
Fig. 160

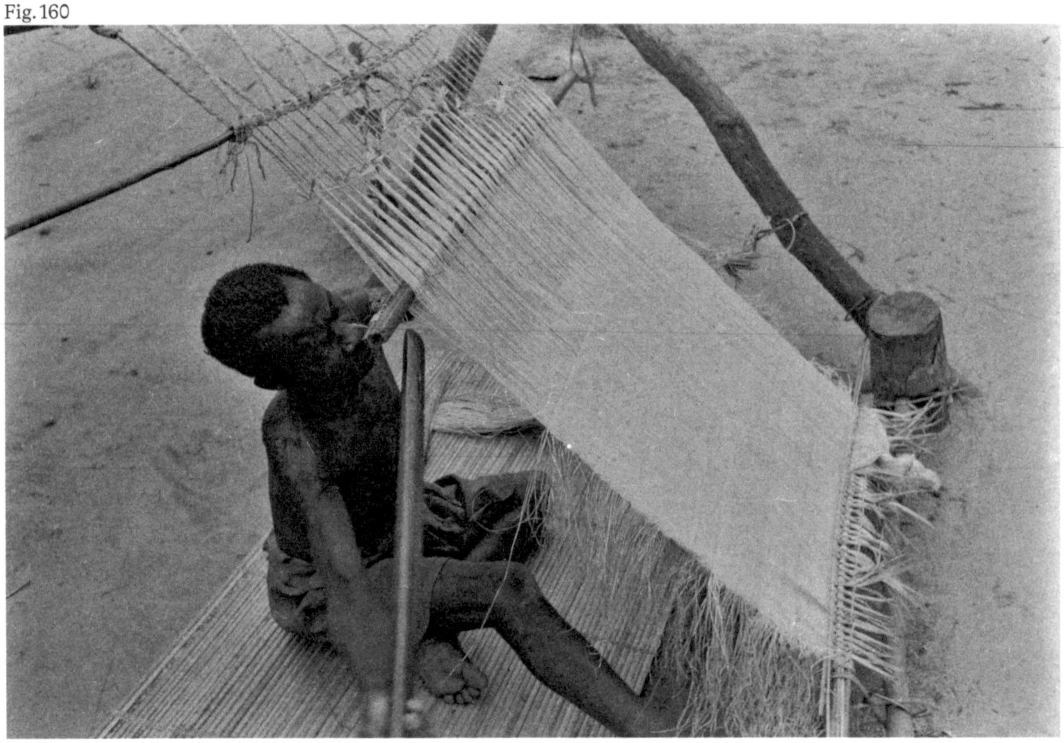
Fig. 161

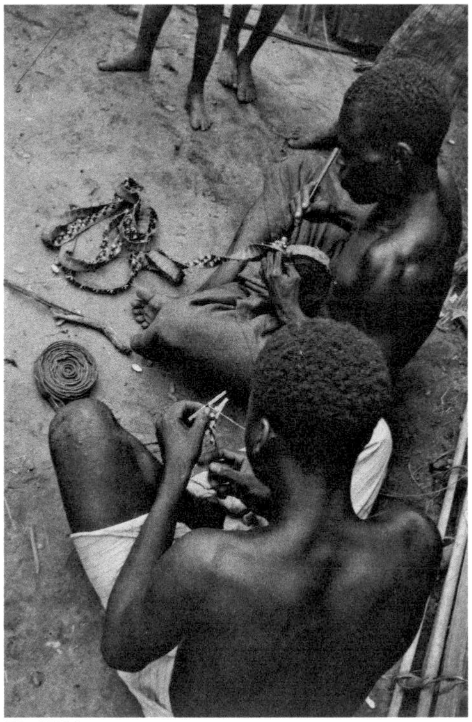

Fig. 162.1

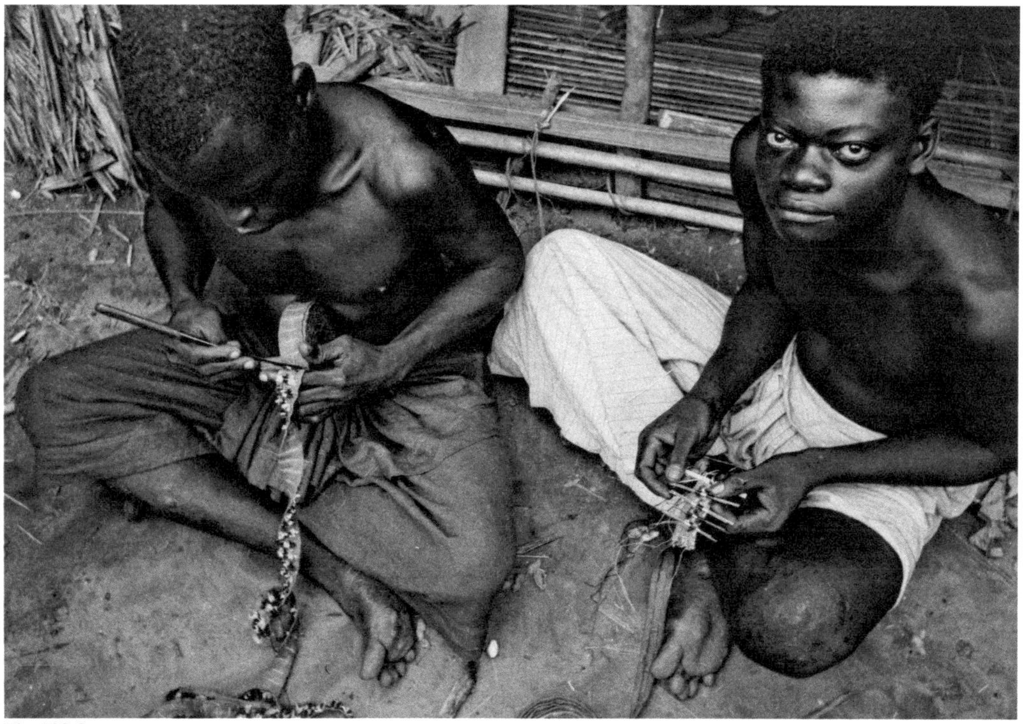

Fig. 162.2

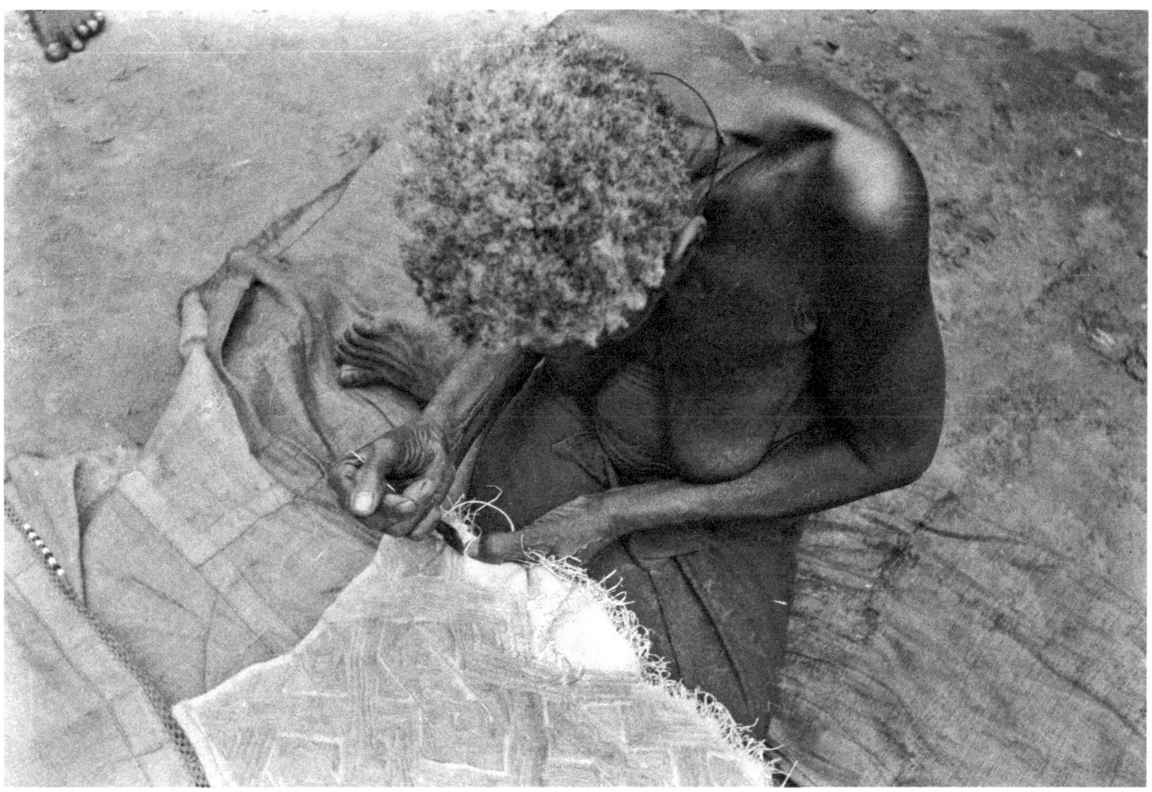

Fig. 163

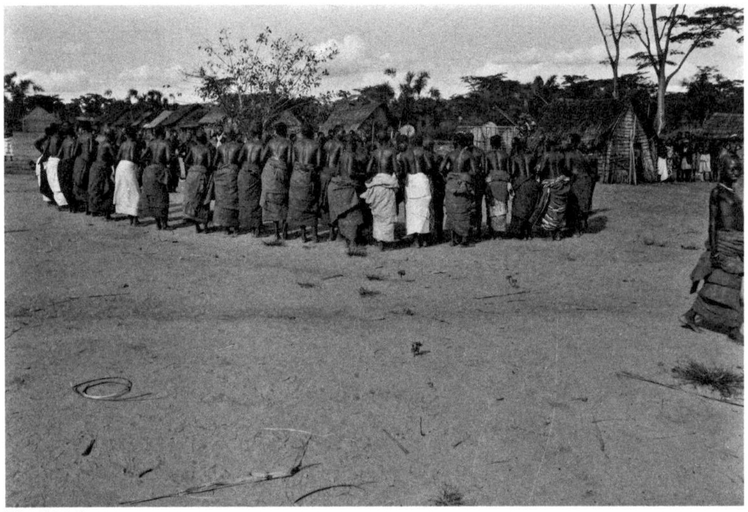
Fig. 164.1

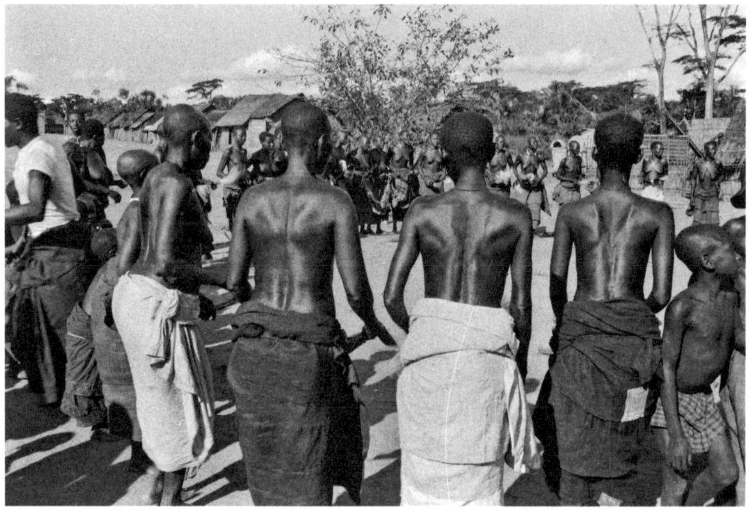
Fig. 164.2

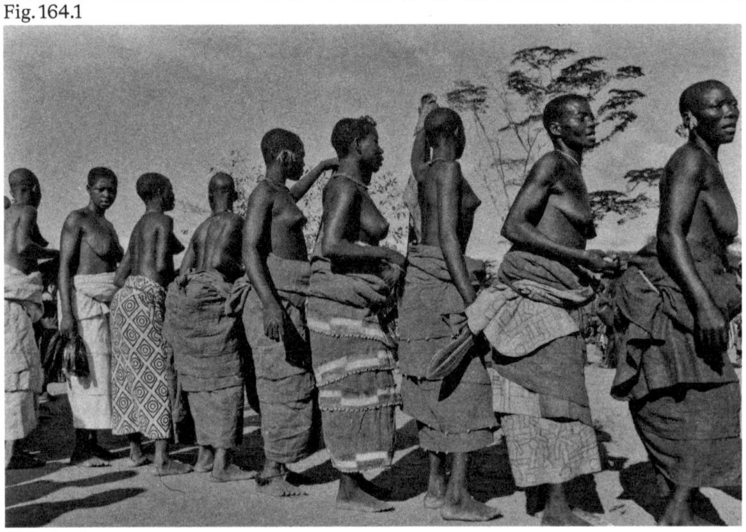
Fig. 164.3

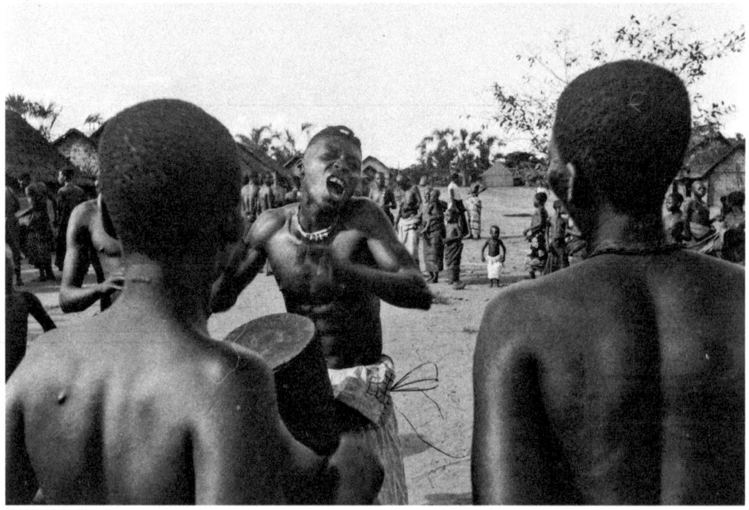
Fig. 164.4

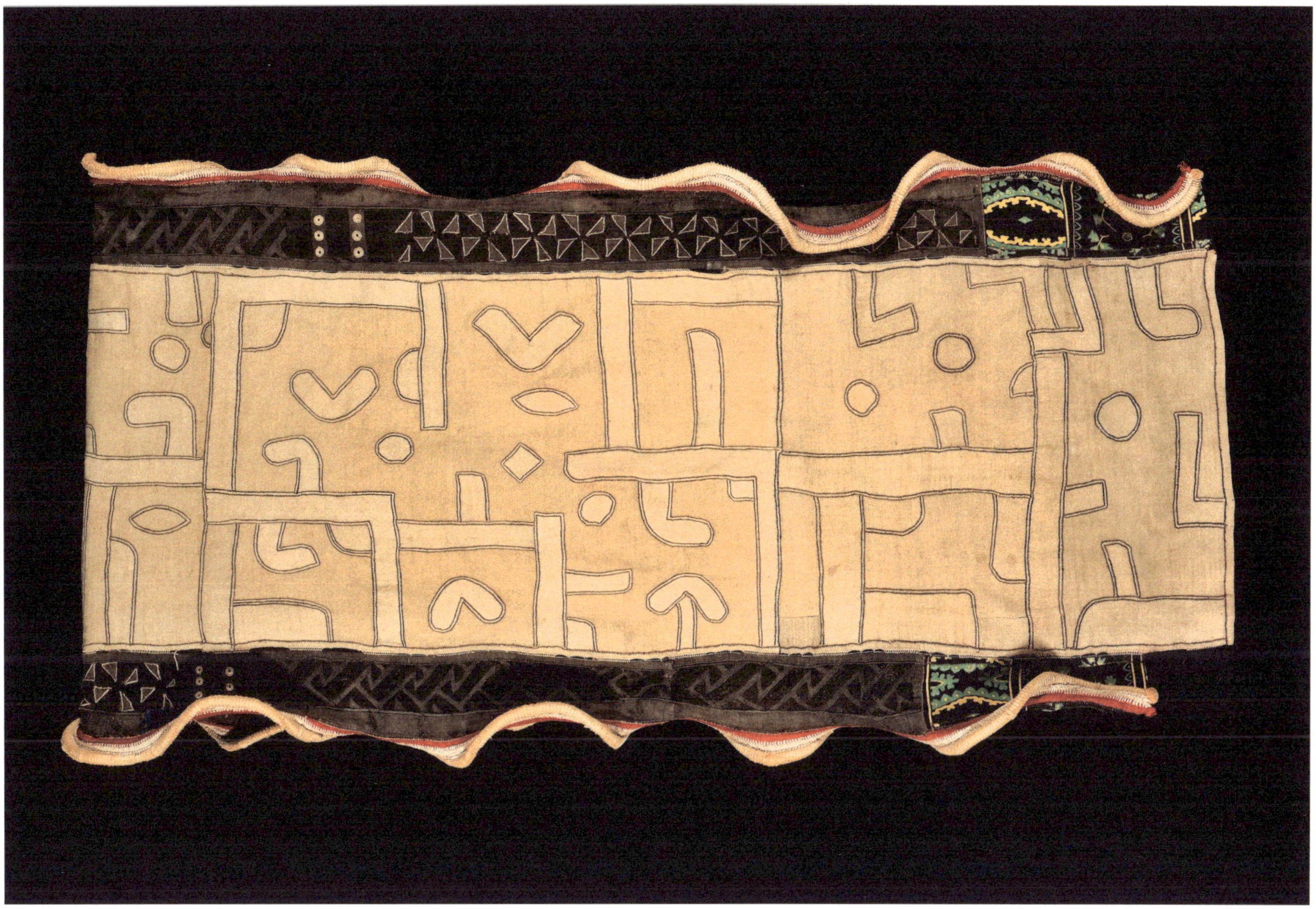
Fig. 165

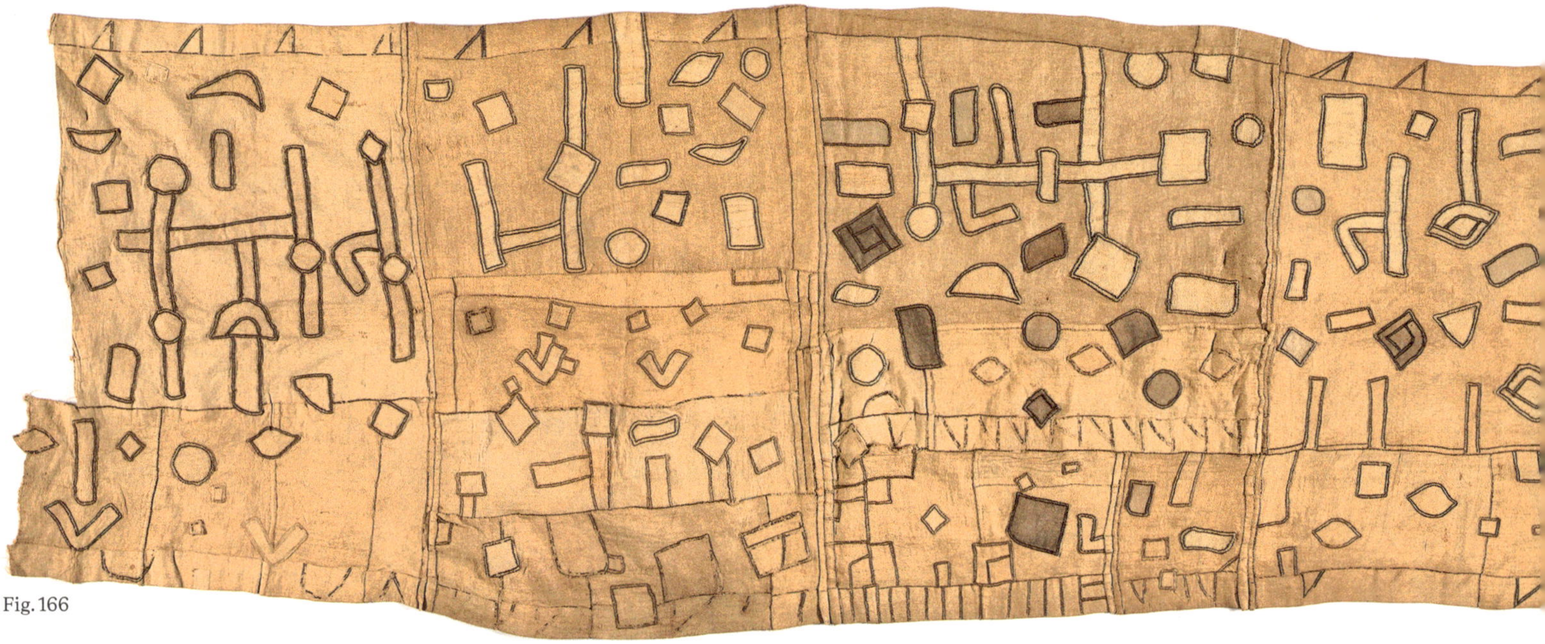

Fig. 166

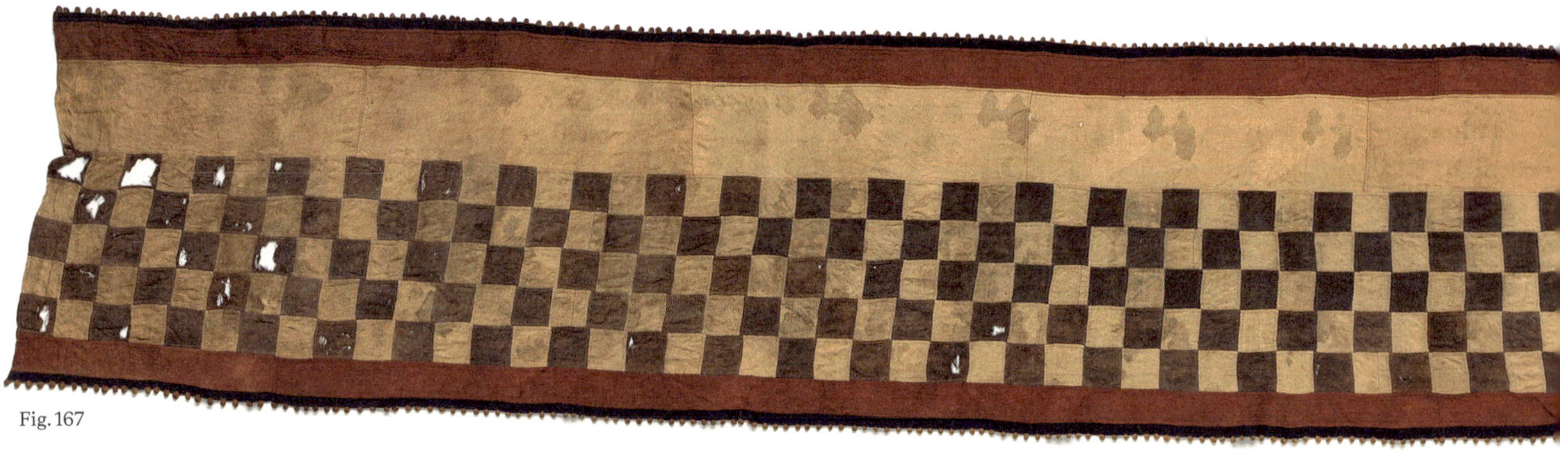

Fig. 167

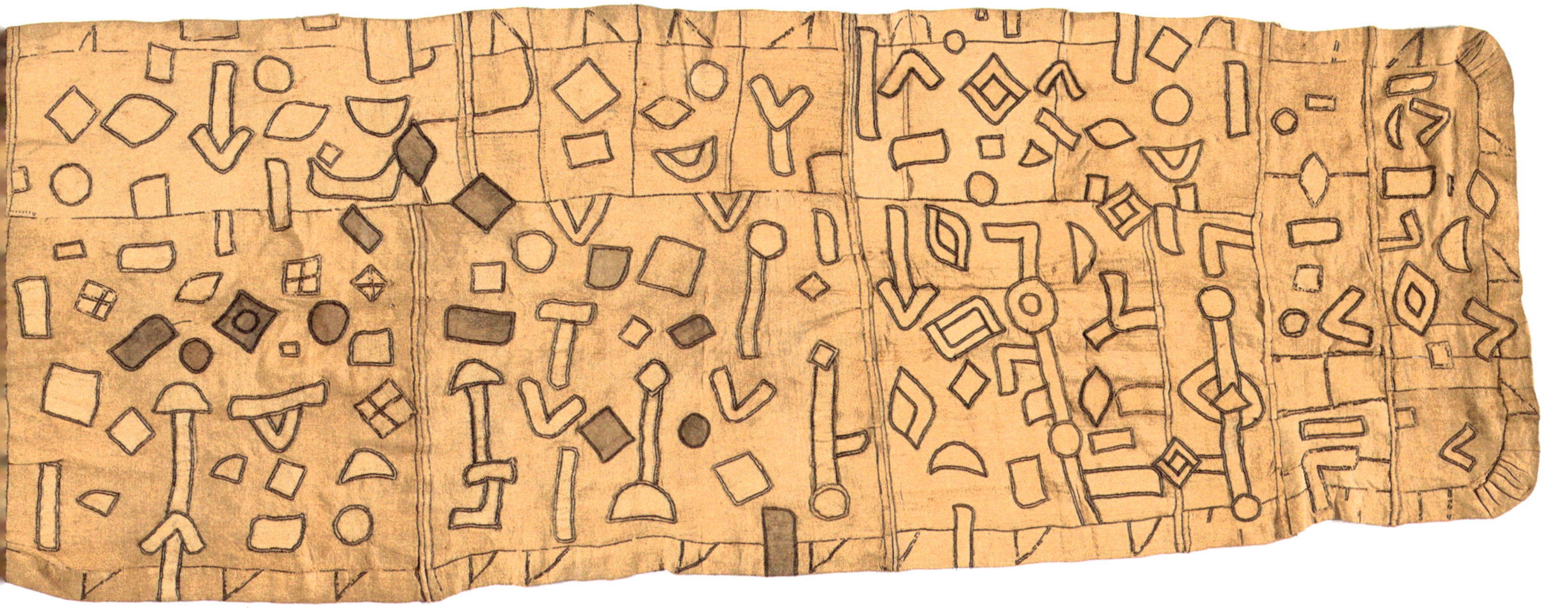

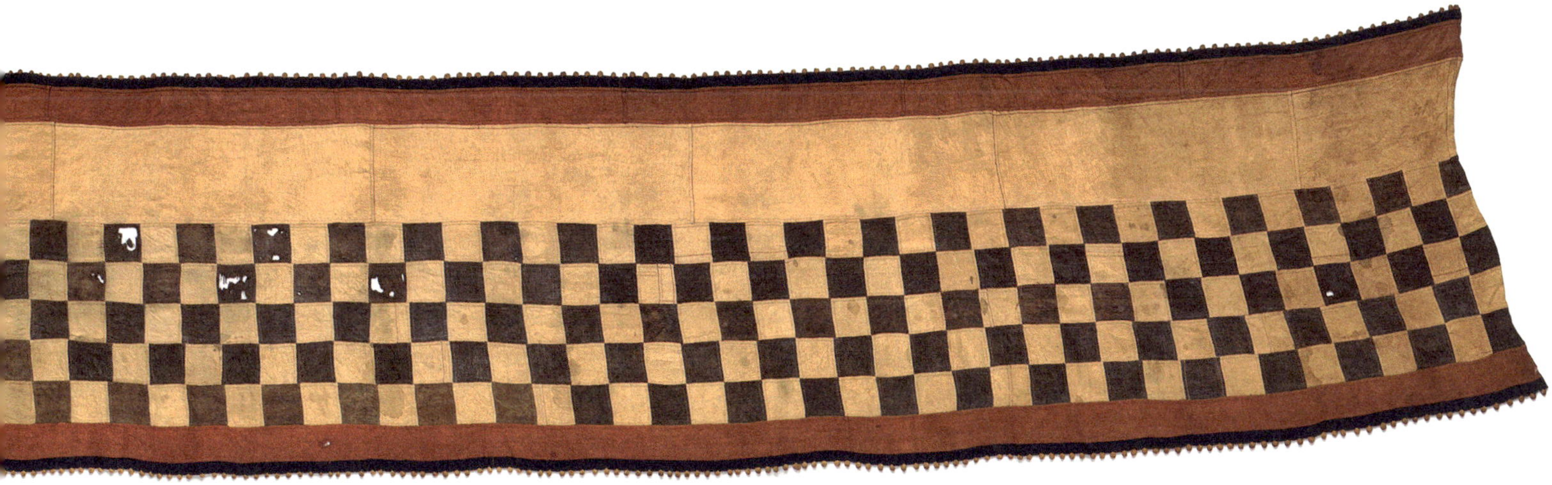

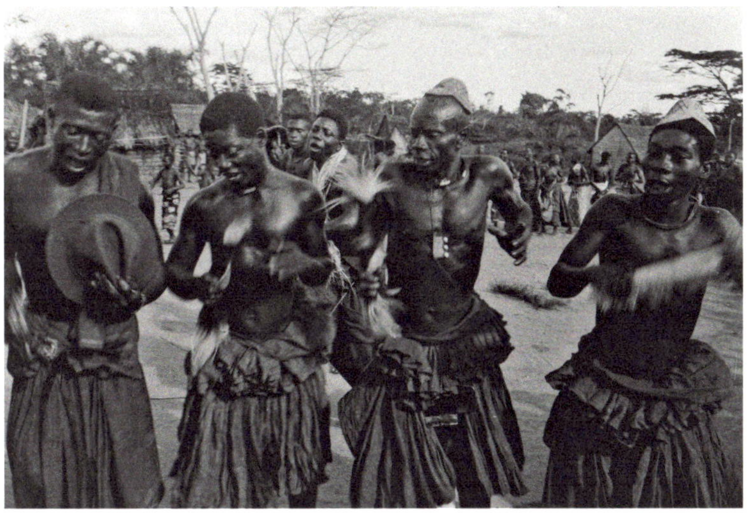

Fig. 168

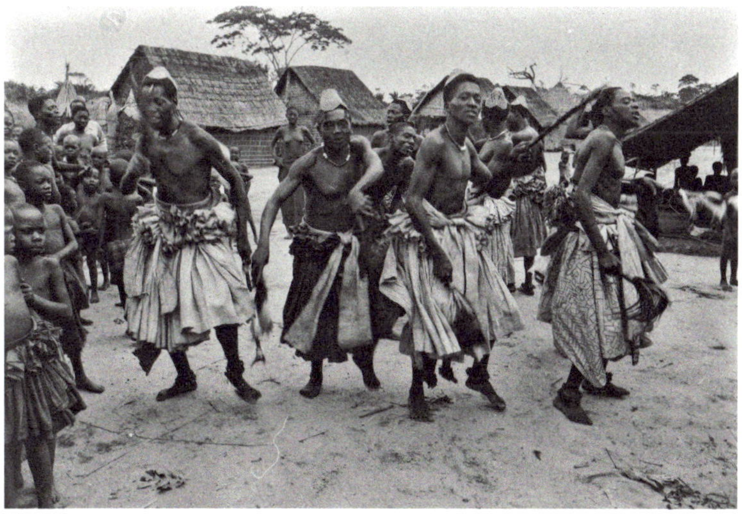

Fig. 169

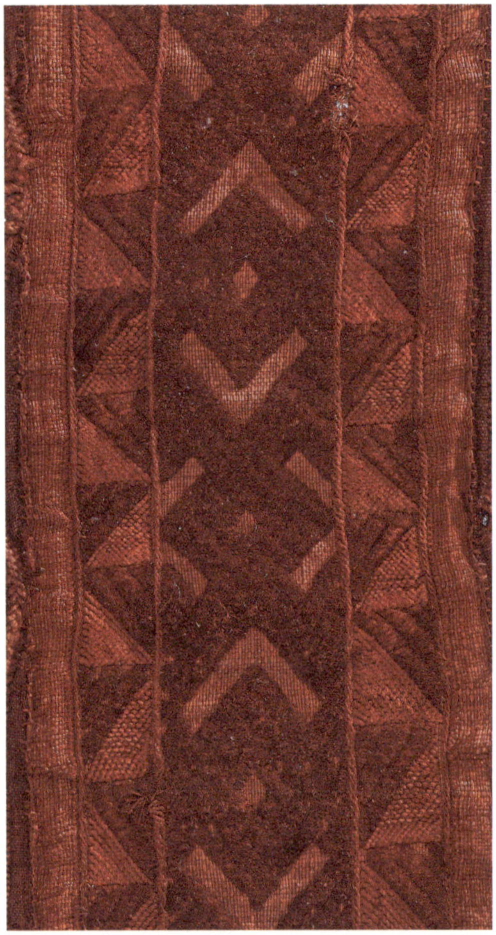
Fig. 170

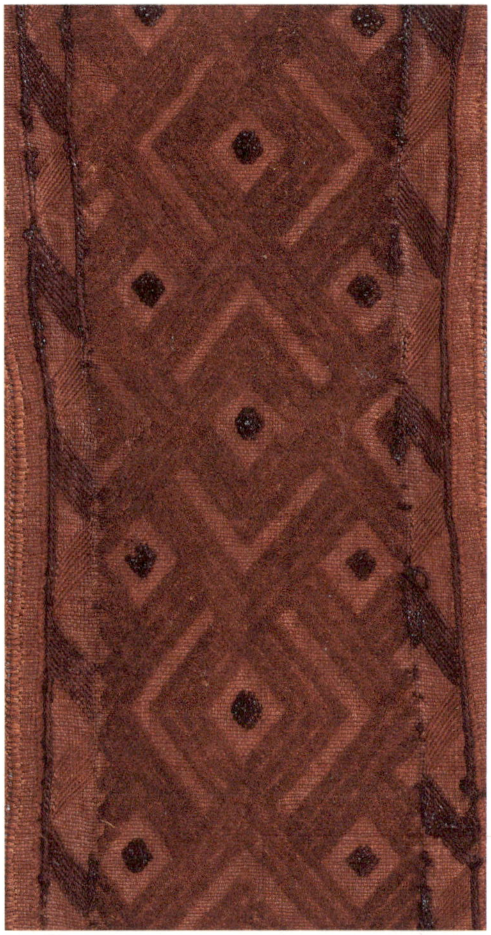
Fig. 171

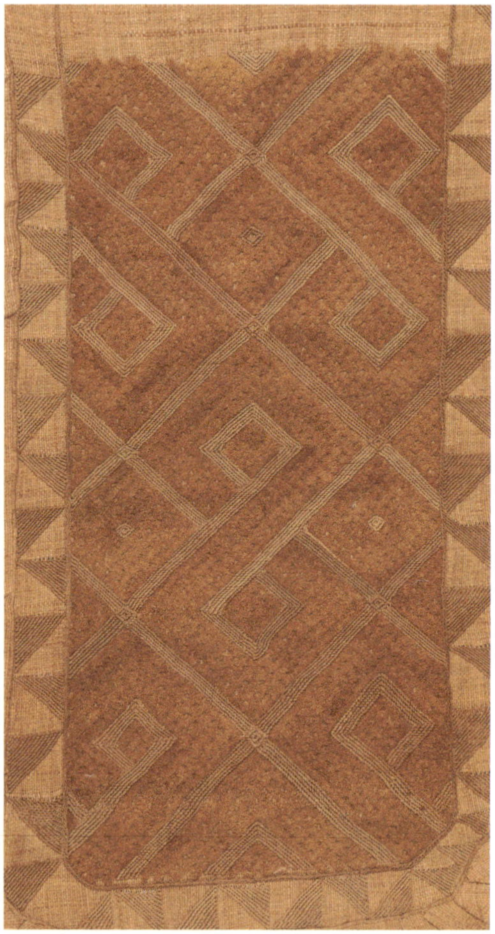
Fig. 172

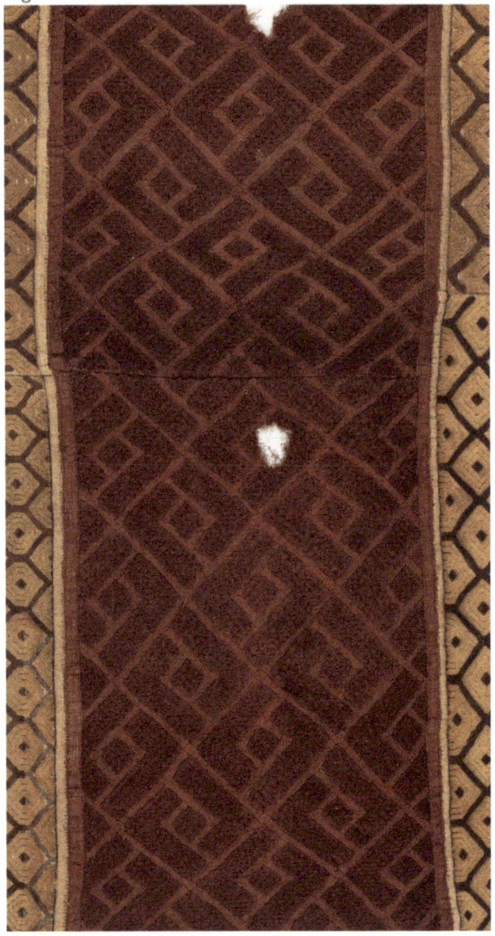
Fig. 173

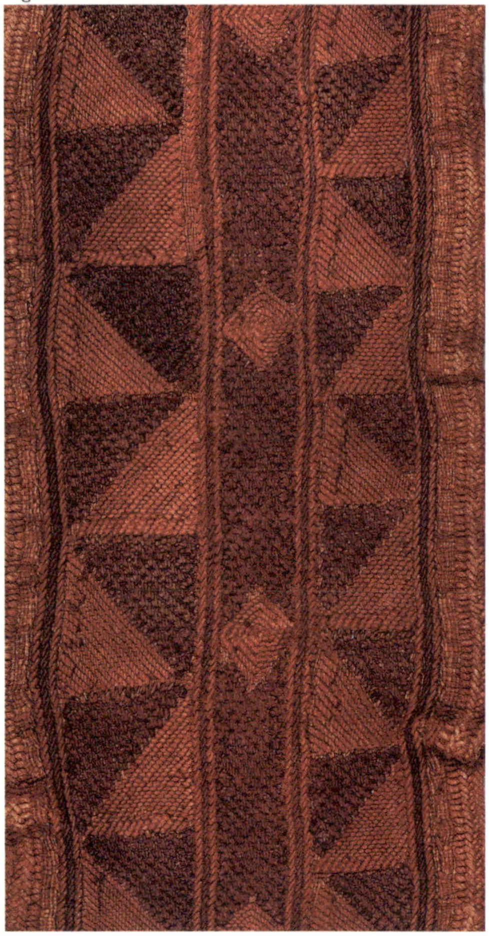
Fig. 174

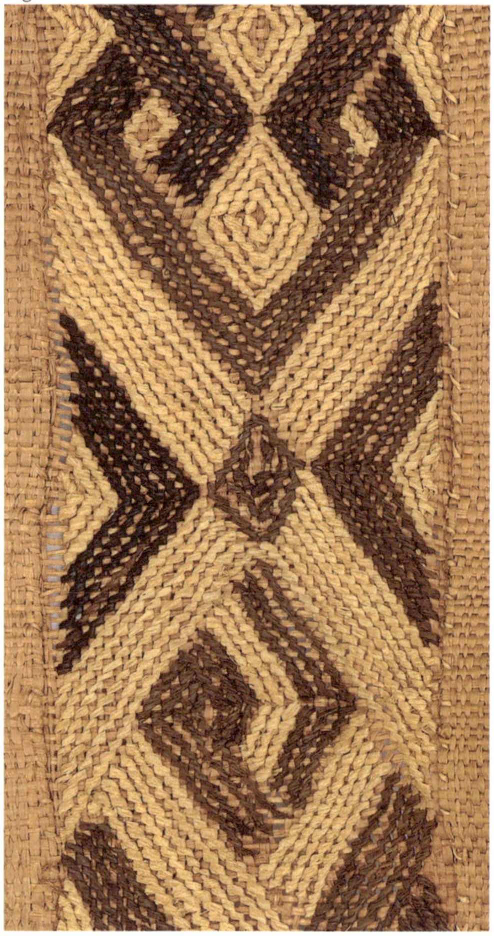
Fig. 175

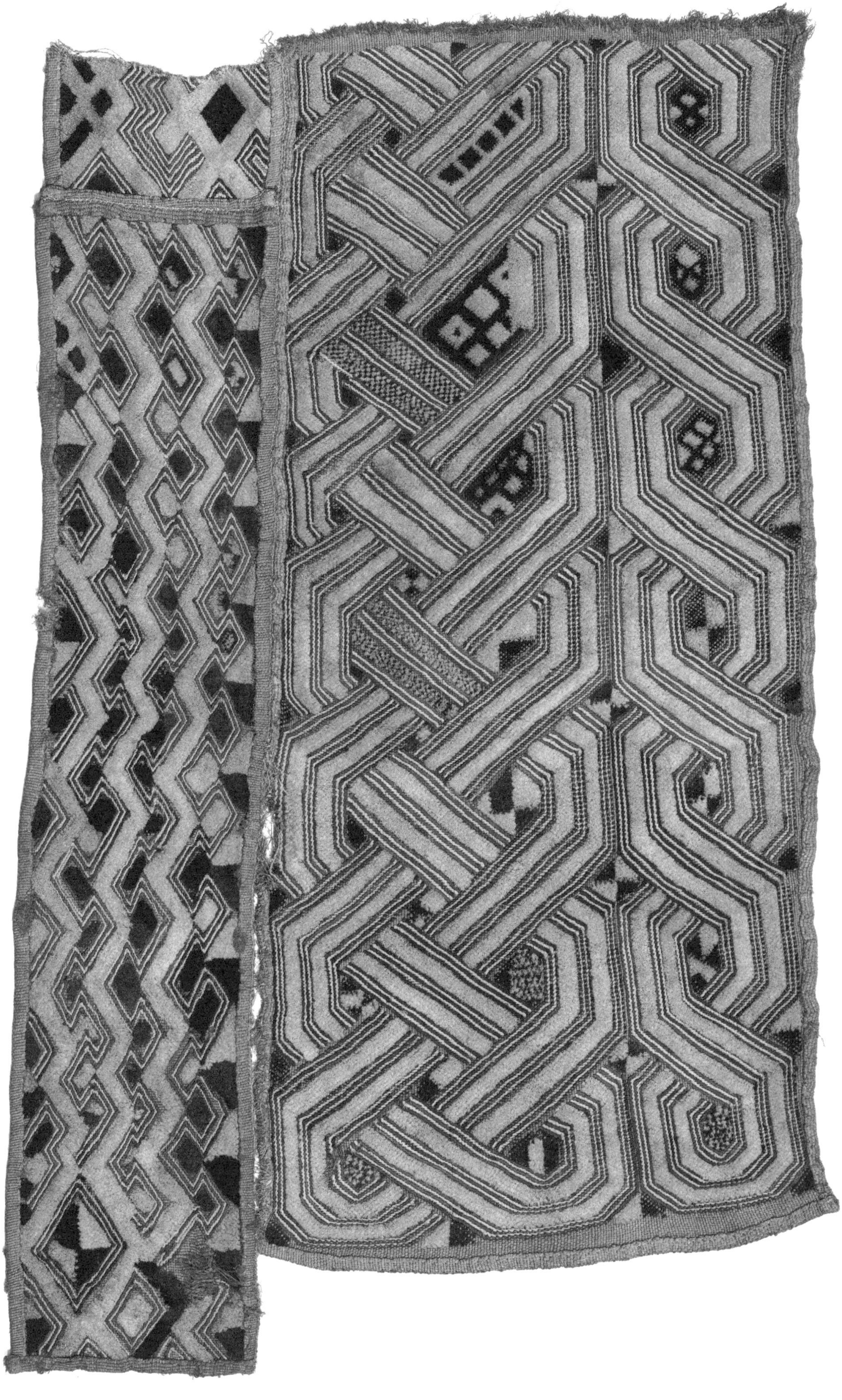

Fig. 176

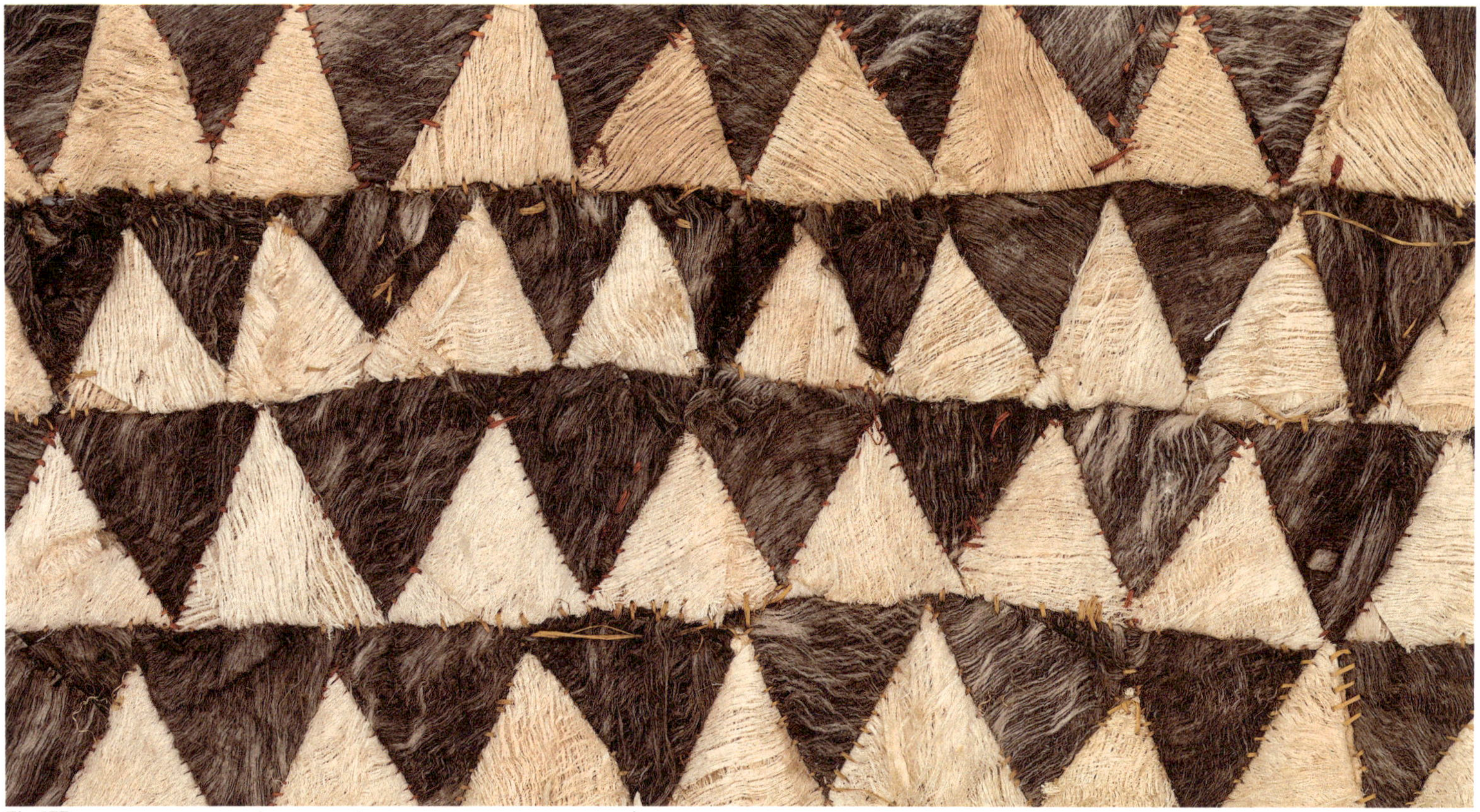
Fig. 177

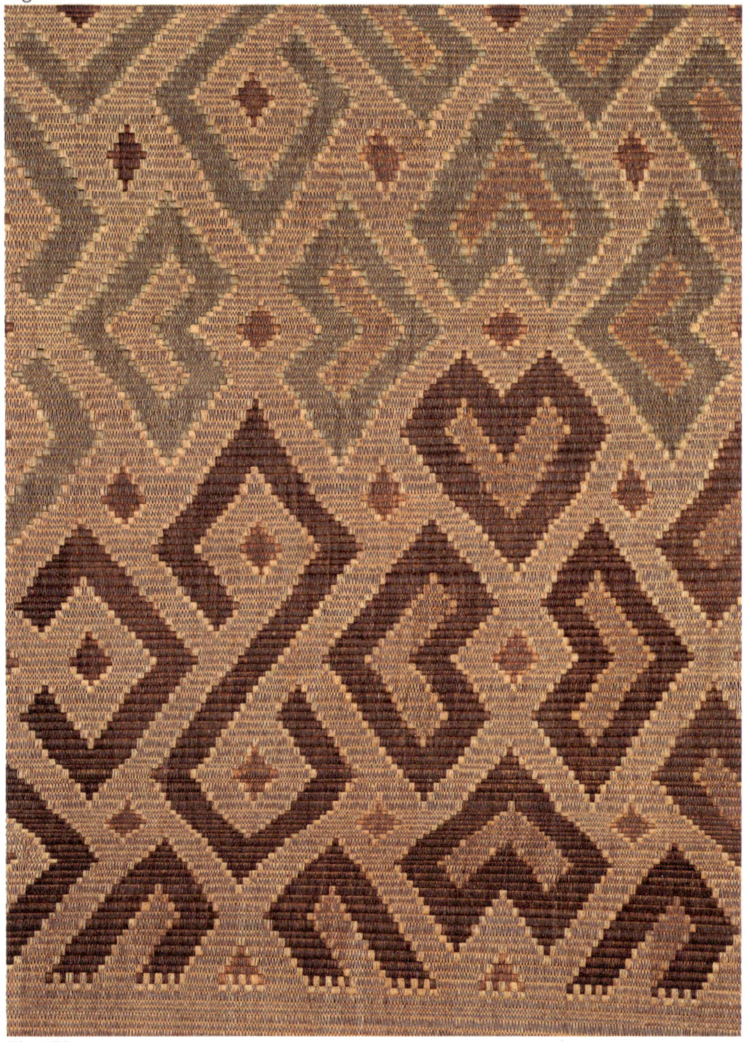
Fig. 178

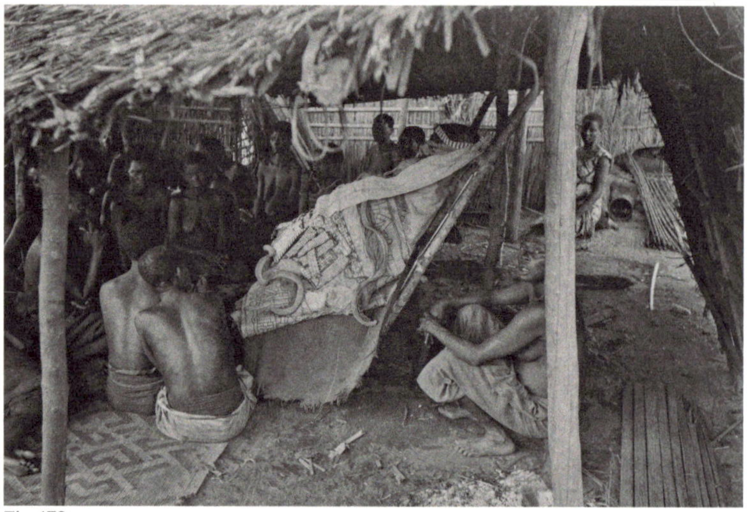
Fig. 179

Fig. 180

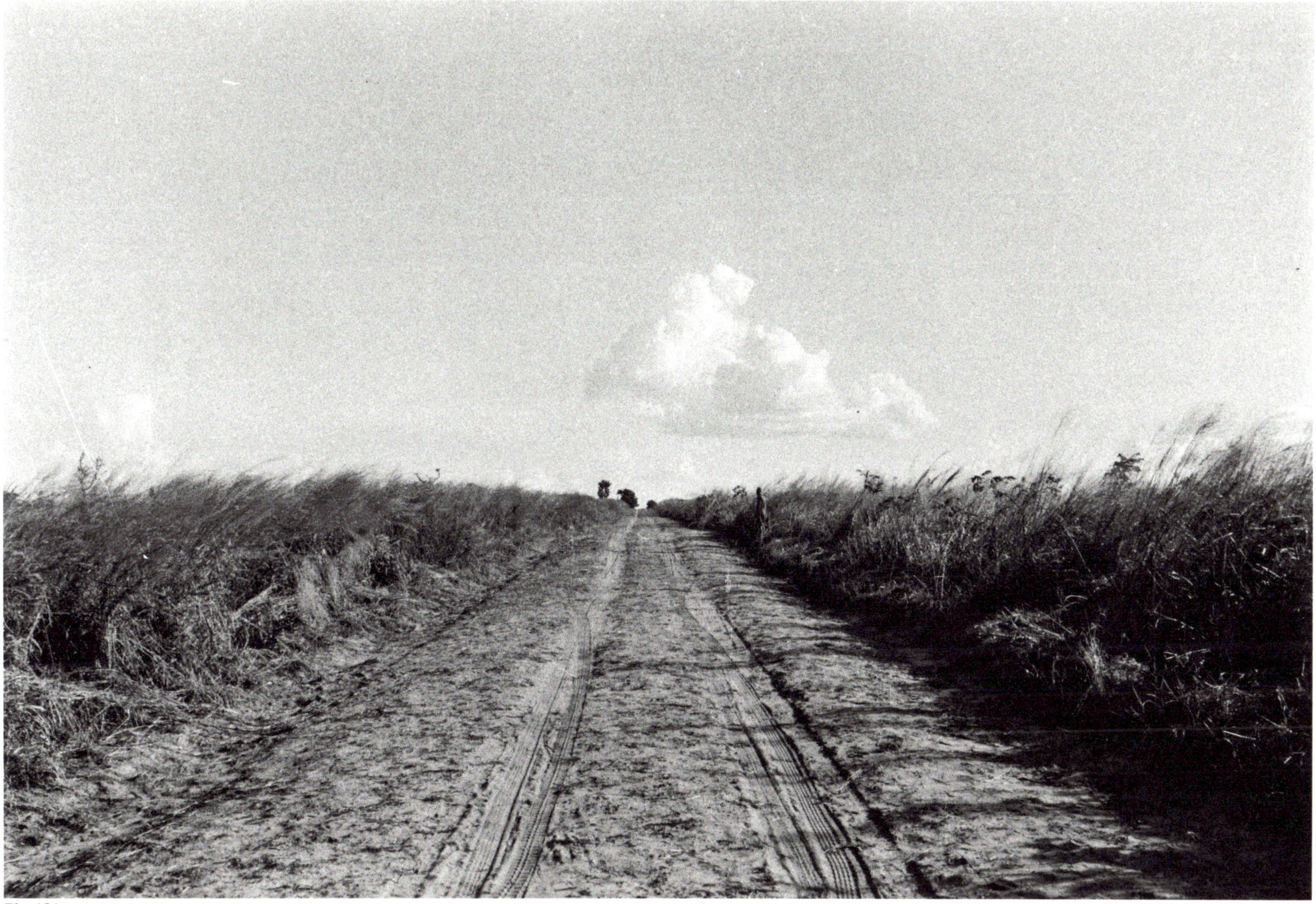

Fig. 181

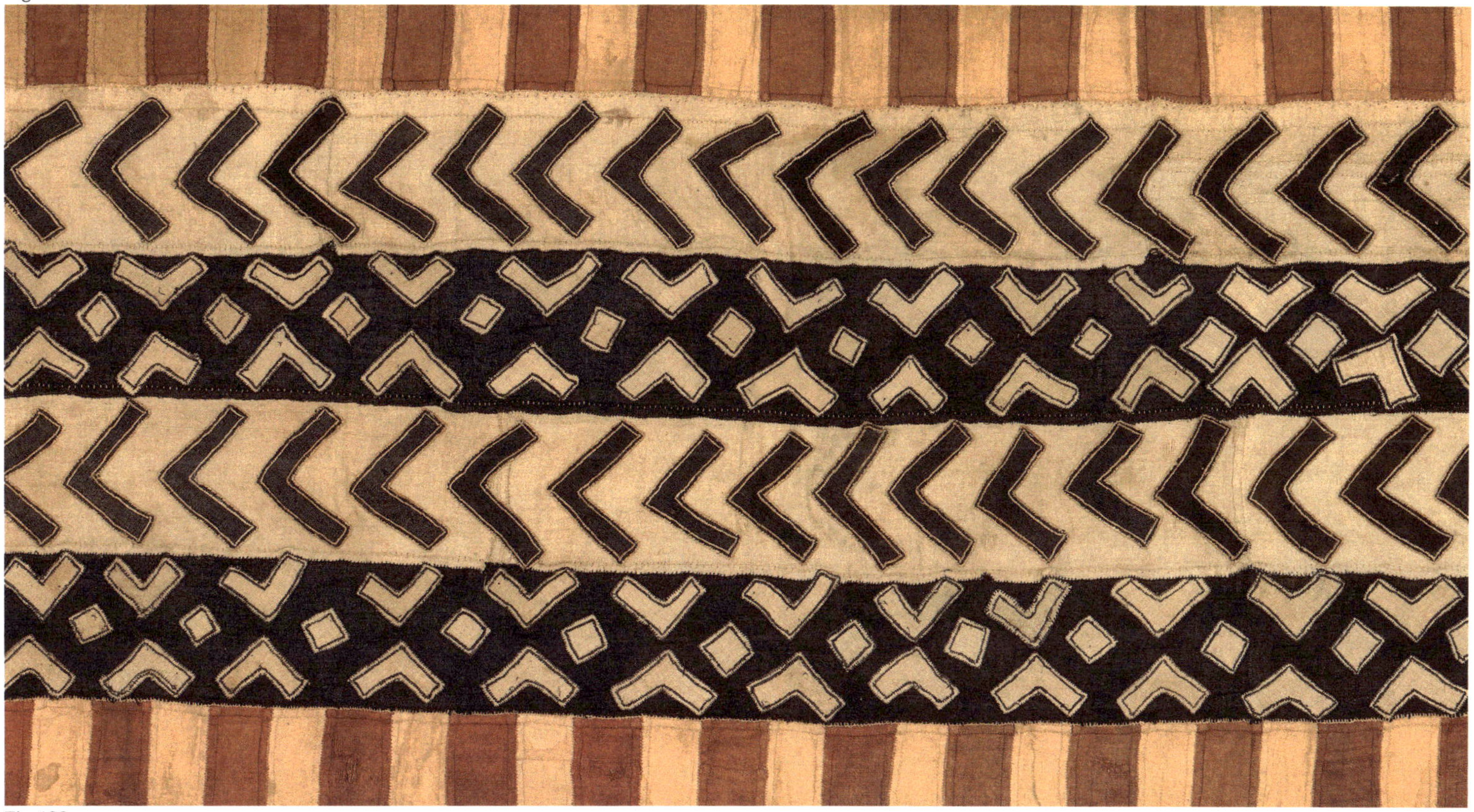

Fig. 182

Figs. 160/161
Hans Himmelheber
Men's vertical loom used to produce raffia fabrics
Lele and Kuba region, 1939, b/w negatives
Museum Rietberg Zürich, FHH 178-27, FHH 184-6

Fig. 162
Hans Himmelheber
Production of borders
Mushenge, January 24, 1939, b/w negatives
Museum Rietberg Zürich, FHH 183-8, FHH 183-9

Fig. 163
Hans Himmelheber
Elderly woman embroidering a raffia textile
Kuba region, 1939, b/w negative
Museum Rietberg Zürich, FHH 184-5

Fig. 164
Hans Himmelheber
Dancing women at a funeral
Ichala, January 10, 1939, b/w negatives
Museum Rietberg Zürich, FHH 181-4, FHH 181-6 and 7, FHH 181-18 and 19, FHH 181-31

Fig. 165
Male and female artist of the Bushoong region
***Ncák minen'ishushuna* overskirt for women**
Before 1924, raffia, cotton, and wool, 72 × 191 cm
RMCA Tervuren, EO.0.0.27927
Acquired by René Paul Preys

Fig. 166
Male and female artist of the Kuba region
***Mapel* skirt for men**
Early twentieth century, raffia, 130 × 653 cm
Museum Rietberg Zürich, 2019.417
Acquired with municipal funds

Fig. 167
Male and female artist of the Kuba region
***Mapel* skirt for men**
Early twentieth century, raffia, 90 × 435 cm
Museum Rietberg Zürich, 2019.416
Acquired with municipal funds

Fig. 168
Hans Himmelheber
Dancing men at a woman's funeral
Ichala, January 10, 1939, b/w negative
Museum Rietberg Zürich; FHH 181-10

Fig. 169
Hans Himmelheber
Dancing men at a funeral
Near Mweka, January 16, 1939, b/w negative
Museum Rietberg Zürich, FHH 182-19

Fig. 170
Male and female artist of the Kuba region
Panels of a skirt
Before 1939, raffia, 43 × 16.5 cm
Museum Rietberg Zürich, 2013.6
Gift of Barbara and Eberhard Fischer
Acquired by Hans Himmelheber

Fig. 171
Male and female artist of the Kuba region
Panels of a skirt
Before 1939, raffia, 23 × 56 cm
Museum Rietberg Zürich, 2013.2
Gift of Barbara and Eberhard Fischer
Acquired by Hans Himmelheber

Fig. 172
Male and female artist of the Kuba region
Fragment of a skirt
Before 1939, raffia, 46 × 25 cm
Museum Rietberg Zürich, 2013.29
Gift of Barbara and Eberhard Fischer
Acquired by Hans Himmelheber

Fig. 173
Male and female artist of the Kuba region
Women's skirt
Before 1939, raffia, 137 × 57 cm
Museum Rietberg Zürich, 2013.35
Gift of Barbara and Eberhard Fischer
Acquired by Hans Himmelheber

Fig. 174
Male and female artist of the Kuba region
Fragment of a skirt
Before 1939, raffia, 65 × 12 cm
Museum Rietberg Zürich, 2013.37
Gift of Barbara and Eberhard Fischer
Acquired by Hans Himmelheber

fig. 175
Male and female artist of the Kuba region
Border for a skirt
Before 1939, raffia, 10 × 181 cm
Museum Rietberg Zürich, 2013.163
Gift of Barbara and Eberhard Fischer
Acquired by Hans Himmelheber

Fig. 176
Male and female artist of the Kuba region
Skirt
Before 1939, raffia, 82 × 54 cm
Museum Rietberg Zürich, 2013.27
Gift of Barbara and Eberhard Fischer
Acquired by Hans Himmelheber

Fig. 177
Male and female artist of the Kuba region
Bark cloth *ncák ishyiin*
Before 1939, plant fibers, 200 × 38 cm
Museum Rietberg Zürich, 2013.154
Gift of Barbara and Eberhard Fischer
Acquired by Hans Himmelheber

Fig. 178
Artist of the Bushoong region
Mat
Before 1927, raffia, 110 × 302 cm
RMCA Tervuren, EO.0.0.29214
Acquired by René Paul Preys

Fig. 179
Hans Himmelheber
Woman's body covered with valuable raffia textiles
Ichala, January 10, 1939, b/w negative
Museum Rietberg Zürich, FHH 181-22

Fig. 180
Hans Himmelheber
Funeral with mat as covering
Near Mweka, January 16, 1939, b/w negative
Museum Rietberg Zürich, FHH 182-22

Fig. 181
Hans Himmelheber
Tire tracks
Songye region, 1939, b/w negative
Museum Rietberg Zürich, FHH 188-28

Fig. 182
Male and female artist of the Kuba region
Dance skirt with tire track motif
First half of the twentieth century, woven raffia, applications, 290 × 67 cm
Museum der Kulturen Basel, III 26550

Fig. 183
Male and female artist of the Kuba region
Border for a skirt
Before 1939, raffia, 11 × 528 cm
Museum Rietberg Zürich, 2013.165
Gift of Barbara and Eberhard Fischer
Acquired by Hans Himmelheber

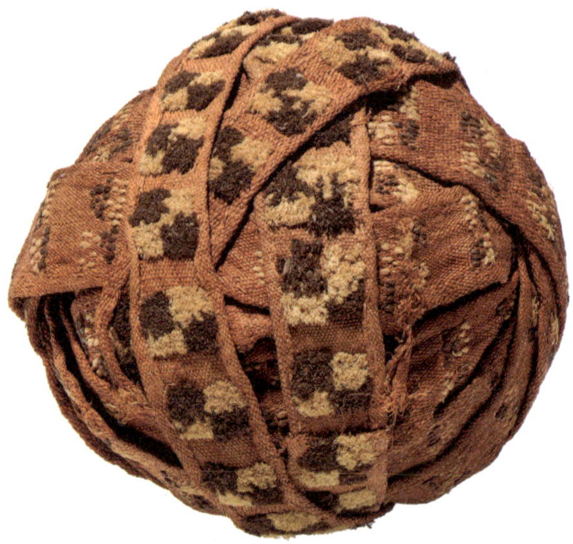

Fig. 183

CREATIVITY AND INNOVATION IN KUBA TEXTILES — Among the various subgroups of the Kuba, architecture, masks, and body art, as well as everyday and prestigious objects, were decorated with geometric motifs.[1] Yet the Kuba are most famous for their textile art. Due to their graphic patterns, these raffia fabrics became popular among painters like Gustav Klimt, Paul Klee, Pablo Picasso, and Henri Matisse. Not only Kuba men but also Kuba women were engaged in the production of raffia textiles, with the men focused on the preproduction. They worked on a vertical loom [figs. 160/161] whose dimensions were determined by the approximately one-meter-long fibers obtained from the raffia palm. Even the borders were made by men [fig. 162]. However, the fine embroidery and appliqué were produced by women, who would sometimes spend months working together on one piece [fig. 163]. The cut pile technique was particularly time-consuming, as the threads had to be drawn through the woven base material using a curved needle and then cut off shortly above the surface.[2]

When Hans Himmelheber visited the Kuba region in 1939, not only was he able to observe an active creative industry in the villages, but he also noted that the wearing of raffia clothing was still commonplace. The square pieces of fabric were sewn together in long strips, decorated, and worn as skirts on special occasions, such as funerals [fig. 164]. The women wrapped their skirt—called *ncák*—layer by layer around their hips and in some cases wore a shorter overskirt with a border over the top [fig. 165]. The men's wraparound skirts (*mapel*) were sometimes over ten meters long [figs. 166/167], but they were worn differently from those of the women. The men folded the long length of fabric around their hips and fastened it with a belt, over which the upper edge of the fabric was turned [figs. 168/169]. In this way the men's legs had enough space for their energetic dance moves. While the women's silhouettes remained slender, the men's were wide and dynamic.

Textiles indicated the wearer's social standing and wealth. Particularly fine and old embroideries with pile—of which Hans Himmelheber was able to purchase a number of examples—used to be worn only by the women of the Kuba king's court [figs. 170–176]. To pay homage to the deceased, it was customary to lay several layers of raffia fabric over the body at funerals [fig. 179]. In a few villages one of the burial objects was also a bark cloth (*ncák ishyiin*) sewn together from small light and dark triangles [fig. 177]. While Western clothing was gradually replacing traditional fabrics in everyday life, these elaborately decorated textiles were still used at funerals into the 1980s.

Kuba design is characterized by irregularities and asymmetries, as well as the juxtaposition of blocks of different colors and motifs. An especially attractive example is the mat shown here, which was displayed at funerals, among other occasions [figs. 178/180]. The invention of new design variants increased the artist's prestige. For example, after a missionary's visit in the 1920s, the Kuba king was inspired to create a new pattern by his motorbike's tire tracks [figs. 181/182][3] — Michaela Oberhofer

1 As Hans Himmelheber rightly noticed, the term "Bakuba" or "Kuba" is a foreign appellation given by the neighboring Luba (1940, pp. 18f.). The various Kuba subgroups had their own chiefs but they all recognized the authority of the Bushoong king (*nyimi*) and called themselves "the king's people." According to Himmelheber, subgroups famous for their textile art were the Shoowa ("Bashowa"), Bushoong ("Bushongo"), and Ngoombe ("Bangombe"). On Kuba textiles, see Brincard 2015 and Mack 2012.

2 Owing to their fluffy surface, the Kuba textiles were also called "velours," "velvets," and "plush."

3 According to Mack 2012, p. 8.

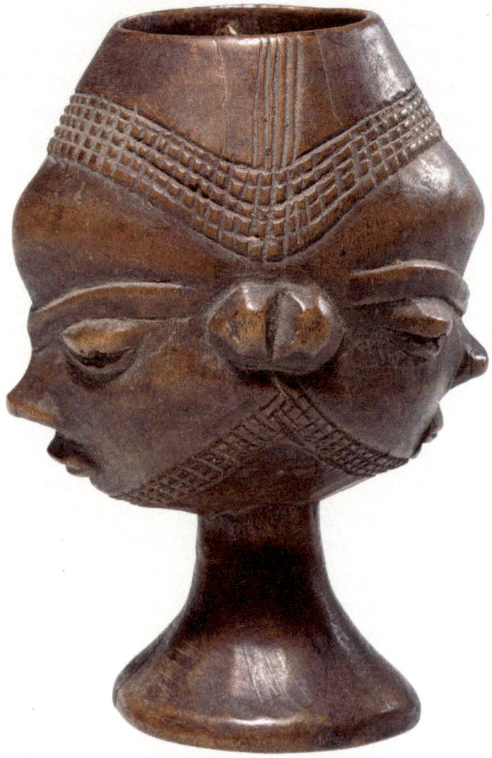

Fig. 184

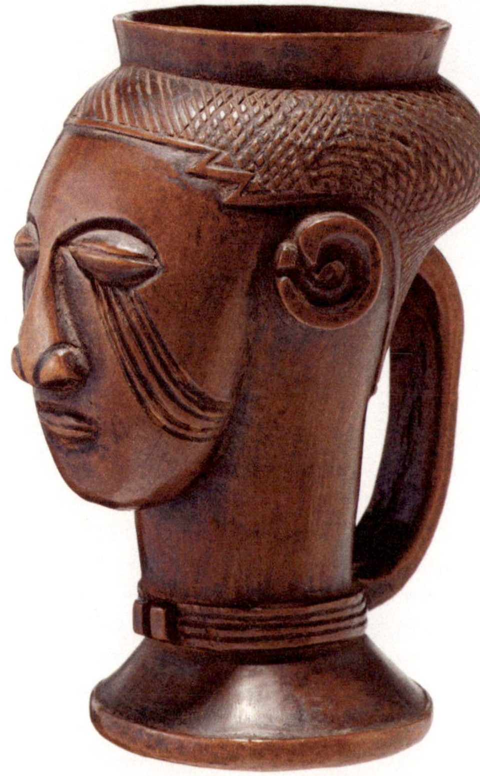

Fig. 185

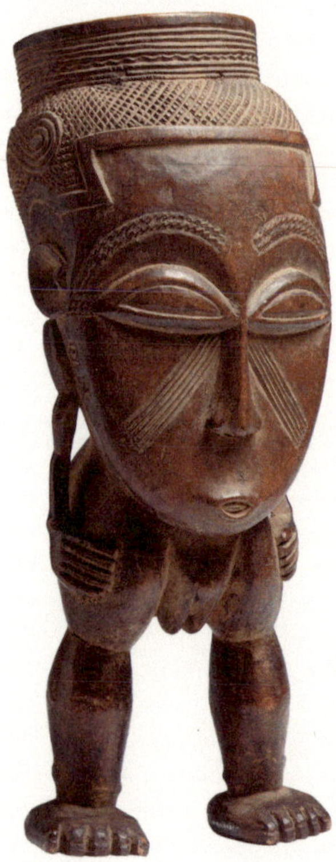

Fig. 186

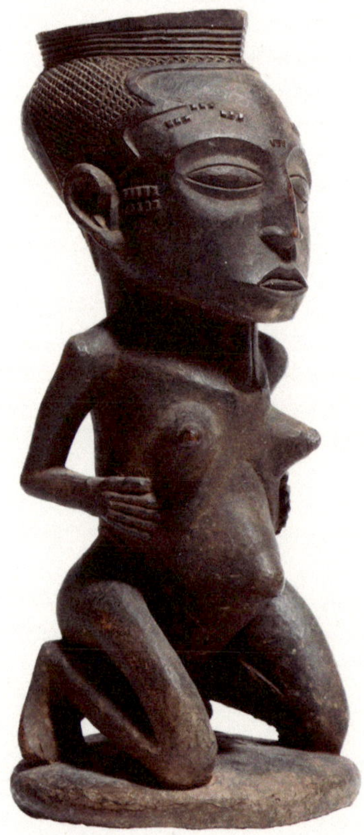

Fig. 187

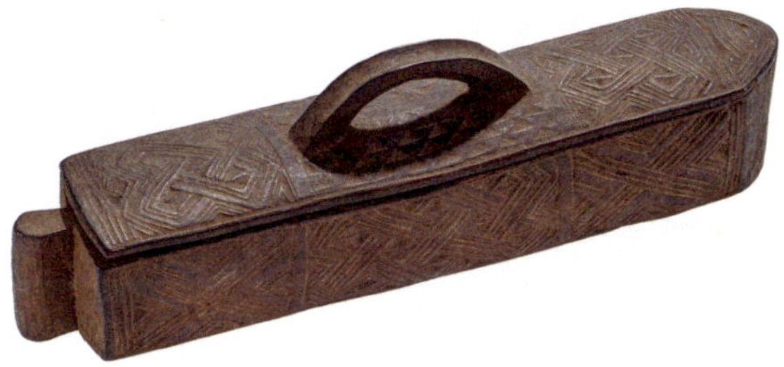

Fig. 190

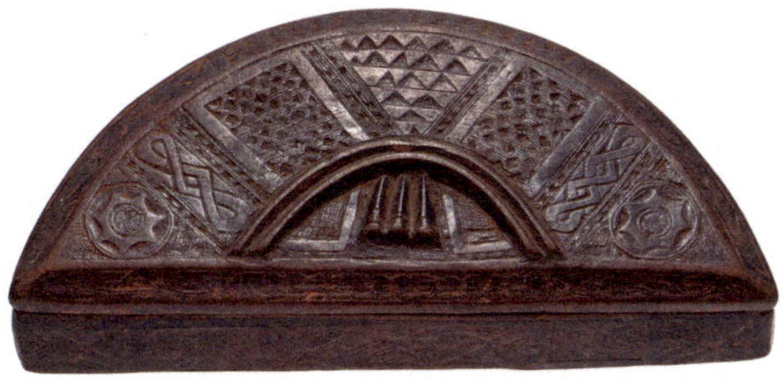

Fig. 191

Fig. 188

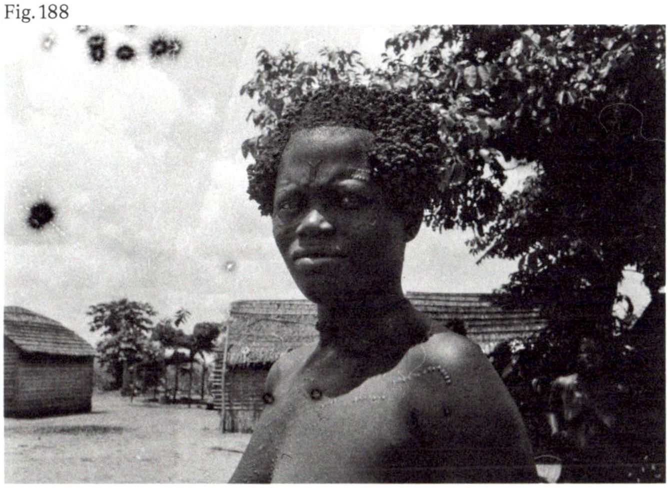

Fig. 189

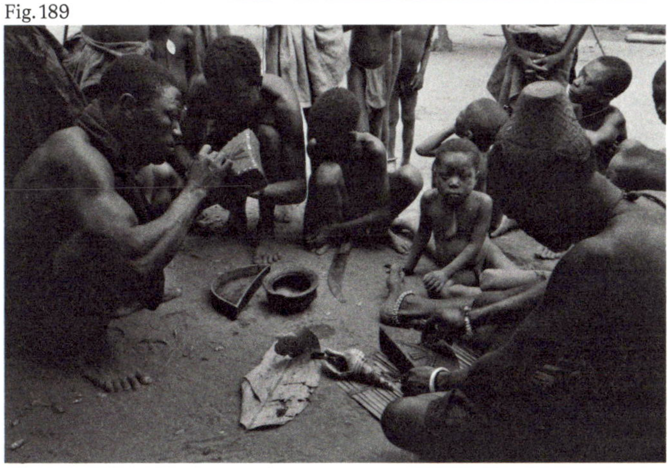

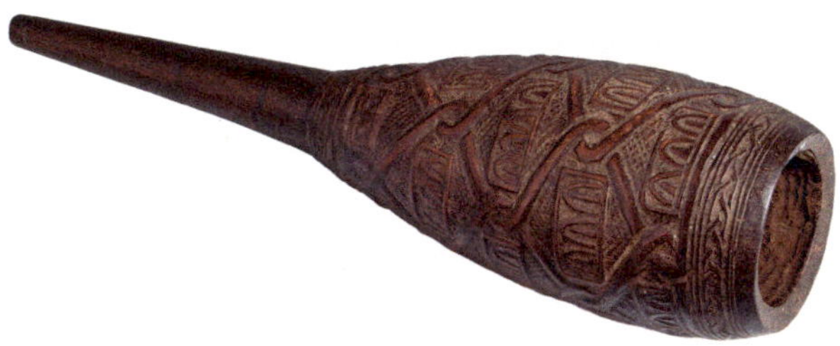

Fig. 192

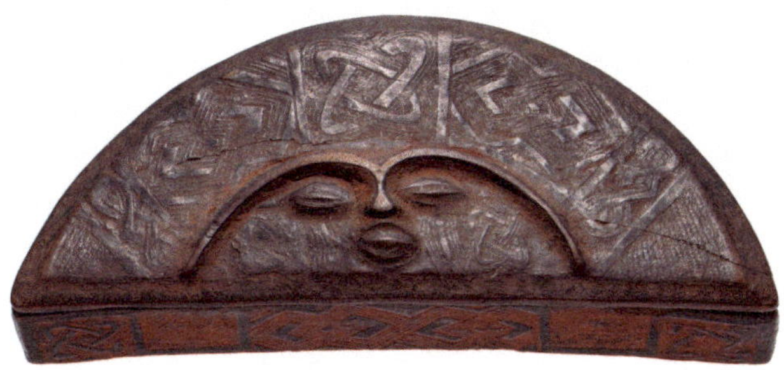

Fig. 193

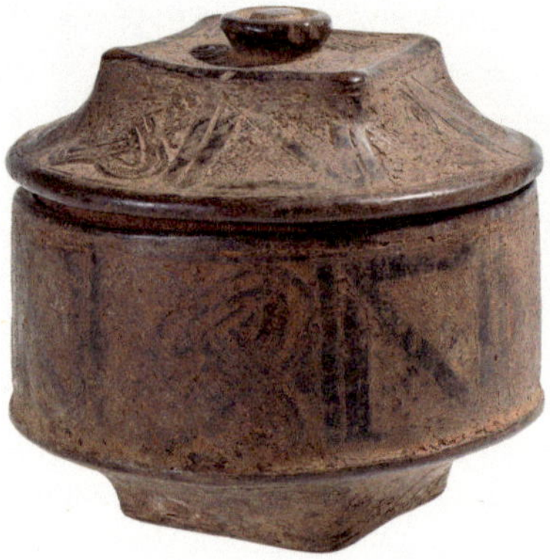

Fig. 194

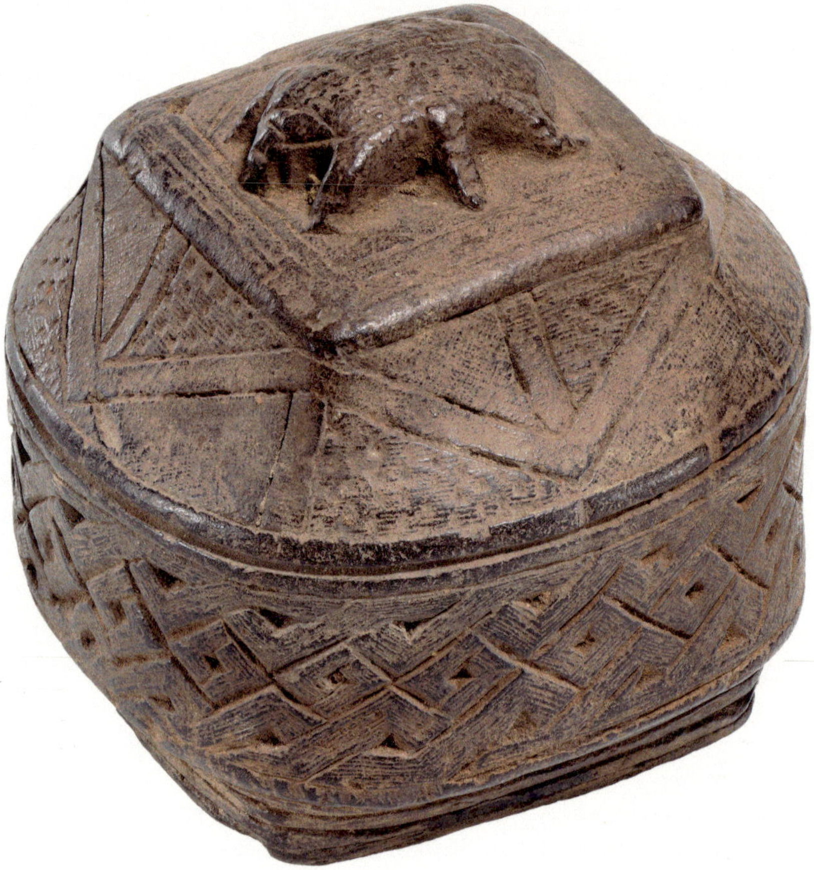

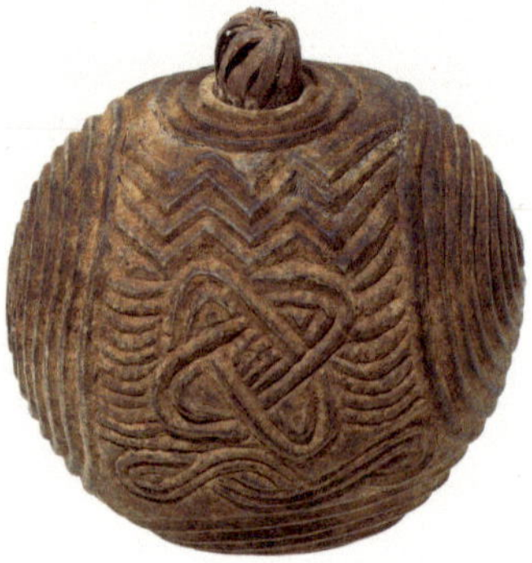

Fig. 195

Fig. 196

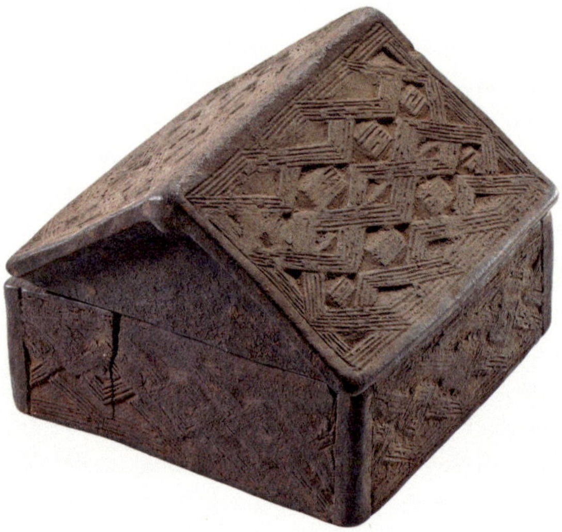

Fig. 197

Fig. 198

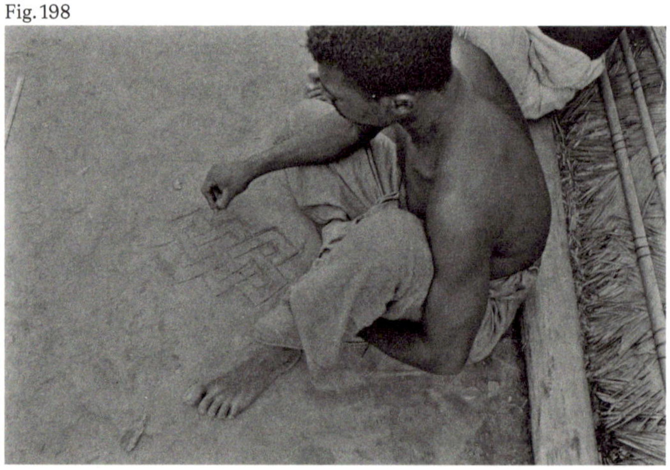

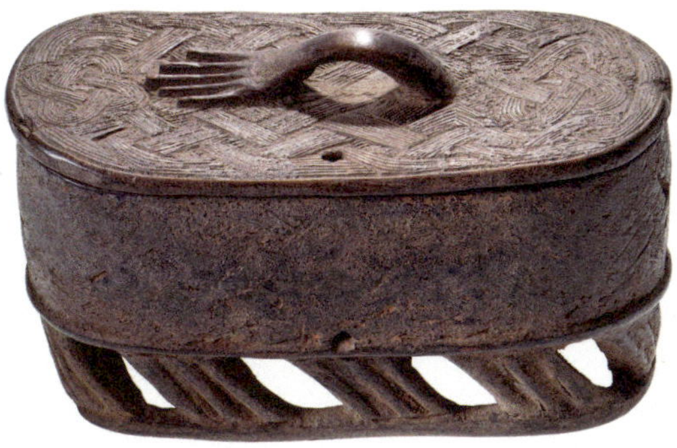

Fig. 199

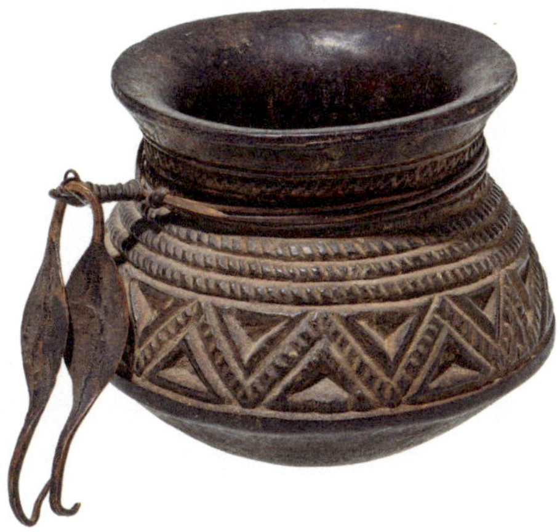

Fig. 200

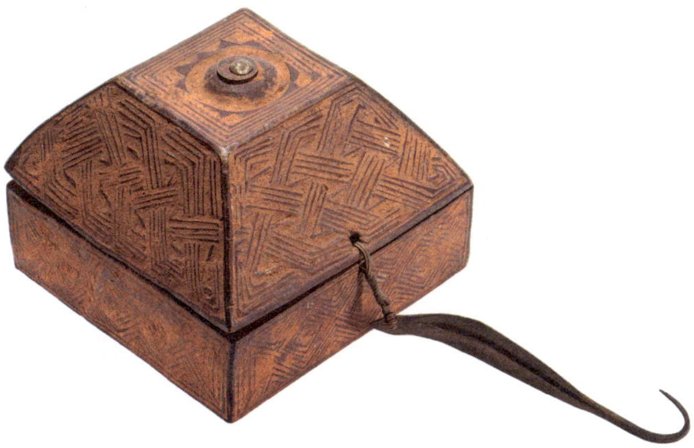

Fig. 201

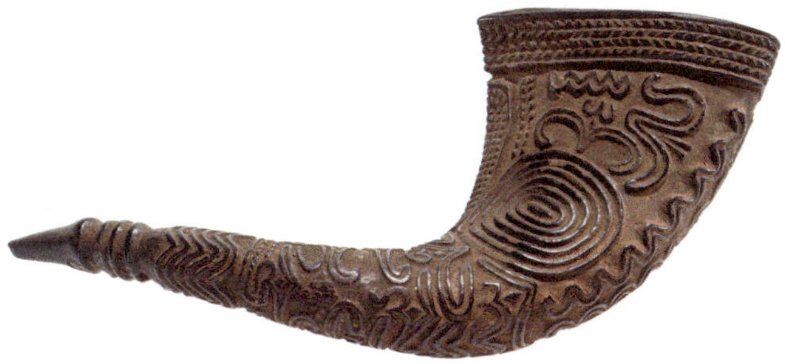

Fig. 202

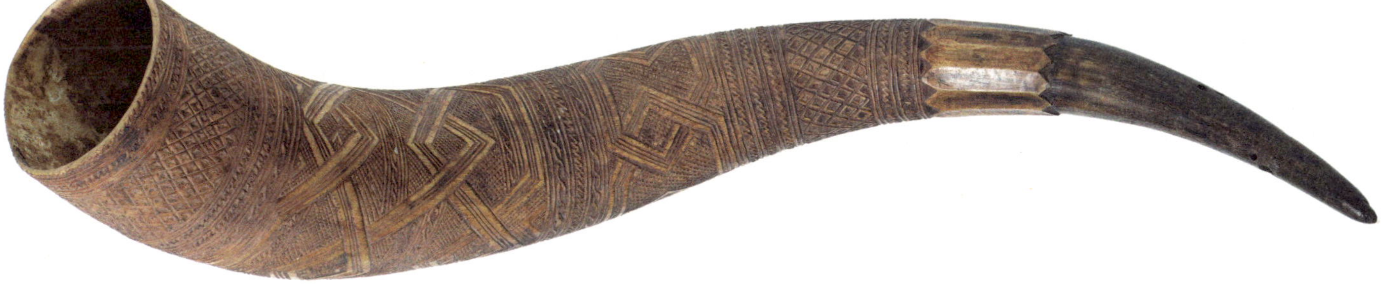

Fig. 203

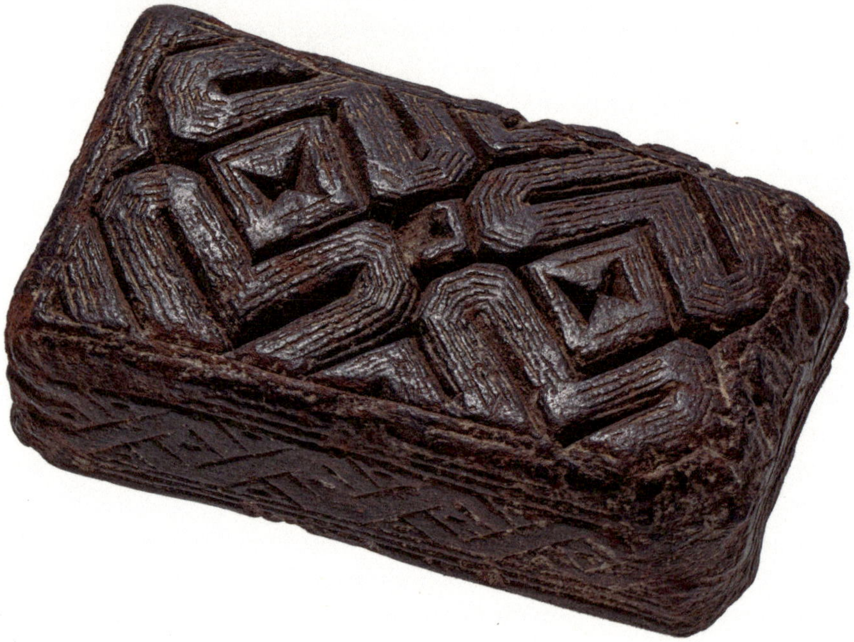

Fig. 204

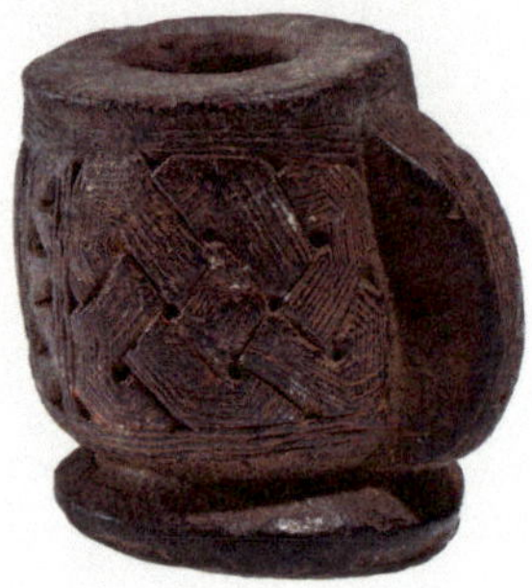

Fig. 205

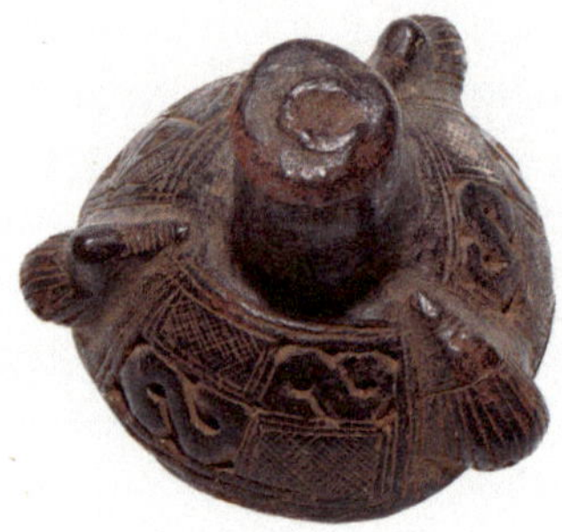

Fig. 206

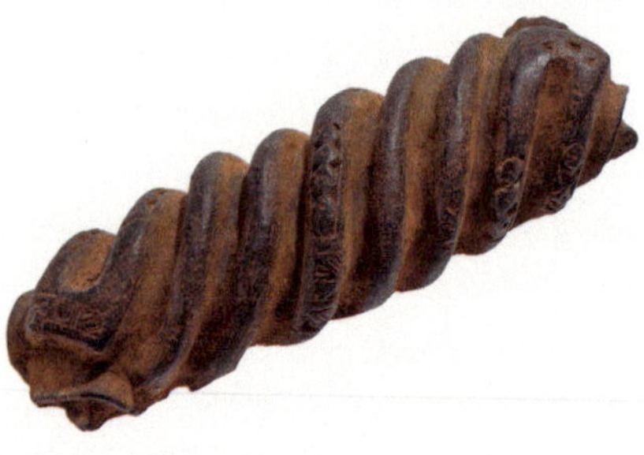

Fig. 207

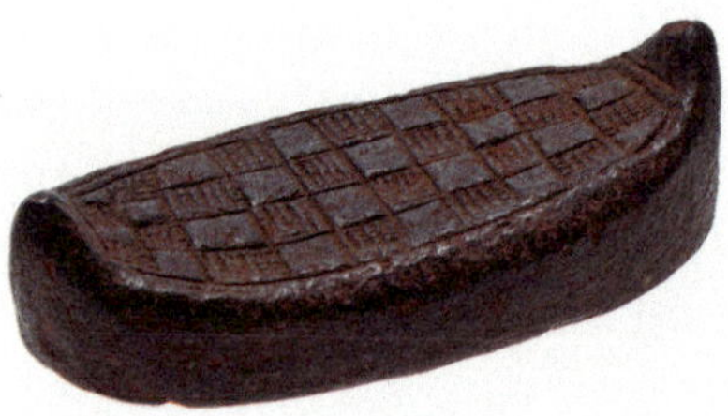

Fig. 208

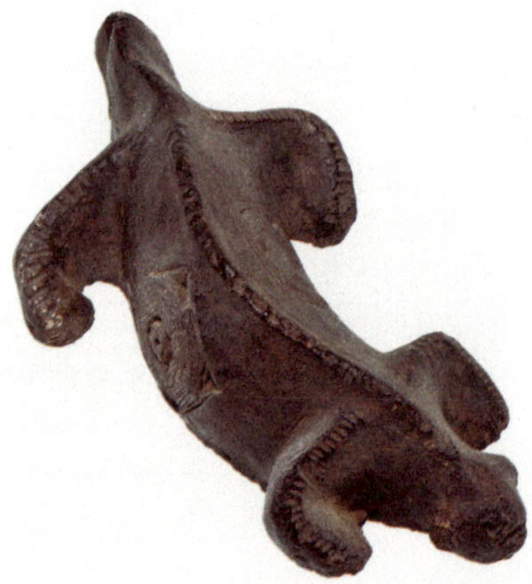

Fig. 209

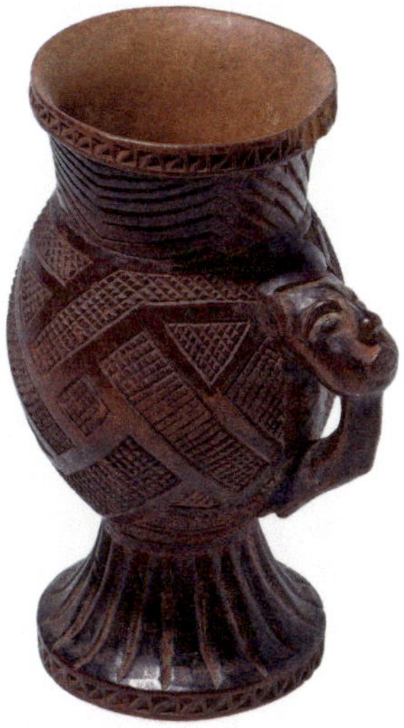

Fig. 210

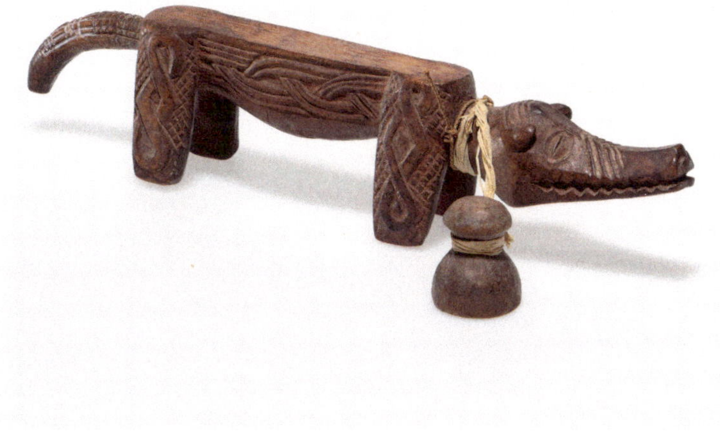

Fig. 213

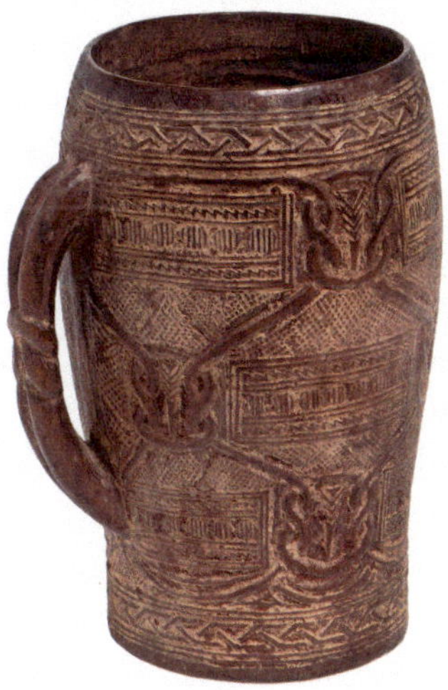

Fig. 211

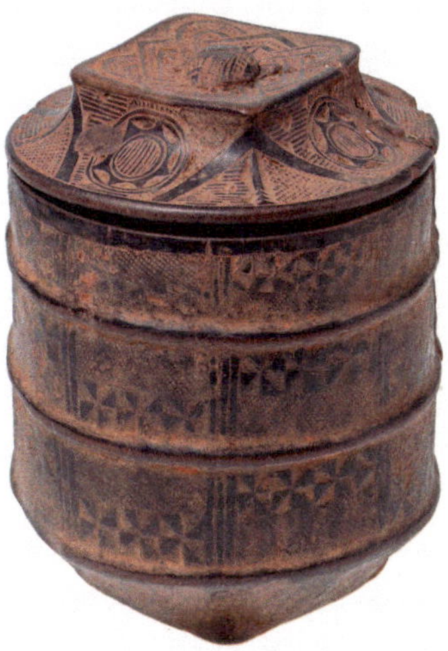

Fig. 212

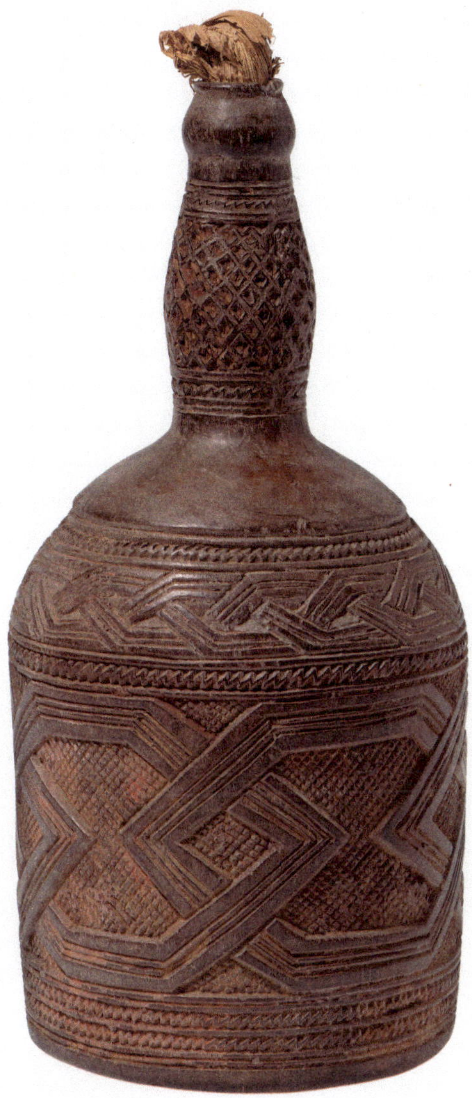

Fig. 214

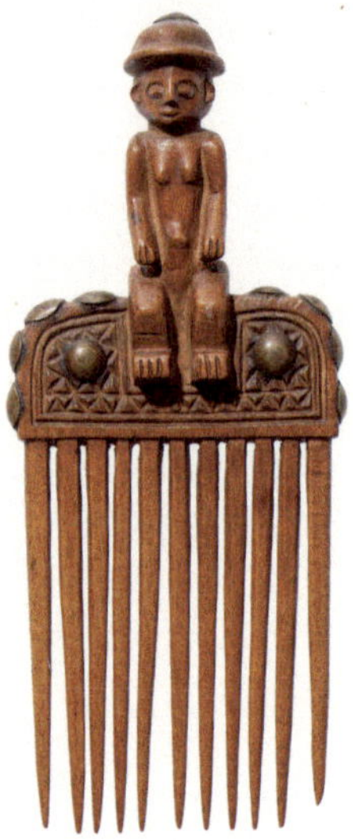

Fig. 215

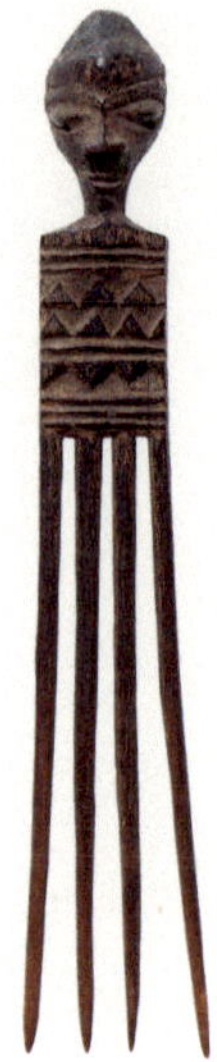

Fig. 216

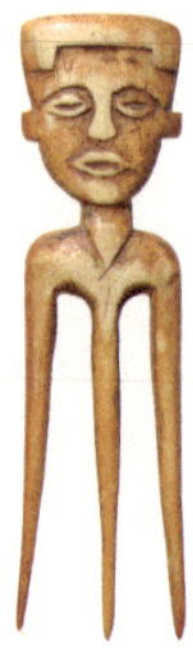

Fig. 217

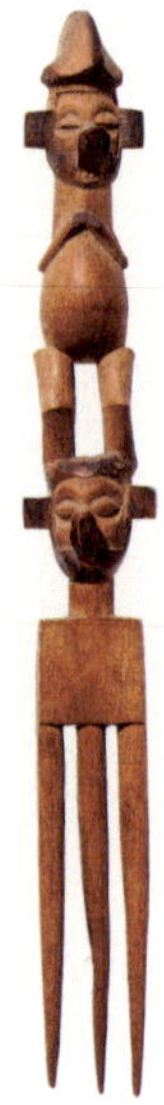

Fig. 218

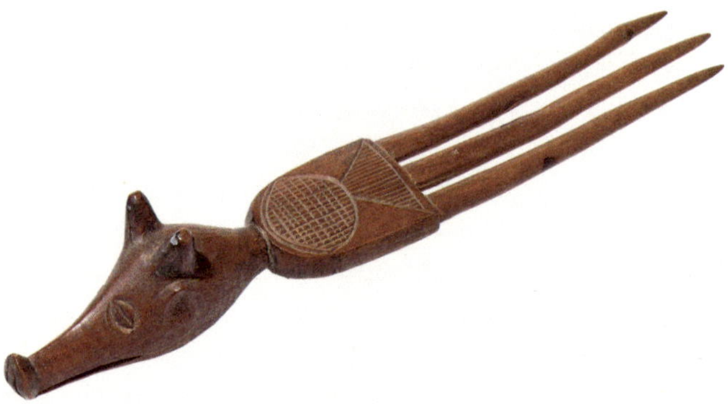

Fig. 219

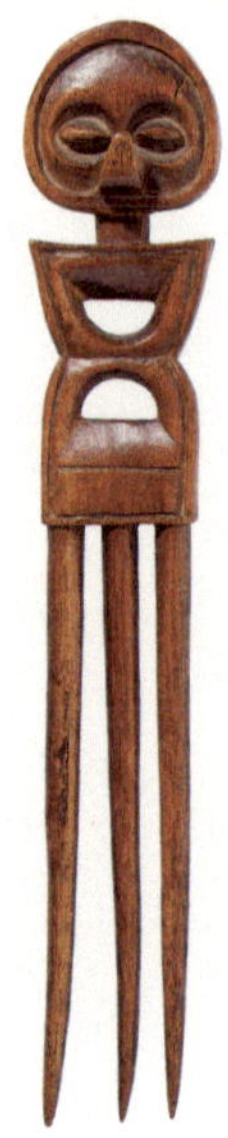

Fig. 220

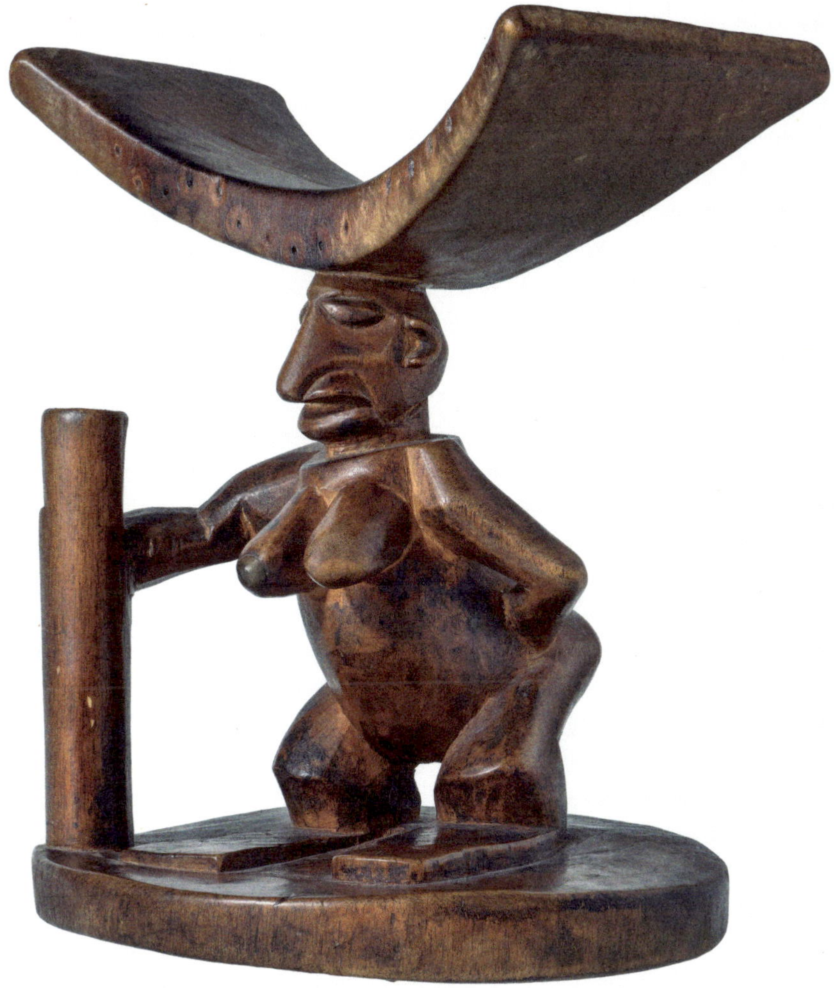

Fig. 221

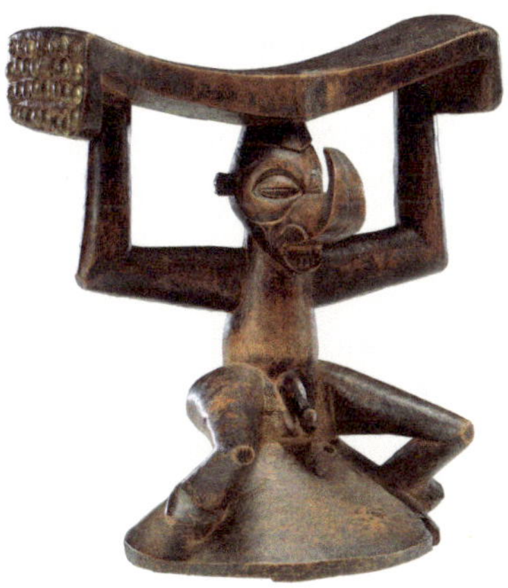

Fig. 222

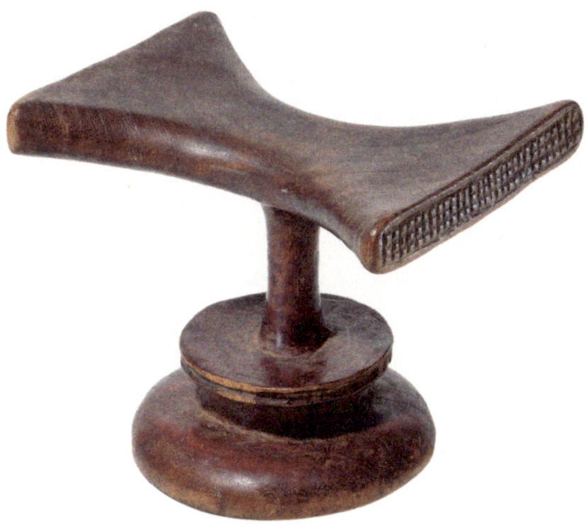

Fig. 223

Fig. 184
Artist of the Pende region
from Nioka Munene
Palm wine cup with two human faces
Before 1939, wood, 11 × 8 × 6 cm
Museum Rietberg Zürich, 2018.36
Gift of Martin Himmelheber
Acquired by Hans Himmelheber

Fig. 185
Artist of the Kuba region
Palm wine cup in the form of a head
Before 1939, wood, 19 × 12 × 15 cm
Museum Rietberg Zürich, 2015.237
Gift of Hans Himmelheber's heirs
Acquired by Hans Himmelheber

Fig. 186
Artist of the Kuba region
Figural cup
Before 1939, wood, 27 × 11 × 10 cm
Museum Rietberg Zürich, HH 10
Gift of Barbara and Eberhard Fischer
Acquired by Hans Himmelheber

Fig. 187
Artist of the Kuba-Kele region
Cup in the form of a female figure
Before 1939, wood, 26.5 × 11 × 11 cm
Museum Rietberg Zürich, HH 12
Gift of Barbara and Eberhard Fischer
Acquired by Hans Himmelheber

Fig. 188
Hans Himmelheber
Portrait of a woman with striking hairline
Kuba region, 1939, b/w negative
Museum Rietberg Zürich, FHH 185-6

Fig. 189
Hans Himmelheber
Production of wooden boxes
Mushenge, 1939, b/w negative
Museum Rietberg Zürich, FHH 184-32

Fig. 190
Artist of the Kuba region
Oblong box for razors
Before 1939, wood, 28 × 8 × 6 cm
Museum Rietberg Zürich, 2018.20
Gift of Martin Himmelheber
Acquired by Hans Himmelheber

Fig. 191
Artist of the Kuba region
Crescent-shaped box
Before 1939, wood, 30 × 14 × 6.5 cm
Museum Rietberg Zürich, 2018.22
Gift of Martin Himmelheber
Acquired by Hans Himmelheber

Fig. 192
Artist of the Kuba region
Rectal syringe
Before 1939, wood, 31 × 8 cm
Museum Rietberg Zürich, 2018.35
Gift of Martin Himmelheber
Acquired by Hans Himmelheber

Fig. 193
Artist of the Kuba region
Crescent-shaped box with face
Before 1939, wood, 36 × 15.5 × 8 cm
Museum Rietberg Zürich, 2018.42
Gift of Martin Himmelheber
Acquired by Hans Himmelheber

Fig. 194
Artist of the Kuba region
Cylindrical box in the form of a small basket
Before 1939, wood, 17 × 19 cm
Museum Rietberg Zürich, 2018.97
Gift of Martin Himmelheber
Acquired by Hans Himmelheber

Fig. 195
Artist of the Kuba region
Spherical ointment vessel
Before 1939, wood, 14.5 cm
Museum Rietberg Zürich, 2018.83
Gift of Martin Himmelheber
Acquired by Hans Himmelheber

Fig. 196
Artist of the Kuba region
Solid copy of a box
Before 1939, wood, 13.9 × 14.5 × 14.5 cm
Barbara and Eberhard Fischer Collection
Acquired by Hans Himmelheber

Fig. 197
Artist of the Kete region
Box in the form of a house
Before 1939, wood, 18 × 18 × 13.5 cm
Museum Rietberg Zürich, 2018.120
Gift of Martin Himmelheber
Acquired by Hans Himmelheber

Fig. 198
Hans Himmelheber
Young man painting patterns in the sand
Kuba region, 1939, b/w negative
Museum Rietberg Zürich, FHH 183-23

Fig. 199
Artist of the Kuba region
Box with hand as the handle
Before 1939, wood, 17 × 31 × 14.5 cm
Museum Rietberg Zürich, 2018.104
Gift of Martin Himmelheber
Acquired by Hans Himmelheber

Fig. 200
Woman artist of the Kuba region
Vessel
Before 1939, clay, 8.5 × 10 × 10 cm
Museum Rietberg Zürich, 2015.236
Gift of Hans Himmelheber's heirs
Acquired by Hans Himmelheber

Fig. 201
Artist of the Kete region
Square box with hook
Before 1939, wood and metal, 14 × 14.5 × 15.6 cm
Museum Rietberg Zürich, 2018.15
Gift of Martin Himmelheber
Acquired by Hans Himmelheber

Fig. 202
Artist of the Kuba-Bindji region
Drinking horn
Before 1939, horn, 28.5 × 16.5 × 8.5 cm
Museum Rietberg Zürich, 2018.40
Gift of Martin Himmelheber
Acquired by Hans Himmelheber

Fig. 203
Artist of the Kuba-Kete region
Drinking horn
Before 1939, cow horn, 78 × 9.5 × 9.5 cm
Museum Rietberg Zürich, 2019.439
Gift of Eberhard and Barbara Fischer/ Susanne Himmelheber
Acquired by Hans Himmelheber

Fig. 204
Woman artist of the Kuba region
***Mboong itool* in the form of an ingot**
Before 1939, redwood powder, 37 × 11 × 4 cm
Museum Rietberg Zürich, 2018.109
Gift of Martin Himmelheber
Acquired by Hans Himmelheber

Fig. 205
Woman artist of the Kuba region
***Mboong itool* in the form of a palm wine cup**
Before 1939, redwood powder, 6 × 6 cm
Museum Rietberg Zürich, 2018.106
Gift of Martin Himmelheber
Acquired by Hans Himmelheber

Fig. 206
Woman artist of the Kuba region
***Mboong itool* in the form of an anvil with small birds**
Before 1939, redwood powder, 5 × 7.5 cm
Museum Rietberg Zürich, 2018.105
Gift of Martin Himmelheber
Acquired by Hans Himmelheber

Fig. 207
Woman artist of the Kuba region
***Mboong itool* in the form of an ingot**
Before 1939, redwood powder, 20 × 6.5 × 4.5 cm
Museum Rietberg Zürich, 2018.19
Gift of Martin Himmelheber
Acquired by Hans Himmelheber

Fig. 208
Woman artist of the Kuba region
***Mboong itool* in the form of a small headrest**
Before 1939, redwood powder, 2.7 × 9 × 4.3 cm
Museum Rietberg Zürich, 2018.107
Gift of Martin Himmelheber
Acquired by Hans Himmelheber

Fig. 209
Woman artist of the Kuba region
***Mboong itool* in the form of a lizard**
Before 1939, redwood powder, 19 × 9.5 × 5.5 cm
Museum Rietberg Zürich, 2018.34
Gift of Martin Himmelheber
Acquired by Hans Himmelheber

Fig. 210
Artist of the Kuba region
Palm wine cup with human face on the handle
Before 1939, wood, 15 × 10.5 × 9 cm
Museum Rietberg Zürich, 2018.102
Gift of Martin Himmelheber
Acquired by Hans Himmelheber

Fig. 211
Artist of the Kuba region
Palm wine cup
Before 1939, wood, 17.5 × 13 × 11 cm
Museum Rietberg Zürich, 2018.95
Gift of Martin Himmelheber
Acquired by Hans Himmelheber

Fig. 212
Artist of the Kuba region
Cylindrical box
Before 1939, wood, 20 × 17.5 cm
Barbara and Eberhard Fischer Collection
Acquired by Hans Himmelheber

Fig. 213
Artist of the Kuba region
Crocodile figure for divination
Before 1939, wood, 30 × 6.2 × 5 cm
Barbara and Eberhard Fischer Collection
Acquired by Hans Himmelheber

Fig. 214
Artist of the Kuba region
Sculpture in the form of a bottle
Before 1939, wood and plant fibers, 26.3 × 12.8 × 12.8 cm
Barbara and Eberhard Fischer Collection
Acquired by Hans Himmelheber

Fig. 215
Artist of the Songye region
Comb with colon figure
Nineteenth/twentieth century, wood, metal, 17.2 × 7.3 × 2.6 cm
Museum Rietberg Zürich, RAC 918
Gift of Wally and Udo Horstmann

Fig. 216
Artist of the Pende region
Figural decorative comb
Before 1939, wood, 17.2 × 3 × 1.5 cm
Museum Rietberg Zürich, 2018.86
Gift of Martin Himmelheber
Acquired by Hans Himmelheber

Fig. 217
Artist of the Kuba region
Decorative comb with man's face
Nineteenth/twentieth century, ivory, 9.1 × 2.5 × 1 cm
Museum Rietberg Zürich, RAC 240
Gift of Eduard von der Heydt

Fig. 218
Artist of the Yaka region
Figural decorative comb
Nineteenth/twentieth century, wood, 18 × 2 × 2.5 cm
Museum Rietberg Zürich, RAC 524
Gift of Eduard von der Heydt

Fig. 219
Artist of the Yaka region
Zoomorphic decorative comb
Nineteenth/twentieth century, wood, 20.2 × 3.2 × 3.4 cm
Museum Rietberg Zürich, RAC 523
Gift of Eduard von der Heydt

Fig. 220
Artist of the Yaka region
***Yisanuna* figural decorative comb**
Before 1925, wood, 17.5 × 3.1 × 1.7 cm
Private Collection Lausanne
Paul Guillaume, André Lhote

Fig. 221
Artist of the Yaka region
Headrest with female figure
Nineteenth/twentieth century, wood, 18.5 × 16.6 × 14.1 cm
Museum Rietberg Zürich, RAC 528
Han Coray Collection

Fig. 222
Artist of the Yaka region
Headrest with male figure
Before 1938, wood and brass upholstery nails, 22.8 × 21.6 × 14.6 cm
Virginia Museum of Fine Arts, 84.81
Adolph D. and Wilkins C. Williams Fund
Acquired by Hans Himmelheber

Fig. 223
Artist of the Yaka region
Headrest
Before 1939, wood, 12.8 × 15.5 × 12.5 cm
Barbara and Eberhard Fischer Collection
Acquired by Hans Himmelheber

KUBA DESIGN: TRANSFORMING THE WORLD IN LINE WITH AESTHETIC PRINCIPLES — In the third article based on his research in the journal *Brousse*, Hans Himmelheber reveals himself to be fascinated by the diversity and vibrancy of the art by the various Kuba subgroups. The desire to aesthetically transform the world was the credo of the Kuba's visual culture.[1] Regardless of age, gender, or rank, making art was important and improved a person's reputation [fig. 198]. The more carefully an object was realized, the more valuable it was in the eyes of the Kuba. Richly decorated everyday and prestigious objects denoted a person's social standing in the hierarchical society of the Kuba and also played a central role in celebrations and in ceremonies like funerals.

Among the most famous types of object that were acquired in large numbers by collectors for European museums are the carved wooden cups from which palm wine was drunk. Their iconography varied from purely geometric patterns to anthropomorphic shapes [figs. 184–187]. Even drums were reproduced [fig. 107]. Vessels in the form of a human face or a mask with horns were the preserve of the royal family. The cups designed as fine faces with hairlines shaved in angular shapes were believed by Himmelheber to be portraits [figs. 185/188]. Whether some forms could be traced back to European models, as Himmelheber speculated, has not been proven conclusively [fig. 210].[2] Even Islamic scrolls were used as ornaments and, as on the cup and rectal syringe shown here, transformed into Kuba iconography [figs. 192/211].

Equally popular as collectors' items were richly decorated, lidded wooden boxes in a wide range of shapes, whether oval, square, or crescent-shaped [figs. 191/193/199/201]. The architecture (houses), masks, and basketwork of the Kuba were likewise recreated in the form of boxes [figs. 194/197]. Himmelheber purchased numerous examples and also documented their production in detail [fig. 189]. In the vessels, blended redwood powder was used both for hair and body care and to dye fabrics or carvings. Furthermore, it served ritual purposes, for example at funerals.[3] The oblong containers were intended for storing razors [fig. 190]. In compliance with the *horror vacui* that is characteristic of Kuba art, the entire surface was covered with geometric, entwined patterns that are reminiscent of the Kuba's textile art. Other everyday objects, too—like the small ointment jar[fig. 195], the wonderfully curved drinking horn [fig. 203], and the little clay pot [fig. 200]—were adorned all over with motifs. The latter was produced by a woman potter.

Another type of object created by women is the so-called *mboong itool* (called *bongotol* by Himmelheber).[4] These are small geometric or figurative sculptures shaped from the powder of redwood, sand, and water, dried, and then smoked over a fire [figs. 204–209]. At funerals *mboong itool* served as gifts for the deceased that were laid under their heads and bodies—and later alongside them in their graves. These miniatures were an expression of social status and economic wealth. In Himmelheber's eyes, they were small artworks created by women—very unusual in African art. Made of redwood, the imitation of a wooden box as a sculpture in the round whose lid would no longer open was an object that he classified as purely *l'art pour l'art* [fig. 196]. — Michaela Oberhofer

1 Himmelheber 1940, p. 22. On the art of the Kuba, see Binkley/Darish 2009.
2 Himmelheber 1960, p. 374.
3 The red paint that was widespread in the Belgian Congo as *tukula* or *ngula*, was either plant or mineral-based. The Kuba used redwood (Pterocarpus) that they imported from the north. See Volper 2015.
4 See Volper 2015.

SAPEURS THEN AND NOW IN PHOTOGRAPHY

Yves Sambu, Hans Himmelheber

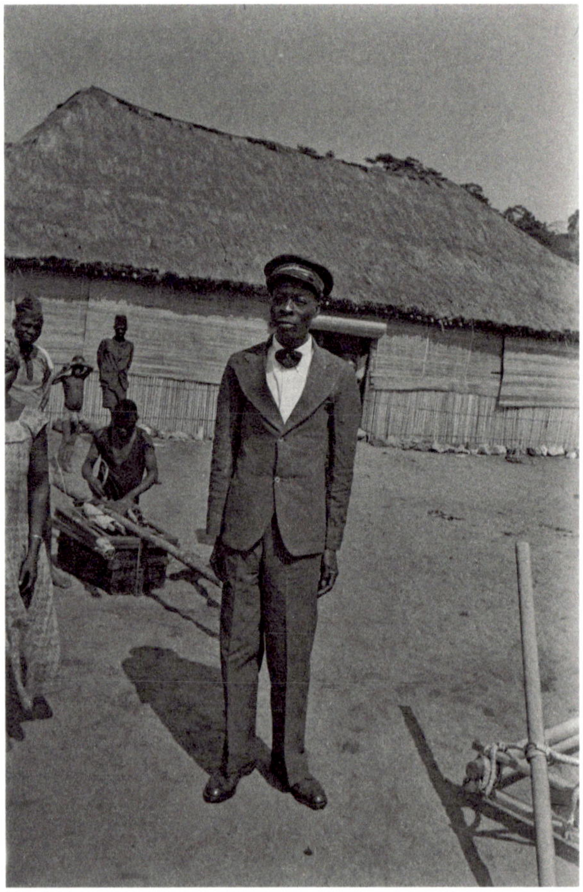

Fig. 224

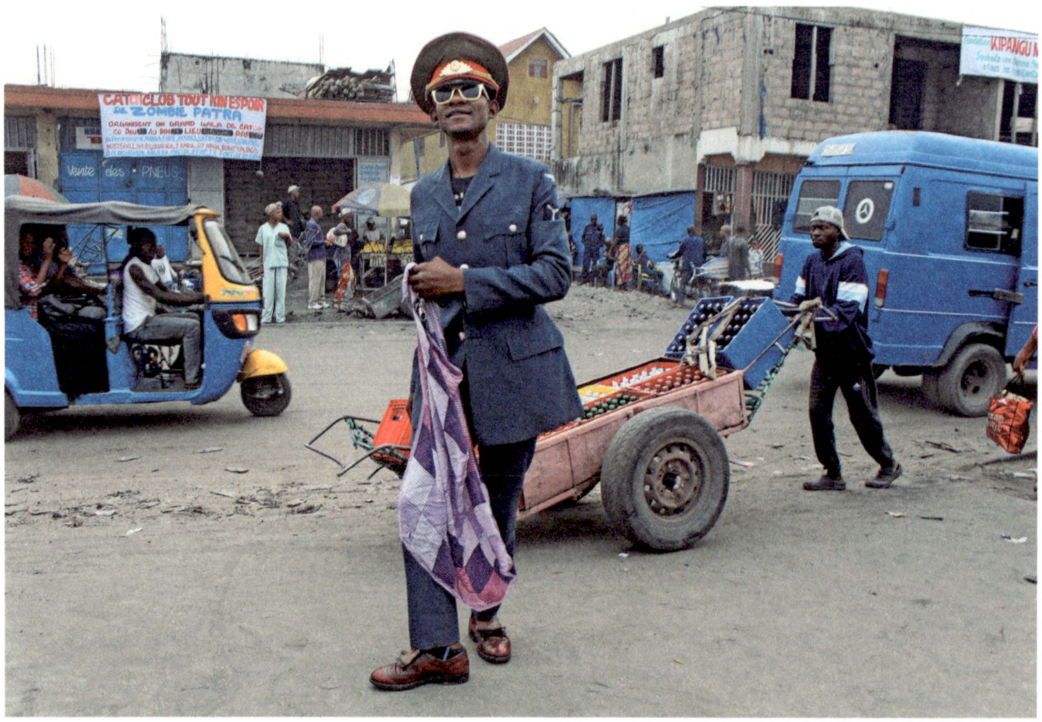

Fig. 225

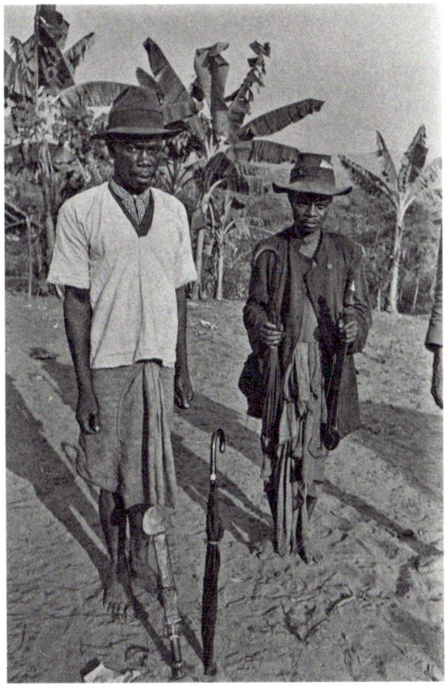

Fig. 226

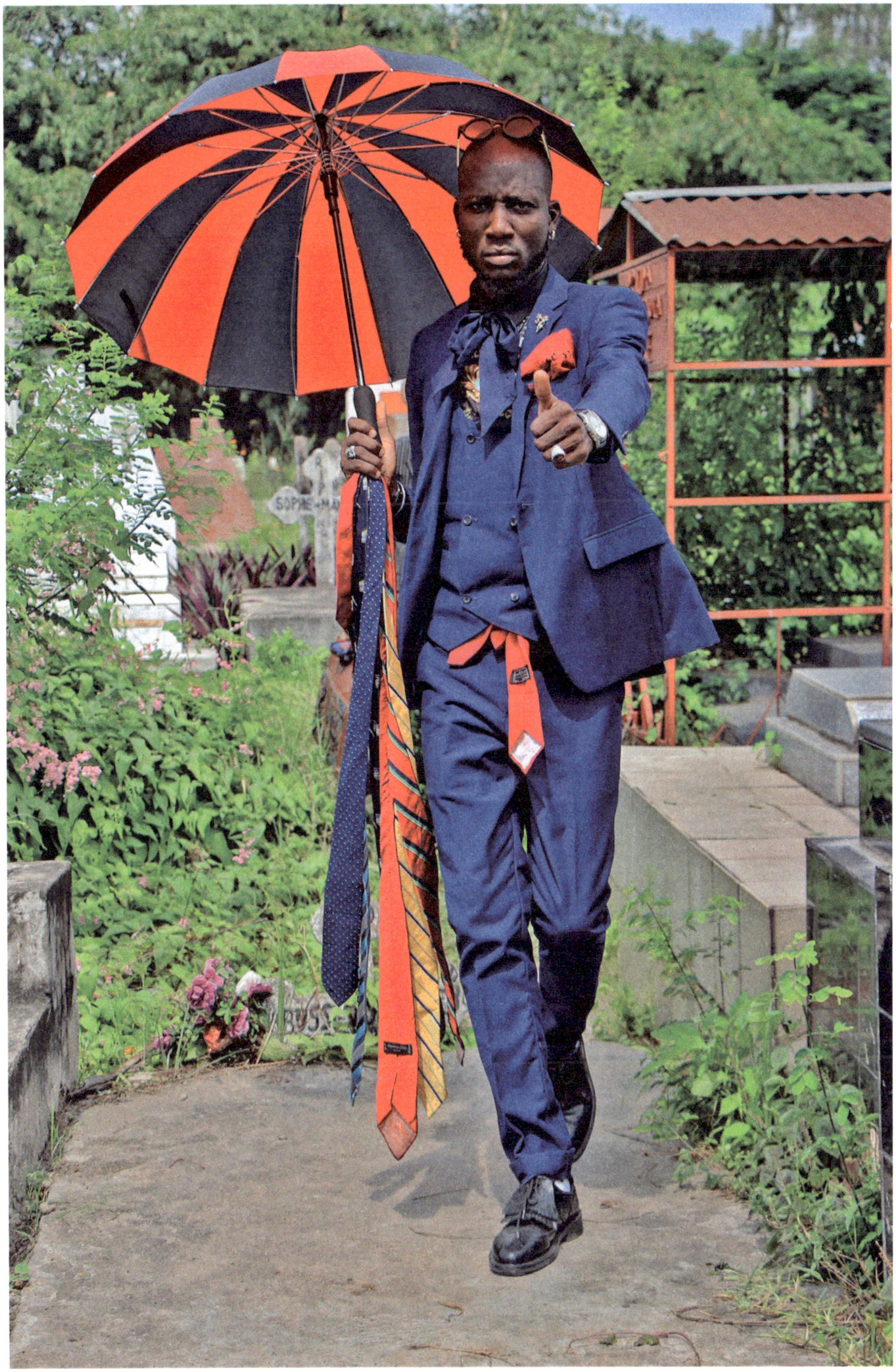

Fig. 227

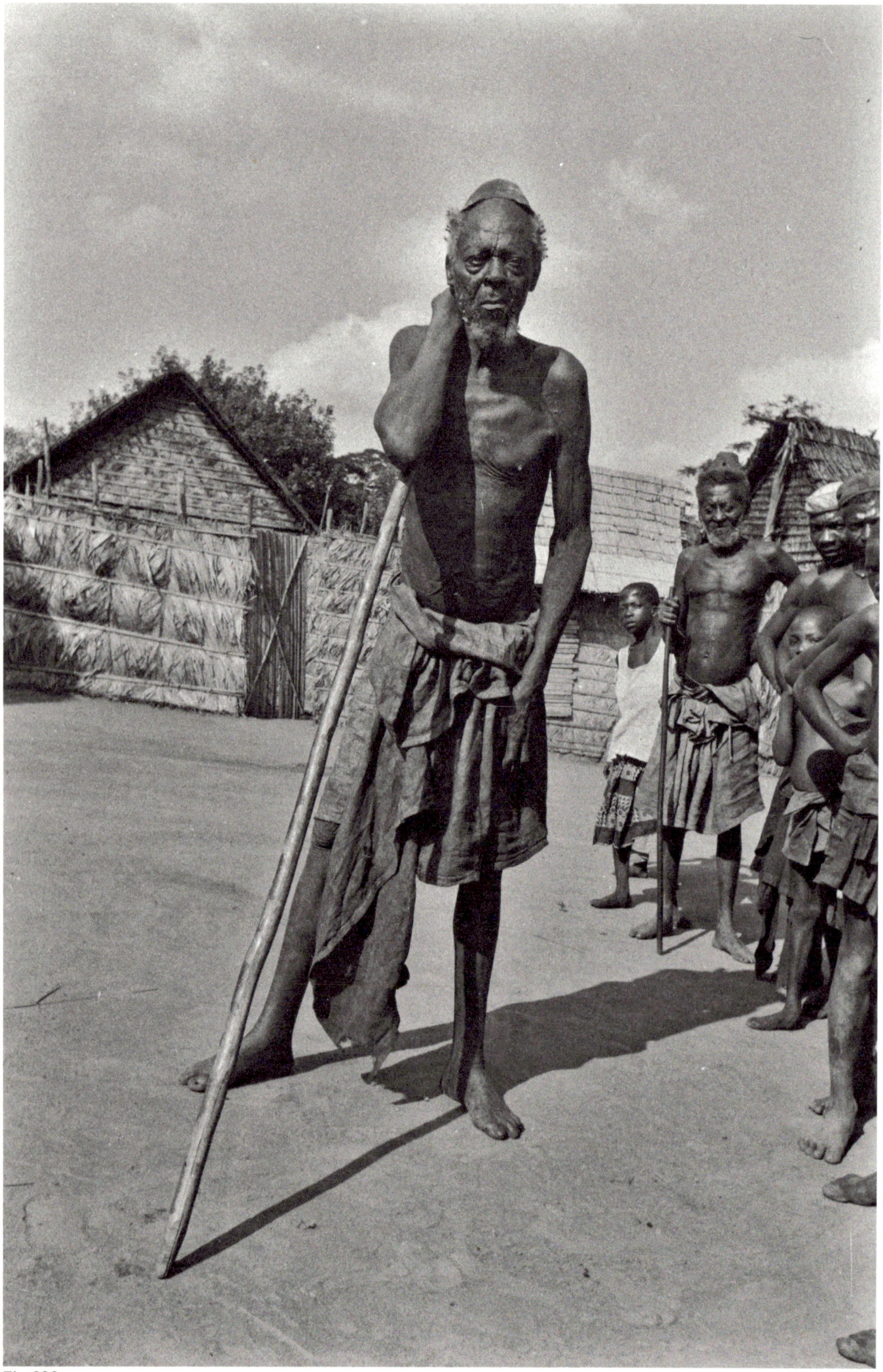

Fig. 228

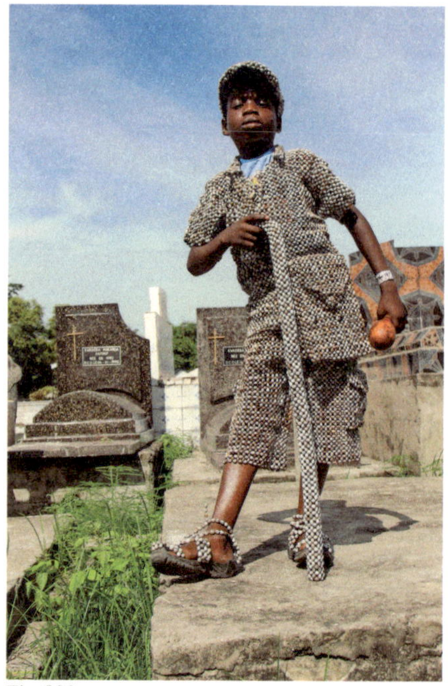

Fig. 229

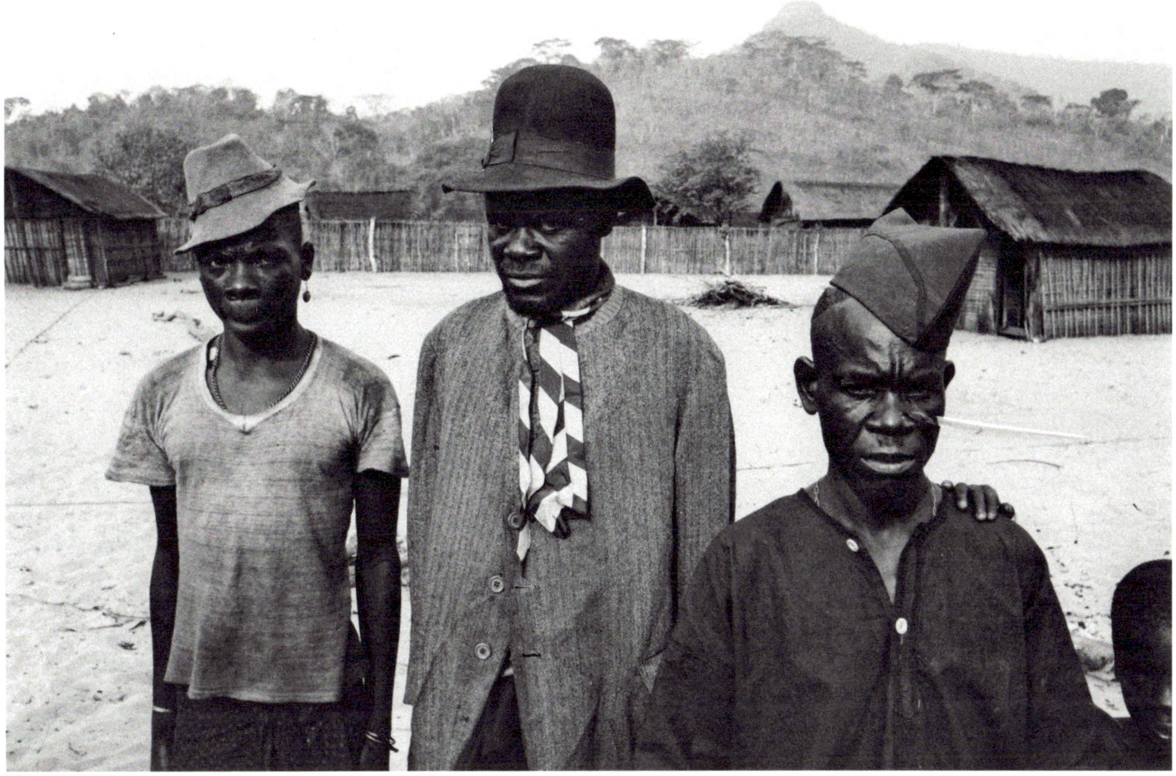

Fig. 230

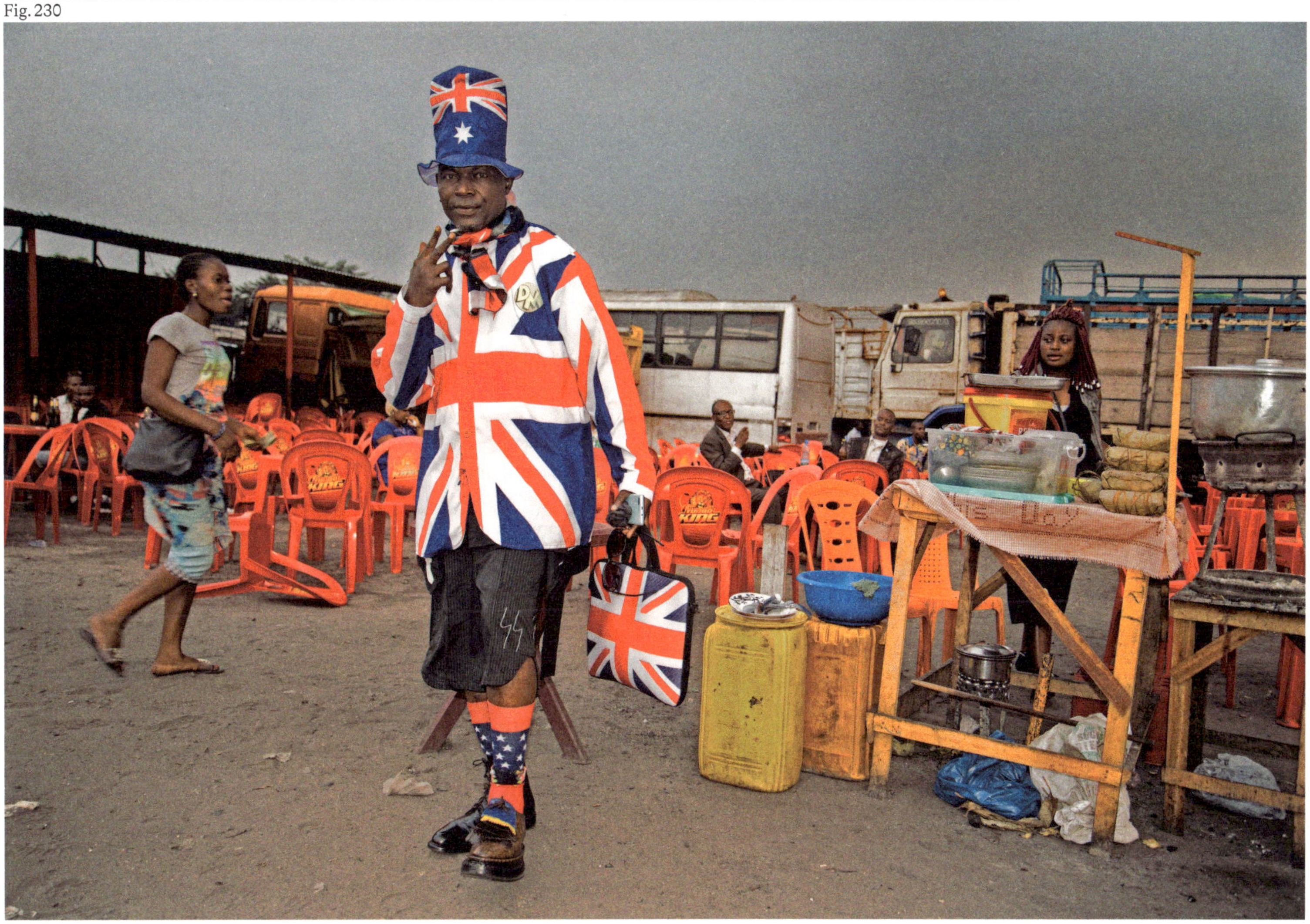

Fig. 231

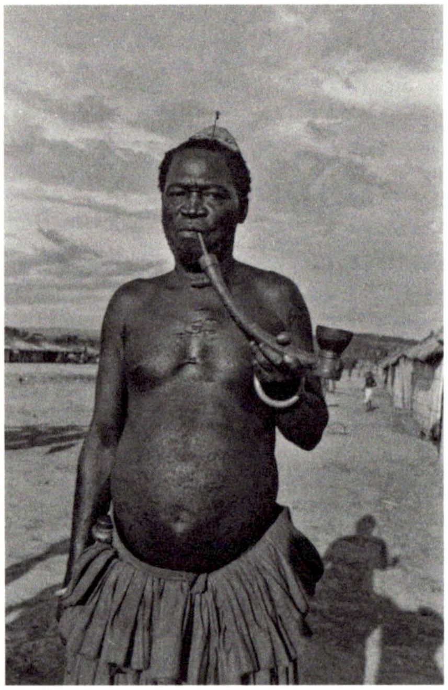
Fig. 232

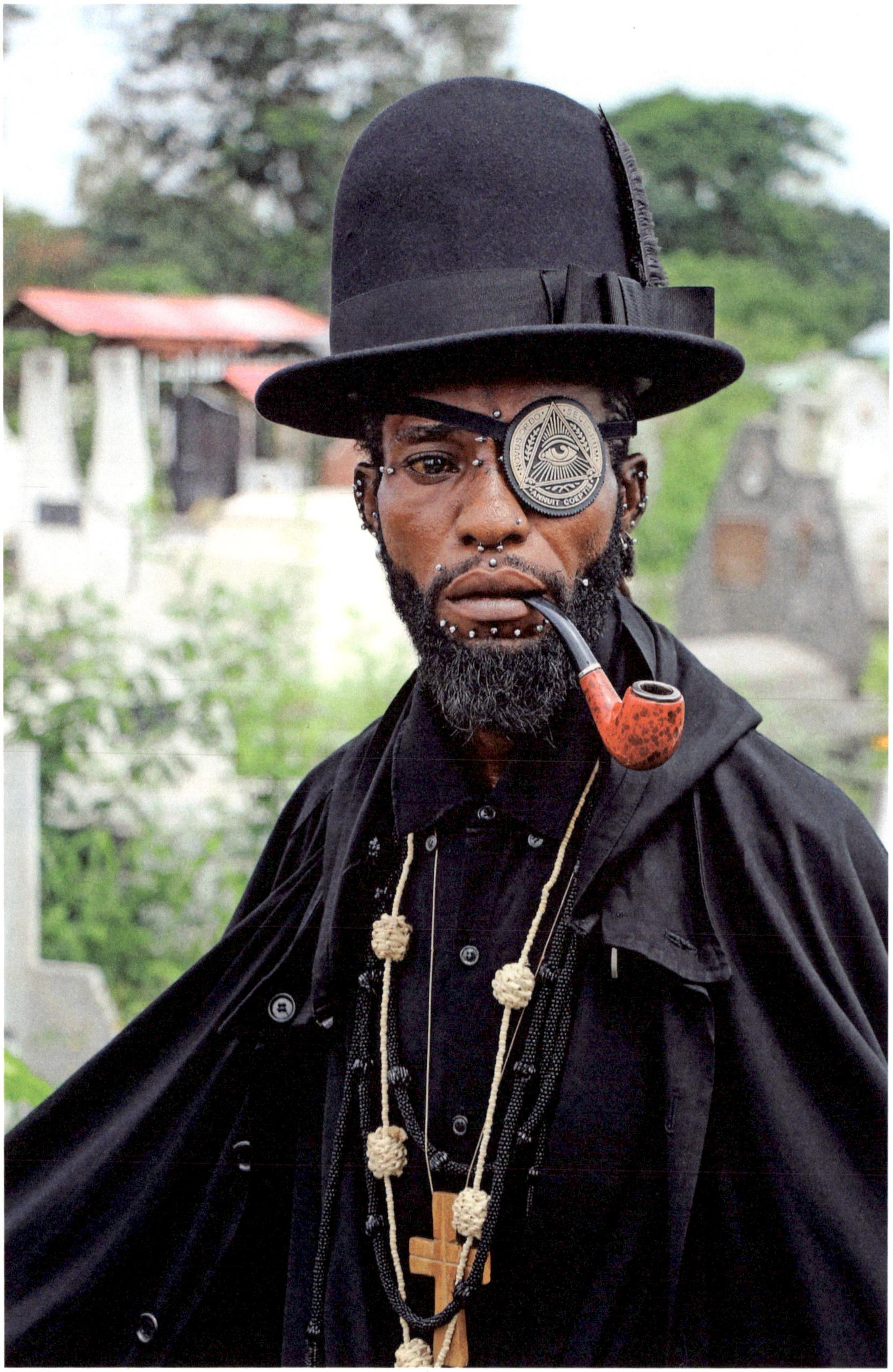
Fig. 233

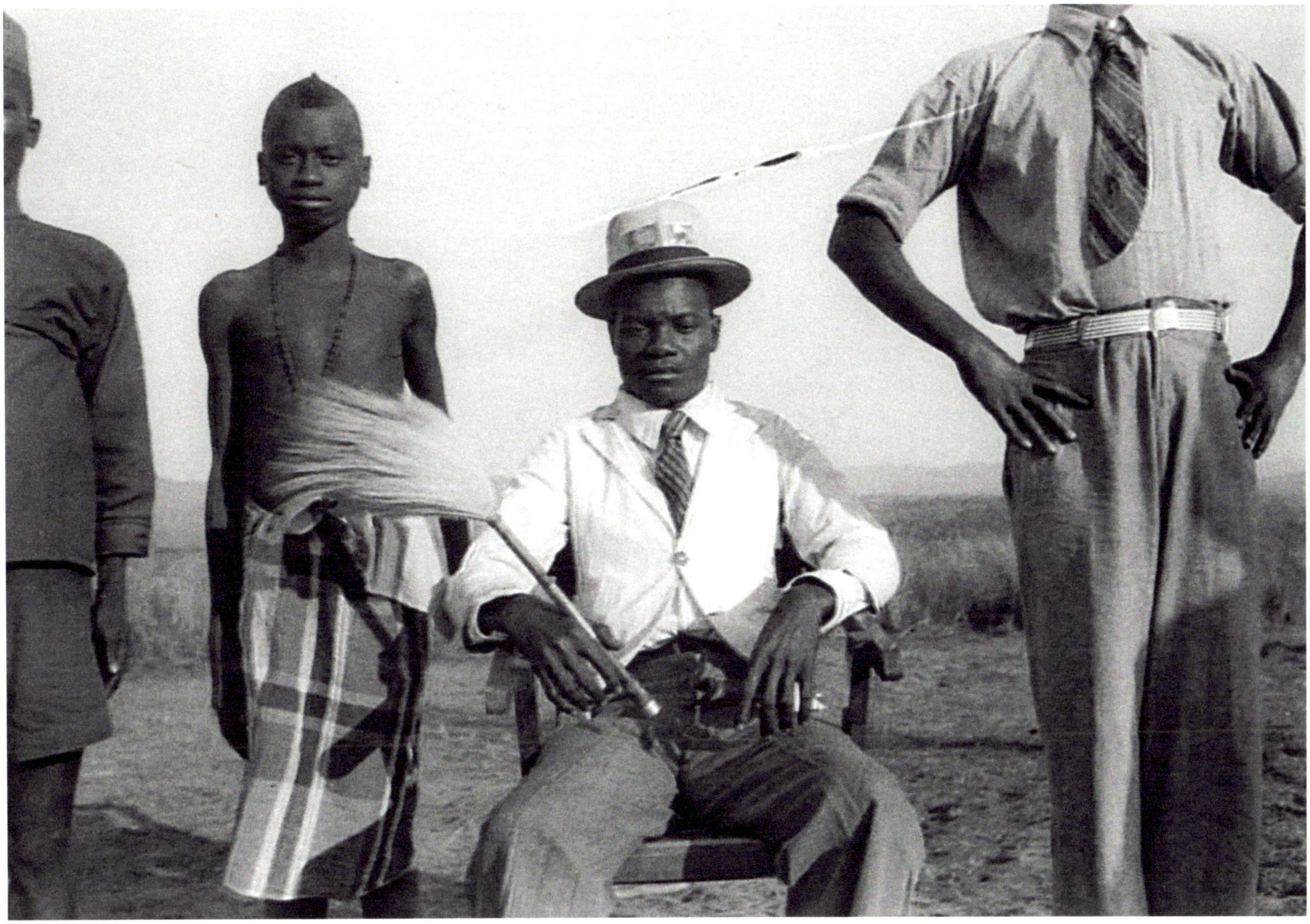
Fig. 234

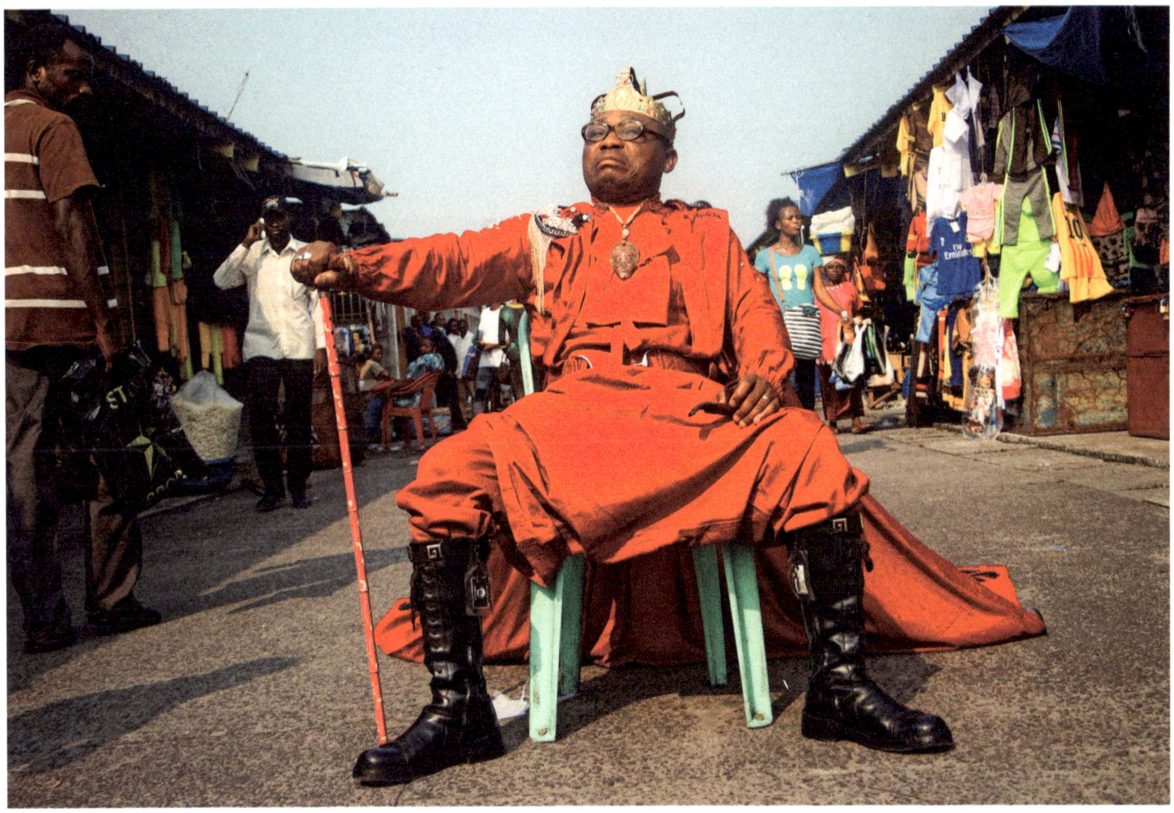
Fig. 235

Fig. 224
Hans Himmelheber
Portrait of King Kasongo Lunda
Yaka region, 1938, b/w negative
Museum Rietberg Zürich, FHH 155-21

Fig. 225
Yves Sambu
Mobutu
From the series *Vanité apparente*
Kinshasa, 2015, photograph, 80 × 120 cm
Yves Sambu

Fig. 226
Hans Himmelheber
Two Bayaka chiefs with sword and umbrellas
Yaka region, 1938, b/w negative
Museum Rietberg Zürich, FHH 155-22

Fig. 227
Yves Sambu
Parasoleil
From the series *Vanité apparente*
Kinshasa, 2018, photograph, 120 × 80 cm
Yves Sambu

Fig. 228
Hans Himmelheber
Old dignitary with cane
Kuba region, 1939, digitized b/w negative
Museum Rietberg Zürich, FHH 184-17

Fig. 229
Yves Sambu
Untitled [young *sapeur* with suit and cane]
From the series *Vanité apparente*
Kinshasa, 2016, photograph, 120 × 80 cm
Yves Sambu

Fig. 230
Hans Himmelheber
Three men with head coverings
Yaka region, 1938/39,
digitized b/w negative
Museum Rietberg Zürich, FHH 169-4

Fig. 231
Yves Sambu
Sapeur Nd'jili
From the series *Vanité apparente*
Kinshasa, 2019, photograph, 75 × 130 cm
Yves Sambu, commissioned by Museum Rietberg Zürich

Fig. 232
Hans Himmelheber
King Pero of the Lele
Kuba region, 1939, b/w negative
Museum Rietberg Zürich, FHH 177-26

Fig. 233
Yves Sambu
Untitled [man with pipe]
From the series *Vanité apparente*
Kinshasa, 2018, photograph, 120 × 80 cm
Yves Sambu

Fig. 234
Hans Himmelheber
Portrait of a chief
Yaka region, 1938, digitized b/w negative
Museum Rietberg Zürich, FHH 157-3

Fig. 235
Yves Sambu
Kadhitoza Imperator
From the series *Vanité apparente*
Kinshasa, 2016, photograph, 80 × 120 cm
Yves Sambu

The *sapeurs'* daily public appearances make Kinshasa and Brazzaville "spectacle cities" and *la sape* (the abbreviation of *Société des Ambianceurs et des Personnes Élégantes*) a veritable art of living. *Sapeurs* are extravagantly dressed men and women from the megalopolis of Brazzaville/Kinshasa whose external appearance contrasts with their living conditions. Unlike the rather reserved Brazzaville, an eclectic style has developed in Kinshasa in which the finest fabrics by Versace are combined with the best Japanese leather and chunky English boots.[1] At fashion competitions and funerals, the Congolese photographer and artist Yves Sambu shot impressive portraits of such eccentrically clad men and women from Kinshasa that make them look like heroic urban figures [figs. 225/227/229/231/233/235]. Thanks to their clothing and poses, the *sapeurs* in Sambu's photos have a strong presence that goes beyond mere vanity.[2] After all, *la sape* is much more than just clothing: with their outer and public appearance, the *sapeurs* are articulating their need for a new social identity that the cities deny them.[3]

The origins of the *sapeur* movement can be found in the colonial period, when chiefs and domestic staff received used clothing from Europeans as gifts and as wages. In the 1920s men known as *popos* from West Africa who were employed by the palm oil companies in the Belgian Congo set new trends with their clothing style. Even Hans Himmelheber photographed men during his travels whose poses and appearance are in no way inferior to the modern *sapeurs* [figs. 224/226/228/230/232/234]. When Yves Sambu first saw the photos of the men shown here, he exclaimed: "Mais ils sont contemporain!" The historical and contemporary photographs are indeed uncannily similar. Just like the present-day *sapeurs*, the chiefs used clothing, attributes, and Himmelheber's camera to give expression to a modern self. A connection between *sapeurs* then and now is also revealed by the example of the "king" dressed in red [fig. 235]. He is wearing a pendant around his neck that is modeled on a Chokwe mask. This is reminiscent of men in the Pende region who wore similar pendants in the 1930s as a symbol of resistance to the colonial regime [see story, p. 206]. — Nanina Guyer

1 Gondola 2019, p. 188.
2 Gondola 2019, p. 207.
3 Gondola 1999, p. 23.

MVUATU-MBOKA NA BISO – ET LA SUISSE: THE CONGOLESE DIASPORA ON FASHION AND IDENTITY IN SWITZERLAND

Fiona Bobo

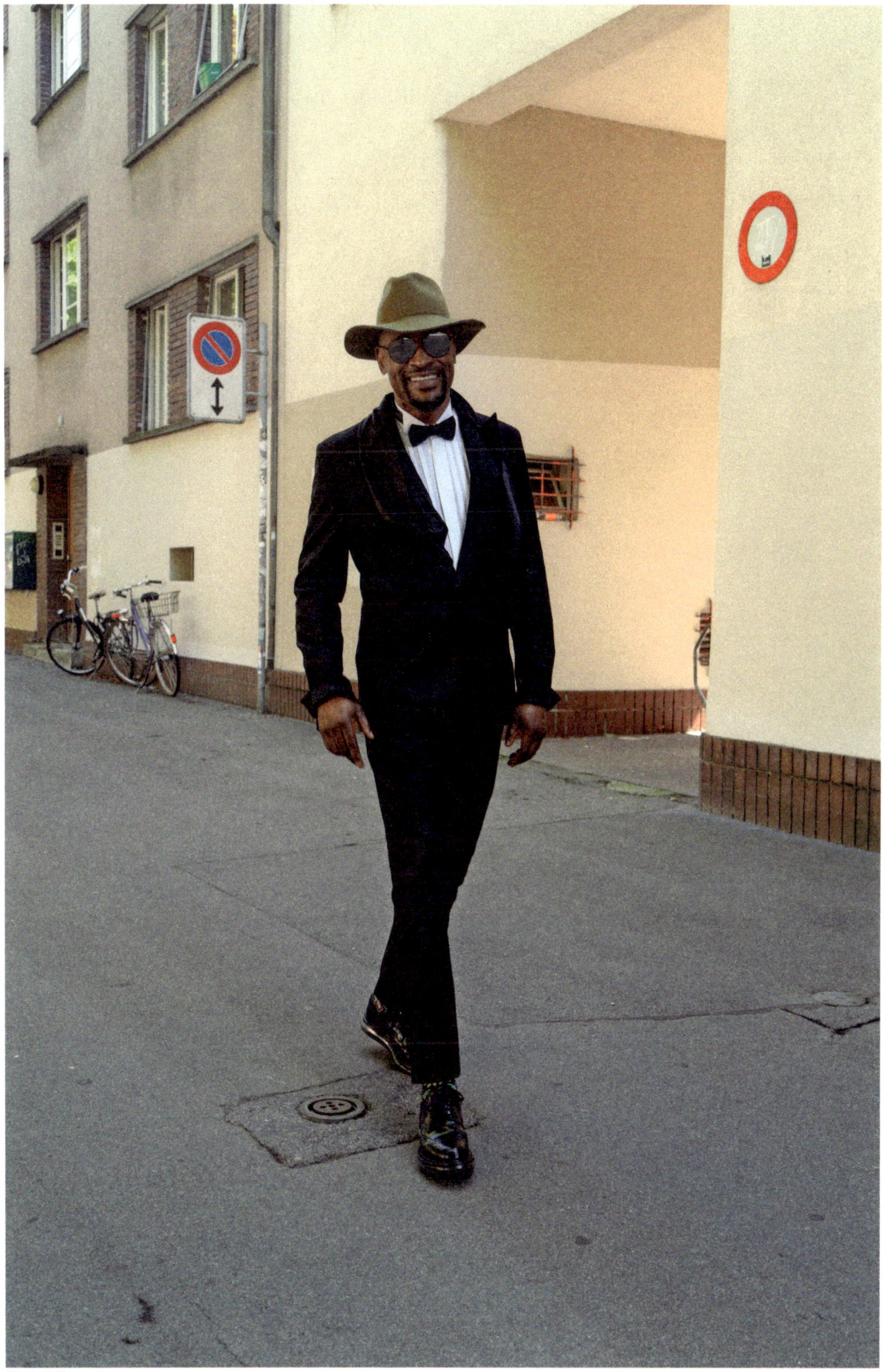

Fig. 236

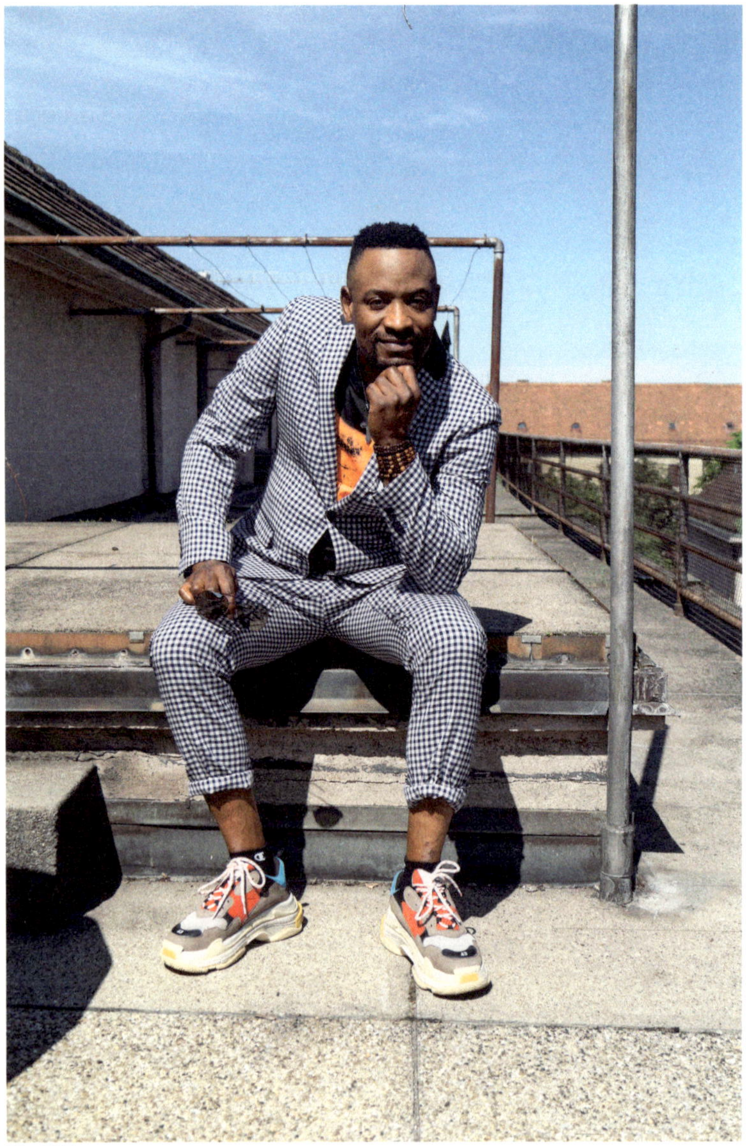

Fig. 237

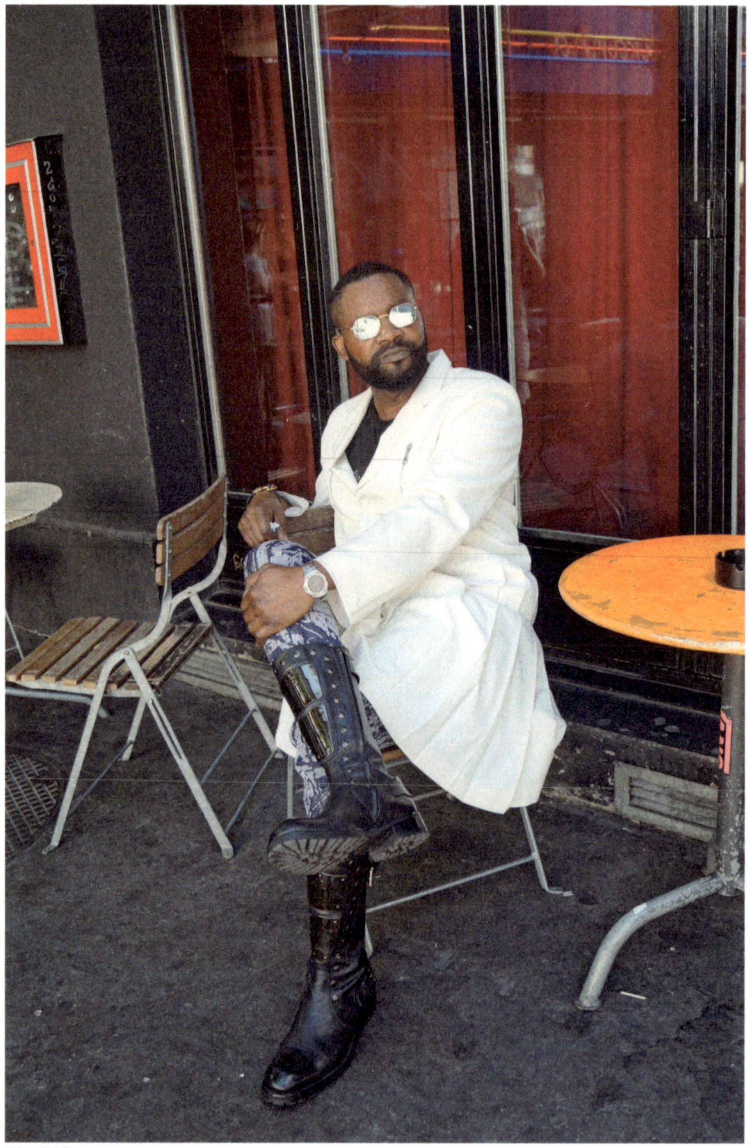

Fig. 238

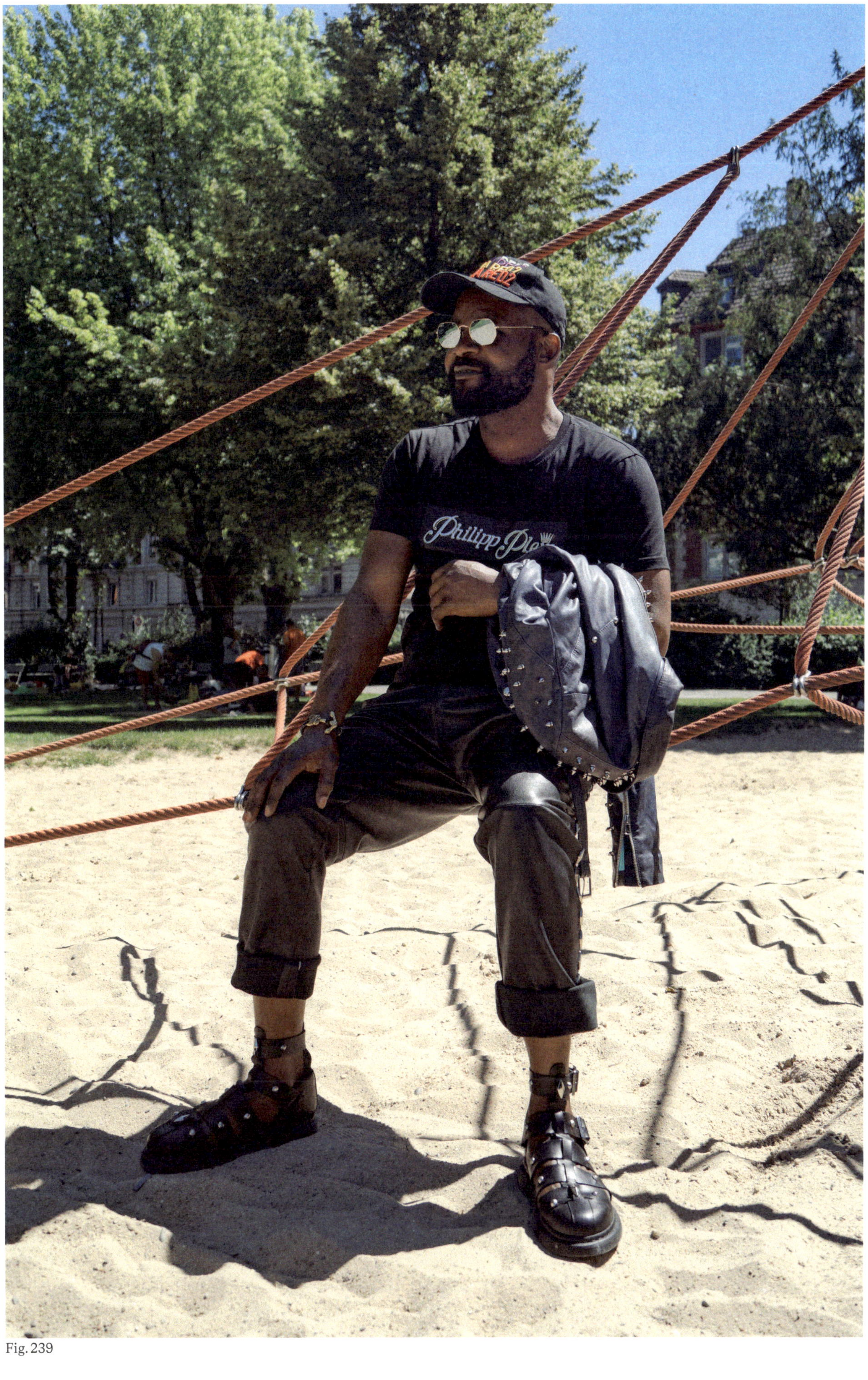

Fig. 239

Fig. 236
Fiona Bobo
Kabongo
From *Mvuatu-Mboka Na Biso—et la Suisse*
2019, photograph
Fiona Bobo, commissioned by Museum Rietberg Zürich

Fig. 237
Fiona Bobo
Kabongo
From *Mvuatu-Mboka Na Biso—et la Suisse*
2019, photograph
Fiona Bobo, commissioned by Museum Rietberg Zürich

Fig. 238
Fiona Bobo
Toko
From *Mvuatu-Mboka Na Biso—et la Suisse*
2019, photograph
Fiona Bobo, commissioned by Museum Rietberg Zürich

Fig. 239
Fiona Bobo
Toko
From *Mvuatu-Mboka Na Biso—et la Suisse*
2019, photograph
Fiona Bobo, commissioned by Museum Rietberg Zürich

The multimedia installation *Mvuatu-Mboka Na Biso—et la Suisse* (*Style, Our Country, and Switzerland*) is the work of the Zurich-based artist Fiona Ndetani Bobo (1992) in collaboration with Fabrice Mawete (1983) and Antonin Wittwer (1992). It addresses fashion as a cultural aspect of the Congolese diaspora in Switzerland and hence is part of the "Design and Elegance" section of the *Congo as Fiction* exhibition. *Mvuatu-Mboka Na Biso—et la Suisse* [figs. 236–239] is the result of several months' research into the Congolese community in Zurich and environs. It soon became clear that external appearances and their presentation play a prominent part in Congolese society and are a way of asserting oneself in the community—not only in the Democratic Republic of the Congo but also in the European and Swiss diaspora. Yet how is this phenomenon manifested and what are the differences between the DRC and the diaspora in Switzerland?

Raised in the canton of Zürich, Fiona Bobo has a Congolese father and a Swiss mother. She is studying social work at the ZHAW (Zurich University of Applied Sciences), and from 2012 to 2016 she was a student of media arts in the Department of Art & Media at the ZHdK (Zurich University of the Arts). During her art degree she mainly focused on issues surrounding her Congolese roots and the cultural differences between Switzerland and Congo. Fiona Bobo's interest in people and their histories has always been crucial and served as her key to these respective spheres. When she traveled to Kinshasa with her father and brother in 2012, she was fascinated by the urban architecture and lifestyle in the capital. Over the following years she increasingly explored this kind of subject. Her journey and family connections have led to close communication with friends and relatives in Congo with whom she collaborates across national borders on her art projects. This is how the work *Chaises bleues* [figs. 240/241] emerged, for example, for which she asked her cousin via Facebook to take photographs of all the blue plastic chairs that stand on every corner in Kinshasa and have a formative influence on the cityscape. Central to this work is her cousin's unique view of the objects, as well as his approach to the task and handling of the camera. In a sense, the artist's final project at university, *BWANIA* [figs. 242/243], is a combination of her earlier works that now features herself more prominently as an individual. At the core of this installation is a video of her grandmother's funeral in Kinshasa [fig. 244]. Commissioned by her relatives, the video shows the entire twenty-four-hour burial ceremony, at which all family members wear custom-made mourning clothes cut from the same fabric [fig. 245]. At her request, one of the artist's aunts made her a dress from the fabric and sent it to her in Switzerland. Fiona Bobo portrayed herself wearing this dress in various photos, which are likewise part of the installation [fig. 246]. Another element of the artwork focuses on the way the Congolese population presents itself. Here her cousin photographed people on the street in conspicuous branded clothing [figs. 247/248].

The themes of fashion, presentation, and identity are a recurring theme in Fiona Bobo's work and to a certain extent constitute the red thread in her oeuvre. Her collaboration with others and the participatory approach as an explicit creative practice are key to her artworks and are also expressed in her cooperation with the Congolese diaspora in Switzerland.

Fig. 240
Fiona Bobo
Chaises bleues
2015, installation view
Fiona Bobo

Fig. 241
Fiona Bobo
Untitled
From *Chaises bleues*
2015, cellphone photo, C-print, approx. 20 × 14 cm
Fiona Bobo

Fig. 242
Fiona Bobo
BWANIA
2015, installation view
Fiona Bobo

Fig. 243
Fiona Bobo
BWANIA
2015, installation view
Fiona Bobo

Fig. 244
Fiona Bobo
Untitled
From *BWANIA*
2015, video still
Fiona Bobo

Fig. 245
Fiona Bobo
Untitled
From *BWANIA*
2015, video still
Fiona Bobo

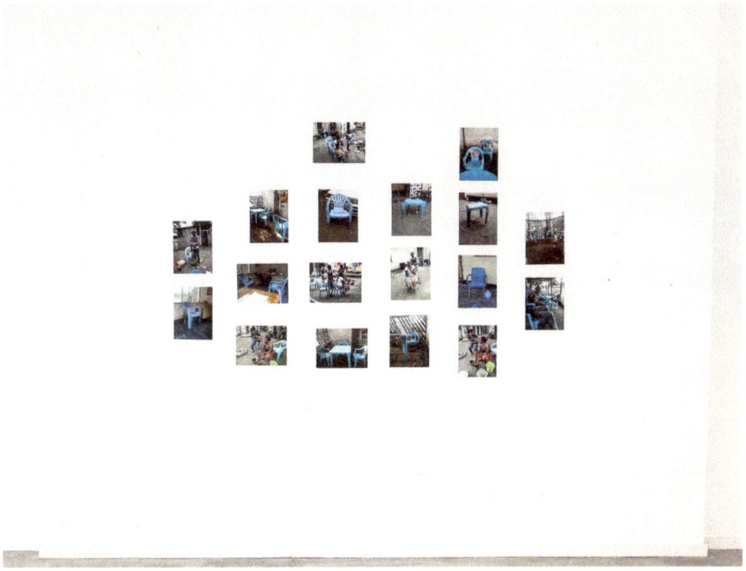
Fig. 240

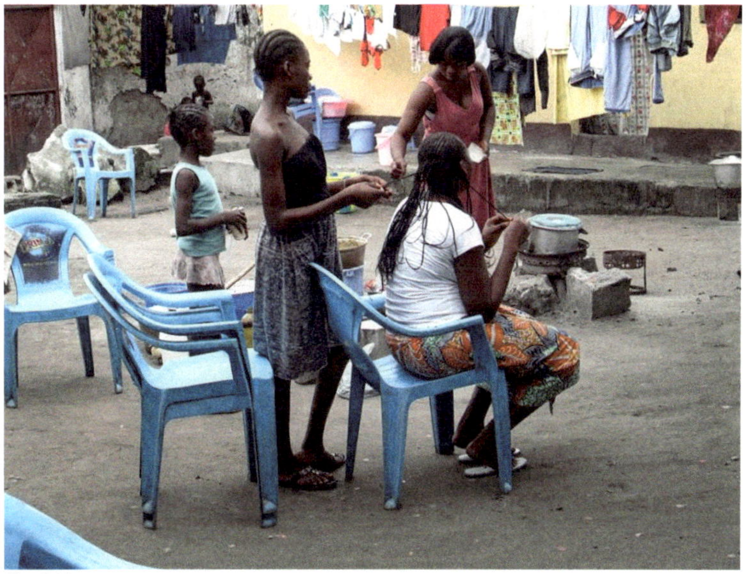
Fig. 241

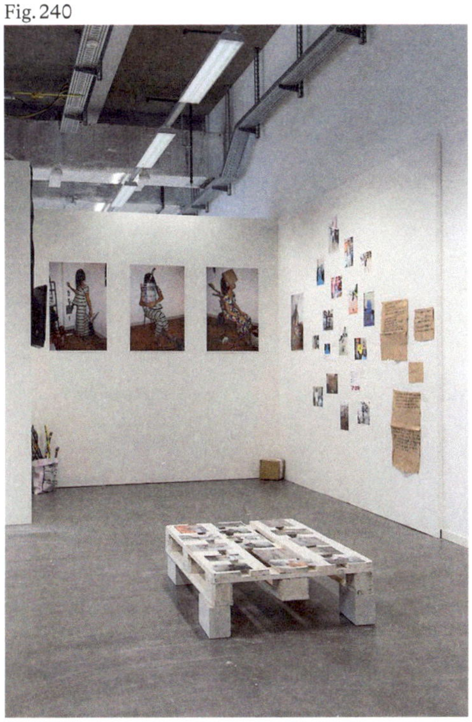
Fig. 242

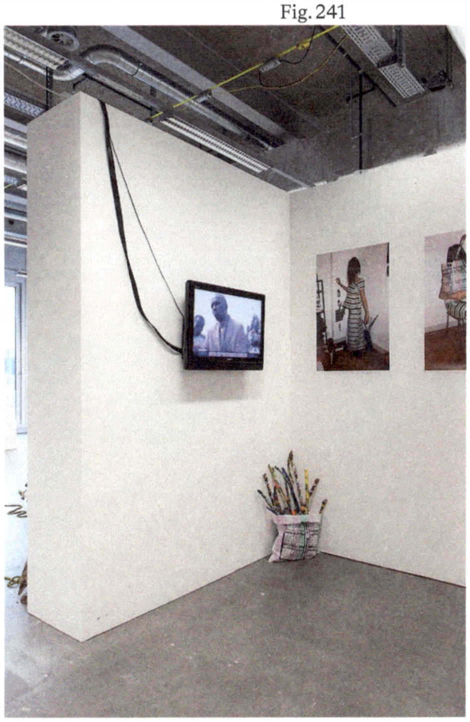
Fig. 243

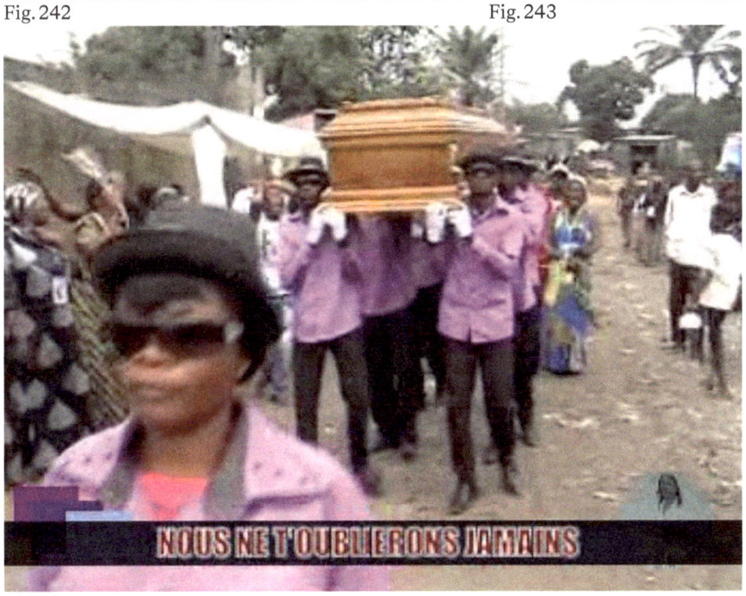

Fig. 244

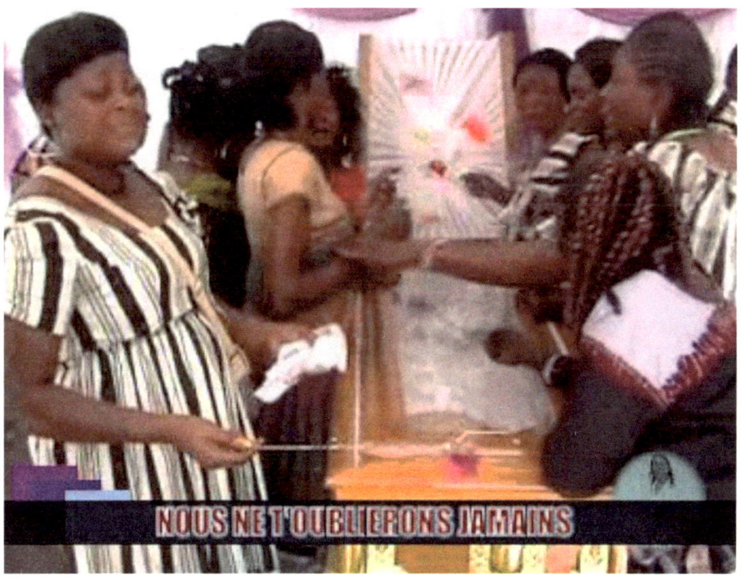

Fig. 245

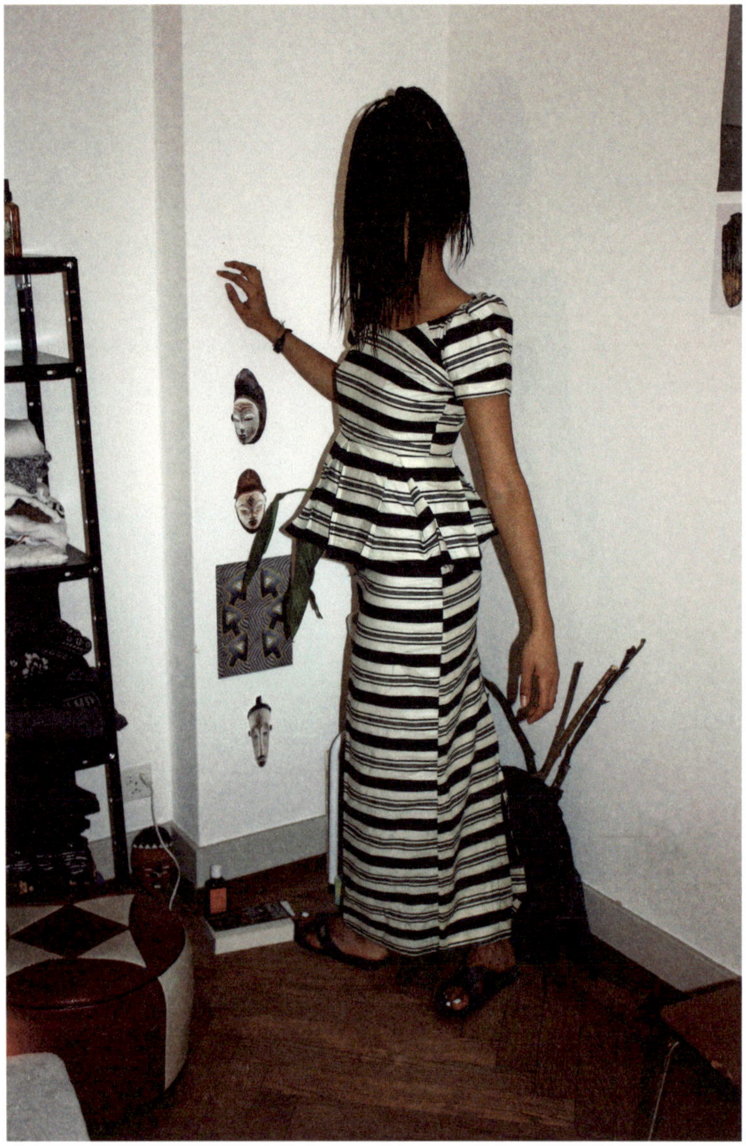

Fig. 246

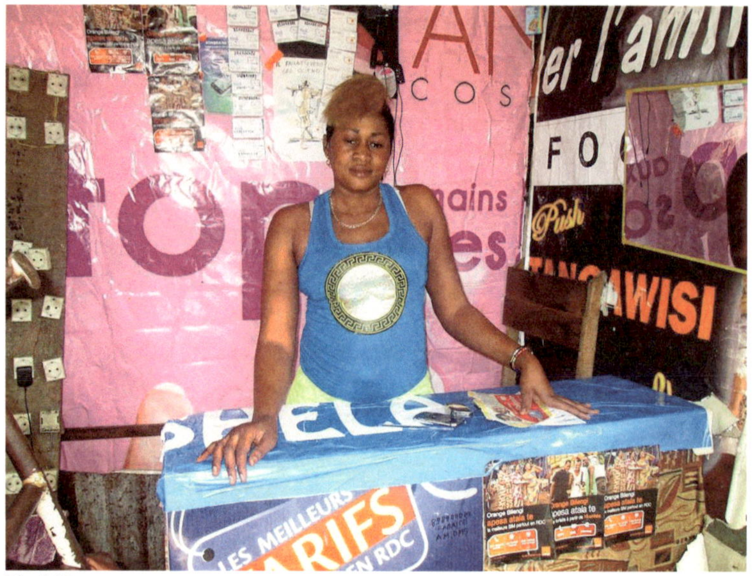

Fig. 247

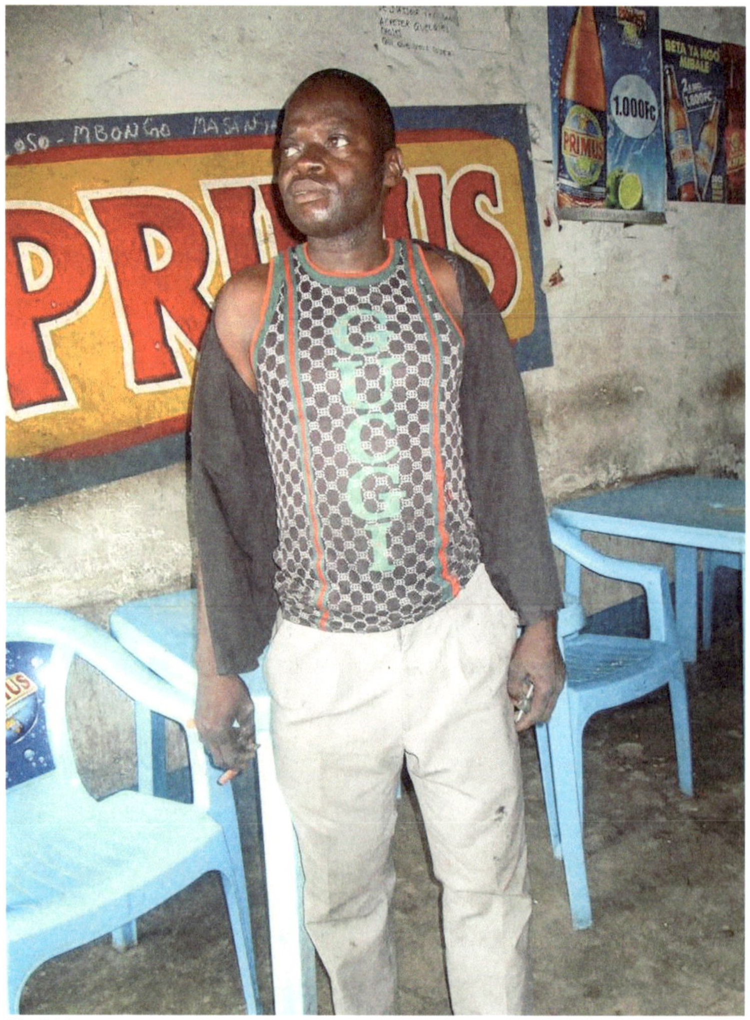

Fig. 248

Fig. 246
Fiona Bobo
Me in African dress
From *BWANIA*
2015, C-print
Fiona Bobo

Fig. 247
Fiona Bobo
Marques
From *BWANIA*
2015, cellphone photo, C-print
Fiona Bobo

Fig. 248
Fiona Bobo
Marques
From *BWANIA*
2015, cellphone photo, C-print
Fiona Bobo

Raised in the canton of Schwyz as the son of Congolese parents, Fabrice Mawete is a qualified social pedagogue with a HEB coaching diploma. During his collaboration with the Congolese people living in the diaspora here for the exhibition *Congo as Fiction,* he took on the important role of mediator: he established contact with Congolese representatives of *la sape* and with other members of the Congolese community in Switzerland and conducted conversations with them in French/Lingala to elicit their attitudes to the topic of the *sapeur* in the Swiss-Congolese community. Starting points for his research were key community meeting places, such as the Flory hairdressing salon and other establishments in Zurich's Langstrasse district. Via this work Fabrice Mawete saw the community from a different angle and was able to explore his own identity in more depth.

Antonin Wittwer, who completed a bachelor's degree in Design, Film and Art at the Lucerne University of Applied Sciences and Arts, was responsible for the filming of the project. He focuses on developing documentary film portraits of people in extraordinary circumstances. For example, in his final degree project *Anders Als Andere* (Different than Others, documentary film, 20 minutes), he portrayed the regulars at his grandmother's pub. During his many years of freelance work, he also gained experience in documentary filmmaking and music videos. For this project he captured on film the opinions and voices of the Congolese community, as well as his impressions of community life and festivities.

At the foreground of *Mvuatu-Mboka Na Biso—et la Suisse* was the question of what value is given to style and elegance in the diaspora, how these aspects are expressed, and to what extent they might form a cultural identity. On the basis of interviews with "key figures" like the *sapeurs*, but also more generally by attending the community's parties and weddings with their ostentatiously dressed guests, those involved in the project attempted to gain an insight into the subject. This process is a subjective approach.

La sape (*Société des Ambianceurs et des Personnes Élégantes*) is a fashion phenomenon from the urban centers of Brazzaville and Kinshasa. The members of this fictitious society call themselves *sapeurs* and feel obliged to dress elegantly or outlandishly. Their history can be traced back to the mid-nineteenth century, to the age of the first encounters with the French and Belge in a colonial context. Given the Europeans' debasement of the African body, Western clothing was seen as an opportunity to increase one's status in colonial society. On the other hand, even at that time items of clothing were used as a medium of exchange between the local population and diverse European expedition leaders. By the 1920s at the latest, Congolese domestic workers were increasingly being remunerated in secondhand clothing. Viewed in this light, today's generation is actually the fourth or even fifth generation of *sapeurs*.[1]

The *sapeurs* in the Congo-Kinshasa enjoy an almost heroic status that is often associated with Christian moral values, as Daniele Tamagni writes: "Non-violence, good education, the dialogue of generous spirit and a passion for all the values that must be integral to be a true *sapeur*."[2] Consequently, among the Congolese *la sape* represents an elegant attitude accompanied by equally elegant behavior and appearance, as Tamagni explains: "In the Congo elegance is very important. Perhaps in no other

1 Gondola 2010, pp. 157–173.

2 Tamagni 2009, unpaged.

country is a sense of style so crucially identified with its own cultural history. A significant part of this heritage is the *sape* and the *sapeurs*."[3] *La Sape* embodies the pride and self-confidence of Congolese culture and is an influential aspect of identity and belonging in the community. The reportage photography *Gentlemen of Bacongo* by Daniele Tamagni and the impressive photo series *Vanité apparente* by Yves Sambu provide an authentic insight into the *sape* scene in Congo [see story, p. 166]. The viewer soon becomes aware that the aesthetic and visual contrast between the *sapeur* and their tidy surroundings here in Switzerland is very different from that in the Congo, where the elegance of the *sapeurs* clearly contrasts with the urban context of the cities where infrastructure is sometimes lacking. In Switzerland the contrast is instead between the *sapeurs* and even other members of the Congolese diaspora and the local, rather modest clothing culture.

3 Tamagni 2009, unpaged.

During the project there was also a discussion of the—in part fierce—criticism of the *sapeurs* that comes from the members of the diaspora themselves. For many Congolese people living in the diaspora, *la sape* symbolizes a degree of superficiality and they disapprove of the fact that fashion seems to be considerably more important to the *sapeurs* than family and community values.

What became apparent during the research was that the Swiss *sapeurs* have perhaps adopted a touch of local restraint: although their outfits come from the latest collections of the big fashion brands and are very elegant, they also conform to the contemporary clothing style in Switzerland. Perhaps the *sape* movement ultimately lives off paradoxes, and possibly it is the contrasting backdrop that lets creativity bloom, as Paul Goodwin states: "It is at once a throwback to a lost world of precolonial elegance and decadence. At the same time it is also futuristic and even a little freakish given the extremity of the urban conditions in which many of the *sapeurs* live, particularly in the Congo. *La sape* is a movement of contradictions and paradoxes."[4]

4 Tamagni 2009, unpaged.

Finally, the project aims to open our eyes to society and culture:

Mvuatu-Mboka Na Biso—et la Suisse offers an opportunity to amplify the voice of local Congolese people about the subject of design and elegance and to gain an overview of this very prominent community in Switzerland. From this, a thought-provoking work emerged: thoughts about individual stories of identity, migration, and local coexistence—and even moral issues. Maybe the project will even succeed in making us aware of extravagance in new contexts in our everyday lives. —— Laura Falletta

POWER AND POLITICS

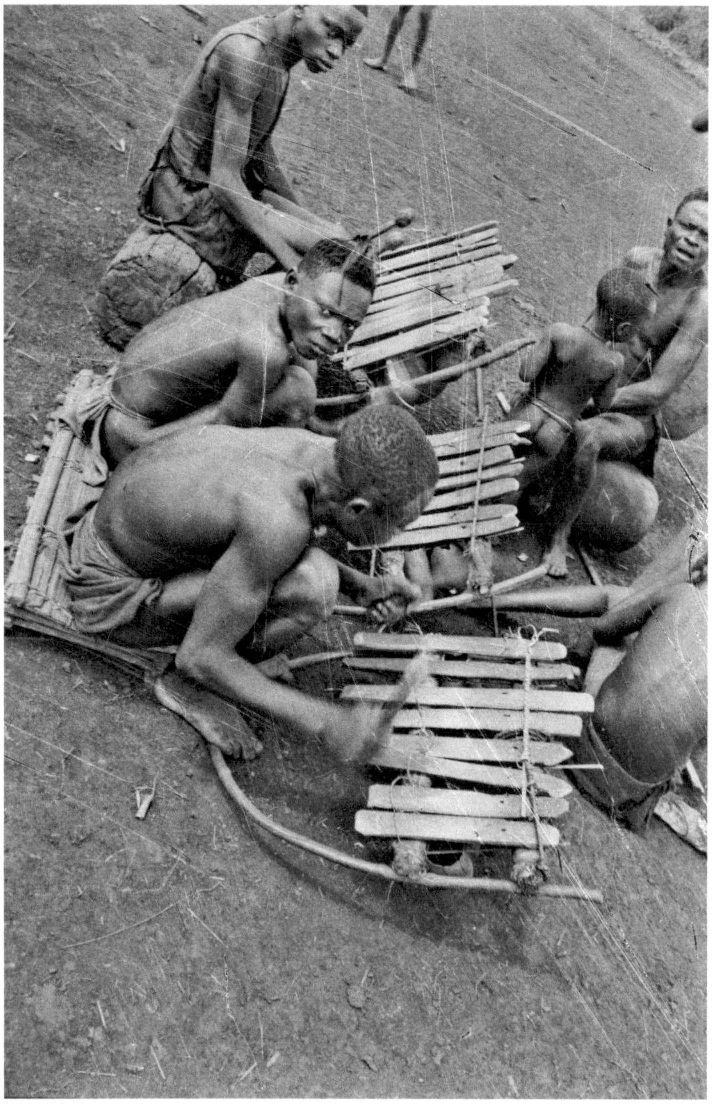
Fig. 249

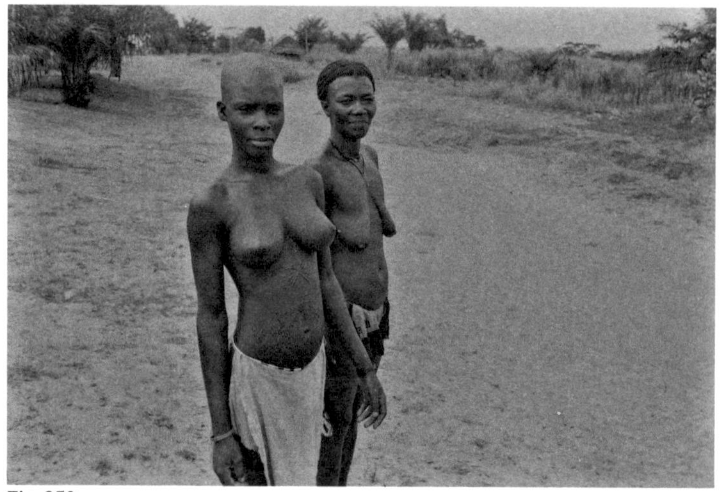
Fig. 250

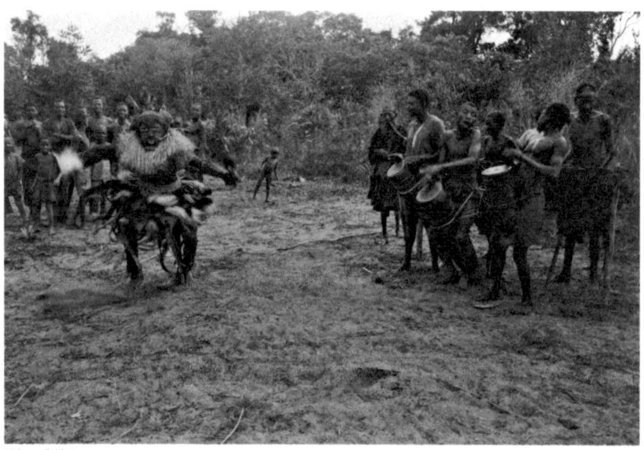
Fig. 251

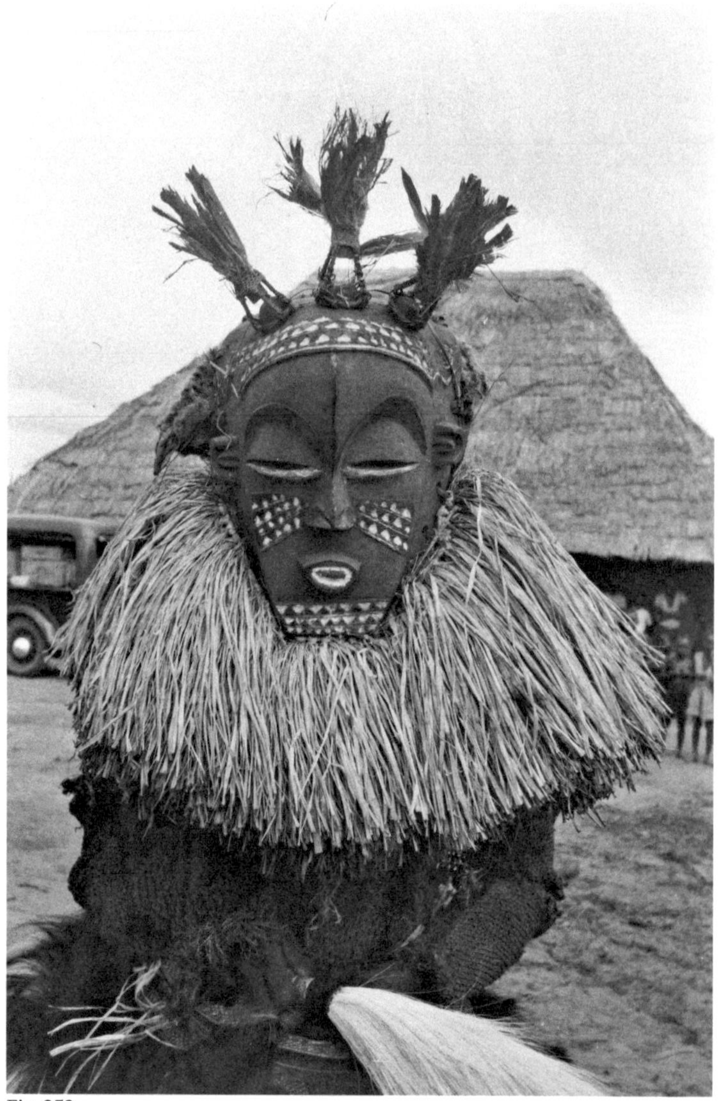
Fig. 252

Fig. 249
Hans Himmelheber
An instrumental ensemble
Luluwa region, 1939, b/w negative
Museum Rietberg Zürich, FHH 186-40

Fig. 250
Hans Himmelheber
Two women
Luluwa region, 1939, b/w negative
Museum Rietberg Zürich, FHH 186-9

Fig. 251
Hans Himmelheber
***Cimwana* masker and musicians**
Byombo region, May 20–22, 1939, b/w negative
Museum Rietberg Zürich, FHH 189-18

Fig. 252
Hans Himmelheber
***Cimwana* masker**
Byombo region, May 20–22, 1939
Museum Rietberg, FHH 189-31

HANS HIMMELHEBER IN LULUWALAND, MARCH 24 – MAY 22, 1939

Constantine Petridis

Although the Museum of Ethnology in Berlin and the Museum of the Belgian Congo in Tervuren, today's AfricaMuseum, had already established the essence of their impressive and comprehensive Luluwa collections, when Hans Himmelheber visited the region in 1939, research on the (Beena) Luluwa and their art had been limited and publications on the subject were barely available. Obviously, Himmelheber was familiar with the published accounts of the late nineteenth-century German explorers Hermann von Wissmann and his co-travelers in which Luluwa art is occasionally mentioned and illustrated.[1] These writings and the Luluwa works Wissmann and his team members had acquired in the late 1880s, which ended up in the museums of Berlin, and to a lesser extent Leipzig, must have inspired Himmelheber as he undertook his Congo voyage.[2]

What has survived from Himmelheber's field notes is limited but the works he acquired during his travels along with the data that accompany them are invaluable documents for our understanding of the history of Luluwa art. And even though the first European exploration of the country's interior had happened half a century earlier, in-depth art-focused research in the Congo, whether by anthropologists or art historians, had only just started at the time of Himmelheber's visit. As such, Himmelheber's pioneering work constitutes an important precursor of the later research conducted by Albert Maesen (1982) and by Paul Timmermans (1966).[3] Adding further to the merits of his legacy, Himmelheber's photographic record comprises a few interesting images of musicians playing various instruments during some type of performance, possibly specifically organized for the entertainment of the German visitor, and a set of photographs of two Luluwa women with striking abdominal scarifications [figs. 249/250].

His photographic record is most interesting for the set it contains of images of a masquerade scene, possibly taken in a village named Ngandu, with wooden masks called *cimwana* ("tshimoana") and *mulwala* ("muluala") and a type of hood from knotted fibers of a genre identified as *munyinga*—Himmelheber[4] spells it "munjinga" [figs. 251–256].[5] Attributed to the (Beena) Byombo (Biombo), the masks captured in these photographs were actually acquired by Himmelheber, with much of their accoutrements intact and a handsome dusty red surface coloring preserved on the wooden examples.[6] Himmelheber[7] noted a stylistic connection with the carved masks of the Eastern Pende and those of the Chokwe. And the wooden *mulwala* type with striking chameleon-like eyes belonged to a genre that Himmelheber had already witnessed among neighboring peoples, such as the Kuba, Bindi, and others.[8]

Field-based documentation on Byombo masking is meager but thanks to research by David Binkley in the 1980s among the Northern Kete and the Southern Bushoong, close neighbors of

1 Himmelheber knew of the work on the Luluwa and their art by Leo Frobenius, who had visited the area during his expedition of 1905/06, and whose field collections were primarily deposited in the Hamburg Museum of Ethnology (today's Museum am Rothenbaum. Kulturen und Künste der Welt), but Frobenius's research is never cited in Himmelheber's writings. We should of course not forget that Frobenius's field notes, which have proven of such great help to Congo art scholars, were not published until the late 1980s in the series edited by Hildegard Klein.

2 Part of the extensive Luluwa holdings of what is today the Royal Museum for Central Africa, or AfricaMuseum, in Tervuren, and largely synchronic with Himmelheber's acquisitions, the hundreds of works field-collected by the Belgian medical doctors Jules-Auguste Fourche and Henri Morlighem between 1933 and 1936, were not offered to the museum until 1946, and were therefore not accessible to Himmelheber prior to his Congo travels. And the many writings by the prolific author duo, with their sporadic references to Luluwa art, were apparently not known to Himmelheber either. See, e.g., Fourche and Morlighem 1937, pp. 189–202; Fourche and Morlighem 1938, pp. 616–672; Fourche and Morlighem 1939.

3 Timmermans's 1966 article is based on research he conducted among the Luluwa and other peoples in the Kasai region from 1955 to 1962. Maesen's research in Luluwaland in 1954 was conducted in the context of the collecting expedition he organized for his employer at the time, the Tervuren museum, from 1953 to 1955. In addition to his 1982 essay and some other succinct contributions in various collective publications, Maesen's unpublished notebooks from this expedition have proven valuable resources for the study of the arts of many of the peoples he visited.

4 Himmelheber 1960, p. 354.

5 Even though the name Ngandu is not cited in Himmelheber's 1960 publication and does not appear in his diaries, I located Himmelheber's photographs of this village on the basis of documentation accompanying a Byombo *cimwana* mask that, according to William Fagg (1980, p. 140) was probably acquired in the field by Himmelheber before it was purchased by the Barbier-Mueller Museum in Geneva through Charles Ratton in 1939. It should also be noted that in Himmelheber's 1960 text, the name *munyinga* is erroneously given to a wooden mask of this *cimwana* type ("tshimoana" in his spelling).

6 Himmelheber 1960, figs. 277 and 278, p. 355.

7 Himmelheber 1960, p. 353.

8 Himmeheber 1960, p. 354.

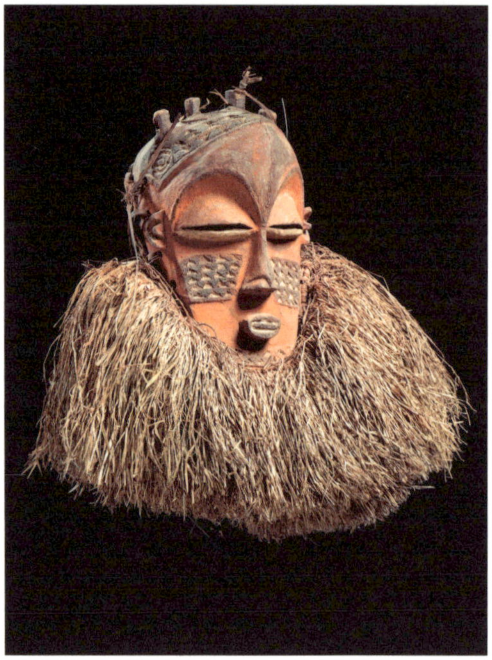
Fig. 253

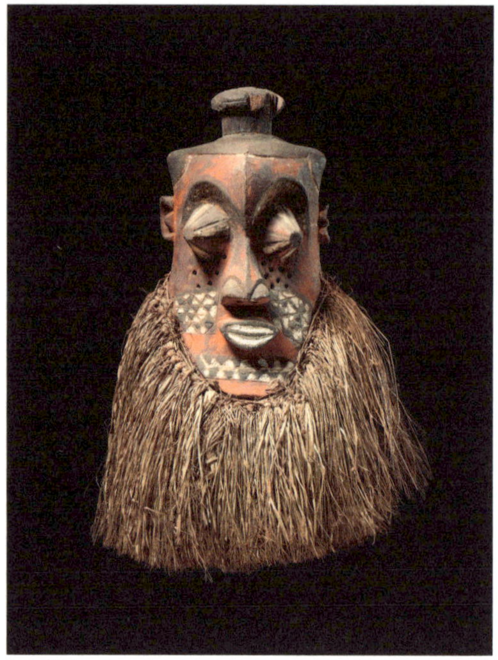
Fig. 254

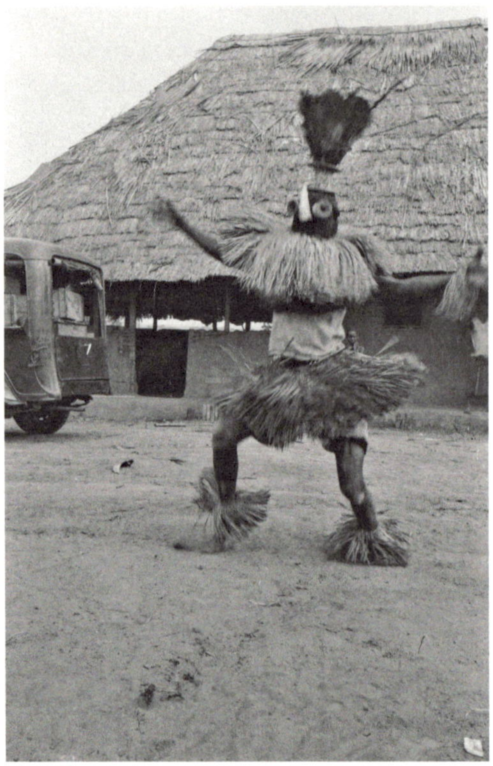
Fig. 255

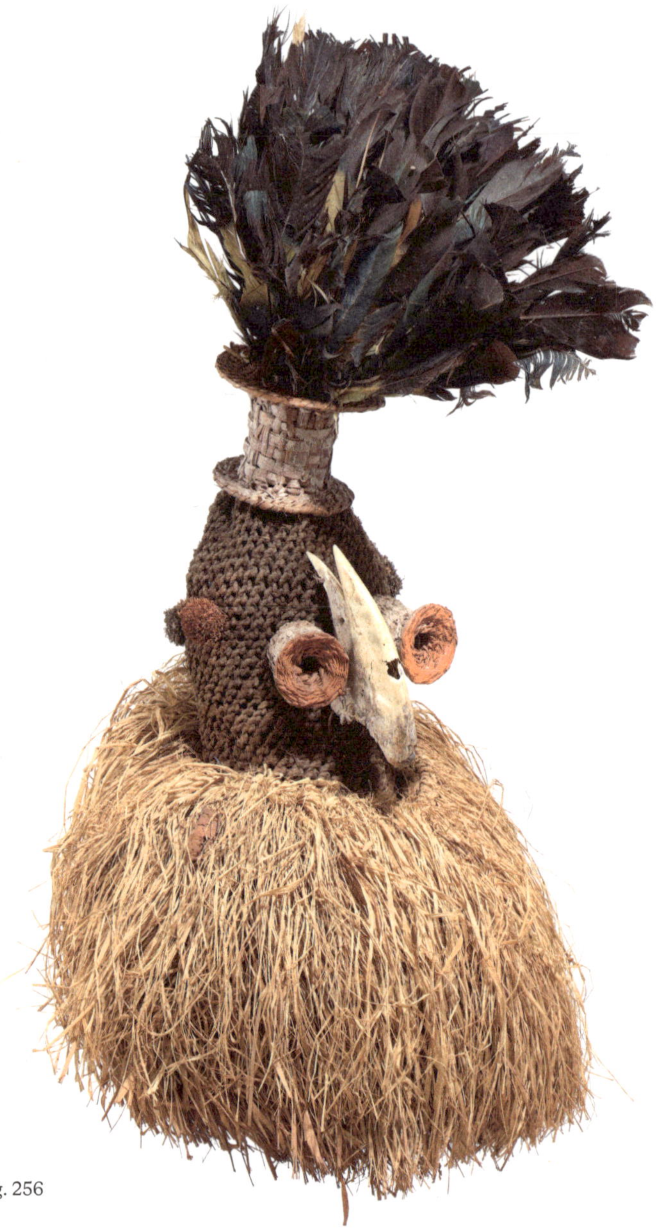
Fig. 256

Fig. 253
Artist of the Byombo region
Mask with collar, *cimwana*
Pre-1939, wood, plant fibers,
50 × 47 × 40 cm
Museum Rietberg Zürich, HH 21b
Gift of Barbara and Eberhard Fischer
Acquired by Hans Himmelheber

Fig. 254
Artist of the Byombo region
Large mask with collar, *mulwala*
Pre-1939, wood, plant fibers,
79 × 40 × 34 cm
Museum Rietberg Zürich, HH 22
Gift of Barbara and Eberhard Fischer
Acquired by Hans Himmelheber

Fig. 255
Hans Himmelheber
Masked figure with beak and crown of feathers, *munyinga*
Byombo region, May 20–22, 1939,
b/w negative
Museum Rietberg Zürich, FHH 189-32

Fig. 256
Artist of the Byombo region
Mask with beak and feather crown, *munyinga*
Pre-1939, plant fibers, horn, feathers,
90 × 55 × 50 cm
Museum Rietberg Zürich, 2019.426
Gift of Barbara and Eberhard Fischer
Acquired by Hans Himmelheber

the Byombo, we know that *munyinga* presides over the hierarchy of masks that comprise *mulwala* and its female counterpart *cimwana*, which together play a central role in the boys' puberty ritual named *buadi* among the Northern Kete and *nkaan* among the Southern Bushoong.[9] Also documented and field-collected by Leo Frobenius in 1905/06,[10] the culture to which masks of this style belong was actually presented as a Luluwa subgroup in Frobenius's field notes. Today, however, the Byombo are generally considered an autonomous group with closer ties to the Kuba confederacy than to the Luluwa. In fact, while the writings on the Luluwa by Frobenius as well as by later authors such as Maesen and Timmermans place great emphasis on the various subgroups that form the Luluwa culture or ethnic group, none of these subdivisions appears in Himmelheber's writings.

COLLECTING POWER OBJECTS

Although he apparently did not acquire any Luluwa masks other than these Byombo examples of wood and knotted fibers, his diaries indicate that during his relatively short visit in Luluwaland of less than two months, Himmelheber field-collected about 200 figure sculptures, or perhaps even more.[11] According to his notes, which indicate that he was indeed primarily interested in the Luluwa peoples' figures, in addition to those he shipped home for his personal collection, the works he collected in the field were sent off to the dealer Charles Ratton in Paris and the Weyhe Gallery in New York and to the museums of Geneva and Basel.[12] From the catalogue cards for various figures in the Basel Museum of Cultures (e.g., III 6819 and 6885), we learn that such sculptures were only carved in six of the Luluwa villages Himmelheber visited.[13] The collector also comments that at the time, Luluwa people did not bear scarifications any longer and that the coiffures as seen in the figures were also of the past.

Generally speaking, Luluwa figure sculptures pertain to the broad class of power objects, once pejoratively labeled as "fetishes," which comprise both human-made and natural receptacles or recipients, such as horns, snail shells, gourds, or even animal skulls, meant to be filled with substances or ingredients that provide them with special, supernatural powers. The local term for such power objects, *bwanga* (singular of *manga*), is the equivalent of the terms *nkisi* (singular of *minkisi*) and *nkishi* (singular of *mankishi*) used in other parts of Central Africa. Most of these power objects are considered to possess both positive and negative qualities, and can serve to protect and help as much as they have the capacity to harm and damage. Ambivalence and ambiguity indeed seem to be a power object's most pertinent characteristics. In addition to the power object, the term *bwanga* also relates to the cult surrounding the object, a system of magico-religious beliefs and practices that centers on communication between the living and the spirits (of the dead). Power figures among the Luluwa, as among many other Central African peoples, acquired their special status as conduits between the world of humans and that of spirits only after they were charged by a ritual expert with ingredients or substances known as *bishimba*. Comprising materials of mineral, plant, animal, or even human origins (e.g., bits of hair, nail clippings, and teeth), the *bishimba* that defined the power object's efficacy and success had to be

9 Binkley 1990, pp. 157–176.

10 Frobenius 1988, pp. 7/126, fig. 129.

11 Himmelheber, diary, March 24 – May 22, 1939. His trip brought him to Demba, Luluabourg (present-day Kananga), Lwebo, and Charlesville (now Djokupunda). Other than the (Beena) Luluwa (or Bashilange, as they preferred to call themselves at the time) and the (Beena) Byombo, Himmelheber also encountered the related Luba and (Beena) Kosh peoples. However, despite his desire to do so, he did not succeed in meeting with the most powerful Luluwa chief of the day, Kalamba-Mukenge.

12 On Himmelheber's role as collector and trader, see the essay by Oberhofer in the present publication.

13 See the card catalogue at the Museum der Kulturen Basel.

recharged regularly, most notably at the appearance of a new moon, a sign of hope and renewal after a period of darkness and uncertainty. *Mupaki wa manga* or *mpaka manga* was the title of the said ritual expert with the special knowledge capable of manipulating the life-force or life-energy contained within the *bwanga*. This man or woman was considered the real creator of the charged figures and it was their name that was remembered more commonly than that of the carver who had provided the wooden receptacle to contain the *bishimba*.

Of the Luluwa figures included in this publication—six of which were field-collected by Himmelheber—a few are remarkably different in style and iconography from what we have come to consider more typical examples. One is the burned fragment of what must have been a chiefly figure, which he acquired on May 18, 1939, in a village named Basangana [fig. 10]. This sculpture belongs to a genre called *bwanga bwa bukalenga*, a rare category of male figures charged with magico-medicinal substances that are responsible for the protection and guidance of the ruler they portray, and by extension, of the people under his authority.[14] These figures might be interpreted as commemorative portraits that refer to historical individuals. Several examples of this rare genre are to be found in the Tervuren museum, but one of the most famous is undoubtedly the imposing figure acquired in the village of Tshiweewe in 1885 by Ludwig Wolf, one of Hermann von Wissmann's travel companions, now in the Berlin museum [fig. 257].

Interestingly, Himmelheber[15] noted the name *kalongo*—in his diary he notes "kalombo" (May 18, 1939)—for the figure he acquired, a proper name that has also been associated with figures of the female gender belonging to a different genre or typological category.[16] That this *kalongo* figure was owned by a priest, as Himmelheber reports, is difficult to confirm. Rather, such figures were most typically the exclusive property of a high-ranking chief of the distinctive *mukalenga wa nkashaama*, or leopard rank, whose image they portrayed. Upon his investiture into this prestigious title, such a leopard chief was believed to be capable of partaking in the special and fearsome powers of the animal, which lent him special supernatural qualities that enabled him to intervene on behalf of his community. Although they were largely damaged as a result of the fire the Himmelheber *kalongo* figure suffered from, various attributes in addition to the helmet indicate the sculpture's relationship with the leopard rank, including the carved imitation of a leopard skin (or the spotted skin of another feline), a cutlass or sword, and the attachment of a medicine-filled gourd or a shell on the figure's back or chest. The *bwanga bwa bukalenga* was indeed one of the Luluwa people's most important cults and related power objects with collective responsibilities. Like among the neighboring Songye, the Luluwa distinguish between small *manga* for personal use and large *manga* for communal purposes; that the former category is better represented in collections in the West reflects its wide popularity.

14 Much of the contextual information provided here stems from my recent monograph (Petridis 2018), which summarizes my doctoral dissertation and many of my earlier publications on the subject, and also includes many of the illustrations reproduced here.

15 Himmelheber 1960, p. 399.

16 The succinct data presented in Himmelheber's unpublished French essay destined for the now defunct colonial magazine *Brousse* are basically the same as those published in his *Negerkunst und Negerkünstler* of 1960.

Fig. 257
Artist of the Beena Beele Luluwa region
Male figure, *bwanga bwa bukalenga*
Pre-1885, wood, pigment, 73.5 × 19.5 × 17.5 cm
Ethnologisches Museum, Staatliche Museen, Preussischer Kulturbesitz, Berlin, III C 3246
Acquired by Ludwig Wolf

Fig. 258
Artist of the Luluwa region
Stool in the form of a human figure (detail of fig. 105)
Pre-1939, wood, 42 × 19 × 18 cm
Museum Rietberg Zürich, 2018.110
Gift of Martin Himmelheber
Acquired by Hans Himmelheber

Fig. 259
Artist of the Luluwa region
Caryatid stool
Possibly late nineteenth or early twentieth century, wood, pigment, and fiber, 43.2 cm
Paul Tishman (by 1968), current collection unknown

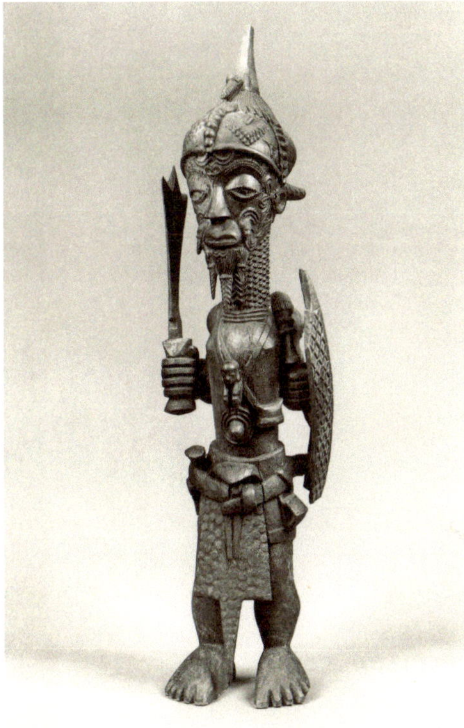

Fig. 257

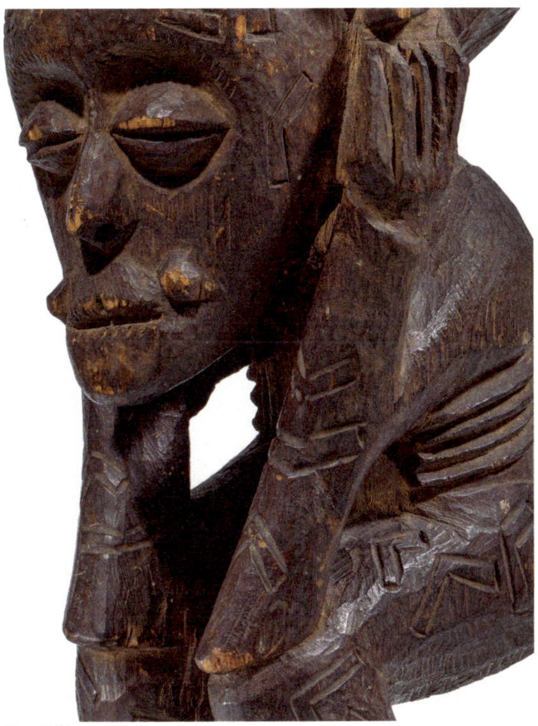

Fig. 258

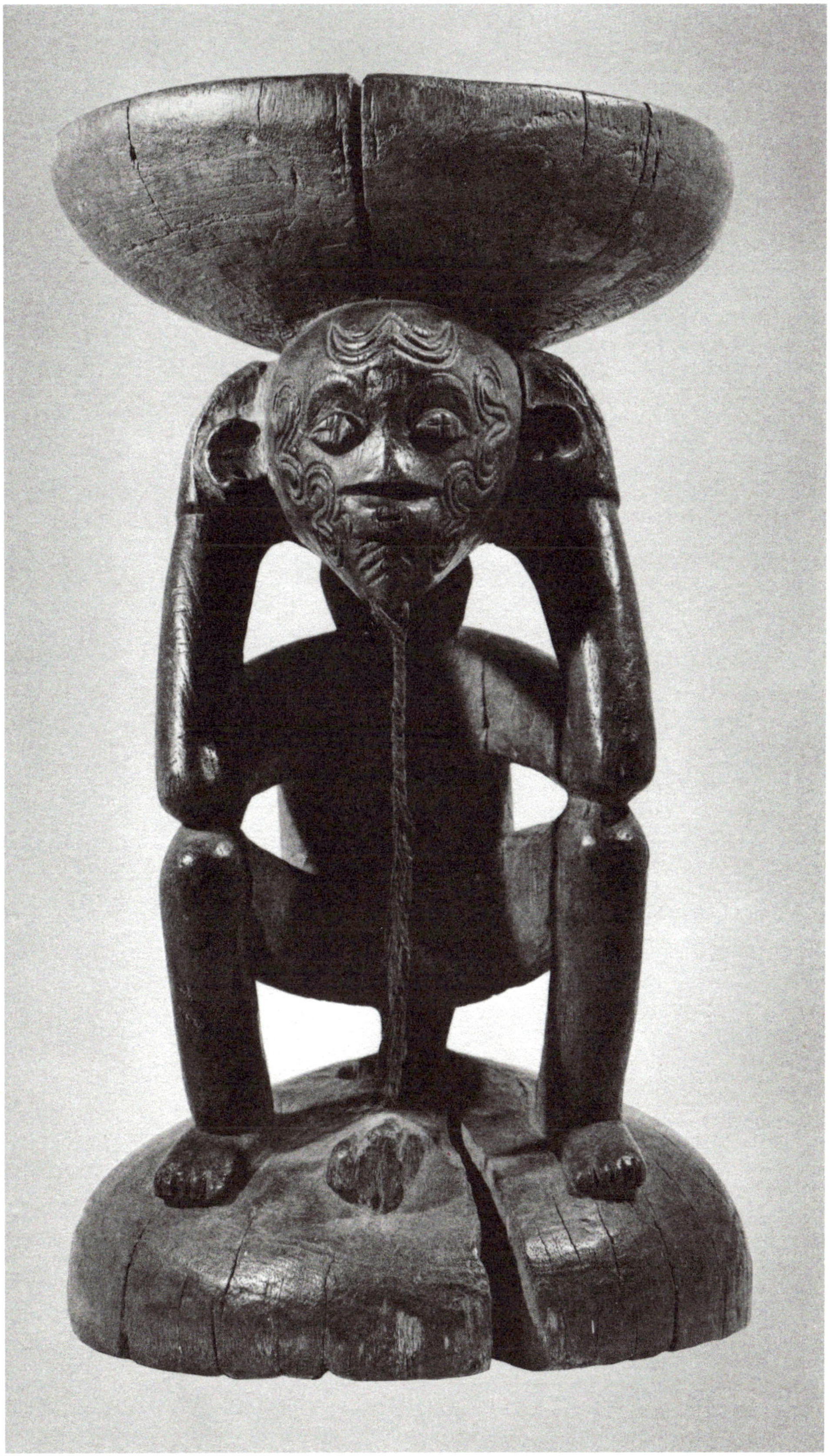

Fig. 259

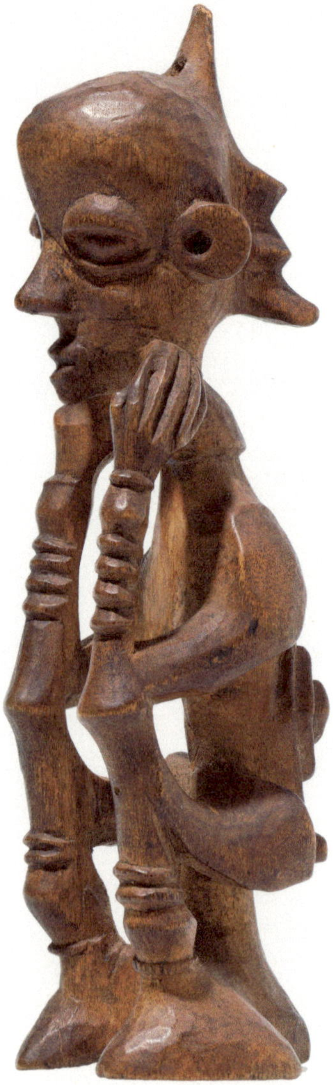

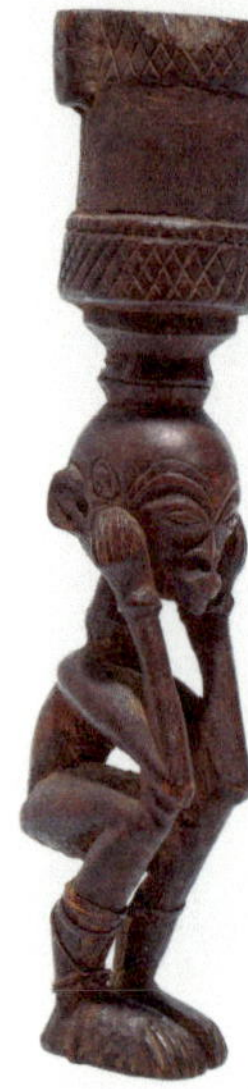

Fig. 261

Fig. 260

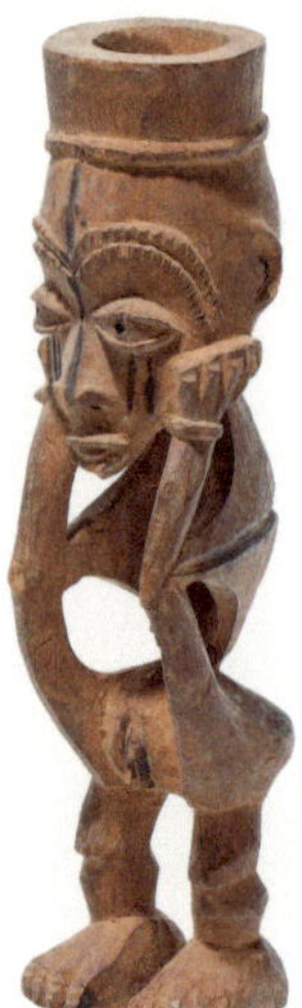

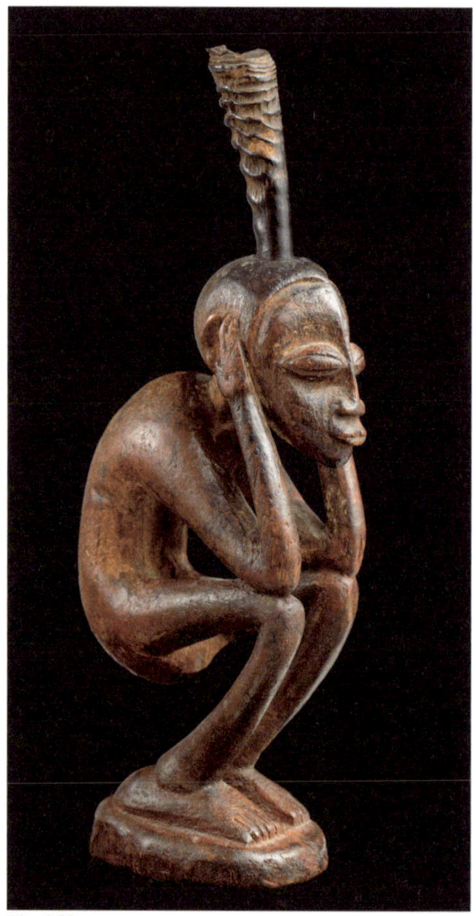

Fig. 262

Fig. 263

Fig. 260
Artist of the Luluwa region
Crouching figure
First half of the twentieth century, wood, 13.5 × 4.2 × 4 cm
Museum Rietberg Zürich, RAC 314
Gift from Eduard von der Heydt

Fig. 261
Artist of the Luluwa region
Tobacco mortar
Pre-1950s/60s, wood, 16.6 × 3.7 × 4 cm
Museum Rietberg Zürich, 2017.706
Bequest Dr. François Bochud
Acquired by Paul Timmermanns

Fig. 262
Artist of the Luluwa region
Tobacco mortar
Nineteenth/early twentieth century, wood, 16.5 × 4 × 5.5 cm
Museum Rietberg Zürich, RAC 315
Gift from Eduard von der Heydt

Fig. 263
Artist of the Luluwa region
Crouching figure, possibly *bwanga bwa cilembi*
Possibly late nineteenth or early twentieth century, wood, pigment, and antelope horn, 24 cm
Musée Barbier-Mueller, Geneva, 1026-11
Former Essayan Collection

CARYATID STOOLS AND CARYATID MORTARS

A strikingly unusual Luluwa acquisition by Himmelheber is the caryatid stool with a crouching supporting figure [fig. 258]. The only other Luluwa caryatid stool we know of is the one formerly in the collection of Paul and Ruth Tishman in Los Angeles [fig. 259]. The genre of stool to which the Himmelheber example belongs was quite widespread in southern Congo. Aside from the Songye and to a lesser extent the Chokwe, we are especially familiar with the diverse range of sculptures of this type that stem from the Luba king- and chiefdoms in southeastern Congo. Despite the lack of any field-based information to confirm this, such stools most probably had the same connotations of rank and prestige among the Luluwa as they had among their neighbors. That only few stools in Luluwa style have been acquired possibly underscores their rarity and elite status but it may also suggest that such chiefly attributes were more frequently imported from neighboring cultures rather than locally produced. Thus, when I traveled in the region in the mid-1990s, I actually witnessed a similar practice with regard to other political emblems, such as axes of Songye origin, skirts of Kuba origin, and staffs of Luba origin. When these works of various origins are acquired without any first-hand data, as is so often the case when they end up in museums or private collections, they are not automatically associated with the Luluwa.

A remarkable trait of the Himmelheber Luluwa stool is the rendering of ribs on the chest of the supporting caryatid figure. The same pronounced bones can actually be observed in several of the miniature sculptures of crouching or squatting figures for which the Luluwa are quite famous. Some of these figures, with their elbows touching or resting on the knees and their hands holding the cheeks, are integrated in what the literature has commonly identified as mortars for either tobacco or cannabis, or a combination of both [figs. 261/262]. Daniel Biebuyck[17] and other scholars in his wake have suggested that such mortars, filled with medicinal or magical substances, may actually have been used as power objects for therapeutic purposes with their contents being snuffed, inhaled, or otherwise consumed by the patient. It is not impossible that pounded dried tobacco leaves were part of such therapeutic concoctions. Ever since its introduction from the Americas to Africa by the Portuguese in the sixteenth century, tobacco has actually been praised for its medicinal and magical properties. According to this viewpoint, the image of a caryatid figure with skeletal features would hint at the health issues that the mortar as a power object was meant to cure. It is perhaps not a coincidence that Wissmann already named the mortars "fetish snuff tobacco boxes."[18]

17 Biebuyck 1992, p. 315.

18 Wissmann 1891, p. 218.

In some of the earlier literature the depiction of an emaciated figure has specifically been related to the health problems caused by the excessive use of cannabis (or marijuana; *Cannabis sativa*). However, while the reports on the damaging effects of cannabis consumption cannot be dismissed, the recognition of this causal relationship in Luluwa carving, though appealing, is not based on first-hand data. In fact, even if one were to reject the possible therapeutic use of such mortars, it cannot be determined that the mortars were indeed used for cannabis, known as *dyamba*, rather than for tobacco, called *mfwanka*. For the same reason, it is difficult to assert the connection between the popularity of caryatid mortars and the religious movement called *bwanga bwa dyamba* that centered around the consumption of cannabis promoted in the late nineteenth century by the chief Kalamba-Mukenge. Truth is, the smoking of cannabis, most typically with a water pipe made of a gourd, has always had religious meaning among the Luluwa and occurred in the context of ancestor worship up to at least the 1960s.

The knee-to-elbow position with hands on the cheeks that is shared between these miniature carvings and the two known stools is not unique to the Luluwa corpus. But because it seems to have been more prominent here than among some of their neighbors, it is mostly associated with the Luluwa. Even though crouching is a common way of resting in places where stools or chairs are not widely used, various meanings have been proposed to explain this striking posture. One opinion is that it represents a chief or someone of high rank who reflects on his duties and responsibilities. Another opinion views it as an expression of pain and sickness or even sorrow. A more popular interpretation associates it with a hunting ritual imitating how a hunter crouches in front of the sculpture and blows smoke on it in order to activate the inhabiting spirit and to ensure its positive intervention. Small caryatid figures with this position were carried attached to a hunter's belt for continued protection and good luck or, like in the case of the Berlin figure illustrated earlier [fig. 257], to a necklace. Crouching figures that are slightly taller than those integrated into the average mortars and that bear a small antelope horn inserted in their head, are typically identified as power figures for the hunt, known as *manga wa cilembi* (plural of *bwanga bwa cilembi*) [fig. 263].

BWANGA BWA BWIMPE: FOR BEAUTY AND GOOD HEALTH

The four other standing figures included in this publication are different examples of the broad *bwanga* power object category. Three specifically pertain to a genre known as *bwanga bwa bwimpe* [figs. 264/265/267]. Recognizable by the little cup in one hand that was originally filled with chalk, this is perhaps the most popular genre of Luluwa power object. The fourth example [fig. 266] is somewhat unusual in that it holds a hard-to-identify tool in one hand and carries a child in the other. Indeed, the maternity theme is typically reserved for yet another type of power cult known as *bwanga bwa cibola* that addresses questions of childbirth and fertility. Mother-and-child figures related to this *cibola* cult are among the best-represented and most beloved Luluwa sculptures in collections in the West. Still, the categories of *cibola* and *bwimpe* (I will return to them later) share a common philosophy that is actually encapsulated by the term *bwimpe*. Uniting our Western notions of ethics or morality, and aesthetics or beauty, the fusion of the *bwimpe* and *cibola* categories into one single work with the intention to protect unborn or new life, should not come as a surprise.

According to Himmelheber,[19] smaller figures of the *bwimpe* type were owned by almost every man and woman, and his informants told him that they were "idols" carved upon the recom-

19 Himmelheber 1960, pp. 395–399.

Fig. 264
Artist of the Luluwa region
(probably Bakwa Mushilu)
Female (?) figure, *bwanga bwa bwimpe*
Probably early to mid-nineteenth century, wood and pigment, 45 cm
Royal Museum for Central Africa, Tervuren, EO.0.0.7158
Acquired by De Bruyn

Fig. 265
Artist of the Luluwa region
(probably Bakwa Mushilu)
Male figure with stamper, *bwanga bwa bwimpe*
Pre-1939, wood, 30 × 6.5 × 8 cm
Museum Rietberg Zürich, HH 8
Gift of Barbara and Eberhard Fischer
Acquired by Hans Himmelheber

Fig. 266
Artist of the Luluwa region
Mother with child, *bwanga bwa bwimpe* or *bwanga bwa cibola*
Pre-1939, wood, 28 × 5.5 × 7 cm
Museum Rietberg Zürich, HH 7
Gift of Barbara and Eberhard Fischer
Acquired by Hans Himmelheber

Fig. 267
Artist of the Luluwa region
Male figure, *bwanga bwa bwimpe*
Pre-1939, wood, 37.1 cm
Jan Calmeyn, Sint-Niklaas
Acquired by Hans Himmelheber

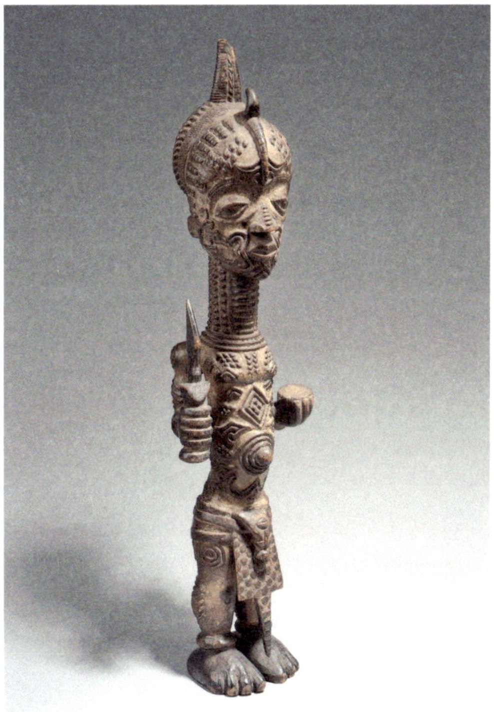

Fig. 264

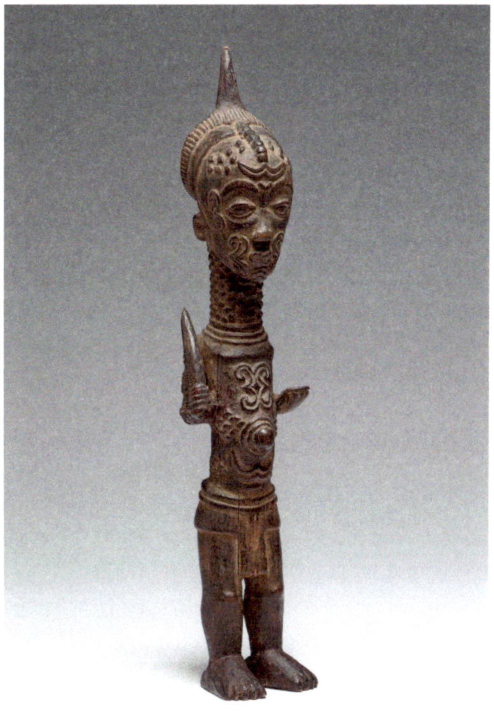

Fig. 265

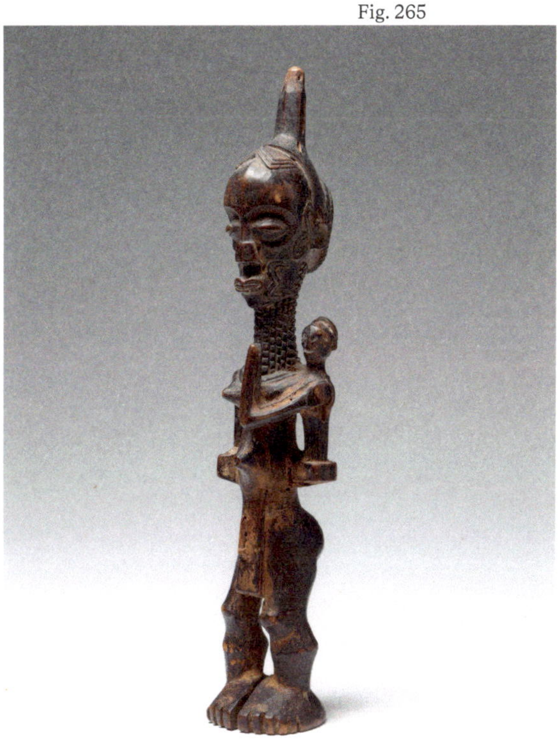

Fig. 266

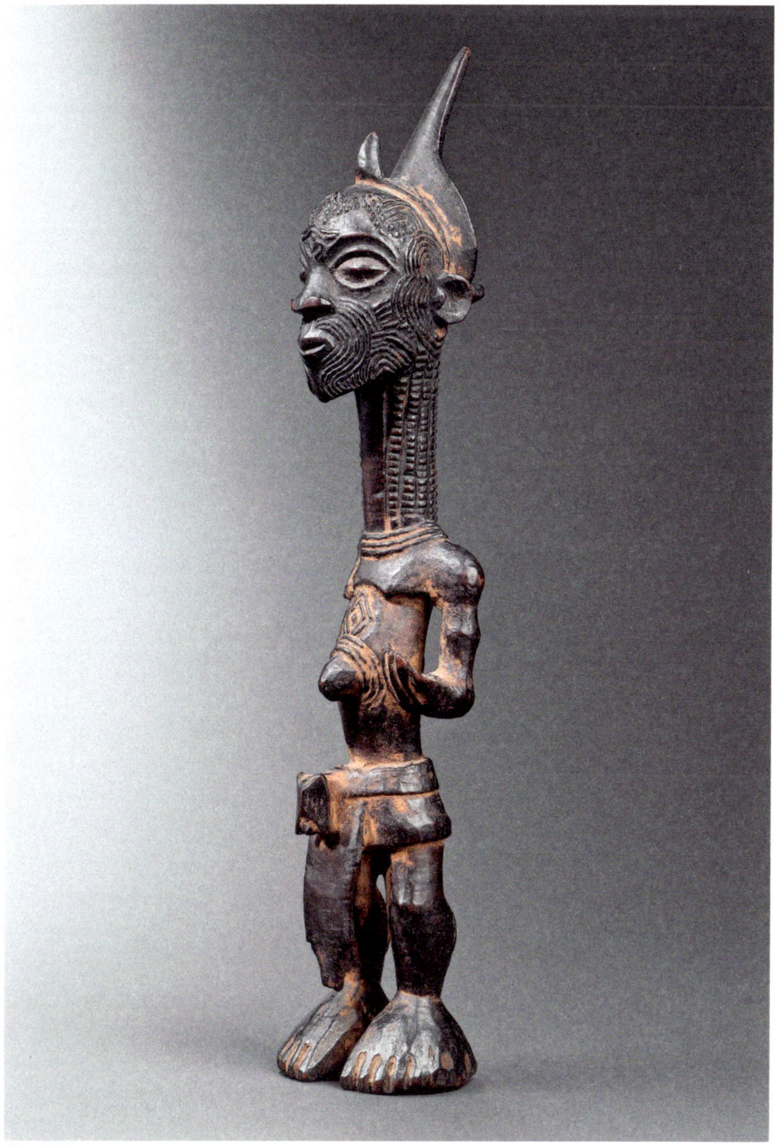

Fig. 267

mendation of a "sorcerer."[20] Each figure would originally have been made for a specific purpose but could subsequently be used to help with any possible challenge or concern. In order to activate it, the figure was rubbed with red camwood powder while white chalk was placed in the cup it held. Its most important task was to intervene at the time of a woman's pregnancy and to assist with the delivery. The last day before a future mother would give birth, she placed the figure in front of her house so that passersby might sprinkle white chalk in its hand-held cup to ensure that the woman would be supported during the painful process.

One of the Himmelheber *manga wa bwimpe* examples illustrated here [fig. 265] is stylistically very similar to a figure currently in the Tervuren museum, which was acquired in the field by a man called De Bruyn by 1912 [fig. 264]. The Tervuren and Rietberg sculptures are in a popular substyle called Bakwa Mushilu, which originated in the region around the town of Demba in northern Luluwaland, where Himmelheber spent the night on March 27, 1939. The Tervuren example, which is possibly female rather than male but also slightly taller and more refined, may in fact be a generation older than the Rietberg one. Perhaps the latter was even especially carved as a replacement for the former. Although the practice of replacing works that were discarded, sold, or otherwise relinquished has not been recorded in the Luluwa literature, it seems reasonable to assume that it was done here as it was elsewhere in Central Africa.

The name which Himmelheber recorded for the figures he acquired of this general type, *bulenga*, is currently also used as a synonym of *bwimpe* but it appears to have originally been proper to the neighboring Luba-Kasai culture. Both terms, *bulenga* and *bwimpe*, have the same meaning in that they both combine our Western notions of beauty and goodness. What the concept of *bwimpe/bulenga* implies is the human or cultural intervention in a person's biological or natural appearance and anatomy. Among the means to accomplish the realization of this aesthetico-moral ideal are the application of various body beautifications in the shape of elaborate hairdos and hairstyles, jewelry and other accessories, and, most significantly, scarifications, locally known as *nsalu*. The often complex curvilinear and geometric patterns incised into the skin that decorate the surfaces of wooden figures imitates the practice of cicatrization that was in vogue until a recent past. Rubbing the skin with a paste made of red camwood powder and clay mixed with chalk, water, and palm oil in order to make it look healthier and thus more attractive, was also copied on the wooden figures.

The leadership attributes, overall size, and male gender of the *bwimpe* sculptures illustrated here, however, suggest that these figures had a purpose that extended beyond the protection of the beauty and health of a mother and her offspring. Indeed, the spotted feline skirt along with the cutlass or sword that replaces the more common pestle or stamper, are references to prestige and status similar to the carved accessories of the category of power objects called *bwanga bwa bukalenga* mentioned earlier in this essay. Himmelheber[21] actually also distinguished such figures of larger size (20 to 30 centimeters) from the smaller works that made up the *bwimpe* category stricto sensu, and he associated them instead with the term *mukenge*. Based on earlier speculations offered by the then Tervuren museum curator Joseph Maes

20 The conception of such figures as idols in the sense of the representations of gods that are used as objects of worship has long been dispelled in the scholarly literature, and the character Himmelheber identified as a sorcerer was most likely a diviner, locally known as *mubuki* or *mwena lubuku*.

21 Himmelheber 1960, p. 399.

(1940), Himmelheber identified them as ancestral figures that belonged to chiefs and their spouses.[22]

Because of their status as power objects, that is, as sculptures charged with supernatural qualities that could serve defensive or offensive purposes, Luluwa figures were not only persecuted by local religious reform movements, during the Belgian colonial period they were also targeted by Church and State. As expressions of a society that colonial officers and missionaries believed had to be "civilized" and liberated from "paganism," they were likely driven underground to adopt a new, secret life, out of public view. Even more often, however, they were either destroyed or seized and exported to Europe and later the USA. We lack descriptions of any of these iconoclastic activities when the country was under Belgian rule but when Albert Maesen explored the region in the mid-1950s, much of the local art production had already waned. And by the time of my own visits in 1994 and 1996, there were hardly any traces of traditional sculpture to be found, except for some masks. In light of such historical transformations and their negative impact on Luluwa culture, the art-historical interest of survivals, such as the objects acquired by Hans Himmelheber and now preserved in the museums of Basel and Zurich, and the documentation that accompanies them, can simply not be overstated.

22 Himmelheber cannot be faulted for his reliance on Maes's writings as it would not be until much later that the latter's problematic analyses and interpretations would be questioned, critiqued, and ultimately rejected.

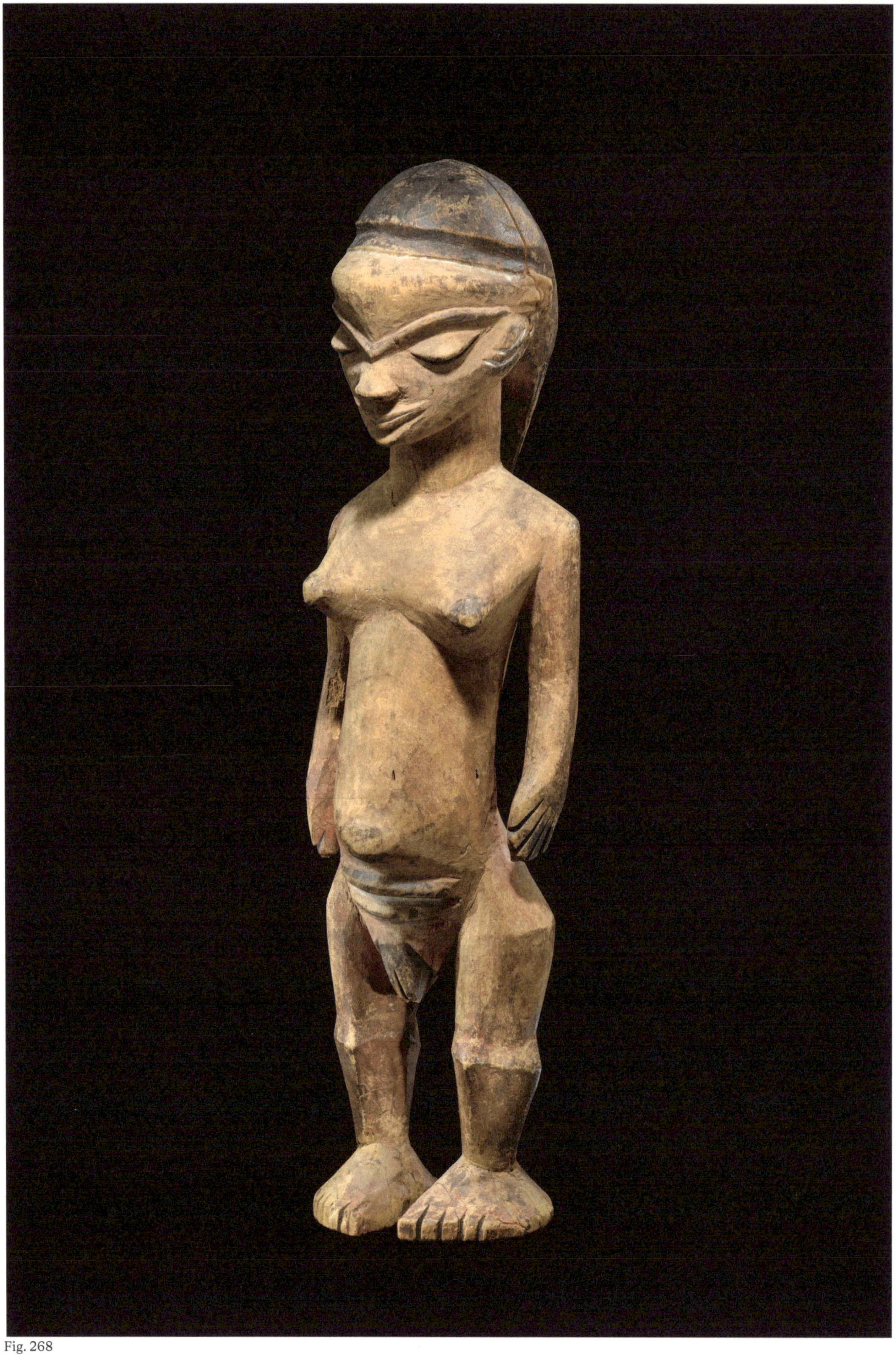

Fig. 268

Fig. 268
Artist of the Pende region
Female figure
Early twentieth century, wood, pigments, 56.8 × 15.5 × 15.6 cm
Museum Rietberg Zürich, RAC 802
Gift of Eduard von der Heydt

BETWEEN INSIDE AND OUTSIDE: A FEMALE POWER OBJECT BY THE CONGOLESE CENTRAL PENDE

Michaela Oberhofer, David Mannes and Jens Stenger

Above all, the Pende people are famous for their spectacular masks. Freestanding, anthropomorphic sculptures by them are comparatively rare. The latter are often power objects owned by high-ranking chiefs.[1] While masks should not resemble any living people, the Pende's power figures had a relatively naturalistic design. In the context of the Pende revolt during the colonial period, some power figures emerged that were furnished with bundles of animal or plant materials. This "medicine"—and most importantly the words uttered by the ritual expert—invoked the vital energy or the spirit of a deceased person. Charged with these supernatural powers, a power object identified various tasks related to the concerns and hardships of both individuals and communities. Until now it was these two aesthetic principles—the relative naturalism and accumulation of materials—that had been typical of the Pende's power objects. Both were aimed at eliciting from the viewer a combination of astonishment, awe, and fear. While the power objects' external features immediately catch the eye, their interiors long remained concealed.

At the heart of this essay is a female sculpture from the central Pende region that is owned by the Museum Rietberg.[2] Enabled by modern imaging techniques, the view into its interior yielded surprising findings.[3] Previously acclaimed above all for its balanced design, this sculpture is a power object filled with substances. Only its holistic study in the context of a complementary art historical and scientific analysis has been able to reveal new insights into the material, technical, and cultural processes used for the Pende's power objects [figs. 268/269].

SEEN FROM OUTSIDE: THE EPITOME OF COOL FEMININITY

The Museum Rietberg's Pende figure was part of the collection of Eduard von der Heydt, who had acquired it from the Parisian art dealer Charles Ratton. It was published by Eckart von Sydow as early as 1932 in *Kunst der Naturvölker*, which means that it was made in the 1920s or earlier [fig. 270].[4] The first female director of the Museum Rietberg, Elsy Leuzinger used effusive terms to describe the sculpture's beauty: "The statue, a felicitous stylistic combination of realism and schematism, stands out for its expressive head and very summarily treated limbs. [...] The simplicity of the body, the frontality, and not least the simplified, straight fall of the arms, which emphasize the cohesive silhouette, lend the statue its great composure and concentration."[5] Seen from the side, the balance between rising and sinking forms and the zigzag line of the body are striking.

1 On power objects among the Pende, see Strother 1993, 2014/15, 2016. Power objects could have very diverse forms. In the 1980s there were, e.g., miniature portrayals ranging from airplanes and cars to small robot-like sculptures (Strother 2014/15, p. 140).

2 We would like to express our huge gratitude to Z. S. Strother for so generously sharing with us her knowledge of the art of the Pende. The elaborations on the Pende are based in large part on her comprehensive publications (Strother 1993, 1998, 2000, 2014/15, 2016). We would also like to thank Kilian Anheuser (Geneva Fine Art Analysis GmbH, Lancy), Martin Ledergerber (Museum Rietberg), Adriana Rizzo (Metropolitan Museum), Richard Woodward and his team (Virginia Museum of Fine Arts), and the Paul Scherrer Institut in Villigen.

3 See the findings of similar analyses in Bouttiaux and Marc Ghysels 2008; Hersak 2013; Howe and Rizzo 2015 and LaGamma 2008.

4 In this first publication from 1932, the figure was still wearing a necklace made of blue and green glass beads, which was later removed (e.g., Leuzinger 1963).

5 Leuzinger 1963, p. 204, figs. 153 a, b.

The compact body emphasizes the expressive face, which has numerous parallels with the design of mask faces. Among the Pende the physiognomy of masks is especially important.[6] Gender roles and characteristics are expressed in the facial features that cover a spectrum from female to male to hypermasculine. In the Museum Rietberg's Pende figure, we can identify the typical attributes of a feminine mask face, such as the downward gaze with lowered eyelids known as *zanze* and the heart-shaped face with a small chin and slightly curved forehead. Though the closed mouth with thin lips is unusual, it is reminiscent of a female mask in the AfricaMuseum in Tervuren that was acquired by the Belgian colonial official Delhaise prior to 1924.[7] The smooth hairstyle is reminiscent of the *mukoto* style.[8]

Like the masks, the Rietberg figure represents the ideal of femininity and beauty that the Pende associate with "coolness."[9] The essence of femininity that is expressed in the sculpture's face is stressed by its unusually erotic and youthful body with its shapely breasts, pronounced vulva, rounded stomach that perhaps indicates a pregnancy, and the scarifications under the navel that served the sexual pleasure of men and women alike.[10] Its interpretation as a "fertility figure," as advocated by Elsy Leuzinger, seems obvious. Women were revered by the matrilineal Pende as givers of life, in relation to both their own progeny and their work cultivating the land.

However, Léon de Sousberghe had already conjectured that the Rietberg figure might be a child figure that accompanied female masks.[11] We thank Z. S. Strother for drawing our attention to a photograph of a village mask (*mbuya jia kifutshi*) performance taken by Vanden Bossche before the Second World War [fig. 271]. In contrast to initiation masks, village masks generated an atmosphere of joy and gratitude as a link between the living and the dead.[12] The female gendered mask on the photo is holding a child figure in its arm that constitutes an exact copy of herself, down to the white fabric slung around the hips, the face painting, and even the wig.[13] During her field research in the late 1990s, Z. S. Strother documented the Pende's memories of female masked performances with such figures known as *mona* (child) or *gakishi* (small three-dimensional carving).[14] Occasionally, the dance of the mother and child ensemble portrayed a woman being initiated into the women's health society after the birth of her child. The female audience in particular was fond of this performance that commented on their own realm of experience.

The body and face of the Pende figure from the Museum Rietberg are very similar to the child figure on the photo. There are also temporal and regional congruencies, which indicates that it could be just such an entertaining accessory for masquerades. However, the naturalistic design and the latest scientific analyses suggest that the sculpture was in fact a power object owned by a chief. The clue came from the discovery of small holes in the Rietberg object that resemble those of the power figure of a colonial officer at the Virginia Museum of Fine Arts in Richmond.

6 See e.g., Strother 1998, chapters 5 and 6 in this catalogue.

7 Cf. de Sousberghe 1958, fig. 37.

8 Using the example of a mother and child figure from the Cleveland Museum of Art, the art historian Constantine Petridis (2002) discovered that many Pende carvings had been erroneously attributed to the Mbala on the basis of the lobed coiffures, even though this headdress can also be found in sculptures from the Kwilu-Pende region.

9 See Strother 1998, 2016.

10 Many thanks to Z. S. Strother for this information (email from May 3, 2019).

11 See de Sousberghe 1958, p. 151.

12 See Strother 2008, p. 18.

13 Mother and child depictions were also popular for the wooden figures (*kishikishi*) on the roofs of powerful chiefs from the 1940s at the latest, after the artist Kaseya Tambwe Makumbi had invented the subject—possibly inspired by the Virgin Mary with child (Strother 2014/15). However, *kishikishi* were unclothed and did not wear any wigs.

14 Our thanks to Z. S. Strother for these references.

RELATIVE NATURALISM: RESISTANCE AND DETERRENCE

In the Museum Rietberg's Pende figure, which can be seen from the outside, there are seven holes slightly above the navel, whose almond shape and measurements resemble the vertical holes in the figure from Richmond [cf. fig. 279]. The latter is a depiction of a Belgian colonial officer that is unique among the Pende.[15] Z. S. Strother's research led to the surprising finding that this is in fact a naturalistic portrait of Maximilian Balot. The Belgian colonial administrator was embroiled in a dispute between the Pende chief Matemo a Kelenge and the territorial agent Edouard Burnotte. Burnotte had abused Matemo's wife in order to impose forced labor during a tour of inspection. Shortly thereafter Balot was instructed to investigate this sadistic incident. In the process he was killed by Matemo—who probably mistook him for Burnotte—on June 8, 1931 in Kilamba near Gungu. Balot's death was the catalyst for the Pende revolt, which was led by Matemo. The Belgian colonial government reacted ruthlessly and sent an armed punitive expedition to the insurrectionary region.

There are various reasons why the death of a lowly colonial official was able to trigger a revolt. The Pende in the Kwilu and Kasai region suffered particularly severely under the economic conditions of colonial rule and the global financial crisis, which made the price of palm oil plummet. For this reason, the Pende in rural regions in particular resisted the pecuniary per capita taxation and the labor for the Belgian colonial government. After Balot's death the revolt spread quickly. At first the religious movement against the whites (*Tupelepele*) was very successful. Its followers believed that they could regain control of their country and lives. Collection points for European goods were established in the hope that the ancestors would replace these wares with products of African design. Only a few months later Belgium quelled the revolt with incredible severity.

In remembrance of this historical event, a carver created this portrait of Maximilien Balot. His long, thin face, his angular chin, parted hair, and large eyes have been faithfully reproduced. Even the uniform with buttons, belt, collar, and insignia has been recreated with utmost care. Yet at the same time, the artist depicted Balot as a *ngunza* (killer), meaning as a violent man, characterized according to the aesthetic criteria of the Pende by an especially long face and wide-open *meso abala* (dangerous eyes). The sculpture of Balot is a power object to transform the Belgian aggressor's spirit into a watchman and to use it for the benefit of the community.

A characteristic feature of anthropomorphic power objects by the Pende is their style, which Z. S. Strother describes as "relative naturalism."[16] Visible to everyone, figures over a meter high (*kishikishi*) were installed on the roofs of important chiefs' houses. They signaled to the visitor that s/he was entering a dangerous place protected by a spiritual being. Another category of freestanding, figurative sculptures was the *tungulungu* (sing. *kangulungu*), which were likewise reserved for high-ranking chiefs and were stored inside the ritual buildings (*kibulu*).[17] It was their task to stand watch over the homestead and to catch thieves, as well as to heal gynecological disorders. The portrait-like appearance was intended to remind the viewer that the figures were

15 On the history of the Balot figure and the Pende revolt, cf. Weiss, Woodward, and Strother 2016 and Strother 2016, pp. 219–234. The American political scientist Herbert F. Weiss was able to purchase the old figure along with a female sculpture in Gungu during his research in 1972. The owner informed him that the figure—stored in the clan house as a sacred object—represented a white man who was killed in 1931.

16 Strother 2014/15, p. 140.

17 It was possible for the outside of the ritual building to be adorned with other carvings. On ancestral shrines in the chief's house, head sculptures (*mahamba*) were also installed, but these are not categorized as power objects.

containers for the spirit of a deceased family member, mostly a younger relative, whose journey to the next world had been interrupted in order to protect the community for a limited time. The relative naturalism of power objects among the Pende emphasized this ambivalent position of the chiefs with their connection to the spirit world and evoked anxiety in the viewer. The realistically designed Pende figure from the Museum Rietberg could also be a power object that had served a chief as the vessel for the spirit of a female relative.

INSIDE INSIGHTS: CHANNELS AND CHARGES

In addition to this stylistic and art historical analysis, the Pende figure was examined using scientific methods. X-ray tomography[18] is a noninvasive, nondestructive investigative method that makes the internal structure of the object visible: Fig. 272 contrasts a conventional photograph with the three-dimensional surface visualization of the X-ray tomography data set and a longitudinal section. The grayscale variations visible in the middle image arise from greater absorption of the X-radiation depending on the chemical composition and density of the material in the respective area. Light areas suggest the presence of materials that absorb more X-radiation. In this way it is possible to identify the wood grain created by growth rings, as well as paint residues on some uneven surfaces.

Wood grain and paint residues likewise emerge in the longitudinal section on the right of the illustration, and in addition the internal structure of the object becomes visible. A vertical channel runs along the entire height of the sculpture from which several horizontal channels branch off at navel height. This arrangement is consistent with the type of wood known as *Alstonia boonei*.[19] About halfway up, the main channel is sealed with a material that absorbs more X-radiation. The inside wall of the channel above this point is covered throughout with a material that exhibits grayscale values comparable to this sealed section, which indicates the material's similar or same composition. Chemical analyses confirm this hypothesis.

Three samples—from the upper entrance to the channel and from the points above and below the seal—have been analyzed.[20] All three have proven to be a combination of kaolin, quartz sand, and triterpene resin. It was possible to identify the latter element as the resin of the tree *Symphonia globulifera*, thanks to reference data[21] from the Metropolitan Museum of Art in New York. This substance was also found on a nineteenth-century Yombe sculpture in the Musée d'ethnographie de Genève.[22] In the white, black, and red paint residues on the surface of the figure, this resin could not be detected; instead, a binding agent that contains carbohydrate (probably gum) was discovered. The pigments have been proven to be kaolin and red ocher.

Fig. 273 shows another longitudinal section through the upper section of the sculpture. The mass formed by the approximately three-centimeter-long seal in the chest area exhibits great inhomogeneity, which suggests that the individual components were not well mixed. Continuing downward this section ends with a concave area. Above the seal it is possible to identify a screw-like structure in the hollow space. In order to better illus-

18 The X-ray tomographic data were recorded at the Paul Scherrer Institut. The X-ray source was operated with 100 kV and 15 A. The analysis of the sculpture took place in two rounds of tomography (first section: head and thorax, second section: abdomen and legs). For every tomography scan 375 radiographies were detected by a scintillator digital camera system with 2160 x 2560 pixels at an exposure time of 15 s. The individual projections were reconstructed using the software Muhrec and the two tomography data sets combined with Kiptool. The subsequent evaluation and visualization were conducted with VG Studio max.

19 Our thanks go to Casey Mallinckrodt from the Virginia Museum of Fine Arts for this information.

20 Analyses of this and other samples were carried out with Fourier-transform infrared spectroscopy (Perkin Elmer Spotlight 400—Frontier), gas chromatography—mass spectrometry (Focus GC, coupled with Thermo Electron DSQ II instrument), and Raman spectroscopy (Renishaw inVia). We would like to thank Carolina Zanchet and Nadim Scherrer for their assistance.

21 Our thanks to Adriana Rizzo for the FTIR reference spectra.

22 See http://www.ville-ge.ch/meg/musinfo_public.php?id=021316, accessed June 20, 2019.

Fig. 269
Radiograph and photograph as additional levels of analysis.
The radiographs are transmission images; the more X-radiation is absorbed by a picture area, the lighter it appears. Higher absorption can be attributed to a higher density and/or the presence of "heavier" elements.

Fig. 270
First publication of the Pende figure, with the necklace still in place.
Eckart von Sydow, *Kunst der Naturvölker* 1932, p. 73.

Fig. 271
Adrien Vanden Bossche
Female mask with child figure
Pende region, 1950s, b/w negative
Charles Hénault, Marc Felix, Archives du Congo Basin Art History Research Center

Fig. 272
From left: conventional photograph, three-dimensional surface visualization of the X-ray tomography data set, longitudinal section
2018, Paul Scherrer Institut Villigen, Museum Rietberg Zürich

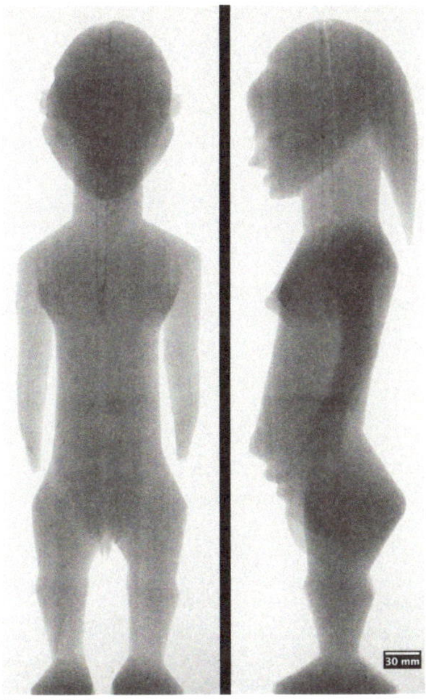

Fig. 269.1

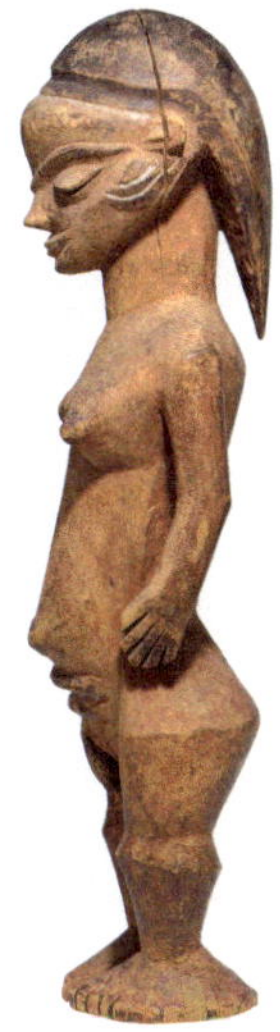
Fig. 269.2

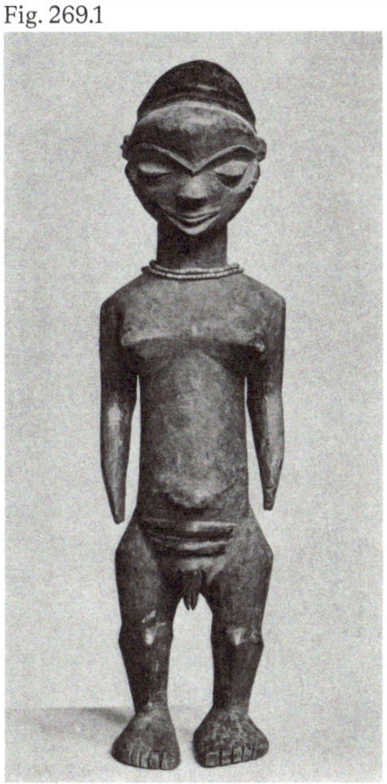
Fig. 270

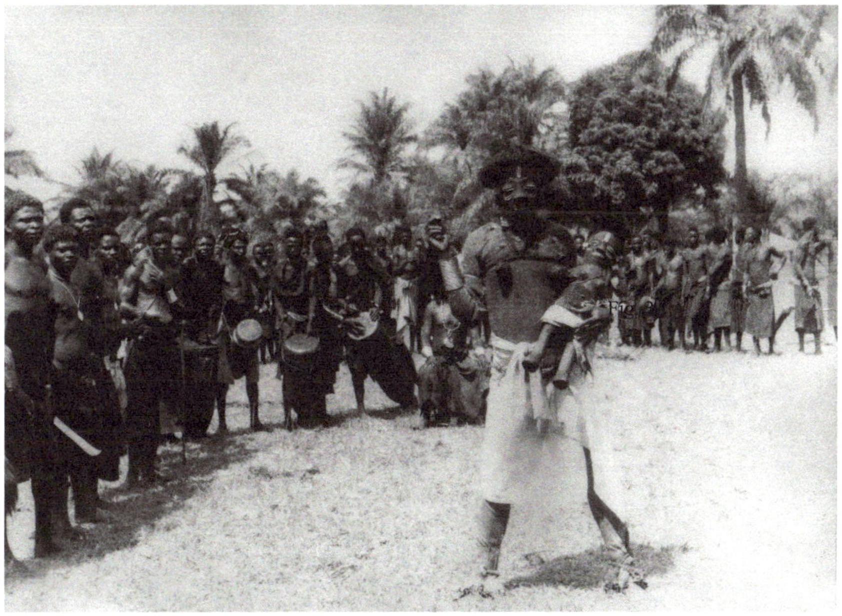
Fig. 271

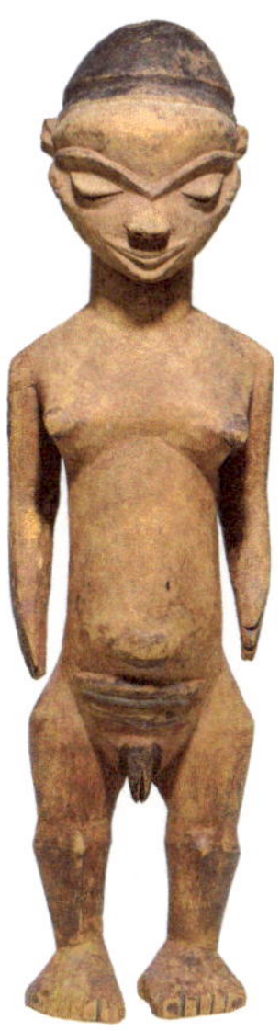
Fig. 272.1

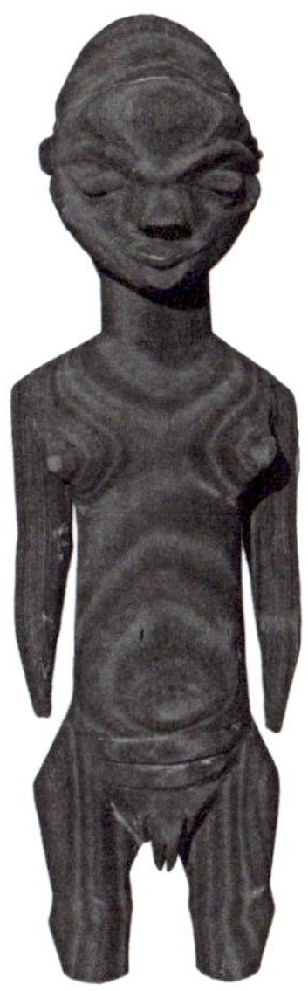
Fig. 272.2

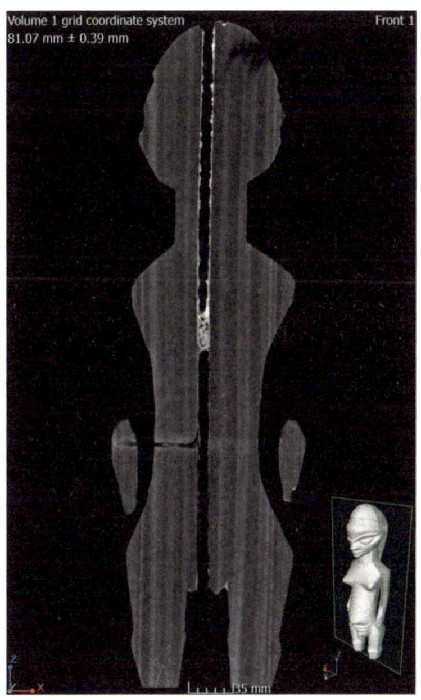

Fig. 272.3

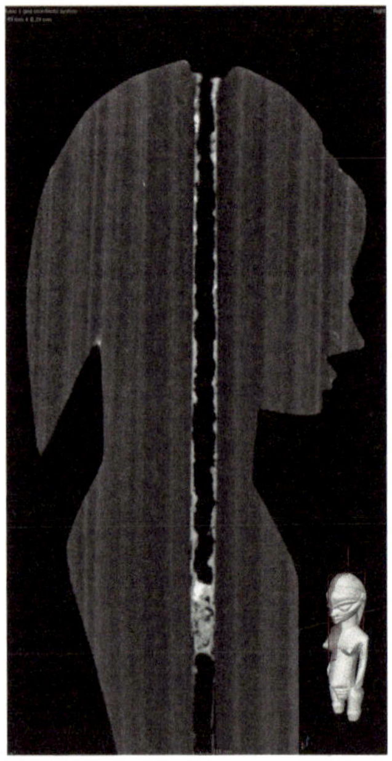
Fig. 273

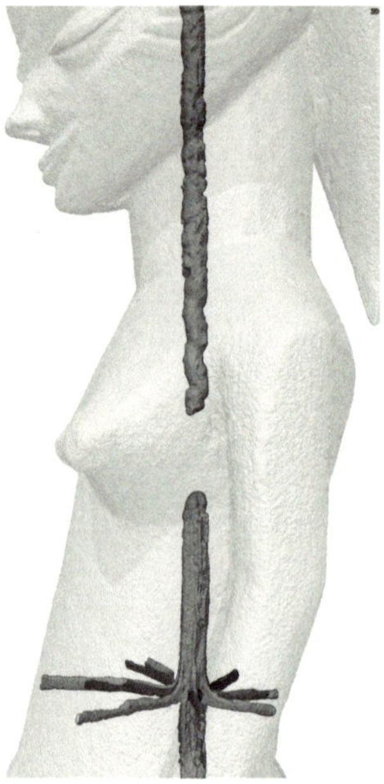
Fig. 274

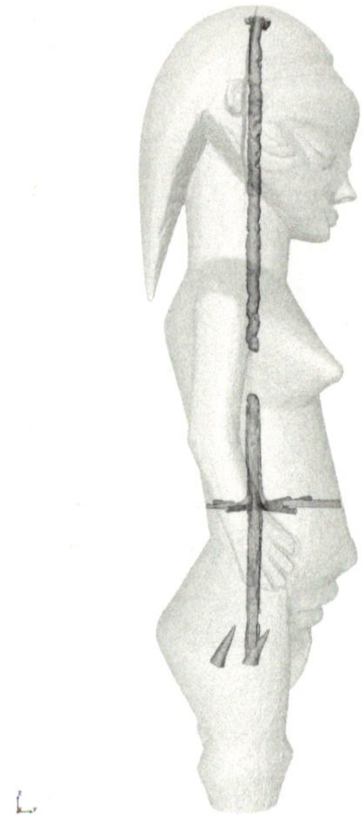
Fig. 275

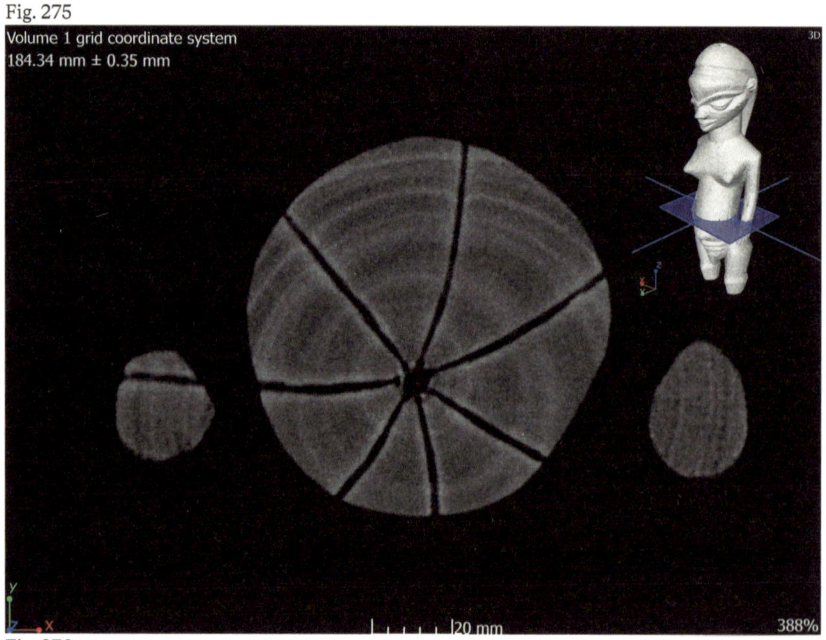

Fig. 276

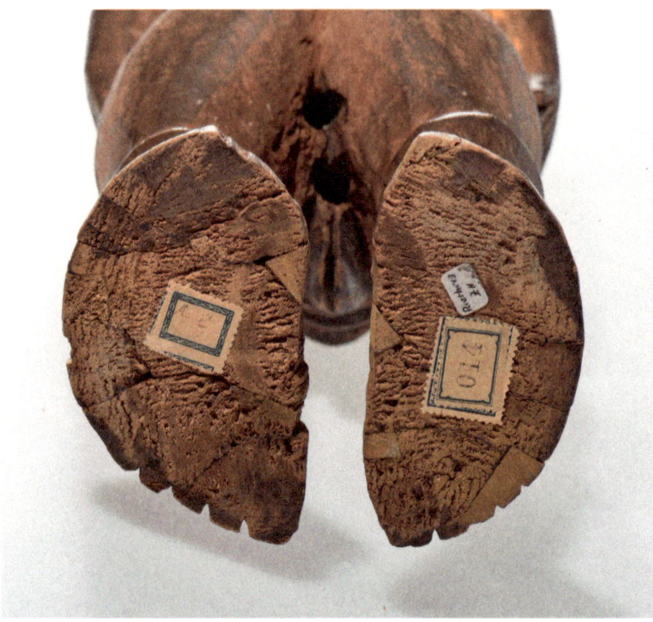
Fig. 277

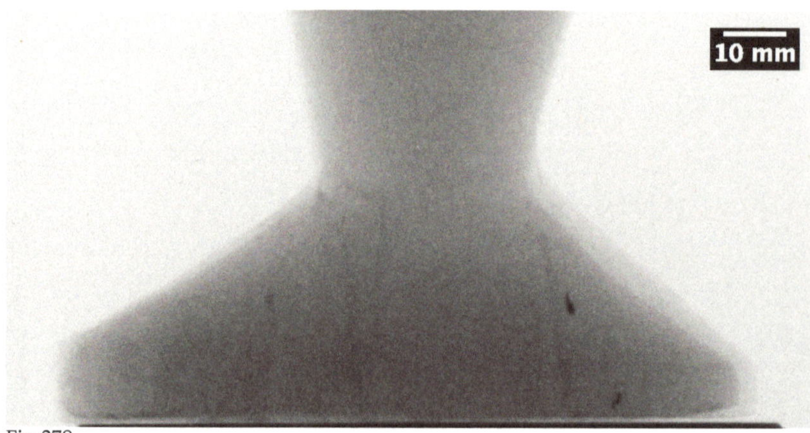

Fig. 278

Fig. 273
X-ray tomographic longitudinal section, detail

Fig. 274
Visualization of the hollow spaces inside the figure

Fig. 275
Visualization of the hollow spaces inside the figure, overview

Fig. 276
X-ray tomographic cross section at navel height.
Seven horizontal bent channels radially converge on the central vertical channel.

Fig. 277
Photograph of the sculpture from below
In addition to the two openings in the genital region, the restorations to the feet can also be seen.

Fig. 278
X-ray of the feet, lateral
2018, Paul Scherrer Institut Villigen, Museum Rietberg Zürich

trate this and the other hollow spaces, figs. 274/275 show negative forms. Here the corkscrew-like geometry of the upper cavity is particularly clear.

Furthermore, below the seal it is possible to see how the vertical channel splits off into seven horizontal branches at navel height that protrude up to the surface. These branches have a spindle-shaped cross section and are bent upward toward the central channel. Fig. 276 shows a cross section of these branches. Here it becomes clear that the horizontal channels are not straight but bent. One of the channels continues in one of the figure's arms, while another ends at the surface with a thread-like structure. This image also makes plain that the wood's growth rings run concentrically around the vertical channel.

On the lower exit of the central channel, two conical holes have been drilled in the genital region as the vagina and anus. These openings have the same shape, the same length, and are at the same angle to the vertical channel, which implies that the same tool was used.

Figs. 277/278 show a photograph of the sculpture from below and an X-ray of the feet from the side. In the photograph one can see supplementary wooden restorations that have been inserted with glue. In the X-ray numerous light lines are visible, probably material from the glue that absorbs more X-rays than the wood. An analysis under the stereomicroscope also suggests that large parts of the feet have been restored and little original material remains here. A chemical analysis identified the glue as protein. The use of wood and protein glue does not provide any clue—at least at this time—as to when and where the restoration was carried out.

SUMMARY

The combination of art-historical and scientific analysis emphasizes just how much effort went into manipulating the sculpture. This indicates that the Museum Rietberg's Pende figure is indeed a power object. When comparing the object's outer appearance with its internal channel structure, it is noticeable how closely the carver correlated his composition with the natural anatomy of the wood. The central vertical main channel is aligned with the sculpture's axis from the part in the hair to the lower exit between the legs. This channel along with the seven horizontal branches was not made artificially but rather corresponds to the way the wood grew. Perhaps the carver intentionally positioned the small holes at the height of the stomach in order to foreground it as the spiritually important center. It is probable that soft, natural material was initially removed from these cavities.[23]

The carver or ritual expert used the vertical channel, which he positioned centrally, for other purposes, too. On the lower end he expanded the channel's opening with a tool to create a kind of vagina and also added an anus. Such artificial channels were previously known from figures by the Songye, for example, but not by the Pende. Among the Songye, *mankishi* serve as containers that are activated with supernatural powers by substances applied outside and inside. These powers are concentrated in the head or stomach, whose openings were closed, whereas the channels from the mouth, ears, and anus were left open in order to admit libations or medicine, for example.[24] In our Pende figure the upper vertical cavity was filled with a mixture of kaolin, sand

23 In contrast, the channel in the Balot figure runs slightly obliquely and ends in the foot. The cavity is filled, though the analysis of the filling material is not yet complete.

24 Hersak 2013

and the resin from another tree. The plug in the chest area was likewise thickened with these materials. The mixture now only sticks to the walls of the upper channel. The corkscrew-shaped impression inside suggests that the filling was twisted in and out like a screw.[25]

However, it is not only the inside but also the surface of the figure that was elaborately treated, with the latter being painted red, black, and white. The white highlights the body decoration, such as the scarifications on the cheek and the lower abdomen, as well as the line of the head and the mouth. Black was applied to emphasize the hair, eyebrows, nipples, navel, scarifications, and vagina; yet it was also used to paint the insides of the two openings in the genital region, even though they are not visible. The body was covered in a red paint of which only residues remain. Red (*misege*) was obtained from redwood of the genus *Pterocarpus* and used to be rubbed into the skin to make it shine, and with reference to this cosmetic effect is was also applied in several layers to masks or figures. In addition to redwood, the pigment *mungundu*—as in the case of the Pende figure—was also extracted from ocher, i.e., red soil containing clay, which was easier to obtain and longer lasting.

Among the Pende, kaolin, called *pemba*, is frequently used for ritual purposes. The kaolin, which comes from riverbeds, features in healing rituals, for example.[26] It is said that its white color has a positive "cooling" effect, whether for a healer to reduce his patient's fever or to bless someone with good wishes before a journey. Moreover, as a color from another world that is associated with a positive connection to the ancestors, kaolin can also be used to weaken or "cool off" the powers of a dangerous opponent. Indeed, chiefs kept pieces of kaolin in their house so as to be ready for any emergency.[27] We consider the kaolin mixture inside the Rietberg figure to be more evidence of it having been used as a chief's power object in the ritual context.

The restoration of the feet is another argument for the Pende figure being less a child figure for a masked performance than a power object. As power figures (*tungulungu*) were stored on a kind of shrine on the floor of the chiefs' ritual building, some of them bear evidence of termite damage or have been eroded by moisture. The feet of the Rietberg figure had probably also been damaged up to the ankles and had thus been restored—perhaps prior to the figure's purchase.

The findings of the scientific analysis in combination with the stylistic evaluation of the relative realism of the figure from the Museum Rietberg suggest that it was a power object that belonged to a high-ranking Pende chief. Yet the new insights into the inside of the figure have also given rise to questions that it has not been possible to answer in full. Thus while it is clear that the inside of the figure was filled with something, precisely how this was carried out is unknown. Perhaps further complementary examinations of similar figures in other museums and collections in the future will deliver new findings that will enable us to see the connection between the visible and invisible, the outside and inside of Pende sculptures in an entirely new light.

25 It might have been a cord or a soft, oblong object. If it had been a stick or a metal rod, the corkscrew structure would have been destroyed when it was removed.

26 See Strother 1998, p. 149.

27 Our thanks to Z. S. Strother for this information (email from May 20, 2019).

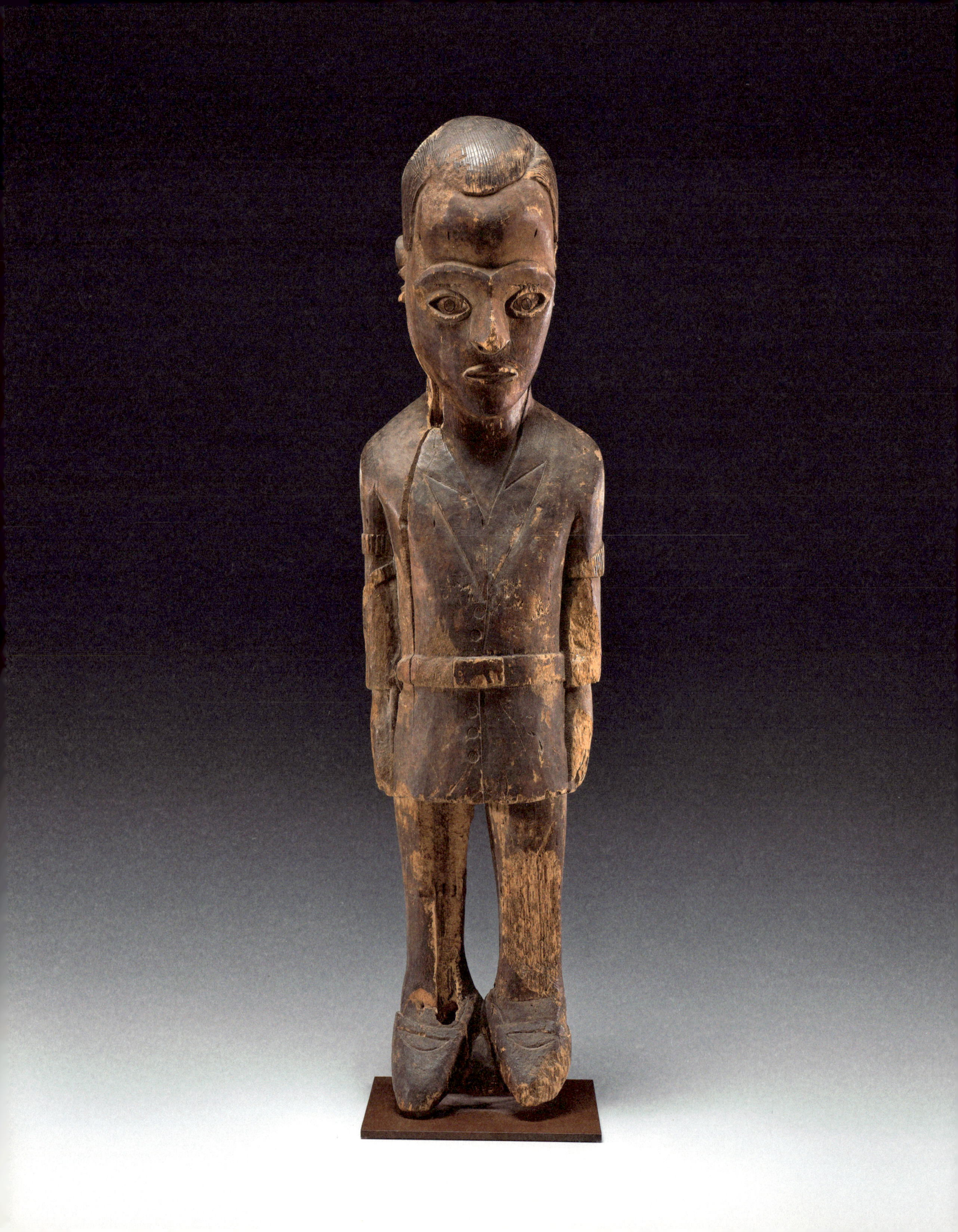

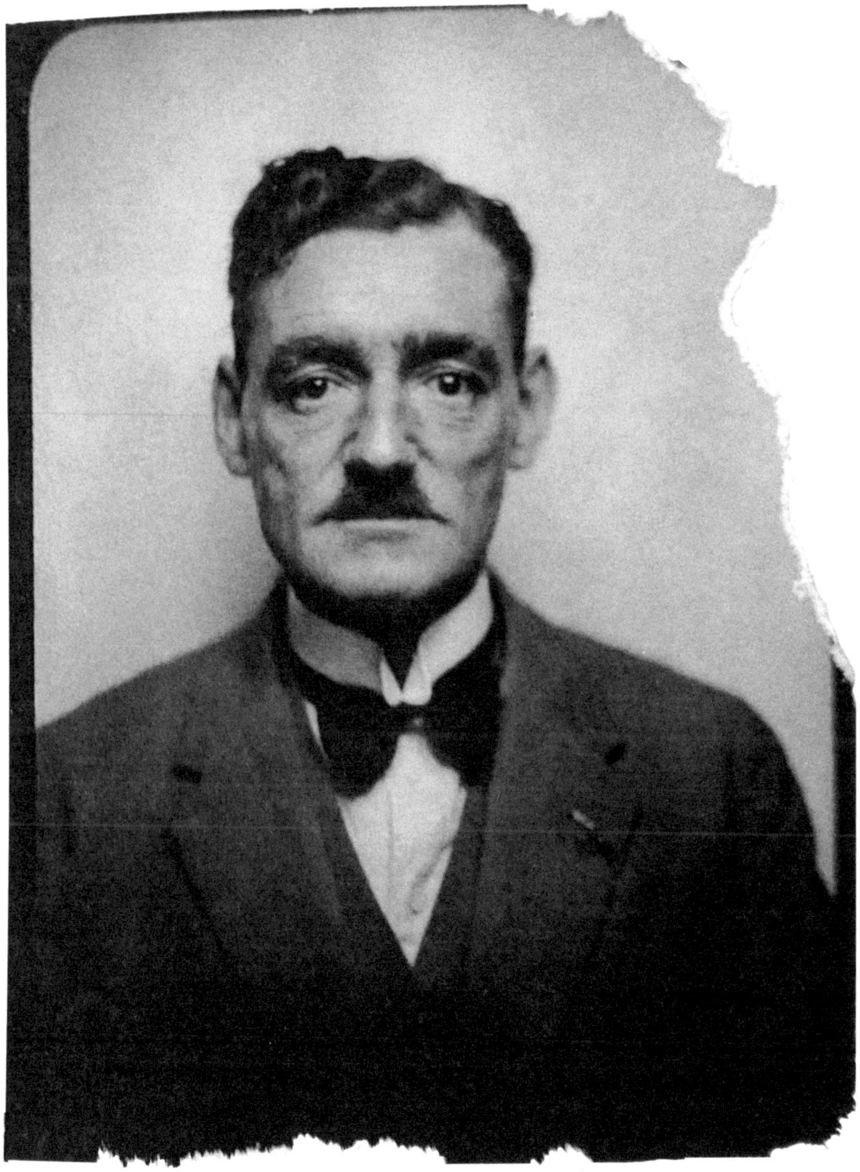
Fig. 280

Fig. 279

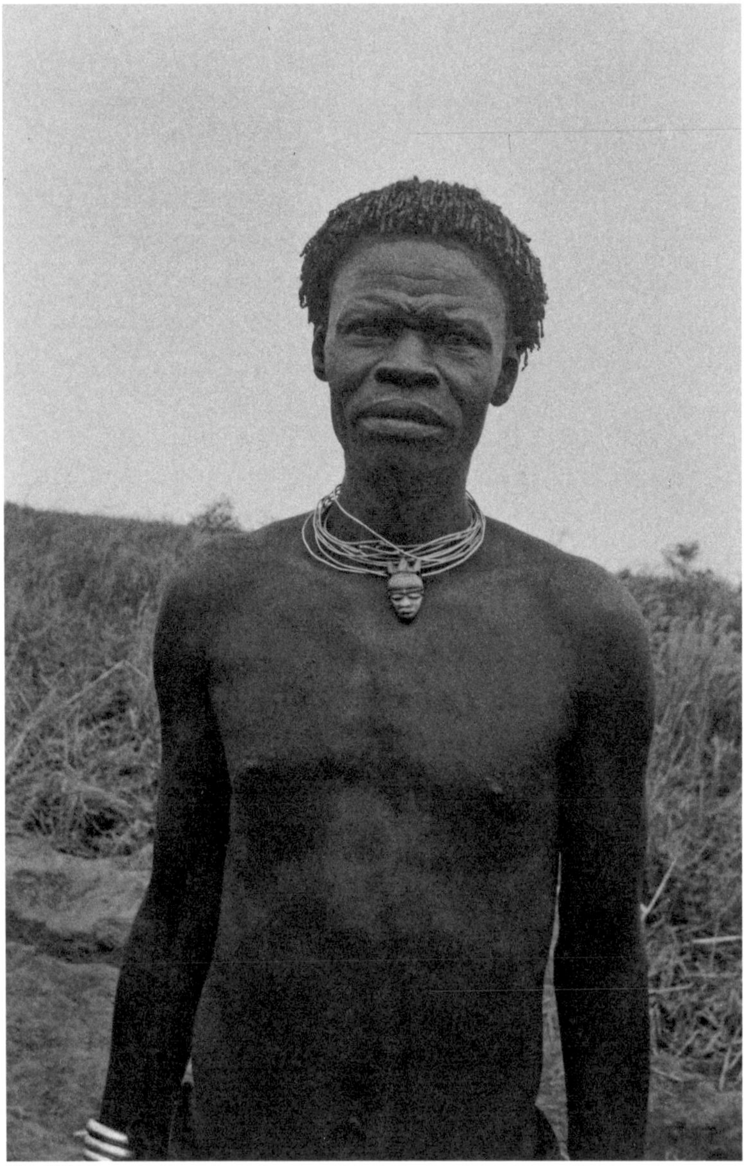
Fig. 281

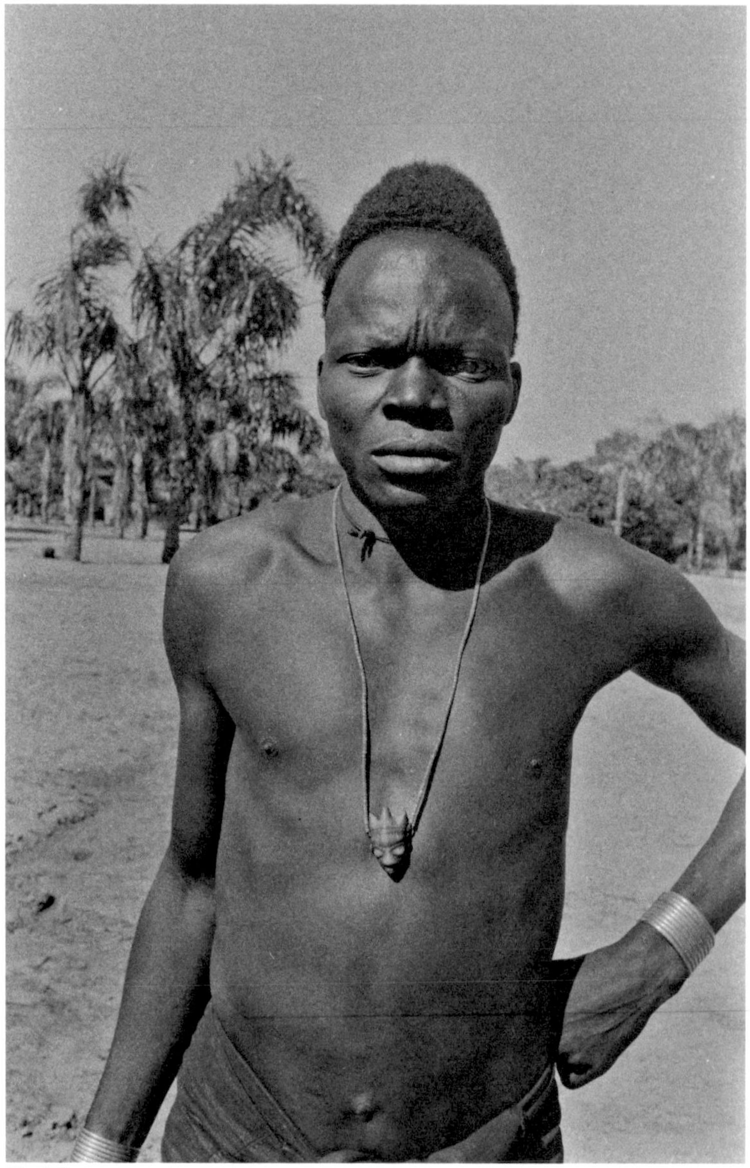
Fig. 282

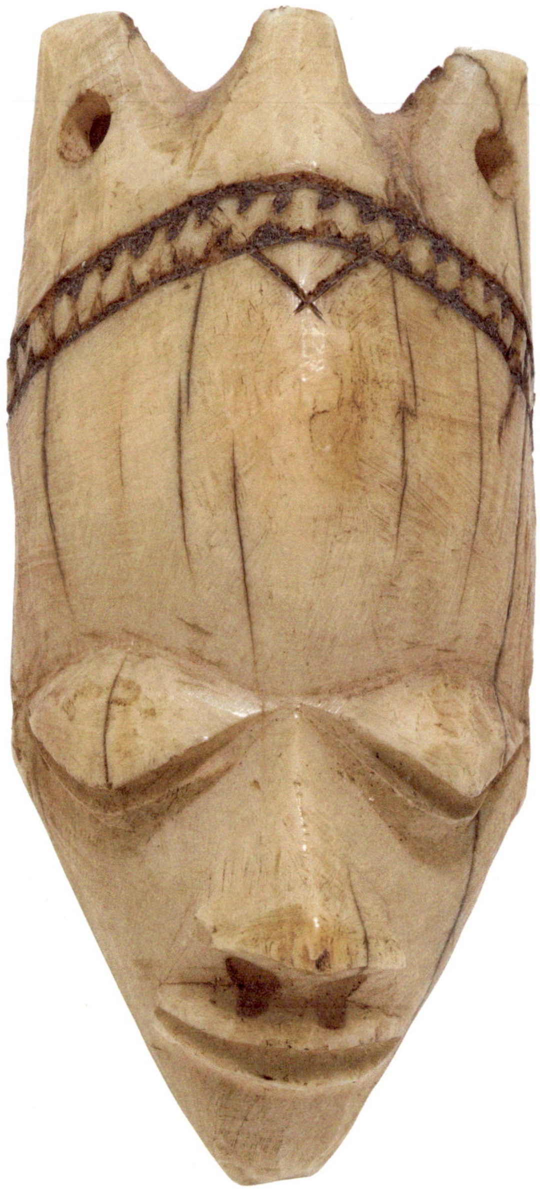

Fig. 283

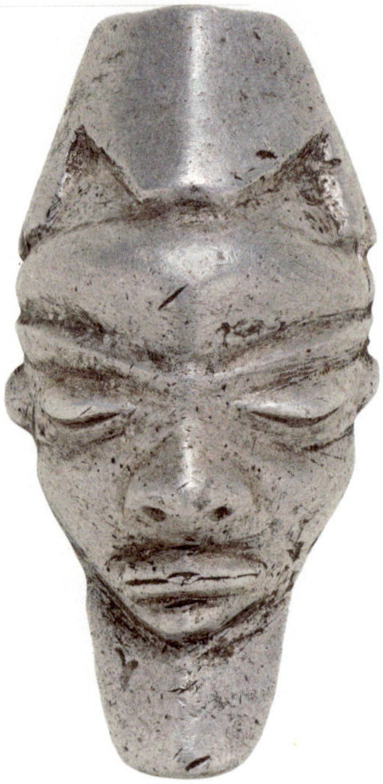

Fig. 284

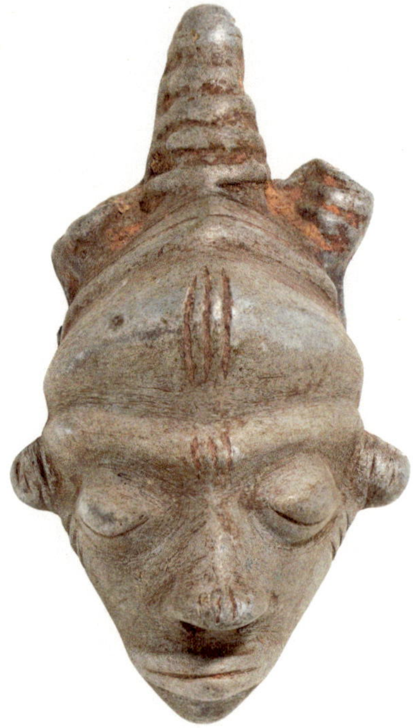

Fig. 285

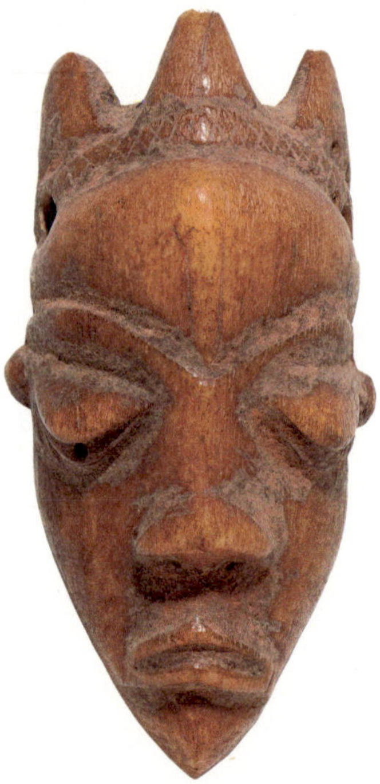

Fig. 286

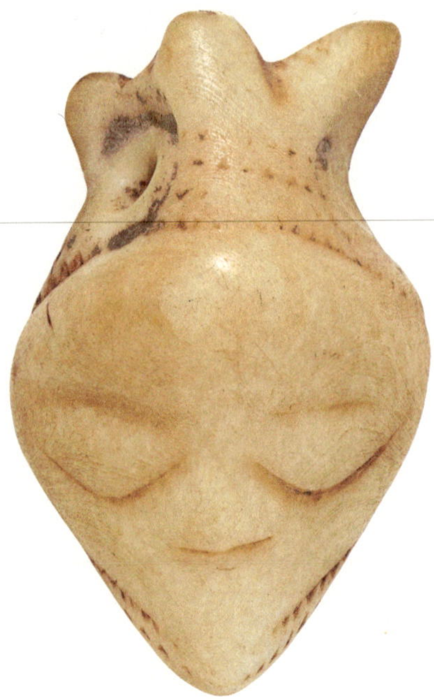

Fig. 287

ART AS EXPRESSION OF RESISTANCE: PENDE POWER FIGURES AND PENDANTS — In the 1920s the Congo population's dissatisfaction with the colonial state grew and manifested in open revolts like those of the Pende. The resistance to the Belgian colonial power was also expressed in art. This is especially clear in the wooden Pende figure that is a portrait of the Belgian colonial official by the name of Maximilien Balot [fig. 279]. His side part, high forehead, and uniform have been faithfully reproduced [fig. 280]. In 1931 Balot was involved in a conflict between the Pende chief Matemo a Kelenge and the cruel territorial agent Edouard Burnotte and was killed as a result.[1] Among the Pende, sculptures were rarely designed naturalistically—and if so, they were intended to elicit awe and fear. Thus, in the figure Balot is depicted as a *ngunza* (killer) with wide-open eyes—considered dangerous—and an angry expression. The sculpture is a power object to capture the spirit of the Belgian aggressor in a guardian figure and use it for the benefit of the community [see essay Oberhofer]. Balot's murder marked the beginning of the Pende revolt, which was directed against the colonial power's reprisals; it lasted only a few months before being brutally crushed by the Belgian army in 1931.

After the Pende rebellion, chains with pendants in the form of small faces became widespread until the country's independence. Cherished for their beauty, they were simultaneously a symbol of the newly fortified Pende identity and of solidarity in the face of the colonial rulers.[2] Himmelheber photographed two men with such pendants and was able to purchase an array of miniature masks. According to him, the pendants were also used to heal diseases.[3] In one case he suspected that the face might be a portrait of the man wearing the necklace [fig. 281]. Nevertheless, these faces were not true portraits, which the Pende associated with witchcraft. For this reason, the carvers avoided any close resemblance to living persons. Instead, the pendants represented various types of Pende masks, which could be identified by their different "hairstyles" [fig. 282]. The majority of the miniature masks were made from ivory or hippopotamus bones, in addition to which there were also examples made of wood or imported materials like aluminum or lead [figs. 283–286]. Sometimes the faces have been completely worn away because their owners rubbed them with sand for years in order to prevent the ivory from turning yellow and to attain a brilliant white—a sign of appreciation for these small carvings [fig. 287]. — Michaela Oberhofer

1 See Weiss/Woodward/Strother 2016.
2 Strother 2008, p. 52.
3 Himmelheber, diary, Djingila, May 25, 1939 (archive of the Museum Rietberg).

Fig. 279
Artist of the Pende region
Portrait figure of the Belgian colonial officer Maximilien Balot
1931, wood with metal repair clamp, 62.5 cm
Virginia Museum of Fine Arts, Richmond, 2015.3
Aldine S. Hartman Endowment Fund
Acquired by Herbert F. Weiss

Fig. 280
Unknown photographer
Personnel card of Maximilien Norbert Balot
1930, Brussels, Archives générales du Royaume 2 (dépôt Cuvelier), Service du Personnel d'Afrique, Série Colonie, K2615, n°15988, p. 1.

Fig. 281
Hans Himmelheber
According to Hans Himmelheber, this miniature mask is a portrait
Pende region, 1939, b/w negative
Museum Rietberg Zürich, FHH 191-5

Fig. 282
Hans Himmelheber
Pende man with miniature mask as pendant
Pende region, 1939, b/w negative
Museum Rietberg Zürich, FHH 191-16

Fig. 283
Artist of the Pende region
***Ikhoko* pendant in the form of a mask**
First half of the twentieth century, ivory, 5.9 × 2.7 × 2.1 cm
Museum Rietberg Zürich, RAC 850
Gift of Eduard von der Heydt

Fig. 284
Artist of the Pende region
***Ikhoko* pendant in the form of a mask**
First half of the twentieth century, aluminum, 4.9 × 2.5 × 1.7 cm
Museum Rietberg Zürich, RAC 872
Gift of Elsy Leuzinger

Fig. 285
Artist of the Pende region
***Ikhoko* pendant in the form of a mask**
Before 1939, lead, 5.8 × 3 × 2.2 cm
Museum Rietberg Zürich, 2018.478
Gift of Martin Himmelheber
Acquired by Hans Himmelheber

Fig. 286
Artist of the Pende region
***Ikhoko* pendant in the form of a mask**
Before 1939, bone, 5.7 × 2.9 × 2.2 cm
Museum Rietberg Zürich, 2018.479
Gift of Martin Himmelheber
Acquired by Hans Himmelheber

Fig. 287
Artist of the Pende region
***Ikhoko* pendant in the form of a mask**
First half of the twentieth century, ivory, 5.6 × 3.5 × 1.9 cm
Museum Rietberg Zürich, RAC 867
Gift of Eduard von der Heydt

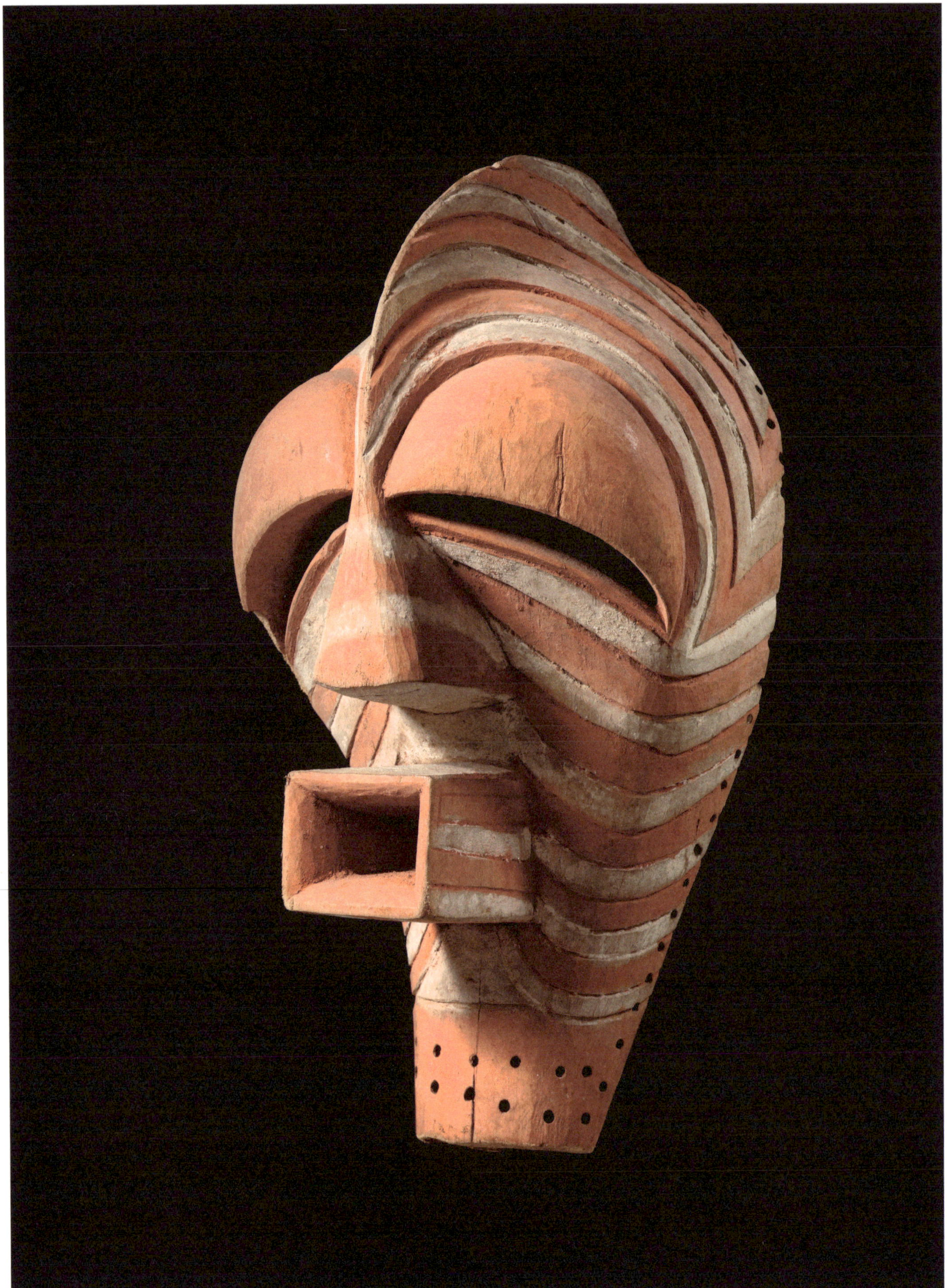
Fig. 288

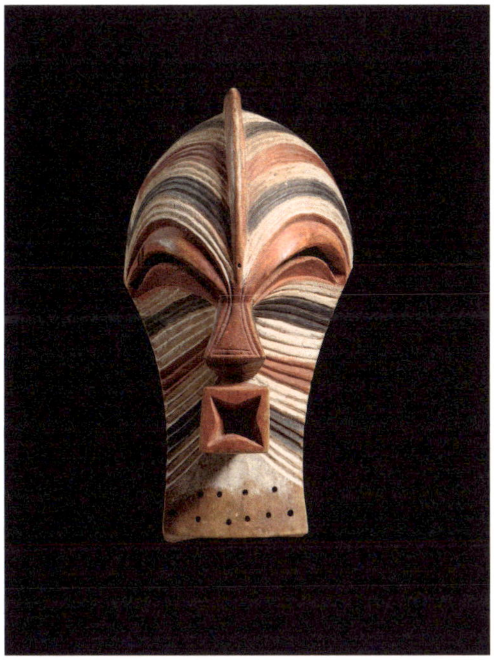
Fig. 289.1

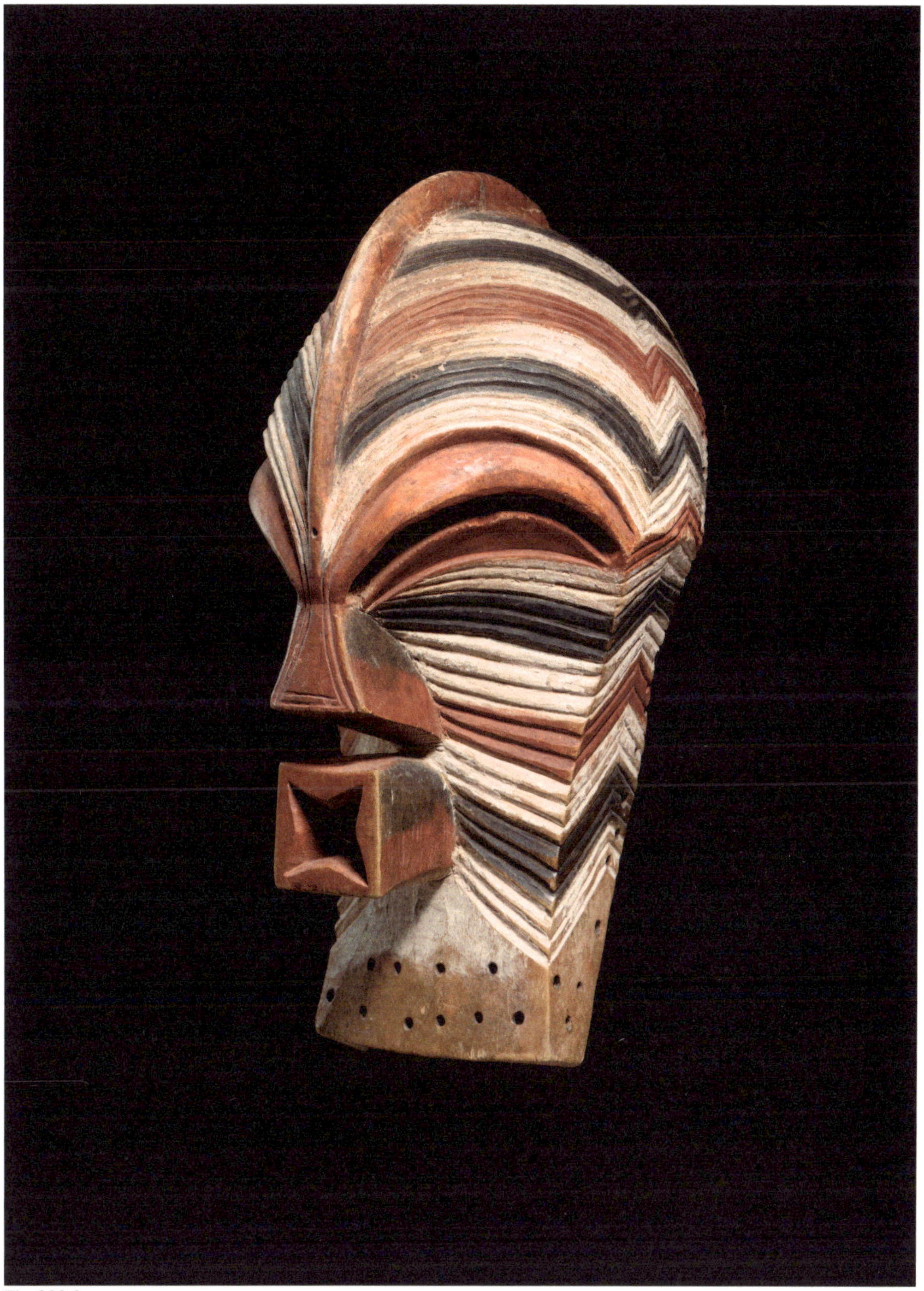
Fig. 289.2

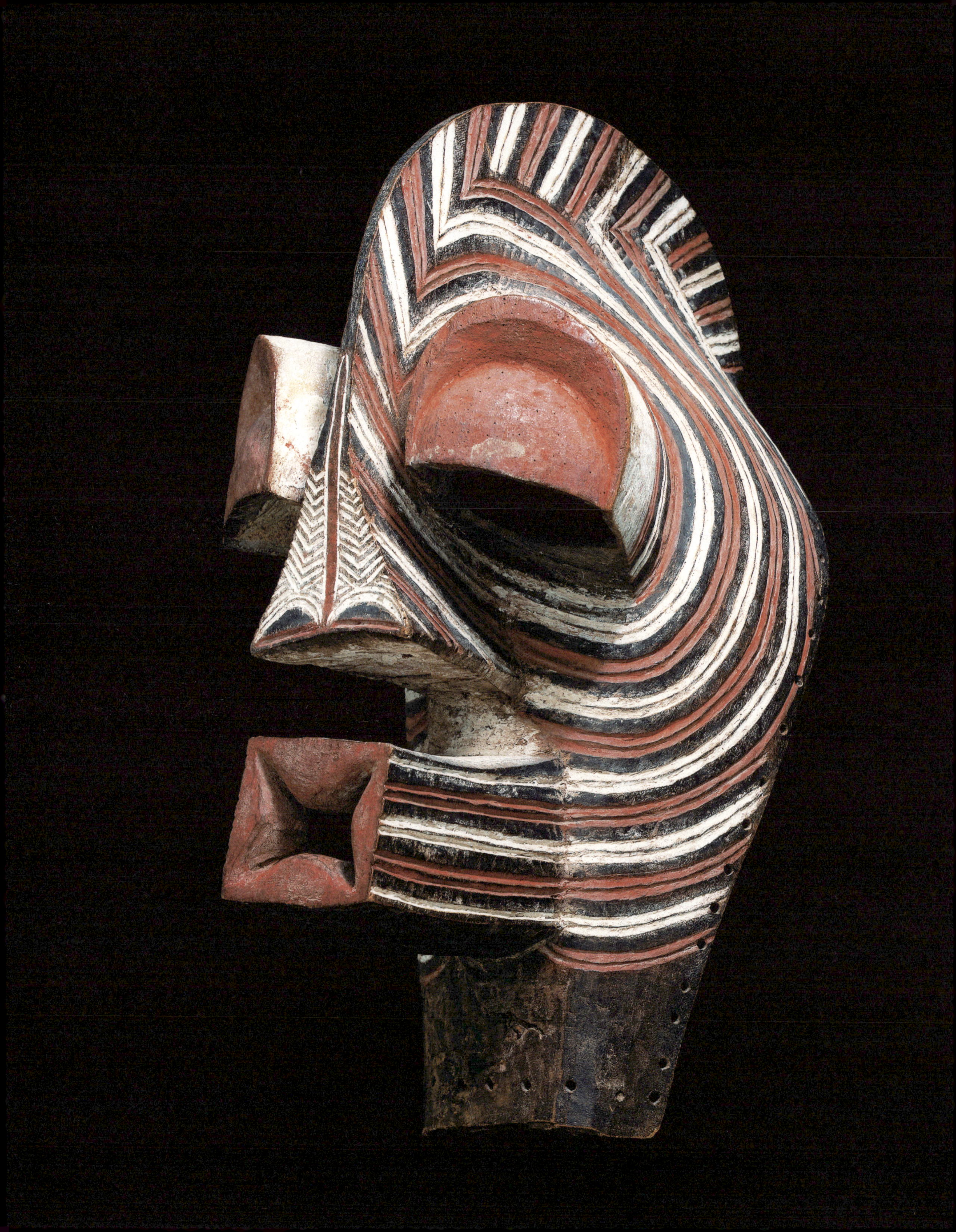

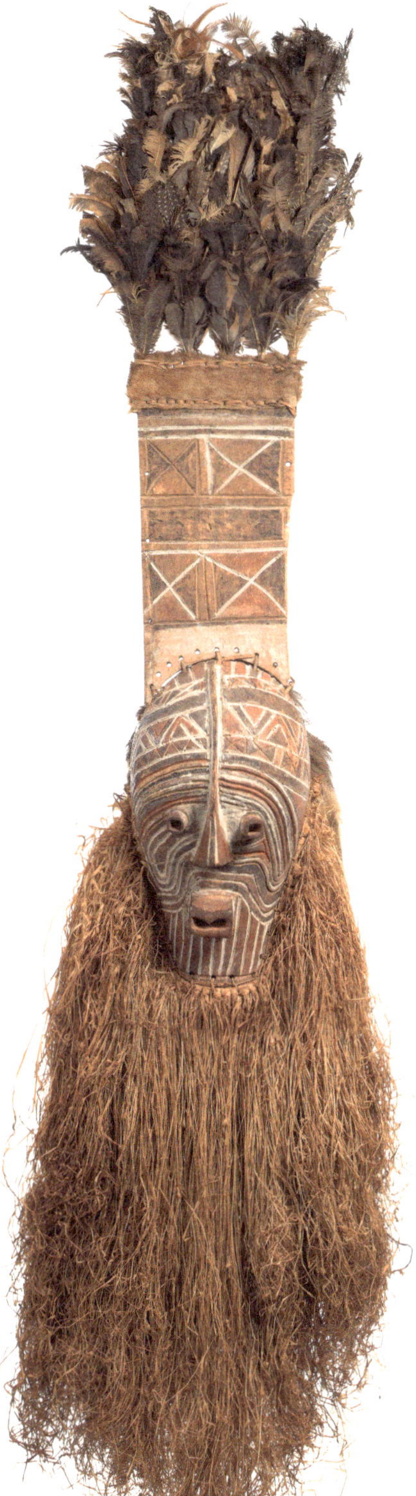

Fig. 291

Fig. 290

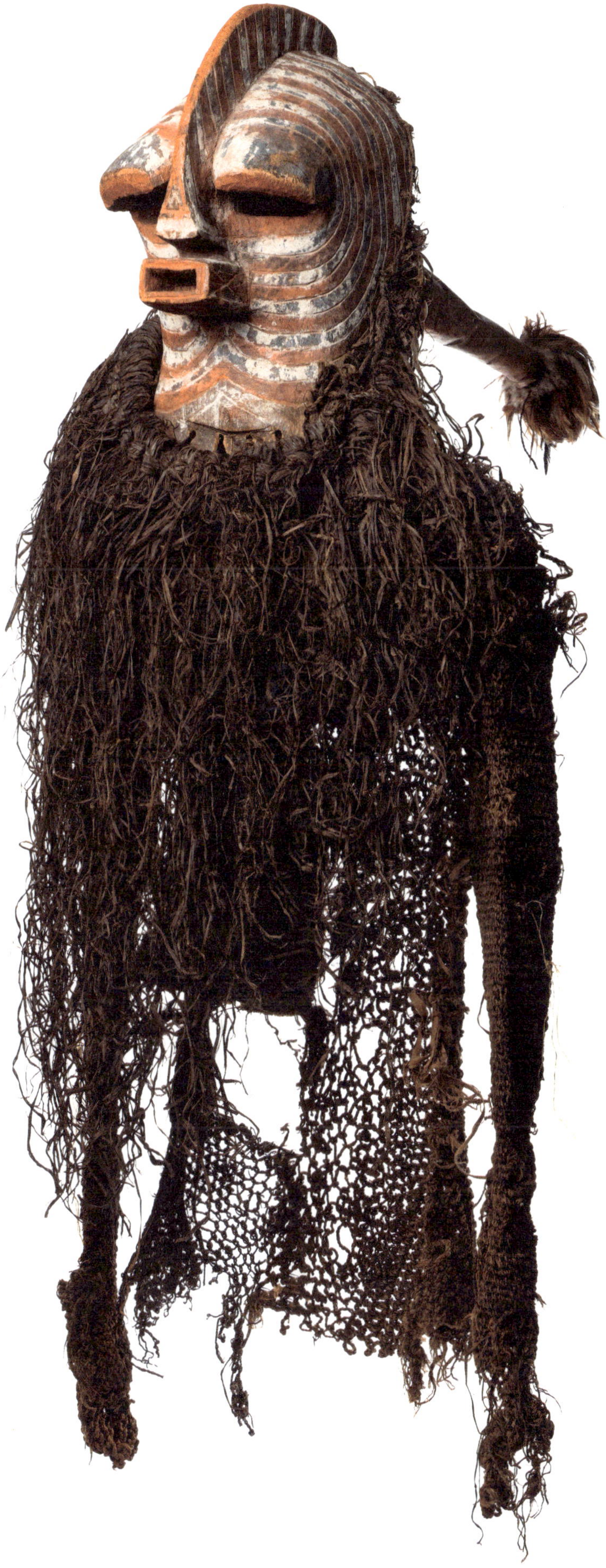

Fig. 292

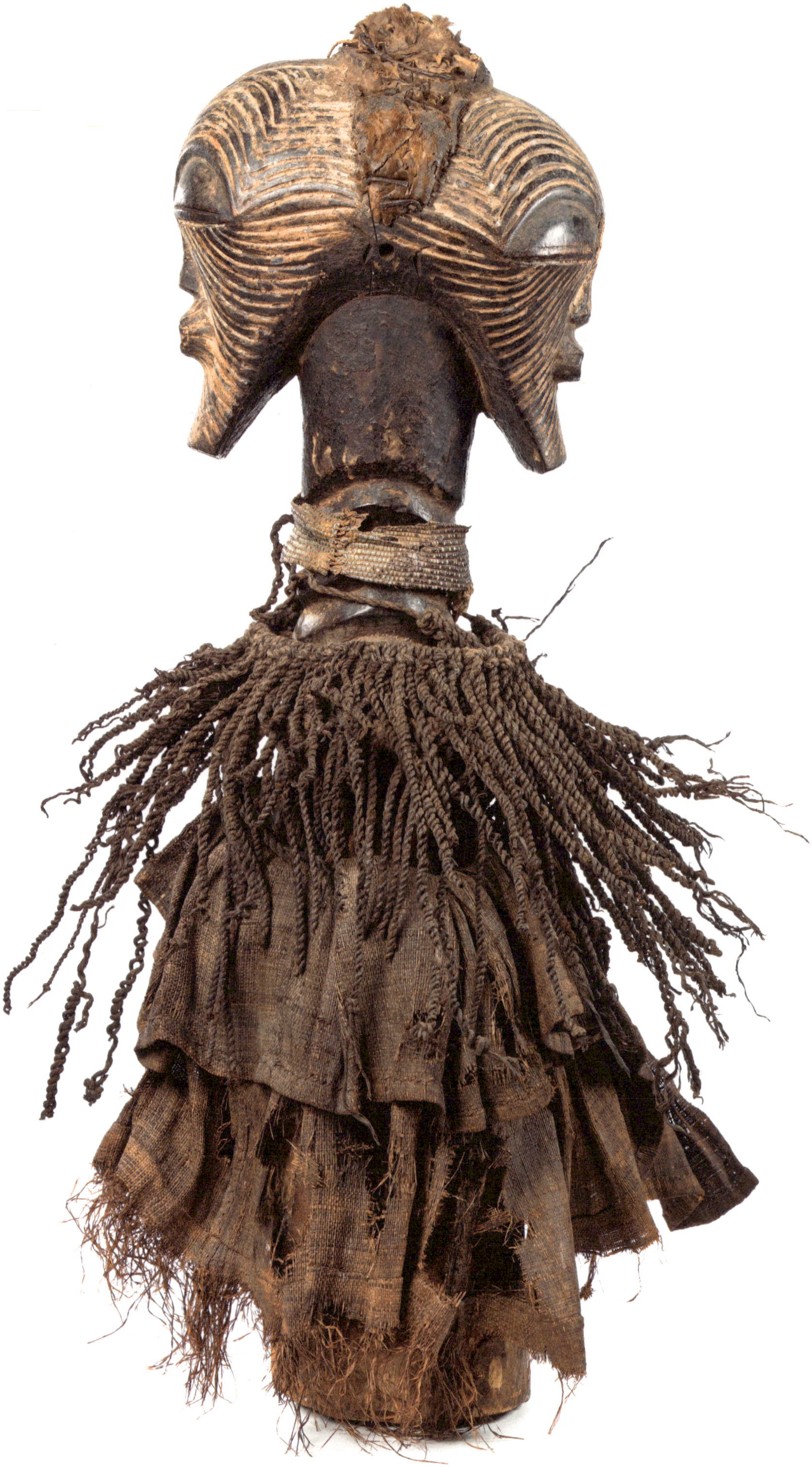

Fig. 293

Fig. 288
Artist of the Songye region
***Kifwebe* mask**
Before 1939, wood, pigments, 45.5 × 22.5 × 20.5 cm
Museum Rietberg Zürich, HH 25
Gift of Barbara and Eberhard Fischer
Acquired by Hans Himmelheber

Fig. 289
Artist of the Songye region
***Kifwebe* mask**
Before 1939, wood, pigments, 43 × 22 × 21 cm
Museum Rietberg Zürich, HH 24
Gift of Barbara and Eberhard Fischer
Acquired by Hans Himmelheber

Fig. 290
Artist of the Songye region
***Kifwebe* mask**
Nineteenth/early twentieth century wood, pigments, 57 × 27.5 × 32 cm
Museum Rietberg Zürich, RAC 302
Gift of Eduard von der Heydt

Fig. 291
Artist of the Songye region
***Kalengula* mask**
Before 1939, wood, paint, raffia fibers, fur, feathers, leather, 166.5 × 40 × 24 cm
Museum der Kulturen Basel, III 9507
Acquired by Hans Himmelheber

Fig. 292
Artist of the Songye region
***Kilume* mask**
Before 1939, wood, raffia, beans, feathers, leather, pigments, 135 × 25 × 50 cm
Museum der Kulturen Basel, III 9506
Acquired by Hans Himmelheber

Fig. 293
Artist of Kabashilange, Songye region
Figure with Janus head
Before 1939, wood, fur, raffia, reptile skin, 73 × 27 × 29 cm
Museum der Kulturen Basel, III 9514
Acquired by Hans Himmelheber

FEARED MASKS, CUBISTIC ICONS: *KIFWEBE* FROM THE SONGYE REGION — The histories of the *kifwebe* masks in the Congo and the West could not be more different: as emissaries of the local elite, the *kifwebe* masked figures of the *bwadi bwa kifwebe* male society in the territory of the Songye were responsible for political and social control over the community in the early twentieth century. Even during the colonial period, the masks remained influential. For this reason, the Belgian colonial government had the masks banned and confiscated in the 1920s.

At the same time, artists and art collectors in the geographic north declared these abstractly carved masks painted with red, white, and black lines icons of Cubism [figs. 288–290]. In the Songye region, the masks' visual codes and their significance constituted the core of the secret knowledge that the boys learned during their initiation. This knowledge was connected to cosmology, animals, and mythical heroes.

While in their place of origin the masks were stored in secret places and could only be accessed by a select few, today the objects are presented as highlights in museum vitrines, brightly lit and visible to everyone. Between these poles of hidden and forbidden, secret and sought-after, Hans Himmelheber went in search of such masks around the administrative center of Kabinda. His search proved extremely difficult, as he notes in his diary:

> "But in every village the same answer: the père of Kongolo had taken the masks away or burned them. Until I arrive at the big chief's village of Sangua, where I am eagerly shown a mask kept in a ruin in the bush, then another—and very pretty figures, too. Finally. The masks are actually very beautiful, precisely the style for which I have been hunting for so long [...] and which was recently shown to me in the mission. [...] Just twenty of these very highly paid masks make the long journey worthwhile."[1]

Hans Himmelheber, who always had an eye for unusual items, also purchased artworks that did not conform to the Western *kifwebe* canon. These pieces may not have yielded high profits, but they continue to demonstrate the full spectrum of artistic production in the region. For example, he not only acquired the wooden face masks that were sought after in the West, but also the associated mask costumes [fig. 292]. Among his most unusual finds is a two-headed figure whose face is carved in the style of the *kifwebe* masks [fig. 293]. Himmelheber gives us the following information about the figure: he purchased it in the village Kabashilange, where it was standing in an inconspicuous square. Due to its two faces, it could see everywhere from this position. Corroded by woodworms, the base of the figure had been repaired by its former owners.[2] — Nanina Guyer

1 Himmelheber, diary, April 24, 1939 (archive of the Museum Rietberg).
2 Index card III 9524, (archive of the Museum der Kulturen Basel); Himmelheber, diary, May 7, 1939 (archive of the Museum Rietberg).

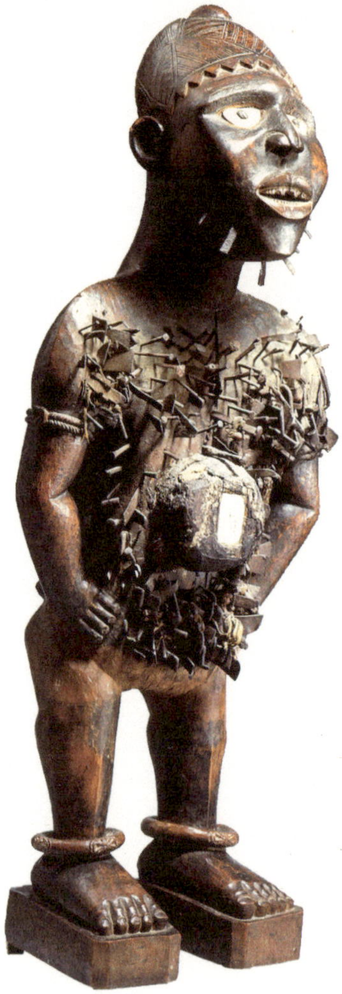

Fig. 294

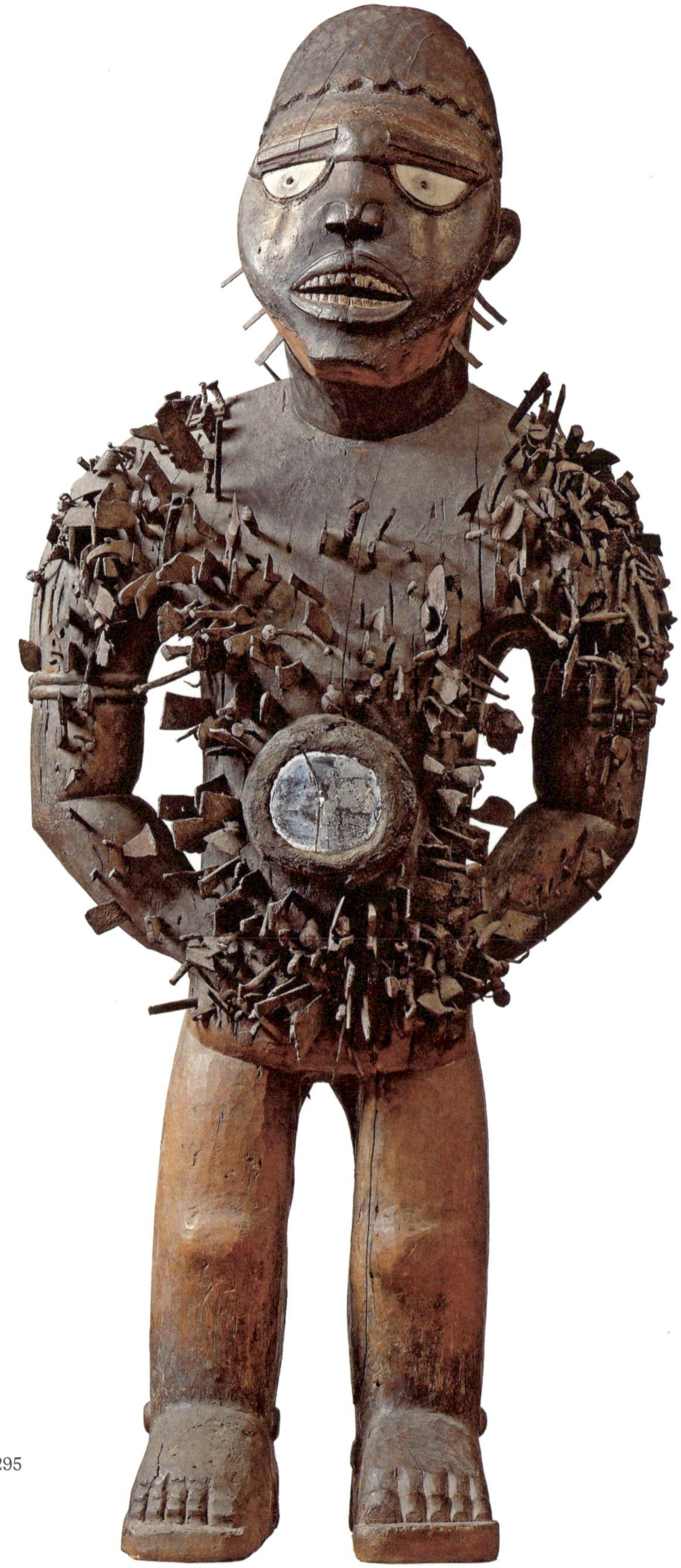

Fig. 295

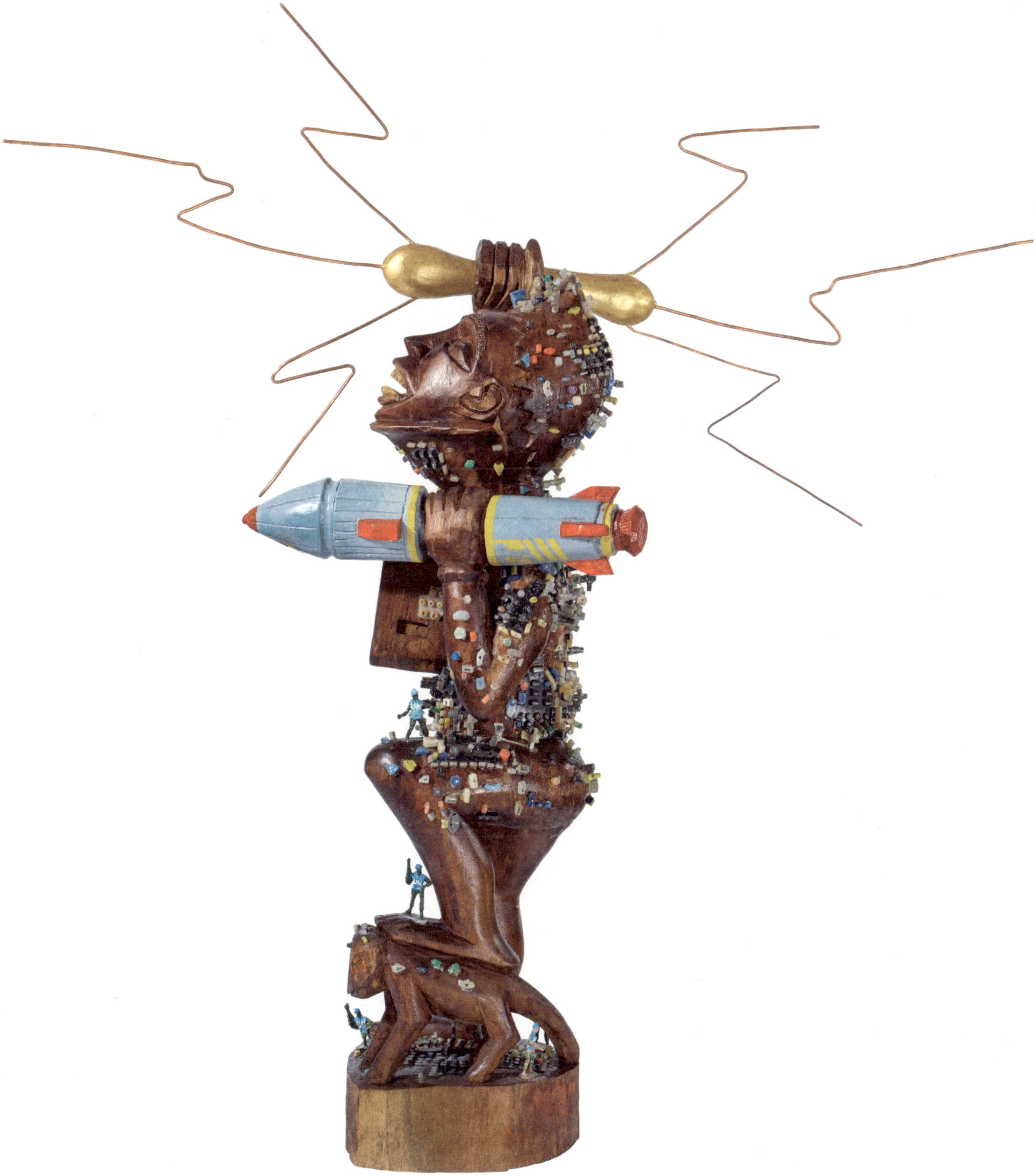

Fig. 296

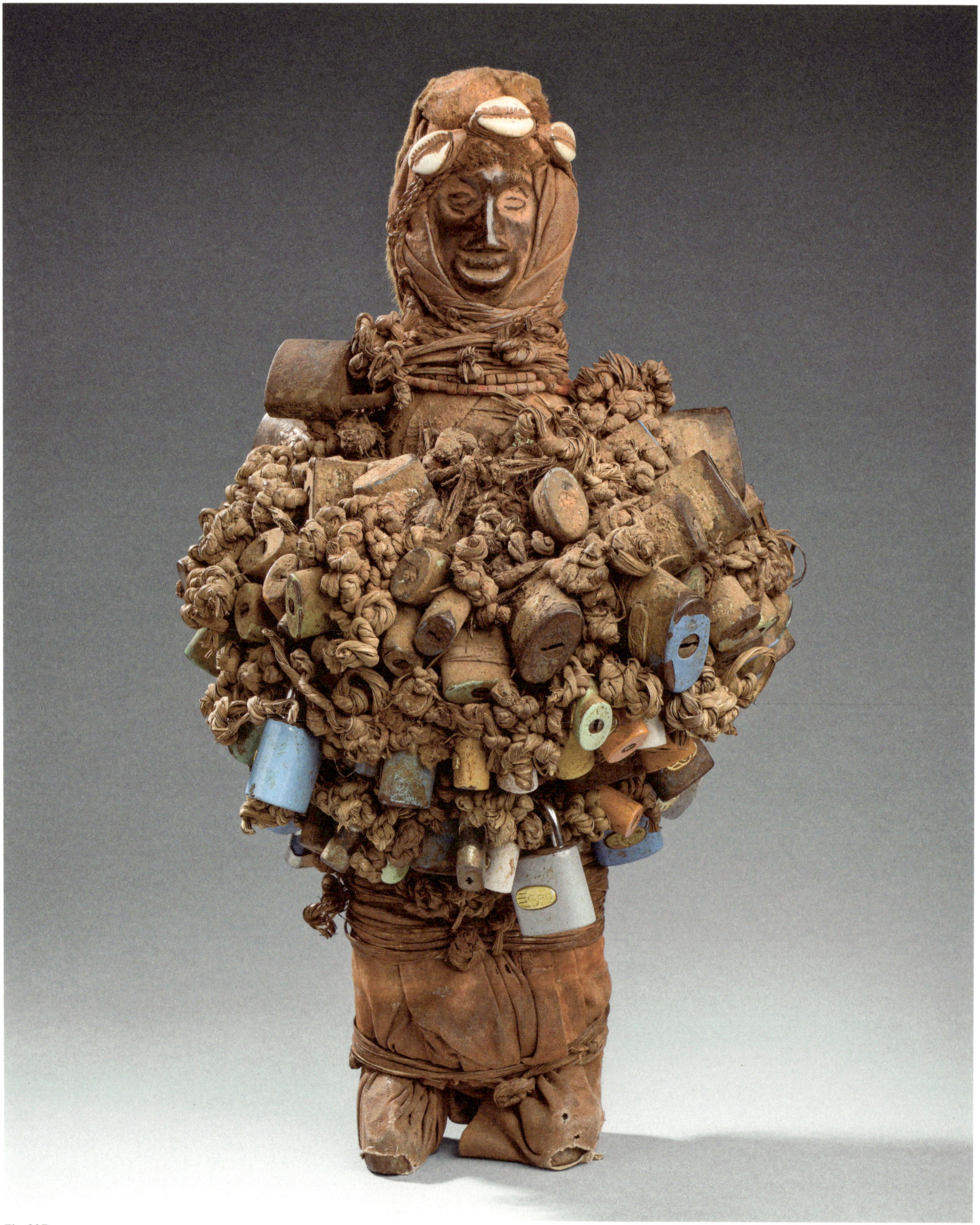

Fig. 297

Fig. 294
Artist from the Kingdom of Kongo
***Mangaaka* power figure**
Nineteenth century, wood, iron, metal, plate glass, ceramic, plant fibers, textiles, and pigments, 115 × 45 × 37.5 cm
Horstmann Collection, Zug

Fig. 295
Artist from the Kingdom of Kongo
***Mangaaka* power figure**
Nineteenth century, wood, iron, metal, plate glass, ceramic, plant fibers, textiles, and pigments, 110 cm
Private Collection, Zug

Fig. 296
Hilaire Balu Kuyangiko
Nkisi numérique
2017, various media, 109 × 50 × 50 cm
Nuno Crisostomo Collection,
The Bujas-Crisostomo Family Collection

Fig. 297
Artist from the Kongo region
***Mpungu* figure with Chinese locks**
Before 1991, wood, skin, pigments, plant fibers, nut, metal, cowries, textiles, 38.5 × 22 cm
RMCA Tervuren, EO.1991.21.5
Acquired by A. Mieke Van Damme

(IM)BALANCE OF POWERS: *MANGAAKA* FIGURES THEN AND NOW — Transcending cultural barriers, the majestic power figures (*mangaaka*) from the Kingdom of Kongo that are charged with metal and other substances continue to evoke mixed feelings today [figs. 294/295]. Indeed, the aesthetic of accumulation is intented to inspire awe and to astonish.[1] First, a carver would create the voluminous sculpture from a piece of wood. Much more important, however, was the ritual specialist (*nganga*), who would insert plant, animal, or mineral substances (*bilongo*) into the abdomen or head of the figure. Nails and iron blades activated the powers with which a *mangaaka* could administer justice, seal agreements, settle conflicts, and restore morality in a community. Beyond our conceptual separation of subject and object, power figures possessed social agency in the sense of Alfred Gell[2] because they were attributed a positive and occasionally negative effect on other people.

Over the course of the nineteenth century, the colonial powers' pressure on local political structures constantly increased.[3] On the Loango coast the Kingdom of Kongo lost its authority and ultimately collapsed. In these uncertain times *mangaaka* power figures acquired particular importance. With their help, the chiefs attempted to maintain control of trade and politics—in competition with the Europeans. Trade agreements or oaths were sealed with a nail and those who did not keep their side of the bargain were punished. New power figures emerged as a reaction to the regime implemented by the Europeans and were a means of resistance against colonization. This was a thorn in the side of the colonial government, which destroyed these powerful protectors in order to dominate the economy and politics. The Christian missionaries likewise branded these charged objects as the work of the devil and had them burnt.

However, the practices of activating power figures did not disappear completely. Today they may seem much less conspicuous and more incidental or be charged with symbols of modernity, such as Chinese locks [fig. 297]. Even contemporary artists like Hilaire Balu Kuyangiko have applied themselves to the subject. In his hybrid sculpture *Nkisi numérique*, the Kinshasa-based artist reappropriates the historical carving technique and imagery while simultaneously criticizing the idolization of capitalism and consumption in modern society [fig. 296]. Painted with Chinese characters, the rocket in the colors of the Congolese flag alludes to China's economic and trade offensive on the continent and African dependence on Chinese investment. The assemblage of electronic waste is all the more horrifying when one is aware that the inhumane conditions in mines of minerals in Congo supplies the rest of the world with coltan, the foundation on which digitization is built. — Michaela Oberhofer

1 See MacGaffey 1993.
2 See Gell 1998.
3 LaGamma 2008, 2015.

THE LORD IS DEAD, LONG LIFE TO THE LORD
Sinzo Aanza

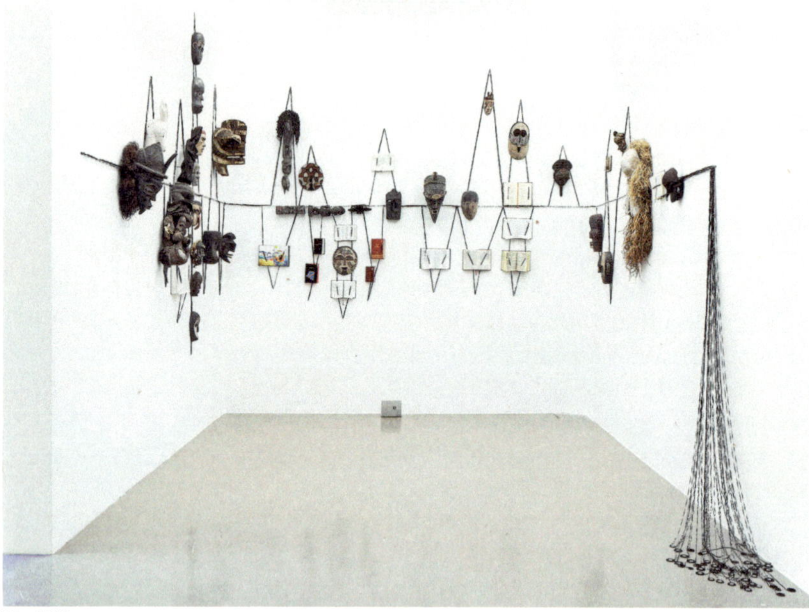
Fig. 298

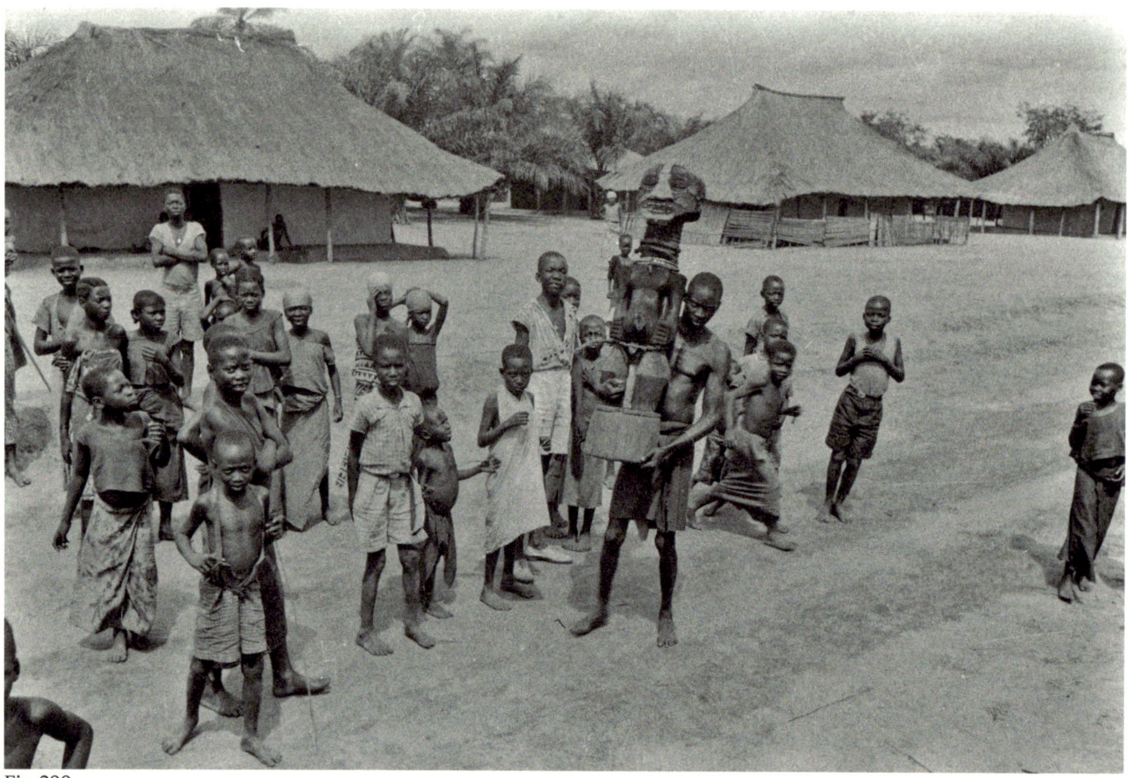
Fig. 299

Fig. 298
Sinzo Aanza
Le Royaume des Cieux
2017, different materials
Sinzo Aanza and Galerie Imane Farès, Paris

Fig. 299
Hans Himmelheber
The power figure is carried over
Songye region, April 28, 1939, b/w negative
Museum Rietberg Zürich, FHH 188-20

Fig. 300
Sinzo Aanza
Untitled
2018, different materials
Sinzo Aanza and Galerie Imane Farès, Paris

Fig. 301
Sinzo Aanza
Sans titre 7
2018, photograph, 80 × 137 cm
Sinzo Aanza and Galerie Imane Farès, Paris

Fig. 302
Sinzo Aanza
Sans titre 8
2018, photograph, 80 × 137 cm
Sinzo Aanza and Galerie Imane Farès, Paris

Hans Himmelheber's photographs bear witness to the waning subjection to traditional power structures, whose cosmogony and materiality of discourse summoned different figures offering power and protection relative to the powers held by others, all gravitating around the tutelary figure of a chief. Thereafter, subjection to a new world began, the one that colonization had brought into being and stabilized with its institutions after the great adventures of the explorers, navigators, and conquerors. I was especially drawn to the image of this man carrying a large power figure—large power figures being supposed to concentrate more power or have the ability to ward it off—to sell to the art dealer [fig. 299]. His motives were certainly, as so often during the period, the need to pay taxes or simply to meet the new demands of life in the so-called *groupements extra-coutumiers*, groups outside traditional jurisdictions where people aligned with the colonial project, in which they had served, still served or hoped to serve as porters, soldiers, workmen, collection clerks, etc., lived. For these people, the encounter with the West had just produced the equivalent of an economic Great Depression. Almost overnight, the items that stood for wealth in the imaginary of their societies had come to be perceived as junk. The photograph speaks to the magnitude of the upheavals produced by a colonial process that sought to reorganize spiritual existence—substituting for the invisible, to which the large power figure on the shoulders of the man offered a form of access—a poetic and political consensus supposed to contain spirituality, education and enlistment in the project of colonial exploitation. The Pentateuch, the nucleus of Christianity, is made up of an origin story, Genesis, followed by divine and human legends that conclude upon the law, the necessity of hierarchy, or, better put, of obedience to the new established order. It is, therefore, for the pursuit of power, the most accommodating form of the legal state, which explains the global reach of this story that still undergirds most state-controlled organizations today.

As an art dealer, Himmelheber inevitably found himself on the outside of events. His photographs were taken in the same way that Joseph Conrad's famous novella *Heart of Darkness* was written, offering an overview of a situation whose sole interest lay in the story that would be drawn from it. However, this space was in the process of transformation. It would continue after these stories drawn from it; indeed, it would feed on them for its transformation. After the "heart of darkness," this space would become the "empire of silence" in the eyes of the colonial administration. Its artistic productions, like its commercial activity in the nascent urban, so-called detribalized areas, would follow the trajectory of what we can see in Hans Himmelheber's photographs, that is to say, a market would emerge without order or any real law and defined by nervous instability and anxiety.

This operation followed the stories the West told itself about the rest of the world, with the great adventures of commercial maritime voyages and worldwide exploration. Such stories would contribute to the colonial labor of indoctrination, relaying to the very places they described new imaginaries and a new way of being in the world, the new identity of peoples the world over being bound from then on to the commercial needs of the largest economic powers.

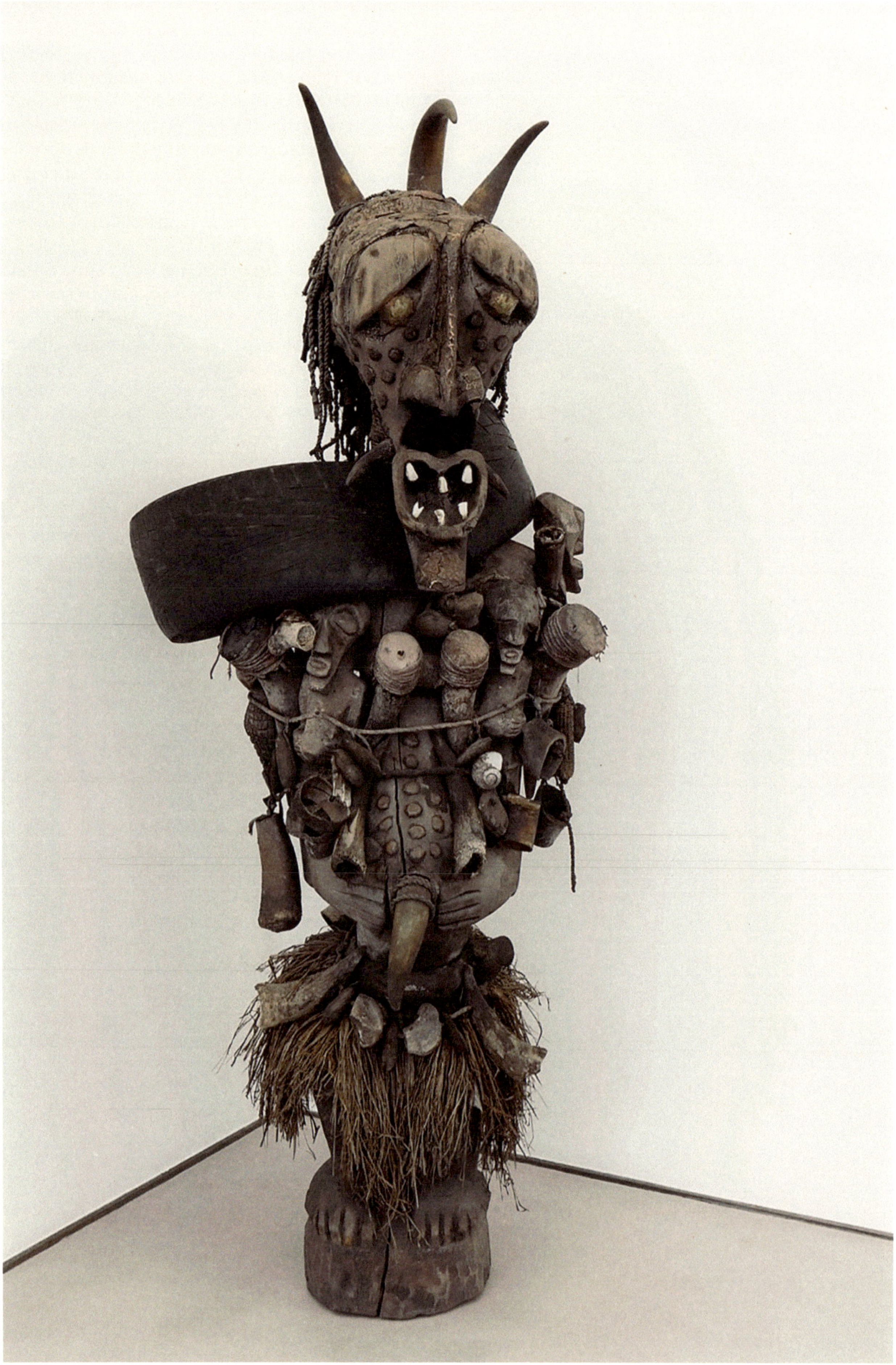

Fig. 300

THE ROADS ARE SERPENTS

They bite like serpents
They hiss, they suffocate, they snap, they swallow,
They defecate, they vomit
And you are no longer the same
Their story is one of a snakeskin being sloughed
The first to grab you is a path
It puts a stitch in your side, you quell its breath
It's windy
A little dusty wind, but dense and swirling
Triumphing over the receding forest

Men here have become the gods they slew

A python swallows you up as soon as the path releases you
A highway of beaten earth
Carrying trucks and human bodies
Loaded with logs
Bags of cinders and mineral sludge
Vegetables that wither under a harsh sun
Livestock dead and living

Heavy-footed shadows trudge ahead
Under a storm of mediatized spittle
A trail of rags and bent forms

They say they knocked their attainment of humanity out of commission
They refused to work
What man refuses to work choosing instead to slaughter the good souls that beg him to work for his own good?
What man says no, when he is told, work, my good friend?
What man says no when he is told, from now on, you're no longer a child?
When he is told, you're no longer an animal?
Work!
For your own good!
For mine too, but above all for yours!
Put your heart in it, exploit the emanations of your newly attained humanity
Work for yourself!

They killed with machete blows, arrows, and pestles
They were felled by cannon and submerged in a pagan death
Then they came back to life
Having no name, no face, they emerged from the mud in a mishmash of decay

Children
Indolent
Inert
Dying
Dead
Anecdotal women
Displaying an atrophied breast
And dusty as the wind
And flat ... like the wings of officious flies
And empty ... like the look they cast on suckling indolence

They too have taken their neighbors' babies by the knees and
smashed their skulls against the sides of their impatience
Anger is an incomplete story
It is out of impatience they heckled humanity the world over
The humanity of dust
The humanity of water
The humanity of hills
The humanity of forests
The humanity of the firmament
It is out of impatience they threatened with their frail finger
And out of impatience they abandoned their bodies in this *scavenging* dust

There are
Children
Women, men as well
Indolent
Inert
Dying
Dead

The shadows debauch the meaning of the journey
And people gather for the victim
At the hangman's feet
In the epic of his glory
The hangman is the nation builder
And his life and his death, the only echo of common history

It was the hangman who built the roads
Then said, come, you must live on the roads
You must feed the roads and feed on roads

Without the roads, railroads, and ships,
We are nothing but a pile of mud waiting to dry up

Come, parasites, wandering in the night of time and consciousness
Today your animal life comes to an end,
No more existential quietude
Let's open up this land to the world!

The python vomits you out on a muddy road that defies the fever of a low sky
And a somersaulting village

The sky draws near like it was damnation
It tosses and turns, twists in pain, groans, and slobbers
The sky cries out and sweats
The sky furrows the road and fields and bellies

And men are digging along the road
They have stripped the gods
Stuck an obscene finger in all their holes
Suffocating the sacred fire of their guts

Fig. 301

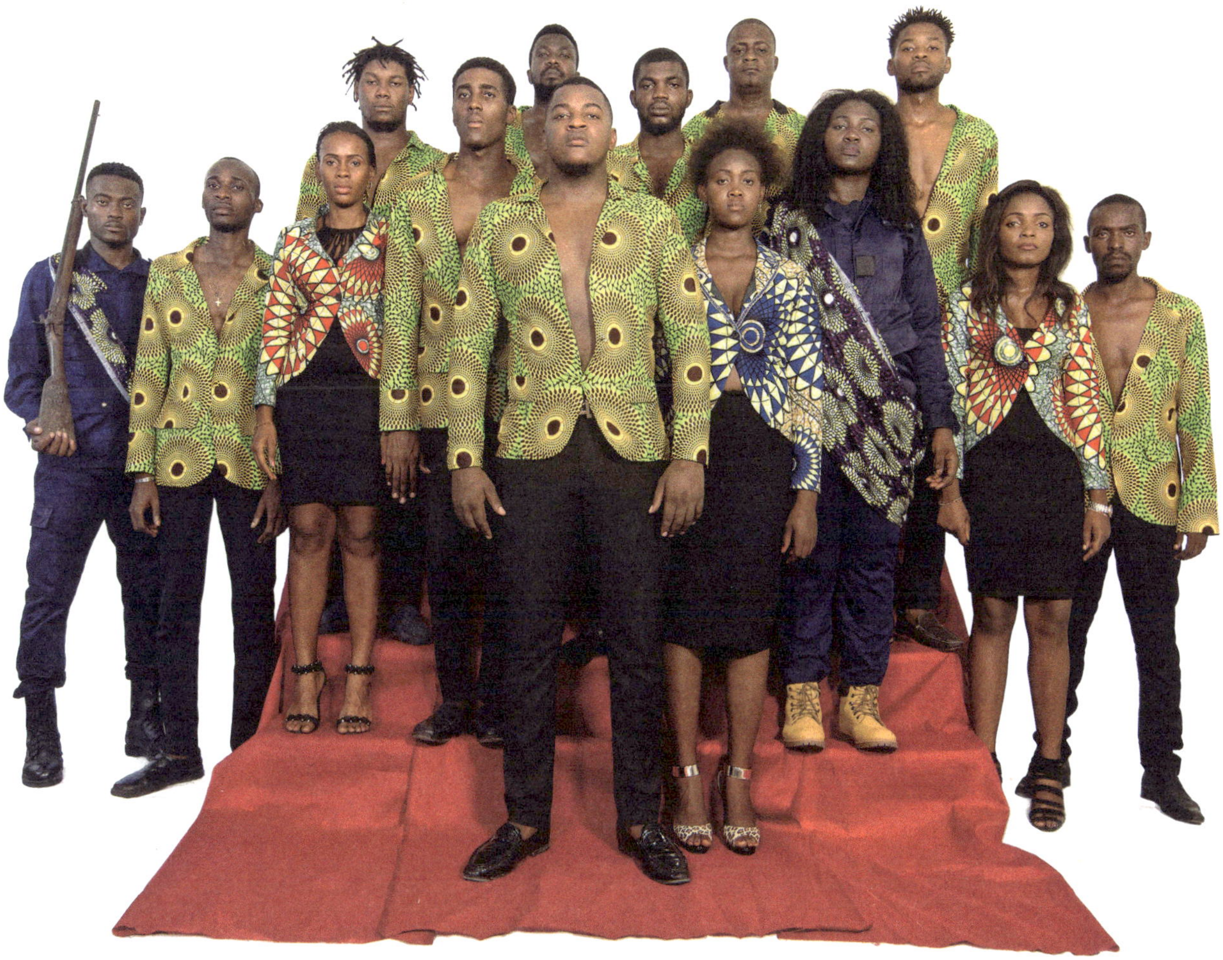

Fig. 302

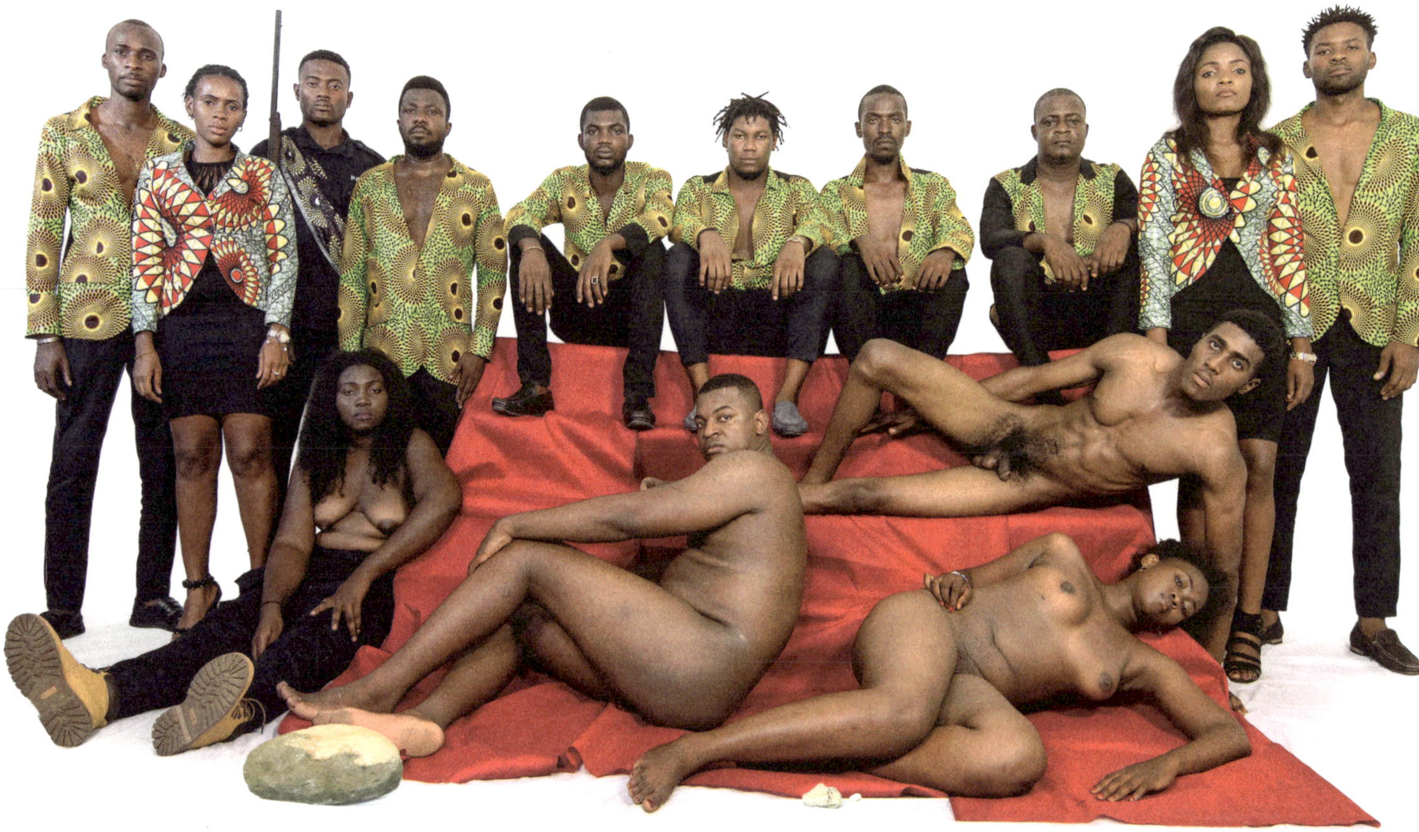

They are naked
Head held high
Arms determined
Genitals erect
They search the land
They search with their treacherous gaze
They search with their heads leashed to an immature hope
They search with their sacrilegious arms
They search with their eager genitalia

The sky has come so low
The sky coughs so hard
The sky spits out burst pieces of its tubercular clouds
It is the dirty blue of political promises
The dirty blue of the new economic order
The dirty blue of the right to stipulate, to command, to extract, to rectify, to tame…
The dirty blue of the infinitely big and the infinitely trivial
The dirty blue of the promised land and the rediscovered country
The dirty blue of the water that pools with seed thrown on the ground
The dirty blue of the gospel according to the missionaries

Blue of the flood, of indoctrination, of tax collection
Blue of the pious idea of homeland and clothes hiked up to rape the gods

Here, God is man's thirst
The hunger of men
The insatiable appetite of men
Here, God is a dead end

Here the shadows feed on each other
With corn fufu and palm wine

Kera loves Ndabi the way one loves a boy
She dresses up for him each morning
Each morning, he gazes at her in silence, but with ardent eyes
Each morning, she gives thanks to the God of eyes, for all eyes that can speak such volumes
Each morning, Ndabi draws palm wine and takes it to Kera's father
In the hope of seeing her again so beautiful, so beautiful for him
The village listens to Ndabi gazing
The entire village can read in his palm wine the torture of a shy passion
Kera loves Ndabi the way one loves a shy boy
The moons pass and still Ndabi says nothing
The village grows impatient and Ndabi says nothing
The village tells Kera to make the first move: "smile at him more often, more openly, for longer…
Tell him to lower into his mouth the jubilation of his eyes…
Tell him to raise up the words from his palm wine…
Tell him flowers are born of flowers and of the embrace of bees…
That even mountains said to be lonely hold hands in the valley… Tell him…"
Kera loves Ndabi the way one loves a boy
This boy, her mother tells her, who speaks with his eyes and palm wine, is a gift from God
Mothers speak even better than palm wine
It is they who judge the beauty of the flame and fan it with their breath
Men are the last to know
For the paperwork and more palm wine
The village flocks to the feast that breaks Ndabi's silence, the sole fervor of his eyes, the forenoon excuse of palm wine…

Men say yes after women do
Ndabi smiles with his lips that say nothing and his ardent eyes
Kera loves him the way one loves a shy boy
Night falls with song, dancing, laughter, drunkenness ... and soldiers' boots!
The boots fire on the brawny men
The boots burn the thatched huts
The boots build cages, confine the women and Kera there
The boots tie up the others with the goats
The boots say they're all set, the perimeter is secure ...
Kera prays for Ndabi, for the ardent flame in his eyes, for their honeymoon

She pleads with the God of ardent eyes, weddings and palm wine
that he may choose as he likes the children's names
The children she will bear Ndabi
She prays the village may sing, dance, and smile on the birth of children
The children she will bear Ndabi
The rugged boots yank her from the cage, after her maid of honor and Ndabi's mother
Kera is adorned for Ndabi's eyes
The rugged boots cut off her necklaces with a knife and put the blade to her throat
Kera is heartsick
She knows she shouldn't cry, but she is so heartsick
Kera cries on the blade that slides under her chin
She weeps
Not for herself ...
But for all the pain she causes Ndabi
For her mother who howls like a storm, her face hid by trembling hands
For her father whose grief is tied up with the goats
Kera can see her blood mingle with her tears in the gleam of the blade
Kera can see Ndabi close his eyes
She can hear him moan
Her heart swells with love and anguish
Kera loves Ndabi the way one loves a shy boy
To hear him moan hurts her more than the blade
Kera closes her eyes
The rugged boots lift her from the ground
Undress her
Turn her around
Flip her over
Cut her in pieces
Mix her together with her maid of honor
Mix her together with Ndabi's mother
Rub her with chili pepper
Salt her
Season her some more
And some more
Douse her with oil
With water
With sweet peppers
With leeks ...
With more chili pepper
With more salt ...
Carry her to the fire made for her by the village
For Ndabi and for the children to whom the God of ardent eyes and palm wine, boots and victories
will give a name in some putrefied memory of his divinity of ardent eyes and palm wine, boots and
victories ...
Kera loves Ndabi the way one loves a boy

Here the shadows are scattered turds in the bush
After the passage of the boots

I don't know if we love
Like the wave and the cliff
Or the air and the bird
I don't know if our gazes
Struck in unison
The innocence of our hearts
If the zeal of your uncovered hair
can wash clean the conventions around us
If the game of our misguided laughter
Frightens the birds in the trees

We are so mad, so alone
So lost, so far away...

You don't know if we love like blood and wine
If our arms are wings
Barricades or bridges
You don't know if the sound of the wind
Is a distant metaphor
Perhaps we'll live again
We'll set the moon to dance in our hands
We'll be alive
We'll seal up the sky in our glances
And the four winds in our sighs
We'll be the hurricane's upheaval
and I'll make love to you in a reversal of our cries of terror
And juddering of our bodies fallen
in the blood, dust, and bullets...

Here...
Love stories
have no beginning

The mirrors of life are eyes that do not see you
And the roads are serpents

Translated by J. Bret Maney

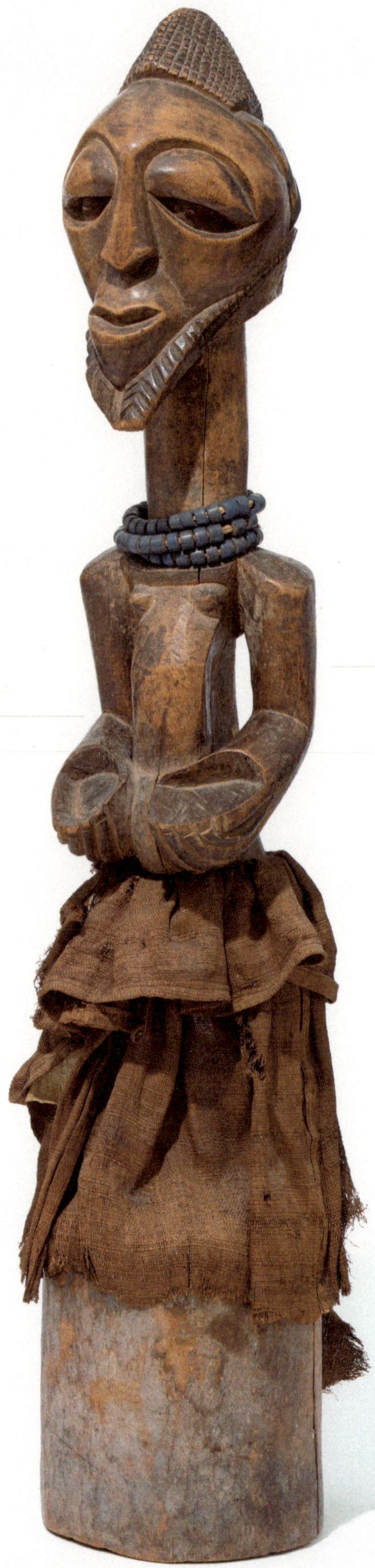

Fig. 303

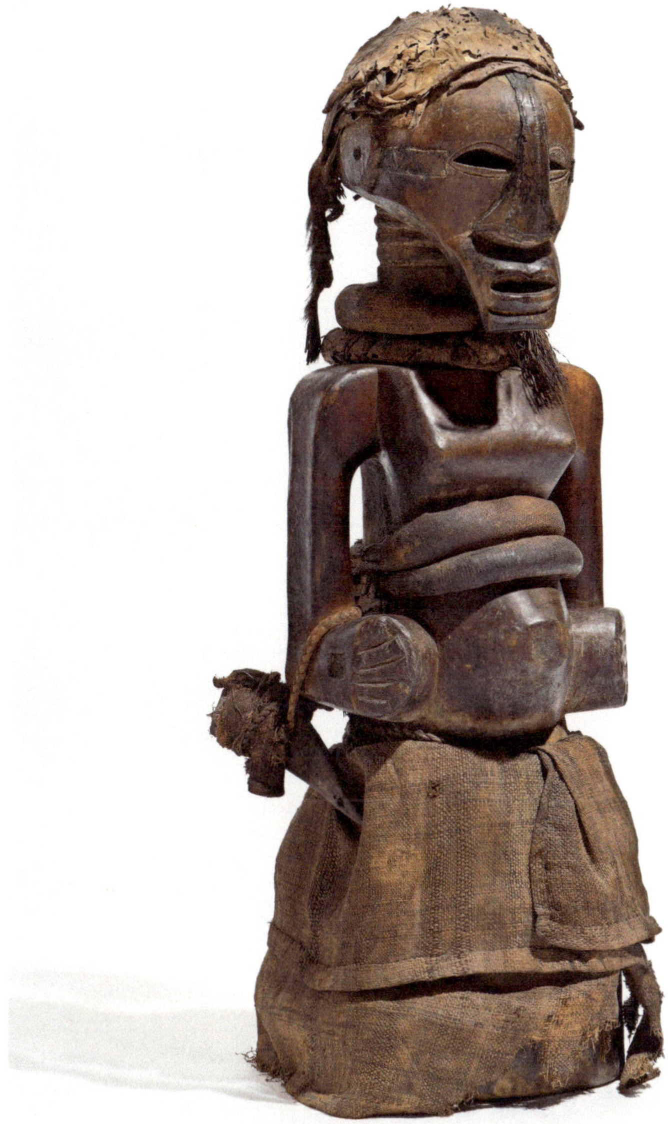

Fig. 304

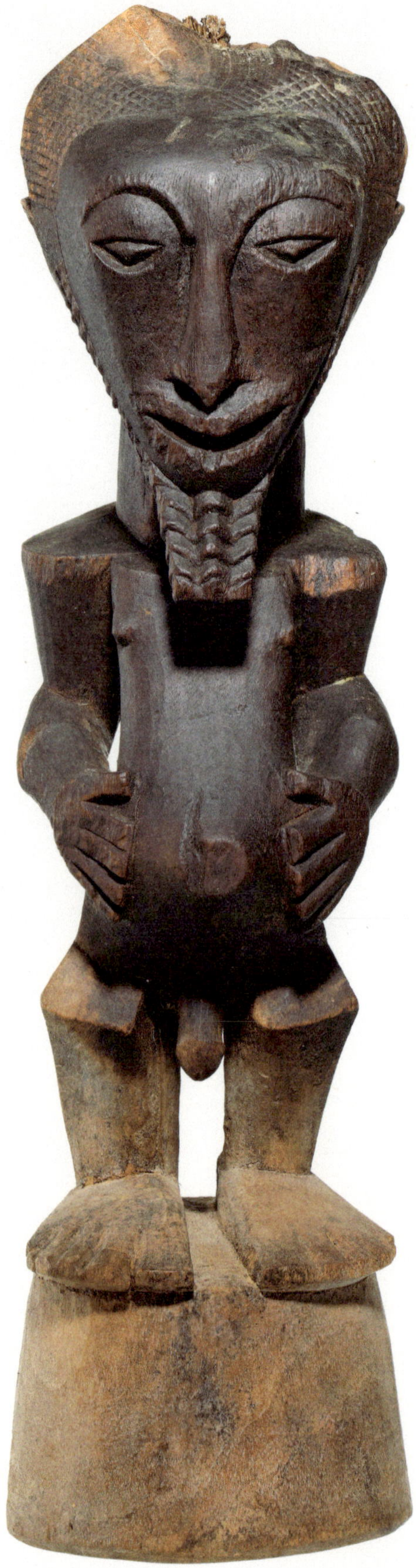

Fig. 305

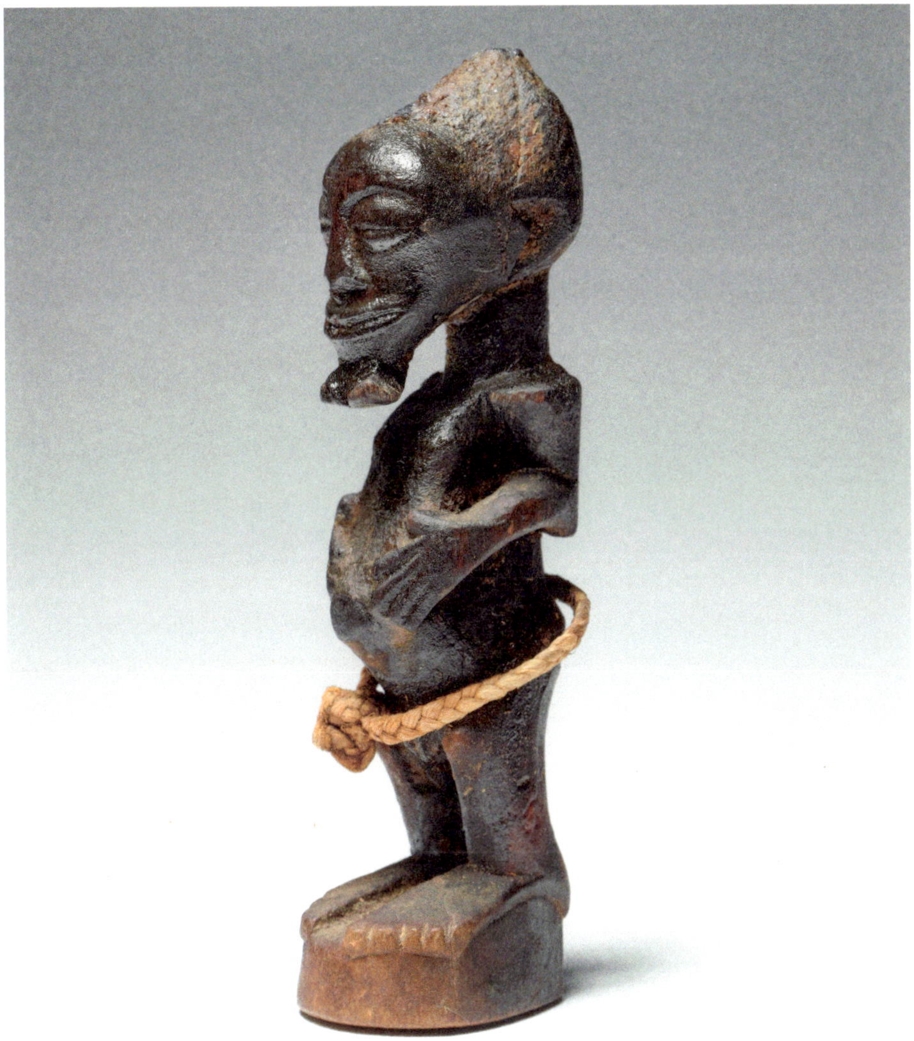

Fig. 306

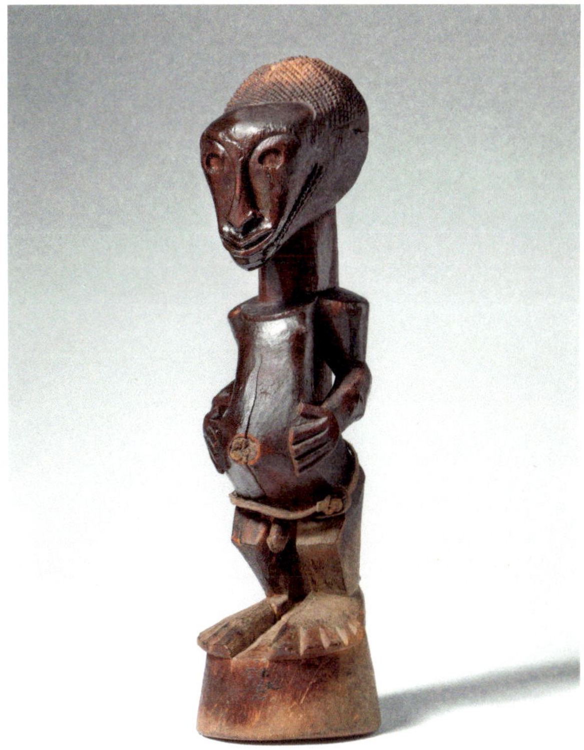

Fig. 307

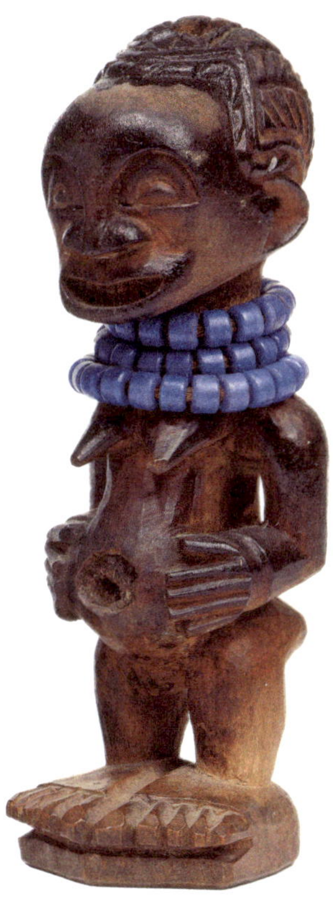

Fig. 308

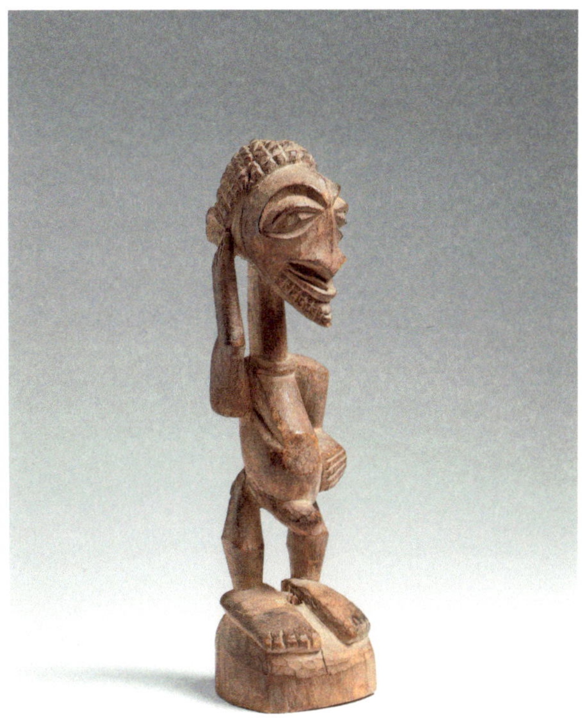

Fig. 309

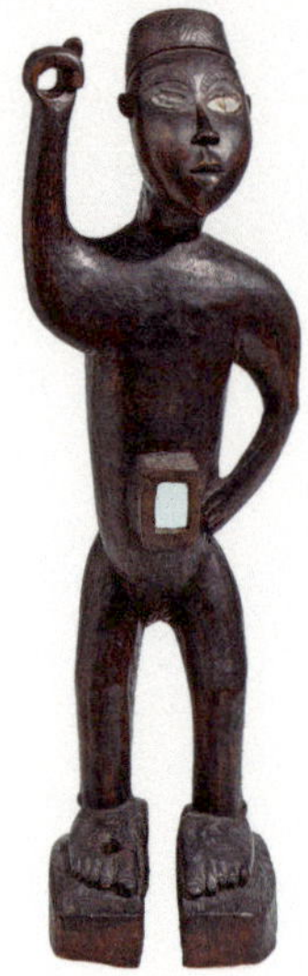

Fig. 311

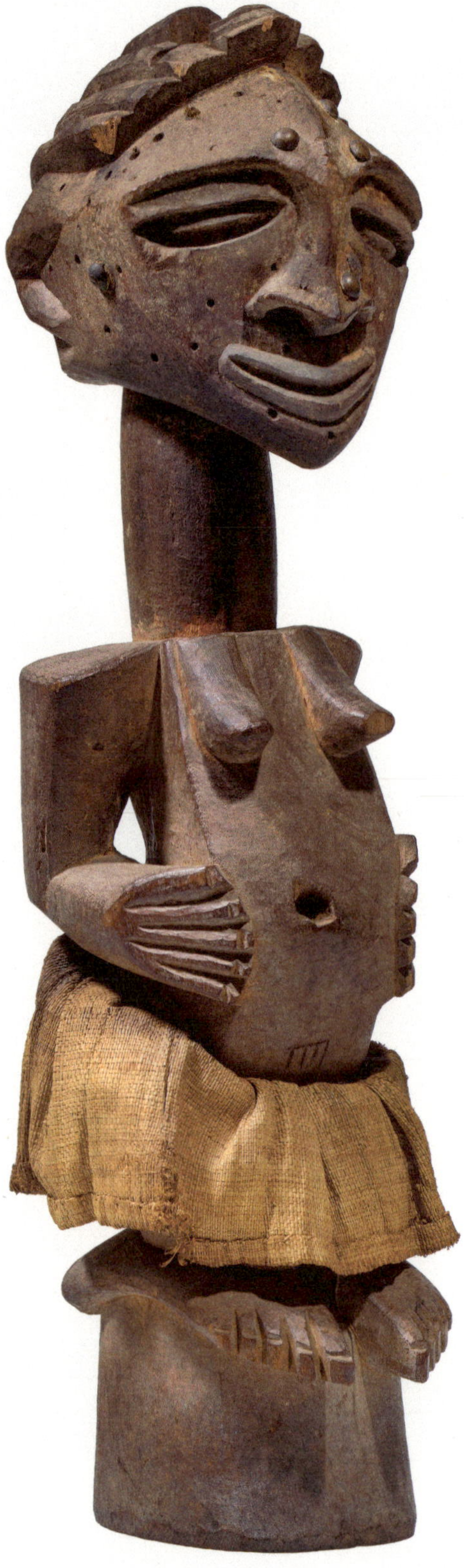

Fig. 310

VISIBLE AND INVISIBLE WORLDS: SONGYE POWER FIGURES

—— Already Hans Himmelheber differentiated between the Songye's small power figures made for personal use and the impressive, large sculptures used by communities. When it was necessary to produce a power figure (sing. *nkishi*, pl. *mankishi*), first a chief or an elder would commission a carver with the wooden corpus.[1] Then a ritual expert (*nganga*) would apply substances (*bishimba*) of plant, animal, or mineral materials to the outside and inside of the figure. His words and sacrifices would then activate the powers (*kikudi*) of the spirits of the deceased, which could ward off diseases, infertility, or other evil dangers associated with witchcraft. The Songye believed that the *kikudi* were located in a person's abdomen or head—which is where the potent substances are applied to the figures. *Mankishi* were vessels for these supernatural powers that were bound in time and space. They are the expression of the complementarity between the living and the dead, between the visible and the invisible or rather the outside and the inside.

Due to their size and accumulation of materials, the community figures elicited a combination of awe and fear. A Bekalebue sculpture described by Himmelheber as an ancestral figure [fig. 303] exudes exceptional calm and harmony as a result of its dignified face and unusual gesture of suppliant palms. The large figures were given their own names and bore insignia of wisdom and power, such as a beard, headdress, glass necklace, or raffia skirt. In contrast, materials like snakeskin, leopard teeth, or antelope horns [fig. 304] were intended to act as a deterrent and be reminiscent of characteristics associated with these wild animals, such as strength or speed. Metal arrows and staffs were associated with the culture heroes of the hunter and blacksmith, but also symbolized the lightning that a warlock or a witch could use against enemies. In the colonial period the importance of the *mankishi* grew as they seemed to guarantee continuity and cohesion in an age of economic and social insecurity and power imbalance.[2]

Both the large and the small power figures of the Songye are characterized by a V-shaped face, half-closed eyes, and a triangular nose that merges into the distinctive arches of the eyebrows [figs. 305–309]. The torso—with the hands often at the sides of the abdomen—is composed of angular shapes and volumes whose Cubistic appearance was very popular among European collectors. Few *mankishi* survive in their original condition with all their substances. In these two examples [figs. 312–315], only an X-ray tomography reveals the invisible load, such as a metal arrow or the veins inside the head and the abdomen. Far more commonly, the sculptures were "uncharged" [fig. 310]—by the original owners prior to sale or by later owners—so that they would correspond to the aesthetics of the Western art market. The artist of this sculpture that was carved in the Kongo style [fig. 311] went one step further, creating a smooth and dark surface—entirely in line with the classic taste of collectors at the time—and reducing the "charge" to a small mirror. —— Michaela Oberhofer

1 See Hersak 2013.
2 Hersak 2010, p. 41.

Fig. 303
Artist of the Bekalebue-Songye region
Male figure
Before 1939, wood, glass beads, and plant fibers, 92.4 × 19.7 × 24.5 cm
Museum Rietberg Zürich, EFA 13
Permanent loan from Barbara and Eberhard Fischer
Acquired by Hans Himmelheber

Fig. 304
Artist of the Songye region
Large power figure *nkishi*
Before 1938, wood, metal, plant and animal substances, fur, horn, 80 cm
Private collection
Acquired by Hans Himmelheber

Fig. 305
Artist of the Songye region
Power figure *nkishi*
Before 1939, wood, 52 × 16 × 13 cm
Museum Rietberg Zürich, 2019.440
Gift of Barbara and Eberhard Fischer/ Susanne Himmelheber
Acquired by Hans Himmelheber

Fig. 306
Artist of the Songye region
Power figure *nkishi*
Before 1939, wood, plant fibers, 19 × 5 × 6 cm
Museum Rietberg Zürich, HH 2
Gift of Barbara and Eberhard Fischer
Acquired by Hans Himmelheber

Fig. 307
Artist of the Songye region
Power figure *nkishi*
Before 1939, wood, leather, 42 × 12 × 12 cm
Museum Rietberg Zürich, HH 6
Gift of Barbara and Eberhard Fischer
Acquired by Hans Himmelheber

Fig. 308
Artist of the Songye region
Power figure *nkishi*
Before 1939, wood, glass, 18 cm
Horstmann Collection, Zug
Acquired by Hans Himmelheber

Fig. 309
Artist of the Songye region
Power figure *nkishi* with raised arm
Before 1939, wood, 24 × 6.5 × 6.5 cm
Museum Rietberg Zürich, HH 3
Gift of Barbara and Eberhard Fischer
Acquired by Hans Himmelheber

Fig. 310
Artist of the Songye region
Female power figure *nkishi*
Before 1939, wood, textile, and metal alloy, 54 × 15 × 16 cm
Museum Rietberg Zürich, 2018.112
Gift of Martin Himmelheber
Acquired by Hans Himmelheber

Fig. 311
Artist of the Congo region
Power figure for the art market
1920s/1930s, wood, plate glass, 75.2 × 25 × 20 cm
Museum Rietberg Zürich, RAC 725
Han Coray Collection

Fig. 312
Artist of the Songye region
Power figure *nkishi*
Before 1939, wood, copper, iron, glass beads, textile, plant fibers, encrusted patina, bone, snake, and horn, 43 × 26 × 26 cm
Museum Rietberg Zürich, 2016.155
Gift of Barbara and Eberhard Fischer
Acquired by Hans Himmelheber

Figs. 313/314
Pictures of the inside of the two Songye power figures
2018, X-ray tomography
Paul Scherrer Institut, Villigen

Fig. 315
Artist of the Songye region
Power figure *nkishi*
Before 1939, wood, textile fibers, leather, plant fibers, snake, copper alloy, patina, horn, and plant seeds, 33.5 × 12 × 14 cm
Museum Rietberg Zürich, EFA 21
Gift of Barbara and Eberhard Fischer
Acquired by Hans Himmelheber

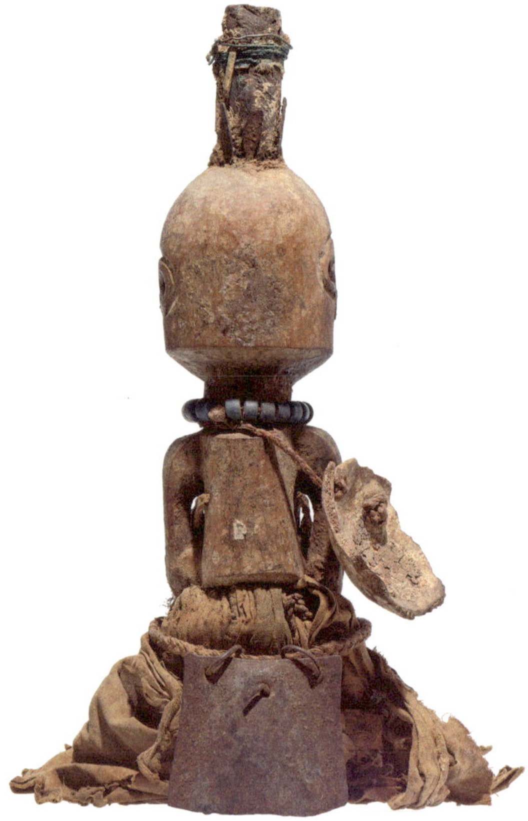

Fig. 312.1

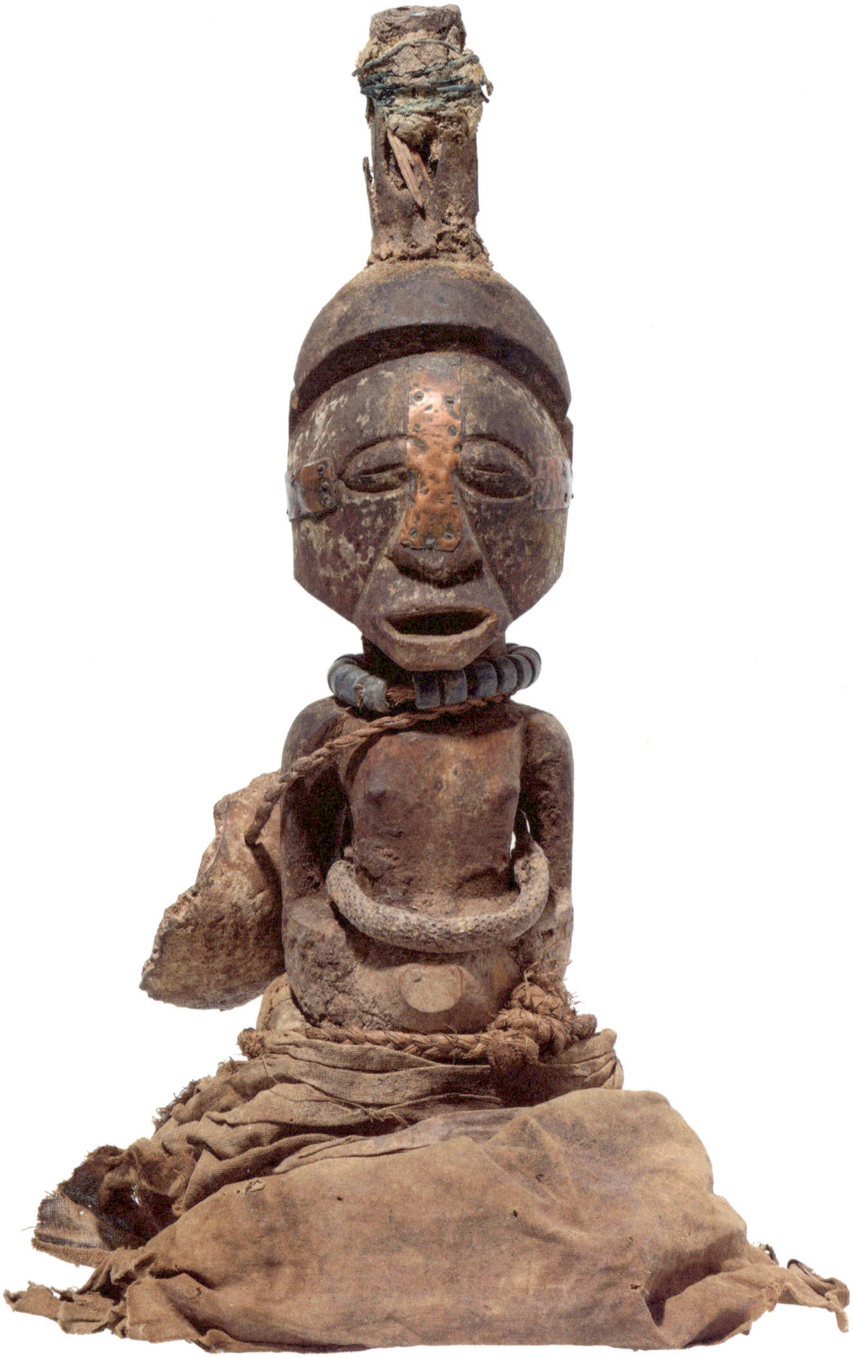

Fig. 312.2

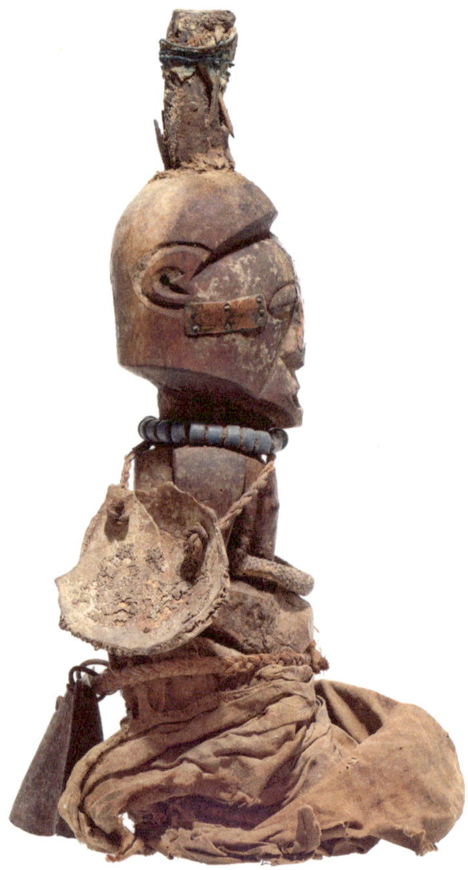

Fig. 312.3

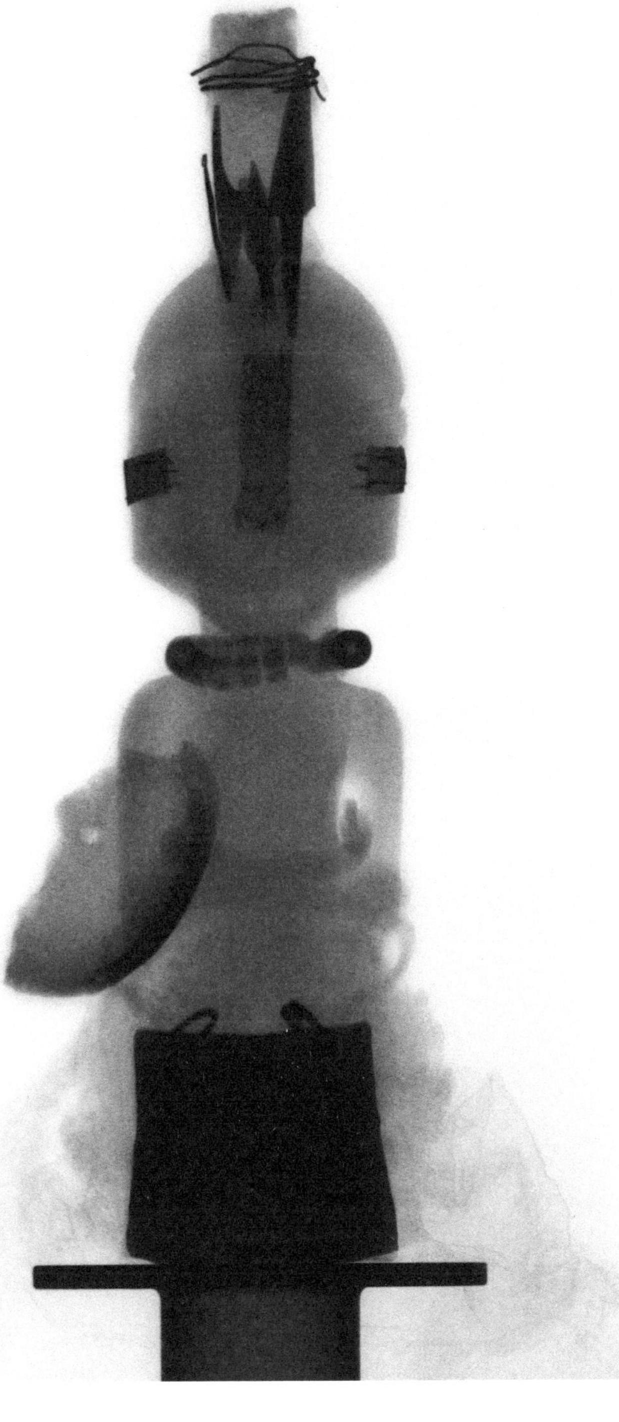
Fig. 313.1

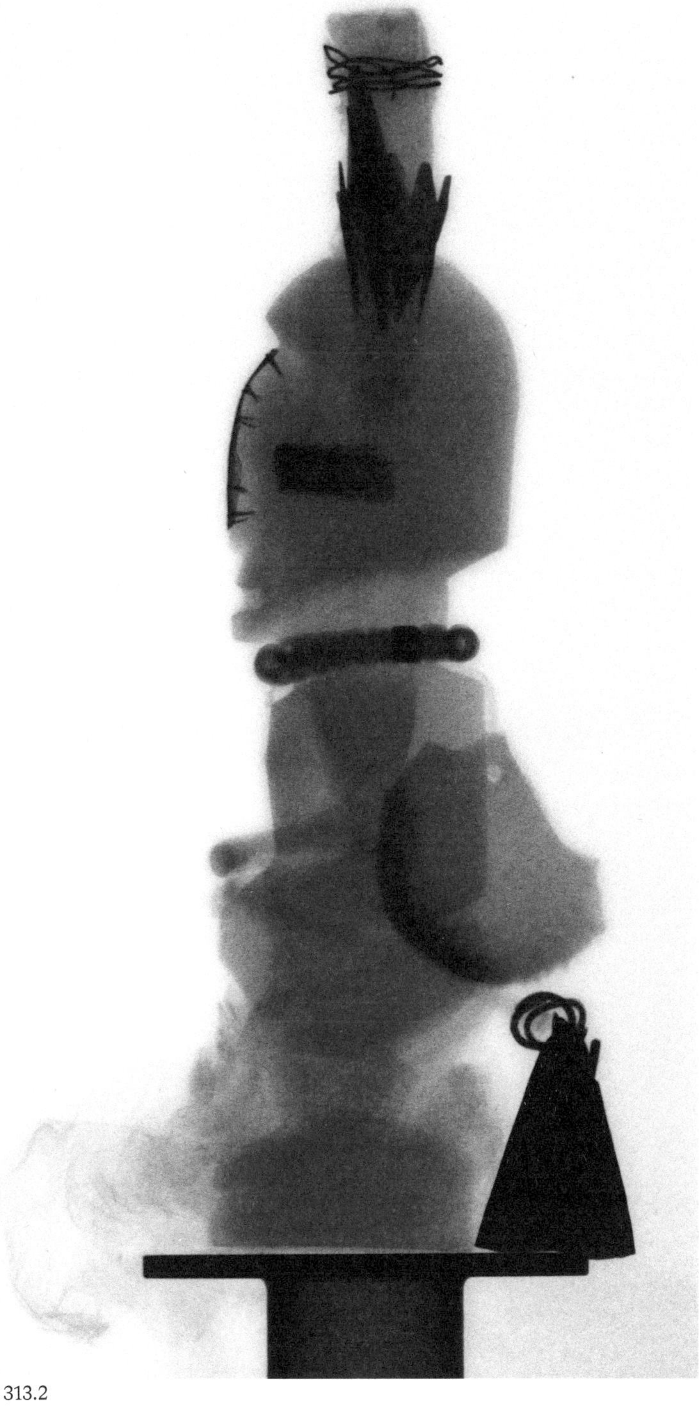
Fig. 313.2

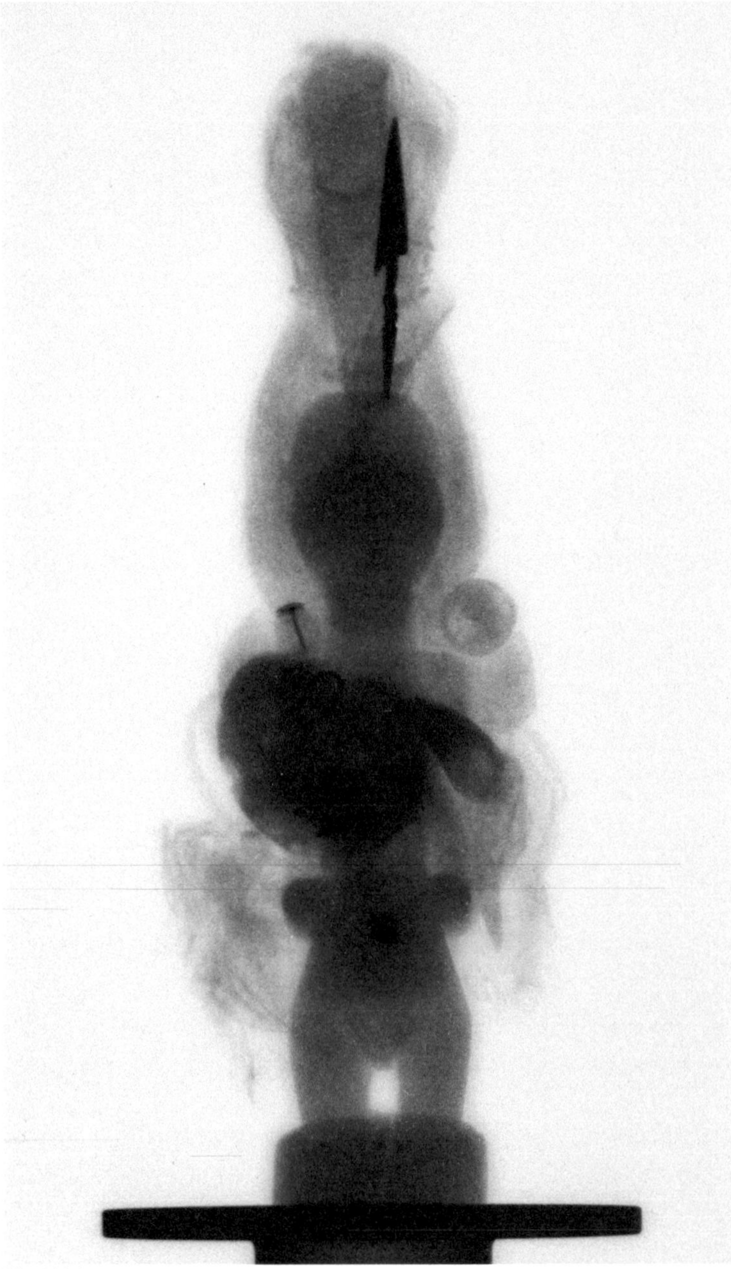

Fig. 314.1

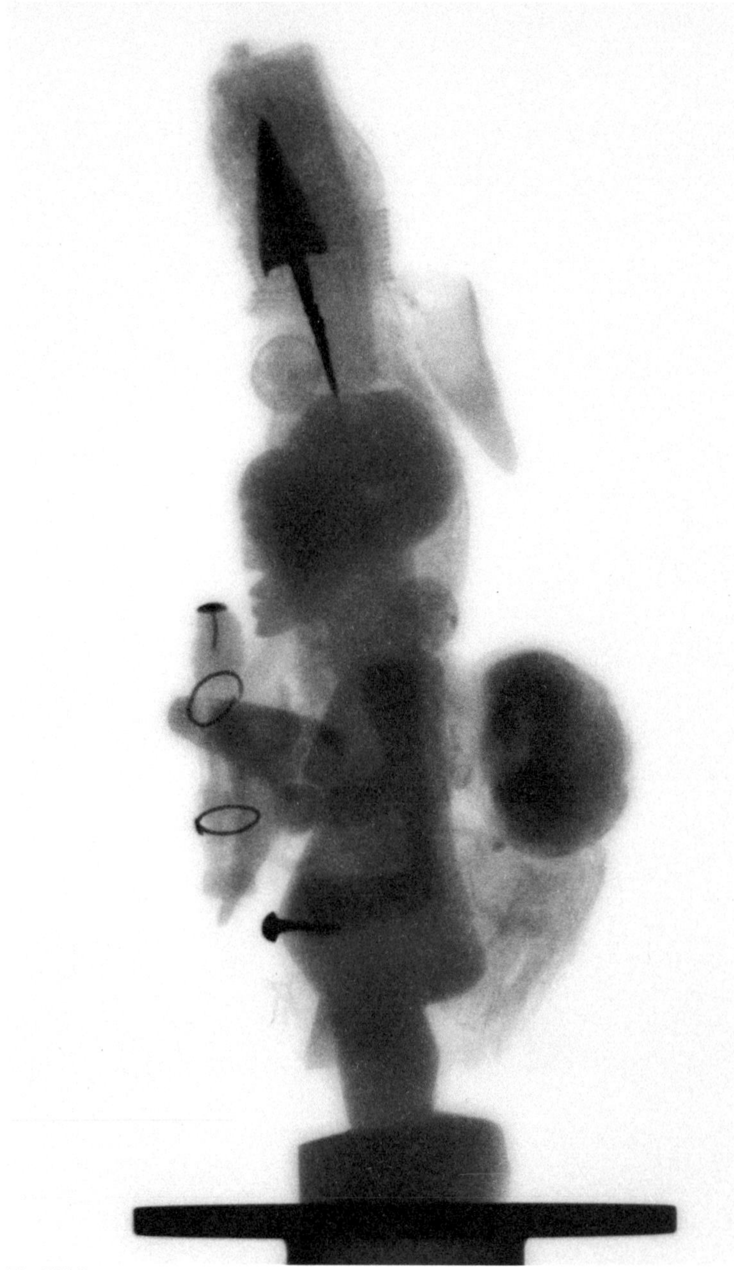

Fig. 314.2

Fig. 315

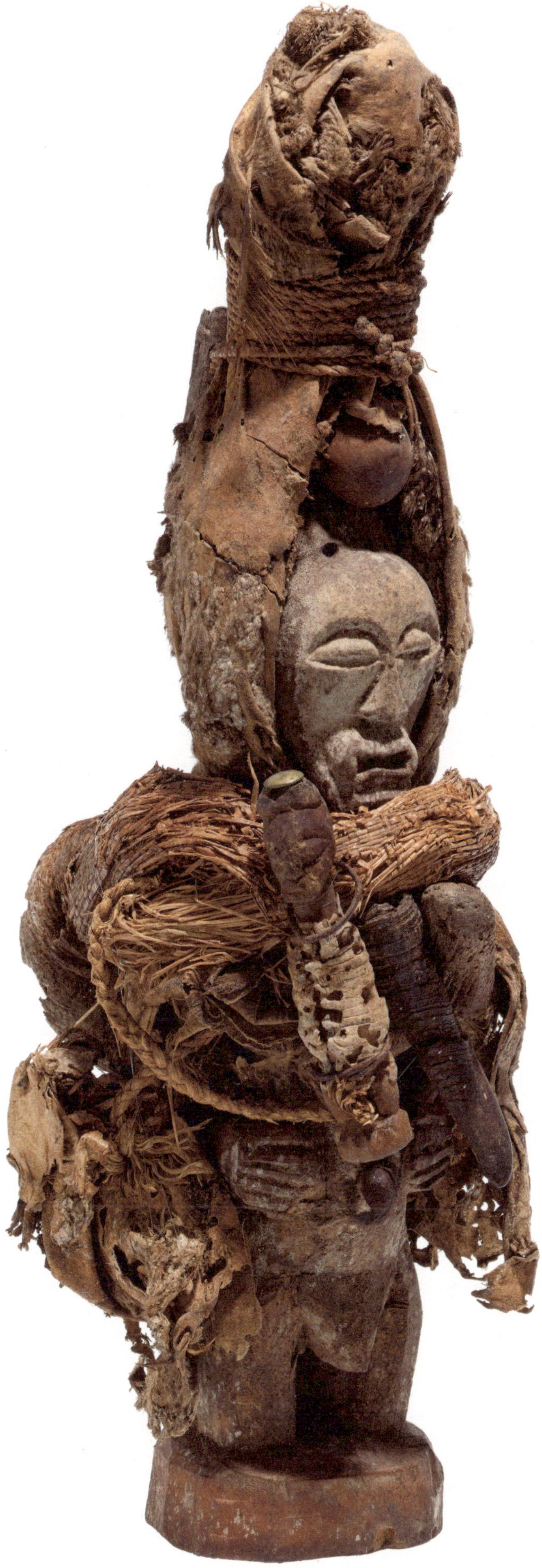

KASALA: THE SLAUGHTERHOUSE OF DREAMS OR THE FIRST HUMAN, BENDE'S ERROR

Sammy Baloji
with texts by Fiston Mwanza Mujila

"When men die, they go down in history. When statues die, they go down in art. This botany of death is what we call culture.

An object is dead when the living gaze that was cast on it has disappeared, and when we will have disappeared, our objects will go where we send those of the Negroes: to the museum."

Alain Resnais, Chris Marker, and Ghislain Cloquet
Excerpts from the film *Statues Also Die*.
1953, film Révue Présence Africaine
Tadé Cinéma Production

KASALA 78
the masquerade
or the rancid concerto
of the carnivores
of the carrion feeders
of the cutthroats
of the first rain
avid for blood and sperm
goes on forever

KASALA 22
dreams nipped in the bud?

KASALA 28
the masquerade
of the carnivores
blows up in our face
the masquerade
of the traffickers
incites financial collapse
in the sickly spiral
of this broken beautiful word

KASALA 11
before memory begins to play
its tricks on us
shall we spike the djudju juice
with some liquor
or name off the entire genealogy
gunned down?

KASALA 12
the diggers of Katekelayi
cut down in broad daylight
for having committed a single crime
mining the precious stone
in their own country
drift in the streets of Grand Kasai

KASALA 8
not even twenty suns suffice
the night continues its frantic farandole

KASALA 33
the Congo River is filled to the brim
with corpses and other seeming suicides

KASALA 81
should Bende, the first Human, have to stomach
the whole mess?
if he'd known what was to follow from his scheming
would he have had the nerve to take Mvidi Mukulu, the Elder
Spirit's measure?

KASALA 29
Patrice Emery Lumumba
Rossy Mukendi Tshimanga
Floribert Chebeya
Fidèle Bazana
Thérèse Kapangala
the list of so-called suicides
is as long as the Mississippi

KASALA 44
the night
still rings with the laughter
of the children of Katekelayi
their breath
their heaving chests
their seared voices
in a cerebral cacophony
blending with the uproar
of others who perished during the full moon

KASALA 15
because of one man: Bende
the universe went off the rails

KASALA 85
the mass graves of Maluku
what a lovely story!
holes stuffed with meat
an ancient stench

KASALA 64
Central Africa is a slaughterhouse

KASALA 86
in the mines of Shinkolobwe
the kids, with their wasted faces
bellies bloated from disease
dig, measles imprinted on their bodies
they stink of excrement and gasoline
their dirty, yellow, loose teeth
rip the carpet, scrape the floor
without fearing a collapse

KASALA 73
we had the sun in our mouths

KASALA 25
and Bende's curse sticks to our skin

KASALA 68
what was Bende thinking
when clumsily pulling the strings
that Mvidi would resume creation?
a second begetting
to satisfy the creature's swollen ego
a farce that dare not speak its name

KASALA 51
take this as a warning
by catching epilepsy
from these sclerotic nights
forsaken by the good God
weaned from mother's milk
affected by scurvy
infested with mosquitos
and other cockroaches
we've become a nomadic people
headless, spineless
scattered in the bush
party animals in Hong Kong
boozers in Moscow
club dancers in Malaga
night watchmen in Prague
errand boys in Casablanca
carwash guys in Brazza

KASALA 1
the trains still carry
kids and ore
in the backcountry of Katanga

KASALA 38
it all began in Nsanga-a-Lubangu
departure of my Kaku and his family
followed by other migrations
then, return to Katanga for the mines
then exodus in great haste
the skeleton balled up in pain

KASALA 67
the false copies
not unlike the cutthroats of the full moon
can think of nothing but a good pogrom
without that, and the masquerade that drips from it
they succumb to nervousness
smash everything that comes to hand

KASALA 4
the carnivores in Beni never lose their hard-on
they perform with passion
an excremental orgy

KASALA 63
Central Africa's favorite spot
its mass graves
those it never tires of digging
at this rate, it may well squash all its kiddies
half of them already can barely stay on their feet

KASALA 56
in whose cabinet of curiosities
do my Kaku's amulets gather dust?

KASALA 42
since we are there
Lumumba's teeth

KASALA 53
I, Mukalenga Mwanza
Mwanza Mujila Tshimankinda
Mwanza Nkongolo
Mwanza wa ba Tshibamba
Mwanza wa Mwanza
will part the ocean
for whoever brings me
arms and legs trussed
one of these dinner-jacketed spies

KASALA 14
who's got the goods
on Kalambayi's offspring?
who knows in what podunk town squat Mukendi's issue?
Kanjinga wa Mukendi
Mulumba wa Mukendi
Ntumba wa Mukendi
Kongolo wa Mukendi

KASALA 2

and to think that even death
no longer speeds one's return to Mwene-Ditu

KASALA 3

now this nourishing land
is no longer what she was
in the time of Tshimbalanga and Mujinga
Kabwanga and Mukengeshayi Alphonse
Mulanga Judith and Mbombo Antoinette
the land of Baloji Kabambi
is but a shadow of herself
a barren sepulcher
she is spitting blood
her belly barks with diamonds
the brambles thicken
the trees grow stunted
the rivers are gumming up
worse, the waters of Lake Munkamba
despite being our only lifeline
can no longer manage
to remove the stain
they augur trouble ahead
the waters of the lake

KASALA 52

in desperation
we fling open our mouths
our pleadings to Mvidi Mukulu
lose their bite in the sky
we implore Mvidi Mukulu
to stop driving us to suicide in our sleep
we implore Mvidi Mukulu
to stop punishing us with diarrhea
we implore Mvidi Mukulu
to stop unleashing
famine and her sisters-in-arms: nausea, madness, sleeping sickness, amnesia, schistosomiasis, typhoid, measles
Mvidi, stop reducing us to beggary
Mvidi, stop condemning us to exile
to vicarious wandering
to pointless transhumance
to death by asphyxiation
Mvidi, stop abandoning us
in the very middle of the unwinding
without food or pets
at the mercy of the cutthroats of the full moon
Mvidi Mukulu, we implore Mvidi Mukulu
to delay the lightning
to delay tuberculosis
to delay the heat wave
to delay the flood
to issue a permanent injunction against malaria

KASALA 45

here we come
and here we are, slobbering
having reached the chapter of despair
Pithecanthropi
the wretched of the earth
pot-bellied
rags on our backs
bodies wasted by
primordial exile
slumped over, bodies transmuted
from one region to another
as dictated by hunger
the mines
wars of liberation
and as always
scurvy

KASALA 71

Who's responsible?
us or Mvidi?
us or the Celestial Animals?
us or Bende?
we were the first
to usher in the devil-may-care dance
we were the blacksmiths
of our own malediction
the assiduous artisans
of defection
now we are left to pick up the pieces
of a collective heresy
and incidentally an unneeded one
first, we called Mvidi
every name in the book
then we stopped praying
boycotting at the same time the kutshipulula rite
we weren't exactly heading down a good path
we had scorned the Elders
on the samc impulse
we hammered down
what Kaku, our great-grandfathers, had built up
by the sweat of their brow
as if that was not enough
we lost all control
we danced stark naked
we pounded the pavement
we uttered sarcasm, miasma, invective
we flaunted ill-gotten opulence
in the midst of uncontrolled chaos
on every corner
stunned by bottles of djudju juice
and potations of the same ilk
we abandoned the homeland
to its own pathetic fate
exile in Saint Louis
itinerancy in Moscow
exodus to Baltimore
banishment to Prague
just like Mansemba, thirty years before

KASALA 40
while we wait for Mvidi
to feel like redeeming us
to suspend the lightning and the fire
to slow down the fury of the Bakishi
what remains for us is to try and force Mvidi's hand
to supplicate Mvidi
to implore Mvidi
to extricate us
from this hell
what remains is to haggle with the Lesser Spirits
those who have kept company with Mvidi
from a time before the Stone Age

KASALA 31
the years have pulverized memory
they've turned it into laughable dust
who remembers Mujinga wa Tshimankinda?
Tshisungu Mutamba
or even Lwamba François
son of the late lamented Lwambo and Ntumba Bernadette
Lwamba the giant
Lwamba the caterpillar-eater
Lwamba, with hands hardened by the pickaxe
Lwamba, lighter on his feet than a gazelle
Lwamba, burlier than a rhinoceros at the watering hole
Lwambo, he of the hoarse voice
Lwamba, the first to leave Mbuji-Mayi
("goat-water" or "water-goat")
climbing onto the first locomotive
in search of an umpteenth chore
in the slag heaps of Katanga
at the acme of his eighteen years
Lwamba who roamed throughout the Colony
Lwamba who stayed two months in Stanleyville
Lwamba who called the shots in Banningville
Lwamba and his endless trips to Thysville
Lwamba the pilgrim
Lwamba the explorer
Lwamba the mapper of the backcountry
Lwamba and his restless feet that never got a cramp
Lwamba who sent the whole world packing
Lwamba who pushed the logic to its very end
Lwamba who pilloried the holy rollers, gigolos and their
nephews
Lwamba who danced the rumba in the bistros of Leopoldville
Lwambo who toiled for the first whites in the country
Lwamba, valet for the Italians
Lwamba, driver for the Belgians
Lwamba, gardener for the Portuguese
Lwambo and his Greek friends
Lwambo who whispered secrets in the ears of the Americans
Lwamba who knew the colonial prison
and the splendid jails of the Second Republic
Lwamba, yes, still him
Lwamba and his dynasty
Lwamba, three times shambuyi
first pregnancy:
Lwamba and his wife give birth to two girls
second pregnancy:
Lwamba and his wife
give birth to a girl and a boy
third pregnancy:
Lwamba and his wife
give birth to a girl and a boy
Lwamba, the male with 67 grandchildren
Lwamba, the man who lived into his one hundred and
twenty-second year
Lwamba the patriarch
Lwamba and his bluffing
Lwamba and his head-scratching gossip
Lwamba, who read and wrote in the language of the Europeans
supreme euphoria when Lwamba got his first bike
Lwamba, still him, posing with his first car

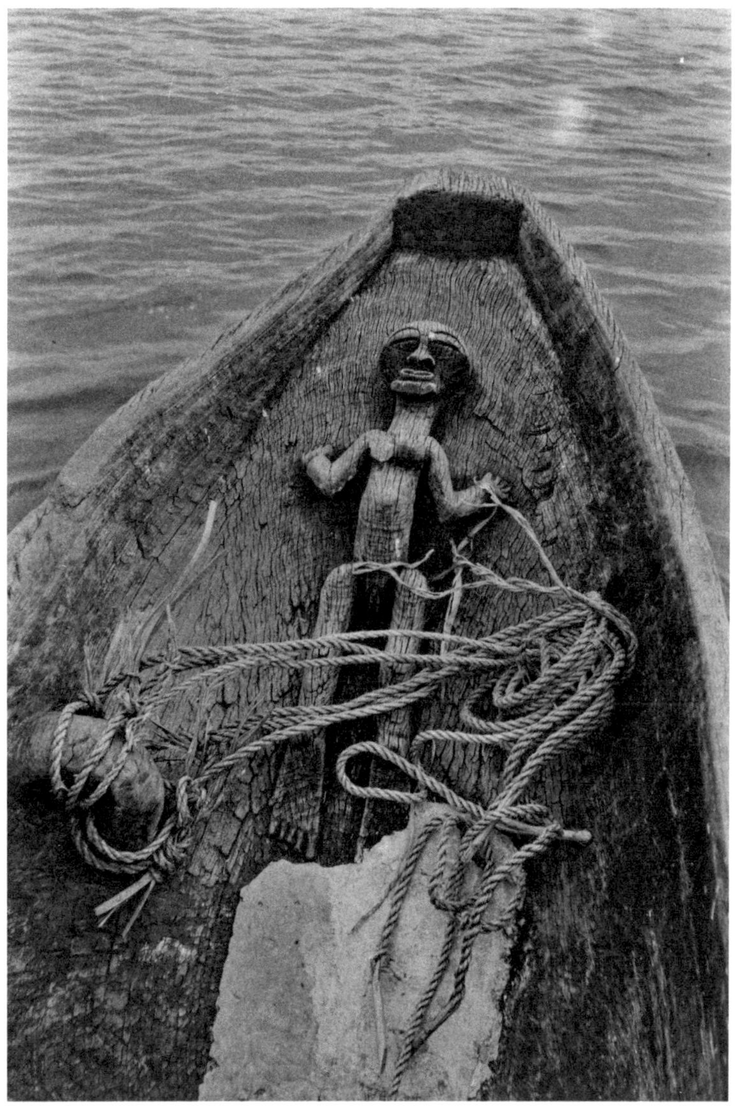
Fig. 316

Fig. 316
Hans Himmelheber
Figure on the bow of a dugout
Songye region, 1939, b/w negative
Museum Rietberg Zürich, FHH 188-25

Fig. 317
Sammy Baloji
Mine à ciel ouvert noyée de Banfora. Lieu d'extraction artisanale
2010, ink, paper
Sammy Baloji

Fig. 318
Hans Himmelheber
Congo river at Léopoldville (Kinshasa)
Kinshasa, 1938, b/w negative
Museum Rietberg Zürich, FHH 160-5

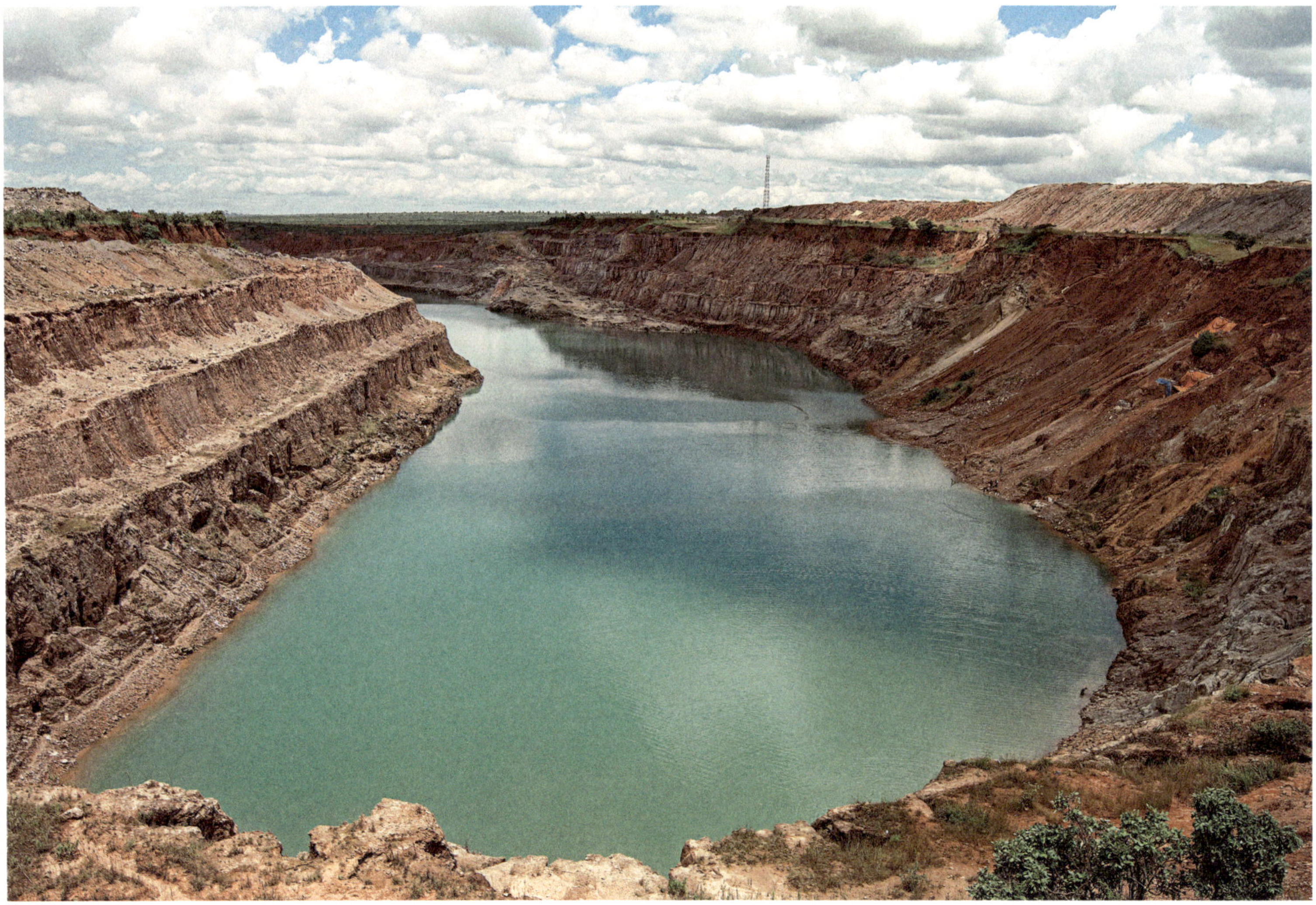
Fig. 317

KASALA 36
who remembers
Mulowayi wa Kalala François
The uncle of many nicknames
the Ancestor
the Golden Voice
the Chief
the Warrior
solitude, when you lead us by the nose
in the time of Mulowayi wa Kalala
a descendant of the Tshisumpa line
exile was but a dim lure
the carats accumulated
day followed night
and night winked out before the sun
we possessed a homeland
where we sought our way
without pissing our pants

KASALA 10
Mumbu
Dilenge
Mululu
Kapolowayi
Muabi
Tree-Spirits
once invoked by Tshimbalanga
the second youngest of my uncles
give us the strength to subdue the sun

KASALA 79
Bende's nerves cracked
and here we are floundering in the mud

KASALA 65
the isolate
Kongolo Kaa Mukanda who thought he was pulling the rug
out from under Mvidi Mukulu's feet
came to at the bottom of a ravine
metamorphosed into a snake, among reptiles
a pathetic destiny
for one who once was a Great Lord

KASALA 83
were it not for Bende's embezzlements
we might still be in High Heaven
cozier than ever

KASALA 74
the tragedy of Kongolo Kaa Mukanda is to have been
from his apparition neither Man, nor Thing, nor Animal
is that reason enough to envy other creatures
to lobby until hoarse for an artificial beauty?
what happens next, we well know

KASALA 17
country of surfeit and excess: diamonds, oil, forests, river,
copper, mass graves

KASALA 87
let's leave the creature
to his homely ruminations

KASALA 88
don't think we'll rush for the exits
go wake up Kabambi Baloji Mutambayi Mwena Shabanza,
Mukua Mulumba too,
just because Bende shot himself in the neck
or went on a bender for the umpteenth time
in the same damn week

KASALA 89
the city has the feel of a public flophouse
kids high on diamba and other hallucinogens
skid through the streets, fast and loose
cardboard boxes do duty as mattresses
the kids get carried away, wear the same plague-stricken faces
as their cousins digging in the mines of Shinkolobwe

KASALA 90
biso nionso tosa bikelemu ya Nzambe
he who makes a big show of disbelief has but to craft his own
world
with its whores, its rivers, its pampas, its filth, its pimps, its
mass graves, its midlife crises, its latrines, its shit show and
all the rest

KASALA 92
a poor bedfellow?
Bende gulps down his lutuku moonshine
without feeling the slightest buzz
The zealot burps and struts about in the crowd
he forgets he's just a puppet
a shit, nothing more

KASALA 93
we won't visit the King of the Animals
under penalty of peopling his pantry

KASALA 95
you could give Bende centuries to repent
the result wouldn't change
give or take a few utterances
the same legendary shenanigans and the birth of brats

KASALA 69
every fabrication is a work of consolation
not excluding the creation of Man
overcome by pity, Mvidi created the Spirits (hermaphrodites),
the Animals, Men and Things
what happens next we well know
a bloodbath

KASALA 91
mass graves still have a bright future
the jesters doze with their Kalashnikovs under the pillow

KASALA 106
it would be too good to be true
if their too subtle scheming ended in defenestration
a leech, can you picture it eating pizza?
even in your dreams!
it's like mistaking the ocean for the Kalahari

KASALA 5
one struggles to unhear
the stinging cries of the Katekelayi diggers

KASALA 76
Mulunda wanyi
your children are still digging mass graves
lash us with the flood or stomach sickness
they've been digging for twenty years

KASALA 39
Ntete
Tshiame
Mukulumpe
Ancestors of the dawn of dawns
if you showed yourselves to us
we might get out of the Zairean wood

KASALA 82
the longest cemetery stretches
between Lubumbashi and Mbuji-Mayi
thousands of bodies crammed along the tracks
a corridor of ethnic cleansing
in every station, the trains stopped
to unload the corpses
and if you're looking for the graves
(if still visible to the naked eye)
of Kabeya Jean, Mujinga Marie or even Kaniki Alphonse
take the train from Mwene-Ditu or Katanga

KASALA 54
the Bakishi watch over me
rejoice in my offhandedness
almost lose hope
uncork the epilepsy and syphilis
come to their senses at the last second

KASALA 49
winter is fast approaching
and my Kaku is missing

KASALA 58
in his rocking chair
Kaku, my great-grandfather
looks even older
as ancient as the river
as old as the Lubumbashi-Mwene-Ditu railroad

KASALA 59
Kaku can no longer move his legs
only his jaws work
he repeats forgotten names
one after the other

KASALA 60
Mvidi Mukulu wa Mukulumpe
Mvidi Mukulu wa Bende
Mvidi Mukulu wa Tshiana Tshikulu
Mvidi Mukulu wa Tshilele
Mvidi Mukulu wa Tshiame
your creature that I am
has a toad spinning in his head
credit his deep dives in the djudju juice.

KASALA 84
the Bakishi are still upset
about my body pitted with smallpox
is Bende to blame?

KASALA 41
the genealogy of Mwanza Nkongolo
is unused to a scarcity of masks
is Bende to blame?

KASALA 61
the kids gasp for breath in a copper mine
they look like zombies
is Bende to blame?

KASALA 94
ba meli, ba tondi, ba buaki ngunda
it's Aunt Konde who should kick herself
the creatures cut the cord
is Bende to blame?

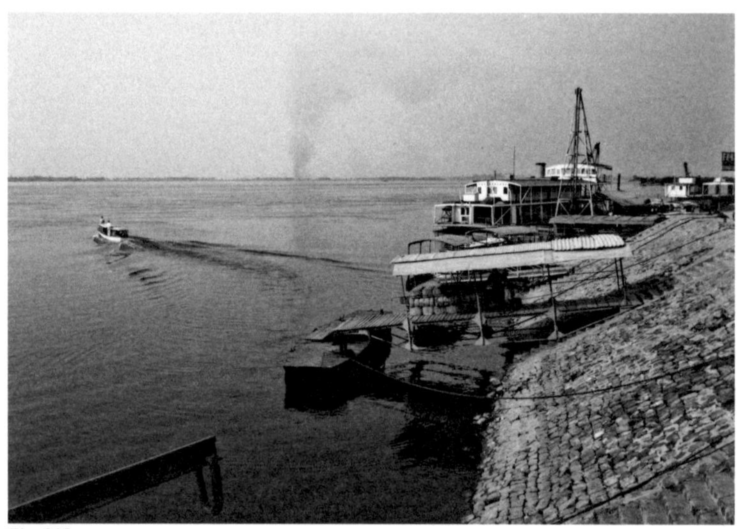
Fig. 318

KASALA 18
Kaku and me, we lie about
drink nothing the entire evening
not a sip of beer, no djudju juice, not even Chibuku
the masks, the masks
is Bende to blame?

KASALA 46
Kaku comments on the events
gets riled up
even if age keeps him from brawling
he curses the cutthroats down to the sixth generation
gives in to collective reproach
is Bende to blame?

KASALA 34
every time he gets a cavity
Kaku brings up Lumumba's teeth
is Bende to blame?

KASALA 55
the diggers of Katekelayi await...
a resurrection, their own
is Bende to blame?

KASALA 57
the cutthroats of the full moon are busy
gulp down the last chalice of sperm
before rushing out for fresh meat
is Bende to blame?

KASALA 47
from Nsanga-a-Lubangu
we trot behind a fictional country
is Bende to blame?

KASALA 70
mua Ntumba mourns her twins,
Mbuyi and Kabanga, shouting themselves hoarse in the cells
of the ANR
is Bende to blame?

KASALA 26
Mwanza wa Mwanza
is waiting for his Kaku's bracelets
is Bende to blame?

KASALA 100
from wanting democracy too much
we end up with a country that pisses blood

KASALA 98
kids barely weaned from their mothers' milk
toil in the hole
they stink of shit
is Bende to blame?

KASALA 96
on top of the trains bound for Mbuji Mayi
the kids are rolling with laughter
once past the slag heap, will they track down some ancestor
or invoke Mvidi to Kaku, to the Spirit of their
Great-Grandmothers
to release them from the curse
once and for all?

KASALA 101
kids, bellies full of roundworms
dig by hand
in the quarries of Fungurumu
is Bende to blame?

KASALA 97
the masks that cross the ocean
are valued at less than trinkets
is Bende to blame?

KASALA 99
the kids continue to go down the mine
they cry out to the God of Foremother Tshiame
to spare them from a collapse
from yet more measles
or the sleeping sickness

KASALA 107
the child miners
have a beaut of a hangover
they all shave their heads
in imitation of army recruits
sport second-hand sneaks
to cut a fine figure in the mines of Dimbelenge
is Bende to blame?

KASALA 108
even with a gun to our heads
we won't go to Prague, Moscow or Kingakati
but to Tshikapa
to perform the Tshishimbi dance
to make offerings of "nzolo" to the ancestors

KASALA 106
in this country where the intelligence services are run better
than hospitals, whorehouses, and nursery schools
the kids who go down the hole
still foster dreams
to find enough stones to launch themselves out of the mud

KASALA 102
the kids, suffering, what's more, from smallpox
or is it a lingering trace of tuberculosis?

KASALA 23
without Mvidi Mukulu wa Mukulumpe
we'd still be mired in shit
body of grimy mornings
mouth filled with grass

KASALA 7
they won't defenestrate themselves as quick as all that
no offense to the false copies

KASALA 32
am I so much to be pitied
to be pushed to suicide in the river?
just me or my whole line
Kaku's, that is, my great-grandfather?

KASALA 77
and if we traded my Kaku's teeth
for Lumumba's?

KASALA 37
I won't line up
for a bowl of bloodstained soup
if I sell out my genealogy
let Mvidi Mukulu wa Mwanza strike me with venereal disease
a heart attack
and let the Bakishi unstep my erection
for the next two hundred years and forty rainy seasons

KASALA 9
you may impound my hand
if it means the sun
and also the moon
will rise in my mouth
this afternoon
no offense to Bende

KASALA 16
I refuse to sit down
with the cutthroats
of the first rain
they reek of fresh blood

KASALA 19
I'd pick exile
over the cabal
no offense to Bende

KASALA 20
I refuse with my belly
I refuse with my balls
I refuse with my protozoan mug
choose madness over
dishonoring my Kaku
no offense to Bende

KASALA 43
I die, my belly cut open
oh death!, the good death, what is it?
you get inured to the machete
the cutthroats, the cutthroats
they have a yen for the pubic mound

KASALA 30
theater of the absurd?
the cutthroats of the full moon
speak of Peace and Love for one's neighbor
they listen to Brahms and Mozart
but still despair over the lack of new victims

KASALA 35
everlasting nostalgia for Tshimbalanga
the second youngest of my uncles
he left to get his share of diamonds
in the mines of Dimbelenge
is Bende to blame?

KASALA 13
we dispersed
according to the railway's whims
is Bende to blame?

KASALA 96
what are these jokes about a pimp past his prime
is Bende to blame?

KASALA 6
insane prices
masks sold at auction
the crowd presses in
snaps them up without batting an eye
is Bende to blame?

KASALA 21
a great country was ours
vast, green, lush, gigantic
stretching from Kinshasa to Katanga
from Luebo to Gbadolite
is Bende to blame?

KASALA 72
Kongolo Kaa Mukanda wonders:
does Mvidi Mukulu regret
having deposed me
extorted forever my insignia of a Great Lord
and dumped me like a criminal on Earth?

KASALA 48
years after the carnage
the Katekelayi diggers ranted
in the nameless tongue of the dead

KASALA 86
what we do best
mass graves
shall we blame it on Bende?
has anyone actually seen him digging for us?
is it Bende who rapes the Kivu women and girls?
is it the black hand of Bende at work in the Kamuina Nsapu massacre?
is it Bende meddling in the merry carnage of the Bundu dia Kongo followers?
the bodies in the river, still Bende?

KASALA 27
the assegais, bracelets, masks, statuettes, drums, rugs, spears, and other ornaments of Mwanza wa Mwanza still loiter in the museums
is Bende to blame?

KASALA 24
names are a roving museum
when I whistle my kasala
I cease to be alone
I am with my mother and father
my aunts and Uncle Tshimbalanga, the Congo River and the Celestial Animals, the railroads and mountains, the sun and the rain, Munkamba Lake and the Lubilanji River, my Kaku always at my side, my Kaku and his rocking chair, my Kaku and his long beard, my bespectacled Kaku

KASALA 62
this wild night
the urge to do something foolish rises in my chest
I'll go dance the rumba and the tshikuna-fou
until I crush my spine
my Kaku would truly deserve that
an exhilarating thwocking of the hips in honor of mukishi

KASALA 50
I summon 347 horses
I summon the earthquake
I summon the solar eclipse
I summon the flood
I summon the stars
I summon 560 luxury rides
I summon 345 rhinoceroses
I summon 67 tigers
I summon the Mississippi, I summon the Maningoza, I summon the Maroni, I summon the Brahmaputra, I summon the Okavango and the Jordan and the Niger and the Saloum and the Essequibo and the Euphrates and the Mackenzie and the Rio Grande and the Kamchatka and the Yangtze and the Santa Cruz and the Suriname and the Amu Darya and the Ganges and the Congo and the Indus and the Charente and the Dnieper and the Dordogne and the Irrawaddy and the Guadalquivir and the Meuse and the Volga and the Mokau and the Sepik and the Tiber and the Yser and the Lena and Lake Tanganyika and the Orinoco and the Mekong and Lake Tshangalele and the Danube, and the Amazon and the Rhine and the Limmat and the Nile and the Limpopo and the Zambezi
to celebrate a Woman
my mother, Ma'Nanga

Translated by J. Bret Maney

Glossary

KASALA: Praise song or poem for oneself, a relative, a dignitary, or even a fictional character.

MVIDI MUKULU: Literally meaning Elder Spirit, or Supreme Spirit, a reference to God. A title often combined with other terms in order to underline one of God's characteristics. In this way, many names arise, such as Mvidi Mukulu wa Tshiame, Mvidi Mukulu wa Tshiana Tshikulu, Mvidi Mukulu wa Tshimpanga…

NSANGA-A-LUBANGU: The mythical place from which the Luba people dispersed. They emigrated to the Kasai region and established themselves in Katanga. Also considered as the place of origin of the Luba people of Katanga and Kasai.

BAKISHI, in the singular MUKISHI: The spirits or manes of the departed. Deceased relatives acquire this title and remain reference points for the living.

BENDE: A highly polysemous word. 1. It is used to denote belonging when it is not used as a proper noun. For example, "Mbuji wa bende," someone else's goat. 2. It is a name of God since Bende holds a privileged place in the divine lineage and Maweja Nangila, God, is also invoked with the names of illustrious persons. 3. The word designates the ancestor of all Human Beings. 4. It applies to the human ancestor brought into creation in the form of the twin, or couple, formed by one man and one woman. 5. In genealogies, Bende is also identified as one of the founders of the clan or bakole. 6. Bende appears in legends as the equal or double of God. Bende orchestrates the world with Maweja Nangila but also contradicts his authority (Van Caeneghem, *La Notion de Dieu chez les BaLuba du Kasaï*, 1956).

KONGOLO KAA MUKANDA: "The Lawgiver" or "The Spiral of the Law." Brother of the rain, a being who is half-man, half-animal, he reproached Maweja Nangila due to his imperfect physiognomy. He went further by trying to trick Maweja Nangila, which led to his "defenestration" from the High Heavens (Fourche and Morlighem 2002).

PERFORMANCE AND INITIATION

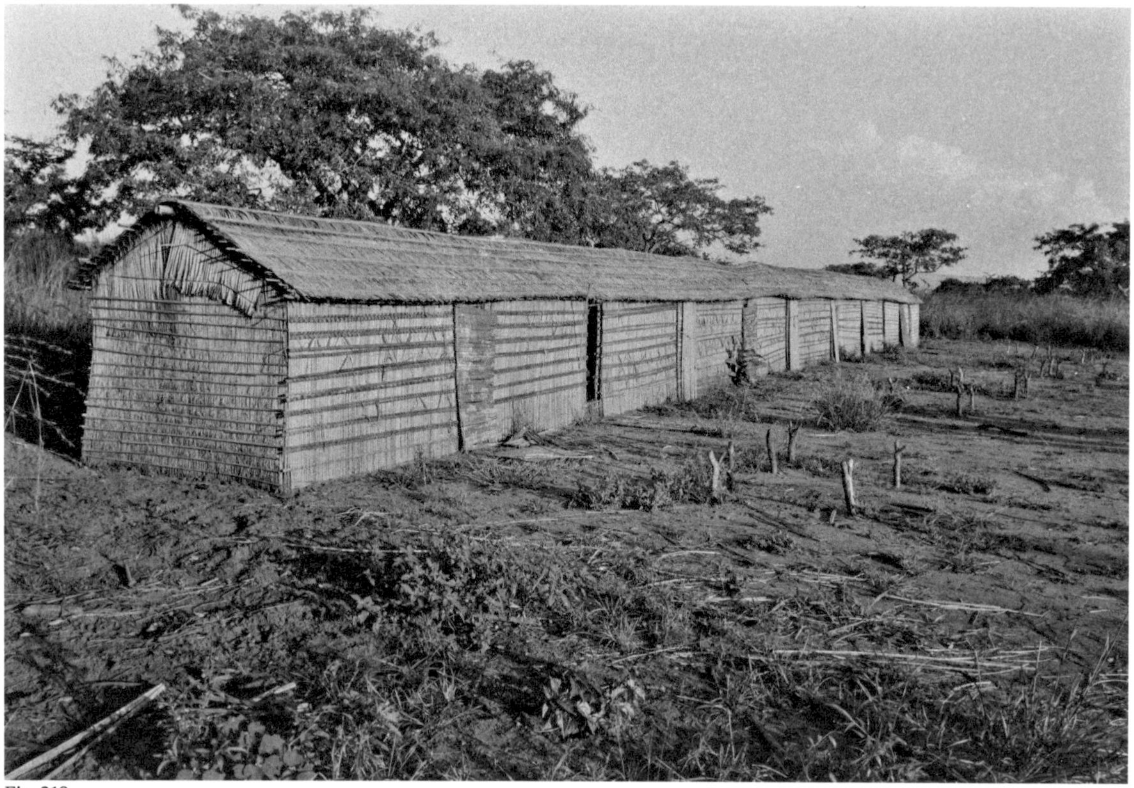
Fig. 319

Fig. 319
Hans Himmelheber
Long house in a *mukanda* camp
Pende region, May 24, 1939, b/w negative, Museum Rietberg Zürich, FHH 190-28

PHOTO ESSAY: THE ROLE OF MASKS IN THE EASTERN PENDE *MUKANDA*

Z. S. Strother,
Nzomba Dugo Kakema

In memory of Chief Kombo-Kiboto (Mukanzo Mbelenge) (d. 1987) and Mukishi Loange (d. 1996), who sent the authors to *mukanda* to learn about Pende art and culture (*ima jia Apende*).

In 1939, while searching for sculpture on the southern savanna of what is now the Democratic Republic of the Congo (DRC), Hans Himmelheber stumbled upon *mukanda* camps among Yaka, Chokwe, and eastern Pende peoples. The *mukanda* is or was many things, including a men's fraternity, a puberty initiation, and, a woods-and-crafts camp. The *mukanda* turns boys into men and in the past, the protracted initiation created tight bonds of solidarity within a generation so that its members developed a lifetime *esprit de corps*, aiding one another in conflicts but also in social tasks, such as building houses or laying new fields. As an institution, the *mukanda* probably began in central Angola but spread north in the seventeenth century into what is today the DRC. It survived during the colonial occupation as a rite of passage, although it sometimes faced fierce opposition from the Roman Catholic Church by clerics who regarded it as "immoral." In particular, they disapproved of the songs used for sex-education and of what they called "stealing," i.e., confiscating domestic animals to feed the boys during their seclusion. Despite the criticism, the *mukanda* continued to expand. For example, during the 1930s, Lunda enclaves adopted it from Chokwe. Perhaps holding onto the *mukanda* was a form of resistance during the colonial period. It is striking that many communities only dropped the initiation after independence in 1960. The regime of Mobutu Sese Seko (1971–1997) left it to chiefs to decide about the value of the *mukanda* as long as the initiation did not encroach on the school calendar. It seems that the *mukanda* was disrupted in Angola following protracted unrest and civil war; however, waves of refugees introduced it or reinforced its importance in Zambia.

The *mukanda* is an institution central to the transmission of social values; however, what this essay will show is that it is structured from beginning to end through the use of masks and it is the charisma of the masks that helps it survive. The institution remains strong among the eastern Pende and the text is based on exhaustive documentation by Z. S. Strother of two different initiations in 1987 and 1988 (funded by Fulbright Predoctoral Grants issued by the US Information Agency). Participating in a government-sponsored exchange program allowed Strother to secure the necessary research clearance (including the right to take photographs) in order to prepare an art history dissertation. It was one thing to work among the central Pende in Bandundu Province, but quite another to study the arts of the eastern Pende who lived in the Western Kasai in a highly regulated "mining zone." In the late 1980s, during the repressive regime of Mobutu Sese Seko, there was a window when research was tolerated—although closely monitored—on topics of cultural "authenticity." That window closed in the 1990s and Strother was unable to make a follow-up visit until 2007. Fresh interviews were conducted by Nzomba Dugo Kakema in 2018/19, which bring the research up to date.

Although an academic treatise will follow one day, this photo essay is an opportunity to share with readers the emotional intensity of *mukanda*. With the addition of a little context, they will be able to see the little smile playing on the face of the blacksmith as he works, the boys cringing in fear at what they are asked to do, the tenderness of a mother showing love to her son in a stolen moment, the precision and discipline of initiates marching to the beat, and a man laughing to hear a young man belt out a sassy song in public. It is not a matter of going through the motions or checking rituals off of a master list. The *mukanda* is absorbing and elicits the entire gamut of emotions from joy to loss to fear to pride of accomplishment. Nzomba Dugo Kakema wrote that his interviewees felt nostalgia in recalling the *mukanda*, and we did, too, in reliving it.

According to the conventions of photo essays, the text is written for the most part in the historical present unless it is important to underscore a break or adaption of practice. (For more on the photographs, see the "Photo Research Note" at the end of the essay.)

[Fig. 319] Sponsoring a *mukanda* was one of the prerogatives most jealously guarded by paramount chiefs. Himmelheber photographed one of the long houses built to house the initiates (*tundanda*), which he estimated to be twenty meters long. Men initiated in the 1930s recalled how boys would sleep together in rooms organized according to their home villages. Judging from the number of doors visible, the house illustrated probably sheltered boys from eight to nine villages. Some estimate that by the end, eighty to two hundred young men might be brought together. The *mukanda* now exists more as a rite of passage than as a fraternity, a social institution providing men with assistance throughout their lives. Furthermore, the initiation, which once lasted for many months, has been abridged to accommodate the school vacation period. Its length now ranges from six to ten weeks.

Ideally, initiations should be launched by the boys themselves. The stated goal of *mukanda* is to turn spoiled children, boys who have never been spanked, into a community of men. In the village, the experience is made to sound as disagreeable as possible. There are bogus claims that the initiates shiver from cold because they have no fire at night, that they sleep without shelter, that they eat raw food, etc. On the other hand, it is true that every small infringement of discipline will be punished by the blow of a whip. Therefore, it is an important point that the boys themselves ask for *mukanda* because it means that they are old enough and brave enough to face their childhood terrors in order to gain the status of adulthood.

[Fig. 320] A couple of boys go to the chief's house and begin to sing the infectious tune: "Fathers, why are you silent? Let *ngolo* arrive." *Ngolo* is the symbol of the initiation. The word itself

Fig. 320
Artist of the central Pende region
***Ngolo* mask with horns**
Before 1939, wood, plant fibers, pigments, 67 × 29 × 36 cm
Museum Rietberg Zürich, HH 19
Gift of Barbara and Eberhard Fischer
Acquired by Hans Himmelheber

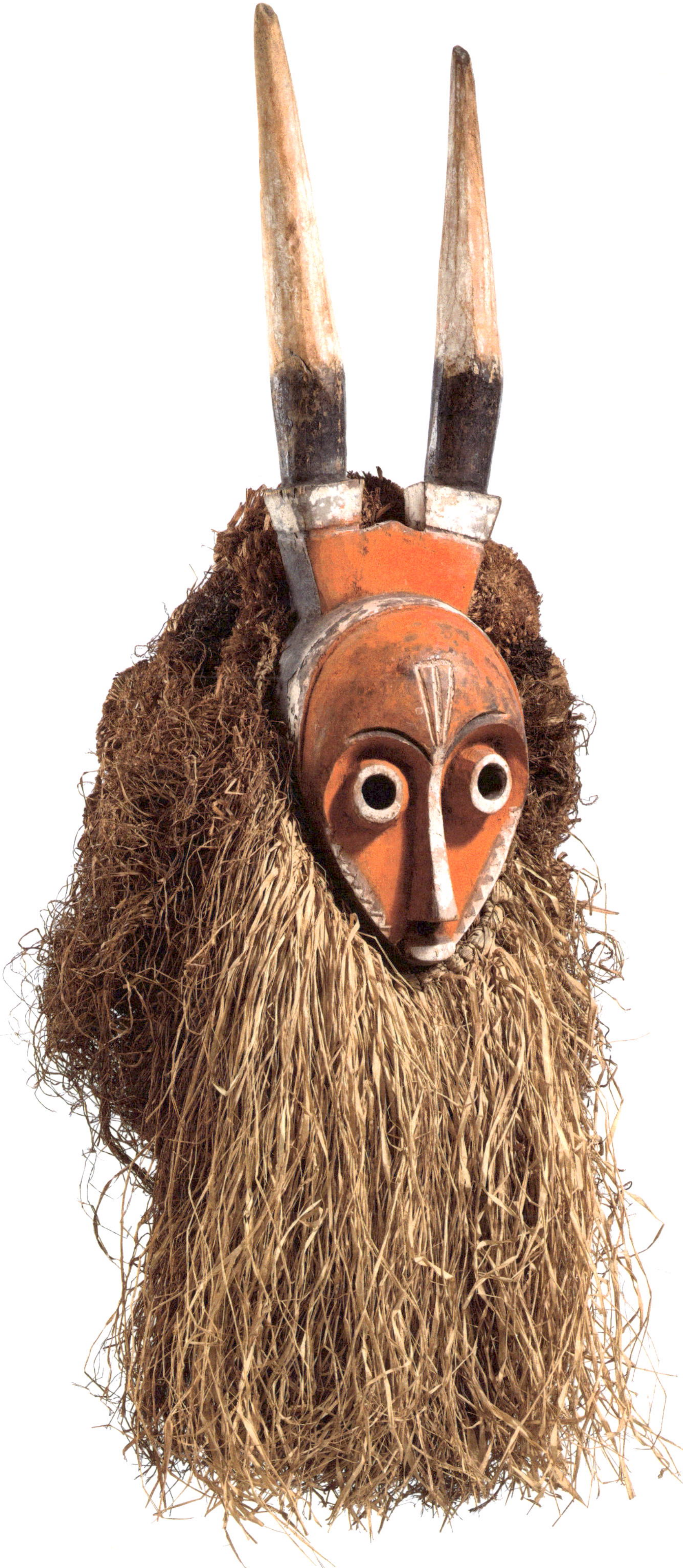

Fig. 320

signifies "strength" and "health" and is used as the name for any generic horned mask with white protruding eyes. If enough boys join the call, the chief will be obliged to respond. A given community will hold an initiation approximately every ten to twelve years, but the camps are staggered around the region. In 1987, there were at least twenty-something camps active among the eastern Pende. In 1988, there were another couple of dozen. In 1989, there were more. It takes five to six years for an entire generation to be initiated.

[Fig. 321] When the community agrees, the first thing that the chief must do is commission a series of masks. Chief Kende Kakele (Katshivi Koji) hired blacksmith Ngoma Kandaku Mbuya, who worked around the clock for six days to carve three masks so that the process could get started. Behind, the chief keeps a watchful eye on his progress. There is a chicken dinner in the pot to encourage him in his work.

[Fig. 322] On the tenth day, the first major rite of *mukanda* began. The nine boys cannot believe their eyes; the smallest cringes in fear. They see four masqueraders raising a cloud of dust, leaping and pirouetting. Boys who have run from masks all their lives are told to their horror that they must "touch the mask," i.e., run over and pull off the headpiece from one of the masqueraders, who is guarded by three others, all of them well-built young men much bigger than the boys who are, on average, twelve years old. And they all carry whips!

[Fig. 323] The chief points, "Go! Go! Grab that one!" But they huddle together, paralyzed.

[Fig. 324] Finally, Luya (who is fourteen years old) runs out and tries to pull off the headpiece from the target (who wears an overskirt of shiny green leaves). His courage inspires the other boys, who race out to help. However, Luya is just not big enough. One of the other masqueraders charges forward, whip raised to give him a terrific blow across the back, hard enough to raise a welt. Luya's father (Sh'a Lamba) can't stand it any longer. He races to his son's rescue and it is he who actually pulls off the headpiece while another father wrestles with the bodyguards.

It is strictly forbidden for the fathers to intervene, but they often do so because the young men running the camp can become overly enthusiastic about their new role in administering discipline. In fact, the fathers break the rules all the time and it is one of the means by which adolescents bond with their fathers. When things grow calmer, the boys who were more timid are obliged to pull a leaf from the costume of the target mask and to receive a symbolic blow on the back. In the end, the experience is designed to increase the boys' self-confidence because each of them has wrestled with his worst fear and emerged triumphant. As in martial arts training, the boys learn that they are tougher than they realized.

Boys will continue to join the camp up until the end. No matter when they arrive, each individual will have to undergo a personal ritual of "touching the mask" (what Westerners would call "unmasking") when he must pull off the headpiece or a piece of the costume off a masquerader and receive a small blow in punishment. Once a boy has done this, he must not leave the camp until he graduates. The parallel is made between the secrets of *mukanda* and the secrets of childbirth as men historically were not allowed to be present at a delivery.

Fig. 321
Z. S. Strother
Sculptor Ngoma Kandaku Mbuya carves a mask with such speed and assurance that his adze has blurred out of sight.
Mukanda of Chief Kende Kakele, Ndjindji, July 6, 1987
Z. S. Strother

Fig. 322
Z. S. Strother
"Touch the mask!" The opening ritual of the boys' initiation.
Mukanda of Chief Kende Kakele, Ndjindji, July 11, 1987
Z. S. Strother

Fig. 323
Z. S. Strother
"Go! Grab the one in the middle"
Mukanda of Chief Kende Kakele, Ndjindji, July 11, 1987
Z. S. Strother

Fig. 324
Z. S. Strother
A father runs to the aid of his son.
Mukanda of Chief Kende Kakele, Ndjindji, July 11, 1987
Z. S. Strother

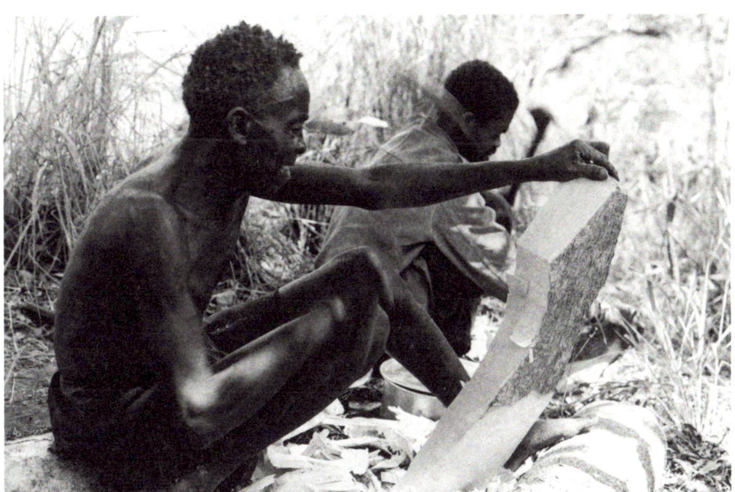

Fig. 321

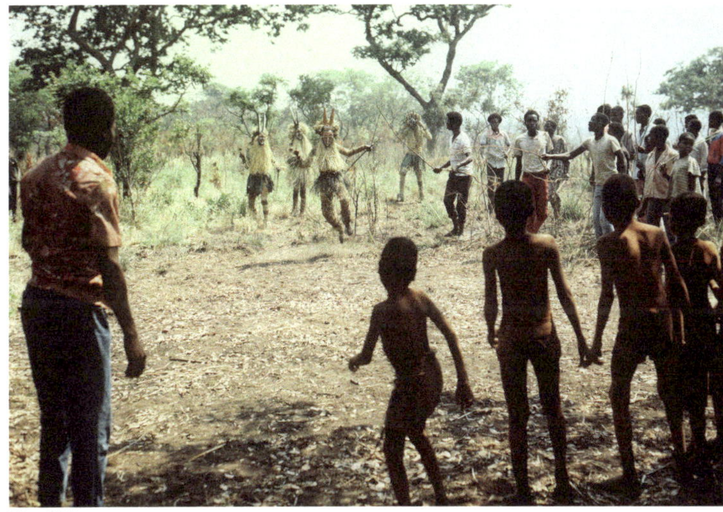

Fig. 322

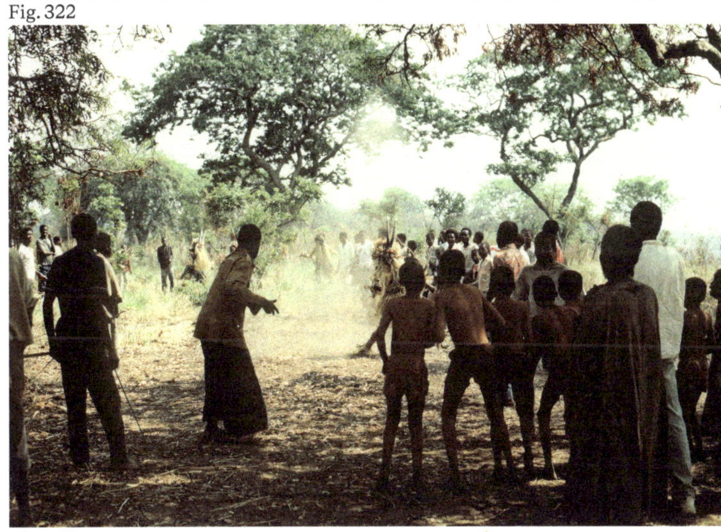

Fig. 323

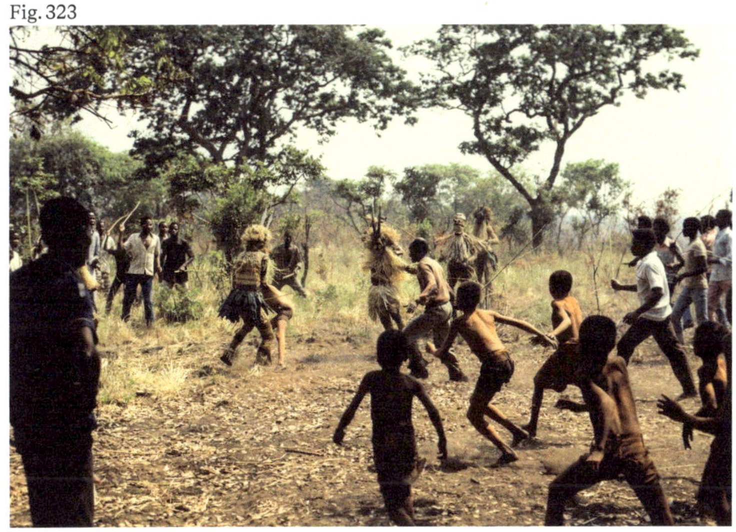

Fig. 324

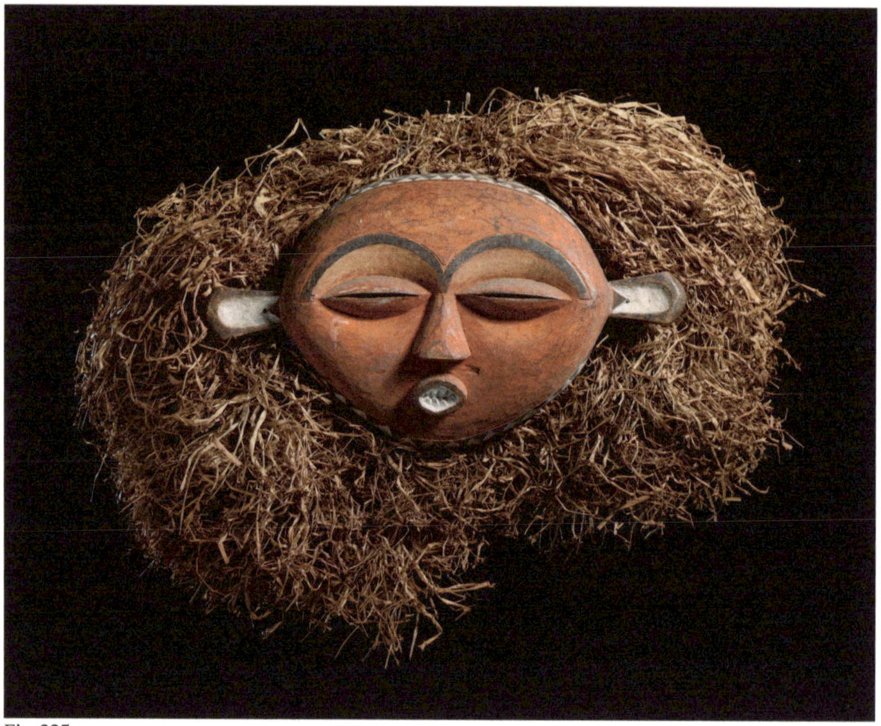

Fig. 325

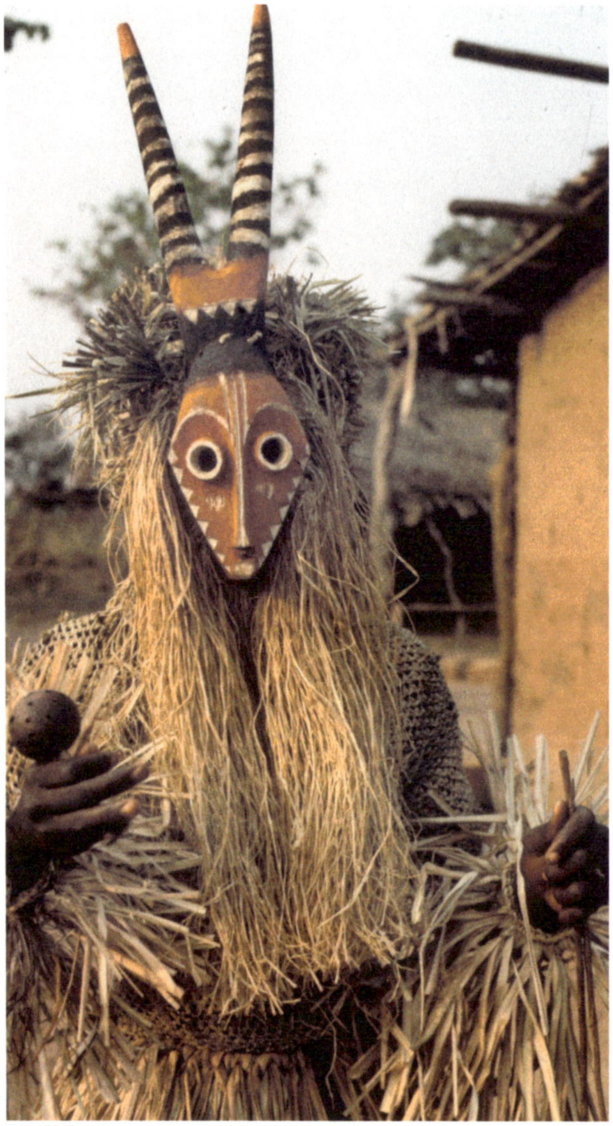

Fig. 326

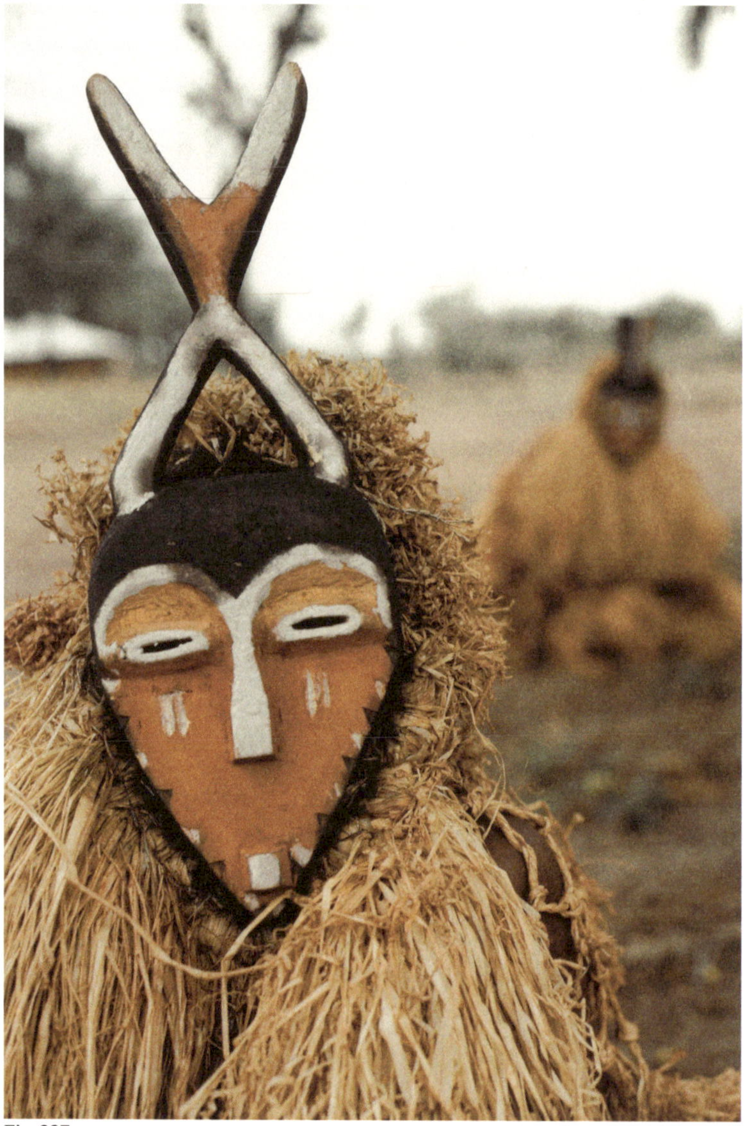

Fig. 327

Fig. 325
Artist of the eastern Pende region
***Panya ngombe* mask**
Before 1939, wood, pigments, and plant fibers, approx. 35 × 67 × 26 cm
Museum Rietberg Zürich, EFA 23
Gift of Barbara and Eberhard Fischer
Acquired by Hans Himmelheber

Fig. 326
Z. S. Strother
***Thengu ya lukumbi* is named after the roan antelope which is notorious for goring hunters who think that they have killed it (this example was commissioned from Ngoma Kandaku Mbuya for the *mukanda* of Chief Mukunzu.)**
Ndjindji, August 1987
Z. S. Strother

Fig. 327
Z. S. Strother
Once the *tundanda* master the dances, some will be allowed to don masks and to take them into the villages.
Mukanda of Chief Kime (Mayimbi a Mulenda), August 1988
Z. S. Strother

The penalty for "touching the mask" used to be circumcision, an operation that was painful for adolescents. In 1939, Himmelheber photographed the last generation to be universally circumcised in the camps. Increasingly, the Belgian colonial state required that the operation take place in birthing centers for reasons of health and safety. As a result, some felt that the *mukanda* had lost its raison d'être with the suppression of the central ritual marking the transformation of a boy into a man able to marry and father children. The Kwilu Pende abandoned the *mukanda* in the 1930s and the central Pende in the 1950s. On the other hand, the eastern Pende believed that the *mukanda* was a multi-facetted institution too valuable to lose. Instead, they made the unmasking, which had always preceded the circumcision, the central transformative ritual.

The one mask that dropped out of the eastern Pende *mukanda* repertoire was *panya ngombe* [fig. 325]. This unique helmet mask once appeared in the villages in the interim period after the boys had been circumcised and before they were healed. It was a tense period because infections occasionally cost a boy his life. The appearance of *panya mgombe* distracted people but also expressed their anxieties. According to one witness, the masquerader was restrained by a cord and would whirl and cut it at the climax of its performance after which it searched for a chicken or goat to kill before it could retire. Himmelheber collected one of these masks, which is extremely rare today, although it still appears carved in relief on the lintel of the door of chiefs who enjoy the honor of being authorized to host a *mukanda*.

[Fig. 326] The symbol of the initiation, of its pleasures as well as its terrors, is the mask and the whip. During the initiation, masks erupt from the bush to run through the village, carrying switches made from branches. Their main targets are mothers of initiates and adolescents. However, there are many rules that ensure a raucous atmosphere reminiscent of "tag," where the would-be victims taunt the masqueraders before they dash to safety, screaming with laughter. Because the masqueraders carry rattles, it is difficult for them to take anyone unaware.

One of the horned masks that Himmelheber collected [figs. 101/320] is extraordinary for being carved with the face deliberately off-kilter from the upright horns. What the sculptor was mimicking is the way that dancers of *ngolo* will often tilt their faces to the side to make their audience smile at their curiosity. Since no one can run with their head on the side, adopting the pose is a strategy to put the viewer at ease and to keep him or her within range of the whip until the performer suddenly snaps back into character for the chase. In this case, because the dancer does not actually need to tilt his head, he will be able to pursue his targets without a moment's hesitation.

[Fig. 327] The forms of the masks can be quite varied as long as they play with the idea of the initiates as creatures of the savanna. Some of the horns metamorphose into knives or swords. In the village of Kime, they reserved the more fanciful shapes for the younger boys who were not allowed to strike anyone.

[Fig. 328] The *mukanda* masks are also described as police (*pulushi*) and their main function is to make sure that most people keep a distance from the camp and the initiates. After not being seen for over three weeks, the initiates are brought into the town under masked guard to demonstrate the dances that they've learned. In the past, the celebration called *mimba* marked a major transition because it reassured the mothers that their sons had survived circumcision. Even today, there is concern that the boys are vulnerable during this period; they are supposed to avoid all eye contact and no one is supposed to touch them—with one exception.

A woman past menopause greets the initiates on behalf of their mothers, rubbing red cosmetic powder on them, which is prepared from a bark powder mixed with water. Today, *miseke* identifies someone in a liminal, ritual state because it is rare and expensive but it is first and foremost a beauty product, a superb skin conditioner that gives the skin a coppery glow.

Kavula and Kibi, the first two boys in the line, are spotted like leopards to acknowledge their status as sons of the chief. The mask with protruding white-rimmed eyes intimidates people from approaching too closely. It is named *Mabeu* ("He who looks every which way") and the dancer makes a point of jerking his head to stare in different directions. The crocheted style of western Pende *mukanda* masks (*minganji*) is becoming popular because the dancers can breathe more easily and therefore run faster.

[Fig. 329] The initiates (*tundanda*) are careful to obey the rules and to keep their eyes lowered. The day is poignant for mothers. They are relieved to see their sons performing and in good health. However, it drives home to them that they are moving into a new phase of life. Although a festive occasion, the mothers dress in rags to show psychic solidarity with the suffering of their sons. The photo shows a mother sneaking a bonbon into her son's mouth. Although forbidden, the counselors turn a blind eye. Her son quickly swallows without acknowledging her in any way. Meanwhile, Kashala (in a new dress) dances alongside her nephew Kibi to show her love and support.

[Fig. 330] During *mimba*, the initiates (*tundanda*) display their mastery of the signature *mukanda* dances. For *sh'a khulu*, they should be able to gyrate their hips so that the cords of their tutus fly straight out (level with the hips). The crowd encourages them, chanting "*kosa!*" (Get it up!), a ribald *double entendre* for a puberty ritual. The argument for circumcision is that it will ensure the fertility and potency of the initiates.

[Fig. 331] There is an infectious joy about *mimba* with the masks dancing on the rooftops and the women enjoying the music. In Kende village, food and millet beer was offered to over 300 guests.

[Fig. 332] During the initiation, the boys eat better than they ever have in their lives thanks to heavy taxes exacted on the community for meat. As a result, they grow before everyone's eyes and put on muscle mass thanks to the strenuous physical training. Although enjoyable, the hours of stamping and twisting of shoulders and hips also strengthen the boys' stamina and breathing. During an exit poll conducted by one of the authors, the boys were asked what they liked most about *mukanda*. Fifty percent said the eating and fifty percent the dancing.

In order to help pay for the initiation, the initiates (*tundanda*) are requisitioned for community chores, e.g., gathering firewood. Today, coppery red *miseke* is reserved for festivals. Most days, the initiates and their guardians rub their bodies with red ocher clay (*khundzu*). The layer of clay helps protect them from mosquitoes

Fig. 328
Z. S. Strother
The *tundanda* welcomed to the village for *mimba*.
Mukanda of Chief Kende Kakele, Ndjindji, July 26, 1987
Z. S. Strother

Fig. 329
Z. S. Strother
A mother sneaks a bonbon into her son's mouth—*mimba* celebration.
Mukanda of Chief Kende Kakele, Ndjindji, July 26, 1987
Z. S. Strother

Fig. 330
Z. S. Strother
Get it up! The *sh'a khulu* dance—*mimba* celebration.
Mukanda of Chief Kende Kakele, Ndjindji, July 26, 1987
Z. S. Strother

Fig. 331
Z. S. Strother
***Mimba* is a day of joy.**
Mukanda of Chief Kende Kakele, Ndjindji, July 26, 1987
Z. S. Strother

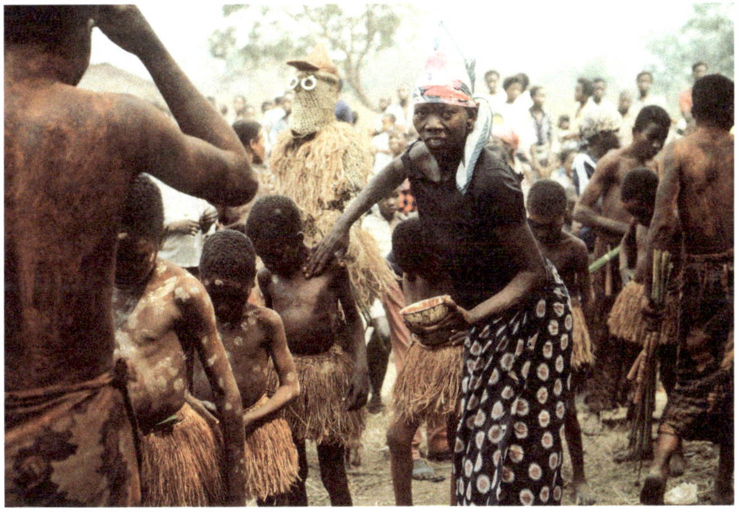
Fig. 328

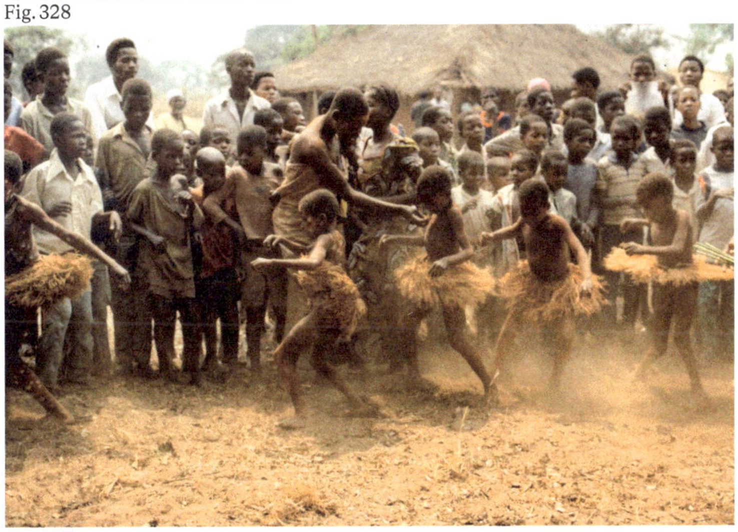
Fig. 329

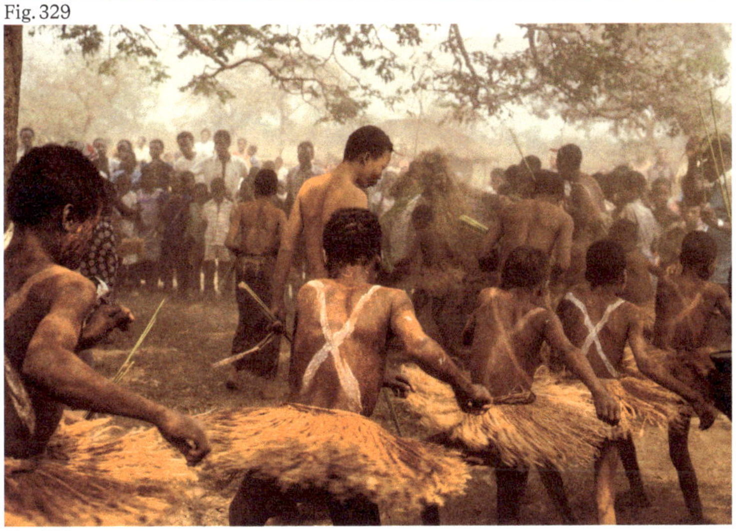
Fig. 330

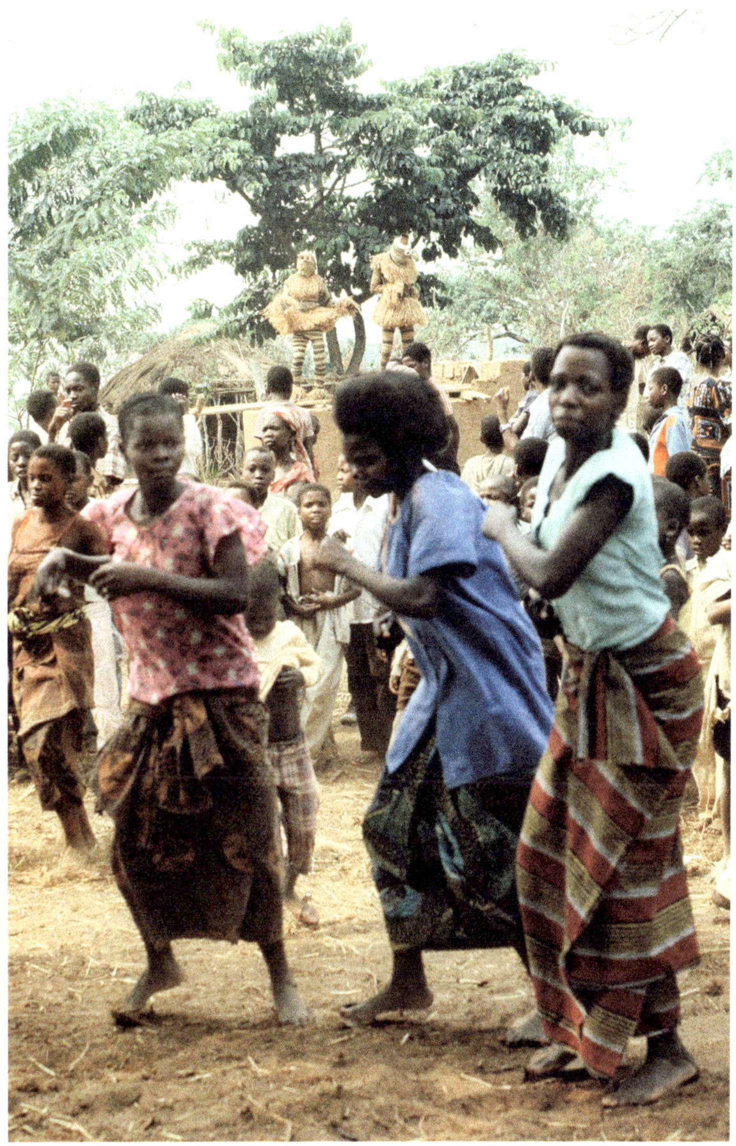
Fig. 331

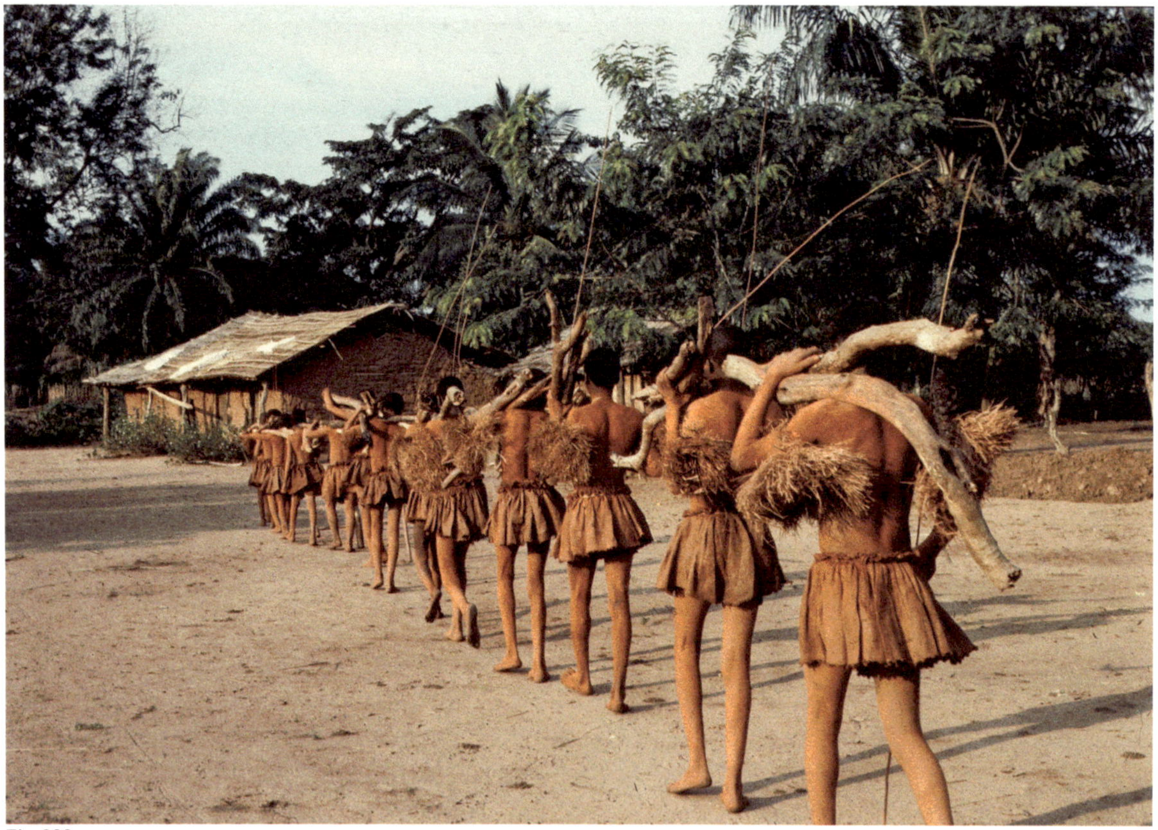
Fig. 332

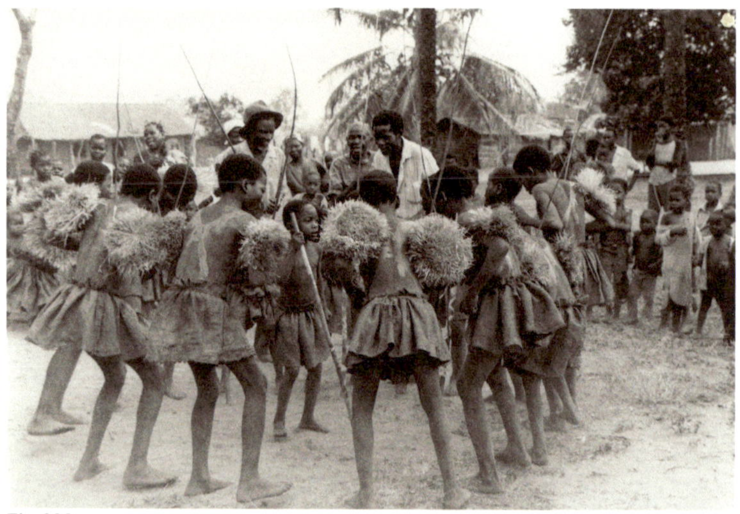
Fig. 333

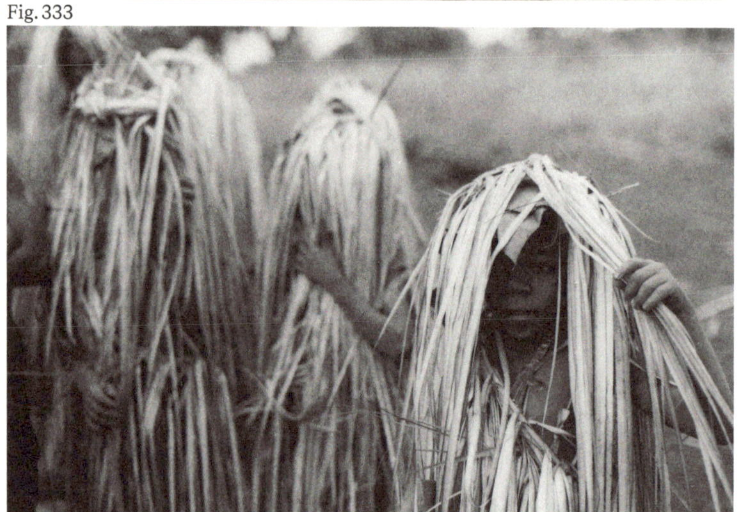
Fig. 334

Fig. 332
Z. S. Strother
***Tundanda* carry firewood into the village.**
Mukanda of Chief Kime (Mayimbi a Mulenda), August, 1988
Z. S. Strother

Fig. 333
Z. S. Strother
***Tundanda* in circle sing *mitodio* (*mukanda songs*) and dance.**
Mukanda of Chief Kime (Mayimbi a Mulenda), August, 1988
Z. S. Strother

Fig. 334
Z. S. Strother
Toto sneaks a peek.
Mukanda of Chief Kime (Mayimbi a Mulenda), September 7, 1988
Z. S. Strother

in the bush and from the scratches they get from going barefoot. Moreover, *khundzu* is dark red in color, reminiscent of blood. For this reason, it is a constant reminder that the initiates should have fortitude (*unzui*) in the face of adversity. At Kime, the initiates dug themselves a pit from which to mine *khundzu*. Each day they ground it up in a mortar to apply to themselves.

[Fig. 333] Rather than do calisthenics to improve their strength and stamina, the boys spend at least seventy-five minutes both morning and evening singing and dancing in a circle. In call and response, the boy in the center will shout a cheer and begin a song, which the others follow. Guardians behind make sure that they match steps. The photo shows a rare occasion at Kime when the boys brought their singing into the community. Usually, they sing on a dance floor (*kilombo*) close to the village so that everyone can hear them although few have access to the camp itself.

[Fig. 334] Toto (seven years old) was the youngest in a camp of twenty-six boys, in which the average age was fourteen. His father forced him to go because a chief must have a son in the camp. Initially, it was hard for him to sing some of the ribald songs because he was embarrassed that his mother might recognize his voice. And yet, within a few weeks, he began taking pleasure in shouting out the naughty words at the top of his lungs. He was developing audacity (*umbunzudi*). Nonetheless, he and the other young boys would seek out their mothers when allowed to visit the village disguised for various rituals, hoping that she would guess who they were. A mother may be simultaneously smiling and teary-eyed after such encounters. While it reassures her to see her son healthy and mischievous, she cannot help feeling a little sad that she cannot talk to him. The experience of proximity and separation drives home the reality that her son has moved beyond her domain into the realm of men.

After *mimba*, when the initiates show off their mastery of the dances for the *mukanda* masks, they begin to practice the technically more difficult dances for the village masks (*mbuya jia kifutshi*), the most important of Pende masks, those that bring the living and the dead together in celebration. Knowing what is to come, sculptors circulate in the region offering masks for sale and chiefs also begin to place commissions for masks missing from their collections.

Himmelheber was fortunate to arrive in Pende country during this period and acquired a number of pristine, beautifully colored, ready-to-dance village masks, such as *kindjinga* [fig. 341]; *kambanda* [fig. 343]; and *kiwoyo* [fig. 350]. The chiefs were probably willing to sell them to help defray the heavy costs of the comingout ceremonies and figured that they had time to replace them at a more nominal cost.

[Fig. 335] The ritual of "touching the mask" introduced the boys to the *mukanda* masks. During one of the closing rituals, the initiates (*tundanda*) will be reconciled with the village masks. At Kende, the *tundanda* are told to lie down so that they cannot see what is happening. One of the guardians brushes some medicine on the back of the initiate. *Kipoko* (the chief of the village masks) [fig. 351] steps on the back to strengthen the spine and to release sperm from the sack believed to be located at the base of spine. Then he taps the boy with a flywhisk. His assistant brushes some kaolinite on the initiate's legs.

Once everyone has been blessed, the ritual closes with a test of the boys' virility. The initiates are lined up and (one by one) they grab the ears of *kipoko*, the chief of the village masks, and eat a bite of food from the shelf on the bottom of the mask (or sometimes from the tip of his nose). Once the boy has eaten, he must turn and dash through a gauntlet of whips. If he can do so without incident, he is judged capable of intercourse. However, sometimes a boy will vomit from anxiety. If so, he will be pushed aside and required to repeat the ritual at another camp before he can graduate.

Later that afternoon, the initiates showed off for the community their mastery of some of the dances of the village masks (*mbuya jia kifutshi*) as a group. (The whip-toting *mukanda* masks are banned from this joyous event.) Three of the oldest and most accomplished initiates appeared in full costume to perform to great acclaim. The village masks must dance to close a *mukanda* but some chiefs prefer to wait for some months to give the community time to rest and gather their resources for a three- to five-day extravaganza. This strategy can backfire as the months pass because the *tundanda* are not considered fully initiated until they eat from the mask *kipoko*.

[Fig. 336] The initiates are told that the *mukanda* cannot end until they hunt and kill an elephant. Near the end, the camp, by now grown to its maximum size, is marched into the forest, where they met the "elephant": an umbrella tree (*musengedi*). They learn that "killing the elephant" really involves felling this tree and keeping fires burning around the clock in secret to dry the trunk so that it will resonate as a talking drum. The boys also collect leaves from the tree, which will be incorporated into a medicine to ensure their potency.

Kidinda, the boy on the right, ran off to *mukanda* when he heard songs mocking the uninitiated. His father proposed paying a fine to withdraw him, arguing that he needed Kidinda to babysit his other children. Everyone knew that the real reason was that they were Malembists (a charismatic Protestant denomination) opposed to the initiation. The chief probably would have agreed but the camp counselors threatened to go on strike and the boy himself adamantly refused, telling his father: 1) you're responsible for babysitting; 2) you were able to have children because you were initiated yourself; and 3) that's your church, not mine! The matter went to trial, but without the boy's assent, nothing could be done. Although not a natural dancer, Kidinda worked hard to master the songs and dances. At the comingout ceremony, he surpassed himself and received a huge ovation from the crowd.

[Fig. 337] Eleven days later, when the "elephant "was ready, the non-initiates were locked up in their houses. As many as forty men with sticks joined the initiates to play the dry tree trunk as a drum throughout the night, carousing and singing war songs,

Before the men began, the camp counselors gathered the masquerading costumes and headpieces and had the initiates sweep up all the straw surrounding the camp to throw onto the roof of their house. At this point, in 1987, there was quite a dispute. The young men running the camp wanted to follow the rules and to throw all the masks on the fire. The fathers felt that the masks could be hidden in a burlap bag and sold on the sly to help defray the costs of the camp.

Fig. 335
Z. S. Strother
***Kipoko* mask at *Kibetelo* ritual during Chief Kende's boys' initiation into the *mukanda*.**
Ndjindji, August 9, 1987
Z. S. Strother

Fig. 336
Z. S. Strother
Hunting the elephant
Mukanda of Chief Kende Kakele
Ndjindji, August 11, 1987
Z. S. Strother

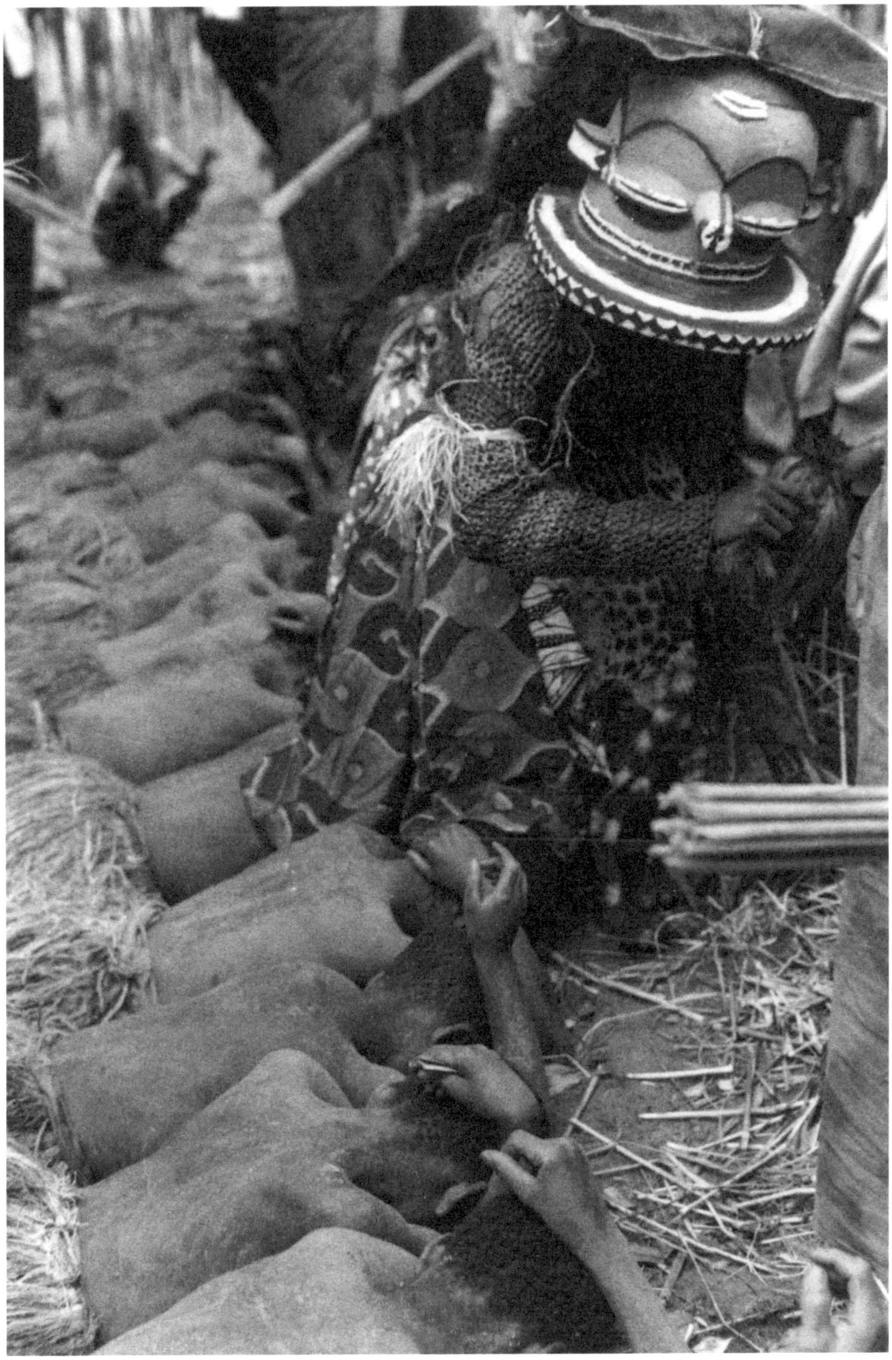

Fig. 335

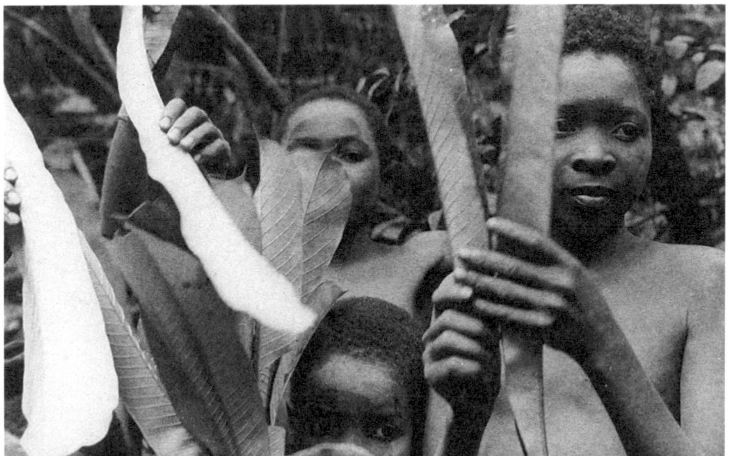

Fig. 336

Once the singing was finished, the organizers collected some chunks of dry wood to serve as replicas for the masks and disguised them by putting them in burlap bags. They had chosen a moonless night for the ceremony and when the drill sergeant set the "elephant" and house ablaze, the size of the conflagration was impressive. One could feel the heat on one's face. And when they threw the bags into the blaze, the dry wood hissed and popped as it exploded into a shower of sparks.

Why go to *mukanda* in 2018? Whereas the Catholic Church vehemently opposed the *mukanda* for much of the twentieth century, many of their representatives accepted it in the 2000s, sometimes even organizing graduation parties. On the other hand, Congolese charismatic churches (*églises de réveil*) take a hard line and will excommunicate parents who allow their sons to go. Many young men also oppose the *mukanda*, not seeing its value in the contemporary economy. The boys who continue to call for *mukanda* do so to avoid being teased. They do not want to have to run from the *mukanda* masks and some would like to be allowed to dance the village masks. Boys must also be initiated in order to be eligible to become the chief of a lineage or the chief of a village. It is striking that, despite growing resistance, some of the camps are far larger than they were in the late 1980s. Kende, who had around twenty boys in 1987, had sixty in 2000 and forty-six in 2011. Even during a period of uncertainty in the region, in 2018 documented camps ranged from thirteen to thirty-two boys. One turnaround from the 1980s was that it was chiefs and fathers who were responsible for launching most of the camps rather than the boys themselves.

Why go to *mukanda*? Ironically, only two people out of the dozens interviewed over the years have cited what the boys in fact spend most of their time doing: singing. In 1987 and 1988, I recorded eighty-five to 120 different songs for each of two camps. Some were teasing ("Whoever stays in the village is a child!"); many teach morals through the escapades of birds and animals; some were outrageously bawdy; and the most memorable were historical songs with haunting melodies. For example,

Ngenze a Panda udi kale ku mbongo ya Loange,
Muna Munzadi wamakana ha pambu ya Khoyi,
Ita ngayisha mu Mbinda. Tsumienu ngenji, jiyile Makumbi a Lubunda,
Wasala kungima.
Mbimbi tsuayidile kilako, Makumbi a Panda azuele milonga, mbimbi tuaitshikina.
Kisanga kia Muna Mumbanda!

In the voice of a messenger of Chief Kisanga:

Ngenze a Panda has already gone downriver,
The Child of Munzadi stopped at the crossroads at Khoyi,
I left the war on the savanna called Mbinda, [at the border].
Send someone, let him go get Mukumbi a Lubunda,
Who stayed behind.
We were agreed on what Makumbi a Panda said, what he said was what we wanted to do.
Kisanga, Child of Mumbanda!

Sometimes in wishing to justify the *mukanda*, foreigners describe it as a "school." However, the situation is far more complex than this analogy allows. Yes, the boys learned to sing the song as they concentrated on their dance steps. Nonetheless, on examination, it turned out that the words were as opaque to them as they were to the authors of this essay. Nor did anyone attempt to explain the song to the initiates. Instead, the boys were turned into unconscious tape recorders for the community's use.

While the boys learn nothing about the history recorded in the songs, it is the people listening at leisure in the village who may ask someone knowledgeable: who or what was "Ngenze a Panda"? What war are we talking about? It is at this point, divorced from the stress of initiation, that the motivated will learn that, at one time, men of Kisanga agreed to go to war with the people of Kombo-Kiboto. However, at the last moment, the three lieutenants scattered and did not follow through on the plan worked out by Makumbi a Lubunda with the result that the chief himself was killed.

While referring to an actual conflict (probably in the late nineteenth century), the song carries a moral: Make a plan and stick together, or you will lose. In everyday life, the song is launched during trials for one witness to remind another: we agreed; follow through or we will lose.

Most often, the *mukanda* is valued because of the transformation that it achieves. In the 1980s, many said that the raison d'être of *mukanda* was to make the boy *kutema*, aware, resourceful, on his toes, resilient, hard-working, independent, and able to earn his own living. In 2018, Nzomba found through extensive interviews that the parents believed "that the uninitiated are not awake [*éveillés*]: they do not have the courage to express themselves or to initiate projects, they have no stamina, no courage or audacity. Certain families find that these qualities can only be cultivated in the field. And that these qualities will help the boy to defend himself and his family [...] because the initiate will not recoil from a situation when he swears an oath in the name of his generation." Many parents share the point of view that the boys who are not yet initiated are "timid, unformed, lazy, dull, preferring to stick close to their mothers and sisters. They avoid groups of boys and are unable to speak up for themselves in a crowd."

The *mukanda* masks first appear to children in nightmares but then they will woo them, tease them, plead for them [fig. 338], and the boys will finally have the opportunity to lay hands on them, an action that is identical linguistically to "taking ownership" of them. According to Chief Malombo Kalongela, the *mukanda* is important because it brings together young men from different families and teaches them to live together as they share and negotiate certain intense experiences. Confronting the masks is central to that process.

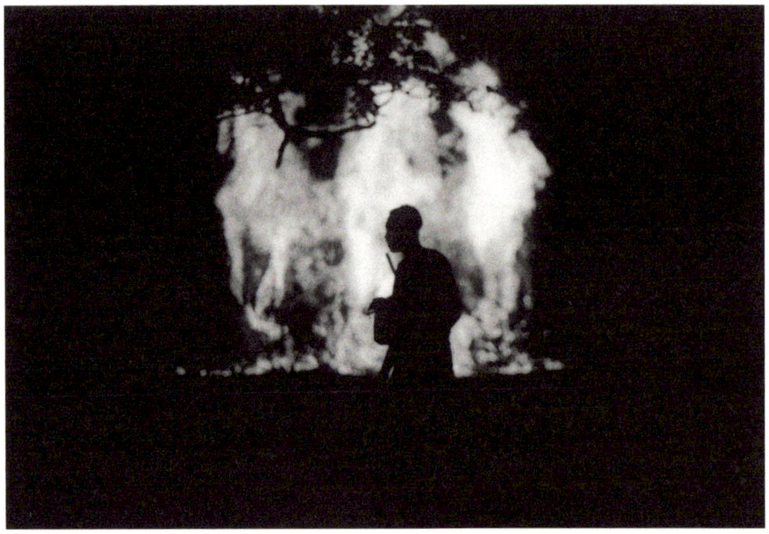

Fig. 337

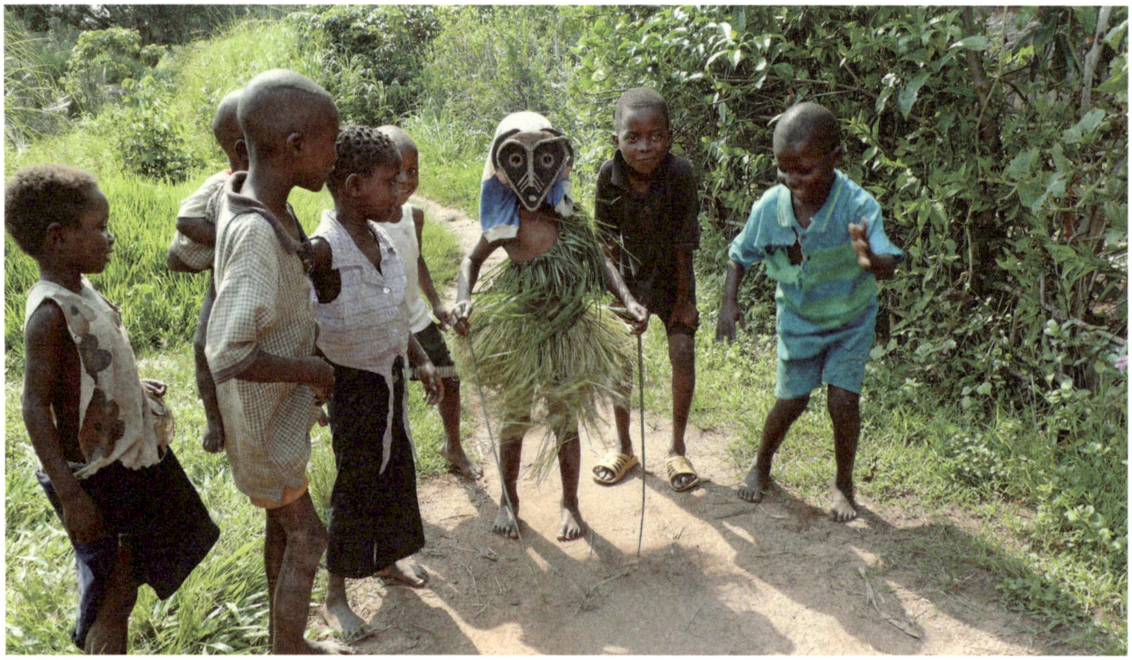

Fig. 338

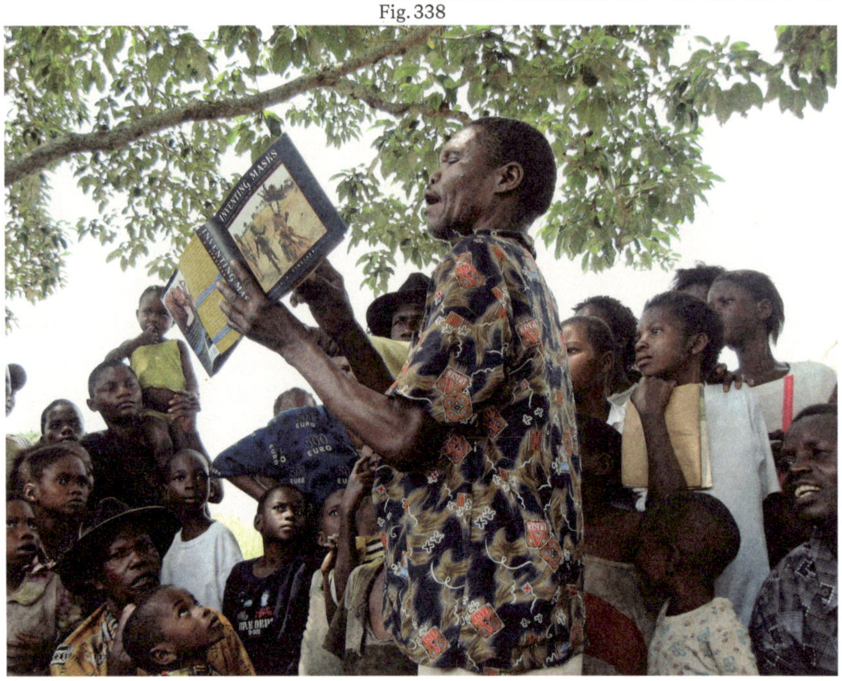

Fig. 339

Fig. 337
Z. S. Strother
In theory, everything is destroyed at the end of *mukanda*—a sentinel watches over the fire and makes sure that no one is able to pluck anything out before it burns to ash.
Mukanda of Chief Kende Kakele, Ndjindji, August 23, 1987
Z. S. Strother

Fig. 338
Z. S. Strother
The masks still attract children to *mukanda*—some children play with a ram's mask from a previous *mukanda*, which was hidden away to sell when the opportunity arises; in the past, it would have been burned at the end of the initiation.
Nyanga, January 6, 2007, digital photograph
Z. S. Strother

Fig. 339
Marvin Goertz
The sculptor Mashini Gitshiola shows pictures of himself to a crowd.
Nyoka-Munene, January 2007, digital photograph
Marvin Goertz

Z. S. Strother — The photographs in this essay were conceived as documentation for future publications and slide lectures. I used a Nikon F3. Several photographers had recommended using Kodachrome slide film because it was sensitive to reds and greens and would complement the red soil and lush foliage of tropical Africa. Most of the photos in this particular essay were taken with Kodachrome; however, I ended up throwing away quite a few rolls because Kodachrome was a slow film and masquerades or other strenuous physical activity are usually scheduled late in the day when it is cooler. Ektachrome was faster, essential on overcast days, but tinted blue.

There were no photo processing laboratories for color film in the country. At the time, Nzomba Dugo Kakema was working as an itinerant portrait photographer and he had to send his black-and-white film roll by roll to Kinshasa to be developed and printed. From reviewing his prints and negatives, I could see that the labs would "push" their chemicals to save money. If one's order arrived when the chemicals were weak, then the quality of the negative and associated prints would be thin. It was clear that all my film would need to be sent out of the country to be developed.

An unexpected trip home at the end of one year allowed me to see my photos for the first time and confirmed that, as predicted, black-and-white negative film was far more tolerant of being stored for months in tropical conditions before and after exposure. For most of my work, I relied on black-and-white. I carried back pre-paid mailers addressed to laboratories in Europe or the USA and would wait long months until I met someone leaving the country to ask him or her to mail them for me from abroad.

In the late 1980s, every adult was required by the Mobutu regime to affix a photograph to his or her identity card. There was great hunger for portrait photographs and people were accustomed to long delays between the taking of the photos and the delivery of black-and-white prints for the reasons outlined above. They preferred their own portraits to be full figure and carefully posed. Most people were pleased to be photographed and rarely refused. The same was true in 2007 during a follow-up visit. Occasionally, an individual might hesitate because she was dressed in ritual or work clothes and feared (as one woman worded it) that "people in America will think that I am poor." However, they accepted when I promised to explain the circumstances. (The pirating of my photos on the internet sometimes proves a problem in my keeping this promise.) Occasionally, a young chief would wonder if a certain object or site should be photographed but his elders always agreed, asking "What harm could it do?" It was never an issue with the *mukanda*. The chiefs and elders had given their permission. The discipline and emotional intensity during rituals was such that both initiates and organizers seldom seemed aware of my presence as they were concentrating on anticipating what would come next and doing what was expected of them.

Because of the difficulties in conducting research in a restricted zone, I am embarrassed by how long it has taken to present the publications sought-after by my hosts. In 2007, I carried back as many copies as I could and found field associates nostalgic to see pictures of themselves from their youth and eager to show young people why Pende art and culture (*ima jia Apende*) should be valued [fig. 339]. Nzomba and I look forward to distributing copies of the present catalogue for their delectation.

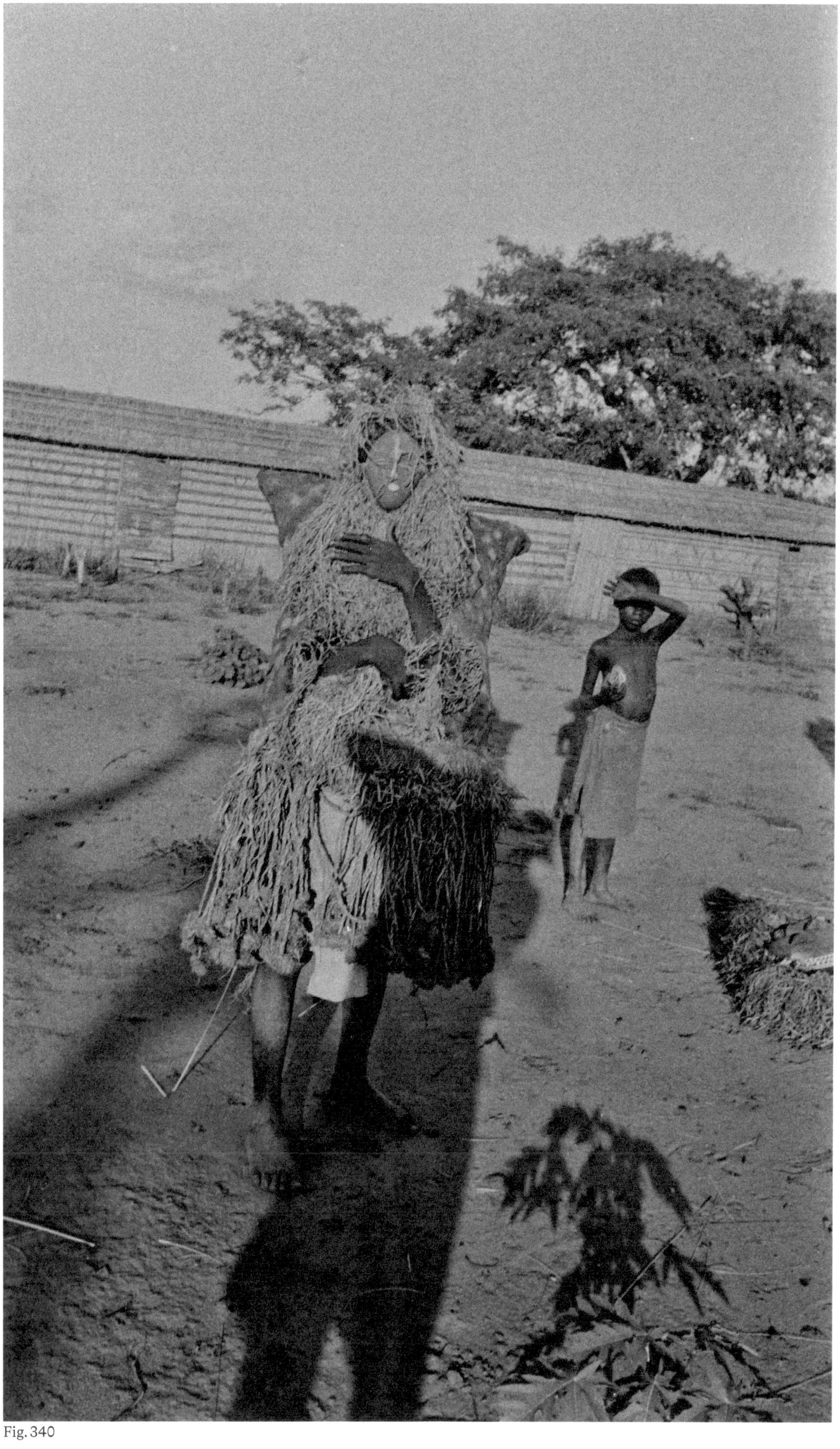

Fig. 340

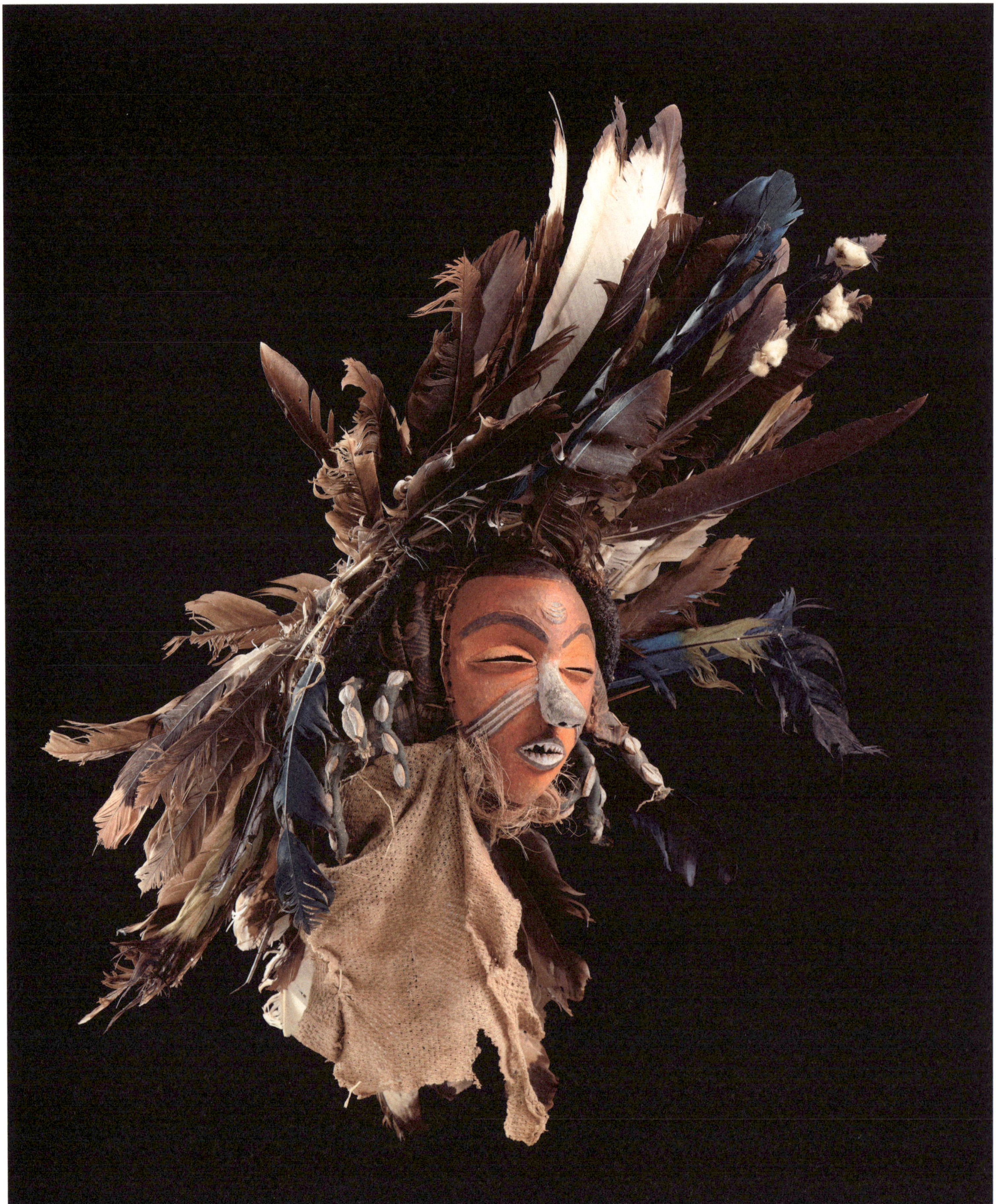

Fig. 341

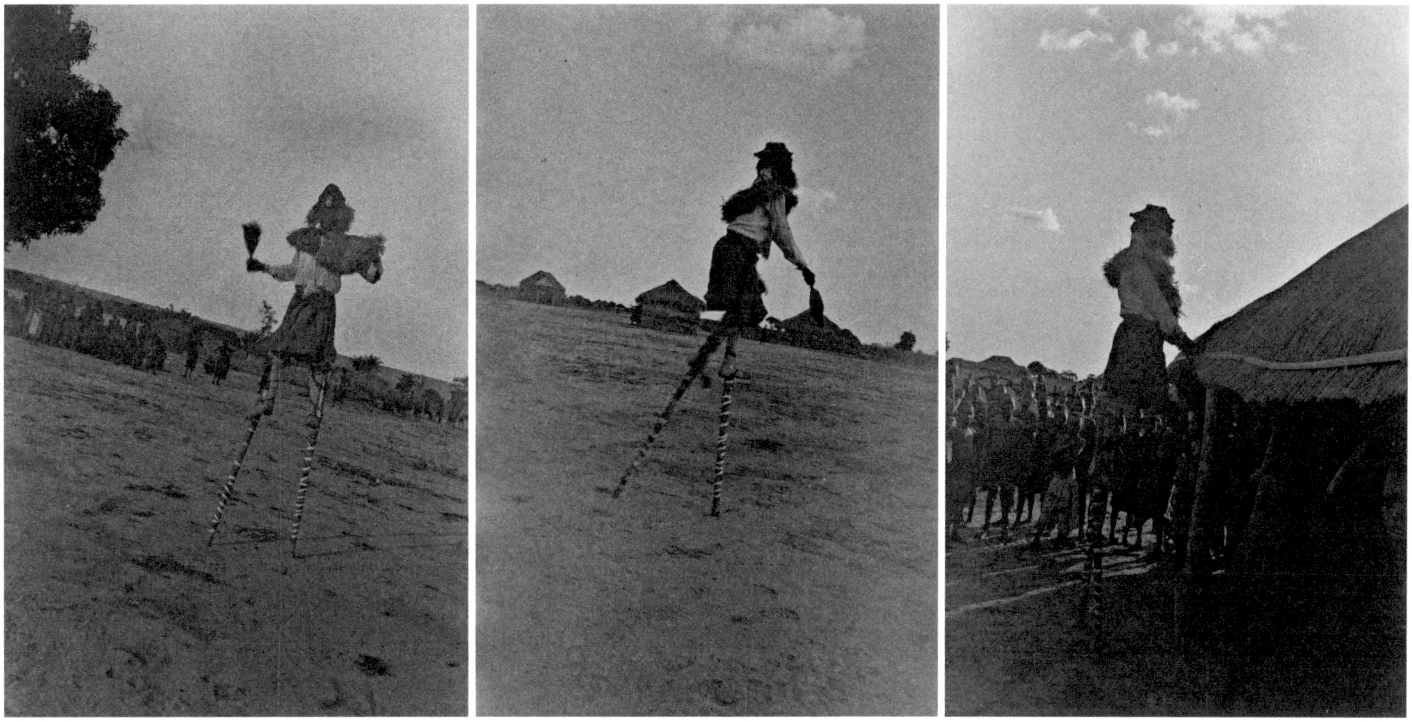

Fig. 342

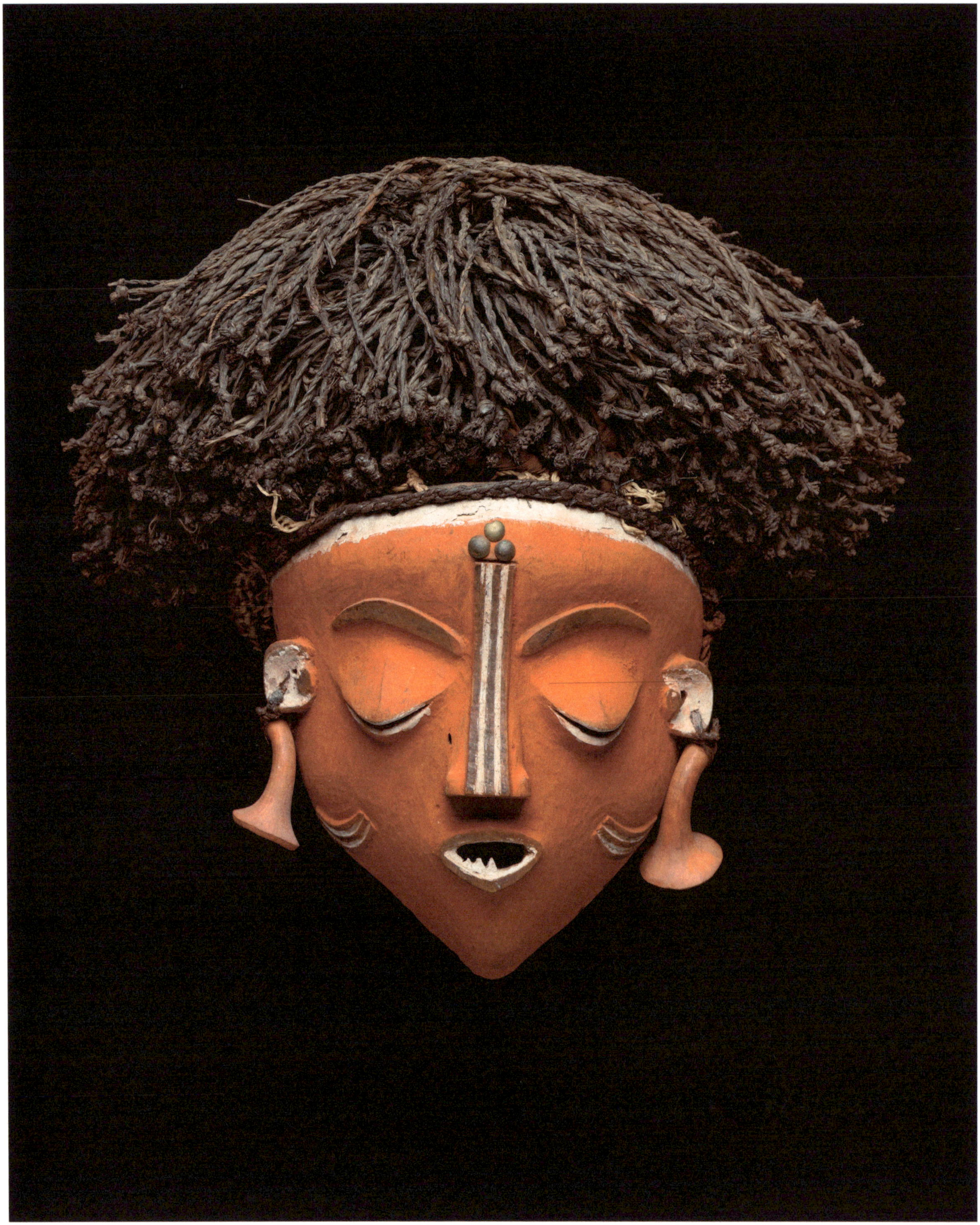

Fig. 343

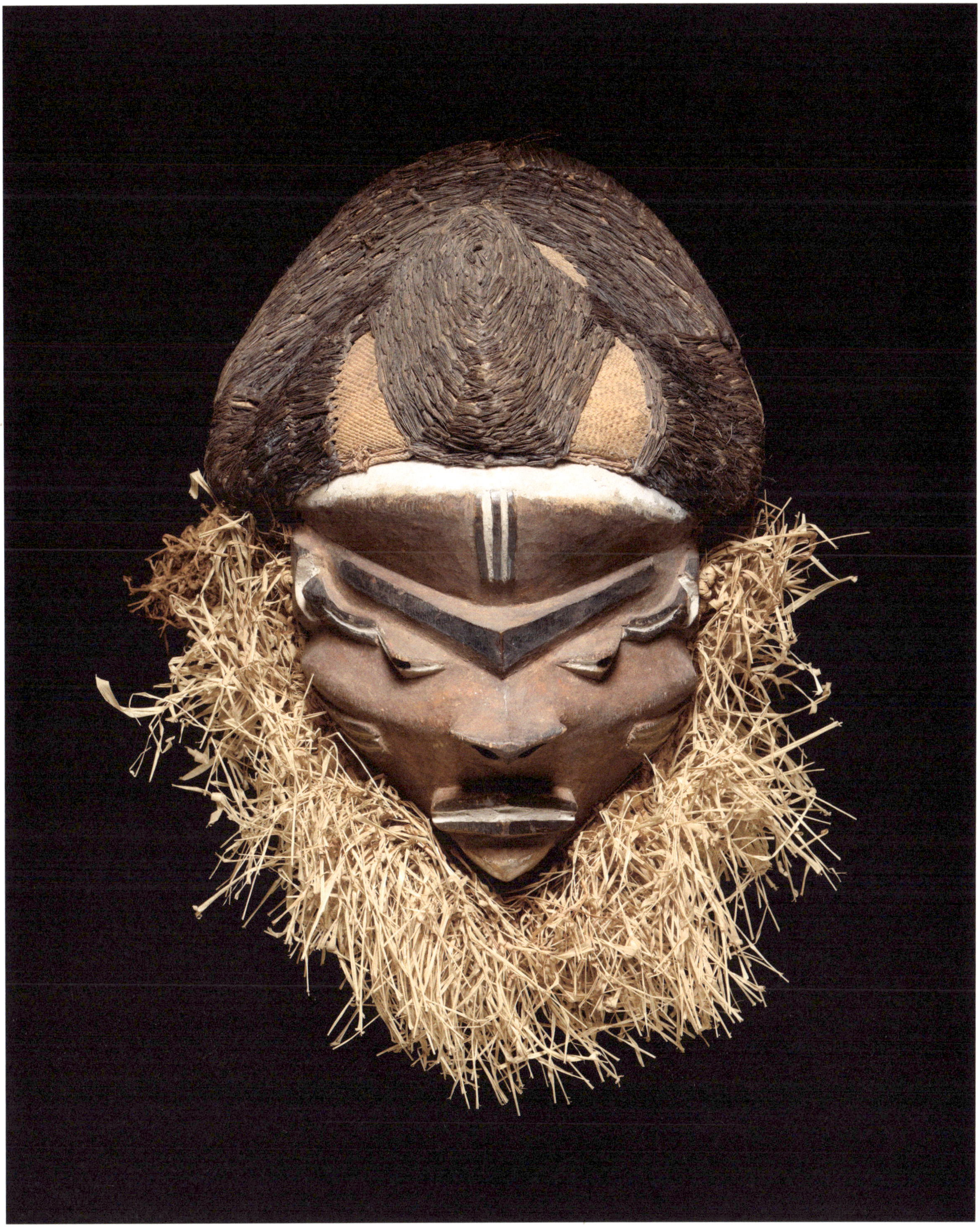

Fig. 344

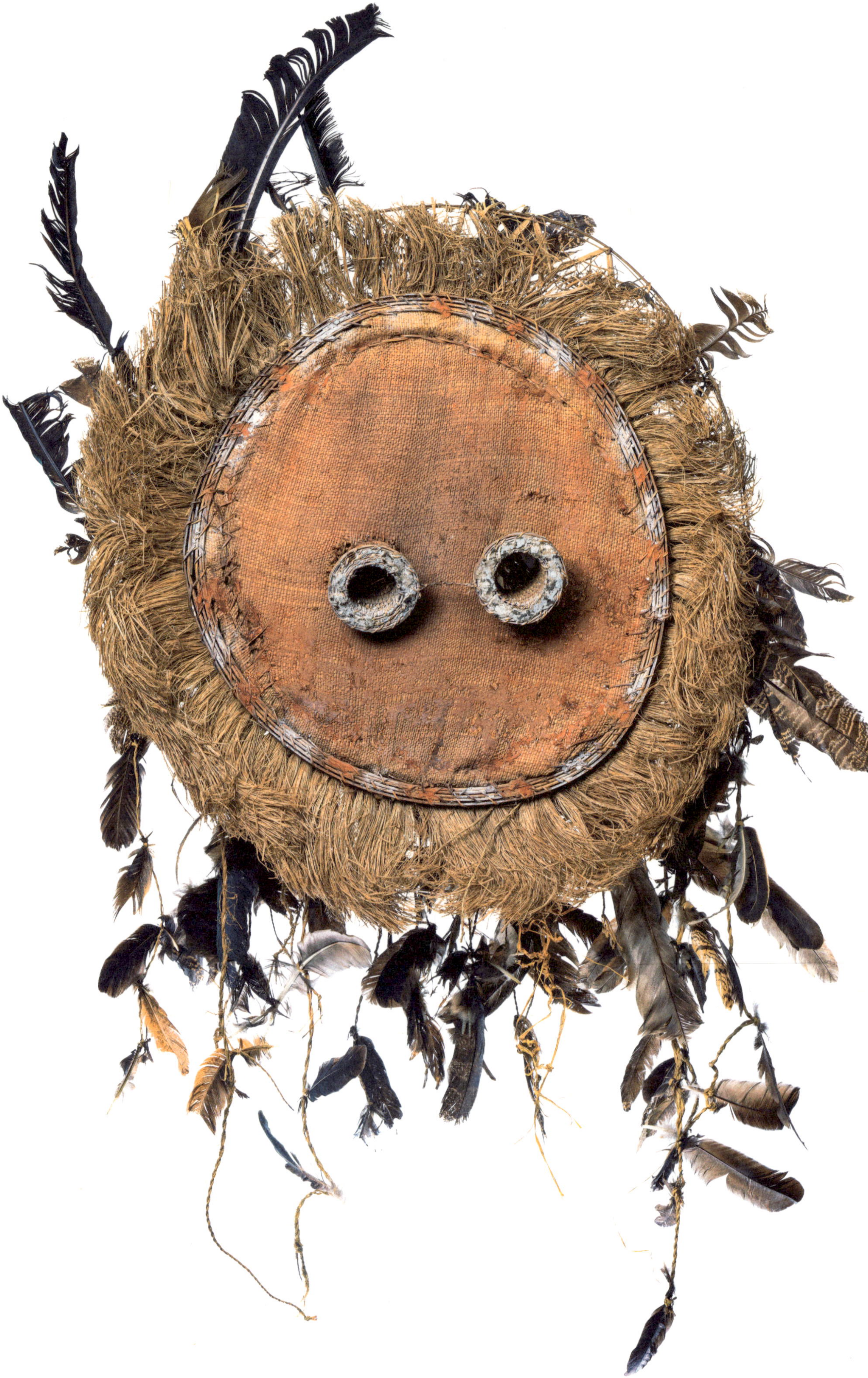

Fig. 345

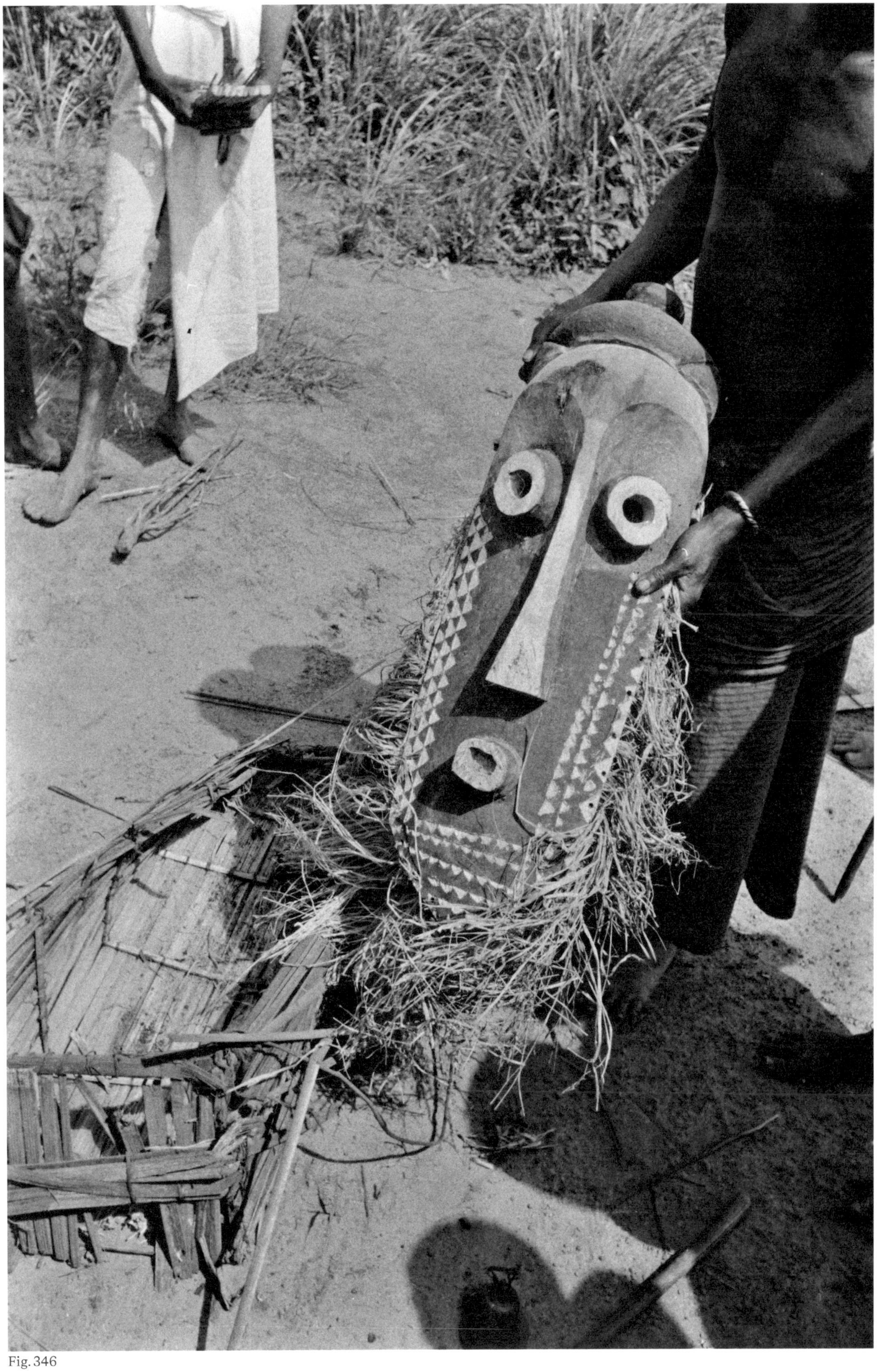

Fig. 346

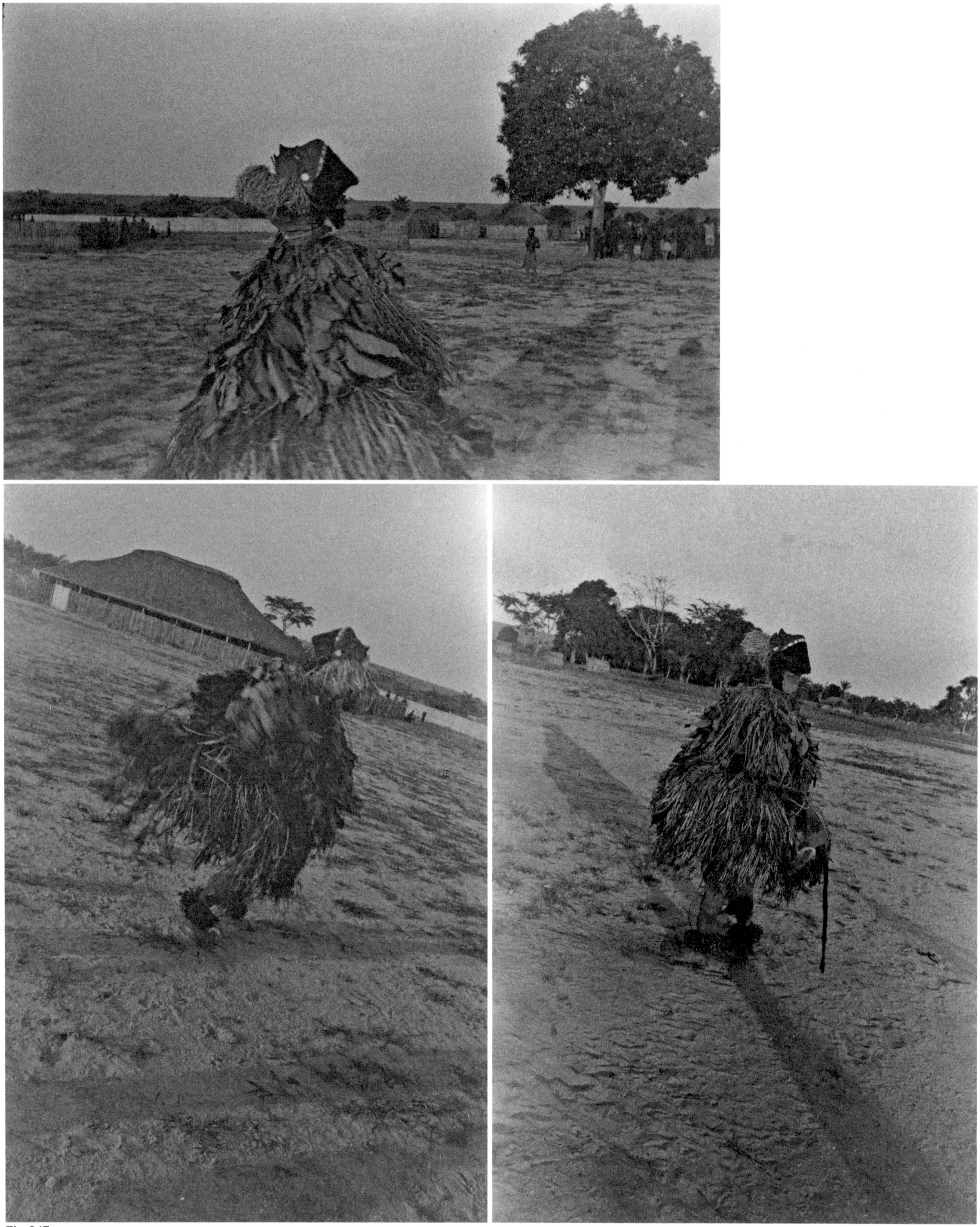

Fig. 347

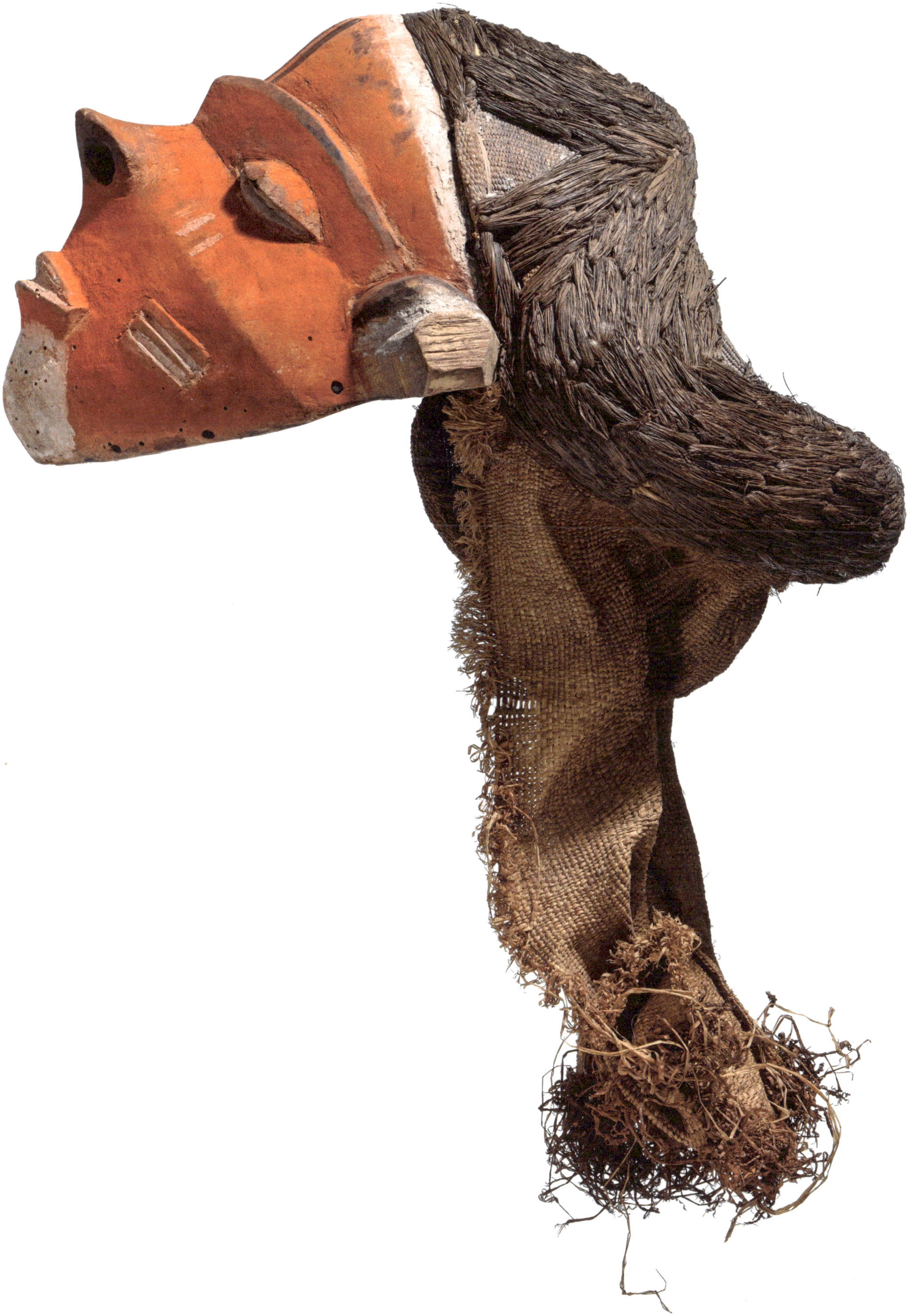

Fig. 348

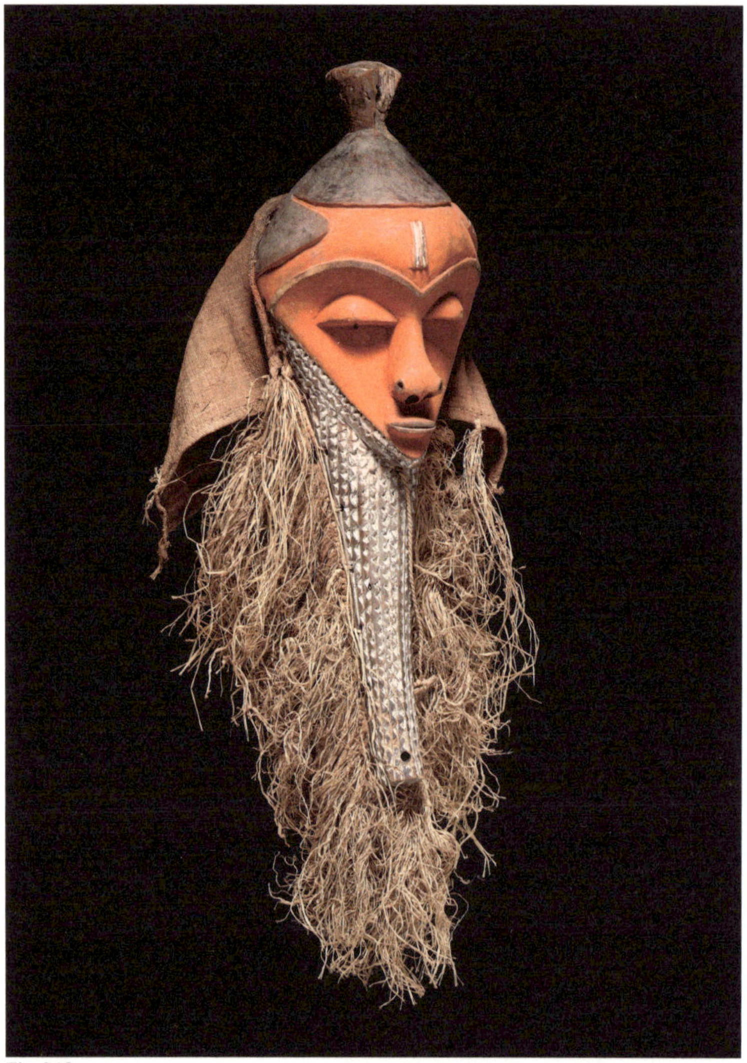
Fig. 349

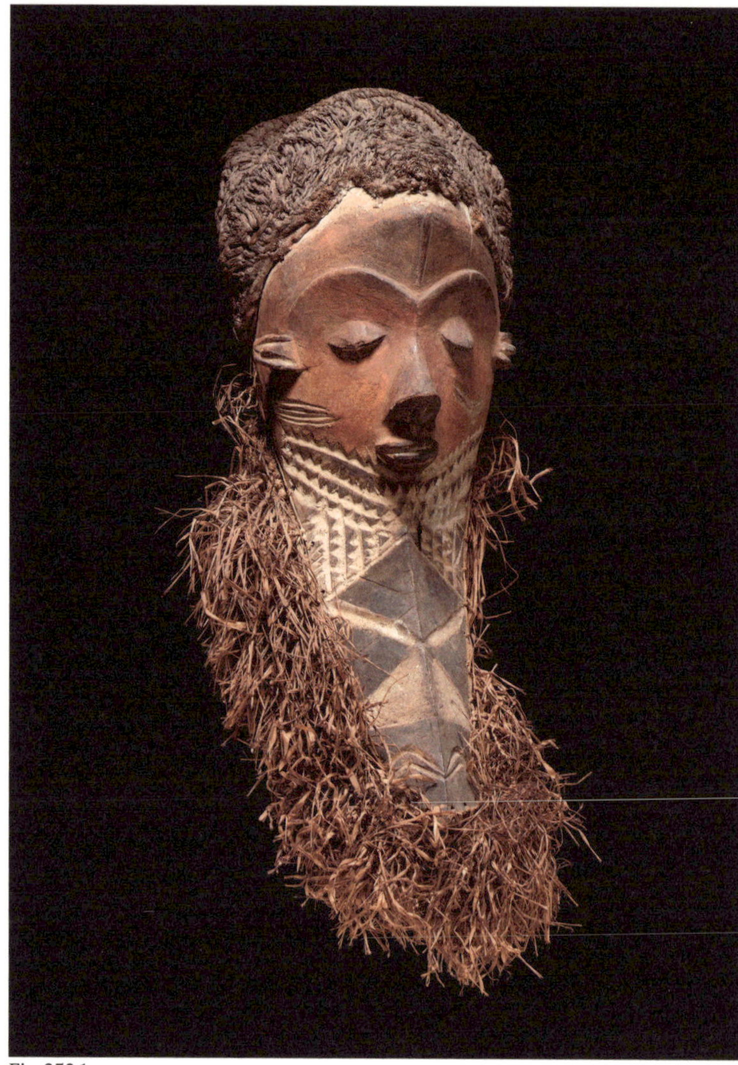
Fig. 350.1

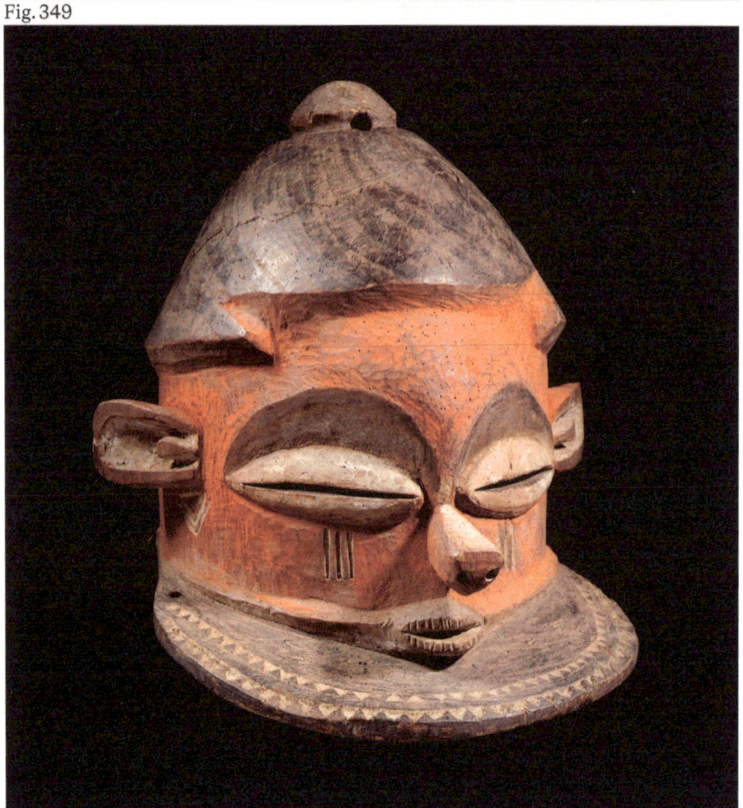
Fig. 351

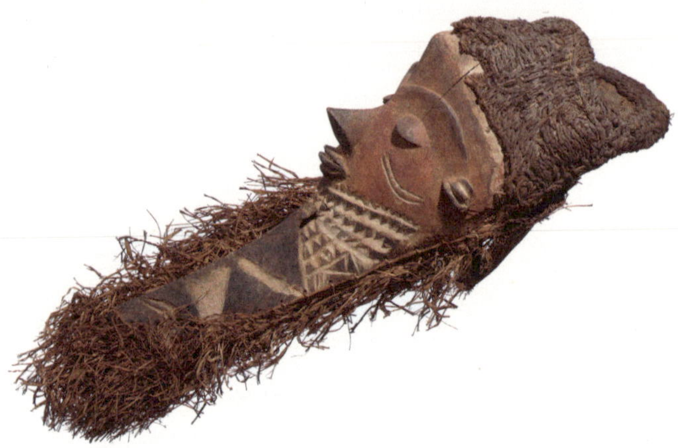
Fig. 350.2

PENDE INITIATION MASKS: ART THAT MAKES MEN OUT OF BOYS — Hans Himmelheber's visit to the Congo in 1938/39 happened to coincide with the initiation ceremony (*mukanda*) in the Pende region, which only takes place once every ten years. The young boys would live in the bush, away from their mothers and separated from the civilized world of the villages, where they would learn dances, songs, or craft skills while also acquiring the secret knowledge that was the preserve of the men [see essay Strother]. At the end of their communal experiences, the boys were prepared for their role as men in society. Various types of masks accompanied the boys during this long period of trials and dangers.[1] Hans Himmelheber visited the camp where the circumcisions were carried out and photographed the dances of these masked figures [figs. 340/342]. As the masks were considered worthless after use, he was able to purchase whole series of these bright red initiation masks.

It is possible to differentiate between female, male, and hypermasculine Pende masks.[2] The feminine is idealized as peaceful, self-controlled, and social. Hot energy, creativity, and strong emotions are seen as male—extending to uncontrolled rage and aggression in the case of the hypermasculine. These characteristics are also identifiable in the masks. The female mask shown here has a flat forehead, round eyebrows, and most importantly the expression with lowered lids known as *zanze*, which was considered particularly beautiful and seductive [fig. 343]. In contrast, the male mask conveys an aggressive impression [fig. 344]: the face is angular and chiseled, the eyes look out vigilantly from under their lids, and the lip is pursed as if the mask—according to the Pende's interpretation—was about to start yelling.

A mask of which one had to be much more wary is the *gitenga* mask in the form of a disk [fig. 345]. The round, open eyes were described as "dangerous." Armed with a whip like all initiation masks, the *gitenga* mask had not only social responsibilities but also police duties, and was able to punish the initiands and villagers if they breached the rules. The *pumbu* mask of the eastern Pende was reserved for especially powerful chiefs and its wide-open eyes made it exceptionally terrifying [fig. 346].

Photographs show that many Pende masks, such as this male mask [fig. 348], were worn horizontally—contrary to our viewing habits. This also applies to *kiwoyo* or *giwoyo* masks [figs. 349/350]. Often mistaken for a beard by Western observers, the latter in fact depict a body laid out horizontally as for burial. This type of mask was naturally associated with the realm of the dead.

Among the most important village masks by the eastern Pende were the chiefs' *kipoko* helmet masks [fig. 351]. *Kipoko* danced at important community rituals like the appointment of a new village chief and represented the connection to the world of the dead. Furthermore, the *kipoko* also played an important role in the circumcision camps. At the end of the initiation, the boys had to grab something to eat from the edge of this imposing mask—the ultimate test—in order to be accepted in society as full-fledged men. — Michaela Oberhofer

1 Strother 1988.
2 See Strother 2008, pp. 23–28.

Fig. 340
Hans Himmelheber
The long building of the circumcision camp can be seen behind the mask
Pende region, 1939, b/w negative
Museum Rietberg Zürich, FHH 190-27

Fig. 341
Artist of the eastern Pende region
***Kinjinga/munyangi* mask with feathers**
Before 1939, wood, pigments, feathers, cowries and textiles, 69 × 42 × 62 cm
Museum Rietberg Zürich, HH 30
Gift of Barbara and Eberhard Fischer
Acquired by Hans Himmelheber

Fig. 342
Hans Himmelheber
Masked performance on stilts
Pende region, 1939, b/w negatives
Museum Rietberg Zürich,
FHH 192-4 to FHH 192-6

Fig. 343
Artist of the eastern Pende region
***Kambanda* mask with woman's face**
Before 1939, wood, pigments, plant fibers, and brass nails, 32 × 35 × 30 cm
Museum Rietberg Zürich, HH 21a
Gift of Barbara and Eberhard Fischer
Acquired by Hans Himmelheber

Fig. 344
Artist of the central Pende region
Male mask
Before 1939, wood, pigments, and plant fibers, 40 × 26 × 24 cm
Museum Rietberg Zürich, HH 20
Gift of Barbara and Eberhard Fischer
Acquired by Hans Himmelheber

Fig. 345
Artist of the Kwilu-Pende region
***Gitenga* mask**
Before 1939, rattan, raffia, feathers, 94 × 64 × 12 cm
Museum der Kulturen Basel, III 9178
Acquired by Hans Himmelheber

Fig. 346
Hans Himmelheber
Big, white eyes were equated with unbound anger
Pende region, May 24, 1939, b/w negative
Museum Rietberg Zürich, FHH 190-29

Fig. 347
Hans Himmelheber
Performance of a *mbuya* mask with leaves and raffia costume
Pende region, 1939, b/w negatives
Museum Rietberg Zürich,
FHH 192-12 to FHH 192-14

Fig. 348
Artist of the central Pende region
Male mask
Before 1939, wood, pigments, and plant fibers, 31 × 23 × 17 cm
Museum Rietberg Zürich, 2016.152
Gift of Barbara and Eberhard Fischer
Acquired by Hans Himmelheber

Fig. 349
Artist of the eastern Pende region
***Kiwoyo* horizontal mask**
Before 1939, wood, pigments, and plant fibers, 64 × 18 × 22 cm
Museum Rietberg Zürich, HH 18
Gift of Barbara and Eberhard Fischer
Acquired by Hans Himmelheber

Fig. 350
Artist of the central Pende region
Horizontal mask in the style of *giwoyo*
Before 1939, wood, pigments and plant fibers, 53.5 × 22 × 37 cm
Museum Rietberg Zürich, HH 17
Gift of Barbara and Eberhard Fischer
Acquired by Hans Himmelheber

Fig. 351
Artist of the eastern Pende region
***Kipoko* helmet mask**
Before 1939, wood, pigments, 28.5 × 30 × 35 cm
Museum Rietberg Zürich, 2016.151
Gift of Barbara and Eberhard Fischer
Acquired by Hans Himmelheber

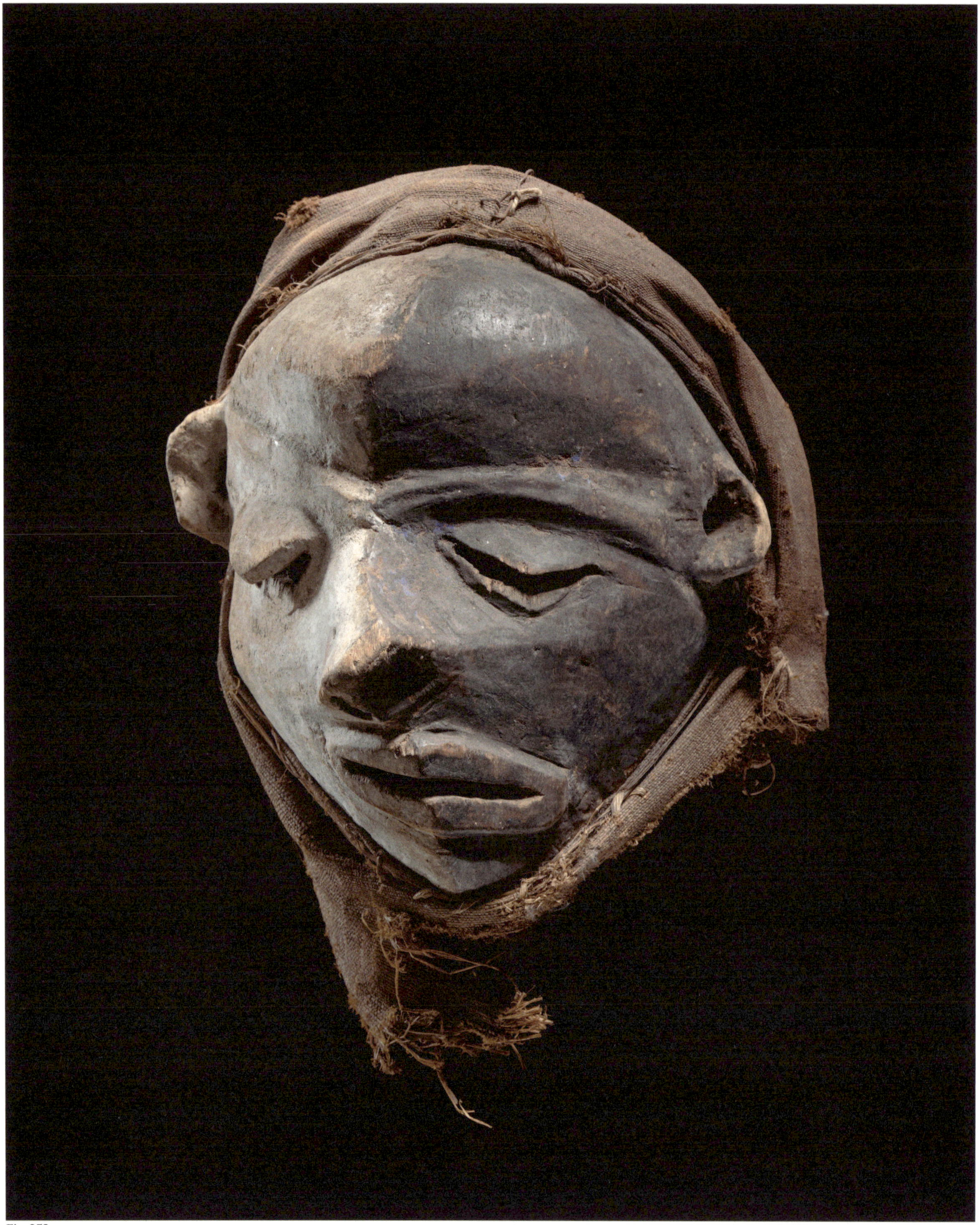

Fig. 352

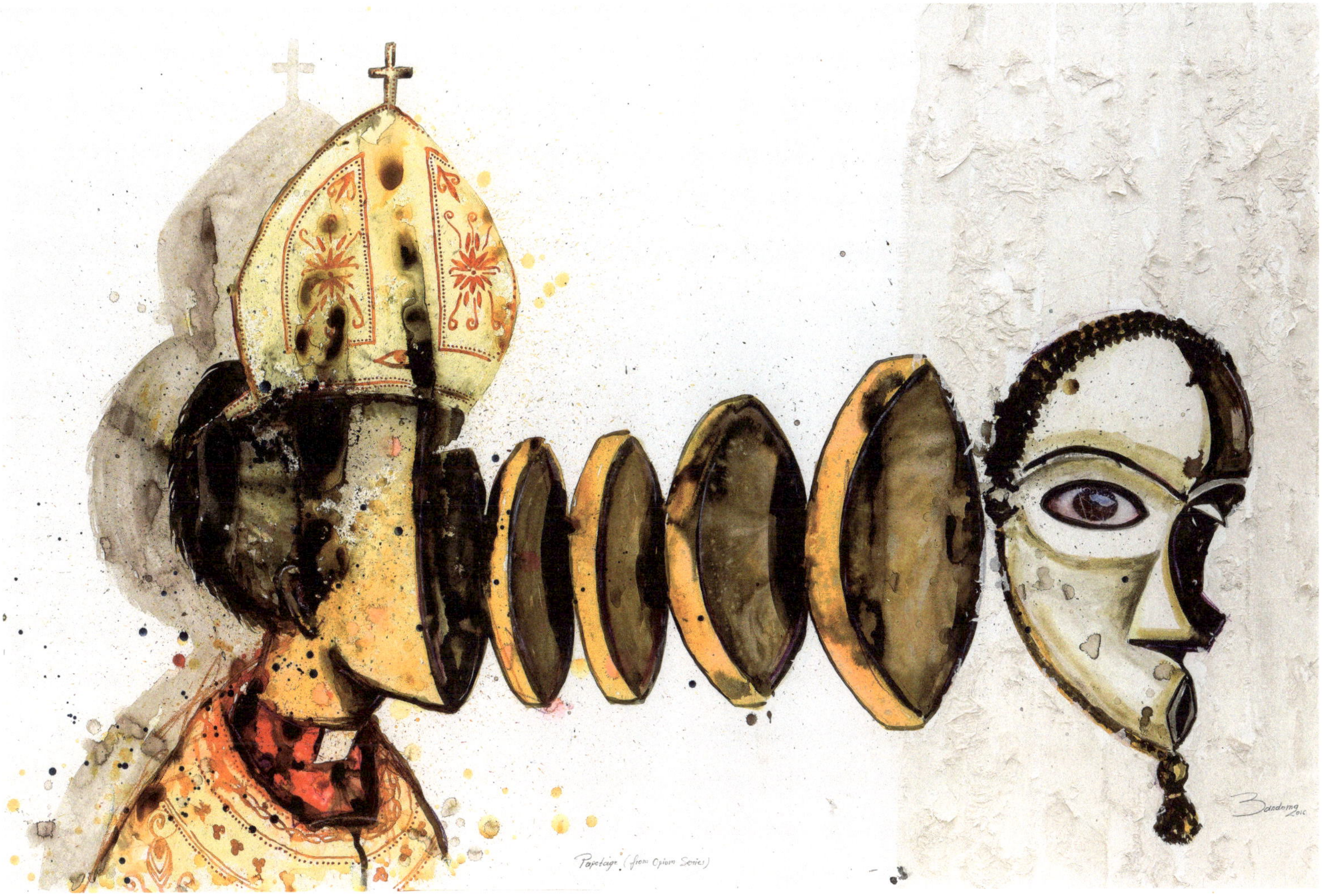

Fig. 353

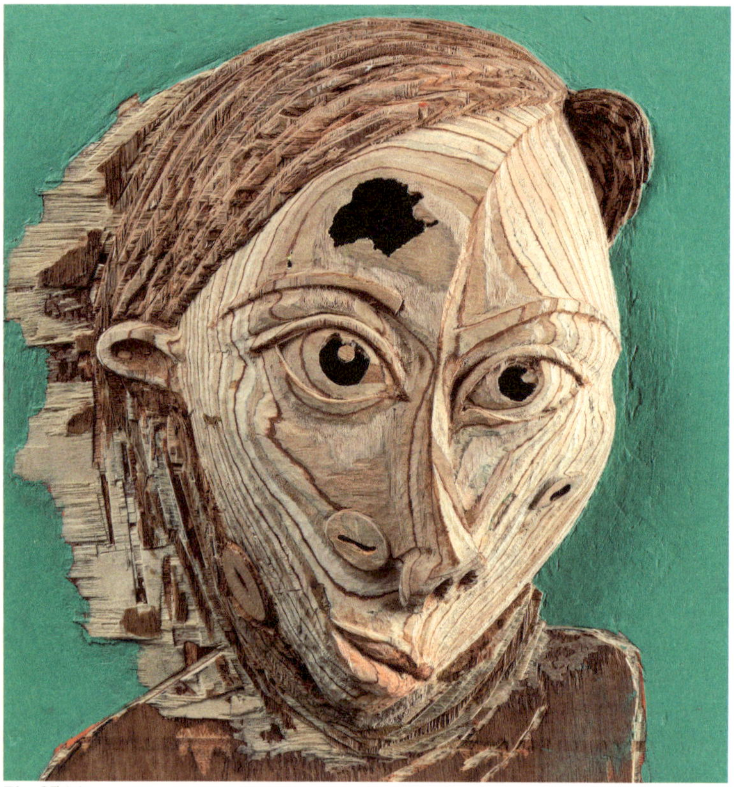
Fig. 354.1

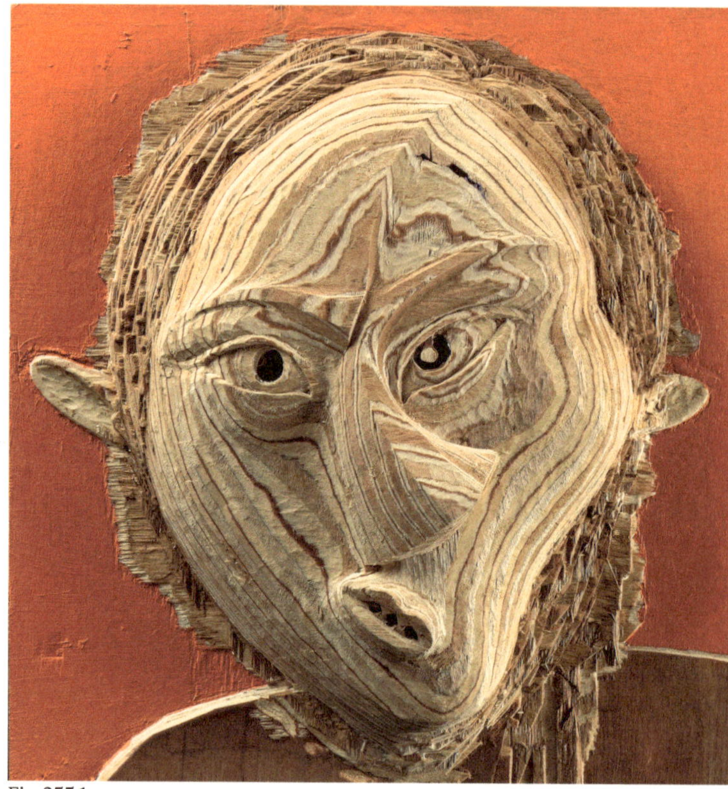
Fig. 355.1

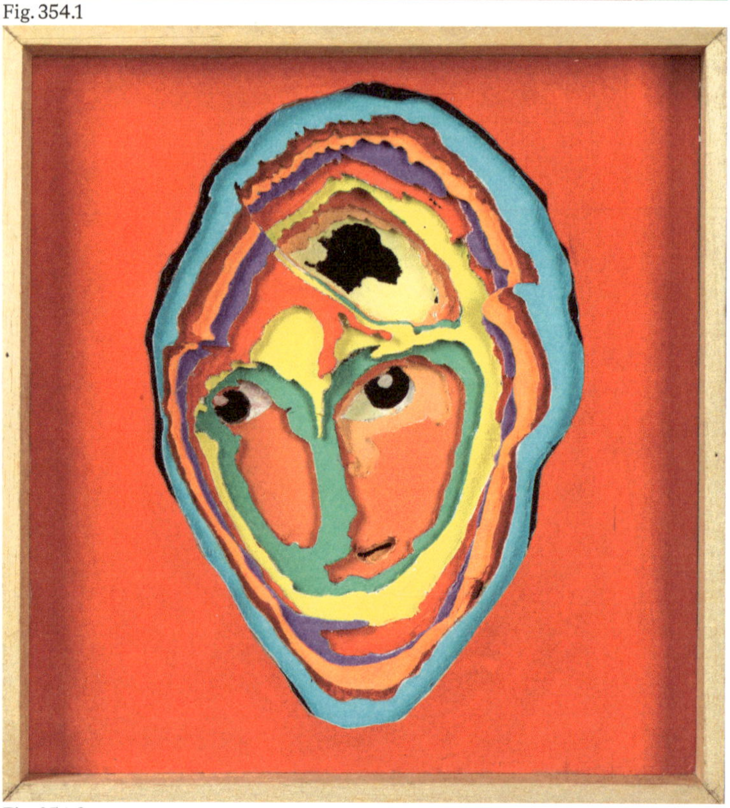
Fig. 354.2

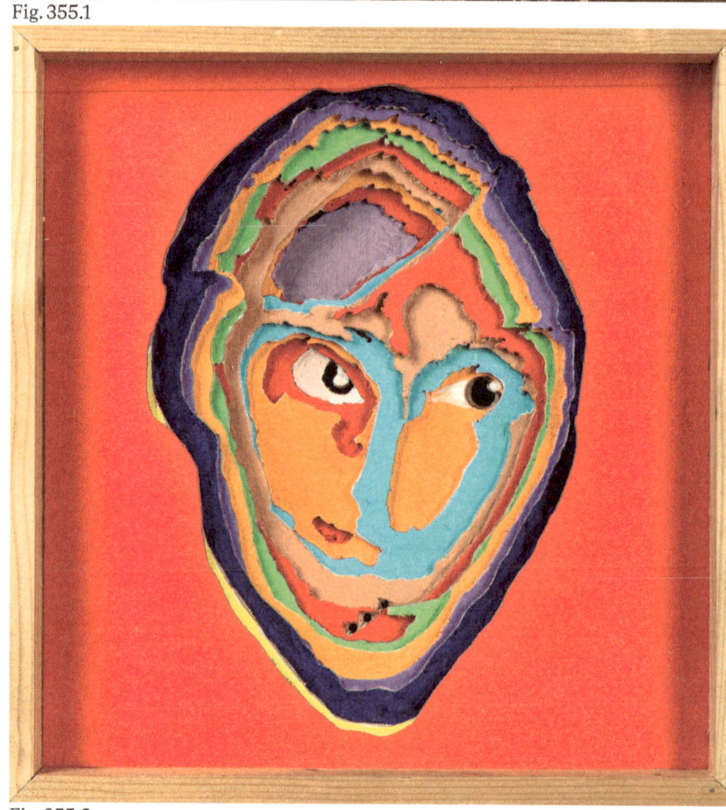
Fig. 355.2

Fig. 352
Artist of the central Pende region
***Mbangu* mask**
Before 1939, wood, textile and plant fibers, pigments, 31 × 21 × 13 cm
Museum Rietberg Zürich, EFA 25
Gift of Barbara and Eberhard Fischer
Acquired by Hans Himmelheber

Fig. 353
Steve Bandoma
Papotage
from the series *Opium*
2016, acrylic, ink, and collage on paper, 180 × 120 cm
Gallery MAGNIN-A, Paris

Fig. 354
Aimé Mpane
La Demoiselle Picasso-Minso
2018, acrylic and mixed media on wood, 31 × 32 × 7 cm
Nomad Gallery, Brussels,
Aimé Mpane Collection

Fig. 355
Aimé Mpane
La Demoiselle Picasso-Mputu
2017, acrylic and mixed media on wood, 31 × 32 × 7 cm
Nomad Gallery, Brussels,
Aimé Mpane Collection

LIGHT AND DARK SIDES: THE PENDE MASK *MBANGU* IN CONTEMPORARY ART — One of the most famous yet most unusual masks is the so-called *mbangu* mask by the central Pende. This is one of the very rare masks in African art that has an asymmetric design [fig. 352]. This initiation mask's potency lies in its strong black-and-white contrast. *Mbangu* was associated with disease, misfortune, and physical shortcomings, which were ascribed to witchcraft.[1] The mouth, nose, and eye on the dark, "sick" side are distorted. In contrast, the white side bears typical features of a male Pende mask, like the distinctive forehead and pronounced cheekbones—symbols of strength and health. *Mbangu* was "bewitched" but was also searching for the source of its curse. With its simultaneously harmonious and asymmetrical design, *mbangu* symbolized illness and cure, suffering and hope.

Both Congolese artists Steve Bandoma and Aimé Mpane reference this unusual mask type in their artworks. In his painting *Papotage* ("chitchat") from the series *Opium*, Steve Bandoma questions the missionary work from the fifteenth century to the present day [fig. 353]. With this title and the subject of the *mbangu* mask, he is criticizing the Church's two-faced behavior and promise of salvation. Instead of exchange and syncretism, the missionaries often demanded the rejection of traditional religious practices. This was sadly accompanied by the destruction of old masks and figures, which Hans Himmelheber also documented on his travels.

In his series *Demoiselles* the artist Aimé Mpane created two-faced portraits that can be seen on the recto and verso of the supporting material [figs. 354/355]. Drawing on Pende masks among other things, three-dimensional faces emerge from several layers of plywood. While the carved faces on the one side are reminiscent of the topographies and reliefs of a landscape, the strong colors and abstract forms on the other side allude to Cubism. With the title Aimé Mpane makes direct reference to Picasso's iconic picture *Les Demoiselles d'Avignon* from 1907, which was modeled on African masks. Mpane is paying tribute to Picasso, but he is also criticizing the avant-garde's appropriation of African art. Being able to see through the masks from both sides raises the question of what is the front and the back, what is public and private. — Michaela Oberhofer

1 Strother 2008, pp. 27f.

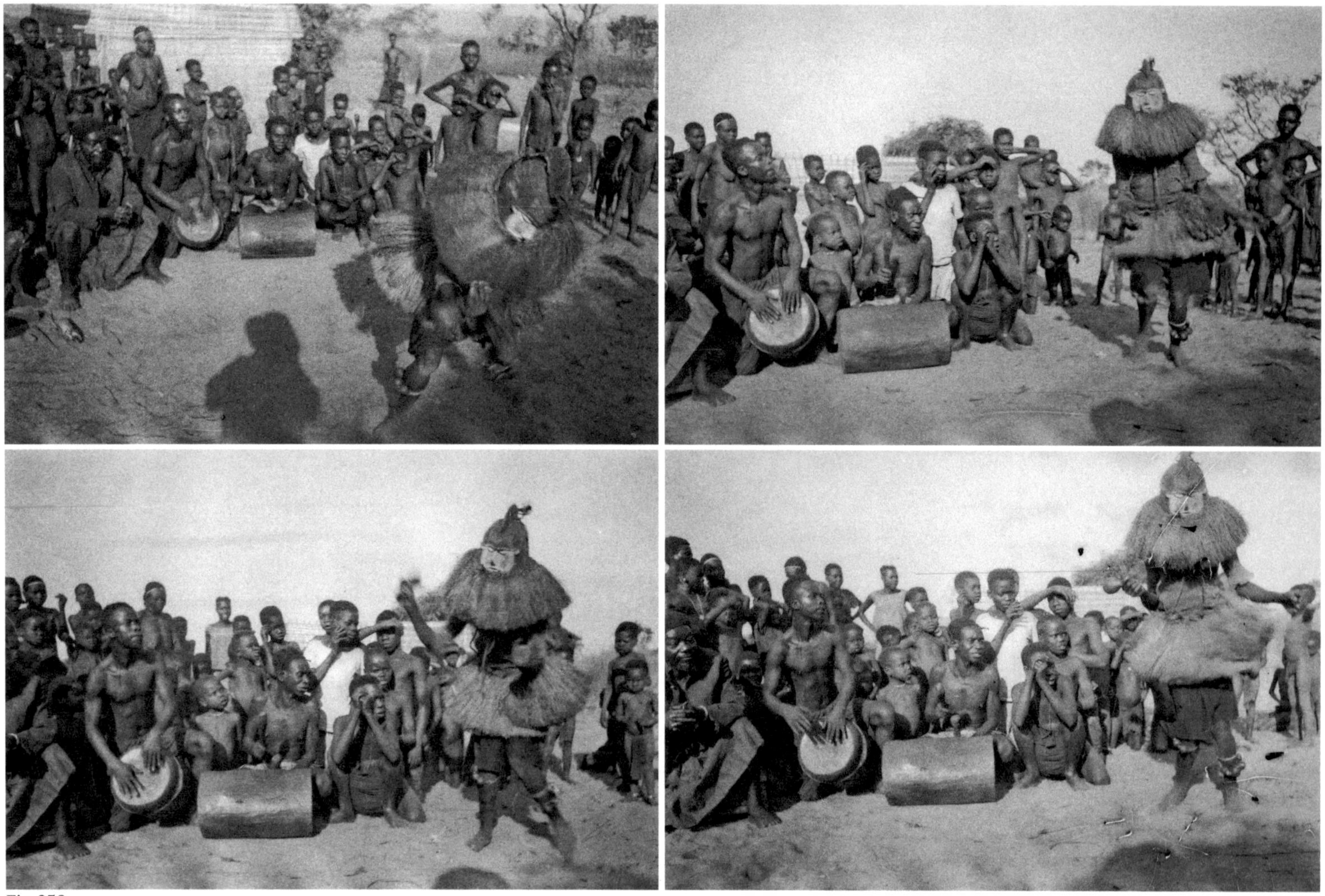

Fig. 356

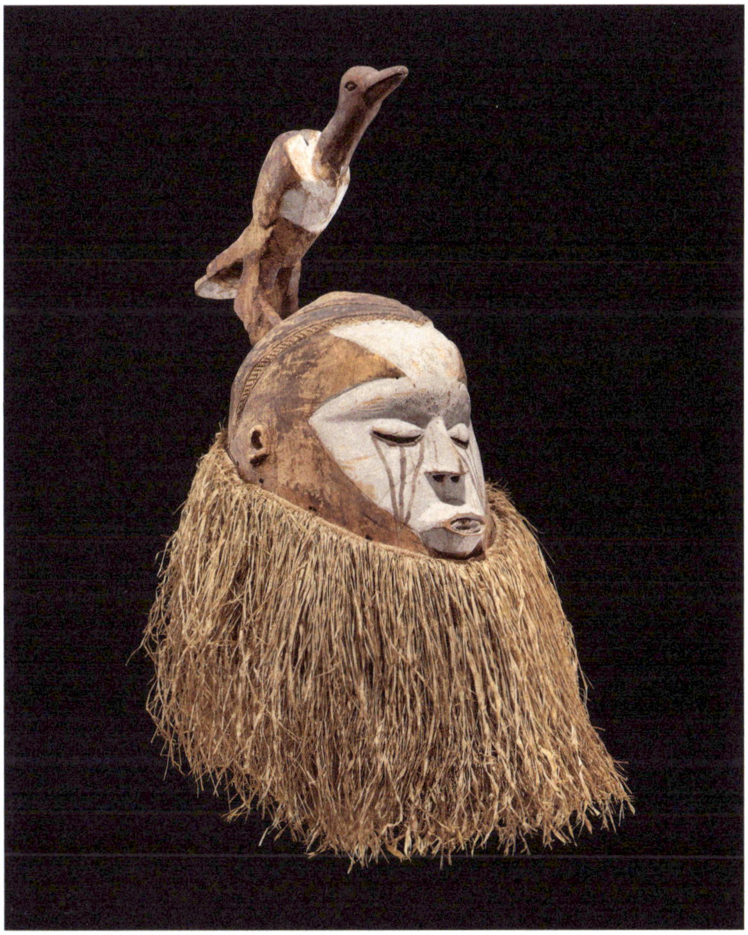
Fig. 357

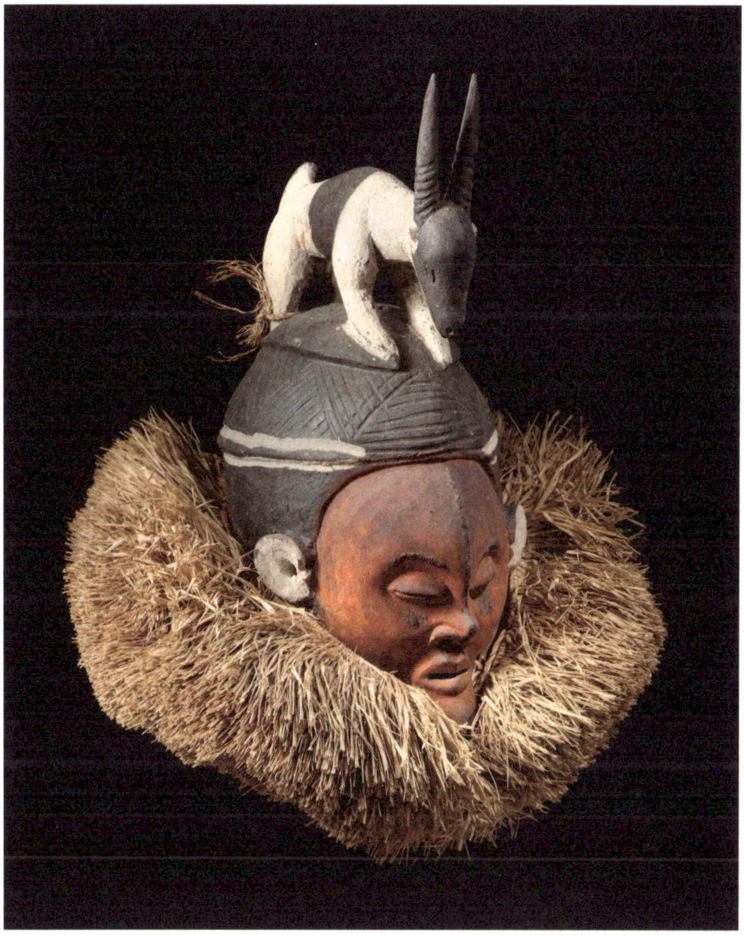
Fig. 358

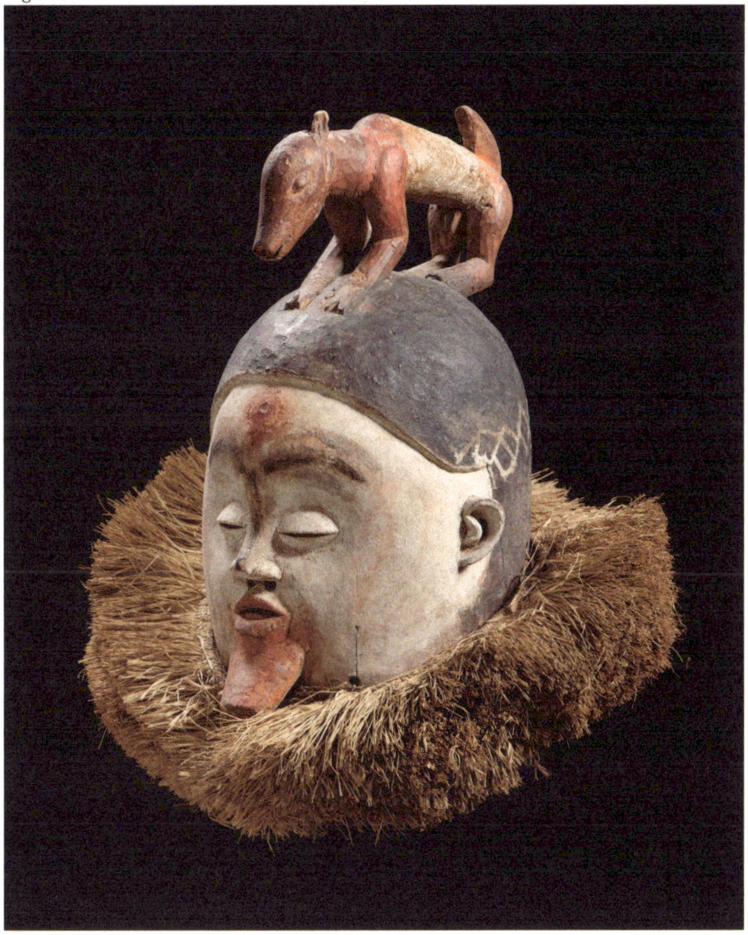
Fig. 359

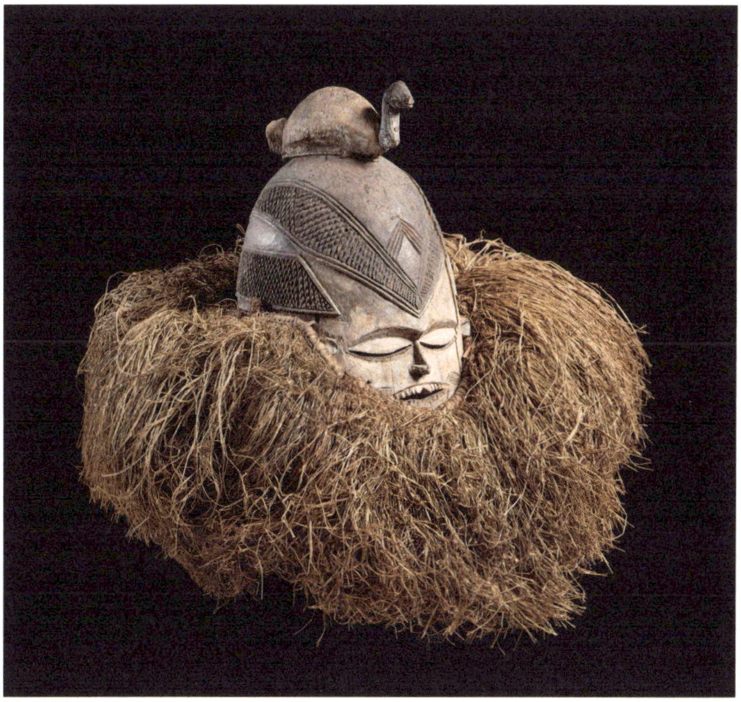
Fig. 360

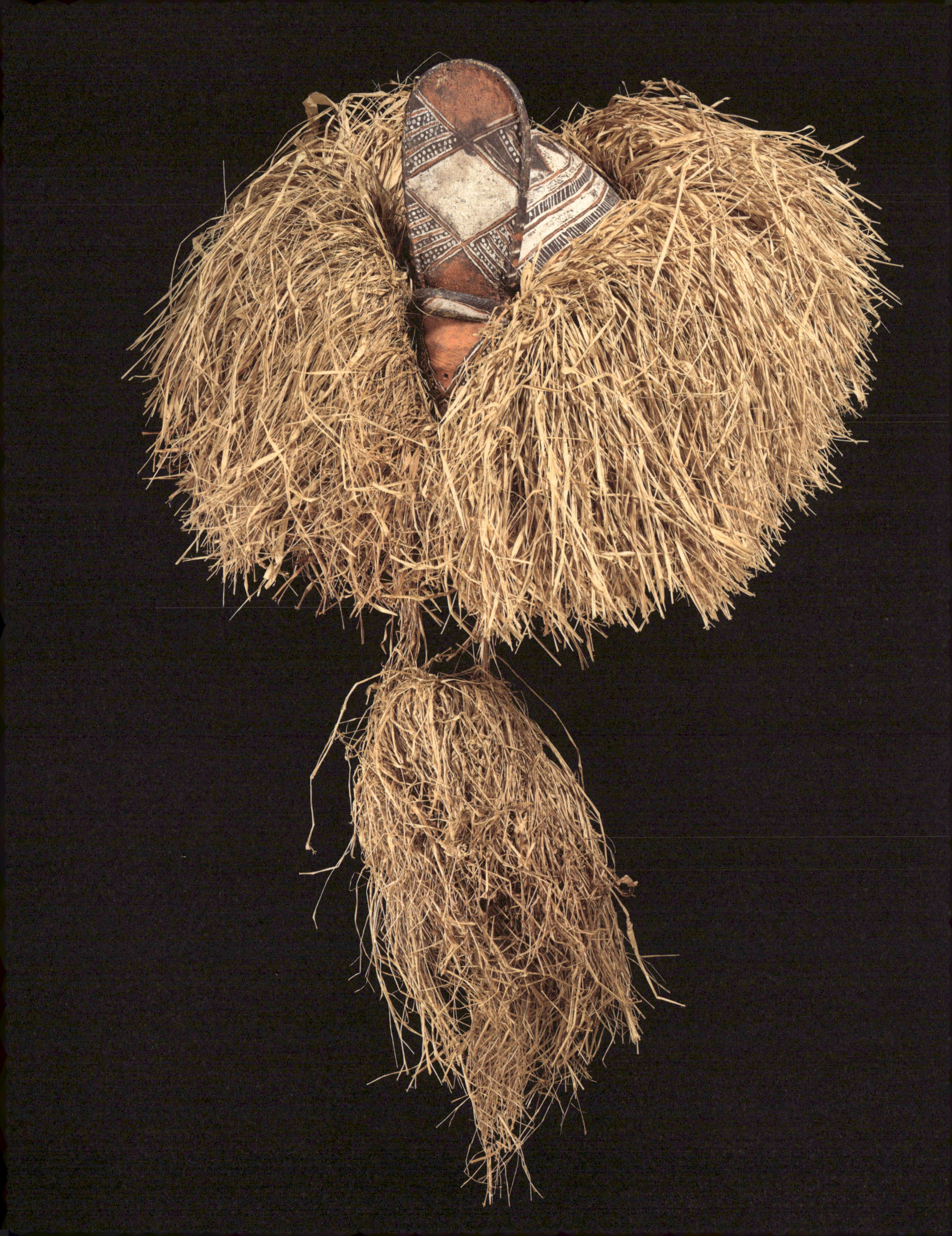

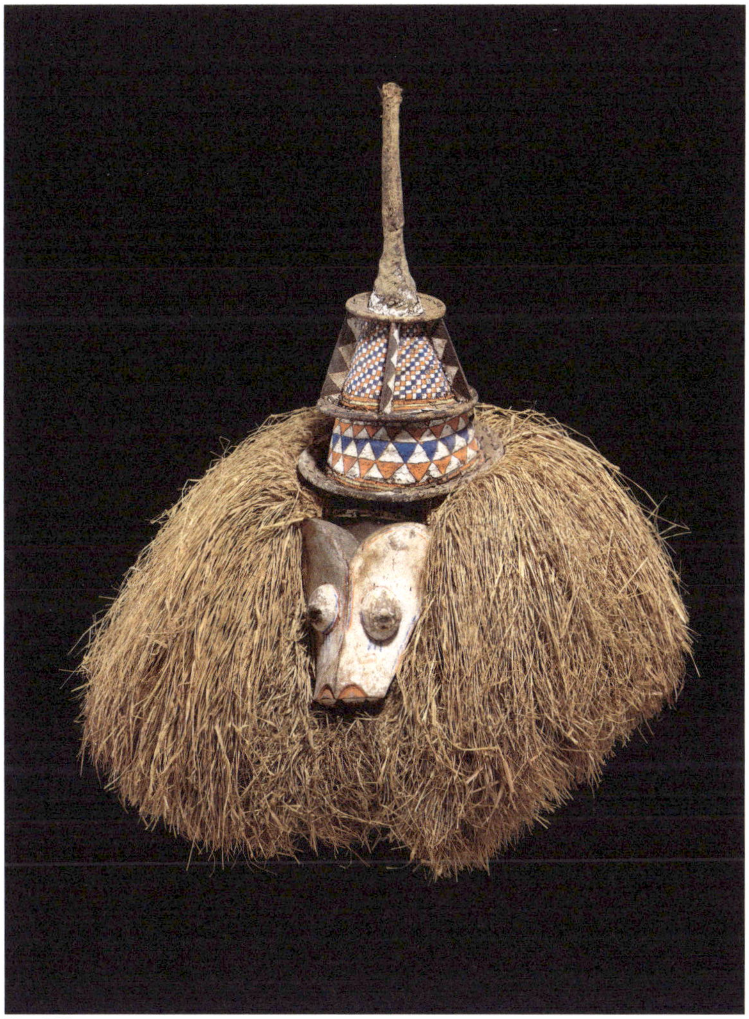
Fig. 362

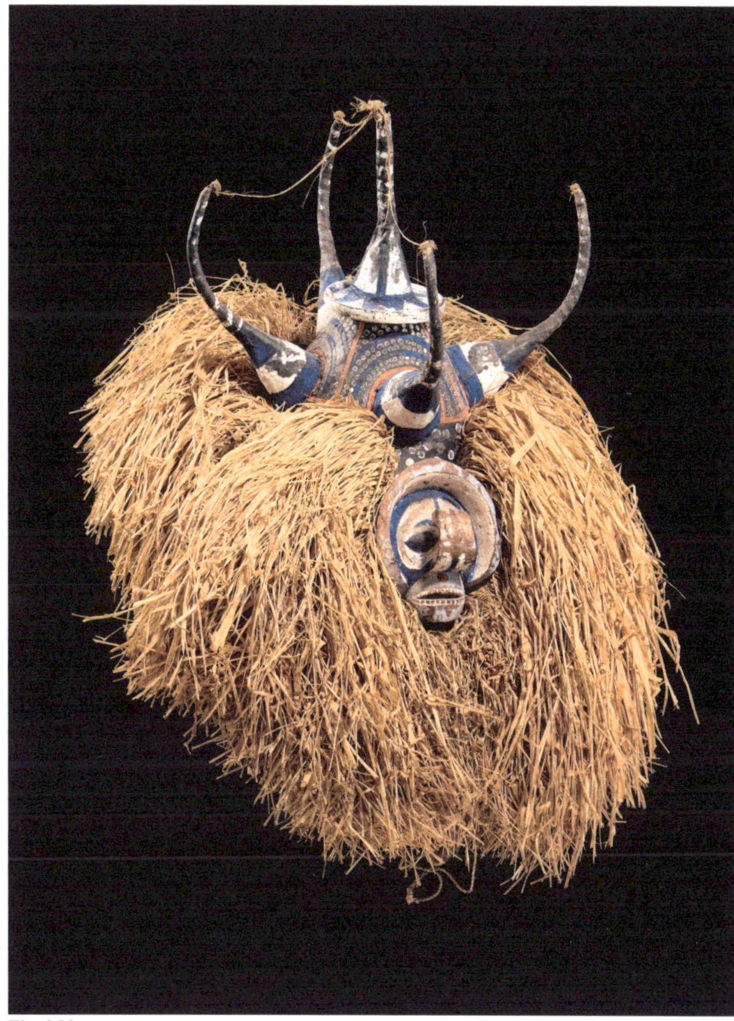
Fig. 363

Fig. 361

Fig. 366

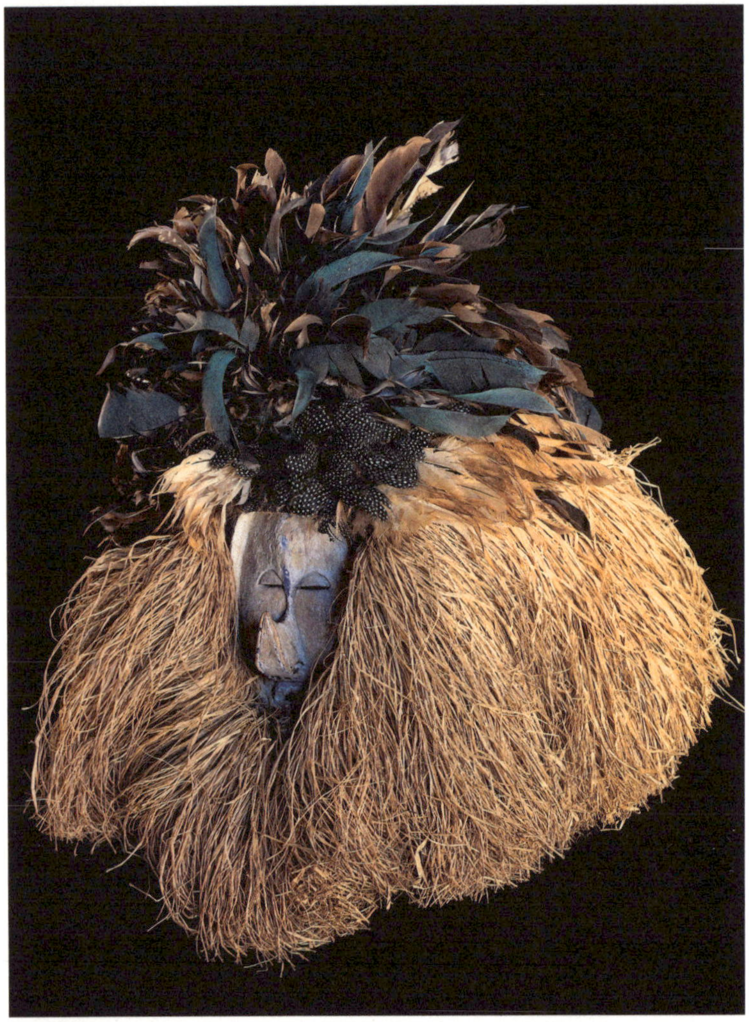

Fig. 364

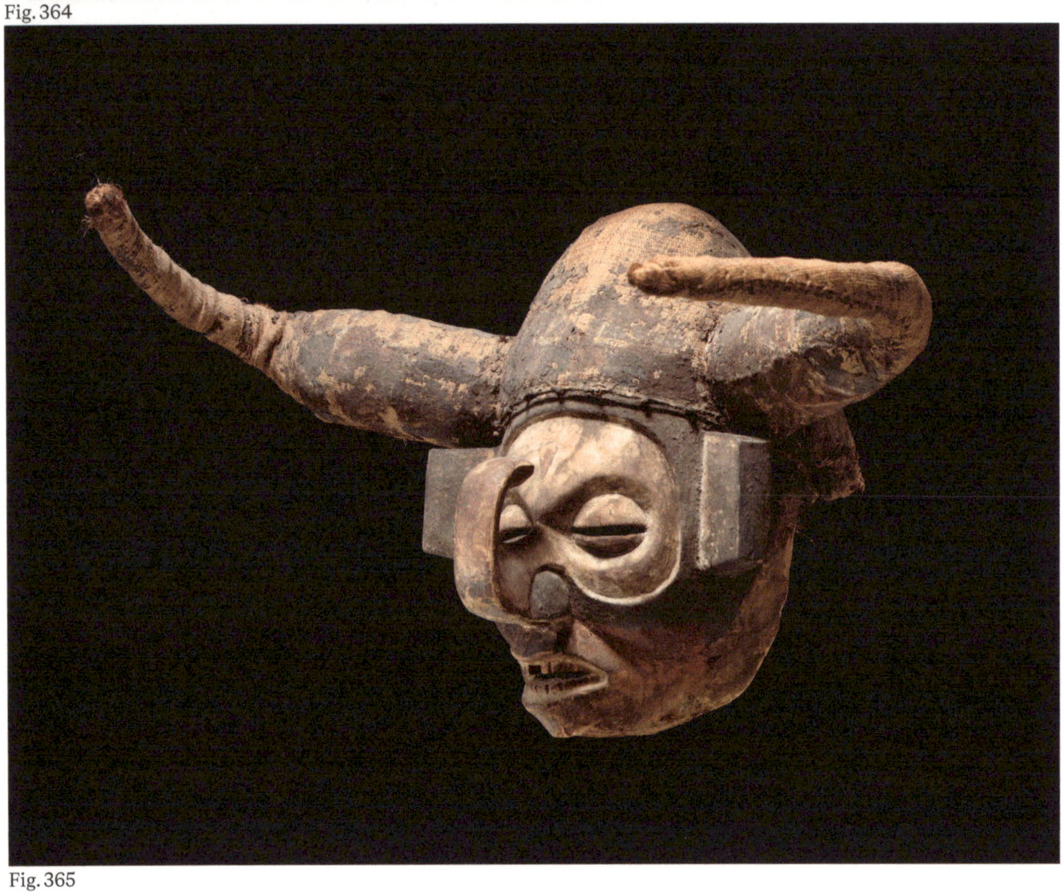

Fig. 365

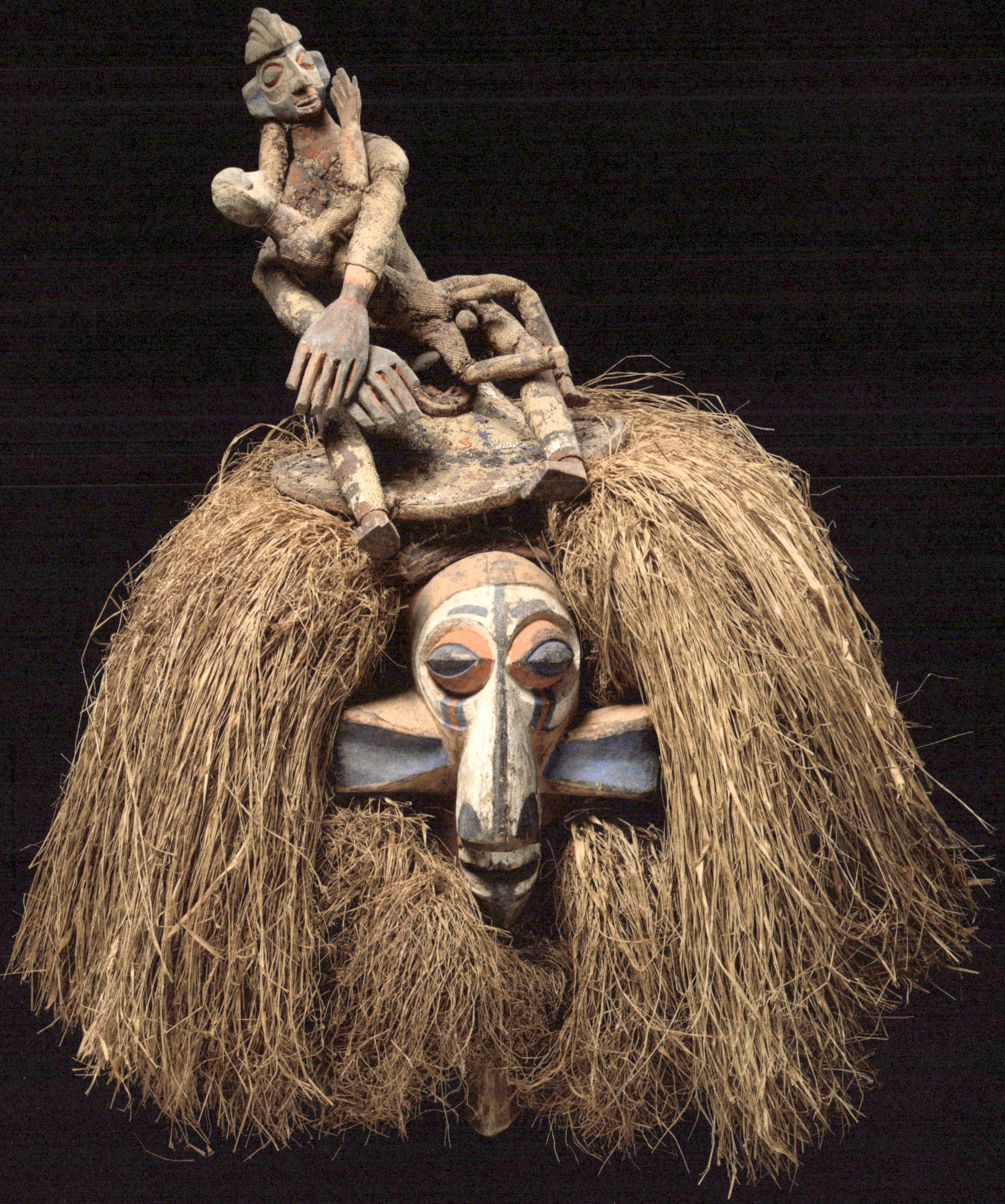

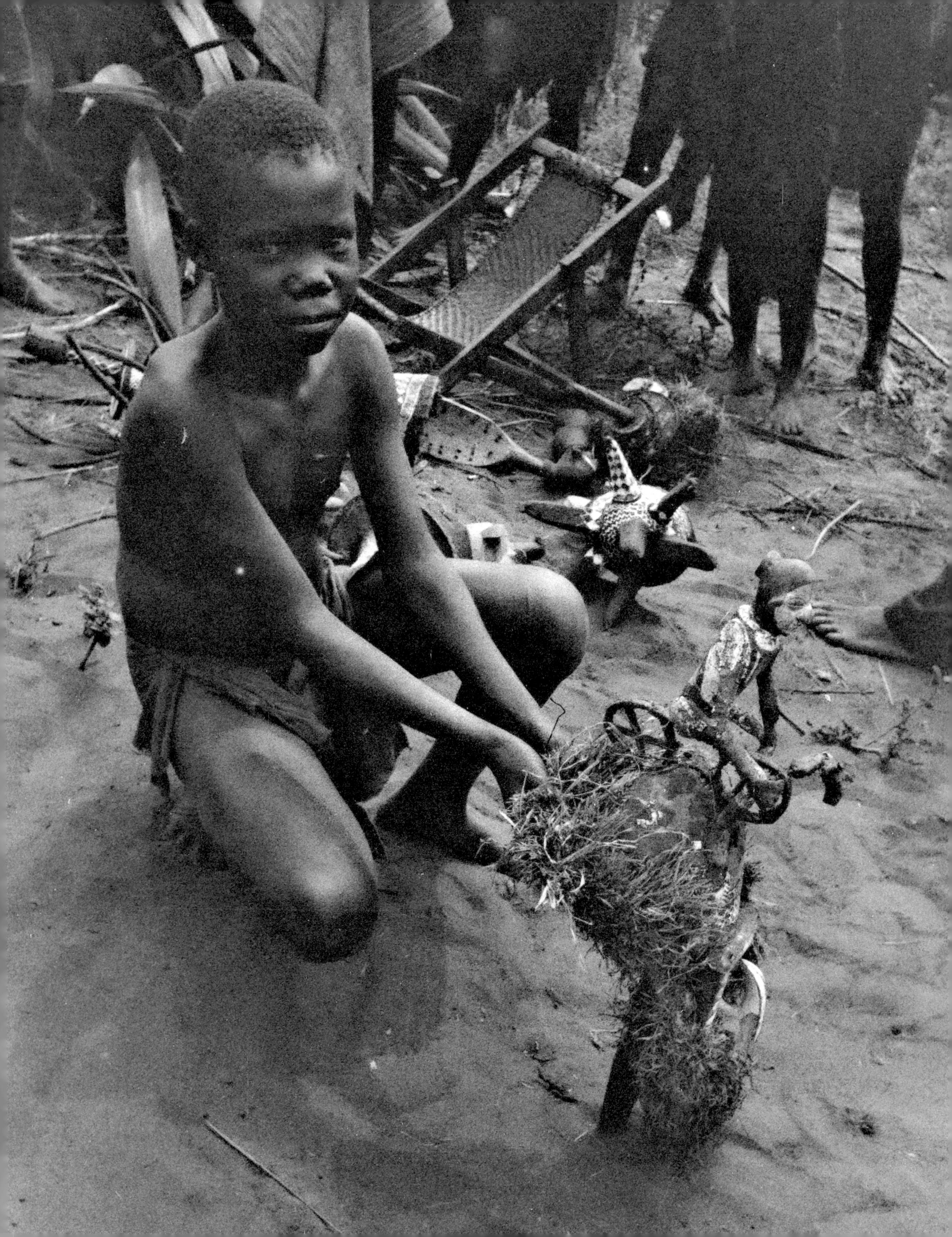

Fig. 367

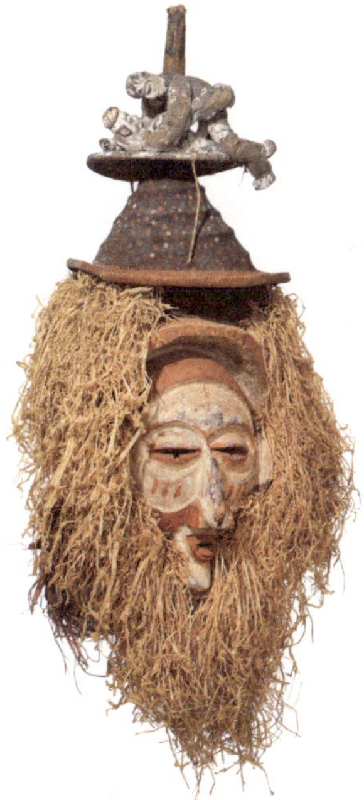

Fig. 368

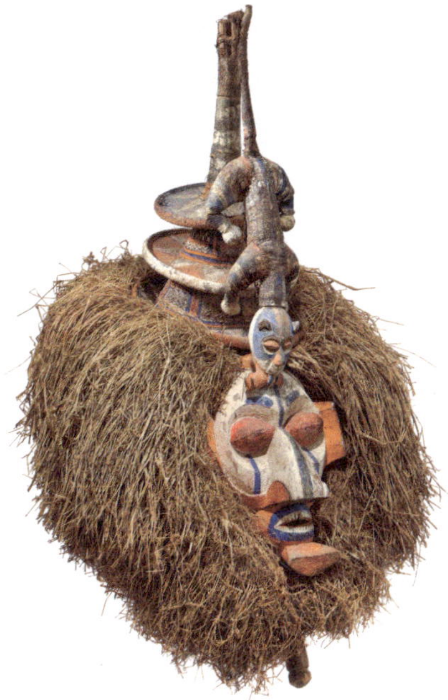

Fig. 369

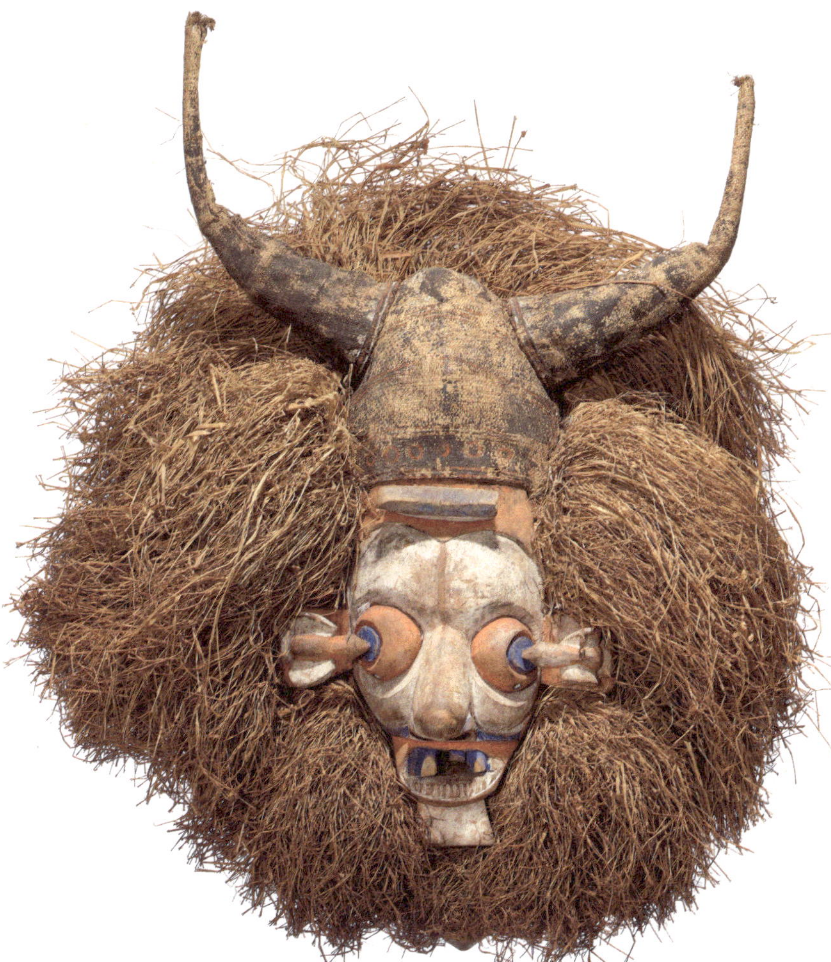

Fig. 370

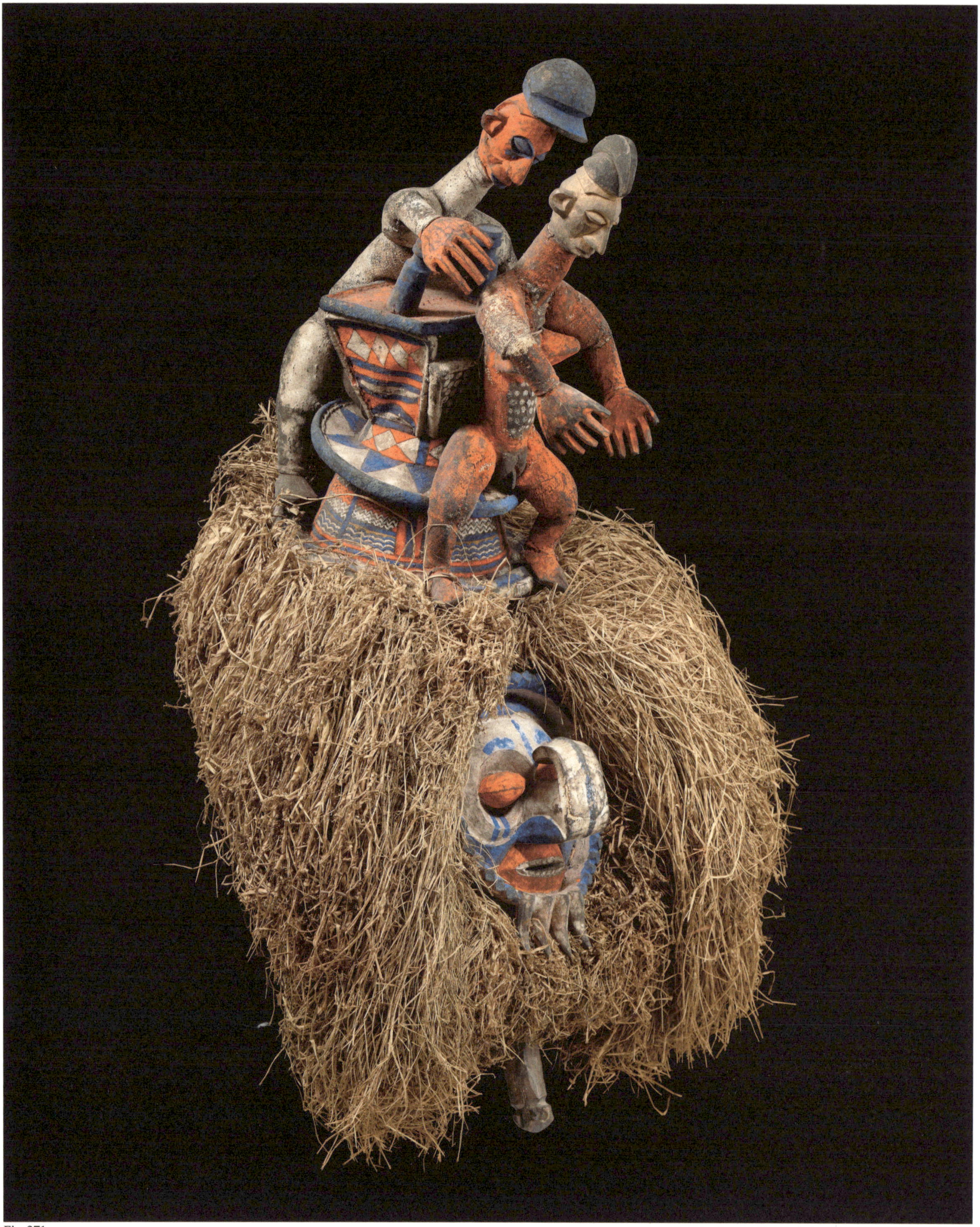

Fig. 371

Fig. 356
Hans Himmelheber
Performance of the *hemba* mask
Kiala, June 24, 1938, b/w negatives
Museum Rietberg Zürich,
FHH 157-38 to FHH 157-41

Fig. 357
Artist of the Suku region
Mask with bird crest
Circa 1900, wood, plant fibers,
pigments, 70 × 35 × 48 cm
Museum Rietberg Zürich, RAC 506
Gift of Eduard von der Heydt

Fig. 358
Artist of the Suku region
Helmet mask with antelope
Before 1939, wood, plant fibers,
pigments, 57 × 45 × 47 cm
Museum Rietberg Zürich, EFA 2
Gift of Barbara and Eberhard Fischer
Acquired by Hans Himmelheber

Fig. 359
Artist of the Suku region
Helmet mask
Before 1939, wood, plant fibers,
pigments, 49 × 35 × 41 cm
Museum Rietberg Zürich, EFA 1
Gift of Barbara and Eberhard Fischer
Acquired by Hans Himmelheber

Fig. 360
Artist of the Suku region
Helmet mask
Before 1939, wood, plant fibers, pigments,
approx. 40 × 50 × 50 cm
Museum Rietberg Zürich, EFA 4
Gift of Barbara and Eberhard Fischer
Acquired by Hans Himmelheber

Fig. 361
Katomi from Kapuna
Mask *kambaandzya* as protection
Before 1938, Kingulu, plant fibers,
pigments, 28 × 60 × 46 cm
Museum Rietberg Zürich, 2019.430
Gift of Barbara and Eberhard Fischer
Acquired by Hans Himmelheber

Fig. 362
Artist of the Yaka region
Mask with cone crest
Before 1938, wood, plant fibers,
pigments, approx. 80 × 60 × 50 cm
Museum Rietberg Zürich, 2019.429
Gift of Barbara and Eberhard Fischer
Acquired by Hans Himmelheber

Fig. 363
Artist of the Yaka region
Mask with five-pronged crest
Before 1938, wood, plant fibers,
pigments, approx. 54 × 51 × 32 cm
Museum Rietberg Zürich, 2019.428
Gift of Barbara and Eberhard Fischer
Acquired by Hans Himmelheber

Fig. 364
Mukelenge Yamfu from Moanauta
***Ndeemba* mask**
Before 1938, wood, raffia textile,
feathers, white, black, and blue
pigments, 50 × 50 × 49 cm
Museum der Kulturen Basel, III 1337
Acquired by Hans Himmelheber

Fig. 365
Artist of the Yaka region
***Kisokolo* mask with horns**
Before 1938, wood, plant fibers,
pigments, 36 × 60 × 50 cm
Museum Rietberg Zürich, HH 26
Gift of Barbara and Eberhard Fischer
Acquired by Hans Himmelheber

Fig. 366
Artist of the Yaka region
Mask with lovemaking couple
Before 1938, wood, plant fibers,
pigments, 67 × 41 × 35 cm
Museum Rietberg Zürich, HH 28
Gift of Barbara and Eberhard Fischer
Acquired by Hans Himmelheber

Fig. 367
Hans Himmelheber
***Mbala* mask with bicycle**
Yaka region, 1938, b/w negative
Museum Rietberg Zürich, FHH 168-12

Fig. 368
Artist of the Yaka region
Mask with lovemaking couple
Early twentieth century, wood, woven
bast, plant fibers, 100 × 30 × 30 cm
Private Collection Lausanne
John Torres Jr.

Fig. 369
Artist of the Yaka region
Mask with animal crest
Before 1938, wood, plant fibers,
pigments, 90 × 56 × 44 cm
Museum Rietberg Zürich, HH 29
Gift of Barbara and Eberhard Fischer
Acquired by Hans Himmelheber

Fig. 370
Artist of the Yaka region
Mask with birds pecking out the eyes
Before 1938, wood, plant fibers,
pigments, 60 × 50 × 20 cm
Museum Rietberg Zürich, 2018.7
Gift of Martin Himmelheber
Acquired by Hans Himmelheber

Fig. 371
Artist of the Yaka region
Mask with two figures
Before 1938, wood, plant fibers,
pigments, 77 × 44 × 43 cm
Museum Rietberg Zürich, HH 27
Gift of Barbara and Eberhard Fischer
Acquired by Hans Himmelheber

A SNAPSHOT OF ARTISTIC PRACTICES AROUND 1938: THE YAKA'S *MUKANDA* MASKS — Right at the beginning of his travels, Hans Himmelheber came across the dances performed east of Kinshasa in connection with the Yaka's *mukanda* circumcision camp. In these camps boys spent a year undergoing their initiation to become full-fledged men. They learned craft skills and practiced dancing and singing. The artist *kalaueni* produced three to eleven masks for each camp; with the exception of the leader, they would then always perform in pairs. They were danced by the newly initiated with a privileged status. Himmelheber was able not only to document these dances in numerous photographs but also to purchase mask ensembles. These comprised very distinct masks, ranging from faceless ones worked entirely from raffia [fig. 361] to ones with carved wooden faces and simple headdresses like antennal extensions [figs. 362/363] or feathers [fig. 364] to horned masks [fig. 365]. As a costume, the masked figures wore dancing shirts made of woven cord [fig. 32]. At the dances the plainer masks performed first [fig. 59]. The largest and most attractive mask, the *mbala*, made its appearance at the end of the performance and was the leader's mask. *Mbala* were the public's clear favorites and were intended to astound the viewers with surprising scenes that were reenacted with marionettes on the head section. The artists were inspired by sex, humor, and current events. For example, Himmelheber purchased masks that show a couple lovemaking [fig. 366/368]. Modern subjects were also popular and Himmelheber photographed a mask bearing a cyclist [fig. 367]. Humor played a big part in the selection of subjects for *mbala* masks. Parodies of colonial officials were popular, such as an *agent sanitaire* on his motorbike, a nurse at the microscope, or another doctor's assistant examining a woman on a gynecological chair [fig. 371].[1] One genuine discovery is the mask with birds carved on the sides of the face section that are pecking out the mask's eyes [fig. 370]. Before now this subject had not been described for the Yaka, but it testifies to the artists' inventiveness. Yaka artists created new masks for every *mukanda* camp; in this respect, the mask ensembles acquired by Himmelheber constitute a snapshot of artistic practices in 1938.
— Nanina Guyer

1 Himmelheber 1939a, p. 11.

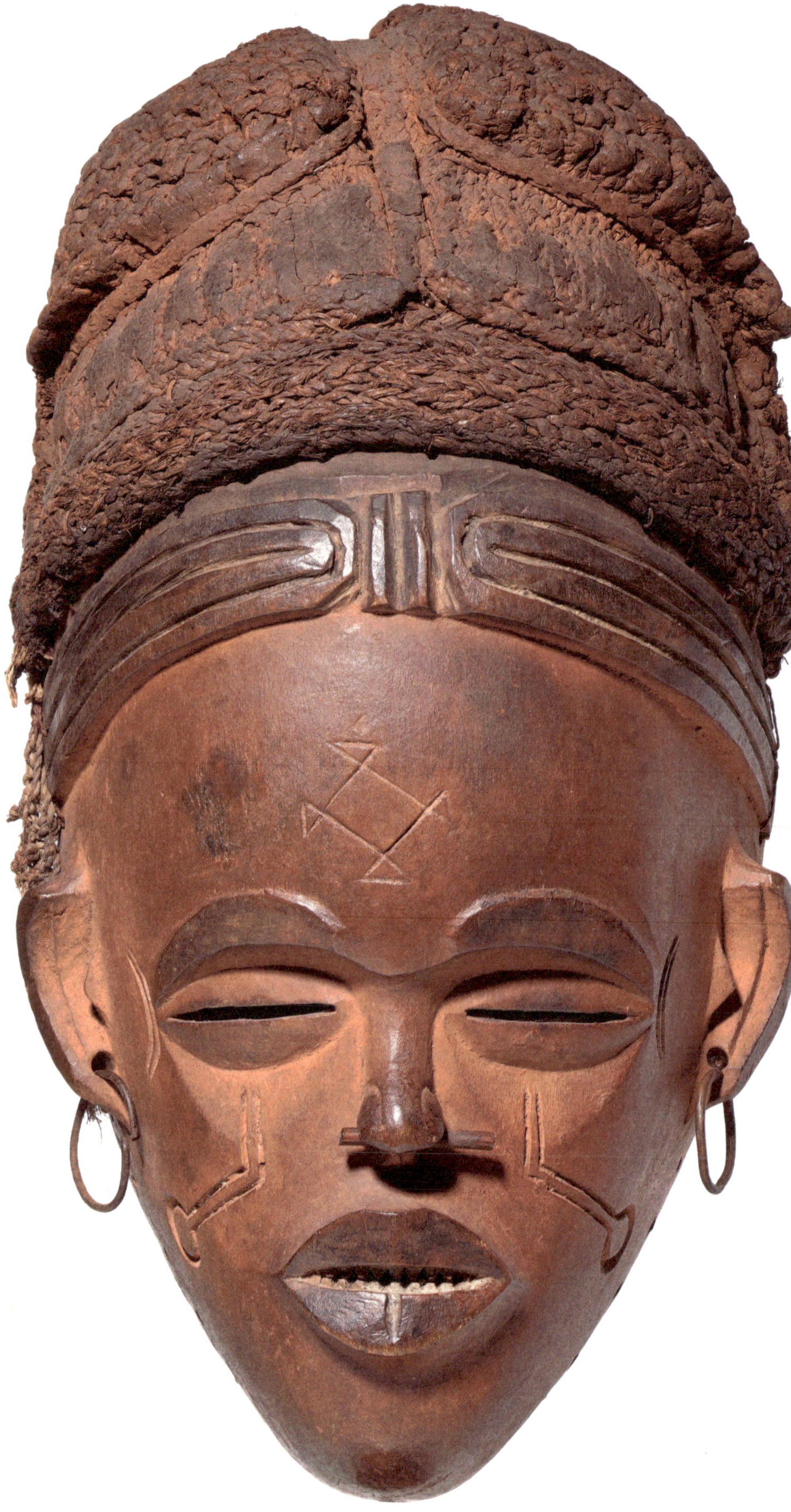

Fig. 372

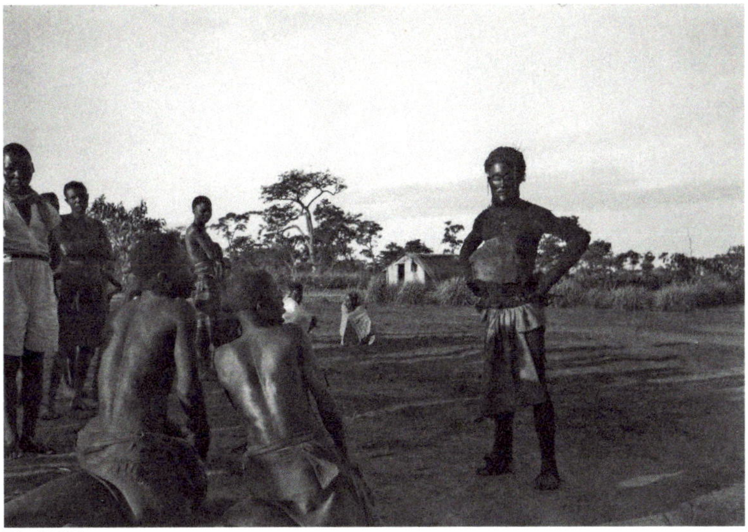
Fig. 373.1

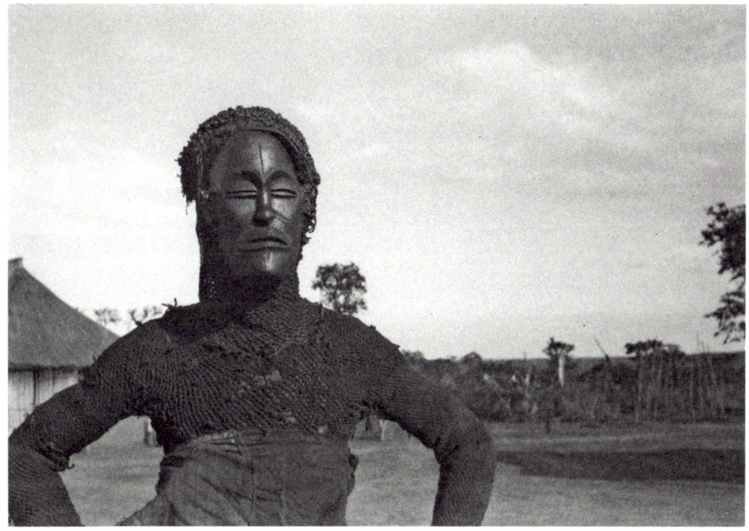
Fig. 373.2

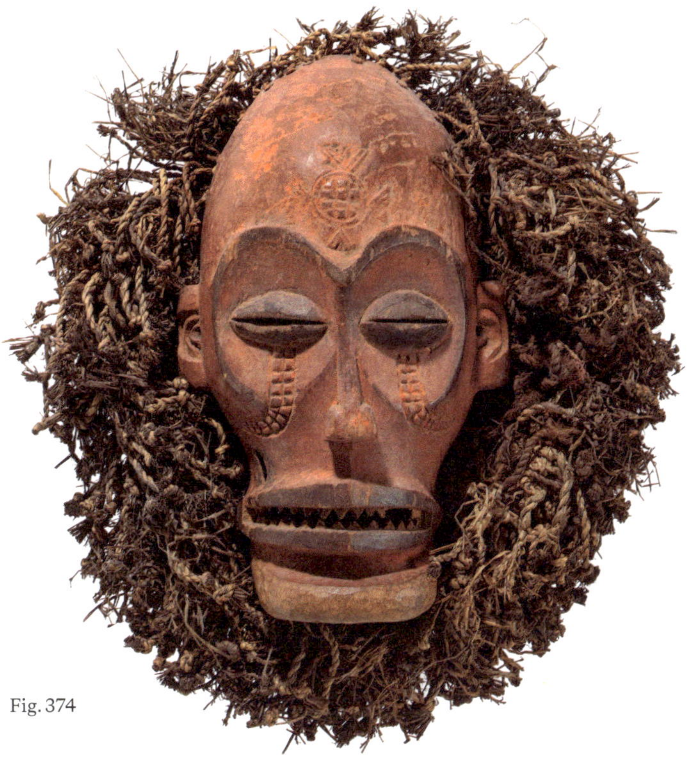
Fig. 374

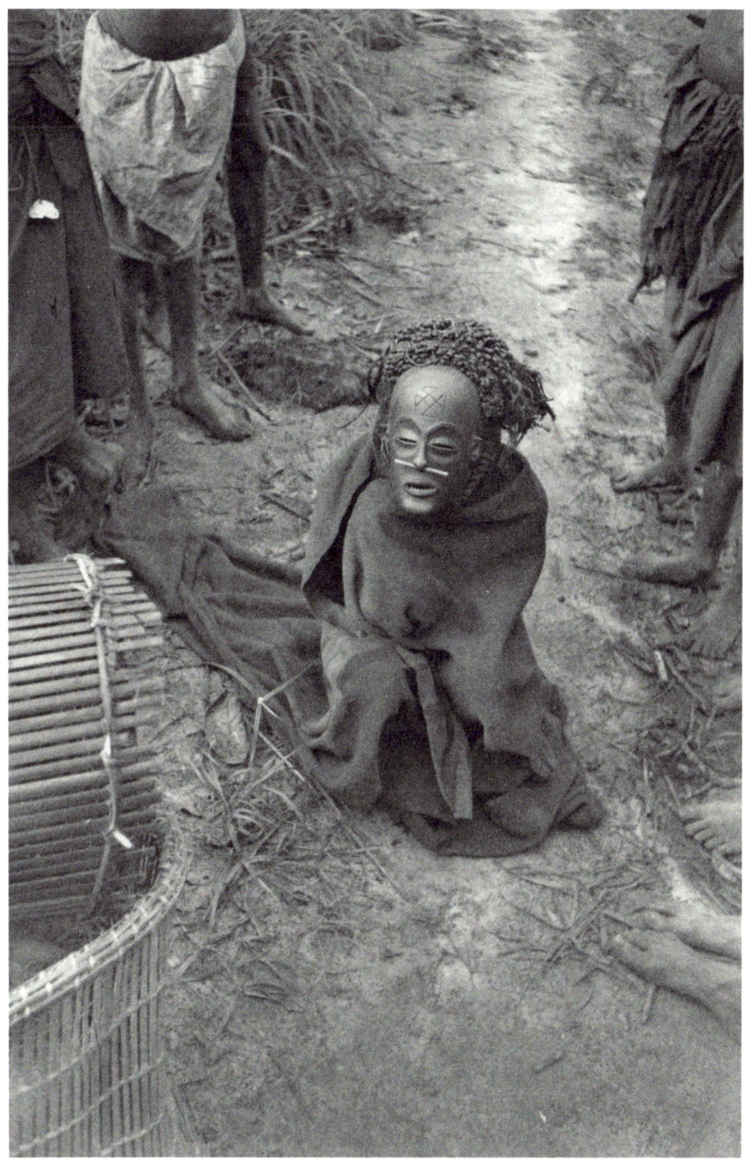
Fig. 375

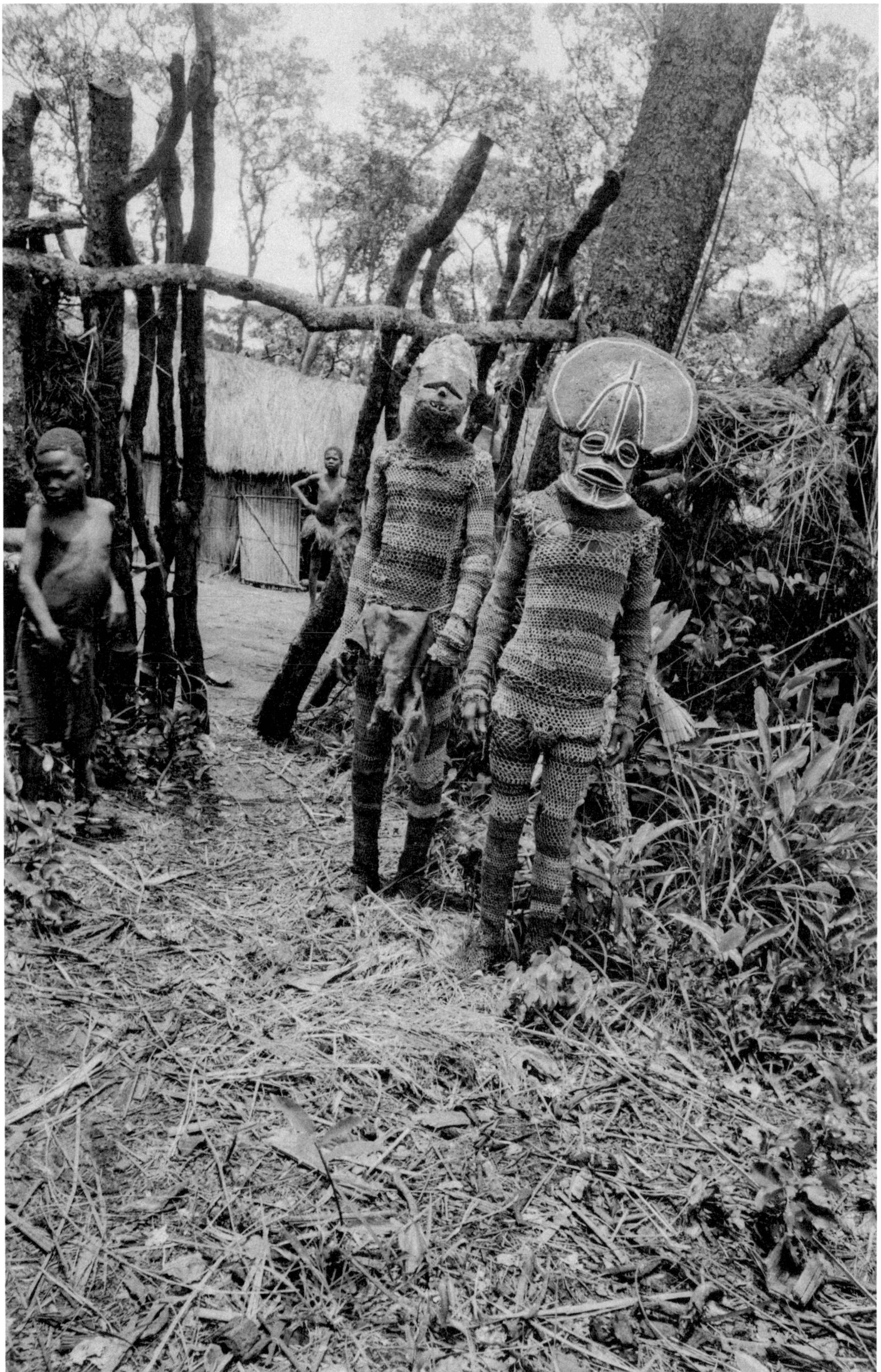

Fig. 376

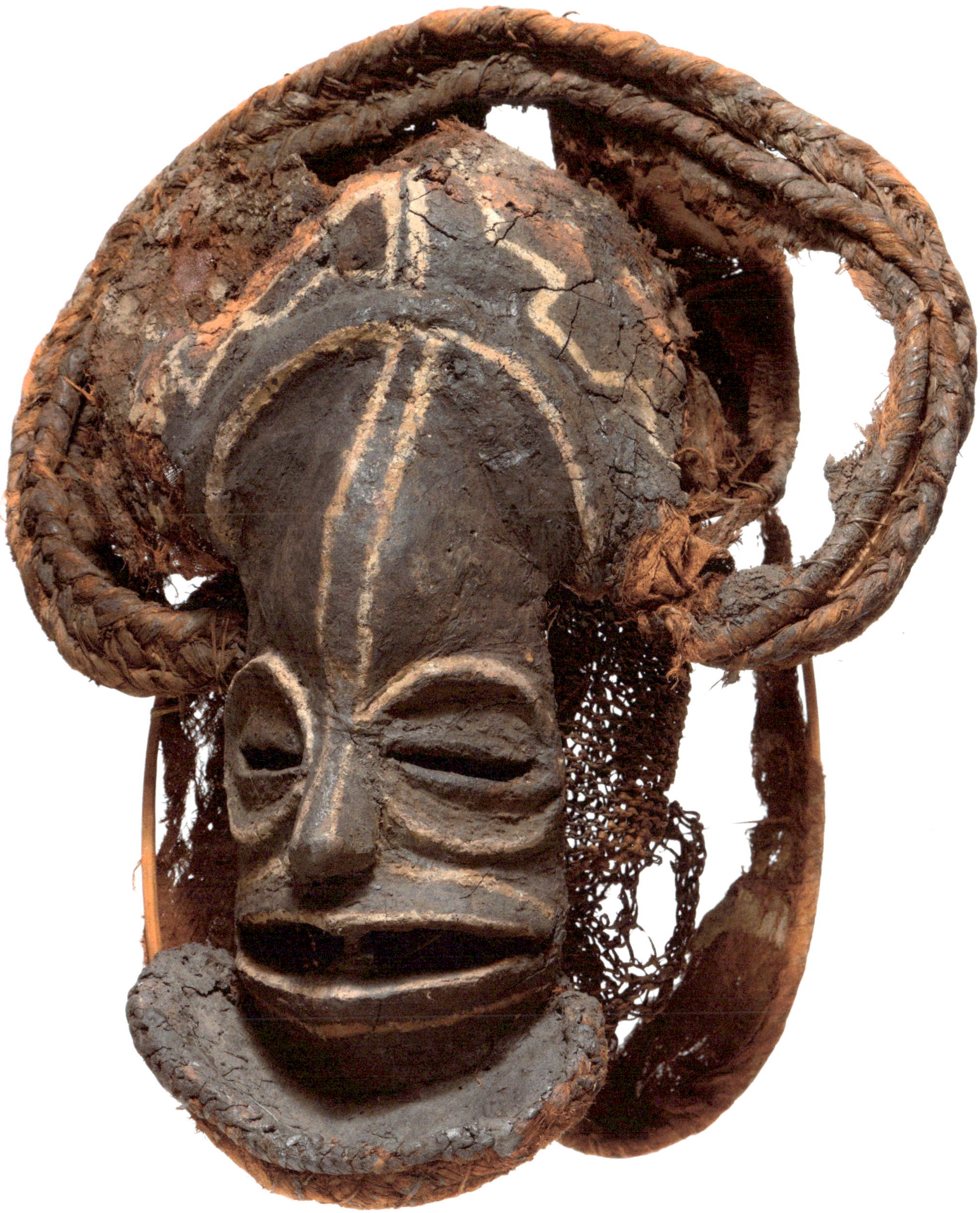

Fig. 377

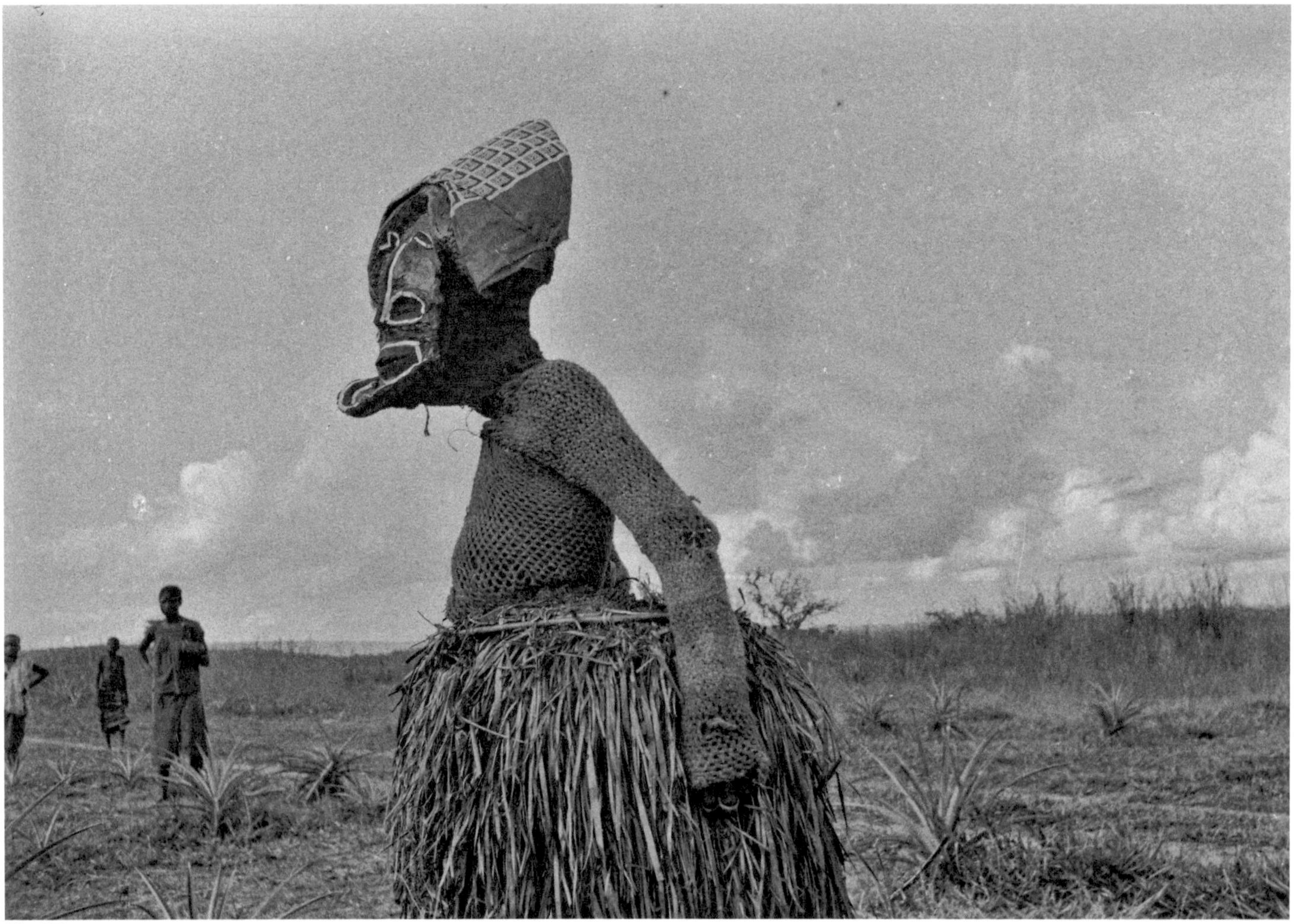
Fig. 378

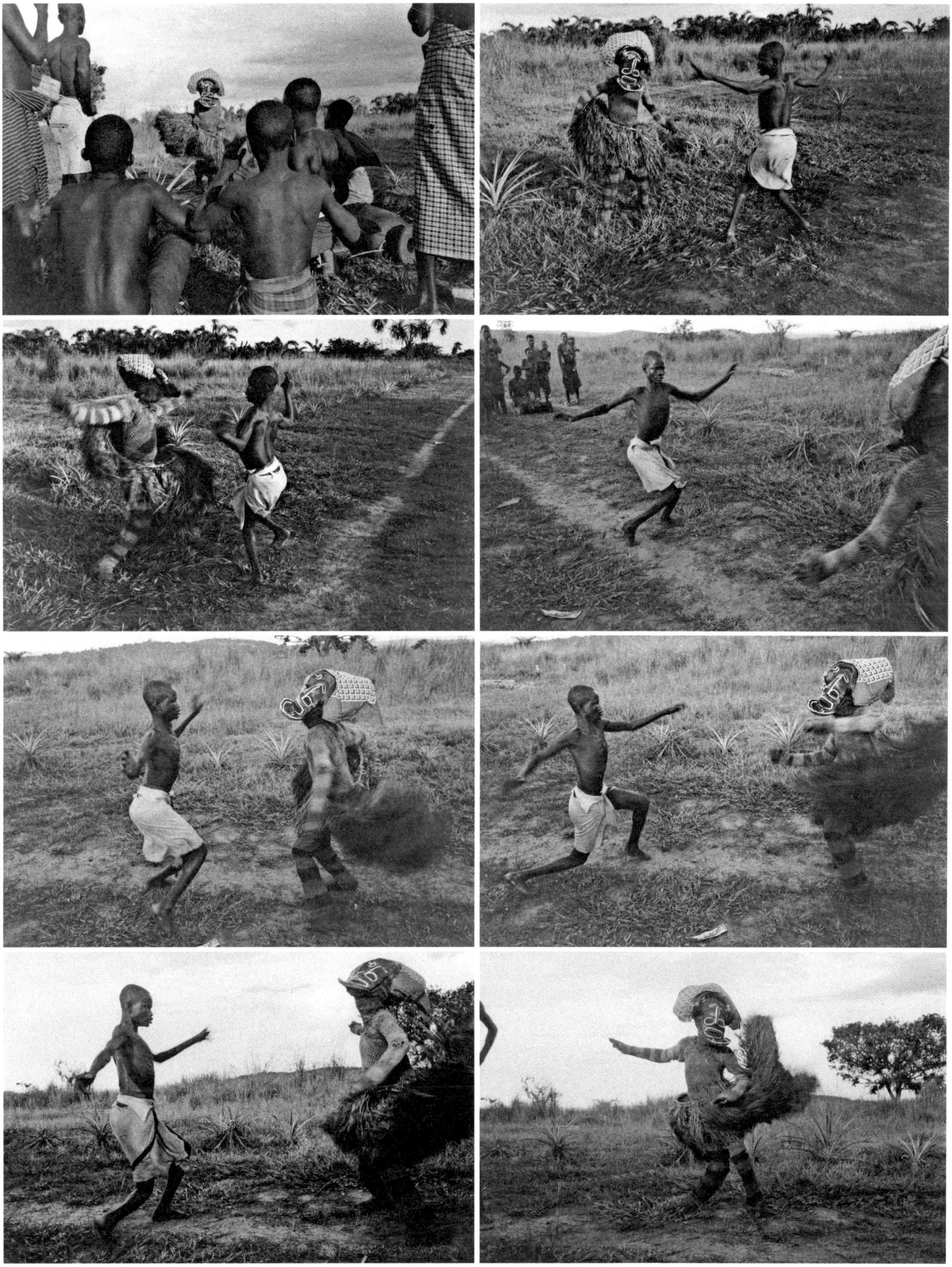

Fig. 379

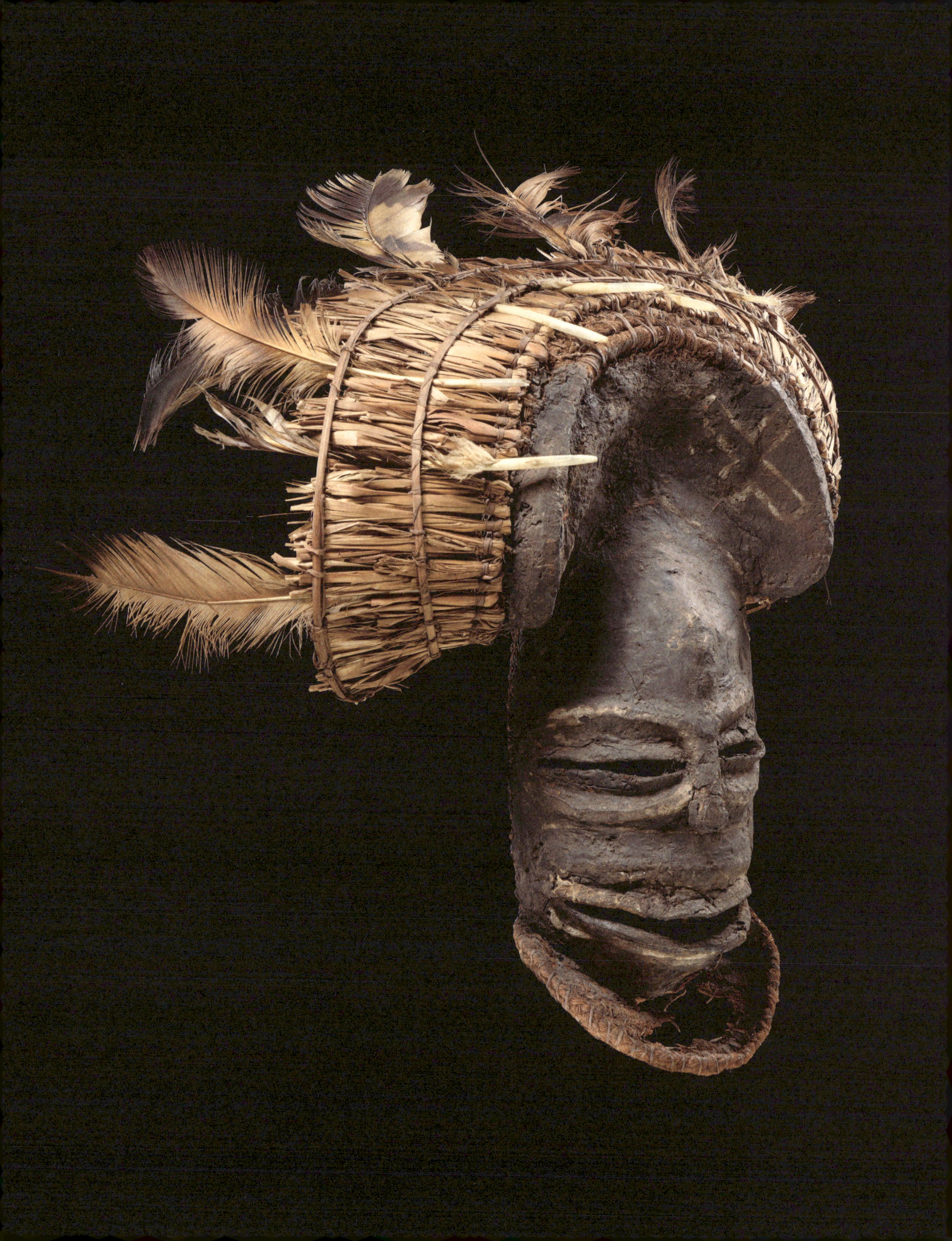

Fig. 372
Artist of the Chokwe region
Female *pwo* mask
Before 1939, wood, pigments, plant fibers, iron, copper alloy, 34 × 19 × 21 cm
Museum Rietberg Zürich, 2019.423
Purchased with funds from the Rietberg-Kreis
Acquired by Hans Himmelheber

Fig. 373
Hans Himmelheber
***Pwo* masked figure**
Northern Suku region (?), 1938/39, b/w negatives
Museum Rietberg Zürich, FHH 173-15, FHH 173-35

Fig. 374
Artist of the Chokwe region
Mask with wig
Before 1939, wood, plant fibers, 29 × 24 × 12 cm
Museum Rietberg Zürich, HH 16
Gift of Barbara and Eberhard Fischer
Acquired by Hans Himmelheber

Fig. 375
Hans Himmelheber
Crouching *pwo* masked figure
Northern Suku region (?), 1938/39, b/w negative
Museum Rietberg Zürich, FHH 172-7

Fig. 376
Hans Himmelheber
Two *chihongo* guardian masks at the entrance to the *mukanda* camp
Northern Suku region (?), 1938/39, b/w negative
Museum Rietberg Zürich, FHH 174-2

Fig. 377
Artist of the Chokwe region
***Chihongo* mask**
Before 1939, wood, plant fibers, resin, pigments, 55 × 42 × 33 cm
Museum Rietberg Zürich, EFA 5
Gift of Barbara and Eberhard Fischer
Acquired by Hans Himmelheber

Fig. 378
Hans Himmelheber
***Chihongo* guardian mask**
Lele region, January 6, 1939, b/w negative
Museum Rietberg Zürich FHH 178-36

Fig. 379
Hans Himmelheber
Dance of the *chihongo* guardian mask
Lele region, January 6, 1939, b/w negatives
Museum Rietberg Zürich, FHH 179-13 to FHH 179-20

Fig. 380
Artist of the Chokwe region
***Chihongo* mask**
Before 1939, wood, plant fibers, resin, feathers, pigments, 58 × 58 × 34 cm
Museum Rietberg Zürich, EFA 29
Gift of Barbara and Eberhard Fischer
Acquired by Hans Himmelheber

BEAUTY AND THE BEAST: CHOKWE MASKS — With colonization the Chokwe's tradition of eternalizing wealthy men as wooden figures, in the style of the cultural hero Chibinda Ilunga, died out [see fig. 7]. Instead the artists concentrated on producing masks. We know of two different types of mask: dance masks whose facial sections are carved naturalistically from wood, and the guardian masks from the *mukanda* camps that are shaped from resin.

During his travels Hans Himmelheber regularly came across these various masked figures of the Chokwe, photographed their performances, purchased masks, and interviewed their creators. He also noted down their names: Maliboka from Kambaganungu, Allone from Sakuhindika, Mamukepe.[1] In these interviews Himmelheber makes a significant discovery for the history of art. Embodying the ideal woman with their graceful facial features, tattoos, and hairstyle, the *pwo* dance masks are actually a kind of semi-portrait because their proportions are modeled on a real woman's face [figs. 372/373/375]. An artist told Himmelheber how he tricked the woman into giving him these measurements without realizing what he was doing. According to the artist, he went up to a pretty girl and said: "Oh, your face is much longer than mine." She would then protest, they would compare their faces with a stick, and *voilà*—he had his first measurement. This was followed by the distance between the eyes, between the nose and the mouth, etc. "Once I have done a portrait of my wife, my fiancée, and my girlfriend in this way," said one of the artists interviewed by Himmelheber, "then I can use another man's wife as my model. I just ask her husband to provide me with her measurements."[2]

Pwo, the ideal woman, is danced by a man. To do so he wears a woven, full-body dress and artificial breasts. On one occasion Himmelheber even saw a dancer who had chastely concealed his wooden breasts "à la mode de la mission" with a little chiffon scarf [fig. 373].[3] Such dance masks can also depict men, in which case they generally have more angular carvings. Himmelheber purchased one of these onto which, curiously enough, a carefully worked female wig has been attached [fig. 374].

The second type of mask by the Chokwe, *chihongo*, was produced in the *mukanda* camps from a blackened resin compound and plant fibers. A woven head basket adorned with stork feathers sits on the modeled face [fig. 380]. They were the guardian masks of the *mukanda* camps. With their towering face masks, the masked figures made an impression even from a distance [fig. 376]. One of their tasks was to scare off the women with their terrifying appearance, because the freshly circumcised boys were not allowed to see any women. For the performance these masks' feather hairstyle was adorned with a scarf [fig. 378]. In the village of King Pero, Himmelheber witnessed the performance of a *chihongo* mask and captured the tremendous vitality of its dance in stunning photographs [fig. 379]. After the performance, he was able to purchase the mask. Despite its now faded colors and missing costume, this mask still gives an impression of its original impact [fig. 377]. — Nanina Guyer

1 Himmelheber 1939b.
2 Himmelheber 1960, pp. 340–341.
3 Fischer and Mayer-Himmelheber 1993, p. 150.

Fig. 380

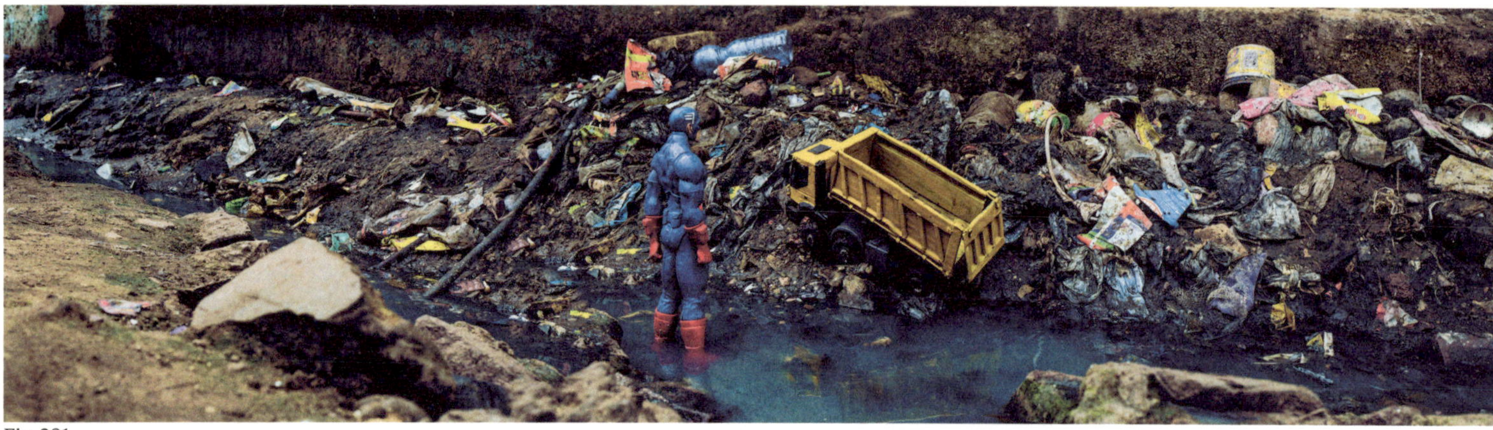

Fig. 381

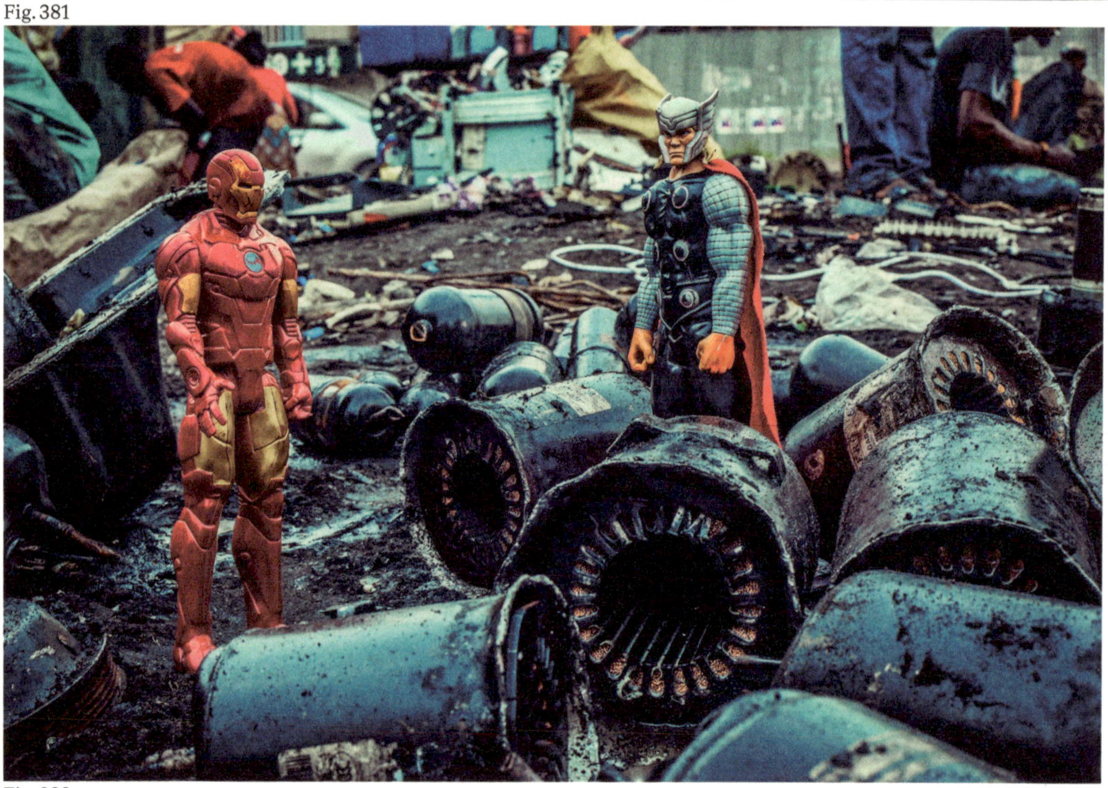

Fig. 382

Fig. 381
Nelson Makengo
Sans-titre
From *Théâtre Urbain*
2017, photograph, 40 × 150 cm
Nelson Makengo

Fig. 382
Nelson Makengo
Sans-titre
From *Théâtre Urbain*
2017, photograph, 60 × 120 cm
Nelson Makengo

"MANY ARTISTS MAKE AN ACERB CRITIQUE OF WHAT THEY PERCEIVE AS THE UNINTERRUPTED COLONIZATION OF THEIR COUNTRY BY CAPITALIST AND GEOPOLITICAL INTERESTS." A conversation on the Contemporary Art Scene of the Democratic Republic of Congo

Sandrine Colard, Nanina Guyer

Sandrine Colard is an art historian, writer, and curator based in New York and Brussels. A specialist in modern and contemporary African arts (PhD Columbia University), Colard is a professor at Rutgers University-Newark and has been appointed artistic director of the 6th Lubumbashi Biennale 2019, Democratic Republic of Congo (DRC). Her writings include contributions to exhibition catalogues such as *Sammy Baloji: Hunting and Collecting* (2016) and *The Expanded Subject: New Perspectives in Photographic Portraiture from Africa* (2016). In addition to the Biennale, she is also curating *The Way She Looks: A History of Female Gazes in African Photography* in collaboration with the Artur Walther Collection (Ryerson Image Center, Toronto, 2019). Colard is currently working on her book about the history of photography in the DRC.

NANINA GUYER The contemporary art scene in the Congo and its diaspora is thriving. What makes it unique and what are the core themes that today's artists are working on?

SANDRINE COLARD The vastness of the country makes it difficult to speak about "one" scene, but the cities of Kinshasa, the capital, and Lubumbashi, the second most important city in the southeast Katanga province, have produced and attracted the largest number of internationally recognized contemporary artists. Historically, both cities became the seats of the two national and formal art schools founded in the 1940s and the 1950s under Belgian colonialism, and they retain the position of art poles to the present day. However, the young generations of Congolese artists often position themselves independently or against the "academicism" of these schools, and they came of age after the period of state-sponsored art put in place during the 1970s by President Mobutu. Therefore, these artists' practices are often supported and nourished by the incredible energy of artist-based initiatives and collectives, such as Picha and Centre Waza in Lubumbashi, or KinArt Studio and Eza Possible in Kinshasa. Simultaneously exhibition spaces, intellectual hubs, art organizations, and sponsors, these spaces have become central to the dynamism of the Congolese artistic ecosystem, and ensure networks of collaboration and support that have contributed to the growth of the national scene. This necessity for artistic self-reliance parallels the resilience of the larger Congolese society, for which political and economic instability and episodes of violence are part of everyday life. Naturally, these preoccupations lie at the heart of many contemporary artists' practices.

The drastic transformation of a city like Kinshasa, the harshness of its urban environment and of its infrastructures, are recurrent themes, as is the transcendence of these difficulties. The posthumous retrospective of the utopian *maquettes* by Bodys Isek Kingelez at the New York Museum of Modern Art in 2018 has probably provided the most well-known example of this, but younger artists like Mega Mingiedi also create quasi frescoes of futurist versions of Congolese cities. The photographer and video artist Nelson Makengo has made a trademark of using superhero toys and figurines that he films as *kinois* prevailing over their circumstances [fig. 381/382], or again, the performance artists of KinAct and their annual festival intervene directly on the streets of the megalopolis. All address the urban "chaos" but ultimately sublimate and re-enchant it. The photographs of the late Kiripi Katembo are beautiful examples of this, turning Kinshasa's flooded potholes into poetic mirrors of the city.

The long tradition of so-called "popular" Congolese painting, often charged with a social, moral, and political critique, is pursued by the famous painter Chéri Samba. But younger painters also experiment with different approaches, creating portraits of a less figurative nature. Often composite collages, the subjects of painters such as Steve Bandoma, Hilaire Balu Kuyangiko, or Eddy Kamuanga Ilunga evoke fragmented subjectivities of twenty-first-century Congolese.

Many more topics occupy Congolese artists, but the question of mobility and migration is certainly an important one, too. In recent years, Jean Katambayi has produced a magnificent series of drawings entitled *Visafrolampes* (2018), which is the result of his reflections on the numerous impediments to travel for Africans [figs. 383/384].

N.G. The archival turn, or the appropriation of archival material as a major artistic practice has profoundly influenced the work of artists worldwide. How has this trend affected Congolese artists?

S.C. In the Democratic Republic of the Congo as in the rest of the world's contemporary art scene, the turn to the twenty-first-century has seen the rise of the so-called "archival turn." Here, it also coincided with the approach of the fiftieth anniversary of the country's independence from Belgium in 1960, as well as with the publication of a few best-sellers about the country's history, for instance, Adam Hochschild's *King Leopold's Ghost*. Therefore, the first decade of the 2000s saw a "rediscovery" of the colonial era and its massive photographic archives, both in Bel-

Fig. 383
Jean Katambayi
Visafrolampes
2019, installation view
Multiple Transmissions: Art in the Afropolitan Age,
WIELS

Fig. 384
Jean Katambayi
Visafrolampes
2018, ten drawings, different pens on paper, A3 (29.7 × 42.3 cm, unframed)
Trampoline Gallery, Antwerp

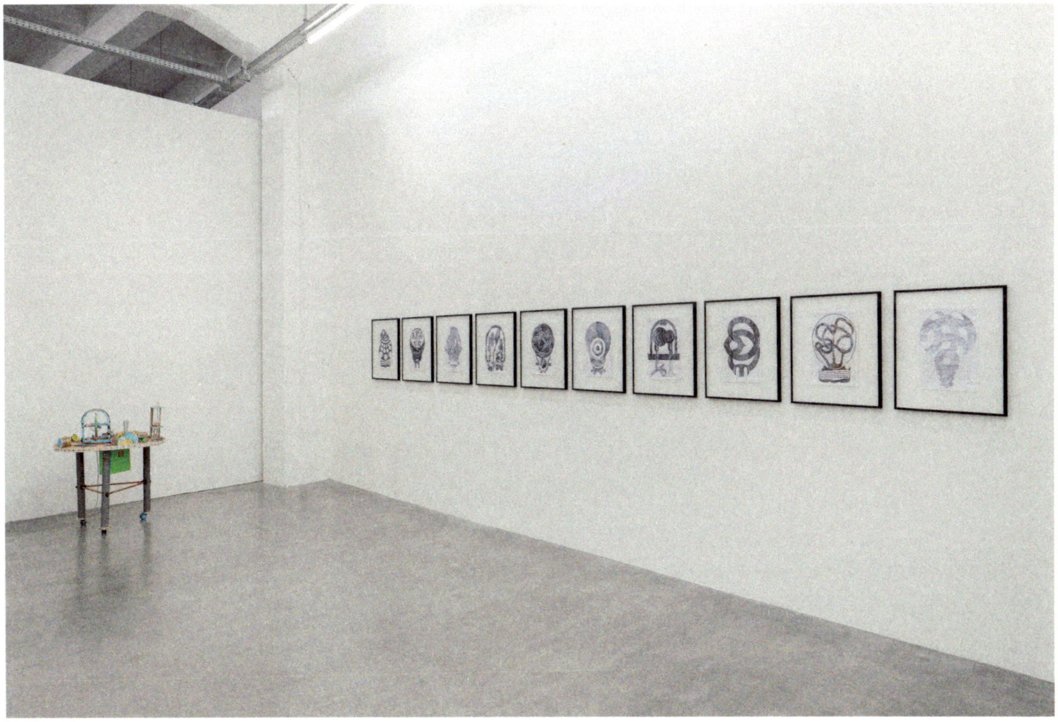

Fig. 383

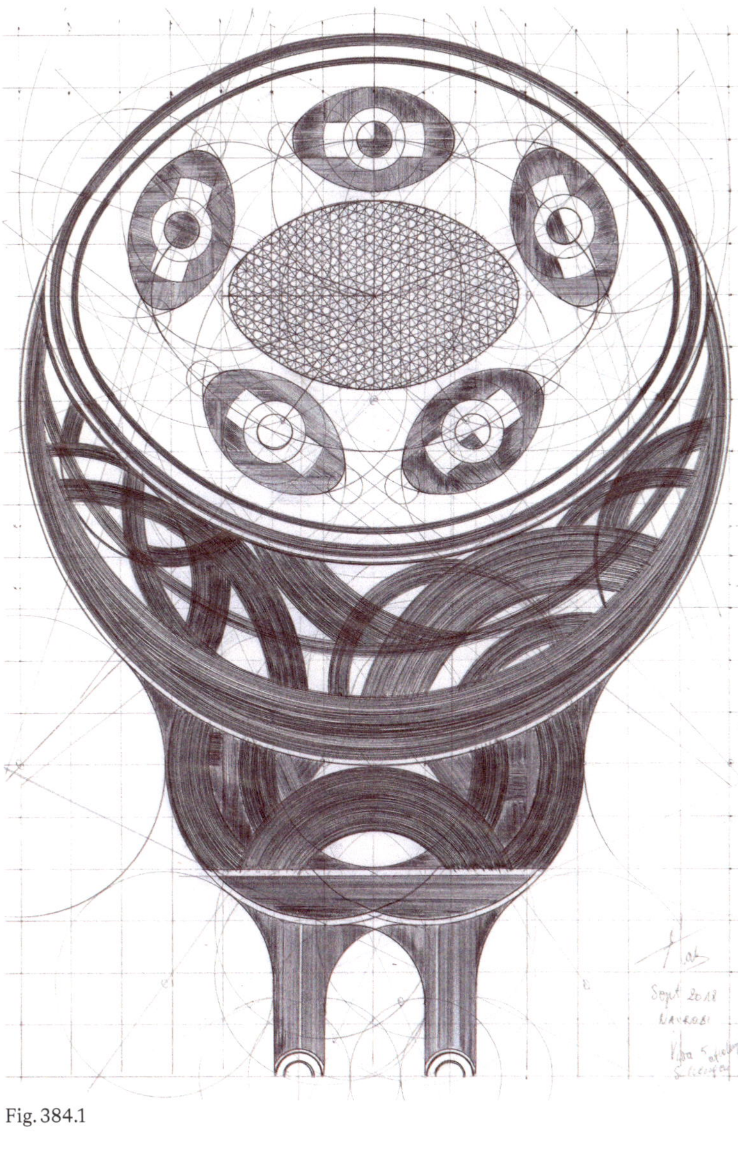

Fig. 384.1

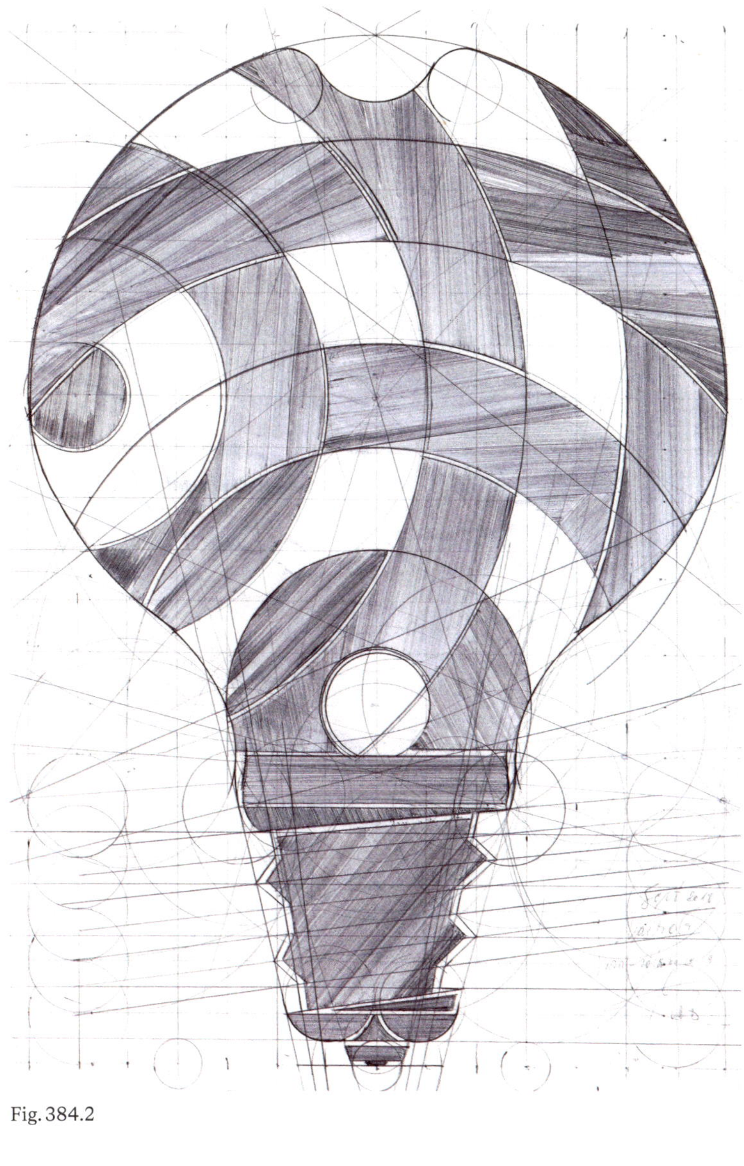

Fig. 384.2

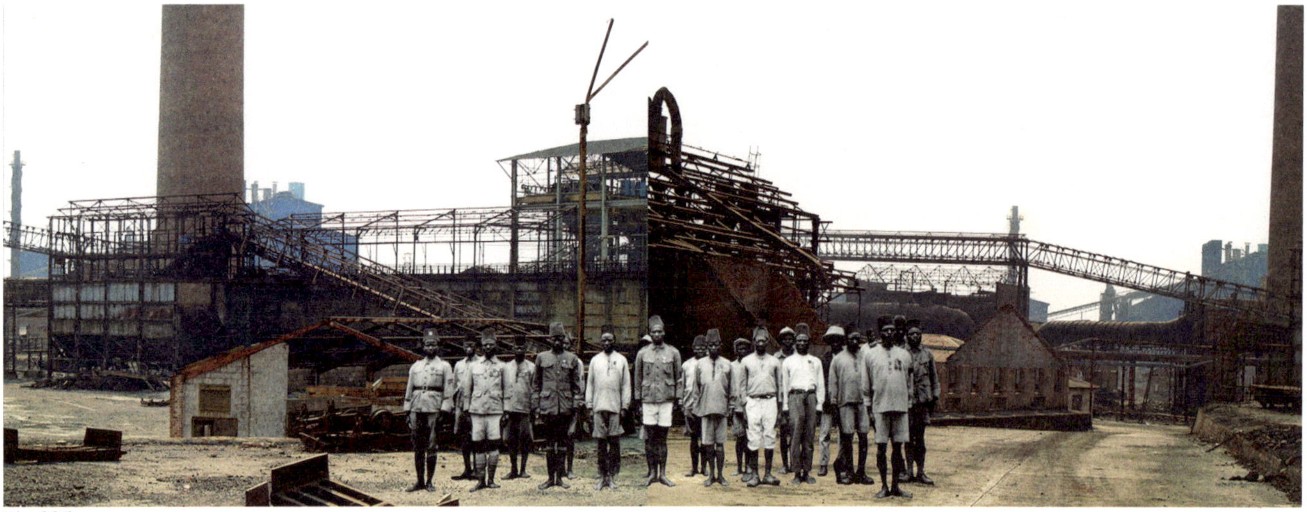
Fig. 385
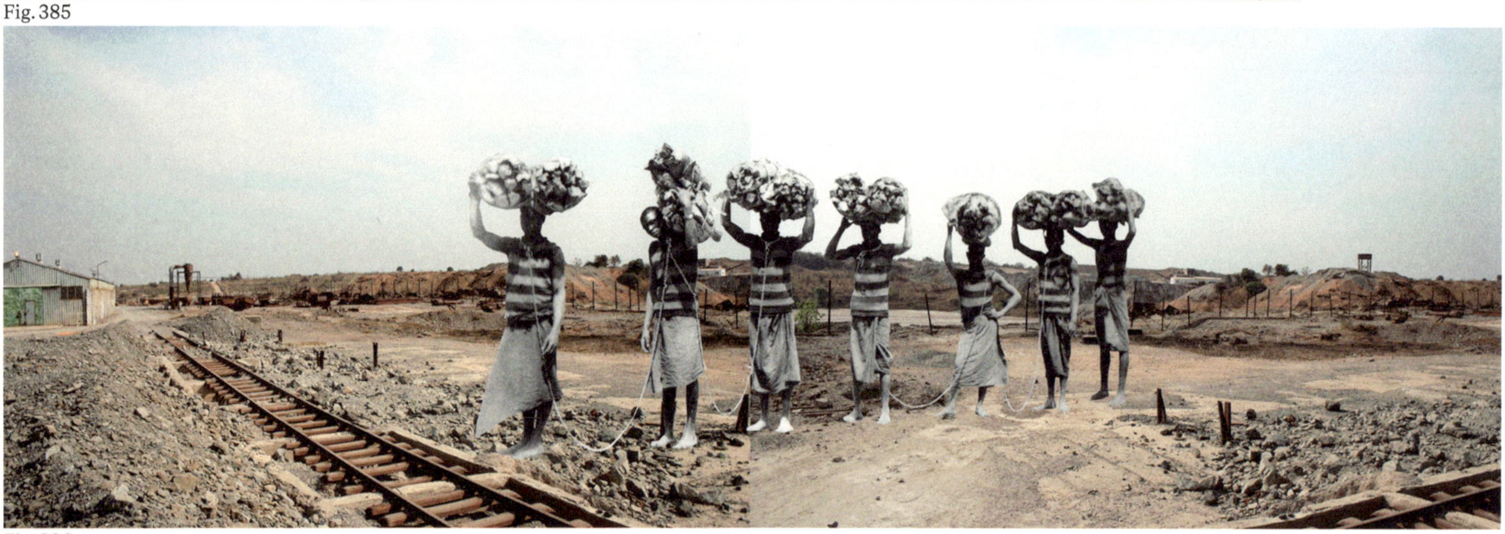
Fig. 386
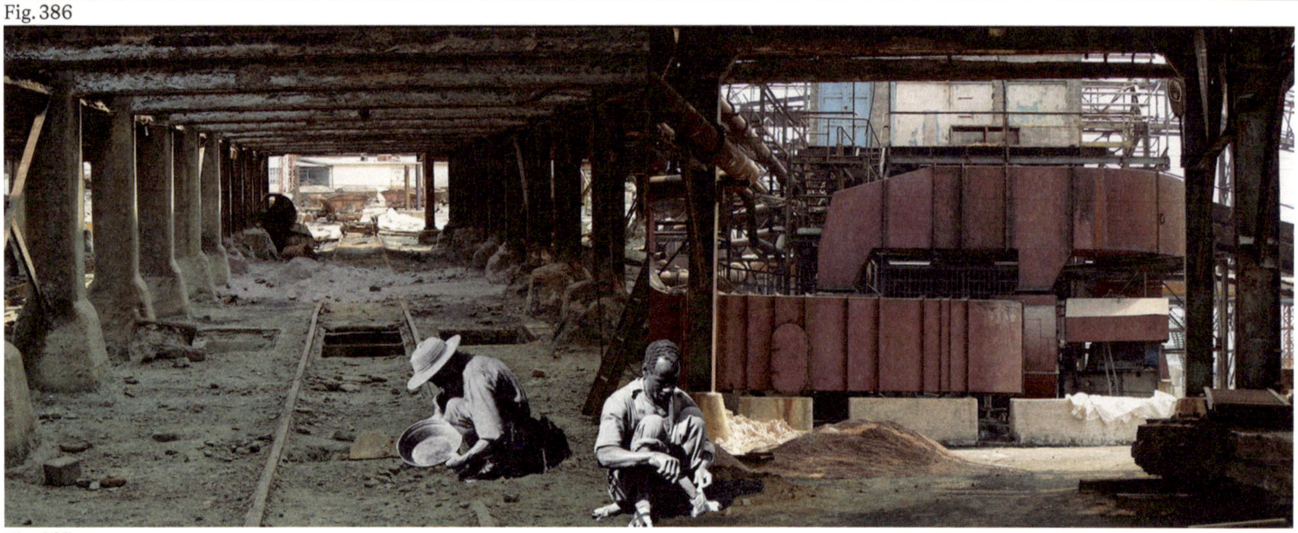
Fig. 387

Fig. 385
Sammy Baloji
Untitled #18
2006, archival photograph on satin matte paper, 60 × 160 cm
Galerie Imane Farès, Paris

Fig. 386
Sammy Baloji
Untitled #12
2006, archival photograph on satin matte paper, 60 × 181 cm
Galerie Imane Farès, Paris

Fig. 387
Sammy Baloji
Untitled #19
2006, archival photograph on satin matte paper, 60 × 160 cm
Galerie Imane Farès, Paris

gium and in the DRC. Different efforts at digitization made large numbers of pictures that had not been circulating for a long time more readily available. This was particularly palpable in Lubumbashi, which is a city that still visibly bears the traces of its colonial past. The preserved colonial architecture and the imposing slagheap and chimney of the former *Union Minière du Haut Katanga* company still dominate the cityscape. The company produced its own important photographic archive, which was rescued and digitized by the local Institut Français. This is how an artist like Sammy Baloji was able to discover these images and create his first series of collages, *Mémoire* (2006/07), which launched his career. That work digitally juxtaposed contemporary views of the run-down mining setting onto which the artist pasted cutouts of vintage photographs, which showed figures from the colonial period, particularly (forced) laborers [figs. 385–387]. As the series' title indicates, the work is about retrieving the memory of the city and its inhabitants and commemorating the labor carried out by the ancestors, which is often forgotten to the profit of the industrial know-how brought by the Europeans. In the Congo, the archival turn was about reappropriating a history that was largely forgotten, and connecting it to the country's present situation. The younger generations and artists born after independence do not really know that history and are seldom educated on the subject.

In 2017, I led an artists' workshop about the history of colonial photography, parallel to the last edition of the Lubumbashi Biennale curated by Toma Muteba Luntumbue. The great interest and will to further work on those archives among young Congolese artists was evident. Following the workshop, for instance, Nelson Makengo produced a video, *E'ville*, which incorporates some of the photographs that we discussed.

Interestingly, European museums of ethnography or natural sciences own large collections of colonial artifacts and photographs, and there is a growing tendency to invite Congolese artists to reflect upon them. In a sense, then, the "archival turn" has put Africans and Europeans in dialogue around the colonial history. Long before its renovation, Sammy Baloji and the Congolese writer Patrick Mudekereza were invited by the AfricaMuseum in Tervuren (Belgium) in 2008 to mine and reinterpret their collections in order to create new artworks from an African point of view. This resulted in the *Congo Far West* exhibition and book (2011). Similarly, for the exhibition *Congo as Fiction*, the artist David Shongo is using Museum Rietberg's collection of photographs by the ethnographer Hans Himmelheber. While these residencies have had the great merit of sharing collections and perspectives, some scholars such as Lotte Arndt have also warned against putting the weight of these institutions' "decolonial" task in dealing with their past exclusively on the shoulders of African artists.[1]

N.G. Artists like Sinzo Aanza, Sammy Baloji, Michèle Magema, and David Shongo make use of a variety of archival material such as objects, sound recordings, photographs, films, and texts. Especially the use of colonial photographs is a recurring theme in the works of these artists, and is striking.

S.C. The dominance of colonial photographs is explained by the very large production that was created by the Belgian admin-

1 Arndt 2013.

istration, but also by their easier circulation through digital platforms and the internet. Many of the official archives from the colonial period are not held in the DRC, but in Belgium. Even if photographs, because of their reproducibility, have remained present in the Congo, the institutions that hold them are not always easily accessible, or their collections are just not listed. But when they do not have direct access to collections, artists source their material on the internet. A good example is the series of diptychs by the Lubumbashi photographer Georges Senga, *Une Vie après la mort* (2012) [fig. 388]. That work consists in imagining what Patrice Lumumba, the first prime minister of the Congo and martyr of independence, would have become had he not been assassinated in 1961. Several portraits of a present-day Lumumba admirer and lookalike are coupled with archival images and portraits, newspaper clippings, etc., and all of them have been retrieved from the web. In the same way, the Kinshasa-born, Belgium-based artist Freddy Mutombo also works on colonial photographs that he has recuperated online. This says a lot about the democratization of resources that the internet has brought about for African artists, and also about the unequal access and continued effort still necessary for the sharing of collections.

Fig. 388
Georges Senga
Une Vie après la mort
2012, photographs, different formats
Georges Senga

N.G. Perhaps connected to this and as a follow-up question: can you elaborate on the ways that artists have engaged with colonialism and called for a decolonization of minds?

S.C. I have rarely heard Congolese artists use the term "decolonization." This does not mean that it is not an issue of interest to them, but in my opinion, it translates differently than in the European and American diasporas, where the notion has recently regained a powerful attraction after its initial coining by Walter Mignolo. A precursor of the decolonizing awareness in the DRC is the resonant "authenticity" (*authenticité*) campaign promoted by President Mobutu starting in the 1970s. Because he believed that post-independence Congolese still suffered from mental and cultural colonialism—they were *mundele ndombe*, that is, white people with black skin—Mobutu implemented "decolonial" cultural policies *avant la lettre* that pervaded all aspects of society. The way people dressed was modified: dresses and suits were abandoned in favor of *pagnes* and *abacost* (short for "à bas le costume," that is, "down with the costume.") Christian names were officially changed to indigenous ones. Artistically, this campaign largely favored and sponsored classical or "traditional" African arts and motifs. Today, artists in the Congo regard that authenticity campaign with ambivalence, for the mold that it imposed on artistic practices and for the political propaganda tool that it became in the hands of Mobutu. Also, today's Congolese artists are so conversant with the global contemporary art scene that questions of authenticity seem to be of little concern. However, the necessity for African self-pride is a preoccupation that remains, for instance, in the photographs of Alain Nsenga [fig. 389]. In a series entitled *Métamorphoses*, the artist has documented the imposing billboards that advertise skin-bleaching products in the streets of the city of Lubumbashi. Because a lighter complexion is often regarded as more beautiful than dark skin tones, these cosmetics enjoy great popularity and testify to the pervasiveness of Western beauty standards in Africa. Nsenga denounces this aesthetic colonialism that he counteracts by creating portraits of

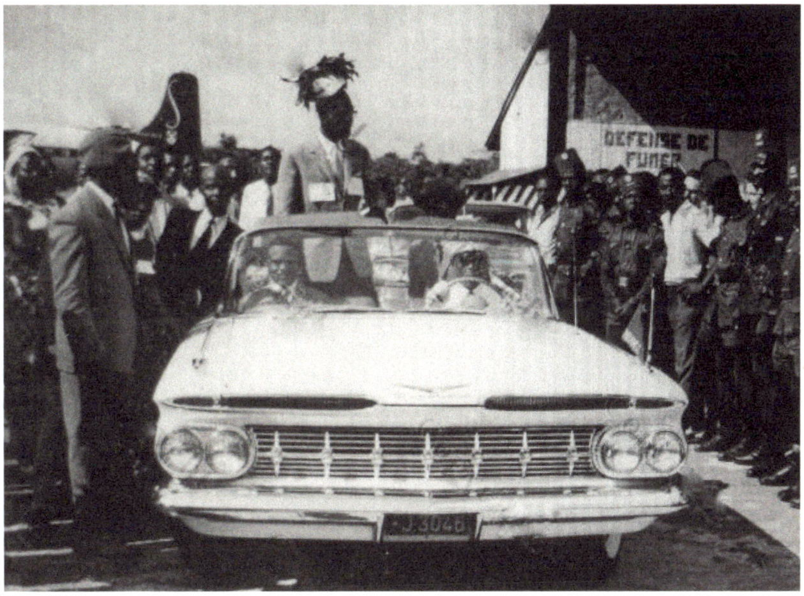

Fig. 388.1

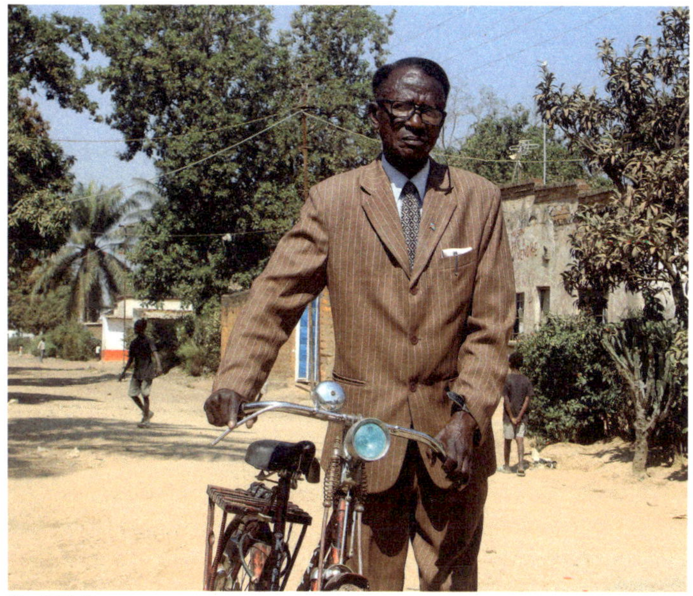

Fig. 388.2

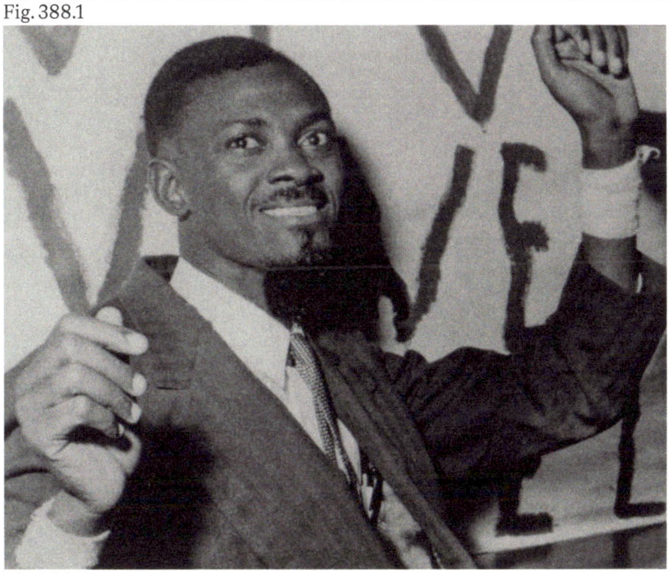

Fig. 388.3

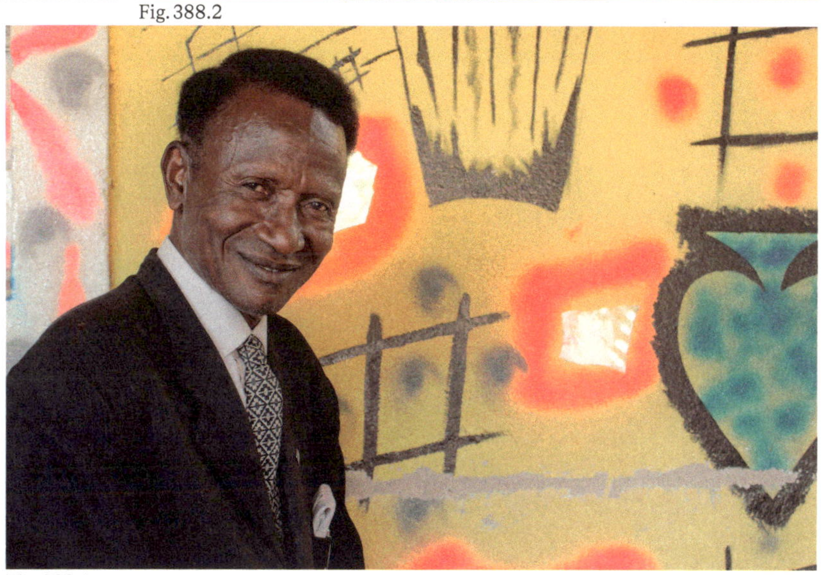

Fig. 388.4

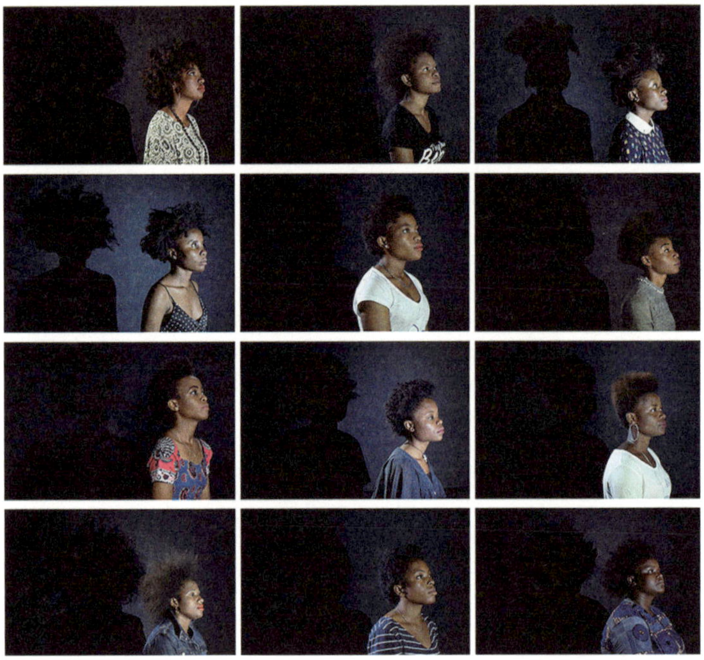

Fig. 389.1

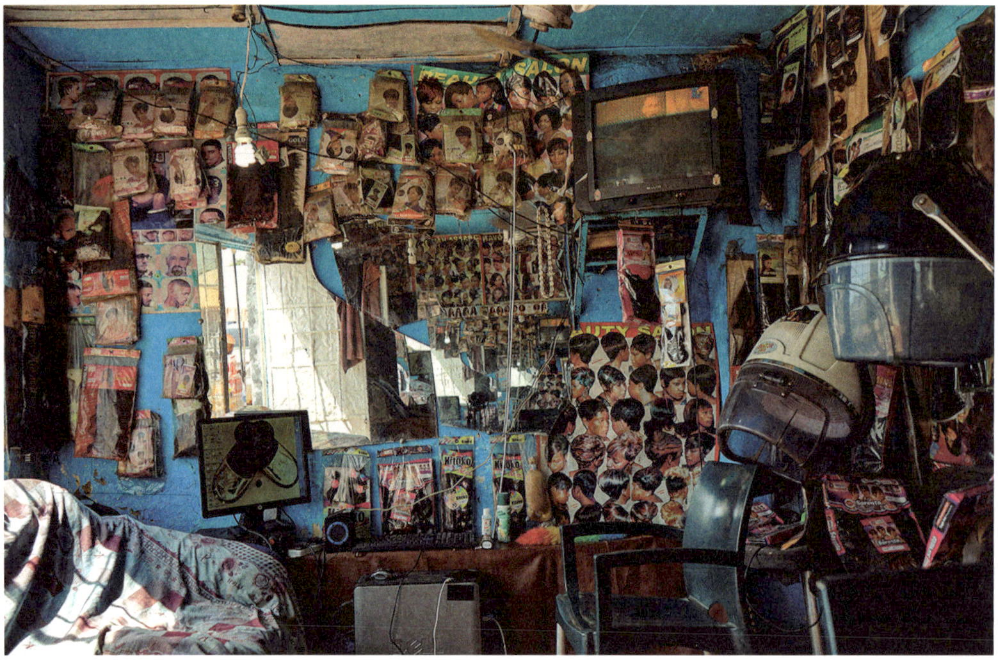

Fig. 389.2

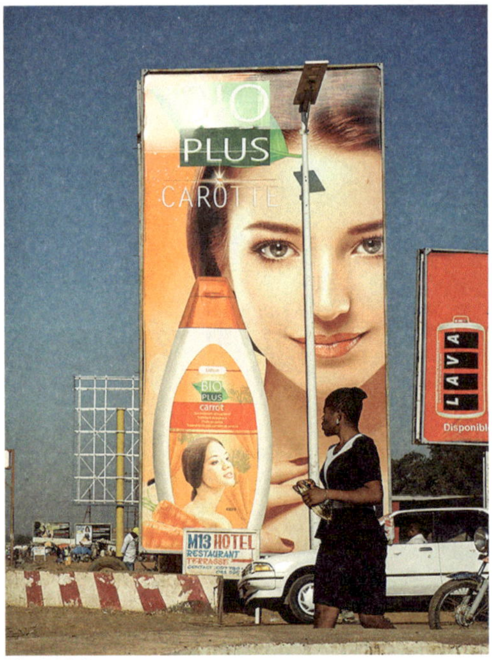

Fig. 389.3

Fig. 389
Alain Nsenga
Métamorphoses
2018, photographs, different formats
Alain Nsenga

black women with their natural hair, in dramatic lighting, as a sort of localized Black is Beautiful movement launched in the USA by the African-American photographer Kwame Brathwaite.

More generally, many artists make an acerb critique of what they perceive as the uninterrupted colonization of their country by capitalist and geopolitical interests. The way that the industrial and financial world sucks out the natural resources of the DRC to the detriment of the local population constitutes the backdrop or overt subject of many Congolese art practices. Visual arts but also literary works address that situation frontally, such as the unambiguously titled novel *Congo Inc.* by Jean Bofane. In the same way, Sinzo Aanza is a writer and an artist for whom global capital's stranglehold on Congolese national sovereignty is a recurrent question. For instance, in his installation, photographic series, and video *Pertinences Citoyennes* (2018), [figs. 301/302] Aanza deconstructs what he calls the "institutional national fiction" that is the Congo. As a creation of the 1884/85 Berlin Conference and a continuous financial playground for the international community, the country and its politicians are reduced to puppets of what the artist calls the "feudality of the capital." In Katanga, Sammy Baloji has worked on similar issues by documenting the economy of soil extractions and the consequences for local people and artisanal miners, for instance, in his series *Kolwezi* (2011).

N.G. Many artists participating in the exhibition *Congo as Fiction* connect the past with the present and the future in their works. As the curator of the Biennale of Lubumbashi, you have chosen the leitmotif *Future Genealogies—Tales from the Equatorial Line* [figs. 390/391]. To me, the themes utopia, fiction, and the quest for a new geographical centering of art history resonate here.

S.C. The decentering of art history that started in the 1980s with groundbreaking exhibitions like *Magiciens de la Terre* is undergoing a new acceleration. At the institutional level, a geographical shift back to the African continent is undeniable. Museums such as Zeitz Mocca, or le Musée des Civilisations in Dakar, and art fairs like 1:54 that takes place in Marrakech, in addition to its London and New York editions, are some of the examples that testify to that continental grounding. In the West, the call for decolonizing art institutions have started to make collections that are much more inclusive of non-Western arts. The recent donation by the famous contemporary African art collector Jean Pigozzi to MoMA is striking, as the museum has long represented a fortress of Euro-American modernism and contemporary art. In that context, the existence of African biennales like the one in Lubumbashi play an important role, as it participates in the creation of an African discourse around African art. For the coming year alone, three biennales are planned in the DRC: *Lubumbashi*, but also *Young Congo* in Kinshasa, and the second edition of *Yango*, founded by the late Kiripi Katembo.

What interested me about the oxymoron in the title of the biennale *Future Genealogies* was to express the impossibility of thinking about the present and the future of the arts separately from their past history. As you rightly point out, many Congolese artists conflate various time periods in their work, as the Congo is a place where different layers of time coexist. The country still lives in the aftermath of colonialism, but the Congolese are simultaneously at the forefront of future technologies and development due to the presence of a multitude of companies sourcing necessary raw materials. For instance, *On-Trade-Off*, is an ongoing artistic project led in collaboration between Congolese and Belgian artists. It raises awareness about environmental and economic implications of the extraction and processing of lithium, the main raw material needed for the global production of green energy, and for the construction of Tesla cars. One of the pieces created for that project is *Tesla Crash, A Speculation* (in progress), by Jean Katambayi, Sammy Baloji, and Daddy Tshikaya. It is a handmade, 1:1 model of the Tesla Model × in recycled copper wires, based on the model that children often make in the Congo [fig. 392]. Another good example of this layering of time is the works by the painter Eddy Kamuanga Illunga, who mixes tall, elongated figures with Congo cosmogony and electric circuits.

N.G. What is your vision of the Congo's art scene in 2050?

S.C. Other cities are contributing more and more to the contemporary art scene, and I expect a multiplication of Congolese art poles. Kisangani has long been another center of art production, particularly with the Studios Kabako of Faustin Linyekula. Lately, also the city of Goma's burgeoning art scene has attracted lots of attention. Women still represent a minority of the practitioners, but this is rapidly changing. In a few years, young female artists like Michèle Magema, Géraldine Tobé, Pamela Tulizo, Gosette Lubondo, and Hadassa Ngamba, just to name a few, have risen.

My wish is for a well-rooted Congolese art ecology to bloom, one that can critically sustain and accompany the formidable artists who thrive there. Only with local art critics and institutions, curators, patrons, and audiences can the Congolese art scene continue to grow.

Fig. 390
Pierre-Philippe Dûchatelet
Généalogies Futures
Lubumbashi Biennale VI
October 24 – November 24, 2019
Poster French/English

Fig. 391
Pierre-Philippe Dûchatelet
Mazazi Ya Baadaye
Lubumbashi Biennale VI
October 24 – November 24, 2019
Poster Swahili/French

Fig. 392
Sammy Baloji, Jean Katambayi Mukendi, and Daddy Tshikaya
Tesla Crash, a Speculation
2019, Mixed media, 60 × 50 × 50 cm, view of the installation
Galerie Imane Farès, Paris

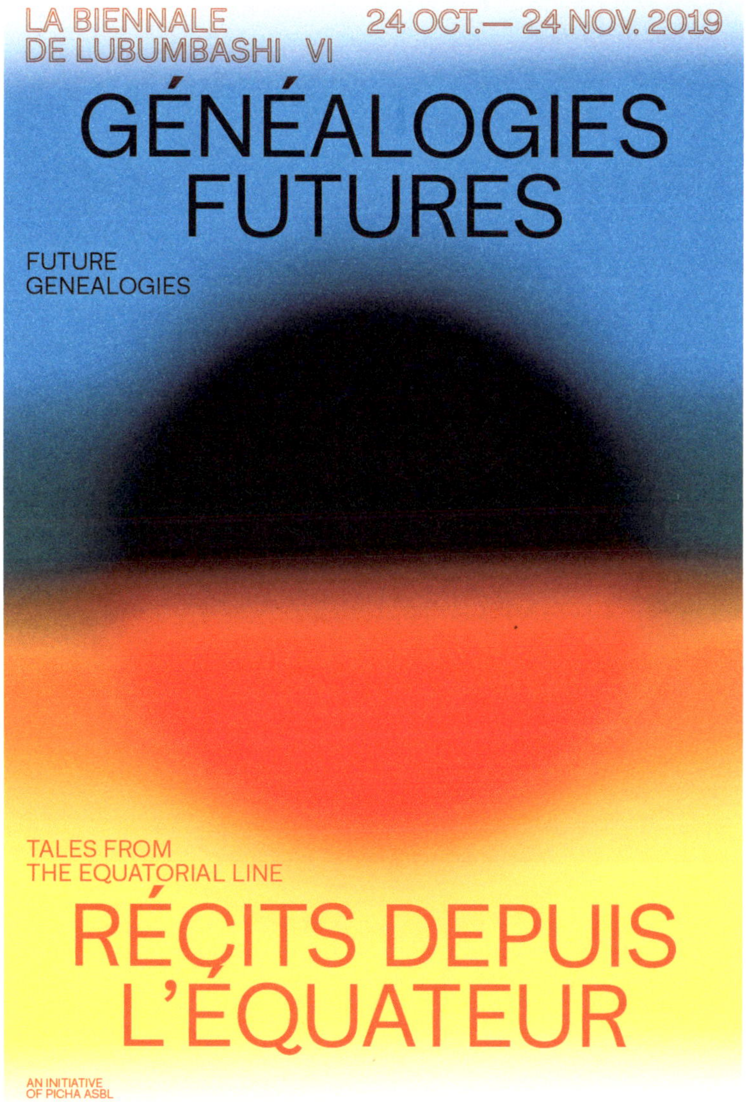

Fig. 390

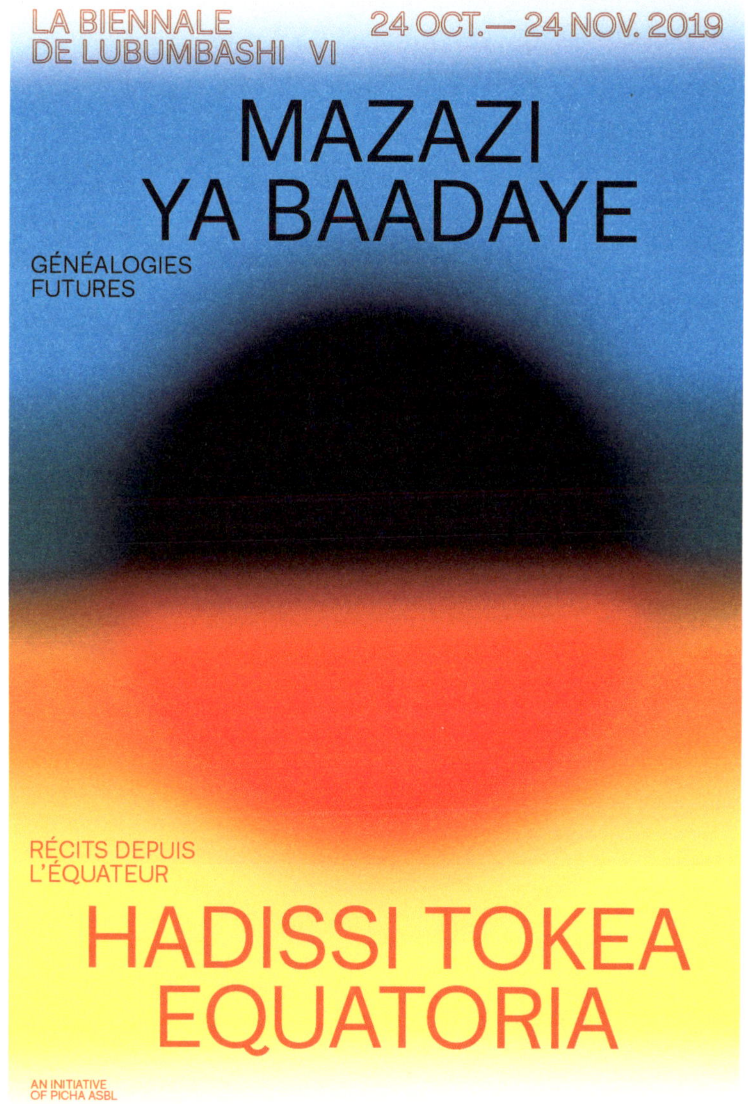

Fig. 391

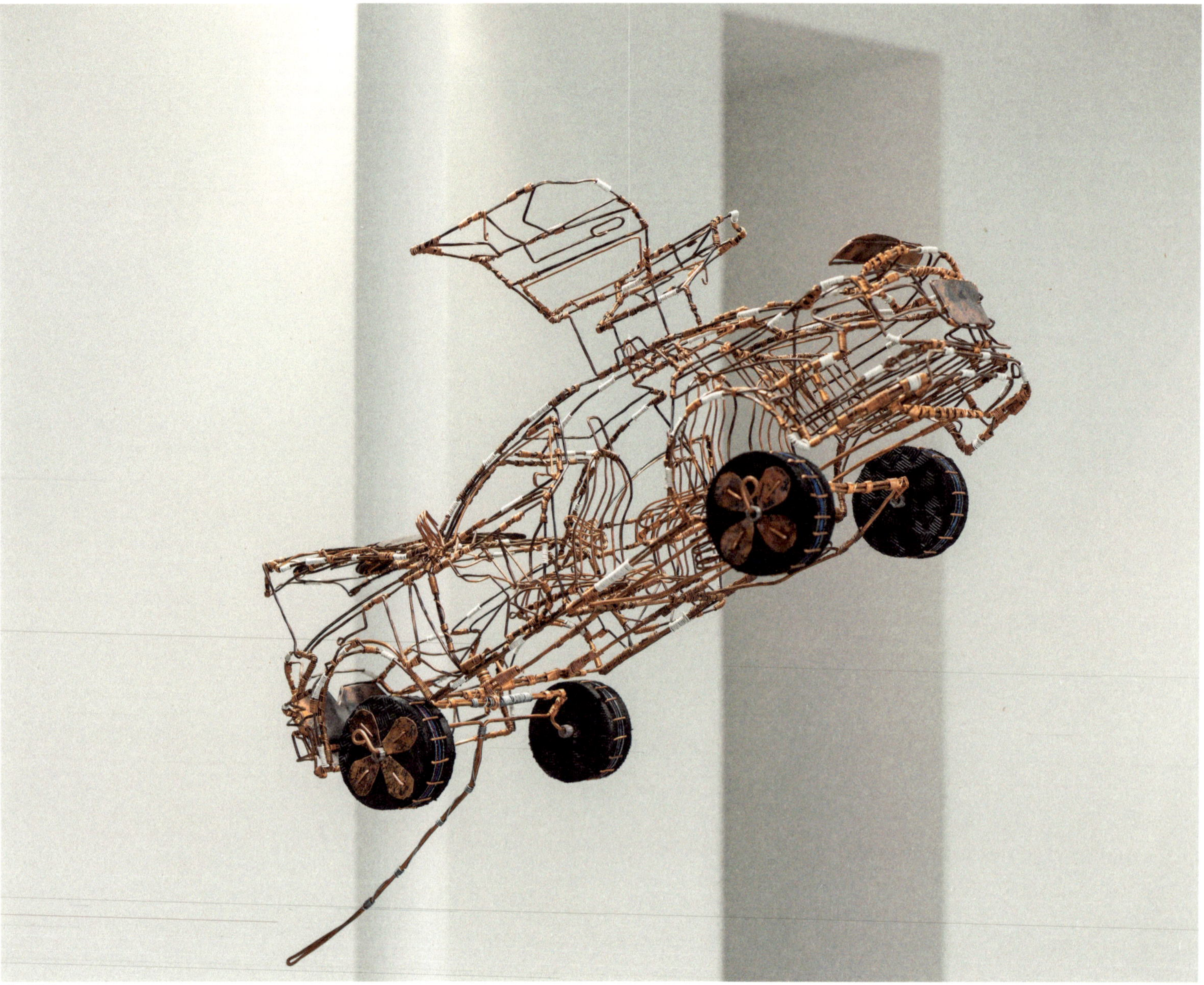

Fig. 392

APPENDIX

AUTHORS

LAURA FALLETTA is a graduate student of art history in a global context and of Portuguese language and literature at the University of Zürich. Her interests lie in the field of cultural transfer within a global understanding of art history, focusing on the lusophone world and a gender-sensitive reappraisal of the art historiography. She is currently completing a curatorial internship at the Museum Rietberg in Zürich.

CHRISTRAUD M. GEARY is an independent scholar and Teel Senior Curator Emerita of African and Oceanic Art at the Museum of Fine Arts, Boston. A cultural anthropologist, she conducted research on history and arts of the Cameroon Grassfields, a highland region in the western part of the country. She also focused on early colonial photography in Cameroon and other parts of the African continent, and in the 1980s joined a cohort of scholars who began pioneering research on the history of photography and Africa, including the work of African practitioners. From 1990 to 2003, before joining the MFA Boston, she was curator of the Eliot Elisofon Photographic Archives at the National Museum of African Art, Smithsonian Institution, Washington DC. Geary has organized photographic exhibitions and published catalogues, books, and numerous essays.

NANINA GUYER is curator for photography at the Museum Rietberg in Zürich. Her special interests include the global history of photography and its local forms of expression. She earned her PhD with a thesis on historical photographs from Sierra Leone and Liberia. Currently she is working on the history of photography in the Democratic Republic of the Congo in the 1930s, with special emphasis on the photographs of Hans Himmelheber. Additionally, she is preparing an exhibition on early African photographers.

NZOMBA DUGO KAKEMA is a photographer based in Tshikapa, Democratic Republic of the Congo.

DAVID MANNES is a scientist in the research group for Neutron Imaging and Applied Materials at the Paul Scherrer Institut (PSI) in Villigen. He assists domestic and international researchers in their experiments with neutron imaging and both advises and supervises clients from the industry. His main interest is in the nondestructive analysis of art historical objects using imaging techniques.

MICHAELA OBERHOFER is curator for Africa and Oceania and head of Collection Services at the Museum Rietberg. Her exhibitions (e.g., *Dada Africa, Bead Art*) highlight the entangled history of creative production in Africa as well as the reception of non-Western art in Europe. Together with Professor Gesine Krüger (University of Zürich) she has headed the research project Hans Himmelheber since 2018. At the Ethnologisches Museum in Berlin and at GRASSI Museum für Völkerkunde in Leipzig, she carried out studies and realized exhibitions on the history of acquisitions and collectors. A further focus of her work is on cooperations with museums in Africa.

CONSTANTINE PETRIDIS is chair of the department of the Arts of Africa and the Americas and curator of African Art at the Art Institute of Chicago. His recent book *Luluwa: Central African Art Between Heaven and Earth* (Brussels: Mercatorfonds, 2018) derives from his doctoral dissertation on the same subject for Ghent University in his native Belgium.

JENS STENGER is a physicist and has been working in the field of art research for fifteen years. His research into the materials and production techniques used in works of art took him from the Harvard Art Museum to the Institute for the Preservation of Cultural Heritage at Yale University and then to the Swiss Institute for Art Research. His main interest is in matters of art history at the intersection of materiality and imaging techniques.

Z.S. STROTHER is Riggio Professor of African Art at Columbia University, New York. She is the author of *Inventing Masks: Agency and History in the Art of the Central Pende* and *Humor and Violence: Seeing Europeans in Central African Art*.

ARTISTS

SINZO AANZA (*1990) lives and works in Kinshasa. In his poetic texts, the writer questions the political conditions under colonial rule as far as the present power relations in the DR Congo. In his installations, he addresses the ruthless exploitation of his country's mineral resources, the representation of national identity, as well as the construed postcolonial image of the Congo. Most recently he displayed his work at the group exhibition *Kinshasa Chroniques Urbaines* in Sète (France) and is to appear at the Biennale in Lubumbashi (2019). Together with Sammy Baloji, he took part in an artist-in-residence programme for the exhibition *Congo as Fiction* at the Museum Rietberg. In the process, Sinzo Aanza concerned himself with the photographs of the art anthropologist Hans Himmelheber, focussing on the far-reaching changes brought about by the realignment of space and power at the hands of the colonial regime.

SAMMY BALOJI (*1978) lives and works in Brussels and Lubumbashi. He ranks among the most renowned Congolese artists. Baloji has not only taken part in notable art biennales (Dakar 2016, Venice 2015, Lyon 2015), *documenta* 2017, and various photo festivals (Bamako 2007, 2015), his works are also held by museums in Lyon, Paris, Tervuren, Ulm, Washington, Virginia, and as far as Luanda (Angola) and Ouidah (Benin). His work has been shown in numerous exhibitions; he has also served as curator (*Congo Art Works* 2016, *Congo Stars* 2019) and is one of the cofounders of the Biennale in Lubumbashi. In 2008 he received the Prince Claus Award.

In his photographs, videos, and installations, Baloji is concerned with historical archives and enquires into the impact of Belgian colonial rule on Congolese society to this day. The multimedia installation he created for *Congo as Fiction* focuses on the reinterpretation of traditional Luba remembrance practices to which the Graz-based writer Fiston Mwanza Mujila has added the vocal background.

HILAIRE BALU KUYANGIKO (*1992) is a painter and sculptor. He lives and works in his native city of Kinshasa. His sculptures are based on *mangaaka* power figures and are invested with modern symbols of consumption and globalization. His works have been shown in exhibitions in Austria, France, and Germany, as well as in his home country.

STEVE BANDOMA (*1981) born in Kinshasa, now lives and works in South Africa. After his art degree in Kinshasa he moved to South Africa, where he developed the painting style comprising *objets trouvés*, fashion magazines, and watercolors for which he has become famous. In his pictures, collages, and installations he addresses politics, religion, history, and many other aspects of postcolonial Africa. Bandoma, who was awarded the American ArtBuzz prize in 2009, has exhibited his work in solo and group shows in Europe, the Congo, and South Africa.

FIONA BOBO (*1992) lives and works in Zürich. In her degree thesis *BWANIA* at the Department of Art & Media of the Zürich University of the Arts, she dealt with her Congolese roots. This has resulted in a multimedia installation that addresses the issue of identity and sets Western visual culture against that of the Congo. She uses photographs to illustrate the significance of fashion and designer clothes in modern Congolese society.

MICHÈLE MAGEMA (*1977) is a Congolese-French video, performance, and photography artist. She was born in Kinshasa, Democratic Republic of the Congo. She emigrated to Paris, France in 1984, where she currently resides. Michèle Magema has participated in exhibitions such as *Africa Remix* and *Global Feminism* (Brooklyn Museum), and her work can be found in museums and collections worldwide. She locates her work within an intermediate zone, a sort of a mental space or a frontier that she created, which she situates between the Global South and the Global North. The exploration of her feminine identity displaced through time, memory, and history reflects the image of a woman with a new identity that is totally detached from exoticism. A key focus for her is articulating a permanent exchange between individual stories, collective memory, and history. Michèle Magema walks the line between the limits of personal experience and the wider outlook shared by collective anxieties.

AIMÉ MPANE (*1968) is an internationally successful artist who lives and works in Brussels and Kinshasa. In addition to his paintings, Mpane creates sculptures and portraits out of wood, in which he links the colonial history of the Congo to the reception of African art in the avant-garde, among other things.

FISTON MWANZA MUJILA (*1981) was born in Lubumbashi and lives in Graz as a French-speaking writer. He writes poetry, plays, and prose and teaches African literature at the university. His award-winning novel *Tram 83* was published in 2014. The plot is set in "Tram 83," a nightclub and vibrant center in a run-down fictional Congolese city and the starting point for the story of two very different friends who meet up there.

CHÉRI SAMBA (*1956) is one of the most famous contemporary artists from Africa. Numerous solo and group exhibitions have been dedicated to the painter, whose works can be found in art collections worldwide. In his humorous and ironic pictures that often feature a self-portrait, Samba takes a critical approach to Congolese and Western society and questions the collection practices of European museums in Africa.

YVES SAMBU (*1980) lives and works in Kinshasa. He has presented his photography in solo exhibitions (Brussels, Graz, Fribourg) and also participated in group shows in Berlin, Brussels, Dortmund, and Paris. Since 2007, he has been a member of the artist collective SADI (*Solidarité des Artistes pour le Développement Intégral*). In his work, the visual artist deals with urban phenomena such as the *sapeurs* and Kimbanguism. For the *Congo as Fiction* exhibition, Sambu selected motifs from his series *Vanité Apparente* in which he addresses the ostentatious display of elegance and vanity. Remarkably, the pictures also bear surprising reference to Hans Himmelheber's photographs shot roughly eighty years ago.

DAVID SHONGO (*1994) lives and works in Lubumbashi. In his work the young composer and artist questions the colonial images that persist in modern-day Congo to this day. He combines music, film, and colonial photography to create works that deal with the psychological repercussions of the colonial era, the social and economic effects of technological change, the impact of coltan mining on the country, and the reinvention of imagery. In a joint residency programme for the 2019 Lubumbashi Biennale and the *Congo as Fiction* exhibition in Zürich, Shongo has created a piece in which he reinterprets Hans Himmelheber's historical photographs with the aid of blackout poetry, thus catapulting the images into the present.

MONSENGO SHULA (*1959) lives and works in Kinshasa. Like many popular artists, he is inspired by everyday life and politics in the capital and is interested above all in social inequality. Monsengo Shula's paintings differ from those by other masters of popular art due to their unique choice of color, which lends his images a mythical character and transports the viewer to unworldly spheres. He has participated in various group exhibitions, most recently exhibiting in *Beauté Congo—1926–2015—Congo Kitoko* at the Fondation Cartier pour l'art contemporain as well as in *Congo Stars* in Tübingen and Graz.

PATHY TSHINDELE KAPINGA (*1976) lives and works in Kinshasa. The trained sculptor was a founding member of the artist collective Eza Possible in 2003. His work can be located between contemporary art and popular painting. In his pictures that capture revolts, language, life, streets, and light, he links his personal story to the history of the Congo.

BIBLIOGRAPHY

A

Arndt, Lotte, "Vestiges of Oblivion—Sammy Baloji's Works on Skulls in European Museum Collections," in *Darkmatter*, November 18, 2013, http://www.darkmatter101.org/site/2013/11/18/vestiges-of-oblivion-sammy-baloji's-works-on-skulls-in-european-museum-collections, accessed on August 19, 2019.

B

Baumann, Hermann, Lunda, *Bei Bauern und Jägern in Inner-Angola: Ergebnisse der Angola-Expedition des Museums für Völkerkunde,* Berlin, 1935.

Becker, Howard Saul, *Art World,* Berkeley, 1982.

Bernatzik, Hugo Adolf, *Afrika. Handbuch der angewandten Völkerkunde,* Innsbruck, 1947.

Biebuyck, Daniel, "Tobacco Mortar," in eds. Erna Beumers; Hans-Joachim Koloss, *Kings of Africa: Art and Authority in Central Africa,* Maastricht, 1992, p. 315.

Binkley, David A., "Masks, Space, and Gender in Southern Kuba Initiation Ritual," in *Iowa Studies in African Art* vol. 3 (1990), pp. 157–176.

Binkley, David A., Darish, Patricia, *Kuba,* Milan, 2009.

Bouttiaux, Anne-Marie; Ghysels, Marc, "Probing Art with CT Scans: A New Look at Two Masterpieces from Central Africa," in *Arts & Cultures* (2008), pp. 230–249.

de Bouveignes, Olivier, *Poëtes et conteurs noirs,* Anvers, 1948.

Brincard, Marie-Thérèse, *Kuba Textiles: Geometry in Form, Space, and Time,* Neuberger Museum of Art, New York, 2015.

C

Colard, Sandrine, *Pre-Figuring Kinshasa City Dwellers in the Streets of Léopoldville: The Photography of Jean Depara,* February 21, 2019, https://post.at.moma.org/content_items/1248-pre-figuring-kinshasa-city-dwellers-in-the-streets-of-leopoldville-the-photography-of-jean-depara?fbclid=IwAR3-6eBPnDO7jJsL1MhmqHTXKelD5lHP0bEwP3-JHo9AVAd-eQOlCnYnDBg, ESSAYS, accessed on July 15, 2019.

D

Darish, Patricia, "Kuba Art and Culture," in Brincard 2015.

E

Edwards, Elizabeth; Fischer, Robert, *Anthropology and Photography, 1860–1920,* London, 1992.

Enwezor, Okwui; Zaya, Octavio, "Colonial Imaginary, Tropes of Disruption: History, Culture, and Representation in the Works of African Photographers," in Clare Bell, *In/sight: African Photographers, 1940 to the Present: Solomon Guggenheim Museum, May 24 – September 29, 1996.* New York, 1996, pp. 17–48.

Etambala, Zana, "Notes sur le Tipoye en Afrique noire," in *Ngonge, Carnets de Sciences Humaines,* 6 (2011), pp. 7–15; 7 (2012), pp. 14–23.

F

Fabian, Johannes, *Time and Other: How Anthropolgy Makes its Object,* New York, 1983.

Fabian, Johannes, *Out of Our Minds: Reason and Madness in the Exploration of Central Africa.* Berkeley, 2000.

Fagg, William, *Masques d'Afrique dans les collections du Musée Barbier-Müller,* Paris, 1980.

Fall, N'Goné (ed.), *Photographies Kinshasa,* Paris, 2001.

Fischer, Eberhard; Clara Mayer-Himmelheber (eds.), *Zaire 1938/39: Hans Himmelheber. Photographic Documents on the Arts of the Yaka, Pende, Tshokwe and Kuba / Fotodokumente zur Kunst bei den Yaka, Pende, Tshokwe und Kuba,* Zürich, 1993.

Fourche, Jules-Auguste; Morlighem, Henri, "Conceptions des indigènes du Kasai sur l'homme et la mort," in *Journal de la Société des africanistes* vol. 7, no. 2 (1937), pp. 189–202.

Fourche, Jules-Auguste; Morlighem, Henri, "Architecture et analogie des plans des mondes, d'après les conceptions indigènes du Kasai et d'autres régions," in *Bulletin de l'Institut royal colonial belge* vol. 9, no. 3 (1938), pp. 616–672.

Fourche, Jules-Auguste; Morlighem, Henri, *Les communications des indigènes du Kasai avec les âmes des morts,* Brussels, 1939.

Fourche, Jules-Auguste; Morlighem, Henri, *Une Bible Noire. Cosmogonie Bantu,* Paris, 2002.

Frobenius, Leo, *Ethnographische Notizen aus den Jahren 1905 und 1906. III: Luluwa, Süd-Kete, Bena-Mai, Pende, Cokwe,* Wiesbaden, 1988.

Fromont, Cécile, *The Art of Conversion. Christian visual culture in the Kingdom of Kongo,* Chapel Hill, 2014.

G

Gagliardi, Susan Elizabeth, *Senufo Unbound,* Cleveland Museum of Art, 2015.

Gardi, Bernhard, *Zaire Masken – Figuren,* Basel, 1986.

Garner, Virginia, *Images Out of Africa: The Virginia Garner Diaries of the Africa Motion Picture Project,* edited with an introduction by Glenn Reynolds, foreword by J. M. Burns, photos by Virginia and Ray Garner, Lanham, Maryland, 2011.

Gell, Alfred, *Art and Agency, an Anthropological Theory,* Oxford, 1998, pp. 17ff.

Geary, Christraud: "Two Days in Mushenge Eliot Elisofon's Images of the Kuba," in *African Arts* 26, no. 2 (1993), pp. 72–77.

Geary, Christraud M., *In and Out of Focus: Images from Central Africa, 1885–1960,* with an essay by Krzysztof Pluskota, London, 2002.

Geary, Christraud M., "Creating and Disseminating Images of the Kuba and Their Arts, 1885–1971," in Brincard, 2015, pp. 56–67.

Geary, Christraud M., *Postcards from Africa. Photographers of the Colonial Era.* Selections from the Leonard A. Lauder Postcard Archive, Boston, 2018.

Gondola, Didier, "La Sape Exposed! High Fashion among Lower-Class Congolese Youth," in eds. Suzane Gott; Kristyne Loughran, *Contemporary African Fashion,* Bloomington, Indianapolis, 2010, pp. 157–173.

Gondola, Didier, "Ego, Identity, Illusion: Metamorphoses of a Fantasy: La Sape in Kinshasa," in ed. Dominique Malanquais, *Kinshasa Chroniques,* Montreuil, 2019, pp. 186–207.

Guyer, Nanina, "Extending the Stage: Photography and Sande Initiates in the Early Twentieth-Century," in Jan-Lodewijk Grootaers; Alexander Bortolot, *Visions from the Forests: The Art of Liberia and Sierra Leone,* Minneapolis, 2014, pp. 42–55.

Guyer, Nanina, "Unvertraute Anblicke, unerwartete Einblicke. Zur Geschichte und Rezeption von Postkarten aus Westafrika," in eds. R. Burmeister; M. Oberhofer; E. Tisa-Francini, *Dada Afrika. Dialog mit dem Fremden,* Zürich, 2016, pp. 109–113.

H

Hahn, Hans Peter, "On the Circulation of Colonial Pictures, Polyphony and Fragmentation," in eds. Sissy Helff; Stefanie Michels, *Global Photographies, Memory – History – Archives,* Bielefeld, 2018, pp. 89–101.

Halen, Pierre, "Une revue coloniale de culture congolaise: Brousse (1935–1939–1959)," in *Actes de la 1ère Journée d'études consacrée aux littératures «européenes» à propos ou issues de l'Afrique centrale (Bayreuth, 21 juillet 1993).* Documents de travail réunis par János Riesz et Pierre Halen, Bayreuth, 1994, pp. 68–91.

Hersak, Dunja, "Beyond the Naked Eye: Ethnography Screened through the Scientific Lens," in *Critical Interventions* 11 (2013), pp. 95–104.

Hersak, Dunja, "Reviewing Power, Process, and Statement: The Case of Songye Figures," in *African Arts* 43, 2 (2010), pp. 38–51.

Himmelheber, Hans, *Negerkünstler. Ethnographische Studien über den Schnitzkünstler bei den Stämmen der Atutu und Guro im Innern der Elfenbeinküste. Ergebnisse einer Forschungsexpedition,* Stuttgart, 1935.

Himmelheber, Hans, *Eskimokünstler. Ergebnis einer völkerkundlichen Reise in Alaska,* Stuttgart, 1938.

Himmelheber, Hans, "Les Masques Bayaka et leurs sculpteurs," in *Brousse* no. 1 (1939a), pp. 3–23.

Himmelheber, Hans, "Art et Artistes Batshiok," in *Brousse* no. 3 (1939b), pp. 17–31.

Himmelheber, Hans, "Arts et artistes 'Bakuba,'" in *Brousse* vol. 2, no. 1 (1940), pp. 17–30.

Himmelheber, Hans, *Negerkunst und Negerkünstler. Mit Ergebnissen von sechs Afrika-Expeditionen des Verfassers,* Brunswick, 1960.

Himmelheber, Hans, "Das Portrait in der Negerkunst. Bericht über eine Versuchsreihe," in *Baessler-Archiv,* 20 (1972), pp. 261–311.

Howe, Ellen; Rizzo, Adriana, https://www.metmuseum.org/exhibitions/listings/2015/kongo/blog/posts/materials-that-make-mangaaka (2015), accessed on August 22, 2019.

K

Kasfir, Sidney Littlefield, "One Tribe, One Style? Paradigms in the Historiography of African Art," in *History in Africa,* 11, 1984, pp. 163-193.

Kasfir, Sidney Littlefield, "Cast, Miscast: The Curator's Dilemma," in *African Arts,* vol. 30, no. 1 (Winter, 1997), pp. 1, 4, 6, 8f., and 93.

Kwete Mwana, Georges, *Souvenir d'un prince Kuba du Congo (1913–1970).* Présenté et annoté par Jan Vansina, Paris, 2010.

L

LaGamma, Alisa, "The Recently Acquired Kongo Mangaaka Power Figure," in *Metropolitan Museum Journal* 43 (2008), pp. 201–210.

LaGamma, Alisa, *Heroic Africans. Legendary Leaders, Iconic Sculptures,* New York, 2011.

LaGamma, Alisa; Howe, Ellen G.; Rizzo, Adriana, "Mangaaka," in ed. Alisa LaGamma, *Kongo: Power and Majesty,* New York, 2015, S. 221–265.

Leuzinger, Elsy, *Afrikanische Skulpturen,* Museum Rietberg, Zürich, 1963.

Loos, Pierre; Buch, Pierre (eds.), *A Passage to Congo: Photographs by Doctor Émile Muller 1923–1938,* Milan, Brussels, 2007, pp. 74–79.

M

MacGaffey, Wyatt, "The Eyes of Understanding: Kongo Minkisi," in *Astonishment and Power,* Washington, 1993, pp. 19–103.

Mack, John, *Emil Torday and the Art of the Congo,* London, 1990.

Mack, John, "Documenting the Cultures of Southern Zaire: The Photographs of the Torday Expeditions 1900–1909," in *African Arts* vol. 24, no. 4 (1991), pp. 60–69, 100.

Mack, John, "Making and Seeing: Matisse and the Understanding of Kuba Pattern," in *Journal of Art Historiography* 7 (2012), pp. 1–19.

Maes, Joseph, "Figurines 'phemba' dites maternités des Bena Lulua," in *L'Illustration congolaise* vol. 220 (1940), pp. 29–31.

Maesen, Albert, "Statuaire et culte de fécondité chez les Luluwa du Kasaï (Zaïre)," in *Quaderni Poro* vol. 3 (1982), pp. 49–58.

Mbeme, Achille, "Decolonizing Knowledge and the Question of the Archive," lecture, University of the Witwatersrand, 2015, https://wiser.wits.ac.za/system/files/Achille%20Mbembe%20-%20Decolonizing%20Knowledge%20and%20the%20Question%20of%20the%20Archive.pdf, accessed on August 30, 2019.

Monroe, John Warne, "Surface Tensions: Empire, Parisian Modernism, and 'Authenticity' in African Sculpture, 1917–1939," in *American Historical Review,* (April 2012), pp. 445–475.

Morton, Christopher, "Double alienation Evans-Pritchard's Zande and Nuer photographs in comparative perspective," in ed. Richard Vokes, *Photography in Africa: Ethnographic Perspectives,* Woodbridge, 2012, pp. 33–55.

Mudimbe, Valentin Y., *The Invention of Africa: Gnosis, Philosophy and the Order of Knowledge,* Bloomington, 1988.

O

Oberhofer, Michaela, "'Der Wert von Stroh, Eisen und Holz' – Leo Frobenius als Händler und Sammler," in eds. Jean-Louis Georget; Hélène Ivanoff; Richard Kuba, *Kulturkreise. Leo Frobenius und seine Zeit,* Berlin, 2016, pp. 217–237.

Oberhofer, Michaela; Tisa Francini, Esther, "Han Coray zwischen Dada und Afrika. Ein Leben für die Kunst," in eds. R. Burmeister; M. Oberhofer; E. Tisa Francini, *Dada Afrika. Dialog mit dem Fremden,* Zürich, 2016, pp. 114–123.

Oberhofer, Michaela (ed.), *Perlkunst aus Afrika. Die Sammlung Mottas,* Zürich, 2018.

P

Petridis, Constantine, "Mbala, Tsaam, or Kwilu Pende? A Mother-and-Child Figure from the Kwango-Kwilu Region of the Democratic Republic of the Congo," in *Cleveland Studies in the History of Art* 7 (2002), pp. 126–141.

Petridis, Constantine, *Luluwa: Central African Art Between Heaven and Earth,* Brussels, 2018.

Pluskota, Krzysztof, "Atelier PHOTO Cinématographique – C. Zagourski," in Geary 2002, pp. 58–67.

R

Raymaekers, Jan, "The Musée de la vie inidgène in Leopoldville," lecture presented at the sitting of the class of Human Sciences of the Royal Academy of Overseas Sciences of Brussels, March 21, 2017, http://www.kaowarsom.be/documents/PDF%20BULLETIN/RAYMAEKERS.pdf, accessed on July 12, 2019.

Reynolds, Glenn, "'Africa Joins the World': The Missionary Imagination and the Africa Motion Picture Project in Central Africa, 1937–9," in *Journal of Social History,* vol. 44, no. 2, *The Arts in Place* (2010), pp. 459–479.

S

Saint Léon, P. M., *Anthologie de la photographie africaine et de l'Océan Indien,* 2nd ed., Paris, 1999.

Sarr, Felwine, *Afrotopia,* Berlin, 2019.

Schildkrout, Enid, "The Spectacle of Africa through the Lens of Herbert Lang: Belgian Congo Photographs 1909–1915," in *African Arts* vol. 24, no. 4 (1991), pp. 70–85, 100.

Schildkrout, Enid; Keim, Curtis A., "Objects and Agendas: Re-Collecting the Congo," in eds. Enid Schildkrout; Curtis A. Keim, *The Scramble for Art in Central Africa,* Cambridge, 1998, pp. 1–36.

Schneider, Jürg, "Portrait Photography: A Visual Currency in the Atlantic Visualscape," in eds. John, Peffer; Elisabeth L. Cameron, *Portraiture & Photography in Africa,* Bloomington, 2013, pp. 35–65.

Sheppard, Rebekha, *A History of Encounter, an Encounter with History. The Emil Torday Expedition 1907–1909,* Phd thesis, Sainsbury Research Unit, Norwich UK, 2017.

Sheppard, William H., *Presbyterian Pioneers in the Congo,* Richmond, Virginia, 1917.

de Sousberghe, L., *L'art Pende,* Gembloux, 1958.

Strother, Z. S., "Eastern Pende Constructions of Secrecy," in ed. Robert Nooter, *Secrecy: African Art that Conceals and Reveals,* New York, 1993, pp. 156–178.

Strother, Z. S., *Inventing Masks. Agency and History in the Art of the Central Pende,* Chicago, 1998.

Strother, Z. S., "From Performative Utterance to Performative Object: Pende Theories of Speech, Blood Sacrifice, and Power Objects," in *Res: Journal of Anthropology and Aesthetics* 37 (2000), pp. 49–71.

Strother, Z. S., *Pende,* Milan, 2008.

Strother, Z. S., "A Terrifying Mimesis: Problems of Portraiture and Representation in African Sculpture (Congo-Kinshasa)," in *Res: Journal of Anthropology and Aesthetics* 65-66 (2014/15), pp. 126–145.

Strother, Z. S., *Humor and Violence. Seeing Europeans in Central African Art,* Bloomington, 2016.

von Sydow, Eckart, *Kunst der Naturvölker. Afrika, Ozeanien, Indonesien,* Berlin, 1932.

T

Theye, Thomas, *Der Geraubte Schatten. Photographie als ethnographisches Dokument.* Munich, 1989.

Thoss, Michael, "Spotted Vision, Fotografische Fantasien und Visionen," in eds. Annette Czekelius; Michael Thoss, *Porträt Afrika, Fotografische Positionen eines Jahrhunderts.* Berlin, 2000, pp. 8–20.

Timmermans, Paul, "Essai de typologie de la sculpture des Beena Luluwa du Kasai," in *Africa-Tervuren* vol. 12, no. 1 (1966), pp. 17–27.

Torday, Emil, *Causeries Congolaises,* Brussels, 1925.

Torday, Emil, *On the Trail of the Bushongo. An Account of a Remarkable and Hitherto Unknown African People,* London, 1925.

Traeger, Verena, "Gustav Klimt and African Art: Kuba Affinities," in Brincard 2015, pp 68–79.

V

Van Beurden, Sarah, *Authentically African. Arts and the Transnational Politics of Congolese Culture,* Athens, 2015.

Van Caeneghem, R., *La notion de Dieu chez les baLuba du Kasai*, Brussels, 1956.

Vanhee, Hein, "Maîtres et serviteurs. Les chefs médaillés dans le Congo colonial," in eds. Jean-Luc Vellut et al., *La mémoire du Congo. Le temps colonial,* Musée royal de l'Afrique centrale, Tervuren, 2005, pp. 79–82.

Vansina, Jan, "Photographs of the Sankuru and Kasai River Basin Expedition undertaken by Emil Torday (1876–1931) and M.W. Hilton Simpson (1881–1936)," in Elizabeth Edwards; Robert Fischer, *Anthropology and Photography, 1860–1920,* London, 1992, pp. 193–205.

Vansina, Jan, "La survie du royaume Kuba à l'époque coloniale et les arts," in *Annales Aequatoria,* vol. 28 (2007), pp. 5–29.

Vansina, Jan, Being Colonized. *The Kuba Experience in Rural Congo, 1880–1960.* Madison, 2010.

Van Reybrouck, David, *Kongo, Eine Geschichte,* Berlin, 2012.

Volper, Julien, "Women in Red. The Kuba Art of Tukula," in Brincard, 2015, pp. 51–55.

W

Wannijn, Jeanne, "Le grand chef Lukengo est mort," in *L'Illustration Congolaise. Journal bimensuel de propagande colonial,* vol. 219 (1939), pp. 7612–7614.

Weiss, Herbert F.; Woodward, Richard B.; Strother, Z. S., "Art with Fight in It: Discovering that a Statue of a Colonial Officer Is a Power Object from the 1931 Pende Revolt," in *African Arts* 49/1 (2016), pp. 56–69.

Wendl, Tobias; Behrend, Heike (eds.), *Snap me one! Studiofotografen in Afrika,* Munich, 1998.

Wendl, Tobias; von Lintig, Bettina, *Black Paris, Kunst und Geschichte einer schwarzen Diaspora,* Wuppertal, 2006.

von Wissmann, Hermann von, et al., *Im Innern Afrikas: Die Erforschung des Kassaï während der Jahre 1883, 1884 und 1885,* 3rd ed., Leipzig, 1891.

Y

Yelengi, Nkasa T., "The PFB Railroad, Society and Culture in Rural Katanga (Colonial Zaire)," in *Africa: Revista trimestrale di studi e documentazione dell'Istituto italiano per l'Africa e l'Oriente* vol. 52, no. 2 (1997), pp. 182–211.

LENDERS

Aimé Mpane and NOMAD GALLERY BRUSSELS
Barbara and Eberhard Fischer
Boris Kegel-Konietzko, Hamburg
CAAC – The Pigozzi Collection, Geneva
Christraud M. Geary Collection
Gallery MAGNIN-A, Paris
Henri and Farida Seydoux Collection, Paris
Horstmann Collection
Jan Calmeyn, Sint-Niklaas
Marc Felix, Brussels
Michèle Magema
Museum der Kulturen Basel
Musée d'ethnographie de Genève – MEG
Musée royal de l'Afrique centrale, Tervuren
Nuno Crisostomo, The Bujas-Crisostomo Family Collection, Lisbon / New York / France / Kinshasa, Democratic Republic of the Congo
Private Collection Lausanne
Private Collection, Zug
Virginia Museum of Fine Arts, Richmond VA
Zentralbibliothek Zürich
and private collectors who prefer to remain anonymous

WORKS COMMISSIONED BY THE MUSEUM RIETBERG

David Shongo
Fiona Bobo
Fiston Mwanza Mujila
Michèle Magema
Sammy Baloji
Sinzo Aanza
Yves Sambu

IMAGE CREDITS

© Alain Nsenga: fig. 389
© Angelo Turconi: fig. 40
© bpk / Ethnologisches Museum, SMB; photo Waltraut Schneider-Schütz: fig. 257
© Carlsen Verlag GmbH Hamburg: fig. 91
© Charles Hénault, Marc Felix, Archives du Congo Basin Art History Research Center: fig. 217
© Chéri Samba / photo courtesy CAAC – The Pigozzi Collection, Geneva: fig. 1
© Collection Christraud M. Geary: figs. 92–94, 98, 99, 128, 131, 134, 137
© Collection Marc Felix; photo Maureen Vincke: fig. 89
© Collection Pierre Loos, Brussels: figs. 129, 130
© Collection RMCA Tervuren: fig. 90/ photo Ch. Delhaise, ca 1923: fig. 136/photo J.-M. Vandyck: figs. 165, 178/photo J. Van de Vyver: fig. 297
© David Shongo: figs. 21, 124.1, 124.3, 125.2, 126.2, 127.2
© Dr. David Mannes, Neutron Imaging and Applied Materials Group (NIAG), Laboratory for Neutron Scattering and Imaging, Paul Scherrer Institut: figs. 269.1, 272.2, 272.3, 273–276, 278, 313, 314
© Eliot Elisofon Photographic Archives, National Museum of African Art, Smithsonian Institution: fig. 149
© Farida and Henri Seydoux Collection; Photo westudio.fr: endpapers
© Fiona Bobo: figs. 236–248
© Fondation Musée Barbier-Mueller; Photo studio Ferrazzini-Bouchet: fig. 263
© Gallery MAGNIN-A, Paris; photo Cyrille Martin: figs. 159, 353
© Gay Garner Mackintosh: fig. 139
© Georges Senga: fig. 388
© Jan Calmeyn; photo H. Dubois: fig. 267
© KEYSTONE Pictures USA: fig. 97
© Los Angeles County Museum of Art: fig. 259
© Marvin Goertz: fig. 339
© Michèle Magema, figs. 115–119
© Michèle Magema, courtesy Kunsthaus Graz; photo N. Lackner: figs. 8.1, 8.2
© Ministère des Affaires étrangères, Archives Africaines, fig. 280
© Musée d'ethnographie de Genève MEG; photo J. Watts: fig. 13
© Museum der Kulturen Basel; photo Omar Lemke 2019: figs. 5, 32, 111, 114, 150, 182, 292, 293/photo Omar Lemke 2017: fig. 291/photo Markus Gruber 2008: fig. 364/ photo Markus Gruber 2006: fig. 41
© Museum of Fine Arts, Boston: fig. 138
© Museum Rietberg: figs. 9, 11, 14–19, 22–24, 26, 28–31, 33–39, 42–82, 84, 85, 95, 102–104, 109, 110, 112, 114, 120–123, 124.2, 125.1, 126.1, 127.1, 132, 133, 135, 143, 144, 148, 160–164, 168, 169, 179–181, 188, 189, 198, 224, 226, 228, 230, 232, 234, 249–252, 255, 261, 262, 269.2, 281, 282, 299, 316, 318, 319, 340, 342, 346, 347, 356, 367, 373, 375, 376, 378, 379
© Museum Rietberg; photo Rainer Wolfsberger: figs. 2–4, 6, 10, 20, 25, 27, 88, 100, 101, 105, 106–108, 140–142, 145–147, 151–156, 157, 158, 166, 170–177, 183–187, 190–197, 199–221, 223, 253, 254, 256, 258, 264, 265, 266, 268, 269.2, 272.1, 277, 283–290, 296, 303–307, 309–312, 315, 320, 325, 341, 343–345, 348–352, 357–363, 365, 366, 368–372, 374, 377, 380
© Nelson Makengo: figs. 381, 382
© NOMAD GALLERY BRUSSELS, collection Aimé Mpane; photo Vincent Everarts: figs. 354, 355
© Pierre-Philippe Dûchatelet: figs. 390, 391
© Private collection: fig. 295
© Revue Noire: fig. 83
© Sammy Baloji: fig. 317
© Sammy Baloji, courtesy of the artist and Galerie Imane Farès, Paris: figs. 385–387
© Sinzo Aanza and Galerie Imane Farès, Paris: figs. 298, 300–302
© Sputnik: fig. 96
© Tadzio, courtesy of On-Trade-Off and Galerie Imane Farès, Paris: fig. 392
© Trampoline Gallery, Antwerp and Jean Katambayi: fig. 384
© Virginia Museum of Fine Arts; Photo Travis Fullerton: figs. 222, 279
© Wally and Udo Horstmann: figs. 294, 308
© WIELS; Photo Hugard & Vanoverschelde Photography: fig. 383
© Yves Sambu: figs. 225, 227, 229, 231, 233, 235
© Zentralbibliothek Zürich, figs. 86, 87
© Z. S. Strother: figs. 321–324, 326–338

Despite best efforts, we have not been able to identify the holders of copyright and printing rights for all the illustrations. Copyright holders not mentioned in the credits are asked to substantiate their claims, and recompense will be made according to standard practice.

IMPRINT

This book was published on the occasion of the exhibition *Congo as Fiction—Art Worlds between Past and Present* at the Museum Rietberg Zürich from November 22, 2019 to March 15, 2020.

Edited by Nanina Guyer and Michaela Oberhofer, Museum Rietberg

Catalogue assistance: Laura Falletta, Daniela Müller

Translations:
From German: Lisa Rosenblatt, Maria Slater
From French: Bridget Mason

Copy editing: Charlotte Eckler, Lisa Rosenblatt

Proofreading: Colette Forder

Project manager publishing house: Muriel Blancho, Chris Reding

Design: Hi – Megi Zumstein & Claudio Barandun

Lithography, printing and binding: DZA Druckerei zu Altenburg GmbH, Thuringia

Museum Rietberg Zürich
Gablerstrasse 15
8002 Zurich
Switzerland
www.rietberg.ch

Verlag Scheidegger & Spiess
Niederdorfstrasse 54
8001 Zurich
Switzerland
www.scheidegger-spiess.ch

Scheidegger & Spiess is being supported by the Federal Office of Culture with a general subsidy for the years 2016–2020.

ISBN 978-3-85881-835-5

German edition:
ISBN 978-3-85881-643-6

MUSEUM RIETBERG

Mayor: Corine Mauch

Director: Albert Lutz / Annette Bhagwati

Exhibition curators: Michaela Oberhofer and Nanina Guyer

Curatorial internship: Laura Falletta and Daniela Müller

Scenography: Martin Sollberger

Graphic design: Jacqueline Schöb

Registrar: Andrea Kuprecht

Conservator: Martin Ledergerber and Nanny Boller

Lighting, photography: Rainer Wolfsberger

Multimedia: Inlusio Interactive, Masus Meier

Art education: Maya Bührer, Christiane Ruzek, Suy Ky Lim, Robert Ashley

Guided tours: Damian Christinger, Linda Christinger, Gabriela Blumer Kamp, Sylvia Seibold, Anja Soldat, Penelope Tunstall

Communications: Elena DelCarlo, Nicola Morgan, Pascal Schlecht, Alain Suter

Events: Caroline Delley, Monique Schuler

Translation, copy editing: Nigel Stephenson, Nicole Viaud, Mark Welzel

Rietberg-Gesellschaft, Rietberg-Kreis: Annelis Huber

Shop: Régine Illi, Frauke Freitag, Theres Marty

HR: Sabine Brenner, Patrizia Zindel

Accounting: Michael Busse, Christine Hunziker

Library: Josef Huber

Publications: Mark Welzel

Reception, security, museum guards: Fani Buchholz, Randolph Egg, Sandra Gomez, Peter B. Gröner, Noorjahan Haupt, Michael Hoffmann, Xi Hu, Annelis Huber, Christina Hunziker, Laura Jones, Valentin Magaro, Maka Mamporia, Tanja Michel, Olivia Pajarola, Davide Pellandini, Ramses Rapadas, Pema Ribi, Soraya Stindt, Ursula Tanner, Isabelle Torelli

Café: Urban Högger, Fabian Kaiser, Rebecca Lüscher, Nico Lutziger, Daiana Mandato, Lea Pasinetti, Leroy Ramseier, Alexi Rapeaud, Deborah Schneider, Daniela Tau, Daniela Zgraggen

Facility management: Silvan Bosshard, Sandra Gomez

Shipping: Ly Xuong Long

Facility maintenance: Gönül Akalin, Aljbine Bajrami, Cirila Blocher, Pashije Hamidi, Katerina Kara, Mesut Kara, Zejnije Sherifi, Selam Seifu Tola, Oğuz Turhan

Partner / Sponsors: With the support of Rietberg-Gesellschaft and Accentus

Monsengo Shula
Roi satellite
2012, acrylic and sequins
on canvas, 140 × 140 cm
Henri and Farida Seydoux
Collection

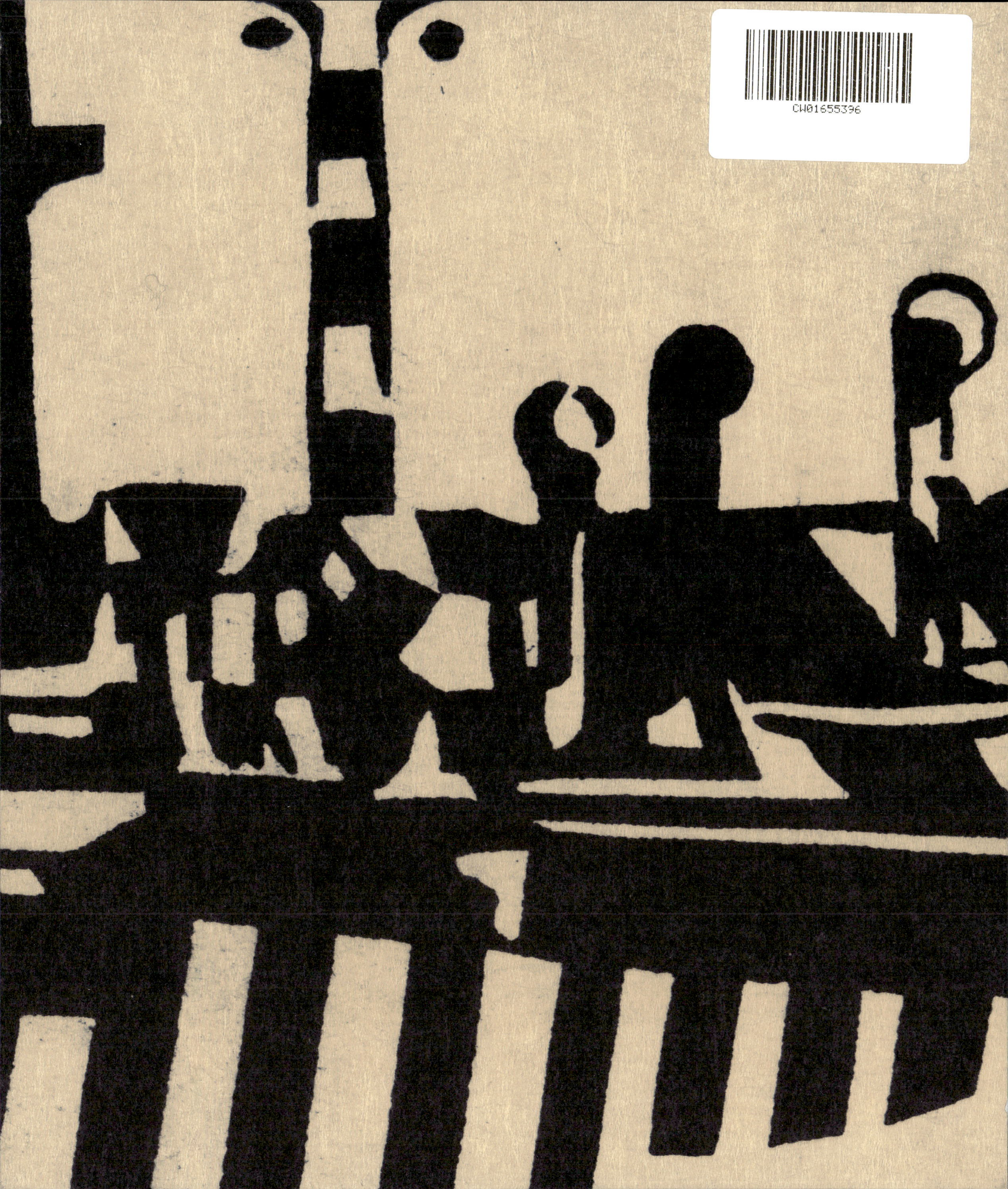

MODERN TIMES

BRITISH PRINTS, 1913–1939

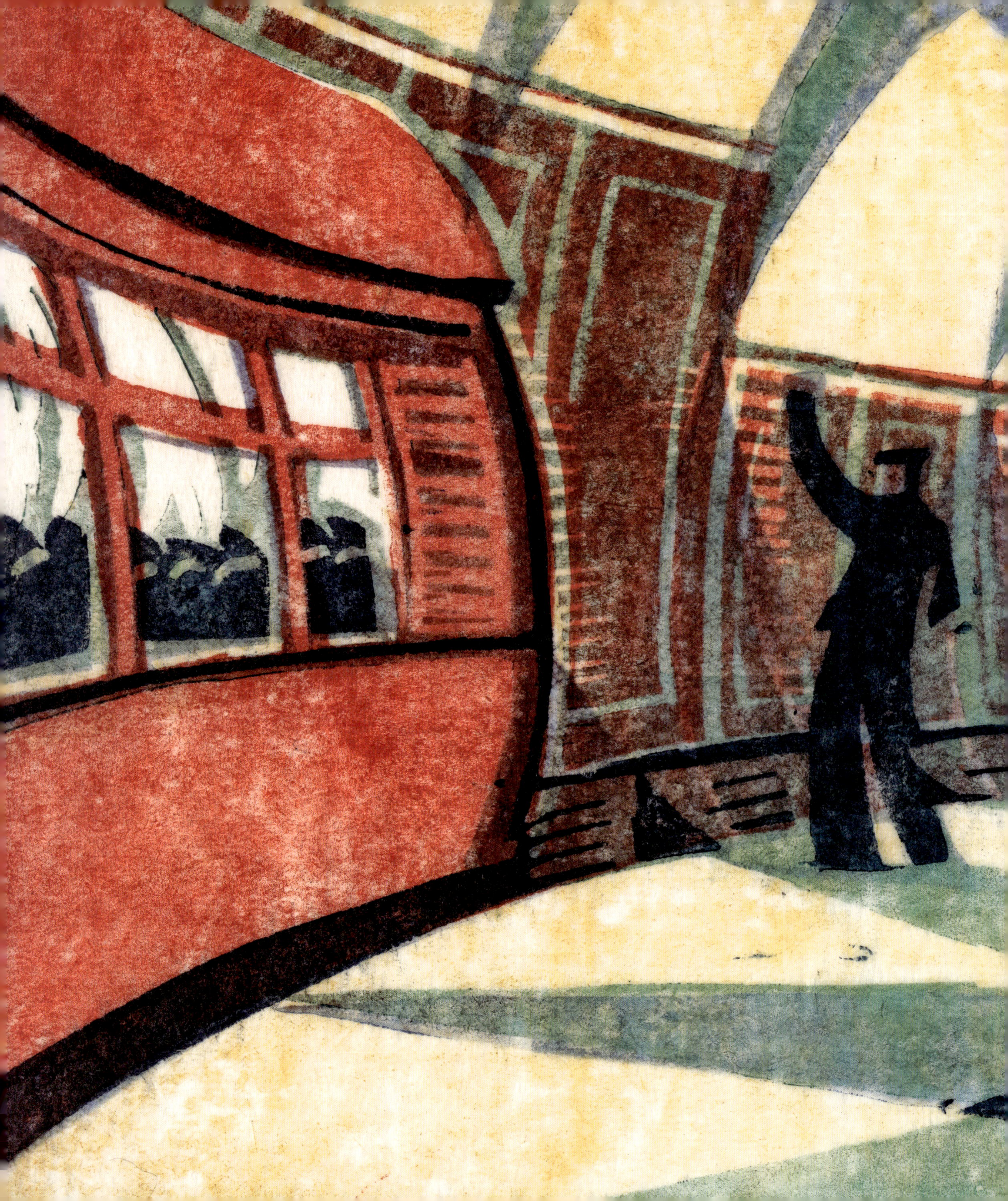

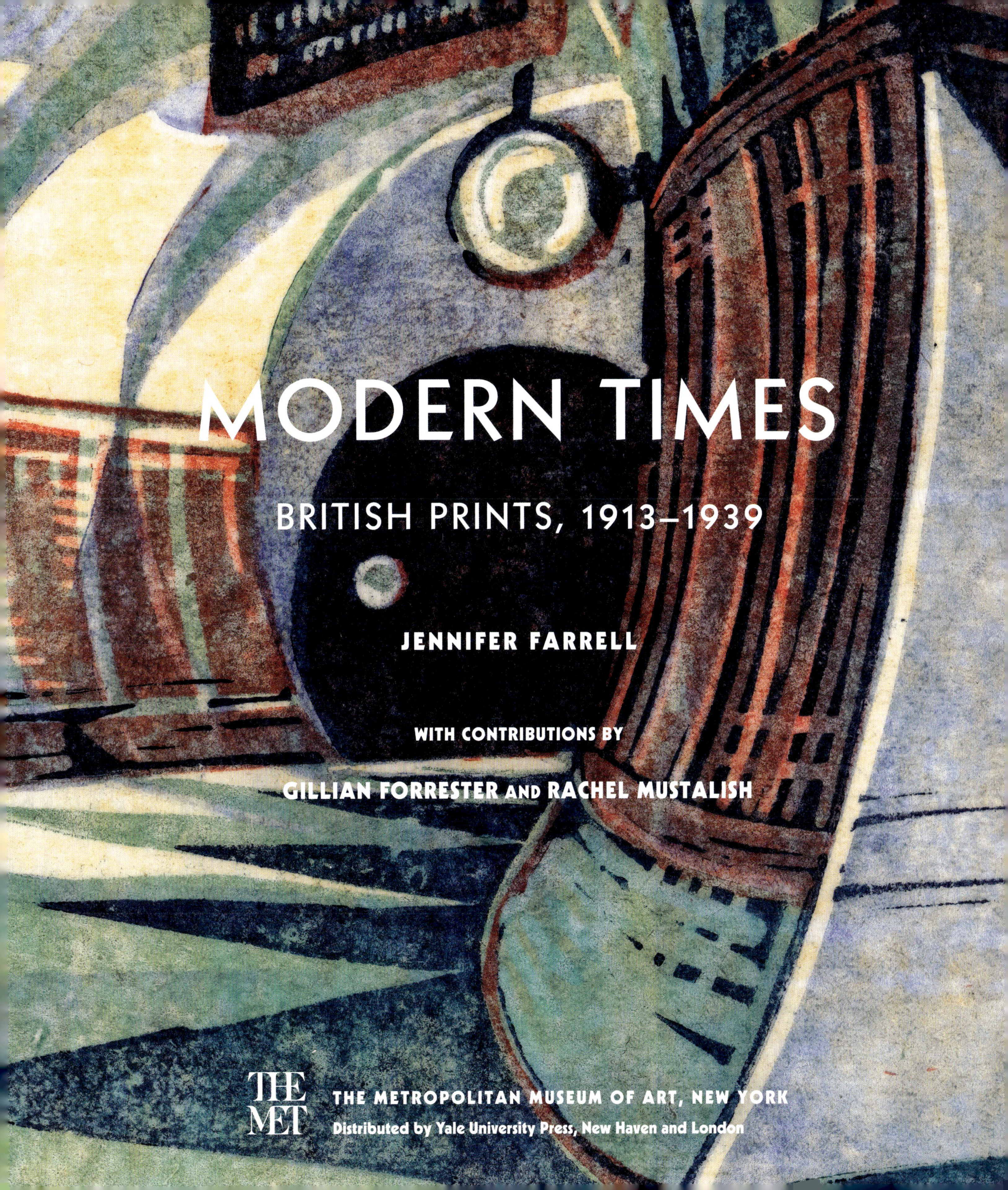

MODERN TIMES

BRITISH PRINTS, 1913–1939

JENNIFER FARRELL

WITH CONTRIBUTIONS BY

GILLIAN FORRESTER AND RACHEL MUSTALISH

THE MET
THE METROPOLITAN MUSEUM OF ART, NEW YORK
Distributed by Yale University Press, New Haven and London

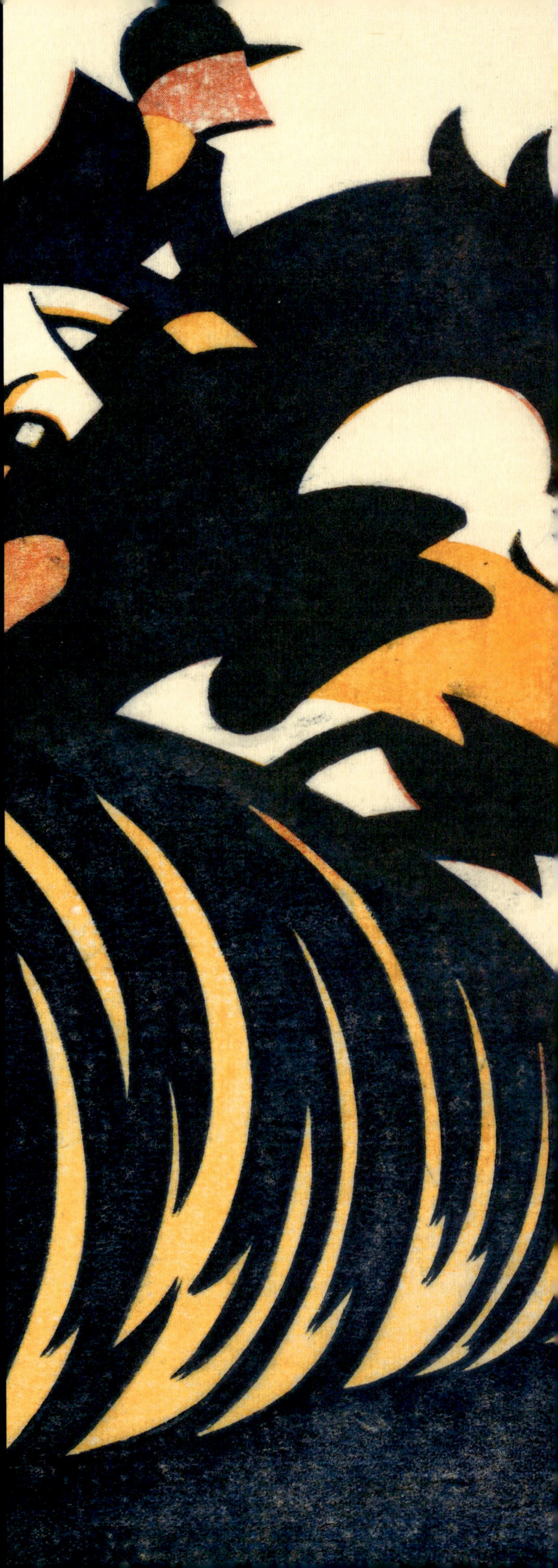

"In Full Cry" 38/50

Sybil Andrews

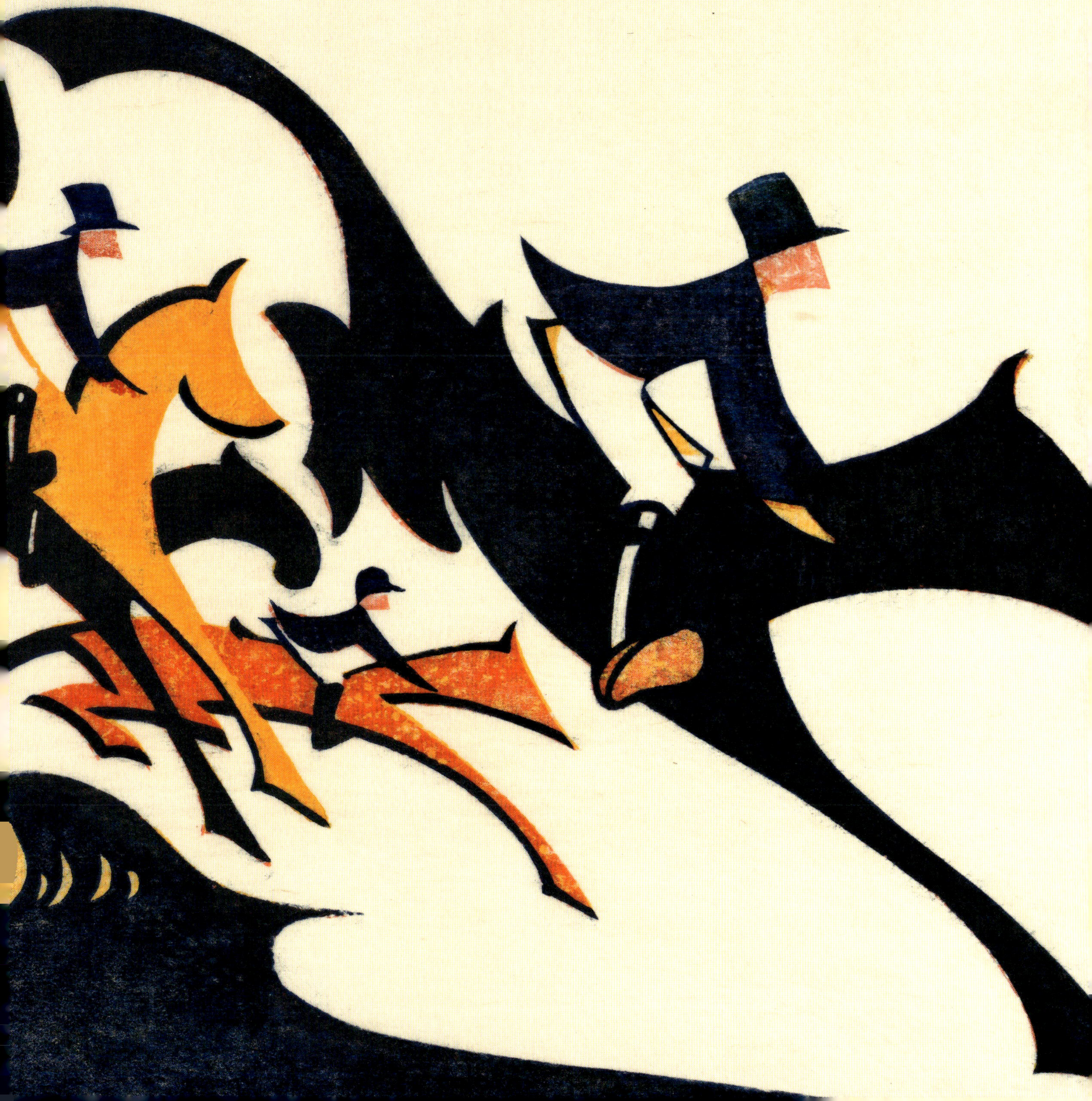

Director's Foreword

The bold graphic images made by artists affiliated with Vorticism, British Futurism, and the Grosvenor School of Modern Art capture the optimism and anxiety of early twentieth-century Britain. It was a period marked by two world wars, the fall of four empires, a global pandemic, the Great Depression, the rise of Fascism and Communism, and the expansion of colonial rule. At the same time, many people—including women in Britain and many other parts of the world—gained the right to vote; new technologies transformed experience and perception; and leisure, entertainment, and art expanded in profound ways to become accessible to more people. Through their powerful images, numerous artists sought to redefine printmaking by depicting quotidian life during the machine age with suitably modern techniques and visual styles.

Over the course of six decades, Leslie and Johanna Garfield have built an extraordinary collection, which includes images by German Expressionists and Provincetown Printers, as well as midcentury and contemporary prints, with a focus on such innovative figures as Richard Hamilton, Jasper Johns, and Dieter Roth. This book and exhibition celebrate The Met's acquisition of more than seven hundred rare and important British modernist works on paper from Leslie and Johanna's remarkable collection. The acquisition establishes The Met as a leading institution for British prints and drawings from this period and provides us with unparalleled opportunities to reconsider an expanded and more complex history of modernism. These works join the British modernist prints the Garfields donated in 2005.

This project highlights the achievements of British artists working from roughly 1913 to 1939. Some of the earliest examples are the prints by Edward Wadsworth, who, with other Vorticists, revolutionized a new graphic language. Equally compelling are the Futurist-inspired prints by Christopher Richard Wynne Nevinson, who captured the violence and destruction of the First World War and, in the process, redefined the possibilities for war art. At the heart of the study are the colorful linocuts made by artists associated with London's celebrated Grosvenor School of Modern Art. The visually striking compositions by Sybil Andrews, Claude Flight, Cyril E. Power, and Lill Tschudi, among others, convey the vitality of contemporary interwar life, from the changes brought by industrialization to metropolitan centers to the survival of traditional activities, the return of music, fairs, and sporting events, and the rhythms of the countryside.

We are grateful to Nadine M. Orenstein, Drue Heinz Curator in Charge of the Department of Drawings and Prints, for her support of this exhibition, publication, and acquisition—one of the largest in the history of the Department of Drawings and Prints. Curator Jennifer Farrell proposed and guided the acquisition and developed the book and exhibition, collaborating with colleagues while the Museum was closed due to the COVID-19 pandemic. We extend our deepest gratitude to everyone for their incredible dedication, professionalism, and creativity. The Roswell L. Gilpatric Publications Fund has our gratitude for its support of this catalogue. We also want to acknowledge the generosity that made this acquisition possible, with particular thanks to Leslie and Johanna Garfield, for their enthusiasm for this project and for providing The Met with this opportunity to become the home to their collection of British modernist works on paper.

Max Hollein
Marina Kellen French Director
The Metropolitan Museum of Art, New York

Acknowledgments

Modern Times: British Prints, 1913–1939 explores the myriad responses of a select group of British artists to the complex and often contradictory nature of this period. The project was inspired by the recent acquisition of British modernist works on paper from the collection of Leslie and Johanna Garfield, an acquisition that has been transformative for the Department of Drawings and Prints.

This publication and related exhibition benefited from the wisdom and encouragement of many individuals. First and foremost, I gratefully acknowledge Leslie and Johanna Garfield for their extraordinary generosity and their continuous support of this project and related programs, and of The Met in general. Profound thanks are due to Heather Hess, curator of the Garfield collection, for her assistance and good humor. I am indebted to Gillian Forrester and Rachel Mustalish for their original and thoughtful essays, as well as their comments and encouragement; one could not ask for better or more collaborative colleagues. In particular, our writings build on the scholarship of Stephen Coppel, whose *Linocuts of the Machine Age: Claude Flight and the Grosvenor School* (1995) is an invaluable resource.

At The Met, Max Hollein, Marina Kellen French Director, was a wonderful advocate for this acquisition, exhibition, and publication. Daniel H. Weiss, President and Chief Executive Officer, offered important early support for this endeavor. Andrea Bayer, Deputy Director for Collections and Administration, provided valuable counsel at critical moments and enthusiasm throughout.

Nadine M. Orenstein, Drue Heinz Curator in Charge of the Department of Drawings and Prints, was a tireless champion of this project. I sincerely thank her, as well as my present and former colleagues in Drawings and Prints. Special thanks go to David del Gaizo, Clara Goldman, Sarah Jane Kim, Arielle Schraeter Llupa, Ricky Luna, Kirsten Rendina, and Elizabeth Zanis.

In addition to contributing a fascinating essay, Rachel Mustalish gave expert advice on the care and presentation of these works, along with Marjorie Shelley, Sherman Fairchild Conservator in Charge, Rebecca Capua, and Martin A. Bansbach in the Department of Paper Conservation.

Several people went to great lengths to produce this book and install the show. I wish to acknowledge the Exhibitions Department, in particular Quincy Houghton, Deputy Director for Exhibitions, Amy Bogansky, and Marci King, for their organizational skills and aid. Alicia Cheng, Daniel Kershaw, Alexandre Viault, and Kamomi Solidum, in the Design Department, created a beautiful presentation reflective of the era and were assisted by Maanik Singh Chauhan, Clint Ross Coller, Grace Mennell, Amy Nelson, Josh C. Nusbaum, and Christopher DiPietro. Taylor Miller, Matthew Lytle, and Maria Nicolino, in Buildings, helped with all aspects of the installation. In the Counsel's Office, Sharon H. Cott, H. Sujin Kim, and Caroline Y. Chang provided vital assistance, as did Bryanna O'Mara in the Registrar's Office. In Communications, Kenneth Weine and Micol Spinazzi generated excitement about this project, and in Development, Clyde B. Jones III, Jason Herrick, and Katherine Lester Thompson played a crucial role in fundraising.

In addition to the authors, I am very grateful to my colleagues in Publications and Editorial, led by Mark Polizzotti, Peter Antony, and Michael Sittenfeld, for their strong support of the catalogue and exhibition-related material. I also thank Anne Blood Mann for her keen eye, patience, and sharp editorial skills, as well as Livia Tenzer for her thoughtful comments. Jean Wilcox created the gorgeous design of the catalogue, while Christopher Zichello expertly managed the book's production and Shannon Cannizzaro gathered the images and permissions. Elizabeth Benjamin and Frances Malcolm skillfully edited the exhibition texts and labels.

Erica Allen and Mark Morosse, in the Imaging Department, created the stunning photographs for the book, capturing the works' dynamism and complexity. I also wish to thank Merrill Berman and Jolie Simpson of the Merrill C. Berman Collection, the Tate, and Hauser & Wirth for allowing us to reproduce works from their collections.

With libraries around the world closed due to the COVID-19 pandemic, the staff of the Thomas J. Watson Library truly went above and beyond. I am grateful to Kenneth Soehner, Arthur K. Watson Chief Librarian, for making so much accessible and to Robyn Fleming, Dana Keith, and Jessica Ranne-Cardona for their dedication in tracking down books and texts.

Numerous people enabled the acquisition of this collection. Special thanks go to the Garfields for their largesse and encouragement at every stage, as well as for sharing their deep passion for prints and British modernism. I offer my heartfelt gratitude to Lila Acheson Wallace, Charles and Jessie Price, David T Schiff, The Elisha Whittelsey Collection, The Elisha Whittelsey Fund, Dolores Valvidia Hurlburt, the Peco Foundation, and the Friends of Drawings and Prints, who made gifts in support of the acquisition. I would also like to acknowledge the following donors: Jeffrey F. and Maud Welles, Ellen Peckham, Diana Wege, Christie's, Evelyn and David Lasry, the Cristea Roberts Gallery, Janice C. Oresman, Margaret Conklin and David Sabel, the Jockey Hollow Foundation, Katherine Michel, the Susan Sheehan Gallery, Mary Ryan and Jeffrey Lee, Kirk Kellogg, and Andrew Allen.

It is through the generosity of the Roswell L. Gilpatric Publications Fund that this catalogue is made possible.

I am indebted to friends and colleagues who shared advice and materials. Particular thanks go to Ágnes Berecz, Diana Bush, Samantha Deutch, Lisa Hodermarsky, Marcel Just, and Clayton Press for their intellectual feedback, probing questions, and insightful comments. I also wish to acknowledge the early enthusiasm of Carrie Rebora Barratt and Mark Fisch for this acquisition, which was much appreciated.

Finally, to Tom, Elizabeth, and Vivienne, with gratitude for everything.

Jennifer Farrell
Curator, Department of Drawings and Prints
The Metropolitan Museum of Art, New York

FORCES IN FLUX

Transformation and Experimentation in British Printmaking

Jennifer Farrell

In Sybil Andrews's vibrant color linocut *The New Cable*, a small group of men strains to push, turn, and pull a giant cable and the massive drum around which it is coiled (fig. 1). Even though the first transatlantic telegraph cable was laid in the 1850s, during the reign of Queen Victoria, thus accelerating communication between Great Britain and the world—in particular, the lands of the British Empire—Andrews's image, made in 1931, signifies more than imperial technological power. The rows of jagged teeth indicating layers of cable recall mechanized elements seen in earlier depictions of industrialization and modernity, such as the sawtooth and zigzag forms found throughout *Newcastle* of 1913, Edward Wadsworth's abstract woodcut made with somber black ink on gray wove paper (see fig. 5). Produced just before the First World War and named for the northern port, *Newcastle* can be read as representing Britain's perceived position as "the workshop of the world."[1] *The New Cable*, by contrast, was created in the interwar period, when the carnage and trauma of the first modern war, one enabled by industrialization and its mechanized weaponry, was still being processed. It was also an era in which British exports dropped precipitously and unemployment soared in the midst of a global depression. Nevertheless, Andrews chose to celebrate connectivity, labor, and the frequently overlooked, unglamorous actions that were essential to modern life. Rather than monumentalize the cold, hard elements that testified to the superhuman power of the machine as Wadsworth had done in *Newcastle*, she highlighted the teamwork of the anonymous and expressionless figures, who, with their angular forms, blank faces, and green-and-brown

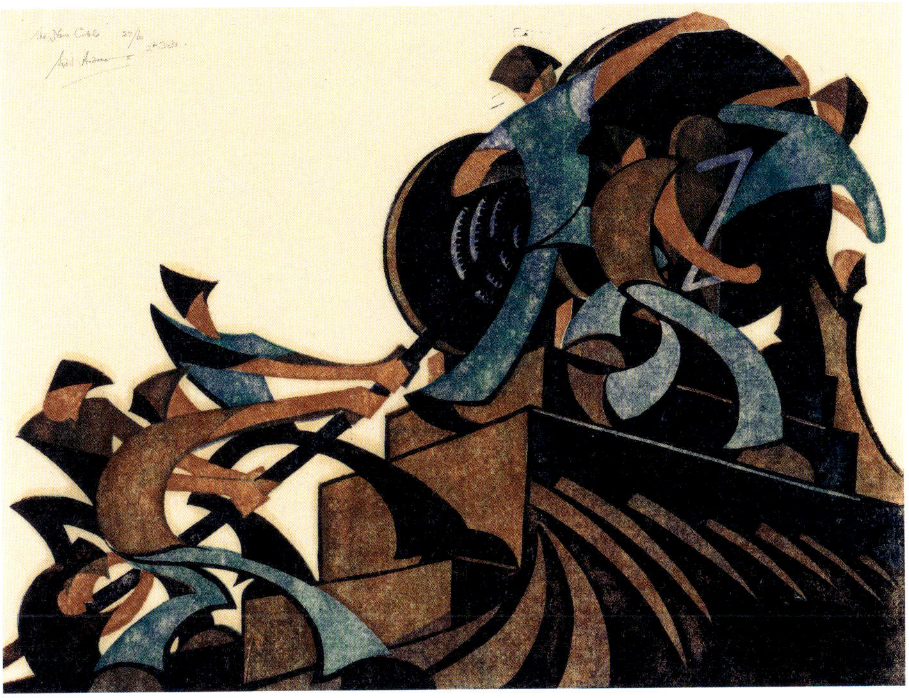

Fig. 1 **Sybil Andrews** (British, 1898–1992). *The New Cable*, 1931. Linocut on Japanese paper, image $12\frac{5}{16} \times 16\frac{3}{4}$ in. (31.2 x 42.6 cm). The Metropolitan Museum of Art, New York (2019.592.322)

uniforms, resemble interchangeable machine products themselves. Their contorted bodies emphasize and laud the human toil and raw physicality that underpinned telegraphy, telephony, and other systems that marked the new age.

These two images bracket the period on which this book and the related exhibition focus. The artists featured in *Modern Times: British Prints, 1913–1939* depicted the structures, forms, and experiences of contemporary life, with a particular interest in representations of speed, motion, and power. Their subjects were diverse and included city life, factories, underground trains, airplanes, race cars, elevators, and escalators, as well as lines of soldiers charging to the front, war-torn landscapes, and exhausted and frightened young men (fig. 2). At the same time, they also depicted leisure, the countryside, and traditional activities, such as farming, sports, and festivals, all through a modern lens.

The first half of the twentieth century witnessed dramatic political, economic, and cultural changes shaped by two world wars, the collapse of four empires, Communism, a deadly pandemic, the rise of Fascism, and a global depression. In Great Britain, while entire industries were decimated and large portions of the population suffered from deprivation, there were also enormous technological and social advances, including the expansion of voting rights and education, especially for women. The prints made by British artists reflect their search for appropriate visual styles and techniques via which to capture the often paradoxical character of the times.

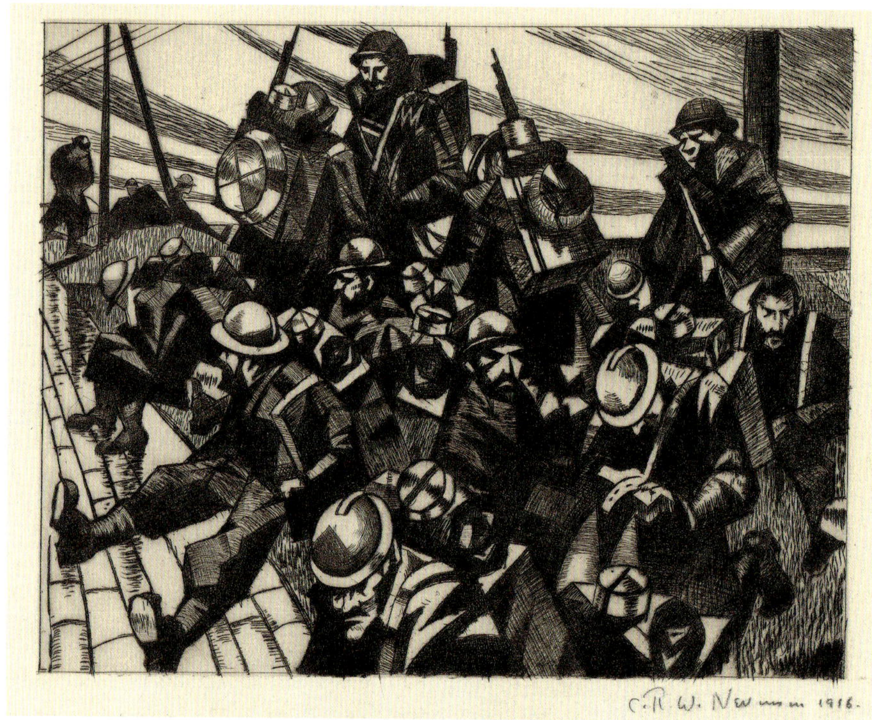

Fig. 2 Christopher Richard Wynne Nevinson (British, 1889–1946). *Troops Resting*, 1916. Drypoint on Western paper, plate 7 5/16 x 9 1/4 in. (18.5 x 23.5 cm). The Metropolitan Museum of Art, New York (2019.592.628)

Much attention has been paid to modernism in continental Europe; however, British art from the early twentieth century and the interwar period, and the graphic arts, in particular, have not received the same level of critical examination.[2] There are several reasons for this omission, including a long-standing, predominant interest in prewar abstraction. Greater consideration has also been given to artists who explicitly tied their formal experimentations with radical political ideology or used new technologies (such as photography and film), strategies (such as performance and installation), and methods (such as collage and montage). Many studies have been devoted to larger and more prominent movements outside of Britain that were accompanied by stronger markets and related networks of collectors, curators, critics, and dealers. There has also been a tendency to exclude printmaking from broader artistic and cultural histories that have relied more heavily on other arts, such as painting and literature.[3] By contrast, this book aims to highlight the innovation of British printmaking during these tumultuous decades. The authors analyze why a number of British artists—and closely affiliated international artists—turned to printmaking in an era when many contemporaries were embracing film, photography, collage, and constructions. Through their unique, distinctive artworks, we examine how they responded to and reflected both modernity and British culture.

Around 1914, the London-based modernists associated with Vorticism and Futurism were attracted to the potential of the machine, fetishizing speed,

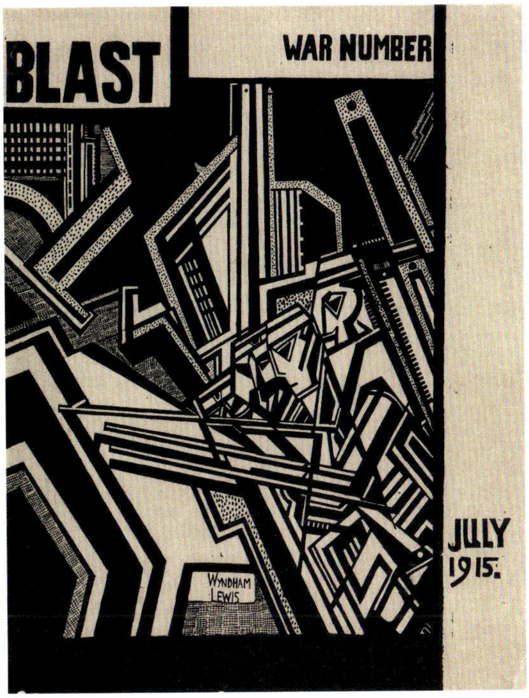

strength, industrialization, and even conflict (fig. 3). Like their countrymen, many of these figures would later serve in the First World War as soldiers, volunteers, or war artists. The experience led several of them to change their style, subject matter, politics, and—significantly—their choice of media, a topic Gillian Forrester explores in her essay in this volume. Artists such as Christopher Richard Wynne Nevinson and Paul Nash redefined the possibility for war art, with Nevinson, in particular, striving to portray the brutality of modern combat that destroyed both people and the landscape. Not surprisingly, public response was sharply divided: Some called for Nevinson's work to be censored, whereas others praised his haunting images for their honesty.

Fig. 3 Wyndham Lewis's *Before Antwerp* reproduced on the cover of *BLAST* no. 2 (July 1915), published with John Lane, London. The Metropolitan Museum of Art, New York, The Elisha Whittelsey Collection, The Elisha Whittelsey Fund, 1967 (67.804.13[2])

During the interwar years there was a changing conception of the appropriate role and form of the visual arts and even of the cultural field itself. While some scholars have argued that British art institutions and artistic production were in crisis in the early to mid-twentieth century, others have proposed that the era was one of expansion, citing the concerted effort—often with government support—to increase opportunities to engage directly with art, especially beyond metropolitan centers. There was also a shift in the art market as new patrons, such as the London Passenger Transport Board, commissioned pieces not only to promote public transportation but also to make commuting a pleasant, even enlightening experience. Such projects enabled artists to redefine their practice and reach a wider, more diverse audience. In retrospect, it is this very contradiction—between crisis and expansion—that informed artistic production during these decades.

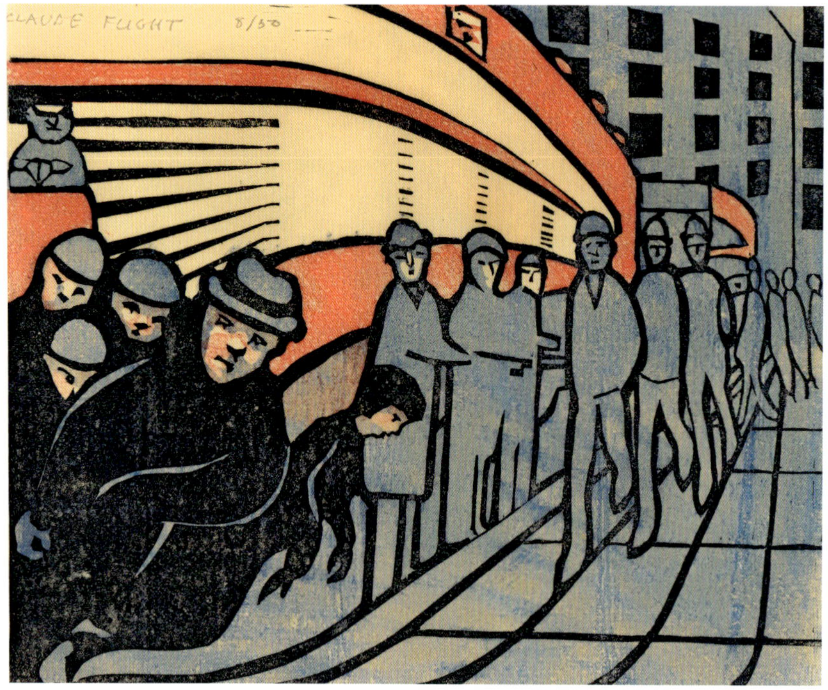

Fig. 4 Claude Flight (British, 1881–1955). *Three Speeds*, ca. 1922. Linocut on tracing paper, image 9 1/16 x 11 3/16 in. (23 x 28.4 cm). The Metropolitan Museum of Art, New York (2019.592.357)

In their quest to explore the possibilities for printmaking, artists created innovative works that portrayed in subject, form, material, and technique the vibrant quality of contemporary life. While Nevinson used overlapping Futurist shapes to convey swift movement and force, other figures, such as Dorothy Burroughes (p. 103), employed a stark, angular vocabulary that, when combined with the flat forms of linocut, conveyed what she praised as the new beauty of the "age of machinery."[4] Several printmakers adopted the disorienting viewpoints and dynamism found in contemporary avant-garde photographs and films. However, while they embraced effects that reflected the heightened visual sensations generated by cameras—such as capturing bodies and forms in motion—they avoided using machine technology to produce their works.[5] In the age of mechanical reproduction, these artists—especially those associated with London's Grosvenor School of Modern Art (1925–40)—created and advocated for prints that were resolutely handmade, a quality indicated by the irregularities and differences within a single edition.

Related to woodcut, the earliest form of printmaking, a linocut is created by carving a design into a block of linoleum, an inexpensive, mass-produced product. For the artist Claude Flight and his students at the Grosvenor School, the material enabled them to reflect the modern era not only in the visual effects found in their works but also in their pricing and distribution, as I explore in my essay in this volume. In addition, the linocut challenged artistic and cultural hierarchies, especially as it could be made using tools—such as a kitchen knife or an umbrella rib—that could be found in most households. The Grosvenor School artists believed that this form of printmaking would allow them—and others who adopted the technique—to create "an unusual experience from a commonplace subject," in the words of Flight (fig. 4).[6]

Color linocuts were perceived by many critics, artists, and other contemporaries as a representation of, and a reaction to, both the positive and negative aspects of modernity. They allowed artists to make a more affordable and democratic art by using cheap industrial materials associated with craft, decoration, and the art of children. It was these same qualities, however, that led detractors to minimize the work and dismiss the technique. Yet, while they promoted the accessibility of the linocut, the Grosvenor School artists themselves created complex, meticulously planned prints. Rachel Mustalish examines this topic in her essay in this volume, shedding light on their process and formal choices.

The extraordinary opportunity to study these powerful works in depth is due to the vision and commitment of the collectors and philanthropists Johanna and Leslie Garfield. The Garfields are widely respected for their internationally renowned collection of modern and contemporary prints. Built over the course of six decades with the help of a dedicated curator, their collection is deep and broad and expresses a range of interests. For over thirty years, the Garfields worked tirelessly on assembling the world's premier collection of early modern British prints and related material. This book is published on the occasion of an exhibition to celebrate The Met's recent acquisition of more than seven hundred rare and important British modernist prints, sketches, and works on paper from the Garfield collection, which establishes the Museum as a global center for works on paper from this dynamic period. Providing close readings of the art made in Great Britain slightly before the First World War to the start of the Second World War, this publication frames the production, promotion, and circulation of these works against the cultural, political, and social contexts in which they were created.

In 1932, Paul Nash asked "whether it is possible to 'Go Modern' and still 'Be British.'" This, he noted, was "a question vexing quite a few people to-day."[7] While Nash was referring to the debates concerning an appropriate form for British art and the tension between British artists' relationship with avant-garde movements in continental Europe and national traditions, it is our hope that this publication and the related exhibition will also address these issues in order to promote more inclusive, often contradictory definitions of modernism and of what it was to "be British" at this tumultuous moment in time.

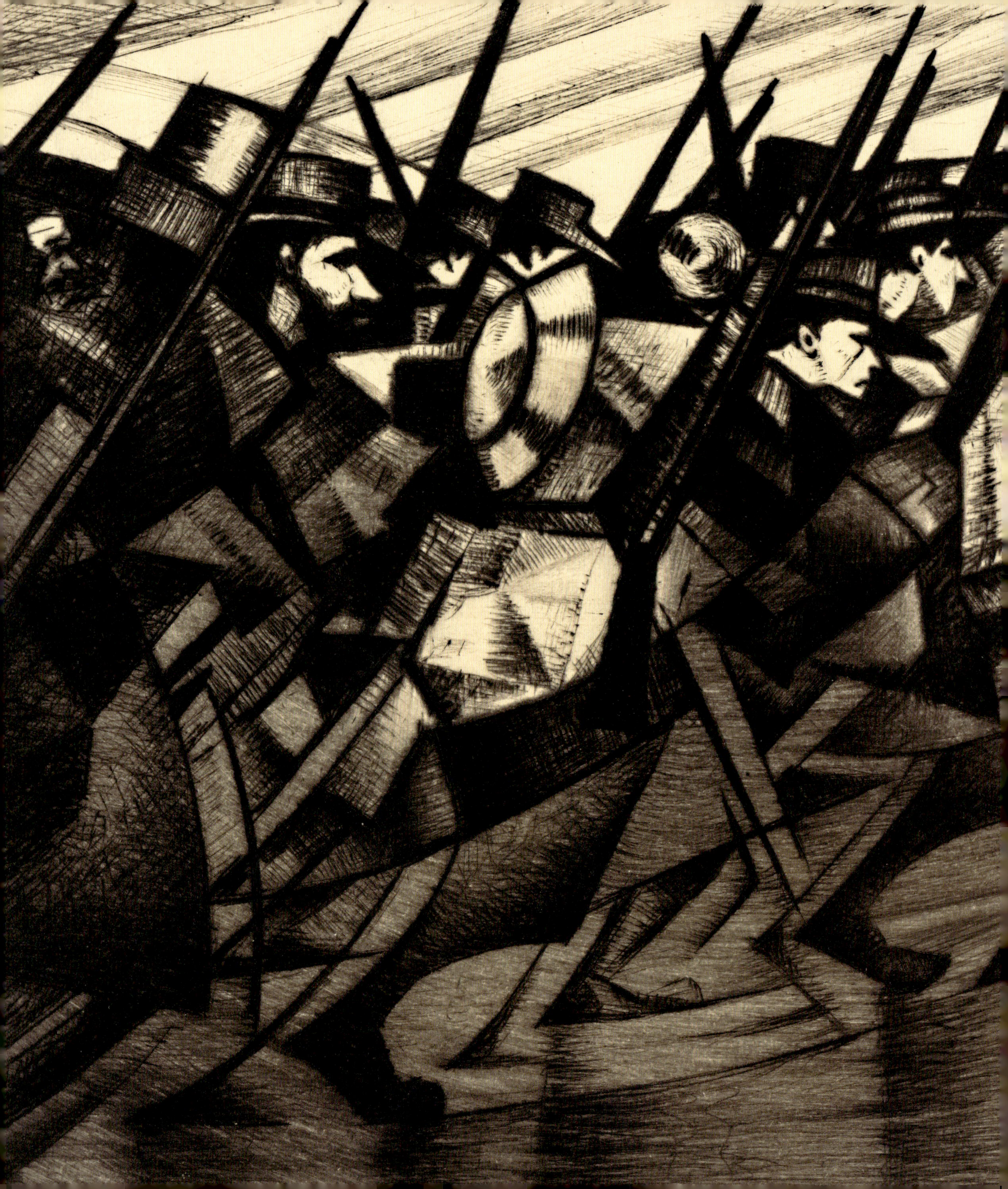

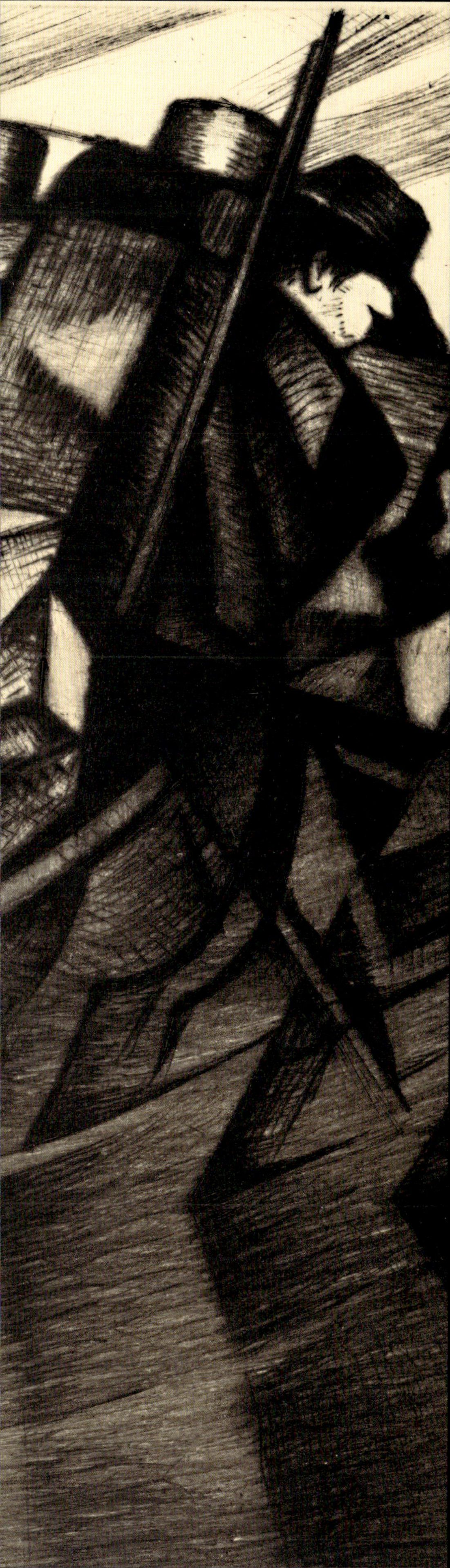

THE SHADOW LINE

British Printmakers and the First World War

Gillian Forrester

The First World War fomented a burgeoning visual culture in Britain. Painted, drawn, carved, cast, and printed, many images were commissioned from artists for official purposes to bolster patriotic feeling and attract new recruits; some were intensely personal statements, often made as eyewitness accounts. This rich archive enables us to reimagine the intensity of the experience of troops and civilians who endured the physical and psychological ravages of what is often described as the first modern war.

Of all the images produced during and in the immediate aftermath of the war, prints were the most compelling.[1] Printmaking offered artists an intimate relationship with the materials of production and the immediacy of drawing with the possibilities of creating multiple iterations of a design. The act of applying etching needle to copper plate, crayon and wash to lithographic stone, and gouge to wooden block provided a sensory experience that united the activity of hand and mind. Their insistent choice of monochrome inks—either black or deep brown hues—for these prints indicates that their repudiation of color was strategic and inevitable when making art in the midst of carnage and destruction. In particular, three remarkable artists, who all worked in other media, excelled at printmaking: Paul Nash, Christopher Richard Wynne Nevinson, and Edward Alexander Wadsworth.[2] Two of these men experienced periods of mental illness during and after the war; I suggest they may have found printmaking therapeutic, a method of alleviating trauma at a time of immense stress. Certainly, the expressive directness of the medium made possible the visceral articulation of emotion that characterizes British prints of the First World War.

FROM THE EDWARDIAN ERA TO MODERNISM

The British King Edward VII died on May 6, 1910, having reigned for just nine years, and his son George ascended to the throne. The Edwardian decade has been characterized as a pivotal moment between the Victorian and the modern eras, remarkable primarily for the wealth of the leisured classes, the production and consumption of luxury goods, and the triumph of society portraits, of which the American expatriate artist John Singer Sargent was the most distinguished exponent. The period, however, has been increasingly recognized as a time of momentous political, economic, social, and technological transformation. The trade union and labor movements gained momentum, and in 1906 the Conservative government was toppled by the Liberal Party.[3] The campaign for women's suffrage became more vocal and militant, and in 1918 the passage of the Representation of the People Act would enfranchise over 8 million women.[4] Profound if subtle changes were also taking place in the world order: the Austro-Hungarian Empire was disintegrating and, with the Ottoman, German, and Russian Empires, would collapse by the end of the war. The British Empire, although ostensibly at the height of its powers, was undermined by Independence movements in India and Ireland, and would vanish within fifty years.[5]

In this crucible of social, political, and technological transformation, the visual and plastic arts, architecture, music, and literature flourished. The second half of the nineteenth century was a site of contention between tradition and the avant-garde. The former was represented by the Royal Academy of Arts, founded in 1768, and the latter by new initiatives, including the Pre-Raphaelite Brotherhood, the Aesthetic movement, the Arts and Crafts Exhibition Society, and the New English Art Club, which from 1886 introduced French avant-garde practices into British painting. While many British artists in the Edwardian era adhered to conventional methods, some created works that were highly experimental, both formally and in terms of subject matter, and that were often in dialogue with photography and the new medium of film. The American expatriate artist James Abbot McNeill Whistler, who died in 1903, exerted great influence in late nineteenth-century Britain, and the work of his favorite pupil and assistant, Walter Richard Sickert, in turn attracted both critical acclaim and notoriety. Whistler and Sickert, significantly, were insistent on the importance of printmaking, which was held in low esteem by the Royal Academy. Each produced a remarkable body of innovative prints, predominantly etchings and lithographs.[6]

The Georgian art world was animated by restless energy. Alliances were formed and often broken, and artists' groups and exhibiting societies proliferated. Ambitious artists eschewed the conservative Royal Academy Schools, opting to enroll instead at newer and more dynamic art institutions, notably the Slade School of Fine Art, which opened in London in 1871. In the 1890s, Philip Wilson Steer and Henry Tonks transformed the school, establishing a rigorous curriculum with a particular stress on life drawing. Although Tonks's pedagogy was notoriously disciplinarian, the atmosphere at the Slade was stimulating; friendships and rivalries were constantly in flux, and some were to prove significant for the trajectory of British art between 1910 and 1914.[7]

Nevinson and Wadsworth were classmates at the Slade between 1909 and 1912; Nash studied there in 1910. They joined a remarkable cohort that included David Bomberg (p. 87), Dora Carrington, Mark Gertler, Benedict (Ben) Nicholson, and Stanley Spencer.[8] Wyndham Lewis, who studied at the Slade between 1898 and 1901, was to exert considerable influence on some of this cohort and to play a key role in the development of the British art scene.[9]

Nevinson (known as Richard) was born in Hampstead, North London, into an affluent and liberal family.[10] His father, Henry Woodd Nevinson, was a successful journalist who specialized in war reportage, and his mother, Margaret Wynne Nevinson, was a high-profile social reformer and supporter of women's suffrage. Exposure to modern warfare would have a shattering effect on Richard, who had experienced a childhood of emotional neglect. He oscillated between hyperactive enthusiasm and catatonic depression; Henry Nevinson frequently noted in his journal that his son was experiencing episodes of "nerves," a commonplace generic diagnosis of mental illness at the period.[11] Nevinson distinguished himself at the

Slade by his flamboyance, ebullience, and enthusiastic espousal of the avant-garde. After graduation he continued his studies in Paris, where he shared a studio with Amedeo Modigliani and familiarized himself with the work of Henri Matisse, Pablo Picasso, and Vasily Kandinsky.

Wadsworth was born in the town of Cleckheaton, in West Yorkshire, where his father, Frederick, owned a flourishing textile factory.[12] His mother, Hannah, died soon after his birth. From the age of thirteen, he attended Fettes College, a private boarding school in Scotland that valorized sports, which he loathed. After leaving school at seventeen, he was sent to Munich by his father to learn German and machine drawing in preparation for joining the family business. Wadsworth was captivated by the cultural and intellectual vitality of Munich. He studied drawing, painting, and woodcutting at the Knirr School of Art, avidly read the German satirical magazine *Simplicissimus*, and acquired a deep knowledge of German music. Returning to Yorkshire in 1907, he announced his intention to become a painter. His father very reluctantly agreed, and Wadsworth went to the Bradford School of Art, and then to the Slade.

Nash was born in London.[13] When he was three, his family moved to Iver Heath, a village in Buckinghamshire, on the periphery of London, where he developed a love of landscape. His mother, Caroline, had a mental illness and spent much of Nash's childhood living in care homes and psychiatric hospitals; she died in 1910. Nash attended St Paul's, a prestigious London private school, and, having resolved to become an illustrator, he went on to study at the South-Western Polytechnic in Chelsea and subsequently took evening classes at the London County Council School of Photo-engraving and Lithography. In 1910, Nash enrolled at the Slade, but he found the focus on life drawing challenging and the atmosphere uncongenial, noting that it resembled a private school (he had very much disliked St Paul's). Nash preferred to work independently; he designed bookplates, made landscape drawings that were influenced by Romantic British artists, such as William Blake and Samuel Palmer, and had a solo exhibition at the Carfax Gallery in London in 1912.[14]

BLASTING

The year 1910 was a watershed for British art. The exhibition *Manet and the Post-Impressionists* opened at the Grafton Galleries in London. Organized by the artist and critic Roger Fry with the critic Desmond MacCarthy, the show included over two hundred paintings, drawings, and sculptures by Paul Cézanne, Paul Gauguin, Edouard Manet, Henri Matisse, and Vincent van Gogh, and a smaller representation of works by such artists as Paul Signac, Georges Seurat, André Derain, and Pablo Picasso.[15] Prints, however, were apparently not included. Conservative critics were disturbed by the radical nature of the Fauvist works; art students, however, found them to be a revelation, as did members of the Bloomsbury Group, whom Fry first met in 1910.[16]

Two years later, in his *Second Post-Impressionist Exhibition*, Fry displayed French works, notably Matisse's *Red Studio*, alongside Russian and English contemporary art, with prominence given to Matisse and Picasso. The 1912 exhibition was formative for modernist taste in Britain.[17] In his catalogue introduction for the English section, the critic Clive Bell noted, "We have ceased to ask, 'What does this picture represent?' and ask instead, 'What does it make us feel?' We expect a work of plastic art to have more in common with a piece of music than with a coloured photograph."[18] The association of specific colors with certain feelings and states of mind was not original, as it has existed since antiquity, but it was to resonate with artists in the years preceding and during the First World War.[19]

In March 1912, the first London Futurist exhibition was held at the Sackville Gallery. The Futurist movement had been founded in 1909 by the Italian poet Filippo Tommaso Marinetti, who published his manifesto on the front page of the French newspaper *Le Figaro* on February 20 of that year. Marinetti repudiated the freight of past cultures, proposing an art that was engaged with industry, technology, motion, speed, violence, misogyny—and war.[20] He was joined soon by a group that included Giacomo Balla, Umberto Boccioni, and Gino Severini. The Futurists made paintings and sculptures, published manifestos, and staged performances intended to confront and shock their audiences.[21]

The Sackville Gallery exhibition was popular with the public but received a skeptical reception from critics. Futurism was to gain more traction in Britain when Severini's work was featured at London's Marlborough Gallery the following year. Around the same time, Nevinson, recently returned from Paris, was exhibiting poetic cityscapes painted under the influence of Neo-Impressionism in London with the Camden Town Group, but his style was soon to take a more radical turn when he saw Severini's show and met the artist, who recommended him to Marinetti. Nevinson, who relished manic activity, shattering bourgeois conventions, and self-publicity, was greatly attracted to the Futurist modus operandi. He participated in the *Post-Impressionist and Futurist Exhibition* in the fall of 1913 at the Doré Gallery, London, his standout submission a Cubo-Futurist painting titled *The Departure of the Train de Luxe*.[22]

In November 1913, Marinetti came to London to give a series of readings, and Nevinson and Lewis hosted a dinner for him. In March of the next year, Lewis founded the Rebel Art Centre at 38 Great Ormond Street in London as a hub for avant-garde British artists, in rivalry with Fry's Omega Workshops at 33 Fitzroy Square in Bloomsbury. Lewis invited Nevinson to join.[23] The following month, Marinetti returned to London to perform with Nevinson for three nights at the Doré Gallery.[24] The two artists collaborated on "Vital English Art: Futurist Manifesto," which was published in the *Observer* newspaper in June 1914.[25] Their statement proclaimed the virtues of machines, speed, and violence, calling for "an English art that is strong, virile and anti-sentimental."[26] Lewis, likely annoyed by his exclusion, repudiated Futurism and founded a new movement, Vorticism,

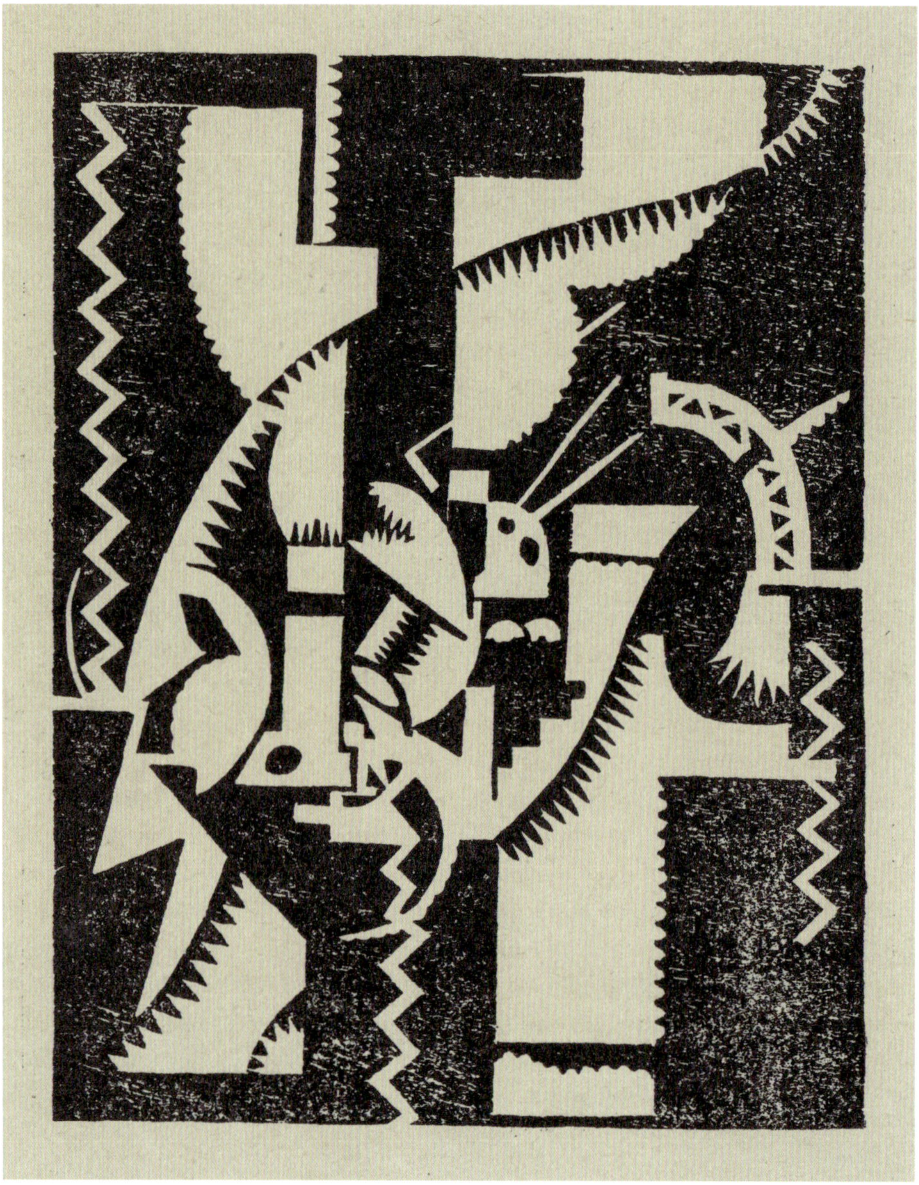

Fig. 5 **Edward Alexander Wadsworth** (British, 1889–1949). *Newcastle*, 1913. Woodcut on Western paper, block 5 ½ x 3 ¹⁵⁄₁₆ in. (14 x 10 cm). The Metropolitan Museum of Art, New York (2019.592.298)

which, he claimed, would liberate British culture from the repressive legacy of Victorianism and celebrate the machine age.[27] Lewis was joined by others associated with the Rebel Art Centre (including the pioneering women abstract artists Jessica Dismorr and Helen Saunders, the French sculptor Henri Gaudier-Brzeska, and Wadsworth), leaving Nevinson as the sole British proponent of Futurism.[28]

Lewis announced the arrival of Vorticism in 1914 with the journal *BLAST*.[29] The publication contained two manifestos that were signed by eleven artists and writers, including Gaudier-Brzeska and the American poet Ezra Pound, reviews, opinion pieces, and poetry, set in Elisha Pechey's distinctive typeface Grotesque No. 9.[30] Its illustrations shared certain characteristics: visual clarity, hard-edged forms, and fragmented space that connected to Vorticism's preoccupation with mechanization, warfare, and the urban experience. Wadsworth contributed *Newcastle*, a woodcut named for the industrial port city in the northeast of England (fig. 5).[31] His first published print, it seems to function as a visual autobiography, alluding to his origins as the son of a textile mill owner in the north of England, his training in machine drawing and woodcutting in Munich, and his recent adoption of abstraction. The distinctive zigzag forms likely reference the first standard screw thread invented by the Manchester textile magnate Sir Joseph Whitworth in 1841, which became an essential component for industrial machinery throughout the world.[32]

BOMBARDIERING

On July 28, 1914, the First World War broke out as if in fulfillment of the wishes of the Futurists and Vorticists. It had increasingly seemed an inevitable event for some years, foreshadowed by an arms race between Germany and Britain. The theory that war would act as a stimulus to artistic production had been prevalent even outside of avant-garde circles; C. H. Collins Baker, the keeper of the National Gallery, London, and critic for the *Saturday Review* opined, "Art will benefit if the war be great enough to engrave the world's mind deeply," a phrase that, albeit inadvertently, predicted the powerful emotional impact of printmaking.[33]

Many artists enlisted. Gaudier-Brzeska immediately returned to France to fight with the French army. Nevinson, who had rheumatic fever when he was a child, was deemed unfit for combat, but his father, Henry, who seems to have been more at home in a war zone than in Hampstead, arranged for them both to travel to France, under the aegis of the Quaker Friends' Ambulance Unit, to work in the field hospitals. Their first posting was at the Shambles, a covered goods yard near Dunkirk where wounded French and German soldiers were deposited on arrival from the front. The work was physically and mentally demanding, and the younger Nevinson's health deteriorated rapidly. Traumatized by the experience, he later commemorated the suffering soldiers that he nursed in two paintings, *La Patrie* and *The Doctor*, the latter of which he also engraved in drypoint.[34]

Nevinson returned to London in January 1915 and was discharged "for business reasons." Conscious of the need to rehabilitate his reputation, he submitted an article to the *Daily Express* with the arresting title "Painter of Smells at the Front: A Futurist's View of the War." His view of Futurism seemed more ambivalent than formerly; he asserted that "there is no beauty except in strife, no masterpiece without aggressiveness," yet also noted that he could not accept the Futurists' doctrine "that war is the only health-giver."[35] The following day, the newspaper published an open letter by Nevinson that stated that he was "in no way suffering from any form of nerve trouble."[36] The importance of "manliness" was a constant

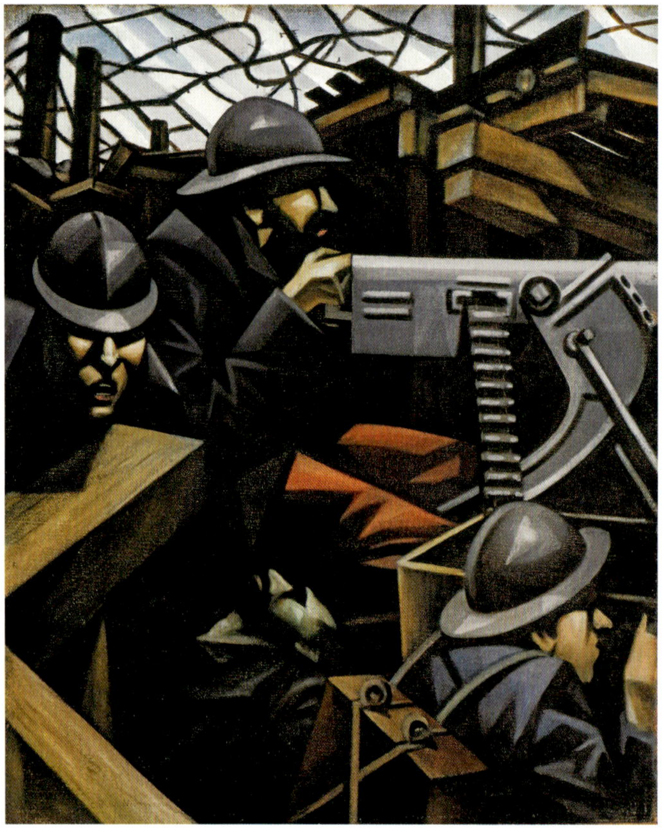

Fig. 6 **Christopher Richard Wynne Nevinson** (British, 1889–1946). *La Mitrailleuse*, 1915. Oil on canvas, 24 x 20 in. (61 x 50.8 cm). Tate, Presented by the Contemporary Art Society 1917 (N03177)

refrain in recruiting propaganda, and Nevinson likely felt under pressure to meet the expectations of his father, who in his son's words "worshipped the Man of Action."[37] In his autobiography, *Paint and Prejudice*, published long after, in 1937, Nevinson confessed that "I crocked up and was sent home" from France.[38]

After an extended period of sick leave, Nevinson enlisted as a private in the Royal Army Medical Corps. In June 1915, he was assigned to the Third London General Hospital, which had been requisitioned for military use. As in France, he found the experience of nursing wounded men harrowing. He assisted in operating theaters and was particularly affected by a stint working in a shell-shock ward. He also contributed a series of striking black-and-white drawings that resembled woodcuts to the hospital's *Gazette*.[39]

In July 1915, Lewis published the second issue of *BLAST* to accompany the Vorticist exhibition at the Doré Gallery. The cover featured his drawing *Before Antwerp*, depicting automaton-like soldiers wielding rifles, and was inscribed with the words "War Number" (see fig. 3). Lewis, carefully distancing himself from Futurism, noted in one of his short essays that "as to Desirability, nobody but Marinetti, the Kaiser, and professional soldiers WANT War. And from that little list

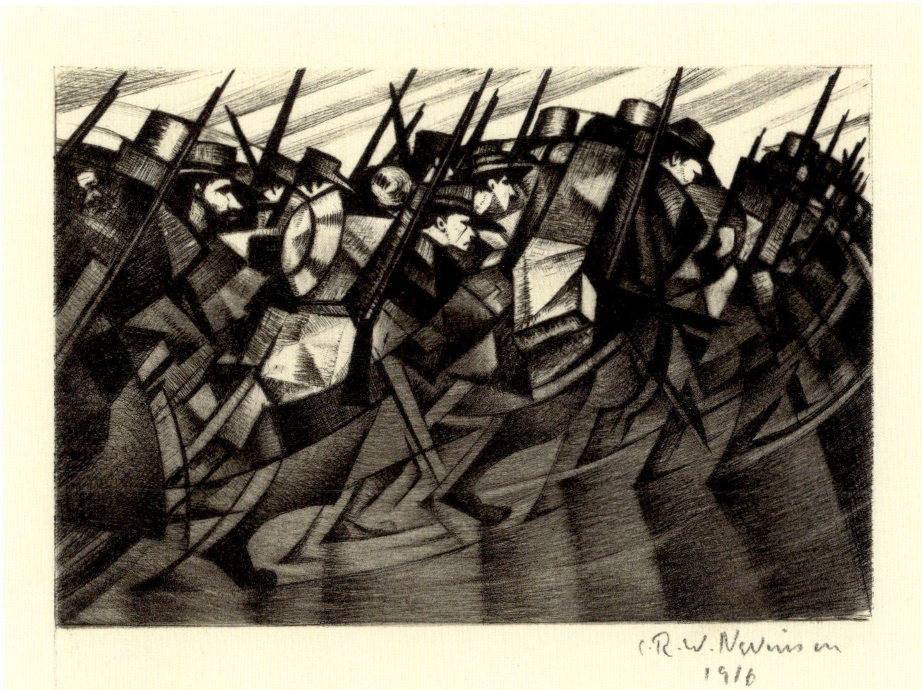

Fig. 7 **Christopher Richard Wynne Nevinson** (British, 1889–1946). *Returning to the Trenches*, 1916. Drypoint on Western paper, plate 6 x 8 1/16 in. (15.2 x 20.5 cm). The Metropolitan Museum of Art, New York (2019.592.425)

the Kaiser might have to be extracted."[40] The journal also included a reflection on war and art titled "Vortex Gaudier-Brzeska," written by the sculptor from the trenches.[41] Underneath the author's name was a bleak announcement that must have been added shortly before the journal went to press, framed with a single black line, stating that Gaudier-Brzeska had been killed in battle at Neuville St.-Vaast on June 5. Lewis joined the army as a gunner the following year, upon which he abandoned his commitment to Vorticism and to *BLAST*.

In January 1916, Nevinson was released from active service due to illness. He was nonetheless able to work, and in September he had a solo exhibition of paintings, drawings, prints, and a single sculpture at the Leicester Galleries, a high-profile commercial gallery in Leicester Square founded in 1902, which specialized in modern British and French art.[42] No longer an ardent Futurist, Nevinson now practiced a skillful and readily intelligible synthesis of an avant-garde aesthetic influenced by abstraction and realism. The exhibition was acclaimed by critics, the general public, and those in the armed forces.[43] The standout work was *La Mitrailleuse* (Machine Gun), an arresting painting depicting a French gunner in action, as if welded to his gun, flanked by two soldiers, with a fourth lying dead (fig. 6).

Sickert predicted that the work "will probably remain the most authoritative and concentrated utterance on the war in the history of painting."[44]

The prints, the first that Nevinson exhibited, were drypoints, which he made by scratching into a copper plate with a sharp needle.[45] All based on paintings, the drypoints were translations rather than reproductions; each constituted a new and distinctive statement, its power deriving from the stark outlines incised deeply by the needle, dense areas of darkness produced by insistent working of the plate, and the viscous black and sepia printing inks. Nevinson later wrote:

> It happened that I was the first artist to paint war pictures without pageantry without glory, and without the over-coloured heroic that had made up the tradition of all war paintings up to this time. I had done this unconsciously. No man saw pageantry in the trenches.[46]

Nevinson's eschewal of the "over-coloured heroic" was both metaphorical and literal. Some of the paintings exhibited at the Leicester Galleries demonstrated that he had already begun to restrict his palette, increasingly using muted grays and earth tones, rather than the strong, metallic primary colors that were the vestiges of his Futurist aesthetic, exemplified by slightly earlier works, such as *La Mitrailleuse*, *Returning to the Trenches*, and *A Dawn, 1914*.[47] Visitors to the exhibition would have been able to compare the second painting with Nevinson's compelling drypoint translation, in which the laborious mark making expressed more powerfully the exhaustion of the conscripted French soldiers, inexorably driven onto the battlefields by the machine of war (fig. 7).[48] The critic of the *Manchester Guardian* was evidently moved by the exhibition and wrote that "Nevinson gives you the black gloom, the horror, the feeling of despair that make even death and mutilation seem trivial incidents in an epoch of horror."[49]

The repetition of the word "horror" might have evoked in readers' minds Joseph Conrad's *Heart of Darkness*, published in 1899.[50] The novella is a searing, if ambiguous, critique of Belgium's brutal colonial regime in the Congo, and, by implication, a condemnation of the British imperial project. Conrad, incidentally, attended the exhibition, though he does not seem to have expressed an opinion of Nevinson's work.

After war broke out, Wadsworth continued to develop his woodcutting skills, experimenting with Vorticist compositions.[51] He sometimes included woodcuts in the care packages he regularly sent to Gaudier-Brzeska, who was then fighting in Flanders, and who in exchange mailed him drawings. The woodcuts offered some respite to Gaudier-Brzeska; on November 18, 1914, he wrote to Wadsworth, "I have your letter with the woodcuts—it's a great relief to touch civilisation in its tender mood now and then."[52]

Wadsworth joined the Royal Naval Volunteer Reserve in 1915, after Gaudier-Brzeska's death, and in June of the following year he was sent to the Aegean to

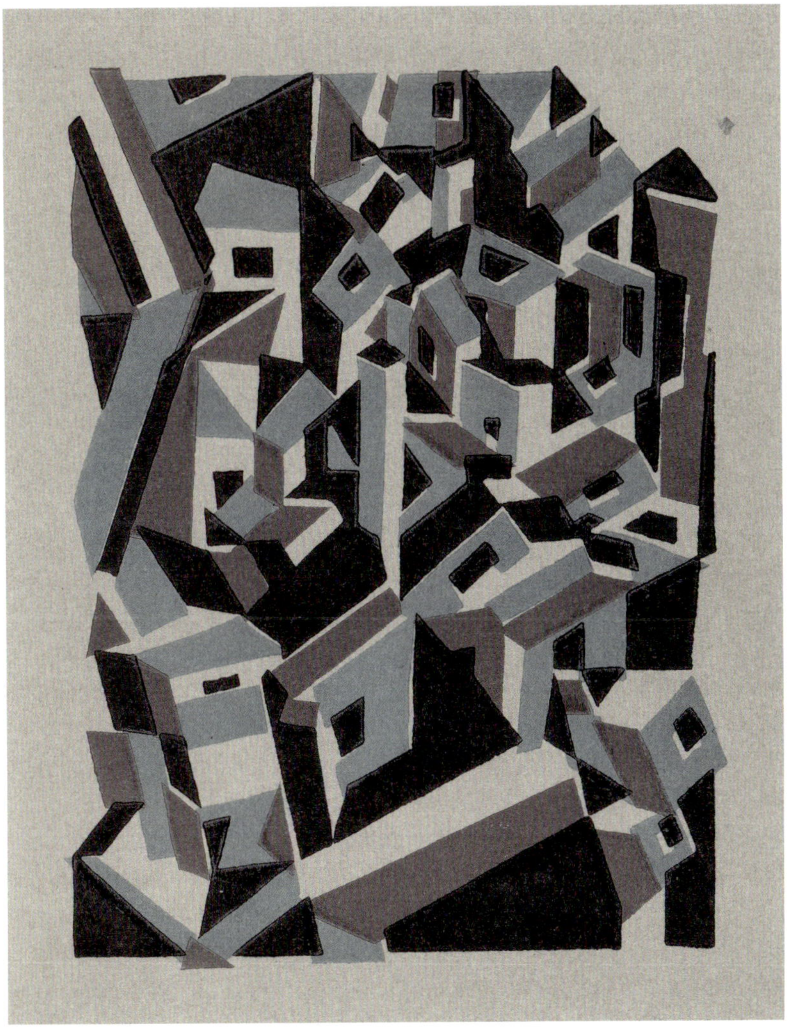

work as an intelligence officer. Based on the Greek island of Ispatho near Mudros, which was not a combat zone, Wadsworth had a quite different experience of war than Gaudier-Brzeska, Lewis, and Nevinson, and he felt no impetus to disavow either abstraction or a Vorticist aesthetic. Wadsworth drew designs for woodcuts on blocks, which he carved after he returned to England in 1917, suffering from ill health. Before he left for Greece, Wadsworth had experimented with printing in different color variations on various shades of paper, and he developed this practice after his return. Seven color variants are known for *Riponelli: A Village in Lemnos*; some, like figure 8, are in a muted range of grays with black, but one impression exists in purple and orange.[53] That Wadsworth's choice of colors and papers was strategic rather than impulsive is revealed by a letter he wrote to the

Fig. 8 Edward Alexander Wadsworth (British, 1889–1949). *Riponelli: A Village in Lemnos*, 1917. Woodcut on Western paper, block 4 x 3 in. (10.2 x 7.6 cm). The Metropolitan Museum of Art, New York (2019.592.299)

New York lawyer and collector John Quinn, who was avidly buying British modernist works. Quinn had mentioned how much he admired Wadsworth's woodcuts. In response, the artist wrote, "The woodcut, I must say, appeals to me more than any of the other similar mediums (etchings, lithographs, mezzotints etc.): it leaves nothing at all to accident."[54]

After his return to England, Wadsworth was assigned to supervise the painting of warships with strongly contrasting bands of color. This "dazzle camouflage" had just been invented in 1917 by the marine artist Norman Wilkinson, who theorized that the form of the ships would be broken up by the designs and would confuse enemy submarine operators.[55] Whether this strategy was successful is debatable, but, in any case, the ships provided perfect material for a Vorticist woodcutter. Wadsworth, who worked in Bristol and Liverpool, kept photographic records of the ships from which he produced a series of eight optically challenging woodcuts that includes *S.S. Jerseymoor* and *Liverpool Shipping* (pp. 91, 93).[56]

When war broke out, Nash joined the Artists Rifles, a volunteer regiment founded in 1859 that was popular with actors, artists, musicians, and writers. After months spent drilling in the courtyard of the Royal Academy of Arts in London, Nash was commissioned in the 15th Hampshire Regiment and sent to the Ypres Salient in February 1917. He arrived during a lull in fighting and was enthralled by the springtime landscape of war-torn France and Belgium. In late May, he fractured a rib when he fell in a trench and was sent back to England. Several days later, his unit was almost decimated in the Battle of Messines, on Hill 60, a notorious German-held position. During his time at the front, Nash had made twenty drawings using pencil, watercolor, and pastels, and in July the Goupil Gallery in London showed them in a solo exhibition, *Landscapes of the Ypres Salient*, to critical and popular acclaim.[57] One critic noted that Nash's drawings possessed "an actuality, an immediacy, that brought to life everything about the front which people had read and heard, but had found themselves quite unable to visualize."[58] While Nash did not disguise the war-ravaged landscape, he also celebrated the regenerative capability of nature. Yet viewers, including the perceptive critic Laurence Binyon, who noted "a kind of brooding vision, with a sense of hurt in the landscape," intuited a sense of bleakness.[59] Nash's vision of war was to darken significantly when he returned to Flanders in November.

BRITAIN'S EFFORTS AND IDEALS

In 1916, an official war artists' scheme was established under the aegis of Wellington House, a government propaganda bureau headed by the Liberal Party politician C. F. G. Masterman. The scheme's stated objective was to provide a pictorial record of the sites and events of the First World War, both for posterity and for immediate propagandistic purposes. The initiative was pressing, as there had been official reluctance to send photographers to the battlefields, and, consequently, few visual records existed, aside from drawings and maps made for strategic military use.

Masterman's selection method was scattershot; there was no formal application process, and artists were either invited or lobbied themselves for inclusion. Twenty-six artists participated, but only one was a woman, the pioneering photographer Olive Edis, who was not permitted to visit the battlefields until the war had ended.[60] The first appointee was the veteran printmaker Muirhead Bone, who was sent to France, and other established artists, including William Orpen and John Singer Sargent, followed. In February 1917, Wellington House was subsumed into the new Department of Information, headed by the politician and novelist John Buchan. The following month, the War Cabinet approved a proposal to create a national museum to house records of the war; this provided a further impetus to the war artists' program, and Masterman soon recognized the need to include younger artists who had firsthand experience of the conflict.[61]

Nevinson had been grappling with chronic anxiety, but he and his father nonetheless lobbied hard for his inclusion. While he was impatiently waiting for Masterman's decision, Nevinson, along with fellow artist Eric Henri Kennington and others, was commissioned to contribute to an official propaganda publication. Kennington, who had fought in France and Flanders until he was injured in June 1915, was also keen to return as an official war artist.[62] *The Great War: Britain's Efforts and Ideals* was a hybrid project, positioned between the commercially printed poster and the artist's print.[63] It contained sixty-six lithographs by eleven artists and was printed in an edition of two hundred. The "Efforts" section, consisting of fifty-four monochromatic prints, in thematic suites of four or six, celebrated the war work on the home front, including the significant role performed by women, whereas the larger "Ideals" lithographs portrayed allegorical subjects, often drawing on chivalric tropes, and were printed in color. The lithographs were intended both for display in museums and civic spaces around Britain to boost flagging civilian morale and for circulation in neutral countries, notably the United States, to encourage them to join the conflict in support of the Allies. The project had been pitched to Masterman by the artist Thomas Derrick; Campbell Dodgson, the keeper of Prints and Drawings at the British Museum; and F. Ernest Jackson, the master lithographer, teacher, and designer. Jackson had been advising Wellington House on the use of lithography for printing recruitment and propaganda posters since the outbreak of war.[64]

Kennington and Nevinson were allotted the subjects, respectively, of "Making Soldiers" and "Building Aircraft." Working between late May and mid-June 1917, they drew their designs in charcoal on paper and handed them over to Jackson, who supervised the transfer to the lithographic stone and printing.[65] Kennington documented the three-month training program of conscripts and was careful to depict the new instructional regime that the British army had introduced in February 1917. Although Kennington had returned from the front injured and angered by the incompetence of the military command, he had a profound admiration for the fortitude and intelligence of his comrades. This is evident in his powerful

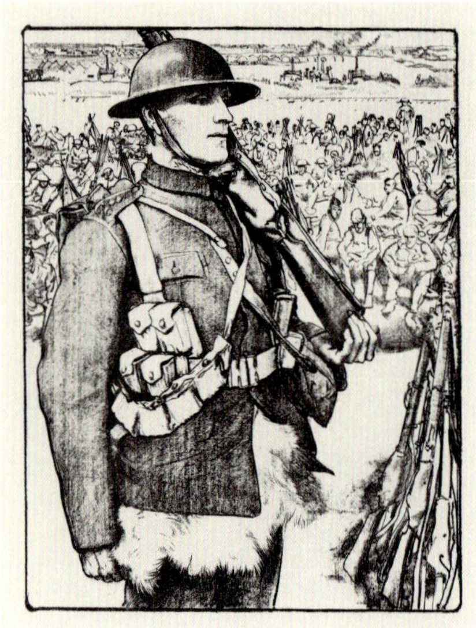

Fig. 9 **Eric Henri Kennington** (British, 1888–1960). "Ready for Service," from *Making Soldiers* portfolio, part of *The Great War: Britain's Efforts and Ideals*, 1917. Lithograph on Western paper, image 18 5/16 x 14 3/16 in. (46.5 x 36 cm). The Metropolitan Museum of Art, New York (2019.592.314)

delineation of the heroic bodies of the recruits in the *Making Soldiers* portfolio (fig. 9).[66] Nevinson undertook research in aircraft factories in London and East Anglia, and he was taken for his first flight in a two-seater biplane piloted by Major-General Sir Sefton Brancker. Three of his designs depict different stages of the manufacturing process, including a compelling image of women acetylene welders; the other three, aerial views from the cockpit of a plane, evoke the exhilarating experience of flight, suggesting that Nevinson had retained his Futurist appetite for the sensory experiences that modern technology offered (p. 96).[67] The airplane became an essential tool for military surveillance, and, by extension, a potent symbol of the power of the British state.

Britain's Efforts and Ideals was exhibited at the Fine Art Society in London in July 1917 and subsequently toured around Britain, France, the United States, Canada, and Australia.[68] The lithographs were offered for sale for ten guineas for a set of "Efforts" and two guineas for single prints.[69] "Efforts," in particular Nevinson's aerial designs, were well received, but there was little enthusiasm for the insipid pastel-colored "Ideals," which seemed to exemplify what Nevinson disparagingly had termed the "over-coloured heroic."[70]

VOID OF WAR

Nash, Kennington, and Nevinson were commissioned as official war artists in the second half of 1917. Nevinson evidently had managed his nerves; in a letter to Buchan, Masterman described him with approval as a "desperate fellow and without fear" and "only anxious to crawl into the front line and draw things full of violence and terror."[71] He flew to France on July 5, 1917, three weeks before the Passchendaele campaign began.[72]

Nevinson wrote Masterman about his extensive field trips, "all about the line North & South in trenches, balloons, aeroplanes, batteries dug-outs + most of the roads behind the lines,"[73] but he privately fretted about the restrictions imposed on him and about his ability to satisfy Masterman, who had not provided the artists with a brief. Masterman seems to have been ambivalent, expecting them to produce images that were suitable for propaganda purposes and did not disclose classified information to the enemy but would also appeal to those with more avant-garde tastes. When Nevinson asked if there were any subjects he should avoid, Masterman replied, "No, no, paint anything you please."[74] Occupying a landscape ravaged by shelling, populated by disheveled, exhausted, and traumatized soldiers living in trenches alongside decomposing bodies, the artists were confronted with a representational crisis. In late August, Nevinson was reprimanded for venturing too close to a battle zone at Ypres and sent back to London.

On his return to the capital, Nevinson was dejected, but nonetheless he embarked on a series of paintings using his field drawings and translated some into prints, using drypoint, lithography, and, in two cases, woodcut. In March 1918, Nevinson's solo exhibition *Pictures of War* opened at the Leicester Galleries. There

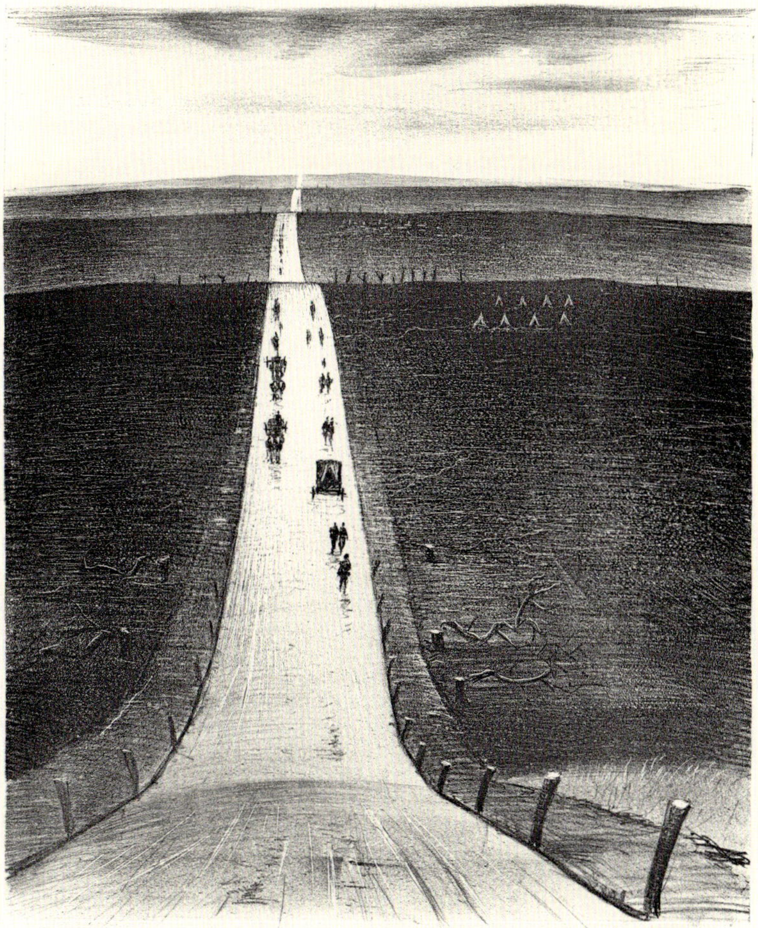

Fig. 10 **Christopher Richard Wynne Nevinson** (British, 1889–1946). *The Road from Arras to Bapaume*, 1918. Lithograph on Western paper, image 18 9/16 x 15 3/16 in. (47.2 x 38.5 cm). The Metropolitan Museum of Art, New York (2019.592.426)

were fifty-six works, of which twenty were prints. Nevinson wrote a trenchant introduction to the catalogue, in which he justified his abandonment of modernist styles of image making and declared that he had "now attempted to synthesize all the human activity" of the British campaign in France and Belgium.[75] A painting depicting two dead British soldiers lying on the muddy ground had been censored by the Department of Information when it was still in the artist's studio the previous November. Nevinson, however, defiantly exhibited the painting with the title *Paths of Glory*, having covered the soldiers' bodies with a piece of brown paper on which he had scrawled the word "Censored." His dramatic gesture generated a flurry of publicity as well as official disapproval.[76] Critical reaction to the exhibition was generally appreciative, though subdued, but Nevinson's work was greeted with enthusiasm by the popular press and by the public, many of whom had had firsthand experience of the conflict and could relate to his empathetic vision.[77] Nevinson's experience of war had pushed him to forge a new idiom of art that was radical in its democratic appeal, though it appeared conservative to the majority of his peers.

Nevinson used a very restricted tonal range for the paintings, as if to underscore the utter banality of war, but his compositions became even more desolate when translated into monochrome prints. Nevinson had mastered lithography; *The Road from Arras to Bapaume* depicts a seemingly endless and dreary highway stretching toward the horizon, dotted with human figures and horse-drawn carts, and cutting through a brooding landscape punctuated only by stricken trees and army bell tents (fig. 10).[78] He achieved the print's abraded surface by scraping the lithographic stone. For the drypoint *That Cursèd Wood* (p. 99), Nevinson articulated the blackened mud and tortured trees by digging deep into the engraving plate with needle or gouge. The sky, featureless apart from the faint forms of birds and military airplanes surveying the ravaged landscape, was rendered ominously dull through his use of plate tone, that is, by leaving a film of ink on the plate before printing.[79]

Nash went to the front as an official war artist in early November 1917, when the second battle of Passchendaele was ending. He stayed six weeks, traveling around the battlefields and compulsively making drawings, using chalk, graphite, ink, and watercolor on brown paper. Nash's experience of war changed him profoundly. As the art historian David Alan Mellor has noted, Nash's fascination with the supernatural was transformed into a state of existential horror precipitated by exposure to a German gas attack soon after his arrival.[80] On November 13, he wrote a letter to his wife, Margaret, from "somewhere near the Western Front," in which he voiced his revulsion and sense of alienation:

> I have just returned (last night) from a visit to Brigade HQ up the line & I shall not forget it as long as I live. I have seen the most frightful nightmare of a country ever conceived by Dante or Poe—unspeakable, utterly indescribable. . . . Sunset & sunrise are blasphemous mockeries to man; only the black rain out of the bruised & swollen clouds or thro' the bitter black of night is fit atmosphere in such a land. The rain drives on; the stinking mud becomes more evilly yellow, the shell holes fill up with green white water, the roads & tracks are covered in inches of slime, the black dying trees ooze & sweat and the shells never cease. They whine & plunge over head, tearing away the rotting tree stumps, breaking the plank roads, striking down horses & mules; annihilating, maiming, maddening; they plunge into the grave which is this land, one huge grave, and cast up the poor dead. O it is unspeakable, Godless, hopeless. I am no longer an artist interested & curious, I am a messenger who will bring back word from men fighting to those who want the war to last for ever. Feeble, inarticulate will be my message but it will have a bitter truth and may it burn their lousy souls.[81]

Nash's drawings of the battlefields were visual counterpoints to this horrific vision of a world devoid of humanity. The surfaces were violently scratched and scored, evincing a method of mark making that the painter and writer Paul Gough has termed "a new calligraphy of war."[82] After his return to London, Nash made six crayon lithographs based on drawings, with the help of Nevinson.[83] For Nash, lithography was a natural extension of his drawing practice, and he incised the surface of the stone to articulate the surface of the muddy craters and express the effect of driving rain. He gave these works plain, but resonant, titles, such as *Void*. Nash used a seventh print, a wash lithograph that resembled a woodcut, on the poster for his exhibition *Void of War* (fig. 11), which opened at the Leicester Galleries in May 1918.[84] The image signified that the war had reduced human existence to a state of absolute nullity and that viscous black printing ink could express that state most powerfully. Nash had entered the heart of darkness.

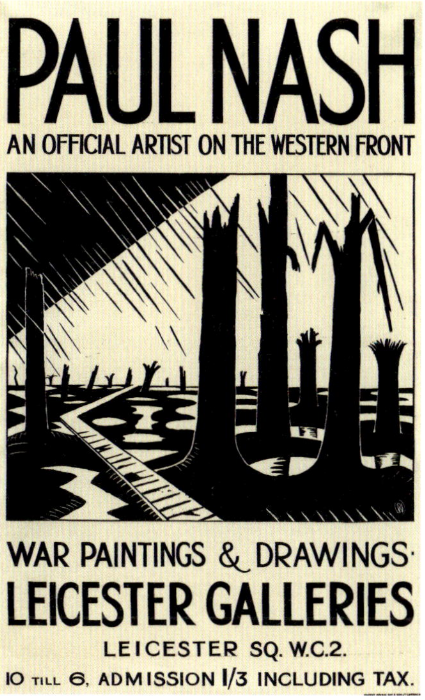

Fig. 11 **Paul Nash** (British, 1889–1946). Exhibition poster for *Void of War. Paul Nash: An Official Artist of the Western Front*, 1918. Lithograph on Western paper, sheet 29 ½ x 19 in. (74.9 x 48.3 cm). Collection of Merrill C. Berman

NERVES OF AN ARMY

In November 1918, Nevinson exhibited a remarkable drypoint in *Modern Masters of Etching* at the Leicester Galleries. *Nerves of an Army*, based on a painting that Nevinson had included in his solo exhibition earlier that year, depicts four Royal Engineers balancing precariously on a utility pole, attempting to repair broken wires (fig. 12).[85] The telegraph and telephone were the chief means of communication between the front line and their commanders, yet wires were continually severed by machine-gun fire and exploding shells, leading to tactical errors and disastrous outcomes on the battlefields. In a perceptive review of Nevinson's exhibition, the critic Jan Gordon, writing as John Salis, singled out the painting, noting:

> An army is like an electric current. It has its generating station, its wires carrying the current, and the points where the current is turned into active work, and its return wires. Mr. Nevinson's picture, 'The Nerves of the Army' [*sic*], has thus a double meaning and might stand as a symbol of the whole show. . . . As the saying is, these pictures speak for themselves; before them one is no longer a spectator, one is a partaker, one is brought into a far closer touch than mere imagination will bring one.[86]

The choice of the word "touch" is telling, implying a haptic quality to Nevinson's works. Gordon did not go on to speculate on the significance of the severed wires, but Nevinson's meaning is inescapable; the nervous system of the British army was broken.

As has already been noted, Nevinson was frequently afflicted with chronic anxiety, or "nerves," and he may have intended the drypoint to allude to his own mental illness and that of many soldiers traumatized by their experiences in the trenches. Charles Samuel Myers, a British psychologist, coined the term "shell shock" in 1915 to describe what is now known as post-traumatic stress disorder.[87]

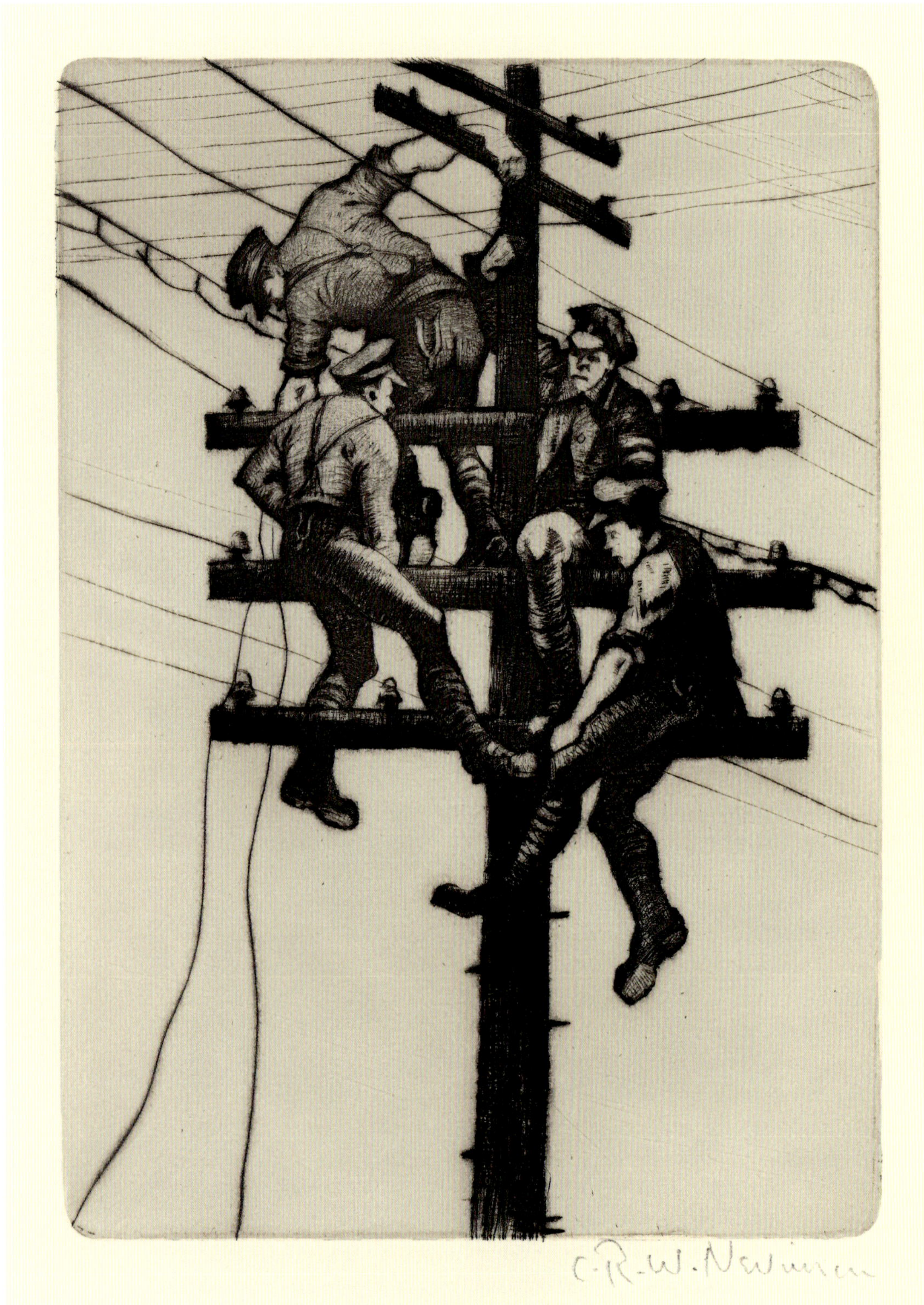
C.R.W. Nevinson

Soldiers with shell shock were often disciplined, and occasionally executed. Nevinson's experience of working in a shell-shock ward at the Third London General Hospital affected him profoundly. He exhibited *In the Observation Ward* in his 1916 Leicester Galleries exhibition, a painting which depicts a wild-eyed, shell-shocked soldier with saliva dripping from his open mouth.[88] At the time, critical reaction was polarized between accusations of sensationalism and praise for his willingness to confront this controversial topic.[89] *Nerves of an Army* may have been a further, if oblique, attempt to address the ravages of war on the minds of a generation of men.

Nevinson may have also made the drypoint to assuage his own feelings of what he later called the "black pessimism to which I am always liable."[90] In summer 1918, he wrote to Masterman that making prints, and particularly drypoints, helped him to "ward off my fits of melancholy which end in sleeplessness."[91] Nevinson would have been familiar with the current theory that creating and viewing art and handicrafts contributed to injured and shell-shocked soldiers' rehabilitation; he lent three paintings and a sculpture to an exhibition held in 1915 at the Third London General Hospital intended for the soldiers, and to which the public was not admitted.[92]

In 1917, Nevinson experimented with mezzotint, a technique that works from dark to light. The plate is first prepared using a tool known as a rocker, and a fully rocked plate will print as a rich, velvety area of darkness. The light areas are gradually introduced using a variety of instruments, including burnishers and scrapers. The bringing-forth of an image out of darkness has a powerful metaphysical dimension that may not have been lost on Nevinson, and the repetitious act of rocking is often described by artists as self-soothing. His adoption of the technique also marked a departure from war subjects in favor of civilian ones, in particular figurative city views and landscapes that look back to the Edwardian era.[93] Such drypoints as *Ebb Tide on the Camber* (fig. 13) and *Sussex Downs* have an elegiac affect and resonate with the state of collective mourning in the postwar era.[94] In his cityscapes, even London, New York, and Paris seem evacuated, and the gaiety of modern metropolitan life hollow.[95] Nevinson made his last print, *Spirit of Progress*, in 1933 during a period of physical and mental illness, and when fears of a second war were escalating. A medley of earlier images, this lithograph hints at an apocalyptic future.[96]

In March 1919, Wadsworth had a successful exhibition of woodcuts at the Adelphi Gallery in London organized by the critic Frank Rutter. Earlier that year he had visited the Black Country, the highly industrialized area around Birmingham, named for its aerial pollution and mounds of coal refuse, known as slag heaps. On his return to London, Wadsworth cut a series of blocks, printing them in black inks on different colored papers. These arresting woodcuts included *Black Country*, which was printed on buff, orange, and pink papers (p. 100), and *Ladle Slag, Old Hill I* and *II*.[97] Wadsworth found industrial landscapes "beautiful,"[98] but, for those who

Fig. 12 Christopher Richard Wynne Nevinson (British, 1889–1946). *Nerves of an Army*, 1918. Drypoint on Western paper, plate 7¾ x 5¾ in. (20 x 14.2 cm). The Metropolitan Museum of Art, New York (2019.592.633)

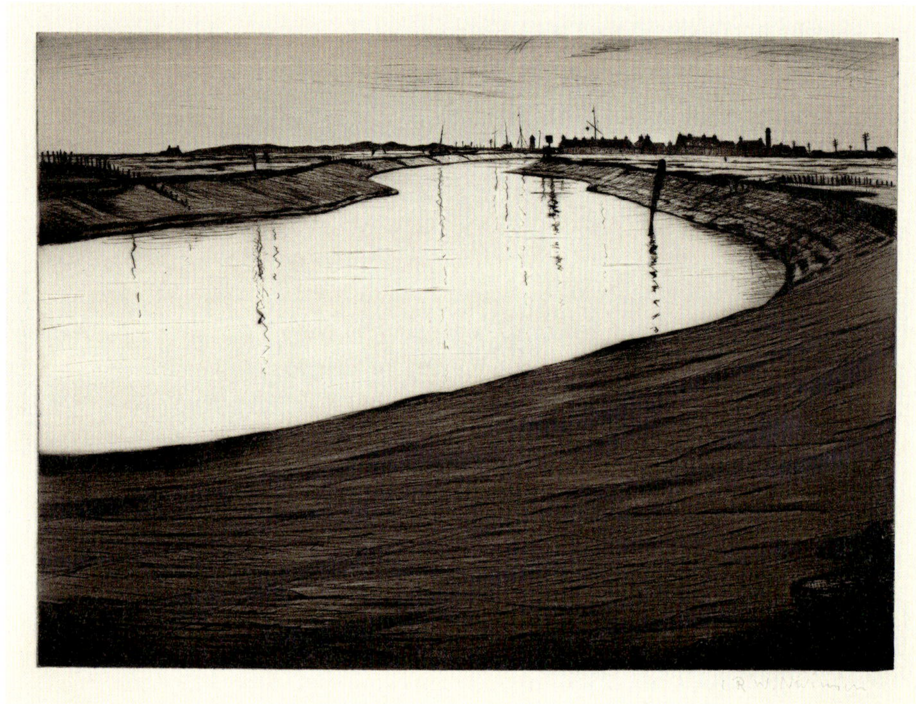

Fig. 13 **Christopher Richard Wynne Nevinson** (British, 1889–1946). *Ebb Tide on the Camber*, 1918. Drypoint on Western paper, plate 10 5/16 x 14 5/16 in. (26.2 x 36.3 cm). The Metropolitan Museum of Art, New York (2019.592.182)

had fought on the Western Front, these woodcuts may have triggered recollections of the nightmarish blackened landscapes of France and Flanders. Wadsworth had not experienced active warfare, but he likely was aware of the dark feelings these bleak postwar works might evoke. In his 1924 volume *The Modern Woodcut*, the art critic and writer Herbert Furst perceptively categorized the Black Country woodcuts as "emotional abstraction," going on to note, "the landscape is seen not so much as what it *looks* like but as what it *feels* like."[99]

Nash was devastated by his experience of Passchendaele in 1917. After the success of his Leicester Galleries exhibition in 1918, his mental and physical health deteriorated, and he was diagnosed with "war strain." In 1920, he and his wife, Margaret, decided to leave London and move to Dymchurch on the southern coast of England, where they lived for five years. In 1919, Nash had taken up woodcutting, perhaps in an attempt to assuage his psychological distress, and he continued to work with the medium in Dymchurch. He became obsessed with the enormous seawall originally constructed by the Romans to protect Romney Marsh, and it inspired a large group of drawings, paintings, and woodcuts. Some, including the woodcut *Promenade No. 1* (fig. 14), depict spectral figures walking on the wall while waves break menacingly below.[100] The figures' shadows fall darkly behind them,

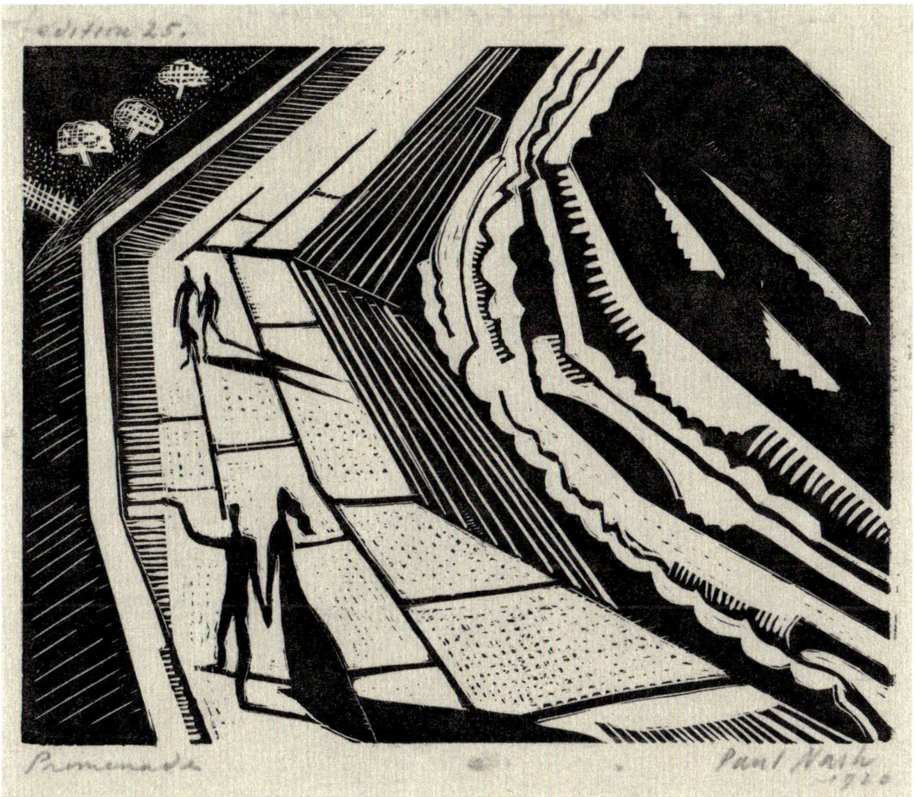

and the image speaks of profound alienation. Nash abandoned printmaking in 1930 to concentrate on drawing and painting.

In fall 1916, Joseph Conrad published the first installment of a new novella—*The Shadow-Line: A Confession.* Set on a merchant ship at sea, and somewhat autobiographical, the book is an allegory signifying the passage from adolescence to manhood.[101] Although not explicitly about the war, it was dedicated "To Borys and all others / who like himself have crossed / in early youth the shadow-line / of their generation / with love." Borys, Conrad's eldest son, was seventeen and about to fight on the Western Front. Borys would survive the war, but in October 1918, a month before the Armistice, he was gassed and injured, and while recovering in hospital was diagnosed with shell shock, a condition to which Conrad could relate, as he frequently had depressive episodes.[102] Conrad had not seen prints by Nevinson, Nash, or Wadsworth when he wrote the novella, but its title offers a perfect summation of their graphic memorials to the First World War.

Fig. 14 **Paul Nash** (British, 1889–1946). *Promenade No. I*, 1920. Wood engraving on Japanese paper, block 4 ½ x 5 ¾ in. (11.4 x 14.6 cm). The Metropolitan Museum of Art, New York (2019.592.172)

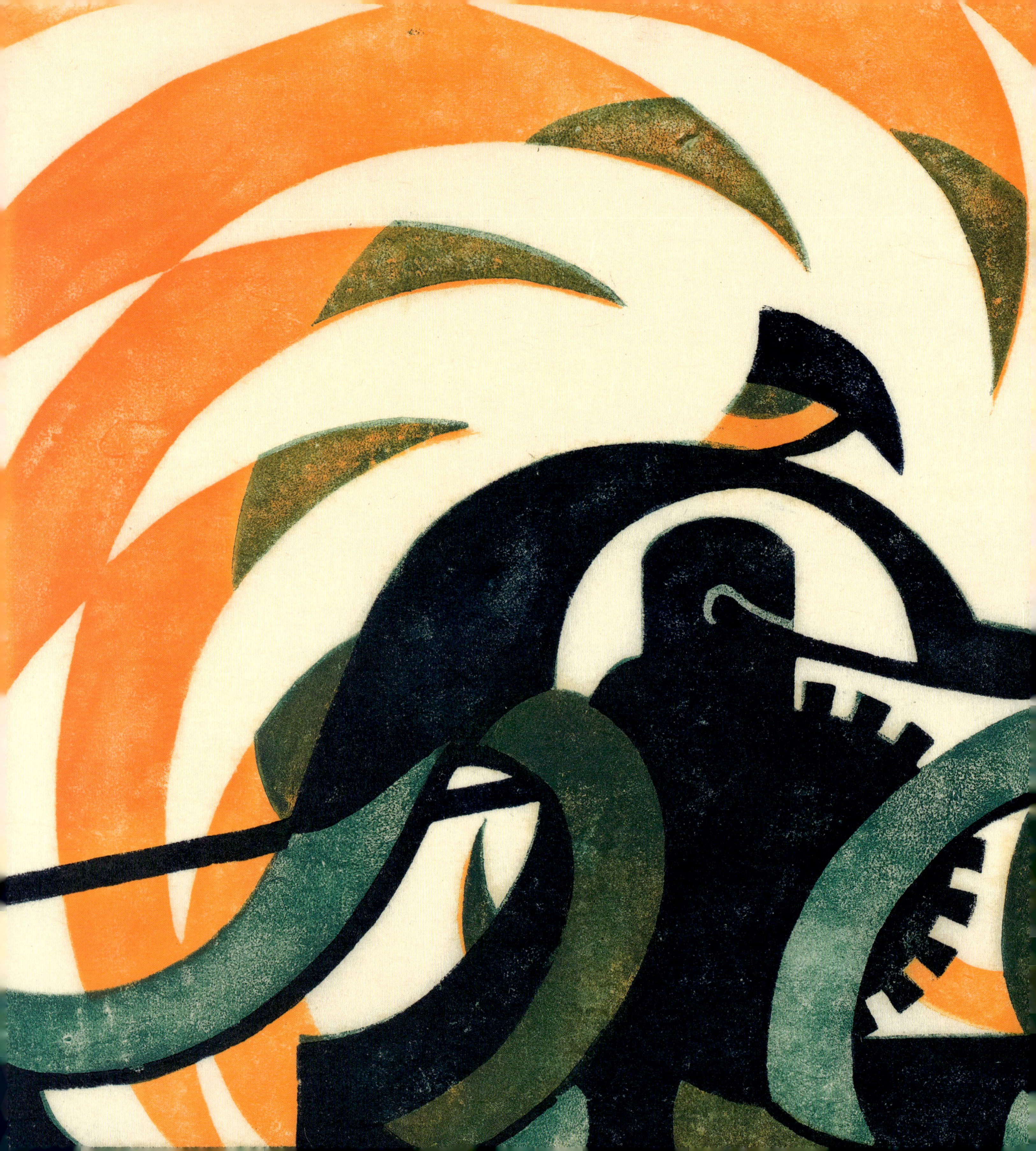

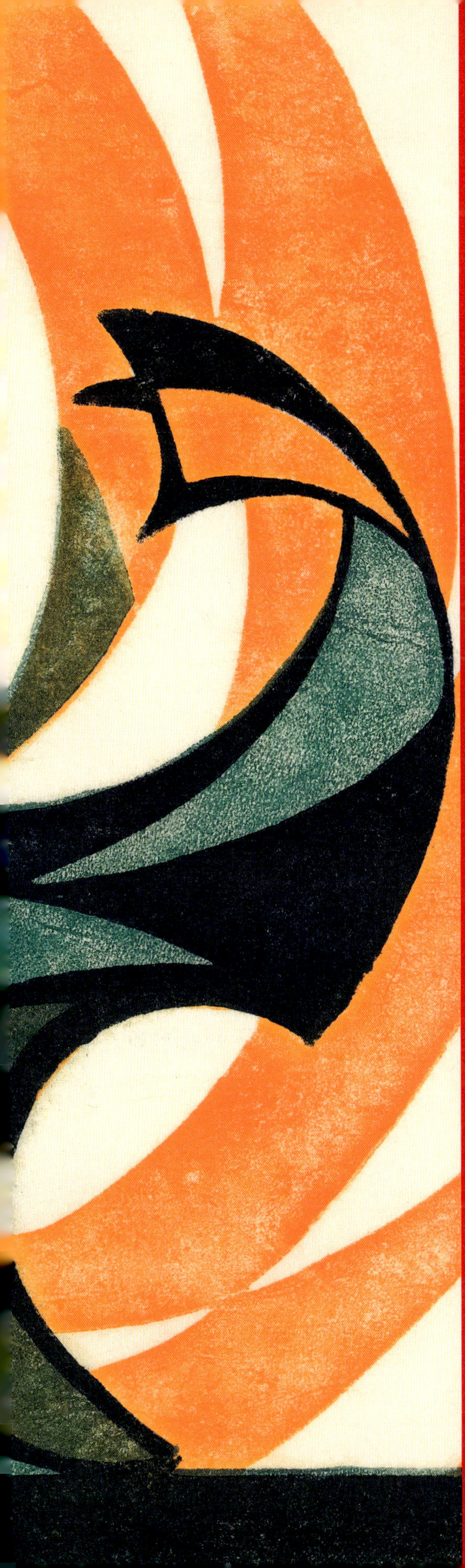

THE ART OF TO-DAY

British Modernist Linocuts in the Interwar Years

Jennifer Farrell

In his book *Culture and Society, 1780–1950*, published in 1958, the influential Welsh literary critic Raymond Williams analyzed how political, economic, and social changes in Britain since the Industrial Revolution had led to the transformation of the meaning and usage of certain key words—industry, democracy, class, art, and culture—to reflect the ways in which contemporary life was experienced, described, and theorized.[1] Williams contrasted his argument for the democratization of culture—that it encompassed "a whole way of life, material, intellectual and spiritual"[2]—with the more limited and elite conception the London-based American poet and essayist T. S. Eliot presented in his *Notes towards the Definition of Culture* of 1948. There, Eliot wrote that culture "includes all the characteristic activities and interests of a people: Derby Day, Henley Regatta, Cowes, the twelfth of August, a cup final, the dog races, the pin table, the dart board, Wensleydale cheese, boiled cabbage cut into sections, beetroot in vinegar, nineteenth-century Gothic churches and the music of Elgar."[3] Williams noted the narrowness of "this pleasant miscellany" and argued that a more accurate account of culture required a broader frame of reference: "The 'characteristic activities and interests' would also include steel-making, touring in motor-cars, mixed farming, the Stock Exchange, coalmining and London Transport. Any list would be incomplete, but Eliot's categories are sport, food and a little art— a characteristic observation of English leisure."[4]

Although Williams wrote it more than a decade after the end of the Second World War, his list is significant for this essay because in his quest to provide a more comprehensive definition of culture—one that included labor as well as leisure—he highlighted multiple subjects found in the linocuts made by artists affiliated with London's Grosvenor School of Modern Art in the 1920s and 1930s. In addition to their desire to create an art that would be representative of everyday life, the artists sought to make their work attainable for a larger section of the public. Their art, and its links to craft and decoration, and their method, a do-it-yourself approach involving low-cost common materials of the type frequently employed in children's art making, likely contributed to the artists and their prints not receiving an appropriate level of attention and critical support and, consequently, their omission from many histories of the period.[5] Their colored linocuts, however, were firmly of the moment in which they were made. They reflected the aspirations and fears of the interwar era and both celebrated the potential social and cultural advances offered by modernity and expressed the anxieties of the age.[6]

ART FOR ALL

In 1925, the Grosvenor School of Modern Art opened in the Pimlico neighborhood of London.[7] It was founded by Iain Macnab, a Scottish wood engraver and former principal at London's Heatherley School of Fine Art. Unlike "Heatherleys," which opened in 1845 and promoted portraiture and life studies, the Grosvenor School was not aligned with a particular aesthetic style or technique. Instead, Macnab assembled a faculty that would, in the words of the school prospectus, "encourage students to express their own individual ideas rather than be forced to accept worn-out academic theories."[8] Among the teachers was Frank Rutter, a prominent curator, critic, editor, and supporter of both modern art and the suffragist movement, who taught art history. The progressive institution had neither entrance requirements nor fixed terms; thus students could attend according to their own schedules.[9] Such freedom made the school attractive to a wide number of people, including international students, such as the Swiss artist Lill Tschudi and the Australian artists Dorrit Black, Ethel Spowers, and Eveline Syme. The school was also flexible with regard to financial arrangements, and, in an advertisement that ran in *Artwork*, it announced "Special terms to Artists wishing to work without tuition."[10] The philosophy appealed to the British artists Cyril E. Power and Sybil Andrews. Both studied and worked at the Grosvenor School: Power, a trained architect, taught architectural history, and Andrews was the school secretary.

The Grosvenor School offered courses in lithography and etching, life drawing, painting, composition, and other subjects, with each discipline outfitted with the appropriate equipment and material.[11] The most popular course, and the one that had the greatest impact, was a seminar on color linoleum cutting or linocut (a relief-printmaking technique related to the woodcut) that the British artist Claude Flight taught from 1926 to 1930.[12] Although Flight worked in a variety of media, he promoted the color linocut with evangelical devotion through his art, publications, teaching, and exhibitions, many of which traveled internationally.

Like other British art schools at the time, the Grosvenor School admitted a number of women students and allowed equal access to classes, including life drawing from models. Indeed, women, notably Andrews and Tschudi, were key figures in the interwar color linocut movement, and Flight featured their prints in exhibitions, books, and catalogues along with those of their male colleagues. Before transferring to the Grosvenor School with her partner Power, Andrews studied with private instructors and at Heatherleys. Tschudi attended the Grosvenor School between 1929 and 1930, when she was eighteen years old, before moving to Paris, where she trained with such artists as Fernand Léger, André Lhote, and Gino Severini, all of whom influenced her desire to use repetitive geometric forms and portray movement in her art. Despite her short time at the Grosvenor School, Tschudi was profoundly impacted by her experience there. She maintained a close connection with Flight and regularly sent him pieces for commentary and inclusion in the linocut exhibitions he organized.

Flight was well connected in British artistic and intellectual circles by the time Macnab hired him to teach at the Grosvenor School: he was a member of the Royal Society of British Artists and knew numerous avant-garde figures, including the British Futurist Christopher Richard Wynne Nevinson, whom he had met when they were both training in London (Nevinson at the Slade School of Fine Art and Flight at Heatherleys).[13] Flight was also well aware of international artistic developments, especially as he spent summers in France and had exhibited abroad as early as 1922.[14]

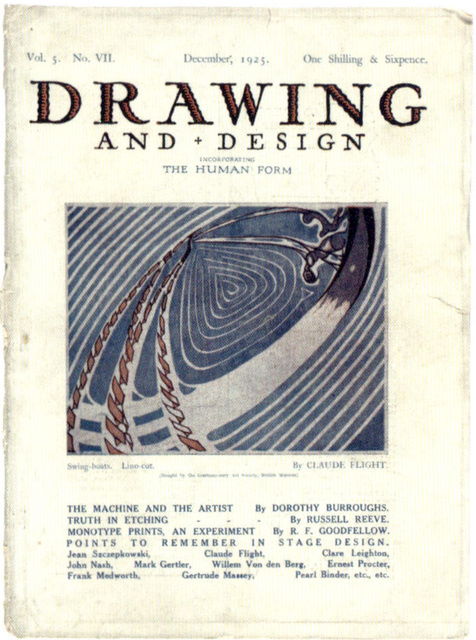

Vol. 5. No. VII. December, 1925. One Shilling & Sixpence.

DRAWING
AND + DESIGN
INCORPORATING
THE HUMAN FORM

Swing-boats. Lino-cut. By CLAUDE FLIGHT.

THE MACHINE AND THE ARTIST By DOROTHY BURROUGHS.
TRUTH IN ETCHING - - - By RUSSELL REEVE.
MONOTYPE PRINTS, AN EXPERIMENT By R. F. GOODFELLOW.
POINTS TO REMEMBER IN STAGE DESIGN.
Jean Szczepkowski, Claude Flight, Clare Leighton,
John Nash, Mark Gertler, Willem Von den Berg, Ernest Procter,
Frank Medworth, Gertrude Massey, Pearl Binder, etc., etc.

Fig. 15 **Claude Flight's** *Swing-Boats* (p. 138) as reproduced on the cover of *Drawing and Design* 5, no. 7 (December 1925). The Metropolitan Museum of Art, New York

Flight developed his linocut technique and a passionate belief in its potential to transform both art and education (and through them, society) after learning of the contemporary writings, teachings, and exhibitions by the Austrian artist Franz Cižek, who promoted the linocut, particularly for children.[15] German Expressionists, such as Erich Heckel and Christian Rohlfs, had created black-and-white linocuts earlier, as had the London-based French Vorticist Henri Gaudier-Brzeska and the London Group artist Horace Brodzky, but the method was not widely practiced in the early twentieth century, especially for color printing (with the notable exception of the work of Vasily Kandinsky). Flight made his first linocut in 1919, and by 1921 he was producing mature color linocuts, such as *Swing-Boats*, which was featured on the December 1925 cover of *Drawing and Design* (fig. 15). The print shows a funfair ride in motion and captures the velocity and dynamism Flight and the Grosvenor School artists sought to portray in their art. Below the image is information about the print: "Swing-boats. Lino-cut. By CLAUDE FLIGHT" and, in much smaller type and in parentheses, "Bought by the Contemporary Art Society, British Museum," revealing that Flight had already achieved institutional recognition and support for his prints.[16]

Flight's linocut *Speed* of 1922 (p. 114) captures the bustling energy and movement of both buses and pedestrians on Regent Street, a busy commercial hub in London's West End. The closest red double-decker bus has the lettering "SPEE" on its side, which, combined with the curving forms of the buildings and roads, conveys the sensation of speed.[17] This depiction of contemporary urban activity evokes comments by the Italian Futurists Filippo Tommaso Marinetti ("London itself is a Futurist City! Look at those brilliant-hued motor-'buses, these enormous, glaring posters") and Gino Severini ("London is a city where movement and order reign. . . . Motor-omnibuses passing and re-passing rapidly in the crowded streets covered with letters—red, green, white—are far more beautiful than the canvases of Leonardo or Titian, and closer, too, to Nature"), artists whose work Flight knew and whom he may have met when they were in London.[18]

Speed was closely associated with Flight, particularly after he featured it on the cover of his 1934 manual *The Art and Craft of Lino Cutting and Printing* (fig. 16). Its long sinuous lines, simplified shapes, spare decorative elements, and flat planes of color showed that linocut was an ideal technique via which artists could create dynamic images of contemporary life. Linoleum—machine-made, inexpensive, readily available, representative of domestic life (it was a common flooring material at the time), and new to fine art—exemplified his belief in democratizing art production.[19] Furthermore, linocuts were something that amateur artists of all ages could make in their homes, with materials at hand, such as a knife or an umbrella rib, and a sheet of soft linoleum, without the expertise of professional printers.

Curiously, linocut is not mentioned by name in Grosvenor School advertisements (just the broader term "block printing" to refer to relief prints: see fig. 17), despite its prominence in the curriculum and that of Flight, who also minimized his relationship to prints and linocuts in his essay of 1925, "Claude Flight: By Himself." There he wrote about "a new approach in picture making," but rather than extol the virtues of linocut, as he would do later, he made numerous references to paintings and drawings.[20] Art, he claimed, should reflect "new eyes and a new vision, or shall we say the eyes of a child, and a vision unhampered by tradition and use—these are necessary if one would paint the world of to-day, the spirit of this great international force which is at the root of all modern art."[21]

The connection between "new eyes" and the "eyes of a child" can be interpreted as a nod to Cižek and his work with children's art, exhibitions of which had toured Britain and attracted large crowds. "A new vision" connotes heightened perception and an unorthodox approach to the modern world and the technologies, structures, and materials found in it. The term was used in the late 1920s and 1930s in different contexts, perhaps most notably by filmmakers, photographers, and those who used photo-based processes to capture disorienting viewpoints, such as the Hungarian artist and teacher László Moholy-Nagy.[22] Artists, especially those affiliated with progressive institutions, such as the Bauhaus in Germany and Vkhutemas in the Soviet Union, sought to use machines—namely cameras—to produce a different way to encounter the world, with the hope that this radical mode of perception would lead to a new consciousness. However, despite the ubiquity of photography, which was then found in both avant-garde and everyday sources, such as journals, newspapers, and advertisements, Flight did not mention it in his essay, nor did he mention films. Rather, he named paint and stone as the materials with which artists could express their emotions and experiences. It is notable that he praised painting when others were declaring its demise and embracing techniques and materials in which the hand of the artist is absent. In parallel, it testifies to his desire to rethink the possibilities for what many considered to be a more traditional form of art—the relief print—and to make it modern, although he does not discuss this technique in the text.

In 1926, Flight published "The Art of To-Day," in which he outlined not only the function and criteria for contemporary British art but also the obligation

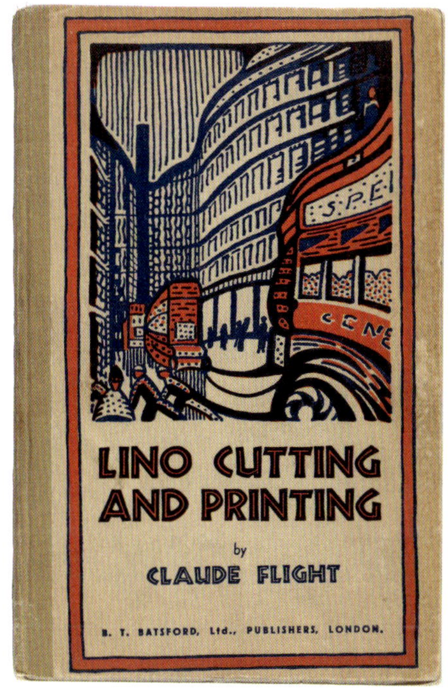

Fig. 16 **Claude Flight's** *Speed* (p. 114) as reproduced on the cover of *The Art and Craft of Lino Cutting and Printing* (1934). The Metropolitan Museum of Art, New York (2019. 592.339)

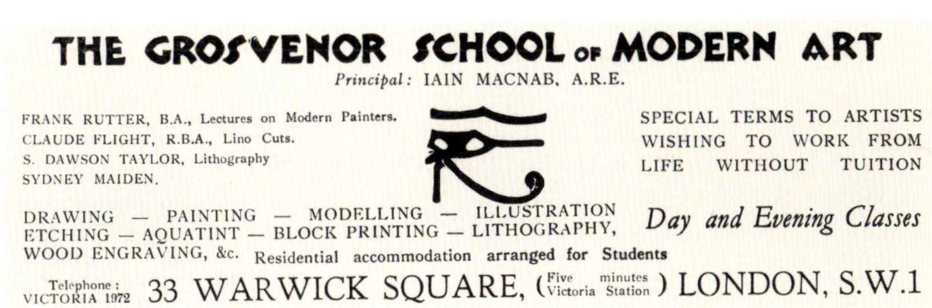

Fig. 17 An advertisement for the Grosvenor School of Modern Art published in the *Studio* 96, no. 427 (October 1928). The Metropolitan Museum of Art, New York

for art to reflect contemporary politics and labor.[23] While Flight acknowledged the economic and cultural "difficulties" that led artists to seek refuge in "the ghosts of heredity, of custom, of habit," he argued that "the art of to-day must be in relation to the life of to-day, and, art being *the most universal expression of the most universal emotion*, the art of to-day must be the expression of this collective spirit in terms of simplicity, of unity, and of harmony." His declaration was informed by his support for socialism, as was his criticism that "even to-day the 'modern' artist does not realize the reason of his being, does not understand that the expression of the great social upheaval which is going on so rapidly all over the world to-day is his for the taking. The painter of to-day still looks to the art of the last hundred years or so for inspiration . . . he still lives a life remote from the people whom he ignores or despises and whose outlook he does not trouble to understand."[24]

Flight and the Grosvenor School artists worked at a time that remains contested, contradictory, and difficult to categorize.[25] The interwar years were shaped by the trauma of the First World War and the rise of Fascism and bore witness to numerous hunger marches and strikes, high levels of unemployment, and a global economic depression. Yet during this period there were also substantial progressive societal changes, such as legislation that increased the electorate, resulting in significantly more men being eligible to vote and, for the first time, women, as well as growing opportunities for women in education and employment.[26] Government investments in home building and the expansion of public transportation led to a higher standard of living for many in the middle and working classes.[27] These contradictions can be read as informing Flight's belief in the need for a more democratic art. The linocut, he proposed, could appeal to a wide range of consumers, especially new homeowners, who might have enough disposable income to acquire goods, such as art, which previously had been less accessible due to price and because many works, especially those that used a more modern visual language and bold colorful forms, were unique objects and thus in limited supply. While members of the middle class would most likely compose the majority of his audience (especially as many sought modern designs for their new housing), Flight hoped linocuts would be sold at a price on a par with those of other consumer items aimed at a mass audience.

Flight was not alone in his goal to make art more accessible. As early as 1916, under the influence of the minister of education Herbert Fisher, the British government expanded its support for art education and institutions, an effort further cemented with the Education Act of 1918. The postwar Liberal government of the British prime minister David Lloyd George saw educational as well as financial reasons to devote attention to the arts, particularly in light of the nation's rebuilding after the war and the desire to produce a greater number of exports. The Ministry of Reconstruction bluntly stated in 1919, in language that could have been Flight's:

> Art is indispensible in life, and therefore in education and in work. Art has become limited in meaning. It is generally understood to be a thing apart, the product of picture painters and craftsmen and similarly gifted and lucky persons. It is spelt with a big A. It is a decorative and purchasable luxury, to be hung up, stood about, and applied to things. It is "applied" or "fine" (two of the most ignorant and misleading terms ever invented) according as it is useful or not; but it concerns the people only so far as they can afford to buy some of it as a demonstration of the possession of taste—or money. We must work for the restoration of the broader meaning of art, for the reunion of the many subdivisions of Art into art—one and indivisible in its association with life and work. It must be recognised as a necessity to give us a truer appreciation and use of our country and ourselves.[28]

While the economic recession prevented many of these grand plans from being realized, the concept of expanded art education, as well as greater opportunities to encounter and even acquire art, had a profound influence on a number of cultural figures. Such ideals were also reflected in the rise of interwar arts organizations, such as the Arts League of Service. Created in 1919, it sought to "awaken public opinion to the importance of the Arts" and to "bring Art within the reach of all."[29] As noted by the art historian James Fox, the organization's lectures, exhibitions, and other initiatives—such as the distribution of drawings to schools, often in the provinces—were primarily devoted to British modern art. In addition to aiding contemporary artists and promoting education, these programs sought to help unify and rebuild the nation by creating links between the public and artists.[30]

In the 1920s, there was a boom in the British print market, when etchings, drypoints, lithography, and wood engravings found a strong reception, both domestically and internationally. Prints were acquired by institutions, such as London's British Museum and the Victoria and Albert Museum, as well as individuals, including new collectors outside the upper class. As the curators Frances Carey and Antony Griffiths write, "The typical prosperous middle-class home of the 1910s and 1920s would be likely to have hung in the hall and minor rooms a line of etchings and drypoints, all surrounded by a sea of white mount and a thin black frame."[31] The 1929 crash in the print market reflected not only bleak economic conditions affecting the country but also a profound change in collectors' taste as younger generations moved away from black-and-white etchings and more traditional works.

It was during this period that Flight first wrote of his goal that linocuts would be available to the public for rent ("like a lending library") or for acquisition at a more affordable price than paintings and drawings. Flight argued that linocuts were uniquely suited for the moment. Not only did they reflect a more modern visual language but, since linoleum was durable, artists could pull several color prints without compromising quality; the resultant prints could be sold at lower prices, fulfilling the artists' aspirations to create a more collective and equitable art market. As Flight noted in *Lino-Cuts: A Hand-Book of Linoleum-Cut Colour Printing* of 1927:

> Being born about the same time as our ultra-modern development of industry, modern art shows very clearly the same tendencies of combining and of simplifying, after very careful analysis and the suppression of unnecessary details, those things which are indispensable, and it does this with almost industrial efficiency.
>
> Mass production in business is essential to our very existence. Living as we do in closely packed communities mass production brings down the price of our goods to a reasonable and saleable rate.
>
> Pictures both in oil and water-colour can never be painted so as to be sold at a price which appeals to the pocket of the average man, pockets already taxed to such an extent by the State that the only relaxation which he can afford is of the cheapest kind.
>
> Linoleum-cut colour prints could be sold, if only the interest in and the demand for them could be stimulated, at a price which is equivalent to that paid by the average man for his daily beer or his cinema ticket.
>
> Given the right art education in the elementary schools and their equivalent institutions on the continents of Europe and America, the average man will buy these colour prints, for he will realize that the satisfaction to be obtained from their possession has a greater lasting quality than that derived from the taste and exhilaration from the beer or the excitement and comfort from the cinema; knowing also that aesthetic pleasure surmounts creature comforts, and that the harmony, the intensity, and the vision which a good work of art affords would be his for the asking.[32]

Flight's quest for a more democratic art was shared by many of his peers, and by 1924 it was already a common cause among British artists, even those with more conservative views.[33] That year, the artist and teacher Frank Morley Fletcher published "The Woodblock Colour-Print: A Democratic Art," in which he praised the color woodblock as being both accessible and suitable for contemporary houses, which were smaller in scale and reflected a different design aesthetic.[34] The color woodblock would be "a democratic art—an art whose character was both expressive, and decorative, and yet sufficiently prolific as to be so moderate in cost that the new prints might be within the means of art loving persons of whatever class." He lamented that the public had not yet embraced color prints despite these favorable conditions, a problem he attributed to the general public's lack of discrimination and belief that color prints were not "personal" but reflected "some kind of mechanical production." He blamed this misunderstanding on the "harmful influence . . . [of] the flood of coarse work that has appeared under the name of wood-block printing, most of it printed from linoleum." Linoleum, he claimed, "is not suited for printing a beautiful surface of colour nor for giving the finer qualities of line, and when it is used for colour the result is poor. Linoleum work illustrates very clearly the rule that when the tools and materials of an Art are made easy, the tendency is for design to deteriorate, and for the Art to become base. Witness the effect on handwriting of the invention of the steel pen, or the effect on popular painting and music of the technical facilities of to-day."[35]

Fletcher's article reflected an unfounded prejudice the Grosvenor School artist faced, especially from those affiliated with more traditional printmaking methods, such as etching, woodcut, and wood engraving. Despite their engagement with machine-age imagery (and despite the allegations of critics such as Fletcher), color linocuts were resolutely handmade and required a great deal of time and physical labor to produce. In addition to developing a composition through sketches, studies, and related drawings, the artists carved the design on each block used for a color in the composition, and for every print, they lined up the paper on the freshly inked blocks in a precise order.[36] To avoid the flatness and mechanical quality created by printing presses, as well as to dispel prejudices such as Fletcher's, Flight and the Grosvenor School artists were adamant that linocuts be printed by hand. Tschudi, in fact, noted in inscriptions on the front of her prints—often in proximity to her signature, the edition number, and title—that her linocuts were hand printed ("*handdruck*").[37] The handmade quality is visible in the irregularity of tones and the differences, both slight and profound, among the prints in an edition, as well as the ink splatters and stains that reveal the layering of colors, visible just slightly beyond the perimeter. In addition, because individual linocuts were often created on demand with gaps in their production, prints within an edition are not identical.[38]

The insistence on the handmade and craft—which Flight made explicit in the title of his 1934 manual *The Art and Craft of Lino Cutting and Printing*—linked the linocut with decoration, which was often cause for criticism, particularly due to its association with women and domestic space.[39] This association was felt even more strongly as women artists were key members of the Grosvenor School and were heavily featured in exhibitions and publications. As the curator Jay A. Clarke noted, during the interwar period when the linocuts were first exhibited, "It was customary for critics to condescendingly refer to so-called women's work, namely, flower paintings, watercolors, and craft work, or, conversely, to argue that a work of art was 'so good' one would never know it was produced by a woman. Neither of these negative characterizations are present in the contemporary criticism on female linocut artists. Rather . . . the medium itself was gendered."[40] Because of this prejudice, the linocuts were dismissed by many.

The emphasis on the handmade, craft, and decoration also connected linocuts to the earlier Arts and Crafts movement and to the more recent legacy of the Omega Workshops in Britain, despite critical differences. The Arts and Crafts movement, which emerged in the late nineteenth century, reflected a deep anxiety about industrialization and therefore sought to elevate craft and the handmade in an effort to reform society. The artists associated with the Omega Workshops, founded by the artist and critic Roger Fry and in operation from 1913 to 1919, strove to erase distinctions between the fine and decorative arts, and created expensive decorative items for wealthy clients.[41] While Flight and his partner, the artist Edith Lawrence, owned an interior design business, the Grosvenor School artists worked individually in their own studios (as opposed to a workshop), and they signed their works, unlike the Omega Workshops artists, who often chose to remain anonymous. Moreover, it was imperative to Flight and others that their art be affordable and available to a broad public.

The Grosvenor School linocuts reflected a way of making art and engaging with a world that had experienced the positive and negative effects of industrialization after the First World War. The artists believed their prints corresponded with contemporary life and would, in the words of Flight, allow them to "express some experience of to-day in the technique of to-day." Flight also argued that the linocut offered a fresh beginning: "The lino-cut is different to the other printing mediums, it has no tradition of technique behind it, so that the student can go forward without thinking of what Bewick or Rembrandt did before, he can make his own tradition, and coming at a time like the present when new ideas and ideals are shaping themselves out of apparent chaos, he can do his share in building up a new and more vital art of to-morrow."[42] In order to create "a new and more vital art of to-morrow," the Grosvenor School artists used a spare language composed of bold planes of solid color, rhythmically repeated lines, and simplified forms to depict symbols of modernity encountered in everyday life, frequently in an urban center.[43] Within this subject, they often focused on systems of circulation—such as buses and subways, elevators and escalators, telephones and telegraphs—that both signified the era and allowed it to thrive.

CITY LIGHTS

An engagement with public metropolitan spaces as sites that were concurrently created by, and producers of, modernism informed many other artists, writers, filmmakers, and intellectuals of the period.[44] In Virginia Woolf's essay "Street Haunting: A London Adventure," published in 1927, the narrator, an independent woman from an elite background, freed from the demands of working inside the home, goes into town on an errand to purchase a lead pencil and discovers that it is the perfect moment to "indulge safely in the greatest pleasure of town life in winter—rambling the streets of London," an experience that would have been denied to her and many women less than a generation earlier. It is at this time, she claims, that "we . . . become part of that vast republican army of anonymous trampers, whose society is so agreeable after the solitude of one's own room."[45] Despite the specificity of the mission and the setting, Woolf acts mainly as a flaneur commenting on merchandise, materials, and memories, rather than one partaking in the revolutionary act of the *dérive*, the aimless yet engaged drift through diverse spaces within a city as a means to interact with, even transform, urban space and one's experience.[46] As opposed to the characters in her 1925 novel *Mrs. Dalloway*, who navigate a metropolis bustling with cars, buses, and people from various backgrounds and socio-economic positions on an early summer day, the narrator in "Street Haunting" responds to the empty city; she contrasts the "republican army of anonymous trampers" with the glories of the surfaces (of buses, food, and flowers) she encounters.[47]

The city as portrayed by Grosvenor School artists was full of people, the majority of whom were in movement. Flight described the modern artist's responsibility to capture the city and its energy in his article "Dynamism and the Colour Print," published in 1925, where he wrote:

> Traffic problems, transport problems; everybody is on the rush either for work or pleasure: business is hustle, the Cinema, all movement, is killing the more stationary Music Hall.
>
> The Painter cannot but be influenced by the restlessness of his surroundings; he notes the strivings everywhere, he sees the little ant people jostling one another over their endless tasks and he too turns to the individual movements that appeal to him. He sees the 'buses rushing down the street, the swift swirl of a taxi round a corner, the swaying, breaking and re-forming of the crowds in a busy highway; he feels the wind, the rain and the snow as they work their will on the street, and follows their individual rhythmic curves.[48]

Many of the people in motion and "jostling one another" were commuters, who took advantage of the expansion of public transportation networks after the First World War. In 1933, a public company, the London Passenger Transport Board (LPTB, better known as London Transport), was established to oversee all the subways, trains, buses, trams, and coaches that served nearly 9.5 million people in London and its environs. As the London Transport executive Frank Pick famously noted, in the interwar period, the London Underground became "the framework of the town," shaping and underpinning the daily life of what was still the world's largest city, now spreading well beyond its traditional borders.[49] Artists frequently chose the Underground as a subject because it signified modernity, speed, efficiency, and the intermingling of classes and genders in metropolitan centers.

Pick, who had been involved with the city's transportation system before the formation of London Transport, was also an enthusiastic patron of modern art and design. Beginning in 1908, he used modernist posters to promote the Underground. Seven years later, he helped create the Design and Industries Association and served as its president between 1932 and 1934. In 1934, he was named the inaugural chairman of the government's Council for Art and Industry. Indeed, Pick

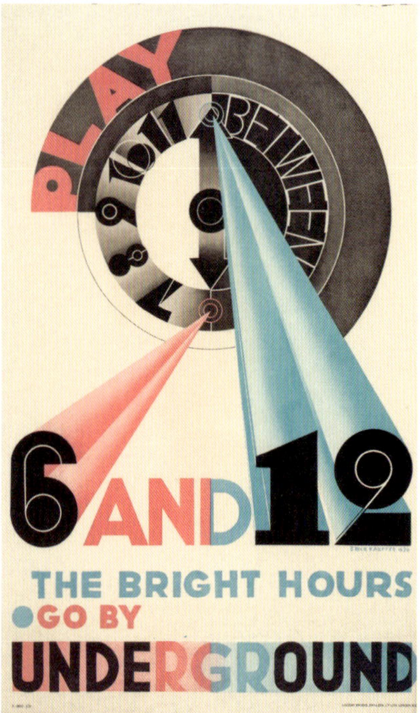

Fig. 18 Edward McKnight Kauffer (American, 1890–1954). *Play Between 6 and 12, The Bright Hours*, 1930, printed 1931. Lithograph on Western paper, sheet 40 x 25 in. (101.6 x 63.5 cm). The Metropolitan Museum of Art, New York (2019.592.171)

was so respected for his support of modern art in all its forms that in 1942 the art historian Nikolaus Pevsner described him as "the greatest patron of the arts whom this century has so far produced in England, and indeed the ideal patron of our age."[50]

In order to both promote mass transit and make the Underground into a public art gallery, Pick sought out architects, designers, and artists to design stations and create posters, logos, and other such pieces for the network.[51] He commissioned a range of artists, including those associated with commercial design (such as the American expatriate Edward McKnight Kauffer), fine art (such as Nevinson, Paul Nash, and Edward Wadsworth), the avant-garde (such as Man Ray), and illustration (such as Dorothy Burroughes), before his retirement in 1940. Posters, in particular, were essential to his mission to educate the public and democratize art. They were also a great way to bring modern art to the people, both in London and the provinces, whether through public installations and traveling exhibitions or as gifts to art schools.[52] Notably, the works from these projects were so admired that in 1949 the Victoria and Albert Museum staged an exhibition of art made for the London Transport titled *Art for All*.

One of the artists most associated with Pick was Kauffer, whose posters, such as *From Winters Gloom to Summers Joy* of 1927 and *Play Between 6 and 12, The Bright Hours* of 1930 (printed 1931; fig. 18), evoke prewar styles, such as Futurism, Vorticism, and Cubism.[53] In the former work, Kauffer depicted the transition from winter to spring and summer through sharp edges, geometric forms, and stark contrasts between the dark tones of winter and the brighter colors of summer, while in the latter, he captured the machine forms and sense of velocity associated with the Underground.

The Grosvenor School artists were well aware of these works, including Kauffer's posters, which they found "marvelous."[54] And, as Frank Rutter noted, "The whole nation is much less affected by what pictures are shown in the Royal Academy than by what posters are put up on the hoardings. A few thousand see the first, but the second are seen by millions. The art galleries of the People are not in Bond Street, but are to be found in every railway station."[55] In addition to being widely distributed and placed in public spaces, some posters were even sold for approximately one shilling in a shop run by the London Transport.[56] Because they were neither handmade nor restricted by a limited edition, these posters achieved the accessibility and popularity that the Grosvenor School artists and many of their peers sought.

In the early 1930s, Pick commissioned Andrews and Power to create posters promoting excursions using public transportation. The artists credited the eight posters they made for the London Transport to "Andrew Power," in reference to their two surnames, but according to Andrews, the labor was divided: Power secured the commission, and she designed the posters.[57] Many of these posters celebrate sporting events, from ice skating and hockey to the Wimbledon tennis tournament and cricket at Lord's and the Oval. *To Hire a Bus or Coach* of 1934 focuses exclusively on the vehicles themselves, with red representing the city buses and green the country coaches (fig. 19). Intriguingly, Power approached the subject of travel differently in the near-contemporary print *The Sunshine Roof* of about 1934 (fig. 20). Here, Power, as if a passenger himself, depicted the interior of the bus with geometric patterns created by yellow shafts of light on the viridian seats and strong contrasts between dark and light tones. He used simplified forms for the passengers, almost all of whom wear hats that shield much of their faces and render them unknowable.[58]

The Grosvenor School artists made numerous sketches and prints of the Underground, focusing variously on the architectural elements of the stations, the trains and their interiors, and the commuters. While some prints, such as Tschudi's *Underground* of 1930 (p. 115) or Power's *The Tube Station* of about 1932 (p. 123), project an optimism that recalls Pick's belief in the potential of the Underground,[59] other works feel more ominous. For instance, Power's linocut *The Escalator*, of about 1929, which shows a man framed against an extraordinarily steep and potentially dangerous moving staircase, has a menacing hallucinatory quality that inspired the art writer Philip Vann to describe the figure as "a vulnerable urban Everyman at odds with the wider social and existential System."[60]

Reflecting both the modernity of the machine-age environment of the subway and the rigor demanded by industrialized life, many of Power's prints and drawings of the Underground have a hard-edged quality. Vertiginous escalators and staircases appear inhospitable to humans, with their steps resembling the toothed forms of metal traps. *The Tube Staircase* of 1929 (p. 113) shows a tight metal coil, more like a corkscrew than a platform designed for human use. The people depicted in such spaces frequently appear to be brittle as well, their bodies and faces marked by sharp angles. In *The Tube Train* of about 1934 (p. 121), Power presented a crowded London subway car in even more dramatic terms, highlighting the positive aspects of modernity—such as speed and efficiency, and the intermingling of classes and genders in urban centers—as well as feelings of alienation.[61] The passengers' mask-like visages mirror the guarded and artificial faces evoked by Eliot in his poem "The Love Song of J. Alfred Prufrock" of 1915.

In Power's linocut *Whence & Whither?* of about 1930 (p. 119), faceless commuters descend to the platform in a manner that evokes the work's original title *The Cascade*. The size of the crowd suggests rush hour, especially as the uninterrupted row of people seems to extend beyond the edge of the paper, thus implying an assembly line rather than speed and force. This conveyor belt funneling anonymous and interchangeable bourgeois passengers emphasizes reification and repetition, monotony and standardization. The commuters in Power's linocut recall the seemingly endless line of French soldiers in Nevinson's *Column on the March* of 1916 (p. 95); yet, rather than projecting a sense of shared purpose like the men in the latter's "human tank" charging to the front, the people in Power's print seem to be full of ennui and passivity.

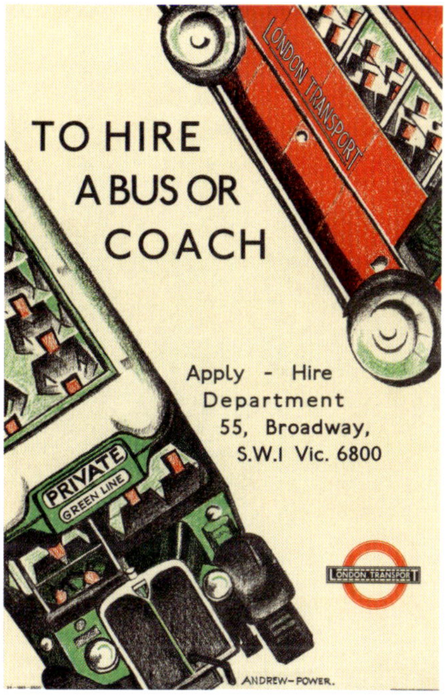

Fig. 19 **Andrew Power**. *To Hire a Bus or Coach*, 1934. Lithograph on Western paper, sheet 30 x 19¾ in. (76.2 x 50.2 cm). The Metropolitan Museum of Art, New York (2019.592.320)

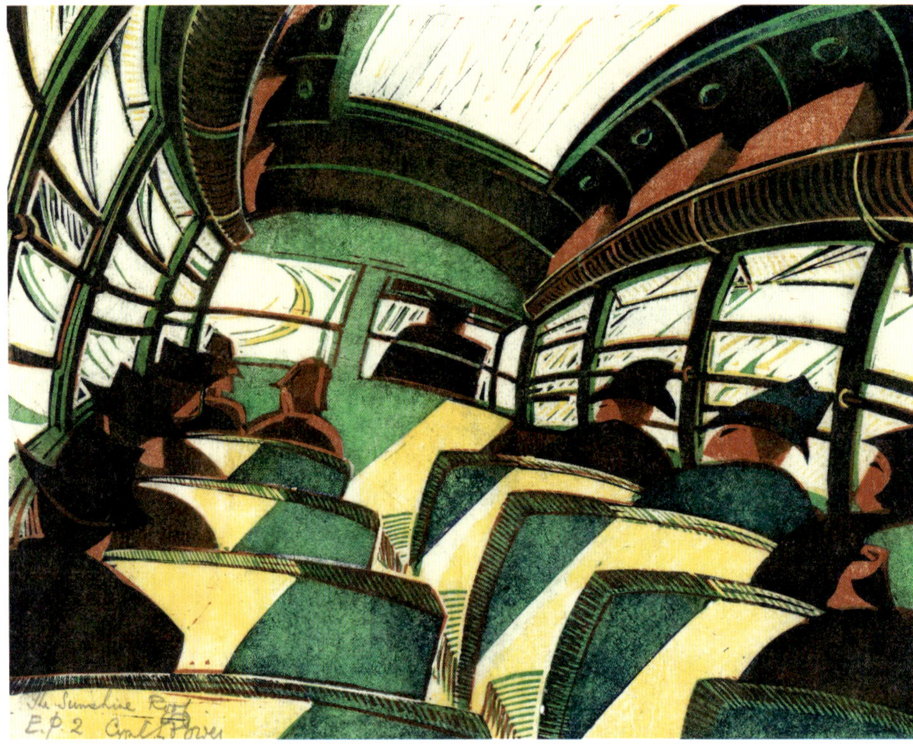

Fig. 20 **Cyril E. Power** (British, 1872–1951). *The Sunshine Roof*, ca. 1934. Linocut on Japanese paper, image 10 ¼ x 13 ⅛ in. (26 x 33 cm). The Metropolitan Museum of Art, New York (2019.592.463)

Power made numerous sketches for *Whence & Whither?*, including drawings of the escalators at the Tottenham Court Road station begun in 1928. An inscription on one such work reads, "THE ROBOTTOMLESS PIT, HOMO MECHANIENS," conveying a sense of anxiety, even doom, generated by the subterranean world with its long, winding tunnels and automated stairs. In this and several of his drawings, Power portrayed the Underground stations as monumental neo-Gothic structures, where rib-like vaults and pointed arches combine with steep escalators, and shadows act as architectural elements (fig. 21). Such images testify to Power's training as an architect and to his lifelong interest in medieval constructions.[62]

Andrews also set works in the Underground. She used a palette similar to Power's and depicted similar subjects, but her works were decidedly more cheerful. She also went even further than Flight and Power in eliminating details that would detract from the pulsating rhythm of modernity. In *Straphangers* of 1929 (p. 120), a work an anonymous critic described as capturing "the very soul of modern London," Andrews used just a sharp curve to represent the torsos and arms of passengers packed onto a subway car as they hold straps for stability.[63] *Rush Hour* (p. 120), made a year later, can be read as a reverse of *Straphangers*. Andrews flipped the crescent shape from the bottom of the sheet to the top, and, rather than their upper bodies, she showed anonymous passengers of both sexes from the knees down as they navigate the spiky orange points that represent the wooden steps of the escalator.

POVERTY IN THE MIDST OF PLENTY

During the interwar years, alongside vast technological advances, as reflected in transportation and new methods for communication, labor was a major political and social issue. After a brief period of economic growth, prosperity faltered, and, by the summer of 1921, there were almost 2 million people unemployed. The General Strike, the first ever such event in Britain, occurred in May 1926. Led by coal miners, it soon expanded to other industries, resulting in 1.7 million workers on strike for nine days. The economic situation only worsened with the Wall Street Crash of 1929, which led to a global depression. The historian Richard Overy framed the devastation for many British people as existential, writing, "Knowledge of what had happened in other countries was widespread so that the recession was viewed not just as a national disaster but as a possibly terminal crisis of world capitalism. The economic crisis was the greatest single issue facing British society during the inter-war years, and became the reference point in the 1930s not just in discussions about the economic viability of capitalism but in all assessments of the future course of civilization."[64]

In 1932, the nadir of what was known as the "Great Slump," almost 3 million people were jobless in Britain,[65] and unemployment numbers stayed above a million until the first year of the Second World War. As summarized by the historians John Stevenson and Chris Cook, "For almost twenty years there were never fewer than a million people out of work in Great Britain, representing a tenth of the insured working population."[66] While the figures were grim, they did not reach the levels of other nations and, despite the widespread belief that the slump signaled the end of capitalism, paradoxically, for many people, the quality of life improved substantially during this period. That contradiction inspired the era's slogan "Poverty in the midst of plenty."[67]

One of the reasons for these contradictory experiences was that unemployment and poverty were not distributed evenly across the nation, with areas such as Wales, the north of England, and Northern Ireland hit hardest, and industries such as coal, textiles, shipbuilding, iron, and steel most negatively impacted by fewer exports.[68] Wages fell for many, including civil servants, teachers, the police, and even the Royal Navy (which went on strike in 1931). At the same time, however, new areas of employment—such as the electric industry, home building, and car manufacturing—were growing, and areas like London and the southeast of England did not feel the devastating economic effects as intensely. Moreover, the cost of living fell by as much as a third during this period, providing a greater standard of living for the middle class. As the historian A. J. P. Taylor later observed, "Most English people were enjoying a richer life than any previously known in the history of the world: longer holidays, shorter hours, higher real wages. They had motor cars, cinemas, radio sets, electrical appliances. The two sides of life did not join up."[69] The gap that separated the classes—and the class structure itself—was increasingly visible due to this disparity.

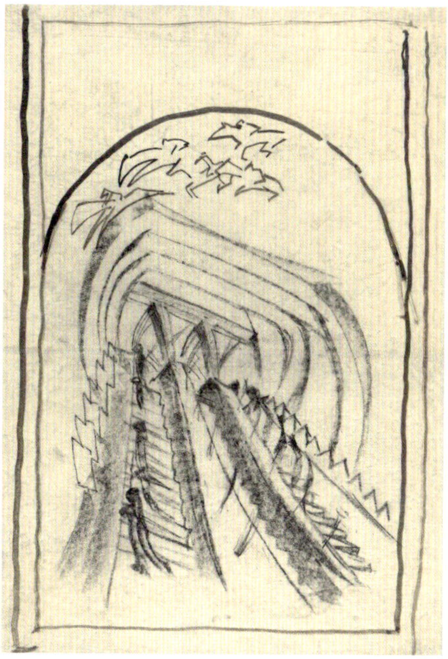

Fig. 21 **Sybil Andrews** (British, 1898–1992) and **Cyril E. Power** (British, 1878–1951). Sketches for *Steeplechasing* and *Whence & Whither?*, 1930. Ink and pastel on tracing paper, 20 x 14½ in. (50.8 x 36.8 cm). The Metropolitan Museum of Art, New York (2019.592.328)

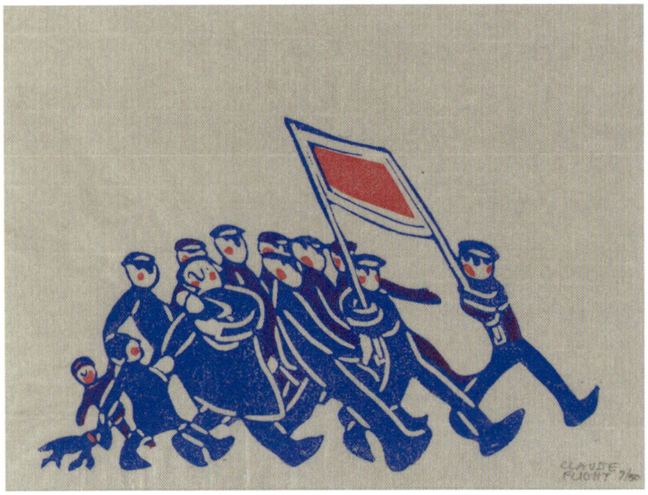

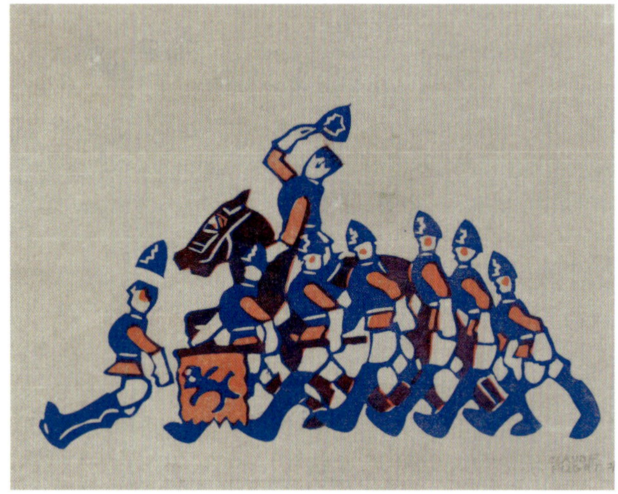

Fig. 22 **Claude Flight** (British, 1881–1955). *Unemployed*, ca. 1934. Linocut on gray Japanese paper, image $7\frac{13}{16} \times 10\frac{1}{4}$ in. (19.9 x 26.1 cm). The Metropolitan Museum of Art, New York (2019.592.359)

Fig. 23 **Claude Flight** (British, 1881–1955). *Employed*, ca. 1934. Linocut on gray Japanese paper, image $7\frac{11}{16} \times 10\frac{7}{16}$ in. (19.6 x 26.5 cm). The Metropolitan Museum of Art, New York (2019.592.344)

Despite their interest in portraying contemporary life, scenes of unemployment, protests, and other references to the "Great Slump" were largely absent from Grosvenor School works. An exception was Flight's pair of linocuts *Unemployed* and *Employed* of about 1934 (figs. 22, 23), which, according to the curator Stephen Coppel, was "a political comment on the effects of the Great Depression."[70] *Unemployed* contains a group of men and women workers with children and a dog in tow carrying a large banner with a red rectangle. Unified, they stride forward and face off against the all-male group in *Employed*, whose ceremonial uniforms and rigidity give the impression that the figures are toy soldiers from another era.[71]

Of the Grosvenor School artists, it was Andrews and Tschudi who focused the most on scenes of labor, from agricultural production and local markets to industrial and urban work. The labor was almost exclusively that of men; labor traditionally associated with women—office work, domestic labor (such as childcare by either a parent or a governess), or housework undertaken by an inhabitant or a professional—was not a topic of interest.[72]

Andrews praised hard work, both professionally and in art production. In addition to taking care of her younger brothers and sisters after her father left the family, Andrews was a schoolteacher, a secretary, and a welder constructing airplanes during the First World War. *Sledgehammers* of 1933 (p. 111) was based on a memory from her wartime work of seeing blacksmiths at the forge. In this linocut, she extended and contoured the blacksmiths' bodies to convey a feeling of monumentality at odds with the limited dimensions of the paper and eliminated the anvil, metal, and anything that might detract from the image of pure physical force. Arms and hammers appear as a single instrument of power, and the sensation of repeated blows and coiled energy radiates across the surface, while the circular formation recalls Futurist pieces, such as Umberto Boccioni's *The City Rises* (1910).

Andrews explored similar depictions of manual labor in *Haulers* of 1929 (p. 110), *The Winch* of 1930 (fig. 24), and *The New Cable* of 1931 (see fig. 1).[73] Her work *Oranges* of 1929 (p. 106) shows a line of men moving boxes of imported produce. As oranges were not grown in Britain, their presence and that of the crates evoke both the presence of imported goods in the Britain during the interwar period and the global reach of the British Empire.

In *Fixing the Wires* of 1932 (p. 109),Tschudi portrayed labor alongside key signifiers of modernity: the telegraph and telephone.[74] By the early twentieth century, new modes of communications, from telephones to radio towers, were frequently encountered in daily life as well as in movies, literature, and art.[75] In contrast to Nevinson's 1918 *Nerves of an Army* (see fig. 12), an image of four Royal Engineers trying to repair damage and maintain a safe position, *Fixing the Wires* shows two trained professionals skillfully adjusting loose wires while adroitly balancing like taut acrobats.[76] Their gracefulness is reinforced by the delicate arc of the dangling wires Tschudi engraved into the linoleum block.[77] One can compare both the Nevinson and the Tschudi to Ursula Fookes's *Poplar Trees and Telegraph Poles* of about 1930 (p. 108). In Fookes's print, no people are present; instead, it features a row of wooden utility poles that mirror in form and orientation a line of poplar trees, creating a new kind of allée that reflected the alteration of the landscape by contemporary technologies.

Fixing the Wires also foreshadows Tschudi's *Sticking Up Posters* of 1933 (p. 112), a depiction of Parisian workers wheat-pasting advertisements. In both the linocut

Fig. 24 **Sybil Andrews** (British, 1898–1992). *The Winch*, 1930. Linocut on Japanese paper, image 7 ¼ x 11 13⁄16 in. (18.4 x 28.4 cm). The Metropolitan Museum of Art, New York, Gift of Johanna and Leslie Garfield, 2005 (2005.470.4)

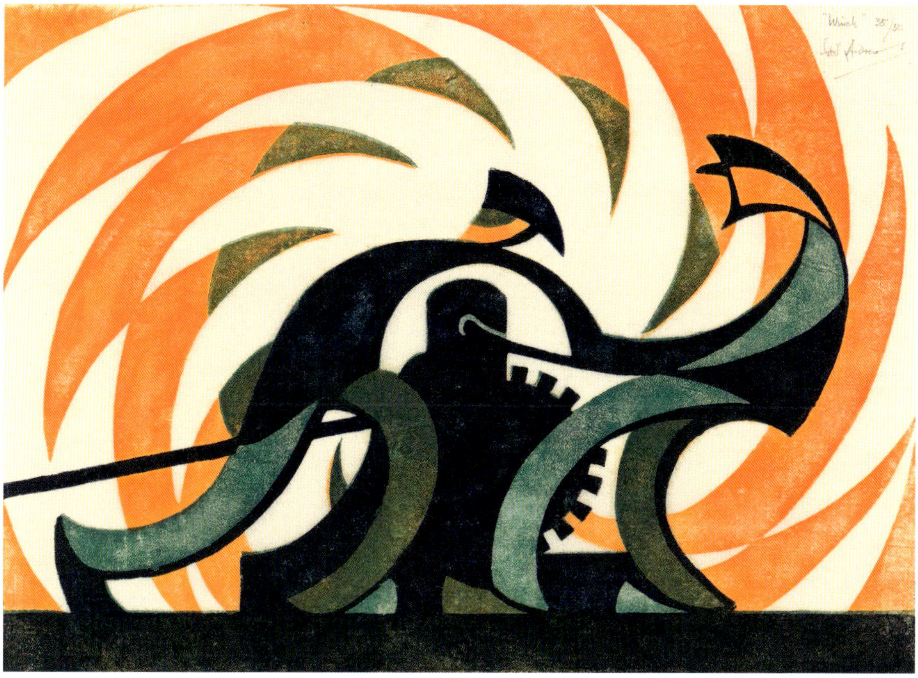

and preparatory sketch (see fig. 33a. b), she eliminated details, including text, branding, and even the object or event being promoted (with the exception of a packet of cigarettes rendered as three tubular forms extending from a rectangle); the composition is composed almost exclusively by sharp-edged, repeated geometric forms. Flight's description of *Fixing the Wires* is broadly applicable to the Grosvenor School: "As far as the subject goes [it] is commonplace, the experience is an unusual one, an unusual experience from a commonplace subject." In regard to the viewer, he continued, "We who view the print, find a commonplace subject translated in such a manner that we derive from it a new way of viewing a certain aspect of nature, it gives us a new phase of consciousness."[78]

THE COUNTRY AND THE CITY

A large number of the Grosvenor School linocuts portray more timeless images set in rural environments and small towns.[79] Andrews, in particular, made numerous prints devoted to her hometown of Bury St Edmunds, with scenes of planting (*Michaelmas*, 1935), mowing (*The Mowers*, 1937), harvesting (*Haysel*, 1936), plowing (*Fall of the Leaf*, 1934), and market stalls (*Market Day*, 1936). Many of these pieces feature traditional farm equipment and horses. In *Tillers of the Soil* of 1934 (fig. 25) and *The Timber Jim* of 1932 (p. 161), teams of Shire horses dominate the compositions. As opposed to the elongated, elegant equine forms that leap seemingly without effort in such prints as *Water Jump* of 1931 and *Steeplechasing* of 1930, these

Fig. 25 **Sybil Andrews** (British, 1898–1992). *Tillers of the Soil*, 1934. Linocut on Japanese paper, image 10½ x 13⁹⁄₁₆ in. (26.6 x 34.4 cm). The Metropolitan Museum of Art, New York (2019.592.71)

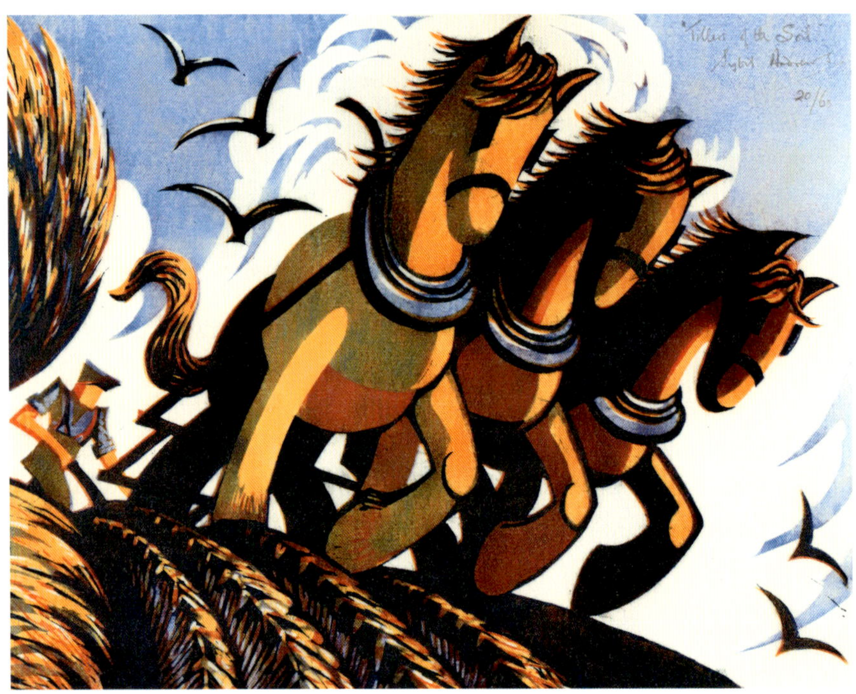

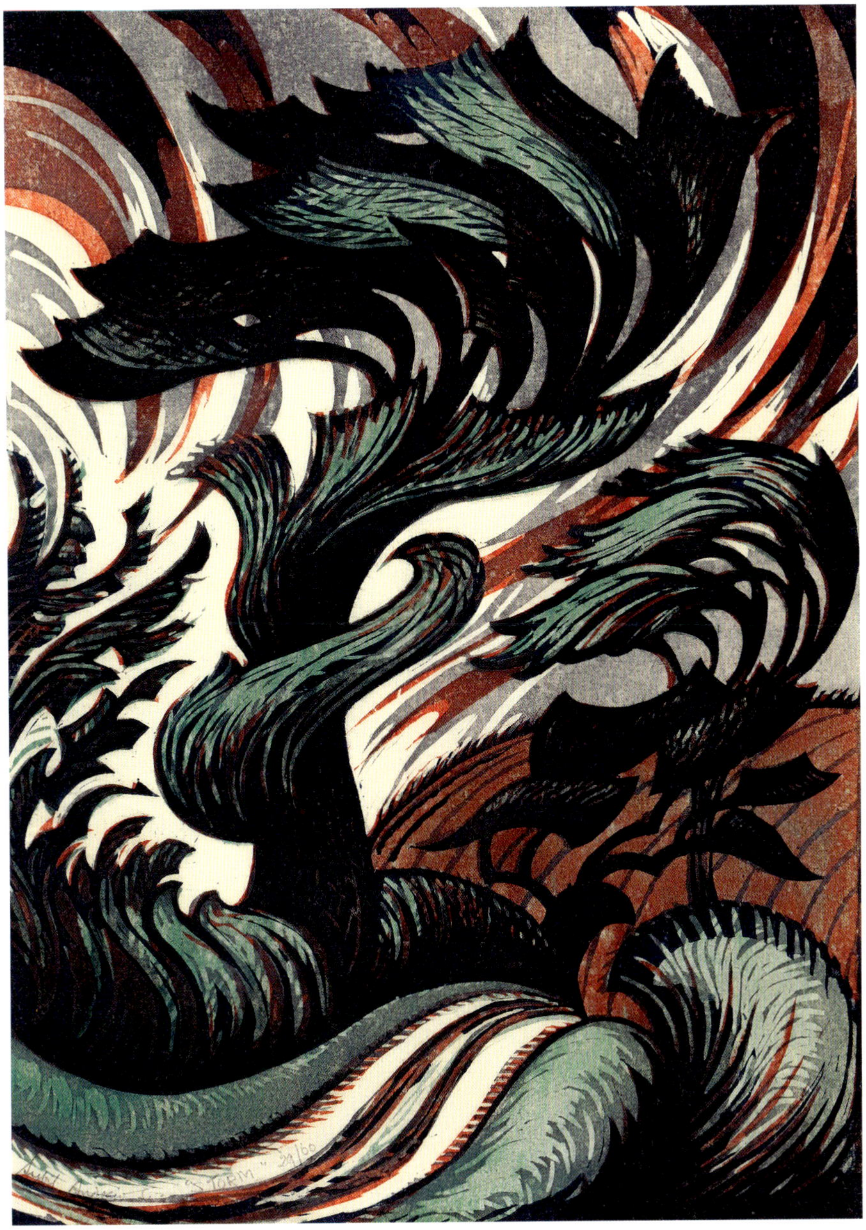

Fig. 26 **Sybil Andrews** (British, 1898–1992). *Storm*, 1935. Linocut on Japanese paper, image 13 x 9 ⅛ in. (33 x 23.2 cm). The Metropolitan Museum of Art, New York (2019.592.65)

massive farm animals have sturdy, thick bodies, which connect them to the land. Their legs, raised in unison, and the prominent yokes around their necks indicate the rigor of the chores they perform. The horses are designated as laborers engaged in grueling physical work in tandem with the farmers, as opposed to the pedigreed horses used in leisure activities enjoyed by the middle class and wealthy.

At times, Andrews's prints express nostalgia, particularly in *Fall of the Leaf* (p. 162), an idealized scene of harmony between man and nature. While it initially appears to be pure landscape, on closer inspection one sees, underneath the fanned-out trees, a man at a plow led by three horses whose forms mirror the patterning of the fields. The linocut is dominated by decorative and textural elements and composed by multiple tones, with overlapping curving shapes. Nevertheless, as the British historian Eric J. Hobsbawm and others have noted, by the 1930s British agriculture was no longer central to the economy and "had become a very minor factor indeed."[80] In fact, there was such a crisis that the government had to intervene to save the British agricultural industry.[81]

Andrews often focused on the natural elements, particularly in pastoral settings. *The Windmill* of 1933 (p. 160) and *Storm* of 1935 (fig. 26) convey nature's magnificent power and its potential for destruction, a duality seen earlier in Nevinson's *The Blue Wave* of 1917 (p. 147). While *The Windmill* shows nature harnessed, *Storm*, with its violent, twisting forms, captures its extraordinary beauty and danger. By contrast, *The Gale* of 1930 (p. 151), likely set in an urban site, portrays blustery winds and rain as an everyday occurrence, with the people depicted more inconvenienced than either endangered or awestruck. *The Gale* also recalls Flight's earlier linocut *Autumn* of about 1926 (p. 150), though critical differences exist. Both works show a pair of figures, their bodies curved as they brace themselves against the elements, yet *Autumn*, like the other prints in Flight's series *The Four Seasons*, has more abstracted figures that appear outside of a specific time or place and evoke traditional bather imagery.

PLAYTIME

The Grosvenor School artists also explored the diverse leisure activities of the interwar period and their attraction to people from different economic, political, social, and cultural classes.[82] In addition to pastimes that embraced new media (such as movies) and new machinery (such as car races), more traditional activities (such as visiting funfairs and the circus, participating in sports, and going to concerts, theaters, and music halls) remained popular. Andrews's first published linocut, *Concert Hall* of 1929 (p. 154), was based on sketches made of London's Queen's Hall, a premier venue for classical music due to its excellent acoustics.[83] Andrews used a cool palette to depict the dramatic curves and nearly abstract shadows of the balconies; the tightly packed rows of people point to the venue's notoriously cramped conditions. While the image might evoke exclusivity, the Queen's Hall was known for hosting the Proms, a concert season with lower-priced tickets and a more relaxed experience that sought to make "high art" more accessible.[84] In 1927, the British Broadcasting Corporation (BBC) took over the concerts, which were also broadcast on the radio, thus extending their reach.

Music and concerts were a recurring theme: Power and Tschudi made images of classical orchestras and trios, while Flight and Tschudi produced linocuts showing less formal contemporary musical performances, ranging from jazz and the rhumba to street singers. In *Jazz Band* of 1930 (fig. 27), the compressed

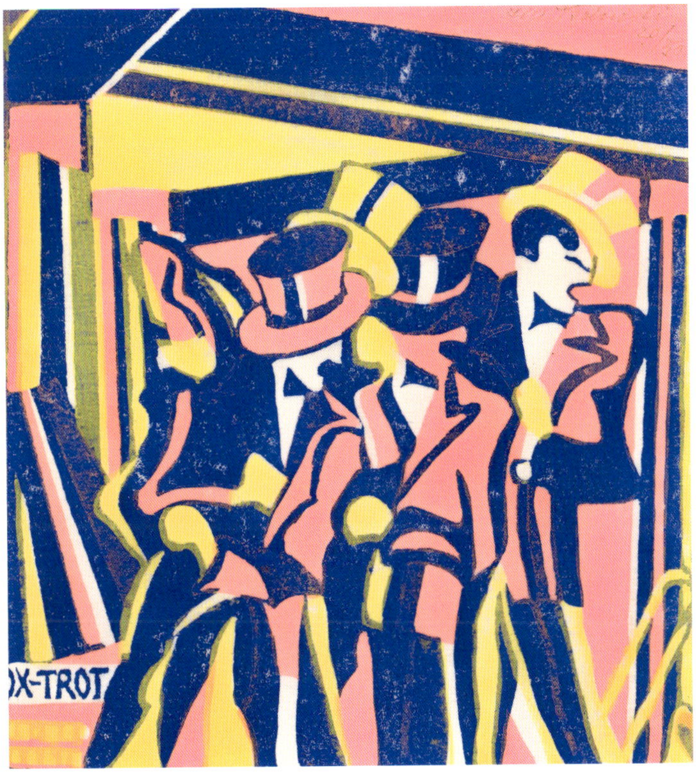

Fig. 27 **Lill Tschudi** (Swiss, 1911–2004). *Jazz Band*, 1930. Linocut on Japanese paper, image 7 ⅜ x 6 $^{11}/_{16}$ in (18.8 x 17 cm). The Metropolitan Museum of Art, New York (2019.592.507)

figures in formal wear, rendered in a range of acidic tones of blue, pink, and yellow, reflect the vitality and rhythm of the music. The letters "OX-TROT," visible in the bottom corner, are short for foxtrot, the popular ballroom dance performed to jazz music. In one of her sketchbooks, Tschudi made several color preparatory drawings in which she tested the composition. One sketch has a lighter palette with visible pencil lines, while another more closely mirrors the linocut with darker tones, whose development is indicated by multiple color swatches at the top of the page, and a similar orientation to the print; both contain snippets of text ("X TROT") that she would later expand in the print.[85]

The circus mesmerized numerous British authors and artists during the interwar period and was promoted aggressively in advertisements and editorials. This attention not only reflected the circus's dramatic growth (including the rise of traveling circuses) but also its extreme popularity among people of various classes, ages, economic positions, and regions. The belief that "the modern circus was very much an English invention and an important aspect of the nation's history and character" was upheld widely in Britain, as was the concept of the circus as a particularly democratic institution and form of entertainment. Such a framing was intended to challenge the American claim for inventing democracy and modern popular leisure, as well as to contrast the circus with both more recent forms of recreation—such as movies, which were dominated by American studios—and rising nondemocratic forms of government in Europe.[86]

Power and Tschudi both made images featuring circus acrobats in which they portrayed dynamism, speed, exhilaration, and risk. Tschudi's *In the Circus* of 1932 (p. 148) has three performers distorting their bodies into angular forms that echo the shafts of light that run diagonally through the composition. While Tschudi's figures convey stability and strength, those in Power's *Acrobats* of about 1933 (p. 145) seem nearly weightless. Rather than depict performers in the midst of their routine, as seen in Edgar Degas's *Miss La La at the Cirque Fernando* of 1879 and Nevinson's *The Acrobat, Montmartre* of 1921–22, Power rendered his performers as silhouettes framed against the circus tent. They curve into tumbling concave and convex forms and sharp angles as they fly through the air. Power was inspired by trapeze artists at the celebrated Bertram Mills Circus in London, and while his work captures the excitement of the act, it also anticipates by about two years his linocut *Air Raid* and the related monotype *Aerial Combat* based on his memories of the First World War. These images of circus performers and dogfights carry a sense of precariousness and danger, and they were likely a reflection of the political situation in Europe, which was increasingly fraught with the threat of Fascism and another world war.

As with *Acrobats*, Power deployed a mixture of festivity and danger in his images of funfairs. In about 1930, a few years after visiting the Wembley Exhibition Funfair in London, he created *The Merry-Go-Round* (p. 144) and *The Giant Racer* (fig. 28).[87] The merry-go-round projects an almost manic energy that captures the heightened experience of being on the ride while also anticipating the dynamic force found in his nearly abstract linocut *The Vortex* (p. 141). In *The Merry-Go-Round*, Power restricted his palette to orange and blue—contrasting colors that produced the maximum visual impact. While festive flags atop the roof provide a bit of levity, sharp-edged spikes, found throughout the composition, add a sense of menace. By contrast, *The Giant Racer* is dominated by elongated curving forms, culminating with the vertiginous drop outlined in red.

The motion in Power's linocuts like *'Appy 'Ampstead* of about 1933 (p. 142) recalls that in works by Futurist artists, such as Giacomo Balla's 1912 *Dynamism of a Dog on a Leash*. Rather than create an image that was composed of a series of movements, as in the time-lapse photographs of Eadweard Muybridge, in *'Appy 'Ampstead*, Power conveyed a sense of frenetic activity by repeating lines and other visual elements to express speed and the feeling of time itself, using only four blocks of color (yellow, red [see fig. 35], viridian, and dark blue). While Flight had engaged with the same subject—a fairground ride—a decade earlier, focusing on the form of a single swing-boat reduced to its geometrical essence, Power depicted several swing-boats (four in a pencil sketch).[88] He multiplied arcs and looping forms and compressed them into a vertical format to exaggerate the dynamism of the composition. The soaring swing-boats cast shadows on the ground that merge

Fig. 28 **Cyril E. Power** (British, 1872–1951). *The Giant Racer*, ca. 1930. Linocut on Japanese paper, image 10⅞ x 7$\frac{9}{16}$ in. (27.6 x 19.2 cm). The Metropolitan Museum of Art, New York (2019.592.444)

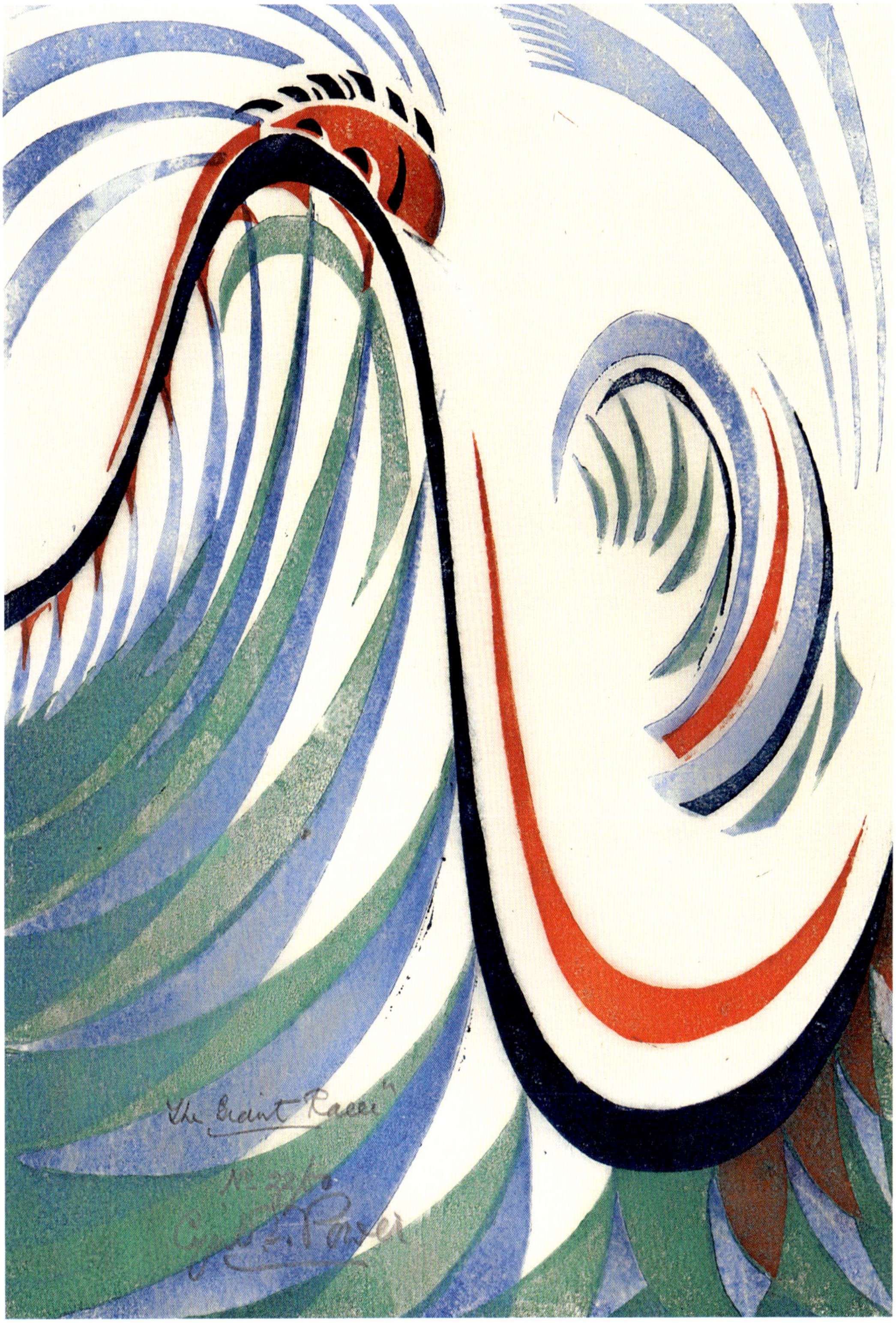

with the decorative patterning of the tents and flags flying behind them to achieve a sense of optical confusion. The riders are abstracted to such a degree that they become unrecognizable; the groups of people on the ground, including a woman with children, serve as an entry point for the viewer and draw attention to the vertiginous heights achieved by the swing-boats.

In addition to concerts, circuses, and funfairs, physical activity and sports received great attention between the wars. Britain was not alone in this focus, nor in the depiction of athletics in art and culture. While for some it was part of rehabilitation prescribed in the wake of the First World War (and in anticipation of another conflict), for others it was a leisure activity or form of entertainment. The Grosvenor School artists presented images of sports from the vantage point of the spectator more than that of the athlete. Andrews set her sporting scenes in rural environments, highlighting elite equestrian activities, such as steeplechases and hunts, traditionally associated with the landed gentry. Yet, she reinvented this genre and applied a machine-like aesthetic to her subjects. One finds a similar sense of velocity in *Speedway* of 1934 (p. 125) and *In Full Cry* of 1931 (p. 129). In the former, riders on motorbikes furiously circle a track, while in the latter, riders and horses are captured midjump, likely following hunting dogs (who are not visible) in pursuit of a fox. Andrews amplified this feeling of speed in *Racing* of 1934 (p. 128), a nearly abstract composition of riders, their bodies distended, mounted on orange-toned horses. Here, the impression of motion and time unfolding recalls the photographs of Muybridge, as well as contemporary films showing the movement of animals and people.[89]

Intriguingly, even Andrews's scenes of sports show a kind of aesthetic of labor that often evokes the ideas of factory production, such as Taylorization and Fordism. Numerous similarities exist, for instance, between *Haulers* of 1929, *Oranges* of 1929, and *Bringing in the Boat* of 1933 (p. 131): the single line of workers from the earlier linocuts is echoed and expanded in the later print in the two receding lines of rowers, whose sharp angles and jagged lines are mirrored by the boat's metal spokes. One can also compare Andrews's industrialized aesthetic with that found in Power's *The Eight* of 1930 (p. 133), which shows a boat racing along the River Thames as seen from the Hammersmith Bridge.[90] Here, he eliminated figures (such as the coxswain) and details (such as facial features) to create an image that recalls the organic world through its rounded forms and palette of greens, blues, and oranges. At the same time, the synchronized movement of standardized figures link the image to mechanization.

The glorification of speed was not exclusive to artists; indeed, there was great interest in racing events and record breaking during the period.[91] In *Brooklands* of about 1929 (p. 117), Flight depicted the six-hour endurance race at Brooklands track, an event widely covered in the press. The rhythmic movement of the three race cars reflects what Italian Futurists termed "the beauty of speed." Flame-like strips of color and curving forms amplify the feeling of velocity and mechanical force while also conveying the exhilaration of the spectators. Power's *Speed Trial* of about 1932 (p. 122) features the Bluebird, a Bentley driven by Malcolm Campbell that, after shattering numerous world records, came to symbolize speed and mechanical force.

Tschudi's *Tour de Suisse* of 1935 (p. 126) shows a bicycle race that required cyclists to travel the narrow and vertiginous Klausen Pass, located in the mountains near where Tschudi lived. By compressing the riders and emphasizing the undulating Alpine path they navigate, she expressed the sheer physical endurance and strength necessary for this endeavor rather than speed. A decorative border mirrors the interior patterns; it refers to the artist's plan to print the image on fabric and marks this impression as a rare example from the edition. As with the artists of the Omega Workshops and the Vorticist-affiliated Rebel Art Centre, the Grosvenor School artists did not separate art from either decoration or craft; in fact, in 1927, Flight and Edith Lawrence opened a decorating business to promote these connections. By selling home accessories, they not only supplemented their income but were able to fulfill their prime mission of integrating art into daily life.

A BRAVE NEW WORLD?

In the summer of 1935, Tschudi went to London for an exhibition organized by Flight that featured works by her and other Grosvenor School artists. There, she encountered the celebrations in honor of the Silver Jubilee of King George V that she would commemorate in *Street Decoration* (p. 169). Made in April 1937 in tones of red and blue, the festive print reflects the colors of the Union Jack while also testifying to Britain's political, social, and cultural power. The image is dominated by flags, banners, and other decorations, which seem to extend beyond the edge of the composition to lead the viewer into the scene. Tschudi altered scale and perspective, cropping the image and compressing space to evoke a sense of exuberance and disorientation.[92] By the time Tschudi created the print, King George V had died and his son Edward VIII had assumed the throne. Edward would rule for less than a year before he abdicated to marry the American divorcée Wallis Simpson, causing a great scandal and crisis within the country, which some worried predicted a decline in the power of the British Empire.[93]

Grosvenor School prints dominated the linocut exhibitions Flight organized to promote the medium. The *First Exhibition of British Lino-Cuts* was held in July 1929 at London's Redfern Gallery with the support of the gallerist Rex Nan Kivell.[94] Flight continued to mount annual shows at Redfern through 1931 and then at London's Ward Gallery between 1933 and 1937.[95] He also sent touring exhibitions throughout Britain and to venues in the United States, Canada, Australia, and China in the 1930s. Through his efforts, linocuts were acquired by numerous British and international institutions. The same year *Street Decoration* was published, the Ward Gallery held the eighth and final annual "British Lino-Cuts" exhibition. To the disappointment of the artists and the gallery, the show did not sell well.

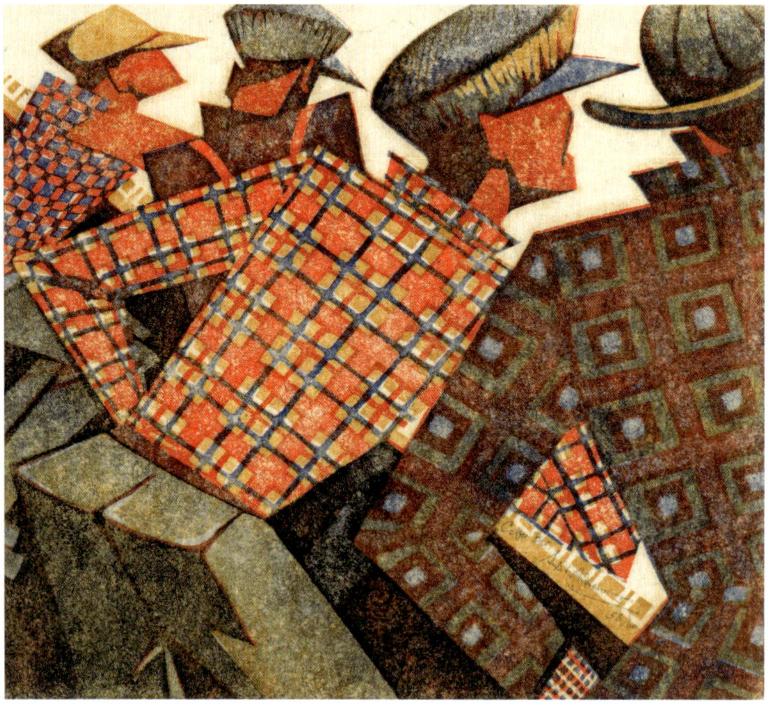

Fig. 29 **Sybil Andrews** (British, 1898–1992). *Coffee Bar*, 1952. Linocut on Japanese paper, image 8 1⁄16 x 9 in. (20.5 x 22.9 cm). The Metropolitan Museum of Art, New York (2019.592.665)

Flight's last major linocut exhibition was at the City of Birmingham Museum and Art Gallery in 1939.

The curator Stephen Coppel and art historian Hana Leaper have noted the problem inherent in Flight's aspirations for the linocut as a democratic art.[96] The artists usually planned to produce editions of only fifty or sixty prints, a limited run that contradicted "their specific intention of making the linocut available to all."[97] And, although linocuts were markedly cheaper than paintings and other art forms, they were still too expensive for the average person, in particular the "working man" to whom Flight hoped to impart a greater understanding and appreciation for modern art.[98] The linocuts were generally priced at one to three guineas (with each guinea—an outdated currency that continued to be used for luxury purchases, such as art, land, jewelry, and racehorses—equivalent to twenty-one shillings, or one British pound and one shilling), an amount significantly higher than what "the average man [paid] for his daily beer or his cinema ticket," both of which would have been under a shilling at between 6 and 10 pence.[99] At the same time, the price was too low for the artists, who could only produce a limited number of linocuts a year and, even if they sold an entire edition, could not earn enough to support themselves through their art.[100]

An additional problem, as Leaper astutely observed, was that the main platforms Flight used to promote his ambitions—art books and journals—had a small, high-brow readership.[101] Furthermore, while Flight arranged numerous exhibitions in galleries both within Britain and abroad, such venues had a limited reach due to numerous factors, including geographic distances from the venues, limited awareness of the shows, and the belief that art was an exclusive activity for a particular cultural class. The narrow dissemination of his message contrasts sharply with the self-promotion of other movements like Futurism, which often published its manifestos in newspapers and organized public demonstrations, and with the various British poster projects, which reached a broader audience composed of people from different classes and regions. However, Flight's publications, especially his linocut manuals, had a great influence on several artists, as did his exhibitions. For example, after reading *Lino-Cuts* in Melbourne, the Australian artist Eveline Syme was inspired to travel to London to study with Flight. After leaving London, Syme, along with Ethel Spowers and Dorrit Black, was instrumental in bringing linocuts to Australia through exhibitions, publications, and lectures, thus continuing their influence.

The 1930s can be seen as the prime of the linocut movement, yet attention waned as the decade progressed. As Europe was increasingly menaced by Fascism and political refugees arrived in Britain,[102] taste turned toward pure abstraction, Surrealism (especially after the 1936 *London International Surrealist Exhibition*), and a romantic realism based on portraiture and landscapes.[103] Members of the Grosvenor School also began pursuing other interests, both personal and artistic. While Tschudi and Andrews would produce linocuts for decades, others abandoned the practice—and printmaking in general—such as Power in 1938, when he ended his partnership with Andrews and returned to his family. That same year, Andrews left London and moved to the Hampshire woods, fearful of the looming conflict; when war arrived, she was conscripted and worked in a shipyard. There, she met her future husband, with whom she would emigrate to Canada, where she made prints that reflected her new home, such as *Coffee Bar* (fig. 29), and taught local artists the linocut technique. Flight was also fearful and in 1938 wrote a letter to Tschudi describing his concern about the rising forces of Fascism in Europe, declaring, "it is too terrible and we could all be so happy if only there were a few people in power who weren't absolutely mad."[104] His London studio was bombed during the Blitz in 1941 and most of its contents were destroyed; in 1947, Flight had a stroke that left him unable to make prints. Tschudi, who returned to Switzerland in 1935, served in the Swiss Women's Auxiliary Military Service (FHD) during the war. She continued to produce linocuts, but her style became more abstract, a result, she told Flight, of the war preventing her from creating optimistic images.[105] Tschudi's linocut *London Buses* of 1949 (fig. 30) depicts a city that had recently survived a second world war and a barrage of bombing. It is more figurative and representational than her early works or that of the other Grosvenor School artists, such as Flight's *Speed*, with its bright red buses flying down a distorted Regent Street. In Tschudi's print and the related drawings, the buses appear more solid and to be moving more slowly, constrained by the

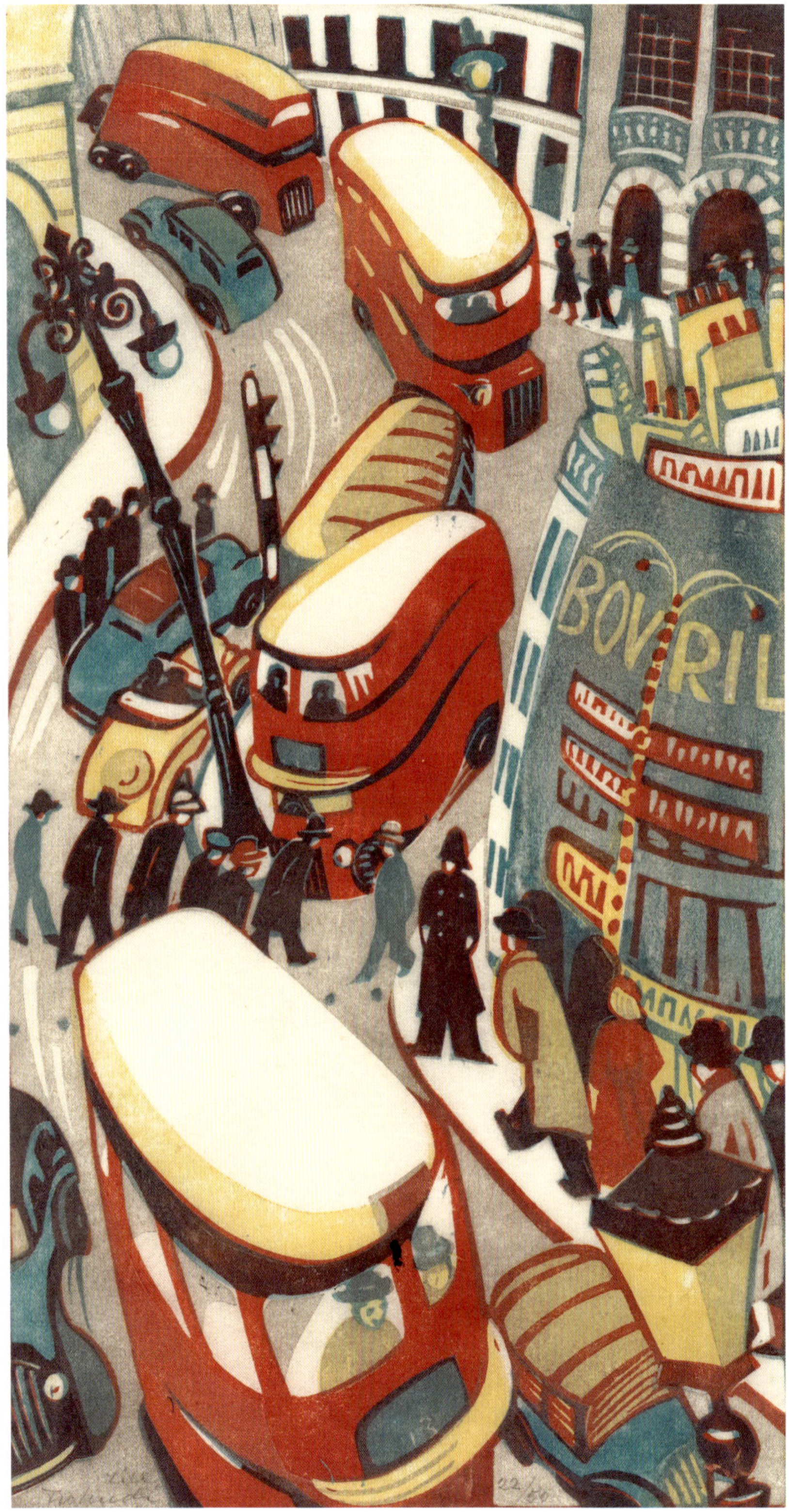

Fig. 30 **Lill Tschudi** (Swiss, 1911–2004). *London Buses*, 1949. Linocut on Japanese paper, image 13 7/16 x 7 1/8 in. (34.1 x 18.1 cm). The Metropolitan Museum of Art, New York (2019.592.513)

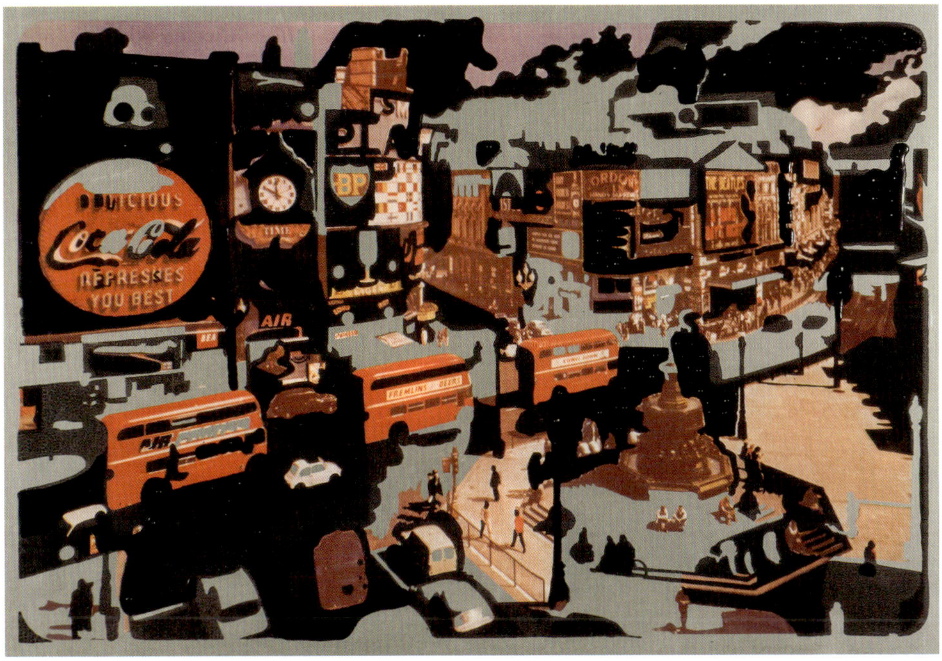

Fig. 31 **Dieter Roth** (Swiss, 1930–1998). Untitled from *6 Piccadillies*, 1969–70. Double-sided screenprint on offset lithograph from a portfolio of six double-sided screenprints on offset lithographs with a screenprinted box, $19\,^{5}/_{8}$ x $27\,^{1}/_{2}$ in. (50 x 70 cm). Courtesy Hauser & Wirth and Dieter Roth Foundation, Hamburg

congested street, while somnolent figures in overcoats plod in an orderly file on the sidewalks underneath a sign promoting "Bovril," a British meat extract. Set in Piccadilly Circus in the direction of Regent Street, this image of everyday life in a busy London seems to anticipate the Swiss artist Dieter Roth's *Piccadillies* series, which he began in 1968 and continued in various forms and configurations for several years (fig. 31). Roth, like Tschudi, adopted a bird's-eye view to show a stream of red buses in Piccadilly Circus traveling on expanded boulevards under giant billboards for Coca-Cola, Guinness, British Petroleum (BP), Air India, and other such advertisements for multinational corporations. Using an image derived from a picture postcard, Roth presented a view of London again transformed, and with it, concepts of modernity.

Through their linocuts, the Grosvenor School artists captured both the optimism and anxiety of the interwar years in Britain. Their depictions of the everyday and the communal experience reflected new possibilities, as did their pursuit of the democratization of art. In the midst of "the machine age," they embraced craft and the handmade, while also employing a modernist vocabulary. Although the color linocut movement only existed for a little more than a decade, a study of its art and methods, as well as of the utopian beliefs that informed it, encourages a more complex, complicated, and expansive understanding of both the era and modernism broadly considered.

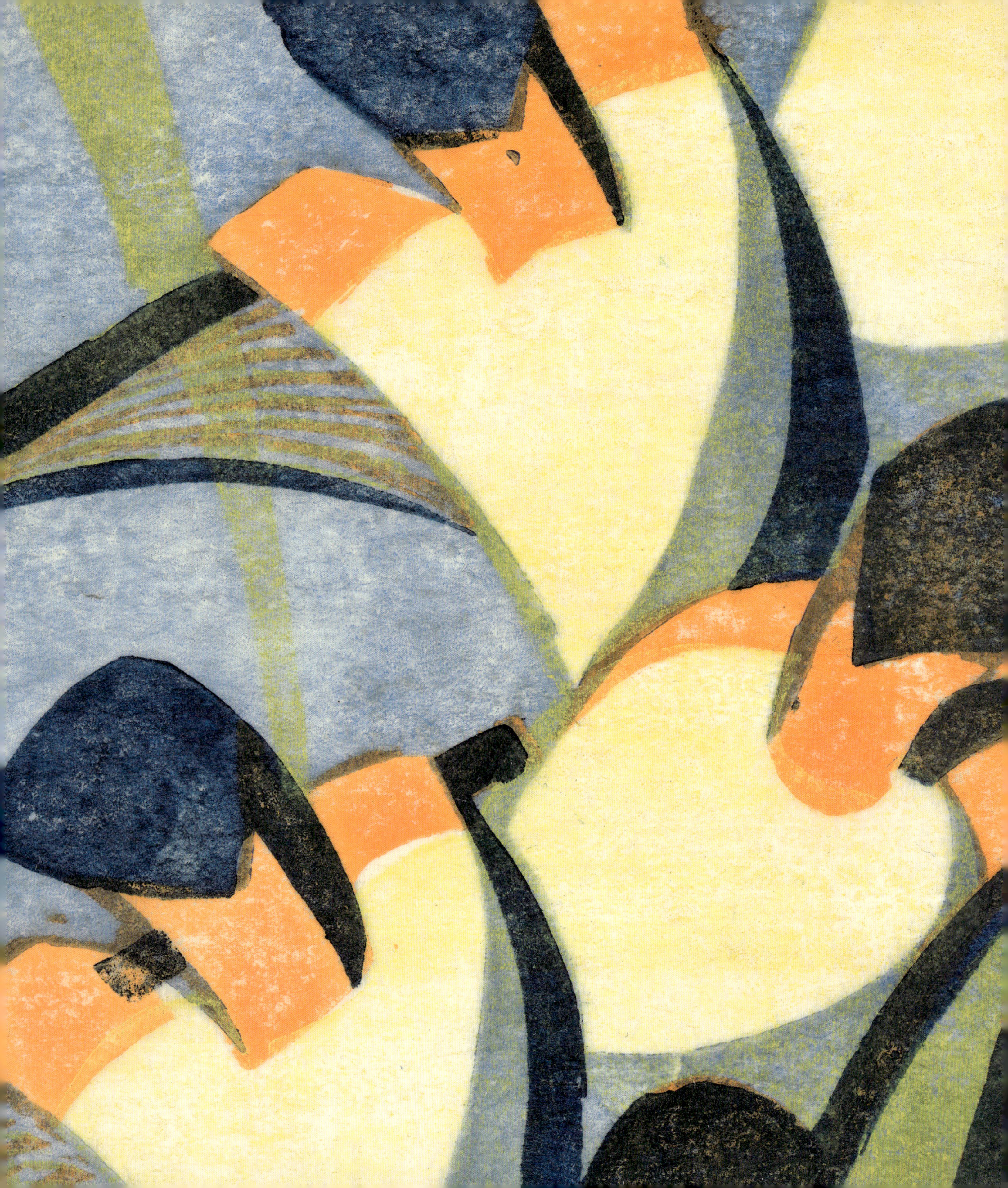

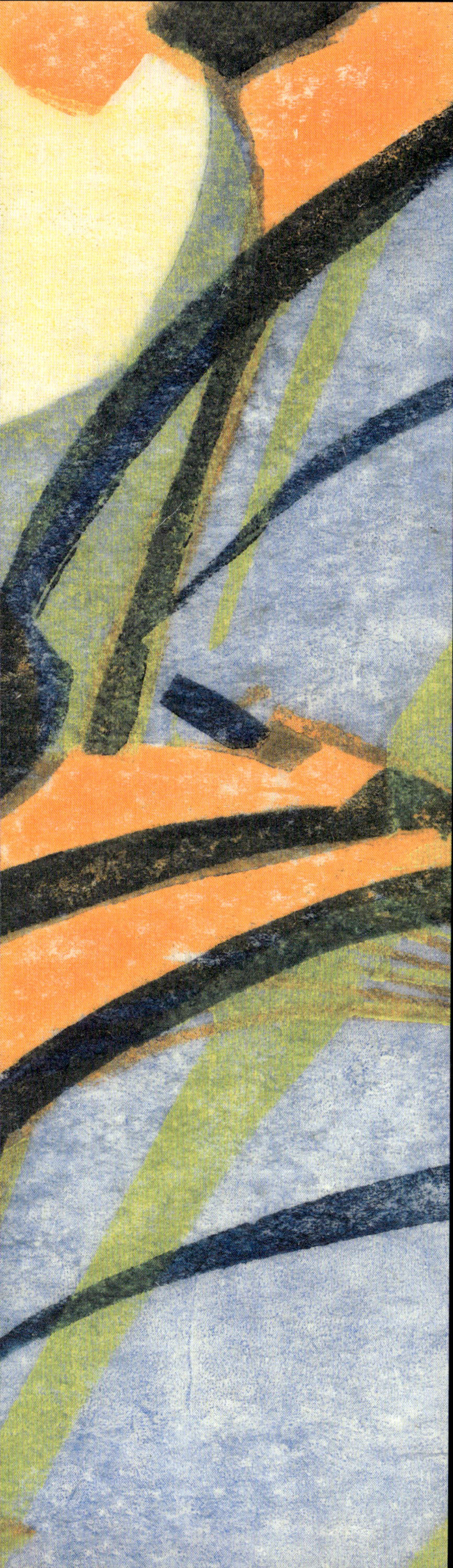

CAPTURING MODERN

Cyril E. Power's *The Eigh*
from Sketch to Print

Rachel Mustalish

During the early twentieth century, modern artists sought new materials and techniques for producing works of art, driven by a desire to make a conscious break from traditional practices. Illustrative of this movement, in 1926, Claude Flight began to teach linocut printmaking at the Grosvenor School of Modern Art in London. There, teachers, students, and staff, including Cyril E. Power, Sybil Andrews, Lill Tschudi, Eileen Mayo, Dorrit Black, William Greengrass, Eveline Syme, and Ethel Spowers, practiced and promoted innovative printmaking techniques that stretched the boundaries of the medium to produce works that married their materials and processes with their artistic philosophy.

Flight's 1927 and 1934 instruction manuals on the linocut, *Lino-Cuts: A Hand-Book of Linoleum-Cut Colour Printing* and *The Art and Craft of Lino Cutting and Printing*, introduced the technique to beginners and explained why linocuts—as well as the cutting tools, linoleum, inks, paints, and papers used to make them—were ideal for the creation of modern art.[1] The Grosvenor School artists believed that their use of new materials and methods freed their creative spirit from the confines of past aesthetics, subjects, and processes, resulting in a body of work that was wholly of their time: the "experience of to-day in the technique of to-day."[2] An examination of Power's remarkable print *The Eight* of 1930 (p. 133), and the sketches and preparatory drawings he executed for it, illuminates how Power strove to depict the dynamism of modern life not only through his composition and color choices but also by exploiting the unique technical properties of the linocut.

A linocut, also called a linoleum cut or linoleum print, is created by carving a design into a block of linoleum; the uncarved areas left in relief are inked and then printed onto a support, often paper, to produce a print. Linoleum, a floor covering invented in the mid-nineteenth century, is made from solidified linseed oil mixed with fillers and pigments and often mounted on wood or strong canvas. In comparison with wood or metal, two materials commonly used for creating relief prints, linoleum is significantly softer and thus easier to carve, and inexpensive. Individuals can also print linocuts by hand without expensive, large, complicated equipment, such as a printing press, or the need for a professional printer. These factors led Flight and others to praise the linocut as a printing technique that was accessible to people across a wide range of skill levels, including children; this quality aligned with the Grosvenor School's belief that art could be made outside of the academy system, where, liberated from the old ideas that governed artistry, artists would find greater creative freedom.

While the basics of linocut printmaking seem simple, the works created by the Grosvenor School artists were anything but. The production of their prints required remarkable skill in understanding not only how to cut the blocks, layer the forms, and balance the colors but also how to use oil paints and printing inks in nuanced ways and to pull prints by hand onto the very thin, tissue-like paper that these artists preferred, in editions up to sixty.[3] As in many other multicolor printing processes, linocuts were formed with one color per carved block. Flight advocated that the number of blocks be kept to a minimum (typically three or four). This was a departure from the process employed for some late nineteenth-century color lithographs, which used as many as forty stones or blocks to compose an image. Grosvenor School artists rejected the older practice, believing that it had been enlisted to produce images that mimicked other media, such as watercolor or oil painting, and that linocuts should openly and unabashedly embrace the process by which they were made.

A prime example of the technique is Power's *The Eight*, which depicts a team of rowers in movement along the River Thames, likely by Hammersmith Bridge in London, near his studio at this time.[4] The title refers to a rowing event in which eight persons, each with one oar, row in synchronization to propel a low, narrow boat across the water. Boat racing was a popular fixture of urban culture in the early twentieth century; there were numerous rowing clubs along the Thames, and every Saturday of the season, races were watched by tens of thousands of spectators. Rowing featured in newsreels and subway advertising, and even the American film star Buster Keaton, in his 1927 film *College*, took a position in an eight boat.

The Eight is composed of four colors: orange, yellow, and two different blues. Power layered these colors in a particular order during the printing, deploying his great knowledge of pigments and inks to realize a broad color range with a small number of blocks. For example, Power used the yellow block to give the inside of the boat and the shirts of the rowers some texture and to reduce the overall contrast between the white paper and the printed areas. He conveyed the disturbance of the water with a very bright acid yellow-green, achieved by printing the more translucent yellow over the light blue, imparting to it a greenish hue. In the curved bowlike forms that emanate from the pivot points of the oars, he added thin strips of yellow and orange at slightly different angles to produce both regular

Fig. 32 Photomicrograph (12x magnification) of *The Eight* (p. 133), showing how Power layered color and positioned the lines to convey the visual effects of movement

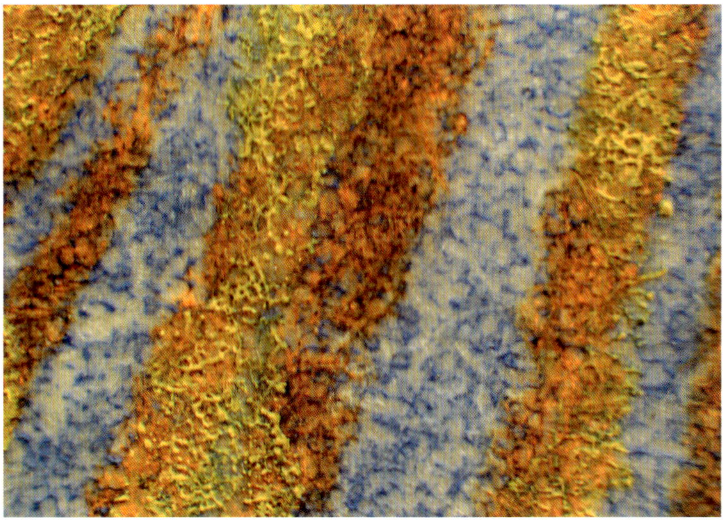

and irregular alignments that emphasize the rowing action (fig. 32). He then augmented the dynamic interaction of these thin lines with a pale blue tone to increase the variability of their color and density, making the space appear to vibrate and thereby strengthening perceptions of speed, sound, and motion.[5]

The two blues, one a Prussian blue and the other a synthetic ultramarine, were printed from separate blocks. The pale blue (Prussian blue) dominates *The Eight*; it was intentionally applied in a variable fashion to capture the dappled watery background on which the rowing takes place. The dark blue (synthetic ultramarine) accents parts of the boat and the swooshes that run along the backs of the left-side rowers, highlighting their motion as they prepare to stroke. In The Met's impression of *The Eight*, the rowers' heads on the left side are blue while those on the right appear black, a detail that reflects Power's ability to capture how the angle of the light modulates color. A close examination of the print reveals that the artist achieved this black hue by layering all four pigments—the orange, the yellow, and both blues; no black ink is present in the print. In total, Power produced seven distinct colors from the four inks, a consequence of careful planning, skillful block carving, practiced printing, and a highly developed understanding of how pigments interact when printed.

Oil paints and oil-based printing inks were central to the Grosvenor School's practice. These materials helped distinguish their output from another popular form of color printing that was having a resurgence in Europe during the early twentieth century—Japanese woodcuts. These prints and the Japanese-inspired works that followed (part of a trend known as Japonisme) used a water-based printing ink that soaks into the paper, creating even fields of color and adding no texture to the resulting image, which can resemble a watercolor. In contrast, the oil-based printing technique produces vivid colors, considerable tonal variation across a single printed field, and a palpable texture, seen dramatically in Power's linocut *Speed Trial* of about 1932 (p. 122), which also depicts movement and sound. Moreover, in another conscious departure from the Japanese woodcut, Grosvenor School artists rarely used a key block, a printing element that defines forms and outlines fields of color. Although Flight did employ this mechanism in such works as *Speed* of 1922 (p. 114), he and others typically relied only on the colored fields and their clever overlapping to create a design.

To achieve a coherent image from multiple carved blocks, it was essential to have a system of transferring the design to the linoleum that would ensure that, even without a key block, forms and colors were properly aligned. Artists developed various methods to guarantee that each block/color would line up correctly during printing, a process called registration. Andrews used a carbon-paper system to copy the same design to each block prior to carving. Flight and Tschudi used an incision method by which the preparatory design was laid onto a block and then traced with a pencil or stylus that indented the soft linoleum to indicate where the block should be cut (fig. 33a, b). Tschudi also oiled her paper before tracing to

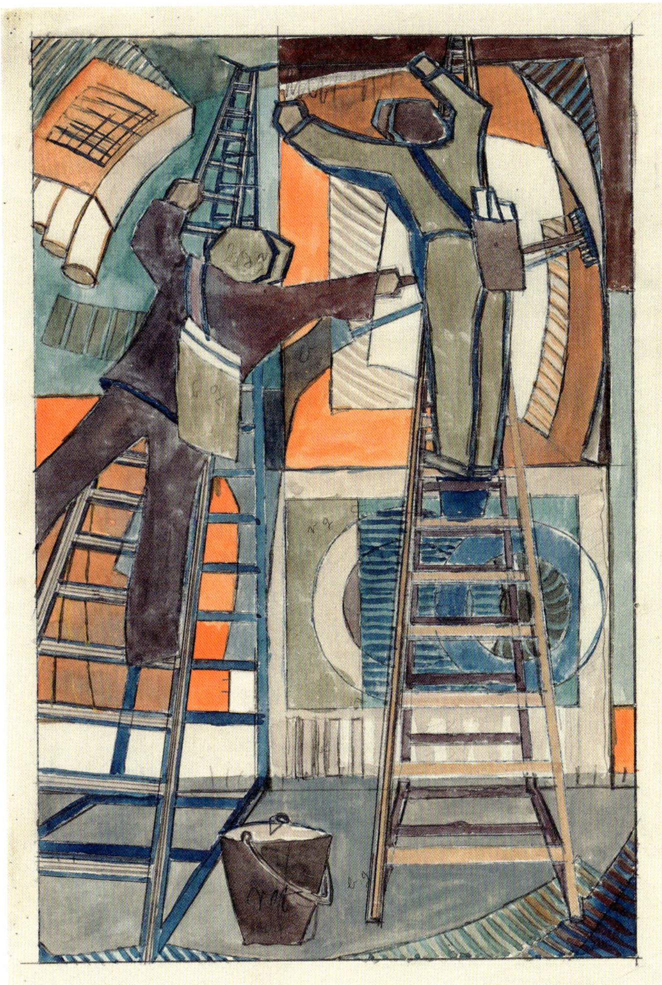

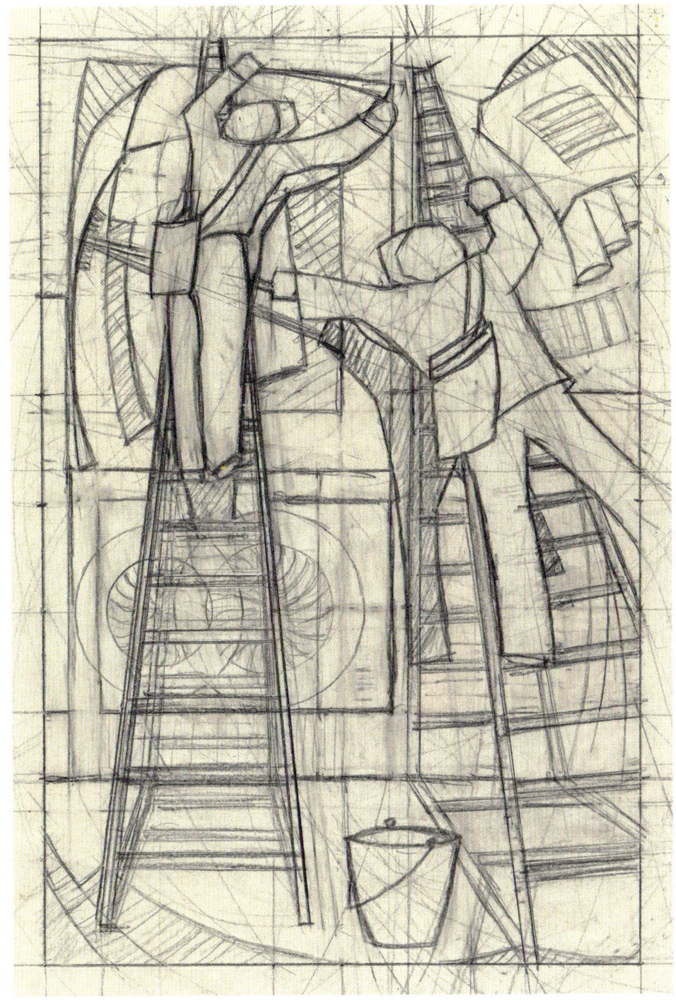

enable continuous contact between the design drawing and the linoleum, and to increase the transparency of the paper, allowing her to see her intended colors as she transferred the design.

To print the final work, oil paint or oil-based printing ink was applied to each carved block with a brayer (a small handheld roller). Flight preferred a brayer made from gelatin, but rubber was also common. The Grosvenor School artists did not mix colors before applying them to the block but rather used them straight from the tube (albeit occasionally thinned). Paper was pressed down upon the inked block, and because proper placement was essential, the carved blocks always included a mark, divot, or notch that ensured the precise alignment of the paper and permitted the correct registration of colors and forms. The back of the paper was rubbed with a baren (a flat disk wrapped in leather or another natural material), the back of a spoon, or one's hands and fingers to cause the ink to

Fig. 33a, b Recto and verso of a preparatory drawing for printing. A preliminary pencil sketch was done first. Watercolor and gouache were added on the recto to suggest the color scheme for printing. Hard, dark pencil lines on the verso were used to transfer the design and the color fields to the linoleum block. **Lill Tschudi** (Swiss, 1911–2004). Preparatory drawing for *Sticking Up Posters*, 1933. Watercolor, pencil, and gouache on Western paper, 13 ⅛ x 9 in. (33.3 x 22.9 cm). The Metropolitan Museum of Art, New York (2019.592.538)

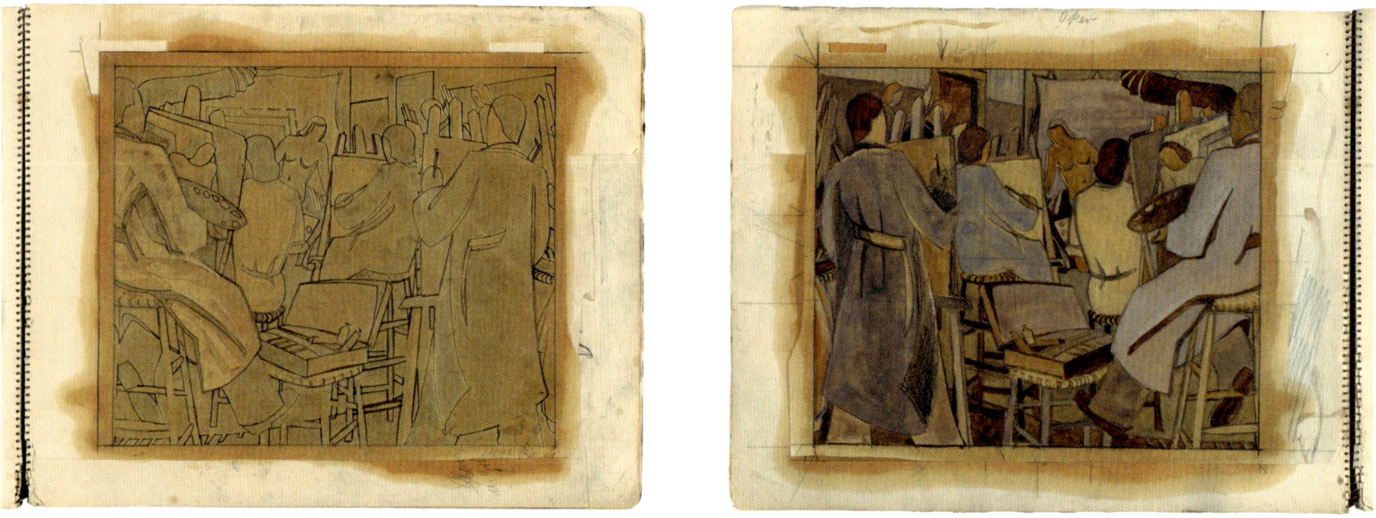

Fig. 34a, b Recto and verso of a preparatory drawing for *Life Class*, 1938, showing how Tschudi cut registration notches in the corners of the drawing and oiled the sheet (now aged and appearing as brown blotches) to increase the transparency of the paper. These steps helped her to transfer the design to the linoleum block properly and insure alignment. **Lill Tschudi** (Swiss, 1911–2004). Sketchbook, 1937. Watercolor, pencil, and gouache on Western paper. The Metropolitan Museum of Art, New York (2019.592.531)

transfer to the paper support. This process was repeated for each block/color that was necessary to make the print. The amount of pressure applied dictated the amount of printing ink that transferred to the paper and therefore the density of the color in the final print.

Many Grosvenor School artists kept notebooks and/or sketchbooks that provide clues to their complex working processes and the evolution of their prints. Tschudi's extant sketchbooks reveal not only how she tested her subjects, from quickly dashed line drawings of a gesture or shape to fully worked-out designs complete with color, but also how she prepped her designs for transfer and created guides for block cutting (fig. 34a, b). Power also swiftly put down sketches and logged his printing activities, but unfortunately, after his death in 1951, most of his preparatory material was destroyed.[6] However, a few books of his sketches and notes that were in the possession of Sybil Andrews, with whom he shared a studio in London, have survived. A cooperative endeavor between Power and Andrews, these Print Books, as they are known, document the techniques, materials, and experiments the pair undertook while making their prints.[7] The two artists obsessively recorded information on the number and order of blocks employed, the paper chosen, the type and brand of ink or oil paint used, and the pressure with which each block was printed. The books also contain color samples and cast-off printing samples. It was important to keep such detailed notes because the chemical compositions of different pigments, as well as their method of manufacture, can change the characteristics of inks and paints, resulting in varied appearances, textures, and working properties. In his notations for *The Eight*, Power wrote that he used chrome orange, permanent blue (also known as Prussian blue) from the paint manufacturer and art-supply company Winsor & Newton, pale (a shade of chrome yellow), and Chinese blue (synthetic ultramarine) tube oil paints. These particular choices allowed Power to fulfill his aesthetic goals in his print.

In his notes on *The Eight*, Power specified different degrees of pressure for specific areas—for example, "Chinese blue rather light pressure except for accent of heads" and "Chrome orange medium pressure on oars / fairly heavy on men."[8] Different impressions of this print illustrate the individuality that hand printing made possible; some have areas left in reserve or extra lines,[9] and most feature variations of color intensity of the pale blue background. The ability to alter the saturation of the color during printing further expanded the range of perceived colors that was achievable with a small number of blocks. The saturation and color variations of *The Eight* grant solidity to the rowers, oars, and water, and simultaneously capture the motion and sounds of the boat and the flickering reflections and fleeting shadows across the scene. Another of Power's prints, *The Merry-Go-Round* of about 1930 (p. 144), also displays the finesse of his linocut technique. The foreground of the work—created from two color blocks, one orange and one deep blue—was printed heavily, producing nearly solid fields of color that depict the titular machine and its riders. The surrounding area, representing the noise and motion of the active equipment, printed with the same colors but with less pressure, allowed Power to illustrate both the fixed and the ephemeral. Power often used areas of similar tone to illustrate the transient aspects of motion.

But even before the artists embarked on pulling the final print, they tested and evaluated the colors and textures through a process called proofing. Proofing allowed the artists to analyze each block's printed appearance as they developed the design and color schemes and to understand how the forms and colors manifested as they were layered, as seen in Power's red proof of *'Appy 'Ampstead* of about 1933 (fig. 35). Power also produced trial impressions, which enabled him to evaluate different colorways of his prints, as illustrated by the many versions of *The Tube Station* of about 1932 (fig. 36), which, while printed from the same blocks, have a varied appearance and feel.

While developing the design for *The Eight*, Power made at least ten studies of an eight-man rowing configuration as he worked through issues of light, shadow, gesture, color, and composition. He intentionally selected friable media and thin tissue or tracing-type papers for his preparatory studies. Friable media, which include charcoal, pastel, crayon, and graphite and colored pencils, have little or no binder and function by transferring small particles of color from the drawing implement to the paper via the act of mark making. Power chose thin, finely textured papers for his drawings, which have similar attributes to the higher-quality Japanese paper used for his prints, as they allow light to pass through the colors, imparting a diaphanous nature to the drawing that is particularly critical to simulating the final appearance of the print.[10] By using friable media on these papers, Power could thus predict the transparent and pebbled effect that could be achieved by printing with oil-based media on Japanese paper (figs. 37, 38).[11]

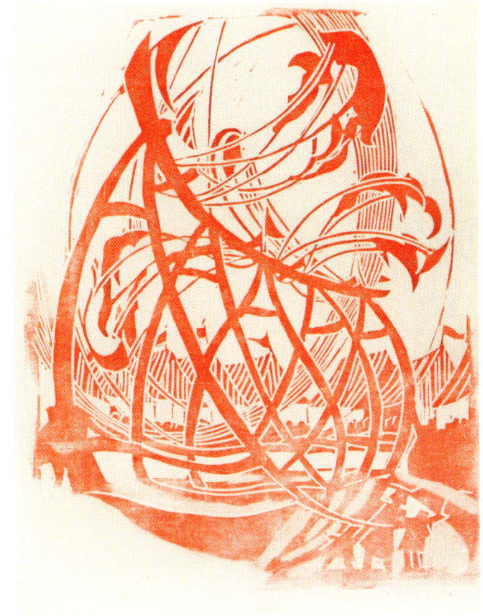

Fig. 35 **Cyril E. Power** (British, 1872–1951). *'Appy 'Ampstead* (proof in red), ca. 1933. Linocut on Japanese paper, image 13 9/16 x 10 13/16 in. (34.5 x 27.5 cm). The Metropolitan Museum of Art, New York (2019.592.17)

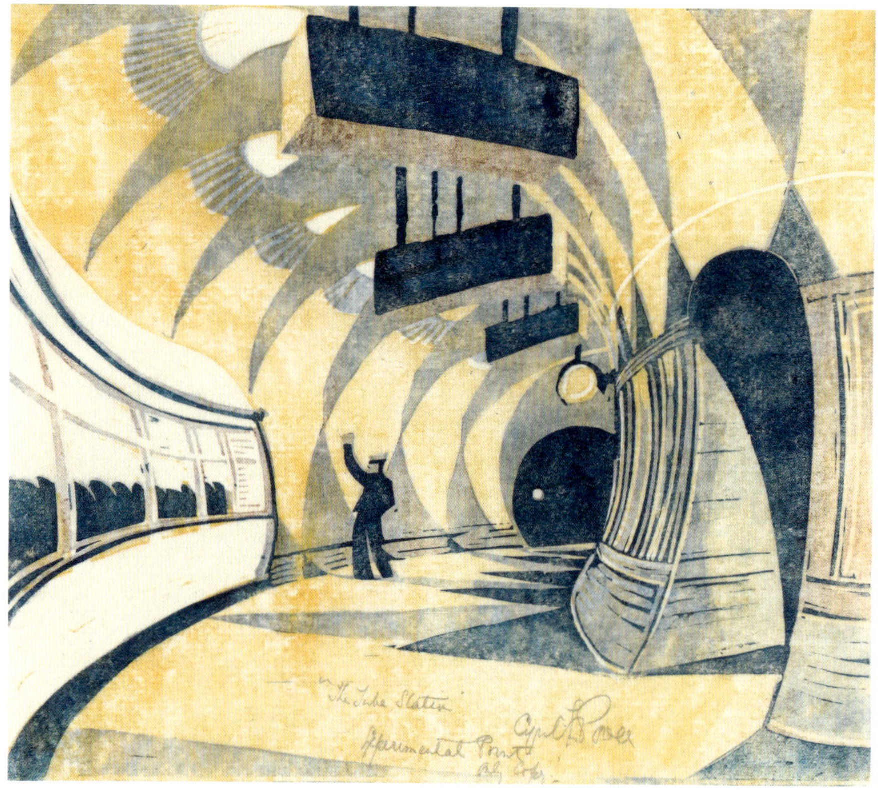

Fig. 36 **Cyril E. Power** (British, 1872–1951). *The Tube Station* (unique experimental proof), ca. 1932. Linocut on Japanese paper, image 10 3/16 x 11 5/8 in. (25.8 x 29.5 cm). The Metropolitan Museum of Art, New York (2019.592.469)

Power captured the nuances of rowing, its effects on the surrounding water and air, and the experience of spectating the sport from several vantage points. One rowing study shows a team of rowers from a low angle; deliberate yet lightly applied graphite pencil lines suggest the figures, boat, and water, while red crayon colors the flesh of the rowers, leaving in reserve and thereby accentuating the typical rowing uniform of a white shirt and shorts (fig. 39). Though the rowers are faceless, Power rendered them in a variety of postures, and he gave the coxswain (the figure who directs the rowing team and steers the boat) his characteristic flat cap and megaphone and bent-arms pose. In a second rowing study, the subject is seen from a river-level perspective; the water and boat are barely articulated, and the figures have become angular blocks—forms that emphasize their mass (fig. 40). Power drew this study with a soft graphite pencil and a red colored pencil, and added deep black ink lines that strongly define the edges of the shapes and the specific details of the scene, such as the oars, megaphone, and boat. In the upper right corner of this sheet, in both pencil and ink, Power made small sketches that convey the bodily gestures of rowers at the moment just before they take one of the large, powerful strokes that drive the boat. Comprising thin, crisp lines, these small sketches have the appearance of mechanical drawings, and they emphasize the machine-like nature of the rowers' movements. They also helped Power, as did most of the black lines in the study, to determine how the blocks should be cut to best capture the forms.

Other drawings portray boats and rowers from above as the subject is rendered in the final print. These images highlight Power's ability to play with the vertical stacking of space. Some of these studies focus on the water and its movement between several boats,[12] while others concentrate on the movements of the rowers.[13] Power executed one drawing for *The Eight* primarily with sweeping strokes made from the side of the pastel stick, which simultaneously produced a crisp line on one side of the stroke and a wide swath of graded color on the other; this action froze the motion that Power was attempting to render (fig. 41). These fields of color dominate the scene and exemplify an integral Grosvenor School idea of defining a design with color masses, rather than lines. This technique is seen in many of Power's preparatory drawings for other prints, such as the studies for *Whence & Wither?* of about 1930 (fig. 42), in which the people, arches, and escalator are composed of fixed masses of motion.

Details in *Study VIII for "The Eight"* (fig. 43), such as the semicircles that appear where the oars enter the water, as well as the circular ripples that form in the disturbed water a few seconds later (visible in the upper left by the boat that is nearly out of frame), highlight Power's desire to render accurately the real-life appearance of his subject (fig. 44). In this study, Power used colored crayons to draw curvilinear geometric shapes that abut and overlap to create the complex composition of rowers, water, and boats. He also employed black ink and graphite pencil lines to work through issues of symmetry in his design and to create hard edges that were vitally important to the later steps of block cutting and printing alignment. In the upper right of this drawing, Power identified the colors he required (red, blue,

Fig. 37 Photomicrograph (12x magnification) of figure 40, showing how Power applied color to achieve a pebbled effect in the preparatory drawing that he would mimic in the final print

Fig. 38 Detail of *The Tube Station* (p. 123), showing how Power could achieve pebbled textures in prints

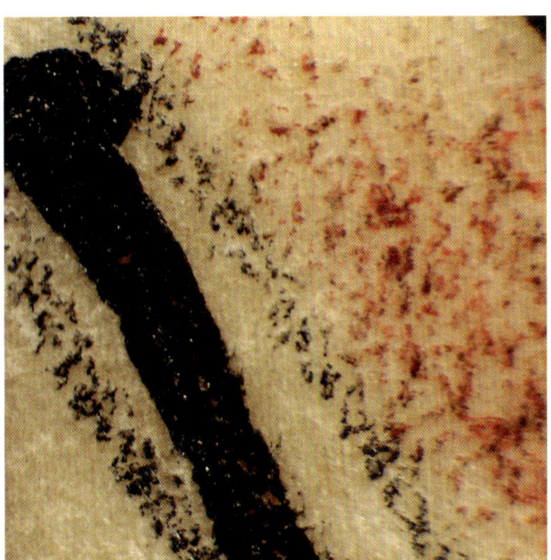

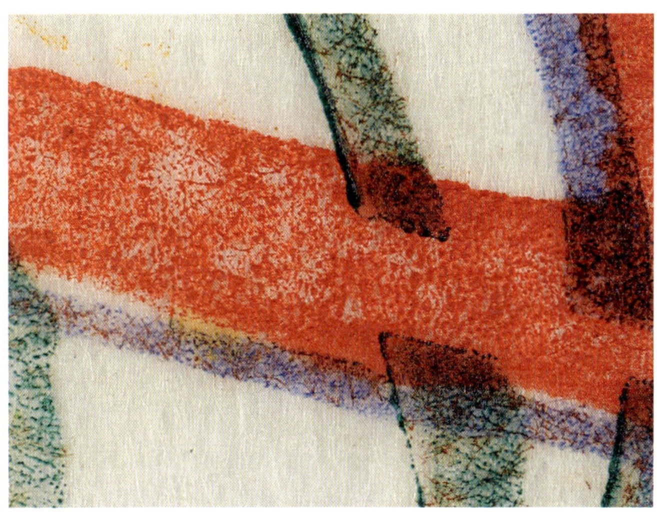

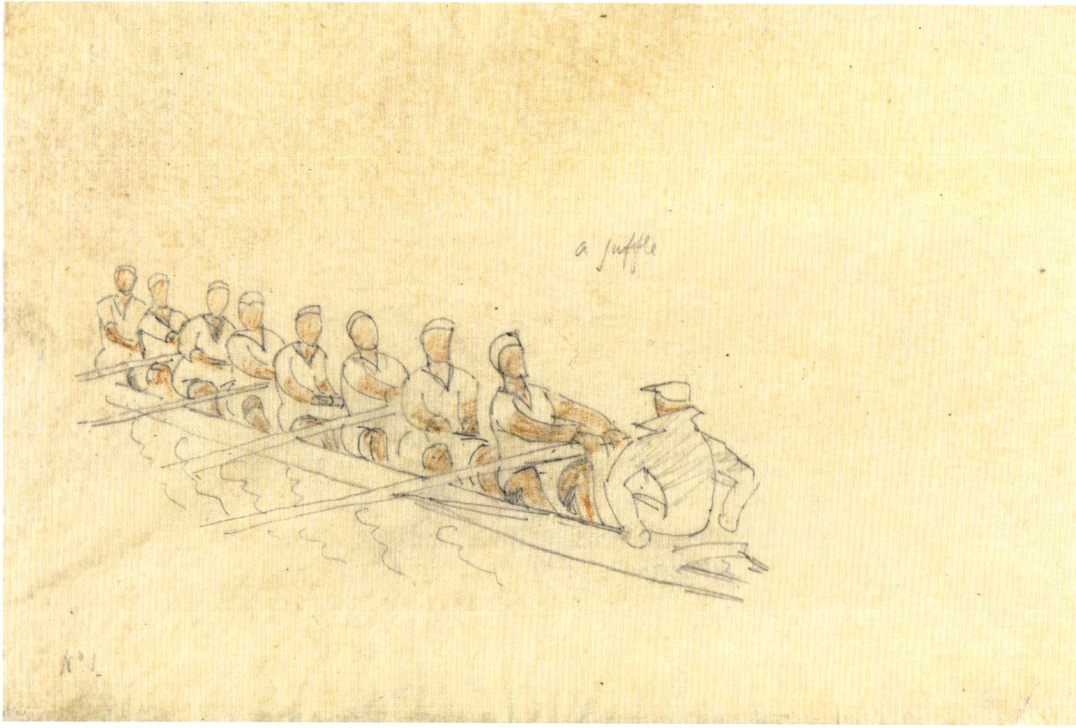

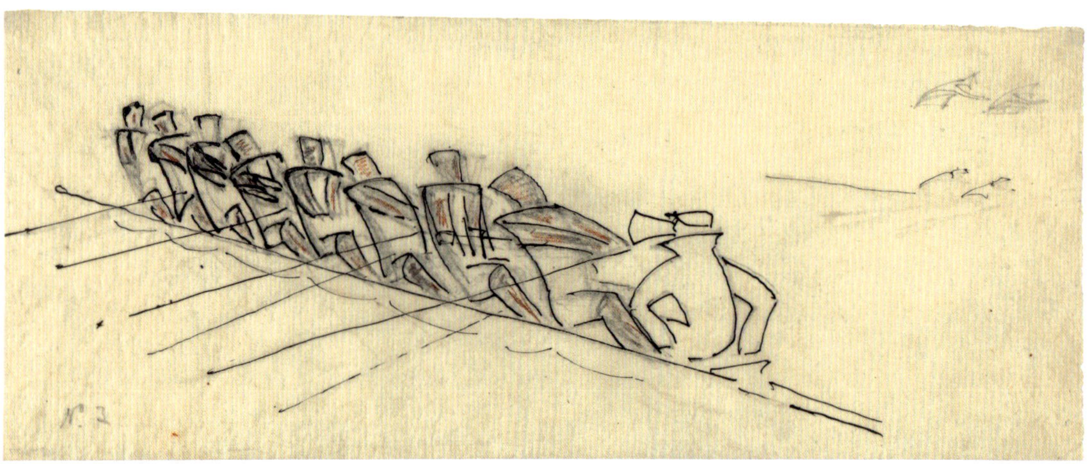

Fig. 39 Cyril E. Power (British, 1872–1951). *Rowing Study*, ca. 1930. Pencil and crayon on tracing paper, 9 15⁄16 x 16 1⁄8 in. (25.2 x 41 cm). The Metropolitan Museum of Art, New York (2019.592.222)

Fig. 40 Cyril E. Power (British, 1872–1951). *Rowing Study*, ca. 1930. Ink, pencil, and colored crayon on tracing paper, 5 15⁄16 x 14 7⁄8 in. (15.1 x 37.8 cm). The Metropolitan Museum of Art, New York (2019.592.223)

Fig. 41 Cyril E. Power (British, 1872–1951). Drawing for *The Eight*, ca. 1930. Pastel on tracing paper, 15 x 10 in. (38.1 x 25.4 cm). The Metropolitan Museum of Art, New York (2019.592.439)

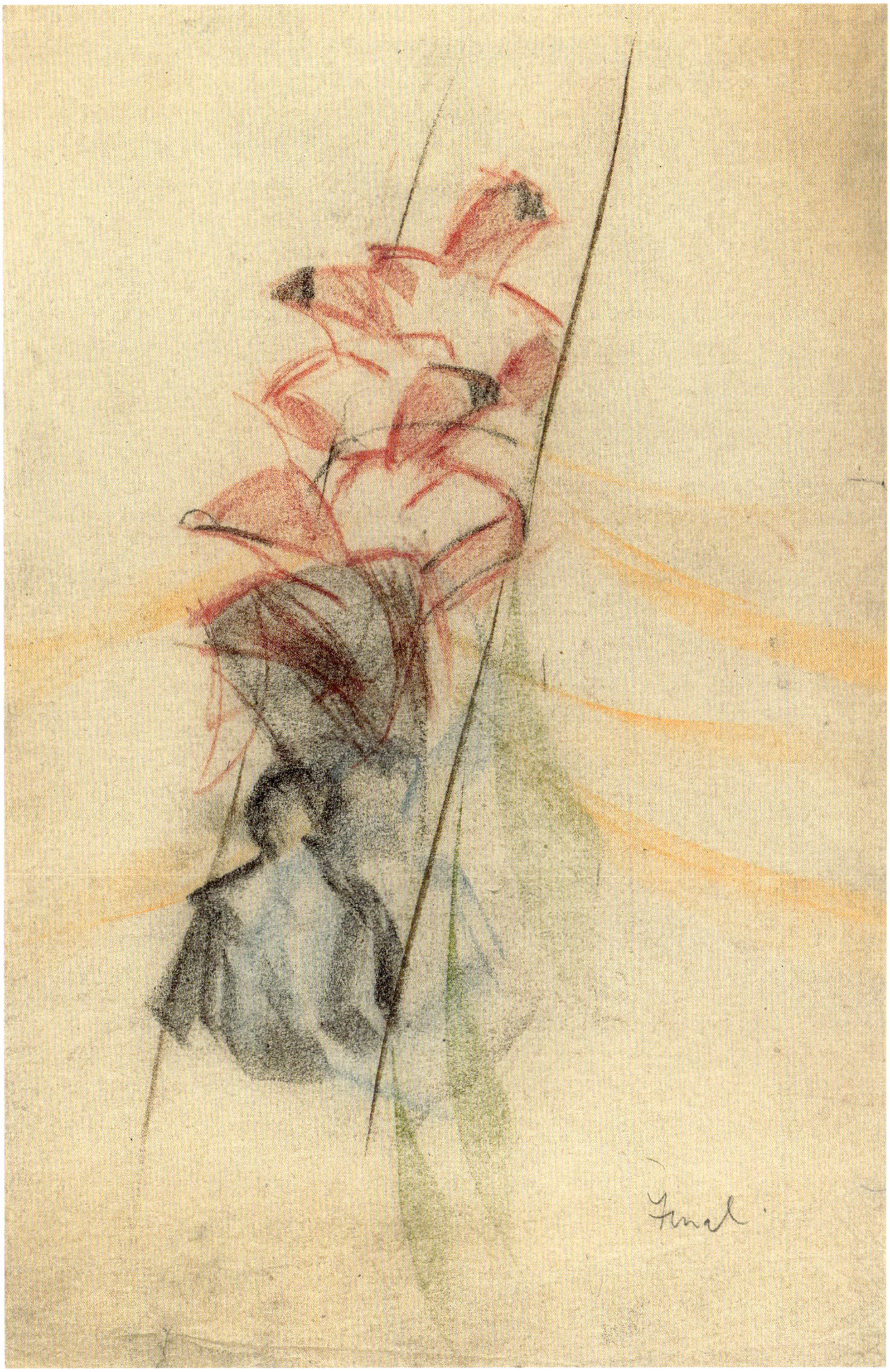

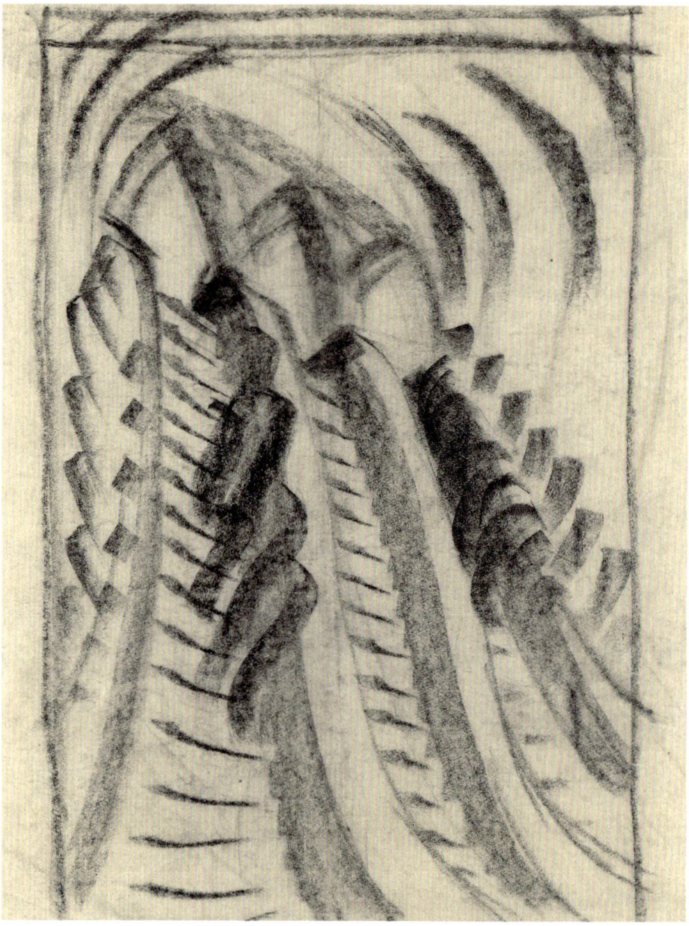

Fig. 42 **Cyril E. Power** (British, 1872–1951). Study for *Whence & Whither?* (Study of escalators IV), ca. 1930. Pastel on tracing paper, image 13 ½ x 8 ½ in. (33 x 21.6 cm). The Metropolitan Museum of Art, New York (2019.592.442)

green, and yellow) and how they should overlap to create the additional shades (brown, orange, purple, and "dark"[14]) he needed to render the subject.

It is interesting to note, however, that the color scheme and the orientation of the subject is different in the final print of *The Eight*, in which Power eliminated the coxswain, cropped the oars, and rotated the viewpoint 180 degrees to focus on the backs of the rowers. In this way, Power draws viewers' attention to the human engine of the rowing endeavor, emphasizing the alternating positions of the rowers' bodies, poised at the moment before they take a stroke. This interest in movement is also found in Andrews's work *Sledgehammers* of 1933 (p. 111), in which the focus is on the people depicted, the motions they make, and the noises they create when working—and not on the object of their hammers, which is out of the frame of the composition.

Power and other Grosvenor School artists created prints that have a unique aesthetic; they are richly colored despite being made with a small number of inks, composed of curving and linear masses, precisely organized, and often printed

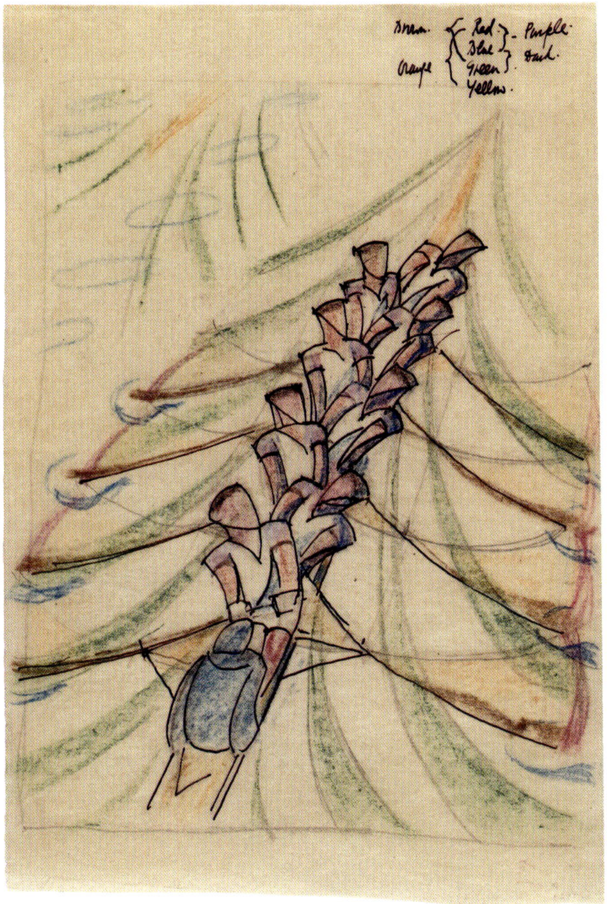

on thin, smooth papers that enhance movement and light effects. Their appearance directly reflects the materials and techniques by which they are made: the soft linoleum allowed for ease in carving long, smooth curves, and the oil-based inks could realize both solid and mottled fields of vivid color. Free of the technical demands of past techniques, the linocut was a perfect vehicle for modern artistic expression. The mixture of the human and the mechanical, inherent in the act of printing that creates these works, is reflected in the subject matter, and it makes each print perpetually thought-provoking. Power's numerous preparatory drawings show how he was able to understand, and analyze, his subject. Power captures a complete experience in *The Eight*: the rowers and the spectator (the viewer of the print) are encompassed in a swirl of sound, light, movement, and color. Yet, it is neither a chaotic nor a nature-driven scene but an organized, constructed, and human-made experience that imposes itself on the modern world, much like the linocut technique itself.

Fig. 43 **Cyril E. Power** (British, 1872–1951). *Study VIII for The Eight*, ca. 1930. Pencil, pen and black ink, and colored crayon on tracing paper, 14 ¹⁄₁₆ x 10 ¹⁄₁₆ in. (37.6 x 25.5 cm). Museum of Fine Arts, Boston, Gift of Johanna and Leslie Garfield (2005.1104)

Fig. 44 Oxford and Cambridge Boat Race, near Hammersmith Bridge, London, 1926–27

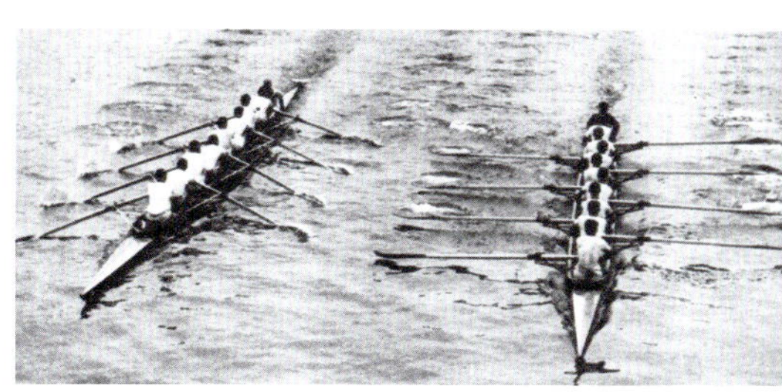

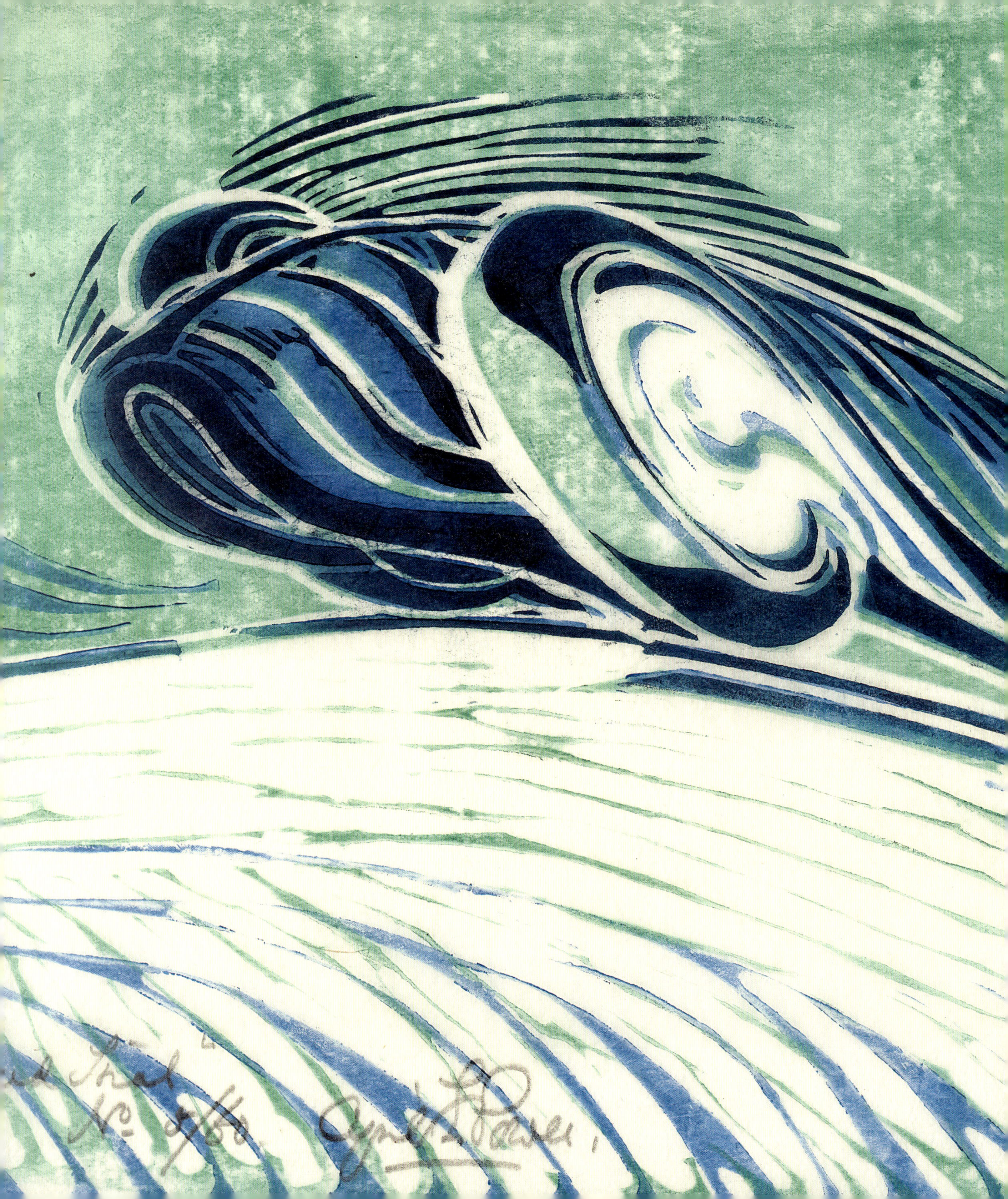
Trial
No 5/60
Cyril E Power

PLATES

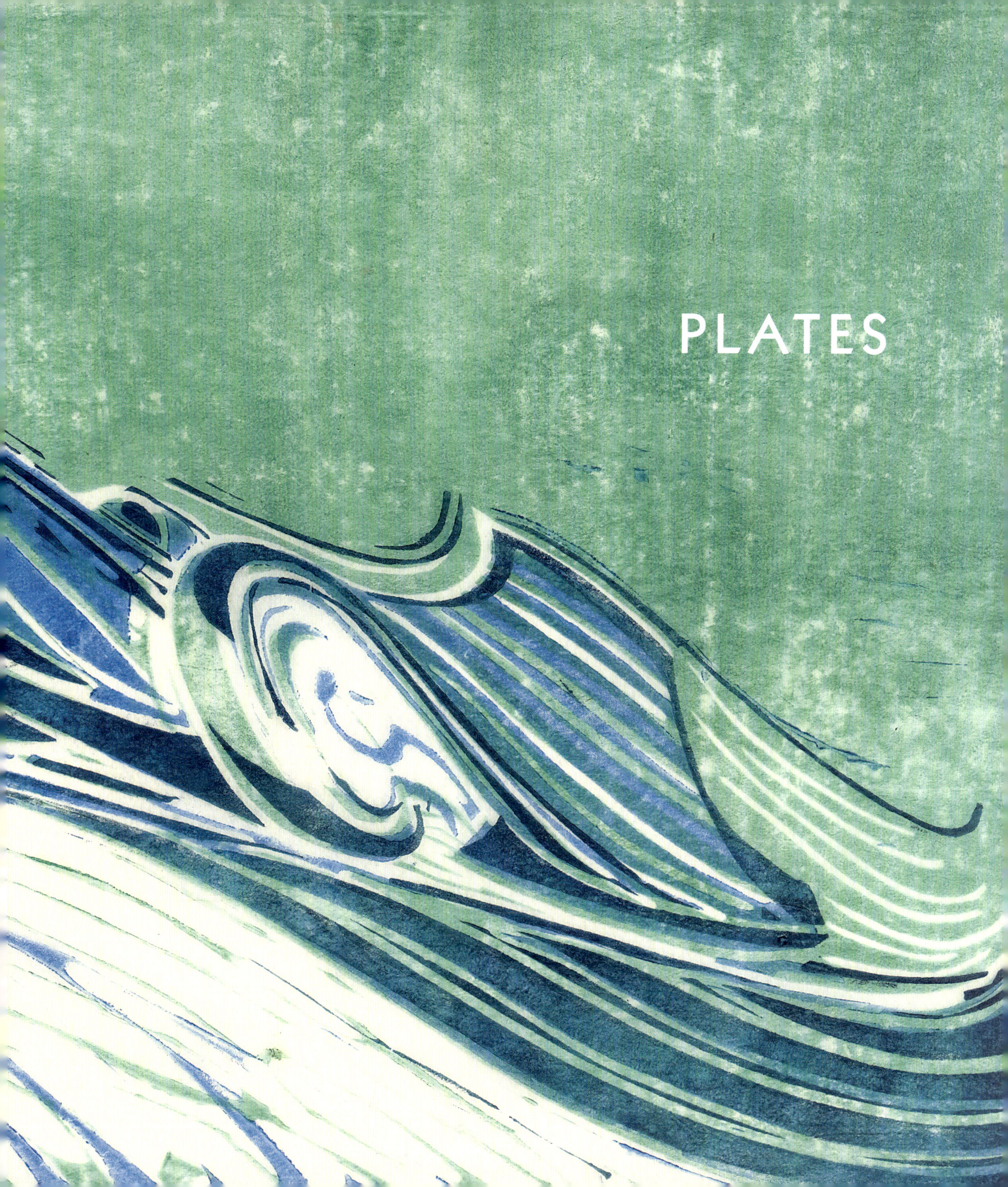

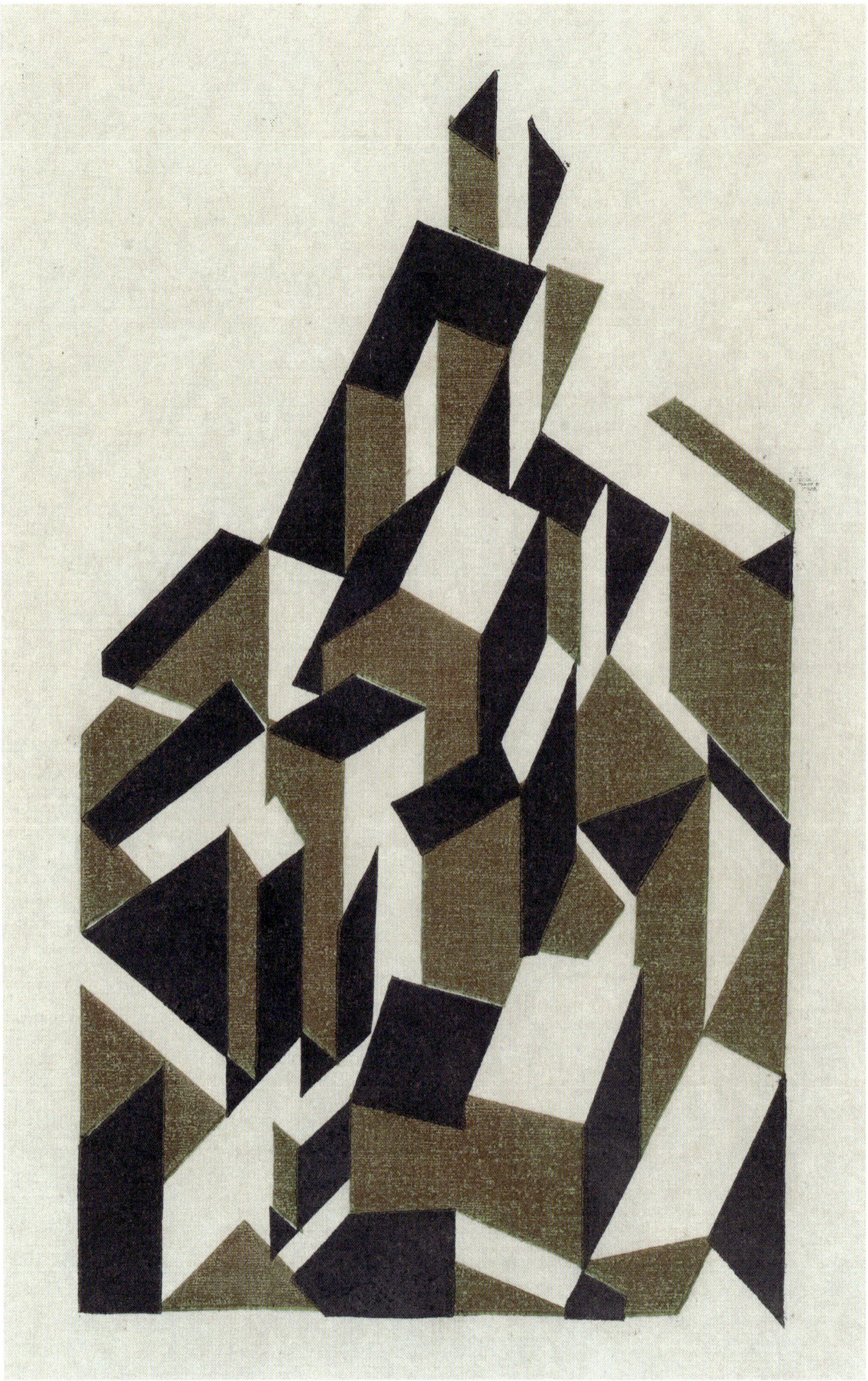

Edward Alexander Wadsworth *Yorkshire Village*, 1914

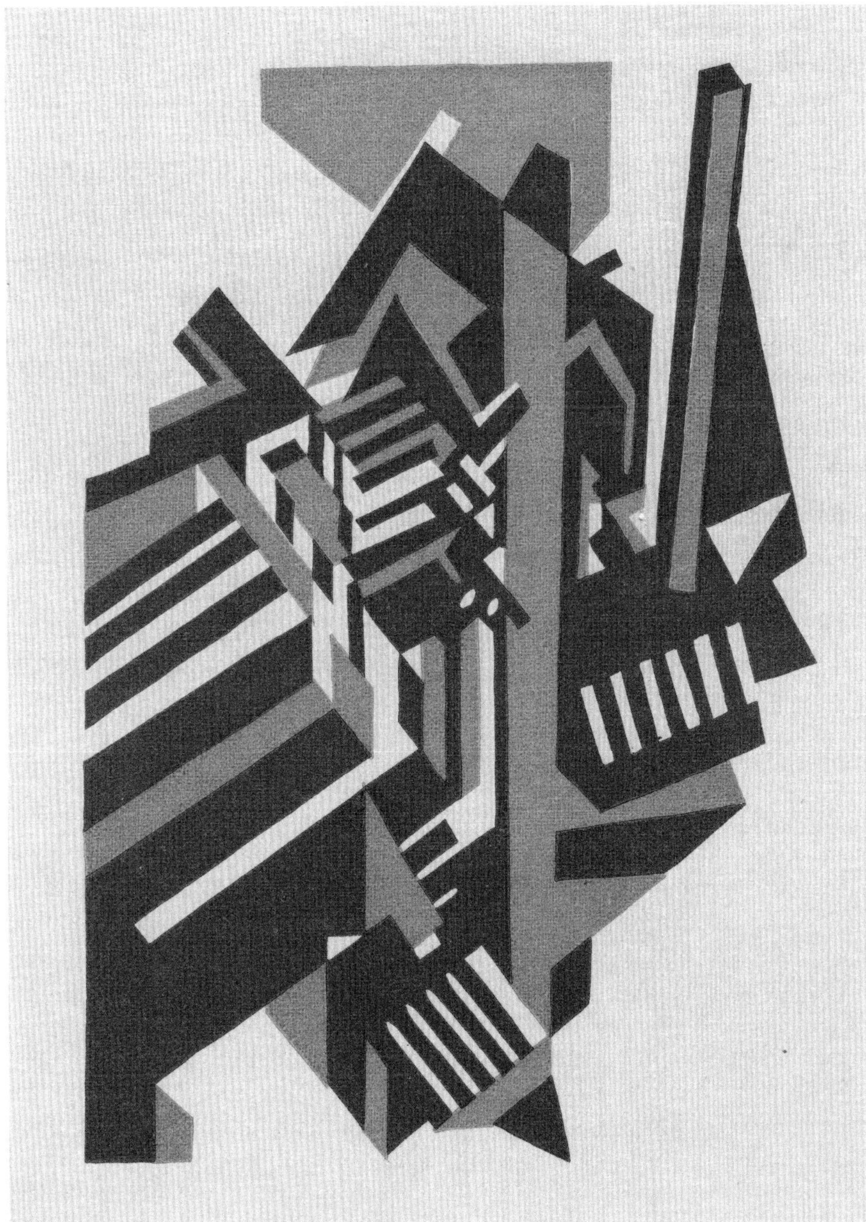

Edward Alexander Wadsworth *Bradford: View of a Town*, 1914

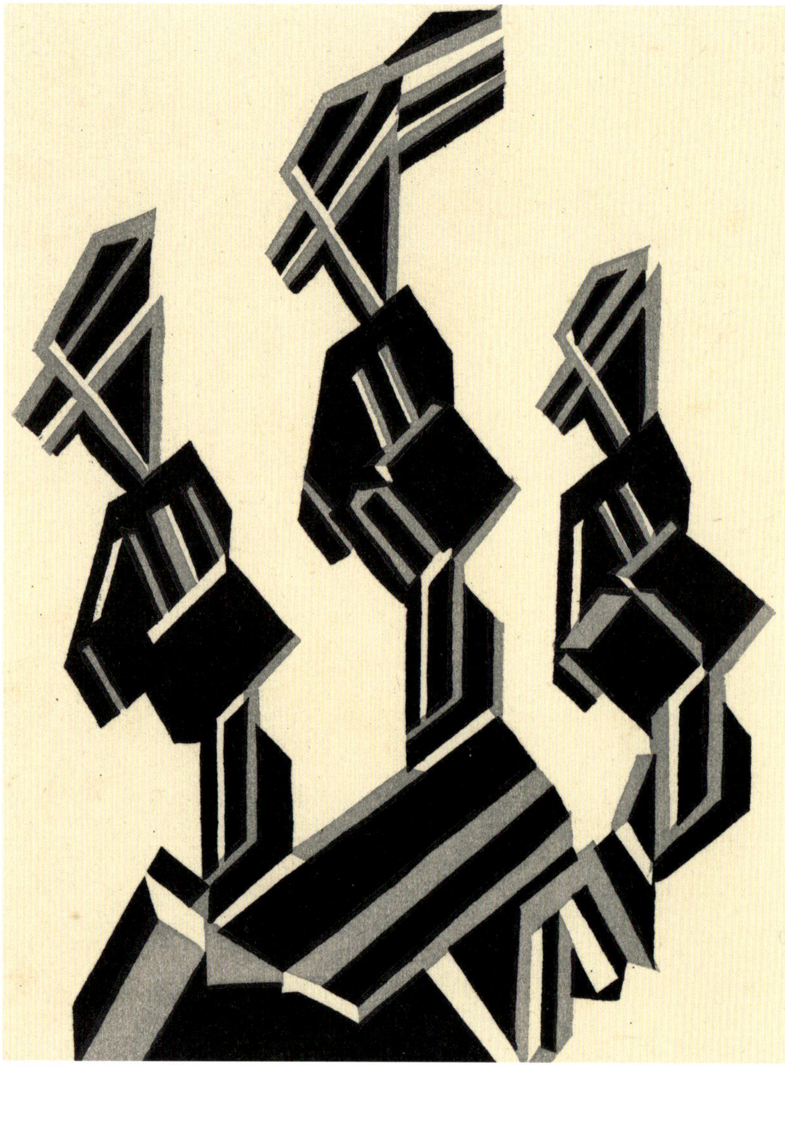

Edward Alexander Wadsworth *Street Singers*, ca. 1914

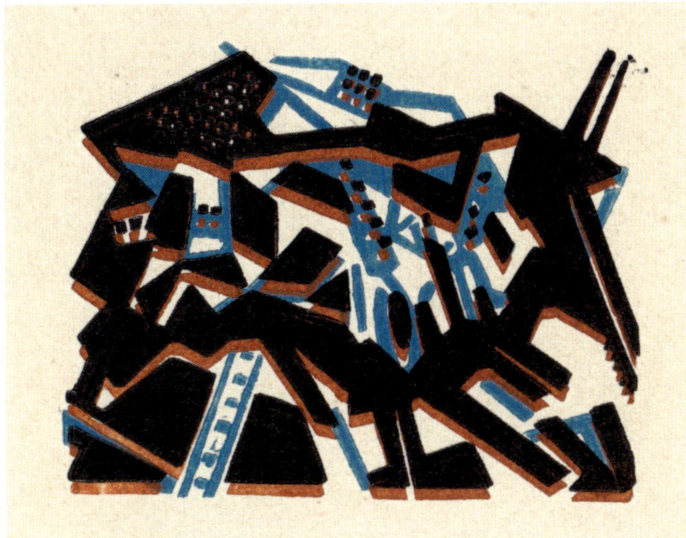

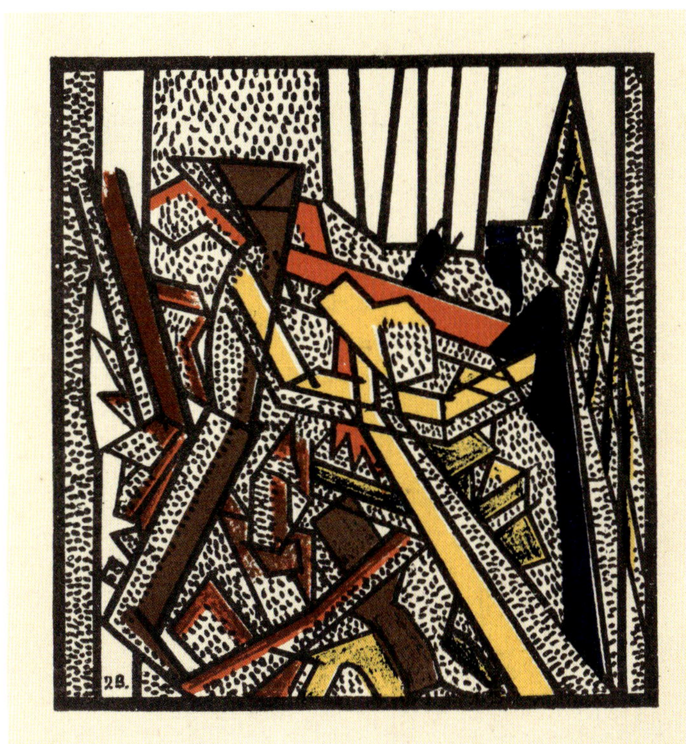

Edward Alexander Wadsworth *Landscape*, 1914

David Bomberg Detail from *Russian Ballet*, published 1919

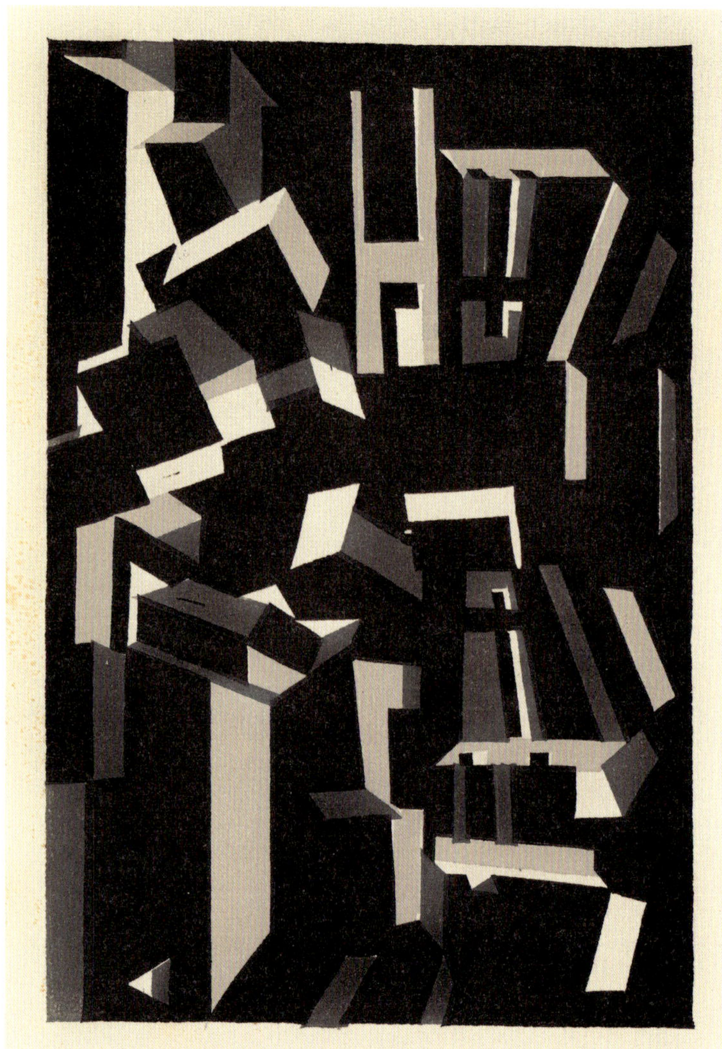

Edward Alexander Wadsworth *Interior*, 1917

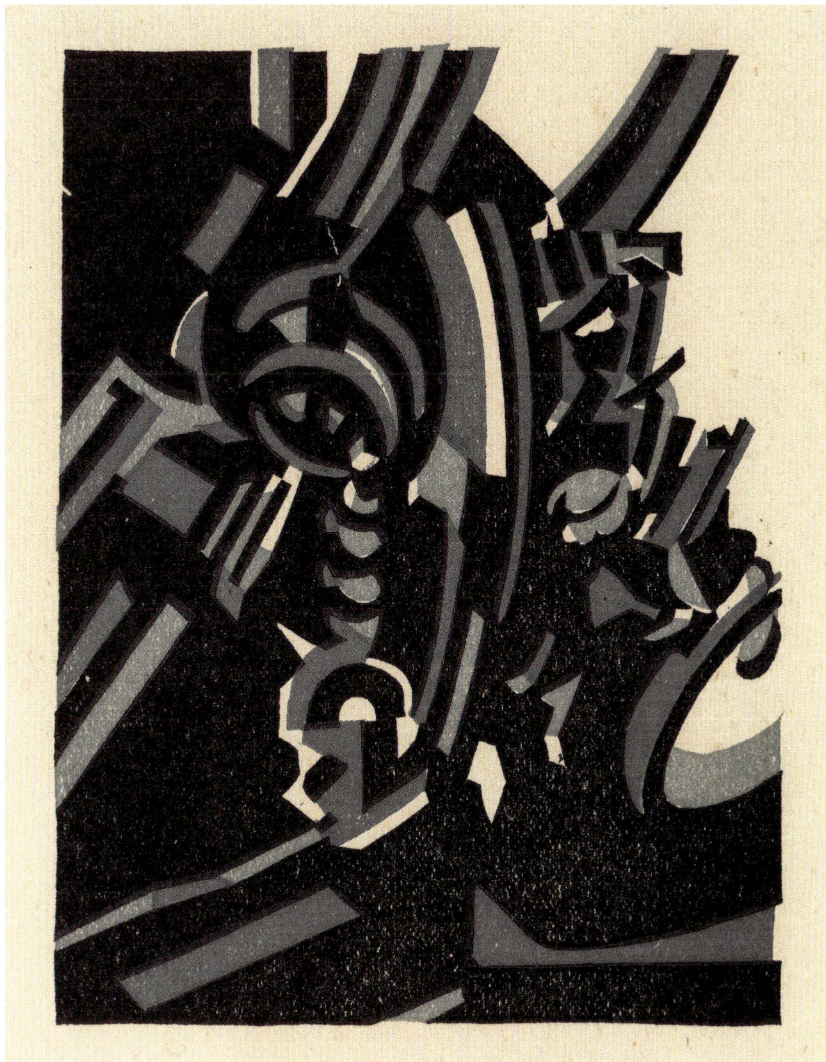

Edward Alexander Wadsworth *Invention*, 1917

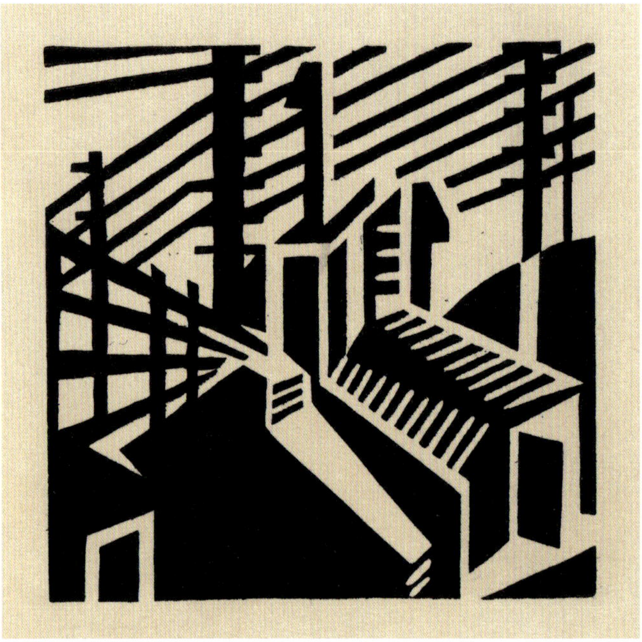

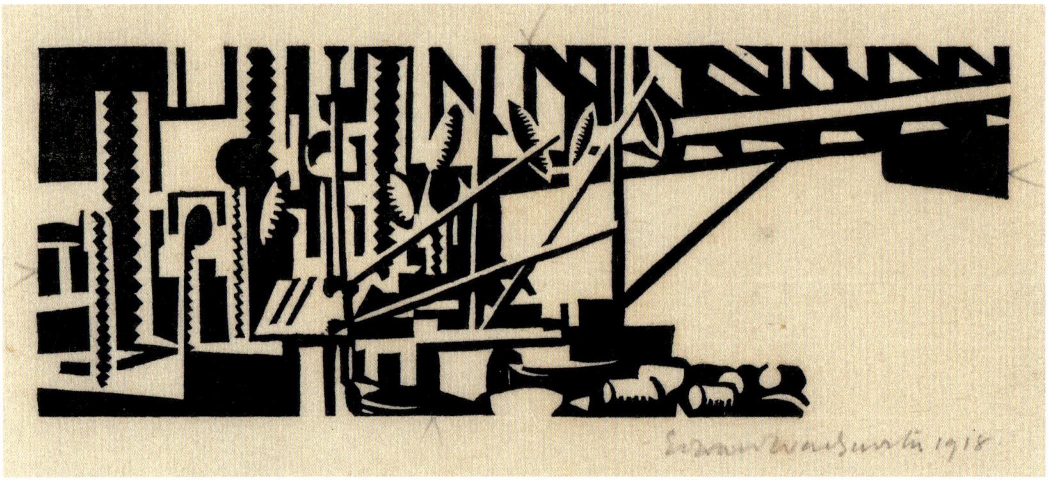

Edward Alexander Wadsworth *Platelayers' Sheds*, 1914/ca. 1918

Edward Alexander Wadsworth *Minesweepers in Port*, 1918

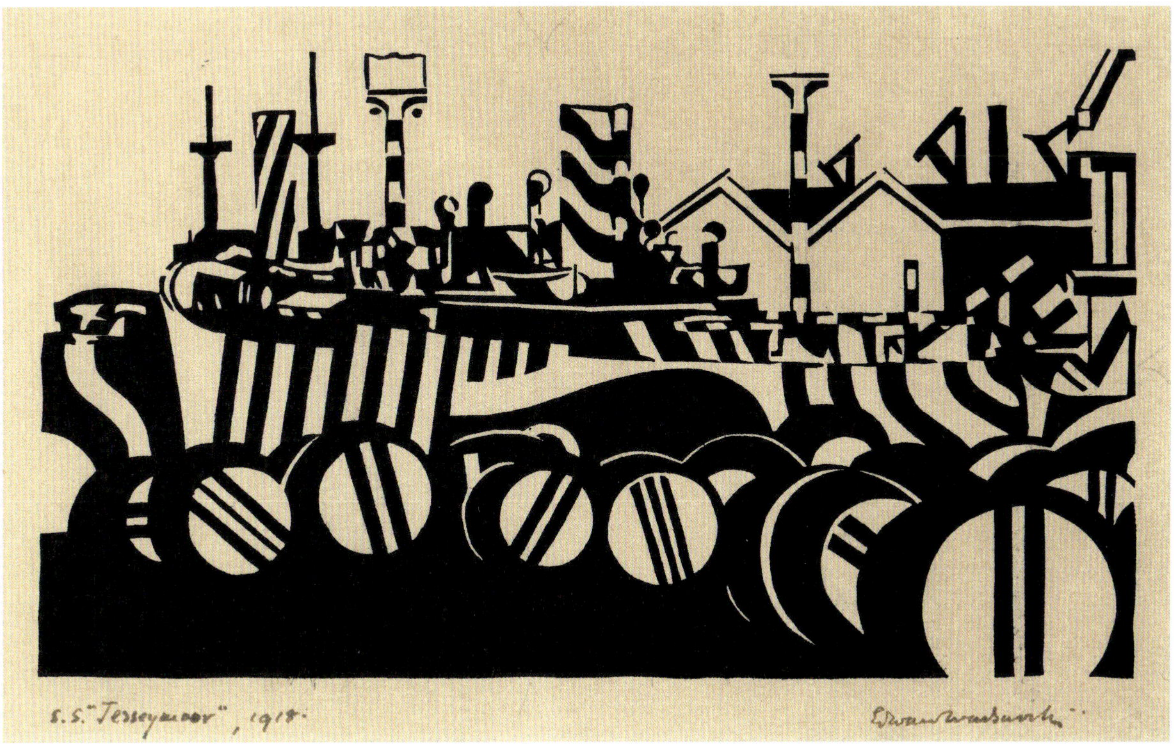

Edward Alexander Wadsworth *S.S. Jerseymoor*, 1918

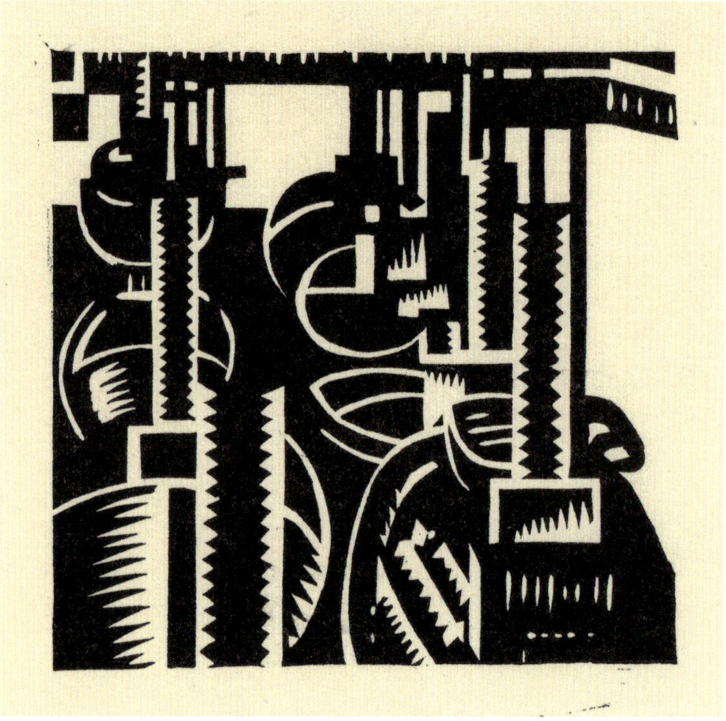

Edward Alexander Wadsworth *Tugs,* 1918

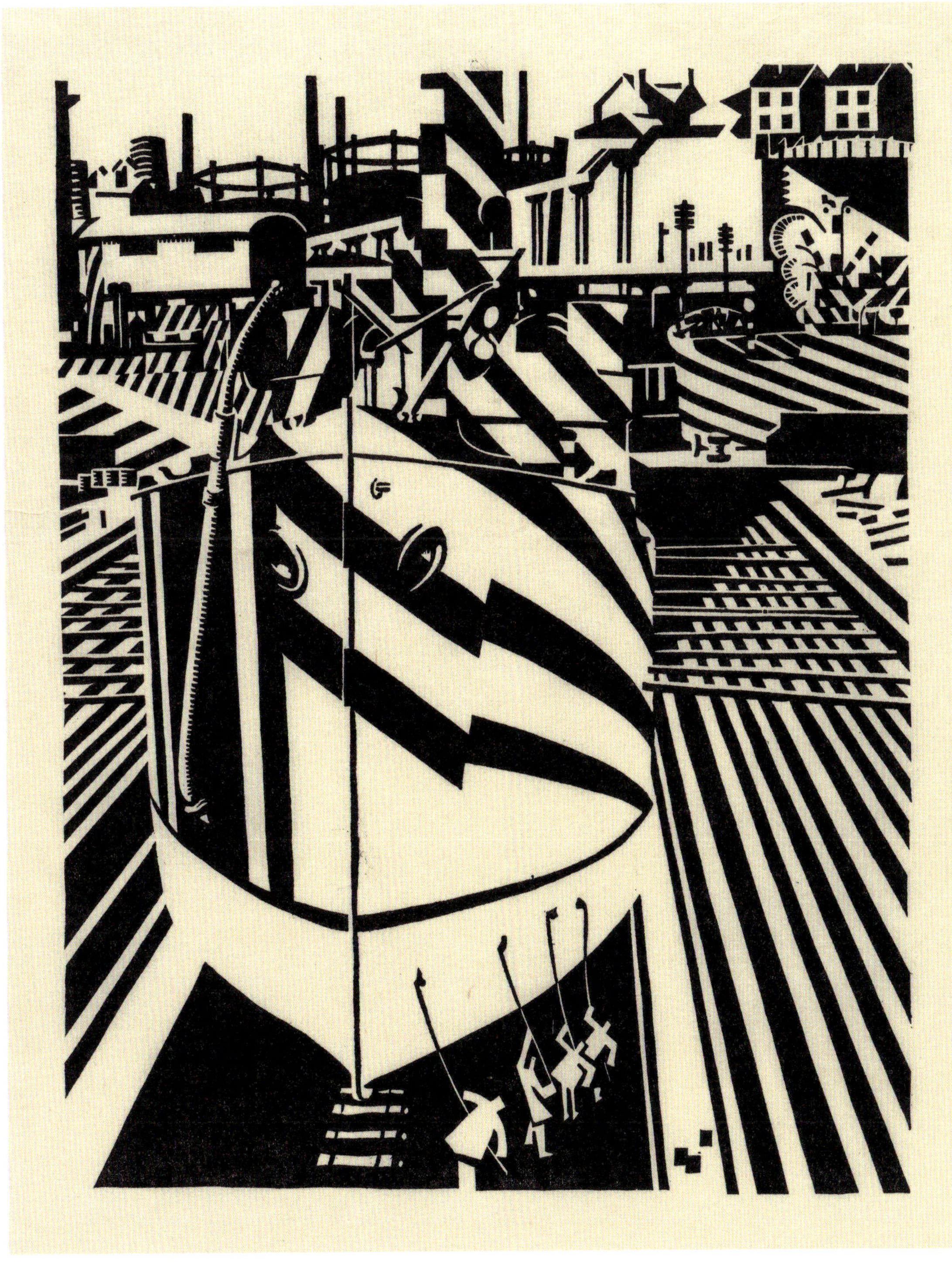

Edward Alexander Wadsworth *Liverpool Shipping*, 1918

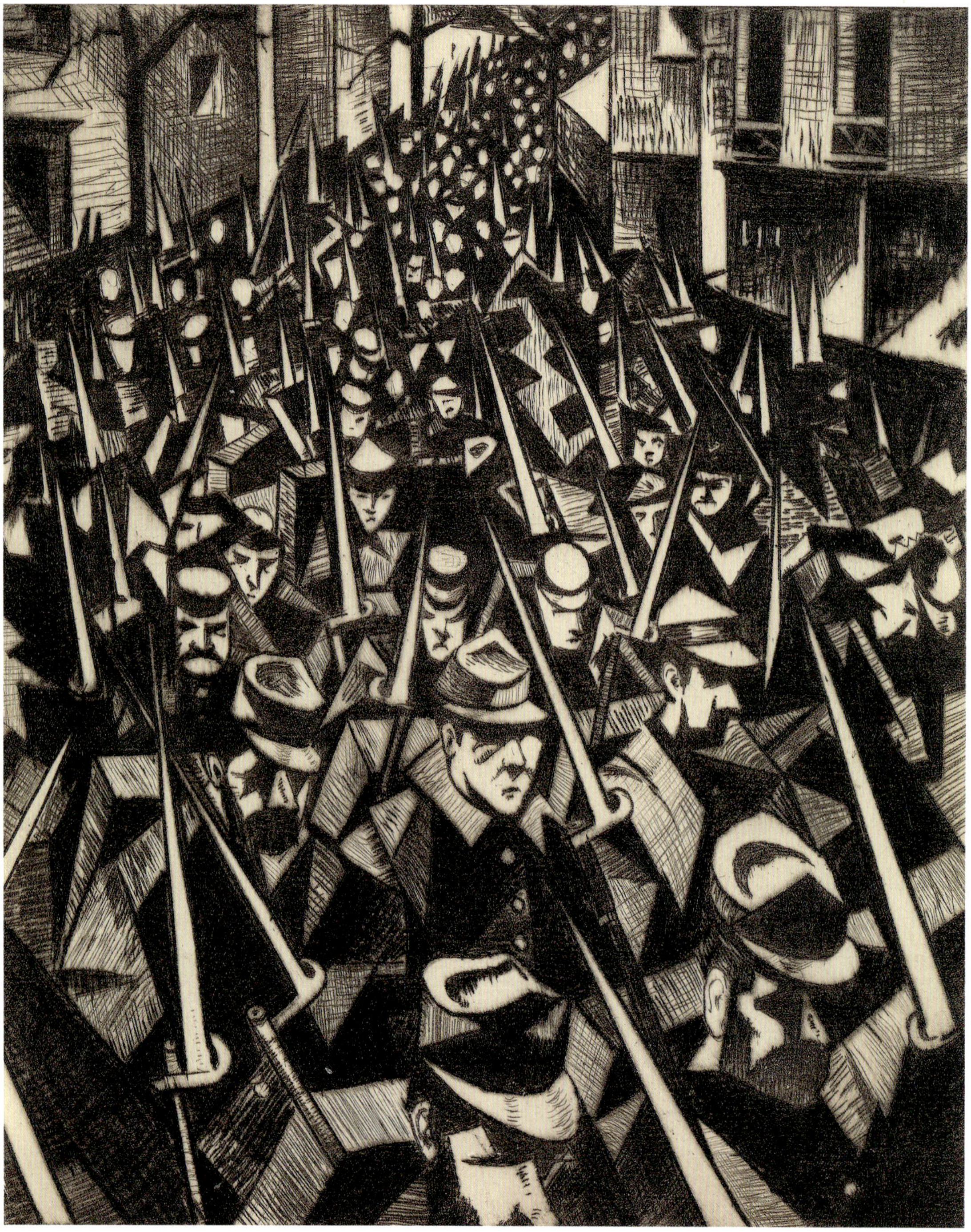

Christopher Richard Wynne Nevinson *A Dawn, 1914*, 1916

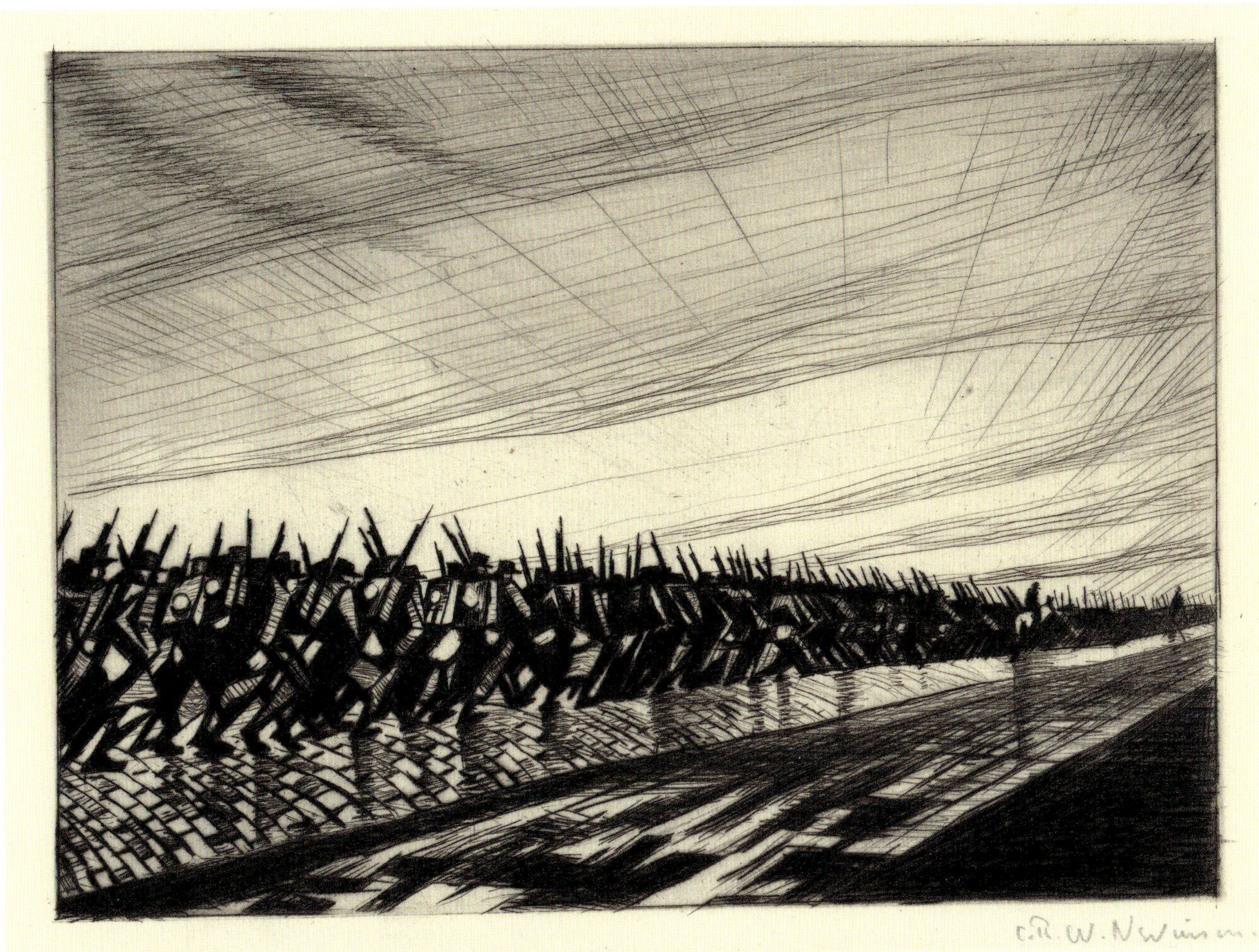

Christopher Richard Wynne Nevinson *Column on the March*, 1916

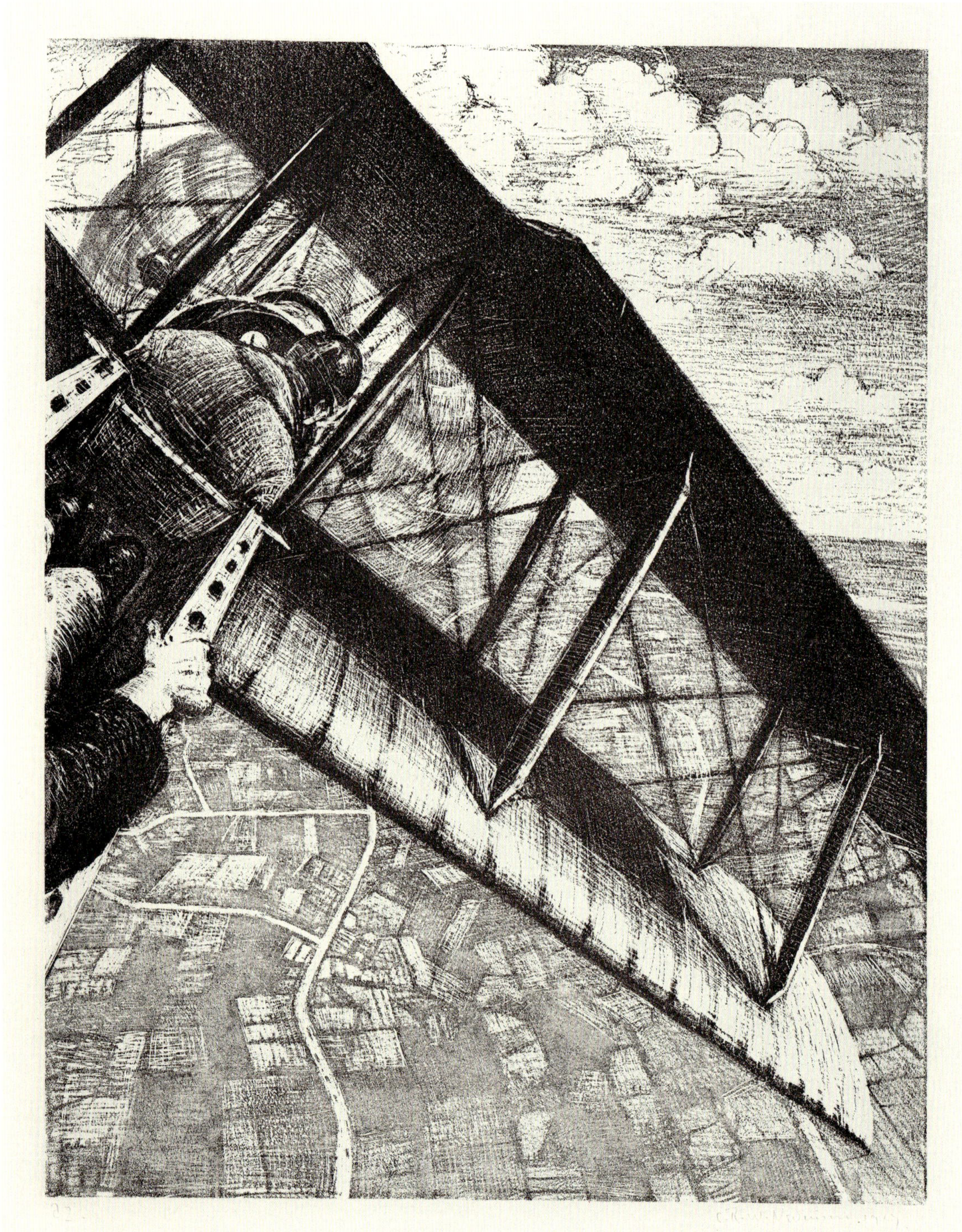

Christopher Richard Wynne Nevinson *Banking at 4,000 Feet*, from *Making Aircraft* portfolio, part of *The Great War: Britain's Efforts and Ideals*, 1917

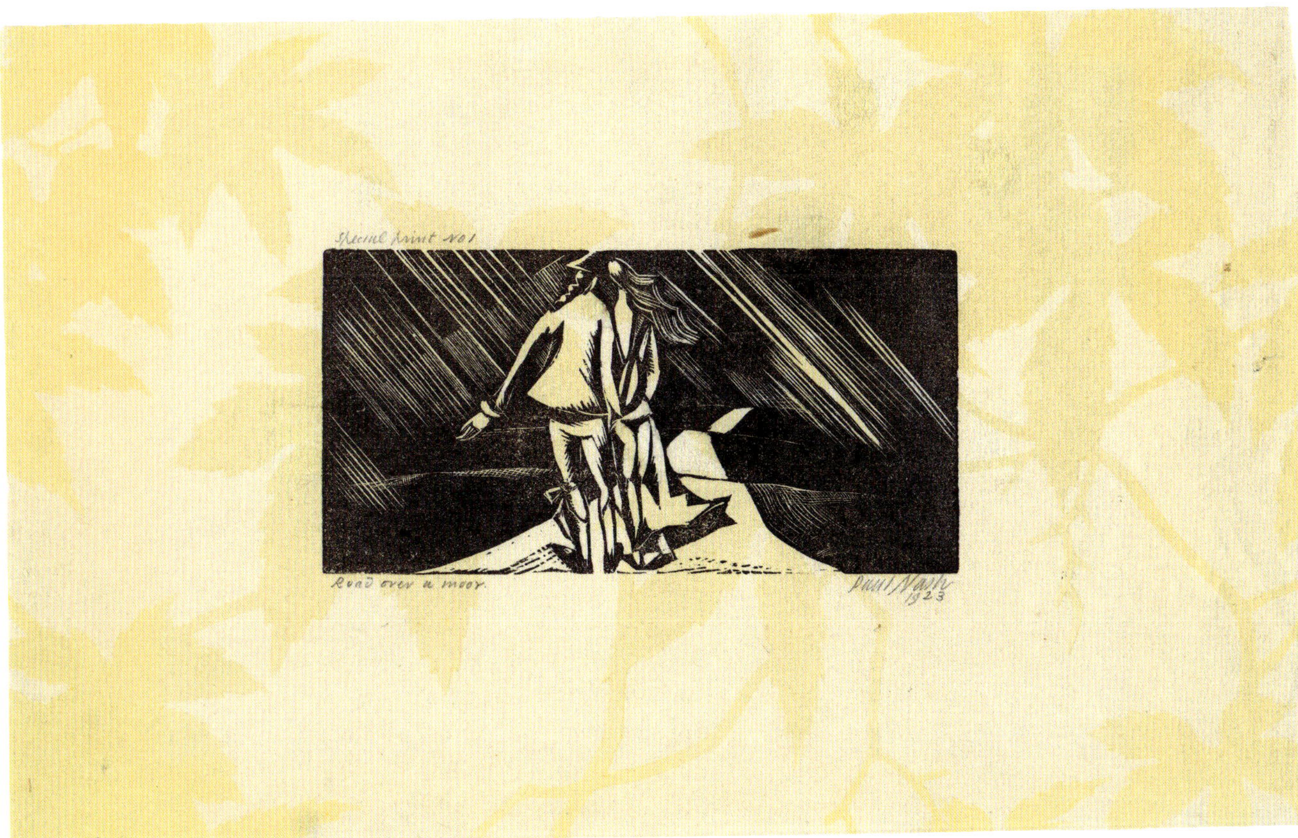

Paul Nash *A Road, Perhaps Over a Moor*, 1923

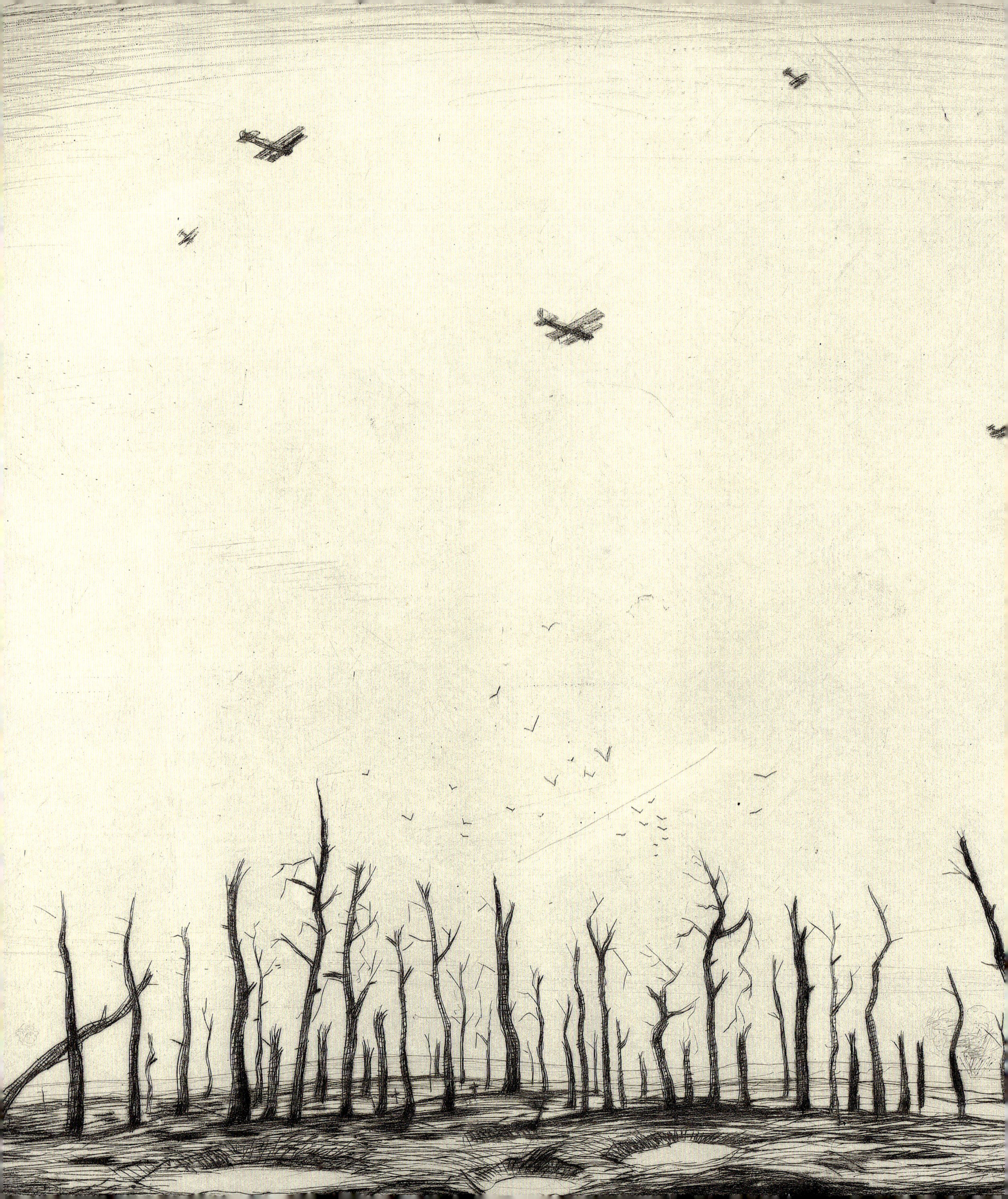

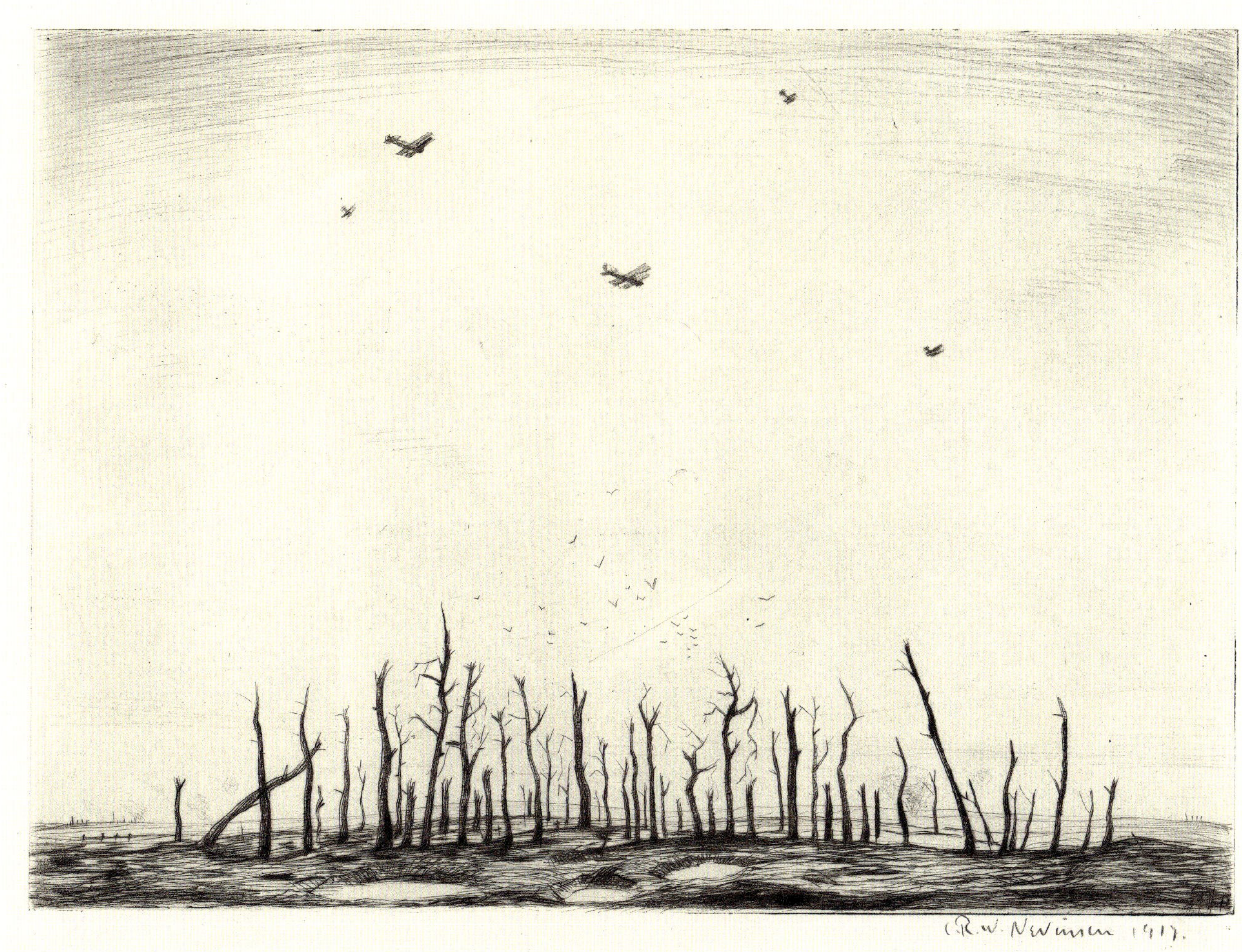

Christopher Richard Wynne Nevinson *That Cursèd Wood*, 1918

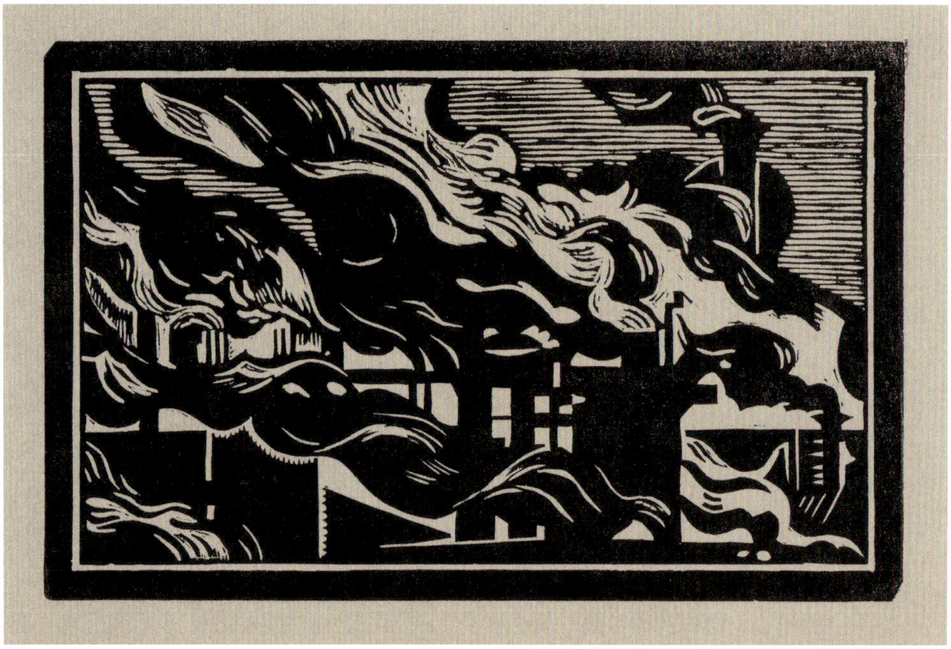

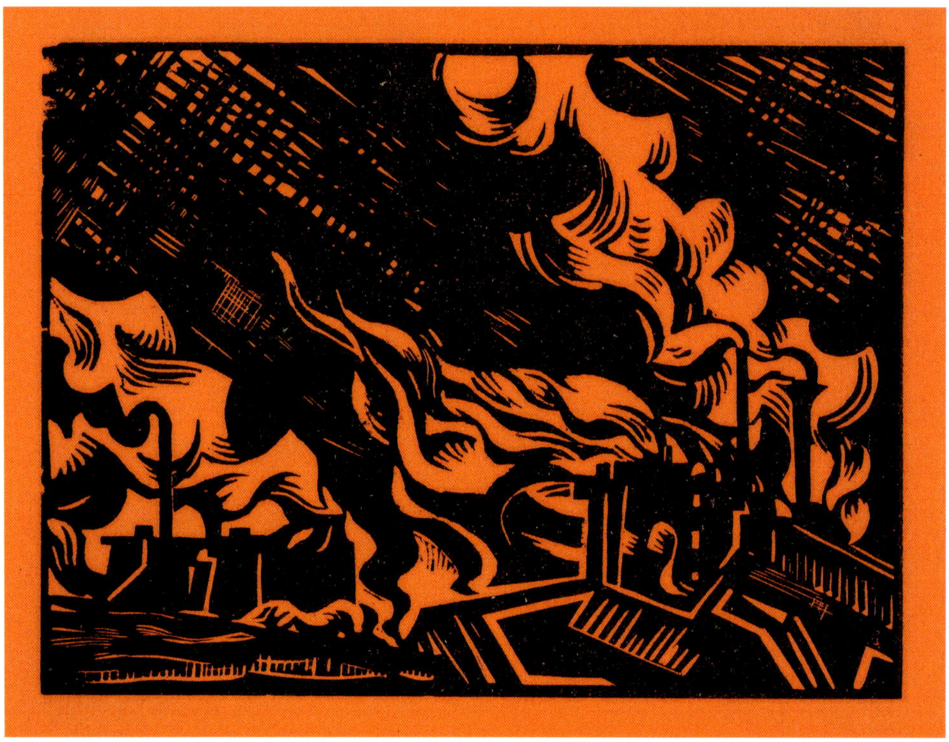

Edward Alexander Wadsworth *Blast Furnaces I (Netherton Furnaces)*, 1919

Edward Alexander Wadsworth *Black Country*, 1919

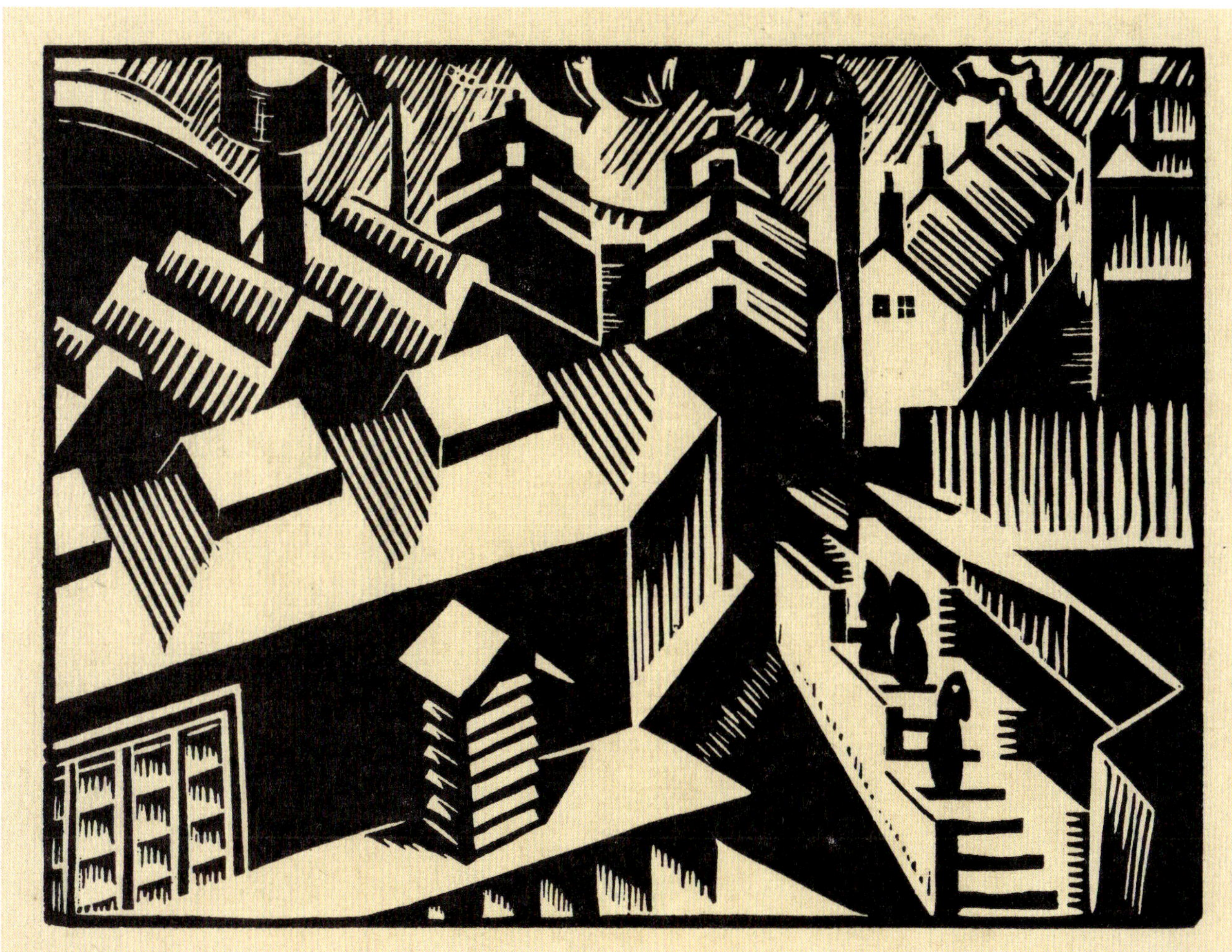

Edward Alexander Wadsworth *Yorkshire*, 1920

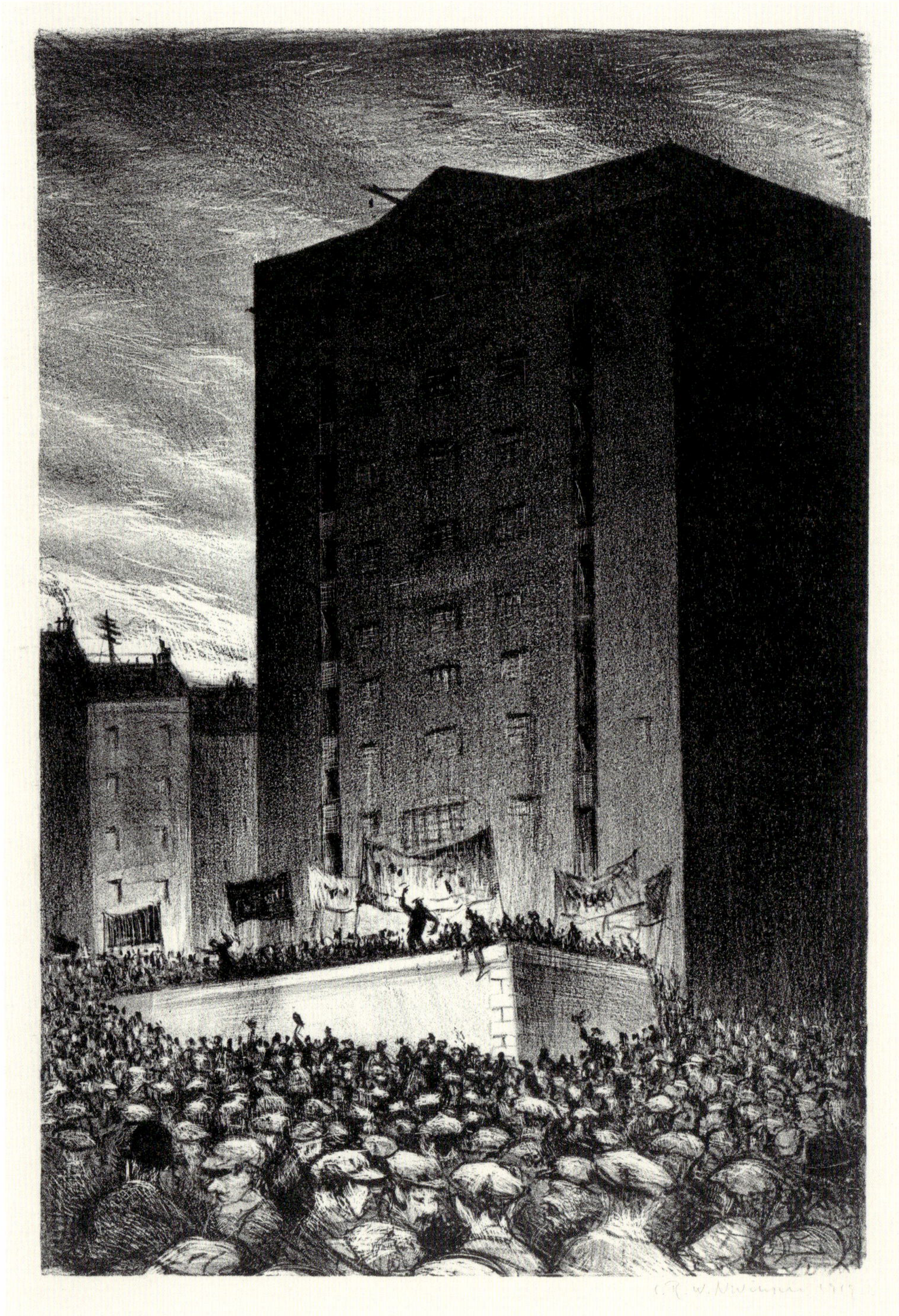

Christopher Richard Wynne Nevinson *The Workers*, 1919

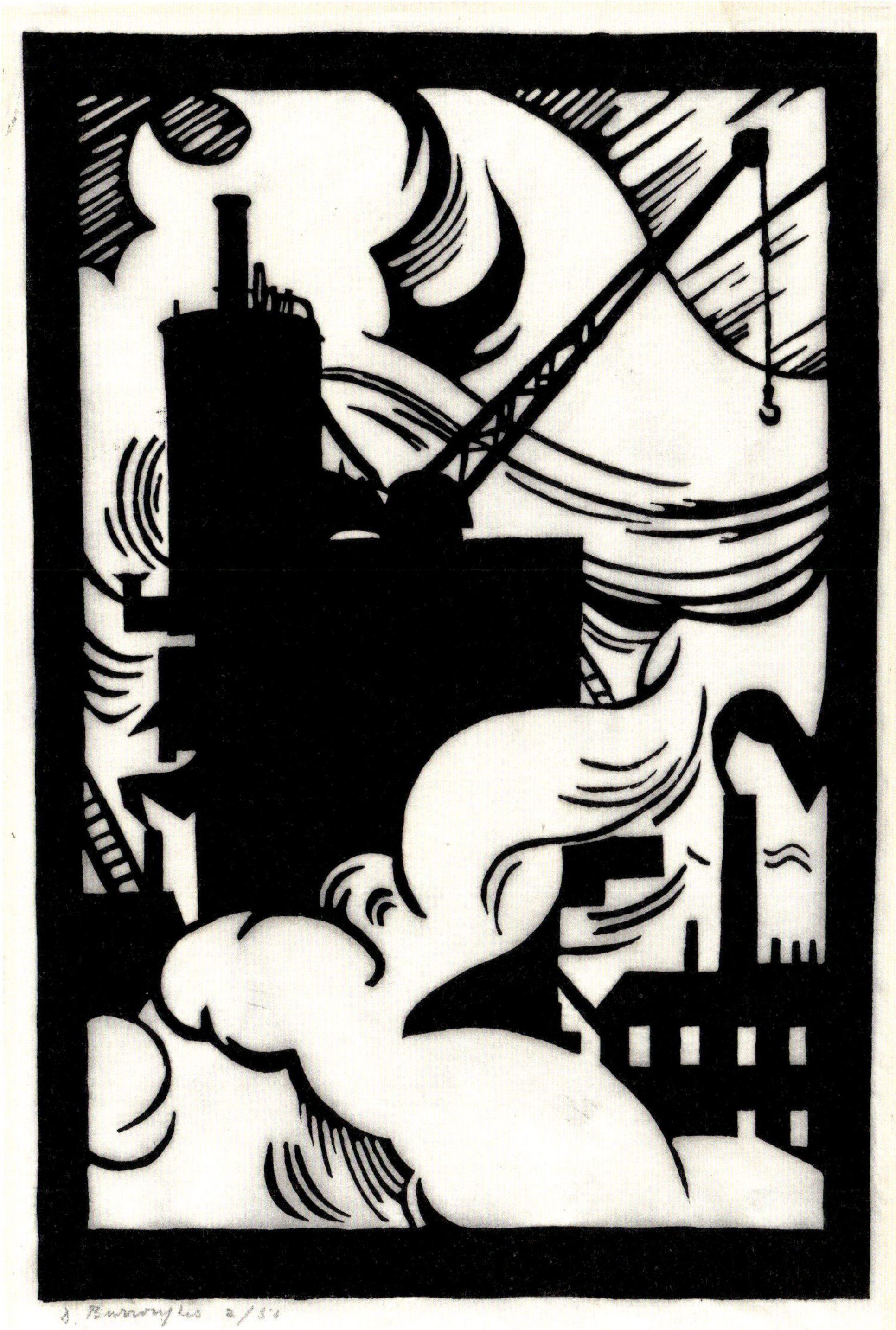

Dorothy Burroughes *The Factory*, ca. 1925

Edith Lawrence *Port*, ca. 1930

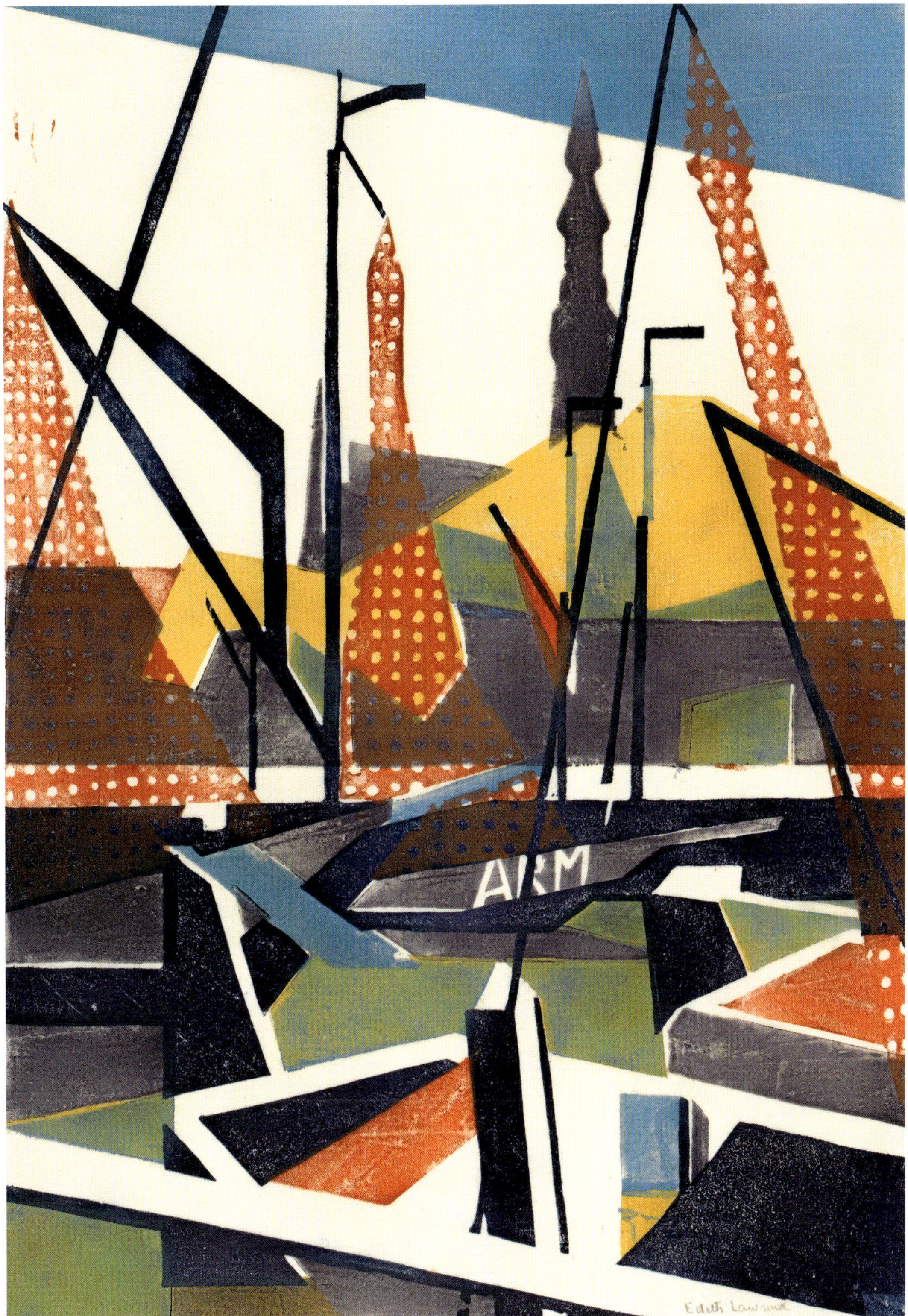
ARM

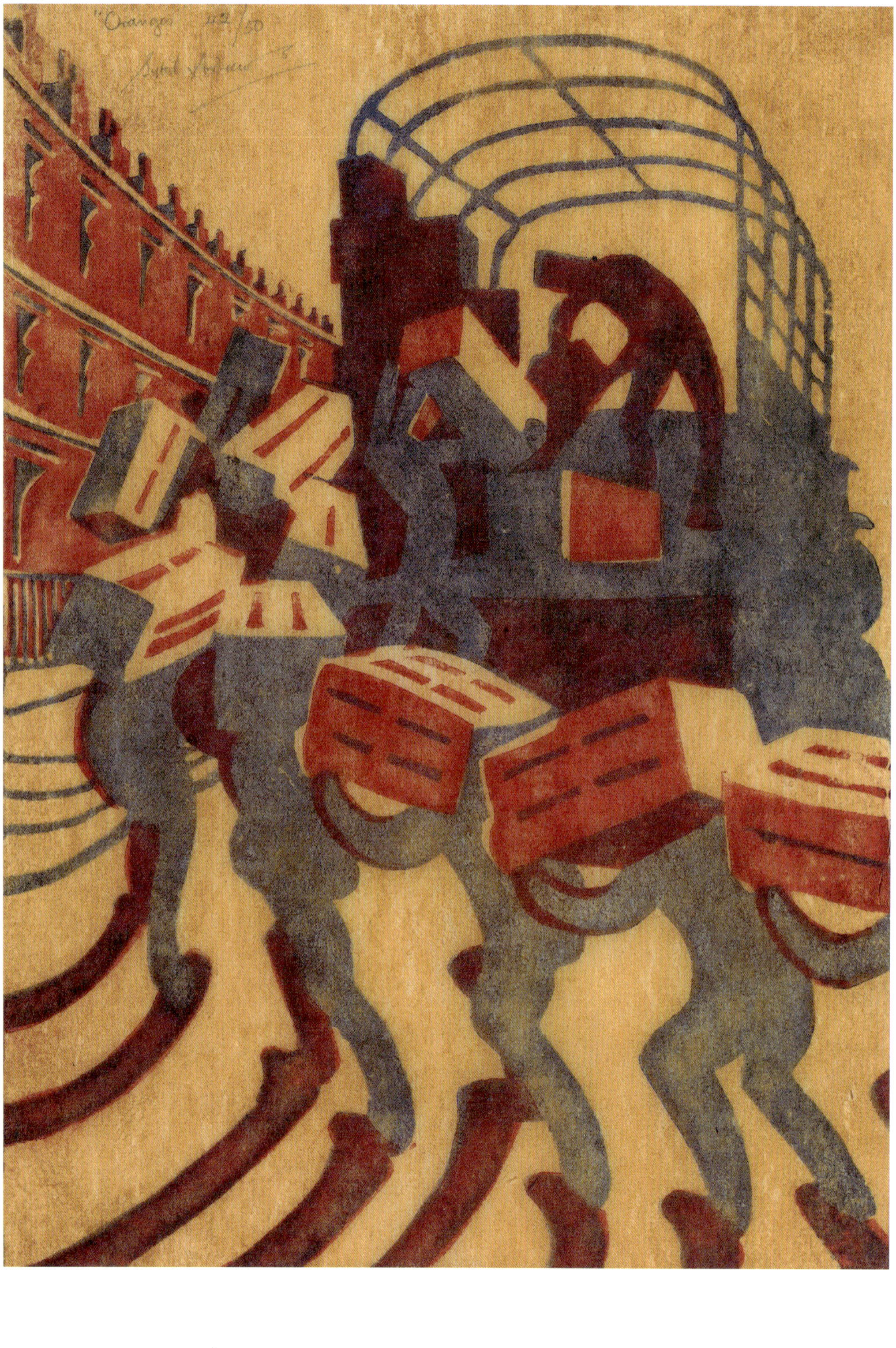

Sybil Andrews *Oranges*, 1929

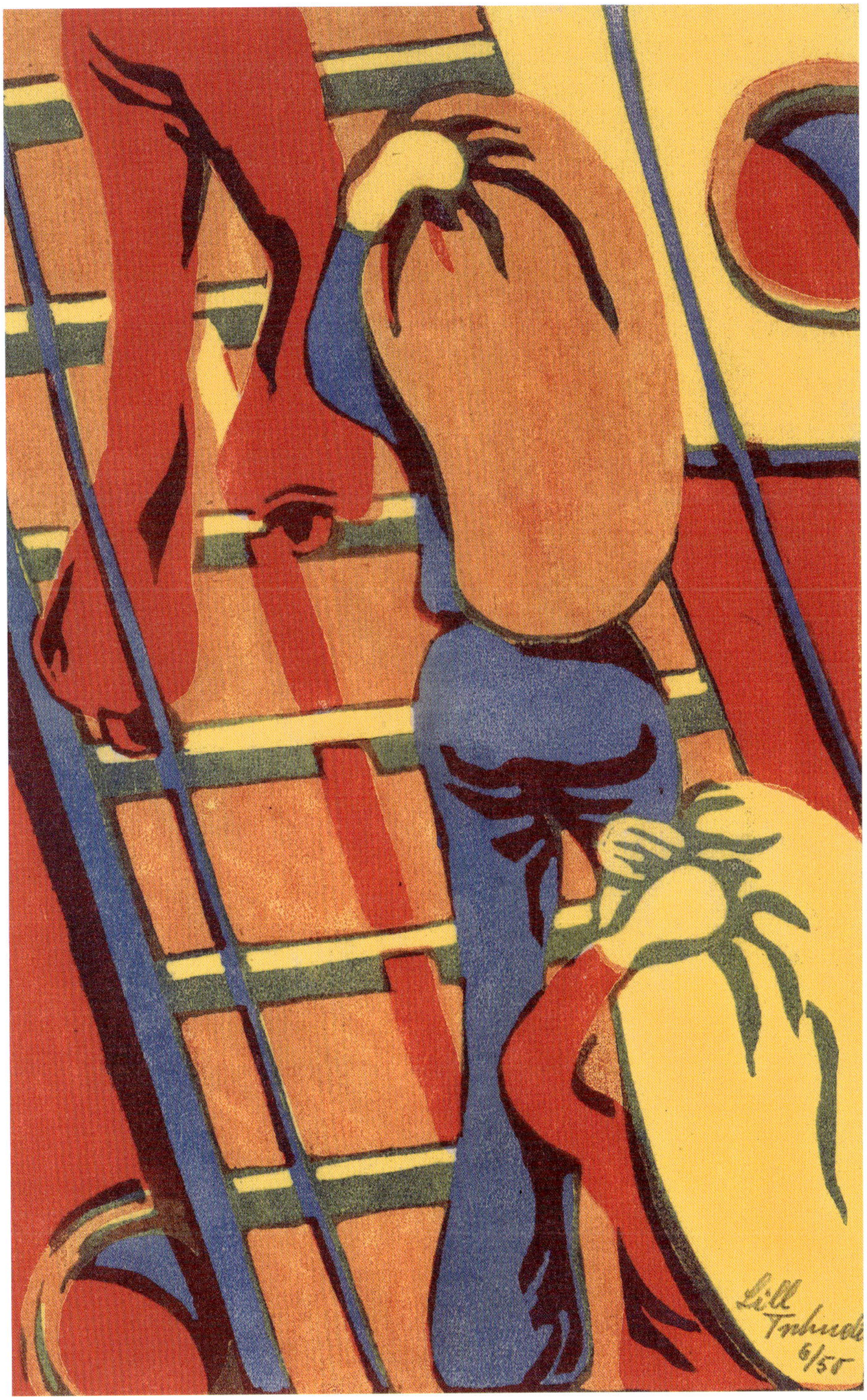

Lill Tschudi *Sailors*, 1930

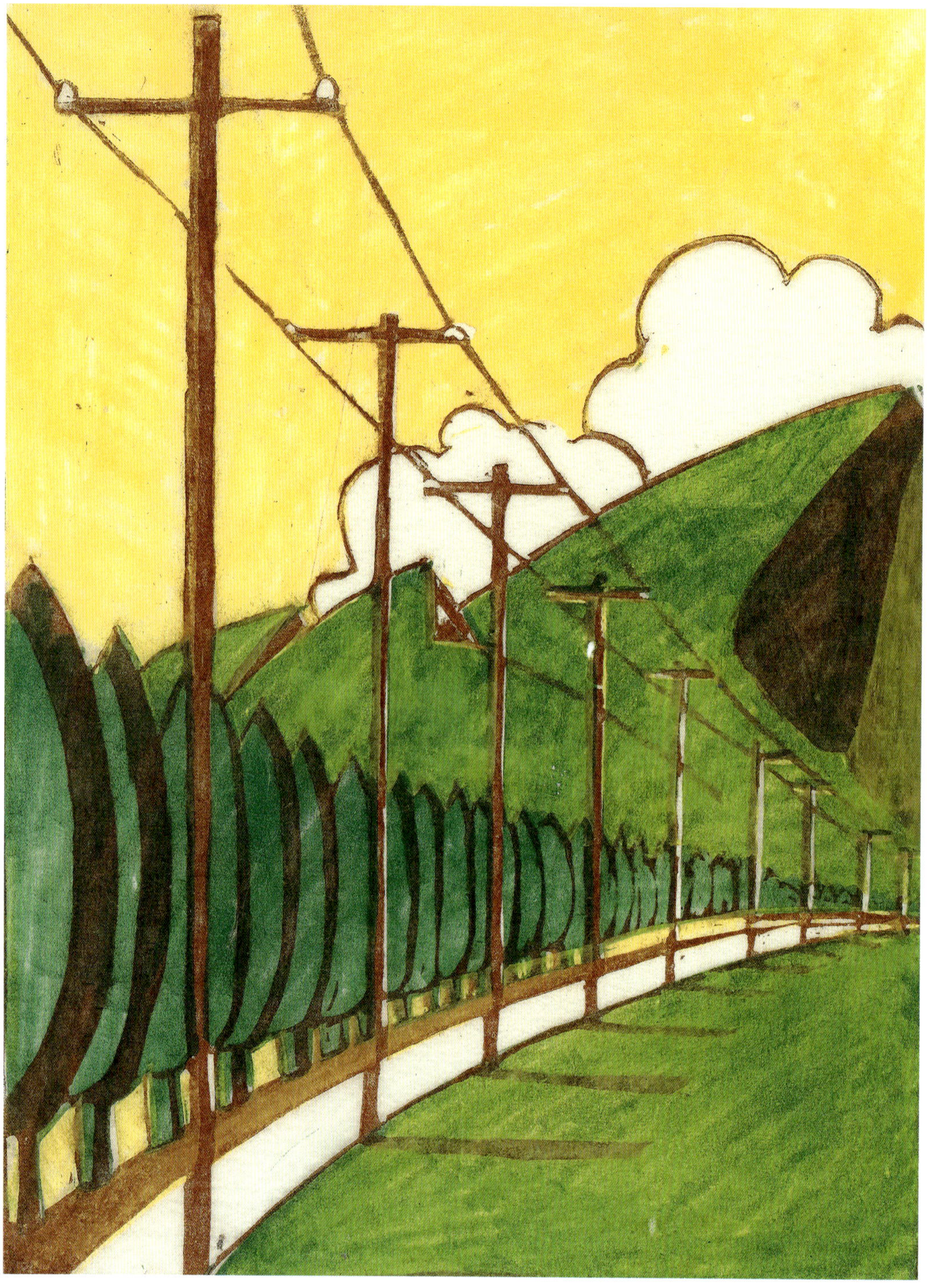

Ursula Fookes *Poplar Trees and Telegraph Poles*, ca. 1930

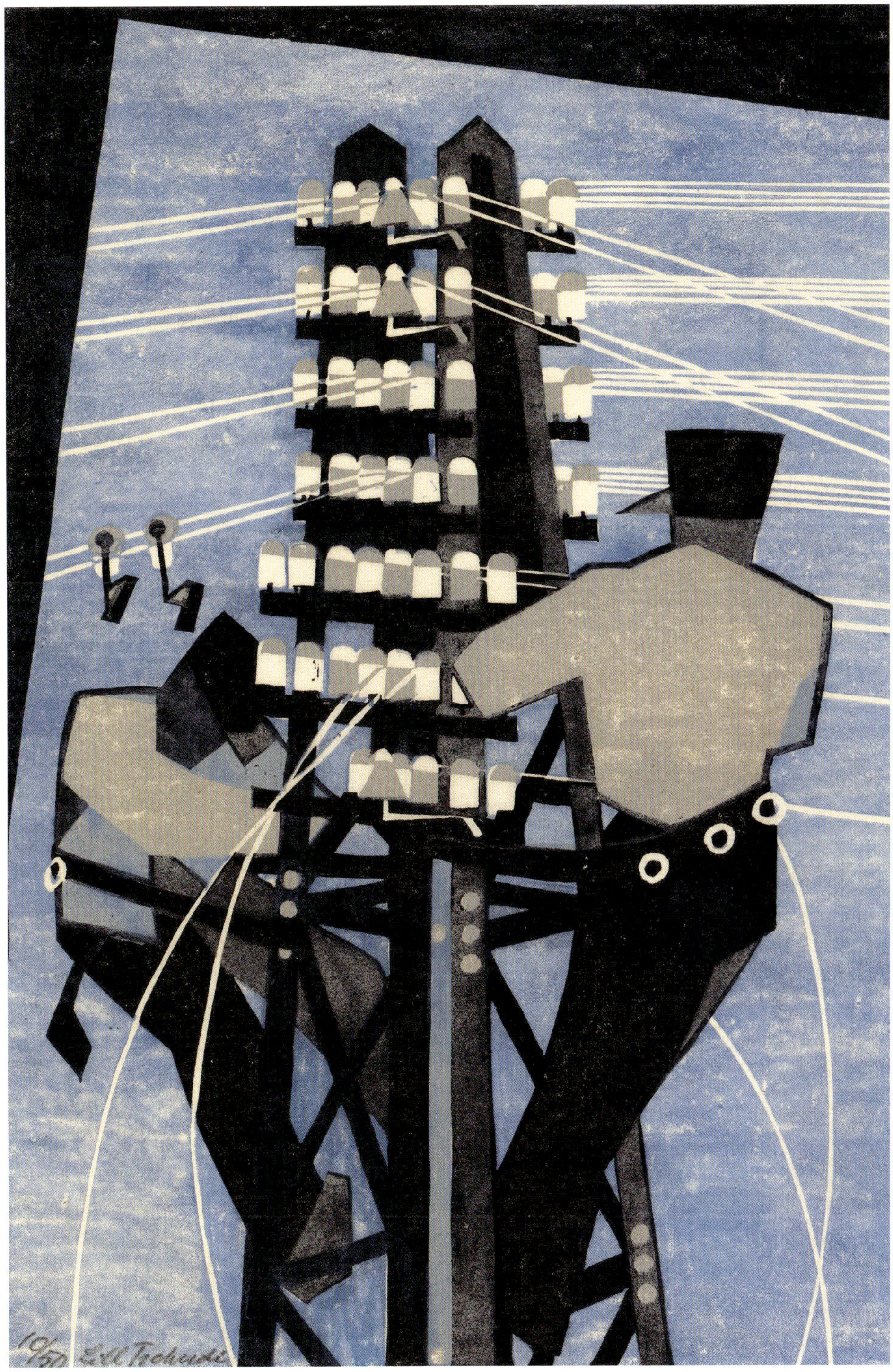

Lill Tschudi *Fixing the Wires*, 1932

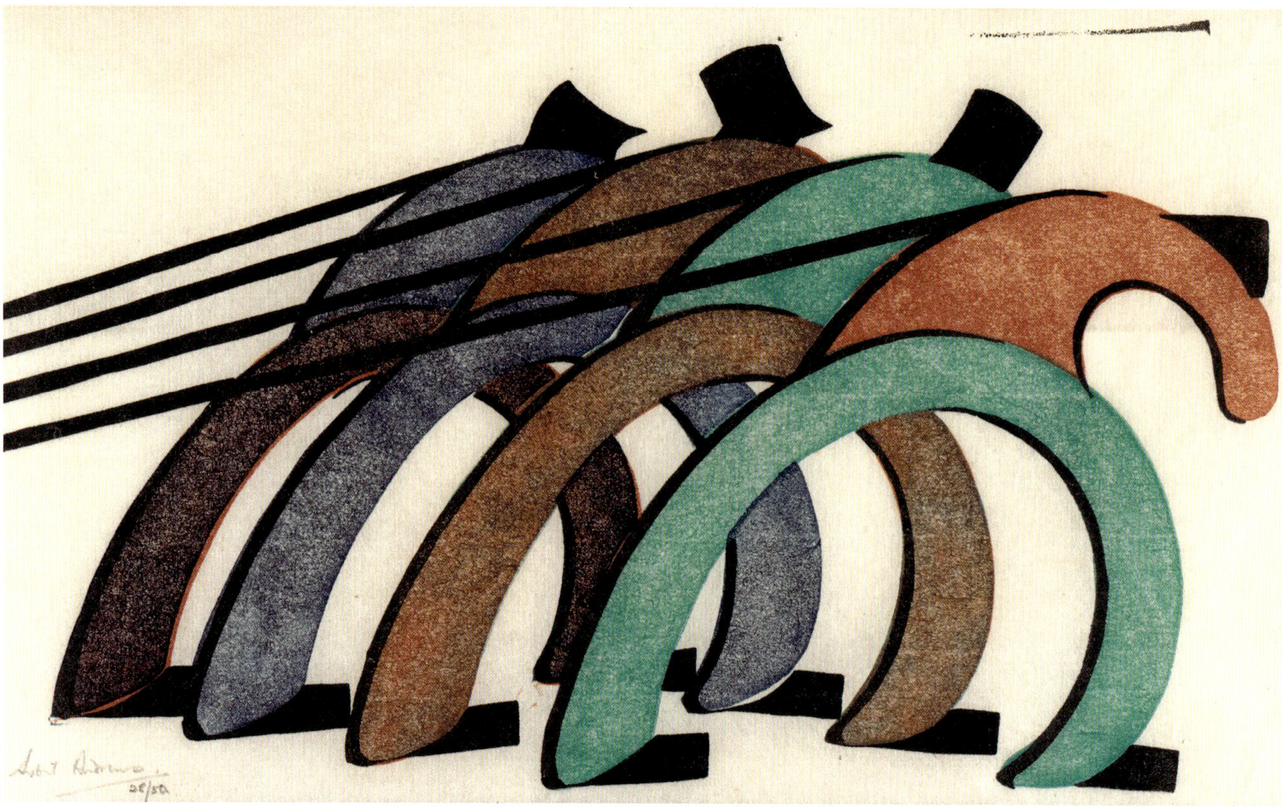

Sybil Andrews *Haulers*, 1929

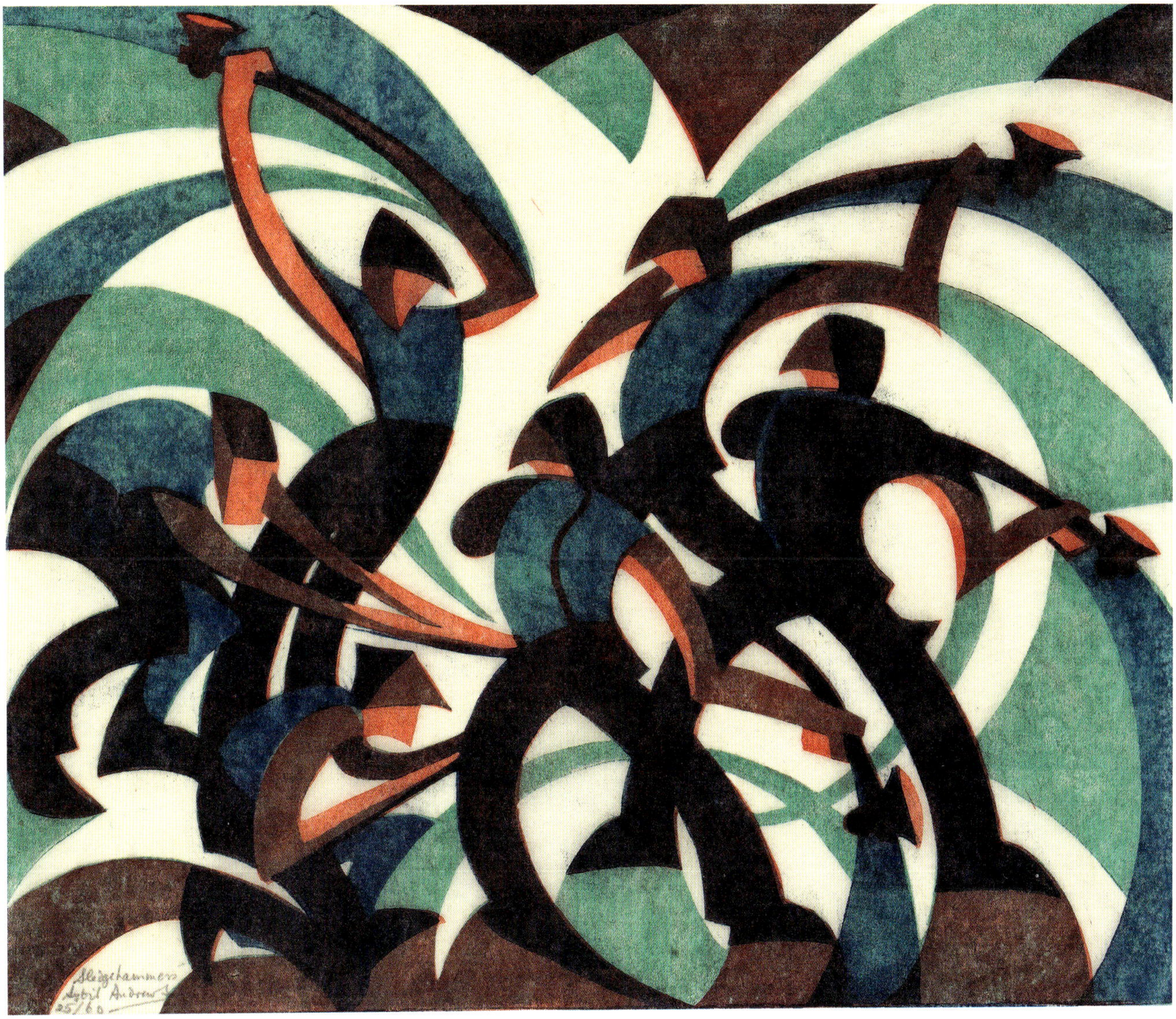

Sybil Andrews *Sledgehammers*, 1933

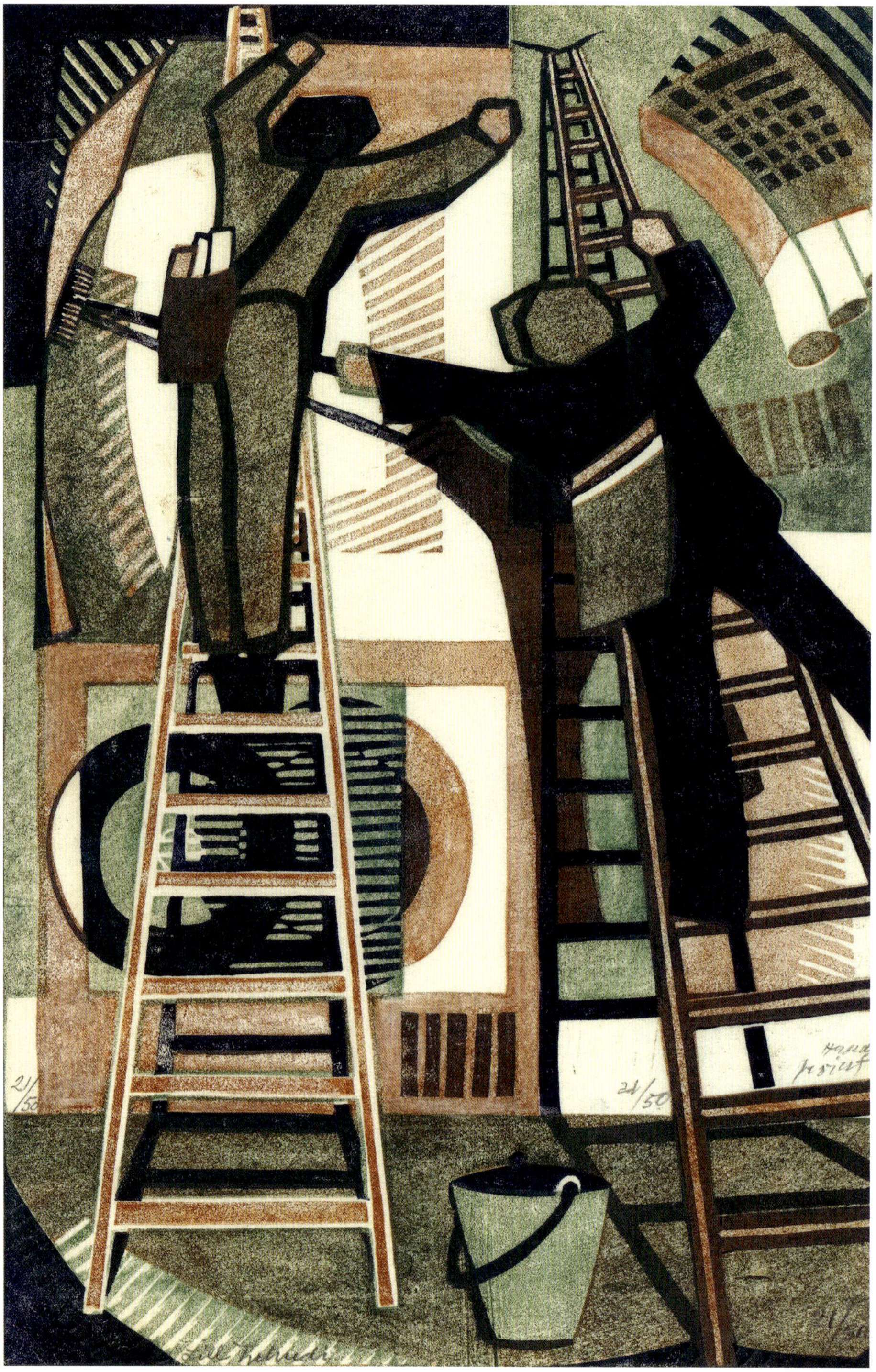

Lill Tschudi *Sticking Up Posters*, 1933

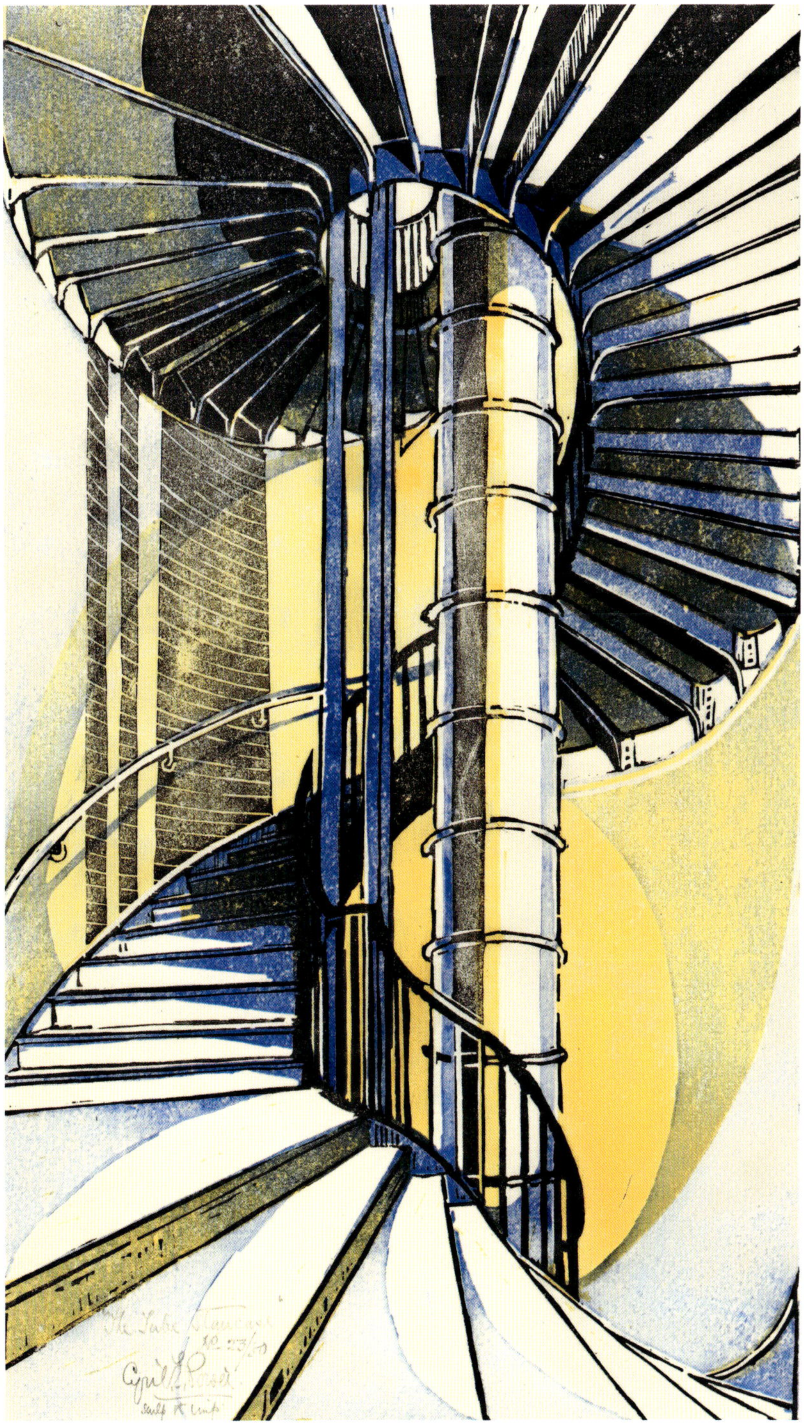

Cyril E. Power *The Tube Staircase*, 1929

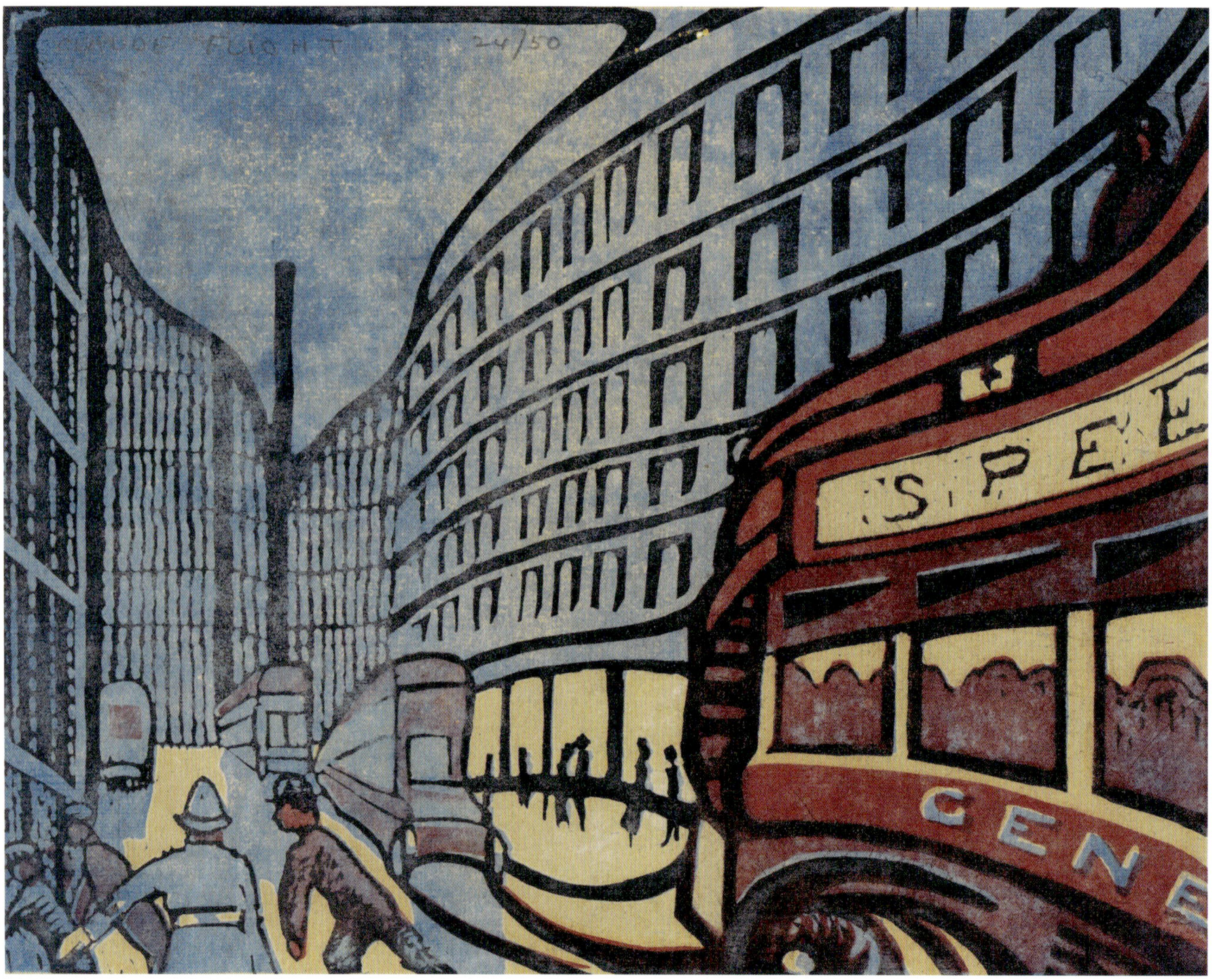

Claude Flight *Speed*, 1922

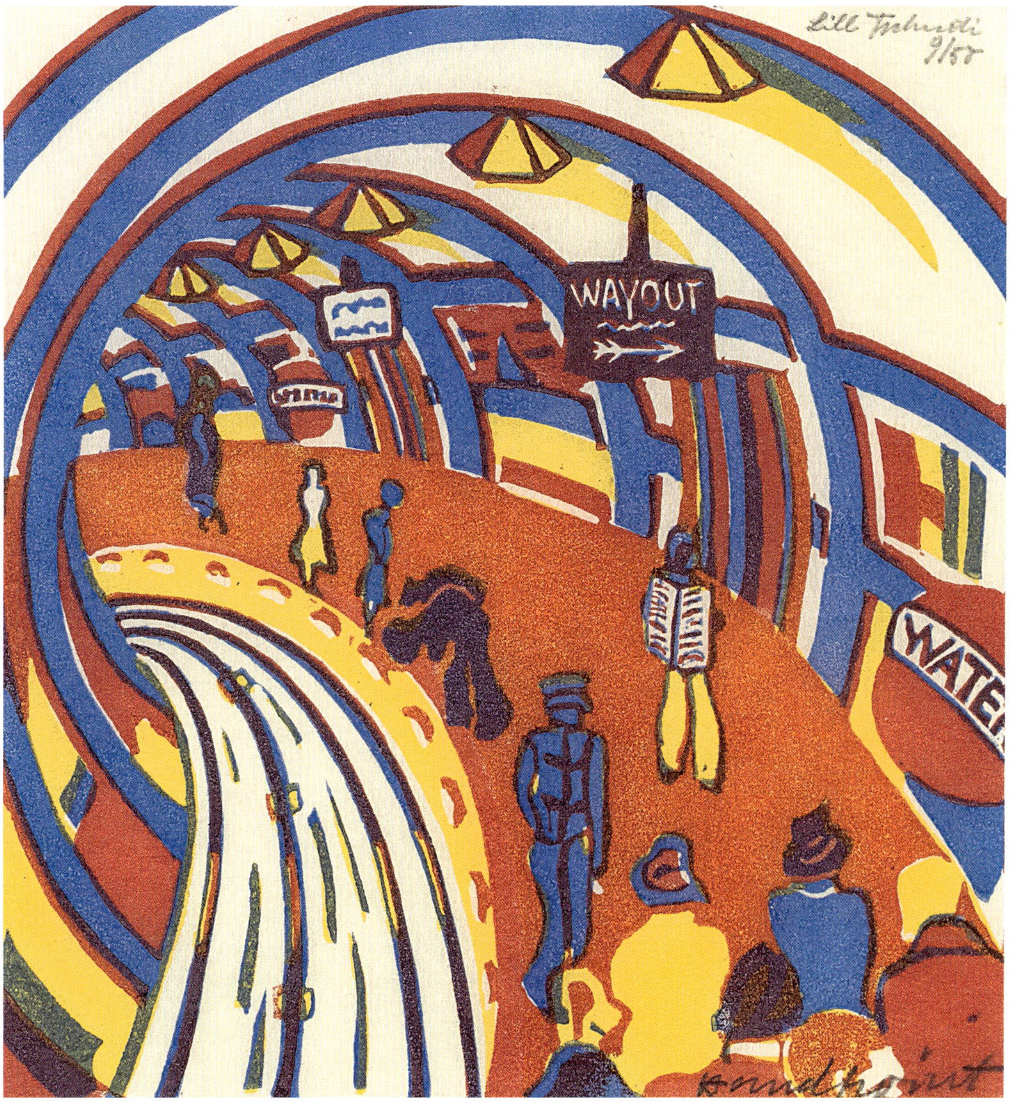

Lill Tschudi *Underground*, 1930

Claude Flight *Brooklands*, ca. 1929

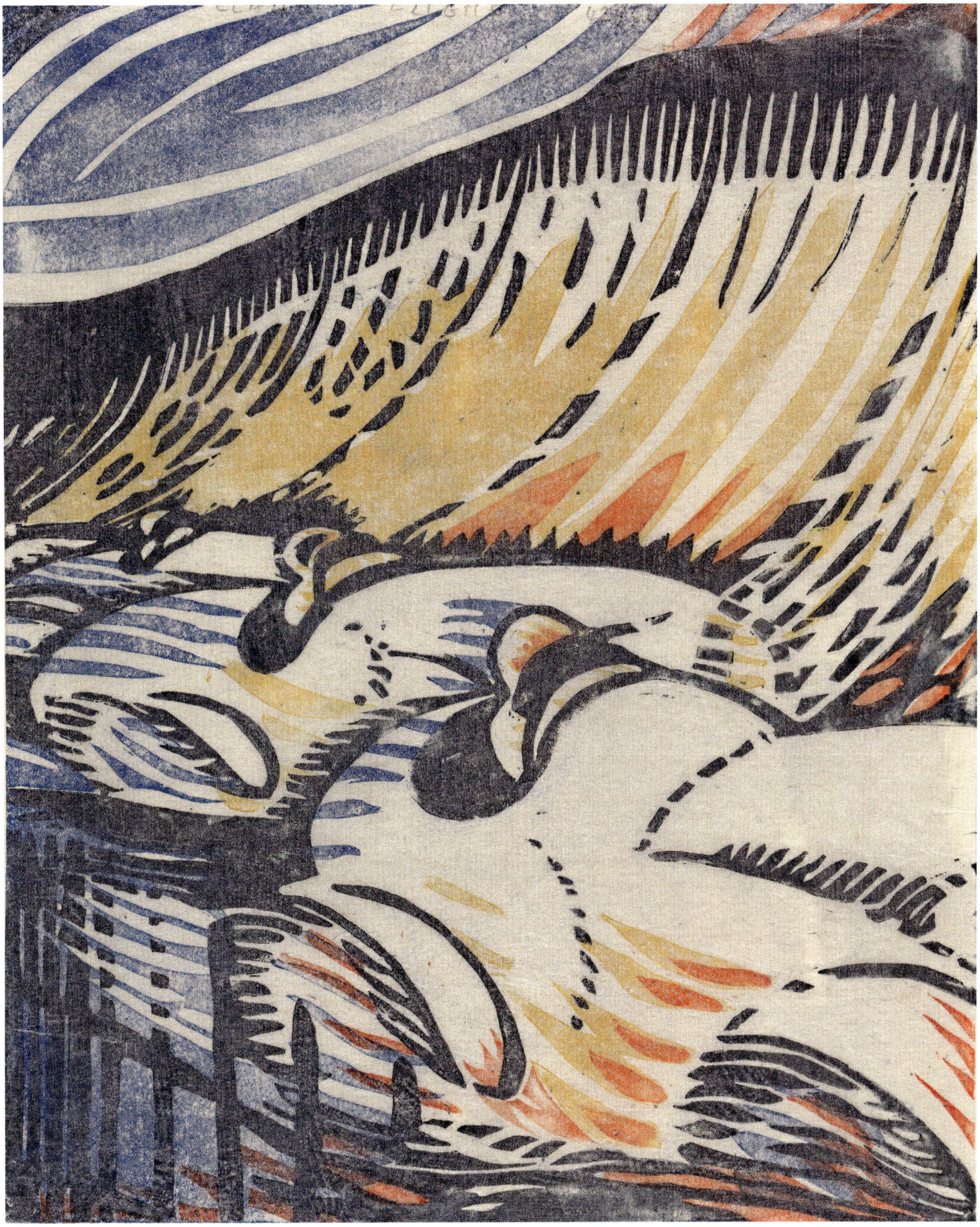

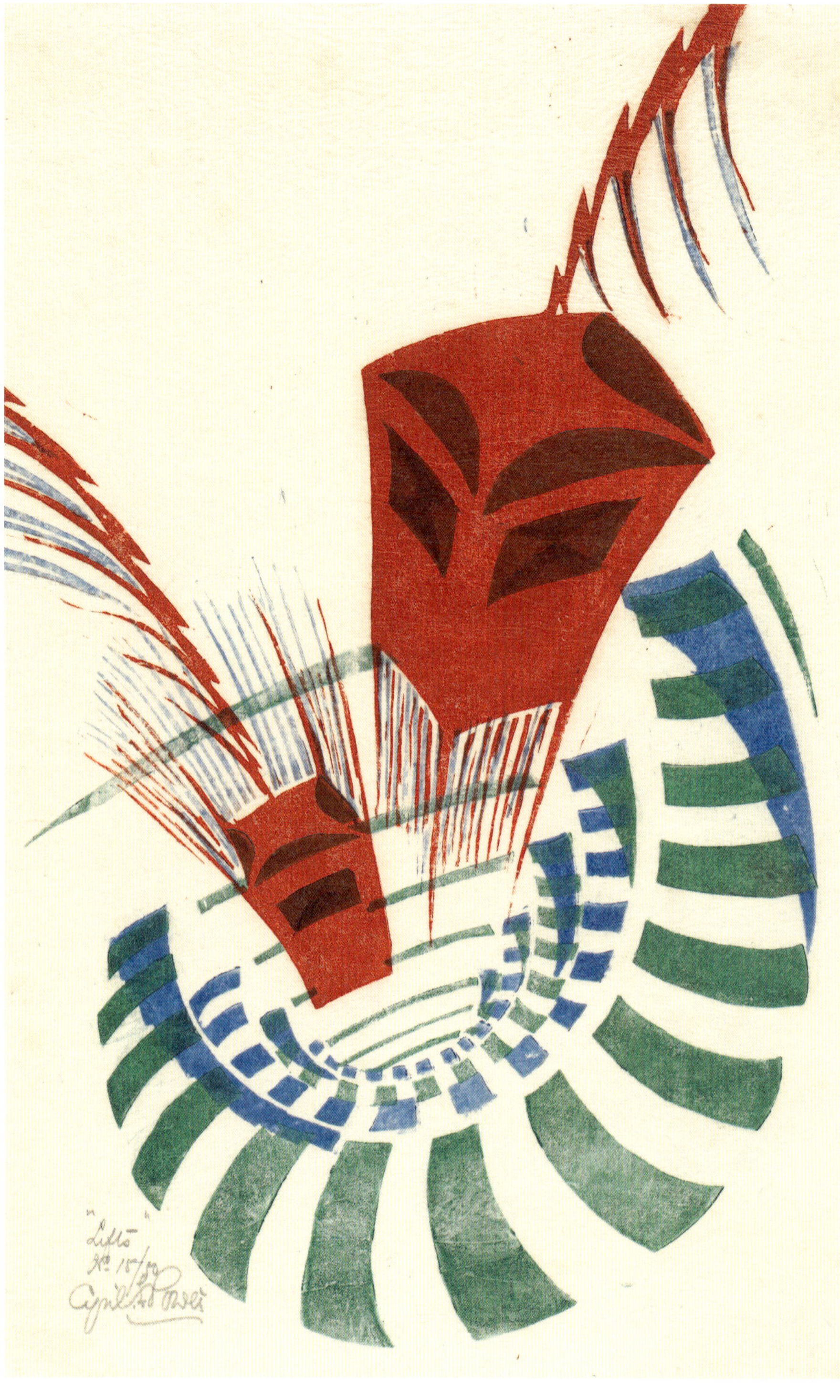

Cyril E. Power *Lifts*, ca. 1930

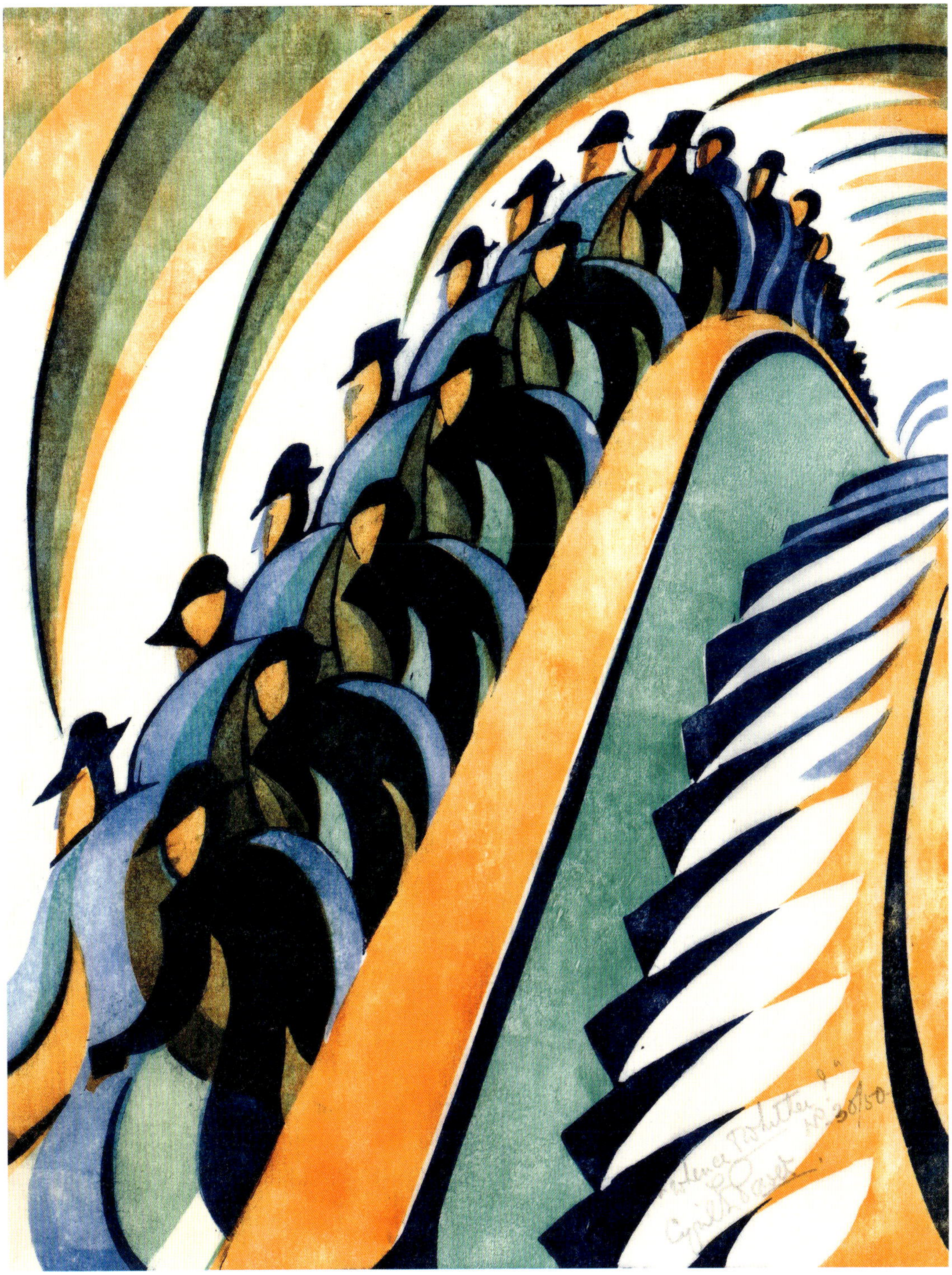

Cyril E. Power *Whence & Whither?*, ca. 1930

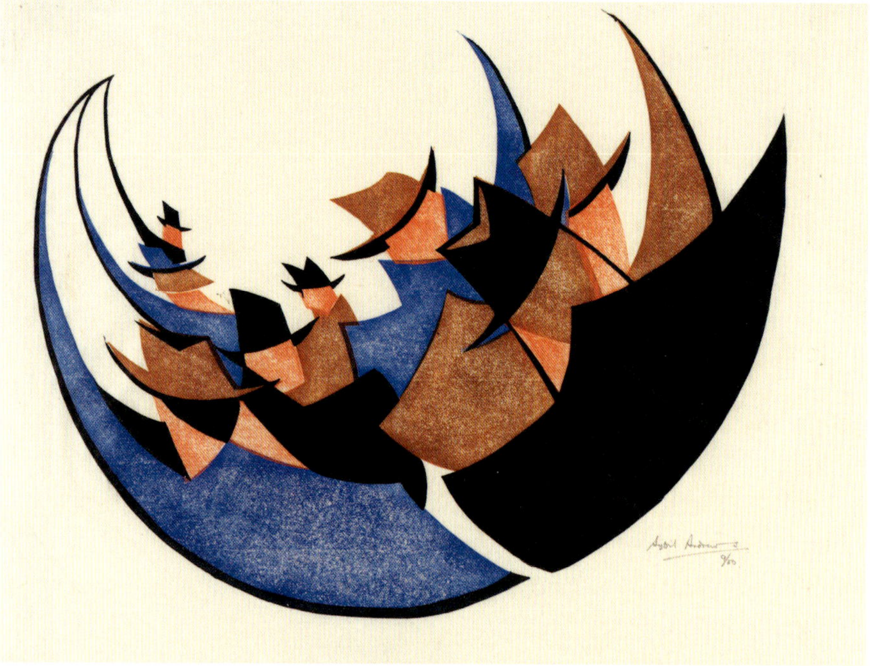

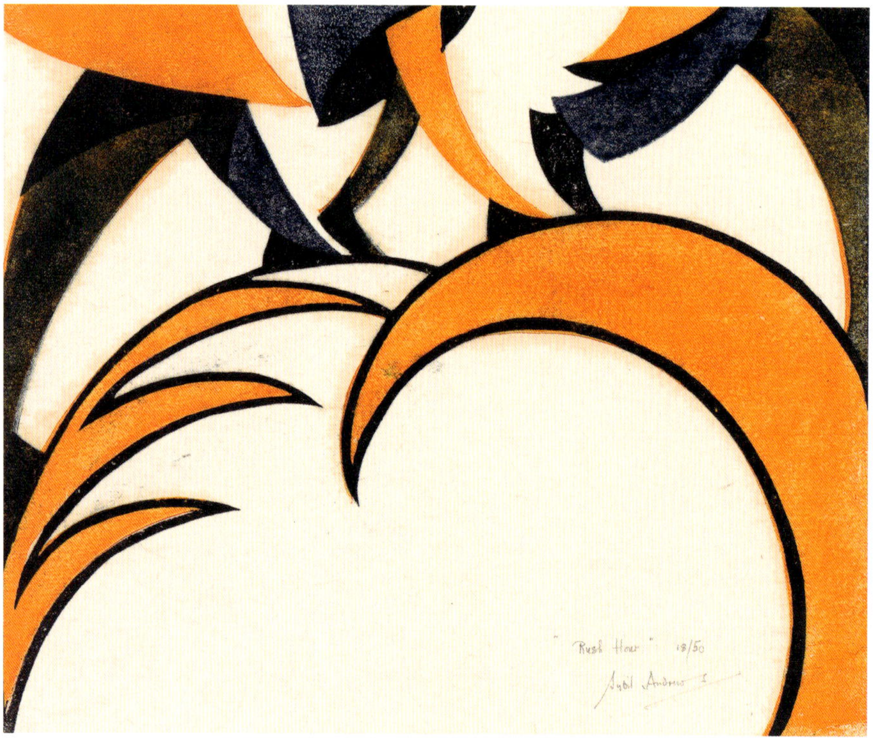

Sybil Andrews *Straphangers*, 1929

Sybil Andrews *Rush Hour*, 1930

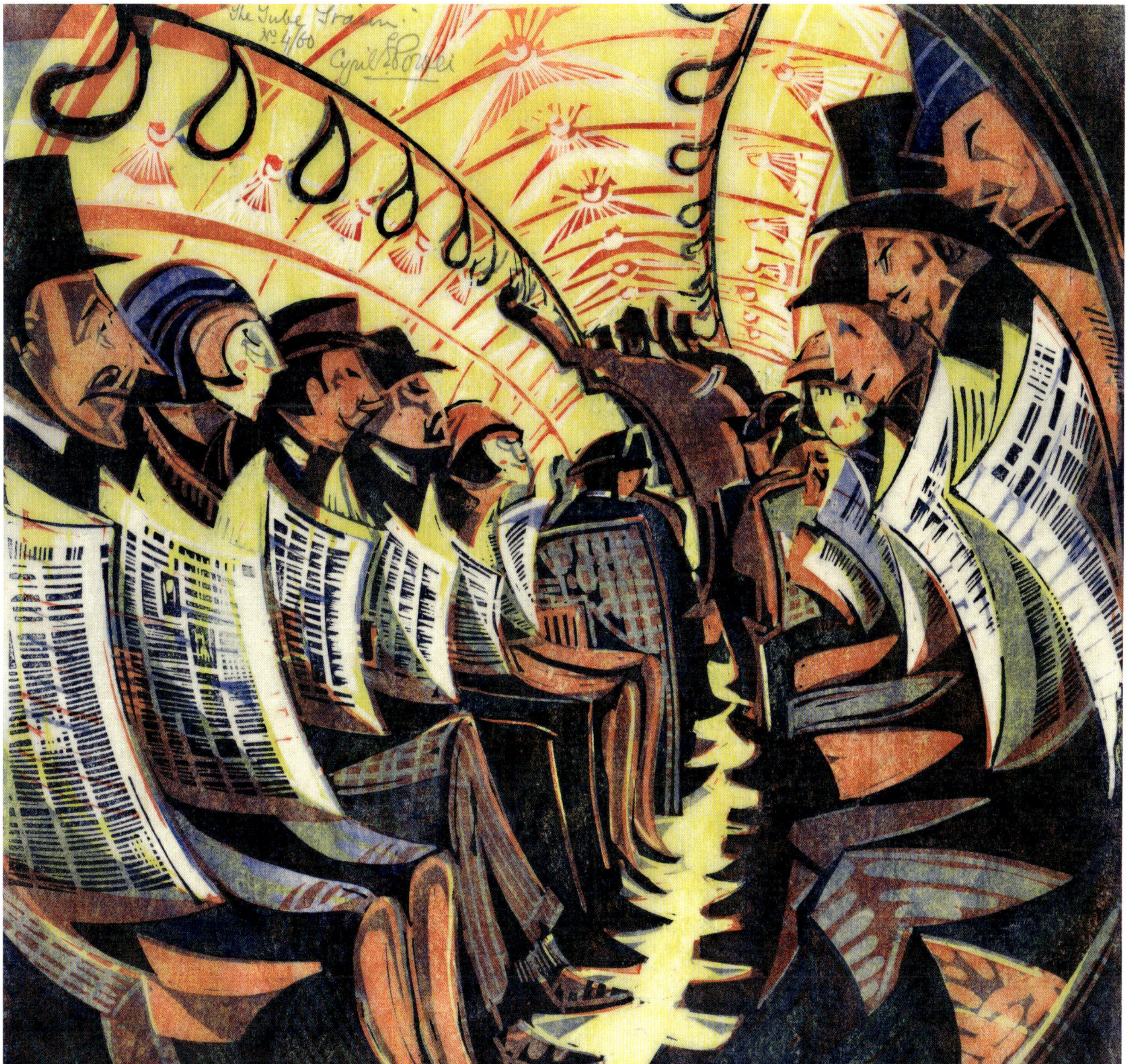

Cyril E. Power *The Tube Train*, ca. 1934

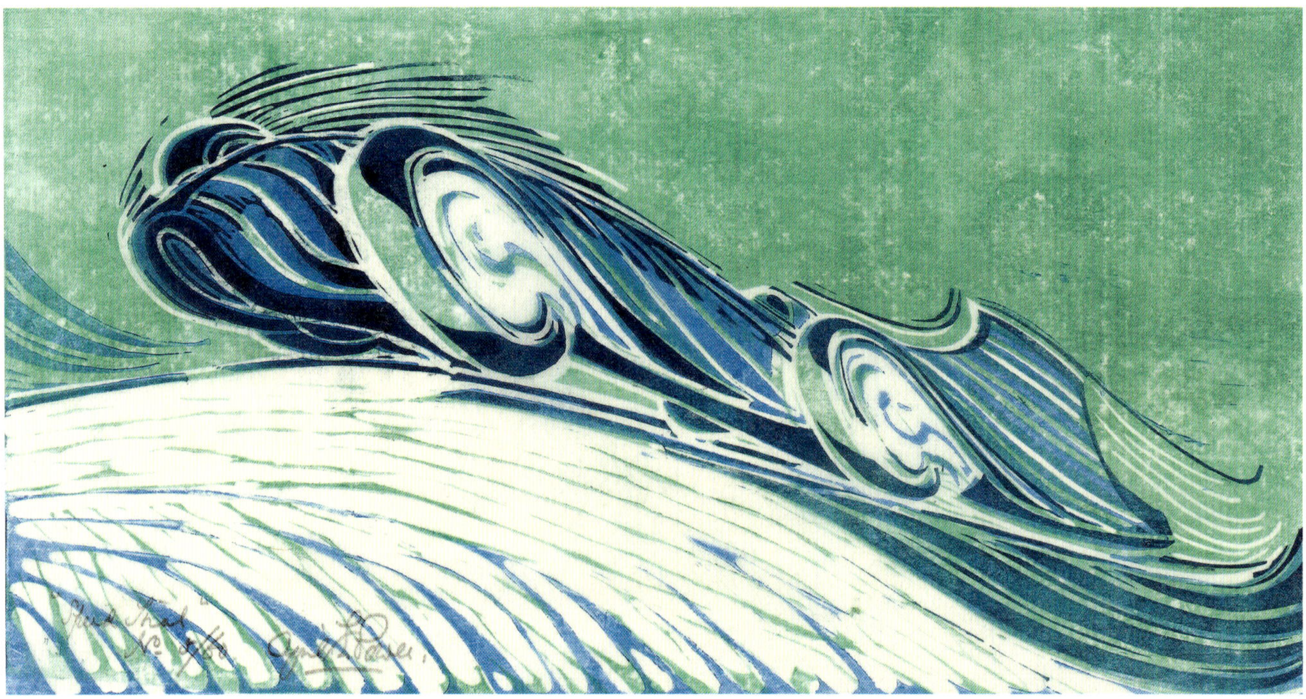

Cyril E. Power *Speed Trial*, ca. 1932

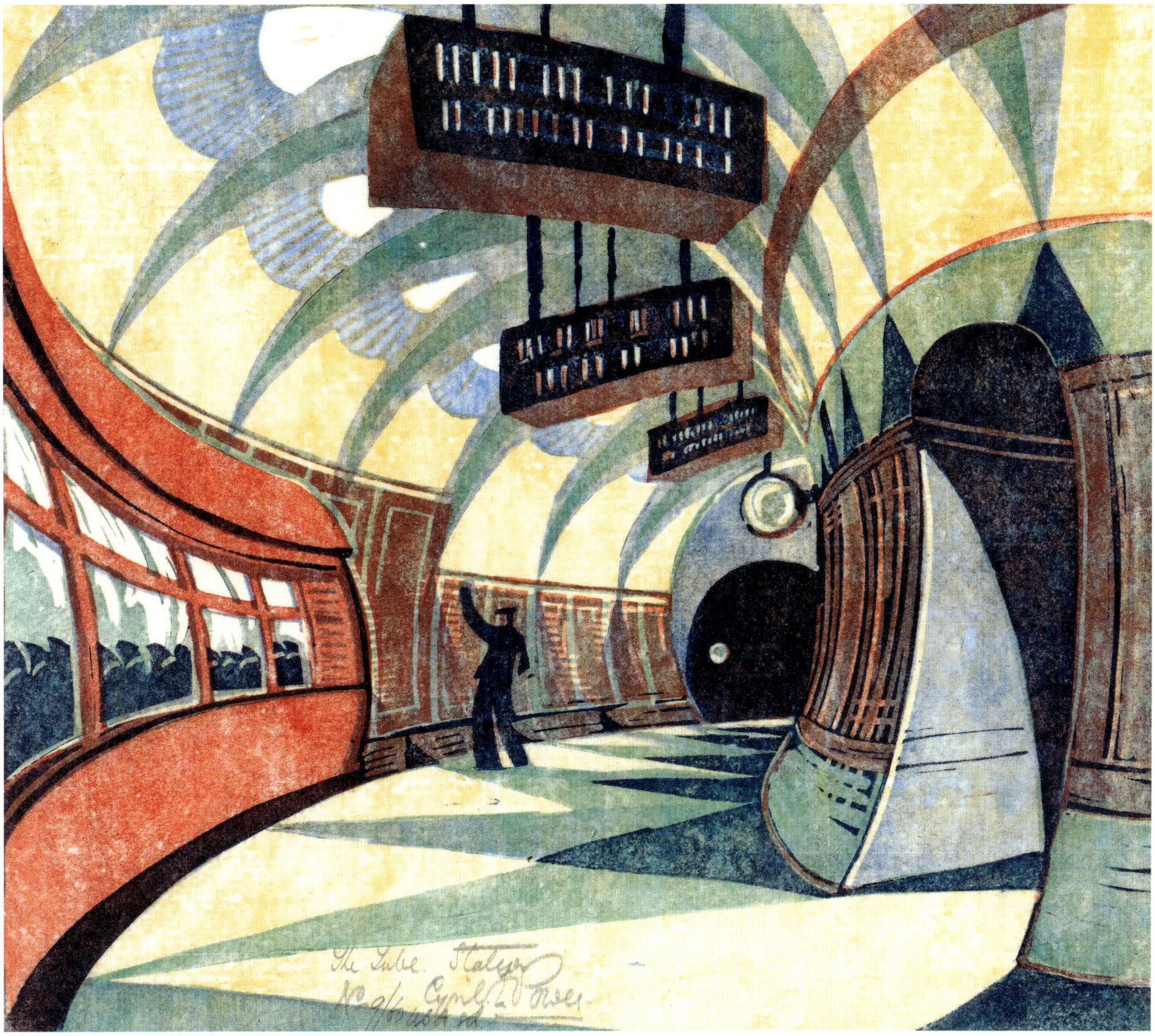

Cyril E. Power *The Tube Station*, ca. 1932, printed ca. 1935

Sybil Andrews *Speedway*, 1934

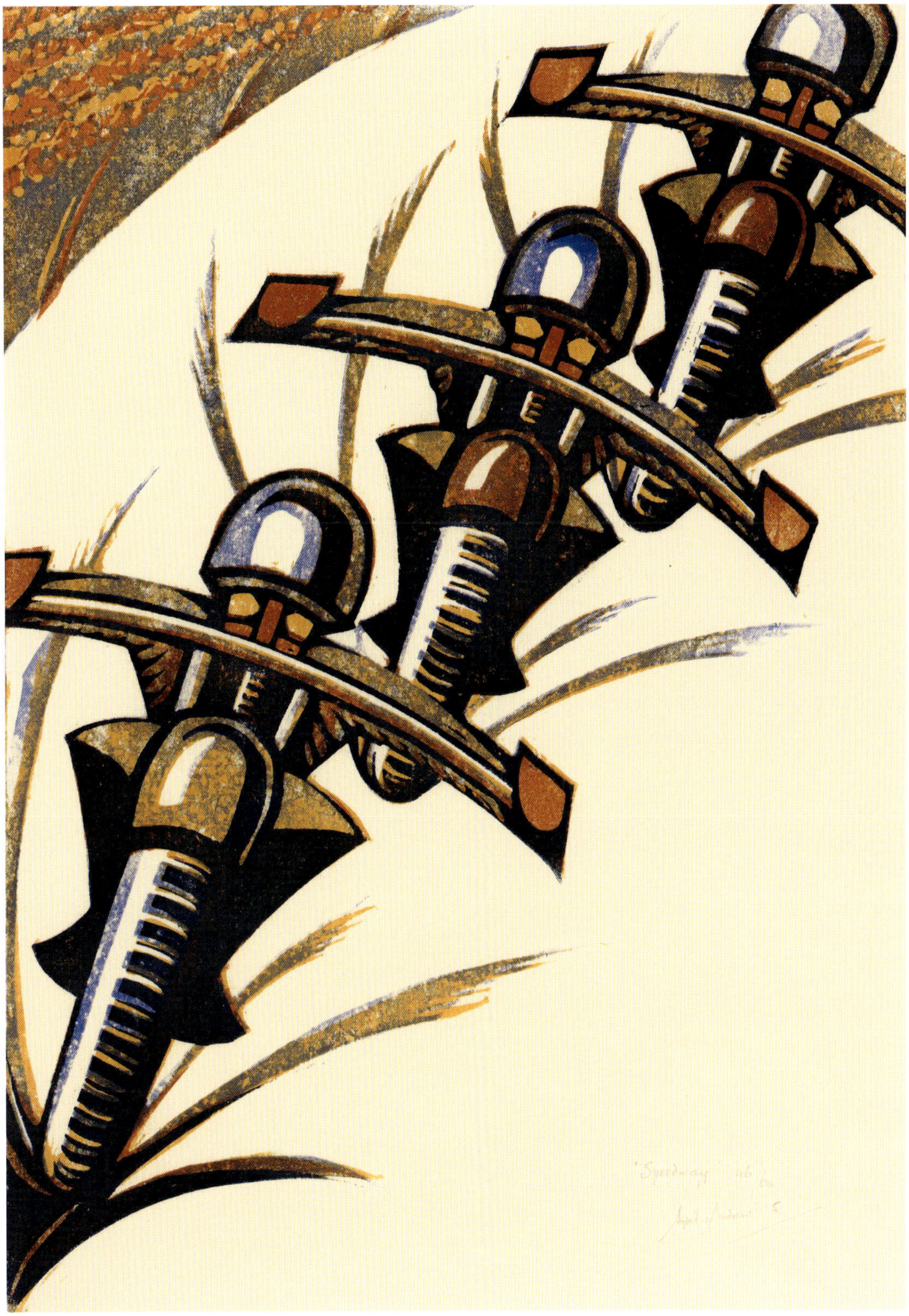

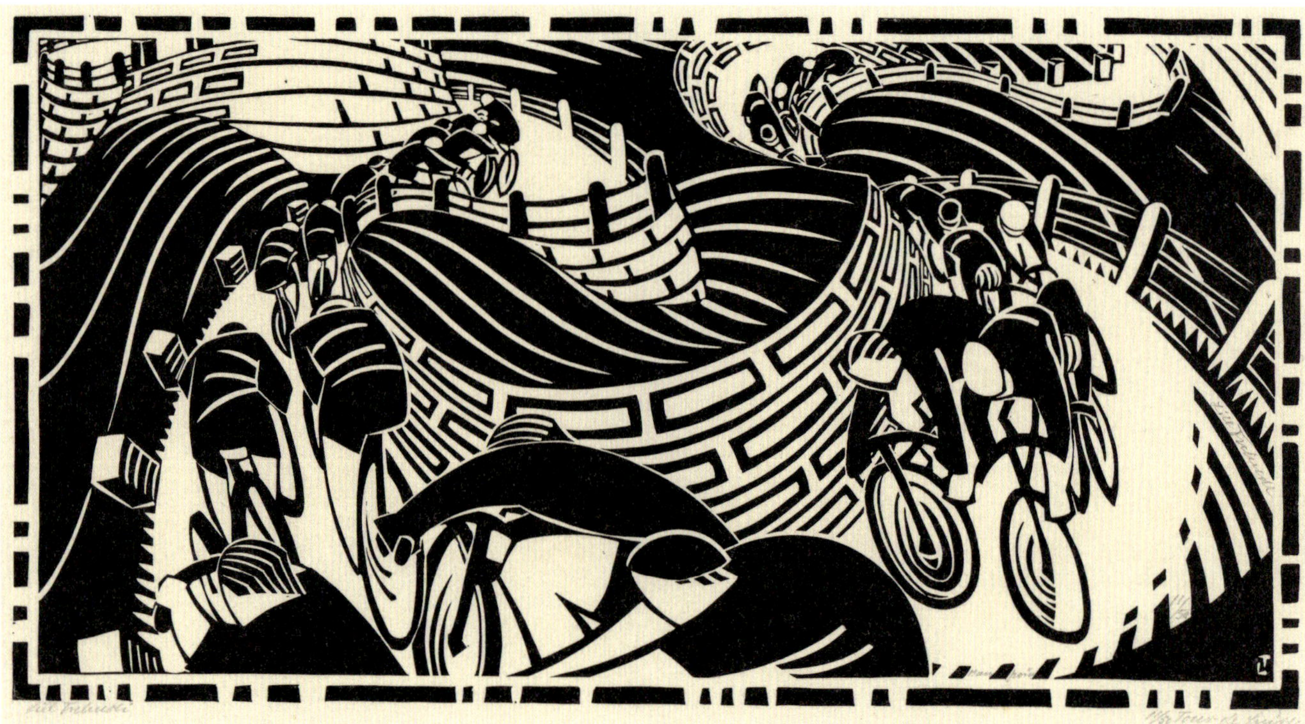

Lill Tschudi *Tour de Suisse*, 1935

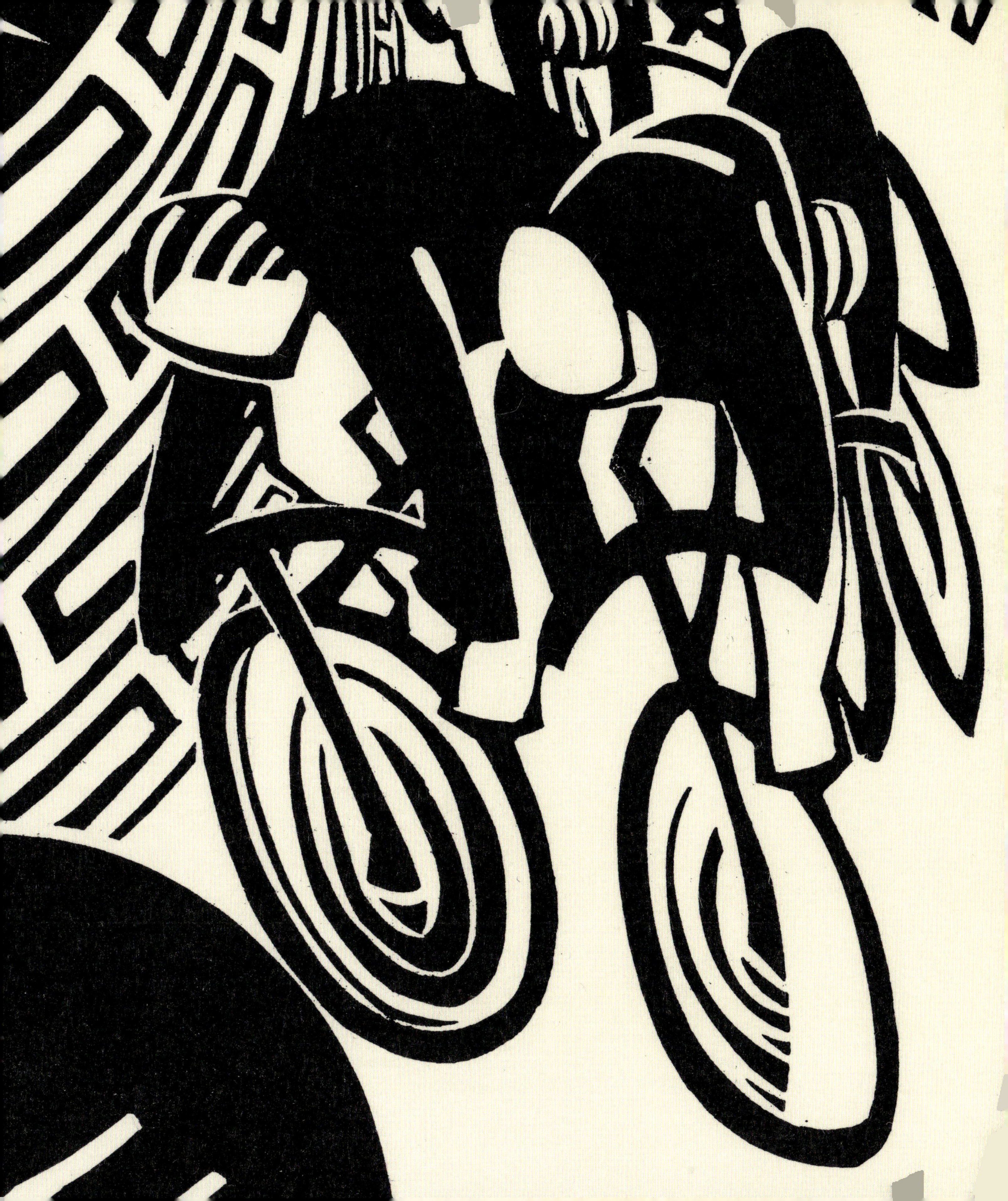

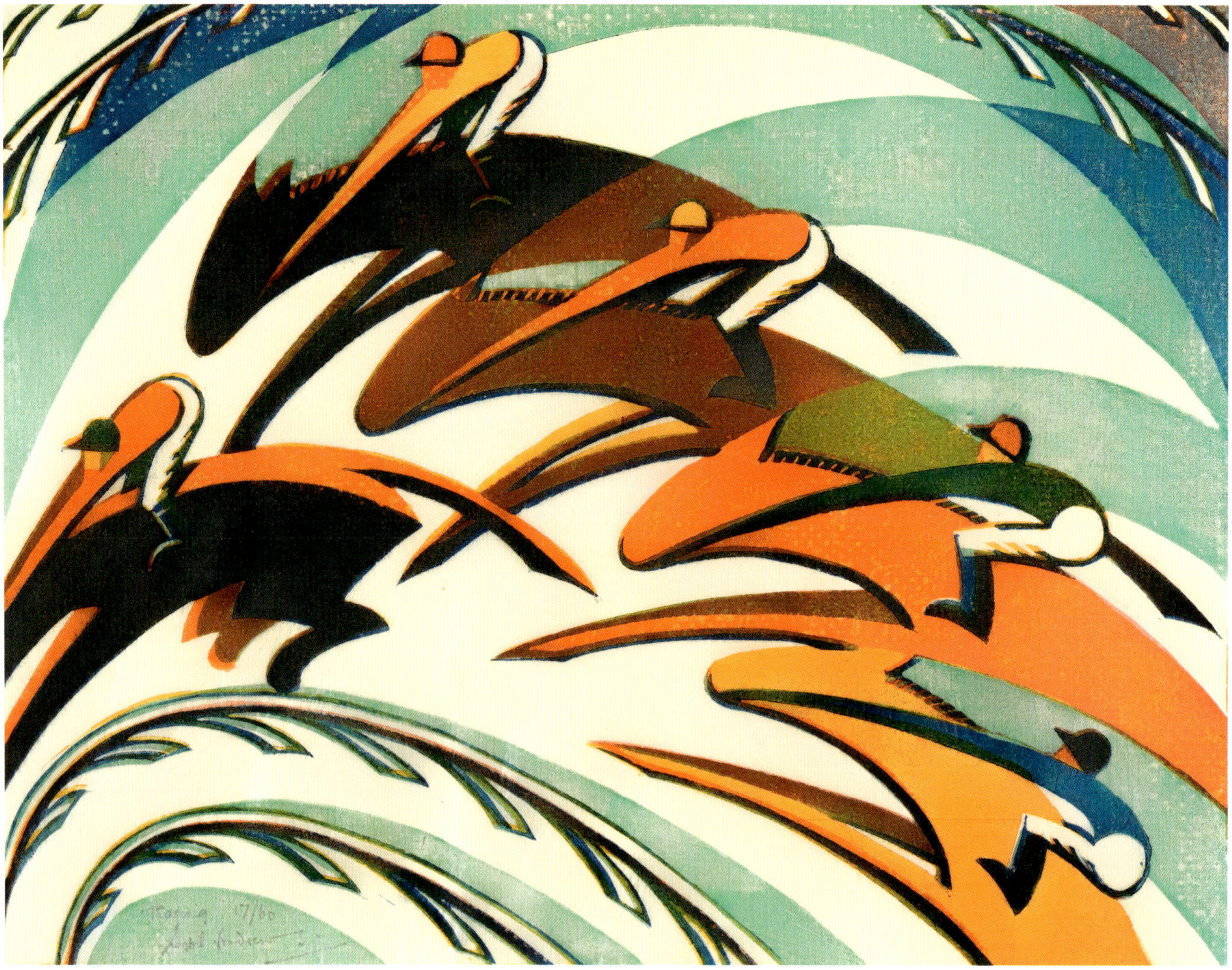

Sybil Andrews *Racing*, 1934

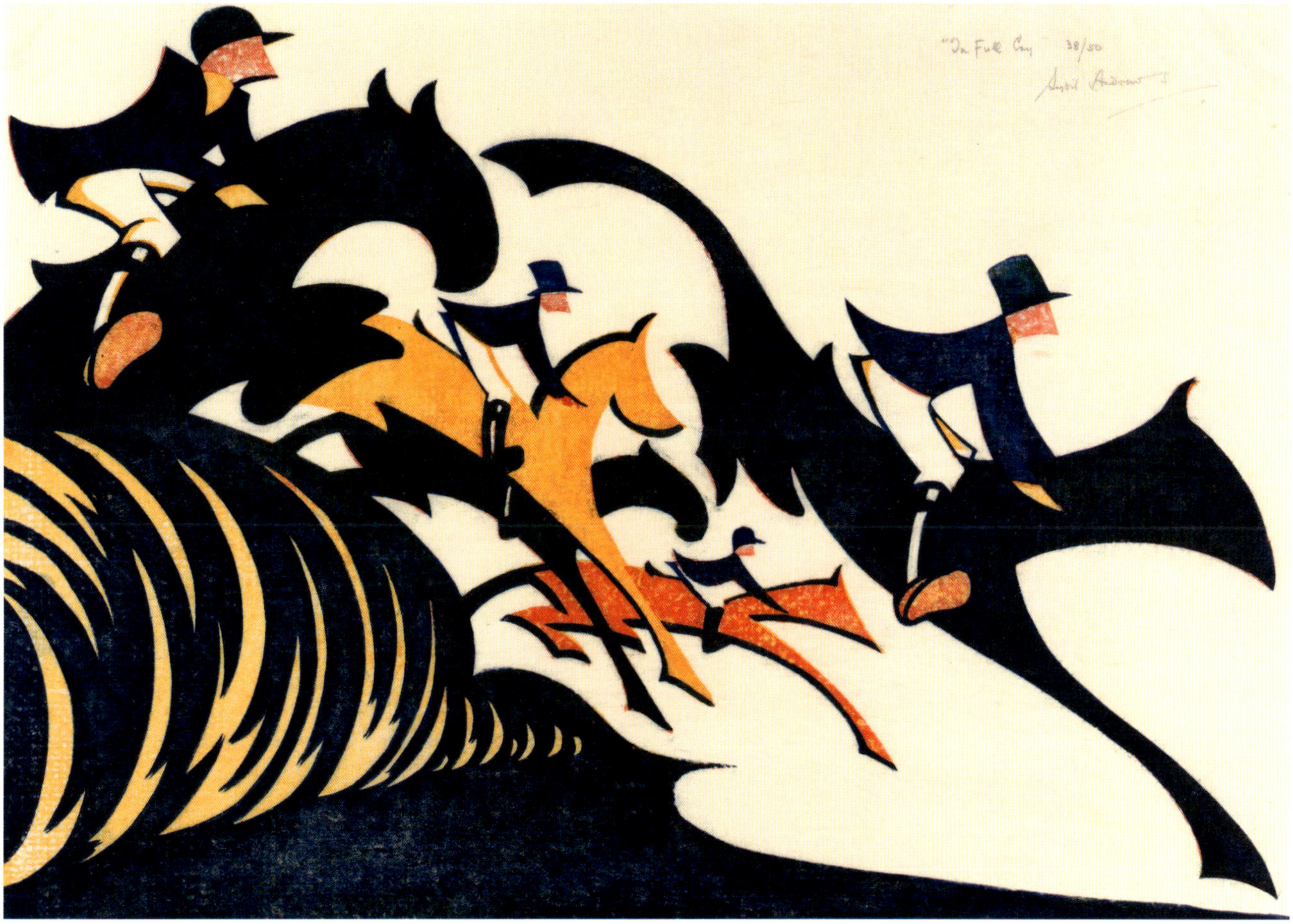

Sybil Andrews *In Full Cry*, 1931

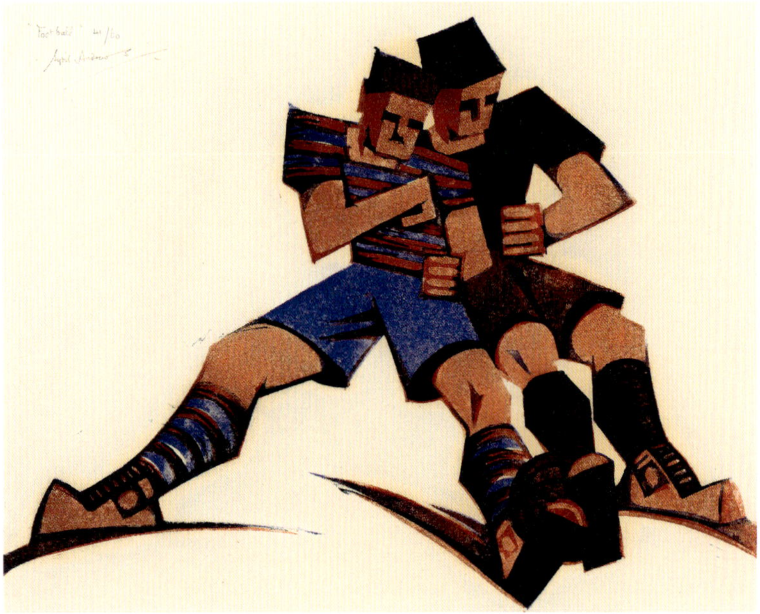

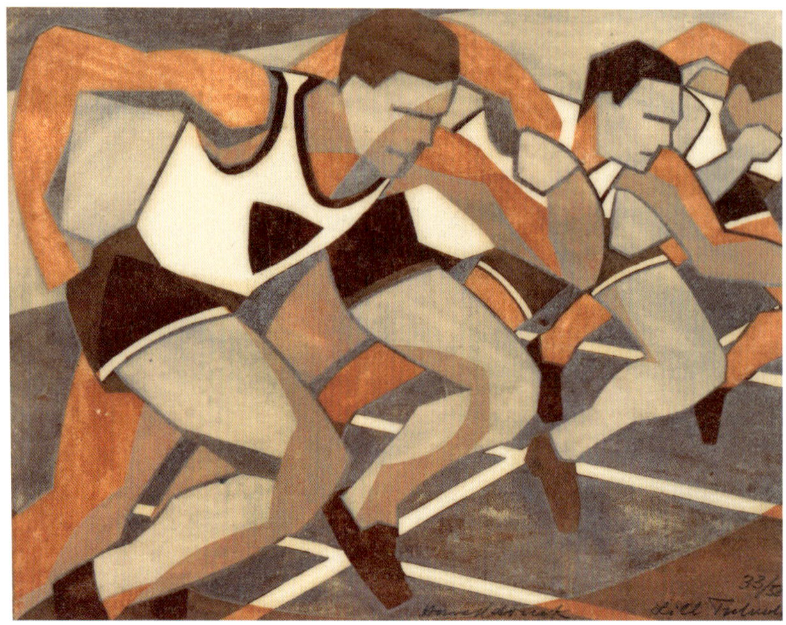

Sybil Andrews *Football*, 1937

Lill Tschudi *Just Off*, 1932

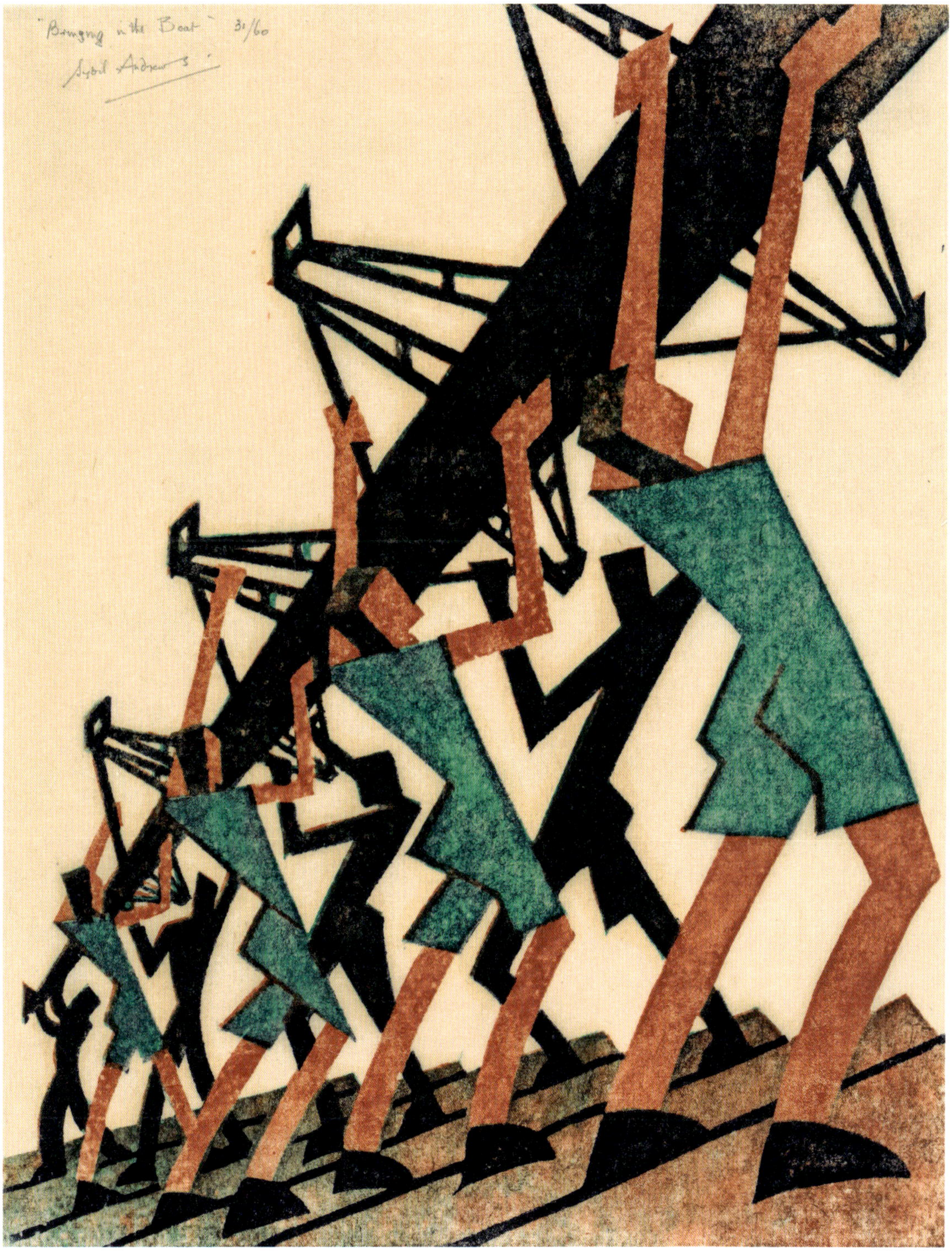

Sybil Andrews *Bringing in the Boat*, 1933

Cyril E. Power *The Eight*, 1930

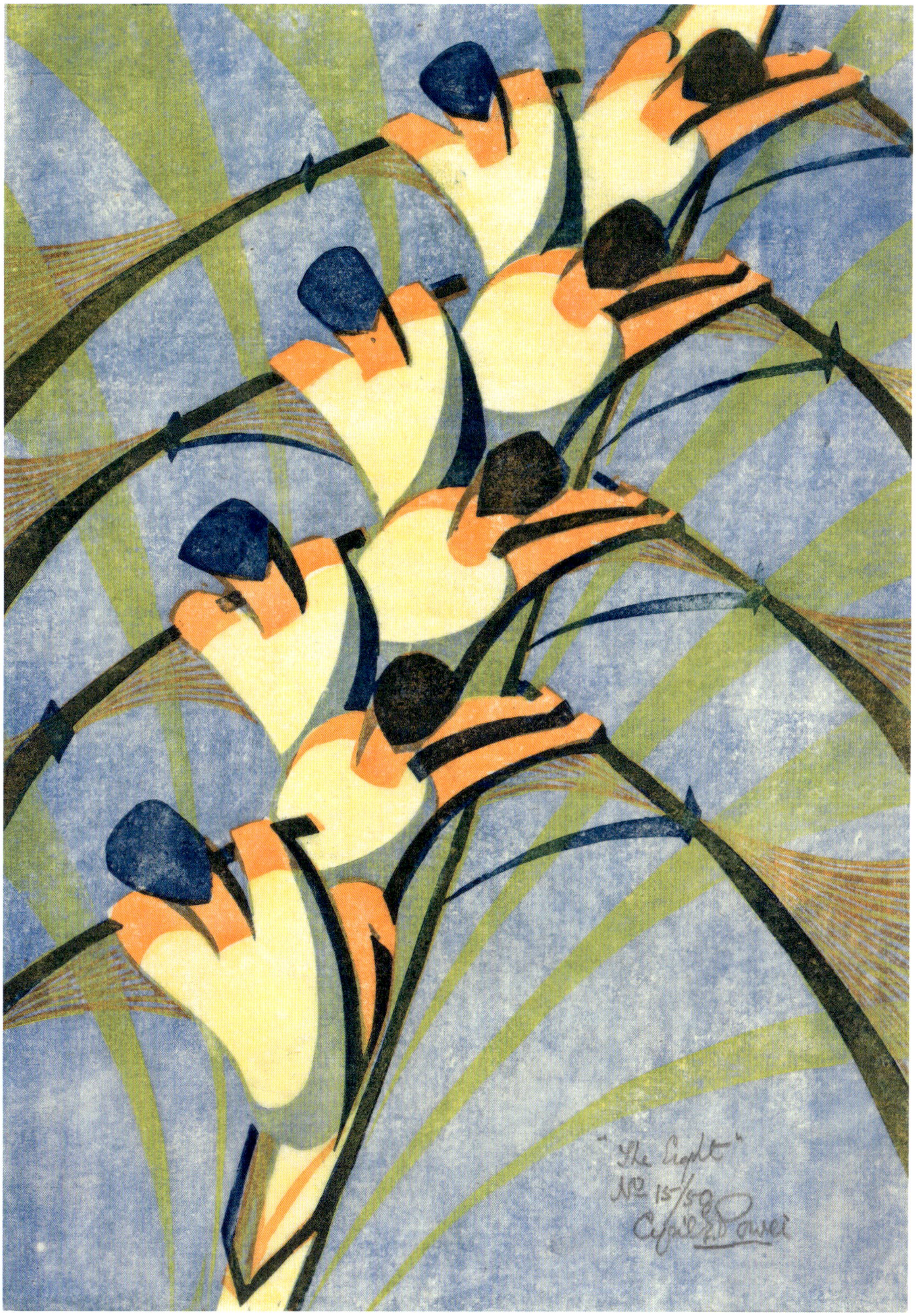
"The Eight"
No 15/50
Cyril E Power

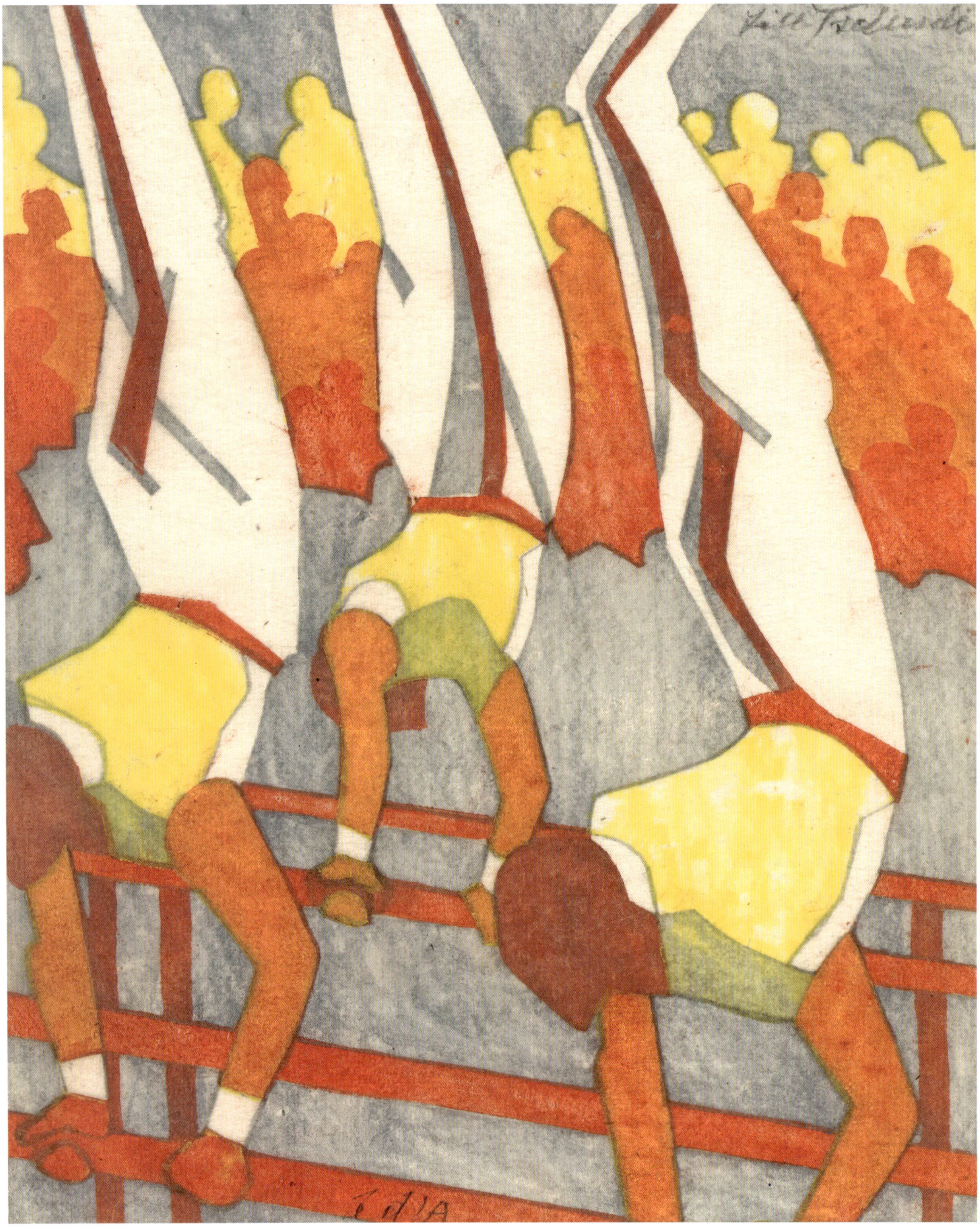

Lill Tschudi *Gymnastic Exercises*, 1931

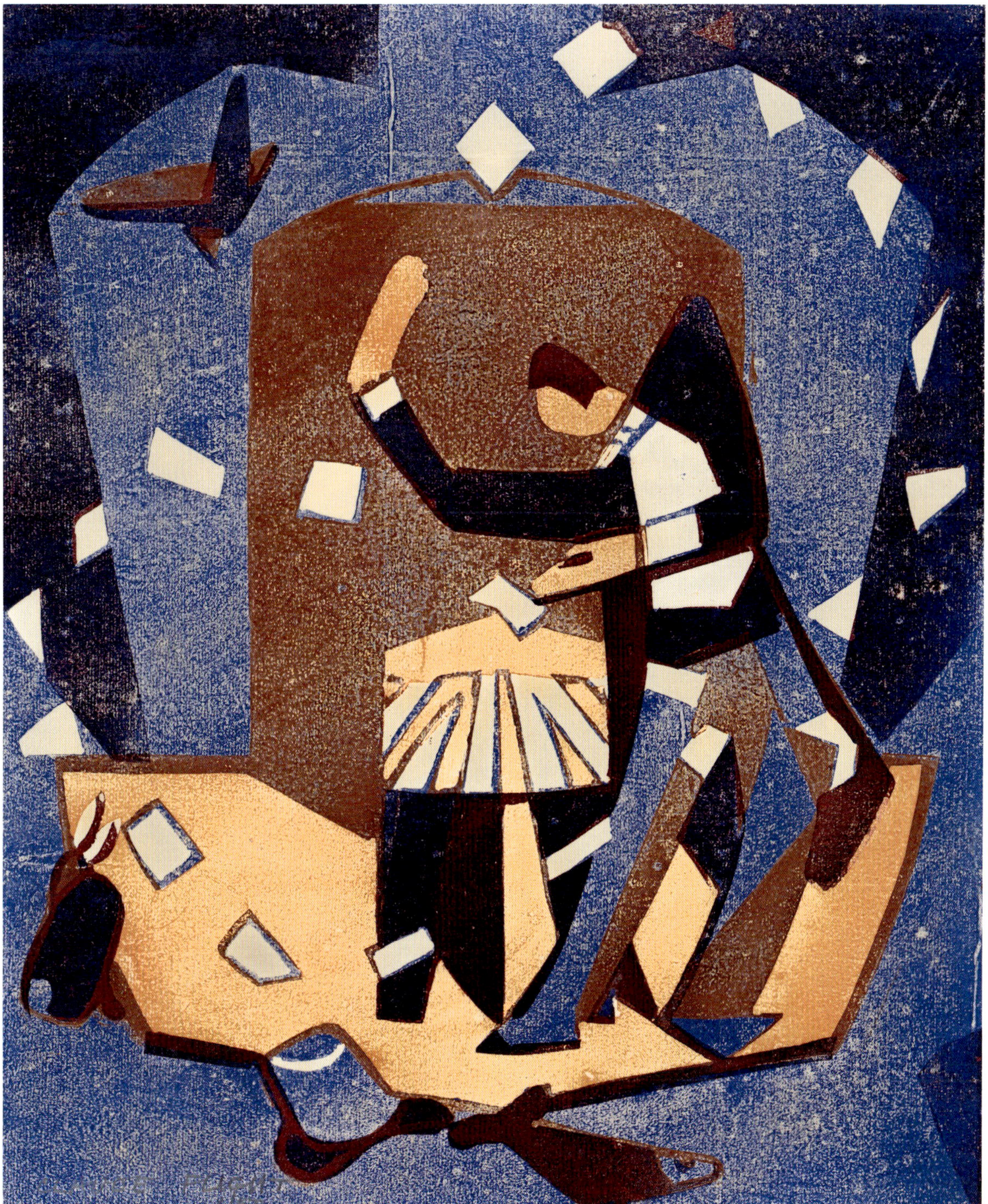

Claude Flight *The Conjuror*, ca. 1933

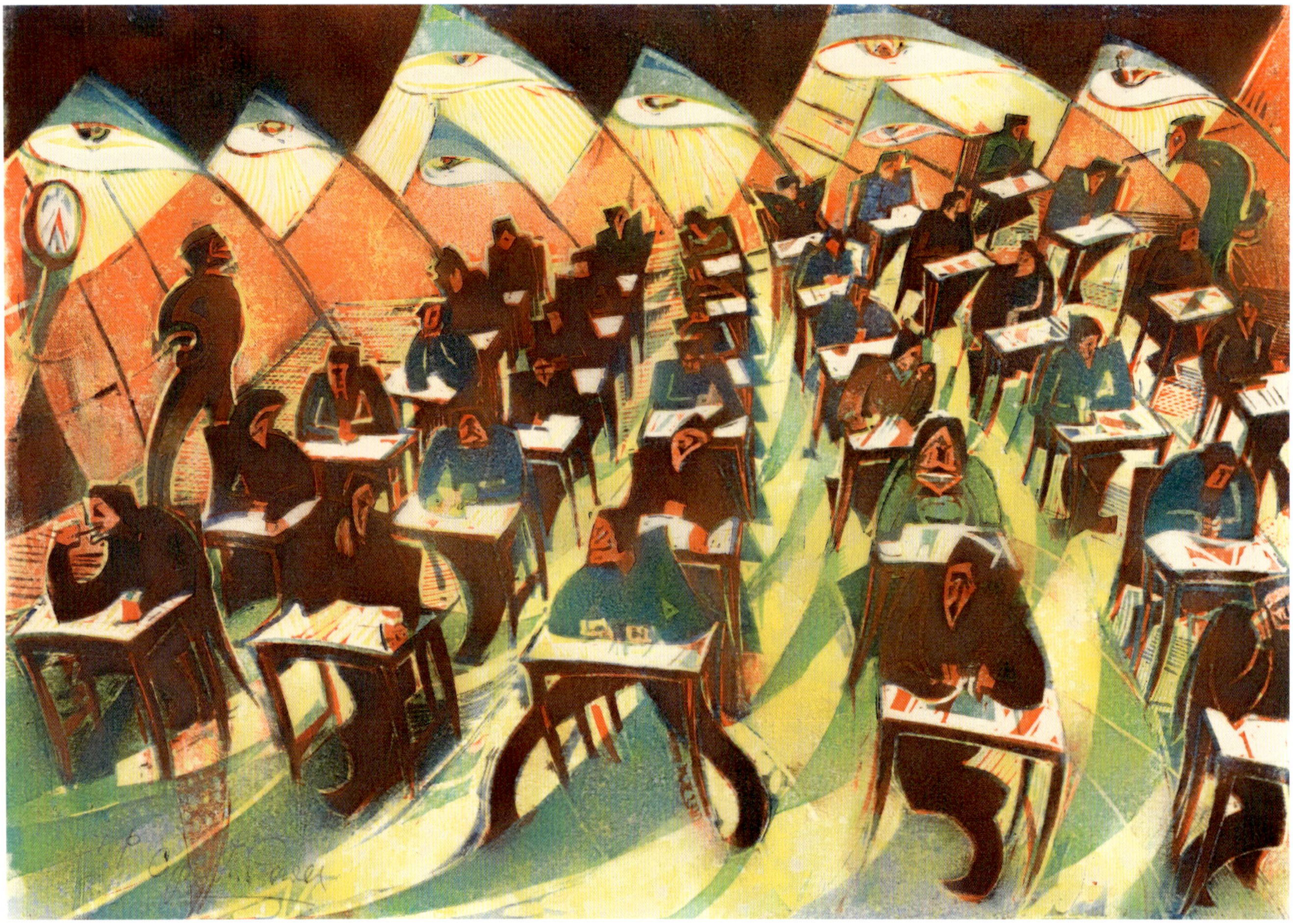

Cyril E. Power *The Exam Room*, ca. 1934

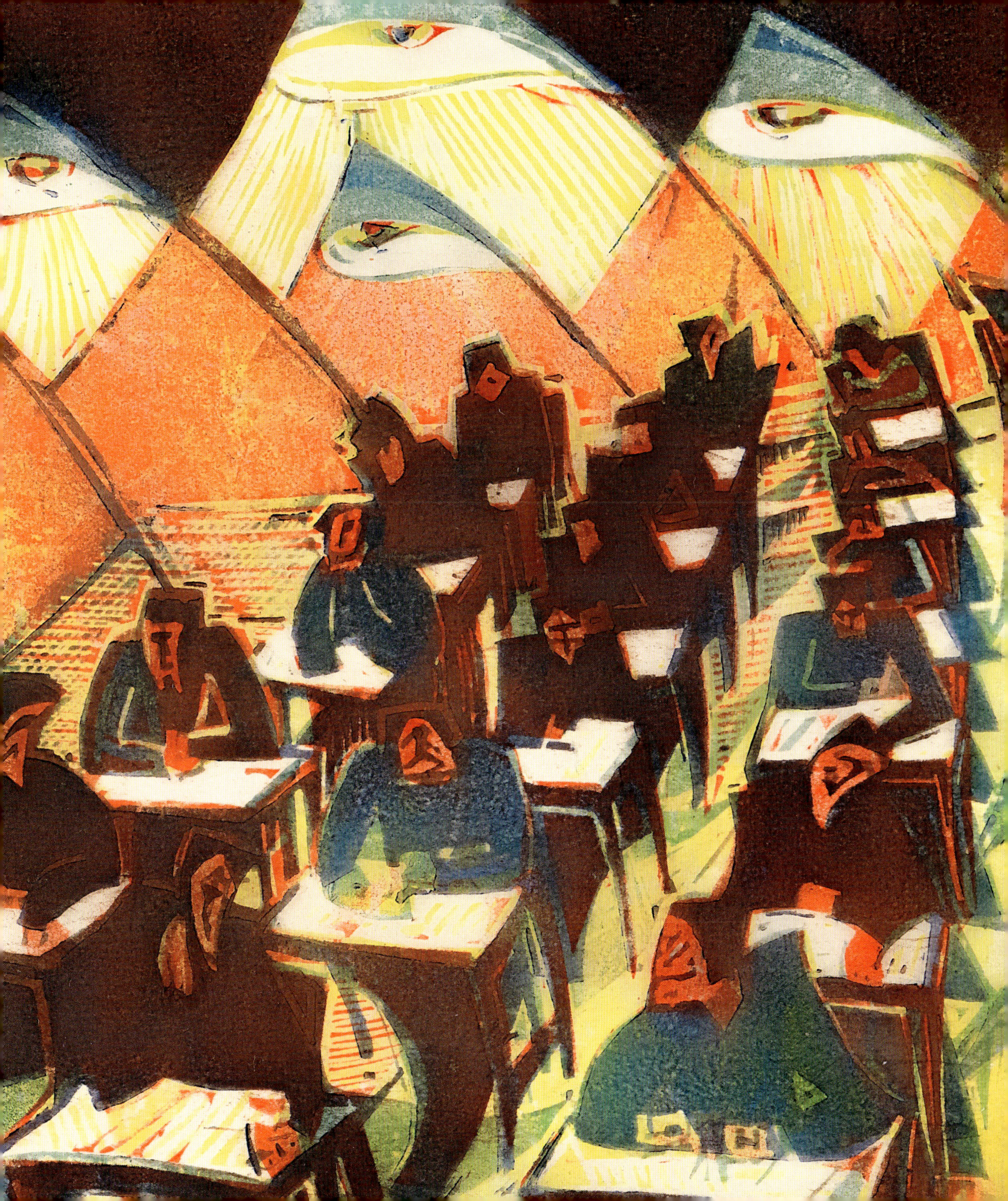

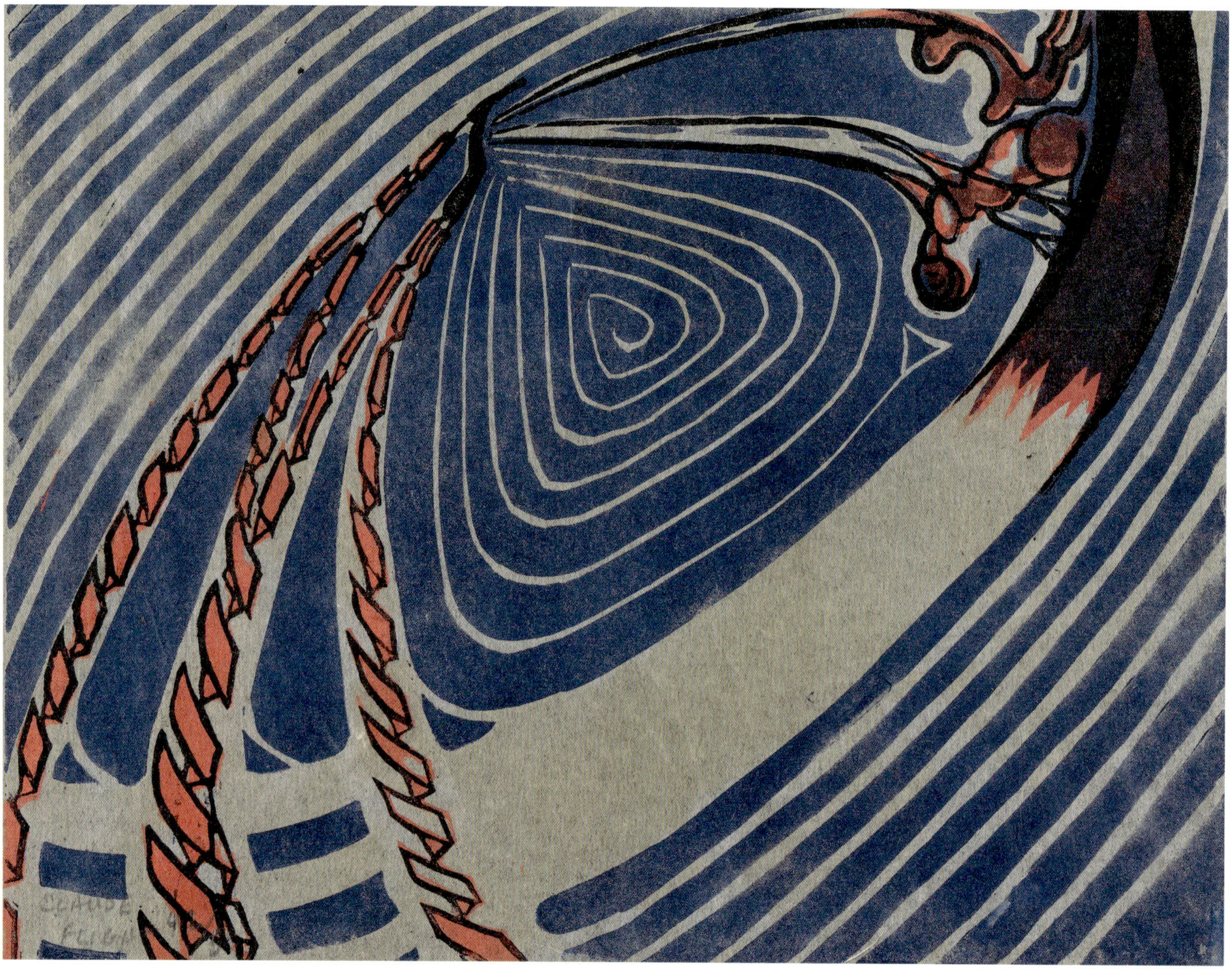

Claude Flight *Swing-Boats*, 1921

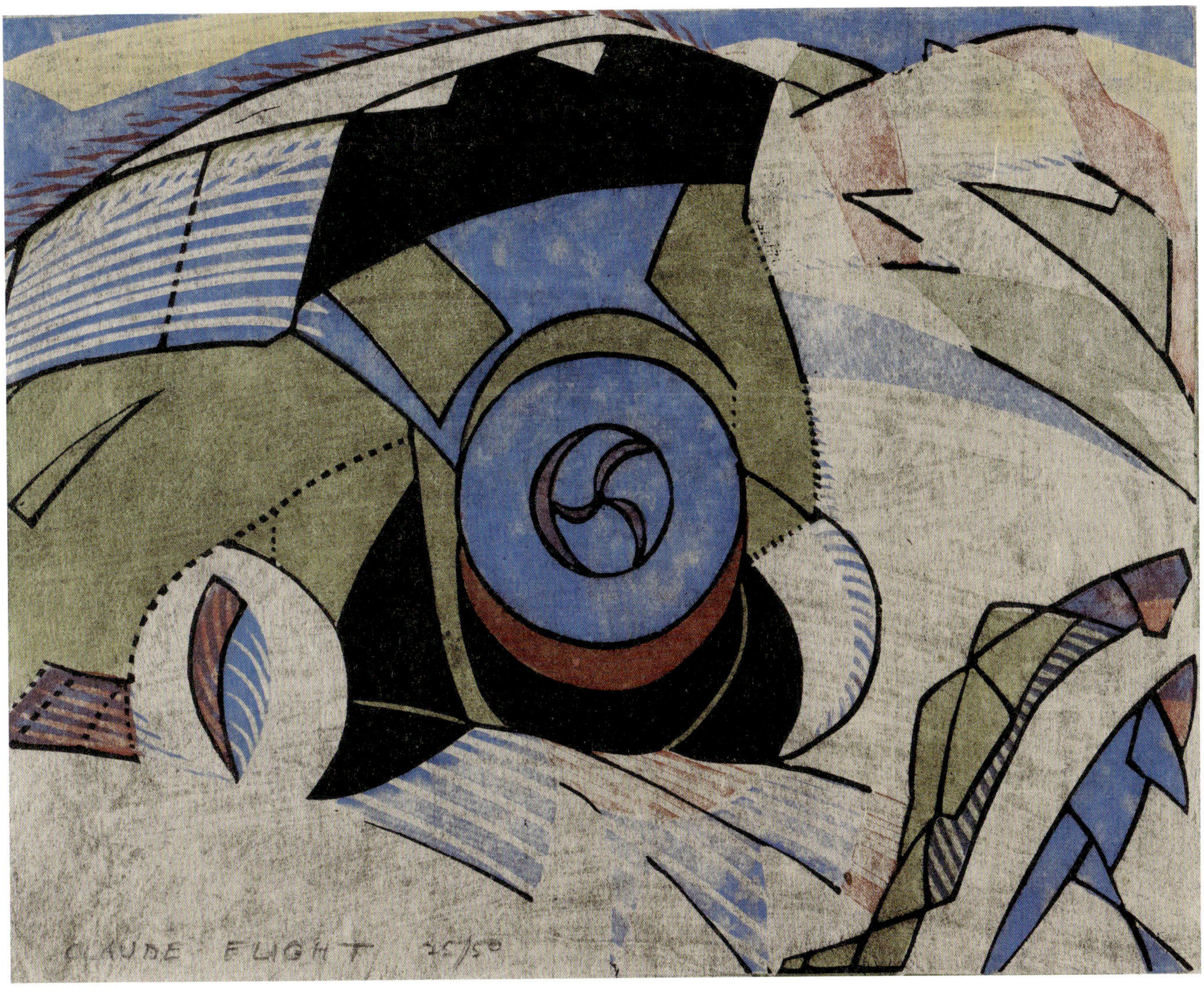

Claude Flight *Paris Omnibus*, 1923

Cyril E. Power *The Vortex* (experimental proof before the 1931 edition), 1929

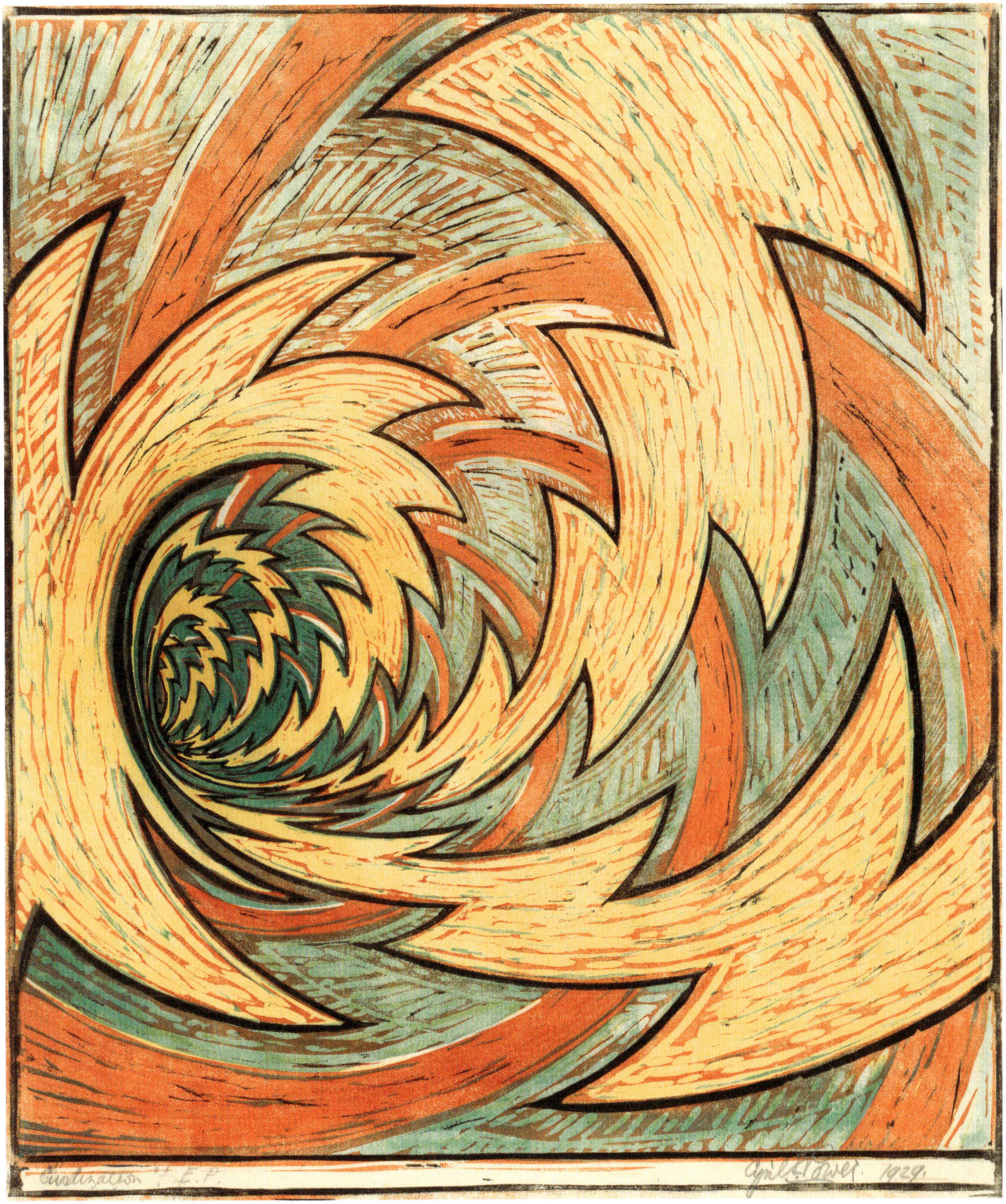
E.P.
1929.

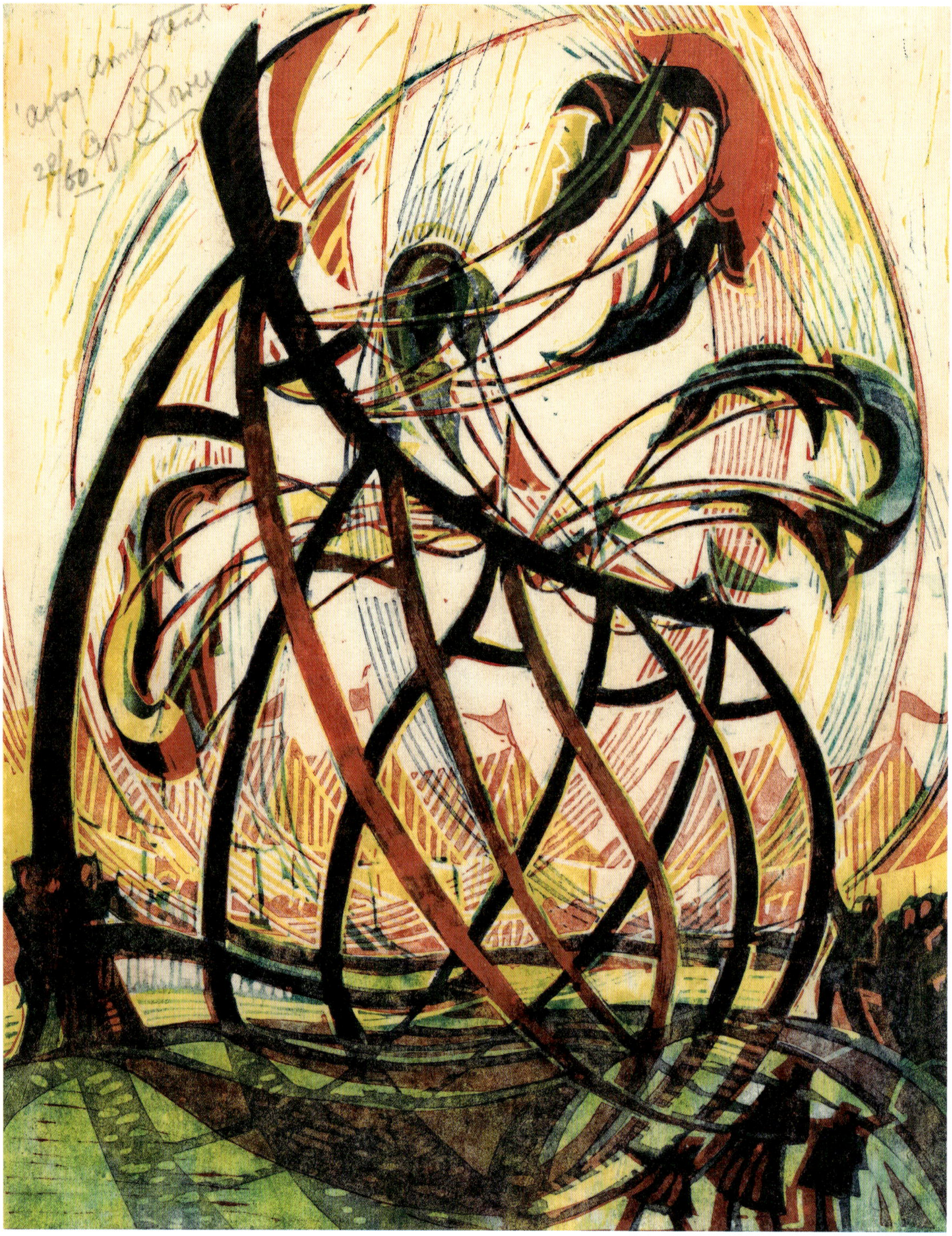

Cyril E. Power *'Appy 'Ampstead*, ca. 1933

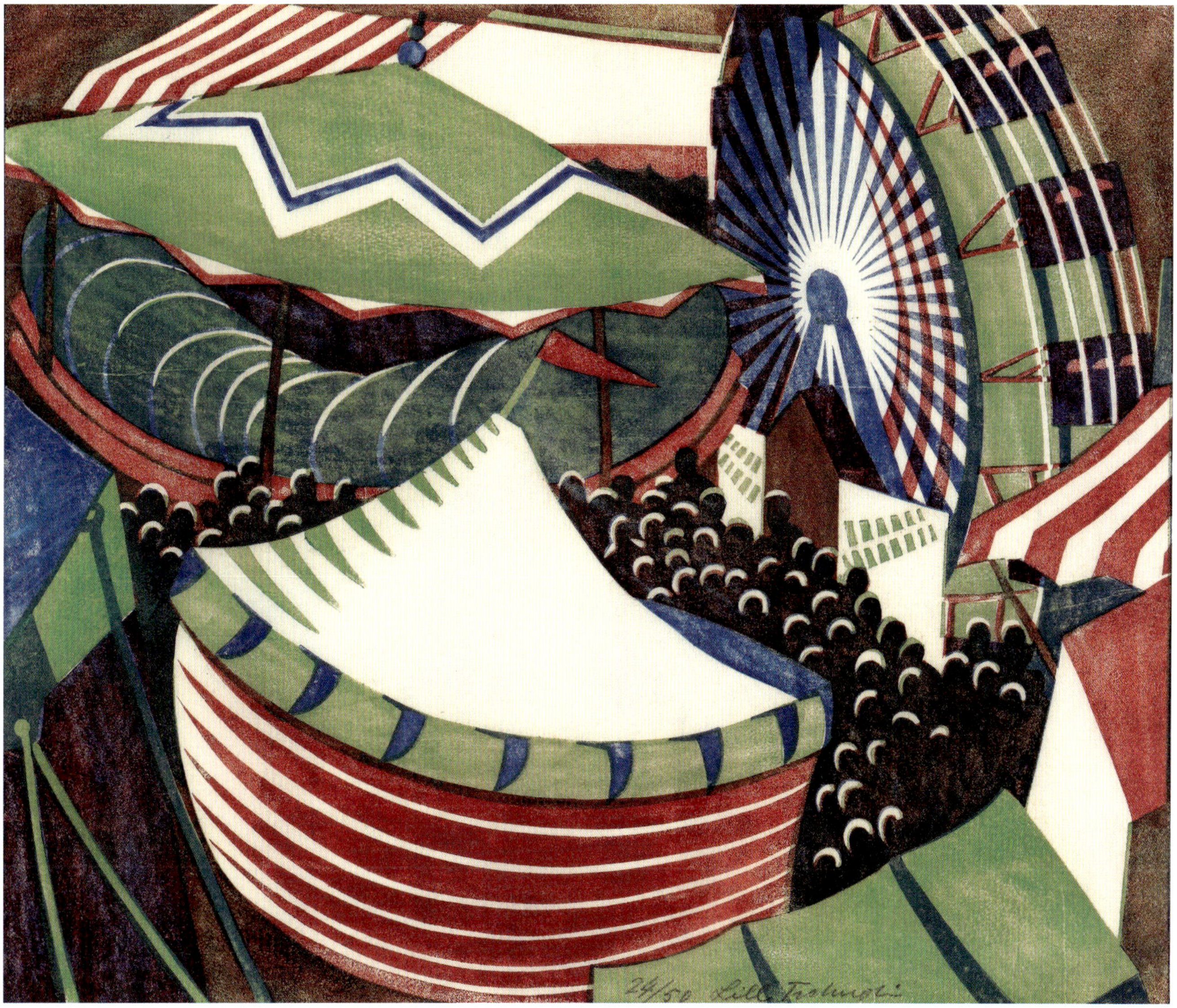

Lill Tschudi *Village Fair I*, 1934

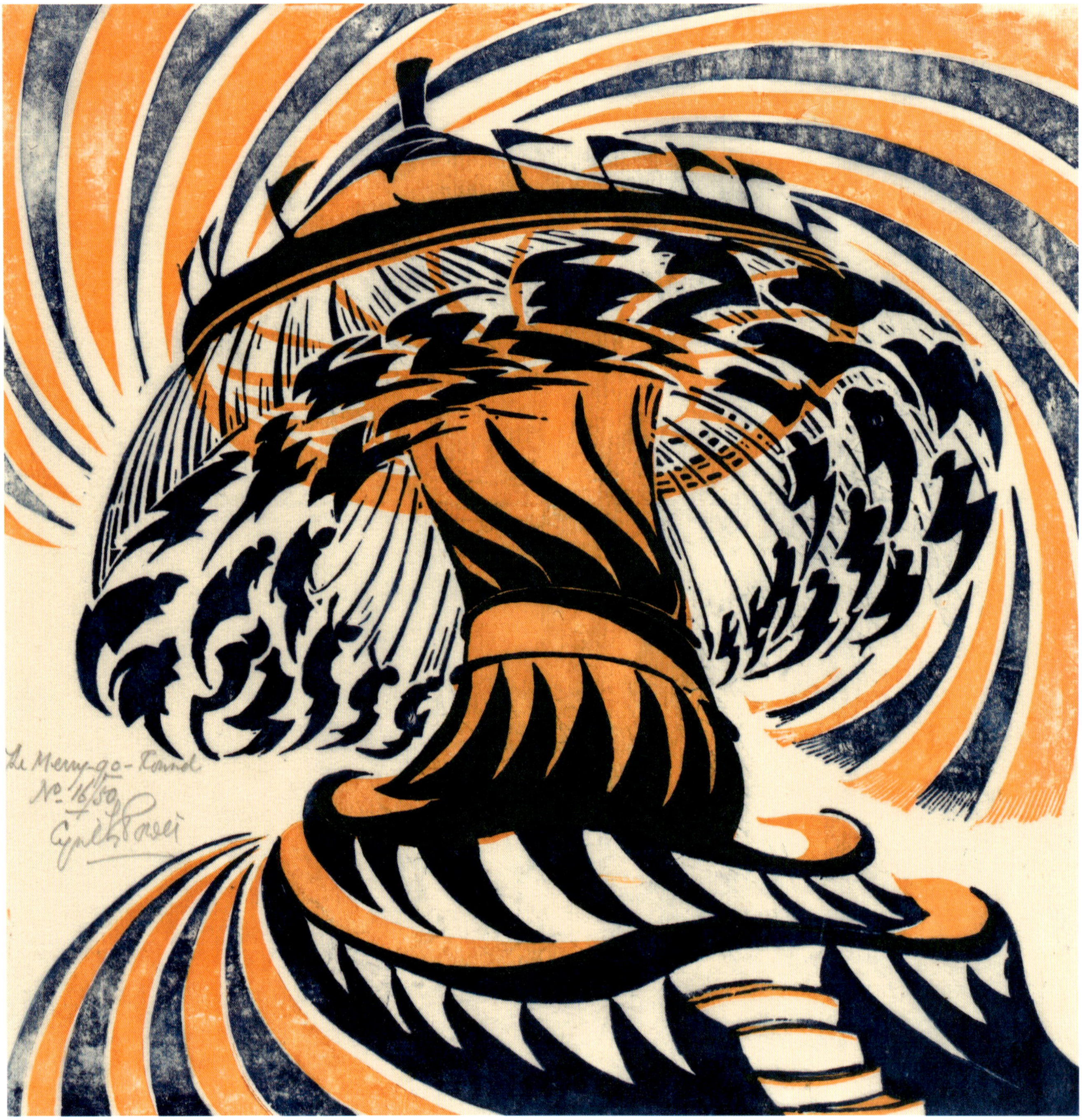

Cyril E. Power *The Merry-Go-Round*, ca. 1930

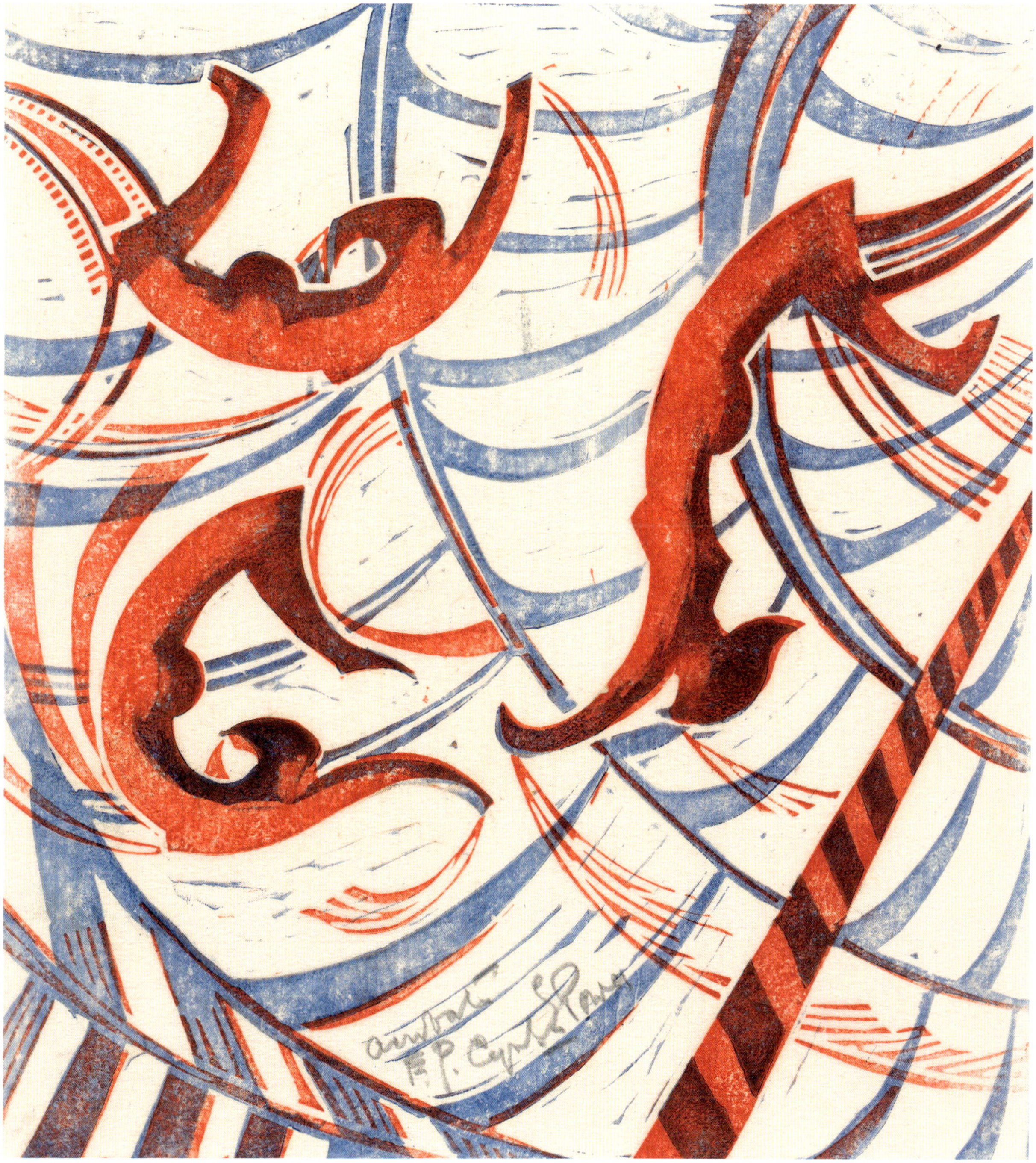

Cyril E. Power *Acrobats* (experimental proof), ca. 1933

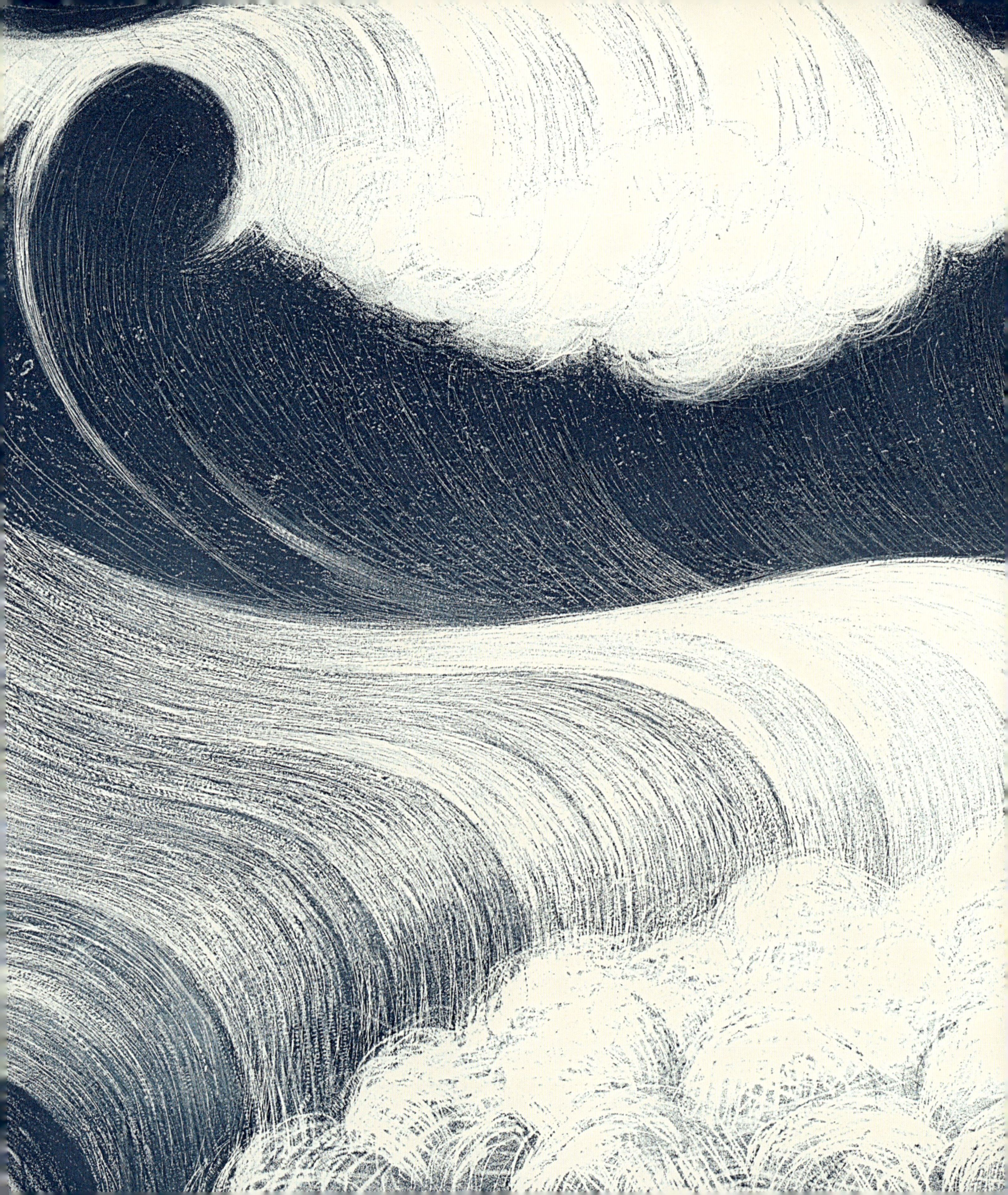

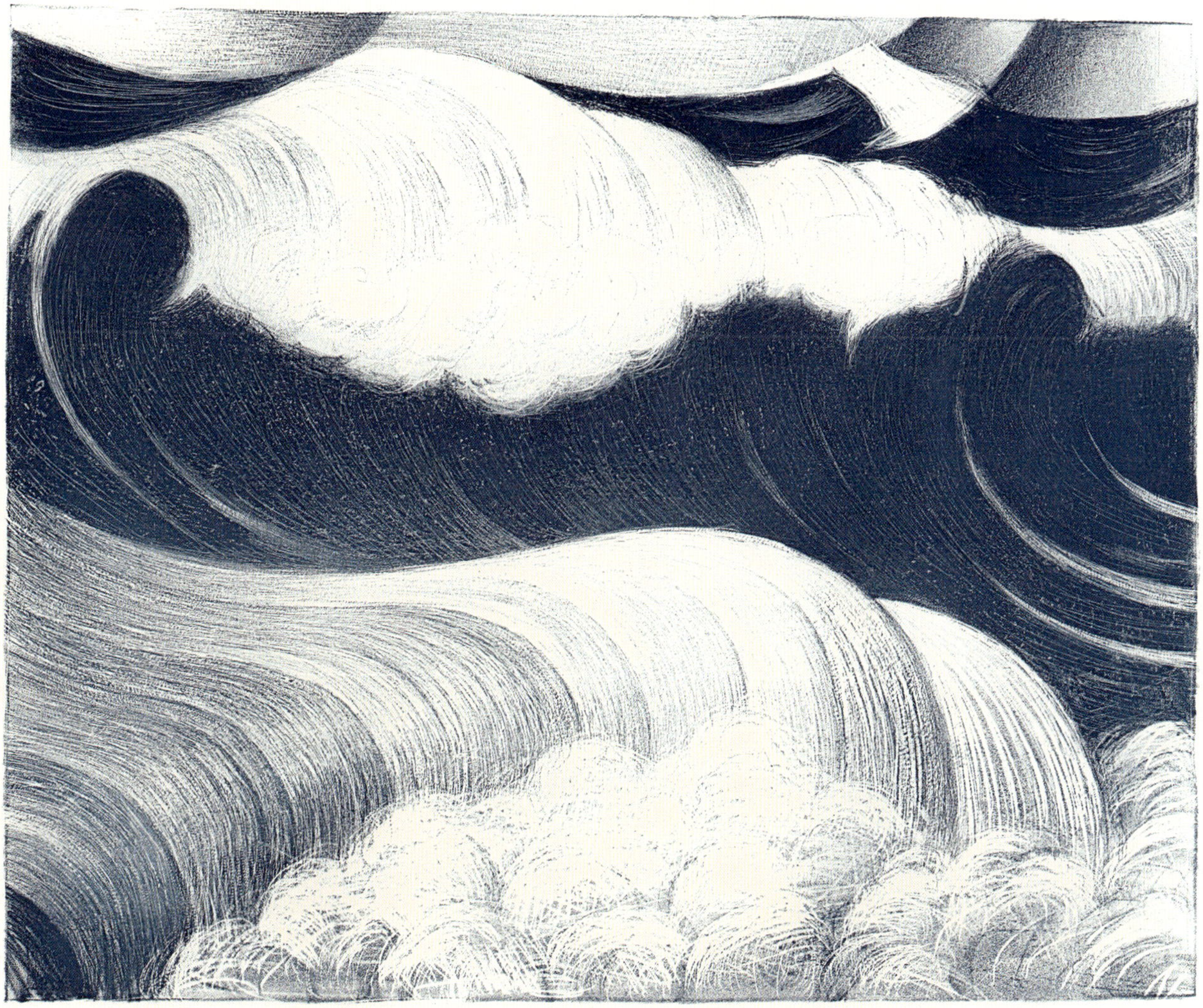

Christopher Richard Wynne Nevinson *The Blue Wave*, 1917

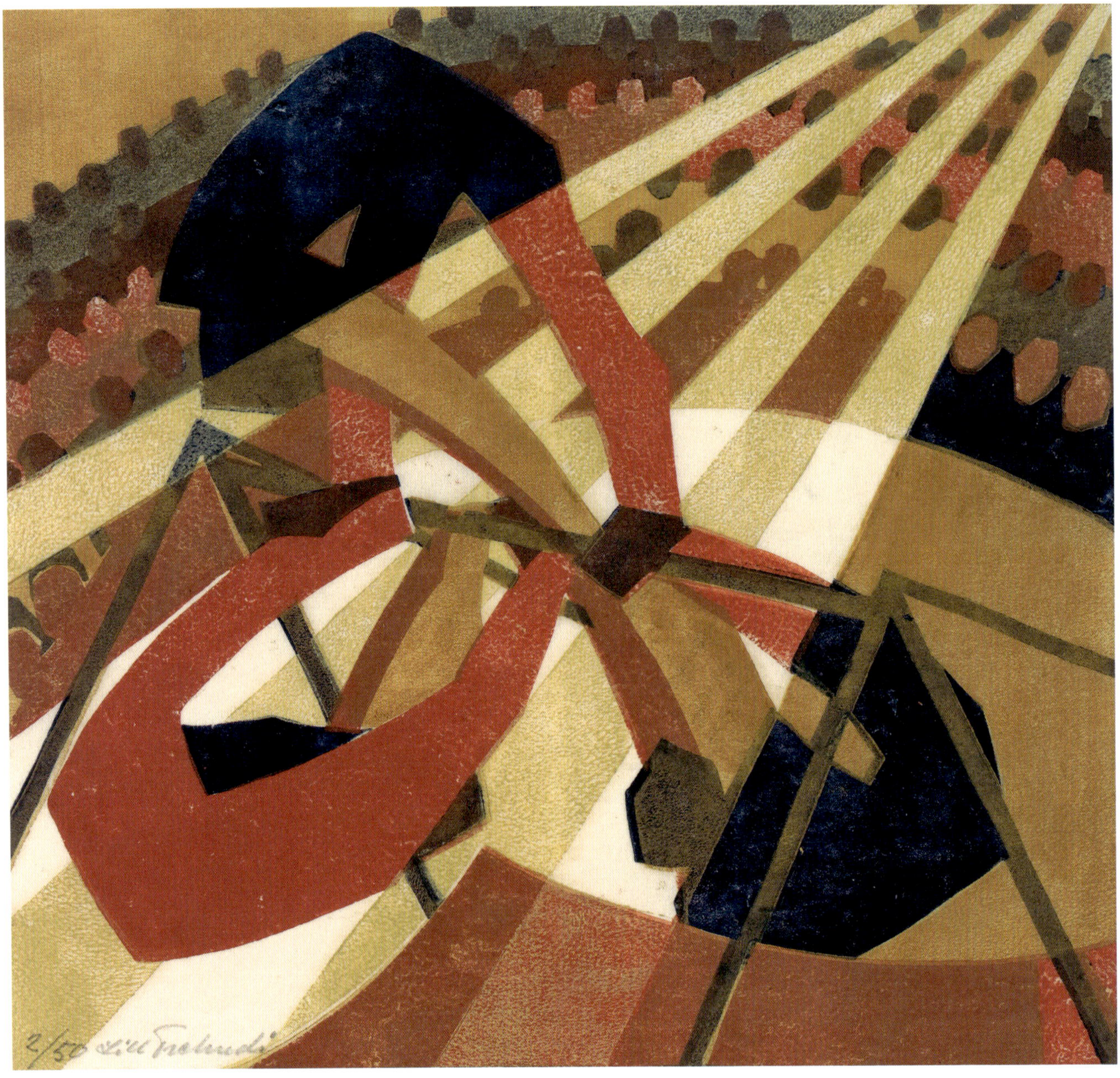

Lill Tschudi *In the Circus*, 1932

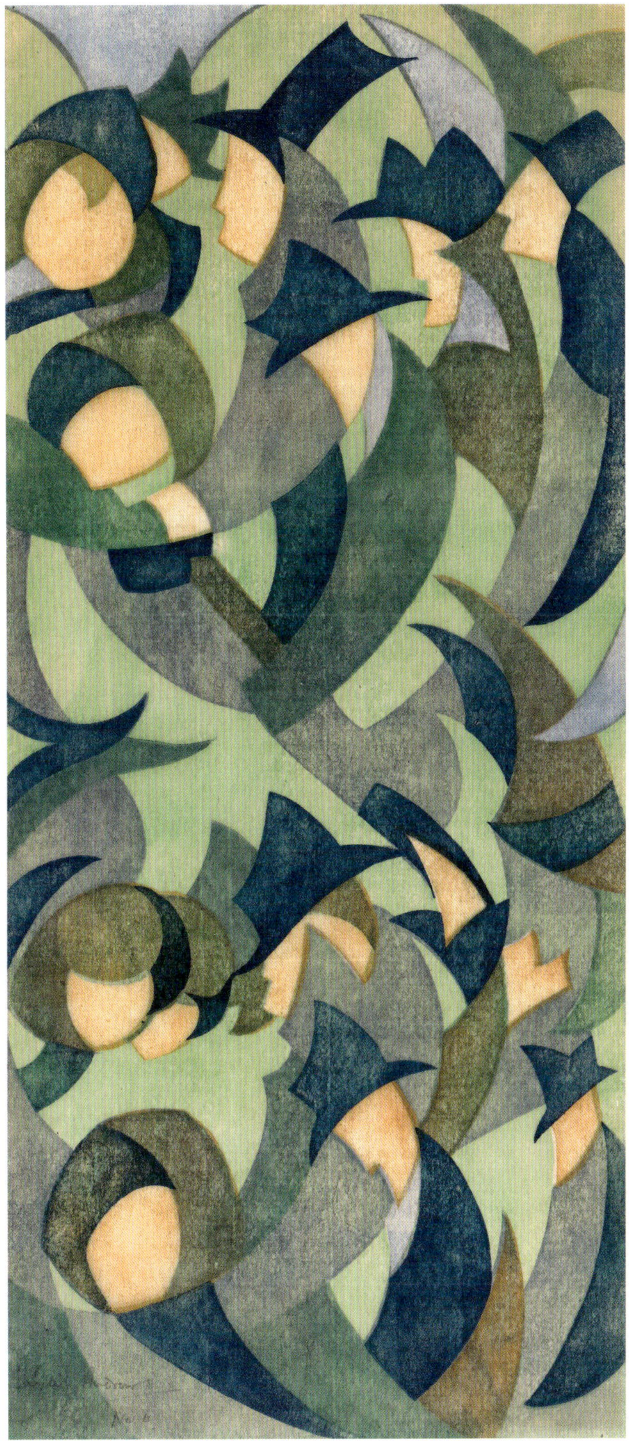

Sybil Andrews *Hyde Park*, 1931

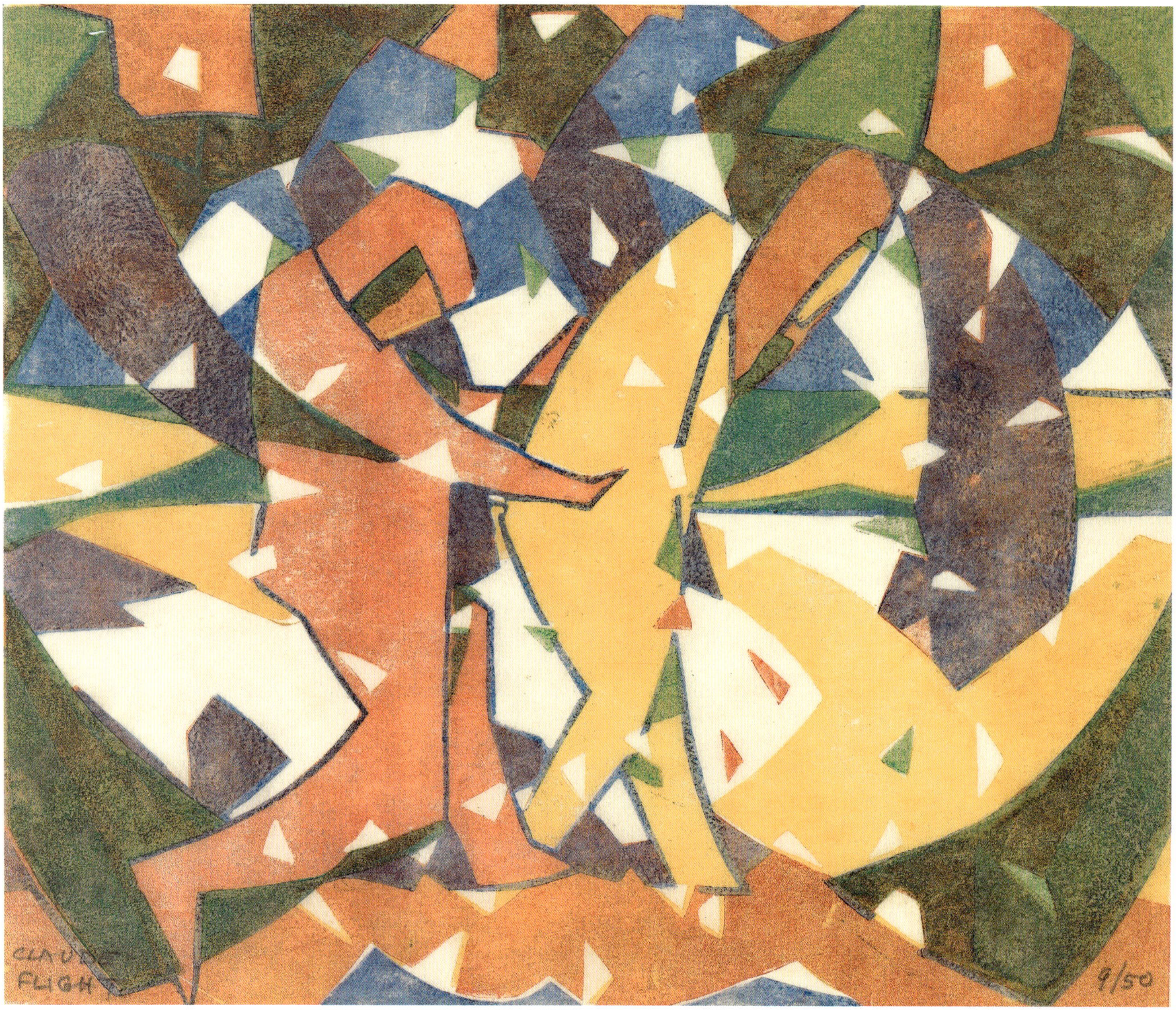

Claude Flight *Autumn*, from *The Four Seasons*, ca. 1926

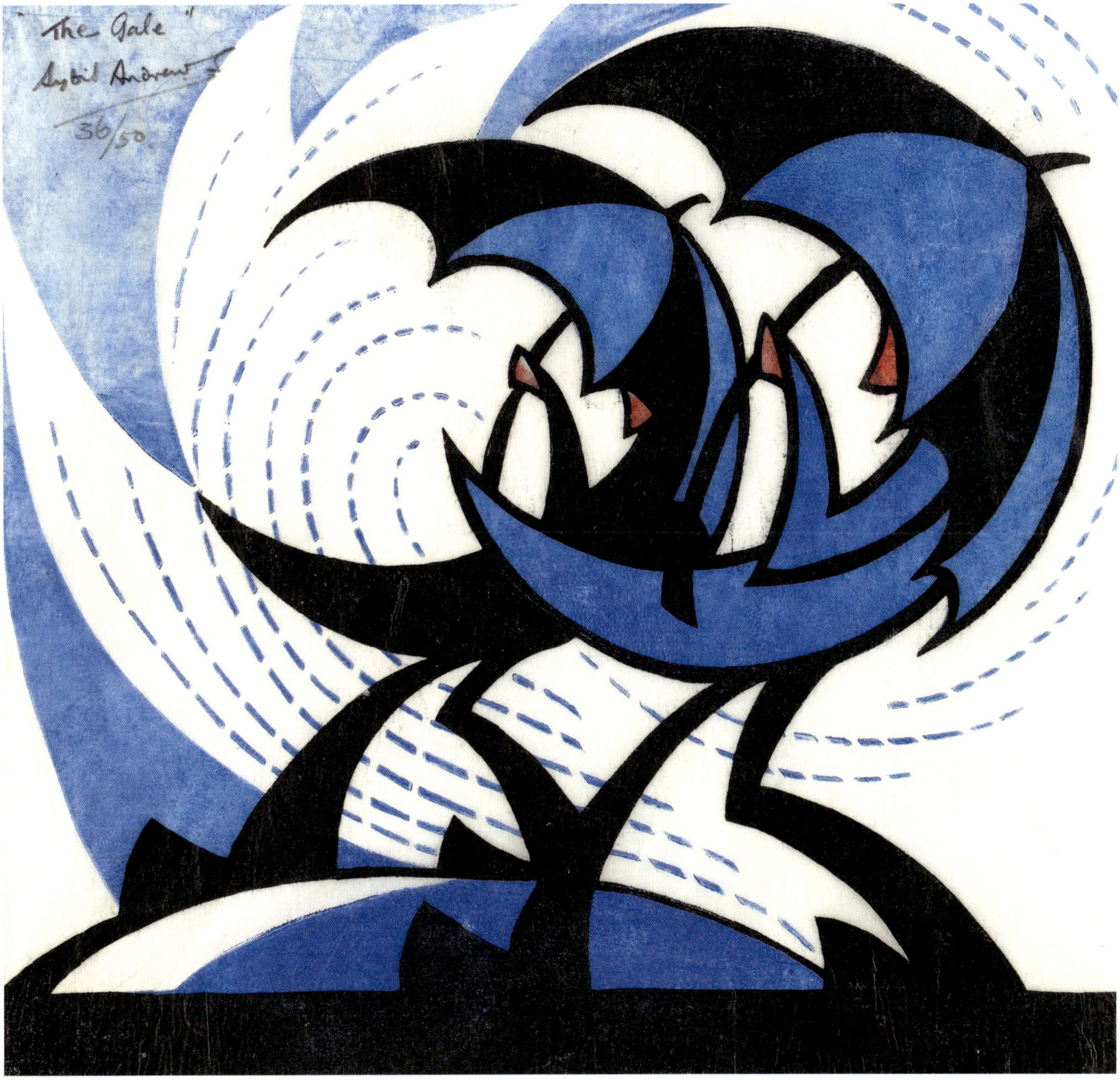

Sybil Andrews *The Gale*, 1930

Claude Flight *Street Singers*, 1925

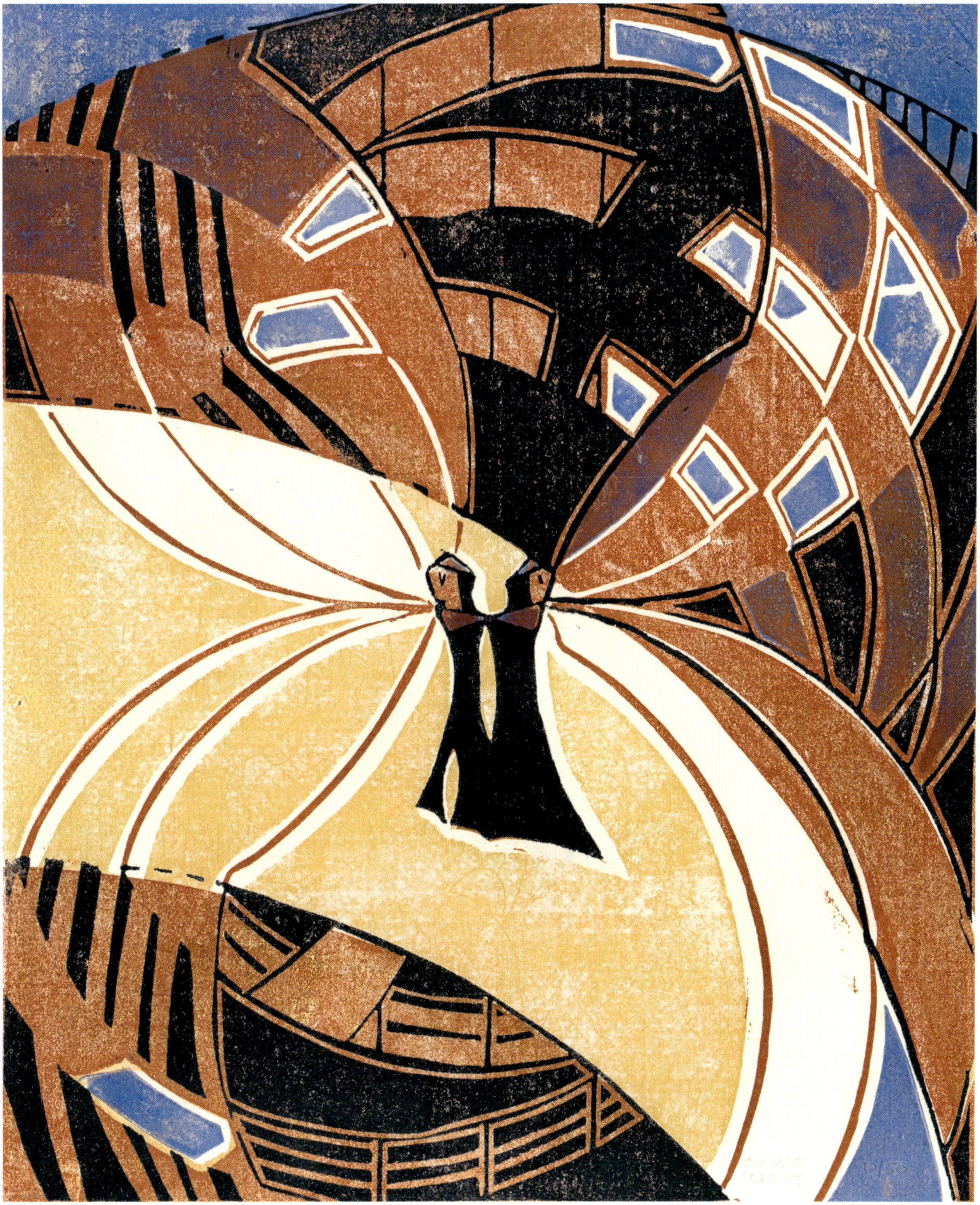

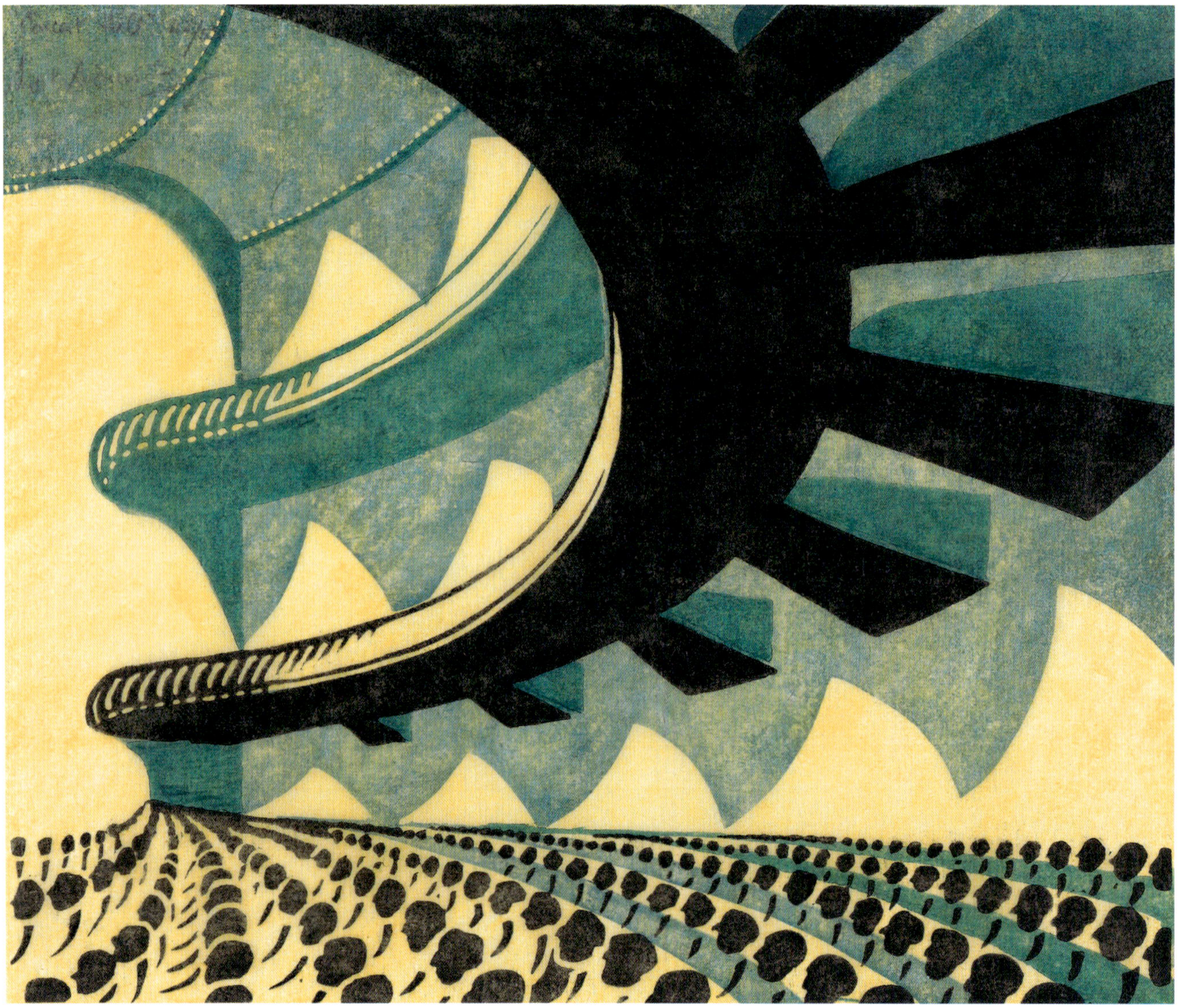

Sybil Andrews *Concert Hall*, 1929

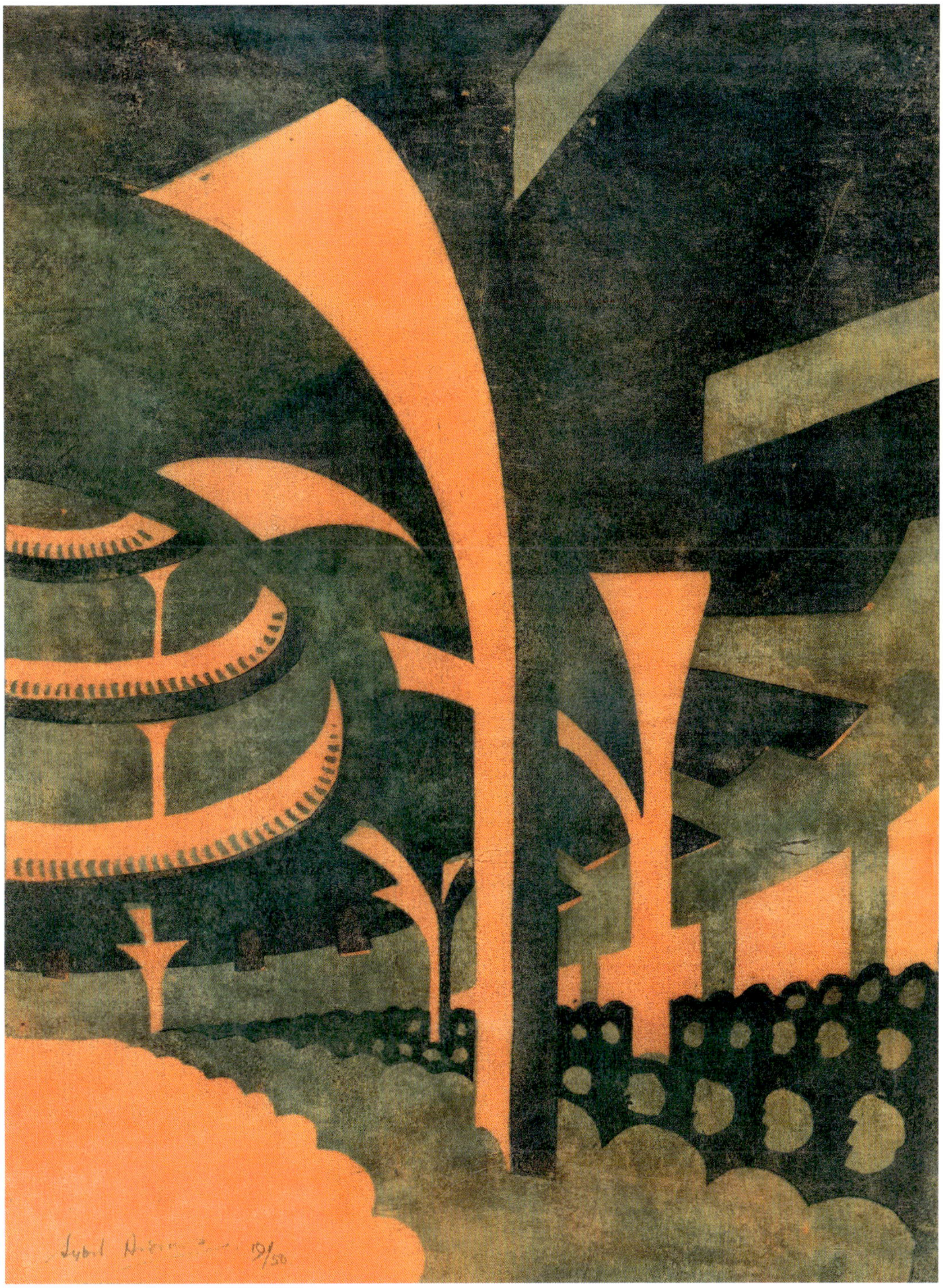

Sybil Andrews *Theatre*, 1929

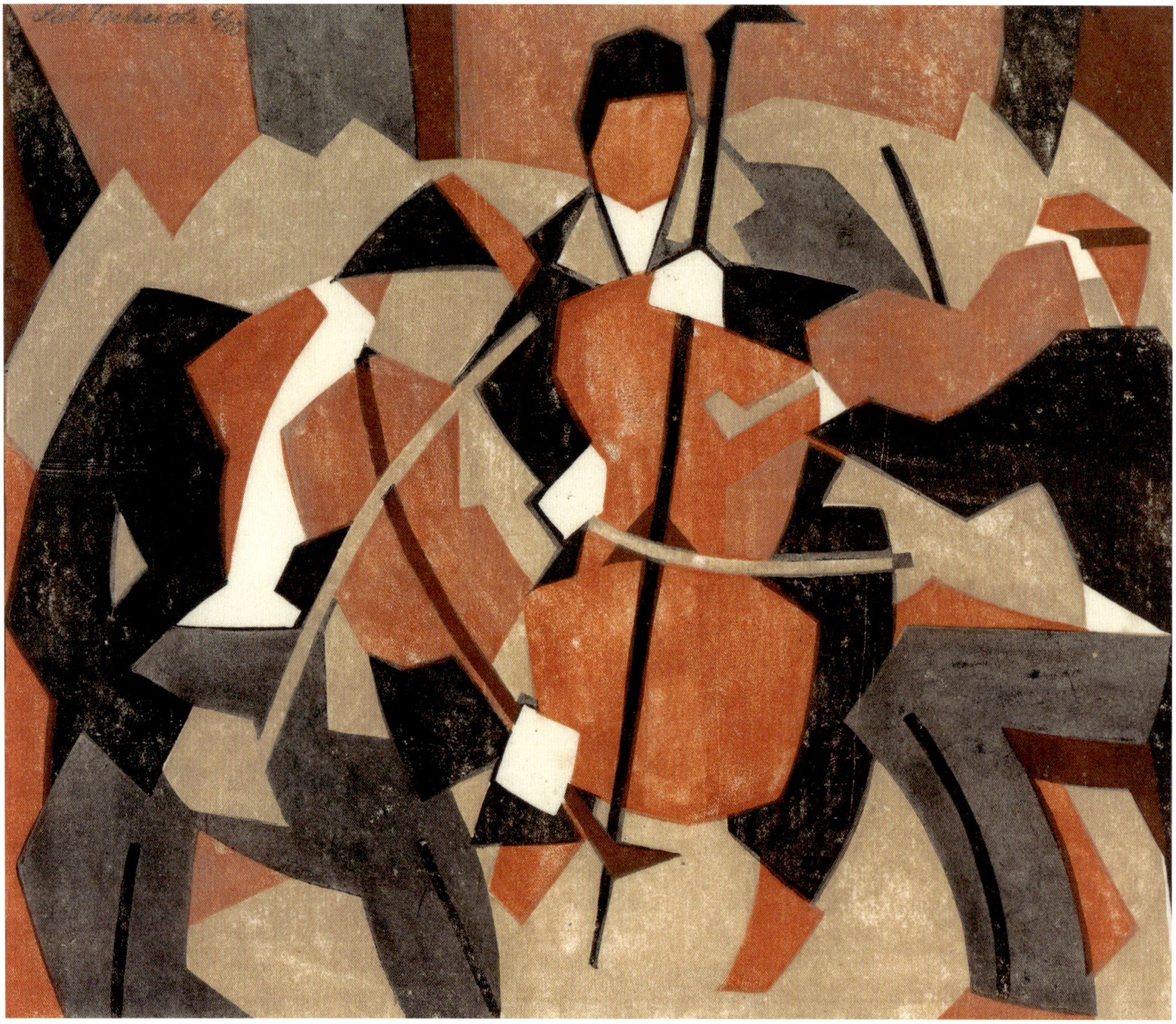

Lill Tschudi *Trio*, 1931

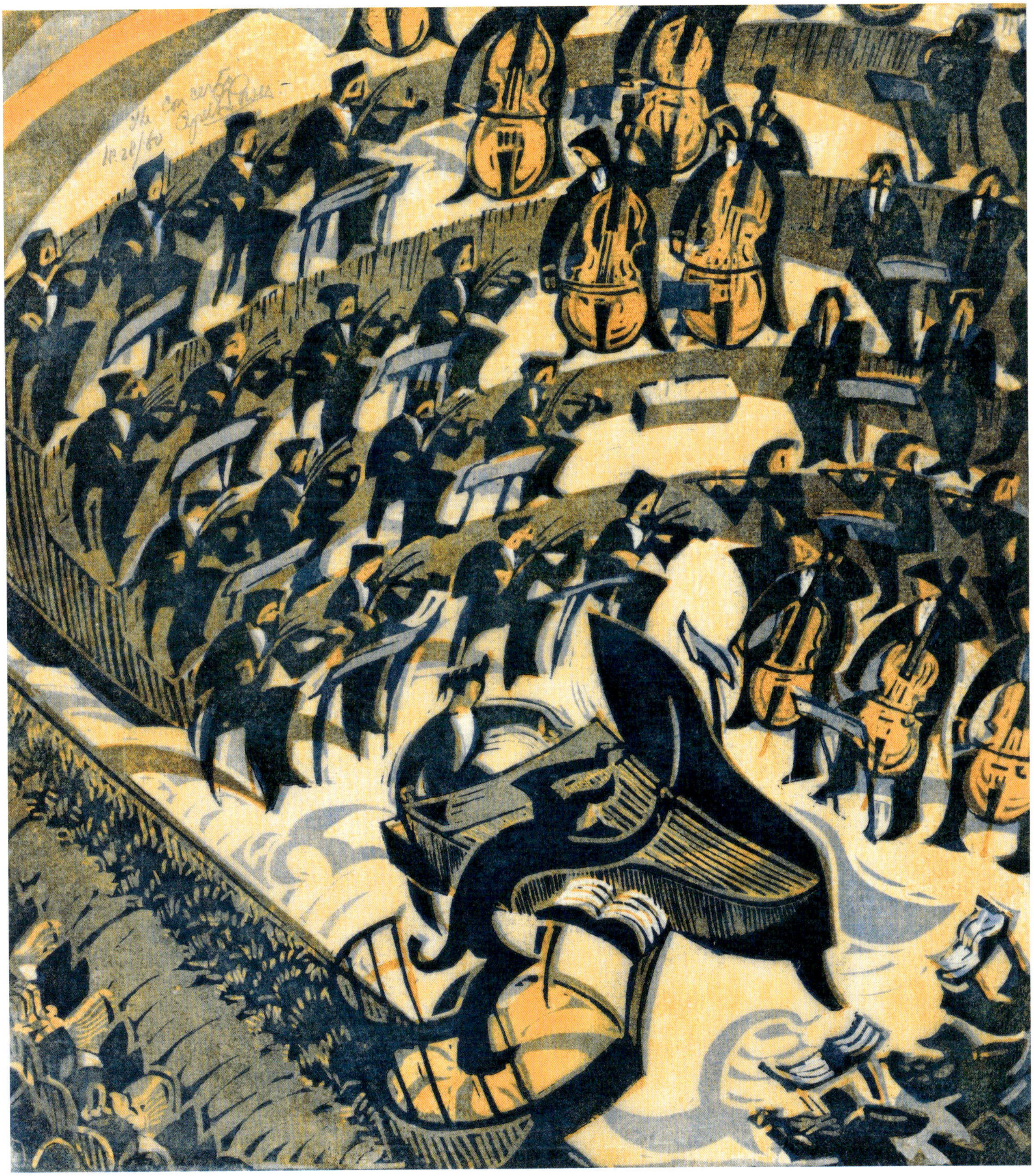

Cyril E. Power *The Concerto*, ca. 1935

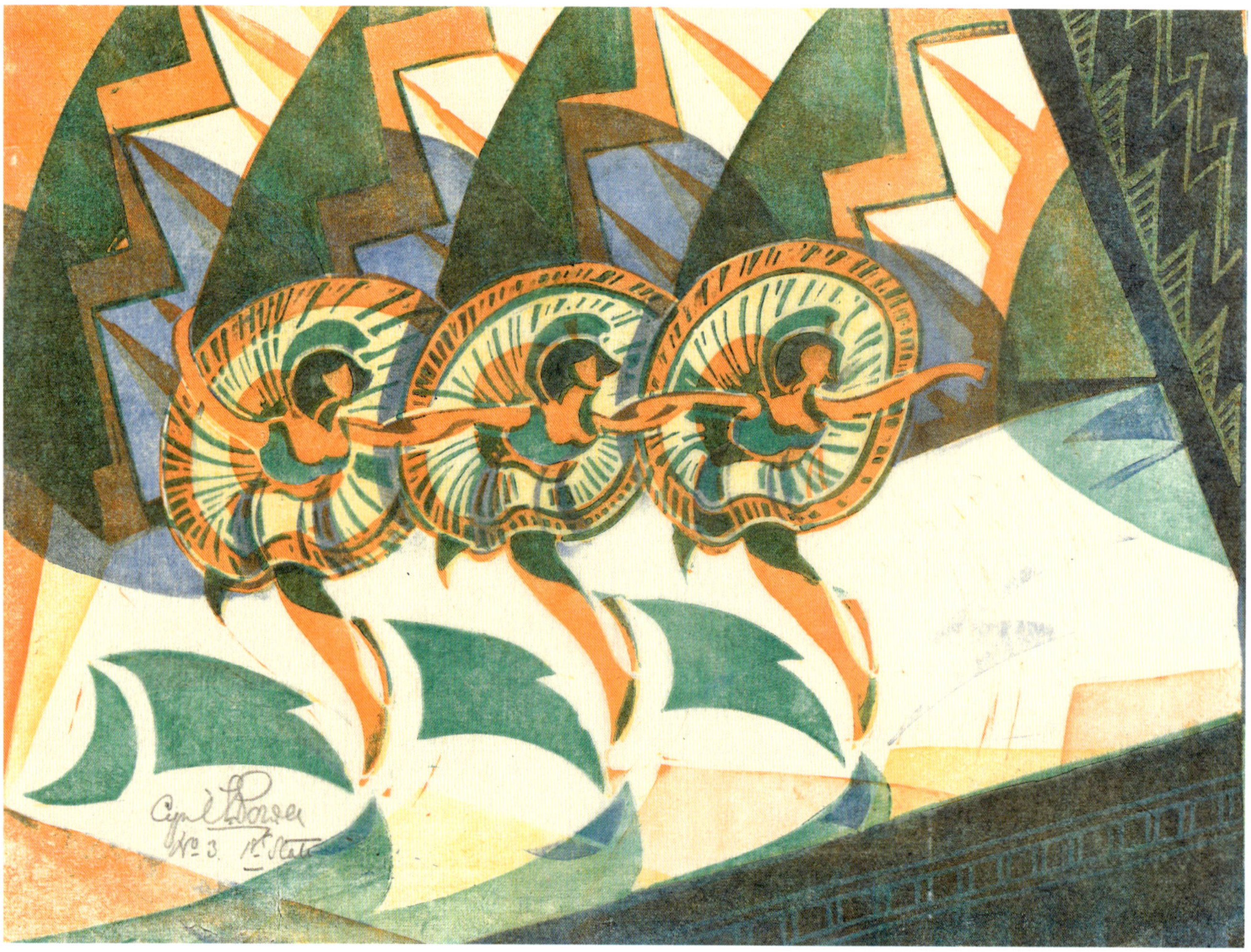

Cyril E. Power *Divertissement*, ca. 1932

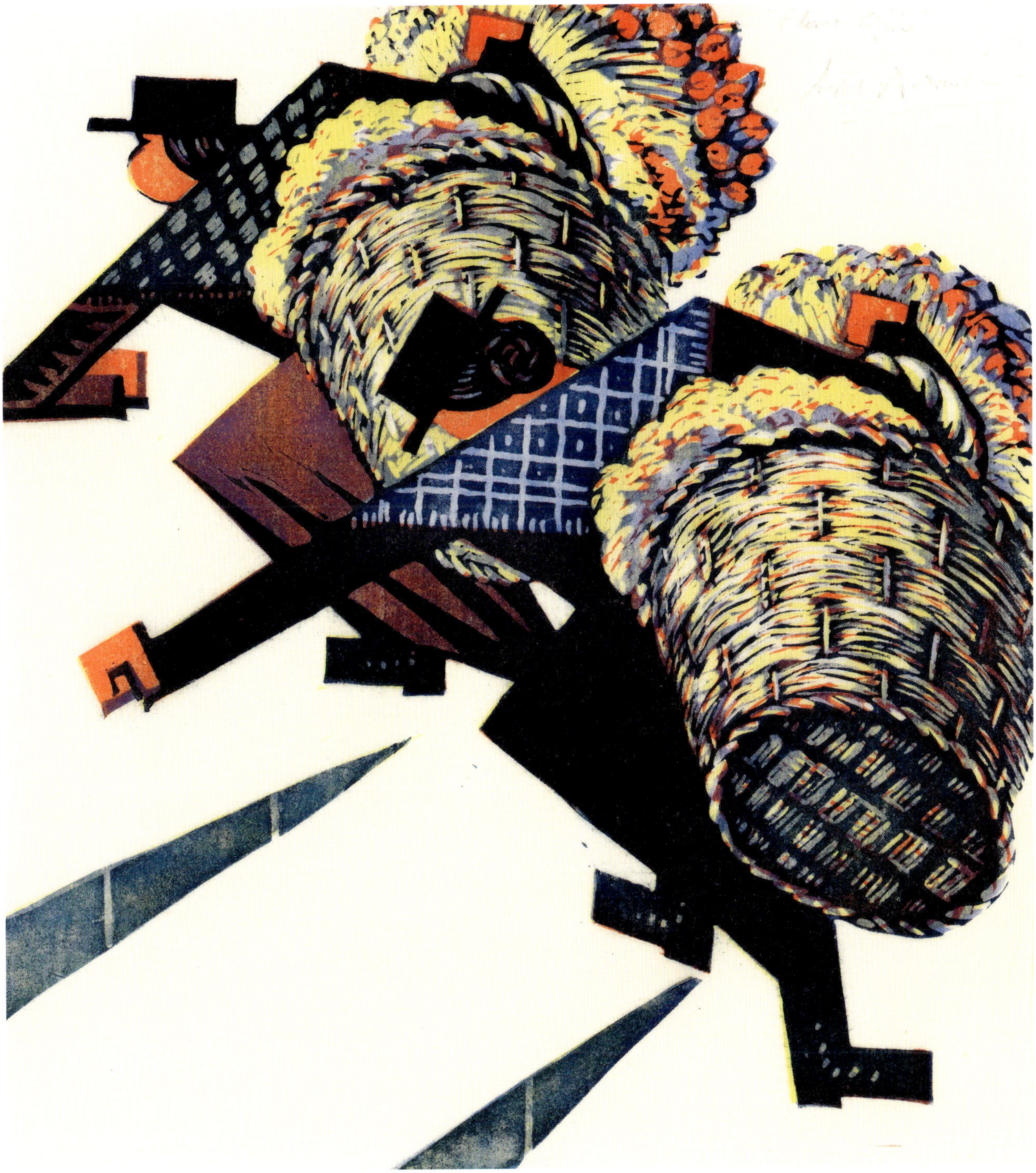

Sybil Andrews *Flower Girls*, 1934

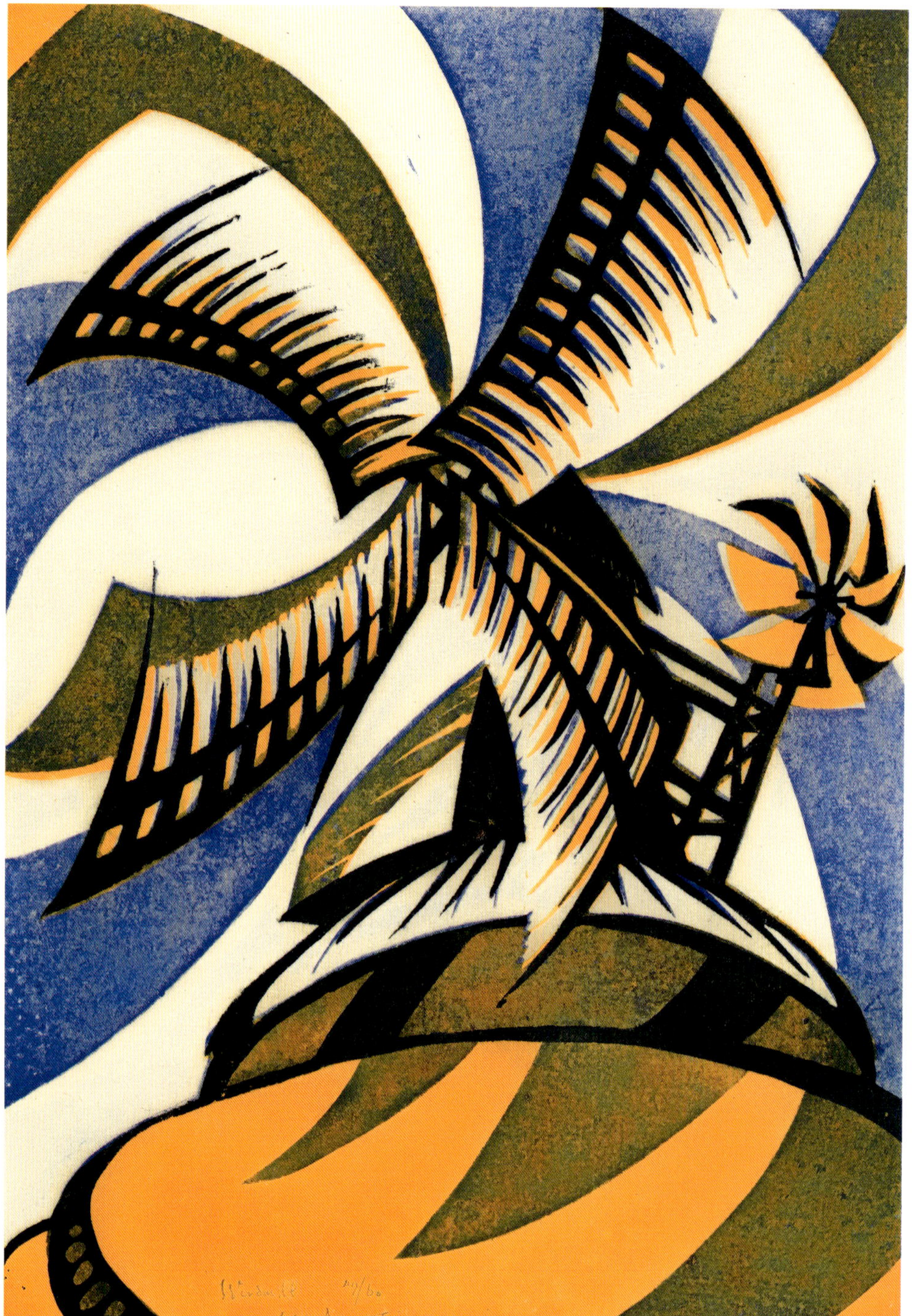

Sybil Andrews *The Windmill*, 1933

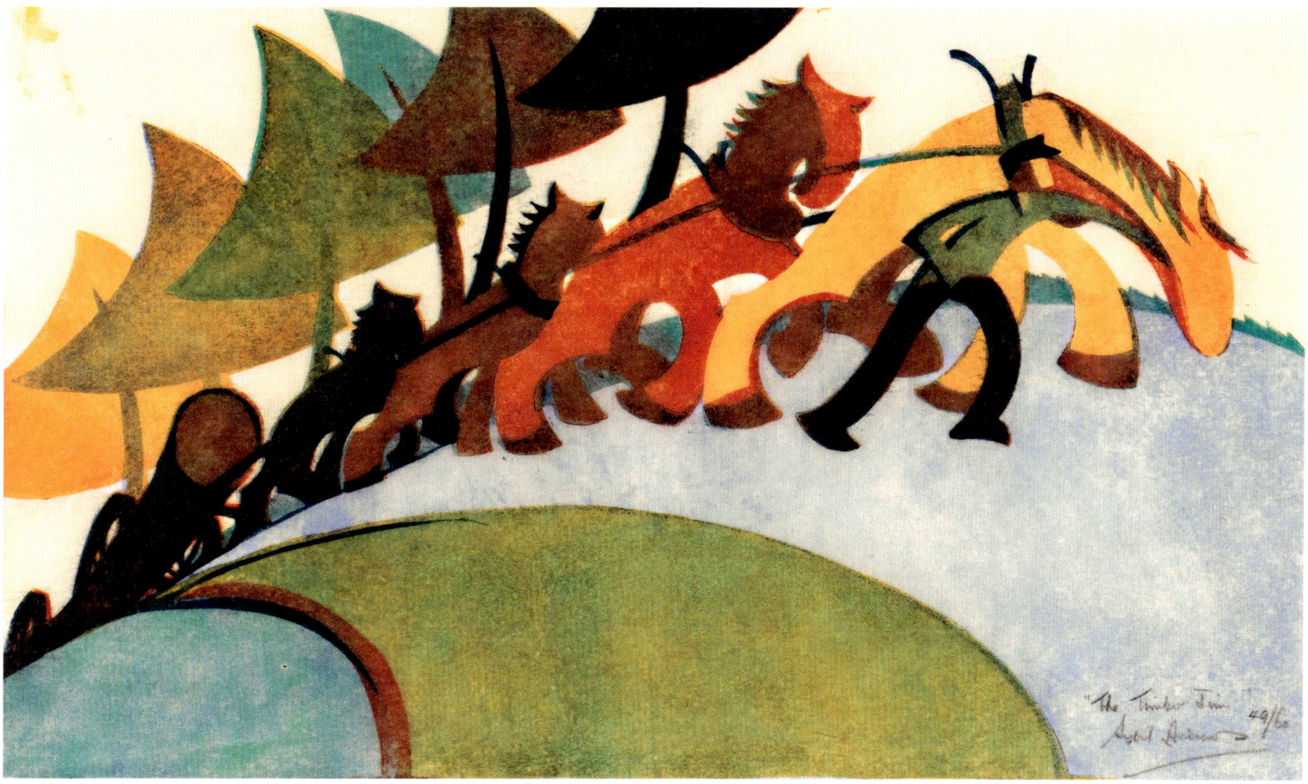

Sybil Andrews *The Timber Jim*, 1932

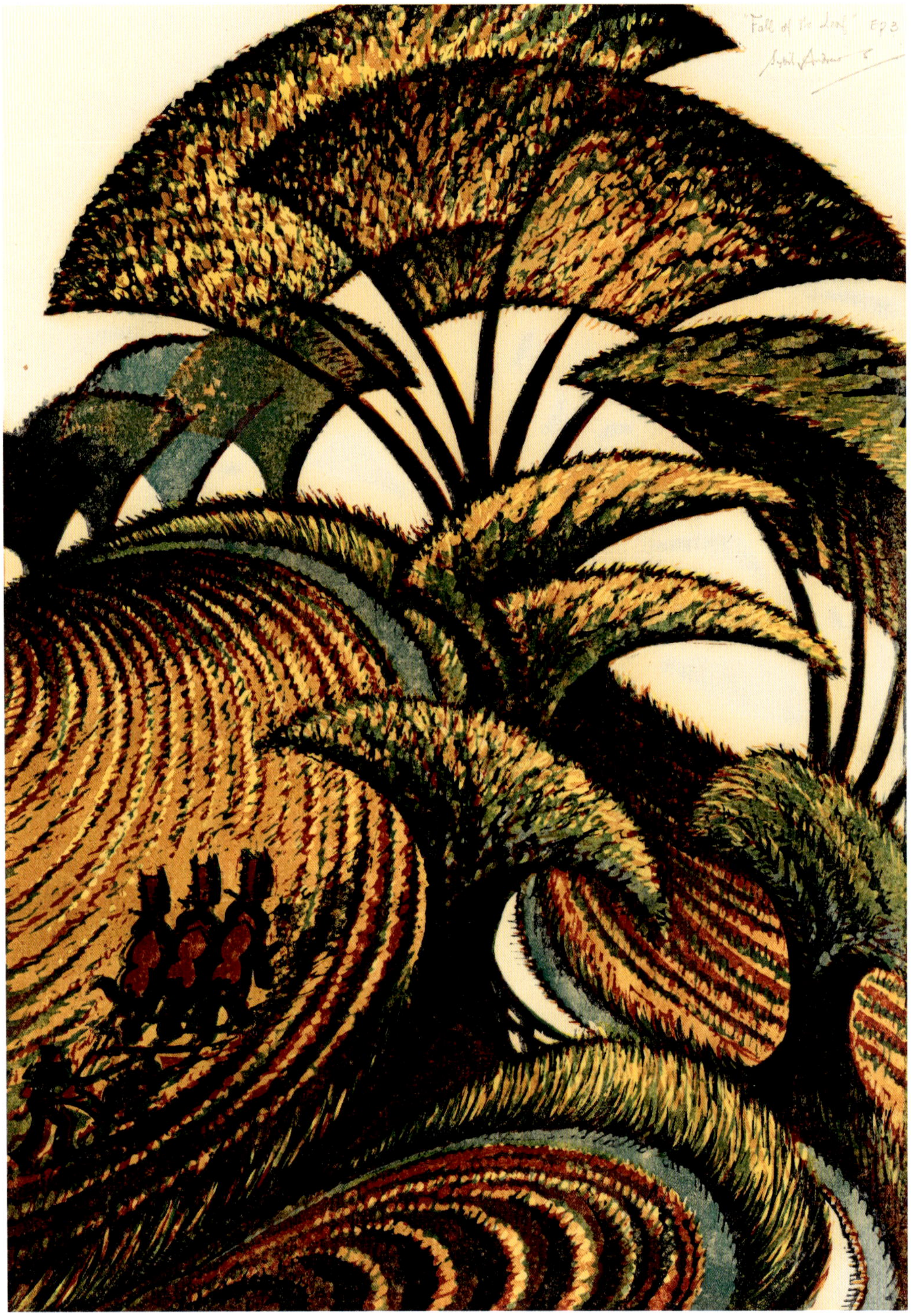

Sybil Andrews *Fall of the Leaf*, 1934

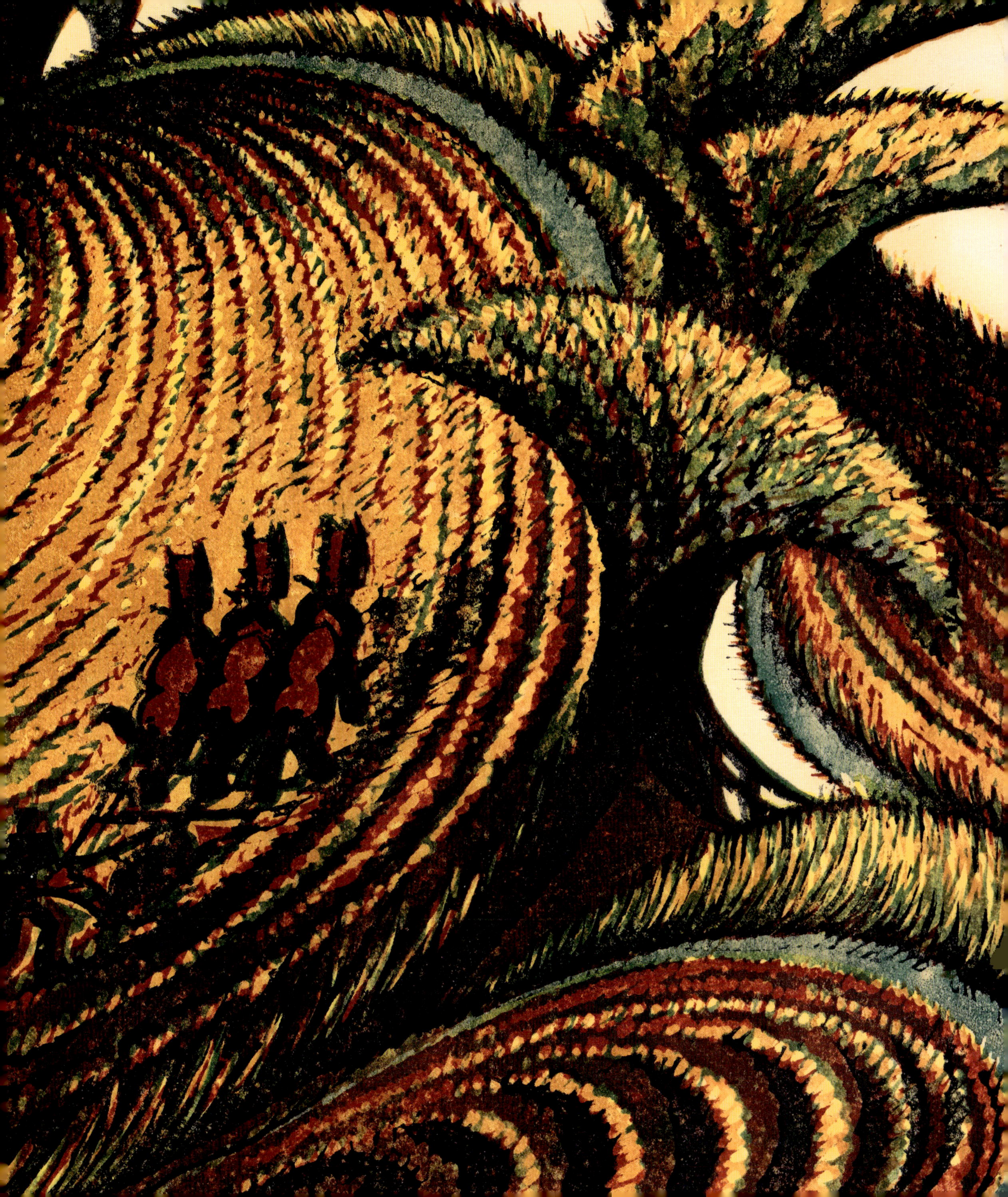

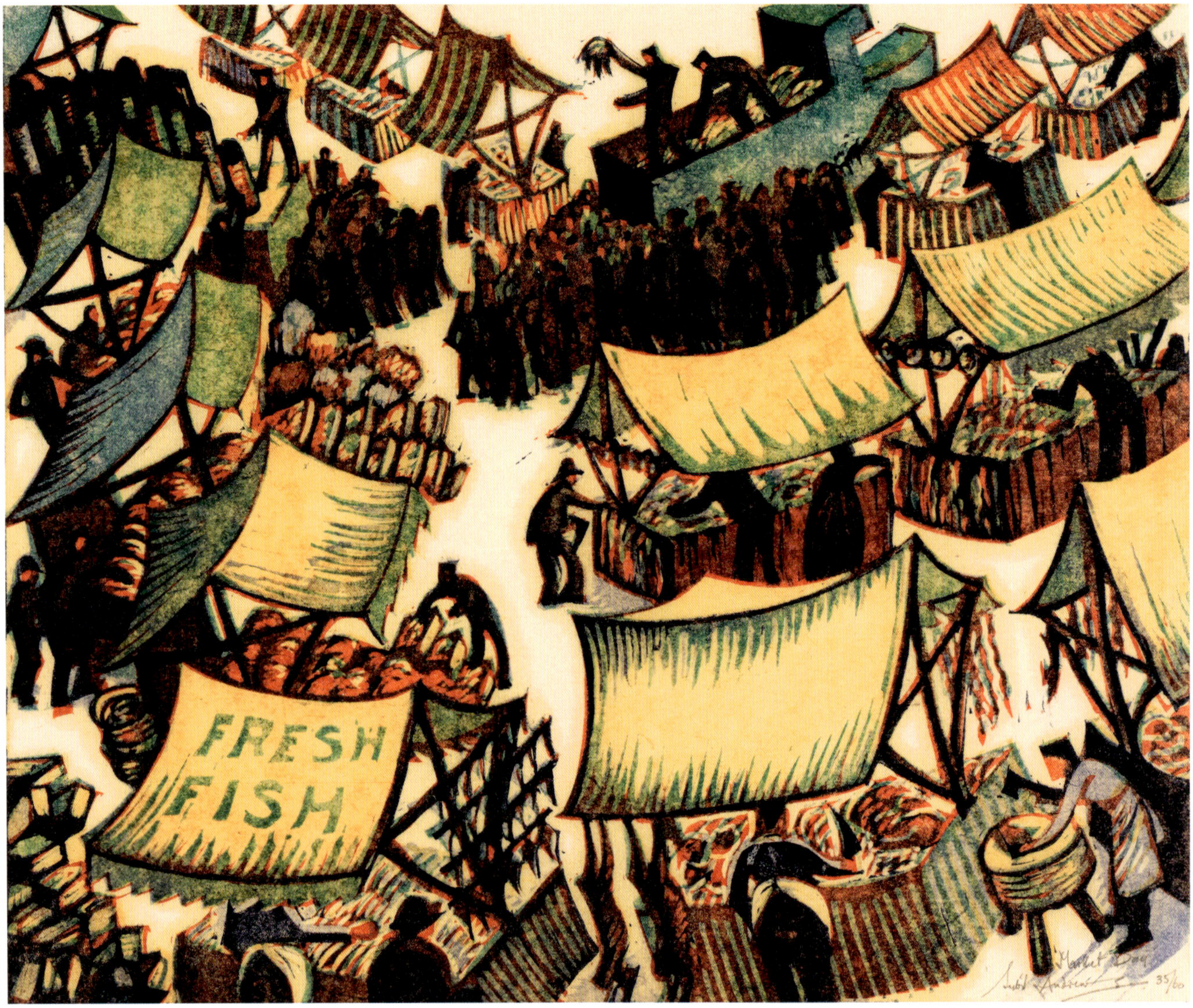

Sybil Andrews *Market Day*, 1936

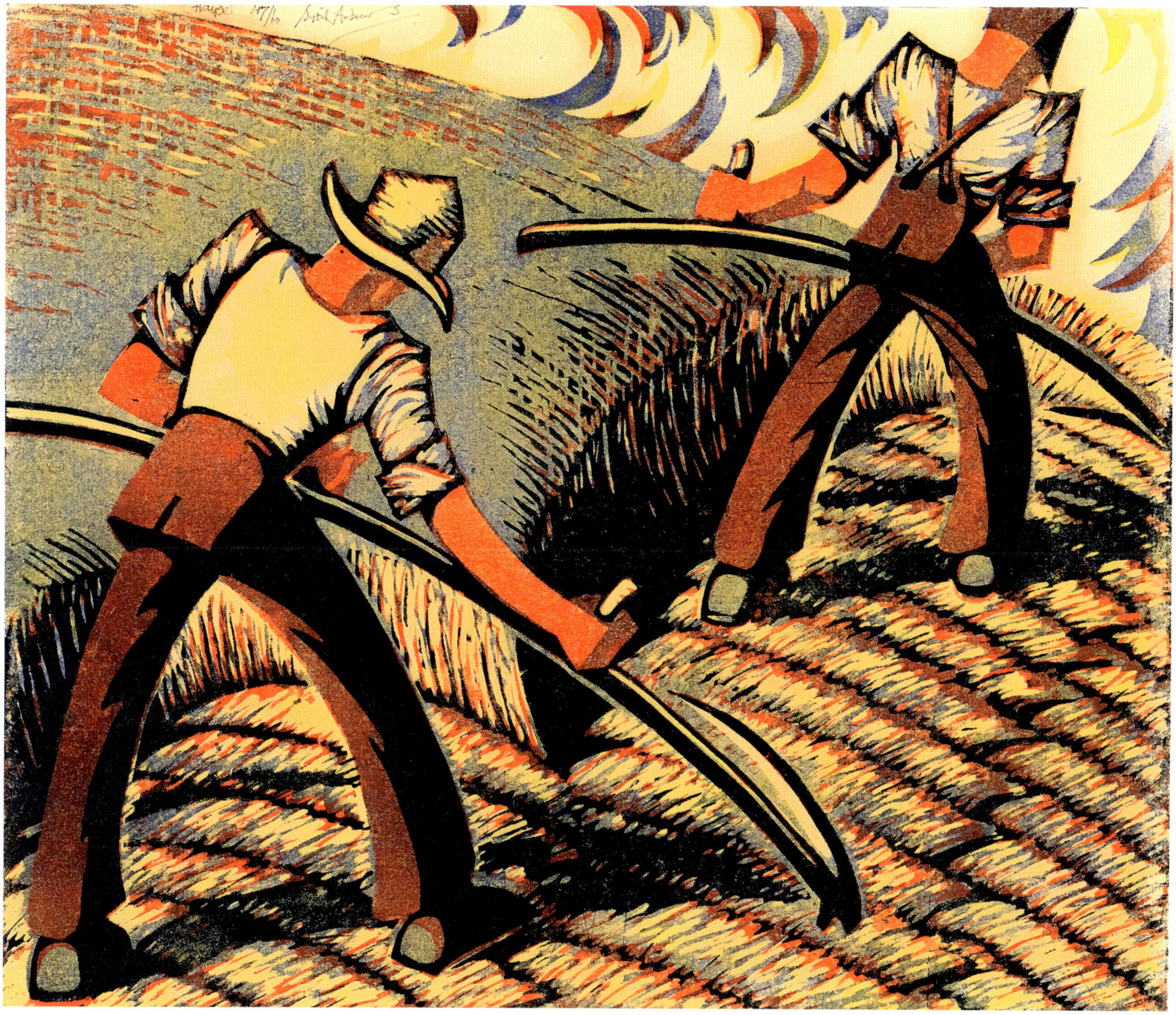

Sybil Andrews *Haysel*, 1936

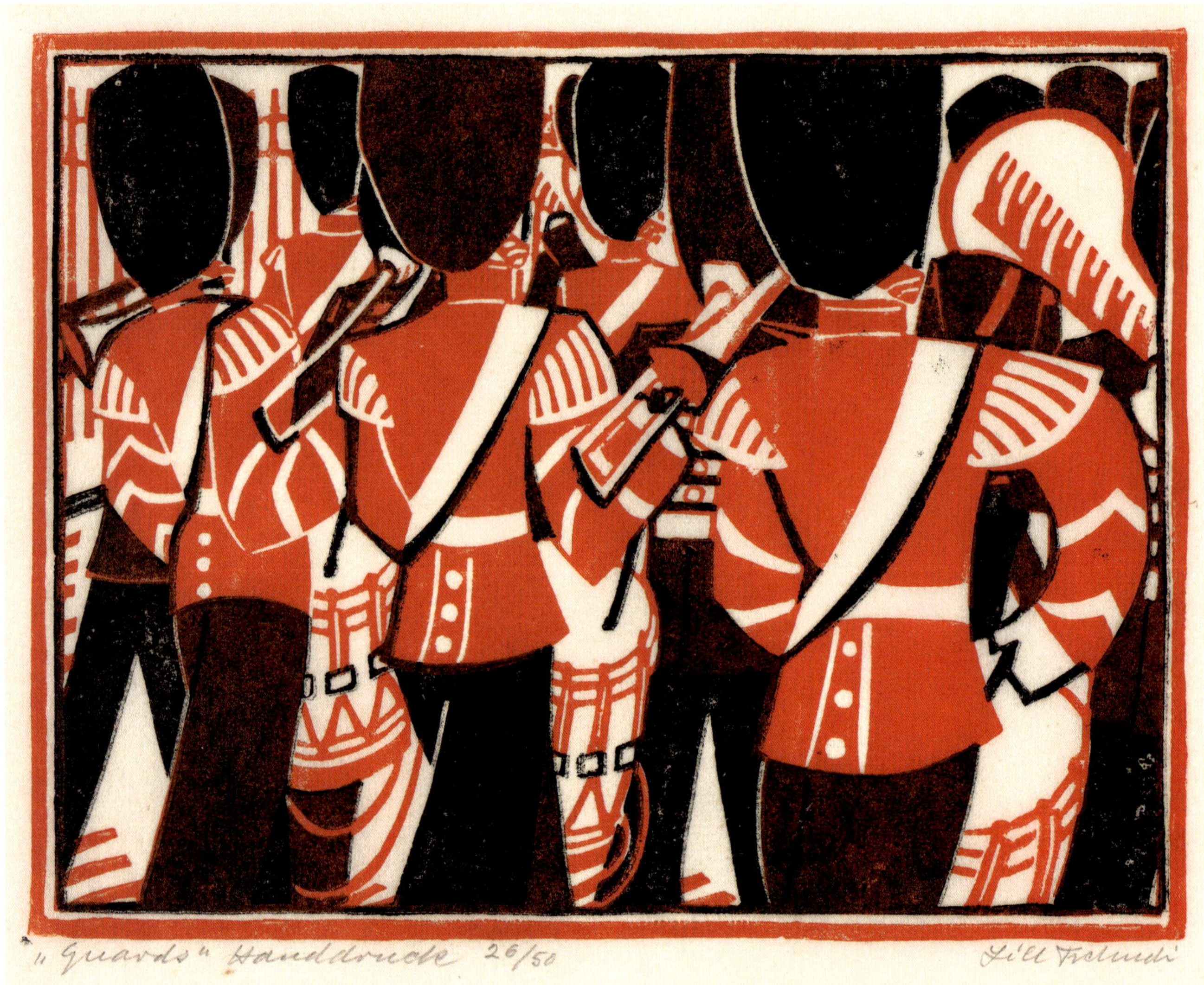

Lill Tschudi *Guards*, 1936

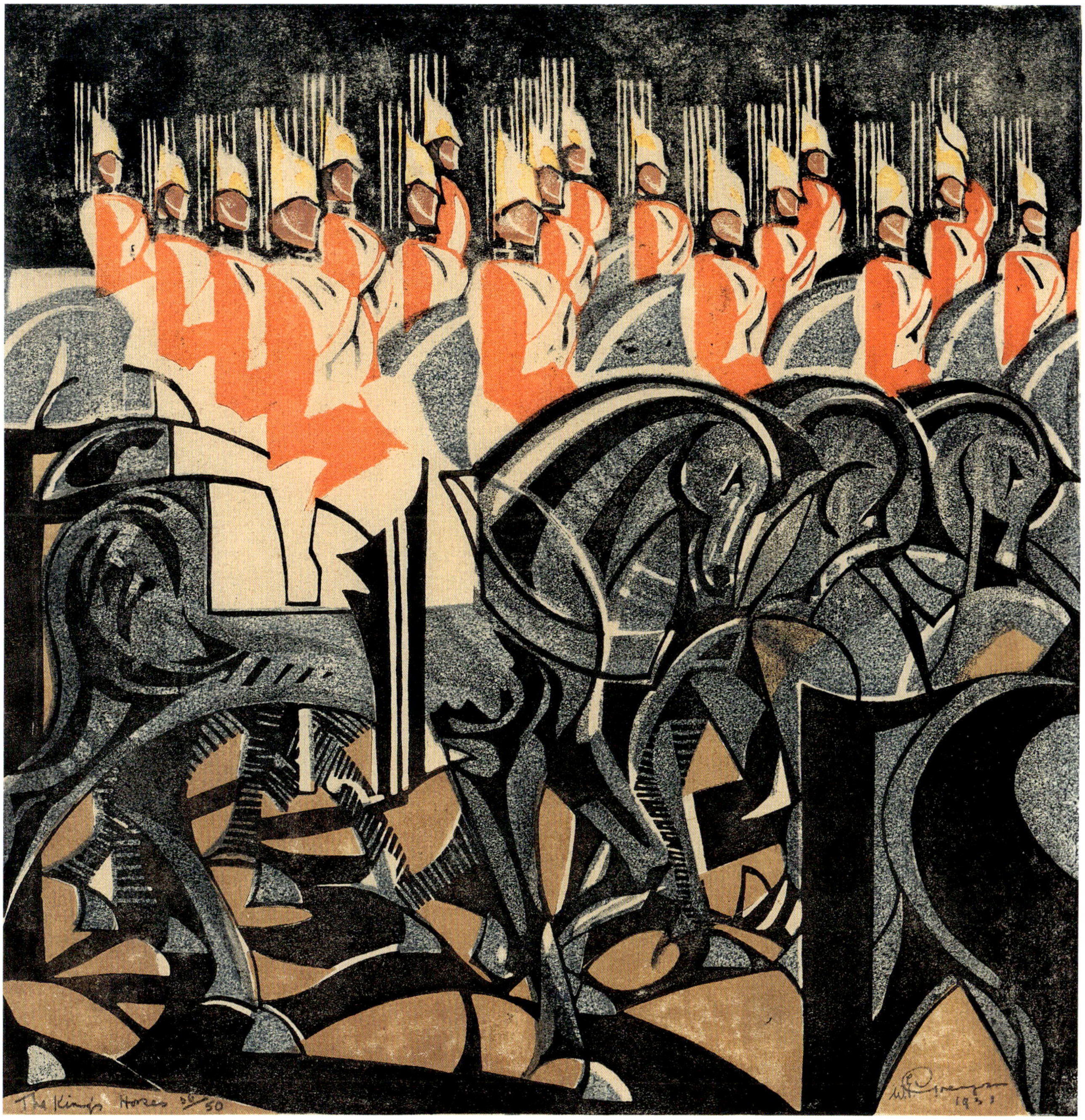

William Greengrass *The King's Horses*, 1931

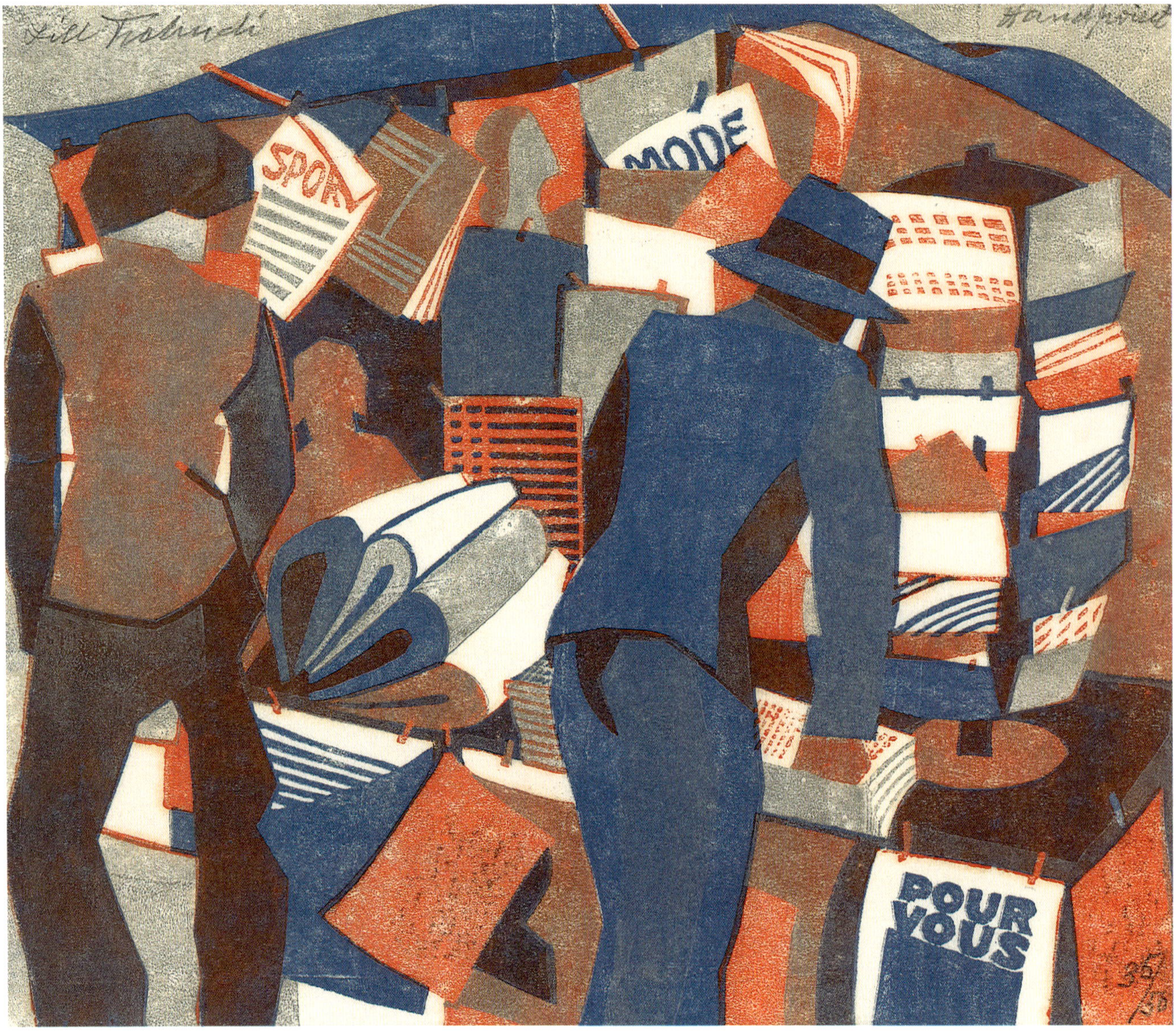

Lill Tschudi *Kiosk in Paris*, 1933

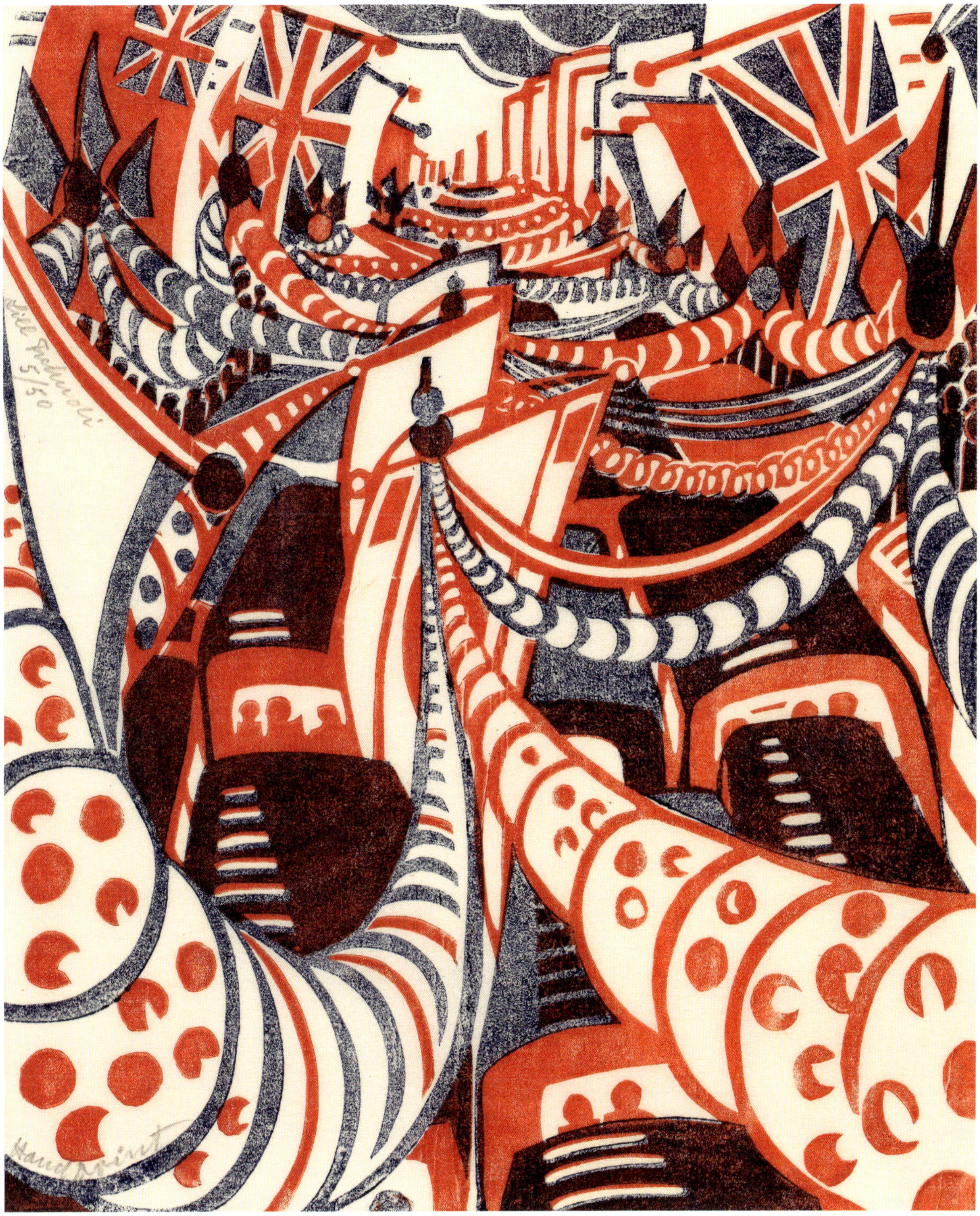

Lill Tschudi *Street Decoration*, 1937

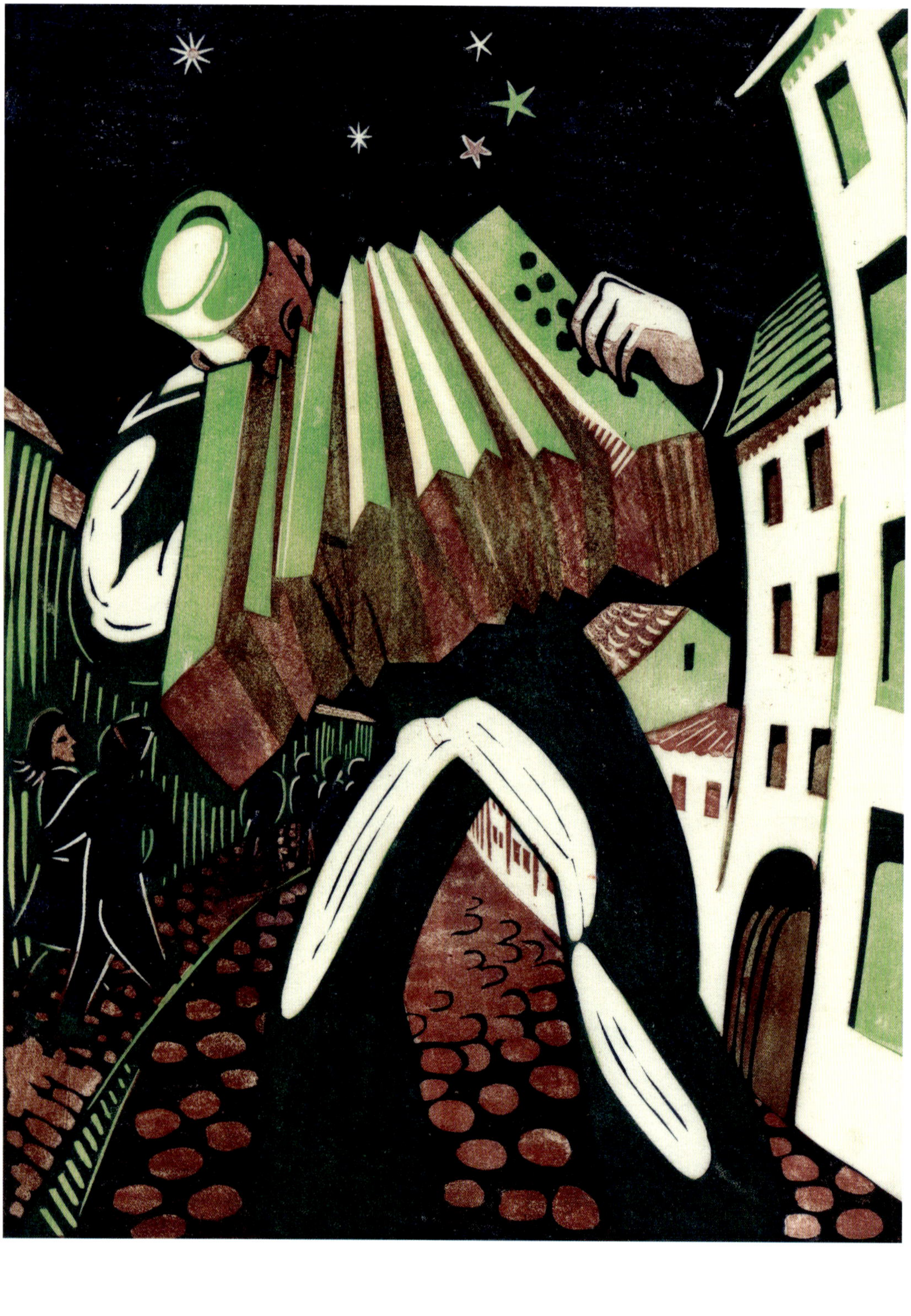

Lill Tschudi *The Lonely Way Home*, 1946

Chronology

1901 January 22: Queen Victoria dies, and Edward VII ascends to the throne.

1906 The Liberal Party wins general election, displacing the Conservative government.

1909 February 20: Filippo Tommaso Marinetti, leader of the Italian Futurists, publishes the group's manifesto on the front page of French newspaper *Le Figaro*.

1909 Christopher Richard Wynne Nevinson and Edward Alexander Wadsworth enroll at the Slade School of Fine Art in London, where they study until 1912.

1910 May 6: King Edward VII dies, and George V ascends to the throne.

1910 Paul Nash enrolls at the Slade School of Fine Art; he leaves after a year. Edith Lawrence also begins her studies at the Slade, where she stays until 1914.

1910–11 November 8–January 15: *Manet and the Post-Impressionists*, organized by Roger Fry with Desmond MacCarthy, is held at the Grafton Galleries, London.

1911 Vasily Kandinsky publishes *Concerning the Spiritual in Art* in Germany. In 1914, the first issue of the Vorticist journal *BLAST* publishes selected passages, translated by Wadsworth, from the book.

1912 March: First exhibition of Italian Futurist works in London is held at the Sackville Gallery.

1912 October 5–December 31: *Second Post-Impressionist Exhibition*, organized by Fry, is held at the Grafton Galleries.

1912 November: Nash has solo exhibition at the Carfax Gallery, London.

1912 Claude Flight enrolls at the Heatherley School of Fine Art in London.

1913 July: Fry establishes the Omega Workshops in London with Vanessa Bell and Duncan Grant.

1913 English translation of Sigmund Freud's *The Interpretation of Dreams* (1899) is published in Britain.

1913–14 October 12–January 16: *Post-Impressionist and Futurist Exhibition* is held at the Doré Gallery, London. The show includes works by Wyndham Lewis, Nevinson, and Wadsworth.

1914 March: Lewis founds the Rebel Art Centre in London in rivalry with the Omega Workshops.

1914 May 8–June 20: *Twentieth Century Art: A Review of Modern Movements* is held at the Whitechapel Art Gallery, London. Exhibitors include Nevinson, Wadsworth, Lewis, Henri Gaudier-Brzeska, Nash, and John Copley.

1914 June 7: Nevinson and Marinetti publish "Vital English Art: Futurist Manifesto" in London's *Observer* newspaper. In April, the two artists had staged several performances at the Doré Gallery.

1914 June 28: Archduke Franz Ferdinand of Austria, heir to the Austro-Hungarian throne, and his wife, Sophie, duchess of Hohenberg, are assassinated in Sarajevo by Gavrilo Princip, a Bosnian Serb and self-described Yugoslav nationalist, setting off a chain of events that leads to the outbreak of the First World War.

1914 July 2: Lewis announces the creation of Vorticism with the publication of the first issue of his journal *BLAST* (dated June 20 but delayed).

1914 July 28: Austria-Hungary declares war on Serbia.

1914 August 2–7: Germany invades Luxembourg and Belgium, and France invades Alsace. Britain declares war on Germany and Austria-Hungary. British forces arrive in France.

1914 August 6: Eric Henri Kennington enlists with the 13th Battalion, London Regiment ("Kensingtons"), and is sent to France.

1914 August 10: Austria-Hungary invades Russia.

1914 September 10: Nash joins the Artists Rifles, a volunteer regiment.

1914 November: Nevinson begins work in field hospitals in France and Belgium. He is discharged in January 1915.

1915 February 18: Germany begins naval blockade of Britain.

1915 May 7: A German submarine sinks the *Lusitania*, a British passenger ship, during its crossing from New York to Liverpool, killing 128 Americans and over 1,000 non-Americans.

1915 May 23: Italy declares war on Austria-Hungary.

1915 June 5: Gaudier-Brzeska is killed in battle at Neuville St.-Vaast.

1915 June: Nevinson begins work as a medical orderly at the Third London General Hospital. He is discharged due to illness in January 1916.

1915 June: Kennington is discharged from the army after being wounded earlier in France.

1915 July: Lewis publishes the second issue of *BLAST*, the "War Number," to accompany a Vorticist exhibition at the Doré Gallery.

1915 Wadsworth joins the Royal Naval Volunteer Reserve.

1915 Charles Samuel Myers, a British psychologist, coins the term "shell shock" to describe what is now known as post-traumatic stress disorder.

1916 April 24–29: The Easter Rising occurs in Ireland against British rule.

1916 June 23: Wadsworth sails to Greece to work as an intelligence officer.

1916 July: Official war artists' scheme is established under the aegis of Wellington House, a government propaganda bureau, with the objective of creating a pictorial record of the First World War.

1916 September 26–November 4: Nevinson's first solo exhibition is held at the Leicester Galleries, London. The show includes a group of drypoints.

1916 Kennington travels to the Somme as an unofficial war artist.

1916 Sybil Andrews, then eighteen, works as a welder building airplanes during the war.

1917 January: Nevinson shows two lithographs in the Senefelder Club's annual exhibition at the Leicester Galleries.

1917 February: Nash receives a commission in the 15th Hampshire Regiment and is sent to the Ypres Salient.

1917 April 6: The United States declares war on Germany.

1917 May 25: Nash returns to London after being injured in service. A few weeks later, his unit is decimated on Hill 60 at the Battle of Messines, which ends with German withdrawal.

1917 Kennington, Nash, and Nevinson receive commissions as official war artists and are all sent to France. Kennington is at the front from May 1917 until March 1918; Nash from early November until mid-December; and Nevinson from early July until late August.

1917 July: *The Great War: Britain's Efforts and Ideals* is published and exhibited at the Fine Art Society, London, and subsequently tours around Britain before traveling to France, the United States, Canada, and Australia.

1917 July: Nash has solo exhibition, featuring twenty drawings made in France, at the Goupil Gallery, London.

1917 Summer: Wadsworth returns to Britain from the Mediterranean and is assigned to supervise painting of "dazzle camouflage" on ships in Bristol and Liverpool.

1917 Fall: The Bolshevik Party seizes control in Russia as part of the October Revolution, which leads to the Russian Civil War that lasts until 1923.

1918 February 6: The Representation of the People Act of 1918 extends the right to vote to men over the age of twenty-one, regardless of if they own property, and to women over the age of thirty. The bill adds over 7.5 million men and 8.5 million women to the electorate.

1918 February: Devastating influenza pandemic begins; it lasts until spring 1920. Over a quarter of the British population is infected, and more than 228,000 people die.

1918 March 1–April 5: Nevinson's solo exhibition *Pictures of War* is held at the Leicester Galleries. The show includes twenty prints.

1918 May: Nash's solo exhibition *Void of War* is held at the Leicester Galleries.

1918 August 11: The Battle of Amiens ends in a decisive Allied victory.

1918 November 11: The First World War ends after armistice is signed by Allied and German representatives in Compiègne, France.

1918 Cyril E. Power and Andrews meet in Bury St Edmunds.

1919 January 21: Sinn Féin forms a breakaway government in Dublin. The new government declares Irish independence and the creation of the Irish Republic, precipitating the Irish War of Independence (Anglo-Irish War), which lasts until July 11, 1921.

1919 March: Wadsworth has solo exhibition of woodcuts and drawings at the Adelphi Gallery, London.

1919 April 29–May 17: Nevinson has solo exhibition of forty-six prints at Frederick J. Keppel Galleries, New York.

1919 June: Allied and German representatives sign the Treaty of Versailles. Britain acquires new colonies in the Middle East and Africa, giving the British Empire governance over the largest amount of land and greatest number of people in its history.

1919 August: The Omega Workshops close.

1919 October: Nevinson has solo exhibition at the Leicester Galleries. The show includes ten prints.

1919 Claude Flight makes his first linocut.

1920 January 10: The League of Nations is formally instituted.

1920 January: Wadsworth has solo exhibition, *The Black Country*, at the Leicester Galleries. He abandons printmaking later in the year, after completing a series of related Black Country woodcuts, begun in 1919.

1920 August: Communist Party of Great Britain forms.

1920 December 23: The Government of Ireland Act, also known as the Fourth Home Rule Bill, divides Ireland into Northern Ireland and Southern Ireland.

1920 Nash moves to Dymchurch, Kent, where he remains for five years. He works intensively on woodcuts until 1929, mainly for publication in books.

1920–21 Britain experiences a postwar recession.

1921 December 6: The British and Irish governments agree to the Anglo-Irish Treaty, which is ratified in January 1922. Ireland is partitioned, creating the Irish Free State, a self-governing dominion (renamed Ireland in 1937).

1921 December: Power and Andrews hold first joint exhibition at Crescent House, Angel Hill, Bury St Edmunds.

1922 February 28: Egypt is granted formal independence from Britain.

1922 October 31: King Victor Emmanuel III names Benito Mussolini, founder of Italy's National Fascist Party, prime minister following the March on Rome (October 27–28).

1922 November 20–December 9: Flight exhibits with the Seven and Five Society in their second annual exhibition, held at the Walker Gallery, London. He is associated with the artistic group until 1928.

1922 Power and Andrews move to London and enroll at the Heatherley School of Fine Art, where they meet Iain Macnab.

1922 Flight meets Edith Lawrence; the two are artistic, business, and romantic partners until Flight's death in 1955.

1922–26 Economic stagnation in Britain is followed by a brief economic downturn in 1926.

ca. 1924 Power and Andrews author unpublished manifesto "Aims of the Art of To-Day."

1925 April: Flight has first solo exhibition at the Mayor Gallery, London. That same month, he publishes "The Modern Colour-Print," in the *Arts and Crafts Quarterly*. He writes several more articles on printmaking between 1925 and 1927, including "Dynamism and the Colour Print" (1925), "Linoleum-Cut Colour Printing" (a six-part series published between March 1926 and May 1927), "The Art of To-Day" (1926), and "Stimulating an Interest in Art: Mr K. Doubleday's School" (1926).

1925 Macnab leaves the Heatherley School of Fine Art to open the Grosvenor School of Modern Art in London.

1926 May 4–12: The Trade Union Congress organizes the first ever general strike in Britain to protest the low pay and adverse working conditions of coal miners. 1.7 million workers go on strike in solidarity.

1926 Britain supports German membership in the League of Nations.

1926 Flight begins teaching linocut technique at the Grosvenor School. He continues to teach his popular linocut courses until 1930. Flight also starts editing the *Arts and Crafts Quarterly*.

1926 Power and Andrews, both of whom are working at the Grosvenor School, enroll in Flight's linocut classes.

1927 June: Flight has solo exhibition of "oils, watercolours, designs, sculpture and linocuts" at Redfern Gallery, London.

1927 Flight publishes *Lino-Cuts: A Hand-Book of Linoleum-Cut Colour Printing*, the first monograph on color linocuts. It is based on articles he wrote for the *Arts and Crafts Quarterly*.

1927 Flight and Lawrence open an interior decorating business in London.

1927–29 Britain experiences a short economic boom.

1928 July 2: The Representation of the People (Equal Franchise) Act extends the right to vote to all women over the age of twenty-one.

1928 November: Flight has solo exhibition of textiles, drawings, and linocuts at Redfern Gallery.

1928 Andrews leaves the Grosvenor School.

1929 July 4–27: *First Exhibition of British Lino-Cuts* is held at Redfern Gallery. The show features ninety-four prints by thirty-three artists, including Flight, Power, and Andrews. Annual British linocut exhibitions are held at Redfern until 1931 and then at the Ward Gallery, London, between 1933 and 1937.

1929 September–October: The stock market crash on Wall Street inaugurates collapse of banking and period of global economic depression. Britain suffers economic crash known as the "Great Slump" until 1932.

1929 October: Flight and Redfern Gallery organize a traveling exhibition for the United States of color linocuts to correspond with the *First Exhibition of British Lino-Cuts*. Flight subsequently begins an international exhibition program that sends shows to China (1931), Australia (1932 and 1937), the United States (1934), and Canada (1935–36).

1929–30 Lill Tschudi studies with Flight at the Grosvenor School. After leaving the school, she maintains connections with Flight, who includes her work in his exhibitions and publications.

1930 July 23–August 23: *British Lino-Cuts*, the second exhibition of British linocuts, is held at Redfern Gallery. The catalogue contains a foreword by Flight.

1930 October: Nevinson has solo exhibition at the Leicester Galleries. The show includes thirty-eight prints and is his last major print show during his lifetime.

1930 Nash makes his last woodcut, a bookplate for the British industrialist and art collector Samuel Courtauld.

1930 Flight leaves the Grosvenor School.

1931 August: Financial crisis in Britain leads treasury to abandon the gold standard.

1931 August: After the Labour government collapses, members of the Conservative, Labour, and Liberal parties form a centrist coalition government with the goal of solving the financial crisis.

1931 Summer: *British Lino-Cuts 1931*, the third exhibition of British linocuts, is held at Redfern Gallery. The catalogue contains a foreword by Flight.

1931 October 1–24: Flight has solo exhibition at Redfern Gallery.

1931–33 Tschudi studies art in Paris with André Lhote, Gino Severini, and Fernand Léger.

1932 August 22: First full televised program airs on the British Broadcasting Corporation (BBC). Experimental broadcasts had begun in 1929. Regular television service begins in 1936.

1932 October 3: Iraq becomes independent from Britain.

1932 The British Union of Fascists, led by Oswald Mosley, forms.

1932–37 The British economy continues to stall.

1933 January 5–28: Two-person exhibition *Sybil Andrews and Cyril E. Power* is held at Redfern Gallery.

1933 January 30: Adolf Hitler becomes chancellor of Germany.

1933 May 17–June 10: *Fourth Exhibition of British Lino-Cuts* is held at the Ward Gallery. The catalogue contains a foreword by Flight.

1933 November: Exhibition of linocuts by Flight, Lawrence, and Tschudi is held at Atelier E. Matter, Montreux, Switzerland.

1933 The London Passenger Transport Board (LPTB), better known as London Transport, is established. Frank Pick is named vice chairman and chief executive.

1933 Numerous refugees emigrate to London from Germany, including the artist Lucian Freud (then eleven) and his family.

1933 Nevinson makes his last print, the lithograph *Spirit of Progress*.

1934 June: *Lino-Cuts 1934*, the fifth exhibition of British linocuts, is held at the Ward Gallery.

1934 Flight publishes *The Art and Craft of Lino Cutting and Printing*.

1935 March: Hitler announces German rearmament.

1935 May 1–15: *Lino-Cuts 1935*, the sixth exhibition of British linocuts, is held at Ward Gallery.

1935 Tschudi returns to Switzerland, living in Schwanden and Zurich until her death in 2004.

1936 January 20: King George V dies, and Edward VIII ascends to the throne.

1936 June 10–July 8: *Lino-Cuts 1936*, the seventh exhibition of British linocuts, is held at the Ward Gallery.

1936 June 11–July 4: *The International Surrealist Exhibition* is held at the New Burlington Galleries, London, and is attended by over 30,000 people.

1936 July: Spanish Civil War begins. The war is fought until 1939, when the Republican forces surrender to the Nationalists under Generalisimo Francisco Franco.

1936 December 11: King Edward VIII abdicates and is succeeded by his brother George VI.

1936 Popular Front governments are formed in France and Spain.

1937 April 26: Franco's Spanish Nationalists forces, aided by Nazi and Fascist militaries and governments, bomb Guernica, a Spanish town.

1937 April: Nevinson publishes his autobiography, *Paint and Prejudice*. The US edition appears in 1938.

1937 Two weeks after the coronation of George VII on May 12, Neville Chamberlain replaces Stanley Baldwin as prime minister.

1937 May 26–June 23: *Lino-Cuts 1937*, the eighth exhibition of British linocuts, is held at the Ward Gallery. It is the last annual British linocut exhibition organized by Flight.

1937 Lewis publishes his autobiography, *Blasting and Bombardiering*.

1938 March 13: Germany occupies Austria.

1938 June 4: Sigmund Freud flees Vienna with his wife, Martha, and daughter Anna to live in London to escape persecution by Nazi regime.

1938 September 30: Britain, France, Germany, and Italy sign the Munich Agreement, ceding the Sudetenland, the German-speaking portion of Czechoslovakia, to Germany. Hitler announces that the region is his last territorial claim in Europe. Although presented as a means of avoiding war, the agreement is soon viewed as a failed attempt at appeasement of Hitler and a betrayal of Czechoslovakia.

1938 Andrews and Power end their relationship. Power returns to his family and abandons linocuts. Andrews leaves London for New Forest, Hampshire, and makes only a few color linocuts until 1946.

1939 February: Chamberlain pledges military support for France.

1939 March 30–April 19: *Modern Lino-Cuts* is held at the City of Birmingham Museum and Art Gallery. Arranged by Flight, it is the last exhibition in which members of the Grosvenor School group participate.

1939 April: Conscription begins for British citizens.

1939 September 3: Britain and France declare war on Nazi Germany; the Second World War begins.

1939 Tschudi joins the Swiss Women's Auxiliary Military Service.

1940 The Grosvenor School of Modern Art closes.

1940 Nash receives a commission as an official war artist for the Air Ministry. He produces a group of paintings and three lithographs.

1940–41 In July 1940, the German air force (Luftwaffe) launches an air campaign against the British Royal Air Force (RAF) and military targets, before turning to London and other cities in the Battle of Britain. The massive bombing campaign focused on London and other British cities, known as the Blitz, kills over 40,000 people.

1941 Flight's London studio is destroyed during the Blitz, resulting in loss of numerous artworks and all his linoleum blocks.

1942 Andrews is conscripted and works in a shipyard during the war. She does not make art during this period.

1945 May 7: Germany surrenders to the Allies, and May 8 becomes known as VE (Victory in Europe) Day.

1945 September 2: Japan formally surrenders to the Allies following atomic bombing of Hiroshima and Nagasaki in August, ending the Second World War.

1947 Andrews and her husband, Walter Morgan, emigrate to Vancouver Island, a logging town in British Columbia, Canada. While being transported, four of her blocks are damaged beyond repair.

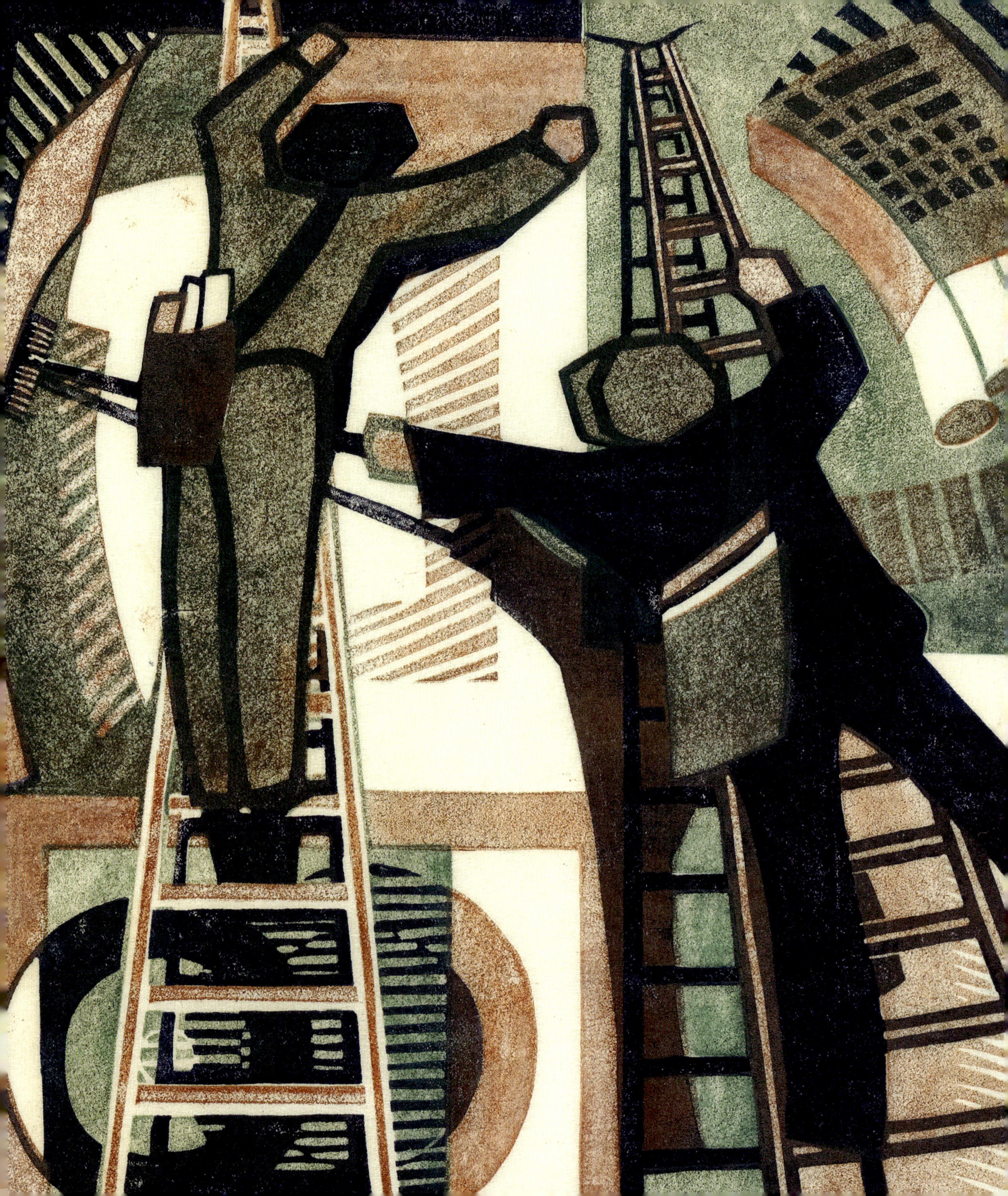

List of Plates

Block, image, or plate dimensions are given instead of sheet dimensions due to the irregular size of many of the sheets.

All works are from The Metropolitan Museum of Art, New York.

Unless otherwise noted, the credit line for these works is as follows: Purchase, Leslie and Johanna Garfield Gift, Lila Acheson Wallace, Charles and Jessie Price, and David T Schiff Gifts, The Elisha Whittelsey Collection, The Elisha Whittelsey Fund, Dolores Valvidia Hurlburt Bequest, Peco Foundation and Friends of Drawings and Prints Gifts, and funds from various donors, 2019.

Plate 9 13/16 × 13 11/16 in. (25 × 34.7 cm)
(2019.592.30)
p. 99

Edward Alexander Wadsworth (British, 1889–1949)
Blast Furnaces I (Netherton Furnaces), 1919
Woodcut on gray Western paper
Block 4 ¾ × 7 ½ in. (12 × 19 cm)
(2019.592.549)
p. 100 (top)

Edward Alexander Wadsworth (British, 1889–1949)
Black Country, 1919
Woodcut on coated Western paper
Block 4 5/16 × 5 11/16 in. (11 × 14.5 cm)
(2019.592.25)
p. 100 (bottom)

Edward Alexander Wadsworth (British, 1889–1949)
Yorkshire, 1920
Woodcut on Western paper
Block 4 ¼ × 5 ¾ in. (10.8 × 14.6 cm)
(2019.592.307)
p. 101

Christopher Richard Wynne Nevinson (British, 1889–1946)
The Workers (alt. titles: *Revolution* and *Strikers on Tower Hill*), 1919
Lithograph on Western paper
Image 20 3/16 × 13 ¾ in. (51.2 × 35 cm)
(2019.592.217)
p. 102

Dorothy Burroughes (British, 1883–1963)
The Factory (published as *Construction on Waterloo Bridge*), ca. 1925
Linocut on Japanese paper
Image 14 ½ × 9 ¾ in. (36.8 × 25.1 cm)
(2019.592.83)
p. 103

Edith Lawrence (British, 1890–1973)
Port, ca. 1930
Linocut on Japanese paper
Image 12 ¼ × 8 ⅝ in. (31.1 × 21.9 cm)
(2019.592.634)
p. 105

Sybil Andrews (British, 1898–1992)
Oranges, 1929
Linocut on Japanese paper
Image 10 5/16 × 7 7/16 in. (26.2 × 18.9 cm)
(2019.592.3)
p. 106

Lill Tschudi (Swiss, 1911–2004)
Sailors, 1930
Linocut on Japanese paper
Image 7 1/16 × 4 ½ in. (18 × 11.4 cm)
(2019.592.257)
p. 107

Ursula Fookes (British, 1906–1991)
Poplar Trees and Telegraph Poles, ca. 1930
Linocut on Japanese paper
Image 8 × 6 in. (20.3 × 15.2 cm)
(2019.592.119)
p. 108

Lill Tschudi (Swiss, 1911–2004)
Fixing the Wires, 1932
Linocut on Japanese paper
Image 11 ⅞ × 7 15/16 in. (30.2 × 20.2 cm)
(2019.592.241)
p. 109

Sybil Andrews (British, 1898–1992)
Haulers, 1929
Linocut on Japanese paper
Image 7 3/16 × 11 13/16 (18.2 × 30 cm)
(2019.592.45)
p. 110

Sybil Andrews (British, 1898–1992)
Sledgehammers, 1933
Linocut on Japanese paper
Image 10 ⅜ × 12 7/16 in. (26.4 × 31.6 cm)
(2019.592.4)
p. 111

Lill Tschudi (Swiss, 1911–2004)
Sticking Up Posters, 1933
Linocut on Japanese paper
Image 11 ⅞ × 7 ⅞ in. (30.2 × 20 cm)
(2019.592.265)
p. 112

Cyril E. Power (British, 1872–1951)
The Tube Staircase, 1929
Linocut on Japanese paper
Image 17 ½ × 10 1/16 in. (44.4 × 25.6 cm)
(2019.592.20)
p. 113

Claude Flight (British, 1881–1955)
Speed, 1922
Linocut on Japanese paper
Image 8 ⅞ × 11 5/16 in. (22.6 × 28.8 cm)
Gift of Johanna and Leslie Garfield, 2005 (2005.470.1)
p. 114

Lill Tschudi (Swiss, 1911–2004)
Underground, 1930
Linocut on Japanese paper
Image 5 15/16 × 5 9/16 in. (15.1 × 14.2 cm)
(2019.592.24)
p. 115

Claude Flight (British, 1881–1955)
Brooklands, ca. 1929
Linocut on Japanese paper coated with a metal-flecked glaze
Image 12 1/16 × 10 3/16 in. (30.6 × 25.8 cm)
(2019.592.6)
p. 117

Cyril E. Power (British, 1872–1951)
Lifts, ca. 1930
Linocut on Japanese paper
Image 14 ⅜ × 9 ⅛ in. (36.6 × 23.2 cm)
(2019.592.449)
p. 118

Cyril E. Power (British, 1872–1951)
Whence & Whither?, ca. 1930
Linocut on Japanese paper
Image 12 3/16 × 9 7/16 in. (31 × 24 cm)
(2019.592.21)
p. 119

Sybil Andrews (British, 1898–1992)
Straphangers, 1929
Linocut on Japanese paper
Image 9 15/16 × 13 in. (25.3 × 33 cm)
(2019.592.66)
p. 120 (top)

Christopher Richard Wynne Nevinson (British, 1889–1946)
The Blue Wave, 1917
Lithograph on Western paper
Image $13\frac{3}{8} \times 16\frac{3}{4}$ in. (34 × 42.5 cm)
(2019.592.404)
p. 147

Lill Tschudi (Swiss, 1911–2004)
In the Circus, 1932
Linocut on Japanese paper
Image $9\frac{7}{16} \times 10\frac{1}{4}$ in. (24 × 26 cm)
(2019.592.506)
p. 148

Sybil Andrews (British, 1898–1992)
Hyde Park, 1931
Linocut on Japanese paper
Image $13\frac{3}{8} \times 6\frac{1}{8}$ in. (34 × 15.5 cm)
(2019.592.49)
p. 149

Claude Flight (British, 1881–1955)
Autumn, from *The Four Seasons*, ca. 1926
Linocut on Japanese paper
Image $10 \times 12\frac{1}{16}$ in. (25.4 × 30.6 cm)
(2019.592.96)
p. 150

Sybil Andrews (British, 1898–1992)
The Gale, 1930
Linocut on Japanese paper
Image $8\frac{1}{4} \times 9\frac{11}{16}$ in. (21 × 24.6 cm)
(2019.592.1)
p. 151

Claude Flight (British, 1881–1955)
Street Singers, 1925
Linocut on Japanese paper
Image $12\frac{5}{16} \times 10\frac{5}{16}$ in. (31.2 × 26.2 cm)
(2019.592.8)
p. 153

Sybil Andrews (British, 1898–1992)
Concert Hall, 1929
Linocut on Japanese paper
Image $9\frac{5}{16} \times 11$ in. (23.6 × 28 cm)
(2019.592.37)
p. 154

Sybil Andrews (British, 1898–1992)
Theatre (alt. title: *Au Théâtre*), 1929
Linocut on Japanese paper
Image $10\frac{13}{16} \times 8\frac{1}{16}$ in. (27.5 × 20.5 cm)
(2019.592.70)
p. 155

Lill Tschudi (Swiss, 1911–2004)
Trio, 1931
Linocut on Japanese paper
Image $8\frac{11}{16} \times 10\frac{1}{4}$ in. (22 × 26 cm)
(2019.592.268)
p. 156

Cyril E. Power (British, 1872–1951)
The Concerto, ca. 1935
Linocut on Japanese paper
Image $12\frac{13}{16} \times 11\frac{13}{16}$ in. (32.6 × 30 cm)
(2019.592.436)
p. 157

Cyril E. Power (British, 1872–1951)
Divertissement, ca. 1932
Linocut on Japanese paper
Image $9\frac{1}{8} \times 12\frac{3}{8}$ in. (23.2 × 31.5 cm)
(2019.592.438)
p. 158

Sybil Andrews (British, 1898–1992)
Flower Girls, 1934
Linocut on Japanese paper
Image $9\frac{7}{16} \times 8\frac{9}{16}$ in. (24 × 21.8 cm)
(2019.592.40)
p. 159

Sybil Andrews (British, 1898–1992)
The Windmill, 1933
Linocut on Japanese paper
Image $12\frac{1}{2} \times 8\frac{11}{16}$ in. (31.8 × 22 cm)
(2019.592.326)
p. 160

Sybil Andrews (British, 1898–1992)
The Timber Jim, 1932
Linocut on Japanese paper
Image $8\frac{3}{4} \times 15\frac{1}{8}$ in. (22.2 × 38.4 cm)
(2019.592.72)
p. 161

Sybil Andrews (British, 1898–1992)
Fall of the Leaf, 1934
Linocut on Japanese paper
Image $14\frac{1}{4} \times 10\frac{3}{16}$ in. (36.2 × 25.8 cm)
(2019.592.39)
p. 162

Sybil Andrews (British, 1898–1992)
Market Day, 1936
Linocut on Japanese paper
Image $11 \times 13\frac{1}{4}$ in. (28 × 33.6 cm)
(2019.592.54)
p. 164

Sybil Andrews (British, 1898–1992)
Haysel, 1936
Linocut on Japanese paper
Image $9\frac{5}{8} \times 11\frac{5}{16}$ in. (24.4 × 28.7 cm)
(2019.592.47)
p. 165

Lill Tschudi (Swiss, 1911–2004)
Guards, 1936
Linocut on Japanese paper
Image $6\frac{5}{16} \times 8\frac{1}{4}$ in. (16 × 21 cm)
(2019.592.245)
p. 166

William Greengrass (British, 1892–1970)
The King's Horses, 1931
Linocut on Japanese paper
Image 10 × 10 in. (25.4 × 25.4 cm)
(2019.592.141)
p. 167

Lill Tschudi (Swiss, 1911–2004)
Kiosk in Paris, 1933
Linocut on Japanese paper
Image $8\frac{11}{16} \times 10\frac{1}{4}$ in. (22 × 26 cm)
(2019.592.250)
p. 168

Lill Tschudi (Swiss, 1911–2004)
Street Decoration, 1937
Linocut on Japanese paper
Image $9\frac{1}{2} \times 7\frac{7}{8}$ in. (24.2 × 20 cm)
(2019.592.22)
p. 169

Lill Tschudi (Swiss, 1911–2004)
The Lonely Way Home (alt. titles: *The Accordionist's Lonely Way* and *The Solitary Homecoming*), 1946
Linocut on Japanese paper
Image $13\frac{1}{2} \times 10\frac{1}{4}$ in. (34.3 × 26 cm)
(2019.592.251)
p. 170

Notes

FORCES IN FLUX

1 The phrase, which became commonly used, was coined by Benjamin Disraeli in a speech to the House of Commons on March 15, 1838, reflecting on England's emerging power as a hub of industry and trade. See Benjamin Disraeli, "Wit and Wisdom of the Earl of Beaconsfield," in *The Works of Benjamin Disraeli, Earl of Beaconsfield: Embracing Novels, Romances, Plays, Poems, Biography, Short Stories and Great Speeches*, [vol. 20] *Endymion*, vol. 2 (London and New York: M. Walter Dunne, 1904), p. 77.

2 As Lisa Tickner has noted, "All histories are a matter of perspective: of inclusions and exclusions fought over at the time and in subsequent accounts. Choosing to study prominent institutions and events has broadened the field in some directions while narrowing it in others"; *London's New Scene: Art and Culture in the 1960s* (London: Paul Mellon Centre for Studies in British Art, 2020), p. 270.

3 Among the most relevant discussions in relation to British art and modernism are Charles Harrison, *English Art and Modernism: 1900–1939* (London: Allen Lane; Bloomington: Indiana University Press, 1981); David Peters Corbett, *The Modernity of English Art, 1914–30* (Manchester and New York: Manchester University Press, 1997); and Lisa Tickner, *Modern Life and Modern Subjects: British Art in the Early Twentieth Century* (New Haven and London: Yale University Press, 2000). On broader questions regarding the production, maintenance, and function of culture, as well as the divisions and hierarchies that govern these fields, see especially Pierre Bourdieu and Alain Darbel with Dominique Schnapper, *The Love of Art: European Art Museums and Their Public*, translated by Caroline Beattie and Nick Merriman (1969; Stanford, Calif.: Stanford University Press, 1990); Pierre Bourdieu, *Distinction: A Social Critique of the Judgement of Taste*, translated by Richard Nice (1979; Cambridge, Mass.: Harvard University Press, 1984); and Raymond Williams, *The Politics of Modernism: Against the New Conformists*, edited and introduced by Tony Pinkney (London and New York: Verso, 1989).

4 Dorothy Burrough[e]s, "The Machine and the Artist," *Drawing and Design* 5, no. 7 (December 1925), pp. 218–20; quotation, p. 218.

5 As an exception, machine technology was used to produce offset lithographic posters commissioned for the London Underground.

6 Claude Flight, *The Art and Craft of Lino Cutting and Printing* (London: Batsford, 1934), p. 52.

7 Paul Nash, "'Going Modern' and 'Being British,'" *Week-End Review*, March 12, 1932, pp. 322–23; quotation, p. 322.

THE SHADOW LINE

This chapter was researched and written during the COVID-19 pandemic in the summer and fall of 2020, and I am extremely grateful to those colleagues, friends, and family members who offered me invaluable assistance during these unusual times. It has been a great privilege and pleasure to work with colleagues at The Metropolitan Museum of Art: I thank Jennifer Farrell for her warm collegiality, very generous assistance with research, and insightful comments on the text; Anne Blood Mann for her exemplary editing and management of the publication; and Livia Tenzer for her meticulous bibliographic work. Tim Barringer also generously read and commented on a late draft. I also thank the following, who have helped in innumerable ways: Ruth Forrester, Sophie Forrester, Tilly Forrester, Michael Harding, Susanna Lawrence, Gordon Samuel, Guilland Sutherland, Amy Tibble, and Ian Warrell. The London Library awarded me a Carlyle Membership, and the exemplary staff mailed out books throughout periods of lockdown when all other libraries were forced to close. The chapter is dedicated to my mother, Sophie Forrester, with all my love.

1 There is a substantial literature on British art and material culture of the First World War, though prints have received less attention than works in other media. Surveys include: Albert Eugene Gallatin, *Art and the Great War* (New York: E. P. Dutton, 1919); Meirion Harries and Susie Harries, *The War Artists: British Official War Art of the Twentieth Century* (London: M. Joseph in association with the Imperial War Museum and the Tate Gallery, 1983); Richard Cork, *A Bitter Truth: Avant-Garde Art and the Great War* (New Haven: Yale University Press in association with Barbican Art Gallery, 1994); Sue Malvern, *Modern Art, Britain, and the Great War: Witnessing, Testimony and Remembrance* (New Haven and London: Yale University Press for the Paul Mellon Centre for Studies in British Art, 2004); Paul Gough, *A Terrible Beauty: British Artists in the First World War* (Bristol: Sansom, 2010); Toby Thacker, *British Culture and the First World War: Experience, Representation and Memory* (London and New York: Bloomsbury Academic, 2014); and James Fox, *British Art and the First World War, 1914–1924*, Studies in the Social and Cultural History of Modern Warfare (Cambridge: Cambridge University Press, 2015). For the role of women artists, see Catherine Speck, *Beyond the Battlefield: Woman Artists of the Two World Wars* (London: Reaktion, 2014). See also Jane Beckett, "(Is)land Narratives: Englishness, Visuality and Vanguard Culture 1914–18," in *English Art 1860–1914: Modern Artists and Identity*, edited by David Peters Corbett and Lara Perry (Manchester: Manchester University Press, 2000), pp. 195–212; and James Fox, "Conflict and Consolation: British Art and the First World War, 1914–1919," *Art History* 36, no. 4 (September 2013), pp. 810–33. For prints, see Frances Carey and Antony Griffiths, *Avant-Garde British Printmaking, 1914–1960*, exh. cat. (London: British Museum, 1990), pp. 50–72; and Jennifer Farrell, "World War I and the Visual Arts," *Metropolitan Museum of Art Bulletin* 75, no. 2 (Fall 2017), pp. 4–39. For posters, see James Aulich and John Hewitt, *Seduction or Instruction? First World War Posters in Britain and Europe* (Manchester and New York: Manchester University Press, 2007); and Leanne Green, "Advertising War: Pictorial Publicity, 1914–1918" (PhD diss., Manchester Metropolitan University, 2015). Green's groundbreaking dissertation focuses on the "War Publicity" collection in the Imperial War Museum, London, and examines posters, press advertisements, badges, flags, and other printed ephemera. For war, identity, and memorialization, see Paul Fussell, *The Great War and Modern Memory* (Oxford: Oxford University Press, 1975); Eric J. Leed, *No Man's Land: Combat and Identity in World War I* (Cambridge and New York: Cambridge University Press, 1979); Samuel Hynes, *A War Imagined: The First World War and English Culture* (London: Bodley Head, 1990); and Jay Winter, *Sites of Memory, Sites of Mourning: The Great War in European Cultural History*, Canto Classics (Cambridge: Cambridge University Press, 1995).

2 For essential biographical data, see Myfanwy Piper and Andrew Causey, "Nash, Paul (1889–1946), painter," in *Oxford Dictionary of National Biography* (Oxford University Press, 2004; online ed., 2011), https://doi.org/10.1093/ref:odnb/35186; Julian Freeman, "Nevinson, Christopher Richard Wynne (1889–1946), painter and journalist," in *Oxford Dictionary of National Biography*, https://doi.org/10.1093/ref:odnb/35205; and Mark Glazebrook, "Wadsworth, Edward Alexander (1889–1949), painter and printmaker," in *Oxford Dictionary of National Biography*, https://doi.org/10.1093/ref:odnb/36674. Nevinson exhibited and published under the name C. R. W. Nevinson, and family and friends typically referred to him as "Richard."

3 The Liberal Party entered into a coalition with the nascent Labour Party and instituted social reforms under the leadership of Henry Campbell-Bannerman, who was succeeded by H. H. Asquith in 1908. Espousing progressive social policies and, above all, deeply committed to free trade, the Liberal Party was formed in opposition to the Conservative Party but occupied a more centrist position than left-wing Labour.

4 The act enfranchised women over the age of thirty who met minimum property qualifications, and men over the age of twenty-one.

5 For the visual and material culture of the Edwardian era, see Jane Beckett and Deborah Cherry, eds., *The Edwardian Era*, exh. cat. (Oxford: Phaidon in association with Barbican Art Gallery, 1987); Morna O'Neill and Michael Hatt, eds., *The Edwardian Sense: Art, Design, and Performance in Britain, 1901–1910*, Studies in British Art 20 (New Haven and London: Yale University Press, 2010); and Angus Trumble and Andrea Wolk Rager, eds., *Edwardian Opulence: British Art at the Dawn of the Twentieth Century*, exh. cat. (New Haven: Yale University Press for the Yale Center for British Art, 2013).

6 For Sickert, see Aimée Troyen, *Walter Sickert as Printmaker*, exh. cat. (New Haven: Yale Center for British Art, 1979); Ruth Bromberg, *Walter Sickert, Prints: A Catalogue Raisonné* (New Haven and London: Yale University Press, 2000); and Wendy Baron, *Sickert: Paintings and Drawings* (New Haven: Yale University Press, 2006). For Whistler, see E[lizabeth] R[obins] Pennell and J[oseph] Pennell, *The Life of James McNeill Whistler*, 5th ed. (London: W. Heinemann; Philadelphia: J. B. Lippincott, 1911); Katharine A. Lochnan, *The Etchings of James McNeill Whistler*, exh. cat. (New Haven: Yale University Press in association with the Art Gallery of Ontario, 1984); and Harriet K. Stratis and Martha Tedeschi, eds., *The Lithographs of James McNeill Whistler* (Chicago: Art Institute of Chicago in association with the Arie and Ida Crown Memorial, 1998).

7 For the Slade School, see D. S. MacColl, *Henry Tonks: Slade Professor of Fine Art, 1917–1930* (London: Eyre and Spottiswoode, 1937); *The Slade Tradition: 1879–1921: A Centenary Contribution*, exh. cat. (London: Fine Art Society, 1971), introduced by T. A. Cross; and Emma Chambers, "The Cultivation of Mind and Hand: Teaching Art at the Slade School of Fine Art 1868–92," in *Governing Cultures: Art Institutions in Victorian London*, edited by Paul Barlow and Colin Trodd (Aldershot, U.K., and Burlington, Vt.: Ashgate, 2000), pp. 98–113.

8 David Boyd Haycock, *A Crisis of Brilliance: Five Young British Artists and the Great War* (London: Old Street, 2009), discusses Slade alumni Dora Carrington, Mark Gertler, Paul Nash, C. R. W. Nevinson, and Stanley Spencer.

9 For Lewis's life, see Paul Edwards, *Wyndham Lewis: Painter and Writer* (New Haven: Yale University Press for the Paul Mellon Centre for Studies in British Art, 2000; and Richard Cork, "Lewis, (Percy) Wyndham (1882–1957), artist and writer," in *Oxford Dictionary of National Biography*, https://doi.org/10.1093/ref:odnb/34517. On his wartime experiences and related art, see his first memoir, *Blasting and Bombardiering* (London: Eyre and Spottiswoode, 1937); Paul Edwards and Catherine Wallace, *Wyndham Lewis: Art and War*, exh. cat., Imperial War Museum, London (London: Lund Humphries, 1992); and David Peters Corbett, ed., *Wyndham Lewis and the Art of Modern War* (Cambridge: Cambridge University Press, 1998).

10 Nevinson's autobiography, *Paint and Prejudice* (London: Methuen, 1937), is the primary source for his life; though riddled with inaccuracies, it provides a fascinating account of his career trajectory and experience of the First World War. In the late twentieth century, interest in Nevinson was refreshed by a chapter dedicated to him in David Peters Corbett, *The Modernity of English Art, 1914–30* (Manchester and New York: Manchester University Press, 1997), pp. 152–91, and an exhibition at the Imperial War Museum, London, and the Yale Center for British Art, New Haven, accompanied by the publication of Richard Ingleby's *C. R. W. Nevinson: The Twentieth Century* (London: Merrell Holberton, 1999). Notable recent scholarship includes Michael J. K. Walsh, *C. R. W. Nevinson: This Cult of Violence* (New Haven and London: Yale University Press, 2002); Jonathan Black, "'Neither Beasts, nor Gods, but Men': Constructions of Masculinity and the Image of the Ordinary British Soldier or 'Tommy' in the First World War Art of: C. R. W. Nevinson (1889–1946); Eric Henri Kennington (1888–1960) and Charles Sargeant Jagger (1885–1934)" (PhD diss., University College London, 2003); Michael J. K. Walsh, ed., *A Dilemma of English Modernism: Visual and Verbal Politics in the Life and Work of C. R. W. Nevinson (1889–1946)*

(Newark: University of Delaware Press, 2007); and Michael J. K. Walsh, *Hanging a Rebel: The Life of C. R. W. Nevinson* (Cambridge, U.K.: Lutterworth, 2008). For the Nevinsons' complex family dynamics, see Angela V. John, "A Family at War: The Nevinson Family," in Walsh, *A Dilemma of English Modernism*, pp. 23–35. For the prints, see Carey and Griffiths, *Avant-Garde British Printmaking*, pp. 50–61; Jonathan Black, *C. R. W. Nevinson: The Complete Prints* (Farnham, U.K., and Burlington, Vt.: Lund Humphries in association with Osborne Samuel, 2014); *CRW Nevinson: A Printmaker in War and Peace*, exh. cat. (London: Osborne Samuel, 2014); and *Nash and Nevinson: Impressions of War and Peace*, exh. cat. (London: Osborne Samuel, 2020), pp. 4–10, 33–67. Nevinson did not typically edition his prints.

11 See Walsh, *C. R. W. Nevinson: This Cult of Violence*, pp. 204–5; and Walsh, *Hanging a Rebel*, pp. 124, 140.

12 On Wadsworth, the key source is the biography by his daughter: Barbara Wadsworth, *Edward Wadsworth: A Painter's Life* (Wilton, U.K.: M. Russell, 1989); the volume includes a checklist (unpaged) of the woodcuts, numbered chronologically with the prefix W/D. See also Jeremy Lewison, ed., *A Genius of Industrial England: Edward Wadsworth, 1889–1949*, exh. cat. (Bradford, U.K.: Arkwright Arts and Bradford Art Galleries and Museums, 1990). There are two catalogues raisonnés of the prints: *Edward Wadsworth, 1889–1949: Paintings, Drawings and Prints*, exh. cat. (London: P. and D. Colnaghi, 1974), which has been superseded by Jeremy Greenwood, *The Graphic Work of Edward Wadsworth* (Woodbridge, U.K.: Wood Lea, 2002). Wadsworth did not edition his prints and some were produced in very small quantities.

13 The main source on Nash is the artist's autobiography, published posthumously in 1949; see Paul Nash, *Outline: An Autobiography*, rev. ed., incorporating Margaret Nash's "Memoirs of Paul Nash, 1913–1946," edited by David Boyd Hancock (London: Lund Humphries, 2016). See also Andrew Causey, *Paul Nash: Landscape and the Life of Objects* (Farnham, U.K., and Burlington, Vt.: Lund Humphries, 2013); and Emma Chambers, ed., *Paul Nash*, exh. cat., Tate Britain (London: Tate Gallery, 2016). For the prints, see Alexander Postan, *The Complete Graphic Works of Paul Nash* (London: Secker and Warburg, 1973); Carey and Griffiths, *Avant-Garde British Printmaking*, pp. 61–67; and *Nash and Nevinson: Impressions of War and Peace*, pp. 4–37. Nash did not typically edition his prints, and the quantities vary.

14 See *Drawings by Paul Nash*, exh. cat. (London: Carfax, 1912). The Carfax was a high-profile gallery that showed both Old Masters and young artists. For Nash's account of the management of the gallery and the opening and reception of his 1912 exhibition, see Nash, *Outline*, pp. 103–9.

15 Fry had been working for The Metropolitan Museum of Art, initially as curator of paintings and subsequently, after his return to London, as European advisor, but was fired in 1910 after a disagreement with the Museum's president of trustees, John Pierpont Morgan. He instead devoted his considerable energies and deep knowledge of the contemporary European market to the curation of the exhibition, collaborating with MacCarthy to source works from artists and dealers in Paris and Munich. See Charles Molesworth, *The Capitalist and the Critic: J. P. Morgan, Roger Fry, and the Metropolitan Museum of Art* (Austin: University of Texas Press, 2016).

16 The Bloomsbury Group was a coterie of artists, writers, and intellectuals that included the painter Vanessa Bell and her critic husband, Clive; Vanessa's sister, Virginia Woolf, and her husband, Leonard; painters Dora Carrington and Duncan Grant; economist John Maynard Keynes; and writers Lytton Strachey and E. M. Forster. Fry became a key member of the group. See Richard Shone, *The Art of Bloomsbury: Roger Fry, Vanessa Bell and Duncan Grant*, exh. cat. (London: Tate Gallery, 1999); and Derek Ryan and Stephen Ross, eds., *The Handbook to the Bloomsbury Group* (London: Bloomsbury Academic, 2018).

17 Matisse's strategy of reversing figure and ground, by painting a thin layer of rust-red pigment onto the canvas and using exposed ground to delineate form, was, like Picasso's Cubist deconstructions and referencing of African art, then categorized as "primitive" and considered highly subversive. For the 1910 and 1912 exhibitions and their influence on British art, see Anna Gruetzner Robins, *Modern Art in Britain, 1910–1914*, exh. cat. (London: M. Holberton in association with Barbican Art Gallery, 1997), pp. 40–41, 78–89; and Anna Greutzner Robins, "'Manet and the Post-Impressionists': A Checklist of Exhibits," *Burlington Magazine* 152, no. 1293 (December 2010), pp. 782–93.

18 Clive Bell, "The English Group," in [Roger Fry, Clive Bell, and Boris von Anrep], *Second Post-Impressionist Exhibition: Grafton Galleries, Oct. 5–Dec. 31, 1912*, exh. cat. (London: Ballantyne, 1912), pp. 9–12; quotation, p. 9.

19 See John Gage, *Colour and Culture: Practice and Meaning from Antiquity to Abstraction* (London: Thames and Hudson, 1993); John Gage, *Colour and Meaning: Art, Science and Symbolism* (London: Thames and Hudson, 1999); and David Batchelor, *Chromophobia* (London: Reaktion, 2000).

20 Filippo Tommaso Marinetti, "Manifeste du futurisme," *Le Figaro*, February 20, 1909, p. 1; reprinted in Lawrence Rainey, Christine Poggi, and Laura Whitman, eds., *Futurism: An Anthology* (New Haven and London: Yale University Press, 2009), p. 51.

21 For Futurism, see Marjorie Perloff, *The Futurist Moment: Avant-Garde, Avant Guerre, and the Language of Rupture* (Chicago: University of Chicago Press, 1986); Christine Poggi, *Inventing Futurism: The Art and Politics of Artificial Optimism* (Princeton: Princeton University Press, 2009); and Vivien Greene, ed., *Italian Futurism, 1909–1944: Reconstructing the Universe*, exh. cat. (New York: Guggenheim Museum, 2014).

22 *Post-Impressionist and Futurist Exhibition* (London: Doré Gallery, 1913), unpaged, no. 67. The location of the painting, reproduced in Walsh, *C. R. W. Nevinson: This Cult of Violence*, p. 58, no. 15, is unknown.

23 Fry founded the Omega Workshops with Vanessa Bell and Duncan Grant in 1913, with the objective of producing and selling fabrics, household objects, and furniture designed and fabricated by artists. They recruited a team that included the architect Frederick Etchells, Henri Gaudier-Brzeska, Lewis, and Wadsworth. The Omega Workshops closed in 1919. For a comprehensive account, see Alexandra Gerstein, ed., *Beyond Bloomsbury: Designs of the Omega Workshops 1913–19*, exh. cat. (London: Courtauld Gallery in association with Fontanka, 2009). For Nevinson and Lewis, see Paul Edwards, "Artists as Activists: C. R. W. Nevinson and Wyndham Lewis," in Walsh, *A Dilemma of English Modernism*, pp. 72–88.
24 Nevinson's contribution was to bang on a drum during Marinetti's rendition of his poem on the siege of Adrianople. For the poem, see Filippo Tommaso Marinetti, *Zang Tumb Tumb: Adrianopoli Ottobre 1912: Parole in libertà* (Milan: Edizioni Futuristi di "Poesia," 1914). The performance is described by Nevinson, *Paint and Prejudice*, p. 82; by Marinetti, in a text reproduced in *Marinetti: Selected Writings*, edited by R. W. Flint, translated by R. W. Flint and Arthur A. Coppotelli (London: Secker and Warburg, 1972), p. 47; and by audience members, including Lewis, in his "Marinetti's Occupation," *BLAST*, no. 2 (1915), p. 26.
25 Filippo Tommaso Marinetti and C. R. W. Nevinson, "Vital English Art: Futurist Manifesto," *Observer* (London), June 7, 1914, p. 7. Nevinson published a transcript of the manifesto in *Paint and Prejudice*, pp. 79–81. There were at least seven versions; see Johann Pillai and Anber Onar, "Tracing the Performative: F. T. Marinetti, C. R. W. Nevinson, and the English Futurist Manifesto," in Walsh, *A Dilemma of English Modernism*, pp. 47–71.
26 Nevinson, *Paint and Prejudice*, p. 80.
27 The term was coined by the American poet Ezra Pound. The standard work on Vorticism is Richard Cork, *Vorticism and Abstract Art in the First Machine Age*, 2 vols. (London: G. Fraser, 1976). See also William C. Wees, *Vorticism and the English Avant-Garde* (Manchester: Manchester University Press, 1972); Paul Edwards, ed., *BLAST: Vorticism 1914–1918* (Aldershot, U.K., and Burlington, Vt.: Ashgate, 2000); and Jonathan Black, *Blasting the Future! Vorticism in Britain 1910–1920*, exh. cat., Estorick Collection of Modern Italian Art, London, and Whitworth Art Gallery, Manchester (London: P. Wilson, 2004).
28 For Dismorr, see Alicia Foster, *Radical Women: Jessica Dismorr and Her Contemporaries*, exh. cat. (London: Lund Humphries in association with Pallant House Gallery, 2019). For Saunders, see Brigid Peppin, *Helen Saunders, 1885–1963*, exh. cat. (Oxford: Ashmolean Museum and Graves Art Gallery, 1996). For Gaudier-Brzeska, see H[arold] S[tanley] Ede, *A Life of Gaudier-Brzeska* (London: W. Heinemann, 1930); and Evelyn Silber, *Gaudier-Brzeska: Life and Art* (London and New York: Thames and Hudson, 1996).
29 *BLAST: The Review of the Great English Vortex*, no. 1 (June 1914). The journal was edited by Lewis and published in London by John Lane, the Bodley Head.
30 The first manifesto consisted of two lists, headed "Blast" and "Bless." Effeteness was to be blasted, along with "years 1837 to 1900," "abysmal inexcusable middle class," "Tonks" (a reference to the Slade School professor), "The Post Office," "Codliver Oil," and numerous artists, clerics, composers, playwrights, and others in public life. In contrast, robust masculinity in the form of Britain's industrial complex, ports, seafarers, and ships was to be blessed, as were many aspects of France's artistic, economic, and social cultures. The second manifesto was a series of bullet points, one of which declared, "We are Primitive Mercenaries in the Modern World." Lewis et al., "Manifesto I," "Manifesto II," *BLAST*, no. 1 (June 1914), pp. 11–28, 30–43; quotations, pp. 18, 21, 30.
31 *BLAST*, no. 1 (June 1914), p. 29; Wadsworth, *Edward Wadsworth*, unpaged, no. W/D1. The issue also contains Wadsworth's translation of extracts from Kandinsky's influential treatise *Über das Geistige in der Kunst: Inbesondere in der Malerie* [Concerning the Spiritual in Art: Especially in Painting] (Munich: R. Piper, 1911), embedded in a review of the book, on pp. 119–25. *Newcastle* can be read as an homage to the Russian artist.
32 For Whitworth, see Thomas Seccombe and R. Angus Buchanan, "Whitworth, Sir Joseph, baronet (1803–1887), mechanical engineer and machine tool manufacturer," in *Oxford Dictionary of National Biography*, https://doi.org/10.1093/ref:odnb/29339.
33 C. H. Collins Baker, "Art and War," *Saturday Review of Politics, Literature, Science and Art*, vol. 118, no. 3069, August 22, 1914, p. 220.
34 *La Patrie*, 1916, oil on canvas, Birmingham Museum and Art Gallery (1988P104); *The Doctor*, 1916, oil on canvas, Imperial War Museum, London (IWM ART 725). For the drypoint *The Doctor*, 1916, see Black, *C. R. W. Nevinson: The Complete Prints*, p. 16, ill; p. 118, no. 11.
35 C. R. W. Nevinson, "Painter of Smells at the Front: A Futurist's View of the War," *Daily Express* (London), February 25, 1915; quoted in Walsh, *C. R. W. Nevinson: This Cult of Violence*, p. 98.
36 C. R. W. Nevinson, "A Futurist's Nerves," *Daily Express* (London), February 26, 1915; quoted in Walsh, *C. R. W. Nevinson: This Cult of Violence*, p. 99.
37 Nevinson, *Paint and Prejudice*, p. 56.
38 Ibid, p. 104. "Crocked up" was a popular expression that denoted mental breakdown.
39 *The Gazette of the 3rd London General Hospital, Wandsworth* was published monthly by the hospital between October 1915 and July 1919. Nevinson's contributions included *Night Arrival of the Wounded*, November 1915, p. 30; and *A Futurist's Impression*, February 1915, p. 115.
40 Wyndham Lewis, "A Super-Krupp or War's End?," *BLAST*, no. 2 (July 1915), pp. 13–14; quotation, p. 14.
41 Henri Gaudier-Brzeska "Vortex Gaudier-Brzeska," *BLAST*, no. 2 (July 1915), pp. 33–34.
42 See *Catalogue of an Exhibition of Paintings and Drawings of War by C. R. W. Nevinson (Late Private R.A.M.C.)*, exh. cat. (London: Leicester Galleries, 1916).

43 The eminent art critic Frank Rutter claimed that Nevinson was "the first British painter to give really profound and pictorial expression to the emotions aroused by the war," and the writer H. M. Tomlinson commented in the popular newspaper the *Star*, "As the wounded man said, 'By Jove, this chap gets there!' And that is all any artist need trouble about." Frank Rutter, *Sunday Times* (London), September 24, 1916, quoted in Black, "Neither Beasts, nor Gods, but Men," p. 9; H. M. T[omlinson], "War Pictures: Mr Nevinson's Work at the Leicester Galleries," *Star* (London), October 3, 1916, quoted in Peters Corbett, *Modernity of English Art*, p. 48.
44 W[alter] Sickert, "O Matre Pulchrâ," *Burlington Magazine for Connoisseurs* 29, no. 157 (April 1916), pp. 34–35; quotation, p. 35.
45 Jonathan Black, in *C. R. W. Nevinson: The Complete Prints*, p. 25, notes that the artist exhibited "a dozen" drypoints at the Leicester Galleries in 1916, but Black's catalogue raisonné only lists eight prints from the exhibition. The catalogue for the Leicester Galleries exhibition (see note 42) does not specify medium.
46 Nevinson, *Paint and Prejudice*, p. 118.
47 *Returning to the Trenches*, 1914, oil on canvas, National Gallery of Canada (4800); *A Dawn, 1914*, 1916, oil on canvas, location unknown (sold, *Modern and Post-War British Art*, sale cat. [Sotheby's, London, November 21, 2017], no. 5).
48 Black, *C. R. W. Nevinson: The Complete Prints*, p. 116, no. 4. Nevinson shared his drypoint and etching techniques with Ernest S. Lumsden when the latter was writing a printmaking manual. It is clear from the resulting account that Nevinson was extremely meticulous; E[rnest] S. Lumsden, *The Art of Etching: A Complete and Fully Illustrated Description of Etching, Drypoint, Soft-Ground Etching, Acquatint and Their Allied Arts*, New Art Library (London: Seeley, Service, 1925), p. 358.
49 "Art and the Soldier," *Manchester Guardian*, September 27, 1916, p. 4.
50 *Heart of Darkness* was serialized in three parts in *Blackwood's Magazine* in 1899; it was subsequently published in the compilation *Youth: A Narrative, and Two Other Stories* (Edinburgh: W. Blackwood and Sons, 1902).
51 These included the remarkable *Illustration (Typhoon)*, inspired by a description of a steamship's engine room in Conrad's novella *Typhoon* (1902); Wadsworth, *Edward Wadsworth*, unpaged, no. W/D18b; *Edward Wadsworth, 1889–1949: Paintings, Drawings and Prints*, p. 115.
52 Quoted in Wadsworth, *Edward Wadsworth*, p. 57. In the same letter, Gaudier-Brzeska asked Wadsworth to print the woodcuts on thin paper in order that he would have space for them in his knapsack; ibid., p. 58.
53 Greenwood, *The Graphic Work of Edward Wadsworth*, p. 49. See also Carey and Griffiths, *Avant-Garde British Printmaking*, p. 35, ill.; p. 36, no. 7.
54 Quoted in Wadsworth, *Edward Wadsworth*, p. 73. For Quinn, see B. L. Reid, *The Man from New York: John Quinn and His Friends* (New York: Oxford University Press, 1968).
55 For dazzle camouflage, see Norman Wilkinson, "The Dazzle Painting of Ships," *Journal of the Royal Society of Arts* 68, no. 3512 (March 1920), pp. 263–73; and Roy R. Behrens, "The Role of Artists in Ship Camouflage during World War 1," *Leonardo* 32, no. 1 (1999), pp. 53–59.
56 Greenwood, *The Graphic Work of Edward Wadsworth*, pp. 55, 58. See also Carey and Griffiths, *Avant-Garde British Printmaking*, pp. 36, 38, nos. 10, 13.
57 Nash, *Outline*, p. 194. For the reception of the exhibition, see Gough, *A Terrible Beauty*, pp. 148–50.
58 Quoted in Gough, *A Terrible Beauty*, p. 148.
59 Quoted in Thacker, *British Culture and the First World War*, p. 179.
60 For Edis, see Shirley Neale, "Edis [married name Galsworthy], (Mary) Olive (1876–1955), photographer," in *Oxford Dictionary of National Biography*, https://doi.org/10.1093/ref:odnb/54348; For women artists' work in the war, see Speck, *Beyond the Battlefield*, pp. 7–105.
61 The National War Museum was founded on March 5, 1917, and renamed the Imperial War Museum later that year.
62 For Kennington, see Julian Freeman, "Kennington, Eric Henri (1888–1960), artist," in *Oxford Dictionary of National Biography*, https://doi.org/10.1093/ref:odnb/34286. See also *British Artists at the Front*, vol. 4, *Eric Kennington*, with introductions by Campbell Dodgson and C. E. Montagu (London: *Country Life* and G. Newnes, 1918); and Black, "Neither Beasts, nor Gods, but Men."
63 The most substantive account of the project is Jonathan Black, "'The Human Element': The Contribution of C. R. W. Nevinson and Eric Kennington to the *Britain's Efforts and Ideals* Lithographic Project of 1917," in *Burning Bright: Essays in Honour of David Bindman*, edited by Diana Dethloff et al. (London: UCL Press, 2015), pp. 234–42. For Nevinson's six prints, see Black, *C. R. W. Nevinson: The Complete Prints*, pp. 120–25, nos. 16–21.
64 Many of those posters were crudely delineated and unattributed, but Jackson also commissioned professional artists, notably the distinguished painter and designer Frank Brangwyn, whose representations of the heroic male body were intended to encourage healthy young men to enlist. For Brangwyn, see Alan Windsor, "Brangwyn, Sir Frank William (1867–1956), artist," in *Oxford Dictionary of National Biography*, https://doi.org/10.1093/ref:odnb/32046; and Tim Barringer, "The Heroic Labour of Frank Brangwyn", in *Frank Brangwyn*, edited by Mina Ōya, exh. cat., National Museum of Western Art (Tokyo: Yomiuri Shimbun, 2010), pp. 225–28.
65 Nevinson had taken classes in lithography before the war with Jackson, but if he had made prints then, none has survived. Lithography was regarded primarily as a commercial medium in early twentieth-century Britain, despite its capability for translating the effects of drawing and painting, which made it attractive to artists. Jackson, a fervent advocate, taught lithography at the London County Council art school. He was a cofounder of the Senefelder Club, which was established in

1912 both to promote lithography as an artist's medium by teaching and staging exhibitions, and to bridge the gulf between professional lithographers and artists. Joseph Pennell, the distinguished American printmaker and illustrator, who was then living in London and taught illustration at the Slade, was appointed president. Pennell encouraged Nevinson to try lithography, and Nevinson exhibited two lithographs at the Senefelder Club's annual exhibition in January 1917. See Black, *C. R. W. Nevinson: The Complete Prints*, pp. 25, 119–20.

66 Kennington may have learned lithography at South London Technical Art School, which was renamed City and Guilds of London Art School in 1932.

67 See Michael J. K. Walsh, "'This tumult in the clouds'; C. R. W. Nevinson and the Development of the 'Airscape,'" *British Art Journal* 5, no. 1 (Spring/Summer 2004), pp. 81–87.

68 The series was exhibited in the United States a year after the country had join the war, at the Jacques Seligmann Galleries in New York in March 1918. It subsequently toured to the National Gallery of Art in Washington, D.C.; the Art Institute of Chicago; and the Anderson Galleries in New York. See Black, "'The Human Element,'" p. 242.

69 A guinea was 1 pound and 1 shilling, or 21 shillings total. A set of six "Efforts" prints therefore cost 210 shillings and a single print 42 shillings. By comparison, the hardback first edition of Joseph Conrad's novella *The Shadow-Line: A Confession*, published in 1917 with an extent of 197 pages, cost 5 shillings.

70 See n. 46.

71 Quoted in Walsh, *C. R. W. Nevinson: This Cult of Violence*, pp. 156–57.

72 Henry Nevinson noted in his diary that Richard was "asking to go by aeroplane wh[ich] shows a fine recovery of nerve." Quoted in Walsh, *Hanging a Rebel*, p. 130.

73 Quoted in ibid., p. 131.

74 Quoted in Walsh, *C. R. W. Nevinson: This Cult of Violence*, p. 162.

75 Quoted in Nevinson, *Paint and Prejudice*, p. 144.

76 *Paths of Glory*, 1917, oil on canvas, Imperial War Museum, London (IWM ART 518). A letter from Nevinson to his publisher, Grant Richards, of December 3, 1917, noted, "I have had another one of my pictures censored—a painting of two soldiers who were dead"; The Metropolitan Museum of Art, Purchase, Leslie and Johanna Garfield Gift, Lila Acheson Wallace, Charles and Jessie Price, and David T Schiff Gifts, The Elisha Whittelsey Collection, The Elisha Whittelsey Fund, Dolores Valvidia Hurlburt Bequest, Peco Foundation and Friends of Drawings and Prints Gifts, and funds from various donors (2019.592.391). See Charles E. Doherty, "Nevinson's Elegy: *Paths of Glory*," *Art Journal* 51, no. 1 (Spring 1992), pp. 64–71.

77 The *Saturday Review* published a trenchant critique on March 16, 1918, headed "Duds for the Imperial War Museum," which resulted in an acrimonious exchange between Nevinson and the editor; cited in Walsh, *Hanging a Rebel*, p. 137. J. Turner, a lieutenant in the Royal Warwickshire Regiment, wrote a letter in response to the review, stating, "Show them [Nevinson's exhibited works] to any fellow who has inhabited a dug-out. Pass them round any mess in France or Flanders. Ask the man next to you in hospital in town what he thinks of them. . . . I think you will find he has a pretty whole-hearted admiration for the Art of the man who has realised it so wonderfully"; *Saturday Review* (London), May 25, 1918; quoted in Walsh, *C. R. W. Nevinson: This Cult of Violence*, p. 170. Turner's appreciative comments typify the responses of the many members of the armed forces who visited the exhibition. More sympathetic reviewers included Jan Gordon, writing as John Salis, and Walter Sickert, who both underscored that the official nature of Nevinson's commission required him to adopt a more realist aesthetic; Gordon, quoted in Walsh, *C. R. W. Nevinson, This Cult of Violence*, p. 170; [Walter] R[ichard] S[ickert], "Pictures of War, by C. R. W. Nevinson, at the Leicester Galleries," *Burlington Magazine for Connoisseurs* 32, no 181 (April 1918), p. 165.

78 Black, *C. R. W. Nevinson: The Complete Prints*, p. 130, no. 30; p. 131, ill.

79 Ibid., p. 32, ill.; p. 134, no. 38.

80 David Alan Mellor, "A Spectral Modernity," in Chambers, *Paul Nash*, pp. 23–33; see p. 27.

81 Nash, *Outline*, pp. 185–87. For the manuscript letter, see Tate Archive, London (TGA 8313/1/1/162).

82 Gough, *A Terrible Beauty*, p. 153.

83 Postan, *Complete Graphic Works of Paul Nash*, unpaged, nos. L1–L6.

84 Ibid., unpaged, no. L7.

85 *Nerves of an Army*, 1918, oil on canvas, Imperial War Museum, London (IWM ART 5287). The drypoint of the same title and date is catalogued in Black, *C. R. W. Nevinson: The Complete Prints*, p. 38, ill.; p. 136, no. 41.

86 John Salis [Jan Gordon], "The Nerves of an Army," *Country Life*, March 2, 1918, pp. 211–12.

87 There is a substantive literature on First World War shell shock, its impact on both male and collective identity, and reflections in art. Notable contributions include Joanna Bourke, *Dismembering the Male: Men's Bodies, Britain and the Great War* (London: Reaktion, 1996); Peter Leese, *Shell Shock: Traumatic Neurosis and the British Soldiers of the First World War* (Basingstoke, U.K.: Palgrave, 2002); Ana Carden-Coyne, *Reconstructing the Body: Classicism, Modernism, and the First World War* (Oxford: Oxford University Press, 2009); Ana Carden-Coyne, David Morris, and Timothy Wilcox, eds., *The Sensory War 1914–2014*, exh. cat. (Manchester, U.K.: Manchester Art Gallery, 2014); Ana Carden-Coyne, "Masculinity and the Wounds of the First World War: A Centenary Reflection," *Revue française de civilisation britannique* 20, no. 1 (2015), pp. 1–7; and Paul Gough, *Dead Ground: War and Peace, Remembrance and Recovery; A Cultural Reading of Memoryscapes from the Great War, 1914–1918* (Bristol, U.K.: Sansom, 2018).

88 *Catalogue of an Exhibition of Paintings and Drawings of War by C. R. W. Nevinson*, p. 9, no. 4. The painting, which is untraced, is reproduced in P. G. Konody, *Modern War: Paintings by C. R. W. Nevinson* (London: G. Richards, 1917), p. 49.

89 For the spectrum of responses, see Black, "Neither Beasts, nor Gods, but Men," pp. 103–7. A typical review in the *Athenaeum* (unattributed) complained that the painting radiated a "cheap sensationalism" (October 1916, p. 489), while critic P. G. Konody, among others, argued for Nevinson's objectivity, assessing the painting as a "terribly realistic study of a man suffering from shell-shock. . . . It is like a page from a medical textbook describing the symptoms of an illness" (*Modern War: Paintings by C. R. W. Nevinson*, p. 26).

90 Nevinson, *Paint and Prejudice*, p. 203. During a period of depression in December 1917 and January 1918, Nevinson had three consultations with the eminent neurologist Sir Henry Head, a close friend of W. H. R. Rivers, the anthropologist and psychiatrist. Rivers was administering pioneering treatments to army officers with shell shock at Craiglockhart War Hospital in Scotland. Head and Rivers had earlier conducted experiments into nerve sensation and regeneration, of which Nevinson likely would have been aware. For a fictionalized but well-researched account of Head's and Rivers's work, see Pat Barker's trilogy of novels: *Regeneration* (New York: Viking, 1991), *The Eye in the Door* (New York: Viking, 1993), and *The Ghost Road* (New York: Viking, 1995).

91 Quoted in Black, *C. R. W. Nevinson: The Complete Prints*, p. 187n2.

92 See P. G. Konody, "Art for the Wounded: Exhibition at 3rd London General Hospital; Futurism v. War," *Observer* (London), September 12, 1915, p. 7. For the therapeutic use of art and craft for First World War casualties, see Ana Carden-Coyne, "Butterfly Touch: Rehabilitation, Nature and the Haptic Arts in the First World War," *Critical Military Studies* 6, no. 2 (2020), pp. 176–203.

93 For the mezzotints, see Black, *C. R. W. Nevinson: The Complete Prints*, pp. 138–40, nos. 46–48; p. 145, no. 57 (p. 69, ill.); p. 157, no. 84.

94 Black, *C. R. W. Nevinson: The Complete Prints*, pp. 141, 160, nos. 51, 102.

95 For example, Nevinson's drypoint *New York: An Abstraction*; see Black, *C. R. W. Nevinson: The Complete Prints*, p. 88, ill.; p. 153, no. 77. Following his second, unsuccessful, visit to New York in 1920, Nevinson retitled the original painting *The Soul of a Soulless City*.

96 Black, *C. R. W. Nevinson: The Complete Prints*, p. 185, no. 148.

97 Greenwood, *The Graphic Work of Edward Wadsworth*, pp. 63, 72–73.

98 Wadsworth, *Edward Wadsworth*, p. 89.

99 Herbert Furst, *The Modern Woodcut: A Study of the Evolution of the Craft* (London: J. Lane, 1924), p. 174; quoted in Carey and Griffiths, *Avant-Garde British Printmaking*, p. 40. For the Black Country series, see also Arnold Bennett, *Edward Wadsworth: The Black Country* (London: Ovid, 1920).

100 Postan, *Complete Graphic Works of Paul Nash*, unpaged, no. W9.

101 *The Shadow-Line* was serialized in *Metropolitan Magazine* (New York), September–October 1916, and in the *English Review* (London), September 1916–March 1917, and was published in a single volume in 1917 (London and Toronto: J. M. Dent & Sons; Paris: J. M. Dent et Fils).

102 In 1917, Conrad confided to John Quinn that he was suffering from a "war-nightmare mood." He also wrote to several friends regarding Borys's condition. See John G. Peters, "Conrad's Literary Response to the First World War," *College Literature* 39, no. 4 (2012), pp. 34–45; quotation and Borys references, p. 42.

THE ART OF TO-DAY

1 In regard to the words "industry," "democracy," "class," "art," and "culture," Williams noted, "The changes in their use, at this critical period, bear witness to a general change in our characteristic ways of thinking about our common life: about our social, political and economic institutions; about the purposes which these institutions are designed to embody; and about the relations to these institutions and purposes of our activities in learning, education and the arts." Raymond Williams, introduction to *Culture and Society, 1780–1950* (1958; New York: Columbia University Press, 1983), pp. xiii–xx; quotation, p. xiii.

2 Ibid., p. xvi.

3 T. S. Eliot, "The Three Senses of 'Culture,'" in *Notes towards the Definition of Culture* (1948; London: Faber and Faber, 1962), p. 31. Quoted in Raymond Williams, "T. S. Eliot," in *Culture and Society, 1780–1950*, pp. 227–43; p. 233.

4 Williams continued, "There is a suggestion that he [Eliot] does not fully accept the sense of 'a whole way of life,' but in this illustration translates the older specialized sense of 'culture' (arts, philosophy) into 'popular culture' (sport, food and the Gothic churches). It is evident elsewhere in the book that at times he reverts to the specialized sense"; ibid., p. 234.

5 For more on the hierarchies within artistic culture and the formation of taste, see the work of Pierre Bourdieu, in particular, *Distinction: A Social Critique of the Judgement of Taste*, translated by Richard Nice (1979; Cambridge, Mass.: Harvard University Press, 1984). Particularly helpful for twentieth-century British modernism are Williams, *Culture and Society, 1780–1950*; Charles Harrison, *English Art and Modernism: 1900–1939* (London: Allen Lane; Bloomington: Indiana University Press, 1981); Raymond Williams, *The Politics of Modernism: Against the New Conformists*, edited and introduced by Tony Pinkney (London and New York: Verso, 1989); David Peters Corbett, *The Modernity of English Art, 1914–30* (Manchester and New York: Manchester University Press, 1997); and Lisa Tickner, *Modern Life and Modern Subjects: British Art in the Early Twentieth Century* (New Haven and London: Yale University Press, 2000), esp. "Afterword: Modernism and Modernity," pp. 184–213.

6 As Lisa Tickner writes, "'Modernism' refers to a range of cultural practices deriving from, and promising expression to, the characteristic beliefs and experiences of modernity. It is thus intimately bound up with 'modernisation'—the technological, economic and political processes following in the wake of the Industrial Revolution—and with 'modernity' as the cumulative effect of these changes on social conditions and modes of experience"; *Modern Life and Modern Subjects*, p. 184.
7 Located at 33 Warwick Square, it was formerly the studio and house of the Victorian artist James Swinton.
8 Quoted in Stephen Coppel, *Linocuts of the Machine Age: Claude Flight and the Grosvenor School* (Aldershot, U.K.: Scolar Press in association with the National Gallery of Australia; Brookfield, Vt.: Ashgate, 1995), p. 12.
9 A Grosvenor School promotion declared, "Students may join the school at any time, for a year or for shorter periods." *Drawing and Design* 5, no. 7 (December 1925), advertisements section, unpaged.
10 *Artwork: The International Quarterly of Arts & Crafts*, no. 14 (Summer 1928), advertisements section, p. xiv.
11 As Ethel Spowers described, "It is in the basement that the rooms for lithography, etching and all its kindred processes, are situated. They are fitted up with the correct presses, and other paraphernalia required, for one can learn all the intricacies of any form of art at the Grosvenor School of Modern Art." Quoted in Coppel, *Linocuts of the Machine Age*, p. 13.
12 For more on the linocut process, see Rachel Mustalish, "Materials and Techniques of the Grosvenor School Artists," in *Rhythms of Modern Life: British Prints, 1914–1939*, edited by Clifford S. Ackley, exh. cat. (Boston: MFA Publications; New York: Distributed Art Publishers/D.A.P., 2008), pp. 189–203.
13 Flight was elected to the Royal Society of British Artists in 1923. See Michael Parkin, "Claude Flight and the Linocut," *Journal of Decorative and Propaganda Arts* 6 (Autumn 1987), p. 28. For more on Nevinson, see Gillian Forrester, "The Shadow Line: British Printmakers and the First World War," in this volume.
14 In 1922, Flight showed at the Salon des Indepéndants in Paris, and in 1924, at the XIV Esposizione Internazionale d'Arte Città di Venezia. He was also featured in the British avant-garde journal *Ray*, published by Sidney Hunt, which included international artists, such as Kurt Schwitters, André Masson, Naum Gabo, and László Moholoy-Nagy. Hunt and Flight were fellow members of the Seven and Five Society, a British art group Flight would leave in 1928, as its aesthetic became increasingly abstract.
15 In November 1920, an exhibition of children's art curated by Cižek was shown at the British Institute of Industrial Art, as well as other venues in Britain.
16 In a 1927 review that drew from Flight's own analysis of his art and technique, the critic Malcolm C. Salaman discussed *Swing-Boats* in terms that are almost exclusively formalist and that draw largely from Cubist and Futurist approaches. "Mr. Flight is concerned not at all with the normal vision of the average man, but his own pictorial vision and its interpretation he explains in this way: 'I analyse the various impressions which have interested me from the point of view of their different forces or rhythmic curves, searching for geometrical forms, such as have for us a subconscious associative appeal, by which I can express the skeleton, or construction, of the picture, for it is, in my opinion, by the selection and application of geometrical forms, and by these only, that we can get the unchangeable and universal, those inherited qualities necessary in a work of art'"; *The Woodcut of To-Day at Home and Abroad* (London: The Studio, 1927), p. 54; quoted in Coppel, *Linocuts of the Machine Age*, p. 72.
17 Philip Vann, who linked *Speed* to contemporary scientific theories, specifically those of Einstein, described the bending forms of the buildings and the compression of space as leading to "a mesmerising sensation on the part of the viewer that time is warping—accelerating and then slowing down, then frantically speeding up again—as if in a claustrophobic dream or vision." Vann continued, "There is an intuitive correlation to be made here with the kind of perception outlined by Einstein just seventeen years earlier in his *Theory of Special Relativity*, in which he elaborated that time and space were interwoven entities so that, say, simultaneous events could be perceived as occurring at different times by two separate observers, and that the passage of large bodies of matter would cause a distortion of, or a kind of dimpling in, the fabric of so-called space-time"; "Pulsating Rhythms: The Radical Achievement of Claude Flight and His Printmaking Pupils," in *Cutting Edge: Modernist British Printmaking*, edited by Gordon Samuel, exh. cat. (London: Philip Wilson Publishers and Dulwich Picture Gallery, 2019), pp. 38–51; quotation, p. 42.
18 Flight is believed to have met Marinetti through Nevinson before the First World War. Quotations: Filippo Tommaso Marinetti, "Futurist London: Leader of New Art School on Our Neglect of Reality," interview, *Evening News* (London), March 4, 1912, p. 3; Gino Severini, "Get Inside the Picture: Futurism as the Artist Sees It," *Daily Express* (London), April 11, 1913, p. 4.
19 Linoleum, invented in the mid-nineteenth century, was a machine-made mixture of oxidized linseed oil, cork, gums, and pigments. For the Grosvenor School artists, it connoted modernity in a way that other materials—such as wood—did not. As Pamela H. Simpson notes, "Practical, durable, economical, and ornamental, they [linoleum and the related Lincrusta] were the products of the new industrial age. It is perhaps not surprising that the newly expanded middle class, largely created by the industrial revolution, would embrace the products of industry. Cheap, quick, and easy to install, these materials were also modern, clean, practical substitutes that democratically expanded the availability of ornamental effects"; "Linoleum and Lincrusta: The Democratic Coverings for Floors and Walls," *Perspectives in Vernacular Architecture* 7, Exploring Every-

day Landscapes (1997), pp. 281–92; quotation, p. 290. For more on the linocut, see Stephanie M. Lussier, "The History and Characteristics of Linoleum Block Prints," in *Rhythms of Modern Life: British Prints, 1914–1939*, edited by Clifford S. Ackley, exh. cat. (Boston: MFA Publications; New York: Distributed Art Publishers/D.A.P., 2008), pp. 177–87; Mustalish, "Materials and Techniques of the Grosvenor School"; and Rachel Mustalish, "Capturing Modern Life: Cyril E. Power's *The Eight* from Sketch to Print," in this volume.

20 Claude Flight, "Claude Flight: By Himself," *Drawing and Design* 5, no. 7 (December 1925), pp. 226–28; quotation, p. 226. The article features illustrations of Flight's paintings *Round and Round*, *Vétheuil Church*, *Seine et Oise*, and the woodcut *The Yacht*. Flight's reference (p. 228) to his work "Paris Omnibus" likely alludes to his 1923 linocut with that title and subject, but no image was included.

21 Ibid., p. 227.

22 See László Moholy-Nagy, *The New Vision, 1928; and, Abstract of an Artist*, 3rd ed., translated by Daphne M. Hoffman, The Documents of Modern Art (New York: Wittenborn, 1946).

23 He began with the statement "To the artist of every age it is given to express in terms of his being, of the life that goes on around him, those big, universal emotions which, though they differ slightly from age to age in the manner of their expression, are fundamentally the same." Claude Flight, "The Art of To-Day," *Colour* 2, no. 4 (April 1926), pp. 7–9, 14; quotation, p. 7.

24 Ibid., p. 8.

25 As Andrew Thorpe writes, "Britain in the 1930s was controversial at the time and has remained controversial ever since. On that, at least, there would be little disagreement. But go beyond the platitudes and there are all manner of debatable issues. In economic terms, there are questions ranging from how far government was responsible for, or could have mitigated the effects of, mass unemployment, to how far 'new' industries were replacing 'old'"; *Britain in the 1930s: A Deceptive Decade* (Oxford and Cambridge, Mass.: Blackwell, 1992), p. 1. There are numerous surveys of the period, often with differing ideas. For an overview of diverse opinions, see Charles Loch Mowat, *Britain between the Wars, 1918–1940* (1955; Boston: Beacon Press, 1971); John Stevenson and Chris Cook, *Britain in the Depression: Society and Politics, 1929–1939* (1977, as *The Slump: Society and Politics during the Depression*; London and New York: Longman, 1994); Martin Pugh, *We Danced All Night: A Social History of Britain between the Wars* (London: Bodley Head, 2008); and Richard Overy, *The Twilight Years: The Paradox of Britain between the Wars* (New York: Viking, 2009), published in Britain as *The Morbid Age: Britain between the Wars*.

26 The Representation of the People Act of 1918, which allowed property-owning women over the age of thirty to vote and abolished the property requirements and other restrictions for British men over twenty-one (over nineteen for men in the military), expanded the number of eligible voters from 8 million to 21 million (8.5 million of whom were women). The Representation of the People (Equal Franchise) Act of 1928 allowed all women over the age of twenty-one to vote, adding an additional 6.5 million women to the pool of eligible voters. The Education Act of 1918 raised the school leaving age for girls, and the Sex Disqualification (Removal) Act of 1919 enabled more women to attend schools, including universities and art schools, thus opening up greater professional opportunities.

27 As Robert James has noted, "The social and demographic changes occasioned by the First World War had helped to create a new class of consumer, and it was from within the working classes where these 'new consumers' were principally drawn. Moreover, it was women, especially working-class women, who were regarded to be the main beneficiaries of these changes to society's consumption patterns"; *Popular Culture and Working-Class Taste in Britain, 1930–39: A Round of Cheap Diversions?* Studies in Popular Culture (Manchester and New York: Manchester University Press, 2010), p. 15.

28 Ministry of Reconstruction, *Art and Industry* (London: HMSO, 1919), p. 6. Quoted in James Fox, *British Art and the First World War, 1914–1924*, Studies in the Social and Cultural History of Modern Warfare (Cambridge: Cambridge University Press, 2015), p. 146.

29 *Arts League of Service Annual* (1921–22), p. 9. Quoted in Fox, *British Art and the First World War: 1914–1924*, p. 149.

30 James Fox notes that the Arts League of Service also built relationships with multiple trade unions; *British Art and the First World War: 1914–1924*, p. 151.

31 Frances Carey and Antony Griffiths, *Avant-Garde British Printmaking, 1914–1960*, exh. cat. (London: British Museum, 1990), p. 15.

32 Claude Flight, *Lino-Cuts: A Hand-Book of Linoleum-Cut Colour Printing* (London: Bodley Head, 1927), pp. 3–4.

33 The desire for art to be more accessible and democratic, even revolutionary, was widely held during this time among a variety of artists, including those affiliated with the Bauhaus and Russian Constructivism.

34 Fletcher wrote, "The conditions of modern life render it a form of art that is appropriate in scale, and in decorative power, to ordinary living rooms." Frank Morley Fletcher, "The Woodblock Colour-Print: A Democratic Art," *Original Colour Print Magazine*, June 1, 1924, pp. 4–5; quotation, p. 5. See also the related unsigned article, pp. 6–7, by the magazine's editor William Giles, titled "The Modern Movement of the Colour Print."

35 Fletcher, "The Woodblock Colour-Print," pp. 4–5.

36 See Mustalish, "Capturing Modern Life," in this volume.

37 Tschudi made similar notations on some prints in English.

38 Editions were not always fully realized, while other times, a second edition was created to meet demand, often from international markets. Such prints were frequently marked "USA" in graphite on the front of the work. In addition, some works were printed with a different palette to distinguish the two editions. Power, Flight, and others also created monotypes, or unique works, but such pieces compose only a small percentage of their oeuvre.

39 Claude Flight, *The Art and Craft of Lino Cutting and Printing* (London: Batsford, 1934). For the prejudice against decoration, see, for example, the dictum of Amédée Ozenfant and Le Corbusier: "Il y a une hiérarchie dans les arts: l'art décoratif est au bas, la figure humaine au sommet" (There is a hierarchy in the arts: decorative art is at the bottom, the human form at the top). [Amédée] Ozenfant and [Charles-Edouard] Jeanneret [Le Corbusier, pseud.], *Après le Cubisme*, Commentaires sur l'art et la vie moderne 1 (Paris: Edition des Commentaires, 1918), p. 59.

40 Jay A. Clarke, "Linocuts between the Wars: The Politics of Style, Process, and Gender, 1918–39," in Jay A. Clarke and Jonathan Black, *Machine Age Modernism: Prints from the Daniel Cowin Collection*, exh. cat. (Williamstown, Mass.: Clark Art Institute, 2015), pp. 39–61; quotation, pp. 54–55.

41 See Arthur S. Marks, "A Sign and a Shop Sign: The Ω and Roger Fry's Omega Workshops," *British Art Journal* 13, no. 1 (Spring/Summer 2012), pp. 18–36.

42 Flight, *Art and Craft of Lino Cutting*, p. 63.

43 As early as about 1924, Power and Andrews wrote "Aims of the Art of To-Day," an unpublished manifesto in which they described the necessity of responding to subjects and inventions of contemporary life; for example: "Look at Nevinson's 'Mitrailleuse' [*Machine Gun*]. To express the revolting horridness and the noisy incessant vibrating, rattle, he has used ugly sharp, angular and square shapes and drabby crude colour which hurt to look at." Quoted in Coppel, *Linocuts of the Machine Age*, p. 52.

44 For modernist understandings of urban space, see Henri Lefebvre, *The Production of Space*, translated by Donald Nicholson-Smith (1974; Oxford: Blackwell, 1991).

45 Virginia Woolf, "Street Haunting: A London Adventure," in *The Death of the Moth and Other Essays* (San Diego, New York, and London: Harcourt Brace, 1970), pp. 20–36; quotations, pp. 20–21.

46 See Guy Debord, "Theory of the Dérive" (1956), in *Situationist International Anthology*, edited and translated by Ken Knabb (Berkeley, Calif.: Bureau of Public Secrets, 1981), pp. 50–54.

47 Woolf, "Street Haunting," p. 23. Woolf's *Mrs. Dalloway* was first published by Hogarth Press, London, in 1925.

48 Claude Flight, "Dynamism and the Colour Print," *Original Colour Print Magazine*, June 1, 1925, pp. 56–58; quotation, p. 56.

49 Quoted in Oliver Green, *London's Underground: The Story of the Tube* (London: White Lion, 2019), p. 105.

50 Nikolaus Pevsner, "Patient Progress: The Life Work of Frank Pick," *Architectural Review* 92 (August 1942), pp. 31–48; quotation, p. 34.

51 During Pick's tenure, Henry (Harry) Beck created his iconic *London Underground Railways Map* (1931, published 1933). On Beck, see Green, *London's Underground*, p. 162. For more on Pick and public art, see Michael T. Saler, *The Avant-Garde in Interwar England: Medieval Modernism and the London Underground* (New York and Oxford: Oxford University Press, 1999).

52 See Saler, *The Avant-Garde in Interwar England*, p. 102.

53 Both posters were made for the Underground Electric Railways Company of London Ltd., which became part of the LPTB. As the art critic and Grosvenor School professor Frank Rutter noted, Kauffer "accomplished the miracle of introducing Cubism into the railway-stations and hoarding[s] of England"; *Art in My Time* (London: Rich and Cowan, 1933), p. 194; quoted in Peter White, *Sybil Andrews: Colour Linocuts/Sybil Andrews: Linogravures en couleur*, exh. cat. (Calgary: Glenbow Museum, 1982), p. 24.

54 Ronald Grierson (printmaker), conversation with Peter White, November 1980; quoted in White, *Sybil Andrews: Colour Linocuts*, p. 24.

55 Rutter, *Art in My Time*, p. 249; quoted in Saler, *The Avant-Garde in Interwar England*, pp. 101–2.

56 Carey and Griffiths, *Avant-Garde British Printmaking*, p. 17.

57 Sybil Andrews, letter to Carol Collier, September 3, 1985, London Transport Museum, 2009/6258. Here Andrews answers a series of questions posed by the curator Oliver Green. Later Green wrote her to confirm that he had understood correctly "the interesting information about Power getting the order but you carrying out the designs"; Oliver Green, letter to Sybil Andrews, December 5, 1985, London Transport Museum, 2009/6265.

58 According to Coppel, the image, based on a trip Power made on the Green Line bus from London to Hertford, was deeply personal, as the bus was driven by his second son Cyril Arthur Power; *Linocuts of the Machine Age*, p. 101.

59 Coppel notes that Tschudi's *Underground*, a vibrant depiction of Waterloo Tube station, cast in acidic tones of orange, yellow, and red, was created as an exercise at the Grosvenor School; ibid., p. 128.

60 Vann, "Pulsating Rhythms," p. 42.

61 It is believed to depict the District line. Coppel, *Linocuts of the Machine Age*, p. 102.

62 Power had published some of his illustrations and writings in a multivolume set, and he would later lecture on the topic at numerous art schools. See Cyril E. Power, *English Mediaeval Architecture: In Two Parts*, 2 vols. (London: Talbot, 1912); *English Mediaeval Architecture: In Three Parts*, 2nd ed., 3 vols. (London: Talbot, 1923). For Power's architectural training and interests, see Philip Vann, *Cyril Power Linocuts: A Complete Catalogue* (Farnham, U.K., and Burlington, Vt.: Lund Humphries in association with Osborne Samuel, 2008), p. 18.

63 *The Star* (London), July 4, 1929; quoted in Coppel, *Linocuts of the Machine Age*, p. 107. For *Straphangers*, see Hana Leaper, *Sybil Andrews: A Complete Catalogue* (Surrey, U.K., and Burlington, Vt.: Lund Humphries in association with Osborne Samuel, 2015), p. 52.

64 Overy, *Twilight Years*, pp. 68–69.
65 Stevenson and Cook, *Britain in the Depression*, p. 9. Thorpe claims unemployment rose from 1.1. million to 2.8 million by 1931; *Britain in the 1930s*, p. 23. This figure, just below 3 million, represented "23 per cent of all insured workers, with a slow process of recovery from 1934"; James Klugmann, "Introduction: Crisis in the Thirties; A View from the Left," in *Culture and Crisis in Britain in the Thirties*, edited by Jon Clark et al. (London: Lawrence and Wishart, 1979), pp. 13–36; quotation, p. 14.
66 Stevenson and Cook, *Britain in the Depression*, p. 8.
67 Klugmann, "Introduction: Crisis in the Thirties," p. 14.
68 Overy, *Twilight Years*, p. 68.
69 A. J. P. Taylor, *English History, 1914–1945*, Oxford History of England 15 (Oxford: Clarendon Press, 1965), p. 317. Quoted in Stevenson and Cook, *Britain in the Depression*, p. 10.
70 Coppel, *Linocuts of the Machine Age*, p. 84
71 One can contrast Flight's almost festive scene with Nevinson's lithograph *The Workers* (1919; alternatively titled *Revolution* and *Strikers on Tower Hill*), in which he portrayed a crowd of strikers and their supporters.
72 The exceptions are works such as Tschudi's *Visiting Day*, made in March 1937, which depicts black-and-white clad nurses in a children's hospital, and the pieces she made when she was a member of the Swiss Women's Auxiliary Military Service (FHD).
73 *The New Cable* is the second state of the print known as *The Giant Cable* (1931), which had a blue background. In the second state, Andrews removed the blue to make the background the color of the paper.
74 *Fixing the Wires* was exhibited frequently both in England and abroad and featured in Flight's *The Art and Craft of Lino Cutting and Printing*. After the first edition sold out, it was printed in a second edition marked "USA" and sold to a largely American audience. Coppel, *Linocuts of the Machine Age*, p. 127.
75 See David Trotter, *Literature in the First Media Age: Britain between the Wars* (Cambridge, Mass.: Harvard University Press, 2013), pp. 30–31. Among the artists he mentions as focusing on telephone wires are the photographer Tina Modotti (*Telephone Wires, Mexico*, ca. 1925), painter Edward Hopper (*Adam's House*, 1928, watercolor), and film director Fritz Lang (*M*, 1931).
76 For Nevinson's print, see Forrester, "The Shadow Line," in this volume.
77 Tschudi made multiple works on the theme, including a watercolor with crayon (1932) and pencil drawings (1933).
78 Flight, *Art and Craft of Lino Cutting*, p. 52.
79 Despite the interest in the Grosvenor School representing "the machine age," such prints "account for less than a third of this body of art." Hana Leaper, "'Old-fashioned modern': Claude Flight's Lino-Cuts and Public Taste in the Interwar Period," *Modernist Cultures* 11, no. 3 (November 2016), pp. 389–408; quotation, p. 399.
80 Hobsbawm also noted that in the 1930s "Agriculture provided work for only about five per cent of the occupied population and less than four per cent of the national income"; *Industry and Empire: The Birth of the Industrial Revolution*, rev. ed. (1968; New York: New Press, 1999), edited by Chris Wrigley, p. 173.
81 Ibid., p. 182.
82 The interwar years saw a blossoming of popular entertainments, with enthusiastic reception by a broad public: "The thirties was the period when the mass media—press, radio, film, gramophone records—first began to assume their full modern shape and importance in people's lives. . . . While the number of workers directly employed in providing entertainment and sport increased from 65,000 in 1930 to 116,000 in 1937, it was also a period when intellectual interests, high-quality books and music came within reach of millions for the first time." Noreen Branson and Margot Heinemann, *Britain in the Nineteen Thirties*, The History of British Society (London: Weidenfeld and Nicolson, 1971), p. 246.
83 The Queen's Hall was destroyed in the Blitz of 1941. Andrews's *Theatre* (alternative title, *Au Théâtre*), based on London's Old Vic theater and also made in 1929, shows a similar interest in depicting soaring balconies and other architectural forms, as well as schematic renderings of crowds.
84 Begun in the mid-nineteenth century, these concerts were played outdoors in pleasure gardens where attendees could walk or "promenade" while listening to music. The first Proms was held in 1895 at the Queen's Hall in London; the concerts continue to be performed several times a year at various London venues.
85 For more on Tschudi's practice of developing compositions through preparatory sketches, see Mustalish, "Capturing Modern Life," in this volume.
86 Sandra Trudgen Dawson, "Selling the Circus: Englishness, Circus Fans and Democracy in Britain, 1920–45," in *Leisure and Cultural Conflict in Twentieth-Century Britain*, edited by Brett Bebber, Studies in Popular Culture (Manchester and New York: Manchester University Press, 2012), pp. 84–108; quotation, p. 84; on the circus's popularity in Britain and its link to national identity, see esp. pp. 101–2.
87 The Wembley Exhibition Funfair was originally part of the British Empire Exhibition held at Wembley Park between spring 1924 and fall 1925. The exhibition was staged to celebrate the British Empire, especially as an industrial power with great access to natural resources, at a moment when many viewed it as being challenged by other countries, as well as weakened after the First World War. Power has sketches for *The Merry-Go-Round* dated September 1927.
88 According to Coppel, Power's swing-boats were from the August Bank Holiday Fair on Hampstead Heath, known as 'Appy 'Ampstead; *Linocuts of the Machine Age*, p. 100.
89 At the time Grosvenor School artists were working, both film and photography—arts that indeed were of the machine and reflective of the machine age—were thriving. Critics saw connections between the prints and movies, and Flight, in an

effort to broaden the public's exposure to art, even showed prints in an exhibition gallery at a movie theater.

90 On *The Eight* and the way in which Power created the linocut, see Mustalish, "Capturing Modern Life," in this volume.

91 As Coppel has noted, "The inter-war period was obsessed with breaking speed records for land, water and air; at different times during the 1930s Britain had held world records for all three"; *Linocuts of the Machine Age*, p. 18.

92 The exuberance was not felt by everyone: many on the left noted that the Jubilee banquet held for the royal family and paid for by the city of London cost approximately 5,000 British pounds, while an unemployed family subsisted on 10 pence a day or less. See "£5,000 Banquet—And Thousands Starve," *Daily Worker* (London), May 22, 1935, https://www.nationalarchives.gov.uk/wp-content/uploads/2014/03/ho144-199721.jpg (accessed January 31, 2021).

93 George V died in early 1936. His son Edward VIII was king from January 20 to December 11, 1936. George VI, Edward's brother, ruled from 1936 until 1952.

94 Redfern Gallery opened in September 1923 on Old Bond Street. Originally an artists' cooperative, the gallery was soon showing early works by modernists, such as Henry Moore and Barbara Hepworth.

95 The Ward Gallery (also known as F. J. Ward) was connected to F. J. Ward's Bookshop, King's Road, which sold books and prints, including reproductions, in addition to being a printer and publisher.

96 Coppel, *Linocuts of the Machine Age*, p. 19; Leaper, "'Old-fashioned modern,'" esp. pp. 392–97.

97 Coppel, *Linocuts of the Machine Age*, p. 20.

98 One can compare the reception of the Grosvenor School linocuts with that of the prints produced by Contemporary Lithographs Ltd. Developed in 1937, the initiative sought to create original, color lithographs in editions of four hundred for schools and households of all financial levels. Priced around one pound for the schools and under two pounds for the public, the lithographs were cheaper than Grosvenor School linocuts. Although artists, including Paul Nash, John Piper, and Graham Sutherland, created original designs for the firm (as opposed to reproductions of works made in other media) and drew on the lithographic stones, the prints were made by craftspeople and were neither signed nor numbered, thereby confusing the public, who could not always distinguish between original and reproductive art. See Carey and Griffiths, *Avant-Garde British Printmaking*, p. 18; and Antony Griffiths, "Contemporary Lithographs Ltd.," *Print Quarterly* 8, no. 4 (December 1991), pp. 308–402, esp. p. 398.

99 Flight, *Lino-Cuts*, p. 4. Flight's reference to the cinema was not gratuitous. Movies achieved great popularity during the interwar period, with many people visiting movie theaters multiple times a week. This activity appealed to all classes and inspired A. J. P. Taylor to describe going to the movies as "the essential social habit of the age." There was variety in prices for movie tickets, depending on the luxury of a given theater; in addition, theaters priced seats at different levels, making movies affordable even for working-class consumers, a group that composed the majority of the movie attendees. See James, *Popular Culture and Working-Class Taste*, pp. 13–14.

100 Coppel, *Linocuts of the Machine Age*, p. 19.

101 Leaper, "'Old-fashioned modern,'" pp. 392–97.

102 More than sixty thousand refugees, including numerous artists and intellectuals, fled Germany and countries occupied by the Nazis during the decade. Britain, in the midst of an economic depression, generally limited its welcome to those who would not need financial assistance, such as Ernst L. Freud (an architect and son of Sigmund Freud) and his family, including son Lucian (the artist-to-be). Overall, Britain accepted fewer refugees than other countries. See Norman Bentwich, *The Refugees from Germany, April 1933 to December 1935* (London: G. Allen and Unwin, 1936), pp. 121–22; and Overy, *Twilight Years*, p. 279.

103 See Harrison, *English Art and Modernism*.

104 Claude Flight, letter to Lill Tschudi, March 18, 1938. Quoted in Coppel, *Linocuts of the Machine Age*, p. 63.

105 Hans Neuburg, *Lill Tschudi: Vom figurativen zur abstrakten Expression* (Glarus, Switzerland: Baeschlin, 1979), pp. 8–9.

CAPTURING MODERN LIFE

1 Claude Flight, *Lino-Cuts: A Hand-Book of Linoleum-Cut Colour Printing* (London: Bodley Head, 1927); and Claude Flight, *The Art and Craft of Lino Cutting and Printing* (London: Batsford, 1934).

2 Flight, *Art and Craft of Lino Cutting*, p. 63.

3 Power and Andrews rarely pulled more than one impression at a time, and while an edition number was specified, generally fifty to sixty, these artists did not always print the full quantity. The process was very time consuming, and the works were often printed on demand. This meant the artists did not have to buy all the supplies necessary for the full edition or store the pulled prints. Very rarely, a second edition of a print was issued for the US market; these often had different colored backgrounds and notations indicating they were for the "USA edition."

4 Power occupied a studio at 2 Brook Green, in what had been the Hammersmith School of Art in London, from 1930 to 1938. See Stephen Coppel's catalogue raisonné of Grosvenor School linocuts, *Linocuts of the Machine Age: Claude Flight and the Grosvenor School* (Aldershot, U.K.: Scolar Press in association with the National Gallery of Australia; Brookfield, Vt.: Ashgate, 1995), p. 54.

5 The points where oars attach to the boat are called rowlocks or oarlocks. The distinct, loud sound made when the oars meet the oarlocks during the act of rowing is remarked upon in the title cards of the silent film *Rowing Eves* (London: British Pathé, 1931), 3 min., about women's races on the Thames; British Pathé and the Reuters Historical Collection, London

(948.08). A film showing male sportsmen, *Rowing*, directed by John Betts (Cricklewood, U.K.: Stoll, 1926), 11 min., reveals a great deal about the technical aspects of the sport, rowers' attire, and the boats of the period; Huntley Film Archives, Hereford (1000213).

6 Coppel, *Linocuts of the Machine Age*, p. 89.

7 See Sybil Andrews, Print Book 1, 1929–33, Glenbow Archives, Glenbow Museum, Canada (M-8411-138). This book is the first of several kept by Andrews and Power, and it records prints first made between 1929 and 1933. Andrews continued to update these books until the 1980s.

8 Andrews, Print Book 1, unpaged.

9 See the impression in the Museum of Fine Arts, Boston (2005.1103).

10 Japanese paper is long-fibered paper made for centuries in east Asia from materials such as kozo (paper mulberry). It is often thin and smooth yet remains strong enough to be used in a variety of art making, including printmaking.

11 For an expanded discussion of the printing techniques and materials of these artists, see Rachel Mustalish, "Materials and Techniques of the Grosvenor School Artists," in *Rhythms of Modern Life: British Prints, 1914–1939*, edited by Clifford S. Ackley, exh. cat. (Boston: MFA Publications; New York: Distributed Art Publishers/D.A.P., 2008), pp. 189–203.

12 One notable example is currently in a private collection.

13 See three drawings in the National Gallery of Australia, Canberra: *Study I for "The Eight,"* ca. 1930 (96.198); *Study III for "The Eight,"* ca. 1930 (96.199); and *Study IV for "The Eight,"* ca. 1930 (96.200).

14 Power's notation "dark" may have indicated the dark blue color that would result from his overlapping of the green and blue inks.

Selected Reading

Ackley, Clifford S. ed. *Rhythms of Modern Life: British Prints, 1914–1939*. With contributions by Stephen Coppel, Samantha Rippner, Thomas E. Rassieur, Stephanie Lussier, and Rachel Mustalish. Exh. cat., Museum of Fine Arts, Boston; The Metropolitan Museum of Art, New York; Wolfsonian-Florida International University, Miami. Boston: MFA Publications; New York: Distributed Art Publishers/D.A.P., 2008.

Andrews, Sybil *Artist's Kitchen*. London: R. K. Hudson, 1985.

Black, Jonathan *C. R. W. Nevinson: The Complete Prints*. Farnham, U.K., and Burlington, Vt.: Lund Humphries in association with Osborne Samuel, 2014.

Carey, Frances, and Antony Griffiths *Avant-Garde British Printmaking, 1914–1960*. Exh. cat. London: British Museum, 1990.

Chambers, Emma ed. *Paul Nash*. Exh. cat., Tate Britain. London: Tate Gallery, 2016.

Clarke, Jay A., and Jonathan Black *Machine Age Modernism: Prints from the Daniel Cowin Collection*. Exh. cat. Williamstown, Mass.: Clark Art Institute, 2015.

Coppel, Stephen "Claude Flight and His Australian Pupils." *Print Quarterly* 2, no. 4 (December 1985), pp. 263–83.

Coppel, Stephen "British Color Linocuts: The Critical Response between the Wars." *Tamarind Papers* 14 (1991–92), pp. 21–30.

Coppel, Stephen *Claude Flight and His Followers: The Colour Linocut Movement between the Wars*. Exh. cat., National Gallery of Victoria, Melbourne; Australian National Gallery, Canberra; Art Gallery of New South Wales, Sydney; Museum of New Zealand te Papa Tongarewa, Wellington; Auckland Art Gallery Toi O Tamaki, Auckland. Canberra: Australian National Gallery, 1992.

Coppel, Stephen *Linocuts of the Machine Age: Claude Flight and the Grosvenor School*. Aldershot, U.K.: Scolar Press in association with the National Gallery of Australia; Brookfield, Vt.: Ashgate, 1995.

Cork, Richard *Vorticism and Abstract Art in the First Machine Age*. 2 vols. London: G. Fraser, 1976.

Cork, Richard *A Bitter Truth: Avant-Garde Art and the Great War*. New Haven: Yale University Press in association with Barbican Art Gallery, 1994.

Edelstein, Teri J. ed. *Art for All: British Posters for Transport*. With essays by Teri J. Edelstein, Oliver Green, Neil Harris, Peyton Skipwith, and Michael Twyman. Exh. cat. New Haven: Yale Center for British Art in association with Yale University Press, 2010.

Farrell, Jennifer with a contribution from Donald J. La Rocca. "World War I and the Visual Arts." *Metropolitan Museum of Art Bulletin* 75, no. 2 (Fall 2017).

Flight, Claude *Lino-Cuts: A Hand-Book of Linoleum-Cut Colour Printing*. London: Bodley Head, 1927.

Flight, Claude *The Art and Craft of Lino Cutting and Printing*. London: Batsford, 1934.

Fox, James *British Art and the First World War, 1914–1924*. Studies in the Social and Cultural History of Modern Warfare. Cambridge: Cambridge University Press, 2015.

Fussell, Paul *The Great War and Modern Memory*. Oxford: Oxford University Press, 1975.

Gallatin, Albert Eugene *Art and the Great War*. New York: E. P. Dutton, 1919.

Greenwood, Jeremy *The Graphic Work of Edward Wadsworth*. Woodbridge, U.K.: Wood Lea, 2002.

Harrison, Charles *English Art and Modernism: 1900–1939*. London: Allen Lane; Bloomington: Indiana University Press, 1981.

Hecker, Judith B. "Sybil Andrews." In *Modern Women: Women Artists at the Museum of Modern Art*, edited by Cornelia H. Butler and Alexandra Schwartz, pp. 97–99. New York: Museum of Modern Art, 2010.

Hynes, Samuel *A War Imagined: The First World War and English Culture*. London: Bodley Head, 1990.

Leaper, Hana *Sybil Andrews Linocuts: A Complete Catalogue*. Farnham, U.K., and Burlington, Vt.: Lund Humphries, 2015.

Leaper, Hana "'Old-fashioned modern': Claude Flight's Lino-Cuts and Public Taste in the Interwar Period." *Modernist Cultures* 11, no. 3 (November 2016), pp. 389–408.

Leed, Eric J. *No Man's Land: Combat and Identity in World War I*. Cambridge and New York: Cambridge University Press, 1979.

Lill Tschudi: Linolschnitte 1930–1997; 15. November 1997 bis 11. Januar 1998, Städtische Galerie Bietigheim-Bissingen. Edited by Herbert Eichhorn and Andrea Tietze with Lieselotte Hahn. Exh. cat. Bietigheim-Bissingen, Germany: Städtische Galerie, 1997.

Malvern, Sue *Modern Art, Britain, and the Great War: Witnessing, Testimony and Remembrance*. New Haven and London: Yale University Press for the Paul Mellon Centre for Studies in British Art, 2004.

Nash, Paul *Outline: An Autobiography*. Rev. ed., incorporating Margaret Nash's "Memoirs of Paul Nash, 1913–1946." Edited and with an introduction by David Boyd Hancock. London: Lund Humphries, 2016.

Neuburg, Hans *Lill Tschudi: Vom figurativen zur abstrakten Expression*. Glarus, Switzerland: Baeschlin, 1979.

Nicol, Janet *On the Curve: The Life and Art of Sybil Andrews.* Halfmoon Bay, Canada: Caitlin, 2019.

O'Mahony, Mike "Imaging Sport at the Grosvenor School of Modern Art (1929–37)." *International Journal of the History of Sport* 28, nos. 8–9 (May–June 2011), pp. 1105–20.

Parkin, Michael "Claude Flight and the Linocut." *Journal of Decorative and Propaganda Arts* 6 (Autumn 1987), pp. 26–33.

Peters Corbett, David *The Modernity of English Art, 1914–30.* Manchester and New York: Manchester University Press, 1997.

Postan, Alexander *The Complete Graphic Works of Paul Nash.* London: Secker and Warburg, 1973.

Saler, Michael T. *The Avant-Garde in Interwar England: Medieval Modernism and the London Underground.* New York and Oxford: Oxford University Press, 1999.

Samuel, Gordon ed. *Cutting Edge: Modernist British Printmaking.* With essays by Hana Leaper, Tracey Lock, Gordon Samuel, and Philip Vann. Exh. cat. London: Philip Wilson; Dulwich Picture Gallery, 2019.

Sybil Andrews and the Grosvenor School Linocuts. Introduced by Gordon Samuel with an essay by Hana Leaper. Exh. cat., Osborne Samuel Gallery. London: Osborne Samuel, 2015.

Thacker, Toby *British Culture and the First World War: Experience, Representation and Memory.* London and New York: Bloomsbury Academic, 2014.

Thirties British Art and Design before the War: An Exhibition Organised by the Arts Council of Great Britain in Collaboration with the Victoria & Albert Museum, Hayward Gallery. Exh. cat., Hayward Gallery. London: Arts Council of Great Britain, 1979.

Tickner, Lisa *Modern Life and Modern Subjects: British Art in the Early Twentieth Century.* New Haven and London: Yale University Press, 2000.

Urbanelli, Lora S. *The Grosvenor School: British Linocuts between the Wars.* Exh. cat. Providence: Museum of Art, Rhode Island School of Design, 1988.

Vann, Philip *Cyril Power Linocuts: A Complete Catalogue.* Farnham, U.K., and Burlington, Vt.: Lund Humphries in association with Osborne Samuel, 2008.

Wadsworth, Barbara *Edward Wadsworth: A Painter's Life.* Wilton, U.K.: M. Russell, 1989.

Walsh, Michael J. K. *Hanging a Rebel: The Life of C. R. W. Nevinson.* Cambridge, U.K.: Lutterworth, 2008.

White, Peter *Sybil Andrews: Colour Linocuts/Sybil Andrews: Linogravures en couleur.* Exh. cat. Calgary: Glenbow Museum, 1982.

Winter, Jay *Sites of Memory, Sites of Mourning: The Great War in European Cultural History.* Canto Classics. Cambridge: Cambridge University Press, 1995.

Index

Italic page numbers refer to illustrations.

Photography Credits

© 2021 Artists Rights Society (ARS), New York: figs. 5, 8, pp. 84, 85, 86, 87 (top), 88, 89, 90 (top and bottom), 92, 93, 100 (top and bottom), 101

© 2021 Artists Rights Society (ARS), New York. Image © The Metropolitan Museum of Art, photo by Katherine Dahab: p. 91

© 2021 Artists Rights Society (ARS), New York / DACS, London: pp. 87 (bottom), 167

© Estate of Claude Flight / Bridgeman Images: pp. 114, 135, 138, 139, 150, 153, figs. 4, 15, 16, 22, 23

© Estate of Claude Flight / Bridgeman Images. Image © The Metropolitan Museum of Art, photo by Katherine Dahab: p. 117

Reproduced with permission of Glenbow Museum: front cover, pp. 4–5, 106, 110, 120 (top and bottom), 125, 128, 129, 130 (top), 131, 149, 151, 154, 159, 160, 161, 162, 163, 164, 165, figs. 1, 25, 26, 29

Reproduced with permission of Glenbow Museum. Image © The Metropolitan Museum of Art: pp. 38–39, 155, fig. 24

Reproduced with permission of Glenbow Museum. Image © The Metropolitan Museum of Art, photo by Katherine Dahab: p. 111

© Wyndham Lewis Memorial Trust / Bridgeman Images. Image © The Metropolitan Museum of Art: fig. 3

Image © The Metropolitan Museum of Art: pp. 98, 99, fig. 2

Image © The Metropolitan Museum of Art, photo by Katherine Dahab: p. 95

Image © The Metropolitan Museum of Art, photo by Mark Morosse: p. 94, figs. 17, 18

© Estate of Cyril Power / Bridgeman Images: back cover, pp. 2–3, 82–83, 113, 118, 119, 122, 123, 136, 137, 142, 144, 145, 157, 158, figs. 20, 28, 35, 36, 39, 40, 41, 42

© Estate of Cyril Power / Bridgeman Images. Image © The Metropolitan Museum of Art: pp. 121, 141

© Estate of Cyril Power / Bridgeman Images. Image © The Metropolitan Museum of Art, photo by Katherine Dahab: pp. 68–69, 133

© Estate of Cyril Power / Bridgeman Images. Photo © 2021 Museum of Fine Arts, Boston: fig. 43

© Estate of Cyril Power / Bridgeman Images. Reproduced with permission of Glenbow Museum: fig. 21

© Estate of Cyril Power / Bridgeman Images. Reproduced with permission of Glenbow Museum. Image © The Metropolitan Museum of Art, photo by Katherine Dahab: fig. 19

© Estate of Cyril Power / Bridgeman Images. Image © The Metropolitan Museum of Art, photo by Rachel Mustalish: figs. 32, 37

© Estate of Cyril Power / Bridgeman Images. Image © The Metropolitan Museum of Art, photo by Adam Neese: fig. 38

The Print Collector / Print Collector / Getty Images: fig. 44

Reproduced with permission from the family of the artist: fig. 9

© Dieter Roth Estate Courtesy Hauser & Wirth and Dieter Roth Foundation, Hamburg: fig. 31

Jolie Simpson: fig. 11

Photo © Tate: fig. 6

© Lill Tschudi Estate, Switzerland: pp. 107, 109, 112, 115, 130 (bottom), 134, 143, 148, 156, 166, 168, 169, 170, 176, figs. 27, 30, 33a, b, 34a, b

© Lill Tschudi Estate, Switzerland. Image © The Metropolitan Museum of Art, photo by Katherine Dahab: pp. 126, 127

This catalogue is published in conjunction with *Modern Times: British Prints, 1913–1939*, on view at The Metropolitan Museum of Art, New York, from November 1, 2021, to January 9, 2022.

This publication is made possible by the Roswell L. Gilpatric Publications Fund.

Published by The Metropolitan Museum of Art, New York
Mark Polizzotti, Publisher and Editor in Chief
Peter Antony, Chief Production Manager
Michael Sittenfeld, Senior Managing Editor

Edited by Anne Blood Mann
Designed by Wilcox Design
Production by Christopher Zichello
Bibliographic editing by Livia Tenzer
Image acquisitions and permissions by Shannon Cannizzaro

Photographs of works in The Met collection are by Erica Allen, Imaging Department, The Metropolitan Museum of Art, unless otherwise noted.

Unless otherwise noted, the credit line for the figures is as follows: Purchase, Leslie and Johanna Garfield Gift, Lila Acheson Wallace, Charles and Jessie Price, and David T Schiff Gifts, The Elisha Whittelsey Collection, The Elisha Whittelsey Fund, Dolores Valvidia Hurlburt Bequest, Peco Foundation and Friends of Drawings and Prints Gifts, and funds from various donors, 2019.

Additional photography credits appear on page 199.

Typeset in Joanna Nova, Kabel, and Gill Sans
Printed on 135gsm GardaPat Bianka
Printed and bound by Trifolio S.r.l., Verona, Italy

Cover illustrations: front, Sybil Andrews, *Concert Hall*, 1929; back, Cyril E. Power, *Whence & Whither?*, ca. 1930
Endpapers: Edward Alexander Wadsworth, *S.S. Jerseymoor*, 1918
Pages 2–3: Cyril E. Power, *The Tube Station*, ca. 1932; pages 4–5: Sybil Andrews, *In Full Cry*, 1931; pages 16–17: Christopher Richard Wynne Nevinson, *Returning to the Trenches*, 1916; pages 38–39: Sybil Andrews, *The Winch*, 1930; pages 68–69: Cyril E. Power, *The Eight*, 1930; pages 82–83: Cyril E. Power, *Speed Trial*, ca. 1932; page 176: Lill Tschudi, *Sticking Up Posters*, 1933

First printing

The Metropolitan Museum of Art
1000 Fifth Avenue
New York, New York 10028
metmuseum.org

Distributed by
Yale University Press, New Haven and London
yalebooks.com/art
yalebooks.co.uk

Cataloguing-in-Publication Data is available from the Library of Congress.
ISBN 978-1-58839-739-3

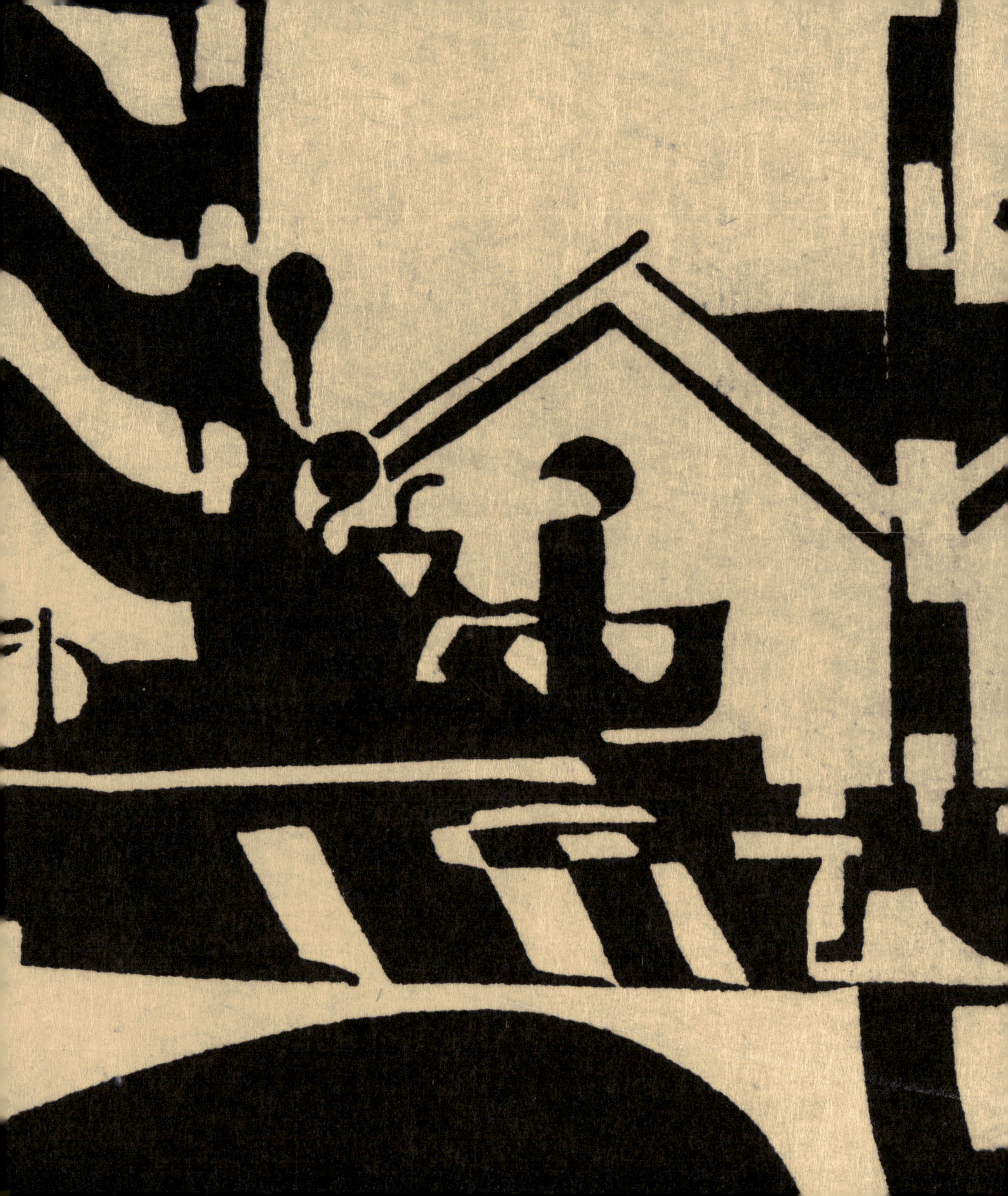